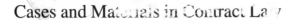
Cases and Materials in Contract Law

Cases and Materials in Contract Law

Max Young BA (Bus Law), MA (Bus Law), MPhil, MIPD
Head of Department of Law, University of Luton

PITMAN
PUBLISHING

London • Hong Kong • Johannesburg • Melbourne • Singapore • Washington DC

PITMAN PUBLISHING
128 Long Acre, London WC2E 9AN
Tel: +44 (0)171 447 2000
Fax: +44 (0)171 240 5771

A Division of Pearson Professional Limited

First published in Great Britain in 1997

ISBN 0 273 62570 5

British Library Cataloguing in Publication Data
A CIP catalogue record for this book can be obtained from the British Library

Typeset by Land & Unwin (Data Sciences) Limited, Bugbrooke
Printed and bound in Great Britain by Bell and Bain Ltd, Glasgow

The Publishers' policy is to use paper manufactured from sustainable forests.

Contents

Preface   xiii
Acknowledgements   xv
Table of cases   xvi
Table of statutes and statutory materials   xxxi

1 Agreement and offer   1
  Preliminary matters   1
  Agreement   1
    Objective appearance of agreement   2
  Offer   5
  Offer or invitation to treat   6
    Examples of invitation to treat   6
  Summary   20

2 Acceptance   21
  Acceptance   21
  Counter-offer   21
  Request for information   26
  Conditional assent is not acceptance   27
  Acceptance may be 'retrospective'   32
  Difficulties in determining acceptance   34
    Sometimes difficult to determine if there has been an acceptance 34
    Difficulty in determining if there has been an acceptance in the case
      of tenders   36
  Communication of acceptance   37
    Exceptions to general rule that acceptance must be communicated 39
  Silence is not consent   45
  Offeree need not personally communicate acceptance   45
  Method of acceptance prescribed by offeror   47
  Speed of communication   52
  The postal rules   56
  Miscellaneous points   60
    Motive irrelevant   62
    Are offer and acceptance always necessary?   62
  Summary   64

3 Ending the offer   **65**
Termination of offer   65
   Offer not terminated merely by acting inconsistently with it   65
Revocation of offer   65
   Exceptions to the general rule that notice of revocation must be
     communicated to the offeree before it takes effect 66
   Rejection and counter-offer   69
   Lapse of offer   69
Summary   71

4 Certainty   **72**
Certainty   72
Vagueness   72
Resolving vagueness   81
   Resolving vagueness on the basis of reasonableness as between
     the parties   81
   Resolving vagueness by discarding meaningless phrases   83
   Resolving vagueness by discarding self-contradictory phrases   85
   Resolving vagueness by reference to the 'machinery' provided in
     the agreement   86
Summary   91

5 Consideration   **92**
Consideration   92
   Explanation of definition of consideration   92
Consideration must move from the promisee   92
What constitutes a valuable consideration?   93
Past consideration   93
Difference between past and executed consideration   95
Consideration need not be adequate   99
Consideration must be real   101
   Motive and consideration   101
   Gift of onerous property   102
   Forbearance to sue   103
   Insufficiency of consideration   106
Summary   121

6 Variation of contracts, promissory estoppel and waiver   **122**
Contract variation   122
Intention to rescind or vary?   122
Have both parties furnished fresh consideration?   123
   Rule in *Pinnel's Case*   124
   Equitable exception - promissory estoppel   126
Features of promissory estoppel   131
   No new rights created   131
   Must there be a pre-existing contractual relationship?   133

There must be an unequivocal representation   135
The party must rely on the statement   136
Must the promissee act to his detriment?   138
Does the promisee need to act differently?   141
Is promissory estoppel suspensory?   143
It must be inequitable for the creditor to go back on his promise   148
Waiver of breach of contract   151
Summary   153

7   Intention to create legal relations   **154**
Intention to create legal relations   154
Social/domestic agreements and commercial agreements   154
    Social and domestic agreements   154
    Commercial agreements   163
    'Ex gratia' compromise   166
    Quasi-commercial agreements   168
Summary   173

8   Privity   **174**
Introduction   174
The imposition of contractual liabilities upon third parties   174
The acquisition of contractual rights by third parties   174
Equitable exceptions to the privity rule   176
    Specific performance in favour of the third party   176
    Trusts of contractual rights   183
    Contracts of insurance   188
    Road Traffic Act 1988   188
    Married Women's Property Act 1882   188
    Marine Insurance Act 1996   189
Exemption clauses and third parties   189
Summary   198

9   Contents of a contract   **200**
Terms and representations   200
    Difficulty of distinguishing terms from representations   200
    Tests to distinguish between terms and representations   206
    Time between the making of the statement and the parties entering
       into the contract   206
    Importance of intention of parties   208
    Later written document   208
    One party an expert   212
    Above tests not conclusive   214
Collateral warranties   214
    Collateral warranties and third parties   217
    Collateral warranties and tenders   219
Express terms   219

Conditions and warranties   219
Innominate terms   223
Implied terms   232
Terms employed by custom   232
Terms implied by statute   232
Terms implied by the courts   233
Summary   245

10 Exemption clauses: the common law   **246**
Exemption clauses   246
Incorporation of an exemption clause into the contract   246
Incorporation by course of dealing   262
Construction   266
Contra proferentem rule   266
Negligence   269
Although the clause will be strictly interpreted, this interpretation must
be a strained one   277
Invalid or inoperative exemption clauses   280
Misrepresentation   280
Overriding oral undertaking   281
Fundamental breach: does it exist?   283
Summary   289

11 Exemption clauses: the Unfair Contract Terms
Act 1977   **290**
The Unfair Contract Terms Act 1977   290
Section 1 Scope of Part I   290
Section 2 Negligence liability   290
Section 3 Liability arising in contract   291
Section 4 Unreasonable indemnity clauses   291
Section 5 'Guarantee' of consumer goods   291
Section 6 Sale and hire-purchase   292
Section 7 Miscellaneous contracts under which goods pass   292
Section 9 Effect of breach   293
Section 10 Evasion of means by secondary contract   293
Section 11 The 'reasonableness' test   293
Section 12 'Dealing as consumer'   294
Section 13 Varieties of exemption clause   294
Section 14 Interpretation of Part I   294
Schedule 1 Scope of sections 2 to 4 and 7   295
Schedule 2 'Guidelines' for application of reasonableness test   295
Scope of the Act   296
Exclusion clauses rendered void   296
Clauses subject to reasonableness test   296
Dealing as a consumer   297
Dealing on the other's written standard terms of business   302

Application of the reasonableness test   303
Exclusion clauses purporting to exclude liability for misrepresentation   310
Evasion of liability by means of a secondary contract   310
Varieties of exemption clauses   313
Unfair Terms in Consumer Contracts Regulations 1994   316
Introduction to the Regulations   317
Article 1 Citation and commencement   317
Article 2 Interpretation   317
Article 3 Terms to which these Regulations apply   318
Article 4 Unfair terms   318
Article 5 Consequences of inclusion of unfair terms in contracts   318
Article 6 Construction of written contracts   318
Article 7 Choice of law clauses   319
Article 8 Prevention of continued use of unfair terms   319
Schedule 1 Contracts and particular terms excluded from the scope
  of these Regulations   319
Schedule 2 Assessment of good faith   319
Schedule 3   320
Summary   321

12 Misrepresentation   **322**
The Misrepresentation Act 1967   322
Section 1 Removal of certain bars to rescission for innocent
  misrepresentation   322
Section 2 Damages for misrepresentation   322
Section 3 Avoidance of provision excluding liability for
  misrepresentation   323
What is misrepresentation?   323
The representation   323
There must be a false representation   323
What if circumstances change?   325
The representation must be one of fact   327
Effect of misrepresentation   337
Fraudulent misrepresentation   338
What constitutes a fraud?   338
Negligence does not amount to fraud   339
Measure of damage for fraudulent misrepresentation   339
Negligent misrepresentation   342
Misrepresentation Act 1967: Section 2(1) Damages for
  misrepresentation   342
Measure for damages   344
Innocent misrepresentation   350
Remedies available to misled person   350
Misrepresentation Act 1967: Section 1 Removal of certain bars to
  rescission for innocent misrepresentation   359
Misrepresentation Act 1967: Section 3 Exclusion of liability   359

Defining liability   360
Application of Misrepresentation Act 1967 section 3   362
Summary   367

13 Mistake   368
Mistake at common law   368
Mistake must exist when the contract was made   368
Common mistake   370
Mistake as to substance or quality   373
Does mistake as to substance avoid the contract?   375
Does mistake as to the quality of the thing contracted for avoid the contract? 380
Failure of consideration   383
Is there a doctrine of common mistake?   386
Unilateral mistake   393
The 'objective test'   393
Four exceptions to the objective test   393
Mistake as to the promise known to the other party   396
Mistake as to the identity of the person with whom the contract is made 397
Mistake in relation to a written document   408
Essentially different transaction   408
Negligence   410
Mistake in equity   411
Refusal of an order for specific performance   411
Rectification   412
Relationship of equity to common law mistake   417
Summary   418

14 Duress, undue influence and inequality of bargaining power   420
Duress   420
Economic duress - does it exist?   421
Establishing economic duress   422
Duress in equity   430
Undue influence   431
Presumption of undue influence   432
Special relationship between the parties   433
Is lender affected by influence?   440
Inequality of bargaining power   453
Inequality of bargaining power - is there such a doctrine?   453
Summary   457

15 Discharge by performance and breach   458
Discharge of the contract by performance   458
Partial performance of an entire contract   458
Doctrine of 'substantial performance'   463
Time of performance   463
Time is not normally the essence of a contract   463

Circumstances in which time will be of the essence   463
Sale of Goods Act 1979: section 10 Stipulations about time   464
Time not originally 'of the essence'   464
Discharge by breach   465
Discharge at option of the injured party   465
Effect of election to accept repudiation   473
Forms of discharge by breach   479
Renunciation before performance due - (anticipatory breach) 484
Summary   488

16 Discharge by frustration   **489**
Introduction   489
Extension of principle to 'frustration of the
  adventure' as opposed to 'literal impossibility'   491
Examples of frustration   493
Limitations on the doctrine   506
Self-induced frustration   506
Events must defeat common intention of the parties   511
Effects of frustration   512
Contract determined automatically   512
Future obligations discharged   513
Unsatisfactory position at common law   515
Law Reform (Frustrated Contracts) Act 1943   516
Section 1 Adjustment of rights and liabilities of parties to
  frustrated contracts   516
Section 2 Provision as to application of this Act   517
Does s 1(3) apply to cases like *Appleby* v *Myers*?   518
Summary   524

17 Remedies for breach of contract   **525**
Introduction   525
Damages   525
Remoteness of damage   525
Compensatory nature of damages   537
For what can damages be recovered?   537
Calculation of damages - difference in value or cost of restoration 545
Difficulty of assessment no bar   550
Penalty clauses and liquidated damages clauses   551
Quantum meruit   554
Requirements for *quantum meruit*   554
Assessment of *quantum meruit*   554
Quasi contract subject to the contract   555
Specific performance   558
Supplementary   559
Discretionary   559
When will specific performance be refused?   559

Specific performance is sometimes available if damages are not an
adequate remedy   567
Contracts requiring constant supervision by court   568
Summary   571

18 Restitution   **573**
Introduction   573
Unjust enrichment: total failure of consideration   573
Equitable rescission   573
Indemnity as a restitutionary remedy   573
Is restitution available for breach of contract?   576
Summary   576

Preface

In writing this book I have had the opportunity to rethink what a contract law course should be in these days of semesters, modules, CATS, student numbers and ever decreasing resources. The modern contract law course now lasts about 22 weeks and even then in many cases it is split into two single semester modules. This book attempts to set out the law of contract in a readable and fairly traditional way so as to enable students to grasp the principles of contract law. As a consequence of re-examining the traditional syllabus in the light of modern demands some old friends have had to go, so such old faithfuls such as *Harvey* v *Facey* (1893) and *Clifton* v *Palumbo* (1944) do not appear in this book. It is hoped that more recent cases showing old principles in more modern circumstances will make contract law more penetrable than in the past with some of the older cases.

I have also tried to include more of the primary sources of the law, i.e. longer extracts from cases, rather than including extracts from secondary sources such as articles and other books.

You will find that unlike other case books if a case is included in this book then, apart from two or three exceptions, there will be a full extract of the case – not just a summary of the case; summaries of cases can be found in your lecture notes and textbooks.

Another feature of this book that distinguishes it from other case books is that, rather than summarise the facts of each case, I have chosen, wherever possible, to include the facts of the case as stated in the judgments.

A final feature of this book is that I have kept commentary on the law and the cases to a minimum; such commentaries you will find in your lecture notes and your textbooks.

Reading 'contract' cases

Although we all try to put 'law' into neat compartments it is not always possible to do so. You'll find that many of the cases that you are given as contract law cases are really criminal law or land law or jurisdiction cases, etc, and that when you come to read the case that has been given to you it doesn't seem to be the right one because it is really, e.g., a criminal law case. This is one of the difficulties that we all experience when we start to study law; we really need to know several areas of law to make sense of some cases. Don't be put off. Before you start to read the case think about the point of law that it illustrates and look for that point in the case. Also make use of the headnote of the case. The headnote is a summary of the facts of the case and the decision of the court. Be warned, though, sometimes the headnote can be misleading and even wrong.

Difficulty in reading and understanding judgments

You will find some of the judgments that you read very difficult to follow or understand; this is part of being a lawyer. Don't be put off – law lecturers and judges, even in the House of Lords, experience the same difficulties from time to time. For example in *Photo Production Ltd* v *Securicor Transport Ltd,* Lord Wilberforce referring to the judgments given in *Suisse Atlantique Société d'Armement Maritime SA* v *NV Rotterdamsche Kolen Centrale* described them as, 'The lengthy, and perhaps I may say sometimes indigestible speeches of their Lordships.' He continued, 'It is only because of Lord Reid's great authority in the law that I have found it necessary to embark on what in the end may be superfluous analysis. For I am convinced that, with the possible exception of Lord Upjohn whose critical passage, when read in full, is somewhat ambiguous, their Lordships, fairly read, can only be taken to have rejected those suggestions for a rule of law which had appeared in the Court of Appeal.'

Again in the *Photo Production* case, Lord Diplock states, 'The fallacy in the reasoning, and what I venture to think is the disarray into which the common law about breaches of contract has fallen, is due to the use in many of the leading judgments on this subject of ambiguous or imprecise expressions without defining the sense in which they are used. I am conscious that I have myself sometimes been guilty of this when I look back on judgments I have given in such cases as *Hong Kong Fir Shipping Co Ltd* v *Kawakasi Kisen Kaisha Ltd.'*

Thanks

Although only the author gets the credit for writing a book, the creation of a book is a team effort. I would like to express my gratitude to the teams who helped me produce this book. The away team, the University of Luton team, who helped in the word processing of parts of the book – Dawn Blackmore, Julie Holding and Lorraine Doyle. The home team, my wife Anne and my children Andrew, Katy and Simon, who put up with me and helped proofread the book with me.

Max Young
January 1997
E-mail: max.young@luton.ac.uk

Acknowledgements

I would like to express my thanks to the following copyright owners, who willingly gave permission for the publishing of extracts:

The Controller of Her Majesty's Stationery Office for permission to reproduce extracts from judgments which are Crown Copyright.

Addison Wesley Longman for permission to reproduce the extract from the Building Law Reports.

Butterworth Law Publishers for permission to reproduce extracts from their reports, including Construction Law Reports, Commonwealth Law Reports, the Law Times Reports and All England Law Reports.

The Estate Gazette Ltd for permission to reproduce extracts from the Estates Gazette Law Reports.

The Incorporated Council of Law Reporting for England and Wales for permission to reproduce extracts from the Weekly Law Reports and The Law Reports.

Jordan Publishing Limited for permission to reproduce the extract from the Family Law Reports.

Lloyd's Reports for permission to reproduce extracts from their reports.

Sweet & Maxwell Ltd for permission to reproduce the extract from the Property Planning and Compensation Reports.

The extract from the United States Law Reports is reproduced with the permission of the copyright holder, Lawyers Cooperative Publishing, a division of Thomson Information Services Inc.

Table of cases

Adams v Lindsell [1818] 1 B & Ald 681   *65, 56*
Addis v Gramophone Co Ltd [1908-10] All ER Rep 1   *54*
Adler v Dickson [1954] 3 All ER 397   *189*
Agar v Bermejo Estancia Co Ltd [1947] 1 All ER 749   *132*
Ailsa Craig Fishing Co Ltd v Malvern Fishing Co Ltd and Securicor (Scotland) [1983] 1 All ER 101   *277, 279*
Ajayi v R T Briscoe (Nigeria) Ltd [1964] 3 All ER 556   *139, 145*
Alan (W J) & Co Ltd v El Nasr Export & Import Co [1972] 2 All ER 127   *137, 138, 141, 146*
Alaskan Trader, The: *see* Clea Shipping Corporation v Bulk Oil International Ltd [1984] 1 All ER 129   *469*
Albion Sugar Co Ltd v Williams Tankers Ltd (The *John S Darbyshire*) [1977] 2 Lloyd's Rep 457   *78*
Alderslade v Hendon Laundry Ltd [1945] 1 All ER 244   *271, 275, 276, 288*
Allcard v Skinner (1887) 36 ChD 145   *432, 434, 435, 436, 437, 439, 455, 456, 457*
Amalgamated Investment & Property Co Ltd v John Walker & Sons Ltd [1976] 3 All ER 509   *368*
Amalgamated Investment & Property Co Ltd v Texas Commerce International Bank Ltd [1982] 1 Lloyd's Rep 27   *134*
Andrews Brothers (Bournemouth) Ltd v Singer and Co Ltd [1934] 1 KB 17   *266*
Andrews v Hopkinson [1956] 3 All ER 422   *218*
Angelia, The: Trade and Transport Inc v Iino Kaiun Kaisha Ltd [1973] 2 All ER 144   *287*
Anns v Merton London Borough Council [1977] 2 All ER 492   *195, 196, 198*
Appleby v Meyers (1867) 36 LJCP 331   *501, 513, 518*
Archdale (James) & Co Ltd v Comservices Ltd [1954] 1 All ER 210   *197, 198, 270*
Associated Japanese Bank (International) Ltd v Credit du Nord SA [1988] 3 All ER 902   *386, 391, 392*
Astley v Reynolds (1731) 2 Stra 915   *422, 424, 454*
Atlantic Baron, The: *see* North Ocean Shipping Co Ltd v Hyundai Construction Co Ltd [1978] 3 All ER 1170   *111, 422, 423, 426*
Atlantic Lines & Navigation Co Inc v Hallam Ltd (The *Lucy*) [1983] 1 Lloyd's Rep 188   *359*
Atlas Express Ltd v Kafco (Importers and Distributors) Ltd [1989] 1 All ER 641   *428*
Attica Sea Carriers Corporation v Ferrostaal Poseidon Bulk Reederei GmbH (The *Puerto Buitrago*) [1976] 1 Lloyd's Rep 250   *470*
Attwood v Lamont [1920] 3 KB 571   *566*
Attwood v Small (1838) 6 Cl & F 232   *336*
Austins of East Ham Ltd v Macey [1941] Ch 338   *477, 478*
Avery v Bowden (1855) 5 E & B 714   *486*
Avon Finance Co Ltd v Bridger (1979) [1985] 2 All ER 281   *447, 450*

Bagot's Executor and Trustee Co Ltd v Coulls (1967) 40 ALJR 471   *178*
Bailey v Bullock [1950] 2 All ER 1167   *538*
Baily v De Crespigny (1869) LR 4 QB 180   *495*
Bainbridge v Firmstone (1839) 8 Ad & El 743   *99, 101*
Bainbrigge v Browne (1881) 18 ChD 188   *446, 449*
Balfour v Balfour [1919] 2 KB 571   *154, 155, 157, 159, 160, 163, 167*
Bank Line Ltd v Arthur Capel & Co [1919] AC 435   *497, 503, 504, 507, 508, 509*
Bank of Baroda v Rayarel [1995] 2 FLR 376   *452, 453*

Bank of Credit and Commerce International SA *v* Aboody [1992] 4 All ER 955 *440, 444, 446, 447, 448*

Bank of Montreal *v* Stuart [1911] AC 120 *437, 438, 439, 445*

Bannerman *v* White (1861) 10 CBNS 844 *204, 208*

Barber *v* Wolfe [1945] 1 All ER 399 *477*

Barclays Bank plc *v* O'Brien [1993] 4 All ER 417 *441, 442, 451, 452*

Barr *v* Gibson (1838) 3 M & W 390 *385*

Barton *v* Armstrong [1975] 2 All ER 465 *426, 427*

Barwick *v* Buba (1857) 2 CBNS 563 *486*

Beck & Co *v* Szymanowski & Co [1923] AC 43 *268*

Behn *v* Burness (1863) 3 B&S 751 *200*

Behzadi *v* Shaftesbury Hotels Ltd [1991] 2 All ER 477 *464*

Bell *v* Gardiner (1842) 4 M & G 11 *105*

Bell *v* Lever Brothers Ltd [1932] AC 161 *370, 375, 378, 379, 380, 383, 384, 386, 387, 388, 389, 390, 392, 418*

Bellgrove *v* Eldridge (1954) 90 CLR 613 *547*

Berry *v* Berry [1929] 2 KB 316 *129*

Beswick *v* Beswick [1968] AC 58 *176, 179, 182, 183*

Bettini *v* Gye (1876) 1 QBD 183 *221*

Birch *v* Paramount Estates (Liverpool) Ltd [1956] 168 EG 396 *201, 202, **207***

Birmingham & District Land Co *v* London & North Western Rail Co (1888) 40 ChD 268 *130, 132*

Bishop & Baxter Ltd *v* Anglo-Eastern Trading & Industrial Co Ltd [1943] 2 All ER 598 *84*

Bisset *v* Wilkinson [1927] AC 177 *327*

Blackburn Bobbin Co Ltd *v* T W Allen & Sons Ltd [1918] 2 KB 467 *511*

Blackpool and Fylde Aero Club Ltd *v* Blackpool Borough Council [1990] 3 All ER 25 *17, 219*

Bolton *v* Mahadeva [1972] 2 All ER 1322 *461*

Boston Deep Sea Fishing & Ice Co Ltd *v* Ansell (1888) 39 ChD 339 *288, 477*

Boulton *v* Jones (1857) 2 H & N 564 *398*

Bourne *v* Mason (1669) 1 Vent 6 *93*

Bowes *v* Shand (1877) 2 App Cas 455 *231*

BP Exploration Co (Libya) Ltd *v* Hunt (No 2) [1982] 1 All ER 925 *518*

Bracewell *v* Appleby [1975] 1 All ER 993 *543*

Branca *v* Cobarro [1947] 2 All ER 101 *27*

Bremer Handelsgesellschaft mbH *v* Continental Grain Co [1983] 1 Lloyd's Rep 269 *509*

Bremer Handelsgesellschaft mbH *v* J H Rayner & Co Ltd [1978] 2 Lloyd's Rep 73 *232*

Bremer Handelsgesellschaft mbH *v* Vanden Avenne-Izegem PVBA [1978] 2 Lloyd's Rep 109 *135, 136*

Brikom Investments Ltd *v* Carr [1979] 2 All ER 753 *141*

Brimnes, The: see **Tenax Steamship Co Ltd *v* Owners of the motor vessel *Brimnes* [1974] 3 All ER 88** *40, 41*

Brinkibon Ltd *v* Stahag Stahl und Stahlwarenhandelsgesellschaft mbH [1982] 1 All ER 293 *41, 43*

British & American Telegraph Co *v* Colson (1871) LR 6 Exch 108 *49*

British and Beningtons Ltd *v* North-Western Cachar Tea Co Ltd [1922] All ER Rep 224 *123*

British Columbia Saw Mill Co *v* Nettleship (1868) LR 3 CP 499 *527*

British Movietonews Ltd *v* London & District Cinemas Ltd [1951] 2 All ER 617 *505*

British Road Services Ltd *v* Arthur V Crutchley & Co Ltd [1968] 1 All ER 811 *22, 25*

British Steel Corporation *v* Cleveland Bridge and Engineering Co Ltd [1984] 1 All ER 504 *78, 556*

British Westinghouse Electric and Manufacturing Co Ltd *v* Underground Electric Railways Co of London Ltd [1912] AC 673 *546*

Brogden *v* Metropolitan Railway Company (1877) 2 App Cas 666 *24, **34**, 44, 61*

Brown *v* Sheen & Richmond Car Sales Ltd [1950] 1 All ER 1102 *219*

Bruner *v* Moore [1904] 1 Ch 305 *48, 59, 139, 152*

Bunge Corporation v Tradax Export SA [1981] 2 All ER 513   *230, 463, 464*
Burges v Wickham (1863) 3 B & S 669   *186*
Burnett v Westminster Bank Ltd [1965] 3 All ER 81   *248*
Burton v Great Northern Railway Co (1854) 9 Ex 507   *37*
Bushwall Properties Ltd v Vortex Properties Ltd [1976] 2 All ER 283   *81, 88*
Butler Machine Tool Co Ltd v Ex-Cell-O Corporation (England) Ltd [1979] 1 All ER 965   *23*
Buttery v Pickard (1946) 174 LT 144   *130, 132*
Byrne & Co v Van Tienhoven & Co (1880) 5 CPD 344   *65, 57*

Cairncross v Lorimer (1860) 3 LJ 130   *215*
Canada and Dominion Sugar Co Ltd v Canadian National (West Indies) Steamships Ltd [1947] AC 46   *147*
Canada Steamship Lines Ltd v R [1952] 1 All ER 305   *277, 278*
Car & Universal Finance Co Ltd v Caldwell [1964] 1 All ER 290   *35, 356*
Carlill v Carbolic Smoke Ball Co [1893] 1 QB 256   *5, 12, 39, 44, 120, 172*
Casey's Patents, *Re*, Stewart v Casey [1892] 1 Ch 104   *95, 98*
Cehave NV v Bremer Handelsgesellschaft GmbH (The *Hansa Nord*)[1975] 3 All ER 739   *227, 231*
Cellulose Acetate Silk Co Ltd v Widnes Foundry (1925) Ltd [1933] AC 20   *551*
Cemp Properties (UK) Ltd v Dentsply Research & Development Corporation [1991] 2 EGLR 197 *358*
Central London Property Trust Ltd v High Trees House Ltd [1947] KB 130;[1956] 1 All ER 256   *128, 132, 133, 137, 139, 141, 148, 150, 152, 215*
Centrovincial Estates plc v Merchant Investors Assurance Company Ltd [1983] Com LR 158   *3, 4*
Chalmers v Pardoe [1963] 3 All ER 552   *560*
Chandler v Lopus (1603) Cro Jac 4   *201, 202*
Chandler v Webster [1904] 1 KB 493   *514, 515*
Channel Home Centers Division of Grace Retail Corp v Grossman (1986) 795 F 2d 291   *78*
Chapelton v Barry UDC [1940] 1 KB 532   *246, 250, 257, 259, 281*
Chaplin v Hicks [1911-13] All ER Rep 224   *549*
Chapman v Westerby (1913) 58 Sol Jo 50   *565*
Chappell & Co Ltd v The Nestlé Co Ltd [1959] 2 All ER 701   *99, 101*
Charles Hunt Ltd v Palmer [1931] 2 Ch 287   *364*
Charles Rickards Ltd v Oppenheim [1950] 1 All ER 420   *132, 139, 151, 463, 464*
Charterhouse Credit Co Ltd v Tolly [1963] 2 All ER 432   *288*
Cheale v Kenward (1858) 27 LJCh 784   *102*
Chesneau v Interhome Ltd (1983) 134 NLJ 341   *348*
Chester Grosvenor Hotel Company Ltd (The) v Alfred McAlpine Management Ltd (1991) 56 Build LR 115   *300, 302, 307*
Chinnock v Marchioness of Ely (1865) 4 DeG J&S 638   *61*
CIBC Mortgages plc v Pitt [1993] 4 All ER 433   *440, 445*
City & Westminster Properties (1934) Ltd v Mudd [1958] 2 All ER 733   *214, 282*
City of Lincoln (Master & Owners) v Smith [1904] AC 250   *190*
Clark v Urquhart [1930] AC 28   *345, 346*
Clarke v Dickson (1858) EB&E 148   *332, 356, 573*
Clarke v The Earl of Dunraven and Mount-Earl (The *Satanita*) [1897] AC 59   *62*
Clea Shipping Corporation v Bulk Oil International Ltd (The *Alaskan Trader*) [1984] 1 All ER 129   *469*
Clydebank Engineering and Shipbuilding Co v Don Jose Ramos Yzquierdo y Castaneda [1905] AC 6   *553*
Coldunell Ltd v Gallon [1986] 1 All ER 429   *447*
Collins v Godefroy (1831) 9 LJOS 158   *106*
Combe v Combe [1951] 1 All ER 767   *131*
Compagnie de Commerce et Commission, SARL v Parkinson Stove Company Ltd [1953] 2 Lloyd's Rep 487   *49*

Cook v Wright (1861) 30 LJQB 321 *104*
Cooper v Phibbs (1867) LR 2 HL 149 *376, 377, 573*
Cort and Gee v Ambergate Nottingham and Boston and Eastern Junction Rly Co (1851) 17 QB 127 *485*
Cory v Thames Ironworks Co (1868) LR 3 QB 181 *528*
Cosgrove v Horsfall (1945) 175 LT 334 *190*
Couchman v Hill [1947] 1 All ER 103 *201, 204, **210**, 213, 214, 282*
Couldery v Bartrum (1881) 19 ChD 394 *150*
Courtney and Fairbairn Ltd v Tolaini Brothers (Hotels) Ltd [1975] 1 All ER 716 *75, 77, 78*
Couturier v Hastie (1856) 5 HLC 673 *383, 384, 385*
Craig deceased, *In Re* [1970] 2 All ER 390 *434*
Crane v Hegeman-Harris Co Inc [1939] 1 All ER 662 *413, 414, 415*
Cremdean Properties Ltd v Nash [1977] 244 EG 547 *365*
Crosse v Gardner (1688) Carth 90 *205, 218, 219*
Crowhurst v Laverack (1852) 8 Exch 208 *109*
CTN Cash and Carry Ltd v Gallaher Ltd [1994] 4 All ER 714 *429*
Cullinane v British 'Rema' Manufacturing Co Ltd [1953] 2 All ER 1257 *544*
Cumber v Wane (1721) 1 Str 426 *125, 150*
Cundy v Lindsay (1878) 3 App Cas 459 *375, 398, 400*
Currie v Misa (1875) LR 10 Ex 153 *93, 103*
Curtis v Chemical Cleaning & Dyeing Co Ltd [1951] 1 KB 805 *280*
Cutter v Powell (1795) [1775-1802] All ER Rep 159 *458, 461, 462, 513*

D & C Builders Ltd v Rees [1965] 3 All ER 837 *148, 421, 423, 455*
Dahl v Nelson, Donkin & Co [1881] 6 AC 38 *505*
Dakin (H) & Co Ltd v Lee [1916] 1 KB 566 *461, 462*
Danube and Black Sea Rly and Kustendjie Harbour Co Ltd v Xenos (1863) 13 CBNS 825 *486*
Daulia Ltd v Four Millbank Nominees Ltd [1978] 2 All ER 557 *67*
Davies v Sumner [1984] 1 WLR 1301 *298, 299*
Davis Contractors Ltd v Fareham Urban District Council [1956] 2 All ER 145 *244, 387, 392, **503**, 508, 509*
Davis v Foreman [1894] 3 Ch 654 *565*
Day v McLea (1889) 22 QBD 610 *151*
De Lassalle v Guildford [1900-3] All ER Rep 495 *142*
Deacon v Transport Regulation Board [1958] VR 458 *425*
Decro-Wall International SA v Practitioners in Marketing Ltd [1971] 2 All ER 216 *480*
Denny, Mott & Dickson Ltd v Fraser (James B) & Co Ltd [1944] 1 All ER 678 *503, 505, 509*
Denton v The Great Northern Railway Company (1856) 5 E&B 860 *14*
Derry v Peek (1889) 14 App Cas 337 *338, 339*
Dick Bentley Productions Ltd v Harold Smith (Motors) Ltd [1965] 2 All ER 65 *204, 212, 282*
Dickinson v Dodds (1876) 2 ChD 463 *45, 69, 71*
Dimmock v Hallett (1866) LR 2 Ch App 21 *323, 331*
Doherty v Allman (1878) 3 App Cas 709 *565*
Donoghue v Stevenson [1932] AC 562 *198*
Doyle v Olby (Ironmongers) Ltd [1969] 2 QB 158 *340, 344, 345, 346, 348*
Drimmie v Davies [1899] 1 IR 176 *178*
Drury v Victor Buckland Ltd [1941] 1 All ER 269 *219*
Dunlop Pneumatic Tyre Co Ltd v Selfridge & Co Ltd [1915] AC 847 *174, 179, 192*
Dunlop Pneumatic Tyre Company v New Garage and Motor Company [1915] AC 79 *551, 552*
Dunlop v Higgins (1848) 1 HL 381 *57, 58*
Durham Fancy Goods Ltd v Michael Jackson (Fancy Goods) Ltd [1968] 2 All ER 987 *134*

East Ham BC v Bernard Sunley & Sons Ltd [1965] 3 All ER 619 *546*
East v Maurer [1991] 1 WLR 461 *344*
Edgington v Fitzmaurice (1885) 29 ChD 459 *332, 334*

Edmunds *v* Merchants' Despatch Transportation Co (1883) 135 Mass 283   *401*
Edwards *v* Skyways Ltd [1964] 1 All ER 494   *166, 169, 171, 172*
Elder, Dempster & Co *v* Paterson, Zochonis & Co [1924] All ER Rep 135   *190, 192, 193*
Eliason *v* Henshaw (1819) 1 Wheaton 225   *55*
Empress Engineering Company, *Re* (1880) 16 ChD 125   *184*
England *v* Davidson (1840) 11 Ald & E 856   *106*
Enrico Furst & Co *v* W E Fischer Ltd [1960] 2 Lloyd's Rep 340   *138, 139*
Entores Ltd *v* Miles Far East Corporation [1955] 2 All ER 493   *37, 41, 43, 44*
Erlanger *v* New Sombrero Phosphate Co (1878) 3 App Cas 1218   *377*
Errington *v* Errington [1952] 1 All ER 149   *67*
Esso Petroleum Co Ltd *v* Harper's Garage (Stourport) Ltd [1965] 2 All ER 933   *245*
Esso Petroleum Co Ltd *v* Mardon [1976] 2 All ER 5   *169, 170*
Esso Petroleum Ltd *v* Commissioners of Customs and Excise [1976] 1 All ER 117   *170*
Eugenia, The: see Ocean Tramp Tankers Corpn *v* V/O Sovfracht [1964] 1 All ER 161   *244*
***Eurymedon*, The [1975] AC 154.** *See also* **New Zealand Shipping Co Ltd *v* AM Satterthwaite**
    and Co Ltd [1974] 1 All ER 1015   *24, 119, 183, 194, 195*
Evans & Son (Portsmouth) Ltd *v* Andrea Merzario Ltd [1976] 2 All ER 930   *281*
Evans *v* Llewellin (1787) 1 Cox 333   *454*
Evenden *v* Guildford City Association Football Club Ltd [1975] 3 All ER 269   *133*

F & B Entertainments Ltd *v* Leisure Enterprises Ltd (1976) 240 EG 455   *348*
Federal Commerce and Navigation Ltd *v* Molena Alpha Inc (The *Nanfri*, The *Benfri*, The
    Lorfri*) [1979] 1 All ER 307   *479, 484
Felthouse *v* Bindley (1862) 142 ER 1037   *45*
Fenner *v* Blake [1900] 1 QB 426   *130*
Fercometal SARL *v* Mediterranean Shipping Co SA (The *Simona*) [1988] 2 All ER 742   *471,*
    485
Ferguson *v* John Dawson & Partners (Contractors) Ltd [1976] 3 All ER 817   *241*
Fibrosa Spolka Akcyjna *v* Fairbairn Lawson Combe Barbour Ltd [1942] 2 All ER 122   *513,*
    515, 516, 573
Financings Ltd *v* Stimson [1962] 3 All ER 386   *70*
Firestone Tyre & Rubber Co Ltd *v* Vokins & Co Ltd [1951] 1 Lloyd's Rep 32   *283*
Fisher *v* Bell [1960] 3 All ER 731   *10, 11*
Fitch *v* Snedaker (1868) 38 NY 248   *61*
Foakes *v* Beer (1884) 9 AC 605   *124, 149, 150*
Foley *v* Classique Coaches Ltd [1934] 2 KB 1   *88, 89*
Forman *v* Wright (1851) 11 CB 481   *105*
Forster *v* Mackinnon (1869) LR 4 CP 704   *411*
Foster *v* Robinson [1950] 2 All ER 342   *132*
Frederick E Rose (London) Ltd *v* William H Pim Jnr & Co Ltd [1953] 2 All ER 739   *377, 414*
Freeman *v* Cooke (1848) 2 Ex 654   *382*
Freeth *v* Burr (1874) LR 9 CP 208   *480*
Frost *v* Knight (1872) LR 7 Exch 111   *486, 487*
Fry *v* Lane (1888) 40 ChD 312   *454*

Gabell *v* Same [1874–80] All ER Rep 166   *249*
Gaisberg *v* Storr [1949] 2 All ER 411   *132*
Gardner *v* Coutts & Co [1967] 3 All ER 1064   *240*
Gator Shipping Corporation *v* Trans-Asiatic Oil Ltd SA and Occidental Shipping Establishment
    (The *Odenfeld*) [1978] 2 Lloyd's Rep 357   *470*
George Mitchell (Chesterhall) Ltd *v* Finney Lock Seeds Ltd [1983] 2 All ER 737   *278, 303*
Gerhard *v* Bates (1853) 2 El & Bl 476   *334*
Gibbons *v* Proctor (1891) 64 LT 594   *61*
Gibson *v* Manchester City Council [1979] 1 All ER 972   *15*
Giles (C H) & Co Ltd *v* Morris [1972] 1 WLR 307   *569, 571*

Glamorganshire Coal Co Ltd v Glamorganshire Standing Joint Committee [1916] 2 KB 206 *107*

Glasbrook Bros Ltd v Glamorgan County Council [1924] All ER Rep 579 *107*

Goddard v O'Brien (1882) 9 QBD 37 *149, 150*

Golding v London & Edinburgh Insurance Co Ltd (1932) 43 Lloyd LR 487 *467, 487*

Gompertz v Bartlett (1853) 2 E&B 849 *373, 384*

Gore v Van der Lann [1967] 1 All ER 360 *180*

Gosling v Anderson [1972] EGD 709 *348*

Gould v Gould [1969] 3 All ER 728 *157, 162*

Governors of the Peabody Donation Fund v Sir Lindsay Parkinson & Co Ltd [1985] AC 210 *197*

Grainger & Son v Gough (Surveyor of Taxes) [1896] AC 325 *11*

Grant v Australian Knitting Mills Ltd [1936] AC 85 *536*

Great Northern Railway Company v Witham (1873) LR 9 CP 16 *36, 37, 120*

Greaves & Co (Contractors) Ltd v Baynham Meikle & Partners [1975] 3 All ER 99 *243*

Green (R W) Ltd v Cade Bros Farms [1978] 1 Lloyd's Rep 602 *303*

Green v Duckett (1883) 11 QBD 275 *454*

Green v Russell [1959] 2 All ER 525 *187*

Grigby v Cox (1750) 1 Ves Sen 517 *446*

Grimston v Cuningham [1894] 1 QB 125 *566*

Grist v Bailey [1966] 2 All ER 875 *369, 388, 389, 392*

Gurney v Wormersley (1854) 4 E&B 133 *373, 384*

Hadley v Baxendale (1854) 23 LJ Ex 179 *344, 525, 526, 529, 530, 532, 533, 534, 535*

Hall v North Eastern Railway Co (1895) LR 10 QB 437 *190*

Hall v Ross (1813) 1 Dow 201 *532, 533*

Hall v Wright (1858) EB & E 746 *490*

Hamlin v Great Northern Railway Co (1856) 1 H&N 408 *538*

Hammersley v De Biel (1845) 12 Cl & Fin 45 *160*

Hannah Blumenthal, The: *see* Paal Wilson and Co v Partenreederei Hannah Blumenthal [1983] 1 AC 854 *509*

Hansa Nord, **The [1975] 3 All ER 739.** *See also* **Cehave NV v Bremer Handelsgesellschaft GmbH *227, 231***

Harbutt's Plasticine Ltd v Wayne Tank and Pump Co Ltd [1970] 1 All ER 225 *284, 285, 287, 288*

Hare v Nicoll [1966] 1 All ER 285 *49*

Harling v Eddy [1951] 2 All ER 212 *201, 212, 266*

Harris v Great Western Railway Co (1876) 1 QBD 515 *252*

Harris v Nickerson (1873) 42 LJQB 171 *13*

Harris' Case (1872) LR 7 Ch App 587 *57*

Harrison & Jones Ltd v Bunten & Lancaster Ltd [1953] 1 All ER 903 *378*

Hart v Hart (1881) 18 ChD 670 *178, 560*

Hartley v Ponsonby (1857) 7 E&B 872 *110*

Hartog v Colin & Shields [1939] 3 All ER 566 *396*

Harvela Investments Ltd v Royal Trust Co of Canada (CI) Ltd [1985] 2 All ER 966 *18*

Hebb's Case (1867) LR 4 Eq 9 *58*

Hedley Byrne & Co Ltd v Heller & Partners Ltd [1963] 2 All ER 575 *196*

Heilbut, Symons & Co v Buckleton [1913] AC 30 *169, 172, 201, 202, 203, 206, 209, 214*

Helby v Matthews [1895] AC 471 *73*

Henderson v Stevenson (1875) LR 2 HL Sc 470 *252*

Henrik Sif, **The:** *see* Pacol Ltd v Trade Lines Ltd [1982] 1 Lloyd's Rep 456 *134*

Henthorn v Fraser [1891-94] All ER Rep 908 *48, 59*

Henty v Schroder (1879) 12 ChD 666 *477*

Herne Bay Steam Boat Co v Hutton [1903] 2 KB 683 *498*

Heron II, **The:** *see* Koufos v C Czarnikow Ltd [1967] 3 All ER 686 *529, 534, 535*

Heyman v Darwins Ltd [1942] 1 All ER 337 *287, 467, 473, 476, 477, 487*

Hicks v Gregory (1849) 8 CB 378 *109*

Hill v Harris [1965] 2 QB 601 *392*

Hillas and Co Ltd v Arcos Ltd [1932] All ER Rep 494   *72, 76, 81, 90*
Hirachand Punamchand v Temple [1911] 2 KB 330   *150, 180*
Hirji Mulji v Cheong Yue SS Co Ltd [1926] AC 497   *505, 507, 509, 512*
Hobbs v London & South Western Railway Co [1874–80] All ER Rep 458   *538*
Hochster v De la Tour (1853) 2 E&B 678   *486*
Hoenig v Isaacs [1952] 2 All ER 176   *460, 462*
Hollier v Rambler Motors (AMC) Ltd [1972] 1 All ER 399   *273*
Holwell Securities Ltd v Hughes [1974] 1 All ER 161   *48, 60*
Hong Kong Fir Shipping Co Ltd v Kawasaki Kisen Kaisha Ltd [1962] 1 All ER 474   *222, 223, 228, 229, 230, 231, 232, 480,*
Hopkins v Tanqueray (1854) 15 CB 130   *213, 214*
Horlock v Beal [1916] 1 AC 486   *503, 512*
Horsler v Zorro [1975] 1 All ER 584   *477*
Horton v Horton (No 2) [1961] 1 QB 215   *103*
Houghton v Trafalgar Insurance Company Ltd [1953] 2 All ER 1409   *267*
Hounslow London Borough Council v Twickenham Garden Developments [1971] 1 Ch 233   *469*
Household Fire and Carriage Accident Insurance Company (Ltd) v Grant (1879) 48 LJQB 577   *49, 58*
Howard Marine & Dredging Co Ltd v Ogden & Sons (Excavations) Ltd [1978] 2 All ER 1134   *342*
Howard v Bodington (1877) 2 PD 210   *55*
Howard v Pickford Tool Co Ltd [1951] 1 KB 417   *467, 487*
Howes v Bishop [1909] 2 KB 390   *445*
Hughes v Metropolitan Railway Co (1877) 2 AC 439   *126, 130, 132, 136, 139, 140, 142, 143, 144, 150*
Huguenin v Baseley (1807) 14 Ves Jun 273   *439*
Hussey v Horne-Payne (1879) LR 4 App Cas 311   *30*
Hyde v Windsor (Dean & Canons) (1597) Cro Eliz 552   *490*
Hyde v Wrench (1840) 3 Beav 334   *21, 24, 25, 27*
Hyman v Hyman [1929] AC 601   *133*
Hyman v Nye (1881) 6 QBD 685   *269*

Imodco Ltd v Wimpey Major Projects Ltd (1987) 40 BLR 1   *546*
Ingram v Little [1960] 3 All ER 332   *402, 404, 406, 407*
Interfoto Picture Library Ltd v Stiletto Visual Programmes Ltd [1988] 1 All ER 348   *260*
Intertradex SA v Lesieur-Tourteaux SARL [1978] 2 Lloyd's Rep 50   *510*

Jackson v Horizon Holidays Ltd [1975] 3 All ER 92   *181, 183*
Jackson v Union Marine Insurance Co Ltd (1874) 44 LJCP 27   *224, 225, 491, 503, 512*
Jacob & Youngs Inc v Kent (1921) 230 NY 239   *547*
Jarvis v Swans Tours Ltd [1973] 1 All ER 71   *348, 537*
Jesse v Roy (1834) 1 Cr M&R 316   *513*
John S Darbyshire, The: see Albion Sugar Co Ltd v Williams Tankers Ltd [1977] 2 Lloyd's Rep 457   *78*
Johnson v Agnew [1979] 1 All ER 883   *287, 476*
Johnson v Shrewsbury and Birmingham Ry Co (1853) 3 De GM & G 914   *561*
Johnstone v Milling (1886) 16 QBD 460   *487*
Jones v Barkley (1781) 2 Doug KB 684   *485*
Jones v Padavatton [1969] 2 All ER 616   *157, 158, 163*
Jones v Vernon's Pools Ltd [1938] 2 All ER 626   *165*
Jorden v Money (1854) 5 HL Cas 185   *129, 130*
Joscelyne v Nissen [1970] 1 All ER 1213   *412*
Joseph Constantine Steamship Line Ltd v Imperial Smelting Corporation Ltd [1942] AC 154   *509*
Junior Books Ltd v Veitchi Co Ltd [1982] 3 All ER 201   *196*

Junior K, The: *see* Star Steamship Society *v* Beogradska Plovidba [1988] 2 Lloyd's Rep 583   *78*

Karberg's Case [1892] 3 Ch 1   *328*
Karsales (Harrow) Ltd *v* Wallis [1956] 2 All ER 866   *285*
Kaufman *v* Gerson [1904] 1 KB 591   *421*
Keates *v* The Earl of Cadogan (1851) 20 LJCP 76   *324*
Kemble *v* Farren (1829) 6 Bing 141   *553*
Kennedy *v* Panama, New Zealand and Australian Royal Mail Co Ltd (1867) LR 2 QB 580
371, 373, 387, 574
King Construction Company *v* Smith Electric Co (1966) 350 SW 2d 940   *423*
King's Norton Metal Co Ltd *v* Edridge, Merrett & Co Ltd (1897) 14 TLR 98   *400,* 407, *408*
Kirchner & Co *v* Gruban [1909] 1 Ch 413   *565*
Kleinwort Benson Ltd *v* Malaysia Mining Corp Bhd [1989] 1 All ER 785   *168*
Knupp *v* Bell (1968) 67 DLR (2d) 256   *455*
Koufos *v* C Czarnikow Ltd (The *Heron II*) [1967] 3 All ER 686   *529, 534, 535*
Krell *v* Henry [1903] 2 KB 740   *493, 507*

L'Estrange *v* Graucob Ltd [1934] 2 KB 394   *250,* 280*
Lacey (William) (Hounslow) Ltd *v* Davis [1957] 2 All ER 712   *556, 557*
Lake *v* Simmons [1927] AC 487   *406*
Lampleigh *v* Braithwait (1615) Hob 105   *96, 98*
Langen & Wind Ltd *v* Bell [1972] 1 All ER 296   *560*
Langford & Co Ltd *v* Dutch 1952 SC 15   *466, 468, 470*
Langridge *v* Dorville (1821) 5 B & Ald 117   *105*
Larrinaga & Co Ltd *v* Société Franco-Americaine des Phosphates de Medulla (1923) 39 TLR 316
496, 507
Laurence *v* Lexcourt Holdings Ltd [1978] 1 WLR 1128   *392*
Lauritzen (J) AS *v* Wijsmuller BV (The *Super Servant Two*) [1990] 1 Lloyd's Rep 1   508
Leaf *v* International Galleries [1950] 1 All ER 693   *200, 355, 377, 378*
Ledingham *v* Bermejo Estancia Co Ltd [1947] 1 All ER 749   *132*
Leigh and Sillavan Ltd *v* Aliakmon Shipping Co Ltd [1986] AC 785   *197*
Les Affréteurs Réunis Société Anonyme *v* Leopold Walford (London) Ltd [1919] AC 801
184, 232
Levison *v* Patent Steam Carpet Cleaning Co Ltd [1977] 3 All ER 498   *288*
Lewis *v* Averay [1971] 3 All ER 907   *404*
Lewis *v* Clay (1897) 67 LJQB 224   *411*
Lindsay *v* Cundy (1876-8) 1 QBD 348   *376*
Lister *v* Romford Ice & Cold Storage Co Ltd [1957] AC 555   *238, 244*
Liverpool City Council *v* Irwin [1976] 2 All ER 39   *236, 241, 242, 243, 244*
Lloyd's *v* Harper (1880) 16 ChD 290   *177, 182, 183*
Lloyds Bank Ltd *v* Bundy [1974] 3 All ER 757   *433, 437, 453*
Long *v* Lloyd [1958] 2 All ER 402   *353*
Lord Elphinstone *v* Monkland Iron and Coal Co (1886) 11 App Cas 332   *553*
Lord Strathcona SS Co *v* Dominion Coal Co [1926] AC 108   *565*
Love & Stewart Ltd *v* S Instone & Co Ltd (1917) 33 TLR 475   *30, 84*
Lovell & Christmas Ltd *v* Wall (1911) 104 LT 85   *425*
Lovelock *v* Exportles [1968] 1 Lloyd's Rep 163   *85*
Low *v* Bouverie [1891-94] All ER Rep 348   *147*
Lucy, The: *see* Atlantic Lines & Navigation Co Inc *v* Hallam Ltd [1983] 1 Lloyd's Rep 188   *359*
Lumley *v* Wagner [1843-60] All ER Rep 368   *561, 562, 563, 565*
Luxor (Eastbourne) Ltd *v* Cooper [1941] AC 108   *68, 244*
Lynch *v* Thorne [1956] 1 All ER 744   *233*

Magee *v* Pennine Insurance Co Ltd [1969] 2 All ER 891   *388, 389, 417*
Majik Markets Pty Ltd *v* S & M Motor Repairs Pty Ltd (No 1) (1987) 10 NSWLR 49   *471*

Manchester Diocesan Council for Education *v* **Commercial and General Investments Ltd** **[1969] 3 All ER 1593** *52, 55, 69*
Maredelanto Compania Naviera SA *v* **Bergbau-Handel GmbH (The** *Mihalis Angelos*) **[1970] 3 All ER 125** *226, 229, 230*
Maritime National Fish Ltd *v* **Ocean Trawlers Ltd [1935] AC 524** *506, 509, 510*
Mark Rowlands Ltd *v* Berni Inns Ltd [1986] QB 211 *197*
Marshall *v* Broadhurst (1831) 1 Tyr 348 *490*
Maskell *v* Horner [1915] 3 KB 106 *421, 422, 423, 427, 454*
Maw *v* Jones (1890) 25 QBD 107 *541*
May & Butcher Ltd *v* **The King [1934] 2 KB 17** *74, 87, 90*
Mayson *v* Clouet [1924] AC 980 *477*
McArdle, *Re* **[1951] 1 All ER 905** *94*
McConnel *v* Wright [1903] 1 Ch 546 *340, 344, 345*
McCrone *v* Boots Farm Sales Ltd [1981] SLT 103 *302*
McCutcheon *v* **David MacBrayne Ltd [1964] 1 All ER 430** *257, 264, 273*
McGrath *v* **Shah (1989) 57 P&CR 452** *360*
McKenna *v* Richey [1950] VLR 360 *478*
McNally *v* Welltrade International Ltd [1978] IRLR 497 *348*
McRae *v* **Commonwealth Disposals Commission (1951) 84 CLR 377** *383, 390*
Medina *v* Stoughton (1700) 1 Salk 210 *205, 218, 219*
Mendelssohn *v* Normand Ltd [1969] 2 All ER 1215 *282*
Merritt *v* **Merritt [1970] 2 All ER 760** *156, 163*
Mersey Docks Trustees *v* Gibbs (1866) LR 1 HL 93 *236*
Midland Bank plc *v* **Massey [1995] 1 All ER 929** *451*
Midland Bank plc *v* Shephard [1988] 3 All ER 17 *447*
Mihalis Angelos, **The:** *see* **Maredelanto Compania Naviera SA** *v* **Bergbau-Handel GmbH [1970] 3 All ER 125** *226, 229, 230*
Milner (J H) & Son *v* Percy Bilton Ltd [1966] 2 All ER 894 *556*
Milnes *v* Gery (1807) 14 Ves Jun 400 *87*
Minscombe Properties Ltd *v* Sir Alfred McAlpine & Sons Ltd (1986) 2 Const LJ 303 *546*
Monarch Steamship Co Ltd *v* A/B Karlshamns Oljefrabriker [1949] 1 All ER 1 *527*
Mondel *v* Steel (1841) 8 M & W 858 *461*
Moorcock, **The [1886-90] All ER Rep 530** *234, 237, 238, 240*
Morley *v* Loughnan [1893] 1 Ch 736 *434*
Morris *v* Baron & Co [1918] AC 1 *123*
Morris *v* C W Martin & Sons Ltd [1965] 2 All ER 725 *288*
Morrison *v* Coast Finance Ltd (1965) 55 DLR (2d) 710 *455*
Moschi *v* **Lep Air Services Ltd [1972] 2 All ER 393** *288, 473, 477*
Mountford *v* Scott [1974] 1 All ER 248 *77*
Munro *v* Butt (1858) 8 El & B 738 *513*

Nanfri, **The:** *see* **Federal Commerce and Navigation Ltd** *v* **Molena Alpha Inc [1979] 1 All ER 307** *479, 484*
National Carriers Ltd *v* Panalpina (Northern) Ltd [1981] AC 675 *509*
National Westminster Bank plc *v* **Morgan [1985] 2 WLR 588** *429, 437, 438, 440, 457*
Nema, **The:** *see* Pioneer Shipping Ltd *v* BTP Tioxide Ltd [1981] 2 Lloyd's Rep 239 *509*
New York Star, **The:** *see* Port Jackson Stevedoring Pty Ltd *v* Salmond & Spraggon (Australia) Pty Ltd [1980] 3 All ER 257 *194*
New Zealand Shipping Co Ltd *v* **A M Satterthwaite & Co Ltd (The** *Eurymedon*) **[1974] 1 All ER 1015** *24, 119, 183, 194, 195*
Newbigging *v* **Adam (1886) 34 ChD 582** *351, 573*
Nicholson & Venn *v* **Smith-Marriott (1947) 177 LT 189** *379*
Nickoll *v* Ashton [1901] 2 KB 126 *494*
Nicolene Ltd *v* **Simmonds [1953] 1 All ER 822** *83*

Nile Co for Export of Agricultural Crops *v* H & J N Bennett (Commodities) Ltd [1986] 1 Lloyd's
   Rep 555   *78*
**North Ocean Shipping Co Ltd *v* Hyundai Construction Co Ltd (The *Atlantic Baron*) [1978] 3
   All ER 1170**   *111, 422, **423**, 426*
Norwich City Council *v* Harvey [1989] 1 WLR 828   *196*
Nottingham Patent Brick and Tile Co *v* Butler [1886–90] All ER Rep 1075   *364*
Nunan *v* Southern Railway Co [1923] 2 KB 703   *255*

**Occidental Worldwide Investment Corp *v* Skibs A/S Avanti, Skibs A/S Glarona, Skibs A/S
   Navalis (The *Siboen* and the *Sibotre*) [1976] 1 Lloyd's Rep 293**   *420, 421, 422, 423, 426*
Ocean Tramp Tankers Corpn *v* V/O Sovfracht (The *Eugenia*) [1964] 1 All ER 161   *244*
Odenfeld, The: *see* Gator Shipping Corporation *v* Trans-Asiatic Oil Ltd SA and Occidental
   Shipping Establishment [1978] 2 Lloyd's Rep 357   *470*
Oliver *v* Davis [1949] 2 All ER 353   *133*
Olley *v* Marlborough Court Ltd [1949] 1 All ER 127   *257, **258**, 276, 280*
Ormes *v* Beadel (1860) 2 Giff 166   *424, 439, 440, 455*
Oscar Chess Ltd *v* Williams [1957] 1 All ER 325   ***200**, 205, 212*
OTM Ltd *v* Hydranautics [1981] 2 Lloyd's Rep 211   *81*
Overbrooke Estates Ltd *v* Glencombe Properties Ltd [1974] 3 All ER 511   *364, 366*
Overseas Tankship (UK) Ltd *v* Morts Dock & Engineering Co Ltd (The *Wagon Mound* (No 1))
   [1961] 1 All ER 404   *533, 534*

Paal Wilson and Co *v* Partenreederei Hannah Blumenthal (The *Hannah Blumenthal*) [1983] 1
   Lloyd's Rep 103   *509*
Pacol Ltd *v* Trade Lines Ltd (The *Henrik Sif*) [1982] 1 Lloyd's Rep 456   *134*
Page One Records Ltd *v* Britton (trading as 'The Troggs') [1967] 3 All ER 822   *560, 563*
Pagnan SpA *v* Feed Products Ltd [1987] 2 Lloyd's Rep 601   *29*
Pamela, The: *see* Schelde Delta Shipping BV *v* Astarte Shipping Ltd [1995] 2 Lloyd's Rep 249
   42
Panoutsos *v* Raymond Hadley Corpn of New York [1917] 2 KB 473   *138, 139, 152*
Pao On *v* Lau Yiu [1979] 3 All ER 65   ***96**, 421, 426*
Paradine *v* Jane (1647) Aleyn 26   *224*
Parana, The (1877) 2 PD 118   *529, 533*
Parker *v* Bristol and Exeter Railway Co (1851) 6 Exch 702   *454*
Parker *v* Clark [1960] 1 All ER 93   *159, 160*
Parker *v* South Eastern Railway Co [1874-80] All ER Rep 166   *248, 249, 250, 251, **252**, 254,
   257, 260, 263,*
Parker *v* Taswell (1858) 2 DG & J 559   *560*
Parsons (H) (Livestock) Ltd *v* Uttley Ingham & Co Ltd [1978] 1 All ER 525   *534*
Partridge *v* Crittenden [1968] 2 All ER 421   *11*
Payne *v* Cave (1789) 3 Term Rep 148   *65*
Peek *v* Derry (1887) 37 ChD 541   *340*
Peek *v* Gurney (1873) LR 6 HL 377   *333*
Penarth Dock Engineering Co Ltd *v* Pounds [1963] 1 Lloyd's Rep 359   *543*
Perrott (J F) & Co Ltd *v* Cohen [1950] 2 All ER 939   *132*
Perry *v* Sharon Development Co Ltd [1937] 4 All ER 394   *234*
Pettitt *v* Pettitt [1970] AC 777   *163*
**Pharmaceutical Society of Great Britain *v* Boots Cash Chemists (Southern) Ltd [1952] 2 All
   ER 456; [1953] 1 All ER 482**   *7, 8*
Philips *v* Ward [1956] 1 All ER 874   *540*
Phillips *v* Brooks Ltd [1919] 2 KB 243   ***401**, 404, 406, 407*
Photo Production Ltd *v* Securicor Transport Ltd [1980] 1 All ER 556   *232, 278, 279, **283**,
   308, 310, **474***
Pickering *v* Bishop of Ely (1843) 2 Y & CCh Cas 249   *561*
Pigott's Case: *see* Cartwright *v* Rowley (1799) 2 Esp 723   *454*

Pinnel's Case [1558-1774] All ER Rep 612 *124, 125, 126, 149*
Pioneer Shipping Ltd *v* BTP Tioxide Ltd (The *Nema*) [1981] 2 Lloyd's Rep 239 *509*
Planché *v* Colburn [1824-34] All ER Rep 94 *554*
Plasticmoda Societa Per Azioni *v* Davidsons (Manchester) Ltd [1952] 1 Lloyd's Rep 527 *139*
Pollock (W & S) & Co *v* Macrae 1922 SC (HL) 192 *277*
Poosathurai *v* Kannappa Chettiar (1919) LR 47 IA 1 *437, 439, 440*
Port Jackson Stevedoring Pty Ltd *v* Salmond & Spraggon (Australia) Pty Ltd (The *New York Star*)
    [1980] 3 All ER 257 *194*
Porter (William) & Co Ltd, *Re* [1937] 2 All ER 361 *132*
Portman *v* Middleton (1858) 4 CBNS 322 *527*
Posner *v* Scott-Lewis [1986] 3 All ER 513 *569*
Post Chaser, The: *see* **Société Italo-Belge Pour Le Commerce et L'industrie *v* Palm and**
    Vegetable Oils (Malaysia) Sdn Bhd [1982] 1 All ER 19 *135, 151*
Price *v* Strange [1977] 3 All ER 371 *559*
Public Works Commissioner *v* Hills [1906] AC 368 *553*
Puerto Buitrago, The: *see* Attica Sea Carriers Corporation *v* Ferrostaal Poseidon Bulk Reederei
    GmbH [1976] 1 Lloyd's Rep 250 *470*
Pym *v* Campbell (1856) 6 E&B 370 *5*

R & B Customs Brokers Co Ltd *v* United Dominions Trust Ltd [1988] 1 WLR 321 *297, 301*
R *v* Clarke (1927) 40 CLR 227 *60*
Radford *v* De Froberville [1978] 1 All ER 33 *547*
Raffles *v* Wichelhaus (1864) 2 H&C 906 *394*
Rasbora Ltd *v* JCL Marine Ltd [1977] 1 Lloyd's Rep 645 *301*
Rawlins *v* Wickham (1858) 3 De GLJ 304 *575*
Reardon Smith Line Ltd *v* Yngvar Hansen-Tangen (trading as H E Hansen-Tangen) [1976] 1 WLR
    989 *231*
Redgrave *v* Hurd (1881) 20 ChD 1 *331, 334, 350, 574, 575*
Reese River Silver Mining Company *v* Smith (1869) LR 4 HL 64 *335*
Regalian Properties plc *v* London Dockland Development Corp [1995] 1 All ER 1005 *555*
Reid *v* Hoskins (1856) 6 E&B 953 *486, 487*
Reigate *v* Union Manufacturing Co (Ramsbottom) Ltd [1918] 1 KB 592 *240*
Richardson, Spence & Co *v* Rowntree [1894] AC 217 *251*
Riverlate Properties Ltd *v* Paul [1974] 2 All ER 656 *416*
Roberts (A) & Co Ltd *v* Leicestershire County Council [1961] 2 All ER 545 *415, 416*
Robertson *v* Minister of Pensions [1948] 2 All ER 767 *132*
Robertson *v* Wait (1853) 8 Ex 299 *184*
Robinson (William) & Co Ltd *v* Heuer [1898] 2 Ch 451 *566, 567*
Robinson *v* Harman [1843–60] All ER Rep 383 *545*
Rookes *v* Barnard [1964] 1 All ER 367 *151*
Roscorla *v* Thomas (1842) 3 QB 234 *94*
Rose & Frank Co *v* J R Crompton and Brothers Ltd [1925] AC 445 *164, 165, 167, 169,*
    171, 172
Ross T Smyth & Co Ltd *v* T D Bailey Son & Co [1940] 3 All ER 60 *480*
Routledge *v* Grant (1828) 6 LJCP 166 *57, 65*
Routledge *v* McKay [1954] 1 All ER 855 *201, 202, 203, **206**, 208*
Royscot Trust Ltd *v* Rogerson [1991] 3 All ER 294 *346*
Rust *v* Abbey Life Assurance Co Ltd [1979] 2 Lloyd's Rep 334 *472*
Rutter *v* Palmer [1922] 2 KB 87 *258, 273, 274, 275, 276*
Ruxley Electronics and Construction Ltd *v* Forsyth [1995] 3 All ER 268 *545*
Ryan *v* Mutual Tontine Westminster Chambers Association [1893] 1 Ch 116 *568, 569, 570, 571*
Ryder *v* Woodley (1862) 10 WR 294 *378*

Sabemo Pty Ltd *v* North Sydney Municipal Council [1977] 2 NSWLR 880 *556, 557*
Salisbury *v* Gilmore [1942] 1 All ER 457 *130*

Sanders & Forster Ltd *v* A Monk & Co Ltd [1980] CA Transcript 35 *81*

Santa Clara, **The:** *see* **Vitol SA *v* Norelf Ltd [1996] 3 All ER 193 *471***

Saunders *v* Anglia Building Society (*sub nom* Gallie *v* Lee) [1970] 3 All ER 961 *408, 410*

Scammell & Nephew Ltd *v* Ouston [1941] 1 All ER 14 *72, 84*

Scandinavian Trading Tanker Co AB *v* Flota Petrolera Ecuatoriana (The *Scaptrade*) [1983] 1 Lloyd's Rep 146 *78, 470*

Scaptrade, The: see Scandinavian Trading Tanker Co AB *v* Flota Petrolera Ecuatoriana [1983] 1 Lloyd's Rep 146 *78, 470*

Schebsman, *Re, ex parte* The Official Receiver, The Trustee *v* Cargo Superintendents (London) Limited and Schebsman [1944] 1 Ch 83 *176, 185, 188*

Schelde Delta Shipping BV *v* Astarte Shipping Ltd (The *Pamela*) [1995] 2 Lloyd's Rep 249 *42*

Schuler A G *v* Wickman Machine Tool Sales Ltd [1973] 2 All ER 39 *220*

Scotson *v* Pegg (1861) 30 LJEx 225 *118, 121*

Scott & Sons *v* Del Sel 1922 SC 592 *503*

Scott *v* Dixon (1859) 29 LJ Ex 62 *334*

Scottish Special Housing Association *v* Wimpey Construction UK Ltd [1986] 1 WLR 995 *197, 198*

Scriven Brothers & Co *v* Hindley & Co (1913) 3 KB 564 *395*

Scruttons Ltd *v* Midland Silicones Ltd [1962] AC 446 *179, 191, 195*

Secretary of State for Employment *v* Globe Elastic Trend Co [1979] 2 All ER 1077 *134*

Shadwell *v* Shadwell (1860) 30 LJCP 145 *116, 159*

Shanklin Pier Ltd *v* Detel Products Ltd [1951] 2 All ER 471 *217, 219*

Sharneyford Supplies Ltd *v* Edge [1987] Ch 305 *348*

Sheikh Bros Ltd *v* Ochsner [1957] AC 136 *389*

Shell UK Ltd *v* Lostock Garage Ltd [1977] 1 All ER 481 *243*

Shepheard *v* Broome [1904] AC 342 *349*

Shiloh Spinners Ltd *v* Harding [1973] AC 691 *570, 571*

Ship's Case, *sub nom* Scottish and Universal Finance Bank Ltd, *Re* (1865) 2 De G J&S 544 *373*

Shipley Urban District Council *v* Bradford Corpn [1936] Ch 375 *413, 415*

Shirlaw *v* Southern Foundries (1926) Ltd and Federated Foundries Ltd [1939] 2 All ER 113 *240*

Shuey *v* United States, Supreme Court of the United States (1875) 92 US 73 *66*

Siboen, **The:** *see* **Occidental Worldwide Investment Corp *v* Skibs A/S Avanti, Skibs A/S Glarona, Skibs A/S Navalis [1976] 1 Lloyd's Rep 293 *420,* *421, 422, 423, 426***

Sibree *v* Tripp (1846) 15 M & W 23 *149, 150*

Simona, **The:** *see* **Fercometal SARL *v* Mediterranean Shipping Co SA [1988] 2 All ER 742** *471, 485*

Simpkins *v* Pays [1955] 3 All ER 10 *161*

Sinclair *v* Bowles (1829) 9 B&C 92 *513*

Skeate *v* Beale (1841) 2 Ad & El 983 *420, 422, 423*

Sky Petroleum Ltd *v* VIP Petroleum Ltd [1974] 1 All ER 954 *567*

Slater *v* Jones (1873) LR 8 Exch 186 *180*

Smith New Court Securities Ltd *v* Scrimgeour Vickers (Asset Management) Ltd [1996] 4 All ER 769 *339*

Smith *v* Chadwick (1882) 20 ChD 27 *328, 332, 339*

Smith *v* Eric S Bush [1989] 2 All ER 514 *305, 312*

Smith *v* Hughes (1871) 40 LJQB 221 *2, 323, 371, 376, 380, 393, 396*

Smith *v* Land and House Property Corporation (1884) 28 ChD 7 *328, 329*

Smith *v* UMB Chrysler (Scotland) Ltd 1978 SC 1 HL *277, 278*

Snelling *v* John G Snelling Ltd [1972] 1 All ER 79 *179*

Société Italo-Belge Pour Le Commerce et L'industrie *v* Palm and Vegetable Oils (Malaysia) Sdn Bhd (The *Post Chaser*) [1982] 1 All ER 19 *135, 151*

Solle *v* Butcher [1950] 1 KB 671 *200, 355, 369,* **375,** *378, 384, 388, 389, 390, 392, 393, 417, 418, 573*

South Hetton Coal Co *v* Haswell Shotton and Easington Coal and Coke Co [1898] 1 Ch 465 *20*

South Wales Miners' Federation *v* Glamorgan Coal Co [1905] AC 239 *185*

Southall *v* Rigg (1851) 11 CB 481   *105*
Southern Water Authority *v* Carey [1985] 2 All ER 1077   *194, 197*
Sowler *v* Potter [1940] 1 KB 271   *376, 406*
Spellman *v* Spellman [1961] 2 All ER 498   *156*
Spencer *v* Harding (1870) LR 5 CP 561   *16, 36*
Spurling Ltd *v* Bradshaw [1956] 2 All ER 121   *258, 260, 262*
SSI Investors Ltd *v* Korea Tungsten Mining Co Ltd (1982) 449 NYS 2d 173   *20*
Stacey *v* Lintell (1879) 4 QBD 291   *109*
Stag Line Ltd *v* Tyne Shiprepair Group Ltd (The *Zinnia*) [1984] 2 Lloyd's Rep 211   *308, 309*
Star Steamship Society *v* Beogradska Plovidba (The *Junior K*) [1988] 2 Lloyd's Rep 583   *78*
State Trading Corp of India Ltd *v* M Golodetz Ltd (now Transcontinental Affiliates Ltd) [1989] 2
   Lloyd's Rep 277   *472*
Stedman *v* Swan's Tours (1951) 95 Sol Jo 727   *539*
Steele *v* Williams (1853) 8 Exch 625   *454*
Stephens *v* Cuckfield RDC [1960] 2 All ER 716   *312*
Stevenson (Jaques) & Co *v* McLean (1880) 5 QBD 346   *26*
Stewart Gill Ltd *v* Horatio Myer & Co Ltd [1992] 2 All ER 257   *313*
Stickney *v* Keeble [1915] AC 419   *152*
Stilk *v* Myrick (1809) 2 Camp 317   *106, 110, 112, 114, 115, 429*
Stratford (J T) & Son Ltd *v* Lindley [1964] 2 All ER 209   *151*
Sudagar Singh *v* Nazeer [1978] 3 All ER 817   *478*
Sudbrook Trading Estate Ltd *v* Eggleton [1982] 3 All ER 1   *86*
Suisse Atlantique Société D'Armement Maritime SA *v* NV Rotterdamsche Kolen Centrale [1966]
   2 All ER 61   *222, 284, 285, 286, 287*
Sumpter *v* Hedges (1898) 1 QB 673   *459*
Super Servant Two, The: *see* **Lauritzen (J) AS *v* Wijsmuller BV [1990] 1 Lloyd's Rep 1**   *508*
Surrey County Council *v* Bredero Homes Ltd [1993] 1 WLR 1361   *542, 576*
Symmons (Peter) & Co *v* Cook (1981) 131 NLJ 758   *298*
Synge *v* Synge [1894] 1 QB 466   *160*

Talbot *v* Talbot [1968] Ch 1   *87*
**Tamplin (F A) Steamship Co Ltd *v* Anglo-Mexican Petroleum Products Co Ltd [1916] 2 AC
   397**   *497, 500, 503, 504, 512*
Tamplin *v* James (1880) 15 ChD 215   *397, 411*
Tarrabochia *v* Hickie (1856) 1 H&N 183   *492*
Tate *v* Williamson (1866) 2 Ch App 55   *434, 455*
Tatem (W J) Ltd *v* Gamboa [1939] 1 KB 132   *496*
Taylor (C R) (Wholesale) Ltd *v* Hepworths Ltd [1977] 2 All ER 784   *547, 548*
Taylor *v* Caldwell (1863) B&S 826   *224, 387, 489, 493, 494, 496, 498, 499, 513, 514*
Taylor *v* Merchants Fire Insurance Co 9 How Sup Ct Rep 390   *57*
**Tenax Steamship Co Ltd *v* Owners of the motor vessel *Brimnes* (The *Brimnes*) [1974] 3 All
   ER 88**   *40, 41*
Thomas Bates & Son Ltd *v* Wyndham's (Lingerie) Ltd [1981] 1 All ER 1077   *415, 417*
Thomas *v* Thomas (1842) 2 QB 851   *101*
Thompson *v* London, Midland and Scottish Railway Company [1930] 1 KB 41   *248, 254, 257*
Thorne *v* Motor Trade Association [1937] 3 All ER 157   *427*
Thornett *v* Haines (1846) 15 M&W 367   *14*
Thornton *v* Shoe Lane Parking Ltd [1971] 1 All ER 686   *256, 261*
Tinn *v* Hoffmann & Co (1873) 29 LT 271   *53, 55*
Tito *v* Waddell (No 2) [1977] 3 All ER 129   *543, 548, 570*
Tool Metal Manufacturing Co Ltd *v* Tungsten Electric Co Ltd [1955] 2 All ER 657   *139, 143*
Torrance *v* Bolton (1872) LR 8 Ch 118   *375*
Toteff *v* Antonas (1952) 87 CLR 647   *345*
Trees Ltd *v* Cripps (1983) 267 EG 596   *78*
Trollope & Colls Ltd *v* Atomic Power Constructions Ltd [1962] 3 All ER 1035   *24, 25, 26, 32*

Trollope & Colls Ltd *v* North West Metropolitan Regional Hospital Board [1973] 2 All ER 260 *239*
Trollope and Sons *v* Martyn Brothers [1934] 2 KB 436 *69*
Tsakiroglou & Co Ltd *v* Noblee & Thorl GmbH [1961] 2 All ER 179 *501*
Tudor Grange Holdings Ltd *v* Citibank NA [1991] 4 All ER 1 *310*
Tufton *v* Sperni [1952] 2 TLR 516 *434, 455*
Turnbull & Co *v* Duval [1902] AC 429 *444, 445, 446, 447*
Turnbull (Peter) & Co Pty Ltd *v* Mundas Trading Co (Australasia) Pty Ltd [1954] 2 Lloyd's Rep 198 *232*
Turriff Construction Ltd *v* Regalia Knitting Mills Ltd (1971) 222 EG 169 *80*
Tweddle *v* Atkinson [1861-73] All ER Rep 369 *93, 101, 114, 174, 179, 192*
Twycross *v* Grant (1877) 2 CPD 469 *340*

UGS Finance Ltd *v* National Mortgage Bank of Greece [1964] 1 Lloyd's Rep 446 *285*
United Dominions Corporation (Jamaica) Ltd *v* Shoucair [1969] 1 AC 340 *122*
United Scientific Holdings Ltd *v* Burnley Borough Council [1978] AC 904 *232*
Universal Cargo Carriers Corpn *v* Citati [1957] 2 QB 401 *224*
Universe Tankships Inc of Monrovia *v* International Transport Workers Federation [1982] 2 WLR 803 *425*

Vanden Avenne Case: see Bremer Handelsgesellschaft mbH *v* Vanden Avenne-Izegem PVBA [1978] 2 Lloyd's Rep 109 *135, 136*
Vaswani *v* Italian Motors (Sales and Services) Ltd [1996] 1 WLR 270 *483*
Victoria Laundry (Windsor) Ltd *v* Newman Industries Ltd [1949] 1 All ER 997 *526, 529, 532, 533, 534*
Vince, *ex parte* Baxter, *Re* [1892] 2 QB 478 *84*
Vitol SA *v* Norelf Ltd (The *Santa Clara*) [1996] 3 All ER 193 *471*
Voest Alpine Intertrading GmbH *v* Chevron International Oil Co Ltd [1987] 2 Lloyd's Rep 547 *78*
Vorley *v* Cooke (1857) 1 Giff 230 *411*

Waddell *v* Blockey (1879) 4 QBD 678 *340*
Wagon Mound, The, (No 1): *see* Overseas Tankship (UK) Ltd *v* Morts Dock & Engineering Co Ltd [1961] 1 All ER 404 *533, 534*
Wakefield *v* Newton (1844) 6 QB 276 *420, 423*
Walford *v* Miles [1992] 1 All ER 453 *77*
Walker *v* Boyle [1982] 1 All ER 634 *361, 363*
Wallace *v* Hardacre 1 Camp 45 *431*
Wallis *v* Smith (1882) 21 ChD 243 *553*
Wallis, Son & Wells *v* Pratt & Haynes [1910] 2 KB 1003 *212, 213*
Ward *v* Byham [1956] 2 All ER 318 *108, 112, 474*
Warlow *v* Harrison (1859) 29 LJQB 14 *13, 14*
Warner Brothers Pictures Inc *v* Nelson [1936] 3 All ER 160 *562, 563, 564*
Warren *v* Mendy [1989] 3 All ER 103 *563*
Wathes (Western) Ltd *v* Austins (Menswear) Ltd [1976] 1 Lloyd's Rep 14 *288*
Watkins *v* Rymill (1883) 10 QBD 178 *257*
Watson *v* Swann (1862) 11 CBNS 756 *195*
Watts *v* Morrow [1991] 4 All ER 937 *539*
Watts *v* Spence [1976] Ch 165 *348*
Way *v* Latilla [1937] 3 All ER 759 *523*
Webster *v* Bosanquet [1912] AC 394 *553*
Webster *v* Cecil (1861) 30 Beav 62 *412*
Webster *v* Higgin [1948] 2 All ER 127 *215*
Wentworth *v* Cock (1839) 10 Ad & El 42 *490*
Wertheim *v* Chicoutimi Pulp Co [1911] AC 301 *527*

West Yorkshire Darracq Agency Ltd *v* Coleridge [1911] 2 KB 326   *180*
White & Carter (Councils) Ltd *v* McGregor [1961] 3 All ER 1178   *465*, *469, 470*
White *v* John Warwick & Co Ltd [1953] 1 WLR 1285   *269*
Whittaker *v* Campbell [1983] 3 All ER 582   *2*
Whittington *v* Seale-Hayne (1900) 82 Law Times 49   *350*
Whitwood Chemical Co *v* Hardman [1891] 2 Ch 416   *564, 565*
Whyte *v* Meade 2 Ir Eq Rep 420   *432*
Wickham, *Re* (1917) 34 TLR 158   *130*
Wickman Machine Tools Sales Ltd *v* Schuler AG [1972] 2 All ER 1173   *230*
William Lacey (Hounslow) Ltd *v* Davis [1957] 2 All ER 712   *81*
William Porter & Co Ltd, *Re* [1937] 2 All ER 361   *130, 132, 180, 181, 215*
William Sindall plc *v* Cambridgeshire County Council [1994] 3 All ER 932   *357, 391*
Williams *v* Bayley [1866] LR 1 HL 200   *431*, *455*
Williams *v* Carwardine (1833) 2 LJKB 101   *61, 62*
Williams *v* Moss' Empires Ltd [1915] 3 KB 242   *123*
Williams *v* Roffey Bros & Nicholls (Contractors) Ltd [1990] 1 All ER 512   *113*, *428*
Williams *v* Williams [1957] 1 All ER 305   *112*
Winn *v* Bull (1877) 47 LJCh 139   *31*
With *v* O'Flanagan [1936] 1 Ch 575   *325*
Wolverhampton Corporation *v* Emmons [1901] 1 QB 515   *571*
Wood Factory Pty Ltd *v* Kiritos Pty Ltd [1985] 2 NSWLR 105   *471*
Woodar Investment Development Ltd *v* Wimpey Construction UK Ltd [1980] 1 All ER 571
    182, *481, 483, 484*
Woodhouse AC (Israel) Cocoa Ltd SA *v* Nigerian Produce Marketing Co Ltd [1972] 2 All ER
    271   *146*
Wright *v* Vanderplank (1855) 2 K&J 1   *433*
Wrotham Park Estate Co Ltd *v* Parkside Homes Ltd [1974] 2 All ER 321   *542, 543, 544*

Yates Building Company Ltd *v* R J Pulleyn & Sons (York) Ltd (1976) 237 EG 183   *54*
Yerkey *v* Jones (1939) 63 CLR 649   *446, 447*

Zamet *v* Hyman [1961] 3 All ER 933   *435*
***Zinnia*, The:** *see* **Stag Line Ltd *v* Tyne Shiprepair Group Ltd [1984] 2 Lloyd's Rep 211**   *308,*
    309

Table of statutes and statutory materials

Arbitration Act 1889 *74, 90*
Bills of Lading Act 1855 *193*
Carriage of Goods by Sea Act 1924 *119*
Consumer Credit Act 1974 *457*
Consumer Safety Act 1978 *457*
Copyright Act 1956
  s 8 *99*
Factors Act 1889 *73*
Hire Purchase Act 1938 *73*
Insurance Companies Act 1982 *457*
Law of Property Act 1925
  s 40 *361*
  s 40(1) *360*
  s 41 ***463***
Law Reform (Frustrated Contracts) Act
  1943 *224*
  s 1 ***516***
  s 1(2) *518, 519*
  s 1(3) *518, 519, 520, 521, 522, 523, 524*
  s 2 ***517***
  s 2(3) *518, 523, 524*
Law Reform (Miscellaneous Provisions)
  Act 1970 *49*
Limitation Act 1939 *131*
Marine Insurance Act 1906
  s 14(2) ***189***
Married Women's Property Act 1882
  s 11 ***188***
  s 17 *158*
Merchant Shipping Act Amendment Act
  1862 *63*
Misrepresentation Act 1967 *538*
  s 1 ***322***, *359, 365*
  s 2(1) ***322, 342***, *343, 344, 347, 348,
    349, 365*
  s 2(2) ***322***, *357, 358, 359*
  s 3 ***323***, *357, 358,* ***359***, *360, 361, 362,
    363, 364, 365, 366, 367*
National Assistance Act 1948
  s 42 *109*

Occupiers' Liability Act 1957 *237*
Pharmacy and Poisons Act 1933
  s 18(1) *7, 9*
Police Pensions Act 1980 *107*
Protection of Birds Act 1954
  s 6 *11*
Purchase Tax Act 1963 *171*
Restriction of Offensive Weapons Act 1959
  s 1(1) *10*
Road Traffic Act 1988
  s 148(7) ***188***
Sale of Goods Act 1893 *36, 73, 75, 224,
  225, 385, 387, 475*
  s 6 *385*
  s 11 *203, 355, 220*
  s 11(1) *228, 229, 230, 355*
  s 13 *267*
  s 14 *230, 303*
  s 35 *355*
  s 55(4) *301, 303, 305*
  s 61(2) *229*
Sale of Goods Act 1979
  s 10 ***464***
  s 14 *232, 233, 297*
  s 23 *356*
  s 55 *278, 279, 305*
Supply of Goods (Implied Terms) Act
  1973 *457*
Supply of Goods and Services Act 1982 *457*
Theft Act 1968
  s 12(1) *2, 4*
Trade Descriptions Act 1968 *298, 299*
Unfair Contract Terms Act 1977 *286, 288*
  s 1 ***290***, *296*
  s 2 *191,* ***290***, *296, 305, 309, 311, 312,
    313, 359*
  s 3 ***291***, *300, 309, 311, 312, 314, 315*
  s 4 ***291***, *313*
  s 5 ***291***
  s 6 ***292***, *296, 297, 301, 316*

Unfair Contract Terms Act 1977 (continued)
   s 7 *292, 309, 314, 315, 316*
   s 8 *359, 360, 361, 363*
   s 9 *293*
   s 10 *293, 311, 312, 313*
   s 11 *293, 301, 305, 307, 308, 309, 315,*
      316, 323, 359, 361, 362, 363
   s 12 *294, 297, 298, 299, 301*
   s 13 *294, 314, 315*
   s 14 *294*
   s 17 *302*
   Sch 1 *295, 296, 313*
   Sch 2 *295, 309, 310, 315, 316*

Unfair Terms in Consumer Contracts
   Regulations 1994 *316*
   Art 1 *317*
   Art 2 *317*
   Art 3 *318*
   Art 4 *318*
   Art 5 *318*
   Art 6 *318*
   Art 7 *319*
   Art 8 *319*
   Sch 1 *319*
   Sch 2 *319*
   Sch 3 *320*

1 Agreement and offer

PRELIMINARY MATTERS

The law of contract is the most important subject in law that you will study. It underpins all aspects of commercial law and is relevant even to the criminal law.

Definition: **A contract is an agreement (usually between two persons) giving rise to obligations on the part of both persons which are enforced or recognised by law.**

Warning: Since, for the most part, the law of contract is a common law subject, do not take any definition you are given as being the only definition. Treat it in the above instance as a working definition to help you analyse contract cases.

AGREEMENT

Time and time again you will be brought back to the fact that the fundamental basis of contract law is the *agreement* of the contracting parties.

What distinguishes the law of contract from other branches of law is that it does not lay down a number of rights and duties which the law will enforce. In other words, the law of contract does not lay down a list of what is either legal or illegal, or what must or must not be included in a contract.

The law of contract lays down a general framework of principles, subject to which the parties may create rights and duties for themselves, which the law will uphold.

The parties to a contract, in a sense, make the law for themselves: so long as they do not infringe some legal prohibition, they can make what rules they like in respect of the subject-matter of their agreement, and the law will give effect to their decisions.

For example, if June says to Fred that he can buy her pen for £100 and he agrees, there will be a legally enforceable contract between June and Fred. The fact that Fred may have been foolish in agreeing to buy a pen that is only worth £1 is irrelevant – the parties to the contract have *agreed* to the price of £100.

Whereas it is generally true that agreement is reached when one person accepts the offer of the other person – in other words there is an *actual* agreement between the two persons, there are two qualifications: first, the objective appearance and, secondly, terms implied by law. The first qualification is dealt with below; the second will be dealt with later in this book.

Objective appearance of agreement

The law is also concerned with the *objective* appearance, as well as the actual fact, of agreement.

For example, if Gill makes an offer to Anne and Anne says that she accepts the offer, but secretly she does not intend to accept the offer, there is in fact not an agreement because Anne has not agreed. However, to an outsider viewing the situation, there would appear to be an agreement. In other words objectively there appears to be an agreement between Gill and Anne. In such a case the court would say that there was an agreement between them.

Apply the principle in the next quote, sometimes known as the rule in *Smith* v *Hughes*, to the example just considered.

Smith v Hughes

(1871) 40 LJQB 221 • Queen's Bench

Blackburn J: '. . . If, whatever a man's real intention may be, he so conducts himself that a reasonable man would believe that he was assenting to the terms proposed by the other party, and that other party upon that belief enters into the contract with him, the man thus conducting himself would be equally bound as if he had intended to agree to the other party's terms . . . '

The next case is a more recent one which deals with the objective test. It demonstrates one of the points made at the start of the book about reading contract cases. The 'catchwords' for the case are: crime; theft; taking conveyance without authority; owner's consent obtained by means of fraudulent misrepresentation; whether 'consent' vitiated; and the Theft Act 1968 s 12(1). To the inexperienced eye it looks only as if it is a criminal law case, but contract law is used by the judge to help resolve the criminal issues.

Whittaker v Campbell

[1983] 3 All ER 582 • Queen's Bench

Whittaker, who did not hold a full driving licence, told Robson, the director of a vehicle-hire business, that he was Dunn and presented him with Dunn's driving licence, which he had found earlier. This misrepresentation led Robson to hire a van to Whittaker, who signed the hire agreement as Dunn. Had Robson known that Whittaker did not possess a driving licence, he would not have hired the van to him. Whittaker was convicted at the magistrates' court of taking the vehicle without the owner's consent or other lawful authority, contrary to the Theft Act 1968 s 12(1). Whittaker's appeal to the Crown Court was dismissed on the ground that Robson had not consented to Whittaker taking the van since Whittaker's deception had rendered Robson's consent invalid.

Whittaker appealed by way of case stated to the Queen's Bench Division of the High Court.

Robert Goff LJ: 'We are concerned in present case with the construction of certain words, viz, "without having the consent of the owner", in their context in a particular subsection of a criminal statute. However the concept of consent is relevant in many branches of the law, including not only certain crimes but also the law of contract and the law of property. There is, we believe, danger in assuming that the law adopts a uniform definition of the word "consent" in all its branches.

Furthermore there is, in our opinion, no general principle of law that fraud vitiates consent. Let us consider this proposition first with reference to the law of contract. In English law, every valid contract presupposes an offer by one party which has been accepted by the offeree. Plainly, there can be no such acceptance unless offer and acceptance correspond: the offer can only be accepted by the offeree, the acceptance must relate to the same subject matter as the offer, and must also be, in all material respects, in the same terms as the offer. But the test whether there has been correspondence between offer and acceptance is not subjective but objective. If there is objective agreement, there may be a binding contract, even if in his mind one party or another has not consented to it – a principle recently affirmed by the Court of Appeal in *Centrovincial Estates plc* v *Merchant Investors Assurance Co Ltd*. Furthermore, putting on one side such matters as the ancient doctrine of *non est factum* and relief from mistake in equity, there is no principle of English law that any contract may be "avoided", i.e. not come into existence, by reason simply of a mistake, whether a mistake of one or both parties. The question is simply whether objective agreement has been reached and, if so, upon what terms. If objective agreement has been reached, in the sense we have described, then the parties will be bound, unless on a true construction the agreement was subject to a condition precedent, express or implied, failure of which has in the event prevented a contract from coming into existence.

What is the effect of fraud? Fraud is, in relation to a contract, a fraudulent misrepresentation by one party which induces the other to enter into a contract or apparent contract with the representor. Apart from the innocent party's right to recover damages for the tort of deceit, the effect of the fraud is simply to give the innocent party the right, subject to certain limits, to rescind the contract. These rights are similar to (though not identical with) the rights of a party who has been induced to enter into a contract by an innocent, as opposed to a fraudulent, misrepresentation; though there the right to recover damages derives from statute, and the limits to rescission are somewhat more severe. It is plain, however, that in this context fraud does not "vitiate consent", any more than an innocent misrepresentation "vitiates consent". Looked at realistically, a misrepresentation, whether fraudulent or innocent, induces a party to enter into a contract in circumstances where it may be unjust that the representor should be permitted to retain the benefit (the chose in action) so acquired by him. The remedy of rescission, by which the unjust enrichment of the representor is prevented, though for historical and practical reasons treated in books on the law of contract, is a straightforward remedy in restitution subject to limits which are characteristic of that branch of the law.

The effect of rescission of a contract induced by a misrepresentation is that property in goods transferred under it may be revested in the transferor (the misrepresentee). But this may not be possible if the goods have been transferred to a third party, for the intervention of third party rights may preclude rescission. In such a case, especially if the misrepresentor has disappeared from the scene or is a man of straw so that damages are an ineffective remedy, the misrepresentee's only practical course may be to seek to establish that there never was any contract (i.e. that the supposed contract was "void"), so that he never parted with the property in the goods and he can claim the goods or their value from the third party. To succeed in such a claim, he has generally to show that there was no objective agreement between him and the representor. For that purpose, however, the misrepresentation (fraudulent or innocent) is simply the origin of a set of circumstances in which it may be shown that there was no objective agreement, e.g. that the offer was, objectively speaking, made to one person and (perhaps as a result of fraud) objectively speaking, accepted by another. Again, it cannot be said that fraud "vitiates consent"; fraud was merely the occasion for an apparent contract which was, in law, no contract at all.

Robert Goff LJ went on to hold that Whittaker's misrepresentation had not vitiated Robson's consent and that, therefore, Whittaker's conviction under Theft Act 1968 s 12(1) should be quashed.

Robert Goff LJ states above 'There is, we believe, danger in assuming that the law adopts a uniform definition of the word "consent" in all its branches'. In his judgment didn't Robert Goff LJ assume that the word 'consent' had a uniform meaning in all branches of law?

Centrovincial Estates plc v Merchant Investors Assurance Company Ltd
[1983] Com LR 158 • Court of Appeal

Centrovincial's solicitors wrote to Merchant Investors, stating 'Our clients and the Board are advised that the appropriate rental value at the review date of 25th December 1982 is £65 000.00 per annum, and you are accordingly invited to agree this figure.' The figure of £65 000 should have read £126 000 but Merchant Investors were not aware of the mistake. Merchant Investors' chartered surveyor wrote back to Centrovincial's solicitors stating, 'I am authorised by Merchant Investors to agree the figure of £65 000.00 per annum as being the appropriate rental value at the review date of 25th December 1982.'

Centrovincial contended that no contract was formed because of the mistake and Merchant Investors contended that a contract had been formed.

Slade LJ: 'In the absence of any proof, as yet, that the defendants either knew or ought reasonably to have known of the plaintiffs' error at the time when they purported to accept the plaintiffs' offer, why should the plaintiffs now be allowed to resile from that offer? It is a well-established principle of the English law of contract that an offer falls to be interpreted not subjectively by reference to what has actually passed through the mind of the offeror, but objectively, by reference to the interpretation which a reasonable man in the shoes of the offeree would place on the offer. It is an equally well-established principle that ordinarily an offer, when unequivocally accepted according to its precise terms, will give rise to a legally binding agreement as soon as acceptance is communicated to the offeror in the manner contemplated by the offer, and cannot thereafter be revoked without the consent of the other party. Accepting, as they do, that they have not yet proved that the defendants knew, or ought reasonably to have known, of their error at the relevant time, how can the plaintiffs assert that the defendants have no realistic hope of establishing an agreement of the relevant nature . . .'

Although the law is concerned with the objective appearance, as well as the actual fact, of agreement, if the intention of the parties is clear then their intention will prevail over any objective appearance.

Pym v Campbell

(1856) 6 E & B 370 • Queen's Bench

Campbell entered into a written agreement with Pym to buy three eighths of the benefits of Pym's invention for £800 'which if Abernethie [an engineer] approved the invention, should be the agreement, but, if Abernethie did not approve, should not be one'. The written agreement was, on the face of it, a clear contract signed by both parties. Abernethie did not approve the invention. Campbell claimed that, despite the existence of a written agreement signed by both parties, there was no contract.

Erle J: 'I think that this rule ought to be discharged. The point made is that this is a written agreement, absolute on the face of it, and that evidence was admitted to shew it was conditional: and if that had been so it would have been wrong. But I am of opinion that the evidence shewed that in fact there was never any agreement at all. The production of a paper purporting to be an agreement by a party, with his signature attached, affords a strong presumption that it is his written agreement; and, if in fact he did sign the paper *animo contrahendi*, the terms contained in it are conclusive, and cannot be varied by parol evidence: but in the present case the defence begins one step earlier: the parties met and expressly stated to each other that, though for convenience they would then sign the memorandum of the terms, yet they were not to sign it as an agreement until Abernethie was consulted. I grant the risk that such a defence may be set up without ground; and I agree that a jury should therefore always look on such a defence with suspicion: but, if it be proved that in fact the paper was signed with the express intention that it should not be an agreement, the other party cannot fix it as an agreement upon those so signing. The distinction in point of law is that evidence to vary the terms of an agreement in writing is not admissible, but evidence to shew that there is not an agreement at all is admissible.'

OFFER

Definition: **an offer is a proposition put by one person to another person made with the intention that it shall become legally binding as soon as it is accepted by the other person.**

An offer may be made to an individual, or a group of persons, or to the world at large.

Carlill v Carbolic Smoke Ball Co

[1893] 1 QB 256 • Court of Appeal

The Carbolic Smoke Ball Company published an advertisement which read '£100 reward will be paid by the Carbolic Smoke Ball Company to any person who contracts the influenza after having used the ball three times daily for two weeks according to the printed directions supplied with each ball. £1,000 is deposited with the Alliance Bank, showing our sincerity in the matter.' Mrs Carlill used the smoke ball as directed but still caught the 'flu. She sued for the £100.

Bowen LJ: 'It was also said that the contract is made with all the world – that is, with everybody; and that you cannot contract with everybody. It is not a contract made with all the world. There is the fallacy of the argument. It is an offer made to all the world; and why should not an offer be made to all the world which is to ripen into a contract with anybody who comes forward and performs the condition? It is an offer to become liable to any one who, before it is retracted, performs the condition, and, although the offer is made to the world, the contract is made with that limited portion of the public who come forward and perform the condition on the faith of the advertisement. It is not like cases in which you offer to negotiate, or you issue advertisements that you have got a stock of books to sell, or houses to let, in which case there is no offer to be bound by any contract. Such advertisements are offers to negotiate – offers to receive offers – offers to chaffer, as, I think, some learned judge in one of the cases has said. If this is an offer to be bound, then it is a contract the moment the person fulfils the condition.'

OFFER OR INVITATION TO TREAT

It can be very difficult to distinguish between an *offer* and an *invitation to treat*. Basically it depends primarily on *the intention* with which a statement is made.

Definition: **An invitation to treat is said to be a statement made by one person asking the other to make the first person an offer.**

An invitation to treat is sometimes described as 'an offer to make an offer'. This is not a very helpful way of describing an invitation to treat.

If a proposition is made by one person *with the intention* that if the other party accepts that proposition there will then be a contract between them, then that proposition is *an offer*.

If a proposition is made by one person *with the intention* that if the other party accepts that proposition there will *not* be a contract between them at that stage, then that proposition is *an invitation to treat*.

In the examples of invitations to treat that follow, consider carefully what proposition or factual situation made the court decide that it was an invitation to treat and not an offer.

Carefully identify the particular elements of the facts of the cases that persuaded the courts that what was intended by one of the parties was an invitation to treat and not an offer.

Examples of invitation to treat

Goods on display

In the following case you are provided with the full text of the judgment in the Queen's Bench Division and in the Court of Appeal. Use this case as an exercise in how to read a case.

1   Summarise the facts of the case, say in about 100 words.
2   Identify the point that the court had to decide.
3   Identify the cases that were cited by the judge.
4   Identify what the judge decided.
5   State who won the case.

When you read the case, think about why the court is treating particular actions as offers or as invitations to treat. What practical difference might it make if the court had decided differently?

Pharmaceutical Society of Great Britain v Boots Cash Chemists (Southern) Ltd

[1952] 2 All ER 456 • Queen's Bench

Lord Goddard CJ: 'This is a Special Case stated under RSC, Ord 34, r 1, and agreed between the parties and it turns on s 18 (1) of the Pharmacy and Poisons Act, 1933, which provides:

> "Subject to the provisions of this Part of this Act, it shall not be lawful – (a) for a person to sell any poison included in Part I of the Poisons List, unless – (i) he is an authorised seller of poisons; and (ii) the sale is effected on premises duly registered under Part I of this Act; and (iii) the sale is effected by, or under the supervision of, a registered pharmacist."

The defendants have adopted what is called a "self-service" system in some of their shops – in particular, in a shop at 73 Burnt Oak Broadway, Edgware. The system of self-service consists in allowing persons who resort to the shop to go to shelves where goods are exposed for sale and marked with the price. They take the article required and go to the cash desk, where the cashier or assistant sees the article, states the price, and takes the money. In the part of the defendants' shop which is labelled "Chemist's dept" there are on certain shelves ointments and drugs, some of which contain poisonous substances but in such minute quantities that there is no acute danger. These substances come within Part I of the Poisons List, but the medicines in the ordinary way may be sold without a doctor's prescription and can be taken with safety by the purchaser. There is no suggestion that the defendants expose dangerous drugs for sale. Before any person can leave with what he has bought he has to pass the scrutiny and supervision of a qualified pharmacist.

The question for decision is whether the sale is completed before or after the intending purchaser has paid his money, passed the scrutiny of the pharmacist, and left the shop, or, in other words, whether the offer out of which the contract arises is an offer of the purchaser or an offer of the seller.

In *Carlill* v *Carbolic Smoke Ball Co* a company offered compensation to anybody who, having used the carbolic smoke ball for a certain length of time in a prescribed manner, contracted influenza. One of the inducements held out to people to buy the carbolic smoke ball was a representation that it was a specific against influenza. The plaintiff used it according to the prescription, but, nevertheless, contracted influenza. She sued the Carbolic Smoke Ball Co for the compensation and was successful. In the Court of Appeal Bowen LJ, said:

> " . . . there can be no doubt that where a person in an offer made by him to another person, expressly or impliedly intimates a particular mode of acceptance as sufficient to make the bargain binding, it is only necessary for the other person to whom such offer is made to follow the indicated method of acceptance; and if the person making the offer, expressly or impliedly intimates in his offer that it will be sufficient to act on the personal without communicating acceptance of it to himself, performance of the condition is a sufficient acceptance without notification."

Counsel for the plaintiffs says that what the defendants did was to invite the public to come into their shop and to say to them: "Help yourself to any of these articles, all of which are priced", and that that was an offer by the defendants to sell to any person who came into the shop any of the articles so priced. Counsel for the defendants, on the other hand, contends that there is nothing revolutionary in this kind of trading, which, he says, is in no way different from the exposure of goods which a shop-keeper sometimes makes outside or inside his premises, at the same time leaving some goods behind the counter. It is a well-established principle that the mere fact that a shop-keeper exposes goods which indicate to the public that he is willing to treat does not amount to an offer to sell. I do not think I ought to hold that there has been here a complete reversal of that principle merely because a self-service scheme is in operation. In my opinion, what was done here came to no more than that the customer was informed that he could pick up an article and bring it to the shop-keeper, the contract for sale being completed if the shop-keeper accepted the customer's offer to buy. The offer is an offer to buy, not an offer to sell. The fact that the supervising pharmacist is at the place where the money has to be paid is an indication that the purchaser may or may not be informed that the shop-keeper is willing to complete the contract. One has to apply common sense and the ordinary principles of commerce in this matter. If one were to hold that in the case of self-service shops the contract was complete directly the purchaser picked up the article, serious consequences might result. The property would pass to him at once and he would be able to insist on the shop-keeper allowing him to take it away, even where the shop-keeper might think it very undesirable. On the other hand, once a person had picked up an article, he would never be able to put it back and say that he had changed his mind. The shop-keeper could say that the property had passed and he must buy.

It seems to me, therefore, that it makes no difference that a shop is a self-service shop and that the transaction is not different from the normal transaction in a shop. The shop-keeper is not making an offer to sell every article in the shop to any person who may come in, and such person cannot insist on buying by saying: "I accept your offer". Books are displayed in a bookshop and customers are invited to pick them up and look at them even if they do not actually buy them. There is no offer of the shop-keeper to sell before the customer has taken the book to the shop-keeper or his assistant and said that he wants to buy it and the shop-keeper has said: "Yes." That would not prevent the shop-keeper, seeing the book picked up, from saying: "I am sorry I cannot let you have that book. It is the only copy I have got, and I have already promised it to another customer". Therefore, in my opinion, the mere fact that a customer picks up a bottle of medicine from a shelf does not amount to an acceptance of an offer to sell, but is an offer by the customer to buy. I feel bound also to say that the sale here was made under the supervision of a pharmacist. There was no sale until the buyer's offer to buy was accepted by the acceptance of the purchase price, and that took place under the supervision of a pharmacist. Therefore, judgment is for the defendants.'

When you now read the judgment of the Court of Appeal look at whether Somervell, Birkett and Romer LJJ agreed with Lord Goddard CJ's judgment. Try to identify two or three sentences from each of their judgments that you think shows whether they agreed or disagreed with Lord Goddard CJ.

Pharmaceutical Society of Great Britain v Boots Cash Chemists (Southern) Ltd

[1953] 1 All ER 482 • Court of Appeal

Somervell LJ, stated the facts and continued: 'One of the duties of the plaintiffs, the Pharmaceutical Society, who were incorporated by Royal Charter, is to take all reasonable steps to enforce the provisions of the Pharmacy and Poisons Act, 1933. The provision of that Act here in question is s 18 (1) which provides:

> "Subject to the provisions of this Part of this Act, it shall not be lawful – (a) for a person to sell any poison included in Part I of the Poisons List, unless . . . (iii) the sale is effected by, or under the supervision of, a registered pharmacist."

The point which is taken by the plaintiffs is this. It is suggested that the purchase is complete if and when a customer going round the shelves in this shop of the defendants takes an article and puts it in the receptacle which he or she is carrying, and, therefore, when the customer comes to the pay desk, the registered pharmacist, even if he is so minded, has no power to say: "This drug ought not to be sold to this customer."

I agree with the Lord Chief Justice in everything he said on the matter, but I will put it shortly in my own words. Whether the plaintiffs' contention is right depends on what are the legal implications of the arrangements in this shop. Is the invitation which is made to the customer to be regarded as an offer which is completed so that both sides are bound when the article is put into the receptacle, or is it to be regarded as a more organised way of doing what is already done in many types of shops – and a bookseller is, perhaps, the best example – namely, enabling customers to have free access to what is in the shop, to look at the different articles, and then, ultimately, having taken the one which they wish to buy, to come to the assistant and say: "I want this"? Generally speaking, the assistant will say: "that is all right", the money passes, and the transaction is completed. I agree entirely with what the Lord Chief Justice says and the reasons he gives for his conclusion that in the case of the ordinary shop, although goods are displayed and it is intended that customers should go and choose what they want, the contract is not completed until the customer has indicated the article which he needs and the shopkeeper or someone on his behalf accepts that offer. Not till then is the contract completed, and, that being the normal position, I can see no reason for drawing any different inference from the arrangements which were made in the present case.

The Lord Chief Justice expressed what I consider one of the most formidable difficulties in the way of the plaintiffs' case when he pointed out that, if they were right, once an article has been placed in the receptacle the customer himself is bound and he would have no right, without paying for the first article, to substitute an article which he saw later of the same kind and which he preferred. I can see no reason for implying from this arrangement any position other than that which the Lord Chief Justice found, namely, that it is a convenient method of enabling customers to see what there is for sale, to choose, and, possibly, to put back and substitute, articles which they wish to have, and then go to the cashier and offer to buy what they have chosen. On that conclusion the case fails, because it is admitted that in those circumstances there was supervision in the sense required by the Act and at the appropriate moment of time. For these reasons, in my opinion, the appeal should be dismissed.'

Birkett LJ: 'I am of the same opinion. The short point of the matter is: At what point of time did the sale in this shop take place? My Lord has explained the system which has been introduced into that shop, and, possibly, other shops since. It is said, on the one hand, that when the customer takes the package from the poison section and puts it into her basket the sale takes place there and then. On the other hand, it is said that the sale does not take place until the customer who has placed that package in her basket comes to the exit. The Lord Chief Justice dealt with the matter in this way, and I would like to adopt his words:

> "It seems to me, therefore, applying commonsense to this class of transaction, there is no difference merely because a self-service is advertised. It is no different really from

the normal transaction in a shop . . . I am quite satisfied it would be wrong to say the shopkeeper is making an offer to sell every article in the shop to any person who might come in and that he can insist by saying: 'I accept your offer'."

Then he goes on to deal with the illustration of the bookshop and continues:

"Therefore, in my opinion, the mere fact that a customer picks up a bottle of medicine from the shelves in this case does not amount to an acceptance of an offer to sell. It is an offer by the customer to buy. I daresay this case is one of great importance, it is quite a proper case for the Pharmaceutical Society to bring, but I think I am bound to say in this case the sale was made under the supervision of a pharmacist. By using the words: 'The sale is effected by, or under the supervision of, a registered pharmacist', it seems to me the sale might be effected by somebody not a pharmacist. If it be under the supervision of a pharmacist, the pharmacist can say: 'You cannot have that. That contains poison'. In this case I decide, first that there is no sale effected merely by the purchaser taking up the article. There is no sale until the buyer's offer to buy is accepted by the acceptance of the money, and that takes place under the supervision of a pharmacist. And in any case, I think, even if I am wrong in the view I have taken of when the offer is accepted, the sale is by or under the supervision of a pharmacist."

I agree with that and I agree that this appeal ought to be dismissed.'

Romer LJ: 'I also agree. The Lord Chief Justice observed that if, on the footing of the plaintiff society's contention, a person picked up an article, once having picked it up he would never be able to put it back and say he had changed his mind, for the shopkeeper could say that the property had passed and the customer would have to pay. If that were the position in this and similar shops, and that was known to the general public, I should imagine the popularity of such shops would wane a good deal. I am satisfied that that is not the position, and that the articles, even though they are priced and put in shops like this, do not represent an offer by the shopkeeper which can be accepted merely by the picking up of the article in question. I agree with the reasons on which the Lord Chief Justice arrived at that conclusion, to which Birkett LJ, has just referred, and to those observations I can add nothing of my own.'

Appeal dismissed.

Now use the same techniques that you have used with the previous case with the following cases; in fact use those techniques with all the cases you read.

Fisher v Bell

[1960] 3 All ER 731 • Queen's Bench

A shopkeeper was convicted of offering for sale a flick knife contrary to the Restriction of Offensive Weapons Act 1959 s 1(1); he had displayed the knife in his shop window. The shopkeeper appealed.

Lord Parker CJ: 'The sole question is whether the exhibition of that knife in the window with the ticket constituted an offer for sale within the statute. I think that most lay people would be inclined to the view (as, indeed, I was myself when I first read these papers), that if a knife were displayed in a window like that with a price attached to it, it was nonsense to say that that was not offering it for sale. The knife is there inviting people to buy it, and in ordinary language it is for sale; but any statute must be looked at in the light of the general law of the country, for Parliament must be taken to know the general law. It is clear that, according to the ordinary law of contract, the display of an article with a price on it in a shop window is merely an invitation to treat. It is in no sense an offer for sale the acceptance of which constitutes a contract. That is clearly the general law of the country . . .'

Advertisements

Partridge v *Crittenden*

[1968] 2 All ER 421 • Queen's Bench

Partridge advertised 'Bramblefinch cocks, Bramblefinch hens, 25s each' in a periodical called *Cage and Aviary Birds*. The words 'offer for sale' were not used but nonetheless Partridge was charged with, and convicted of, unlawfully offering for sale a bramblefinch hen contrary to Protection of Birds Act 1954 s 6(1). Partridge appealed against his conviction.

Ashworth J: 'Having been referred to the decision of this court in *Fisher* v *Bell* the justices nonetheless took the view that the advertisement did constitute an offer for sale . . . Before this court counsel for the appellant, has taken two points, first that this was not an offer for sale . . .

. . . [T]he real point of substance in this case arose from the words "offer for sale", and it is to be noted in s 6 of the Act of 1954 that the operative words are "any person sells, offers for sale or has in his possession for sale". For some reason which counsel for the respondent has not been able to explain, those responsible for the prosecution in this case chose, out of the trio of possible offences, the one which could not succeed. There was a sale here, in my view, because Mr Thompson sent his cheque and the bird was sent in reply; and a completed sale. On the evidence there was also a plain case of the appellant having in possession for sale this particular bird; but they chose to prosecute him for offering for sale, and they relied on the advertisement.

A similar point arose before this court in 1960 dealing, it is true, with a different statute but with the same words, that is *Fisher* v *Bell*. The relevant words of the Act in that case were: "Any person who offers for sale any knife." . . .

The words are the same here "offer for sale", and in my judgment the law of the country is equally plain as it was in regard to articles in a shop window, namely that the insertion of an advertisement in the form adopted here under the title "Classified Advertisements" is simply an invitation to treat . . .

. . . For my part I would allow this appeal and quash the conviction.'

Lord Parker CJ: 'I agree and with less reluctance . . . because I think that when one is dealing with advertisements and circulars, unless they indeed come from manufacturers, there is business sense in their being construed as invitations to treat and not offers for sale. In a very different context Lord Herschell in *Grainger & Son* v *Gough (Surveyor of Taxes)*, said this in dealing with a price-list:

"The transmission of such a price-list does not amount to an offer to supply an unlimited quantity of the wine described at the price named, so that as soon as an order is given there is a binding contract to supply that quantity. If it were so, the merchant might find himself involved in any number of contractual obligations to supply wine of a particular description which he would be quite unable to carry out, his stock of wine of that description being necessarily limited."

It seems to me accordingly that not only is that the law, but common sense supports it.'

What should Partridge have been charged with? Why was he not properly charged in the first place?

Lord Parker CJ said 'I think that when one is dealing with advertisements and circulars, *unless they indeed come from manufacturers*, there is business sense in their being construed as invitations to treat and not offers for sale'. What difference does it make if advertisements come from manufacturers?

An advertisement can be an offer

Sometimes an advertisement can be an offer. Remember the thing that determines whether a statement is an offer or an invitation to treat is the intention of the party who makes the statement: our definition of an offer was 'an offer is a proposition put by one person to another person made with *the intention that it shall become legally binding as soon as it is accepted by the other person*.' So if a proposition, say an advertisement, is made with the intention that if acted upon the person making the advertisement will consider himself legally bound then the advertisement will be an offer and not an invitation to treat.

Carlill v Carbolic Smoke Ball Co

[1893] 1 QB 256 • Court of Appeal

The facts are stated on p 5 above.

Lindley LJ: 'We must first consider whether this was intended to be a promise at all, or whether it was a mere puff which meant nothing. Was it a mere puff? My answer to that question is No, and I base my answer upon this passage: £100 is deposited with the Alliance Bank, showing our sincerity in the matter. Now, for what was that money deposited or that statement made except to negative the suggestion that this was a mere puff and meant nothing at all? The deposit is called in aid by the advertiser as proof of his sincerity in the matter – that is, the sincerity of his promise to pay this £100 in the event which he has specified. I say this for the purpose of giving point to the observation that we are not inferring a promise; there is the promise, as plain as words can make it.'

Bowen LJ: 'Was it intended that the £100 should, if the conditions were fulfilled, be paid? The advertisement says that £100 is lodged at the bank for the purpose. Therefore, it cannot be said that the statement that £100 would be paid was intended to be a mere puff. I think it was intended to be understood by the public as an offer which was to be acted upon.'

AL Smith LJ: 'If I may paraphrase [the advertisement], it means this: "If you" – that is one of the public as yet not ascertained, but who . . . will be ascertained by the performing the condition – "will hereafter use my smoke ball three times daily for two weeks according to my printed directions, I will pay you £100 if you contract the influenza within the period mentioned in the advertisement." Now, is there not a request there? It comes to this: "In consideration of your buying my smoke ball, and then using it as I prescribe, I promise that if you catch the influenza within a certain time I will pay you £100". It must not be forgotten that this advertisement states that as security for what is being offered, and as proof of the sincerity of the offer, £1000 is actually lodged at the bank wherewith to satisfy any possible demands which might be made in the event of the conditions contained therein being fulfilled and a person catching the epidemic so as to entitle him to the £100. How can it be said that such a statement as that embodied only a mere expression of confidence in the wares which the defendants had to sell? I cannot read the advertisement in any such way. In my judgment, the advertisement was an offer intended to be acted upon, and when accepted and the conditions performed constituted a binding promise on which an action would lie, assuming there was consideration for that promise . . .

In my judgment, therefore, this first point fails, and this was an offer intended to be acted upon, and, when acted upon and the conditions performed, constituted a promise to pay.'

Auctions

In an auction the auctioneer normally *intends* to invite *offers* from the public. A bid is an offer to the auctioneer. The auctioneer *accepts* the *offer* when the hammer falls.

Harris v Nickerson

(1873) 42 LJQB 171 • Queen's Bench

Nickerson advertised in the London newspapers that a public auction of certain goods and office fittings would take place in Bury St Edmunds on 14 August 1872. On the faith of the advertisement Harris attended the auction and 'was ready to purchase in pursuance of such request and public notification' but Nickerson 'suddenly and without notice withdrew the goods and office fittings from the sale'. Harris sued for £2 16s 6d (two days' lost time, railway fare and two days' board and lodging).

The issue before the court was whether the advertisement amounted to an offer which Harris had accepted by attending the auction.

Blackburn J: 'It appears that a sale by auction had been advertised, and catalogues distributed, in which it was stated that certain classes of articles would be offered for sale. The plaintiff attended the sale, but it seems that the seller changed his mind, and that certain of the articles were withdrawn from the auction. The plaintiff now says, "As I attended the sale, I am entitled to recover damages for being deprived of the opportunity of purchasing these articles". It has been contended that there was a contract that they should actually be put up for sale, and that the plaintiff should have an opportunity of buying them. But it would be intolerably inconvenient if the law were that any shopkeeper who closed his shop without giving notice, or the proprietor of a theatre who closed the theatre, should be liable to an action at the suit of anyone who had been disappointed. It would be most inconvenient, and there is no authority to lead us to think that it is the law. As for the case of *Warlow* v *Harrison*, I give no opinion as to whether the decision was right or wrong. It may plausibly be argued that where a sale has been advertised 'without reserve' and the auctioneer says, in spite of the advertisement, "I will knock down the articles to their owner, notwithstanding your remonstrances," it may plausibly, I repeat, be argued that in such a case an action is maintainable. But this would not support the present action, unless we go further and extend the decision to a case where the sale is not "without reserve" . . .'

Warlow v *Harrison*

(1859) 29 LJQB 14 • Exchequer Chamber

The facts are stated in the judgment of Martin B.

The issue before the court was whether an auctioneer who advertised that an auction was to be 'without reserve' makes an independent personal offer to the highest bidder.

Martin B: 'The defendant and a Mr Bretherton are auctioneers in partnership in Birmingham, where they have a repository for the sale of horses. In June 1858 they advertised a sale by auction at the repository. The advertisement contained, among other entries of horses to be sold, as follows: – 'The three following horses, the property of a gentleman, without reserve'; one of these was a mare called "Janet Pride". The plaintiff attended the sale, and bid sixty guineas for her; another person immediately bid sixty-one guineas. This person was Mr Henderson, the owner of the mare. The plaintiff having been informed that the last bidder was the owner, declined to bid further, and thereupon the defendant knocked down the mare to Mr Henderson for sixty-one guineas, and entered his name as purchaser in the sale-book, which contained the name of the animals to be sold at the sale, and the name of the proprietor. The plaintiff went at once into the auctioneer's office and saw Mr Bretherton and Mr Henderson, and claimed the mare from Mr Bretherton, as being the highest *bona fide* bidder, and the mare being advertised to be sold without reserve. Mr Henderson said, "I bought her in, and you shall not have her; I gave £130 for her, and it is not likely I am going to sell her for £63". On the same day the plaintiff tendered to the defendant £63 in sovereigns as the price of the mare, and demanded her. The defendant refused to receive the money or deliver the mare, stating that he had knocked her down to the highest bidder, and he could not interfere in the matter . . .

. . . In a sale by auction there are three parties, namely, the owner of the property to be sold, the auctioneer, and the portion of the public who attend to bid, which, of course, includes the highest bidder. In this, as in most cases of sale by auction, the owner's name was not disclosed: he was a concealed principal. The names of the auctioneers, of whom the defendant was one, alone were published, and the sale was announced by them to be 'without reserve'. This, according to all the cases, both at law and in equity, means that neither the vendor nor any person on his behalf may bid at the auction, and that the property shall be sold to the highest bidder, whether the sum bid be equivalent to the real value or not. For this position see the case of *Thornett* v *Haines*. We cannot distinguish the case of an auctioneer putting up property for sale upon such a condition from the case of the loser of property offering a reward, or that of a railway company publishing a time-table stating the times when and the places at which the trains run. It had been decided that the person giving information advertised for, or a passenger taking a ticket, may sue as upon a contract with him – *Denton* v *Great Northern Railway Company*. Upon the same principle, it seems to us that the highest *bona fide* bidder at an auction may sue the auctioneer as upon a contract that the sale shall be without reserve. We think that the auctioneer who puts property up for sale upon such a condition, pledges himself that the sale shall be without reserve, or, in other words, contracts that it shall be so, and is made with the highest *bona fide* bidder, and in case of a breach of it that he has a right of action against the auctioneer.'

Negotiating by correspondence

Where parties are negotiating by correspondence it can sometimes be difficult to determine whether an offer is being made or merely an invitation to treat. The principle is, however, the same; we must look to see whether the writer of the correspondence reasonably appeared to be prepared to be immediately bound by the contract provided the other party agreed.

Gibson v *Manchester City Council*
[1979] 1 All ER 972 • House of Lords

Mr Gibson wished to purchase his council house from the council, who sent him a letter which read:

> ' . . . I refer to your request for details of the cost of buying your Council house. The Corporation may be prepared to sell the house to you at the purchase price of £2180.
>
> If you wish to pay off some of the purchase price at the start and therefore require a mortgage for less than the amount quoted above, the monthly instalment will change; in these circumstances, I will supply new figures on request. The above repayment figures apply so long as the interest rate charged on home loans is $8\frac{1}{2}\%$. The interest rate will be subject to variation by the Corporation after giving not less than three months' written notice, and if it changes, there will be an adjustment to the monthly instalment payable. This letter should not be regarded as a firm offer of a mortgage.
>
> If you would like to make formal application to buy your Council house, please complete the enclosed application form and return it to me as soon as possible.'

Mr Gibson sent in an application and stated that he wished to buy the house. The issue before the House of Lords was whether the council's letter amounted to an offer.

Lord Diplock: '. . . The only question in the appeal is of a kind with which the courts are very familiar. It is whether in the correspondence between the parties there can be found a legally enforceable contract for the sale by the Manchester Corporation to Mr Gibson of the dwelling-house of which he was the occupying tenant at the relevant time in 1971. That question is one that, in my view, can be answered by applying to the particular documents relied on by Mr Gibson as constituting the contract, well settled, indeed elementary, principles of English law . . .

My Lords, there may be certain types of contract, though I think they are exceptional, which do not fit easily into the normal analysis of a contract as being constituted by offer and acceptance; but a contract alleged to have been made by an exchange of correspondence between the parties in which the successive communications other than the first are in reply to one another is not one of these. I can see no reason in the instant case for departing from the conventional approach of looking at the handful of documents relied on as constituting the contract sued on and seeing whether on their true construction there is to be found in them a contractual offer by the council to sell the house to Mr Gibson and an acceptance of that offer by Mr Gibson. I venture to think that it was by departing from this conventional approach that the majority of the Court of Appeal was led into error . . .

My Lords, the words ["*The Corporation may be prepared to sell the house to you at the purchase price of £2725 less 20 per cent = £2180 (freehold). If you would like to make formal application to buy your Council house, please complete the enclosed application form and return it to me as soon as possible.*"] seem to me, as they seemed to Geoffrey Lane LJ, to make it quite impossible to construe this letter as a contractual offer capable of being converted into a legally enforceable open contract for the sale of land by Mr Gibson's written acceptance of it. The words "may be prepared to sell" are fatal to this; so is the invitation, not, be it noted, to accept the offer, but "to make formal application to buy" on the enclosed application form. It is, to quote Geoffrey Lane LJ, a letter setting out the financial terms on which it may be the council would be prepared to consider a sale and purchase in due course.'

Tenders

A tender is an offer in response to an invitation to tender put out by a company. Generally a company which invites tenders is only making an invitation to treat and is not bound to accept any of the tenders.

Spencer v Harding

(1870) LR 5 CP 561 • Common Pleas

Harding sent out a circular which stated 'We are instructed to offer to the wholesale trade for sale by tender the stock in trade of Messrs. G. Eilbeck & Co. amounting as per stock-book to £2503 13s 1d, and which will be sold at a discount in one lot. Payment to be made in cash. The stock may be viewed on the premises, up to Thursday, the 20th instant, on which day, at 12 o'clock at noon precisely, the tenders will be received and opened at our offices'. Spencer claimed that the circular was an offer which he had accepted by submitting the highest tender.

Willes J: 'I am of opinion that the defendants are entitled to judgment. The action is brought against persons who issued a circular offering a stock for sale by tender, to be sold at a discount in one lot. The plaintiffs sent in a tender which turned out to be the highest, but which was not accepted. They now insist that the circular amounts to a contract or promise to sell the goods to the highest bidder, that is, in this case, to the person who should tender for them at the smallest rate of discount; and reliance is placed on the cases as to rewards offered for the discovery of an offender. In those cases, however, there never was any doubt that the advertisement amounted to a promise to pay the money to the person who first gave information. The difficulty suggested was that it was a contract with all the world. But that, of course, was soon overruled. It was an offer to become liable to any person who before the offer should be retracted would happen to be the person to fulfil the contract of which the advertisement was an offer or tender. That is not the sort of difficulty which presents itself here. If the circular had gone on, "and we undertake to sell to the highest bidder", the reward cases would have applied, and there would have been a good contract in respect of the persons. But the question is, whether there is here any offer to enter into a contract at all, or whether the circular amounts to anything more than a mere proclamation that the defendants are ready to chaffer for the sale of the goods, and to receive offers for the purchase of them. In advertisements for tenders for buildings it is not usual to say that the contract will be given to the lowest bidder, and it is not always that the contract is made with the lowest bidder. Here there is a total absence of any words to intimate that the highest bidder is to be the purchaser. It is a mere attempt to ascertain whether an offer can be obtained within such a margin as the sellers are willing to adopt.'

The intention of the party inviting the tenders is all important in determining whether the invitation for tenders is intended as an invitation to treat or an offer.

Blackpool and Fylde Aero Club Ltd v *Blackpool Borough Council*
[1990] 3 All ER 25 • Court of Appeal

Blackpool Borough Council sent an invitation to tender to operate pleasure flights from Blackpool airport to the Blackpool and Fylde Aero Club Ltd (the club) and six other parties. The invitation to tender said that '[t]he Council do not bind themselves to accept all or any part of any tender. No tender which is received after the last date and time specified shall be admitted for consideration.' The club posted its tender in the town hall letter box at about 1100 hrs on Thursday 17 March; this was an hour before the advertised deadline expired. The council's staff failed to empty the letter box at 1200 hrs and as a result the tender was marked late and not considered by the council. The council then accepted the highest tender which was from Red Rose Helicopters. Later the council established that the club's tender had been received in time and so they decided to declare the successful tender invalid and to reissue the invitation to tender. However, Red Rose Helicopters contended that its tender had been accepted and that the council was contractually bound to proceed on that basis. The council decided to honour Red Rose Helicopters' tender. The club brought an action for damages against the council for breach of contract. The club argued that the council had warranted that if a tender was received in good time it would be considered by the council and that the council, having failed to consider its tender, was in breach of contract.

Bingham LJ: 'A tendering procedure of this kind is, in many respects, heavily weighted in favour of the invitor. He can invite tenders from as many or as few parties as he chooses. He need not tell any of them who else, or how many others, he has invited. The invitee may often, although not here, be put to considerable labour and expense in preparing a tender, ordinarily without recompense if he is unsuccessful. The invitation to tender may itself, in a complex case, although again not here, involve time and expense to prepare, but the invitor does not commit himself to proceed with the project, whatever it is he need not accept the highest tender, he need not accept any tender, he need not give reasons to justify his acceptance or rejection of any tender received. The risk to which the tenderer is exposed does not end with the risk that his tender may not be the highest (or, as the case may be, lowest). But where, as here, tenders are solicited from selected parties all of them known to the invitor, and where a local authority's invitation prescribes a clear, orderly and familiar procedure (draft contract conditions available for inspection and plainly not open to negotiation, a prescribed common form of tender, the supply of envelopes designed to preserve the absolute anonymity of tenderers and clearly to identify the tender in question and an absolute deadline) the invitee is in my judgment protected at least to this extent: if he submits a conforming tender before the deadline he is entitled, not as a matter of mere expectation but of contractual right, to be sure that his tender will after the deadline be opened and considered in conjunction with all other conforming tenders or at least that his tender will be considered if others are. Had the club, before tendering, inquired of the council whether it could rely on any timely and conforming tender being considered along with others, I feel quite sure that the answer would have been "of course". The law would, I think, be defective if it did not give effect to that.

It is of course true that the invitation to tender does not explicitly state that the council will consider timely and conforming tenders. That is why one is concerned with implication. But the council does not either say that it does not bind itself to do so, and in the context a reasonable invitee would understand the invitation to be saying, quite clearly, that if he submitted a timely and conforming tender it would be considered, at least if any other such tender were considered.

I readily accept that contracts are not to be lightly implied. Having examined what the parties said and did, the court must be able to conclude with confidence both that the parties intended to create contractual relations and that the agreement was to the effect contended for . . . In all the circumstances of this case . . . I have no doubt that the parties did intend to create contractual relations to the limited extent contended for . . . [C]ounsel for the club was in my view right to contend for no more than a contractual duty to consider. I think it plain that the council's invitation to tender was, to this limited extent, an offer, and the club's submission of a timely and conforming tender an acceptance.'

The order of the High Court was that damages were to be assessed in respect of the council's failure to consider a tender received in accordance with its standing orders. How could this be done? How could the damages be quantified? These difficult questions are dealt with later in the book.

Harvela Investments Ltd v Royal Trust Co of Canada (CI) Ltd

[1985] 2 All ER 966 • House of Lords

Harvela, Sir Leonard Outerbridge and Royal Trust were the shareholders in Harvey & Co Ltd. Royal Trust wished to sell its shares and to this end invited the other two shareholders to make offers to purchase its shares. Whichever of the other two shareholders was successful in its bid would result in it becoming the majority shareholder in Harvey & Co Ltd. The invitation stipulated that offers must be made by sealed tender or confidential telex which would not be divulged by the vendors before the invitation expired at 1500 hrs on 16 September 1981 when the vendors would accept 'the highest offer'. Harvela offered $2 175 000 and Sir Leonard offered $2 100 000 'or C$101 000 in excess of any other offer which you may receive which is expressed as a fixed monetary amount, whichever is the higher'. Royal Trust accepted Sir Leonard's bid. When Harvela learnt of the nature of Sir Leonard's bid it sought an injunction to prevent Royal Trust selling its shares to Sir Leonard. The issue before the court was who had made the highest valid bid.

Lord Diplock: 'The construction question turns on the wording of the telex of 15 September 1981 referred to by Lord Templeman as "the invitation" and addressed to both Harvela and Sir Leonard. It was not a mere invitation to negotiate for the sale of the shares in Harvey & Co Ltd, of which the vendors were the registered owners in the capacity of trustees. Its legal nature was that of a unilateral or "if" contract, or rather of two unilateral contracts in identical terms to one of which the vendors and Harvela were the parties as promisor and promisee respectively, while to the other the vendors were promisor and Sir Leonard was promisee. Such unilateral contracts were made at the time when the invitation was received by the promisee to whom it was addressed by the vendors; under neither of them did the promisee, Harvela and Sir Leonard respectively, assume any legal obligation to anyone to do or refrain from doing anything.

The vendors, on the other hand, did assume a legal obligation to the promisee under each contract. That obligation was conditional on the happening, after the unilateral contract had been made, of an event which was specified in the invitation; the obligation was to enter into a synallagmatic [i.e. reciprocally binding] contract to sell the shares to the promisee, the terms of such synallagmatic contract being also set out in the invitation. The event on the happening of which the vendors' obligation to sell the shares to the promisee arose was the doing by the promisee of an act which was of such a nature that it might be done by either promisee or neither promisee but could not be done by both. The vendors thus did not, by entering into the two unilateral contracts, run any risk of assuming legal obligations to enter into conflicting synallagmatic contracts to sell the shares to each promisee.

The two unilateral contracts were of short duration, for the condition subsequent to which each was subject was the receipt by the vendors' solicitors on or before 3 p m on the following day, 16 September 1981, of a sealed tender or confidential telex containing an offer by the promisee to buy the shares for a single sum of money in Canadian dollars. If such an offer was received from each of the promisees under their respective contracts, the obligation of the promisor, the vendors, was to sell the shares to the promisee whose offer was the higher and any obligation which the promisor had assumed to the promisee under the other unilateral contract came to an end, because the event the happening of which was the condition subsequent to which the vendors' obligation to sell the shares to that promisee was subject had not happened before the unilateral contract with that promisee expired.

Since the invitation in addition to containing the terms of the unilateral contract also embodied the terms of the synallagmatic contract into which the vendors undertook to enter on the happening of the specified event, the consequence of the happening of that event would be to convert the invitation into a synallagmatic contract between the vendors and whichever promisee had offered, by sealed tender or confidential telex, the higher sum . . .'

[Lord Diplock then went on to conclude that the business purpose of a unilateral contract of this type providing for sealed tenders was to exclude referential bids.]

Lord Templeman: 'Thus auction sales and fixed bidding sales are liable to affect vendors and purchasers in different ways and to produce different results. The first question raised by this appeal, therefore, is whether Harvela and Sir Leonard were invited to participate in a fixed bidding sale, which only invited fixed bids, or were invited to participate in an auction sale, which enabled the bid of each bidder to be adjusted by reference to the other bid. A vendor chooses between a fixed bidding sale and an auction sale. A bidder can only choose to participate in the sale or to abstain from the sale. The ascertainment of the choice of the vendors in the present case between a fixed bidding sale and an auction sale by means of referential bids depends on the presumed intention of the vendors. That presumed intention must be deduced from the terms of the invitation read as a whole. The invitation contains three provisions which are only consistent with the presumed intention to create a fixed bidding sale and which are inconsistent with any presumed intention to create an auction sale by means of referential bids.

By the first significant provision, the vendors undertook to accept the highest offer this shows that the vendors were anxious to ensure that a sale should result from the invitation . . .

To constitute a fixed bidding sale all that was necessary was that the vendors should invite confidential offers and should undertake to accept the highest offer. Such was the form of the invitation. It follows that the invitation on its true construction created a fixed bidding sale and that Sir Leonard was not entitled to submit and the vendors were not entitled to accept a referential bid.

. . . The task of the court is to construe the invitation and to ascertain whether the provisions of the invitation, read as a whole, create a fixed bidding sale or an auction sale. I am content to reach a conclusion which reeks of simplicity, which does not require a draftsman to indulge in prohibitions, but which obliges a vendor to specify and control any form of auction which he seeks to combine with confidential bidding. The invitation required Sir Leonard to name his price and required Harvela to name its price and bound the vendors to accept the higher price. The invitation was not difficult to understand and the result was bound to be certain and to accord with the presumed intentions of the vendors discernible from the express provisions of the invitation. Harvela named the price of $2 175 000 Sir Leonard failed to name any price except $2 100 000, which was less than the price named by Harvela. The vendors were bound to accept Harvela's offer.

I am also content to follow the decision . . . in *South Hetton Coal Co* v *Haswell Shotton and Easington Coal and Coke Co* . . . The decision in the *South Hetton* case was followed by a majority of the members of the New York Court of Appeals in *SSI Investors Ltd* v *Korea Tungsten Mining Co Ltd*. The majority judgment succinctly and cogently summarised the reasons for rejecting bids as follows:

"The very essence of sealed competitive bidding is the submission of independent, self-contained bids, to the fair compliance with which not only the owner but the other bidders are entitled . . . to give effect to this or any similar bidding practice in which the dollar amount of one bid was tied to the bid or bids of another or others in the same bidding would be to recognise means whereby effective sealed competitive bidding could be wholly frustrated. In the context of such bidding, therefore, a submission by one bidder of a bid dependent for its definition on the bids of others is invalid and unacceptable as inconsistent with and potentially destructive of the very bidding in which it is submitted."'

SUMMARY

You should now be able to:

- Read a case.
- Appreciate the importance of the concept of *agreement*.
- Appreciate the importance of the intention of the parties.
- Distinguish between an *invitation to treat* and an *offer*.

If you have not mastered the above points you should go through this section again.

2 Acceptance

ACCEPTANCE

Definition: **acceptance is the unconditional consent to the terms of the offer.**

If an acceptance contains any reservations, any variations to the terms in the offer, then the acceptance will be *conditional*. Because it will not be an *unconditional consent* to the terms of the offer it will *not be an acceptance*.

COUNTER-OFFER

A counter-offer is a form of conditional acceptance because it contains different terms from those in the original offer. A counter-offer amounts to the original offeree telling the offeror that the offeror's original offer is unacceptable. The effect of this is that a counter-offer destroys the original offer. In the following cases identify the offer, the counter-offer and the acceptance.

Hyde v *Wrench*

(1840) 3 Beav 334 • Rolls Court

On 6 June Wrench offered to sell his farm to Hyde for £1000. Hyde offered to give Wrench £950 for the purchase of the farm, but Wrench wished to have a few days to consider. On 27 June Wrench wrote to Hyde stating he was sorry he could not feel disposed to accept his offer at present. On 29 June Hyde wrote to Wrench 'I beg to acknowledge the receipt of your letter of the 27th instant, informing me that you are not disposed to accept the sum of £950 for your farm at Luddenham. This being the case I at once agree to the terms on which you offered the farm, viz, £1000 ... by your letter of the 6th instant. I shall be obliged by your instructing your solicitor to communicate with me without delay ...' The issue before the court was whether there was a concluded contract between Hyde and Wrench.

Lord Langdale MR: 'I think there exists no valid binding contract between the parties for the purchase of the property. [Wrench] offered to sell it for £1000, and if that had been at once unconditionally accepted, there would undoubtedly have been a perfect binding contract; instead of that, [Hyde] made an offer of his own, to purchase the property for £950, and he thereby rejected the offer previously made by [Wrench]. I think that it was not afterwards competent for him to revive the proposal of [Wrench], by tendering an acceptance of it; and that, therefore, there exists no obligation of any sort between the parties ...'

British Road Services Ltd v *Arthur V Crutchley & Co Ltd*
[1968] 1 All ER 811 • Court of Appeal

BRS had, under a long-established course of business, warehoused goods with AVC (Arthur V Crutchley). When BRS's lorry drivers arrived at AVC's warehouse they handed to AVC a delivery note which contained their standard terms of business; these terms made the bailees, AVC, wholly liable for any loss of the goods warehoused with AVC. AVC on receiving a delivery note would stamp it 'Received on AVC conditions' and then hand it back to BRS's driver. AVC's terms contained a condition limiting their liability to £800 per ton. A lorryload of whisky, worth £9126, was left with AVC by BRS. The whisky was stolen and the question arose as to whose terms governed the contract. If BRS's terms prevailed then AVC would be liable for the full £9126. If, on the other hand, AVC's terms prevailed then their liability would be limited to £800 per ton which worked out at £6135.

Lord Pearson: 'This case has arisen from the theft of a lorry load of whisky, worth £9126, from a warehouse of the defendants, A V Crutchley & Co Ltd, in the Liverpool dock area. The theft occurred in the early hours of July 30, 1963. The action was brought by the plaintiffs, British Road Services Ltd, as bailors, against the defendants as bailees, for the loss of the goods . . .

Now I come to the terms of the contract between the plaintiffs and the defendants. It was not proved that the plaintiffs' conditions of sub-contracting were ever sent to the defendants, and the defendants in evidence denied that they were sub-contractors to the plaintiffs. The plaintiffs' form of delivery note contained the words:

"All goods are carried on the [plaintiffs'] conditions of carriage, copies of which can be obtained upon application to any office of the [plaintiffs]".

Under the long-established course of business between the parties, however, the plaintiffs' driver brought his delivery note into the defendants' office at the Cotton Street warehouse and asked in effect if he could bring his load into the warehouse. If there were room in the warehouse, the permission would be given, and the delivery note would be rubber-stamped by the defendants with the words "Received under AVC conditions", followed by the date and the address of the warehouse. The delivery note, thus converted into a receipt note, would be handed back to the plaintiffs' driver and he would bring his load into the warehouse as instructed by the warehouse foreman. If this had only happened once, there would have been a doubt whether the plaintiffs' driver was their agent to accept the defendants' special contractual terms. This, however, happened frequently and regularly over many years at this and other warehouses of the defendants. Also the defendants' invoices contained the words: "All goods are handled subject to conditions of carriage copies of which can be obtained on application". It may perhaps be material to add that the defendants' conditions of carriage were not peculiar to them, but were the conditions of carriage of Road Haulage Association Ltd. At any rate, I agree with the decision of the judge that the plaintiffs' conditions were not, and the defendants' conditions were, incorporated into the contract between these parties. The effect was that, while the nature of the defendants' liability as bailees to the plaintiffs was unaffected, the liability was limited in amount to £800 per ton, which, when credit is given for sixty bottles of whisky recovered after the theft, produces a total in this case of £6135 . . .'

Butler Machine Tool Co Ltd v *Ex-Cell-O Corporation (England) Ltd*

[1979] 1 All ER 965 • Court of Appeal

The facts are set out in the judgment of Lord Denning MR.

Lord Denning MR: 'This case is a "battle of forms". The suppliers of a machine, Butler Machine Tool Co Ltd ("the sellers"), on 23 May 1969 quoted a price for a machine tool of £75 535. Delivery was to be given in ten months. On the back of the quotation there were terms and conditions. One of them was a price variation clause. It provided for an increase in the price if there was an increase in the costs and so forth. The machine tool was not delivered until November 1970. By that time costs had increased so much that the sellers claimed an additional sum of £2892 as due to them under the price variation clause.

The buyers, Ex-Cell-O Corpn, rejected the excess charge. They relied on their own terms and conditions. They said: "We did not accept the sellers' quotation as it was. We gave an order for the self-same machine at the self-same price, but on the back of our order we had our own terms and conditions. Our terms and conditions did not contain any price variation clause."

. . . The case was decided on the documents alone. I propose therefore to go through them.

On 23 May 1969 the sellers offered to deliver one "Butler" double column plano-miller for the total price of £75 535, "DELIVERY: 10 months (Subject to confirmation at time of ordering) Other terms and conditions are on the reverse of this quotation". On the back there were 16 conditions in small print starting with this general condition:

"All orders are accepted only upon and subject to the terms set out in our quotation and the following conditions. These terms and conditions shall prevail over any terms and conditions in the Buyer's order."

Clause 3 was the price variation clause. It said:

" . . . Prices are based on present day costs of manufacture and design and having regard to the delivery quoted and uncertainty as to the cost of labour, materials etc during the period of manufacture, we regret that we have no alternative but to make it a condition of acceptance of order that goods will be charged at prices ruling upon date of delivery."

The buyers, Ex-Cell-O, replied on 27 May 1969 giving an order in these words: "Please supply on terms and conditions as below and overleaf". Below there was a list of the goods ordered, but there were differences from the quotation of the sellers in these respects: (i) there was an additional item for the cost of installation, £3100; (ii) there was a different delivery date: instead of 10 months, it was 10 to 11 months. Overleaf there were different terms as to the cost of carriage, in that it was to be paid to the delivery address of the buyers; whereas the sellers' terms were ex-warehouse. There were different terms as to the right to cancel for late delivery. The buyers in their conditions reserved the right to cancel if delivery was not made by the agreed date, whereas the sellers in their conditions said that cancellation of order due to late delivery would not be accepted.

On the foot of the buyers' order there was a tear-off slip:

"Acknowledgement: Please sign and return to Ex-Cell-O Corp (England) Ltd. We accept your order on the Terms and Conditions stated thereon – and undertake to deliver by . . . Date . . . Signed . . . "

In that slip the delivery date and signature were left blank ready to be filled in by the sellers.

On 5 June 1969 the sellers wrote this letter to the buyers:

"We have pleasure in acknowledging receipt of your official order dated 27 May covering the supply of one 'Butler' Double Column Plano-Miller . . . This is being entered in accordance with our revised quotation of 23 May for delivery in 10/11 months, i.e. March/April, 1970. We return herewith, duly completed, your acknowledgement of order form."

They enclosed the acknowledgement form duly filled in with the delivery date, March/April 1970, and signed by the Butler Machine Tool Co Ltd.

No doubt a contract was then concluded. But on what terms? The sellers rely on their general conditions and on their last letter which said "in accordance with our revised quotation of 23 May" (which had on the back the price variation clause). The buyers rely on the acknowledgement signed by the sellers which accepted the buyers' order "on the terms and conditions stated thereon" (which did not include a price variation clause).

If those documents are analysed in our traditional method, the result would seem to me to be this: the quotation of 23 May 1969 was an offer by the sellers to the buyers containing the terms and conditions on the back. The order of 27 May 1969 purported to be an acceptance of that offer in that it was for the same machine at the same price, but it contained such additions as to cost of installation, date of delivery and so forth, that it was in law a rejection of the offer and constituted a counter-offer. That is clear from *Hyde* v *Wrench*. As Megaw J said in *Trollope & Colls Ltd* v *Atomic Power Constructions Ltd*: " . . . the counter-offer kills the original offer". The letter of the sellers of 5 June 1969 was an acceptance of that counter-offer, as is shown by the acknowledgement which the sellers signed and returned to the buyers. The reference to the quotation of 23 May 1969 referred only to the price and identity of the machine.

To go on with the facts of the case. The important thing is that the sellers did not keep the contractual date of delivery which was March/April 1970. The machine was ready about September 1970 but by that time the buyers' production schedule had to be rearranged as they could not accept delivery until November 1970. Meanwhile the sellers had invoked the price increase clause. They sought to charge the buyers an increase due to the rise in costs between 27 May 1969 (when the order was given) and 1st April 1970 (when the machine ought to have been delivered). It came to £2892. The buyers rejected the claim. The judge held that the sellers were entitled to the sum of £2892 under the price variation clause. He did not apply the traditional method of analysis by way of offer and counter-offer. He said that in the quotation of 23 May 1969 "one finds the price variation clause appearing under a most emphatic heading stating that it is a term or condition that is to prevail". So he held that it did prevail.

I have much sympathy with the judge's approach to this case. In many of these cases our traditional analysis of offer, counter-offer, rejection, acceptance and so forth is out-of-date. This was observed by Lord Wilberforce in *New Zealand Shipping Co Ltd* v *A M Satterthwaite*. The better way is to look at all the documents passing between the parties and glean from them, or from the conduct of the parties, whether they have reached agreement on all material points, even though there may be differences between the forms and conditions printed on the back of them. As Lord Cairns LC said in *Brogden* v *Metropolitan Railway Co*:

" . . . there may be a consensus between the parties far short of a complete mode of expressing it, and that consensus may be discovered from letters or from other documents of an imperfect and incomplete description."

Applying this guide, it will be found that in most cases when there is a 'battle of forms' there is a contract as soon as the last of the forms is sent and received without objection being taken to it. That is well observed in Benjamin on Sale (*Benjamin on the Sale of Goods* (9th edn, 1974)). The difficulty is to decide which form, or which part of which form, is a term or condition of the contract. In some cases the battle is won by the man who fires the last shot. He is the man who puts forward the latest term and conditions: and, if they are not objected to by the other party, he may be taken to have agreed to them. Such was *British Road Services Ltd* v *Arthur V Crutchley & Co Ltd* per Lord Pearson; and the illustration given by Professor Guest in *Anson's Law of Contract* (24th edn) where he says that 'the terms of the contract consist of the terms of the offer subject to the modifications contained in the acceptance'. That may however go too far. In some cases, however, the battle is won by the man who gets the blow in first. If he offers to sell at a named price on the terms and conditions stated on the back and the buyer orders the goods purporting to accept the offer on an order form with his own different terms and conditions on the back, then, if the difference is so material that it would affect the price, the buyer ought not to be allowed to take advantage of the difference unless he draws it specifically to the attention of the seller. There are yet other cases where the battle depends on the shots fired on both sides. There is a concluded contract but the forms vary. The terms and conditions of both parties are to be construed together. If they can be reconciled so as to give a harmonious result, all well and good. If differences are irreconcilable, so that they are mutually contradictory, then the conflicting terms may have to be scrapped and replaced by a reasonable implication.

In the present case the judge thought that the sellers in their original quotation got their blow in first; especially by the provision that "These terms and conditions shall prevail over any terms and conditions in the Buyer's order". It was so emphatic that the price variation clause continued through all the subsequent dealings and that the buyer must be taken to have agreed to it. I can understand that point of view. But I think that the documents have to be considered as a whole. And, as a matter of construction, I think the acknowledgement of 5 June 1969 is the decisive document. It makes it clear that the contract was on the buyers' terms and not on the sellers' terms: and the buyers' terms did not include a price variation clause.

Lawton and Bridge LJJ preferred the more traditional approach of offer and counter-offer.

Lawton LJ: 'The rules relating to a battle of [forms] of this kind have been known for the past 130-odd years. They were set out by the then Master of the Rolls, Lord Langdale, in *Hyde* v *Wrench*, and Lord Denning MR has already referred to them; and, if anyone should have thought they were obsolescent, Megaw J in *Trollope & Colls Ltd* v *Atomic Power Constructions Ltd* called attention to the facts that those rules are still in force.

When those rules are applied to this case, in my judgment, the answer is obvious. The sellers started by making an offer. That was in their quotation. The small print was headed by the following words:

"General. All orders are accepted only upon and subject to the terms set out in our quotation and the following conditions. These terms and conditions shall prevail over any terms and conditions in the Buyer's order."

That offer was not accepted. The buyers were only prepared to have one of these very expensive machines on their own terms. Their terms had very material differences in them from the terms put forward by the sellers . . .

As I understand *Hyde* v *Wrench* and the cases which have followed, the consequence of placing the order in that way, if I may adopt Megaw J's words (*Trollope & Colls Ltd* v *Atomic Power Constructions Ltd,* was "to kill the quotation". It follows that the court has to look at what happened after the buyers made their counter-offer. By letter dated 4 June 1969 the sellers acknowledged receipt of the counter-offer, and they went on in this way: "Details of this order have been passed to our Halifax works for attention and a formal acknowledgement of order will follow in due course". That is clearly a reference to the printed tear-off slip which was at the bottom of the buyers' counter-offer. By letter dated 5 June 1969 the sales office manager at the sellers' Halifax factory completed that tear-off slip and sent it back to the buyers.

It is true, as counsel for the sellers has reminded us, that the return of that printed slip was accompanied by a letter which had this sentence in it: "This is being entered in accordance with our revised quotation of 23 May for delivery in 10/11 months". I agree with Lord Denning MR that, in a business sense, that refers to the quotation as to the price and the identity of the machine, and it does not bring into the contract the small print conditions on the back of the quotation. Those small print conditions had disappeared from the story. That was when the contract was made. At that date it was a fixed price contract without a price escalation clause.

As I pointed out in the course of argument to counsel for the sellers, if the letter of 5 June which accompanied the form acknowledging the terms which the buyers had specified had amounted to a counter-offer, then in my judgment the parties never were *ad idem*. It cannot be said that the buyers accepted the counter-offer by reason of the fact that ultimately they took physical delivery of the machine. By the time they took physical delivery of the machine, they had made it clear by correspondence that they were not accepting that there was any price escalation clause in any contract which they had made with the plaintiffs.'

REQUEST FOR INFORMATION

A request for information *does not destroy an offer.*

It can be very difficult to determine whether a statement from the offeree to the offeror regarding the offeror's offer is a mere *request for information* – a request, for example, to clarify certain matters relating to the offer *or* whether the offeree's statement is a *counter offer*.

In the end the test will be – what was the *intention* of the offeree?

Stevenson, Jaques, & Co v McLean
(1880) 5 QBD 346 • Queen's Bench

On Saturday 27 September McLean wrote to Stevenson offering to sell him some iron. The letter stated 'I would now sell for 40s, nett cash, open till Monday'. The letter arrived on Sunday 28 September.

On the Monday 29 September at 09.42 hrs, Stevenson sent a telegram to McLean which said 'Please wire whether you would accept forty for delivery over two months, or if not, longest limit you would give'. This telegram was received by McLean at 10.01 hrs.

McLean then sold the iron for 40s, nett cash, to a third party. At 13.25 hrs McLean sent a telegram to Stevenson which said 'Have sold all my iron here for forty nett today'. This telegram reached Stevenson at 13.46 hrs. However, before it arrived Stevenson had, at 13.34 hrs, sent a telegram to McLean accepting McLean's offer.

The issue before the court was whether the telegram sent by Stevenson at 09.42 hrs on Monday was a counter-offer or merely a request for further information.

Lush J: '. . . [I]t was contended that the telegram sent by Stevenson on the Monday morning was a rejection of McLean's offer and a new proposal on Stevenson's part, and that McLean had therefore a right to regard it as putting an end to the original negotiation.

Looking at the form of the telegram, the time when it was sent, and the state of the iron market, I cannot think this is its fair meaning. The plaintiff Stevenson said he meant it only as an inquiry, expecting an answer for his guidance, and this, I think, is the sense in which McLean ought to have regarded it.

It is apparent throughout the correspondence, that Stevenson did not contemplate buying the iron on speculation, but that their acceptance of McLean's offer depended on their finding someone to take the warrants off their hands. All parties knew that the market was in an unsettled state, and that no one could predict at the early hour when the telegram was sent how the prices would range during the day. It was reasonable that, under these circumstances, they should desire to know before business began whether they were to be at liberty in case of need to make any and what concession as to the time or times of delivery, which would be the time or times of payment, or whether McLean was determined to adhere to the terms of his letter; and it was highly unreasonable that Stevenson should have intended to close the negotiation while it was uncertain whether they could find a buyer or not, having the whole of the business hours of the day to look for one. Then, again, the form of the telegram is one of inquiry. It is not "I offer forty for delivery over two months," which would have likened the case to *Hyde* v *Wrench*, where one party offered his estate for £1000, and the other answered by offering £950. Lord Langdale, in that case, held that after the £950 had been refused, the party offering it could not, by then agreeing to the original proposal, claim the estate, for the negotiation was at an end by the refusal of his counter proposal. Here there is no counter proposal. The words are, "Please wire whether you would accept forty for delivery over two months, or, if not, the longest limit you would give". There is nothing specific by way of offer or rejection, but a mere inquiry, which should have been answered and not treated as a rejection of the offer. This ground of objection therefore fails.'

CONDITIONAL ASSENT IS NOT ACCEPTANCE

As we have seen above, a conditional assent is not an acceptance. However, the courts will look carefully at any words used to determine whether there was an *intention* to accept the offer.

Branca v Cobarro

[1947] 2 All ER 101 • Court of Appeal

On July 15 Cobarro agreed to sell the lease and goodwill of his mushroom farm to Branca for £5000. The agreement concluded 'This is a provisional agreement until a fully legalised agreement drawn up by a solicitor and embodying all the conditions herewith stated is signed.' The question that arose was whether a contract had come into existence on July 15.

Lord Greene MR: 'This case raises the familiar question whether an informal document constitutes a contract or whether it is evidence of mere negotiation in contemplation of a contract coming into existence at some future date . . .

Down to the end of the paragraph preceding the final paragraph there can be no question that the document is a contract. If that final paragraph had not been there, no question could have been raised about it. The sole question is whether that paragraph introduces an element which destroys any contractual efficacy in the rest of the document. It is in rather an unusual form: "This is a provisional agreement until . . ." That the parties contemplated and wished that there should be what they call 'a fully legalised agreement' drawn up and signed is clear, but the first thing to notice about these words is that they are not expressive of a condition or stipulation to that effect. The familiar words "subject to contract" and many other forms of words that one has come across in this class of case are words of condition, but these are not words of condition or stipulation. The word "until" in this context, to my mind, clearly means that what is called "a provisional agreement" is going to have some efficacy until a certain event happens. The efficacy of the document is not made in any sense conditional on the happening of that event. The event puts a term to the operation of what is described as "a provisional agreement" and it is noticeable that the parties describe the thing which is to have that operation until that event happens as "an agreement".

Counsel for the purchaser says: "You must not attach too much importance to the word 'agreement'", and I have already expressed my agreement with that proposition, but it is significant that in this very clause, which is supposed to negative the existence of an agreement, the parties have chosen to use the word "agreement", an agreement which is to have some operation until a certain event happens. If this paragraph is read in its ordinary meaning, if that event does not happen, the document will continue to have for an indefinite period the operation which the parties are giving to it. In other words, the happening of the event, viz, the drawing up of the fully legalised agreement, is not a condition of the operation of this document. On the contrary, it is something which, when it happens, will bring to an end a document which the parties clearly treat as being an operative document. I have used the word "operative" deliberately as a neutral word. The words "fully legalised agreement" must, I think, mean, and I do not think it is disputed, what we generally call a formal agreement. It is agreement which has got to embody 'all the conditions herewith stated.' No other terms or conditions are to appear in that fully legalised agreement.

Denning J decided this case on the construction which he gave to the word "provisional". He said that, in his opinion, it meant "tentative". With the greatest deference, "tentative" is not, I should have thought, the meaning in ordinary English of "provisional". It certainly is not the meaning that is to be found in the Oxford Dictionary, and I should have thought that in this context to change the word "provisional" and substitute "tentative" would be introducing something which is really not contained in "provisional". The idea expressed by "tentative" is something quite different with all respect from that expressed by "provisional". The ordinary meaning of "provisional" is something which is going to operate until something else happens. If I am right that these words are intended to show that the parties regarded themselves as entering into an agreement which was to last only until something else took its place or superseded it, the word "provisional" would be the proper and apt word to describe that intention. An agreement which is only to last until it is replaced by a formal document containing the same terms and drawn up by a solicitor could be described by no more apt word than the word "provisional". If the word "provisional" is linked up with the word "until", the whole thing seems to me to fall into shape.

My reading of this document is that both parties were determined to hold themselves and one another bound. They realised the desirability of a formal document as many contracting parties do, but they were determined that there should be no escape for either of them in the interim period between the signing of this document and the signature of a formal agreement, and they have used words which are exactly apt to produce that result and do not, in my opinion, suggest that the fully legalised agreement is in any sense to be a condition to be fulfilled before the parties are bound, because, as I have said, the word "until" is certainly not the right word to import a condition or a stipulation as to the event referred to. In my judgment, if the parties never signed a fully legalised agreement, the event putting an end to the provisional operation of this agreement would never occur and this document would continue to bind the parties . . .'

Where all of the main terms in a contract have been agreed, and the parties have agreed to be bound thereby, the fact that further terms have still to be negotiated will not prevent there from being a concluded interim contract at that stage.

NB: compare the following case with the cases considered below under the topic of Certainty; especially the cases considered under Vagueness.

Pagnan SpA v Feed Products Ltd
[1987] 2 Lloyd's Rep 601 • Court of Appeal

On Monday 1 February Feed Products offered to sell 30 000 tonnes of feed pellets at $158.50 fob stowed and trimmed for shipment at the rate of 10 000 tonnes per month, 5 per cent more or less at vessel's option during the months May to July 1982 to Agrimec, Pagnan's agent. Agrimec passed on the offer by telephone to Pagnan but he added two further terms of his own which had not been mentioned by Feed Products. These were, first, that the shipping tolerance, that is to say the 5 per cent more or less at vessel's option, should be paid for at contract price, and, secondly, that payment should be cash against documents in New York. Pagnan telephoned Agrimec and told him to book the business. Agrimec telephoned Feed Products and told them that Pagnan had accepted their offer. Agrimec then sent a confirmation telex to each of the parties which read 'We confirm the following business today concluded through our intermediary . . . ' The telex set out the terms which had been agreed on the telephone with Pagnan including the two additional terms which were agreed subsequently with Feed Products. On 2 February Feed Products sent a long telex to Pagnan which made certain amendments to Pagnan's telex of 1 February. On 3 February Pagnan drew attention to these discrepancies. Further telexes were exchanged. Finally Pagnan stated that no contract had been concluded.

The issue before the court was whether a binding contract was made on February 1.

Lloyd LJ: 'We are concerned on this appeal with the perennial question whether the parties reached a concluded contract . . .

I now return to Mr Rokison's [counsel for Pagnan] first and main argument. He submits that it is wrong to look at Agrimec's telex of Feb 1 in isolation. The telex may appear to record a concluded contract, but when you look at the context it takes on a different aspect. Although the parties had reached agreement on the most important terms, such as price, quantity and date of delivery, there were other important terms still to be agreed. The only proper inference, says Mr Rokison, is that the parties were still negotiating and did not intend to become bound until the negotiations were complete.

. . . As to the law, the principles to be derived from the authorities . . . can be summarized as follows:

(1) In order to determine whether a contract has been concluded in the course of correspondence, one must first look to the correspondence as a whole (see *Hussey* v *Horne-Payne*).

(2) Even if the parties have reached agreement on all the terms of the proposed contract, nevertheless they may intend that the contract shall not become binding until some further condition has been fulfilled. That is the ordinary 'subject to contract' case.

(3) Alternatively, they may intend that the contract shall not become binding until some further term or terms have been agreed; see *Love and Stewart* v *Instone*, where the parties failed to agree the intended strike clause, and *Hussey* v *Horne-Payne*, where Lord Selborne said:

> ". . . The observation has often been made, that a contract established by letters may sometimes bind parties who, when they wrote those letters, did not imagine that they were finally settling the terms of the agreement by which they were to be bound; and it appears to me that no such contract ought to be held established, even by letters which would otherwise be sufficient for the purpose, if it is clear, upon the facts, that there were other conditions of the intended act, beyond and besides those expressed in the letters, which were still in a state of negotiation only, *and without the settlement of which the parties had no idea of concluding any agreement.*" [Lloyd LJ's emphasis].

(4) Conversely, the parties may intend to be bound forthwith even though there are further terms still to be agreed or some further formality to be fulfilled (see *Love and Stewart* v *Instone* per Lord Loreburn).

(5) If the parties fail to reach agreement on such further terms, the existing contract is not invalidated unless the failure to reach agreement on such further terms renders the contract as a whole unworkable or void for uncertainty.

(6) It is sometimes said that the parties must agree on the essential terms and that it is only matters of detail which can be left over. This may be misleading, since the word "essential" in that context is ambiguous. If by "essential" one means a term without which the contract cannot be enforced then the statement is true: the law cannot enforce an incomplete contract. If by "essential" one means a term which the parties have agreed to be essential for the formation of a binding contract, then the statement is tautologous. If by "essential" one means only a term which the Court regards as important as opposed to a term which the Court regards as less important or a matter of detail, the statement is untrue. It is for the parties to decide whether they wish to be bound and, if so, by what terms, whether important or unimportant. It is the parties who are, in the memorable phrase coined by the Judge, "the masters of their contractual fate". Of course the more important the term is the less likely it is that the parties will have left it for future decision. But there is no legal obstacle which stands in the way of the parties agreeing to be bound now while deferring important matters to be agreed later. It happens every day when parties enter into so-called "heads of agreement". Mr Rokison submits that that is a special case, but I do not think it is.

Mr Rokison relied heavily on the fact that the Judge described the terms on which the parties had not yet agreed as "terms of economic significance to these buyers". If I am right in the propositions I have stated, and in particular propositions (4) and (6), the fact that the terms yet to be agreed were of economic significance would not prevent a contract coming into existence forthwith if that is what the parties intended. So I can find no error of law in the Judge's approach.

Was the Judge right to draw the inference which he did as to the parties' intentions? [The more important] matters upon which the Judge relied . . . are the following:

(1) Pagnan told Agrimec on Feb 1 to book the business.
(2) Agrimec sent a confirmatory telex the same day referring to the business as – ". . . having been concluded through our intermediary".
(3) Neither party raised any objection to the confirmatory telex.
(4) The plaintiffs thereafter headed their telexes "Contract 1/2/82".
(5) There was no communication of any kind between Feb 8, when the defendants agreed the loading rate, and Mar 9 when Agrimec despatched the documents.
(6) The plaintiffs did not then react as one would have expected if there had been no question of a binding contract.

Mr Rokison argued that the parties' reactions are as irrelevant as their beliefs. I agree of course that the test is objective and the reactions of the parties are not conclusive. But I cannot accept that they are irrelevant. As to the other matters relied on by the Judge, some of the more important of which I have mentioned, Mr Rokison submitted that the Judge gave them altogether too much weight. As for the gap between Feb 8 and Mar 9, Mr Rokison said that there could be several explanations. To choose one rather than another would be mere speculation.

I cannot accept those submissions. The Judge regarded the matters to which I have referred as being – ". . . very strong indications that the parties intended to, and did, make a binding contract on Feb 1".

In my view he was right. Indeed the only indication the other way is that the parties continued with their negotiations after the confirmatory telex of Feb 1. But that is not really an indication at all. Once one accepts that the parties are in law capable of making what I will call an interim agreement, it was only to be expected that they would continue negotiating the terms that remained without delay. This is what they did. In my view the Judge drew the right inference as to the parties' intentions.

. . . For the reasons I have given I would dismiss the appeal.'

The words *subject to contract* are a strong indication that the parties *do not intend* to enter into a contract at this stage.

Winn v Bull

(1877) 47 LJCh 139 • Chancery Division

On 16 March 1877 Winn and Bull signed an agreement whereby Winn agreed to lease a house to Bull for seven years at a yearly rent of £180. The agreement stated 'This agreement is made subject to the preparation and approval of a formal contract.' No 'formal' contract was ever entered into.

Jessel MR: 'In my opinion there is no contract. I think the principle is quite clear. If, on a proposed sale or lease of an estate, two persons agree to all the terms, but say, "We will have the terms put into form", then all the terms being agreed to and put into writing, there is a contract. But if they agree in writing that the terms up to a certain point shall be the actual terms, but that some minor terms shall be settled by solicitors and approved of by them, then there is no contract, because all the terms have not been agreed to . . .

It comes, therefore, to this, when you have an agreement in writing, expressed to be subject to the preparation of a formal contract, it means what it says; it is subject to and conditional upon the preparation of such formal contract. When it is not expressly stated to be so subject, it becomes a question of construction, whether all the terms are really agreed to, but are to be put merely into some formal document, or whether the terms themselves are to be subject to a new agreement not expressed in detail.

I consider that there is no binding contract in this case, and the plaintiff's case therefore fails.'

ACCEPTANCE MAY BE 'RETROSPECTIVE'

In contrast to the parties wishing to postpone the making of the contract, sometimes they wish to get on with things and make the contract later. Although this tends to be an exception rather than a rule it is possible for the parties to carry out certain actions on the basis that they will be regulated by a later contract – the final acceptance will cover these actions.

Trollope & Colls Ltd v Atomic Power Constructions Ltd
[1962] 3 All ER 1035 • Queen's Bench

Trollope and APC (Atomic Power Constructions Ltd) collaborated in the preparation of a tender by the APC with the intention that if the tender was accepted APC would be the main contractors and Trollope would be sub-contractors for the civil engineering part of the work. On 14 February 1959 Trollope submitted a tender to APC for their part of the work. Their tender concluded 'Unless and until a formal agreement is prepared and executed this tender, together with your written acceptance thereof, shall constitute a binding contract between us.' No formal agreement was entered into. The two parties then continued to negotiate about changes in the work Trollope was to carry out for APC. Then on 23 June 1959, by a 'letter of intent', APC stated their intention to enter into a contract agreement for the civil engineering work with Trollope as soon as outstanding matters between the parties were settled, and requested Trollope in the meantime to proceed with the necessary work. Trollope began work on the project. On 11 April 1960 Trollope and APC finally agreed the conditions and entered into a contract.

The issue before the Court was whether the contract of 11 April 1960 governed the parties' rights since 23 June 1959, in other words did the contract of 11 April 1960 have retrospective effect?

Megaw J: 'But, so far as I am aware, there is no principle of English law which provides that a contract cannot in any circumstances have retrospective effect, or that, if it purports to have, in fact, retrospective effect, it is in law a nullity. If, indeed, there were such a principle, there would be many important mercantile contracts which would, no doubt to the consternation of the parties, be nullities. Frequently, in large transactions a written contract is expressed to have retrospective effect, sometimes lengthy retrospective effect: and this in cases where the negotiations on some of the terms have continued up to almost, if not quite, the date of the signature of the contract. The parties have meanwhile been conducting their transactions with one another, it may be for many months, on the assumption that a contract would ultimately be agreed on lines known to both the parties, though with the final form of various constituent terms of the proposed contract still under discussion. The parties have assumed that when the contract is made – when all the terms have been agreed in their final form – the contract will apply retrospectively to the preceding transactions. Often, as I say, the ultimate contract expressly so provides. I can see no reason why, if the parties so intend and agree, such a stipulation should be denied legal effect. Take, as an example, a simple case. Suppose that a contract for the sale of goods is under negotiation. The offeror has said: "I will sell you one thousand tons of coal on such and such terms". While the detailed terms of sale are still under negotiation, the offeree asks for the delivery of five hundred tons and the offeror makes delivery, both parties intending and anticipating that this delivery will count against the contract quantity if and when the contract is made, or perhaps believing wrongly that the contract has already been made. The final terms are then agreed, the offer is accepted, and the contract is made. Even if, in the actual acceptance by the offeree, no express reference is made to the antecedent delivery of the five hundred tons, I should have thought that there would be little room for doubt that the contract was intended to govern, and in law did govern, that antecedent delivery; and that neither party could successfully assert that there was no contract, or that the five hundred tons was delivered on a *quantum meruit* basis; or that the whole one thousand tons still fell to be delivered after the contract. Of course, the position would be different if no contract were ultimately made, as, for example, by the offeror's withdrawal of the offer before acceptance. So here. If a contract was made on 11 April 1960, and if the contract expressly provided, or should in law be assumed to have provided, that its terms as then agreed were to apply retrospectively to previous acts of the parties done since the date of the tender in anticipation of the making of such a contract at a later date, I see no reason why, in law, effect should not be given to such a provision . . .

In the present case, so far, as I have seen, a retrospective effect is nowhere expressly stated or stipulated. Is it to be implied into the contract of 11 April 1960, if contract there was? That, I conceive, is the crucial question on this issue.

It has been said on many occasions that terms are not to be implied merely because they are desirable, or merely because the parties, if they had considered the question, would probably or as reasonable men have agreed such terms. Terms can only be implied where, to use the common phrase, they are necessary in order to give "business efficacy" to the contract. In the present case, in one sense at least, this term of retrospectivity is necessary to give business efficacy to the contract, if contract there was. The submission of counsel for the plaintiffs is in my view right to this extent, that, in the absence of retrospective effect to the variations clauses, an agreement made on 11 April 1960, would not only be devoid of business efficacy but also would not be capable of being a contract at all, because it would pre-suppose a state of affairs (the original specifications and price) which had long since ceased to be realistic or practicable or within the true intentions of either party in relation to the work to be done under an agreement. On the other hand, I do not think that a term such as this can be implied simply for the purpose of upholding the existence of a contract, unless it can clearly be seen that it conforms with what the parties truly intended and with what they both would have accepted as a matter of course had the question been raised in the course of the negotiations or at the moment of the making of the supposed contract. But if those factors are present, in my judgment it is right and necessary that such a term should be treated as being implied.

I am satisfied from all the circumstances that both parties, in all that they did in the course of the negotiations, in the defendants' requests or instructions to the plaintiffs to carry out the work as varied, and in the plaintiffs' acceptance of those instructions, were doing so on the understanding and in the anticipation that, if a contract were made, and whenever it was made, that contract would apply to and govern what was meanwhile being done by the parties. I am satisfied that if, on 11 April 1960 ... the question had been raised, both parties would have said, as a matter of course: "This contract is to be treated as applying, not only to our future relations, but also to what has been done by us in the past since the date of the tender in the anticipation of the making of this contract".'

DIFFICULTIES IN DETERMINING ACCEPTANCE

Sometimes difficult to determine if there has been an acceptance

In the following case look for the offer, the counter-offer and the acceptance.

Brogden v *Metropolitan Railway Company*

(1877) 2 App Cas 666 • House of Lords

From the beginning of 1870 Brogden had supplied MRC with coal and coke for their locomotives. In November 1871 Brogden suggested that the parties should enter into a formal contract. A draft agreement was drawn up which stated 'Brogden shall, at their own expense, as from January 1 1872, supply every week and deliver for the use of the MRC at the Paddington Station 220 tons of coal, and any farther quantity of coal, not exceeding 350 tons per week, at such times and in such quantity as MRC shall from time to time require'. The payment was to be at the rate of 20s per ton of 20 cwt. Either of the parties could 'determine this agreement by giving two calendar months previous notice in writing on November 1 1872.' If no such notice was given the agreement was to continue in force 'for one year from January 1 1873'. If any differences should arise they were to be referred to 'the arbitration of [name of arbitrator to be inserted], and such person or persons as shall be mutually agreed upon'.

The draft agreement was handed to Brogden by MRC for approval by them. Brogden left the date blank. He filled up the part describing the parties by putting in the names of himself and partners. He filled in the arbitration clause with the name, 'William Armstrong Esq of Swindon', and, finally, he appended the word 'approved', and under it signed his own name, 'Alexander Brogden'. He sent the agreement back to MRC to have a formal contract drawn up in duplicate and signed by the respective parties. Brogden never made a copy of the agreement. Mr Burnett, an employee of MRC, put the draft agreement into his drawer where it lay forgotten. Brogden and MRC then conducted business on the basis of the draft agreement for nearly a year until Brogden refused to deliver any more coal. During that year the parties had in most letters between them made reference to 'the contract'.

The issue before the court was whether a concluded contract had ever been entered into between the two parties.

The Lord Chancellor Lord Cairns: 'My Lords ... the parties were approaching to a meeting for a definite and clearly expressed purpose, namely, to make a contract, which was to last for a considerable length of time, and it will be one of the observations in the case, that the view taken by the Appellants in this case leaves your Lordships entirely without any explanation of what ultimately became of that contract which the parties, clearly, were seriously bent upon agreeing to in some form or other.

Now, my Lords, I will call your Lordships' attention to what was done subsequent to this date; but before I do so, there is at the very outset this remarkable circumstance, which your Lordships will bear in mind: these two parties having been in negotiation up to 22 December, both of them clearly bent upon making a contract which was to provide for a supply of coals in the following year, both of them engaged upon it, and so seriously engaged upon it that they had reduced it into writing with very considerable minuteness of detail; according to the view of the Appellants, this agreement, which they were so bent on forming, is said suddenly and without any kind of explanation to have passed entirely out of view, an incomplete and unfinished transaction, as regarded which there never was any *consensus* between them, and no explanation is given in any shape or form of why it was, according to the view of the Appellants, that there never was any reference afterwards to the contract, nor any proceeding taken to have it brought to a definite point. My Lords, it would be, indeed, a very strange matter if, both parties having shewn such earnestness in the business to which they were addressing themselves, they were from the moment of 22 December to be held to have parted without any impression whatever that anything had been done towards accomplishing the object of that act upon which they were bent.

But, my Lords, what took place afterwards was this: On 22 December Mr Burnett, getting this draft, putting it where the contracts of the company were placed for custody, writes in return to Messrs Brogden & Sons. He makes no objection to anything which had been done with regard to that document; he is silent upon that subject, but he says, "We shall require 250 tons per week of locomotive coal, commencing not later than 1st January next" – the very date which was the date mentioned in the contract for the commencement of the supply – "Reply by wire that you will do this, that we may arrange with other collieries accordingly". My Lords, the contract had provided, with regard to the amount of the supply, that it should be "220 tons of coal, and any farther quantity of coal not exceeding 350 tons per week, at such times and in such quantity as the company shall by writing under their agent's hands from time to time require, such notice to be given to the contractors or agents of the contractors for the time being. . . ."

Now, my Lords, what I have to ask myself is this: the draft having been returned with only one variation to which, as far as I can see, any objection could have been taken, namely, that with reference to the arbitrator, and no objection having been made upon the score of the insertion of his name, although any communication which might have been made must distinctly have been made in writing; I have to ask, how is the course of action of the parties – the suppliers of coal and the railway company – during the following year to be accounted for? . . .

[Lord Cairns then gave examples of how the business was conducted between the parties on the basis of the agreement.]

But, my Lords, over and above that, I must say that having read with great care the whole of this correspondence, there appears to me clearly to be pervading the whole of it the expression of a feeling on the one side and on the other that those who were ordering the coals were ordering them, and those who were supplying the coals were supplying them, under some course of dealing which created on the one side a right to give the order, and on the other side an obligation to comply with the order. If it had not been so, I cannot conceive how when there were these repeated complaints against the Messrs Brogden for short or irregular supplies, and when they say more than once that the prices they were receiving from the Metropolitan Company did not make their bargain a good one, or did not make the Metropolitan Company good customers, how it was that if they did not feel that there was a contract somewhere or other entitling the Metropolitan Company to a supply, and binding them (the Brogdens) to supply coal, they did not say "If you do not like the mode in which we are supplying, or the extent to which we are supplying, it is quite easy for you to get your supplies elsewhere, and we are under no obligation to supply you". They do not do that; on the contrary, they go on asking for indulgence and consideration in a way which it appears to me to be impossible to account for, except upon the footing which they recognise in the letter I have read of 25 July, that there was a contract under which there was some maximum or other up to which they were bound to supply the coal.

My Lords, those are the grounds which lead me to think that, there having been clearly a consensus between these parties, arrived at and expressed by the document signed by Mr Brogden, subject only to approbation, on the part of the company, of the additional term which he had introduced with regard to an arbitrator, that approbation was clearly given when the company commenced a course of dealing which is referable in my mind only to the contract, and when that course of dealing was accepted and acted upon by Messrs Brogden & Co in the supply of coals.'

Difficulty in determining if there has been an acceptance in the case of tenders

Tenders are not normally an offer: see *Spencer* v *Harding* above.

Great Northern Railway Company v *Witham*

(1873) LR 9 CP 16 • Common Pleas

In October 1871 GNR advertised for tenders for the supply of goods to be delivered at their station according to a certain specification. Witham sent in a tender which said 'I hereby undertake to supply the Great Northern Railway Company, for twelve months from the 1st of November 1871, to 31st October 1872, with such quantities of each or any of the several articles named in the attached specification as the company's store-keeper may order from time to time, at the price set opposite each article respectively, and agree to abide by the conditions stated on the other side'.

GNR replied 'Sir – I am instructed to inform you that my directors have accepted your tender . . . to supply this company at Doncaster station any quantity they may order during the period ending 31st October, 1872, of the descriptions of iron mentioned on the enclosed list, at the prices specified therein'.

GNR placed several orders for iron with Witham which Witham duly supplied. GNR then placed another order for iron with Witham but Witham refused to supply any more iron.

The issues before the court were first, the relationship that had been brought about by GNR's acceptance of Witham's tender and, secondly, whether Witham's refusal to honour the final order amounted to a breach of contract.

Brett J: 'The company advertised for tenders for the supply of stores, such as they might think fit to order, for one year. The defendant made a tender offering to supply them for that period at certain fixed prices; and the company accepted his tender. If there were no other objection, the contract between the parties would be found in the tender and the letter accepting it. This action is brought for the defendant's refusal to deliver goods ordered by the company; and the objection to the plaintiffs' right to recover is, that the contract is unilateral. I do not, however, understand what objection that is to a contract.

Many contracts are obnoxious to the same complaint. If I say to another, "If you will go to York, I will give you £100," that is in a certain sense a unilateral contract. He has not promised to go to York. But, if he goes, it cannot be doubted that he will be entitled to receive the £100. His going to York at my request is a sufficient consideration for my promise. So, if one says to another, "If you will give me an order for iron, or other goods, I will supply it at a given price", if the order is given, there is a complete contract which the seller is bound to perform. There is in such a case ample consideration for the promise. So, here, the company having given the defendant an order at his request, his acceptance of the order would bind them. If any authority could have been found to sustain Mr Seymour's [counsel for Witham] contention, I should have considered that a rule ought to be granted. But none has been cited. *Burton* v *Great Northern Railway Co* is not at all to the purpose. This is matter of every day's practice; and I think it would be wrong to countenance the notion that a man who tenders for the supply of goods in this way is not bound to deliver them when an order is given. I agree that this judgment does not decide the question whether the defendant might have absolved himself from the further performance of the contract by giving notice.'

In *Great Northern Railway Company* v *Witham*, above, Brett J said 'I agree that this judgment does not decide the question whether the defendant might have absolved himself from the further performance of the contract by giving notice.' Could the defendant have absolved himself from the further performance of the contract by giving notice?

COMMUNICATION OF ACCEPTANCE

General rule: an acceptance has no effect until it is communicated to the offeror.

Entores Ltd v Miles Far East Corporation

[1955] 2 All ER 493 • Court of Appeal

A series of telex messages were sent between Entores Ltd, an English company, and Miles Far East Corporation, a Dutch company. Miles Far East Corporation made an offer to supply cathodes to Entores Ltd. Entores Ltd made a counter-offer to buy cathodes from Miles Far East Corporation at a price of £239 10s a ton. The offer was accepted by Miles Far East Corporation sending a telex from Holland. The issue before the court was 'Where was the contract made?'. This was important because Entores Ltd wished to sue Miles Far East Corporation in the English courts but could only do so if the contract was made in England and not in Holland.

In this case Entores Ltd were not suing for breach of contract but they were seeking the court's permission for leave to serve out of the jurisdiction of the English court under RSC, Ord 11, r 1.

Denning LJ: 'This is an application for leave to serve notice of a writ out of the jurisdiction. The grounds are that the action is brought to recover damages for breach of a contract made within the jurisdiction or by implication to be governed by English law . . .

When a contract is made by post it is clear law throughout the common law countries that the acceptance is complete as soon as the letter of acceptance is put into the post box, and that is the place where the contract is made. But there is no clear rule about contracts made by telephone or by Telex. Communications by these means are virtually instantaneous and stand on a different footing.

The problem can only be solved by going in stages. Let me first consider a case where two people make a contract by word of mouth in the presence of one another. Suppose, for instance, that I shout an offer to a man across a river or a courtyard but I do not hear his reply because it is drowned by an aircraft flying overhead. There is no contract at that moment. If he wishes to make a contract, he must wait till the aircraft is gone and then shout back his acceptance so that I can hear what he says. Not until I have his answer am I bound . . .

Now take a case where two people make a contract by telephone. Suppose, for instance, that I make an offer to a man by telephone and, in the middle of his reply, the line goes "dead" so that I do not hear his words of acceptance. There is no contract at that moment. The other man may not know the precise moment when the line failed. But he will know that the telephone conversation was abruptly broken off, because people usually say something to signify the end of the conversation. If he wishes to make a contract, he must therefore get through again so as to make sure that I heard. Suppose next that the line does not go dead, but it is nevertheless so indistinct that I do not catch what he says and I ask him to repeat it. He then repeats it and I hear his acceptance. The contract is made, not on the first time when I do not hear, but only the second time when I do hear. If he does not repeat it, there is no contract. The contract is only complete when I have his answer accepting the offer.

Lastly take the Telex. Suppose a clerk in a London office taps out on the teleprinter an offer which is immediately recorded on a teleprinter in a Manchester office, and a clerk at that end taps out an acceptance. If the line goes dead in the middle of the sentence of acceptance, the teleprinter motor will stop. There is then obviously no contract. The clerk at Manchester must get through again and send his complete sentence. But it may happen that the line does not go dead, yet the message does not get through to London. Thus the clerk at Manchester may tap out his message of acceptance and it will not be recorded in London because the ink at the London end fails or something of that kind. In that case the Manchester clerk will not know of the failure but the London clerk will know of it and will immediately send back a message "not receiving". Then, when the fault is rectified, the Manchester clerk will repeat his message. Only then is there a contract. If he does not repeat it, there is no contract. It is not until his message is received that the contract is complete.

In all the instances I have taken so far, the man who sends the message of acceptance knows that it has not been received or he has reason to know it. So he must repeat it. But suppose that he does not know that his message did not get home. He thinks it has. This may happen if the listener on the telephone does not catch the words of acceptance, but nevertheless does not trouble to ask for them to be repeated: or if the ink on the teleprinter fails at the receiving end, but the clerk does not ask for the message to be repeated: so that the man who sends an acceptance reasonably believes that his message has been received. The offeror in such circumstances is clearly bound, because he will be estopped from saying that he did not receive the message of acceptance. It is his own fault that he did not get it. But if there should be a case where the offeror without any fault on his part does not receive the message of acceptance – yet the sender of it reasonably believes it has got home when it has not – then I think there is no contract.

My conclusion is that the rule about instantaneous communications between the parties is different from the rule about the post. The contract is only complete when the acceptance is received by the offeror: and the contract is made at the place where the acceptance is received . . .

Applying the principles which I have stated, I think that the contract in this case was made in London where the acceptance was received. It was therefore a proper case for service out of the jurisdiction.'

Parker LJ: 'I have come to the same conclusion, and would only add a few words on the basis that the contract sued on is that created by the Telex messages. As was said by Lindley LJ, in *Carlill* v *Carbolic Smoke Ball Co*:

> "Unquestionably, as a general proposition, when an offer is made, it is necessary in order to make a binding contract, not only that it should be accepted, but that the acceptance should be notified." . . .

Since, however, the requirement as to actual notification of the acceptance is for the benefit of the offeror, he may waive it and agree to the substitution for that requirement of some other conduct by the acceptor. He may do so expressly, as in the advertisement cases, by intimating that he is content with the performance of a condition. Again he may do so impliedly by indicating a contemplated method of acceptance, e.g., by post or telegram. In such a case he does not expressly dispense with actual notification, but he is held to have done so impliedly on grounds of expediency. Thus in *Adams* v *Lindsell* the court pointed out that, unless this were so:

> ". . . no contract could ever be completed by the post. For if the defendants were not bound by their offer when accepted by the plaintiffs till the answer was received, then the plaintiffs ought not to be bound till after they had received the notification that the defendants had received their answer and assented to it. And so it might go on *ad infinitum*." . . .

Where, however, the parties are in each other's presence or, though separated in space, communication between them is in effect instantaneous, there is no need for any such rule of convenience. To hold otherwise would leave no room for the operation of the general rule that notification of the acceptance must be received. An acceptor could say: "I spoke the words of acceptance in your presence, albeit softly, and it matters not that you did not hear me"; or: "I telephoned to you and accepted and it matters not that the telephone went dead and you did not get my message". Though in both these cases the acceptor was using the contemplated, or indeed the expressly indicated, mode of communication, there is no room for any implication that the offeror waived actual notification of the acceptance . . .

So far as Telex messages are concerned, though the dispatch and receipt of a message is not completely instantaneous, the parties are to all intents and purposes in each other's presence, just as if they were in telephonic communication, and I can see no reason for departing from the general rule that there is no binding contract until notice of the acceptance is received by the offeror. That being so and, since the offer – a counter-offer – was made by the plaintiffs in London and notification of the acceptance was received by them in London, the contract resulting therefrom was made in London. I would accordingly dismiss the appeal.'

Exceptions to general rule that acceptance must be communicated

Presumed communication

Definition: **Estoppel is a rule where one person (the representor) makes a statement of fact to another person (the representee). If on reliance of that statement the representee reasonably supposes he is intended to, and does, act to his detriment, then if the representor later sues the representee, the**

representor will not be allowed to say (i.e. he will be estopped from saying) that his representation was untrue, even if it was in fact untrue.

Tenax Steamship Co Ltd v Owners of the motor vessel Brimnes (The Brimnes)

[1974] 3 All ER 88 • Court of Appeal

The shipowners sent a telex message to the charterers at some time between 1730 hrs and 1800 hrs BST withdrawing their ship from the charterers' service. The message was sent and received instantaneously on the charterers' telex machine during their normal business hours at their office and while the member of their staff who was in charge of the machine was present. The charterers claimed that the telex message withdrawing the ship was not seen until the start of the following day. The issue before the court was whether the notice of withdrawal took effect when it was received or not until it was actually read.

Although this case deals with the acceptance of the breach of contract, the principles regarding the communication are the same as the communication of acceptances.

Megaw LJ: [The time of notice of withdrawal] 'The learned judge reviewed with care the acutely conflicting evidence as to the time when the telex notice of withdrawal was despatched from the office of Embiricos SA Ltd and received at the charterers' office on the evening of 2 April. There was no doubt that the telex machine in the charterers' office was in working order and was set so as to invite and receive messages. This telex message, when it was sent, was reproduced in the charterers' office simultaneously with its despatch. The judge held that the telex message was certainly sent, and received on the charterers' machine before 18.00 hours. The time which he found was 17.45 hours . . .

On the assumption that, as I think plainly must be so, this court upholds Brandon J's findings of fact, there was lengthy and elaborate argument, with the citation of numerous authorities, as to the principle applicable for deciding the time at which such notice ought to be treated as having been effectively given.

With all respect, I think the principle which is relevant is this: if a notice arrives at the address of the person to be notified, at such a time and by such a means of communication that it would in the normal course of business come to the attention of that person on its arrival, that person cannot rely on some failure of himself or his servants to act in a normal businesslike manner in respect of taking cognisance of the communication, so as to postpone the effective time of the notice until some later time when it in fact came to his attention.

It was conceded on behalf of the charterers that if Mrs Sayce, an employee of theirs, had seen the telex message when it arrived at the charterers' London office on 2 April, her sight of it would constitute effective notice to the charterers at that moment . . . It follows that if the judge had held that Mrs Sayce saw the telex message that would have been the end of any argument on this point. Notice would have been effectively given before 18.00 hours. But the charterers say that they escape from that conclusion because the judge said that he was inclined to accept that Mrs Sayce was not in fact aware of the telex message, despite the fact that it had arrived and her own emphatic evidence that if it had arrived she could not have failed to see it. The judge was inclined to think that, contrary to her own insistence, either she left the office before 18.00 hours or she neglected to pay attention to the telex machine in the way she claimed it was her practice to do.

I do not think that avails the charterers in the way in which their case was presented.

The shipowners have rebutted the charterers' case that the message had not arrived by 18.00 hours. I do not think that the shipowners were obliged, before the time of the receipt in the charterers' office could be treated as the effective time of the giving of the notice, to go on to establish affirmatively that which the charterers themselves asserted: namely, that a person competent to receive the message was there at that time, and, being there, should have seen it. As I have already said, I do not think that the law regards the effective time of the giving of a notice as liable to be postponed because of some failure by the recipient to see it in the ordinary course of a business competently conducted in a normal businesslike way. I do not think that in the circumstances any burden rested on the shipowners to show that in the ordinary course of business some competent person ought to have been in the office to receive the message when it arrived before 18.00 hours, since the case for the charterers was: "A competent person was there".

I agree with Brandon J that the notice was effectively given when it appeared on the telex machine in the charterers' office before 18.00 on 2 April, when, according to her own evidence, it should have been seen by Mrs Sayce.'

Brinkibon Ltd v Stahag Stahl und Stahlwarenhandelsgesellschaft mbH
[1982] 1 All ER 293 • House of Lords

This case was in many respects similar to the *Entores Ltd* case above. Again the issue was whether the English company could serve a writ out of jurisdiction. The House of Lords followed the *Entores Ltd* case and held that the contract was formed where the acceptance was received, in this case Austria. Since the contract was not an English contract the House of Lords refused to permit service out of jurisdiction.

The quotes from the case that follow develop points made in the *Entores Ltd* case and *The Brimnes* case.

Lord Wilberforce: 'Since 1955 the use of telex communication has been greatly expanded, and there are many variants on it. The senders and recipients may not be the principals to the contemplated contract. They may be servants or agents with limited authority. The message may not reach, or be intended to reach, the designated recipient immediately: messages may be sent out of office hours, or at night, with the intention, or on the assumption, that they will be read at a later time. There may be some error or default at the recipient's end which prevents receipt at the time contemplated and believed in by the sender. The message may have been sent and/or received through machines operated by third persons. And many other variations may occur. No universal rule can cover all such cases; they must be resolved by reference to the intentions of the parties, by sound business practice and in some cases by a judgment where the risks should lie . . .'

Lord Fraser of Tullybelton: 'I have reached the opinion that, on balance, an acceptance sent by telex directly from the acceptor's office to the offeror's office should be treated as if it were an instantaneous communication between principals, like a telephone conversation. One reason is that the decision to that effect in *Entores Ltd v Miles Far East Corp* seems to have worked without leading to serious difficulty or complaint from the business community. Secondly, once the message has been received on the offeror's telex machine, it is not unreasonable to treat it as delivered to the principal offeror, because it is his responsibility to arrange for prompt handling of messages within his own office. Thirdly, a party (the acceptor) who tries to send a message by telex can generally tell if his message has not been received on the other party's (the offeror's) machine, whereas the offeror, of course, will not know if an unsuccessful attempt has been made to send an acceptance to him. It is therefore convenient that the acceptor, being in the better position, should have the responsibility of ensuring that his message is received. For these reasons I think it is right that in the ordinary simple case, such as I take this to be, the general rule and not the postal rule should apply. But I agree with both my noble and learned friends that the general rule will not cover all the many variations that may occur with telex messages.'

Lord Brandon of Oakbrook: 'Since preparing this speech I have had the advantage of reading in draft that of my noble and learned friend Lord Wilberforce. In it he points out that, while the present case, like the *Entores Ltd* case, is concerned only with instantaneous communication by telex between the principals on either side, there may in other cases be a number of variations on that simple theme. He further expresses the view that there can be no general rule capable of covering all such variations, and that, when they occur, the problems posed by them must be resolved by reference to the intention of the parties, sound business practice and in some cases a judgment where the risk shall lie. I agree entirely with these observations.'

Schelde Delta Shipping BV v *Astarte Shipping Ltd (The Pamela)*
[1995] 2 Lloyd's Rep 249 • Queen's Bench

Under the terms of a charter party the owners were to have the right of withdrawing the vessel from the service of the charterers without noting any protest and without interference by any court or any other formality whatsoever if the charterers defaulted in making payment. However, Clause 27, an anti-technicality clause, provided 'If hire is due and not received, the Owners, before exercising the option of withdrawing the vessel will give Charterers forty eight hours notice, Saturday, Sunday and Holidays excluded, and will not withdraw the vessel if the hire is paid within these 48 hours'. On Friday 2 December 1994 the eighth instalment became due. By a telex timed at 23.41 hrs the owners sent a message to the charterers informing them that they were in breach of contract due to non-receipt of hire and that, therefore, the owners were withdrawing their vessel. This telex was received on the charterers' telex machine instantaneously, i.e. at 23.41 hrs, when their office was closed for the weekend and their telex machine was unmanned.

The issue before the court was when did the notice of withdrawal take effect? Was it when it was received, i.e. 23.41 hrs on 2 December, or was it when it was read by an employee of the charterers on the following Monday morning?

Gatehouse J: 'Two specific questions arose on that preliminary hearing and now arise on this appeal. They are:

(1) Whether, in a case where notice is given to the charterer under the anti-technicality clause by means of an instantaneous transmission (telex) but transmitted out of business hours, the notice is to be regarded as "received" by the charterers (a) at the moment when it is recorded on their telex machine, or (b) only at or shortly after the opening of their office on the next business day? . . .

It was not in dispute in the present case that a notice under cl 27 is not effective until it is actually received by the charterer – the "postal rule" referable to the conclusion of a contract has no application. The crucial question is what is meant by "received"? The charterers contended that this must be the moment when it was printed out on their telex machine; that this occurred before the time when they would be in default under cl 7, and accordingly the notice was premature and invalid for that reason, apart from its want of proper form. The owners contended that the moment of receipt was when the telex message was, or must be taken to have been, first read by a responsible member of the charterer's organisation, i.e., at or shortly after 9 am on Monday Dec 5; that the charterers were by then in default of their duty of punctual payment; accordingly the notice was not then premature; it gave the charterers 48 hours from that moment to remedy their default, and the owners were accordingly entitled to withdraw the vessel when they did, at about 9.25 am on the morning of Dec 7, no hire having been received within the 48 hour grace period.

There is no authority on this. The question has not arisen in any reported decision. In *The Afovos* and other similar cases of instantaneous transmission the message was sent during ordinary business hours so the time of sending the notice by the owners and its receipt by the charterers was identical. It is therefore not significant that various Judges have referred to the time when the notice was "sent", or "issued" . . .

What matters is not when the notice is given/sent/despatched/issued by the owners but when its content reaches the mind of the charterer. If the telex is sent in ordinary business hours, the time of receipt is the same as the time of despatch because it is not open to the charterer to contend that it did not in fact then come to his attention (see *The Brimnes* per Mr Justice Brandon, and per the Court of Appeal.

The problem has, of course, been referred to. See the well-known passage in the speech of Lord Wilberforce in *Brinkibon Ltd* v *Stahag Stahl und Stahlwarenhandelsgesellschaft mbH*, a case concerned, *inter alia*, with where a contract was made by telex. After referring to *Entores* v *Miles Far East Corporation*, where the Court of Appeal classified telex communications with instantaneous communications, e.g. by telephone, Lord Wilberforce said:

> "I would accept [the *Entores* rule] as a general rule. Where the condition of simultaneity is met, and where it appears to be within the mutual intention of the parties that contractual exchanges should take place in this way, I think it a sound rule, but not necessarily a universal rule."

Since 1955 the use of telex communication has been greatly expanded and there are many variants on it. The senders and recipients may not be the principals to the contemplated contract. They may be servants or agents with limited authority. The message may not reach or be intended to reach the designated recipient immediately: messages may be sent out of office hours, or at night, with the intention, or upon the assumption, that they will be read at a later time . . . and many other variations may occur. No universal rule can cover all such cases: they must be resolved by reference to the intentions of the parties, by sound business practice and in some cases by a judgment where the risks should lie . . .

Mr Justice Brandon also referred, in passing, to an out-of hours telex in *The Brimnes*.

The charterers in order to found their contention that the telex message was premature, are in fact contending for a universal rule for telex communications which, they say, has the commercial advantage of certainty. But I propose to follow Lord Wilberforce's words and resolve this issue by reference to the particular circumstances. His Lordship's words, quoted above, were spoken with reference to where a contract is to be regarded as having been concluded: hence, as I think, his reference to the intentions of the parties and in some cases, where the risks should lie (both the cases cited were concerned with the risks which arise from a postal acceptance). A notice such as the one with which I am concerned is clearly of a quite different type and does not involve any consideration of the mutual intentions of contracting parties or of where the risks should lie. But I think the tribunal were entitled to find . . . that a notice which arrives at 23 41 on a Friday night is not to be expected to be read before opening hours on the following Monday, and that was a conclusion of fact arrived at by the arbitrators as a matter of commercial common sense . . .

In my judgment the tribunal were right to find that the notice under cl 31 was not received by charterers until the opening of business on Dec 5, and was not premature.'

Waiver of right to receive communication of acceptance

In the *Entores Ltd* case Parker LJ cited with approval Lindley LJ in *Carlill* v *Carbolic Smoke Ball Co* (below) to the effect that offerors can waive their right to receive communication of acceptance.

A good example of a situation in which the offeror intends to dispense with the normal requirement that the offeree must communicate the acceptance is that of unilateral offers.

Carlill v Carbolic Smoke Ball Company
[1893] 1 QB 256 • Court of Appeal

The facts appear on p 5 above.

Lindley LJ: 'But then it is said, "Supposing that the performance of the conditions is an acceptance of the offer, that acceptance ought to have been notified". Unquestionably, as a general proposition, when an offer is made, it is necessary in order to make a binding contract, not only that it should be accepted, but that the acceptance should be notified. But is that so in cases of this kind? I apprehend that they are an exception to that rule, or, if not an exception, they are open to the observation that the notification of the acceptance need not precede the performance. This offer is a continuing offer. It was never revoked, and if notice of acceptance is required – which I doubt very much, for I rather think the true view is that which was expressed and explained by Lord Blackburn in the case of *Brogden* v *Metropolitan Ry Co* – if notice of acceptance is required, the person who makes the offer gets the notice of acceptance contemporaneously with his notice of the performance of the condition. If he gets notice of the acceptance before his offer is revoked, that in principle is all you want. I, however, think that the true view, in a case of this kind, is that the person who makes the offer shows by his language and from the nature of the transaction that he does not expect and does not require notice of the acceptance apart from notice of the performance.'

Bowen LJ: 'Then it was said that there was no notification of the acceptance of the contract. One cannot doubt that, as an ordinary rule of law, an acceptance of an offer made ought to be notified to the person who makes the offer, in order that the two minds may come together. Unless this is done the two minds may be apart, and there is not that consensus which is necessary according to the English law . . . to make a contract. But there is this clear gloss to be made upon that doctrine, that as notification of acceptance is required for the benefit of the person who makes the offer, the person who makes the offer may dispense with notice to himself if he thinks it desirable to do so, and I suppose there can be no doubt that where a person in an offer made by him to another person, expressly or impliedly intimates a particular mode of acceptance as sufficient to make the bargain binding, it is only necessary for the other person to whom such offer is made to follow the indicated method of acceptance; and if the person making the offer, expressly or impliedly intimates in his offer that it will be sufficient to act on the proposal without communicating acceptance of it to himself, performance of the condition is a sufficient acceptance without notification.'

Silence is not consent

Because of the general rule that 'an acceptance has no effect until it is communicated to the offeror' it follows that if the offeree remains silent there will be no communication of the acceptance and therefore no contract will come into existence.

Felthouse v Bindley

(1862) 31 LJCP 204 • Common Pleas

Paul Felthouse wrote to his nephew John Felthouse offering to buy John's horse for £30 15s and added 'If I hear no more about him, I consider the horse mine at £30 15s.' John never replied to the letter. By mistake the horse was sold by John's auctioneer, William Bindley, to a third party. Paul Felthouse brought an action in conversion against William Bindley. (The action was based on the claim by Paul Felthouse that the horse had been sold to him by his nephew and that therefore he was the owner of the horse and that William Bindley had wrongly sold his horse). The court had to decide whether a contract had come into existence between John and Paul.

Wille J: '[I]t is . . . clear that the uncle had no right to impose upon the nephew a sale of his horse for £30 15s unless he chose to comply with the condition of writing to repudiate the offer. The nephew might, no doubt, have bound his uncle to the bargain by writing to him: the uncle might also have retracted his offer at any time before acceptance. It stood an open offer: and so things remained until the 25th of February, when the nephew was about to sell his farming stock by auction . . . It is clear, therefore, that the nephew in his own mind intended his uncle to have the horse at the price which he (the uncle) had named, – £30 15s. but he had not communicated such his intention to his uncle, or done anything to bind himself . . .'

Offeree need not personally communicate acceptance

The general rule is that the acceptance must be communicated. There is generally no requirement that the offeree personally has to communicate the acceptance.

Dickinson v Dodds

(1876) 2 ChD 463 • Court of Appeal

On Wednesday 10 June 1874 Dodds signed and delivered to Dickinson, a memorandum, which read:

"I hereby agree to sell to Mr George Dickinson the whole of the dwelling-houses, garden ground, stabling, and outbuildings thereto belonging, situate at Croft, belonging to me, for the sum of £800. As witness my hand this tenth day of June, 1874. £800. (Signed) John Dodds

PS – This offer to be left over until Friday, 0900 hrs 12 June 1874. (Signed) J Dodds"

In the afternoon of Thursday 11 June Dickinson was informed by Berry that Dodds had been offering or agreeing to sell the property to Allan. Dickinson then went to the house of Mrs Burgess, the mother-in-law of Dodds, where he was then staying, and left with her a formal acceptance in writing of the offer to sell the property: this document never in fact reached Dodds, Mrs Burgess having forgotten to give it to him. In fact on Thursday 11 June Dodds had signed a formal contract for the sale of the property to Allan for £800, and had received from him a deposit of £40.

The issues before the court were firstly was the memorandum of June 10 an offer or a concluded contract? Secondly if it was an offer could Dodds withdraw it before 0900 hrs 12 June? Thirdly if Dodds could withdraw his offer before 0900 hrs 12 June had he effectively done so?

James LJ, after referring to the document of 10 June 1874, continued:

'The document, though beginning "I hereby agree to sell", was nothing but an offer, and was only intended to be an offer, for Dickinson himself tells us that he required time to consider whether he would enter into an agreement or not. Unless both parties had then agreed there was no concluded agreement then made; it was in effect and substance only an offer to sell. Dickinson, being minded not to complete the bargain at that time, added this memorandum – "This offer to be left over until Friday, 9 o'clock am 12 June 1874". That shews it was only an offer. There was no consideration given for the undertaking or promise, to whatever extent it may be considered binding, to keep the property unsold until 9 o'clock on Friday morning; but apparently Dickinson was of opinion, and probably Dodds was of the same opinion, that he (Dodds) was bound by that promise, and could not in any way withdraw from it, or retract it, until 9 o'clock on Friday morning, and this probably explains a good deal of what afterwards took place. But it is clear settled law, on one of the clearest principles of law, that this promise, being a mere *nudum pactum* [a promise not supported by consideration from the other party] was not binding, and that at any moment before a complete acceptance by Dickinson of the offer, Dodds was as free as Dickinson himself. Well, that being the state of things, it is said that the only mode in which Dodds could assert that freedom was by actually and distinctly saying to Dickinson, "Now I withdraw my offer". It appears to me that there is neither principle nor authority for the proposition that there must be an express and actual withdrawal of the offer, or what is called a retraction. It must, to constitute a contract, appear that the two minds were at one, at the same moment of time, that is, that there was an offer continuing up to the time of the acceptance. If there was not such a continuing offer, then the acceptance comes to nothing . . . [I]n this case, beyond all question, Dickinson knew that Dodds was no longer minded to sell the property to him as plainly and clearly as if Dodds had told him in so many words, "I withdraw the offer". This is evident from Dickinson's own statements in the bill.

Dickinson says in effect that, having heard and knowing that Dodds was no longer minded to sell to him, and that he was selling or had sold to someone else, thinking that he could not in point of law withdraw his offer, meaning to fix him to it, and endeavouring to bind him, "I went to the house where he was lodging, and saw his mother-in-law, and left with her an acceptance of the offer, knowing all the while that he had entirely changed his mind". . . . It is to my mind quite clear that before there was any attempt at acceptance by Dickinson, he was perfectly well aware that Dodds had changed his mind, and that he had in fact agreed to sell the property to Allan. It is impossible, therefore, to say there was ever that existence of the same mind between the two parties which is essential in point of law to the making of an agreement. I am of opinion, therefore, that Dickinson has failed to prove that there was any binding contract between Dodds and himself.'

Mellish LJ: 'Then Dickinson is informed by Berry that the property has been sold by Dodds to Allan. Berry does not tell us from whom he heard it, but he says that he did hear it, that he knew it, and that he informed Dickinson of it. Now, stopping there, the question which arises is this – if an offer has been made for the sale of property, and before that offer is accepted, the person who has made the offer enters into a binding agreement to sell the property to somebody else, and the person to whom the offer was first made receives notice in some way that the property has been sold to another person, can he after that make a binding contract by the acceptance of the offer? I am of opinion that he cannot. The law may be right or wrong in saying that a person who has given to another a certain time within which to accept an offer is not bound by his promise to give that time; but, if he is not bound by that promise, and may still sell the property to someone else and if it be the law that, in order to make a contract, the two minds must be in agreement at some one time, that is, at the time of the acceptance, how is it possible that when the person to whom the offer has been made knows that the person who has made the offer has sold the property to someone else, and that, in fact, he has not remained in the same mind to sell it to him, he can be at liberty to accept the offer and thereby make a binding contract? It seems to me that would be simply absurd. If a man makes an offer to sell a particular horse in his stable, and says, "I will give you until the day after tomorrow to accept the offer", and the next day goes and sells the horse to somebody else, and receives the purchase-money from him, can the person to whom the offer was originally made then come and say, "I accept", so as to make a binding contract, and so as to be entitled to recover damages for the non-delivery of the horse? If the rule of law is that a mere offer to sell property, which can be withdrawn at any time, and which is made dependent on the acceptance of the person to whom it is made, is a mere *nudum pactum*, how is it possible that the person to whom the offer has been made can by acceptance make a binding contract after he knows that the person who has made the offer has sold the property to someone else? . . .'

Mellish LJ above said 'If a man makes an offer to sell a particular horse in his stable, and says, "I will give you until the day after tomorrow to accept the offer", and the next day goes and sells the horse to somebody else, and receives the purchase-money from him, can the person to whom the offer was originally made then come and say, "I accept", so as to make a binding contract, and so as to be entitled to recover damages for the non-delivery of the horse?' What is the answer to his question?

Method of acceptance prescribed by offeror

We have already seen that the offeror can dispense with the normal requirement that the offeree must communicate the acceptance. The converse of this is that the offeror can stipulate that an offer can only be accepted in a particular way.

For example the offeror can stipulate that the acceptance has to be received by the offeror.

Holwell Securities Ltd v Hughes

[1974] 1 All ER 161 • Court of Appeal

On 19 October 1971 Hughes granted an option to Holwell Securities to purchase a certain property for £45 000. Clause 2 of the agreement provided: 'THE said option shall be exercisable by notice in writing to Hughes at any time within six months from the date hereof . . . ' On 14 April 1972 Holwell Securities' solicitors wrote to Hughes accepting his offer to sell his property. The letter accepting Hughes's offer was lost in the post. The issue before the court was whether a contract had been formed when the letter was posted on 14 April.

Russell LJ: 'Holwell Securities' main contention below and before this court has been that the option was exercised and the contract for sale and purchase was constituted at the moment that the letter addressed to Hughes with its enclosure was committed by Holwell Securities' solicitors to the proper representative of the postal service, so that its failure to reach its destination is irrelevant.

It is the law in the first place that *prima facie* acceptance of an offer must be communicated to the offeror. On this principle the law has engrafted a doctrine that, if in any given case the true view is that the parties contemplated that the postal service might be used for the purpose of forwarding an acceptance of the offer, committal of the acceptance in a regular manner to the postal service will be acceptance of the offer so as to constitute a contract, even if the letter goes astray and is lost. Nor, as was once suggested, are such cases limited to cases in which the offer has been made by post. It suffices I think at this stage to refer to *Henthorn v Fraser*. In the present case, as I read a passage in the judgment below, Templeman J concluded that the parties here contemplated that the postal service might be used to communicate acceptance of the offer (by exercise of the option); and I agree with that.

But that is not and cannot be the end of the matter. In any case, before one can find that the basic principle of the need for communication of acceptance to the offeror is displaced by this artificial concept of communication by the act of posting, it is necessary that the offer is in its terms consistent with such displacement and not one which by its terms points rather in the direction of actual communication. We were referred to *Henthorn v Fraser* and to the *obiter dicta* of Farwell J in *Bruner v Moore*, which latter was a case of an option to purchase patent rights. But in neither of those cases was there apparently any language in the offer directed to the manner of acceptance of the offer or exercise of the option.

The relevant language here is, "THE said option shall be exercisable by notice in writing to the Intending Vendor . . .", a very common phrase in an option agreement. There is, of course, nothing in that phrase to suggest that the notification to Hughes could not be made by post. But the requirement of "notice . . . to", in my judgment, is language which should be taken expressly to assert the ordinary situation in law that acceptance requires to be communicated or notified to the offeror, and is inconsistent with the theory that acceptance can be constituted by the act of posting, referred to by Anson (*Law of Contract* (23rd Edn) as "acceptance *without notification*".

It is of course true that the instrument could have been differently worded. An option to purchase within a period given for value has the characteristic of an offer that cannot be withdrawn. The instrument might have said "The offer constituted by this option may be accepted in writing within six months"; in which case no doubt the posting would have sufficed to form the contract. But that language was not used, and, as indicated, in my judgment the language used prevents that legal out-come.'

Lawton LJ: 'It is a truism of the law relating to options that the grantee must comply strictly with the conditions stipulated for exercise: see *Hare* v *Nicoll* . . .

Now in this case, the "notice in writing" was to be one "to the Intending Vendor". It was to be an intimation to him that the grantee had exercised the option: he was the one who was to be fixed with the information contained in the writing. He never was, because the letter carrying the information went astray. Holwell Securities were unable to do what the agreement said they were to do, namely, fix Hughes with knowledge that they had decided to buy his property. If this construction of the option clause is correct, there is no room for the application of any rule of law relating to the acceptance of offers by posting letters since the option agreement stipulated what had to be done to exercise the option. On this ground alone I would dismiss the appeal.

Does the [postal] rule apply in all cases where one party makes an offer which both he and the person with whom he was dealing must have expected the post to be used as a means of accepting it? In my judgment, it does not. First, it does not apply when the express terms of the offer specify that the acceptance must reach the offeror. The public nowadays are familiar with this exception to the general rule through their handling of football pool coupons. Secondly, it probably does not operate if its application would produce manifest inconvenience and absurdity. This is the opinion set out in Cheshire and Fifoot's *Law of Contract* (8th Edn). It was the opinion of Bramwell B as is seen by his judgment in *British & American Telegraph Co* v *Colson*, and his opinion is worthy of consideration even though the decision in that case was overruled by this court in *Household Fire and Carriage Accident Insurance Co Ltd* v *Grant*. The illustrations of inconvenience and absurdity which Bramwell B gave are as apt today as they were then. Is a stockbroker who is holding shares to the orders of his client liable in damages because he did not sell in a falling market in accordance with the instructions in a letter which was posted but never received? Before the passing of the Law Reform (Miscellaneous Provisions) Act 1970 (which abolished actions for breach of promise of marriage), would a young soldier ordered overseas have been bound in contract to marry a girl to whom he had proposed by letter, asking her to let him have an answer before he left and she had replied affirmatively in good time but the letter had never reached him? In my judgment, the factors of inconvenience and absurdity are but illustrations of a wider principle, namely, that the rule does not apply if, having regard to all the circumstances, including the nature of the subject-matter under consideration, the negotiating parties cannot have intended that there should be a binding agreement until the party accepting an offer or exercising an option had in fact communicated the acceptance or exercise to the other. In my judgment, when this principle is applied to the facts of this case it becomes clear that the parties cannot have intended that the posting of a letter should constitute the exercise of the option.'

The offeror can also stipulate that only a particular form should be used to communicate the acceptance.

Compagnie de Commerce et Commission, SARL v Parkinson Stove Company Ltd

[1953] 2 Lloyd's Rep 487 • Court of Appeal

Compagnie de Commerce offered to sell some steel sheet to Parkinson Stove. On 5 March Parkinson Stove sent an order form to Compagnie de Commerce which contained the clause 'said offer must be accepted by execution of the acknowledgement in the form attached by Compagnie de Commerce it being expressly understood that no other form of acceptance, verbal or written, will be valid or binding upon Parkinson Stove. There are no agreements or understandings other than those contained in this order.' The formal acceptance slip was never signed by Compagnie de Commerce. Instead Compagnie de Commerce wrote a letter to Parkinson Stove accepting the offer. Parkinson Stove cancelled their order and Compagnie de Commerce sued Parkinson Stove for breach of contract. The issue before the court was whether the offer, the order of 5 March, could only be accepted by using the specified acceptance slip.

Singleton LJ: 'I am prepared to assume that if one party says: 'I want acceptance in a particular form, and unless I get acceptance in that form I will not be bound,' that he is entitled to insist upon that. Still, if the other party accepts in some other way, the party who has made the offer may by word, or by writing, or, indeed, by conduct, so act as to prevent himself from being heard to say: "I insist on the first condition as to acceptance".

. . . if there was an out-and-out acceptance in another form and if they [Parkinson Stove] treated that as being good and acted upon it, I do not think it would be open to them to rely upon the first of the conditions and to say: "You have not sent the slip in". If they stood by while the other party was continuing to manufacture goods for the contract, believing there was a good acceptance, I do not think they [Parkinson Stove] ought to be allowed to say: "We are out of this; we are not bound, because the slip was not sent". The question is, has anything of that kind taken place in fact, and that depends, it seems to me, upon the view one takes of the letter of March 6, that which is said to be an acceptance . . . What is the true construction of the letter of March 6, that which is pleaded by the plaintiffs to be an acceptance of the defendants' offer?

One thing which is more noticeable in this case than in most cases of this kind is that the defendants, by the use of this printed order form, have made clear beyond doubt that they desired an out-and-out acceptance – a clean acceptance. If they had had the slip signed they would have had an acceptance of their order; and the terms of the order are set out . . .

The letter of March 6 acknowledges a letter of February 27, and acknowledges Document No 5, the purchase order, "and for which we thank you". I have looked through this letter of March 6, and I have heard considerable argument upon it. I cannot find in that letter anywhere the words, "We accept your offer", or anything which is equivalent to those words. That is my difficulty in this case. I recognise, as Mr Duveen [counsel on behalf of Compagnie de Commerce et Commission, SARL] submitted, that one or two witnesses said that they thought there was a contract, and I recognise from some of the expressions in later letters that it may well be thought that the defendants thought they had a contract when they wrote: "By reason of difficulties which arose we asked to cancel our order". Mr Duveen submitted that, in view of later correspondence and in view of what was said by one of the plaintiffs' witnesses, Mr Moore, this Court ought to interpret the letter of March 6 as being an acceptance.

I do not think we can interpret the letter in that way . . .'

[Singleton LJ then went on to hold that the letter of March 6 was too uncertain to constitute an acceptance and that therefore no contract had come into existence.]

Hodson LJ agreed with Singleton LJ.

Birkett LJ (dissenting): 'Mr Stenham said: "I can state my case in the broadest possible form; that is to say, that there was a prescribed mode laid down by the defendants for the acceptance of the offer they made; no other mode of any kind, verbal or written, was permissible". It is common ground that that prescribed mode was not followed, and therefore there was no contract; and he said under two subsidiary heads of his main contention that there was no contract at all. He then said by way of precaution: "Assuming that which I submit is quite clear and firm is wrong, or should be held to be wrong, then I say that the letter of March 6, for the reasons I put forward, is not an acceptance in any true sense of the word".

Mr Duveen, on the other hand, said that the document of March 6, to which my Lord has referred, was a clear acceptance of the offer and made a binding contract. He said that in truth the slip was not signed, but that really becomes immaterial because, on the facts of the case, there was clear waiver by the plaintiffs of that term.

It would be quite impossible for me to go into all the detail which has been discussed before the Court, but I agree with Mr Stenham that when you are deciding a case of this kind you are to look not at one or two documents, but if they are interrelated and interconnected you must look at the whole of the documents and see what emerges from them.

. . . So I agree fully with all my Lord has already said, that almost everything turns upon the view to be taken of the letter of March 6, 1952.

In my opinion, that was an acceptance of the offer . . .

Stopping there, I think that letter is itself a plain acceptance. I do not think I need spend many words upon that point, because I hold very clearly that this proviso about signing the slip was manifestly waived, as the subsequent conduct shows. Nothing was ever said by the defendants to the effect: "Well, you know, you have never signed that slip". They were absolutely silent, and everyone was silent, about it until the solicitors came upon the scene and raised this point, perfectly properly and perfectly rightly, but no one else had thought about it up to that minute, and I think that that is some evidence, at any rate, of waiver; and if the subsequent correspondence is looked at, I think it becomes quite clear. I will not read it all, but take, for example, the letter of March 14, which is the first letter of the defendants after receiving the plaintiffs' letter of March 6. What do they say? "We have your letter of March 6, but, you know, you have not signed the slip, and we must insist upon it?" – not a word. All they say is this:

"Further to the correspondence we have had regarding steel sheets, our representative Mr Walters, is in France and proposes calling on you next Tuesday morning, March 18th, when we trust it will be convenient for you to see him.

We should be glad if you could give him the details as to the name and address of the mill, from where the material you are offering will be coming, and also arrange for samples of the material to be made available if possible."

I cannot think when the defendants write a letter like that on March 14, when they are in possession of the letter of March 6, that if they said: "We are going to insist upon that term", they would not have said something about it, but it is perfectly plain that from that point onwards they never made the slightest suggestion about it; and, further, to support the view which I myself take of the letter of March 6, I think myself that the subsequent conduct and what the parties did is an important matter to consider.

. . . I would have dismissed this appeal; but as my brethren think differently, of course the appeal will be allowed.'

Speed of communication

Allied to the point that the offeror can prescribe a particular method of acceptance the offeror can also stipulate the time within which the acceptance must be communicated. This can, of course, be an express stipulation but it might also be implied from the method used in communicating the offer. For example, if the offer is sent by telegram this would imply that the acceptance had to be by an equally fast means of communication.

NB Generally the mode of communication of the offer only fixes the time within which the acceptance must be communicated. It does not fix the actual method of communication to be used.

Manchester Diocesan Council for Education v Commercial and General Investments Ltd

[1969] 3 All ER 1593 • Chancery Division

The Manchester Diocesan Council for Education (M) decided to sell a school by tender. One of the conditions of the tender required tenders to be sent to the M's surveyor on or before 27 August 1964 and stipulated that the sale was subject to the approval of the Secretary of State for Education and Science. Condition 4 stated:

'The person whose tender is accepted shall be the purchaser and shall be informed of the acceptance of his tender by letter sent to him by post addressed to the address given in his tender and every letter sent shall be deemed to have been received in due course of post.'

On 25 August 1964 C (Commercial and General Investments Ltd) completed the form of tender and offered £28 500 for the school.

On 1 September 1964 M's surveyor informed C's surveyor that C's offer was the highest one received and that M's surveyor had recommended its acceptance. In this letter M's surveyor wrote: 'We shall write to you again as soon as we receive formal instructions.' On 14 September C's surveyor replied in a letter in which he wrote: ' ... I look forward to receiving formal acceptance in early course'. This letter was acknowledged by the M's surveyor on 15 September who then wrote:

'The sale has now been approved by M ... [The] Diocesan Registrar ... has been instructed to obtain the approval of the Secretary of State for Education. As soon as this is given he will be getting in touch with [C's] solicitors.'

M relied on this letter as an acceptance of C's offer, notwithstanding that M had failed to comply with their own Condition 4 in that they had not sent a letter to C by post but only to C's surveyor.

On 18 November 1964 the Secretary of State approved the sale. On 23 December 1964 the M's solicitors wrote to C's solicitors:

'We are writing to inform you that this consent has now been obtained and we conclude that the Contract is therefore binding on both parties. Kindly confirm.'

On 5 January 1965 C's solicitors replied:

'We acknowledge receipt of your letter of 23 October upon which we have obtained C's instructions and regret that we cannot confirm that there is a binding contract between the parties in the matter.'

On 6 January 1965 M's solicitors wrote:

'We acknowledge receipt of your letter of yesterday's date and are surprised to hear that C do not consider themselves bound.'

On 7 January they wrote to C giving formal notice of acceptance of C's tender. On the same day the defendant company's solicitors wrote to the plaintiff's solicitors that the defendant company no longer wished to proceed with the purchase.

The issue before the court was whether M were required strictly to comply with their own Condition 4 in order to accept C's offer.

Buckley J: 'The offer contained in the tender was to the effect that in the event of its being accepted in accordance with the conditions of sale on or before the day named therein for that purpose (and none was so named) the defendant company would pay the price and complete the purchase. An offeror may by the terms of his offer indicate that it may be accepted in a particular manner. In the present case the conditions included condition 4 which I have read. It is said on the defendant company's behalf that that condition was not complied with until 7th January 1965; that until that date the offer was never accepted in accordance with its terms; and that consequently nothing earlier than that date can be relied on as an acceptance resulting in a binding contract. If an offeror stipulates by the terms of his offer that it may, or that it shall, be accepted in a particular manner a contract results as soon as the offeree does the stipulated act, whether it has come to the notice of the offeror or not. In such a case the offeror conditionally waives either expressly or by implication the normal requirement that acceptance must be communicated to the offeror to conclude a contract. There can be no doubt that in the present case, if the plaintiff or its authorised agent had posted a letter addressed to the defendant company at 15 Berkeley Street, on or about 15th September informing the defendant company of the acceptance of its tender, the contract would have been complete at the moment when such letter was posted, but that course was not taken. Condition 4, however, does not say that that shall be the sole permitted method of communicating an acceptance. It may be that an offeror, who by the terms of his offer insists on acceptance in a particular manner, is entitled to insist that he is not bound unless acceptance is effected or communicated in that precise way, although it seems probable that, even so, if the other party communicates his acceptance in some other way, the offeror may by conduct or otherwise waive his right to insist on the prescribed method of acceptance. Where, however, the offeror has prescribed a particular method of acceptance, but not in terms insisting that only acceptance in that mode shall be binding, I am of opinion that acceptance communicated to the offeror by any other mode which is no less advantageous to him will conclude the contract. Thus in *Tinn* v *Hoffman & Co*, where acceptance was requested by return of post, Honeyman J, said:

"That does not mean exclusively a reply by letter by return of post, but you may reply by telegram or by verbal message, or by any means not later than a letter written and sent by return of post . . ."

If an offeror intends that he shall be bound only if his offer is accepted in some particular manner, it must be for him to make this clear. Condition 4 in the present case had not, in my judgment, this effect.

Moreover, the inclusion of condition 4 in the defendant company's offer was at the instance of the plaintiff, who framed the conditions and the form of tender. It should not, I think, be regarded as a condition or stipulation imposed by the defendant company as offeror on the plaintiff as offeree, but as a term introduced into the bargain by the plaintiff and presumably considered by the plaintiff as being in some way for the protection or benefit of the plaintiff. It would consequently be a term strict compliance with which the plaintiff could waive, provided the defendant company was not adversely affected. The plaintiff did not take advantage of the condition which would have resulted in a contract being formed as soon as a letter of acceptance complying with the condition was posted, but adopted another course, which could only result in a contract when the plaintiff's acceptance was actually communicated to the defendant company.

For these reasons, I have reached the conclusion that in accordance with the terms of the tender it was open to the plaintiff to conclude a contract by acceptance actually communicated to the defendant company in any way; and, in my judgment, the letter of 15th September constituted such an acceptance. It follows that, in my judgment . . . the parties thereupon became contractually bound.'

The courts will tend to interpret such requests as not being mandatory or obligatory but rather permissive in the absence of evidence to show that the prescribed method of communication and no other, would suffice.

Yates Building Company Ltd v R J Pulleyn & Sons (York) Ltd

(1975) 237 EG 183 • Court of Appeal

Pulleyn gave Yates an option to purchase building land. The option read:

'The option hereby granted shall be exercisable by notice in writing given by or on behalf of Yates to Pulleyns or to Pulleyns' solicitors at any time between April 6 1973 and May 6 1973 such notice to be sent by registered or recorded delivery post to the registered office of Pulleyns or the offices of their said solicitors.'

On Monday April 30 1973 Yates's solicitors posted a letter to Pulleyns' solicitors to formally exercise the option; they enclosed a cheque for £1890 for the deposit. The letter was sent by ordinary post and not by registered or recorded delivery post but it arrived well in time. It was opened by Pulleyn's solicitors at some time on or before Friday May 4 1973. On that Friday Pulleyn's solicitors wrote back to Yates's solicitors returning the cheque for the deposit and said:

'We write to acknowledge receipt today of your letter of April 30 1973 with its enclosure. You will recall that clause 2 of the option agreement provides for notice to be sent by a registered or recorded delivery post. Your letter was not so sent.'

Yates brought proceedings for specific performance, but the judge refused it. He held that this requirement that the letter had to be sent by registered or recorded delivery post was a requirement which must be complied with, and as it had not been complied with, there was no contract. Yates appealed.

Lord Denning MR: 'It seems to me that this depends on the construction of the option clause. The option is an offer: an irrevocable offer. When a person makes an offer, he does sometimes prescribe the method by which it is to be accepted. If he prescribes it in terms which are mandatory or obligatory, the acceptance is only good if it complies with the stated requirements. Thus in the present case the notice of acceptance *must* be in writing, and *must* be given to Pulleyns or to Pulleyns' solicitors, and *must* be given between April 6 1973 and May 6 1973. But the question is whether the words "such notice to be sent by registered or recorded delivery post" are mandatory or directory. That test is used by lawyers in the construction of statutory instruments, but it can also be used in the construction of other documents. The distinction is this: a mandatory provision must be fulfilled exactly according to the letter, whereas a directory provision is satisfied if it is in substance according to the general intent (see *Howard* v *Bodington*). In applying this rule of construction, you must look to the subject-matter, consider the object to be fulfilled, and then see whether the provision must be fulfilled strictly to the letter or whether the substance of it is enough. So in the present case the question is whether the letter of acceptance *must* be sent by registered or recorded delivery post, else it is bad; or whether it is sufficient if it gets there in time, as, for instance, by ordinary post or by special messenger. Orr LJ gave this instance in the course of the argument. Suppose there were a postal strike during the last week, and the buyer, to make sure it was in time, sent the letter by special messenger, would this not be sufficient? Looking at the object of this provision, it seems to be this. It is inserted for the benefit of the buyer so that he can be sure of his position. So long as he sends the letter by registered or recorded delivery post, he has clear proof of postage and of the time of posting. But if the buyer sends it by ordinary post, he will have no sufficient proof of posting, or of the time of posting. In that case, if the seller proves that he never received it, or received it too late, the buyer fails. None of those reasons apply, however, when the seller does receive it in time. So long as he gets the letter in time, he should be bound. So I would hold, simply as a matter of interpretation, that if the letter did reach the sellers in time, it was a valid exercise of the option.

There are only a few cases on the point, and they support what I have just said. There is *Tinn* v *Hoffmann & Co*. There was an offer which contained the words "waiting your reply by return of post". The court held that that did not mean a reply had to be sent by *letter* by return of post. A reply by telegram, or by verbal message, or by any means which arrived not later than a letter sent by post would reach its destination would equally satisfy the requisition. The next case is an old one from the United States, *Eliason* v *Henshaw*, in which the offeror at Harper's Ferry wrote to the offeree at Mill Creek: "Please write by return of wagon whether you accept our offer". The wagon was due to return to Harper's Ferry. The letter of acceptance was not sent by return of wagon to Harper's Ferry. It was sent by ordinary mail to George-town and took longer to get there. The Supreme Court of the United States said:

> "The meaning of the writers was obvious. They could easily calculate by the usual length of time which was employed by this wagon, in traveling from Harper's Ferry to Mill Creek, and back again with a load of flour, about what time they should receive the desired answer, and, therefore, it was entirely unimportant, whether it was sent by that, or another wagon, or in any other manner, provided it was sent to Harper's Ferry, and was not delayed beyond the time which was ordinarily employed by wagons engaged in hauling flour from the defendant's mill to Harper's Ferry . . . . The place, therefore, to which the answer was to be sent, constituted an essential part of the plaintiffs' offer."

The Supreme Court there looked to see what was the essential part of the offer, what was important or not important. It said that the manner of sending was "entirely unimportant", so long as it got to the proper place at the proper time. The only remaining case is *Manchester Diocesan Council of Education* v *Commercial & General Investments*, where this very point was considered by Buckley J. He gave this guide to construction:

> "Where, however, the offeror has prescribed a particular method of acceptance, but not in terms insisting that only acceptance in that mode shall be binding, I am of

opinion that acceptance communicated to the offeror by any other mode which is no less advantageous to him will conclude the contract."

It seems to me that Buckley J was there adopting the same test as I have stated. If the offeror uses terms insisting that only acceptance in a particular mode is binding, it is mandatory. If he does not insist, and it is sufficient if he adopts a mode which is no less advantageous, it is directory. At any rate, adopting Buckley J's test in this case, there were no words insisting that only registered or recorded delivery post would do, and the sending by ordinary post was no less advantageous to the sellers than sending by registered post, so long as it got there in time. In my opinion this option was perfectly well exercised and there was a binding contract accordingly. I would allow the appeal.'

THE POSTAL RULES

The postal rules *only apply* when the acceptance is sent by post. The general rule is that acceptance takes effect when the letter is posted.

Adams v Lindsell

[1818] 1 B & Ald 681 • King's Bench

Action for non-delivery of wool according to agreement. At the trial at the Lent Assizes for the county of Worcester, before Burrough J it appeared that the defendants, who were dealers in wool, at St Ives, in the county of Huntingdon, had, on Tuesday the 2nd of September 1817, written the following letter to the plaintiffs, who were woollen manufacturers residing in Bromsgrove, Worcestershire. 'We now offer you eight hundred tods of wether fleeces, of a good fair quality of our country wool, at 35s. 6d. per tod, to be delivered at Leicester, and to be paid for by two months' bill in two months, and to be weighted up by your agent within fourteen days, receiving your answer in course of post.'

This letter was misdirected by the defendants, to Bromsgrove, Leicestershire, in consequence of which it was not received by the plaintiffs in Worcestershire till 7 pm on Friday, September 5th. On that evening the plaintiffs wrote an answer, agreeing to accept the wool on the terms proposed. The course of the post between St Ives and Bromsgrove is through London, and consequently this answer was not received by the defendants till Tuesday, September 9th. On the Monday September 8th, the defendants not having, as they expected, received an answer on Sunday September 7th (which in case their letter had not been misdirected, would have been in the usual course of the post), sold the wool in question to another person. Under these circumstances, the learned Judge held, that the delay having been occasioned by the neglect of the defendants, the jury must take it, that the answer did come back in due course of post; and that then the defendants were liable for the loss that had been sustained: and the plaintiffs accordingly recovered a verdict.

The Court said that, if this were so, no contract could ever be completed by the post. For if the defendants were not bound by their offer when accepted by the plaintiffs till the answer was received, then the plaintiffs ought not to be bound till after they had received the notification that the defendants had received their answer and assented to it. And so it might go on *ad infinitum*. The defendants must be considered in law as making, during every instant of the time their letter was travelling, the same identical offer to the plaintiffs; and then the contract is completed by the acceptance of it by the latter. Then as to the delay in notifying the acceptance, that arises entirely from the mistake of the defendants, and it therefore must be taken as against them, that the plaintiffs' answer was received in course of post.

Rule discharged.

Byrne & Co v Van Tienhoven & Co

(1880) 5 CPD 344 • Common Pleas

On 1 October Tienhoven wrote from Cardiff offering to sell 1000 boxes of tinplate to Byrne at New York. Byrne received the offer on 11 October and accepted it by telegram on the same day, and by letter on 15 October. On 8 October Tienhoven posted a letter to Byrne withdrawing the offer because there had been a 25 per cent price rise in the tinplate market. This letter reached Byrne on 20 October. The issue before the court was whether a contract had been formed on 11 October when Byrne had sent the telegram or whether Tienhoven's offer of 11 October had been revoked on 8 October when Tienhoven had posted the letter of revocation.

Lindley J: 'These letters and telegram [both of 11 October] would, if they stood alone, plainly constitute a contract binding on both parties . . . The defendants, however, raise . . . [a defence] to the action which remain[s] to be considered . . . [T]hey say that the offer made by their letter of 1 October was revoked by them before it had been accepted by the plaintiffs by their telegram of 11th or letter of 15th . . .

There is no doubt that an offer can be withdrawn before it is accepted, and it is immaterial whether the offer is expressed to be open for acceptance for a given time or not: *Routledge* v *Grant.* For the decision of the present case, however, it is necessary to consider two other questions, viz: 1. Whether a withdrawal of an offer has any effect until it is communicated to the person to whom the offer has been sent? 2. Whether posting a letter of withdrawal is a communication to the person to whom the letter is sent?

It is curious that neither of these questions appears to have been actually decided in this country. As regards the first question . . . an uncommunicated revocation is for all practical purposes and in point of law no revocation at all. This is the view taken in the United States: see *Taylor* v *Merchants Fire Insurance Co* cited in *Benjamin on Sales*, and it is adopted by Mr Benjamin. The same view is taken by Mr Pollock in his excellent work on *Principles of Contract*, ed ii, and by Mr Leake in his *Digest of the Law of Contracts* . . . I pass, therefore, to the next question, viz, whether posting the letter of revocation was a sufficient communication of it to the plaintiff. The offer was posted on 1 October, the withdrawal was posted on 8th, and did not reach the plaintiff until after he had posted his letter of 11th, accepting the offer. It may be taken as now settled that where an offer is made and accepted by letters sent through the post, the contract is completed the moment the letter accepting the offer is posted: *Harris' Case*; *Dunlop* v *Higgins*, even although it never reaches its destination. When, however, these authorities are looked at, it will be seen that they are based upon the principle that the writer of the offer has expressly or impliedly assented to treat an answer to him by a letter duly posted as a sufficient acceptance and notification to himself, or, in other words, he has made the post office his agent to receive the acceptance and notification of it. But this principle appears to me to be inapplicable to the case of the withdrawal of an offer. In this particular case I can find no evidence of any authority in fact given by the plaintiffs to the defendants to notify a withdrawal of their offer by merely posting a letter; and there is no legal principle or decision which compels me to hold, contrary to the fact, that the letter of 8 October is to be treated as communicated to the plaintiff on that day or on any day before 20th, when the letter reached them. But before that letter had reached the plaintiffs they had accepted the offer, both by telegram and by post; and they had themselves resold the tin plates at a profit. In my opinion the withdrawal by the defendants on 8 October of their offer of the 1st was inoperative; and a complete contract binding on both parties was entered into on 11 October, when the plaintiffs accepted the offer of 1st, which they had no reason to suppose had been withdrawn. Before leaving this part of the case it may be as well to point out the extreme injustice and inconvenience which any other conclusion would produce. If the defendants' contention were to prevail no person who had received an offer by post and had accepted it would know his position until he had waited such a time as to be quite sure that a letter withdrawing the offer had not been posted before his acceptance of it. It appears to me that both legal principles, and practical convenience require that a person who has accepted an offer not known to him to have been revoked, shall be in a position safely to act upon the footing that the offer and acceptance constitute a contract binding on both parties.'

Household Fire and Carriage Accident Insurance Company (Ltd) v Grant

(1879) 48 LJQB 577 • Court of Appeal

On 30 September 1874 Grant applied by letter for 100 shares (this was his offer to buy the shares) in the Household Fire and Carriage Accident Insurance Company Ltd. The shares were allotted to him (this was the company's acceptance of his offer), and on 20 October 1874 a letter of allotment was sent to him at the address given by him. Grant said that this letter of allotment never reached him and that he never heard anything about the shares until March 1877 when he received a letter demanding the payment of a call upon 100 shares (the shares had been issued partly paid and the 'call' was the demand by the company for Grant to pay the next instalment due on the shares). The jury found that the letter of allotment of 20 October 1874 had been posted, but that it had never been received by Grant.

The letter of acceptance having never reached Grant the court had to decide whether there was ever a contract between Grant and the company for the sale of the 100 shares.

Thesiger LJ: 'How, then, are these elements of law to be harmonised in the case of contracts formed by correspondence through the post? I see no better mode than that of treating the Post-office as the agent for both parties, and it was so considered by Lord Romilly in *Hebb's Case*, where, in the course of his judgment, he said, "*Dunlop* v *Higgins* decides that the posting of a letter accepting an offer constitutes a binding contract, but the reason of that is, that the Post-office is the common agent of both parties". . . . But if the Post-office be such common agent then it seems to me to follow, that as soon as the letter of acceptance is delivered to the Post-office the contract is made as complete and final, and absolutely binding, as if the acceptor had put his letter into the hands of a messenger sent by the offerer himself as his agent, to deliver the offer and receive the acceptance. What other principle can be adopted short of holding that the contract is not complete by acceptance until and except from the time that the letter containing the acceptance is delivered to the offerer, a principle which has been distinctly negatived? . . .

To me it appears, that in practice a contract complete upon the acceptance of an offer being posted, but liable to be put an end to by an accident in the post, would be more mischievous than a contract only binding upon the parties to it upon the acceptance actually reaching the offerer, and I can see no principle of law from which such an anomalous contract can be deduced. There is no doubt that the implication of complete, final and absolutely binding contract being formed, as soon as the acceptance of an offer is posted, may in some cases lead to inconvenience and hardship. But such there must be at times in any view of the law. It is impossible in transactions which pass between parties at a distance, and have to be carried on through the medium of correspondence, to adjust conflicting rights between innocent parties, so as to make the consequences of mistake on the part of a mutual agent fall equally upon the shoulders of both. At the same time I am not prepared to admit that the implication in question will lead to any great or general inconvenience or hardship. An offerer, if he chooses, may always make the formation of the contract which he proposes dependent upon the actual communication to himself of the acceptance. If he trusts to the post, he trusts to a means of communication which, as a rule, does not fail and if no answer to his offer is received by him, and the matter is of importance to him, he can make enquiries of the person to whom his offer was addressed.'

Bruner v Moore

[1904] 1 Ch 305 • Chancery Division

Moore granted an option (made an offer) to Bruner to purchase a patent of a sewing machine attachment for £400. The option was to last until the end of March 1903.

On 28 March 1903 Bruner sent a telegram from London addressed to Moore at Hotel Genes, Genoa which said 'Have money ready to carry out option in exchange for documents. When can I see you?' On the same day he wrote a letter to Moore at his Paris address confirming and repeating his telegram.

Moore had left Genoa on the morning of 28 March before the telegram arrived. He received both letter and telegram in Paris on 30 March. He shortly afterwards returned to England, and refused to carry out his agreement with Bruner on the ground that the option had not been exercised in time. Bruner brought an action for specific performance of the agreement.

The issue before the court was whether the option had been exercised (accepted) in time.

Farwell J: '. . . [A]ssuming that the option expired on March 29. The facts are these. On March 22 the plaintiff telegraphed for the defendant's address, and on March 23 wrote the letter to which I have already referred. The defendant received this letter on the 26th, on which day he left Rome for Genoa, and telegraphed from Rome to the plaintiff: "Hotel Genes, Genoa, Friday – Paris, Monday". On Saturday the 28th the plaintiff telegraphed to the defendant at Genoa exercising his option under the agreement, but before the telegram arrived the defendant left for Monte Carlo, and proceeded to Paris on Sunday, arriving on Monday, the 30th. The plaintiff wrote a letter on March 28th confirming his telegram and exercising his option, and posted it on the 28th, addressed to the defendant in Paris. This letter would arrive in due course on the 29th, but the defendant did not reach Paris till the 30th. It is now argued that this option, having expired on March 29th, a telegram and letter sent on the 28th, but not reaching the defendant until the 30th, were too late. In my opinion this contention fails also, for the option was duly exercised when the telegram was sent and the letter posted. I take the rule as stated by Lord Herschell in *Henthorn v Fraser*: 'Where the circumstances are such that it must have been within the contemplation of the parties that, according to the ordinary usages of mankind, the post might be used a means of communicating the acceptance of an offer, the acceptance is complete as soon as it is posted". In the present case the parties are American citizens staying temporarily at London hotels when they signed the contract. That contract obviously contemplates the events that in fact happened – that the two parties would separate and would visit various parts of Europe, and would communicate with one another constantly by letter and telegram. If there ever was a case in which the parties contemplated that "the post might be used as a means of communicating" on all subjects connected with the contract, this is that case. I hold, therefore, that the option was duly exercised.'

Possible exclusion of postal rules

In *Holwell Securities Ltd* v *Hughes* (see p 48), Lawton LJ said 'Does the [postal] rule apply in all cases where one party makes an offer which both he and the person with whom he was dealing must have expected the post to be used as a means of accepting it? In my judgment, it does not. First, it does not apply when the express terms of the offer specify that the acceptance must reach the offeror . . . '

MISCELLANEOUS POINTS

Must acceptor have knowledge of offer when accepting? The point here is again the *agreement* and *intention* of the parties.

If the offer is forgotten at the time of acceptance can it be said that the acceptor intends to accept an offer which he does not know exists?

R v Clarke

(1927) 40 CLR 227 • High Court of Australia

The Government of Western Australia offered a reward "for such information as shall lead to the arrest and conviction of the person or persons who committed the murders" of two police officers. Clarke, who knew of the offer, gave the required information in order to clear himself of a false charge of murder and not in order to claim the reward. Later Clarke claimed the reward.

The issue before the court was whether Clarke had accepted the offer of the reward; had he in mind the offer when he 'did the act' required by the unilateral offer?

Higgins J: 'On 6th June, Clarke gave false information in order to screen the murderers; and, as he says, I had no intention then of doing anything to earn the reward . . . On 10th June, I began to break down under the strain. Manning took down my statement on 10th June at my request. I had no thought whatever then of the reward that had been offered. My object was my own protection against a false charge of murder . . . Up to 10th June I had no intention of doing anything to earn the reward. At the inquest (where he gave evidence without asking to be allowed to give evidence) I was committed for trial as an accessory . . . *When I gave evidence in the Criminal Court I had no intention of claiming the reward. I first decided to claim the reward a few days after the appeal had been dealt with.* Inspector Condon told me to make application. *I had not intended to apply for the reward up to that date.* I did not know exactly the position I was in. Up to that time I had not considered the position . . . *I had not given the matter consideration at all.* My motive was to clear myself of the charge of murder. I gave no consideration and formed no intention with regard to the reward. These statements of Clarke show clearly that he did not intend to accept the offer of the Crown, did not give the information on the faith of, or relying on, the proclamation. He did not mentally assent to the Crown's offer; there was no moment of time at which there was, till after the information was given, as between Clarke and the Crown, a *consensus* of mind. Most of the cases turn on the *communication* of assent, from the offeree to the offeror; communication is necessary, and it may be by act as well as by words; but there can be no *communication* of assent until there be assent. If the case so much relied on for Clarke, the case of *Williams* v *Carwardine*, can be taken as deciding that mutual consent to the terms is not necessary, as well as communication of assent by the offeree, I can only point to higher and more recent authority, such as that of Lord Westbury LC in *Chinnock* v *Marchioness of Ely*: "An agreement is the result of the mutual assent of two parties to certain terms, and if it be clear that there is no *consensus*, what may have been written or said become immaterial". This pronouncement is cited by *Leake on Contracts*, 7th ed; and the author adds: "A *consensus ad idem* is a prime essential to the validity of a contract". The distinction should be clear between the essential mental assent, and the essential communication of that assent; as in *In re National Savings Bank Association*; *Hebb's Case*: I am of opinion that an offer does not bind the person who makes it until it has been accepted, and *its acceptance* has been communicated to him or his agent".

But I do not regard *Williams* v *Carwardine* as deciding anything to the contrary of this doctrine. That case seems to me not to deal with the essential elements for a contract at all: it shows merely that the *motive* of the informer in accepting the contract offered (and the performing the conditions is usually sufficient evidence of acceptance) has nothing to do with his right to recover under the contract. The reports show (as it was assumed by the Judges after the verdict of the injury in favour of the informer), that the informer *knew* of the offer when giving the information, and meant to accept the offer though she had also a *motive* in her guilty conscience. The distinguished jurist, Sir Frederick Pollock, in his preface to vol. 38 of the *Revised Reports*, makes comments adverse to the case; but I concur with Burnside J in his view that we cannot treat such comments as equivalent to an overruling of a clear decision. The case of *Gibbons* v *Proctor* is much more difficult to explain. There a policeman was held entitled to recover a reward offered by handbills, for information given to the superintendent of police which led to arrest and conviction, although the policeman did not know of the handbills before he sent the information by his agents, or before the handbills reached the superintendent. This would seem to mean that a man can accept an offered contract before he knows that there is an offer – that knowledge of the offer before the informer supplies the information is immaterial to the existence of the contract. *Anson on Contracts* (16th Ed), thinks that this decision must be wrong. I venture to think so too; and, though we cannot well overrule it, we ought not to follow it for the purposes of this Court. It should be noted in this connection that the great judgment of Lord Blackburn in *Brogden* v *Metropolitan Railway Co* is addressed to the other condition of contract, that acceptance must be communicated; but the whole judgment assumes that consensus of mind pre-existed – "simple *acceptance in your own mind*, without any intimation to the other party, and expressed by a mere private act, such as putting a letter into a drawer", does not complete a contract (and see per Lord Cairns LC). The reasoning of Woodruff J in *Fitch* v *Snedaker* seems to me to be faultless; and the decision is spoken of in *Anson* as being undoubtedly correct in principle: – The motive inducing consent may be immaterial, but the consent is vital. Without that there is no contract. How then can there be consent or assent to that of which the party has never heard? Clarke had seen the offer indeed; but it was not present to his mind – he had forgotten it, and gave no consideration to it, in his intense excitement as to his own danger. There cannot be assent without knowledge of the offer; and ignorance of the offer is the same thing whether it is due to never hearing of it or to forgetting it after hearing. But for this candid confession of Clarke's it might fairly be presumed that Clarke, having once seen the offer, acted on the faith of it, in reliance on it; but he has himself rebutted that presumption.'

Motive irrelevant

The motive for accepting an offer is *irrelevant*. The question is did the acceptor *know of the offer* when accepting the offer?

Williams v *Carwardine*

(1833) 2 LJKB 101 • King's Bench

A handbill stated that 'whoever would give such information as might lead to a discovery of the murderer of Walter Carwardine, should, on conviction, receive a reward of £20.' At the trial it appeared that although Williams was the person who gave the information which afterwards led to the conviction of the murderer her motive in giving the information was not to gain the reward but rather to ease her conscience. The court held that she was entitled to the reward.

On appeal Carwardine argued that Williams was not entitled to the reward because her motive in giving the information was not to obtain the reward but to ease her conscience.

Littledale J: 'It is a general promise held out to the population of the country, that whoever should give information which should lead to the conviction of the murderer, should receive a reward. That gives a right of action, and the Court cannot enter into the motives of the party giving that information.'

Are offer and acceptance always necessary?

Clarke v *The Earl of Dunraven and Mount-Earl, The Satanita*

[1897] AC 59 • House of Lords

The appellant and the respondent entered their yachts, the *Satanita* and the *Valkyrie*, in the Mudhook Yacht Club race. Both parties had signed a letter to the secretary of the club stating that they would be bound by the sailing rules of the Yacht Club Association. Rule 24 stated '. . . If a yacht, in consequence of her neglect of any of these rules, shall foul another yacht, or compel other yachts to foul, she shall forfeit all claim to the prize, and shall pay all damages.' Rule 32 stated 'Any yacht disobeying or infringing any of these rules, which shall apply to all yachts whether sailing in the same or different races, shall be disqualified from receiving any prize she would otherwise have won, and her owner shall be liable for all damages arising therefrom.'

Whilst racing the *Satanita* ran into the *Valkyrie* and sank her. The owner of the *Valkyrie* brought an action in the Admiralty Division against the appellant claiming damages. The appellant paid into court a sum as the amount of damages for which he was answerable under the Merchant Shipping Act Amendment Act 1862, calculated at the rate of 8 shillings per ton on the registered tonnage of the *Satanita*.

The issue before the court was whether there was a contract between the appellant and the respondent and if there was did the words in the rules that the person at fault would pay 'all damages' override the statutory limitation.

Lord Herschell: 'My Lords, I am of the same opinion. I cannot entertain any doubt that there was a contractual relation between the parties to this litigation. The effect of their entering for the race, and undertaking to be bound by these rules to the knowledge of each other, is sufficient, I think, where those rules indicate a liability on the part of the one to the other, to create a contractual obligation to discharge that liability. That being so, the parties must be taken to have contracted that a breach of any of these rules would render the party guilty of that breach liable, in the language of rule 24, to "pay all damage", in the language of rule 32, to be "liable for all damages arising therefrom". The language is somewhat different in the two rules; but I do not think they were intended to have, with regard to payment or liability to damages, any different effect. It is admitted that the appellant broke one of those rules, and, having broken or disobeyed that rule, it is quite clear, on the assumption of a contract such as I have described, that there arose the liability to "pay all damages", or "to be liable for all damages arising therefrom" . . .

My Lords, it has been said that a contract such as the Court below have held to exist is a very unlikely contract for the parties to have entered into. I confess I am not satisfied of that either. The parties here are yacht-owners who are entering their yachts for a race in which other yachts will be engaged. I do not think there is anything extraordinary in their entering for that race upon the terms that they shall be liable for all damages, because the contract gives of course the correlative right of being entitled to all damage. The question to whom that contract would be an advantage would depend on the size of the injured vessel and the injuring vessel in the particular case, which could not be foreseen; therefore it does not seem to me extraordinary that a contract of this sort should be entered into. And again, whilst it is a most uncommon thing for merchant vessels engaged in an adventure to be actually navigated by the owner, that is not at all an uncommon thing in the case of yachts. Of course, if the yacht were navigated by the owner and there were negligent navigation, he would be liable for all damages; and that may have been a consideration which led to a contract of this description being made a condition of yachts entering for the race. It puts upon a level, upon an equity as regards liability to one another, a yacht which is being navigated by the owner and a yacht which is being navigated by some other person on his behalf or employed by him. Therefore, there seems to me to be nothing monstrous, nothing absurd, in the contract which has been held to exist by the Court below, which would justify this House, or any tribunal, in saying that the parties never could have intended to enter into a contract of this description, and that it must have some other interpretation. My Lords, I go no further than that – I do not know whether that was the reason – I do not care whether that was the reason why the provision in question was inserted; but when you seek to cut down what is the *prima facie* meaning of a contract, and to impose a limitation upon the general words which are used in it, if you seek to do so by considerations such as those which have been urged upon your Lordships with great force by the learned counsel for the appellant, then you must make it manifest that it is a contract which there could be no reasonable ground for the parties to have entered into.'

SUMMARY

You should now be able to:

- Distinguish between an *offer* and a *counter-offer*.
- Distinguish between a *counter-offer* and a *request for information*.
- Appreciate the rules relating to the communication of acceptances.
- Determine when an offer has been *accepted*.
- Understand and apply the *postal rules*.

If you have not mastered the above points you should go through this section again.

3   Ending of the offer

TERMINATION OF OFFER

The general rule is that an offer can be withdrawn at any time before it is accepted. However, once an offer has been accepted it becomes irrevocable.

Offer not terminated merely by acting inconsistently with it

See *Adams* v *Lindsell* above (p 56). What act did the defendants claim had terminated their offer?

REVOCATION OF OFFER

Notice of revocation *must be communicated* to the offeree: *the postal rules do not apply to revocation*: see *Byrne* v *Van Tienhoven* (1880) above.

A promise to keep an offer open is not binding unless the offeror has provided consideration.

NB It is probably best to skip the next case until you have studied Section 5 on consideration.

Routledge v *Grant*
(1828) 6 LJCP 166 • Common Pleas

Grant wrote to Routledge offering to purchase the lease of his house. The offer was to remain open for six weeks. Grant then changed his mind about purchasing the lease and, within the six weeks, withdrew his offer. After Routledge had received Grant's letter withdrawing the offer he wrote to Grant, within the six weeks, accepting Grant's offer. The issue before the court was whether Grant could withdraw his offer within the six week period.

Best CJ: '. . . If a party make an offer and fix a period within which it is to be accepted or rejected by the person to whom it is made, though the latter may at any time within the stipulated period accept the offer, still the former may also at any time before it is accepted retract it; for to be valid, the contract must be mutual: both or neither of the parties must be bound by it . . .

. . . So, on the same principle, it was decided in *Payne* v *Cave*, that a bidder at an auction may retract his bidding at any time before the hammer is down; and the Court said, "The auctioneer is the agent of the vendor, and the assent of both parties is necessary to make the contract binding; that is signified on the part of the seller by knocking down the hammer, which was not done here till the defendant had retracted . . .

Every bidding is nothing more than an offer on one side till it is assented to. But, according to what is now contended for, one party would be bound by the offer, and the other not, which can never be allowed". So, here, until both the plaintiff and defendant had agreed to the terms of the contract, either party had a right to repudiate it.'

Exceptions to the general rule that notice of revocation must be communicated to the offeree before it takes effect

Estoppel

See *The Brimnes* case above (p 40).

Unilateral offer

Shuey v United States

Supreme Court of the United States • (1875) 92 US 73

By a proclamation published in the public newspapers on 20 April 1865 the Secretary of War offered a $25 000 reward 'for the apprehension of John Surratt, one of Booth's accomplices' [Booth was President Lincoln's assassin], and that 'liberal rewards will be paid for any information that shall conduce to the arrest of either of the above-named criminals or their accomplices'. On 24 November 1865 the President published an order revoking the reward offered for the arrest of Surratt. In April 1866 Marie informed the American authorities that he had discovered and identified Surratt. At the time of giving the information Marie was ignorant of the fact that the reward offered by the Secretary of War for Surratt's arrest had been revoked by the President. Shuey, Marie's executor, sued to recover the sum of $15 000, being the balance alleged to be due to Marie of the reward of $25 000.

Strong J: 'The offer of a reward for the apprehension of Surratt was revoked on the twenty-fourth day of November 1865; and notice of the revocation was published. It is not to be doubted that the offer was revocable at any time before it was accepted, and before any thing had been done in reliance upon it. There was no contract until its terms were complied with. Like any other offer of a contract, it might, therefore, be withdrawn before rights had accrued under it; and it was withdrawn through the same channel in which it was made. The same notoriety was given to the revocation that was given to the offer; and the findings of fact do not show that any information was given by the claimant, or that he did any thing to entitle him to the reward offered, until five months after the offer had been withdrawn. True, it is found that then, and at all times until the arrest was actually made, he was ignorant of the withdrawal; but that is an immaterial fact. The offer of the reward not having been made to him directly, but by means of a published proclamation, he should have known that it could be revoked in the manner in which it was made.'

When considering the following three cases ask yourself *what is the exact time at which a unilateral offer is accepted*?

Errington v Errington

[1952] 1 All ER 149 • Court of Appeal

The facts are set out in the judgment of Denning LJ.

Denning LJ: 'The facts are reasonably clear. In 1936 the father bought the house for his son and daughter-in-law to live in. The father put down £250 in cash and borrowed £500 from a building society on the security of the house, repayable with interest by instalments of 15s a week. He took the house in his own name and made himself responsible for the instalments. The father told the daughter-in-law that the £250 was a present for them, but he left them to pay the building society instalments of 15s a week themselves. He handed the building society book to the daughter-in-law and said to her: "Don't part with this book. The house will be your property when the mortgage is paid". He said that when he retired he would transfer it into their names. She has, in fact, paid the building society instalments regularly from that day to this with the result that much of the mortgage has been repaid, but there is a good deal yet to be paid. The rates on the house came to 10s a week. The couple found that they could not pay those as well as the building society instalments so the father said he would pay them and he did so.

It is to be noted that the couple never bound themselves to pay the instalments to the building society, and I see no reason why any such obligation should be implied. It is clear law that the court is not to imply a term unless it is necessary, and I do not see that it is necessary here. Ample content is given to the whole arrangement by holding that the father promised that the house should belong to the couple as soon as they had paid off the mortgage. The parties did not discuss what was to happen if the couple failed to pay the instalments to the building society, but I should have thought it clear that, if they did fail to pay the instalments, the father would not be bound to transfer the house to them. The father's promise was a unilateral contract – a promise of the house in return for their act of paying the instalments. It could not be revoked by him once the couple entered on performance of the act, but it would cease to bind him if they left it incomplete and unperformed, which they have not done. If that was the position during the father's lifetime, so it must be after his death. If the daughter-in-law continues to pay all the building society instalments, the couple will be entitled to have the property transferred to them as soon as the mortgage is paid off, but if she does not do so, then the building society will claim the instalments from the father's estate and the estate will have to pay them. I cannot think that in those circumstances the estate would be bound to transfer the house to them, any more than the father himself would have been . . .

In the present case it is clear that the father expressly promised the couple that the property should belong to them as soon as the mortgage was paid, and impliedly promised that, so long as they paid the instalments to the building society, they should be allowed to remain in possession. They were not purchasers because they never bound themselves to pay the instalments, but nevertheless they were in a position analogous to purchasers. They have acted on the promise and neither the father nor his widow, his successor in title, can eject them in disregard of it. The result is that, in my opinion, the appeal should be dismissed and no order for possession should be made.'

Daulia Ltd v Four Millbank Nominees Ltd

[1978] 2 All ER 557 • Court of Appeal

On 21 December 1976 F (Four Millbank Nominees Ltd) promised D (Daulia Ltd) that F would enter into a contract for the sale of a certain property with D if D attended F's offices before 10.00 hrs on 22 December 1976 and there tendered to F D's part of the signed contract together with a banker's draft for £41 250. D did what was required but F refused to exchange their part of the contract for sale with D. The issue before the court was whether a unilateral contract had been formed.

Goff LJ: 'I therefore turn to the . . . question. Was there a concluded unilateral contract by the defendants to enter into a contract for sale on the agreed terms?

The concept of a unilateral or "if" contract is somewhat anomalous, because it is clear that, at all events until the offeree starts to perform the condition, there is no contract at all, but merely an offer which the offeror is free to revoke. Doubts have been expressed whether the offeror becomes bound so soon as the offeree starts to perform or satisfy the condition, or only when he has fully done so. In my judgment, however, we are not concerned in this case with any such problem, because in my view the plaintiffs had fully performed or satisfied the condition when they presented themselves at the time and place appointed with a banker's draft for the deposit and their part of the written contract for sale duly engrossed and signed, and there tendered the same, which I understand to mean proferred it for exchange. Actual exchange, which never took place, would not in my view have been part of the satisfaction of the condition but something additional which was inherently necessary to be done by the plaintiffs to enable, not to bind, the defendants to perform the unilateral contract.

Accordingly in my judgment, the answer to the . . . question must be in the affirmative.

Even if my reasoning so far be wrong the conclusion in my view is still the same for the following reasons. Whilst I think the true view of a unilateral contract must in general be that the offeror is entitled to require full performance of the condition which he had imposed and short of that he is not bound, that must be subject to one important qualification, which stems from the fact that there must be an implied obligation on the part of the offeror not to prevent the condition becoming satisfied, which obligation it seems to me must arise as soon as the offeree starts to perform. Until then the offeror can revoke the whole thing, but once the offeree has embarked on performance it is too late for the offeror to revoke his offer.'

Luxor (Eastbourne) Ltd v Cooper

[1941] AC 108 • House of Lords

Cooper sued two companies for £10 000 commission which he alleged they had agreed to pay him if he introduced a purchaser for two cinemas owned by them. He introduced a potential purchaser who was prepared to pay the minimum price asked by the two companies but they refused to sell the cinemas. Cooper claimed that the two companies had, by not selling the cinemas, broken an implied term in the contract between himself and them that they would 'do nothing to prevent the satisfactory completion of the transaction so as to deprive the respondent of the agreed commission'.

Lord Russell of Killowen: 'A few preliminary observations occur to me. (1) Commission contracts are subject to no peculiar rules or principles of their own; the law which governs them is the law which governs all contracts and all questions of agency. (2) No general rule can be laid down by which the rights of the agent or the liability of the principal under commission contracts are to be determined. In each case these must depend upon the exact terms of the contract in question, and upon the true construction of those terms. And

(3) contracts by which owners of property, desiring to dispose of it, put it in the hands of agents on commission terms, are not (in default of specific provisions) contracts of employment in the ordinary meaning of those words. No obligation is imposed on the agent to do anything. The contracts are merely promises binding on the principal to pay a sum of money upon the happening of a specified event, which involves the rendering of some service by the agent . . .

I do not assent to the view, which I think was the view of the majority in the first *Trollope (George) & Sons* v *Martyn Bros*, that a mere promise by a property owner to an agent to pay him a commission if he introduces a purchaser for the property at a specified price, or at a minimum price, ties the owner's hands, and compels him, as between himself and the agent, to bind himself contractually to sell to the agent's client who offers that price, with the result that if he refuses the offer he is liable to pay the agent a sum equal to or less than the amount of the commission . . . as damages for breach of a term to be implied in the commission contract . . . As to the claim for damages, this rests upon the implication of some provision in the commission contract . . . the object always being to bind the principal not to refuse to complete the sale to the client whom the agent has introduced. I can find no safe ground on which to base the introduction of any such implied term. Implied terms, as we all know, can only be justified under the compulsion of some necessity. No such compulsion or necessity exists in the case under consideration. The agent is promised a commission if he introduces a purchaser at a specified or minimum price. The owner is desirous of selling. The chances are largely in favour of the deal going through, if a purchaser is introduced. The agent takes the risk in the hope of a substantial remuneration for comparatively small exertion. In the case of the plaintiff his contract was made on Sept 23, 1935, his client's offer was made on Oct 2, 1935. A sum of £10 000, the equivalent of the remuneration of a year's work by a Lord Chancellor, for work done within a period of eight or nine days is no mean reward, and is one well worth a risk. There is no lack of business efficacy in such a contract, even though the principal is free to refuse to sell to the agent's client. The position will no doubt be different if the matter has proceeded to the stage of a binding contract having been made between the principal and the agent's client. In that case it can be said with truth that a "purchaser" has been introduced by the agent. In other words the event has happened upon the occurrence of which a right to the promised commission has become vested in the agent. From that moment no act or omission by the principal can deprive the agent of that vested right . . .'

Need offeror communicate the revocation?

See *Dickinson* v *Dodds* above (p 45).

Rejection and counter-offer

We have already seen that a counter-offer destroys an offer. Similarly, if an offeree rejects an offer (i.e. says he will not accept the offer) the offer is destroyed.

Lapse of offer

By passing of time

See *Manchester Diocesan Council for Education* v *Commercial and General Investments Ltd* above (p 52).

By failure of occurrence of condition

If the offer states that it is only 'open' until a certain thing happens, then if that thing happens the offer will automatically lapse.

Financings Ltd v Stimson

[1962] 3 All ER 386 • Court of Appeal

Stimson agreed to buy a car on hire purchase from a car dealer for £350. On 16 March 1961 he signed a hire purchase agreement form which was produced by the car dealer. A clause in the agreement read 'This agreement shall become binding on the owner [Financings] only upon acceptance by signature on behalf of the owner and the hiring shall be deemed to commence on such date of acceptance'. Financings did not sign the acceptance until 25 March 1961. Between Stimson signing the hire purchase agreement on 16 March and Financings' 'acceptance' on 25 March Simson had paid the first instalment of £70 and had been allowed to take the car away. On 20 March Stimson returned the car because he was not satisfied with it. In order to settle the matter he offered to forfeit the £70 he had paid. The car dealer did not get in touch with Financings; nor did Stimson. On the night of 24/25 March the car dealer's premises were broken into and the car was stolen and was badly scratched and damaged. When it was recovered it was returned to Financings who sold it for £240. Financings claimed that Stimson was in breach of the hire purchase agreement. The issue before the court was whether a contract had ever come into existence between Stimson and Financings.

Lord Denning MR: '. . . the crucial matter in the case is whether there was ever a binding agreement between the defendant and the plaintiffs. The document which the defendant signed on March 16 was only an offer. Before it was accepted, he returned the car to the dealer and made it clear that he did not want the car any more. Was that a revocation of the offer? To my mind, that was a clear revocation provided that it was made to a person having authority to receive it. But was the dealer a person authorised to receive the revocation? Was he the agent of the plaintiffs for the purpose?

    . . . It seems to me that, in this transaction before us, as indeed in most of these hire-purchase transactions, the dealer is for many purposes the agent of the finance company . . . It seems to me that, if we take, as we should, a realistic view of the position, the dealer is in many respects and for many purposes the agent of the finance company. I am aware, of course, that the finance companies often put clauses into their forms in which they say that the dealer is not their agent. But these clauses are often not worth the paper they are written on. Nobody can make an assertion of that kind in an agreement so as to bind the courts if it is contrary to the facts of the case . . . In this case we are not troubled by any such clause, for there is none. And, on the facts, I am clearly of opinion that the dealer was ostensibly authorised to receive communications on behalf of the plaintiffs. Just as he was authorised to deliver the car to the defendant in the first place, so he was ostensibly authorised to receive it back when it was returned. Just as he was authorised to receive the offer for the plaintiffs, so, also, he was ostensibly authorised to receive the revocation: and to receive the communication that the defendant had no further use for it.

    I am aware that the defendant did not in terms revoke the offer, for the simple reason that he thought the agreement was concluded. But he made it clear that he did not wish to proceed with the matter and that is all that was necessary. In my judgment, therefore, the offer was revoked on March 20 and there was, for this reason, no concluded contract. Even if I am wrong on that point, there is the second point to be considered which appealed to the county court judge. He said:

> "When this offer was made, it was made on the basis that the car was in good condition, or at all events in the condition in which the defendant had seen it, but, before the offer was accepted (it was accepted on March 25), on the night of March 24/25 it suffered this extra damage which cost £44 to repair, having been scratched and dented by the thieves who stole it. Can a man accept an offer when the condition of the goods has deteriorated in a material respect since the date of the offer?"

It seems to me that, on the facts of this case, the offer made by the defendant was a conditional offer. It was conditional on the car remaining in substantially the same condition until the moment of acceptance. Take the case put by Donovan LJ, in the course of the argument: Suppose an offer is made to buy a Rolls-Royce car at a high price on one day and, before it is accepted, it suffers the next day severe damage. Can it be accepted and the offeror bound? My answer to that is: No, because the offer is conditional on the goods at the moment of acceptance remaining in substantially the same condition as at the time of the offer . . . [T]he offer is made on the understanding that, so long as it remains an offer, it is conditional on the goods being in substantially the same condition as at the time when the offer was made. I agree, therefore, with the county court judge in thinking that, in view of the damage which occurred to this car before the acceptance was given, the plaintiffs were not in a position to accept the offer, because the condition on which it was made had not been fulfilled. So on that ground also there was no contract.

The offer lapsed when the 'thing' happened, i.e. when the car was damaged.

By death

In *Dickinson* v *Dodds*, on p 45 above, Mellish LJ said 'It is admitted law that, if a man who makes an offer dies, the offer cannot be accepted after he is dead . . . for it makes the performance of the offer impossible. I am clearly of opinion that . . . when a man who has made an offer dies before it is accepted it is impossible that it can then be accepted . . .'

SUMMARY

You should now be able to:

* Determine when an *offer* has been *terminated*.
* Determine when an *offer* has been *revoked*.
* Determine when an *offer* has *lapsed*.

If you have not mastered the above points you should go through this section again.

4 Certainty

CERTAINTY

An agreement is not a binding contract if it lacks certainty. An agreement will lack certainty *either* because it is too vague *or* because it is obviously incomplete.

The reason that there will be no contract between the parties goes back to the underlying principle that a contract is an *agreement* between the parties: if the agreement is vague or is not complete, how can the parties say they have agreed? What have they agreed upon?

VAGUENESS

An agreement that is vague will lack certainty and will therefore not be a contract.

Scammell & Nephew Ltd v Ouston

[1941] 1 All ER 14 • House of Lords

Ouston agreed to buy a lorry from Scammell 'on hire-purchase terms'. Before the hire purchase contract was entered into, Ouston decided not to proceed with the purchase. Scammell sued Ouston for breach of contract and Ouston replied that there was no contract of sale because the agreement was void for uncertainty since the words 'on hire-purchase terms' were too vague.

Viscount Maugham: 'It is a regrettable fact that there are few, if any, topics on which there seems to be a greater difference of judicial opinion than those which relate to the question whether, as the result of informal letters or like documents, a binding contract has been arrived at. Many well-known instances are to be found in the books, the latest being that of *Hillas & Co Ltd* v *Arcos Ltd*. The reason for these different conclusions is that laymen unassisted by persons with a legal training are not always accustomed to use words or phrases with a precise or definite meaning. In order to constitute a valid contract, the parties must so express themselves that their meaning can be determined with a reasonable degree of certainty. It is plain that, unless this can be done, it would be impossible to hold that the contracting parties had the same intention. In other words, the consensus *ad idem* would be a matter of mere conjecture. This general rule, however, applies somewhat differently in different cases. In commercial documents connected with dealings in a trade with which the parties are perfectly familiar, the court is very willing, if satisfied that the parties thought that they made a binding contract, to imply terms, and, in particular, terms as to the method of carrying out the contract, which it would be impossible to supply in other kinds of contract: *Hillas & Co Ltd* v *Arcos Ltd* . . .

We come, then, to the question as to the effect of the so-called purchase being on "hire-purchase terms", and here we are confronted with a strange and confusing circumstance. The term "hire-purchase" for a good many years past has been understood to mean a contract of hire by the owner of a chattel conferring on the hirer an option to purchase on the performance of certain conditions: *Helby* v *Matthews*. There is in these contracts – and this is, from a business standpoint, a most important matter – no agreement to buy within the Factors Act, 1889, or the Sale of Goods Act, 1893. There is only an option, and the hirer can confer on a purchaser from him no better title than he himself has, except in the case of sale in market overt. It is inaccurate and misleading to add to an order for goods, as if given by a purchaser, a clause that hire-purchase terms are to apply, without something to explain the apparent contradiction. Moreover, a hire-purchase agreement may assume many forms, and some of the variations in those forms are of the most important character – e.g., those which relate to termination of the agreement, warranty of fitness, duties as to repairs, interest, and so forth.

Bearing these facts in mind, what do the words "hire-purchase terms" mean in the present case? They may indicate that the hire-purchase agreement was to be granted by the appellants, or, on the other hand, by some finance company acting in collaboration with the appellants. They may contemplate that the appellants were to receive by instalments a sum of £168 spread over a period of 2 years upon delivering the new van and receiving the old car, or, on the other hand, that the appellants were to receive from a third party a lump sum of £168, and that the third party, presumably a finance company, was to receive from the respondents a larger sum than £168, to include interest and profit spread over a period of 2 years. Moreover, nothing is said (except as to the 2-years' period) as to the terms of the hire-purchase agreement – for instance, as to the interest payable, and as to the rights of the letter, whoever he may be, in the event of default by the respondents in payment of the instalments at the due dates. As regards the last matters, there was no evidence to suggest that there are any well-known "usual terms" in such a contract, and I think that it is common knowledge that in fact many letters, though by no means all of them, insist on terms which the legislature regards as so unfair and unconscionable that it was recently found necessary to deal with the matter in the Hire-Purchase Act, 1938. These, my Lords, are very serious difficulties, and, when we find, as we do, in this curious case, that the trial judge and the three Lords Justices, and even the two counsel who addressed your Lordships for the respondents, were unable to agree upon the true construction of the alleged agreement, it seems to me that it is impossible to conclude that a binding agreement has been established by the respondents . . .'

Lord Russell of Killowen: 'The oral evidence establishes that the only acquisition by the plaintiffs which was contemplated by the parties was an acquisition by some form of hire purchase which would enable the plaintiffs to spread their payment of £168 over a period of time. This could be brought about in various ways, and by documents containing a multiplicity of different terms. In my opinion, the concluding sentence of the letter of Dec 8, 1937, was not a condition precedent to any contract. It is merely a recording in writing of what had been the common intention of the parties in their discussions and negotiations, with a stipulation, apparently for the first time, for a period of 2 years. However, in view of the numerous forms of hire-purchase transactions, and the multiplicity of terms and details which they involve, the plaintiffs are faced with what appears to me to be a fatal alternative, – namely, either (i) the term of the alleged contract is quite uncertain as to its meaning, and prevents the existence of an enforceable contract, or (ii) the term leaves essential contractual provisions for further negotiation between the parties, with the same result. Accordingly, in my opinion, the action for damages for breach of an alleged contract should have been dismissed, and this appeal should succeed.'

If vital terms (such as the price of the goods) are left to be agreed by the parties there will be no contract: how can the parties say they have *agreed*? What have they agreed upon?

May & Butcher Ltd v *The King*

[1934] 2 KB 17 • House of Lords

May & Butcher Ltd alleged that they had agreed with the Controller of the Disposals Board for the purchase by them of all the tentage that might become available in the United Kingdom for disposal up to 31 March 1923. Clause 3 of the agreement stated 'The price or prices to be paid, and the date or dates on which payment is to be made by the purchasers to the Commission for such old tentage shall be agreed upon from time to time between the Commission and the purchasers as the quantities of the said old tentage become available for disposal, and are offered to the purchasers by the Commission . . .' Clause 10 stated 'It is understood that all disputes with reference to or arising out of this agreement will be submitted to arbitration in accordance with the provisions of the Arbitration Act 1889'. Rowlatt J held that the agreement was not a contract but was merely a series of clauses for adoption if and when contracts were made, because the price, date of payment and period of delivery had still to be agreed; and that the arbitration clause did not apply to differences of opinion upon these questions. The Court of Appeal affirmed Rowlatt J's decision. May & Butcher Ltd appealed.

Lord Buckmaster: 'In my opinion there never was a concluded contract between the parties. It has long been a well recognised principle of contract law that an agreement between two parties to enter into an agreement in which some critical part of the contract matter is left undetermined is no contract at all. It is of course perfectly possible for two people to contract that they will sign a document which contains all the relevant terms, but it is not open to them to agree that they will in the future agree upon a matter which is vital to the arrangement between them and has not yet been determined . . .

The next question is about the arbitration clause, and there I entirely agree with the majority of the Court of Appeal and also with Rowlatt J. The clause refers "disputes with reference to or arising out of this agreement" to arbitration, but until the price has been fixed, the agreement is not there. The arbitration clause relates to the settlement of whatever may happen when the agreement has been completed and the parties are regularly bound. There is nothing in the arbitration clause to enable a contract to be made which in fact the original bargain has left quite open.'

Viscount Dunedin: 'I am of the same opinion. This case arises upon a question of sale, but in my view the principles which we are applying are not confined to sale, but are the general principles of the law of contract. To be a good contract there must be a concluded bargain, and a concluded contract is one which settles everything that is necessary to be settled and leaves nothing to be settled by agreement between the parties. Of course it may leave something which still has to be determined, but then that determination must be a determination which does not depend upon the agreement between the parties. In the system of law in which I was brought up, that was expressed by one of those brocards of which perhaps we have been too fond, but which often express very neatly what is wanted: '*Certum est quod certum reddi potest*'. [That is certain which can be rendered certain.] Therefore, you may very well agree that a certain part of the contract of sale, such as price, may be settled by some one else. As a matter of the general law of contract all the essentials have to be settled. What are the essentials may vary according to the particular contract under consideration. We are here dealing with sale, and undoubtedly price is one of the essentials of sale, and if it is left still to be agreed between the parties, then there is no contract. It may be left to the determination of a certain person, and if it was so left and that person either would not or could not act, there would be no contract because the price was to be settled in a certain way and it has become impossible to settle it in that way, and therefore there is no settlement. No doubt as to goods, the Sale of Goods Act, 1893, says that if the price is not mentioned and settled in the contract it is to be a reasonable price. The simple answer in this case is that the Sale of Goods Act provides for silence on the point and here there is no silence, because there is a provision that the two parties are to agree. As long as you have something certain it does not matter. For instance, with regard to price it is a perfectly good contract to say that the price is to be settled by the buyer. I have not had time, or perhaps I have not been industrious enough, to look through all the books in England to see if there is such a case; but there was such a case in Scotland in 1760, where it was decided that a sale of a landed estate was perfectly good, the price being left to be settled by the buyer himself. I have only expressed in other words what has already been said by my noble friend on the Woolsack. Here there was clearly no contract. There would have been a perfectly good settlement of price if the contract had said that it was to be settled by arbitration by a certain man, or it might have been quite good if it was said that it was to be settled by arbitration under the Arbitration Act so as to bring in a material plan by which a certain person could be put in action. The question then arises, has anything of that sort been done? I think clearly not. The general arbitration clause is one in very common form as to disputes arising out of the arrangements. In no proper meaning of the word can this be described as a dispute arising between the parties: it is a failure to agree, which is a very different thing from a dispute.

As regards the option point, I do not think it can be more neatly put than it was by Rowlatt J when he said: "It is an option to offer terms on terms that are not agreed. An option to offer a contract which is not a contract seems to me not to carry the case any further than the first way of putting it". For these reasons I agree in the motion.'

Courtney and Fairbairn Ltd v Tolaini Brothers (Hotels) Ltd

[1975] 1 All ER 716 • Court of Appeal

Tolaini wanted to develop a site. He got in touch with Courtney, a property developer, who had access to finance for building development. It was proposed that Courtney should introduce someone who would lend money to Tolaini and that in return Tolaini would employ Courtney to do the construction work. On 10 April 1969 Courtney wrote to Tolaini stating

'... I am now in a position to introduce you to those who: (a) are interested in your proposals, (b) have access to the necessary finance ...

Accordingly I would be very happy to know that, if my discussions and arrangements with interested parties lead to an introductory meeting, which in turn leads to a financial arrangement acceptable to both parties you will be prepared to instruct your Quantity Surveyor to negotiate fair and reasonable contract sums in respect of each of the three projects as they arise. (These would, incidentally be based upon agreed estimates of the net cost of work and general overheads with a margin for profit of 5%) which, I am sure you will agree, is indeed reasonable.'

On 28 April 1969 Tolaini wrote to Courtney stating 'In reply to your letter of the 10th April, I agree to the terms specified therein, and I look forward to meeting the interested party regarding finance'. Courtney found a person who provided the finance for the projects. Tolaini appointed his quantity surveyor with a view to negotiating with Courtney the price for the construction work but nothing was agreed so Tolaini instructed other contractors to build the projects.

The issue before the court was 'Whether there was concluded any enforceable agreement in law between the Courtney and the Tolaini, and if yes, who were the parties to the agreement and what were its terms'. Shaw J held that there was an enforceable agreement. Tolaini appealed.

Lord Denning MR: 'I am afraid that I have come to a different view from the judge. The reason is because I can find no agreement on the price or on any method by which the price was to be calculated. The agreement was only an agreement to "negotiate" fair and reasonable contract sums. The words of the letter are "your Quantity Surveyor to negotiate fair and reasonable contract sums in respect of each of the three projects as they arise". Then there are words which show that estimates had not yet been agreed, but were yet to be agreed. The words are: "These [the contract sums] would, incidentally be based upon agreed estimates of the net cost of work and general overheads with a margin for profit of 5%". Those words show that there were no estimates agreed and no contract sums agreed. All was left to be agreed in the future. It was to be agreed between the parties themselves. If they had left the price to be agreed by a third person such as an arbitrator, it would have been different. But here it was to be agreed between the parties themselves.

Now the price in a building contract is of fundamental importance. It is so essential a term that there is no contract unless the price is agreed or there is an agreed method of ascertaining it, not dependent on the negotiations of the two parties themselves. In a building contract both parties must know at the outset, before the work is started, what the price is to be, or, at all events, what agreed estimates are. No builder and no employer would ever dream of entering into a building contract for over £200 000 without there being an estimate of the cost and an agreed means of ascertaining the price.

In the ordinary course of things the architects and the quantity surveyors get out the specification and the bills of quantities. They are submitted to the contractors. They work out the figures and tender for the work at a named price; and there is a specified means of altering it up or down for extras or omissions and so forth, usually by means of an architect's certificate. In the absence of some such machinery, the only contract which you might find is a contract to do the work for a reasonable sum or for a sum to be fixed by a third party. But here there is no such contract at all. There is no machinery for ascertaining the price except by negotiation. In other words, the price is still to be agreed. Seeing that there is no agreement on so fundamental a matter as the price, there is no contract.

But then this point was raised. Even if there was not a contract actually to build, was not there a contract to negotiate? In this case Mr Tolaini did instruct his quantity surveyor to negotiate, but the negotiations broke down. It may be suggested that the quantity surveyor was to blame for the failure of the negotiations. But does that give rise to a cause of action? There is very little guidance in the book about a contract to negotiate. It was touched on by Lord Wright in *Hillas & Co Ltd* v *Arcos Ltd* where he said: "There is then no bargain except to negotiate, and negotiations may be fruitless and end without any contract ensuing". Then he went on:

". . . yet even then, in strict theory, there is a contract (if there is good consideration) to negotiate, though in the event of repudiation by one party the damages may be nominal, unless a jury think that the opportunity to negotiate was of some appreciable value to the injured party."

That tentative opinion by Lord Wright does not seem to me to be well founded. If the law does not recognise a contract to enter into a contract (when there is a fundamental term yet to be agreed) it seems to me it cannot recognise a contract to negotiate. The reason is because it is too uncertain to have any binding force. No court could estimate the damages because no one can tell whether the negotiations would be successful or would fall through; or if successful, what the result would be. It seems to me that a contract to negotiate, like a contract to enter into a contract, is not a contract known to the law. We were referred to the recent decision of Brightman J about an option, *Mountford* v *Scott*; but that does not seem to me to touch this point. I think we must apply the general principle that when there is a fundamental matter left undecided and to be the subject of negotiation, there is no contract. So I would hold that there was not any enforceable agreement in the letters between the plaintiff and the defendants. I would allow the appeal accordingly.'

Walford v *Miles*

[1992] 1 All ER 453 • House of Lords

Walford wished to purchase Miles' business for £2m. Miles told Walford that if Walford provided a letter of comfort from his bank for £2m by 20 March then 'he would terminate negotiations with any third party or consideration of any alternative with a view to concluding agreements with' Walford. Miles further agreed that 'even if he received a satisfactory proposal from any third party before close of business on Friday night he would not deal with that third party and nor would he give further consideration to any alternative'. Walford provided the requested letter of comfort in good time. On 25 March Miles wrote to confirm that, subject to contract, he agreed to the sale of the property and the shares at a total price of £2m. On the same day Miles wrote to the third party informing them that he had concluded terms for the sale of the property and the shares in the company to Walford. On 30 March Miles sold the business to the third party. Walford claimed that there was a concluded contract between himself and Miles whereby Miles had agreed not to deal with a third party and not to give further consideration to any alternative offer. Walford claimed that a term should be implied into their agreement that Miles would continue to negotiate with Walford in good faith so long as Miles continued to want to sell his business.

The issues before the court were: was there a concluded contract as Walford alleged and if there was such a contract was there an implied term of good faith in the contract?

Lord Ackner: '[Counsel for Walford] accepted that as the law now stands and has stood for approaching 20 years an agreement to negotiate is not recognised as an enforceable contract. This was first decided in terms in *Courtney and Fairbairn Ltd* v *Tolaini Bros (Hotels) Ltd* where Lord Denning MR said:

"If the law does not recognise a contract to enter into a contract (when there is a fundamental term yet to be agreed) it seems to me it cannot recognise a contract to negotiate. The reason is because it is too uncertain to have any binding force . . . It seems to me that a contract to negotiate, like a contract to enter into a contract, is not a contract known to the law . . . I think we must apply the general principle that when there is a fundamental matter left undecided and to be the subject of negotiation, there is no contract."

. . . The decision that an agreement to negotiate cannot constitute a legally enforceable contract has been followed at first instance in a number of relatively recent cases: *Albion Sugar Co Ltd* v *Williams Tankers Ltd, The John S Darbyshire, Scandinavian Trading Tanker Co AB* v *Flota Petrolera Ecuatoriana, The Scaptrade, Trees Ltd* v *Cripps, Nile Co for Export of Agricultural Crops* v *H & JN Bennett (Commodities) Ltd, Voest Alpine Intertrading GmbH* v *Chevron International Oil Co Ltd* and *Star Steamship Society* v *Beogradska Plovidba, The Junior K.* . . .

Before your Lordships it was sought to argue that the decision in the *Courtney & Fairbairn Ltd* case was wrong. Although the cases in the United States did not speak with one voice your Lordships' attention was drawn to the decision of the United States Court of Appeals, Third Circuit in *Channel Home Centers Division of Grace Retail Corp* v *Grossman* as being 'the clearest example' of the American cases in the appellants' favour. That case raised the issue whether an agreement to negotiate in good faith, if supported by consideration, is an enforceable contract. I do not find the decision of any assistance. While accepting that an agreement to agree is not an enforceable contract, the United States Court of Appeals appears to have proceeded on the basis that an agreement to negotiate in good faith is synonymous with an agreement to use best endeavours and, as the latter is enforceable, so is the former. This appears to me, with respect, to be an unsustainable proposition. The reason why an agreement to negotiate, like an agreement to agree, is unenforceable is simply because it lacks the necessary certainty. The same does not apply to an agreement to use best endeavours. This uncertainty is demonstrated in the instant case by the provision which it is said has to be implied in the agreement for the determination of the negotiations. How can a court be expected to decide whether, subjectively, a proper reason existed for the termination of negotiations? The answer suggested depends upon whether the negotiations have been determined "in good faith". However, the concept of a duty to carry on negotiations in good faith is inherently repugnant to the adversarial position of the parties when involved in negotiations. Each party to the negotiations is entitled to pursue his (or her) own interest, so long as he avoids making misrepresentations. To advance that interest he must be entitled, if he thinks it appropriate, to threaten to withdraw from further negotiations or to withdraw in fact in the hope that the opposite party may seek to reopen the negotiations by offering him improved terms. [Counsel for Walford] of course, accepts that the agreement upon which he relies does not contain a duty to complete the negotiations. But that still leaves the vital question: how is a vendor ever to know that he is entitled to withdraw from further negotiations? How is the court to police such an "agreement"? A duty to negotiate in good faith is as unworkable in practice as it is inherently inconsistent with the position of a negotiating party. It is here that the uncertainty lies. In my judgment, while negotiations are in existence either party is entitled to withdraw from these negotiations, at any time and for any reason. There can be thus no obligation to continue to negotiate until there is a "proper reason" to withdraw. Accordingly, a bare agreement to negotiate has no legal content.'

British Steel Corporation v *Cleveland Bridge and Engineering Co Ltd*
[1984] 1 All ER 504 • Queen's Bench

BSC (British Steel Corporation) were approached by CBE (Cleveland Bridge and

Engineering Co Ltd) to produce cast-steel nodes for a bank which they were about to build. After further discussions on technical requirements and appropriate specifications CBE sent a letter of intent to BSC which stated 'We are pleased to advise you that it is the intention of [CBE] to enter into a Sub-Contract with your company, for the supply and delivery of the steel castings which form the roof nodes on this project. The price will be as quoted in your telex [which was an estimated price] . . . The form of Sub-Contract to be entered into will be our standard form of sub-contract for use in conjunction with the ICE General Conditions of Contract . . . and we request that you proceed immediately with the works pending the preparation and issuing to you of the official form of sub-contract'. BSC did not reply to the letter because a formal order was expected to follow shortly thereafter and in any case BSC would not have agreed to the ICE conditions of contract which provided for unlimited liability for consequential loss arising from late delivery. Further discussions continued between BSC and CBE and although BSC continued to manufacture and deliver the cast-steel nodes the parties were unable to agree any contract terms other than the price of the nodes. BSC claimed £229 832 as the price of 137 cast-steel nodes sold and delivered to CBE or alternatively they claimed the same sum on a *quantum meruit*. CBE counterclaimed £867 735 on the ground that BSC had broken the contract by delivering the nodes too late and out of sequence.

Robert Goff J: '. . . First, was there any binding contract between the parties at all, under which the nodes were delivered? CBE contended that there was such a contract, which was to be found in certain documents (including a letter of intent issued by CBE dated 21 February 1979) and the conduct of BSC in proceeding with the manufacture of the nodes. BSC's primary contention was that no binding contract was ever entered into, and that they were entitled to be paid a reasonable sum for the nodes on a *quantum meruit*, a claim sounding not in contract but in quasi contract. The motives of the parties in putting their cases in these different ways lay primarily in the fact that, unless there was a binding contract between the parties there was no legal basis for CBE's counterclaim for damages in respect of late delivery or delivery out of sequence . . .

Now the question whether in a case such as the present any contract has come into existence must depend on a true construction of the relevant communications which have passed between the parties and the effect (if any) of their actions pursuant to those communications. There can be no hard and fast answer to the question whether a letter of intent will give rise to a binding agreement: everything must depend on the circumstances of the particular case. In most cases, where work is done pursuant to a request contained in a letter of intent, it will not matter whether a contract did or did not come into existence, because, if the party who has acted on the request is simply claiming payment, his claim will usually be based on a *quantum meruit*, and it will make no difference whether that claim is contractual or quasi-contractual. Of course, a *quantum meruit* claim (like the old actions for money had and received and for money paid) straddles the boundaries of what we now call contract and restitution, so the mere framing of a claim as a *quantum meruit* claim, or a claim for a reasonable sum, does not assist in classifying the claim as contractual or quasi contractual. But where, as here, one party is seeking to claim damages for breach of contract, the question whether any contract came into existence is of crucial importance.

As a matter of analysis the contract (if any) which may come into existence following a letter of intent may take one of two forms: either there may be an ordinary executory contract, under which each party assumes reciprocal obligations to the other or there may be what is sometimes called an "if" contract, i.e. a contract under which A requests B to carry out a certain performance and promises B that, if he does so, he will receive a certain performance in return, usually remuneration for his performance. The latter transaction is really no more than a standing offer which, if acted on before it lapses or is lawfully withdrawn, will result in a binding contract.

The former type of contract was held to exist by Mr Edgar Fay QC, the official Referee, in *Turriff Construction Ltd* v *Regalia Knitting Mills Ltd* and it is the type of contract for which counsel for CBE contended in the present case. Of course, as I have already said, everything must depend on the facts of the particular case but certainly, on the facts of the present case (and, as I imagine, on the facts of most cases), this must be a very difficult submission to maintain. It is only necessary to look at the terms of CBE's letter of intent in the present case to appreciate the difficulties. In that letter, the request to BSC to proceed immediately with the work was stated to be "pending the preparation and issuing to you of the official form of sub-contract", being a sub-contract which was plainly in a state of negotiation, not least on the issues of price, delivery dates, and the applicable terms and conditions. In these circumstances, it is very difficult to see how BSC, by starting work, bound themselves to any contractual performance. No doubt it was envisaged by CBE at the time they sent the letter that negotiations had reached an advanced stage, and that a formal contract would soon be signed but, since the parties were still in a state of negotiation, it is impossible to say with any degree of certainty what the material terms of that contract would be. I find myself quite unable to conclude that, by starting work in these circumstances, BSC bound themselves to complete the work . . .

I therefore reject CBE's submission that a binding executory contract came into existence in this case. There remains the question whether, by reason of BSC carrying out work pursuant to the request contained in CBE's letter of intent, there came into existence a contract by virtue of which BSC were entitled to claim reasonable remuneration i.e. whether there was an "if" contract of the kind I have described. In the course of argument, I was attracted by this alternative (really on the basis that, not only was it analytically possible, but also that it could provide a vehicle for certain contractual obligations of BSC concerning their performance, e.g. implied terms as to the quality of goods supplied by them). But the more I have considered the case, the less attractive I have found this alternative. The real difficulty is to be found in the factual matrix of the transaction, and in particular the fact that the work was being done pending a formal sub-contract the terms of which were still in a state of negotiation. It is, of course, a notorious fact that, when a contract is made for the supply of goods on a scale and in circumstances such as the present, it will in all probability be subject to standard terms, usually the standard terms of the supplier. Such standard terms will frequently legislate, not only for the liability of the seller for defects, but also for the damages (if any) for which the seller will be liable in the event not only of defects in the goods but also of late delivery. It is a commonplace that a seller of goods may exclude liability for consequential loss, and may agree liquidated damages for delay. In the present case, an unresolved dispute broke out between the parties on the question whether CBE's or BSC's standard terms were to apply, the former providing no limit to the seller's liability for delay and the latter excluding such liability altogether. Accordingly, when, in a case such as the present, the parties are still in a state of negotiation, it is impossible to predicate what liability (if any) will be assumed by the seller for, e.g., defective goods or late delivery, if a formal contract should be entered into. In these circumstances, if the buyer asks the seller to commence work "pending" the parties entering into a formal contract, it is difficult to infer from the buyer acting on that request that he is assuming any responsibility for his performance, except such responsibility as will rest on him under the terms of the contract which both parties confidently anticipate they will shortly enter into. It would be an extraordinary result if, by acting on such a request in such circumstances, the buyer were to assume an unlimited liability for his contractual performance, when he would never assume such liability under any contract which he entered into.

For these reasons, I reject the solution of the "if" contract. In my judgment, the true analysis of the situation is simply this. Both parties confidently expected a formal contract to eventuate. In these circumstances, to expedite performance under that anticipated contract, one requested the other to commence the contract work, and the other complied with that request. If thereafter, as anticipated, a contract was entered into, the work done as requested will be treated as having been performed under that contract if, contrary to their expectation, no contract was entered into, then the performance of the work is not referable to any contract the terms of which can be ascertained, and the law simply imposes an obligation on the party who made the request to pay a reasonable sum for such work as has been done pursuant to that request, such an obligation sounding in quasi contract or, as we now say, in restitution. Consistently with that solution, the party making the request may find himself liable to pay for work which he would not have had to pay for as such if the anticipated contract had come into existence, e.g. preparatory work which will, if the contract is made, be allowed for in the price of the finished work (cf *William Lacey (Hounslow) Ltd* v *Davis*. This solution moreover accords with authority: see the decision in *Lacey* v *Davis*, the decision of the Court of Appeal in *Sanders & Forster Ltd* v *A Monk & Co Ltd*, though that decision rested in part on a concession, and the crisp dictum of Parker J in *OTM Ltd* v *Hydranautics* when he said of a letter of intent that "its only effect would be to enable the defendants to recover on a *quantum meruit* for work done pursuant to the direction" contained in the letter. I only wish to add to this part of my judgment the footnote that, even if I had concluded that in the circumstances of the present case there was a contract between the parties and that that contract was of the kind I have described as an "if" contract, then I would still have concluded that there was no obligation under that contract on the part of BSC to continue with or complete the contract work, and therefore no obligation on their part to complete the work within a reasonable time. However, my conclusion in the present case is that the parties never entered into any contract at all . . .

It follows that BSC are entitled to succeed on their claim and that CBE's set-off and counterclaim must fail.'

RESOLVING VAGUENESS

Despite the imperfect wording of some agreements the courts will try to give effect to an agreement wherever possible. As Buckley LJ said in *Bushwall Properties Ltd* v *Vortex Properties Ltd* 'I fully accept that the court should be reluctant to hold any contract void for uncertainty if that consequence can be avoided'. Also, in the same case Sir John Pennycuick said 'The court will uphold a contract if it possible to do so'.

Resolving vagueness on the basis of reasonableness as between the parties

Hillas and Co Ltd v Arcos Ltd
[1932] All ER Rep 494 • House of Lords

By a document of 21 May 1930 Hillas agreed 'to buy 22 000 standards softwood goods of fair specification over the season 1930 under the following conditions'. Clause 9 stated 'Buyers shall also have the option of entering into a contract with sellers for the purchase of 100 000 standards for delivery during 1931'. There was no mention of the kinds, sizes or qualities of softwood timber to be supplied.

The issue before the court was whether the agreement of 21 May was an agreement to agree and therefore void for lack of certainty.

Lord Tomlin: '. . . Commercial documents prepared by business men in connection with dealings in a trade with the workings of which the framers are familiar often by reason of their inartificial forms confront the lawyer with delicate problems. The governing principles of construction recognised by the law are applicable to every document, and yet none would gainsay that the effect of their application is to some extent governed by the nature of the document. On the one hand the conveyance of real estate presenting an artificial form grown up through the centuries and embodying terms of art whose meanings and effect have long since been determined by the courts, and on the other hand the formless document, the product of the minds of men seeking to record a complex trade bargain intended to be carried out, both fall to be construed by the same legal principles, and the problem for a court of construction must always be so to balance matters, that without violation of essential principle the dealings of men may as far as possible be treated as effective, and that the law may not incur the reproach of being the destroyer of bargains. The principles are not in dispute. It is in the application of them to the facts of a particular case that the difficulty arises; and the difficulty is of such a kind as often to afford room for much legitimate difference of opinion and to present a problem the solution of which is not as a rule to be found by examining authorities.

In the present case one or two preliminary observations fall to be made. First, the parties were both intimately acquainted with the course of business in the Russian softwood timber trade and had without difficulty carried out the sale and purchase of 22 000 standards under the first part of the document of the 21st May 1930. Secondly, although the question here is whether clause 9 of the document of the 21st May 1930, with the letter of the 22nd Dec 1930, constitutes a contract, the validity of the whole of the document of the 21st May 1930 is really in question so far as the matter depends upon the meaning of the phrase "of fair specification". Thirdly, it is indisputable, having regard to clause 11, which provides that "this agreement cancels all previous agreements", that the parties intended by the document of the 21st May 1930 to make, and believed that they had made, some concluded bargain.

The case against the appellants is put on two grounds. First it is said that there is in clause 9 no sufficient description of the goods to be sold . . . As to the first point it is plain that something must necessarily be implied in clause 9. The words "100 000 standards" without more do not even indicate that timber is the subject-matter of the clause. The implication at the least of the words "of softwood goods" is, in my opinion, inevitable, and if this is so I see no reason to separate the words "of fair specification" from the words "of softwood goods". In my opinion there is a necessary implication of the words "of softwood goods of fair specification" after the words "100 000 standards" in clause 9.

What then is the meaning of "100 000 standards of softwood goods of fair specification for delivery during 1931"? If the words "of fair specification" have no meaning which is certain or capable of being made certain, then not only can there be no contract under clause 9 but there cannot have been a contract with regard to the 22 000 standards mentioned at the beginning of the document of the 1st May 1930. This may be the proper conclusion; but before it is reached it is, I think, necessary to exclude as impossible all reasonable meanings which would give certainty to the words. In my opinion this cannot be done. The parties undoubtedly attributed to the words in connection with the 22 000 standards, some meaning which was precise or capable of being made precise . . .

Reading the document of the 21st May 1930 as a whole, and having regard to the admissible evidence as to the course of the trade, I think that upon their true construction the words "of fair specification over the season, 1930", used in connection with the 22 000 standards, mean that the 22 000 standards are to be satisfied in goods distributed over kinds, qualities, and sizes in the fair proportions having regard to the output of the season 1930 and the classifications of that output in respect of kinds, qualities, and sizes. That is something which if the parties fail to agree can be ascertained just as much as the fair value of a property. I have already expressed the view that clause 9 must be read as "100 000 standards of fair specification for delivery during 1931" and these words, I think, have the same meaning, *mutatis mutandis*, as the words relating to the 22 000 standards. Thus, there is a description of the goods which if not immediately yet ultimately is capable of being rendered certain.'

Lord Thankerton: '. . . Subject to some doubts that I have felt as to the proper construction of the words "of fair specification" and as to which I desire to add some observations, I find myself in entire agreement with the construction which my noble and learned friend has put upon the document of the 21st May 1930, and I also agree with his conclusion that it is not open to the respondents to maintain that there was no concluded agreement.

The question on which I have had doubt is whether the words "of fair specification", on their proper construction, will enable the subject to be identified by the court. In other words, do they provide a standard by which the court is enabled to ascertain the subject-matter of the contract, or do they involve an adjustment between the conflicting interests of the parties, which the parties have left unsettled and on which the court is not entitled to adjudicate? Does the phrase mean a specification which is fair as between the interests, on the one hand, of the seller in respect of the stock of wood, comprising various kinds of wood and various qualities and sizes, available for sale in the season of 1931, and, on the other hand, the interests of the buyer in respect of the requirements of his trade during that season? Or does the phrase mean a fair selection from the seller's stock of wood available for sale in that season? If the former construction be the proper one, I would be of opinion that the court would not be entitled to adjudicate between the opposing interests of the two parties. If the latter construction be the proper one the ascertainment of a fair selection from the seller's available stock is within the province of the court; in that case the court is applying a standard which is provided by the contract, and is thereby merely identifying the subject-matter of the contract.

While I have had considerable doubt on this question of construction, I am affected by the consideration that the contract is a commercial one and that the parties undoubtedly thought that they had concluded a contract, and I have come to the conclusion in agreement with the noble Lord, that the second alternative construction above stated is the proper one and that there was here a concluded contract.'

Resolving vagueness by discarding meaningless phrases

Nicolene Ltd v *Simmonds*

[1953] 1 All ER 822 • Court of Appeal

Nicolene wrote to Simmonds stating 'We enclose our detailed order and require your written confirmation of acceptance of the order . . .' On 16 August Simmonds replied by letter stating 'I thank you for your letter and order of 10 August . . . As you have made the order direct to me, I am unable to confirm on my usual printed form which would have the usual force majeure and war clauses, but I assume that we are in agreement that the usual conditions of acceptance apply . . .' There were no 'usual conditions' between the parties. Simmonds failed to deliver the goods and claimed that there was no concluded agreement between the parties. Sellers J held that there should be implied into the contract the usual force majeure and war clauses as contained in the 'printed form' referred to by the defendant and that there was a concluded contract between the parties. Simmonds appealed.

Denning LJ: 'This case raises a short, but important, point which can be stated quite simply. There was a contract for the sale of three thousand tons of steel reinforcing bars; the seller broke his contract, and when the buyer claimed damages the seller set up the defence that, owing to a sentence in one of the letters which were alleged to constitute the contract, there was no contract at all. The material words are: "We are in agreement that the usual conditions of acceptance apply". There were no usual conditions of acceptance and so it is said that those words are meaningless, that there is nothing to which they can apply, and that, therefore, there was never any contract between the parties.

In my opinion, a distinction must be drawn between a clause which is meaningless and a clause which is yet to be agreed. A clause which is meaningless can often be ignored, while still leaving the contract good, whereas a clause which has yet to be agreed may mean that there is no contract at all, because the parties have not agreed on all the essential terms. I take it to be clear law that, if one of the parties to a contract inserts into it an exempting condition in his own favour which the other side agrees and it afterwards appears that that condition is meaningless or is so ambiguous that no ascertainable meaning can be given to it, that does not render the whole contract a nullity. The only result is that the exempting condition is a nullity and must be rejected. It would be strange, indeed, if a party could escape every one of his obligations by inserting a meaningless exemption from some of them. The proposition which I have stated is supported by the numerous cases where it has been held that, if a man signs a contract expressly as agent for a named company and there is no such company in existence, the courts do not hold that there is no contract, but only reject the meaningless words "as agent for the company" and hold that the individual himself was a party to the contract. So, also, if a person signs "as agent" and has no principal, the words "as agent" are rejected and the contract is held to be a good contract between the parties.

As I read it, *Re Vince. Ex p. Baxter* is an authority in support of what I have said. The contract of loan itself was good, but the vague and unintelligible clause was rejected. The other cases which were relied on can all be explained on the ground that there was a clause yet to be agreed. In *Love & Stewart, Ltd* v *S Instone & Co, Ltd*, where there was a strike clause yet to be agreed, Lord Sumner said that the case was "one of continuing negotiations broken off *in medio*"; in *G Scammell & Nephew, Ltd* v *Ouston*, where there were hire-purchase terms yet to be agreed, Lord Wright said the "agreement was inchoate, and never got beyond negotiations". In *Bishop & Baxter, Ltd* v *Anglo-Eastern Trading & Industrial Co, Ltd*, where there was a war clause yet to be agreed, this court held that, until the parties agreed on a particular form of war clause, there could be no consensus *ad idem*. As I read them, those were all cases where there was a clause yet to be agreed, the matter was still in negotiation, and there was no concluded contract . . .

In the case before the court there was nothing yet to be agreed. There was nothing left to further negotiation. The parties merely agreed that "the usual conditions of acceptance apply". That clause was so vague and uncertain as to be incapable of any precise meaning. It is clearly severable from the rest of the contract, and can be rejected without impairing the sense or reasonableness of the contract as a whole, and it should be ignored. The parties themselves treated the contract as subsisting, and they regarded it as creating binding obligations between them and it would be most unfortunate if the law should say otherwise. Sellers J interpreted the sentence in the letter somewhat differently. He thought it meant that the usual force majeure and war clauses applied. Even so, the clause is still meaningless, because there are no such usual clauses. It is not a case where the clauses had yet to be agreed, and there was nothing left to further negotiation. On this interpretation, therefore, the same position is reached. The sentence is meaningless and must be ignored, but the contract, nevertheless, remains good. I agree that the appeal should be dismissed.'

Resolving vagueness by discarding self-contradictory phrases

Lovelock v Exportles

[1968] 1 Lloyd's Rep 163 • Court of Appeal

A contract between Exportles and Lovelock contained an arbitration clause which provided that 'Any dispute and/or claim which it may be found impossible to settle amicably shall . . . be referred to [arbitration]' and 'Any other dispute that may arise between the parties . . . shall . . . be referred for final decision to the USSR Chamber of Commerce Foreign Trade Arbitration Commission in Moscow'. A dispute arose and Lovelock commenced an action in the English courts. Exportles applied to the court to stay the action claiming that the dispute should be settled by arbitration in Moscow.

Lord Denning MR: 'The first part of the clause . . . seems to cover "Any dispute and/or claim". Yet when you come to the second part, it says "Any other dispute". It is asked: "What are those other disputes?" Attempts have been made in the Courts below and in this Court to reconcile the two parts. Five suggestions have been made . . .

So all five suggestions seem to me to be untenable. I am forced to the conclusion that the clause is so uncertain that the Court cannot give effect to it. The clause is divided into two parts which are inconsistent with one another: and it is impossible to reconcile them. The first part of this arbitration clause would send "Any dispute and/or claim" to arbitration in England. The second part of the clause would send "Any other dispute" to arbitration in Russia. It is beyond the wit of man – or at any rate beyond my wit – to say which dispute comes within which part of the clause. I think I can see how it has come about. The parties have taken separate clauses from two separate forms and bundled them both together into one clause without stopping to think how they could be applied.

In my opinion the whole clause is meaningless. It must be rejected. The Court cannot give effect to it. The dispute cannot be sent to arbitration. It must be decided by the Court . . .

I would refuse the stay and dismiss the appeal.'

Diplock LJ: 'As my Lord has said, no less than five different attempts have been made to reconcile these two clauses. I share my Lord's inability to find any of those attempts convincing. I think the two clauses are repugnant. The parties have failed to express a common intention. Indeed, it is not uninteresting to notice that when the matter arose, the appellants suggested that the arbitration should take place in Moscow pursuant to the second part of the clause and the plaintiffs, the respondents to this appeal, suggested that it should take place in England pursuant to the first part of the clause.

I can find no common intention expressed by the parties. The clause is of course severable and in the result the dispute between them must take the ordinary course, that is to say it is for the Courts to decide it.'

Resolving vagueness by reference to the 'machinery' provided in the agreement

Sudbrook Trading Estate Ltd v *Eggleton*

[1982] 3 All ER 1 • House of Lords

A clause in a lease conferred on the tenants an option to purchase the property that they had been renting at such price as might be agreed upon by two valuers, one to be nominated by the landlords and the other by the tenants and in default of such an agreement by an umpire appointed by the valuers. The tenant exercised his option under the lease to purchase the property and nominated his own valuer but the landlords refused to appoint a valuer. The tenant claimed (1) that the option clause was valid, (2) that he had validly and effectually exercised the option, (3) that the lease ought to be specifically performed and carried into execution in accordance with the conditions contained in the respective clauses of such leases, (4) that directions be given as to the nomination of a valuer by the landlord, (5) damages in addition to specific performance, and (6) costs.

The issues before the court were first, was there a completed agreement between the parties since a price had not been fixed, and second, could the court appoint a valuer or determine a fair price?

Lord Fraser of Tullybelton: 'My Lords, the appellants are the tenants in four leases, by each of which they were granted an option to purchase the freehold reversion of the leased premises at a valuation. The appellants have exercised the options, but the respondents, who are the landlords, contend that the options are unenforceable. The questions now to be determined, therefore, are whether the options are valid and enforceable, and, if so, how they should be enforced . . .

The lessors contend that the options are void for uncertainty on the ground that they contain no formula by which the price can be fixed in the event of no agreement being reached, and that they are no more than agreements to agree. The respondents have therefore declined to appoint their valuer. The machinery provided in the leases has accordingly become inoperable.

. . . Lawson J decided the question of principle in favour of the appellants, but his decision was reversed by the Court of Appeal which held that the options were unenforceable. Templeman LJ, who delivered the judgment of the Court of Appeal, made a full review of the English authorities and the conclusion which he drew from them was, in my opinion inevitably, adverse to the appellants' contentions. The fundamental proposition upon which he relied was, in his own words –

"that where the agreement on the face of it is incomplete until something else has been done, whether by further agreement between the parties or by the decision of an arbitrator or valuer, the court is powerless, because there is no complete agreement to enforce: . . ."

I agree that that is the effect of the earlier decisions but, with the greatest respect, I am of opinion that it is wrong. It appears to me that, on the exercise of the option, the necessary preconditions having been satisfied, as they were in this case, a complete contract of sale and purchase of the freehold reversion was constituted. The price, which was of course an essential term of the contract, was for reasons which I shall explain, capable of being ascertained and was therefore certain. *Certum est quod certum reddi potest*: see [*May and Butcher Ltd v The King* (p 74)] per Viscount Dunedin.

The courts have applied clauses such as those in the present case in a strictly literal way and have treated them as making the completion of a contract of sale conditional upon agreement between the valuers either on the value of the property, or failing that, on the choice of an umpire. They have further laid down the principle that where parties have agreed on a particular method of ascertaining the price, and that method has for any reason proved ineffective, the court will neither grant an order for specific performance to compel parties to operate the agreed machinery, nor substitute its own machinery to ascertain the price, because either of these clauses would be to impose upon parties an agreement that they had not made. That was decided by Sir William Grant MR in *Milnes v Gery* and his decision has been accepted ever since. The basis of his decision is sufficiently explained by the following sentences from his opinion:

> "The only agreement, into which the defendant entered, was to purchase at a price, to be ascertained in a specified mode. No price having ever been fixed in that mode, the parties have not agreed upon any price. Where then is the complete and concluded contract, which this court is called upon to execute?". . .

While that is the general principle it is equally well established that, where parties have agreed to sell "at a fair valuation" or "at a reasonable price" or according to some similar formula, without specifying any machinery for ascertaining the price, the position is different. As Grant MR said in *Milnes v Gery*:

> "In that case no particular means of ascertaining the value are pointed out: there is nothing therefore, precluding the court from adopting any means, adapted to that purpose."

The court will order such inquiries as may be necessary to ascertain the fair price: see *Talbot v Talbot.*

I recognise the logic of the reasoning which has led to the courts' refusing to substitute their own machinery for the machinery which has been agreed upon by the parties. But the result to which it leads is so remote from that which parties normally intend and expect, and is so inconvenient in practice, that there must in my opinion be some defect in the reasoning. I think the defect lies in construing the provisions for the mode of ascertaining the value as an essential part of the agreement. That may have been perfectly true early in the 19th century, when the valuer's profession and the rules of valuation were less well established than they are now. But at the present day these provisions are only subsidiary to the main purpose of the agreement which is for sale and purchase of the property at a fair or reasonable value. In the ordinary case parties do not make any substantial distinction between an agreement to sell at a fair value, without specifying the mode of ascertaining the value, and an agreement to sell at a value to be ascertained by valuers appointed in the way provided in these leases. The true distinction is between those cases where the mode of ascertaining the price is an essential term of the contract, and those cases where the mode of ascertainment, though indicated in the contract, is subsidiary and non-essential: see *Fry on Specific Performance.* The present case falls, in my opinion, into the latter category. Accordingly when the option was exercised there was constituted a complete contract for sale, and the clause should be construed as meaning that the price was to be a fair price. On the other hand where an agreement is made to sell at a price to be fixed by a valuer who is named, or who, by reason of holding some office such as auditor of a company whose shares are to be valued, will have special knowledge relevant to the question of value, the prescribed mode may well be regarded as essential. Where, as here, the machinery consists of valuers and an umpire, none of whom is named or identified, it is in my opinion unrealistic to regard it as an essential term. If it breaks down there is no reason why the court should not substitute other machinery to carry out the main purpose of ascertaining the price in order that the agreement may be carried out.

In the present case the machinery provided for in the clause has broken down because the respondents have declined to appoint their valuer. In that sense the breakdown has been caused by their fault, in failing to implement an implied obligation to co-operate in making the machinery work. The case might be distinguishable in that respect from cases where the breakdown has occurred for some cause outside the control of either party, such as the death of an umpire, or his failure to complete the valuation by a stipulated date. But I do not rely on any such distinction. I prefer to rest my decision on the general principle that, where the machinery is not essential, if it breaks down for any reason the court will substitute its own machinery.'

Bushwall Properties Ltd v *Vortex Properties Ltd*

[1976] 2 All ER 283 • Court of Appeal

Vortex agreed to sell 51½ acres of land to Bushwall for £500 000. The first two conditions in the agreement stated '(1) The purchase price to be phased as to £250 000 upon first completion, as to £125 000 twelve months thereafter and as to the balance of £125 000 a further twelve months thereafter. (2) On the occasion of each completion a proportionate part of the land shall be released forthwith to [Bushwall].' Vortex claimed that condition (2) of the agreement was uncertain, in that the contract did not provide who was to have the power of selection of the proportionate part of land to be released. Oliver J held that the contract was not void for uncertainty since the expression 'proportionate part' of the land referred to the area of land that was proportionate to the sum to be paid for it. Bushwall appealed.

Sir John Pennycuick: 'The first issue is whether the contract purported to be made by the letters exchanged in June 1968 fails by reason of uncertainty, the uncertainty going to the power of selection of the land to be allocated on each phase. The general approach of the court to that question is not in dispute. The court will uphold a contract if it is possible to do so. On the other hand, as Maugham LJ said in *Foley* v *Classique Coaches Ltd* –

> "It is indisputable that unless all the material terms of the contract are agreed there is no binding obligation. An agreement to agree in the future is not a contract; nor is there a contract if a material term is neither settled nor implied by law and the document contains no machinery for ascertaining it." . . .

Leaving aside the implication of a term, I see no ground on which, under the general law as applied to contracts for the sale of land, where an intending vendor and an intending purchaser enter into a binding contract for sale with completion in phases, the power of selection as to what part of the land is to be included in each phase must be regarded as vested in the purchaser. It will be observed that this is no mere matter of machinery. Should the power of selection be vested in the purchaser, the vendor might be severely prejudiced by the manner in which that power is exercised. The point of course would arise if the purchaser, having completed the first stage, were then to make default in the next phase, leaving part but not the whole of the land with the vendor, the latter having over it the ordinary rights of a vendor where the purchaser has failed to complete. It is possible that in such circumstances the land left with the vendor might not be appropriate for advantageous development, and one can think of extreme instances such as a landlocked corner of land or pieces of land separated by the part taken by the purchaser. It seems to me that this is a point of substance and not a mere matter of machinery. It represents an element in a contract which, if left uncertain, would render the contract as a whole uncertain and for that reason unenforceable. The suggestion was made, but not pursued, that the court in such circumstances might leave it to a third party to determine which land should be selected at each phase. The court might, for instance, direct an enquiry in chambers. The court would no doubt do that if one were concerned with a mere matter of machinery. For instance, if the contract was for the sale of land at the market price but the parties were unable to agree on the market price and there was no provision in the contract for reference to some outside party, then I think the court might well direct an enquiry in chambers. Here, however, this is not a mere matter of machinery, and I do not think that course would be open to the court . . .

For the reasons which I have given, I conclude that the contract purported to be made by the letters of June 1968 was indeed unenforceable by reason of uncertainty; in other words, it was not an effective contract.'

Buckley LJ: 'The first question therefore must be whether the contract contained in the letters of June 1968 is on the face of it a specifically enforceable contract, which involves consideration of the question whether the parties can be seen to have agreed all the essential terms of the bargain. I do not read the terms of the letter again, but it will be remembered that it provides for payment of the purchase price by three instalments at yearly intervals, and that on the occasion of each payment of an instalment there shall be a conveyance of a proportionate part of the land sold. No machinery is expressly provided for identifying the part of the land to be conveyed on any of those three completions. I fully accept that the court should be reluctant to hold any contract void for uncertainty if that consequence can be avoided; but, on the other hand, it is not the function of the court to make or to perfect contracts entered into between members of the public. In the present case, the contract does not provide any means of ascertaining with certainty what land should be conveyed on any of the three occasions when a partial completion is to be carried out; and, for reasons that have already been indicated by Sir John Pennycuick in the judgment which he has delivered, I agree that that is an important term of this contract, for the interests of the vendor are liable to be very substantially affected by the choice of the parcels to be conveyed. The contract (so to call it) itself does not provide any machinery for ascertaining the answer to that question, from which in my judgment it must follow that this contract is not one of which the court would decree specific performance. If the contract is not one of which the court would decree specific performance, the principles of law relied on for supplying the defect in the contract cannot apply to the case, and so it is impossible by that means to arrive at the conclusion that the purchaser ought to be regarded as the person having the power to decree what parcels should be included on each of the occasions when completions are to take place. For that reason, it seems to me to be unavoidable that one must conclude that this is not a contract capable of being specifically performed and is not an enforceable contract.

Foley v *Classique Coaches Ltd*

[1934] 2 KB 1 • Court of Appeal

On 11 April 1930 Classique Coaches entered into a written agreement with Foley by which they agreed to buy petrol and/or oil exclusively from Foley. Clause 1 of the agreement stated 'The vendor shall sell to the company and the company shall purchase from the vendor all petrol which shall be required by the company for the running of their said business at a price to be agreed by the parties in writing and from time to time'. Clause 8 stated 'If any dispute or difference shall arise on the subject matter or construction of this agreement the same shall be submitted to arbitration in the usual way in accordance with the provisions of the Arbitration Act, 1889'. For the next three years Classique Coaches bought petrol from Foley without any problems. Disputes then arose which resulted in Classique Coaches declaring that they were not bound by the agreement of 11 April 1930.

The issue before the court was whether the agreement of 11 April 1930 constituted a concluded contract or was void for uncertainty.

Scrutton LJ: 'A good deal of the case turns upon the effect of two decisions of the House of Lords which are not easy to fit in with each other. The first of these cases is *May & Butcher* v *The King*, which related to a claim in respect of a purchase of surplus stores from a Government department. In the Court of Appeal two members of the Court took the view that inasmuch as there was a provision that the price of the stores which were to be offered from time to time was to be agreed there was no binding contract because an agreement to make an agreement does not constitute a contract, and that the language of clause 10 that any dispute as to the construction of the agreement was to be submitted to arbitration was irrelevant, because there was not an agreement, although the parties thought there was. In the second case, *Hillas & Co* v *Arcos*, there was an agreement between Hillas & Co and the Russian authorities under which Hillas & Co were to take in one year 22 000 standards of Russian timber, and in the same agreement they had an option to take in the next year 100 000 standards, with no particulars as to the kind of timber or as to the terms of shipment or any of the other matters one expects to find dealt with on a sale of a large quantity of Russian timber over a period. The Court of Appeal, which included Greer LJ and myself, both having a very large experience in these timber cases, came to the conclusion that as the House of Lords in *May & Butcher* v *The King* considered that where a detail had to be agreed upon there was no agreement until that detail was agreed, we were bound to follow the decision in *May & Butcher* v *The King* and hold that there was no effective agreement in respect of the option, because the terms had not been agreed. It was, however, held by the House of Lords in *Hillas & Co* v *Arcos* that we were wrong in so deciding and that we had misunderstood the decision in *May & Butcher* v *The King*. The House took this line: it is quite true that there seems to be considerable vagueness about the agreement but the parties contrived to get through it on the contract for 22 000 standards, and so the House thought there was an agreement as to the option which the parties would be able to get through also despite the absence of details. It is true that in the first year the parties got through quite satisfactorily; that was because during that year the great bulk of English buyers were boycotting the Russian sellers. In the second year the position was different. The English buyers had changed their view and were buying large quantities of Russian timber, so that different conditions were then prevailing. In *Hillas* v *Arcos* the House of Lords said that they had not laid down universal principles of construction in *May & Butcher* v *The King* and that each case must be decided on the construction of the particular document, while in *Hillas & Co* v *Arcos* they found that the parties believed they had a contract. In the present case the parties obviously believed they had a contract and they acted for three years as if they had; they had an arbitration clause which relates to the subject matter of the agreement as to the supply of petrol, and it seems to me that this arbitration clause applies to any failure to agree as to the price. By analogy to the case of a tied house there is to be implied in this contract a term that the petrol shall be supplied at a reasonable price and shall be of reasonable quality. For these reasons I think the Lord Chief Justice was right in holding that there was an effective and enforceable contract, although as to the future no definite price had been agreed with regard to the petrol.'

SUMMARY

You should now be able to:

- Identify agreements that are *not binding* because they are *vague*.
- Resolve vague agreements.

If you have not mastered the above points you should go through this section again.

5 Consideration

CONSIDERATION

In English law a contract is considered to be a bargain. What this in effect means is that each party to the contract gives the other party something: for example in contracts for the sale of goods money (something) will be exchanged for goods (something).

The 'something' that is given is referred to in English law as *consideration.*

If both parties do not furnish consideration (give each other something) the contract is said to lack consideration and therefore there is no contract.

Consideration is defined as some detriment to the promisee (in that he parts with something of value) *or* some benefit to the promisor (in that he receives value). Benefit and detriment are alternative ways of testing to see if one party has furnished consideration to the other party.

Explanation of definition of consideration

(1) Consideration is a *detriment or a benefit*.
(2) Both parties *must* furnish consideration to the other party.

Let us look at a sale of goods example, and analyse what happens if Fred sells a pen (goods) to Jane for £5 (the price). Fred's consideration, the giving of the pen to Jane is a *detriment* to him (the promisee) in that he parts with something of value – the pen.

Alternatively, Fred's consideration, the giving of the pen to Jane, is a *benefit* to her (the promisor) in that she receives something of value – the pen. We can therefore say that Fred has furnished consideration to Jane.

We now have to do the same exercise for Jane – to see if she has furnished consideration to Fred. What is Jane's consideration to Fred? Remember to explain it in terms of benefit and detriment.

CONSIDERATION MUST MOVE FROM THE PROMISEE

Note that the heading above states *consideration must move from the promisee*: it does not state that the consideration must move to the promisor.

For example if Fred and Jane both agree to give Max £10 there will be a contract between Fred and Jane. Apply the benefit/detriment test. Both suffer a detriment in that they both part with £10: neither receives a benefit – that is not important.

If, say, Fred pays £10 to Max but Jane refuses to pay Max, Fred will then be able to sue Jane for her breach of contract. Fred will be able to show that *consideration has moved from him (the promisee)*.

Tweddle v Atkinson

[1861–73] All ER Rep 369 • Queen's Bench

Tweddle's father and father-in-law promised to pay him £100 and £200 respectively by way of a marriage settlement. Tweddle sued his father-in-law for the £200 which he had failed to pay.

The issue before the court was whether Tweddle could sue his father-in-law for the £200 having furnished no consideration himself.

Wrightman J: 'No doubt there are some old decisions which appear to support the proposition that a stranger to the consideration for the contract, who stands in the relation of child to one of the contracting parties, and for whose benefit the contract is made, may sue upon it. The strongest case of that kind is *Bourne* v *Mason*, relating to the daughter of a physician. But there is no modern case of the kind, and, on the contrary, it is now well established that at law no stranger to the consideration can take advantage of the contract though made for his benefit. If it were otherwise a child might sue his own father in such a case as this. It is admitted that if the relationship of parent and child did not exist, the plaintiff would have no right to sue.

Here there is no consideration moving from the plaintiff, for the marriage was before the contract sued on, and according to the modern cases the plaintiff cannot sue.'

Crompton J: 'The old cases are inapplicable to the modern action of assumpsit. At the time of those cases the law was not settled as it now is, that natural love and affection are not sufficient to support a contract, and that a stranger to the consideration of a contract cannot sue upon it. The modern cases have in effect overruled the old decisions, and it is now clear law that the consideration must move from the party entitled to sue upon the contract. It would be a monstrous proposition to make a child a party to the contract for one purpose, viz to sue for his own advantage, and not for another to bear the liability.'

WHAT CONSTITUTES A VALUABLE CONSIDERATION?

In *Currie* v *Misa*, Lush J said 'A valuable consideration, in the sense of the law, may consist either in some right, interest, profit or benefit occurring to the one party, or some forbearance, detriment, loss or responsibility given, suffered, or undertaken by the other'.

When we look to see if both parties have furnished consideration we usually look to see if one party has paid the other party for goods or services. However, as the above quote shows, other things such as giving up the right to sue the other party can constitute a valuable consideration. This is because the giving up the right to sue is a *detriment* to the party giving up the right, and a *benefit* to the other party in that he will not now be sued.

PAST CONSIDERATION

The general rule is that the consideration for a promise must be given in return for that promise. Hence the maxim – *past consideration is no consideration.*

For example, a window cleaner cleans Fred's windows without being asked to do so. Fred agrees to pay the window cleaner tomorrow for cleaning the windows. When the window cleaner comes back, Fred refuses to pay.

Is there a contract between Fred and the window cleaner?

The answer is no. The window cleaner has furnished no new consideration in return for Fred's promise to pay. The window cleaner's consideration is past consideration and therefore no consideration.

Roscorla v Thomas
(1842) 3 QB 234 • Queen's Bench

On 28 September 1840 Roscorla's servant bought a horse for his master from Thomas for £30; Roscorla was to pay for the horse at a later date. On the following day Thomas called on Roscorla for payment. Roscorla gave Thomas the £30 and in return Thomas gave Roscorla a memorandum which stated that 'I have this day sold to Roscorla a bay nag for £30 which I warrant not to exceed five years off, and to be sound in wind and limb, perfect in vision, and free from vice.' Roscorla sued Thomas for breach of this warranty claiming that the horse was not free from vice, but, on the contrary, was then very vicious and restive.

The issue before the court was whether the warranty was given before or at the time of making of the contract or whether it was given after the contract had been made.

Lord Denman CJ: 'This was an action . . . for breach of warranty on the soundness of a horse. The first count, on which alone the question arises, stated that in consideration that the plaintiff, at the request of the defendant, *had* bought of the defendant a horse for the sum of £30, the defendant promised the plaintiff that it was sound, and was free from vice. It was objected in arrest of judgment, that the precedent executed consideration was insufficient to support the subsequent promise; and we are of opinion that the objection must prevail. It may be taken as a general rule, subject to exceptions not applicable to this case, that the promise must be co-extensive with the consideration. In the present case, the only promise that would result from the consideration as stated, and be co-extensive with it, was to deliver the horse on request. A precedent sale without a warranty, although at the request of the defendant, imposes no other duty or obligation on him. It is clear, therefore, that the consideration stated would not raise an implied promise by the defendant that the horse was sound and free from vice; but the promise in the present case must be taken to be, as in fact it was, express; and the question is, whether that fact will warrant the extension of the promise beyond that which would be implied by law, and whether the consideration, although insufficient to raise an implied promise, would necessarily support an express one. We think that it will not.'

Re McArdle
[1951] 1 All ER 905 • Court of Appeal

Montague McArdle and his wife Marjorie McArdle lived in a bungalow which formed part of Montague McArdle's father's estate. In 1943 the McArdles carried out certain repairs and decorations to the bungalow. Marjorie McArdle paid for the work which cost £488. In April 1945, after the work had been done, Montague McArdle presented each of his three brothers and his sister with a document which stated 'In consideration of your carrying out certain alterations and improvements to the [bungalow] . . . we the beneficiaries under the will of [our father] . . . hereby agree that the executors . . . shall repay to you from the said estate when so distributed the sum of £488 in settlement of the amount spent on such improvements'. The document was signed by the sister and the four brothers. In 1948 the McArdles' mother died and Marjorie McArdle claimed payment of £488. In the meantime Marjorie McArdle's brothers-in-law and sister-in-law had changed their minds about repaying the £488.

The issue before the court was whether there was a contract between Marjorie McArdle and her brothers-in-law and sister-in-law; had she furnished fresh consideration in return for their promise to pay?

Jenkins LJ: '. . . That document on the face of it purports to be an agreement for valuable consideration under which, when Mrs Montague McArdle has carried out certain alternations and improvements to the property known as Gravel Hill Poultry Farm, and in consideration of her so doing, the five children undertake that she is to be paid £488, representing the cost of the work, out of the testator's estate when distributed. Notwithstanding the argument to the contrary, it is plain, so far as the construction of the document is concerned, that it contemplates the doing by Mrs Montague McArdle of work yet to be done and that her doing that work is to form the consideration by virtue of which she is to be entitled to receive £488 from the estate. If the document had correctly represented the facts, I have no doubt that it would have operated as a valid equitable assignment of £488 subject to Mrs Montague McArdle performing her part of the bargain by providing the consideration she had contracted to provide in the form of doing the work. There might have been room for difficulty and argument whether the work had been properly done or not, but those matters could have been resolved one way or the other, if necessary by an action, and ultimately, if Mrs McArdle showed she had done the work contracted for, her title to the £488 would have been complete, and, the agreement being for valuable consideration, it would not have mattered that further steps had to be taken to perfect her title. The true position, however, was that, as the work had all been done and nothing remained to be done by Mrs McArdle at all, the consideration was wholly past, and, therefore, the beneficiaries' agreement for the repayment to her of the £488 out of the estate was *nudum pactum* – a promise with no consideration to support it . . .'

DIFFERENCE BETWEEN PAST AND EXECUTED CONSIDERATION

Re Casey's Patents, Stewart v Casey

[1892] 1 Ch 104 • Chancery Division

Stewart and Chalton, owners of two patents, entered into arrangements with Casey to market their patents. Casey in accordance with the agreement then spent time and money in pushing, developing, and improving the inventions. On 29 January 1889 Stewart and Chalton signed a document in favour of Casey which read

'Dear Sir, – We now have pleasure in stating that in consideration of your services as the practical manager in working both our patents . . . we hereby agree to give you one third share of the patents . . . the same to take effect from this date . . . '

The issue before the court was whether Casey had furnished fresh consideration in return for Stewart's and Chalton's promise to give him a one third share in the patent or whether Casey's consideration was past consideration.

Bowen LJ: 'But then it was said by Mr Daniel [counsel for Stewart and Chalton], "But there is no consideration, and this document is not under seal". We will see if there is consideration. The consideration is stated, such as it is. It is, "in consideration of your services as the practical manager in working our patents as above for transit by steamer". Then says Mr Daniel, "Yes, but that is a future consideration, and a future consideration, if nothing were done under it or nothing was proved to be done, would fail". The answer to that is that the consideration is not the rendering of the services, as is plain from the fact that the document is to take effect in Equity from the date. The consideration must be something other than rendering services in the future. It is the promise to render them which those words imply, that constitutes the consideration; and the promise to render future services, if an effectual promise, is certainly good consideration. Then, driven from that, Mr Daniel said, "Oh! but it is past services that it means, and past services are not a consideration for anything". Well, that raises the old question – or might raise it, if there was not an answer to it – of *Lampleigh* v *Braithwait*, a subject of great interest to every scientific lawyer, as to whether a past service will support a promise. I do not propose to discuss that question, or, perhaps, I should not have finished this week. I should have to examine the whole state of the law as to, and the history of the subject of, consideration, which, I need hardly say, I do not propose to do. But the answer to Mr Daniel's point is clear. Even if it were true, as some scientific students of law believe, that a past service cannot support a future promise, you must look at the document and see if the promise cannot receive a proper effect in some other way. Now, the fact of a past service raises an implication that at the time it was rendered it was to be paid for, and, if it was a service which was to be paid for, when you get in the subsequent document a promise to pay, that promise may be treated either as an admission which evidences or as a positive bargain which fixes the amount of that reasonable remuneration on the faith of which the service was originally rendered. So that here for past services there is ample justification for the promise to give the third share . . .'

Pao On v Lau Yiu

[1979] 3 All ER 65 • Privy Council

Pao owned a private company, Shing On, which had as its main asset a partly completed building that Lau's company, Fu Chip, wished to purchase. On 27 February the sale was agreed and two written agreements were signed. By the first contract (the main agreement) Pao sold all his shares in Shing On to Fu Chip for $10.5 million worth of Fu Chip's shares. As part of that agreement Pao gave Fu Chip an undertaking that 'Each of the Vendors shall retain in his own right in Fu Chip 60% of the shares allotted to him under this Agreement and shall not sell or transfer the same on or before the end of April 1974'; this undertaking was given to protect the share price in Fu Chip. However, before giving this undertaking Pao wanted a measure of protection against a fall in value of the shares during the year in which he could not sell. Accordingly, a second contract (the subsidiary agreement) was signed on 27 February 1973 under which Pao agreed to sell and Lau agreed to buy on or before 30 April 1974 at a price of $2.50 a share 2.5 million shares in Fu Chip (the 2.5 million shares being 60 per cent of the shares acquired by Pao in Fu Chip). Although this second agreement was supposed to protect Pao against a fall in the price of his shares he realised that if the price went up Lau could buy 60% of his shares at $2.50 a share. Pao, therefore, made up his mind that he would not complete the main agreement unless he could substitute a guarantee by way of indemnity for the subsidiary agreement and informed Lau of his position. Lau agreed to cancel the subsidiary agreement and signed a guarantee which cancelled the original and the subsidiary agreement. There was no suggestion that Lau signed the contract of guarantee under protest. On the contrary, he had present his own legal advisers and, as the trial judge put it, was 'quite prepared to take a calculated risk'. In the next year the shares in Fu Chip fell to 36 cents and Pao therefore requested Lau to purchase the shares back under the guarantee at $2.50 per share; this Lau refused to do contending that neither the subsidiary agreement nor the guarantee of 4 May had legal effect.

The guarantee stated 'IN CONSIDERATION of your having at our request agreed to sell all of your shares . . . in [Shing On] . . . for the consideration of $10.5 million . . . we [Lau] HEREBY AGREE AND GUARANTEE the closing market value for 2.5 million shares . . . of the said Fu Chip . . . shall be at $2.50 per share . . . on the following marketing date immediately after 30 April 1974 AND WE FURTHER AGREE to indemnify and keep you indemnified against any damages, losses and other expenses which you may incur or sustain in the event of the closing market price for the shares of Fu Chip . . . shall fall short of the sum $2.50 . . . '

Lord Scarman read the following judgment of the board.
'The first question is whether on its true construction the written guarantee of 4th May 1973 states consideration sufficient in law to support the Laus' promise of indemnity against a fall in value of the Fu Chip shares . . .

Counsel for the plaintiffs before their Lordships' Board but not below contends that the consideration stated in the agreement is not in reality a past one. It is to be noted that the consideration was not on 4th May 1973 a matter of history only. The instrument by its reference to the main agreement with Fu Chip incorporates as part of the stated consideration the Paos' three promises to Fu Chip: to complete the sale of Shing On, to accept shares as the price for the sale, and not to sell 60% of the shares so accepted before 30th April 1974. Thus, on 4th May 1973 the performance of the main agreement still lay in the future. Performance of these promises was of great importance to the Laus, and it is undeniable that, as the instrument declares, the promises were made to Fu Chip at the request of the Laus. It is equally clear that the instrument also includes a promise by the Paos to the Laus to fulfil their earlier promises given to Fu Chip.

The Board agrees with the submission of counsel for the plaintiffs that the consideration expressly stated in the written guarantee is sufficient in law to support the Laus' promise of indemnity. An act done before the giving of a promise to make a payment or to confer some other benefit can sometimes be consideration for the promise. The act must have been done at the promisor's request, the parties must have understood that the act was to be remunerated either by a payment or the conferment of some other benefit, and payment, or the conferment of a benefit, must have been legally enforceable had it been promised in advance. All three features are present in this case. The promise given to Fu Chip under the main agreement not to sell the shares for a year was at Lau's request. The parties understood at the time of the main agreement that the restriction on selling must be compensated for by the benefit of a guarantee against a drop in price: and such a guarantee would be legally enforceable. The agreed cancellation of the subsidiary agreement left, as the parties knew, the Paos unprotected in a respect in which at the time of the main agreement all were agreed they should be protected.

Counsel's submission for the plaintiffs is based on *Lampleigh* v *Brathwait*. In that case the judges said:

> "First . . . a mere voluntary curtesie will not have a consideration to uphold an assumpsit. But if that curtesie were moved by a suit or request of the party that gives the assumpsit, it will bind, for the promise, though it follows, yet it is not naked, but couples itself with the suit before, and the merits of the party procured by that suit, which is the difference."

The modern statement of the law is in the judgment of Bowen LJ in *Re Casey's Patents, Stewart* v *Casey*. Bowen LJ said:

> "Even if it were true, some scientific students of law believe, that a past service cannot support a future promise, you must look at the document and see if the promise cannot receive a proper effect in some other way. Now, the fact of a past service raises an implication that at the time it was rendered it was to be paid for, and, if it was a service which was to be paid for, when you get in the subsequent document a promise to pay, that promise may be treated either as an admission which evidence or as a positive bargain which fixed the amount of the reasonable remuneration on the faith of which the service was originally rendered. So that here for past services there is ample justification for the promise to give the third share."

Conferring a benefit is, of course, an equivalent to payment: see *Chitty on Contracts* (24th edn).

Counsel for the defendants does not dispute the existence of the rule but challenges its application to the facts of this case. He submits that it is not a necessary inference or implication from the terms of the written guarantee that any benefit or protection was to be given to the Paos for their acceptance of the restriction on selling their shares. Their Lordships agree that the mere existence or recital of a prior request is not sufficient in itself to convert what is *prima facie* past consideration into sufficient consideration in law to support a promise: as they have indicated, it is only the first of three necessary preconditions. As for the second of those preconditions, where the act done at the request of the promisor raises an implication of promised remuneration or other return is simply one of the construction of the words of the contract in the circumstances of its making. Once it is recognised, as the Board considers it inevitably must be, that the expressed consideration includes a reference to the Paos' promise not to sell the shares before 30th April 1974, a promise to be performed in the future, though given in the past, it is not possible to treat the Laus' promise of indemnity as independent of the Paos' antecedent promise, given at Lau's request, not to sell. The promise of indemnity was given because at the time of the main agreement the parties intended that Lau should confer on the Paos the benefit of his protection against a fall in price. When the subsidiary agreement was cancelled, all were well aware that the Paos were still to have the benefit of his protection as consideration for the restriction on selling. It matters not whether the indemnity thus given be regarded as the best evidence of the benefit intended to be conferred in return for the promise not to sell, or as the positive bargain which fixes the benefit on the faith of which the promise was given, though where, as here, the subject is a written contract, the better analysis is probably that of the "positive bargain". Their Lordships, therefore, accept the submission that the contract itself states a valid consideration for the promise of indemnity.'

CONSIDERATION NEED NOT BE ADEQUATE

Although both parties must furnish consideration, there is no requirement in English law that the bargain should be a balanced one. If, for example, Fred sells his car worth £15 000 to Jane for £1 there will be a perfectly valid contract between them. Both parties will have agreed and both parties will have furnished consideration, therefore there is a contract.

Bainbridge v Firmstone

(1839) 8 Ad & El 743 • Queen's Bench

Bainbridge, at the request of Firmstone, allowed Firmstone to weigh two of his boilers. Firmstone promised that he would, within a reasonable time after he had weighed the boilers, return the boilers in a perfect and complete condition. Firmstone took the boilers to pieces, weighed them and then refused to put them back together again. Bainbridge sued Firmstone for breach of his promise to return the boilers in a perfect and complete condition; Firmstone pleaded lack of consideration.

Patteson J: 'The consideration is, that [Bainbridge], at [Firmstone's] request consented to allow [Firmstone] to weigh the boilers. I suppose [Firmstone] thought he had some benefit; at any rate, there is a detriment to [Bainbridge] from his parting with the possession for even so short a time.'

What was F's consideration in the above case?

Chappell & Co Ltd v The Nestlé Co Ltd

[1959] 2 All ER 701 • House of Lords

Nestlé, manufacturers of wrapped chocolate bars, advertised for sale, as part of an advertising campaign, the record 'Rockin' Shoes'. The price of the record was 1s 6d plus three wrappings from their 6d chocolate bars. Chappell, who were the sole licensees of the copyright of 'Rockin' Shoes', claimed that Nestlé had infringed their copyright and sought injunction and damages. Nestlé claimed that they were entitled to supply records without the permission or licence of the appellants because they were authorised to do so by the Copyright Act 1956 s 8 which permitted them to sell the records provided they paid to the copyright owner 'six and one quarter per cent of the ordinary retail selling price of the record'. The House of Lords held by a majority of three to two that the Act required that the consideration for the records be wholly in money.

The issue, then, before the court was whether the wrappers formed part of the consideration for the records.

Lord Reid: 'I can now turn to what appears to me to be the crucial question in this case: was the 1s 6d an "ordinary retail selling price" within the meaning of s 8? That involves two questions, what was the nature of the contract between the respondents Nestlé and a person who sent 1s 6d plus three wrappers in acceptance of their offer, and what is meant by "ordinary retail selling price" in this context. To determine the nature of the contract, one must find the intention of the parties as shown by what they said and did. The respondents Nestlé's intention can hardly be in doubt. They were not setting out to trade in gramophone records. They were using these records to increase their sales of chocolate. Their offer was addressed to everyone. It might be accepted by a person who was already a regular buyer of their chocolate; but, much more important to them, it might be accepted by people who might become regular buyers of their chocolate if they could be induced to try it and found they liked it. The inducement was something calculated to look like a bargain, a record at a very cheap price. It is in evidence that the ordinary price for a dance record is 6s 6d. It is true that the ordinary record gives much longer playing time than the Nestlé records and it may have other advantages. But the reader of the respondents Nestlé's offer was not in a position to know that. It seems to me clear that the main intention of the offer was to induce people interested in this kind of music to buy (or, perhaps, get others to buy) chocolate which otherwise would not have been bought. It is, of course, true that some wrappers might come from chocolate which had already been bought, or from chocolate which would have been bought without the offer, but that does not seems to me to alter the case. Where there is a large number of transactions – the notice mentions 30 000 records – I do not think we should simply consider an isolated case where it would be impossible to say whether there had been a direct benefit from the acquisition of the wrappers or not. The requirement that wrappers should be sent was of great importance to the respondents Nestlé; there would have been no point in their simply offering records for 1s 6d each. It seems to me quite unrealistic to divorce the buying of the chocolate from the supplying of the records. It is a perfectly good contract if a person accepts an offer to supply goods if he (a) does something of value to the supplier and (b) pays money; the consideration is both (a) and (b). There may have been cases where the acquisition of the wrappers conferred no direct benefit on the respondents Nestlé but there must have been many cases where it did. I do not see why the possibility that, in some cases, the acquisition of the wrappers did not directly benefit the respondents Nestlé should require us to exclude from consideration the cases where it did; and even where there was no direct benefit from the acquisition of the wrappers there may have been an indirect benefit by way of advertisement.

. . . But where the qualification is the doing of something of value to the seller, and where the qualification only suffices for one sale and must be re-acquired before another sale, I find it hard to regard the repeated acquisitions of the qualification as anything other than parts of the consideration for the sales. The purchaser of records had to send three wrappers for each record, so he had first to acquire them. The acquisition of wrappers by him was, at least in many cases, of direct benefit to the respondents Nestlé, and required expenditure by the acquirer which he might not otherwise have incurred. To my mind, the acquiring and delivering of the wrappers was certainly part of the consideration in these cases, and I see no good reason for drawing a distinction between these and other cases.'

Lord Somervell of Harrow: 'The question, then, is whether the three wrappers were part of the consideration or, as Jenkins LJ held, a condition of making the purchase, like a ticket entitling a member to buy at a co-operative store. I think that they are part of the consideration. They are so described in the offer. "They", the wrappers, "will help you to get smash hit recordings". They are so described in the record itself –

"all you have to do to get [such new] record is to send three wrappers from Nestlé's 6d milk chocolate bars together with postal order for 1s 6d."

This is not conclusive but, however described, they are, in my view, in law part of the consideration. It is said that, when received, the wrappers are of no value to the respondents The Nestlé Co Ltd. This I would have thought to be irrelevant. A contracting party can stipulate for what consideration he chooses. A peppercorn does not cease to be good consideration if it is established that the promisee does not like pepper and will throw away the corn. As the whole object of selling the record, if it was a sale, was to increase the sales of chocolate, it seems to me wrong not to treat the stipulated evidence of such sales as part of the consideration.'

Viscount Simonds dissenting said: 'In my opinion, my Lords, the wrappers are not part of the selling price. They are, admittedly, themselves valueless and are thrown away . . .'

CONSIDERATION MUST BE REAL

Although as Patteson J said in *Thomas* v *Thomas*, below, that 'Consideration means something which is of some value in the eye of the law' we have seen from *Bainbridge* v *Firmstone* and *Chappell & Co Ltd* v *The Nestlé Co Ltd*, above, that very little can amount to a 'real' consideration.

The following cases examine the limits as to what amounts to a 'real' consideration.

Motive and consideration

In *Tweddle* v *Atkinson*, above (p 93), Crompton J said 'The old cases are inapplicable to the modern action of assumpsit. At the time of those cases the law was not settled as it now is, that natural love and affection are not sufficient to support a contract . . . '

Thomas v *Thomas*

(1842) 2 QB 851 • Queen's Bench

Shortly before his death, John Thomas orally expressed his wish that his wife, Eleanor Thomas, should have his house during her lifetime. In order to carry out John's wishes Benjamin Thomas, John's executor and residuary legatee, entered into an agreement with Eleanor whereby it was witnessed that 'in consideration of such desire' of John 'the executors would convey the house' to Eleanor for her life 'provided . . . that the said Eleanor Thomas . . . shall and will, at all times during which she shall have possession of the said dwelling house . . . pay to the said Benjamin Thomas . . . the sum of £1 yearly towards the ground rent payable in respect of the said dwelling house and other premises thereto adjoining, and shall and will keep the said dwelling house and premises in good and tenantable repair'. Eleanor was allowed to live in the house for some time but then Benjamin tried to turn her out of possession.

The issue before the court was whether there was sufficient consideration on Eleanor's part.

Lord Denman CJ: '. . . the stipulation for the payment of it is not a mere proviso, but an express agreement. (His Lordship here read the proviso.) This is in terms on express agreement, and shews a sufficient legal consideration quite independent of the moral feeling which disposed the executors to enter into such a contract . . .'

Patteson J: 'It would be giving to causa too large a construction if we were to adopt the view urged for the defendant: it would be confounding consideration with motive. Motive is not the same thing with consideration. Consideration means something which is of some value in the eye of the law, moving from the plaintiff: it may be some benefit to the plaintiff or some detriment to the defendant; but at all events it must be moving from the plaintiff. Now that which is suggested as the consideration here, a pious respect for the wishes of the testator, does not in any way move from the plaintiff; it moves from the testator; therefore, legally speaking, it forms no part of the consideration. Then it is said that, if that be so, there is no consideration at all, it is a mere voluntary gift: but when we look at the agreement we find that this is not a mere proviso that the donee shall take the gift with the burthens; but it is an express agreement to pay what seems to be a fresh apportionment of a ground rent, and which is made payable not to a superior Landlord but to the executors. So that this rent is clearly not something incident to the assignment of the house; for in that case, instead of being payable to the executors, it would have been payable to the landlord. Then as to the repairs: these houses may very possibly be held under a lease containing covenants to repair; but we know nothing about it: for any thing that appears, the liability to repair is first created by this instrument. The proviso certainly struck me at first . . . that the rent and repairs there merely attached to the gift by the donors; and, had the instrument been executed by the donors only, there might have been some ground for that construction; but the fact is not so . . .'

Gift of onerous property

Cheale v *Kenward*

(1858) 27 LJCh 784 • Chancery

Cheale became the owner of ten shares in a railway company. At this time Cheale had paid no money to the railway company for the shares. Before payment was due on the shares Cheale agreed to transfer his shares to Kenward in return for Kenward's promise to 'do all acts necessary to relieve Cheale from all liability in respect of the said shares'. Later Kenward refused to take the shares and Cheale sued him for specific performance.

The issue before the court was whether both parties had furnished sufficient consideration.

The Lord Chancellor: '. . . [W]here there was an agreement to transfer property in consideration of the transferee's agreement to do something or to undertake a liability, that was a complete agreement . . .

The consideration on the part of the plaintiff was the agreement to transfer, and on the part of the defendant the agreement to undertake the liability. If so, the question of consideration, so far as the defendant was concerned, amounted to this, whether the agreement to undertake the legal liability of another was a good consideration. Such an agreement was, in his Lordship's opinion, a perfectly good consideration, which would render it competent for this defendant to file a bill for specific performance. It might be assumed that the plaintiff was merely desirous of divesting himself of the shares, but that the defendant was desirous of becoming possessed of them, and was willing to take the liabilities upon himself. That would have been a consideration as much as if the plaintiff had paid the amount on the shares, and the defendant had paid to him such amount. It was said, that if money had been paid on either side, it would have rendered it a good agreement. But what difference, in principle, was there? Supposing the plaintiff had paid the deposit and the defendant had paid that amount to him and undertaken the liabilities, that would have been good; but his Lordship could not see the difference between that and the present case, where no money passed, but the whole consideration was an agreement to undertake the liabilities.'

Forbearance to sue

Lush J, in *Currie* v *Misa*, said that 'A valuable consideration, in the sense of the law, may consist of . . . some forbearance . . . ' This is very common in practice, where, for example, someone gives up a right to sue another person in return for that other person settling the action by making a monetary payment: 'out of court' settlements are an example of this. However, what if the person giving up their right to sue is unsure whether they have a valid claim?

Doubtful claims

Horton v *Horton (No 2)*

[1961] 1 QB 215 • Court of Appeal

On 12 March 1954 the husband entered into a separation agreement under seal with his wife whereby under clause 3 of the agreement he agreed to pay her the monthly sum of £30 'for and towards her maintenance and support'. The husband paid the £30 a month without deducting any income tax. In January 1955 the husband signed a supplemental agreement which stated 'It is hereby mutually agreed between the parties hereto that clause 3 of the within written agreement shall be amended by the insertion after the words "monthly sum", of the words "which after deduction of income tax shall amount to the clear sum of £30 each month". It is further declared that the within written agreement was and always has been interpreted by the parties hereto as if the said amendment had been originally in the said agreement when the same was first executed.'

The issue before the court was whether the second agreement was enforceable against the husband; what consideration, if any, had the wife furnished?

Upjohn LJ: 'It is submitted by [counsel] for the husband . . . that there is no consideration for the memorandum executed in 1955 as it is not under seal, and that, therefore, the wife cannot sue under the memorandum and deed but only under the deed, in which case, of course, she is entitled only to £30 a month less tax.

. . . I understand the [county court] judge . . . [expressed] the view on the facts that he was satisfied that the parties had not in the original deed correctly expressed their intention, and that that intention was, in fact, correctly expressed in the supplemental memorandum. [Counsel for the husband] has submitted that there has been no consideration for this memorandum; it is a mere *nudum pactum* to pay an additional sum, that is, the tax due on each of the instalments. He has submitted that there was no doubt to be resolved, and that the judge was wrong in stating that the consideration could be the removal of a doubt. One must remember that the note of the judge's judgment was made some time later from the notes of others, and it may be that the exact language that he used is not before us. But it seems to me clear that all the judge is saying there is this. There was a genuine doubt what the parties had originally intended, and they discussed the matter. The learned judge thought it was plain that the parties originally intended that the husband was going to pay a sum tax free, and, therefore, they entered into that agreement so as to resolve the doubts as to what the parties had intended. I accept at once [counsel for the husband's] argument that no doubt whatever arose on the effect of the original deed. The doubt which arose was whether the original deed in fact carried out their mutual intention.

[Counsel for the husband] has further submitted that, in any event, the consideration was too nebulous to be enforceable. He points out that, had the true intention originally been to secure that the wife was merely to have £30 a month spending money (as the husband said in evidence) and had rectification proceedings followed, the correct form of the rectification proceedings would be to ask for some order whereby the wife was to get £30 a month after deduction of tax, but that she would undertake to pay to the husband any sums recovered by her from the income tax authorities. That may well be so.

The real truth of the matter is this. The original deed did not carry out the parties' intention, as the learned judge held. The wife could have made some claim to rectification. It may be, as I have just said, that that should be limited in some way. But she thought, and was advised no doubt, that she had some right to obtain more than she was entitled to under the existing deed and she must have done that by means of a suit for rectification. Indeed, [counsel for the husband] has submitted that rectification proceedings ought to have been brought here. But the legal effect of what the parties did was that, the wife believing that she had some good claim for rectification – I do not put it any higher than that – entered into an agreement with her husband to resolve that matter. The agreement they entered into, in those circumstances, is surely plainly an agreement for consideration. If some such document had not been signed by the husband in January, 1955, the wife would have been entitled to take rectification proceedings. Whether or not they would have succeeded does not matter but, on the evidence, she had some prospect of success. But in order to compromise the matter, they executed this agreement, which is not under seal, and in those circumstances, it seems to me, that plainly is a document executed for consideration.'

Bad claims

Cook v Wright

(1861) 30 LJQB 321 • Queen's Bench

The facts are stated in the judgment of Blackburn J.

Blackburn J: 'In this case it appeared on the trial that the defendant was agent for a Mrs Bennett, who was the non-resident owner of houses in a district subject to a local act; works had been done in the adjoining street by the Commissioners for executing the act, the expenses of which, under the provisions of the act, they charged on the owners of the adjoining houses. Notice had been given to the defendant, as if he had himself been owner of these houses, calling on him to pay the proportion chargeable in respect of them. He attended at a board-meeting of the Commissioners, and objected both to the amount and nature of the charge, and also stated that he was not the owner of the houses, and that Mrs Bennett was. He was told that if he did not pay he would be treated as one Gable had been. It appeared that Gable had refused to pay a sum charged against him as owner of some houses; that the Commissioners had taken legal proceedings against him, and he had then submitted and paid with costs. In the result it was agreed between the Commissioners and the defendant that the amount charged upon him should be reduced, and that time should be given to pay it in three instalments. He gave three promissory notes for the three instalments; the first was duly honoured, the others were not, and were the subject of the present action. At the trial it appeared that the defendant was not, in fact, owner of the houses. As agent for the owner he was not personally liable under the act. The Commissioners were therefore not, in point of law, entitled to claim the money from the defendant; but no case of deceit was alleged against them. It must be taken that the Commissioners honestly believed that the defendant was personally liable, and really intended to take proceedings against him as they had done against Gable. The defendant, according to his own evidence, never believed that he was liable in law, but signed the notes in order to avoid being sued as Gable was. Under these circumstances the substantial question reserved (irrespective of the form of the plea) was, whether there was any consideration for the notes. We are of opinion that there was.

There is no doubt that a bill or note, given in consideration of what is supposed to be a debt, is without consideration, if it appears that there was a mistake in fact as to the existence of the debt – *Bell* v *Gardiner*; and according to the cases of *Southall* v *Rigg* and *Forman* v *Wright*, the case is the same if the bill or note is given in consequence of a mistake of law as to the existence of the debt. But here there was no mistake on the part of the defendant, either of law or fact; what he did was not merely the making an erroneous account stated, or promising to pay a debt for which he mistakenly believed himself liable. It appeared on the evidence that he believed himself not to be liable, but he knew that the plaintiffs thought him liable, and would sue him if he did not pay; and in order to avoid the expense and trouble of legal proceedings against himself he agreed to a compromise; and the question is, whether a person who has given a note as a compromise of a claim honestly made on him, and which but for that compromise would have been at once brought to a legal decision, can resist the payment of the note on the ground that the original claim thus compromised might have been successfully resisted.

If the suit had been actually commenced the point would have been concluded by authority. [See] *Langridge* v *Dorville* . . .

. . . We agree that unless there was a reasonable claim on the one side, which it was *bona fide* intended to pursue, there would be no ground for a compromise; but we cannot agree that (except as a test of the reality of the claim) the issuing of a writ is essential to the validity of the compromise. The position of the parties must necessarily be altered in every case of compromise, so that if the question is afterwards opened up, they cannot be replaced as they were before the compromise; the plaintiff may be in a less favourable position for renewing his litigation; he must be at additional trouble and expense in getting up his case; and he may no longer be able to produce the evidence which would originally have proved it. Besides, though he may not in point of law be bound to refrain from enforcing his rights against third persons during the continuance of the compromise to which they are not parties, yet, practically, the effect of the compromise must be to prevent his doing so. For instance, in the present case there can be no doubt that the practical effect of the compromise must have been to induce the Commissioners to refrain from taking proceedings against Mrs Bennett, the real owner of the houses while the notes given by the defendant, her agent, were running: though the compromise might have afforded no ground of defence had such proceedings been resorted to. It is this detriment to the party consenting to a compromise, arising from the necessary alteration in his position, which, in our opinion, forms the real consideration for the promise; and not the technical and almost illusory consideration arising from the extra costs of litigation. The real consideration, therefore, depends not on the actual commencement of a suit, but on the reality of the claim made, and the *bona fides* of the compromise.

In the present case we think that there was sufficient consideration for the notes in the compromise made as it was.'

Insufficiency of consideration

We have seen that 'consideration must be real but need not be adequate'. The following situations deal with instances where one party is already bound to do something for another party either by law or by a contract. The issue in the following cases is whether someone who is already obliged to do a certain thing has gone beyond that duty and therefore provided fresh consideration.

Duty imposed by law

Collins v *Godefroy*

(1831) 9 LJOS 158 • King's Bench

Godefroy subpoenaed Collins to give evidence at a case in which he was involved. Godefroy, who was an attorney, claimed six guineas from Collins for his loss of time.

Lord Tenterden: 'Conceding to the plaintiff, that the offer to pay the six guineas, without costs, was evidence of an express promise by the defendant to pay that sum as a compensation to him for his loss of time, still, if the defendant was not bound by law to pay that sum, the offer to do so, not having been accepted, will not avail the plaintiff. If it be a duty imposed by law upon a party regularly subpoenaed, to attend from time to time to give his evidence, then a promise to give him any remuneration for loss of time incurred in such attendance is a promise without consideration. We think, that such a duty is imposed by law; and on consideration . . . of the cases which have been decided on this subject . . . we are all of opinion that a party cannot maintain an action at law for compensation for his loss of time in attending a trial as a witness.'

England v *Davidson*

(1840) 11 Ald & E 856 • Queen's Bench

Davidson offered a £50 reward to 'whoever would give such information as should lead to the conviction of the offender or offenders' who had broken into his mansion house. England, a police constable, gave such information which led to the conviction of Robson. England claimed his reward but Davidson refused to pay.

Counsel for Davidson said: 'No consideration is shown on this record for the defendant's promise, the plaintiff was bound to do that, the doing of which is stated as the consideration. The duty of a constable is to do his utmost to discover, pursue, and apprehend felons . . . It has been laid down that a sailor cannot recover on a promise by the master to pay him for extra work in navigating the ship, the sailor being bound to do his utmost, independently of any fresh contract . . . explained by Lord Ellenborough in *Stilk* v *Myrick* . . . [Coleridge J. Those cases turn merely on the nature of the contract made by the sailor.] If the duty here incumbent on the plaintiff was to do all that the declaration lays as the consideration, the case is the same as if he had been under a previous contract to do all . . . The contract here declared upon is against public policy.'

In a very short judgment Lord Denman CJ said: 'I think there may be services which the constable is not bound to render, and which he may therefore make the ground of a contract. We should not hold a contract to be against the policy of the law, unless the grounds for so deciding were very clear.'

Littledale, Patteson, and Coleridge JJ all simply concurred.

Glasbrook Bros Ltd v *Glamorgan County Council*

[1924] All ER Rep 579 • House of Lords

During a coal miners' strike the manager of Glasbrook Bros Ltd's coal mine asked the local police authority to supply a resident garrison of police to ensure the protection of the mine. The police authority said that a resident garrison was unnecessary and that a mobile squad of police would provide adequate protection. At the mine manager's insistence the police agreed to provide a resident garrison provided that Glasbrook Bros Ltd paid for the extra costs involved, to which Glasbrook Bros Ltd agreed. Once the strike was over, Glasbrook Bros Ltd refused to pay, claiming that the police authority had done no more than they were already required to do by law.

The issue before the court was whether the police authority had provided fresh consideration for Glasbrook Bros Ltd's promise to pay.

Viscount Cave LC: '. . . [I]t was said . . . that on general principles the police authorities are not entitled, except in the cases specifically provided for by statute, to make a charge for police services . . .

The practice by which police authorities make a charge for "special services", that is to say, for services rendered outside the scope of their obligations, has been established for upwards of sixty years and is constantly followed by every police authority in the country with the approval of the Secretary of State; and it is difficult to understand on what grounds it should now be treated as illegal. No doubt there is an absolute and unconditional obligation binding the police authorities to take all steps which appear to them to be necessary for keeping the peace, for preventing crime, or for protecting property from criminal injury; and the public, who pay for this protection through the rates and taxes, cannot lawfully be called upon to make a further payment for that which is their right. This was laid down by Pickford LJ in *Glamorganshire Coal Co Ltd* v *Glamorganshire Standing Joint Committee* . . .

With this statement of the law I entirely agree, and I think that any attempt by a police authority to extract payment for services which fall within the plain obligations of the police force, should be firmly discountenanced by the courts. But it has always been recognised that, where individuals desire that services of a special kind which, though not within the obligations of a police authority, can most effectively be rendered by them, should be performed by members of the police force, the police authorities may (to use an expression which is found in the Police Pensions Act 1980) "lend" the services of constables for that purpose in consideration of payment. Instances are the lending of constables on the occasions of large gatherings in and outside private premises, as on the occasions of weddings, athletic or boxing contests, or race meetings, and the provision of constables at large railway stations. Of course, no such lending could possibly take place if the constables were required elsewhere for the preservation of order; but . . . an effective police force requires a margin of reserve strength in order to deal with emergencies, and to employ that margin of reserve, when not otherwise required, on special police for payment is to the advantage both of the persons utilising their services and of the public who are thereby relieved from some part of the police charges . . .

I conclude, therefore, that the practice of lending constables for special duty in consideration of payment is not illegal or against public policy; and I pass to the second question – namely, whether in this particular case the lending of the seventy constables to be billeted in the appellants' colliery was a legitimate application of the principle. In this connection I think It important to bear in mind exactly what it was that the learned trial judge had to decide. It was no part of his duty to say – nor did he purport to say – whether in his judgment the billeting of the seventy men at the colliery was necessary for the prevention of violence or the protection of the mines from criminal injury. The duty of determining such questions is cast by law, not upon the courts after the event, but upon the police authorities at the time when the decision has to be taken; and a court which attempted to review such a decision from the point of view of its wisdom or prudence would (I think) be exceeding its proper functions. The question for the court was whether on July 9, 1921, the police authorities, acting reasonably and in good faith, considered a police garrison at the colliery necessary for the protection of life and property from violence, or, in other words, whether the decision of the chief constable in refusing special protection unless paid for was such a decision as a man in his position and with his duties could reasonably make. If in the judgment of the police authorities, formed reasonably and in good faith, the garrison was necessary for the protection of life and property, then they were not entitled to make a charge for it, for that would be to exact a payment for the performance of a duty which they clearly owed to the appellants and their servants; but if they thought the garrison a superfluity and only acceded to Mr James' request with a view to meeting his wishes, then, in my opinion, they were entitled to treat the garrison duty as special duty and to charge for it. On this point the Divisional Superintendent, Col Smith, who was a highly experienced officer, gave specific and detailed evidence, and the learned judge, having seen him in the witness-box and heard his examination and cross-examination, accepted his evidence upon the point . . .'

Ward v *Byham*

[1956] 2 All ER 318 • Court of Appeal

The facts are set out in the judgment of Denning LJ.

Denning LJ: 'This is a claim for the sum of £1 a week in respect of the maintenance of a bastard child. The father and mother lived together unmarried for four or five years, from 1949 until May, 1954, and a little girl was born of that union on Oct. 28, 1950. Whilst the father and mother were living together, the father went out to work and maintained the household; but in May, 1954, the father turned the mother out. He put the child into the care of a neighbour and paid the neighbour £1 a week. The mother meanwhile found work as a housekeeper to a man who was ready to let the child come too. The mother wanted the child with her, and she wrote a letter to the father asking for the child, and £1 a week for her maintenance, which was the sum which the father had been paying the neighbour. We have not got a copy of the letter which the mother wrote, but we have the father's reply, which is the basis of this action. It is dated July 27, 1954, and says:

> "Mildred, I am prepared to let you have [the child] and pay you up to £1 per week allowance for her providing you can prove that she will be well looked after and happy and also that she is allowed to decide for herself whether or not she wishes to come and live with you. She is well and happy and looking much stronger than ever before. If you decide what to do let me know as soon as possible."

On receiving that letter the mother went to see the father, and it was agreed that she could have the child. She took the child with her, and the child has lived with the mother ever since.

In February, 1955, some seven months later, the mother married the man to whom she had been acting as housekeeper, and a few weeks later the father himself married. The father kept up the payments of £1 a week until the mother married, but after that he stopped.

I look on the father's letter as dealing with two things. One is the handing over of the child to the mother. The father agrees to let the mother have the child, provided the child herself wishes to come and provided also the mother satisfies the father that she will be well looked after and happy. The other thing is the future maintenance of the child. The father promises to pay the mother up to £1 per week so long as the mother looks after the child.

The mother now brings this action, claiming that the father should pay her £1 per week, even though she herself has married. The only point taken before us in answer to the claim is that it is said that there was no consideration for the promise by the father to pay £1 a week, because, when she looked after the child, the mother was only doing that which she was legally bound to do, and that is no consideration in law. In support of this proposition, reliance was placed on a statement by Parke B, in the course of argument in *Crowhurst* v *Laverack*.

By statute the mother of an illegitimate child is bound to maintain it, whereas the father is under no such obligation (see s 42 of the National Assistance Act, 1948). If she is a single woman the mother can apply to the magistrates for an affiliation order against the father, and it might be thought that consideration could be found in this case by holding that the mother must be taken to have agreed not to bring affiliation proceedings against the father. In her evidence the mother said, however, that she never at any time had any intention of bringing affiliation proceedings. It is now too late for her to bring them, because she has married and is no longer a single woman. (See *Stacey* v *Lintell*.)

I approach the case, therefore, on the footing that, in looking after the child, the mother is only doing what she is legally bound to do. Even so, I think that there was sufficient consideration to support the promise. I have always thought that a promise to perform an existing duty, or the performance of it, should be regarded as good consideration, because it is a benefit to the person to whom it is given. Take this very case. It is as much a benefit for the father to have the child looked after by the mother as by a neighbour. If he gets the benefit for which he stipulated, he ought to honour his promise, and he ought not to avoid it by saying that the other was herself under a duty to maintain the child.

I regard the father's promise in this case as what is sometimes called a unilateral contract, a promise in return for an act, a promise by the father to pay £1 a week in return for the mother's looking after the child. Once the mother embarked on the task of looking after the child, there was a binding contract. So long as she looked after the child, she would be entitled to £1 a week. The case seems to me to be within the decision of *Hicks* v *Gregory* on which the judge relied. I would dismiss the appeal.'

Morris LJ: 'I agree. I think that the letter of July 27, 1954, shows that there was consideration for the agreement and promise of the father. After the mother was made to leave the home in May, 1954, the child in fact stayed with the father until July. The terms of the father's letter of July 27 suggest that he was animated by a concern for the well-being of the child. The phrases that he uses are evidence of that. When the mother asked for the child, the answer was in the terms of the letter. Counsel for the father submits that there was a duty on the mother to support the child, that no affiliation proceedings were in prospect or were contemplated, and that the effect of the arrangement that followed the letter was that the father was merely agreeing to pay a bounty to the mother.

It seems to me that the terms of the letter negative those submissions, for the father says:

"providing you can prove that [the child] will be well looked after and happy and also that she is allowed to decide for herself whether or not she wishes to come and live with you."

The father goes on to say that the child is then well and happy and looking much stronger than ever before. "If you decide what to do let me know as soon as possible". It seems to me, therefore, that the father was saying, in effect: Irrespective of what may be the strict legal position, what I am asking is that you shall prove that the child will be well looked after and happy, and also that you must agree that the child is to be allowed to decide for herself whether or not she wishes to come and live with you. If those conditions were fulfilled the father was agreeable to pay. On those terms, which in fact became operative, the father agreed to pay £1 a week. In my judgment, there was ample consideration there to be found for his promise, which I think was binding.'

Parker LJ: 'I have come to the same conclusion. I think that the letter of July 27, 1954, clearly expresses good consideration for the bargain, and for myself I am content to adopt the very careful judgment of the learned county court judge.'

Duty imposed by contract with promisor

Stilk v Myrick

(1809) 2 Camp 317 • King's Bench

In the course of the voyage two seamen deserted a ship. The captain, being unable to find replacements for the deserters, entered into an agreement with the rest of the crew whereby the deserters' wages would be divided equally between the remaining crew. On the ship's return to London the captain refused to pay the promised extra wages, claiming that the remaining crew had not provided any new consideration.

Lord Ellenborough: '. . . Here, I say, the agreement is void for want of consideration. There was no consideration for the ulterior pay promised to the mariners who remained with the ship. Before they sailed from London they had undertaken to do all that they could under all the emergencies of the voyage. They had sold all their services till the voyage should be completed. If they had been at liberty to quit the vessel at Cronstadt [where the desertion took place], the case would have been quite different; or if the captain had capriciously discharged the two men who were wanting, the others might not have been compellable to take the whole duty upon themselves, and their agreeing to do so might have been a sufficient consideration for the promise of an advance of wages. But the desertion of a part of the crew is to be considered an emergency of the voyage as much as their death, and those who remain are bound by the terms of their original contract to exert themselves to the utmost to bring the ship in safety to her destined port. Therefore, without looking to the policy of this agreement, I think it is void for want of consideration, and that the plaintiff can only recover at the rate of £5 a month [their previously agreed wages].'

Hartley v Ponsonby

(1857) 7 E & B 872 • Queen's Bench

Ponsonby was the captain of a ship called the *Mobile*; Hartley was a member of her crew of 36. The crew, by their articles, agreed to serve on board the ship 'on a voyage from Liverpool to Port Philip, from thence (if required) to any ports and places in the Pacific Ocean, Indian or China Seas, or wherein freight may offer, with liberty to call at a port for orders, and until her return to a final port of discharge in the United Kingdom: or for a term not to exceed three years'. Hartley's wages were £3 per month. While the ship was at Port Philip, 17 of the crew refused to work, and were sent to prison. Of the remaining 19, there were only four or five able seamen. Ponsonby proposed to sail for Bombay and, to induce the remaining crew to take the ship to Bombay, he promised to pay to some of them a sum in addition to their wages. He gave Hartley a written promise which said

> 'I promise to pay, in Liverpool, to Robert Hartley the sum of forty pounds sterling, provided he assist in taking ship *Mobile* from this port to Bombay with a crew of nineteen hands'.

When the *Mobile* arrived at Liverpool Ponsonby refused to pay the seamen more than the wages originally contracted for. Evidence was given as to the unfitness of so small a crew as 19 to navigate the ship.

The issue before the court was whether Hartley had provided any new consideration in return for the promise of the extra wages.

Coleridge J: '. . . I understand the finding of the jury to be, that the ship was unseaworthy; and that, owing to the excessive labour which would be imposed, it was not reasonable to require the mariners to go to sea. If they were not bound to go, they were free to make a new contract: and the master was justified in hiring them on the best terms he could make. It may be that the plaintiff took advantage of his position to make a hard bargain; but there was no duress.'

Crompton J: 'The jury have found that this was a free bargain. As regards public policy, it would be very dangerous to lay down that, under all circumstances and at any risk of life, seamen are bound to proceed on a voyage. The jury have found in this case (and, I think, upon the evidence, correctly) that it was not reasonable to require the seamen to go on. Where, from a ship being short-handed, it would be unsafe for the seamen to go to sea, they become free to make any new contract that they like.'

North Ocean Shipping Co Ltd v Hyundai Construction Co Ltd (The Atlantic Baron)

[1978] 3 All ER 1170 • Queen's Bench

On 10 April 1972 North Ocean Shipping Co Ltd (the owners) agreed to buy from Hyundai Construction Co Ltd (the yard) a ship named the *Atlantic Baron* (the vessel). The contract required the yard to open a letter of credit to provide security for repayment of instalments in the event of their default in the performance of the contract. The contract also provided that the price of the vessel was not to be increased. On 12 February 1973 the dollar was devalued and the yard claimed a 10 per cent increase on the balance of the outstanding price. The owners needed the vessel because they had entered into a lucrative contract to charter the vessel to a third party and on 28 June they agreed to pay the increase 'without prejudice' to their rights. The yard agreed that in return for the owners agreeing to pay the increase in price they would increase their letter of credit to correspond with the increased price. Subsequently they paid off the balance of the price, including the increase, and took delivery of the vessel. The owners claimed that their agreement to pay the increase in the purchase price was void for lack of consideration or, alternatively, that during June 1973 they were compelled to submit to the yard's illegitimate demand for an increase of 10 per cent in the purchase price of the vessel and that their agreement to do so was made under duress and voidable for that reason. The duress issue is dealt with later in this book.

Mocatta J: 'Counsel's argument for the owners that the agreement to pay the extra ten per cent was void for lack of consideration was based on the well-known principle that a promise by one party to fulfil his existing contractual duty towards his other contracting party is not good consideration; he relied on the well-known case of *Stilk* v *Myrick* for this submission. Accordingly there was no consideration for the owner's agreement to pay the further ten per cent, since the yard were already contractually bound to build the ship and it is common ground that the devaluation of the dollar had in no way lessened the yard's legal obligation to do this. There has of course been some criticism in the books of the decision in *Stilk* v *Myrick*, which is somewhat differently reported in the two sets of reports, but Campbell's reports have the better reputation and what I have referred to as being the law on this point is referred to as "the present rule" in Chitty on Contracts . . .

Counsel for the yard relied on what Denning LJ said in two cases dealing with very different subject matters. The earlier was *Ward* v *Byham*. There the father of an illegitimate child, who had lived with her mother for some years, turned the mother out of the house, retaining the child for a while for himself. Later he made an offer to let the mother have the child and pay an allowance of £1 a week, provided the child was well looked after and happy and was allowed to decide for herself where she wished to live. When the mother married, the father discontinued payment, but on being sued by the mother he was held liable. The mother was by statute bound to maintain her illegitimate child, but Denning LJ said that he thought there was sufficient consideration in the promise to perform an existing duty or in its performance. Apart from the fact that the existing duty on the mother was imposed on her by statute law, which I think differentiates the case, the other two members of the Court of Appeal thought that compliance with the special terms of the father's letter, about keeping the child happy and leaving her freedom of choice constituted ample consideration. Again in *Williams* v *Williams*, whilst Denning LJ said that "a promise to perform an existing duty is, I think, sufficient consideration to support a promise", nonetheless he went on to find two separate grounds for good consideration for the husband's promise. Similarly Hodson LJ and Morris LJ found good consideration for the husband's promise. I do not therefore think either of these cases successfully enables counsel for the yard to avoid the rule in *Stilk* v *Myrick*.

What I have, however, found more difficult is whether the yard did not give some consideration for the extra ten per cent on the contract price . . . I have already mentioned that in [the owner's] important telex of 28 June 1973 the final sentence read "No doubt you will arrange for corresponding increases in the letter of credit . . ." and this was readily and quite naturally accepted and given effect to by the yard. I remain unconvinced, however, that by merely securing an increase in the instalments to be paid of ten per cent the yard automatically became obliged to increase the return letter of credit *pro tanto* and were therefore doing no more than undertaking in this respect to fulfil their existing contractual duty. I think that here they were undertaking an additional obligation or rendering themselves liable to an increased detriment. I therefore conclude, though not without some doubt, that there was consideration for the new agreement.

In view of this conclusion it is unnecessary for me to deal with a number of the additional points which counsel for the yard advanced against the argument that there was no consideration . . . I think, however, that I should say something about [one] of them. One was that acceptance of the increased price enabled the contract to be performed on the basis of amicable relations . . . I cannot think that this can amount to anything the law would regard as consideration moving from the yard.'

Williams v Roffey Bros & Nicholls (Contractors) Ltd

[1990] 1 All ER 512 • Court of Appeal

On 21 January 1986 Roffey and Williams entered into a written contract whereby Williams undertook to provide the labour for the carpentry work to 27 flats for a total price of £20 000. By 9 April 1986 Williams had completed the work to the roof, had carried out the first fix to all 27 flats, and had substantially completed the second fix to nine flats. By this date Roffey had made interim payments totalling £16 200. By the end of March 1986 Williams was in financial difficulty because the agreed price of £20 000 was too low to enable Williams to operate satisfactorily and at a profit (a reasonable price for the job would have been £23 783) and because he had failed to supervise his workmen adequately. Roffey were concerned that Williams would not complete his work on time and that they might incur penalties under the penalty clause in their main contract with the building owners. In order to make sure that Williams completed his work on time Roffey promised to pay Williams a further sum of £10 300, in addition to the £20 000, to be paid at the rate of £575 for each flat in which the carpentry work was completed. Williams and his men continued work on the flats until the end of May 1986. By that date Roffey, after their promise on 9 April 1986, had made only one further payment of £1500. At the end of May Williams ceased work on the flats. Roffey therefore hired other carpenters to complete the work, but in the result incurred one week's time penalty in their contract with the building owners. Williams sued for the extra money that had been promised to him.

Roffey argued that their promise to pay an additional £10 300, at the rate of £575 per completed flat, was unenforceable since there was no consideration for it.

Glidewell LJ: *Was there consideration for the defendants' promise made on 9 April 1986 to pay an additional price at the rate of £575 per completed flat?*

'The judge made the following findings of fact which are relevant on this issue. (i) The subcontract price agreed was too low to enable the plaintiff to operate satisfactorily and at a profit. Mr Cottrell, the defendants' surveyor, agreed that this was so. (ii) Mr Roffey (managing director of the defendants) was persuaded by Mr Cottrell that the defendants should pay a bonus to the plaintiff. The figure agreed at the meeting on 9 April 1986 was £10 300.

The judge quoted and accepted the evidence of Mr Cottrell to the effect that a main contractor who agrees too low a price with a subcontractor is acting contrary to his own interests. He will never get the job finished without paying more money.

The judge therefore concluded:

"In my view where the original subcontract price is too low, and the parties subsequently agree that additional moneys shall be paid to the subcontractor, this agreement is in the interests of both parties. This is what happened in the present case, and in my opinion the agreement of 9 April 1986 does not fail for lack of consideration."

In his address to us, counsel for the defendants outlined the benefits to the defendants which arose from their agreement to pay the additional £10 300 as (i) seeking to ensure that the plaintiff continued work and did not stop in breach of the subcontract (ii) avoiding the penalty for delay and (iii) avoiding the trouble and expense of engaging other people to complete the carpentry work.

[Glidewell LJ then reviewed the authorities.]

'Accordingly . . . the present state of the law on this subject can be expressed in the following proposition: (i) if A has entered into a contract with B to do work for, or to supply goods or services to, B in return for payment by B and (ii) at some stage before A has completely performed his obligations under the contract B has reason to doubt whether A will, or will be able to, complete his side of the bargain and (iii) B thereupon promises A an additional payment in return for A's promise to perform his contractual obligations on time and (iv) as a result of giving his promise, B obtains in practice a benefit, or obviates a disbenefit, and (v) B's promise is not given as a result of economic duress or fraud on the part of A, then (vi) the benefit to B is capable of being consideration for B's promise, so that the promise will be legally binding.

As I have said, counsel for the defendants accepts that in the present case by promising to pay the extra £10 300 his client secured benefits. There is no finding, and no suggestion, that in this case the promise was given as a result of fraud or duress.

If it be objected that the propositions above contravene the principle in *Stilk* v *Myrick* I answer that in my view they do not; they refine, and limit the application of that principle, but they leave the principle unscathed e.g. where B secures no benefit by his promise. It is not in my view surprising that a principle enunciated in relation to the rigours of seafaring life during the Napoleonic wars should be subjected during the succeeding 180 years to a process of refinement and limitation in its application in the present day.

It is therefore my opinion that on his findings of fact in the present case, the judge was entitled to hold, as he did, that the defendants' promise to pay the extra £10 300 was supported by valuable consideration and thus constituted an enforceable agreement.

As a subsidiary argument, counsel for the defendants submits that on the facts of the present case the consideration, even if otherwise good, did not "move from the promisee". This submission is based on the principle illustrated in the decision in *Tweddle* v *Atkinson*.

My understanding of the meaning of the requirement that "consideration must move from the promisee" is that such consideration must be provided by the promisee, or arise out of his contractual relationship with the promisor. It is consideration provided by somebody else, not a party to the contract, which does not "move from the promisee". This was the situation in *Tweddle* v *Atkinson*, but it is, of course, not the situation in the present case. Here the benefits to the defendants arose out of their agreement of 9 April 1986 with the plaintiff, the promisee. In this respect I would adopt the following passage from *Chitty on Contracts*, and refer to the authorities there cited:

"The requirement that consideration must move from the promisee is most generally satisfied where some detriment is suffered by him e.g. where he parts with money or goods, or renders services, in exchange for the promise. But the requirement may equally well be satisfied where the promisee confers a benefit on the promisor without *in fact* suffering any detriment." (Chitty's emphasis)

That is the situation in this case.

I repeat, therefore, my opinion that the judge was, as a matter of law, entitled to hold that there was valid consideration to support the agreement under which the defendants promised to pay an additional £10 300 at the rate of £575 per flat.

For these reasons I would dismiss this appeal.'

Russell LJ reviewed the authorities and then said: 'These citations demonstrate that whilst consideration remains a fundamental requirement before a contract not under seal can be enforced, the policy of the law in its search to do justice between the parties has developed considerably since the early nineteenth century when *Stilk* v *Myrick* was decided by Lord Ellenborough CJ. In the late twentieth century I do not believe that the rigid approach to the concept of consideration to be found in *Stilk* v *Myrick* is either necessary or desirable. Consideration there must still be but, in my judgment, the courts nowadays should be more ready to find its existence so as to reflect the intention of the parties to the contract where the bargaining powers are not unequal and where the finding of consideration reflect the true intention of the parties.

What was the true intention of the parties when they arrived at the agreement pleaded by the defendants in paragraph 5 of the amended defence? The plaintiff had got into financial difficulties. The defendants, through their employee Mr Cottrell, recognised the price that had been agreed originally with the plaintiff was less than what Mr Cottrell himself regarded as a reasonable price. There was a desire on Mr Cottrell's part to retain the services of the plaintiff so that the work could be completed without the need to employ another subcontractor. There was further a need to replace what had hitherto been a haphazard method of payment by a more formalised scheme involving the payment of a specified sum on the completion of each flat. These were all advantages accruing to the defendants which can fairly be said to have been in consideration of their undertaking to pay the additional £10,300. True it was that the plaintiff did not undertake to do any work additional to that which he had originally undertaken to do but the terms upon which he was to carry out the work were varied and, in my judgment, that variation was supported by consideration which a pragmatic approach to the true relationship between the parties readily demonstrates.

For my part I wish to make it plain that I do not base my judgment upon any reservation as to the correctness of the law long ago enunciated in *Stilk* v *Myrick*. A gratuitous promise, pure and simple, remains unenforceable unless given under seal. But where, as in this case, a party undertakes to make a payment because by so doing it will gain an advantage arising out of the continuing relationship with the promisee the new bargain will not fail for want of consideration . . .'

Purchas LJ: 'The question must be posed: what consideration has moved from the plaintiff to support the promise to pay the extra £10 300 added to the lump sum provision? In the particular circumstances which I have outlined above, there was clearly a commercial advantage to both sides from a pragmatic point of view in reaching the agreement of 9 April. The defendants were on risk that as a result of the bargain they had struck the plaintiff would not or indeed possibly could not comply with his existing obligations without further finance. As a result of the agreement the defendants secured their position commercially. There was, however, no obligation added to the contractual duties imposed upon the plaintiff under the original contract. *Prima facie* this would appear to be a classic *Stilk* v *Myrick* case. It was, however, open to the plaintiff to be in deliberate breach of the contract in order to "cut his losses" commercially. In normal circumstances the suggestion that a contracting party can rely upon his own breach to establish consideration is distinctly unattractive. In many cases it obviously would be and if there was any element of duress brought upon the other contracting party under the modern development of this branch of the law the proposed breaker of the contract would not benefit . . . I consider that the modern approach to the question of consideration would be that where there were benefits derived by each party to a contract of variation even though one party did not suffer a detriment this would not be fatal to the establishing of sufficient consideration to support the agreement. If both parties benefit from an agreement it is not necessary that each also suffers a detriment. In my judgment, on the facts as found by the judge, he was entitled to reach the conclusion that consideration existed and in those circumstances I would not disturb that finding . . .

Duty imposed by contract with a third party

Shadwell v Shadwell

(1860) 30 LJCP 145 • Common Pleas

Charles Shadwell wrote to his nephew saying 'I'm glad to hear of your intended marriage with Ellen Nicholl; and, as I promised to assist you at starting, I am happy to tell you that I will pay you one hundred and fifty pounds yearly, during my life, and until your annual income derived from your profession of a Chancery barrister shall amount to six hundred guineas, of which your own admission will be the only evidence that I shall receive or require'. The nephew married Ellen Nicholl and, because his income never exceeded 600 guineas a year his uncle paid him the £150 per year as promised. However, on the death of Charles his estate refused to continue with the payments. The nephew sued the estate for the promised monies.

The issue before the court was whether the nephew had provided any consideration in return for his uncle's promise.

Erle CJ delivered the judgment of himself and Keating J: '[D]o these facts shew that the promise was in consideration, either of the loss to be sustained by the plaintiff, or the benefit to be derived from the plaintiff to the uncle, at his, the uncle's, request? My answer is in the affirmative. First, do these facts shew a loss sustained by the plaintiff at the uncle's request? When I answer this in the affirmative, I am aware that a man's marriage with the woman of his choice is in one sense a boon, and in that sense the reverse of a loss; yet, as between the plaintiff and the party promising an income to support the marriage, it may be a loss. The plaintiff may have made the most material changes in his position, and have induced the object of his affections to do the same, and have incurred pecuniary liabilities resulting in embarrassments, which would be in every sense a loss, if the income which had been promised should be withheld; and if the promise was made in order to induce the parties to marry, the promise so made would be, in legal effect, a request to marry. Secondly, do these facts shew a benefit derived from the plaintiff to the uncle at his request? In answering again in the affirmative, I am at liberty to consider the relation in which the parties stood, and the interest in the *status* of the nephew which the uncle declares. The marriage primarily affects the parties thereto; but in the second degree it may be an object of interest with a near relative, and in that sense a benefit to him. This benefit is also derived from the plaintiff at the uncle's request, if the promise of the annuity was intended as an inducement to the marriage; and the averment that the plaintiff, relying on the promise, married, is an averment that the promise was one inducement to the marriage. This is a consideration averred in the declaration, and it appears to me to be expressed in the letter, construed with the surrounding circumstances . . .

. . . [T]he decision turns on a question of fact, whether the consideration for the promise is proved as pleaded. I think it is, and therefore my judgment on the first demurrer is for the plaintiff.'

Byles J (dissenting): 'I am of opinion that the defendant is entitled to the judgment of the Court . . . It is alleged by the fourth plea, that the defendant's testator never requested the plaintiff to enter into the engagement to marry, or to marry, and that there never was any consideration for the testator's promise, except what may be collected from the letter itself set out in the declaration. The inquiry, therefore, narrows itself to this question – Does the letter itself disclose any consideration for the promise? The consideration relied on by the plaintiff's counsel being the subsequent marriage of the plaintiff, I think the letter discloses no consideration. It is in these words – [his Lordship read it]. It is by no means clear that the words "at starting" mean "on marriage with Ellen Nicholl", or with any one else. The more natural meaning seems to me to be, "at starting in the profession", for it will be observed, that these words are used by the testator in reciting a prior promise, made when the testator had not heard of the proposed marriage with Ellen Nicholl, or, so far as appears, heard of any proposed marriage. This construction is fortified by the consideration that the annuity is not, in terms, made to begin from the marriage, but, as it should seem, from the date of the letter. Neither is it in terms made defeasible if Ellen Nicholl should die before marriage. But even on the assumption that the words "at starting" mean "on marriage", I still think that no consideration appears sufficient to sustain the promise. The promise is one which, by law, must be in writing; and the fourth plea shews that no consideration or request, *dehors* [outside] the letter, existed, and, therefore, that no such consideration, or request, can be alluded to by the letter. Marriage of the plaintiff at the testator's express request would be, no doubt, an ample consideration; but marriage of the plaintiff without the testator's request is no consideration to the testator. It is true that marriage is, or may be, a detriment to the plaintiff; but detriment to the plaintiff is not enough, unless it either be a benefit to the testator, or be treated by the testator as such, by having been suffered at his request. Suppose a defendant were to promise a plaintiff, "I will give you £500 if you break your leg", would that detriment to the plaintiff, should it happen, by any consideration? If it be said that such an accident is an involuntary mischief, would it have been a binding promise, if the testator had said, "I will give you £100 a year while you continue in your present chambers"? I conceive that the promise would not be binding for want of a previous request by the testator. Now, the testator in the case before the Court derived, so far as appears, no personal benefit from the marriage. The question, therefore, is still further narrowed to this point – Was the marriage at the testator's request? Express request there was none. Can any request be implied? The only words from which it can be contended that it is to be implied are the words, "I am glad to hear of your intended marriage with Ellen Nicholl". But it appears from the . . . plea, that that marriage had already been agreed on, and that the testator knew it. These words, therefore, seem to me to import no more than the satisfaction of the testator at the engagement as an accomplished fact. No request can, as it seems to me, be inferred from them. And, further, how does it appear that the testator's implied request, if it could be implied, or his promise, if that promise alone would suffice, or both together, were intended to cause the marriage, or did cause it, so that the marriage can be said to have taken place at the testator's request, or, in other words, in consequence of that request? It seems to me, not only that this does not appear, but that the contrary appears; for the plaintiff before the letter had already bound himself to marry, by placing himself not only under a moral, but under a legal obligation to marry, and the testator knew it. The well-known cases which have been cited at the bar in support of the position, that a promise, based on the consideration of doing that which a man is already bound to do, is invalid, apply to this case; and it is not necessary, in order to invalidate the consideration, that the plaintiff's prior obligation to afford that consideration should have been an obligation to the defendant. It may have been an obligation to a third person . . . The reason why the doing what a man is already bound to do is no consideration, is not only because such a consideration is in judgment of law of no value, but because a man can hardly be allowed to say that the prior legal obligation was not his determining motive. But, whether he can be allowed to say so or not, the plaintiff does not say so here. He does, indeed, make an attempt to meet this difficulty, by alleging, in the replication to the fourth plea, that he married relying on the testator's promise; but he shrinks from alleging, that though he had promised to marry before the testator's promise to him, nevertheless, he would have broken his engagement, and would not have married without the testator's promise. A man may rely on encouragements to the performance of his duty, who yet is prepared to do his duty without those encouragements. At the utmost, the allegation that he relied on the testator's promise seems to me to import no more than that he believed the testator would be as good as his word. It appears to me, for these reasons, that this letter is no more than a letter of kindness, creating no legal obligation.'

Scotson v Pegg

(1861) 30 LJEx 225 • Court of Exchequer

Scotson had entered into a contract with a third party for the sale and delivery of coal. Under the contract Scotson agreed to deliver the coal to the third party or to anyone nominated by the third party. The third party sold the coal to Pegg and instructed Scotson to deliver the coal to Pegg. Scotson and Pegg then agreed, at Pegg's request, that Scotson would deliver the coal which was on board his ship to Pegg in return for Pegg agreeing to unload the coal at the rate of 49 tons of coal each working day. Scotson delivered the coal but Pegg failed to unload the coal at the agreed rate which resulted in Scotson's ship being delayed for five days. Scotson sued Pegg for the losses he had incurred due to the delay. Pegg claimed that Scotson had furnished him with no fresh consideration since Scotson was already contractually bound to deliver the coal to him under Scotson's contract with the third party.

Martin B: 'I am of opinion that the plea is bad, on principles of law and of common sense. It is bad in law, because the ordinary rule is, that any act done, from which the contracting party derives a benefit, is a sufficient consideration for a promise by him. Here the defendant derives an immediate benefit by the contract to deliver the coal to him simply; therefore *prima facie* there is a good consideration. Then, is it any answer that the plaintiffs had agreed with other persons to deliver the same coal to their order, the defendant being a stranger to that agreement? I am of opinion that it is not. In law, therefore, the defendant fails. Then, put the case merely as a question of common sense. Suppose the original parties were insolvent and unable to pay the freight, why should not the plaintiffs make a fresh contract, not inconsistent with the first contract, by which the defendant would get the right to the immediate possession of the goods upon undertaking to unload? Here the defendant does so contract, and has had the benefit of the contract.'

Wilde B: 'I am also of opinion that the plaintiffs are entitled to our judgment. The plaintiffs say, that in consideration that they would deliver to the defendant a cargo of coals then in the plaintiffs' ship, the defendant promised to discharge the cargo in a certain manner. The defendant says, "That is very true; I did so promise, but you had previously promised to other persons to deliver the coals; and therefore there was no consideration for my promise". But why is there no consideration? It is said there is no consideration, because the plaintiffs were already bound to other persons to do the same thing. That, in fact, amounts to saying, that a man cannot have an interest in the performance of a contract made with another; but if a person chooses to promise to pay a sum of money, and so induces another to perform that which he has already contracted with a third person to do, I cannot see why such a promise should not be binding. That is what the defendant has done here. He has induced the plaintiffs to part with the cargo, which they might not otherwise have been willing to do, and he gets the right to the immediate removal, which is a benefit to him. I accede to the proposition, that if a man has already contracted with another to do a certain thing, he cannot make the performance of it a consideration for a new promise to the same individual; but it seems to me that the cases cited do not establish the proposition which has been contended for, and that no case can be found that where there has been a promise to one person to do a certain thing, it is not possible to make a valid promise to another to do the same thing. Deciding this question on principle, I think there was a good consideration for the promise of the defendant, and that the plaintiffs are entitled to judgment.'

New Zealand Shipping Co Ltd v A M Satterthwaite & Co Ltd (The Eurymedon)

[1974] 1 All ER 1015 • Privy Council

In June 1964 a drilling machine was shipped on board the ship *Eurymedon* at Liverpool for transhipment to Wellington, New Zealand. The bill of lading (the contract of carriage between Satterthwaite and the carrier) stated:

> 'It is hereby expressly agreed that no servant or agent of the carrier (including every independent contractor from time to time employed by the carrier) shall in any circumstances whatsoever be under any liability whatsoever to the shipper, consignee or owner of the goods or to any holder of this bill of lading for any loss or damage or delay of whatsoever kind arising or resulting directly or indirectly from any act neglect or default on his part while acting in the course of or in connection with his employment and, without prejudice to the generality of the foregoing provisions in this clause, every exemption, limitation, condition and liberty herein contained and every right, exemption from liability, defence and immunity of whatsoever nature applicable to the carrier or to which the carrier is entitled hereunder shall also be available and shall extend to protect every such servant or agent of the carrier acting as aforesaid and for the purpose of all the foregoing provisions of this clause the carrier is or shall be deemed to be acting as agent or trustee on behalf of and for the benefit of all persons who are or might be his servants or agents from time to time (including independent contractors as aforesaid) and all such persons shall to this extent be or be deemed to be parties to the contract in or evidenced by this bill of lading.'

Further, the rules scheduled to the Carriage of Goods by Sea Act 1924 had been incorporated into the bill of lading contract which meant that the carrier was discharged from all liability in respect of damage to the drill unless suit was brought against them within one year after delivery.

In April 1967 Satterthwaite sued New Zealand Shipping, the stevedore, for negligently damaging the drilling machine. New Zealand Shipping claimed that the time limit of one year in the bill of lading contract protected them even though they were not parties to the contract between Satterthwaite and the carriers.

Lord Wilberforce delivered the majority opinion: 'If the choice, and the antithesis, is between a gratuitous promise, and a promise for consideration, as it must be in the absence of a *tertium quid*, there can be little doubt which, in commercial reality, this is. The whole contract is of a commercial character, involving service on one side, rates of payment on the other, and qualifying stipulations as to both. The relations of all parties to each other are commercial relations entered into for business reasons of ultimate profit. To describe one set of promises, in this context, as gratuitous, or *nudum pactum*, seems paradoxical and is *prima facie* implausible. It is only the precise analysis of this complex of relations into the classical offer and acceptance, with identifiable consideration, that seems to present difficulty, but this same difficulty exists in many situations of daily life, e.g. sales at auction; supermarket purchases; boarding an omnibus; purchasing a train ticket; tenders for the supply of goods; offers of rewards; acceptance by post; warranties of authority by agents; manufacturers' guarantees; gratuitous bailments; bankers' commercial credits. These are all examples which show that English law, having committed itself to a rather technical and schematic doctrine of contract, in application takes a practical approach, often at the cost of forcing the facts to fit uneasily into the marked slots of offer, acceptance and consideration.

In their Lordships' opinion the present contract presents much less difficulty than many of those above referred to. It is one of carriage from Liverpool to Wellington. The carrier assumes an obligation to transport the goods and to discharge at the port of arrival. The goods are to be carried and discharged, so the transaction is inherently contractual. It is contemplated that a part of this contract, viz discharge, may be performed by independent contractors – viz the stevedore. By clause 1 of the bill of lading the shipper agrees to exempt from liability the carrier, his servants and independent contractors in respect of the performance of this contract of carriage. Thus, if the carriage, including the discharge, is wholly carried out by the carrier, he is exempt. If part is carried out by him, and part by his servants, he and they are exempt. If part is carried out by him and part by an independent contractor, he and the independent contractor are exempt. The exemption is designed to cover the whole carriage from loading to discharge, by whomsoever it is performed: the performance attracts the exemption or immunity in favour of whoever the performer turns out to be. There is possibly more than one way of analysing this business transaction into the necessary components; that which their Lordships would accept is to say that the bill of lading brought into existence a bargain initially "unilateral" but capable of becoming mutual, between the shipper and the stevedore, made through the carrier as agent. This became a full contract when the stevedore performed services by discharging the goods. The performance of these services for the benefit of the shipper was the consideration for the agreement by the shipper that the stevedore should have the benefit of the exemptions and limitations contained in the bill of lading. The conception of a "unilateral" contract of this kind was recognised in *Great Northern Railway Co* v *Witham* and is well established. This way of regarding the matter is very close to if not identical to that accepted by Beattie J in the Supreme Court: he analysed the transaction as one of an offer open to acceptance by action such as was found in *Carlill* v *Carbolic Smoke Ball Co.* But whether one describes the shipper's promise to exempt as an offer to be accepted by performance or as a promise in exchange for an act seems in the present context to be a matter of semantics. The words of Bowen LJ in *Carlill* v *Carbolic Smoke Ball Co*: "why should not an offer be made to all the world which is to ripen into a contract with anybody who comes forward and performs the condition?" seem to bridge both conceptions: he certainly seems to draw no distinction between an offer which matures into a contract when accepted and a promise which matures into a contract after performance, and, though in some special contexts (such as in connection with the right to withdraw) some further refinement may be needed, either analysis may be equally valid. On the main point in the appeal, their Lordships are in substantial agreement with Beattie J.

The following points require mention.

1. In their Lordships' opinion, consideration may quite well be provided by the stevedore, as suggested, even though (or if) it was already under an obligation to discharge to the carrier . . . An agreement to do an act which the promisor is under an existing obligation to a third party to do, may quite well amount to valid consideration and does so in the present case: the promisee obtains the benefit of a direct obligation which he can enforce. This proposition is illustrated and supported by *Scotson* v *Pegg* which their Lordships consider to be good law . . .

In the opinion of their Lordships, to give the stevedore the benefit of the exemptions and limitations contained in the bill of lading is to give effect to the clear intentions of a commercial document, and can be given within existing principles. They see no reason to strain the law or the facts in order to defeat these intentions. It should not be overlooked that the effect of denying validity to the clause would be to encourage actions against servants, agents and independent contractors in order to get round exemptions (which are almost invariable and often compulsory) accepted by shippers against carriers, the existence, and presumed efficacy, of which is reflected in the rates of freight. They see no attraction in this consequence.'

SUMMARY

You should now be able to:

- Appreciate the importance of consideration.
- Understand the significance of benefit and detriment.
- Determine what constitutes a valuable consideration.
- Distinguish between *past* and *executed* consideration.
- Understand the concepts of adequacy of consideration, nominal consideration and real consideration.
- Understand how forbearance to sue can amount to a valuable consideration.
- Know when an existing duty can constitute fresh consideration.

If you have not mastered the above points you should go through this section again.

6 Variation of contracts, promissory estoppel and waiver

CONTRACT VARIATION

In the vast majority of cases, once parties have entered into a contract the parties perform their obligations under the contract and the contract comes to an end; this is known as 'discharge by performance' and is dealt with more fully later in this book. However, in some cases the parties wish to vary or change the terms of the contract. The simplest way in which the parties to the original contract can vary that contract is to enter into a completely new contract whereby they agree to vary the terms of the original contract: this is known as variation. (Alternatively the parties may agree to abandon the original contract completely; this is known as rescinding the contract.) In either case provided both parties have agreed (offer and acceptance) to the new terms and provided that both parties have provided fresh consideration then there will be a new contract which either varies the terms of the original contract or rescinds it.

However, two problems may arise in this type of situation. Firstly, what have the parties actually agreed? Secondly, and more usually the problem, what fresh consideration have both parties furnished?

INTENTION TO RESCIND OR VARY?

With rescission the old contract is brought to an end and is completely replaced with a new contract. With variation the original contract still exists but is subject to the terms of the new contract; in other words there are two contracts in existence. Whether a contract has been varied or rescinded depends on the intention of the parties when they enter into the new contract.

United Dominions Corporation (Jamaica) Ltd v Shoucair
[1969] 1 AC 340 • Privy Council

UDC lent £55 000 to Shoucair at 9 per cent interest. Later, the bank rate having gone up by 2 per cent, UDC wrote to Shoucair telling him that they had raised their mortgage rate to 11 per cent. They asked Shoucair to confirm in writing to them that he agreed to the new rate, which he did. However, by the Jamaican Moneylenders Act the new agreement was not enforceable in law. Shoucair then defaulted in making his mortgage repayments so UDC threatened to sell his house unless he paid them all the monies he owed to them.

The issue before the Privy Council was what was the effect of the new agreement? If it destroyed the original contract, then, the new contract being unenforceable, UDC would have no contractual means to recover the interest or the principal loan from Shoucair.

Lord Devlin: 'At the root of the problem there lies the concept of unenforceability . . . If the statute made the amending contract void and of no effect, there would be no problem at all. An attempt at changing the original contract would have failed altogether and so left it quite untouched; but unenforceability creates only a procedural bar. The substance of the [amending] contract is good; yet, although the contract is alive and real, the court will not give effect to it . . . Thus the difficulty about enforcing the original mortgage in this case is that, although itself untouched by the statute, it is no longer the real contract between the parties. In reality, although the statute prevents reality from being proved, there is no longer a mortgage at nine per cent but one at eleven per cent. Since however the real contract is not evidenced in the way required by the moneylending law, it cannot be enforced. This is the approach made by . . . the majority in the Court of Appeal.

Another way of arriving at the same result is to treat a variation of a contract as something that necessarily requires the rescission of the old contract and the substitution of a new one. On this view the old contract cannot be enforced because it has been rescinded and the new contract cannot be enforced because it is not properly evidenced. This was the conclusion reached by the Divisional Court in *Williams* v *Moss' Empires Ltd* . . . As Sankey J put it . . . : "The result of varying the terms of an existing contract is to produce, not the original contract with a variation, but a new and different contract."

The disadvantage of this view is that a minor variation may destroy the effect of the whole of the transaction between the parties. The alternative view, adopted by the House of Lords in *Morris* v *Baron & Co* and again in *British and Beningtons Ltd* v *North-Western Cachar Tea Co Ltd* (where Lord Sumner referred to the former view as possibly correct "as a matter of formal logic") is based on the intention of the parties. They cannot have that which presumably they wanted, that is, the old agreement as amended; so the court has to make up its mind which comes nearer to their intention – to leave them with an unamended agreement or without any agreement at all. The House answered this question by rejecting the strict view propounded by Sankey J and distinguishing between rescission and variation. If the new agreement reveals an intention to rescind the old, the old goes; and if it does not, the old remains in force and unamended.

If the principle in *Morris* v *Baron & Co* applies to this case, the [original] mortgage . . . remains in force. The contrary has not been and could not be argued. It would be impossible to contend that a temporary variation in the rate of interest reveals any intention to extinguish the debt and the mortgage . . .

. . . The Board can see no reason for not following *Morris* v *Baron & Co*.'

HAVE BOTH PARTIES FURNISHED FRESH CONSIDERATION?

Very often when parties agree to vary the terms of a contract what happens is that one party agrees to give up some right under the contract but the other party does not. A common example of this is part payment of a debt.

For example if Eric already owes Kate £300 and says to her 'Will you accept £200 in full settlement and forgo the remaining £100' and Kate agrees, can Kate, once she has got the £200 from Eric, sue him for the remaining £100?

In contract law jargon if one party is already bound by contract to pay the other party, is a promise by him to pay a lesser sum in full settlement good consideration?

Rule in *Pinnel's Case*

A creditor is not bound by an undertaking to accept part payment in full settlement.

Pinnel's Case

[1558–1774] All ER Rep 612 • Common Pleas

Pinnel brought an action of debt on a bond against Cole for payment of £8 10s due on 11 November 1600. Cole pleaded, that he at the instance of Pinnel, before the said day, paid on 1 October £5 2s 9d which Pinnel accepted in full satisfaction of the £8 10s.

The whole Court held, that payment of a lesser sum on the day in satisfaction of a greater, cannot be any satisfaction for the whole, because it appears to the Judges that by no possibility, a lesser sum can be a satisfaction to the plaintiff for a greater sum: but the gift of a horse, hawk, or robe, etc in satisfaction is good. For it shall be intended that a horse, hawk, or robe, etc might be more beneficial to the plaintiff than the money, in respect of some circumstance, or otherwise the plaintiff would not have accepted of it in satisfaction. But when the whole sum is due, by no intendment the acceptance of a parcel can be a satisfaction to the plaintiff.

In the case at Bar it was resolved, that the payment and acceptance of parcel before the day in satisfaction of the whole, would be a good satisfaction in regard of circumstance of time, for peradventure parcel of it before the day would be more beneficial to him than the whole at the day, and the value of the satisfaction is not material: so if I am bound in £20 to pay you £10 at Westminster and you request me to pay you £5 at the day at York, and you will accept it in full satisfaction of the whole, it is a good satisfaction for the whole: for the expenses to pay it at York, is sufficient satisfaction.

But in this case the plaintiff had judgment for the insufficient pleading; for he did not plead that he had paid the £5 2s 9d in full satisfaction (as by the law he ought) but pleaded the payment of part generally; and that the plaintiff accepted it in full satisfaction. And always the manner of the tender and of the payment shall be directed by him who made the tender or payment, and not by him who accepts it.

The rule in *Pinnel's Case* was approved by House of Lords in *Foakes* v *Beer*.

Foakes v Beer

(1884) 9 AC 605 • House of Lords

On the 11 August 1875 Beer successfully sued Foakes for £2090 19s. Foakes asked Beer for time to pay. Beer agreed and they entered into an agreement whereby he agreed to pay Beer £500 on signing the agreement and then £150 on 1 July and 1 January each year until the whole of the £2090 19s had been paid. As part of the agreement Beer agreed 'not to take any proceedings whatever on the said judgment'. Foakes paid off the full amount but then Beer realised that Foakes still owed her interest on the £2090 19s. She sued him for the lost interest. Foakes pleaded that the agreement between them prevented Beer from taking any further action against him.

The issue before the court was whether Foakes had provided Beer with any consideration for her promise 'not to take any proceedings whatever on the said judgment'.

Earl of Selborne LC: '. . . But the question remains, whether the agreement is capable of being legally enforced. Not being under seal, it cannot be legally enforced against the respondent, unless she received consideration for it from the appellant, or unless, though without consideration, it operates by way of accord and satisfaction, so as to extinguish the claim for interest. What is the consideration? On the face of the agreement none is expressed, except a present payment of £500, on account and in part of the larger debt then due and payable by law under the judgment. The appellant did not contract to pay the future instalments of £150 each, at the times therein mentioned; much less did he give any new security, in the shape of negotiable paper, or in any other form. The promise *de futuro* was only that of the respondent, that if the half-yearly payments of £150 each were regularly paid, she would "take no proceedings whatever on the judgment". No doubt if the appellant had been under no antecedent obligation to pay the whole debt, his fulfilment of the condition might have imported some consideration on his part for that promise . . .

The question, therefore, is nakedly raised by this appeal, whether your Lordships are now prepared, not only to overrule, as contrary to law, the doctrine stated by Sir Edward Coke to have been laid down by all the judges of the Common Pleas in *Pinnel's Case* in 1602 . . . but to treat a prospective agreement, not under seal, for satisfaction of a debt, by a series of payments on account to a total amount less than the whole debt, as binding in law, provided those payments are regularly made . . . The doctrine itself, as laid down by Sir Edward Coke, may have been criticised, as questionable in principle, by some persons whose opinions are entitled to respect, but it has never been Judicially overruled; on the contrary I think it has always, since the sixteenth century, been accepted as law. If so, I cannot think that your lordships would do right, if you were now to reverse, as erroneous, a judgment of the Court of Appeal, proceeding upon a doctrine which has been accepted as part of the law of England for 280 years . . .

The distinction between the effect of a deed under seal, and that of an agreement by parol, or by writing not under seal, may seem arbitrary, but it is established in our law; nor is it really unreasonable or practically inconvenient that the law should require particular solemnities to give to a gratuitous contract the force of a binding obligation. If the question be (as, in the actual state of the law, I think it is), whether consideration is, or is not, given in a case of this kind, by the debtor who pays down part of the debt presently due from him, for a promise by the creditor to relinquish, after certain further payments on account, the residue of the debt, I cannot say that I think consideration is given, in the sense in which I have always understood that word as used in our law. It might be (and indeed I think it would be) an improvement in our law, if a release or acquittance of the whole debt, on payment of any sum which the creditor might be content to receive by way of accord and satisfaction (though less than the whole), were held to be, generally, binding, though not under seal; nor should I be unwilling to see equal force given to a prospective agreement, like the present, in writing though not under seal; but I think it impossible, without refinements which practically alter the sense of the word, to treat such a release or acquittance as supported by any new consideration proceeding from the debtor.

. . . What is called "any benefit, or even any legal possibility of benefit", in Mr Smith's notes to *Cumber* v *Wane*, is not (as I conceive) that sort of benefit which a creditor may derive from getting payment of part of the money due to him from a debtor who might otherwise keep him at arm's length, or possibly become insolvent, but is some independent benefit, actual or contingent, of a kind which might in law be a good and valuable consideration for any other sort of agreement not under seal . . .'

Equitable exception – promissory estoppel

Introduction

All that *Pinnel's Case* really shows is that if there is fresh consideration provided by the debtor to the creditor then the creditor will be bound by his promise to forgo the promised part of the debt. If the debtor provides no fresh consideration, then there is no new contract: there being no new contract to bind the creditor, the creditor can enforce the original contract. It is to get around the problem of absence of fresh consideration on the part of the debtor that the equitable doctrine of promissory estoppel has developed.

Promissory estoppel is *not* a form of consideration. What basically happens is that a promise is made by one party to the other party that he will accept less than full performance of the contract by the other party. If then the first party tries to sue the second party for failing to carry out the contract completely the court will estop the first party from going back on his word: promissory estoppel is more akin to an evidential rule than to consideration.

Hughes v *Metropolitan Railway Co*

(1877) 2 AC 439 • House of Lords

The facts are stated in the judgment of Lord Cairns LC.

Lord Cairns LC: 'My Lords, the Appellant was the landlord of certain premises in the Euston Road, the lease of which, an old and a long lease, was vested in the Respondents. There were in the lease covenants to repair, and to repair after notice. Notice had been given and served upon the Respondents by the Appellant on the 22nd of October, 1874; it was a notice to repair the premises within six months; that six months would therefore expire on the 22nd of April, 1875. Nothing was done by the Respondents between the 22nd of October and the 28th of November. On the 28th of November the agents of the Respondents wrote to the solicitors of the Appellant a very important letter. There can be no doubt that the letter refers to the premises in question although it refers also to other premises. It states that the notice to repair had been received, and that the repairs required by the covenants of the lease "shall be forthwith commenced", but then it adds: "It occurs to us that the freeholder may be desirous of obtaining possession of the company's interest, which, as you know, is but a short one, and so we propose to defer commencing the repairs until we hear from you as to the probability of an arrangement such as we suggest". Now, if these two parties, the Appellant and the Respondents, were really minded to treat for the purchase of this lease, of course it was to the interest of both parties that the doing of these repairs should be suspended, and that the property should be bought as it then stood, because it might be desired to apply it to purposes for which the repairs would be useless – and I read this as a definite intimation on the part of the Respondents that they would not proceed to execute the repairs (although they stated their readiness to commence them forthwith), if they found that there was a probability of an arrangement to purchase being come to.

The Appellant, when he received that letter, might have said, I have no intention of becoming a purchaser; or he might have said, I may become a purchaser; but if a negotiation is to be commenced you must understand that it is to be without prejudice to my notice to repair; you must go on and make the repairs as if there was no negotiation; or he might have said simply I will adopt what you propose and enter upon a negotiation, saying nothing farther. That third course is the course which he took, and it is a course which, as it seems to me, when taken, carried with it the intimation that he was satisfied with the footing upon which the matter was put by the letter which he was answering. This is what his solicitors say in their letter of the 1st of December: "if the company are the owners of" certain other houses, "and are willing to sell them all" (that is all the houses), "and give immediate possession, our client will, on learning the price, consider whether it is worth while to acquire the company's interest or not. In mentioning the price, please to give us particulars of the tenancies and rents paid to the company".

Now, that being a letter which, as it appears to me, acceded to the suggestion that the repairs were to be deferred until it was ascertained whether an agreement could be made for the purchase, on the 4th of December that letter of the 1st was replied to, and replied to in this way: "We are in receipt of yours of the 1st instant. The particulars and terms asked for shall be sent in the course of a few days". Again, on the 30th of December, the agents of the Respondents write to the solicitors of the Appellant: "We send you herewith a statement of the company's receipts and payments in respect of the houses in Euston Road as requested by you. The company will agree to surrender the whole of the leases in consideration of a payment of £3000. We shall be glad to hear from you at your early convenience". That is followed by the particulars of the Metropolitan Railway Company's interest in the houses in Euston Road, the property of Mr Hughes. There is a somewhat lengthy schedule, and it is obvious that the preparation of that schedule was a work which would easily account for the lapse of time between the 4th and the 30th of December. It was a schedule which was required by the Appellant. Time was required to prepare it, and your Lordships come therefore to the 30th of December with clear proof that no time whatever had been lost between the 28th of November and that day.

The offer, then, standing upon the letter of the 30th of December, that letter is replied to by the solicitors of the Appellant in these words: "We have duly received your letter of yesterday's date enclosing a statement of the company's receipts and payments in respect of the houses in Euston Road, and at the same time intimating that the company will agree to surrender the whole of the leases in consideration of the payment of £3000. Having regard, however, to the state of repair in which the houses now are, and to the large expenditure which will be required to put them in a proper condition, the whole of which the company are liable to bear under the covenants in the leases, we think the price asked for is out of all reason. We must therefore request you to reconsider the question of price, having regard to the previous observations, and to the fact that the company have already been served with notice to put the premises in repair, and we shall be glad to receive in due course a modified proposal from you."

My Lords, I think it unnecessary to go beyond that letter. That is a letter which, a price of £3000 having been proposed, repudiates that price, refuses to give it, and asks for a modified proposal. No modified proposal, in point of fact, was made. But I will put the matter in the most favourable way for the Appellant. I will assume that in place of asking for a modified proposal that had been a letter which had at once terminated the negotiation. No farther proposal having been made in substance the negotiation then determined. I will assume that the letter, upon the face of it, had terminated the negotiation, and now I ask your Lordships to consider what would be the consequence. There had been a notice in October to repair in six months. The effect of the letter of November, as it seems to me, was to propose to the Appellant, and the farther letter of the Appellant had the effect of an assent by the Appellant, to suspend the operation of that notice in order to enter upon a negotiation for the purchase and sale of the lease. That negotiation was entered upon, and, as I have assumed, came to an end on the 31st of December. My Lords, it appears to me that in the eye of a Court of Equity, or in the eye of any Court dealing upon principles of Equity, it must be taken that all the time which had elapsed between the giving of the notice in October and the letter of the 28th of November was waived as a part of the six months during which the repairs were to be executed, and that all the time from the 28th of November until the conclusion of the negotiation, which I have assumed to be on the 31st of December, was also waived – that it was impossible that any part of that time should afterwards be counted as against the tenant in a six months' notice to repair. The result would be, that it would be on the 31st of December, as the first time, that time would begin to run, for the purpose of repairs, as against the tenant.

Then occurs the question, what time from the 31st of December would be given? My Lords, what a Court of Equity would have done if it had found that the tenant after the 31st of December had taken no steps to make the repairs, and that a period of six months had run from the 31st of December without any repairs having been made, it is not necessary here to consider. In point of fact the repairs were made within six months, from the 31st of December; and my Lords, I cannot but think that the lease having prescribed a period of six months, as that which in the eyes of the contracting parties was a reasonable period, within which to make such repairs as those, a Court of Equity would hold, and could be bound to hold, that the negotiation having been broken off on the 31st of December, the repairs were in this case executed within that which according to the view of the parties was a reasonable time for the execution of such repairs.

My Lords, it is upon those grounds that I am of opinion that the decision of the Court below is correct. It was not argued at your Lordships' Bar, and it could not be argued, that there was any right of a Court of Equity, or any practice of a Court of Equity, to give relief in cases of this kind, by which of mercy, or by way merely of saving property from forfeiture, but it is the first principle upon which all Courts of Equity proceed, that if parties which have entered into definite and distinct terms involving certain legal results – certain penalties or legal forfeiture – afterwards by their own act or with their own consent enter upon a course of negotiation which has the effect of leading one of the parties to suppose that the strict rights arising under the contract will not be enforced, or will be kept in suspense, or held in abeyance, the person which otherwise might have enforced those rights will not be allowed to enforce them where it would be inequitable having regard to the dealings which have thus taken place between the parties. My Lords, I repeat that I attribute to the Appellant no intention here to take advantage of, to lay a trap for, or to lull into false security those with whom he was dealing; but it appears to me that both parties by entering upon the negotiation which they entered upon, made it an inequitable thing that the exact period of six months dating from the month of October should afterwards be measured out as against the Respondents as the period during which the repairs must be executed.

I therefore propose to your Lordships that the decree which is appealed against should be affirmed, and the present appeal dismissed with costs.'

Central London Property Trust Ltd v *High Trees House Ltd*

[1956] 1 All ER 256 • King's Bench

The facts are to be found in the judgment of Denning J.

Denning J: 'On Sept 27, 1937, Central London Property Trust, Ltd, the landlords, let a block of flats to High Trees House, Ltd, the tenants, for a term of ninety-nine years from Sept 29, 1937, at a rent of £2500 a year, the lease being by deed and properly executed. Those two companies were closely linked. The plaintiffs held all the shares of the defendant company (the tenants) and they were linked by directors and secretaries.

This new block of flats had not been fully occupied by the beginning of the war in 1939 owing to the absence of people from London; I think only one-third of it had been let by the outbreak of war. With war conditions prevailing, it was plain to those who ran these companies that the rent payable under the lease could not be paid out of the profits. In those circumstances, as a result of discussions, an arrangement was made between the directors concerned, which was put into writing. On Jan 3, 1940, the landlords wrote to the tenants in these terms:

"We confirm the arrangement made between us by which the ground rent should be reduced as from the commencement of the lease to £1250 per annum";

and at a meeting of the plaintiff company (the landlords) in April, 1940, the resolution was confirmed that the tenants be charged ground rent from Mar 1, 1939, at the reduced rate of £1250 a year in place of the £2500 a year provided in the lease.

I am satisfied that that arrangement was intended simply as a temporary expedient to deal with the exceptional conditions then prevailing, under which the block of flats was only partially let. The arrangement had no reference to events in which the block of flats was wholly let, if they subsequently occurred. Indeed, having regard to the close connection between these two companies, I do not suppose anything would have come before the courts but for the fact that in March, 1941, the debenture-holders of the plaintiff company (the landlords) appointed a receiver, by whom the affairs of the landlords have since been managed.

Before and after his appointment the tenants paid the reduced rent of £1250 a year; in one bad year they could not pay even that, but paid a smaller amount. Otherwise £1250 a year was paid in 1941, 1942, 1943, and 1944. Even when the premises were fully let, at the beginning of 1945, the reduced rent of £1250 was paid. The receiver had not looked into the lease, or realised what the rent was. Only in September, 1945, did he realise that the rent reserved was £2500 a year. Accordingly, on Sept 21, 1945, he wrote to the tenants saying that the £2500 a year must be paid, and also arrears, which he says are £7916.

No payment being received, he brings this action to test the position in law. It concerns two periods, which provide a critical test of the rights of the parties. Rent is claimed of £625 for the quarter ending Sept 29, 1945, and also of £625 for the quarter ending Dec 25, 1945.

The tenants said first that the reduction of £1250 was to apply throughout the term of ninety-nine years, and that the reduced rent was payable during the whole of that time. Alternatively, they said that was payable up to Sept 24, 1945, when the increased rent would start.

If I consider this matter without regard to recent developments in the law there is no doubt that the whole claim must succeed. This is a lease under seal, and at common law, it could not be varied by parol or by writing, but only by deed; but equity has stepped in, and the courts may now give effect to a variation in writing (see *Berry* v *Berry*). That equitable doctrine could hardly apply, however, in this case because this variation might be said to be without consideration.

As to estoppel, this representation with reference to reducing the rent was not a representation of existing fact, which is the essence of common law estoppel; it was a representation in effect as to the future – a representation that the rent would not be enforced at the full rate but only at the reduced rate. At common law, that would not give rise to an estoppel, because, as was said in *Jorden* v *Money*, a representation as to the future must be embodied as a contract or be nothing. So at common law it seems to me there would be no answer to the whole claim.

What, then, is the position in view of developments in the law in recent years? The law has not been standing still even since *Jorden* v *Money*. There has been a series of decisions over the last fifty years which, although said to be cases of estoppel, are not really such. They are cases of promises which were intended to create legal relations and which, in the knowledge of the person making the promise, were going to be acted on by the party to whom the promise was made, and have in fact been so acted on. In such cases the courts have said these promises must be honoured. There are certain cases to which I particularly refer: *Fenner* v *Blake, Re Wickham, Re William Porter & Co, Ltd* and *Buttery* v *Pickard.* Although said by the learned judges who decided them to be cases of estoppel, all these cases are not estoppel in the strict sense. They are cases of promises which were intended to be binding, which the parties making them knew would be acted on and which the parties to whom they were made did act on. *Jorden* v *Money* can be distinguished because there the promisor made it clear that she did not intend to be legally bound, whereas in the cases to which I refer the promisor did intend to be bound. In each case the court held the promise to be binding on the party making it, even though under the old common law it might be said to be difficult to find any consideration for it. The courts have not gone so far as to give a cause of action in damages for breach of such promises, but they have refused to allow the party making them to act inconsistently with them. It is in that sense, and in that sense only, that such a promise gives rise to an estoppel. The cases are a natural result of the fusion of law and equity; for the cases of *Hughes* v *Metropolitan Ry Co, Birmingham & District Land Co* v *London & North Western Ry Co,* and *Salisbury* v *Gilmore,* show that a party will not be allowed in equity to go back on such a promise. The time has now come for the validity of such a promise to be recognised. The logical consequence, no doubt, is that a promise to accept a smaller sum in discharge of a larger sum, if acted on, is binding, notwithstanding the absence of consideration, and if the fusion of law and equity leads to that result, so much the better. At this time of day it is not helpful to try to draw a distinction between law and equity. They have been joined together now for over seventy years, and the problems have to be approached in a combined sense.

It is to be noticed that in the sixth interim report of the Law Revision Committee, it was recommended that such a promise as I have referred to should be enforceable in law even though no consideration had been given by the promisee. It seems to me that, to the extent I have mentioned, that has now been achieved by the decisions of the courts.

I am satisfied that such a promise is binding in law, and the only question is the scope of the promise in the present case. I am satisfied on the evidence that the promise was that the ground rent should be reduced to £1,250 a year as a temporary expedient, while the block of flats was not fully or substantially fully let owing to the conditions prevailing. That means that this reduction of rent applied up to the end of 1944. But early in 1945 the flats were fully let and the rents received from them (many were not caught by the Rent Restrictions Acts) had been increased more than originally anticipated. At all events the revenue from them must have been very considerable. The conditions prevailing when the reduction was made had completely passed away, as I find, by the early months of 1945. I am satisfied that the promise was understood by all parties only to apply in the conditions prevailing at the time of the flats being partially let, and the promise did not extend any further than that. When the flats became fully let early in 1945 the reduction ceased to apply.

In those circumstances under the law as I hold it, it seems to me that the quarter's rents are fully payable for the quarter ending Sept 29, 1945, and the quarter ending Dec 25, 1945, which are the amounts claimed in this action.

If it had been a case of estoppel, it might have been said that the estoppel in any event would end with the ending of the conditions to which the representation applied, or alternatively only on notice. But in either case it is only a way of asking what is the scope of the representation. I prefer to apply the principle that the promise, intended to be binding, intended to be acted on and in fact acted on, is binding so far as its terms properly apply. It is binding as covering the period down to early 1945, and from that time full rent is payable. I therefore give judgment for the amount claimed, credit to be given for the £275 paid and accepted.'

FEATURES OF PROMISSORY ESTOPPEL

No new rights created

Combe v Combe

[1951] 1 All ER 767 • Court of Appeal

The facts are to be found in the judgment of Denning LJ.

Denning LJ: 'In this case a wife who has divorced her husband claims maintenance from him – not in the Divorce Court, but in the King's Bench on an agreement which is said to be embodied in letters. The parties were married in 1915. They separated in 1939. On Feb 1, 1943, on the wife's petition, a decree nisi of divorce was pronounced. Shortly afterwards letters passed between the solicitors with regard to maintenance. On Feb 9, 1943 (eight days after the decree nisi), the solicitor for the wife wrote to the solicitor for the husband:

"With regard to permanent maintenance, we understand that your client is prepared to make [the wife] an allowance of £100 per year free of income tax."

In answer, on Feb 19, 1943, the husband's solicitors wrote:

"The respondent has agreed to allow your client £100 per annum free of tax."

On Aug 11, 1943, the decree was made absolute. On Aug 26, 1943, the wife's solicitors wrote to the husband's solicitors, saying:

"Referring to your letter of Feb 19 last, our client would like the £100 per annum agreed to be paid to her by your client to be remitted to us on her behalf quarterly. We shall be glad if you will kindly let us have a cheque for £25 for the first quarterly instalment and make arrangements for a similar remittance to us on Nov 11, Feb 11, May 11, and Aug 11 in the future."

A reply did not come for nearly two months because the husband was away, and then he himself, on Oct 18, 1943, wrote a letter which was passed on to the wife's solicitors:

". . . regarding the sum of £25 claimed on behalf of Mrs Combe . . . I would point out that whilst this is paid quarterly as from Aug 11, 1943, the sum is not due till Nov 11, 1943, as I can hardly be expected to pay this allowance in advance."

He never paid anything. The wife pressed him for payment, but she did not follow it up by an application to the divorce court. It is to be observed that she herself has an income of her own of between £700 and £800 a year, whereas her husband has only £650 a year. Eventually, after nearly seven years had passed since the decree absolute, she brought this action in the King's Bench Division on July 28, 1950, claiming £675 being arrears for six years and three quarters at £100 a year. Byrne, J, held that the first three quarterly instalments of £25 were barred by the Limitation Act, 1939, but he gave judgment for

£600 in respect of the instalments which accrued within the six years before the action was brought. He held, on the authority of *Gaisberg* v *Storr*, that there was no consideration for the husband's promise to pay his wife £100, but, nevertheless, he held that the promise was enforceable on the principle stated in *Central London Property Trust Ltd* v *High Trees House Ltd* and *Robertson* v *Minister of Pensions*, because it was an unequivocal acceptance of liability, intended to be binding, intended to be acted on, and, in fact, acted on.

Much as I am inclined to favour the principle of the *High Trees* case, it is important that it should not be stretched too far lest it should be endangered. It does not create new causes of action where none existed before. It only prevents a party from insisting on his strict legal rights when it would be unjust to allow him to do so, having regard to the dealings which have taken place between the parties. That is the way it was put in the case in the House of Lords which first stated the principle – *Hughes* v *Metropolitan Ry Co* – and in the case in the Court of Appeal which enlarged it – *Birmingham and District Land Co* v *London & North Western Ry Co*. It is also implicit in all the modern cases in which the principle has been developed. Sometimes it is a plaintiff who is not allowed to insist on his legal rights. Thus, a creditor is not allowed to enforce a debt which he has deliberately agreed to waive if the debtor has carried on business or in some other way changed his position in reliance on the waiver: *Re Porter (William) & Co, Ltd, Buttery* v *Pickard, Central London Property Trust Ltd* v *High Trees House Ltd, Ledingham* v *Bermejo Estancia Co, Ltd, Agar* v *Bermejo Estancia Co, Ltd*. A landlord who has told his tenant that he can live in his cottage rent free for the rest of his life is not allowed to go back on it if the tenant stays in the house on that footing: *Foster* v *Robinson*. Sometimes it is a defendant who is not allowed to insist on his strict legal rights. His conduct may be such as to debar him from relying on some condition, denying some allegation, or taking some other point in answer to the claim. Thus, a government department, who had accepted a disease as due to war service, were not allowed afterwards to say it was not, when the soldier, in reliance on the assurance, had abstained from getting further evidence about it: *Robertson* v *Minister of Pensions*. A buyer who had waived the contract date for delivery was not allowed afterwards to set up the stipulated time as an answer to the seller: *Charles Rickards, Ltd* v *Oppenheim*. A tenant who had encroached on an adjoining building, asserting that it was comprised in the lease, was not allowed afterwards to say that it was not included in the lease: *J F Perrott & Co, Ltd* v *Cohen*. A tenant who had lived in a house rent free by permission of his landlord, thereby asserting that his original tenancy had ended, was not afterwards allowed to say that his original tenancy continued: *Foster* v *Robinson*. In none of these cases was the defendant sued on the promise, assurance, or assertion as a cause of action in itself. He was sued for some other cause, for example, a pension or a breach of contract, or possession, and the promise, assurance, or assertion only played a supplementary role, though, no doubt, an important one. That is, I think, its true function. It may be part of a cause of action, but not a cause of action in itself. The principle, as I understand it, is that where one party has, by his words or conduct, made to the other a promise or assurance which was intended to affect the legal relations between them and to be acted on accordingly, then, once the other party has taken him at his word and acted on it, the one who gave the promise or assurance cannot afterwards be allowed to revert to the previous legal relations as if no such promise or assurance had been made by him, but he must accept their legal relations subject to the qualification which he himself has so introduced, even though it is not supported in point of law by any consideration, but only by his word.

Seeing that the principle never stands alone as giving a cause of action in itself, it can never do away with the necessity of consideration when that is an essential part of the cause of action. The doctrine of consideration is too firmly fixed to be overthrown by a side-wind. Its ill effects have been largely mitigated of late, but it still remains a cardinal necessity of the formation of a contract, although not of its modification or discharge. I fear that it was my failure to make this clear in *Central London Property Trust Ltd* v *High Trees House Ltd* which misled Byrne, J, in the present case. He held that the wife could sue on the husband's promise as a separate and independent cause of action by itself, although, as he held, there was no consideration for it. That is not correct. The wife can only enforce the promise if there was consideration for it. That is, therefore, the real question in the case: Was there sufficient consideration to support the promise?

If it were suggested that, in return for the husband's promise, the wife expressly or impliedly promised to forbear from applying to the court for maintenance – that is, a promise in return for a promise – there would clearly be no consideration because the wife's promise would not be binding on her and, therefore, would be worth nothing. Notwithstanding her promise, she could always apply to the divorce court for maintenance . . . No agreement by her could take away that right: *Hyman* v *Hyman* . . . There was, however, clearly no promise by the wife, express or implied, to forbear from applying to the court. All that happened was that she did, in fact, forbear – that is, she did an act in return for a promise. Is that sufficient consideration? Unilateral promises of this kind have long been enforced so long as the act or forbearance is done on the faith of the promise and at the request of the promisor, express or implied. The act done is then in itself sufficient consideration for the promise . . . If the findings of Byrne J, are accepted, they are sufficient to bring this principle into play. His finding that the husband's promise was intended to be binding, intended to be acted on, and was, in fact, acted on – although expressed to be a finding on the principle of the *High Trees House* case – is equivalent to a finding that there was consideration within this long-settled rule, because it comes to the same thing expressed in different words: see *Oliver* v *Davis*. My difficulty, however, is to accept the findings of Byrne J, that the promise was "intended to be acted on". I cannot find any evidence of any intention by the husband that the wife should forbear from applying to the court for maintenance, or, in other words, any request by the husband, express or implied, that the wife should so forbear. He left her to apply, if she wished to do so. She did not do so, and I am not surprised, because it is very unlikely that the divorce court would have made any order in her favour, since she had a bigger income than her husband. Her forbearance was not intended by him, nor was it done at his request. It was, therefore, no consideration.

It may be that the wife has suffered some detriment because, after forbearing to apply to the court for seven years . . . Assuming, however, that she has suffered some detriment by her forbearance, nevertheless, as the forbearance was not at the husband's request, it is no consideration . . .'

Must there be a pre-existing contractual relationship?

There need not, according to Lord Denning MR in the case below.

Evenden v Guildford City Association Football Club Ltd

[1975] 3 All ER 269 • Court of Appeal

Lord Denning MR: 'Counsel for the appellant referred us, however, to the second edition of Spencer Bower's book on *Estoppel by Representation* by Sir Alexander Turner, a judge of the New Zealand Court of Appeal. He suggests that promissory estoppel is limited to cases where parties are already bound contractually one to the other. I do not think it is so limited: see *Durham Fancy Goods Ltd* v *Michael Jackson (Fancy Goods) Ltd.* It applies whenever a representation is made, whether of fact or law, present or future, which is intended to be binding, intended to induce a person to act on it and he does act on it . . .'

Browne LJ and Brightman J agreed that the appeal should be allowed but preferred a different approach to that of Lord Denning MR.

The Evenden Case was overruled in *Sec of State for Employment* v *Globe Elastic Trend Co* but there was no argument on the pre-existing contractual relationship.

Webster J discussed the issue in the following case.

Pacol Ltd v *Trade Lines Ltd (The Henrik Sif)*

[1982] 1 Lloyd's Rep 456 • Queen's Bench

Webster J: 'Was there a legal relationship between the plaintiffs and the defendants in this case when the representation was made? In my view, whatever be the precise meaning of the expression "legal relationship", it applies to the relationship between two parties engaged in an exchange of correspondence in which one of them intends the correspondence to have legal effect in circumstances in which the other knows of that first party's intention and makes requests or purports to grant extensions of time which could only be of relevance to the first party if the correspondence between them affected their mutual rights and obligations. In my judgment the correspondence between the parties in this case was such a correspondence so that in my view, for the purposes of this point, a legal relationship existed, or is to be taken for that purpose as having existed, between the parties.

Moreover, in my judgment, the representation on their behalf that Trade Lines were the proper party to be sued on the bills of lading, if in fact they were not a party to the bills of lading, constituted a representation that they would not enforce their strict rights against the other; they were saying, for practical purposes; "We will not take against you a point of fact and law upon which we would otherwise be entitled to rely in this legal dispute between us" . . . If there be any doubt about the question whether the relationship between the parties when the representation was made was a legal relationship for the purposes of the requirements in question (the doubt arising because of the non-existence of any binding legal relationship between the parties) I would respectfully adopt and apply the dictum of Mr Justice Robert Goff in *Amalgamated Investment & Property Co. Ltd.* v *Texas Commerce International Bank Ltd* . . . where, he said:

> "Where, as in cases of promissory estoppel, the estoppel is founded upon a representation by a party that he will not enforce his legal rights, it is of course a prerequisite of the estoppel that there should be an existing legal relationship between the parties. But where, for example, the estoppel relates to the legal effect of a transaction between the parties, it does not necessarily follow that the underlying transaction should constitute a binding legal relationship. In such a case the representation may well, as I have already indicated, give rise to an estoppel although the effect is to enlarge the obligations of the representor; and I can see no reason in principle why this should not be so, even if the underlying transaction would, but for the estoppel, be devoid of legal effect."

There must be an unequivocal representation

Société Italo-Belge Pour Le Commerce et L'industrie v *Palm and Vegetable Oils (Malaysia) Sdn Bhd (The Post Chaser)*

[1982] 1 All ER 19 • Queen's Bench

Palm and Vegetable Oils sold 250 tonnes of Malayan palm oil to Société Italo-Belge who in turn sold it to Conti. Under the contract the sellers were to give notice to the buyers of the ship's sailing 'in writing as soon as possible after vessel's sailing'. In breach of this condition the sellers were a month late in giving notice to the buyers. This breach by the sellers entitled the buyers to reject the oil but they made no protest to the sellers about the lateness of the notice. On the same day (10 January 1975) that the buyers received the notice from the sellers they passed on the notice to Conti. On 20 January the buyers telexed the sellers requesting them to present the documents direct to Conti; this the sellers did. Conti informed the buyers that they were rejecting the documents as being out of time and on 22 January the buyers informed the sellers that they were rejecting the documents as being out of time. The sellers had to sell the oil on the open market and obtained only $US 460 per long ton; they claimed the difference between this price and the contract price of $US 792.50 per long ton.

The issue before the court was whether the buyers had, by their actions, waived their right to reject the documents.

Robert Goff J: 'I turn then to the second question in the case, viz whether the buyers waived their right to reject the sellers' tender of documents. Both counsel for the buyers and counsel for the sellers were in agreement that the applicable principles were those of equitable estoppel.

In considering this question, it was common ground between counsel that I had first to consider whether, on the facts found, there was an unequivocal representation by the buyers that they did not intend to enforce their strict legal right to reject the sellers' tender of documents; though it was recognised, having regard in particular to the speech of Lord Salmon in the *Vanden Avenne* case, that such a representation could be inferred from the buyers' conduct if they behaved or wrote in such a way that reasonable sellers would be led to believe that the buyers were waiving the relevant defect. Counsel for the buyers submitted that, on the facts of the present case, there was no such representation by the buyers. He submitted that the mere fact that the buyers, on receipt of the sellers' declaration of the *Post Chaser* on January 10, made no protest or statement that they were accepting under reserve, could of itself give rise to no representation by them. Next he submitted that the request by the buyers to Kievit [the seller's agent] on January 20, to present the documents to Conti, could likewise give rise to no representation; because this request was made against the background of Conti's message of January 17 to the buyers (who passed it on the sellers on the same day) that Lewis & Peat [Conti's buyer] had "declined tender" but that Conti were "insisting tender be accepted and feel everything should be ok" so that it should reasonably have been understood as no more than a request to Kievit to present the documents to Conti to enable them to see if they could persuade Lewis & Peat to accept them.

Now I accept counsel for the buyers' submission that the mere absence of protest or reserve on the part of the buyers when they received the declaration could not of itself give rise to any unequivocal representation on their part that they waived their rights. Of course, I take into account the board's finding that, having regard to the usual length of strings in the particular trade and the duty on each party to pass on the notice as soon as possible, the buyers should have been on notice that the declaration was late; and I also take account of the board's view that the buyers should have challenged the declaration and reserved their rights. Even so, I do not find it possible to conclude that the mere fact of receiving the declaration without protest or reserve constituted an unequivocal representation by the buyers that they waived their rights.

However the buyers' message of January 20 seems to me to fall into a different category. It was in terms an unqualified request to Kievit to present the documents to the buyers' own sub-buyers, Conti. Furthermore, it was accompanied by the buyers' request to debit them in respect of the difference between their purchase price ($792.50) and their sale price to Conti ($605); which reinforced the impression that this was not intended to be a provisional presentation in the hope that Conti could persuade Lewis & Peat to accept the documents, but was a representation by the buyers that they were prepared to accept the documents, thus waiving any defect in the prior declaration of shipment. In my judgment, this was a sufficiently unequivocal representation for the purposes of waiver.'

The party must rely on the statement

The Post Chaser

[1982] 1 All ER 19 • Queen's Bench

The facts are given in the preceding case extract.

Robert Goff J: 'However, there next arises the question whether there was any sufficient reliance by the sellers on this representation to give rise to an equitable estoppel. Here there arose a difference between counsel for the sellers and counsel for the buyers as to the degree of reliance which is required. It is plain, however, from the speech of Lord Cairns LC in *Hughes* v *Metropolitan Railway Co*, that the representor will not be allowed to enforce his rights "where it would be inequitable having regard to the dealings which have taken place between the parties". Accordingly there must be such action, or inaction, by the representee on the faith of the representation as will render it inequitable to permit the representor to enforce his strict legal rights.

On the findings of fact in the award before the Court, there is no finding of any reliance by the sellers on the buyers' representation, save the fact that the documents covering the parcel on *Post Chaser* were accordingly presented by Kievit (who in this context must be taken to have acted on behalf of the sellers) to Conti. That was done on January 20; and by January 22 the sellers were informed by the buyers that NOGA had rejected the documents, following which the documents were passed back up the string to the sellers. The question therefore arises whether such action constituted sufficient reliance by the sellers on the buyers' representation to render it inequitable for the buyers thereafter to enforce their rights to reject the documents.

The case therefore raises in an acute form the question which was posed by Lord Salmon in the *Vanden Avenne* case, but left unresolved by him, viz whether it is sufficient for the purpose that the representee should simply have conducted his affairs on the basis of the representation, or whether by so doing he must have suffered some form of prejudice which renders it inequitable for the representor to go back on his representation. A simple example of the latter could occur where a seller, relying upon a representation by his buyers, arranged his affairs and tendered documents to the buyer and by so doing missed an opportunity to dispose of the documents elsewhere for a price greater than that available when the buyer later rejected the documents. Such a conclusion could only be based upon finding of fact as to the movement of the market over the relevant period . . .

On the other hand in *WJ Alan & Co Ltd* v *El Nasr Export and Import Co*, Lord Denning, while stating the principle of equitable estoppel in terms that it must be inequitable for the representor to be allowed to go back on his representation, nevertheless considered that it might be sufficient for that purpose that the representee had conducted his affairs on the basis of the representation, and that it was immaterial whether he has suffered any detriment by doing so.

In the present case, the facts are different from those in the *Vanden Avenne* case in that the buyers' representation was made on January 20; it was acted upon on the same day, by Kievit presenting the documents to Conti; and on January 22 the buyers intimated to the sellers the rejection of the documents. In these circumstances, it is impossible to say that the sellers expended any money at all in consequence of the representation (the presentation of the documents having been made by Kievit); and the time involved was so short that it is difficult to attribute any importance to it. It is impossible therefore, in my judgment, to decide the present case by saying that the sellers acted to their detriment in spending time and money on appropriations. On the other hand, the sellers did (through Kievit) present the documents; and it can therefore be said that they did conduct their affairs on the basis of the buyers' representation.

I approach the matter as follows. The fundamental principle is that stated by Lord Cairns, viz that the representor will not be allowed to enforce his rights "where it would be inequitable having regard to the dealings which have thus taken place between the parties". To establish such inequity, it is not necessary to show detriment; indeed, the representee may have benefited from the representation, and yet it may be inequitable, at least without reasonable notice, for the representor to enforce his legal rights. Take the facts of *Central London Property Trust Ltd* v *High Trees House Ltd*, the case in which Lord Justice Denning MR, breathed new life into the doctrine of equitable estoppel. The representation was by a lessor to the effect that he would be content to accept a reduced rent. In such a case, although the lessee has benefited from the reduction in rent, it may well be inequitable for the lessor to insist upon his legal right to the unpaid rent, because the lessee has conducted his affairs on the basis that he would only have to pay rent at the lower rate; and a Court might well think it right to conclude that only after reasonable notice could the lessor return to charging rent at the higher rate specified in the lease. Furthermore it would be open to the Court, in any particular case, to infer from the circumstances of the case that the representee must have conducted his affairs in such a way that it would be inequitable for the representor to enforce his rights, or to do so without reasonable notice. But it does not follow that in every case in which the representee has acted, or failed to act, in reliance on the representation, it will be inequitable for the representor to enforce his rights; for the nature of the action, or inaction, may be insufficient to give rise to the equity, in which event a necessary requirement stated by Lord Cairns for the application of the doctrine would not have been fulfilled.

This, in my judgment, is the principle which I have to apply in the present case. Here, all that happened was that the sellers, through Kievit, presented the documents on the same day as the buyers made their representation; and within two days the documents were rejected. Now on these simple facts, although it is plain that the sellers did actively rely on the buyers' representation, and did conduct their affairs in reliance on it, by presenting the documents, I cannot see anything which would render it inequitable for the buyers thereafter to enforce their legal right to reject the documents. In particular, having regard to the very short time which elapsed between the date of the representation and the date of presentation of the documents on the one hand, and the date of rejection on the other hand, I cannot see that, in the absence of any evidence that the sellers' position had been prejudiced by reason of their action in reliance on the representation, it is possible to infer that they suffered any such prejudice. In these circumstances, a necessary element for the application of the doctrine of equitable estoppel is lacking; and I decide this point in favour of the buyers.'

Must the promisee act to his detriment?
W J Alan & Co Ltd v *El Nasr Export & Import Co*
[1972] 2 All ER 127 • Court of Appeal

W J Alan & Co Ltd sold two lots of 250 tons of coffee to El Nasr Export & Import Co at a price of 262 Kenyan shillings per hundredweight. Payment was to be made by a confirmed letter of credit and the currency to be used for payment was Kenyan shillings. The buyers opened a letter of credit in favour of the sellers but the currency was expressed in sterling not in Kenyan shillings. The sellers did not object to the discrepancy in the letter of credit because at the time it did not matter since one sterling shilling was equal to one Kenyan shilling. The first lot of coffee was shipped in September 1967 and the sellers claimed payment in sterling under the letter of credit. The second lot of coffee was shipped on 16 November and on the 18 November, again the sellers claimed payment in sterling of £57 877 15s 9d under the letter of credit. However, earlier on the day of 18 November before the sellers claimed payment under the letter of credit sterling had been devalued against the Kenyan shilling. This meant that the £57 877 15s 9d was now only worth 987 734.50 Kenya shillings whereas the sellers had expected to receive 1 153 264.9 Kenya shillings. The sellers therefore claimed the difference of 165 530.45 Kenya shillings from the buyers. The buyers refused to pay the extra, stating that they had paid for the coffee in full.

Clearly the sellers had been in breach of contract by opening the letter of credit in sterling rather than in Kenyan shillings but they claimed that the sellers by accepting payment under the letter of credit had waived their right as regards that breach.

Lord Denning MR: Variation or waiver.
'All that I have said so far relates to a "conforming" letter of credit; that is, one which is in accordance with the stipulations in the contract of sale. But in many cases – and our present case is one – the letter of credit does not conform. Then negotiations may take place as a result of which the letter of credit is modified so as to be satisfactory to the seller. Alternatively, the seller may be content to accept the letter of credit as satisfactory, as it is, without modification. Once this happens, then the letter of credit is to be regarded as if it were a conforming letter of credit. It will rank accordingly as conditional payment.

There are two cases on this subject. One is *Panoutsos* v *Raymond Hadley Corpn of New York* . . . The other is *Enrico Furst & Co* v *W E Fischer Ltd*. In each of those cases the letter of credit did not conform to the contract of sale. In each case the non-conformity was in that it was not a confirmed credit. But the sellers took no objection to the letter of credit on that score. On the contrary, they asked for the letter of credit to be extended; and it was extended. In each case the sellers sought afterwards to cancel the contract on the ground that the letter of credit was not in conformity with the contract. In each case the court held that they could not do so.

What is the true basis of those decisions? Is it a variation of the original contract or a waiver of the strict rights thereunder or a promissory estoppel precluding the seller from insisting on his strict rights or what else? In *Enrico Furst* Diplock J said it was a "classic case of waiver". I agree with him. It is an instance of the general principle which was first enunciated by Lord Cairns LC in *Hughes* v *Metropolitan Railway Co* and rescued from oblivion by *Central London Property Trust Ltd* v *High Trees House Ltd*. The principle is much wider than waiver itself; but waiver is a good instance of its application. The principle of waiver is simply this: if one party, by his conduct, leads another to believe that the strict rights arising under the contract will not be insisted on, intending that the other should act on that belief, and he does act on it, then the first party will not afterwards be allowed to insist on the strict legal rights when it would be inequitable for him to do so: see *Plasticmoda Societa Per Azioni* v *Davidsons (Manchester) Ltd* per Denning LJ. There may be no consideration moving from him who benefits by the waiver. There may be no detriment to him by acting on it. There may be nothing in writing. Nevertheless, the one who waives his strict rights cannot afterwards insist on them. His strict rights are at any rate suspended so long as the waiver lasts. He may on occasion be able to revert to his strict legal rights for the future by giving reasonable notice in that behalf, or otherwise making it plain by his conduct that he will thereafter insist on them: see *Tool Metal Manufacturing Co Ltd* v *Tungsten Electric Co Ltd*. But there are cases where no withdrawal is possible. It may be too late to withdraw; or it cannot be done without injustice to the other party. In that event he is bound by his waiver. He will not be allowed to revert to his strict legal rights. He can only enforce them subject to the waiver he has made.

Instances of these principles are ready to hand in contracts for the sale of goods. A seller may, by his conduct, lead the buyer to believe that he is not insisting on the stipulated time for exercising an option: see *Bruner* v *Moore*. A buyer may, by requesting delivery, lead the seller to believe that he is not insisting on the contractual time for delivery: see *Charles Rickards Ltd* v *Oppenheim*. A seller may, by his conduct, lead the buyer to believe that he will not insist on a confirmed letter of credit: see *Plasticmoda*, but will accept an unconfirmed one instead: see *Panoutsos* v *Raymond Hadley Corpn of New York* and *Enrico Furst* v *Fischer*. A seller may accept a less sum for his goods than the contracted price, thus inducing him to believe that he will not enforce payment of the balance: see *Central London Property Trust Ltd* v *High Trees House Ltd* and *D & C Builders Ltd* v *Rees*. In none of these cases does the party who acts on the belief suffer any detriment. It is not a detriment, but a benefit to him, to have an extension of time or to pay less, or as the case may be. Nevertheless, he has conducted his affairs on the basis that he has that benefit and it would not be equitable now to deprive him of it.

The judge rejected this doctrine because, he said, "there is no evidence of the [buyers] having acted to their detriment". I know that it has been suggested in some quarters that there must be detriment. But I can find no support for it in the authorities cited by the judge. The nearest approach to it is the statement of Viscount Simonds in the *Tool Metal* case that the other must have been led "to alter his position", which was adopted by Lord Hodson in *Emmanuel Ayodeji Ajayi* v *R T Briscoe (Nigeria) Ltd*. But that only means that he must have been led to act differently from what he otherwise would have done. And, if you study the cases in which the doctrine has been applied, you will see that all that is required is that the one should have "acted on the belief induced by the other party". That is how Lord Cohen put it in the *Tool Metal* case, and is how I would put it myself . . .

Applying the principle here, it seems to me that the sellers, by their conduct, waived the right to have payment by means of a letter of credit in Kenyan currency and accepted instead a letter of credit in sterling . . .'

Megaw LJ: 'The offer made by the confirming bank . . . did not comply, in several respects, with what the sellers were entitled to require. However, the only non-conforming aspect of the offer which I regard as relevant for the purposes of this appeal is the term of the offer in respect of currency. That, in my view, is not only relevant, it is vital. The confirming bank's offer, made to the sellers with the knowledge of, and on the instructions of, the buyers, was an offer which involved sterling, not merely as the currency of payment, but as the currency of account, in respect of that transaction. The sellers accepted the confirming bank's offer, including its terms as to currency, by submitting invoices and drafts with the form and contents which I have already described.

As I see it, the necessary consequence of that offer and acceptance of a sterling credit is that the original term of the contract of sale as to the money of account was varied from Kenyan currency to sterling. The payment, and the sole payment, stipulated by the contract of sale was by the letter of credit. The buyers, through the confirming bank, had opened a letter of credit which did not conform, because it provided sterling as the money of account. The sellers accepted that offer by making use of the credit to receive payment for a part of the contractual goods. By that acceptance, as the sellers must be deemed to have known, not only did the confirming bank become irrevocably bound by the terms of the offer (and by no other terms), but so also did the buyers become bound. Not only did they incur legal obligations as a result of the sellers' acceptance – for example, an obligation to indemnify the bank – but also the buyers could not thereafter have turned round and said to the sellers (for example, if Kenyan currency had been devalued against sterling) that the bank would thereafter pay less for the contractual goods than the promised sterling payment of £262 per ton. If the buyers could not revert unilaterally to the original currency of account, once they had offered a variation which had been accepted by conduct, neither could the sellers so revert. The contract had been varied in that respect . . .

For the buyers it was submitted further that, if there were not here a variation of the contract, there was at least a waiver, which the sellers could not, or did not properly revoke. I do not propose to go into that submission at any length. On analysis, it covers much the same field as the question of variation. In my view, if there were no variation, the buyers would still be entitled to succeed on the ground of waiver. The relevant principle is, in my opinion, that which was stated by Lord Cairns LC in *Hughes* v *Metropolitan Railway Co.* The acceptance by the sellers of the sterling credit was, as I have said, a once-for-all acceptance. It was not a concession for a specified period of time or one which the sellers could operate as long as they chose and thereafter unilaterally abrogate; any more than the buyers would have been entitled to alter the terms of the credit or to have demanded a refund from the sellers if, after this credit had been partly used, the relative values of the currencies had changed in the opposite way.'

Stephenson LJ: '. . . I would leave open the question whether the action of the other party induced by the party who "waives" his contractual rights can be any alteration of his position, as Lord Denning MR has said, or must, as the judge thought, be an alteration to his detriment, or for the worse, in some sense. In this case the buyers did, I think, contrary to the judge's view, act to their detriment on the sellers' waiver, if that is what it was, and the contract was varied for good consideration, which may be another way of saying the same thing; so that I need not, and do not, express a concluded opinion on that controversial question.'

Does the promisee need to act differently?

Brikom Investments Ltd v Carr

[1979] 2 All ER 753 • Court of Appeal

A landlord made an oral promise to his tenants that if they bought a 99 year lease to their flats he would repair the roofs of the flats at his own expense. The leases provided that the landlord would repair and maintain the main structure of the building, including the roof, and that the tenants would reimburse him for the expenses incurred in such maintenance. After the leases had been signed by the tenants the landlord repaired the roof at a cost of £15 000; he then claimed a contribution from the tenants towards the cost of the repairs. The tenants refused to pay because of the promise that had been made to them by the landlord. The landlord claimed that Carr, one of the tenants, could not rely on his promise since she had not acted on his promise because she would have entered into the lease without any such promise having been made.

Lord Denning MR: 'Counsel for the landlords submitted that Mrs Dufton (now Mrs Carr) could not rely on the principle in the *High Trees* case, because it was essential that she should have acted on the representation; and here she had not acted on it. On her own admission, he said, she would have gone on and taken the lease even if she had not been told about the roof. In all the cases, said counsel for the landlords, the courts had said that the party must have acted on the promise or representation in the sense that he must have altered his position on the faith of it, meaning that he must have been led to act differently from what he would otherwise have done: see *Alan & Co* v *El Nasr Export & Import Co*. This argument gives, I think, too limited a scope to the principle. The principle extends to all cases where one party makes a promise or representation, intending that it should be binding, intending that the other should rely on it, and on which that other does in fact rely, by acting on it, by altering his position on the faith of it, by going ahead with a transaction then under discussion, or by any other way of reliance. It is no answer for the maker to say: "You would have gone on with the transaction anyway". That must be mere speculation. No one can be sure what he would, or would not, have done in a hypothetical state of affairs which never took place: see *Halsbury's Laws of England* [26 Halsbury's Laws]. Once it is shown that a representation was calculated to influence the judgment of a reasonable man, the presumption is that he was so influenced. The judge put it quite simply:

> "Mrs Dufton had an assurance from Mr Stacpoole, before she signed the contract on 19th January 1972, that the landlords would repair the roof, and she was aware of the assurance by Mr Jarvis before she signed the lease. The landlords should not be allowed to go back on these assurances." . . .

But I may say there is another way in which the cases can be put which seems to me equally valid. Although this is called a "promise" or "representation", it seems to me that it might also qualify for what we call a "collateral contract" or "collateral warranty". On the faith of it these tenants signed the leases. After the first day in the county court, Miss Hickey and Mr and Mrs Roddy took from their predecessors an assignment of the benefit of the collateral contract or warranty. That enables them to take advantage of it as against the landlords. This seems to me a roundabout way of reaching the same result as the *High Trees* principle. It is a technical way of overcoming technical difficulties. I prefer the simple way which is the way the judge put it . . .'

Roskill LJ. 'I have found this case more difficult than Lord Denning MR. While I agree this appeal should be dismissed, I wish, with respect, to make plain that my reasons differ from the first fact of those given in his judgment. I do not rest my decision on any question of promissory estoppel; and I do not think it necessary on the facts of this case to investigate the jurisprudential basis of that doctrine in order to arrive at what I conceive to be the right decision. It is necessary to do no more than to apply that which was said by the House of Lords and especially by Lord Cairns LC in *Hughes* v *Metropolitan Railway Co* . . .

I would respectfully add to that that it would be wrong to extend the doctrine of promissory estoppel, whatever its precise limits at the present day, to the extent of abolishing in this back-handed way the doctrine of consideration . . .

It seems to me in the present case that counsel for the tenants' argument (in so far as it rests on promissory estoppel) involves taking that doctrine a great deal further than it has hitherto been taken. With great respect, I would not go as far as Lord Denning MR in saying it is now the law that benefits and burdens arising from a promise made in circumstances such as those presently founded by the judge, to quote the phrase he used a few moments ago, "run down both sides". It seems to me that the problem is far more complex. Accordingly, I do not rest my conclusion that this appeal should be dismissed on any question of promissory estoppel . . .

What then is the defence which it is sought to advance? . . . One . . . was a defence of collateral contract or collateral warranty, as it is sometimes called . . .

The question is whether Mrs Carr has a defence to [the landlords'] claim . . . I entertain no doubt . . . that there was a perfectly clear agreement between the landlords and Mrs Carr . . . that those who took these 99-year leases from the landlords would not be liable for their share of the cost of repairing the roofs if the time ever came to do those repairs.

. . . I do not see how the landlords can escape from the bond of the promises which were given and which seem to me to have been given for perfectly good consideration. This case seems to me to fall within the principle laid down by this court in *De Lassalle* v *Guildford*. I will read a passage from the judgment of A L Smith MR:

> "The next question is: Was the warranty collateral to the lease so that it might be given in evidence and given effect to? It appears to me in this case clear that the lease did not cover the whole ground, and that it did not contain the whole of the contract between the parties . . . The present contract or warranty by the defendant was entirely independent of what was to happen during the tenancy."

When two parties are about to enter into an agreement for a lease, a lease which imposes on the lessee a very burdensome obligation in respect to repairs, I can see no reason why one party cannot say to the other: "In relation to those outstanding matters, whatever may be our legal position under the terms of the lease, we will not as landlords enforce that obligation against you". I see no reason why effect should not be given to such a position. I think the evidence shows that that was the position here; there was a perfectly good collateral contract between these two parties.

But if I am wrong about that, I think in relation to Mrs Carr's case, and this applies equally to the other two cases, there was a plain waiver by the landlords of their right to claim the cost of these repairs from these tenants . . .

I think it necessary to go no further than what Lord Cairns LC said in *Hughes* v *Metropolitan Railway Co* where the matter was put not as one of promissory estoppel but as a matter of contract law or equity (call it which you will) . . .

For my own part, I would respectfully prefer to regard that as an illustration of contractual variation of strict contractual rights. But it could equally well be put as an illustration of equity eliding from the consequences of strict adherence to the letter of the lease.

But, whichever is the right way of putting it, ever since *Hughes* v *Metropolitan Railway Co* through a long line of cases of which there are many examples in the books, one finds that where parties have made a contract which provides one thing and where, by a subsequent course of dealing, the parties have worked that contract out in such a way that one party leads the other to believe that the strict rights under that contract will not be adhered to, the courts will not allow that party who has led the other to think the strict rights will not be adhered, suddenly to seek to enforce those strict rights against him. That seems to me to be precisely what the landlords are trying to do here. Having said . . . 'We will do these repairs at our expense', they then subsequently . . . tried to enforce against one of these lessees . . . the strict letter of the contract. I do not think that the common law or equity will allow them to take that step; and for my part, with profound respect to Lord Denning MR, I do not think it is necessary in order to reach that result to resort to the somewhat uncertain doctrine of promissory estoppel.'

Cumming-Bruce LJ. 'I agree that the appeal should be dismissed for the reasons stated by Roskill LJ. I add a word of my own as the appeals have given rise to a discussion of some controversial problems of legal analysis.

The first appeal is the case of Mrs Carr. Before she signed her contract, to which the draft lease was annexed, she received an assurance that the grantor who became her landlord under the lease would not enforce against her a covenant imposing on her the burden of paying for repairs to the roof of the building in which she was proposing to become his tenant. Relying on that assurance, she entered into an agreement for a lease. Before she signed the lease, the landlords by their agent repeated the assurance. Relying thereon, she entered into the lease. Those facts establish a contract collateral to the agreement for a lease and collateral to the lease itself. Consideration moved from Mrs Carr because she entered into the agreement for a lease and then made the deed in reliance on the landlords' assurance. Looking back on the transaction she said in evidence that she would have entered into the lease anyway; nonetheless on her evidence the inducement of the landlords' promise was one of the factors that she relied on. That is enough without giving rise to the necessity of assessing the weight or quantum of each of the factors that between them induced her to agree to enter into the lease. After she had taken possession under the lease she was minded to take action to make the landlords repair the roof as was their obligation under the lease. She stayed her hand because the landlords were still assuring all the tenants that they were going to pay for the roof repairs themselves. A long time afterwards they changed their minds about that, apparently out of resentment over the line taken by some tenants in connection with a planning application. The principle declared in *Hughes* v *Metropolitan Railway* is in point. If I am wrong in holding that she can rely on the contract collateral to her lease, she then acted to her detriment in reliance on the landlords' promise that they would not enforce a covenant in the lease, and equity will not allow them to enforce their legal right.'

Is promissory estoppel suspensory?

Tool Metal Manufacturing Co Ltd v *Tungsten Electric Co Ltd*

[1955] 2 All ER 657 • House of Lords

By a contract dated 2 April 1938 the patent holder, Tool Metal Manufacturing Co Ltd (TMMC), granted Tungsten Electric Co Ltd (TECO) a licence to manufacture a certain quota of metal alloys. TECO paid a royalty to TMMC on the goods they manufactured under licence. A term of the contract provided that if in any month

TECO exceeded their quota they would pay 'compensation' to TMMC. After the outbreak of war in 1939 TMMC voluntarily agreed to forgo the compensation anticipating that a new agreement would be entered into after the war. In July 1945, no new agreement having been entered into, TECO sued TMMC for fraudulent misrepresentation and breach of contract. TMMC replied by counterclaiming compensation payments from 1 June 1945. The Court of Appeal held that the counterclaim failed because TMMC were, according to the principle in *Hughes* v *Metropolitan Ry Co*, estopped from reverting to their strict legal position without giving reasonable notice to TECO. In this present action in 1950 TMMC claimed compensation from 1 January 1947.

The issue before the court was whether the counterclaim in 1945 amounted to sufficient notice to TECO that TMMC was going to revert to their strict legal position under the original contract.

Viscount Simonds: '... [TECO] pleaded that the delivery of the counterclaim in the first action did not operate as notice to terminate the equitable arrangement which, as was held in that action, existed at any rate until such delivery, and that it was a condition of its termination that the notice determining it (a) should be unequivocal, and (b) should specify the date of termination, and, further, that that date should give them a reasonable time to adjust their business affairs to meet the altered circumstances. To this, in effect, TMMC replied that the delivery of the counterclaim was a sufficient intimation of their intention to reassert their legal rights and that, that intimation having been given, equity demanded nothing more than that a reasonable time should be allowed before they sought to enforce them. And they further said (nor was this denied by TECO) that, on this footing, a reasonable time was given, since the counterclaim was delivered in March, 1946, and compensation claimed from January, 1947.

... For my part, I have, after some hesitation, formed the opinion that, as soon as the counterclaim was delivered, TECO must be taken to know that the suspensory period was at an end and were bound to put their house in order ... Equity demands that all the circumstances of the case should be regarded, and I think that the fair and reasonable view is that TECO could not, after they had received the counterclaim, regard themselves as entitled to further indulgence.

It was, however, urged on behalf of TECO that, even if the counterclaim could otherwise be regarded as a sufficient notice that the equitable arrangement was at an end, yet it was defective in that it did not name a certain future date at which it was to take effect. To this the reply was made that equity did not require a future date to be named in the notice, but that what it did require was that a reasonable time should be allowed to elapse before it was sought to enforce it ... Equity is not held in a strait-jacket. There is no universal rule that an equitable arrangement must always be determined in one way. It may, in some cases, be right and fair that a dated notice should be given. But in this case, what was the position in January, 1947, which I take to be the critical date? Then for nine months TECO must, in my opinion, be taken to have been aware that TMMC proposed to stand on their legal rights. It is not denied that those nine months gave them ample time to readjust their position. I cannot regard it as a requirement of equity that, in such circumstances, they should have been expressly notified in March, 1946, that they would have nine months and no more to take such steps as the altered circumstances required ...'

Lord Tucker: '... The sole question, therefore, before the courts on this issue in the present action has been throughout: Was the counterclaim in the first action a sufficient intimation to terminate the period of suspension which has been found to exist? . . .

My Lords, it is difficult to keep these two submissions entirely separate as they both involve consideration of what is necessary to terminate a period of suspension and restore the parties to their previous position. It has been said more than once that every case involving the application of this equitable doctrine must depend on its own particular circumstances. It is, of course, clear, as Pearson, J, pointed out, that there are some cases where the period of suspension clearly terminates on the happening of a certain event, or the cessation of a previously existing state of affairs, or on the lapse of a reasonable period thereafter. In such cases, no intimation or notice of any kind may be necessary. But in other cases, where there is nothing to fix the end of the period which may be dependent on the will of the person who has given or made the concession, equity will, no doubt, require some notice or intimation together with a reasonable period for re-adjustment before the grantor is allowed to enforce his strict rights. No authority has been cited which binds your Lordships to hold that, in all such cases, the notice must take any particular form or specify a date for the termination of the suspensory period. This is not surprising having regard to the infinite variety of circumstances which may give rise to this principle which was stated in broad terms and must now be regarded as of general application. It should, I think, be applied with great caution to purely creditor and debtor relationships which involve no question of forfeiture or cancellation, and it would be unfortunate if the law were to introduce into this field technical requirements with regard to notice and the like which might tend to penalise or discourage the making of reasonable concessions.

My Lords, in the present case I can find nothing which persuades me that equity could require anything further than that which is contained in the counterclaim in the first action. It is true that it does not purport to be putting an end to an existing "agreement" for a temporary suspension. No such agreement had been pleaded. It does, however, contain a clear intimation of a reversal by TMMC of their previous attitude with regard to the payment of compensation and of their intention to enforce compliance with cl. 5 of the agreement and for an account thereunder. It does not, I think, lie in the mouth of TECO . . . now to complain that the notice should have specified a named future date on which the suspensory period was to come to an end.'

Ajayi v R T Briscoe (Nigeria) Ltd
[1964] 3 All ER 556 • Privy Council

Ajayi sued Briscoe for the balance of the purchase price of eleven Seddon Tipper lorries which Briscoe had purchased from Ajayi on hire-purchase. Briscoe's defence was based on promissory estoppel, claiming that Ajayi was estopped from claiming the money owed because Ajayi had written to Briscoe stating '. . . we confirm herewith that we are agreeable to your withholding instalments due on the Seddon Tippers as long as they are withdrawn from active service'. Briscoe argued that since the lorries were still off the road Ajayi could not go back on the promise they had made in their letter.

Lord Hodson: '. . . The principle, which has been described as quasi estoppel and perhaps more aptly as promissory estoppel, is that when one party to a contract in the absence of fresh consideration agrees not to enforce his rights an equity will be raised in favour of the other party. This equity is, however, subject to the qualification (a) that the other party has altered his position, (b) that the promisor can resile from his promise on giving reasonable notice, which need not be a formal notice, giving the promisee a reasonable opportunity of resuming his position, (c) the promise only becomes final and irrevocable if the promisee cannot resume his position.

The difficulty of this case stems in great part from the fact that the equitable defence was never expressly pleaded and no part of the argument at the trial appears to have been directed thereto . . .

. . . The defence was first put forward effectively in the Federal Supreme Court and further elaborated before their lordships on inadequate material. It would not be just to the owners to remit the matter either for a new trial or for a decision to be given at this late stage on facts which have not been expressly found . . .

The question remains whether the hire-purchaser has made good the defence. In their lordships' opinion he has not succeeded in so doing. The hire-purchaser did not alter his position by not putting forward counter proposals after receipt of the letter of July 22, 1957. There is no evidence to support the contention that he did so by organising his business in a different way having regard to the fact that the lorries were out of service, and it cannot be inferred from the evidence given that such reorganisation was necessary. It can be said that the lorries were laid up and there is evidence to support the view that they were laid up after the receipt of the letter of July 22, 1957. Nevertheless, in view of the evidence given by the owners' witness . . . it cannot be said to have been proved that the lorries were not made available for the hire-purchaser after they had been repaired.

Compare the following case with *Alan Ltd* v *El Nasr Co* above.

Woodhouse AC Israel Cocoa Ltd SA v *Nigerian Produce Marketing Co Ltd*
[1972] 2 All ER 271 • House of Lords

Woodhouse and NPM had, until 1966, conducted business in Nigerian pounds. However, on 30 September NPM informed Woodhouse that 'payment can be made in Sterling and in Lagos . . . If you are agreeable to these conditions, you are at liberty to make payment in Sterling not only with contracts already entered into but also with future contracts'. On 18 November the pound sterling was devalued by 15% against the Nigerian pound. Woodhouse claimed that because of NPM's letter of 30 September it could pay for its contracts made before 18 November in pounds sterling (which would have meant that NPM would have received 14% less in £N).

The issue before the court was firstly, whether the letter amounted to a variation of the original contracts; Woodhouse claimed that they had furnished consideration for the promise contained in the letter of 30 September in that they had acted to their detriment by not 'hedging' the currencies or insuring against the possible devaluation; or, secondly the promise contained in the letter of 30 September estopped NPM from going back on their promise without giving sufficient notice of their intention to do so.

Lord Hailsham of St Marylebone LC: 'There is no dispute . . . that the purchase price in all the contracts was expressed to be in Nigerian pounds payable in cash in Lagos for 100 per cent of the invoice amount against presentation and in exchange for shipping documents . . . Thus, if no change had been made in the contractual relationship between the parties after the conclusion of the contracts, the respondents' claim to be paid in a sum to be measured in Nigerian currency would have been unassailable.

. . . [Woodhouse] contended . . . that the effect of [the letter of 30 September] was such as to lead them reasonably to suppose that the purchase price of these contracts was to be measured as if it had been expressed in sterling of the same nominal amount, and not, as was in fact the case, in Nigerian pounds. They claimed that, relying on this construction, they had acted to their detriment, since, believing as they did, that they had nothing any longer to fear from devaluation, they did not, as they would otherwise have done, make an attempt, in the words of the award "to hedge" their contractual commitments or to "attempt to obtain insurance cover so as to protect [them] against their exchange exposure under their contracts with the Respondents" . . . Before the umpire, the appellants argued (i) that the exchange of correspondence amounted to a variation in the contractual terms, and (ii) that in any event the respondents were precluded by way of estoppel from disavowing an obligation to accept payment as if the price had been expressed in sterling of the same nominal amount.

. . . In my view, the letters do not bear the construction sought to be put on them by the appellants. They refer to payment of the purchase price in sterling and not measurement of the purchase price in sterling . . . I do not myself think there was ambiguity. But, on the assumption that there was, I agree with the Court of Appeal, that such cases as *Low* v *Bouverie* and *Canada and Dominion Sugar Co Ltd* v *Canadian National (West Indies) Steamships Ltd* are authority for the proposition that, to give rise to an estoppel, representations should be clear and unequivocal, and that, if a representation is not made in such a form as to comply with this requirement, it normally matters not that the representee should have misconstrued it and relied on it . . .

Counsel for the appellants was asked whether he knew of any case in which an ambiguous statement had ever formed the basis of a purely promissory estoppel, as contended for here, as distinct from estoppel of a more familiar type based on factual misrepresentation. He candidly replied that he did not. I do not find this surprising, since it would really be an astonishing thing if, in the case of a genuine misunderstanding as to the meaning of an offer, the offeree could obtain by means of the doctrine of promissory estoppel something that he must fail to obtain under the conventional law of contract. I share the feeling of incredulity expressed by Lord Denning MR in the course of his judgment when he said:

"If the judge be right, it leads to this extraordinary consequence: a letter which is not sufficient to vary a contract is, nevertheless, sufficient to work an estoppel, which will have the same effect as a *variation*."

There seem to me to be so many and such conclusive reasons for dismissing this appeal that it may be thought a work of supererogation to add yet another. But basically I feel convinced that there was never here any real room for the doctrine of estoppel at all. If the exchange letter was not variation, I believe it was nothing. The appellants asked for a variation in the mode of discharge of a contract of sale. If the proposal meant what they claimed, and was accepted and acted on, I venture to think that the respondents would have been bound by their acceptance at least until they gave reasonable notice to terminate, and I imagine that a modern court would have found no difficulty in discovering consideration for such a promise. Businessmen know their own business best even when they appear to grant an indulgence, and in the present case I do not think that there would have been insuperable difficulty in spelling out consideration from the earlier correspondence. If, however, the two letters were insufficiently unambiguous and precise to form the basis, if accepted, for a variation in the contract I do not think their combined effect is sufficiently unambiguous or precise to form the basis of an estoppel which would produce the result of reducing the purchase price by no less than 14 per cent against a vendor who had never consciously agreed to the proposition.

I desire to add that the time may soon come when the whole sequence of cases based on promissory estoppel since the war, beginning with *Central London Property Trust Ltd* v *High Trees House Ltd*, may need to be reviewed and reduced to a coherent body of doctrine by the courts. I do not mean to say that any are to be regarded with suspicion. But, as is common with an expanding doctrine, they do raise problems of coherent exposition which have never been systematically explored. However this may be, we are not in a position to carry out this exploration here and in the present proceedings. It is sufficient to say here that, for the reasons I have given above, I would dismiss this appeal with costs.'

Lord Pearson: 'My Lords, I have had the advantage of reading in advance the opinion of my noble and learned friend, Lord Hailsham of St Marylebone LC, and I agree with it, and wish to add only a few observations.

Although commercial men may not be familiar with the terminology of the distinction between "money of account" and "money of payment", they must be familiar with the difference between "price" and "terms of payment", which are usual headings in a sale of goods contract.

In this case, as I understand the history, the price payable for the cocoa to be delivered under any of the contracts concerned remained unaltered, being a specified number of Nigerian pounds. The price was never varied. The only alteration was in respect of the terms of payment. Even in that respect I think there was no variation of the contract but only an indulgence or concession, whereby the buyers were at liberty to pay the price in sterling currency. But that did not naturally imply any alteration of the price. Liberty to pay the price in sterling currency would naturally mean liberty to pay a sum of sterling currency equivalent to the number of Nigerian pounds which constituted the price.'

It must be inequitable for the creditor to go back on his promise

D & C Builders Ltd v Rees

[1965] 3 All ER 837 • Court of Appeal

The facts are stated in the judgment of Lord Denning.

Lord Denning MR: 'D & C Builders, Ltd ("the plaintiffs") are a little company. "D" stands for Mr Donaldson, a decorator, "C" for Mr Casey, a plumber. They are jobbing builders. The defendant, Mr Rees, has a shop where he sells builders' materials.

In the spring of 1964 the defendant employed the plaintiffs to do work at his premises, 218, Brick Lane. The plaintiffs did the work and rendered accounts in May and June, which came to £746 13s 1d altogether. The defendant paid £250 on account. In addition the plaintiffs made an allowance of £14 off the bill. So in July, 1964, there was owing to the plaintiffs the sum of £482 13s 1d. At this stage there was no dispute as to the work done. But the defendant did not pay.

On Aug 31, 1964, the plaintiffs wrote asking the defendant to pay the remainder of the bill. He did not reply. On Oct 19, 1964, they wrote again, pointing out that the "outstanding account of £480 is well overdue". Still the defendant did not reply. He did not write or telephone for more than three weeks. Then on Friday, Nov 13, 1964, the defendant was ill with influenza. His wife telephoned the plaintiffs. She spoke to Mr Casey. She began to make complaints about the work: and then said: "My husband will offer you £300 in settlement. That is all you'll get. It is to be in satisfaction." Mr Casey said he would have to discuss it with Mr Donaldson. The two of them talked it over. Their company was in desperate financial straits. If they did not have the £300, they would be in a state of bankruptcy. So they decided to accept the £300 and see what they could do about the rest afterwards. Thereupon Mr Donaldson telephoned to the defendant's wife. He said to her: "£300 will not even clear our commitments on the job. We will accept £300 and give you a year to find the balance." She said: "No, we will never have enough money to pay the balance. £300 is better than nothing." He said: "We have no choice but to accept." She said: "Would you like the money by cash or by cheque. If it is cash, you can have it on Monday. If by cheque, you can have it tomorrow (Saturday)." On Saturday, Nov 14, 1964, Mr Casey went to collect the money. He took with him a receipt prepared on the company's paper with the simple words: "Received the sum of £300 from Mr Rees." She gave him a cheque for £300 and asked for a receipt. She insisted that the words "in completion of the account" be added. Mr Casey did as she asked. He added the words to the receipt. So she had the clean receipt: "Received the sum of £300 from Mr Rees in completion of the account. Paid, Mr Casey". Mr Casey gave in evidence his reason for giving it: "If I did not have the £300 the company would have gone bankrupt. The only reason we took it was to save the company. She knew the position we were in."

The plaintiffs were so worried about their position that they went to their solicitors. Within a few days, on Nov 23, 1964, the solicitors wrote complaining that the defendant had "extricated a receipt of some sort or other" from them. They said that they were treating the £300 as a payment on account. On Nov 28, 1964, the defendant replied alleging bad workmanship. He also set up the receipt which Mr Casey gave to his wife, adding: "I assure you she had no gun on her". The plaintiffs brought this action for the balance. The defendant set up a defence of bad workmanship and also that there was a binding settlement. The question of settlement was tried as a preliminary issue. The judge made these findings:

> "I concluded that by the middle of August the sum due to the plaintiffs was ascertained and not then in dispute. I also concluded that there was no consideration to support the agreement of Nov 13 and 14. It was a case of agreeing to take a lesser sum, when a larger sum was already due to the plaintiffs. It was not a case of agreeing to take a cheque for a smaller account instead of receiving cash for a larger account. The payment by cheque was an incidental arrangement."

The judge decided, therefore, the preliminary issue in favour of the plaintiffs. The defendant appeals to this court. He says that there was here an accord and satisfaction – an accord when the plaintiffs agreed, however reluctantly, to accept £300 in settlement of the account – and satisfaction when they accepted the cheque for £300 and it was duly honoured. The defendant relies on the cases of *Sibree* v *Tripp* and *Goddard* v *O'Brien*, as authorities in his favour.

This case is of some consequence: for it is a daily occurrence that a merchant or tradesman, who is owed a sum of money, is asked to take less. The debtor says he is in difficulties. He offers a lesser sum in settlement, cash down. He says he cannot pay more. The creditor is considerate. He accepts the proffered sum and forgives him the rest of the debt. The question arises: is the settlement binding on the creditor? The answer is that, in point of law, the creditor is not bound by the settlement. He can the next day sue the debtor for the balance, and get judgment. The law was so stated in 1602 by Lord Coke in *Pinnel's Case* and accepted in 1884 by the House of Lords in *Foakes* v *Beer*.

Now, suppose that the debtor, instead of paying the lesser sum in cash, pays it by cheque. He makes out a cheque for the amount. The creditor accepts the cheque and cashes it. Is the position any different? I think not. No sensible distinction can be taken between payment of a lesser sum by cash and payment of it by cheque. The cheque, when given, is conditional payment. When honoured, it is actual payment. It is then just the same as cash. If a creditor is not bound when he receives payment by cash, he should not be bound when he receives payment by cheque. This view is supported by the leading case of *Cumber* v *Wane*, which has suffered many vicissitudes but was, I think, rightly decided in point of law.

The case of *Sibree* v *Tripp* is easily distinguishable. There the plaintiffs brought an action for £500. It was settled by the defendant giving three promissory notes amounting in all to £250. Those promissory notes were given on a new contract, in substitution for the debt sued for, and not as conditional payment. The plaintiff's only remedy thenceforward was on the notes and not on the debt. The case of *Goddard* v *O'Brien* is not so easily distinguishable. There a creditor was owed £125 for some slates. He met the debtor and agreed to accept £100 in discharge of it. The debtor gave a cheque for £100. The creditor gave a written receipt "in settlement on the said cheque being honoured". The cheque was clearly given by way of conditional payment. It was honoured. The creditor sued the debtor for the balance of £25. He lost, because the £100 was paid by cheque and not by cash. The decision was criticised by Fletcher Moulton, LJ, in *Hirachand Punamchand* v *Temple*, and by the editors of *Smith's Leading Cases*. It was, I think, wrongly decided. In point of law payment of a lesser sum, whether by cash or by cheque, is no discharge of a greater sum.

This doctrine of the common law has come under heavy fire. It was ridiculed by Sir George Jessel MR, in *Couldery* v *Bartrum*. It was held to be mistaken by Lord Blackburn in *Foakes* v *Beer*. It was condemned by the Law Revision Committee in their Sixth Interim Report (Cmnd 5449). But a remedy has been found. The harshness of the common law has been relieved. Equity has stretched out a merciful hand to help the debtor. The courts have invoked the broad principle stated by Lord Cairns LC, in *Hughes* v *Metropolitan Ry Co*:

> ". . . it is the first principle upon which all courts of equity proceed if parties, who have entered into definite and distinct terms involving certain legal results . . . afterwards by their own act, or with their own consent, enter upon a course of negotiation which has the effect of leading one of the parties to suppose that *the strict rights arising under the contract will not be enforced*, or will be kept in suspense, or held in abeyance, that the person who otherwise might have enforced those rights *will not be allowed to enforce them where it would be inequitable, having regard to the dealings which have taken place between the parties*."

It is worth noticing that the principle may be applied, not only so as to suspend strict legal rights, but also as to preclude the enforcement of them.

This principle has been applied to cases where a creditor agrees to accept a lesser sum in discharge of a greater. So much so that we can now say that, when a creditor and a debtor enter on a course of negotiation, which leads the debtor to suppose that, on payment of the lesser sum, the creditor will not enforce payment of the balance, and on the faith thereof the debtor pays the lesser sum and the creditor accepts it as satisfaction: then the creditor will not be allowed to enforce payment of the balance when it would be inequitable to do so. This was well illustrated during the last war. Tenants went away to escape the bombs and left their houses unoccupied. The landlords accepted a reduced rent for the time they were empty. It was held that the landlords could not afterwards turn round and sue for the balance: see *Central London Property Trust Ltd* v *High Trees House Ltd*. This caused at the time some eyebrows to be raised in high places. But they have been lowered since. The solution was so obviously just that no-one could well gainsay it.

In applying this principle, however, we must note the qualification. The creditor is barred from his legal rights only when it would be inequitable for him to insist on them.

Where there has been a true accord, under which the creditor voluntarily agrees to accept a lesser sum in satisfaction, and the debtor acts on that accord by paying the lesser sum and the creditor accepts it, then it is inequitable for the creditor afterwards to insist on the balance. But he is not bound unless there has been truly an accord between them.

In the present case, on the facts as found by the judge, it seems to me that there was no true accord. The debtor's wife held the creditor to ransom. The creditor was in need of money to meet his own commitments, and she knew it. When the creditor asked for payment of the £480 due to him, she said to him in effect: "We cannot pay you the £480. But we will pay you £300 if you will accept it in settlement. If you do not accept it on those terms, you will get nothing. £300 is better than nothing." She had no right to say any such thing. She could properly have said: "We cannot pay you more than £300. Please accept it on account." But she had no right to insist on his taking it in settlement. When she said: "We will pay you nothing unless you accept £300 in settlement", she was putting undue pressure on the creditor. She was making a threat to break the contract (by paying nothing) and she was doing it so as to compel the creditor to do what he was unwilling to do (to accept £300 in settlement): and she succeeded. He complied with her demand. That was on recent authority a case of intimidation (see *Rookes* v *Barnard* and *J T Stratford & Son, Ltd* v *Lindley*). In these circumstances there was no true accord so as to found a defence of accord and satisfaction (see *Day* v *McLea*). There is also no equity in the defendant to warrant any departure from the due course of law. No person can insist on a settlement procured by intimidation.

In my opinion there is no reason in law or equity why the creditor should not enforce the full amount of the debt due to him. I would, therefore, dismiss this appeal.

See also *The Post Chaser* (p 135) where Robert Goff J held, that in the particular circumstances of the case, it was not inequitable for the buyers to go back on their word.

WAIVER OF BREACH OF CONTRACT

The term waiver is confusingly used in different contexts. Waiver normally arises where one of the parties has failed to perform his part of the contract, for example where a seller of goods fails to deliver goods in time. Where this occurs the innocent party is entitled to sue the other party for breach of contract (this is discussed fully later in the book). However, the innocent party will often not insist on his strict legal rights, for example by allowing the seller of the goods to deliver the goods at a later time. The problem is what if the innocent party changes his mind and insists on the contract being performed as per the original contract? Again the problem is one of trying to find fresh consideration furnished by both parties. The innocent party's fresh consideration is his promise not to insist on his strict legal rights but where is the contract breaker's fresh consideration? The situation is analogous to the creditor/debtor situation examined above. In the situation of a broken contract the courts tend to use the language of 'waiver' rather than of 'estoppel' but it is doubtful whether waiver is really anything different from promissory estoppel.

Charles Rickards Ltd v *Oppenheim*
[1950] 1 All ER 420 • Court of Appeal

Rickards agreed to build a car for Oppenheim within seven months, time being of the essence of the contract. The seven months began to run from 20 August 1947. The car was not ready by 20 March 1948 (the last date for delivery). Oppenheim did not cancel the contract as he was entitled to do so but instead he waived his right as regards the stipulation of time by asking for delivery in time for Ascot. The car was not ready for Ascot and on 29 June Oppenheim wrote to Rickards saying

'Further to my conversation with Mr Musk today, I regret that I shall be unable, unless my plans change, to accept delivery of the Rolls you are making for me after 25 July. For six months I have had a reservation to take a car abroad on 3 August for my holiday and it would appear to me to be impossible for me to alter this date. I shall therefore have to buy another car.'

The car was still not ready for that date so Oppenheim bought another car.

The issue before the Court of Appeal was whether Oppenheim, having waived his original right as regards the stipulation of time, could go back on that waiver and once again make time the essence of the contract.

Denning LJ: '. . . If the defendant, as he did, led the plaintiffs to believe that he would not insist on the stipulation as to time, and that, if they carried out the work, he would accept it, and they did it, he could not afterwards set up the stipulation in regard to time against them. Whether it be called waiver or forbearance on his part, or an agreed variation or substituted performance, does not matter. It is a kind of estoppel. By his conduct he made a promise not to insist on his strict legal rights. That promise was intended to be binding, intended to be acted on, and was, in fact, acted on. He cannot afterwards go back on it. That, I think, follows from *Panoutsos* v *Raymond Hadley Corpn of New York*, a decision of this court, and it was also anticipated in *Bruner* v *Moore*. It is a particular application of the principle which I endeavoured to state in *Central London Property Trust Ltd* v *High Trees House Ltd*.

Therefore, if the matter stopped there, the plaintiffs could have said that, notwithstanding that more than seven months had elapsed, the defendant was bound to accept, but the matter does not stop there, because delivery was not given in compliance with the requests of the defendant. Time and time again the defendant pressed for delivery, time and time again he was assured that he would have early delivery, but he never got satisfaction, and eventually at the end of June he gave notice saying that, unless the car was delivered by July 25, he would not accept it. The question thus arises whether he was entitled to give such a notice, making time of the essence, and that is the question which counsel for the plaintiffs has argued before us . . . [T]he defendant was entitled to give a notice bringing the matter to a head. It would be most unreasonable if, having been lenient and having waived the initial expressed time, he should thereby have prevented himself from ever thereafter insisting on reasonably quick delivery. In my judgment, he was entitled to give a reasonable notice making time of the essence of the matter. Adequate protection to the suppliers is given by the requirement that the notice should be reasonable.

The next question, therefore, is: Was this a reasonable notice? Counsel for the plaintiffs argued that it was not. He said that a reasonable notice must give sufficient time for the work then outstanding to be completed, and that, on the evidence in this case, four weeks was not a reasonable time because it would, and did, in fact, require three and a half months to complete it. In my opinion, however, the words of Lord Parker of Waddington in *Stickney* v *Keeble* apply to such a case as the present, just as much as they do to a contract for the sale of land. Lord Parker said:

"In considering whether the time so limited is a reasonable time the court will consider all the circumstances of the case. No doubt what remains to be done at the date of the notice is of importance, but it is by no means the only relevant fact. The fact that the purchaser has continually been pressing for completion, or has before given similar notices which he has waived, or that it is specially important to him to obtain early completion, are equally relevant facts . . . "

To that statement I would add, in the present case, the fact that the original contract made time of the essence. In this case, not only did the defendant press continually for delivery, not only was he given promises of speedy delivery, but, on the very day before he gave the notice, he was told by the sub-contractors' manager, who was in charge of the work, that it would be ready within two weeks. He then gave a four weeks' notice. The judge found that it was a reasonable notice and, in my judgment, there is no ground on which this court could in any way differ from that finding. The reasonableness of the notice must, of course, be judged at the time at which it is given. It cannot be held to be a bad notice because, after it is given, the suppliers find themselves in unanticipated difficulties in making delivery.

The notice of June 29, 1948, was, therefore, a perfectly good notice so as to make time of the essence of the contract . . .

The case, therefore, comes down to this. There was a contract by the plaintiffs to supply and fix a body on the chassis within six or seven months. They did not do it. The defendant waived that stipulation. For three months after the time had expired he pressed them for delivery, asking for it first for Ascot and then for his holiday abroad. But still they did not deliver it. Eventually at the end of June, being tired of waiting any longer, he gave a four weeks' notice and said: "At all events, if you do not supply it at the end of four weeks I must cancel", and he did cancel. I see no injustice to the plaintiffs in saying that that was a reasonable notice. Having originally stipulated for six to seven months, having waited eleven months, and still not getting delivery, the defendant was entitled to cancel the contract.'

SUMMARY

You should now be able to:

- Understand the difference between variation of contracts and rescission of contracts.
- Understand how a contract that is still to be performed can be brought to an end, without it being performed, by the agreement of the parties.
- Understand how the terms of a contract may be varied by *waiver*.
- Understand and apply the rule in *Pinnel's Case*.
- Understand and apply promissory estoppel.
- Understand and recognise the features of promissory estoppel.
- Appreciate the difference between promissory estoppel and waiver of breach of contract.

If you have not mastered the above points you should go through this section again.

7 Intention to create legal relations

INTENTION TO CREATE LEGAL RELATIONS

The general rule is that an agreement which is supported by consideration is not binding as a contract if it was made without any intention of creating legal relations.

Again we are back to *intention*. If the parties *did not intend* that there should be a legal binding agreement between them, then although there may well have been an offer, acceptance and consideration, there will be no contract.

SOCIAL/DOMESTIC AGREEMENTS AND COMMERCIAL AGREEMENTS

Generally speaking we distinguish between *social/domestic* agreements and *commercial* agreements.

There are two presumptions: first, social/domestic agreements are not intended to be legally binding; secondly, commercial agreements are intended to be legally binding. Both these presumptions are rebuttable: in other words although the presumption is that social/domestic agreements are not intended to be legally binding it is possible to show that the parties did intend, in a particular case, to make the agreement legally binding. Similarly, although the presumption is that commercial agreements are intended to be legally binding it is possible to show that the parties did intend, in a particular case, not to make the agreement legally binding.

Social and domestic agreements

Most social and domestic agreements do not amount to contracts because they are not intended to be legally binding.

Husband and wife

Since such a relationship is a domestic one the general rule applies and therefore agreements between husband and wife are not intended to be legally binding.

Balfour v Balfour
[1919] 2 KB 571 • Court of Appeal

In November 1915 the Balfours returned from Ceylon on leave. When they were about to return to Ceylon Mrs Balfour decided to stay in England on her doctor's advice. As Mr Balfour was about to sail back to Ceylon he verbally promised to pay his wife £30 per month in maintenance until he returned. In July 1918 Mrs Balfour was divorced from her husband. Mrs Balfour then sued her husband on his promise to pay the £30 per month maintenance. The issue before the court was whether there was a contract between the Balfours.

Atkin LJ: 'The defence of this action on the alleged contract is that the defendant, the husband, entered into no contract with his wife, and for the determination of that it is necessary to remember that there are agreements between parties which do not result in contracts within the meaning of that term in our law. The ordinary example is where two parties agree to take a walk together, or where there is an offer and an acceptance of hospitality. Nobody would suggest in ordinary circumstances that those agreements result in what we know as a contract, and one of the most usual forms of agreement which does not constitute a contract appears to me to be the arrangements which are made between husband and wife. It is quite common, and it is the natural and inevitable result of the relationship of husband and wife, that the two spouses should make arrangements between themselves – agreements such as are in dispute in this action – agreements for allowances, by which the husband agrees that he will pay to his wife a certain sum of money, per week, or per month, or per year, to cover either her own expenses or the necessary expenses of the household and of the children of the marriage, and in which the wife promises either expressly or impliedly to apply the allowance for the purpose for which it is given. To my mind those agreements, or many of them, do not result in contracts at all, and they do not result in contracts even though there may be what as between other parties would constitute consideration for the agreement. The consideration, as we know, may consist either in some right, interest, profit or benefit accruing to one party, or some forbearance, detriment, loss or responsibility given, suffered or undertaken by the other. That is a well-known definition, and it constantly happens, I think, that such arrangements made between husband and wife are arrangements in which there are mutual promises, or in which there is consideration in form within the definition that I have mentioned. Nevertheless they are not contracts, and they are not contracts because the parties did not intend that they should be attended by legal consequences. To my mind it would be of the worst possible example to hold that agreements such as this resulted in legal obligations which could be enforced in the Courts. It would mean this, that when the husband makes his wife a promise to give her an allowance of 30s or £2 a week, whatever he can afford to give her, for the maintenance of the household and children, and she promises so to apply it, not only could she sue him for his failure in any week to supply the allowance, but he could sue her for non-performance of the obligation, express or implied, which she had undertaken upon her part. All I can say is that the small Courts of this country would have to be multiplied one hundredfold if these arrangements were held to result in legal obligations. They are not sued upon, not because the parties are reluctant to enforce their legal rights when the agreement is broken, but because the parties, in the inception of the arrangements, never intended that they should be sued upon. Agreements such as these are outside the realm of contracts altogether. The common law does not regulate the form of agreements between spouses. Their promises are not sealed with seals and sealing wax. The consideration that really obtains for them is that natural love and affection which counts for so little in these cold Courts. The terms may be repudiated, varied or renewed as performance proceeds or as disagreements develop, and the principles of the common law as to exoneration and discharge and accord and satisfaction are such as find no place in the domestic code. The parties themselves are advocates, judges, Courts, Sheriff's officer and reporter. In respect of these promises each house is a domain into which the King's writ does not seek to run, and to which his officers do not seek to be admitted. The only question in this case is whether or not this promise was of such a class or not. For the reasons given by my brethren it appears to me to be plainly established that the promise here was not intended by either party to be attended by legal consequences. I think the onus was upon the plaintiff, and the plaintiff has not established any contract. The parties were living together, the wife intending to return. The suggestion is that the husband bound himself to pay £30 a month under all circumstances, and she bound herself to be satisfied with that sum under all circumstances, and, although she was in ill-health and alone in this country, that out of that sum she undertook to defray the whole of the medical expenses that might fall her, whatever might be the development of her illness, and in whatever expenses it might involve her. To my mind neither party contemplated such a result. I think that the parole evidence upon which the case turns does not establish a contract. I think that the letters do not evidence such a contract, or amplify the oral evidence which was given by the wife, which is not in dispute. For these reasons I think the judgment of the Court below was wrong and that his appeal should be allowed.'

Spellman v *Spellman*

[1961] 2 All ER 498 • Court of Appeal

Mr and Mrs Spellman's marriage was going through a bad patch. They thought that if they purchased a new car their relationship might improve. Mr Spellman purchased a new car on hire-purchase and put his wife's name in the registration book. Mrs Spellman asked if the car was for her and Mr Spellman replied that it was. Within three weeks the parties again fell out and Mr Spellman left his wife taking the car with him. The issue before the court was who owned the car; this depended on whether Mr and Mrs Spellman had entered into a legally binding contract: had they intended to create legal relations?

Danckwerts LJ: 'Another matter which brings me to the conclusion that the wife is not entitled to relief in the present case is the principle which has been discussed in such cases as *Balfour* v *Balfour*. The proper conclusion on all the evidence in the present case is that there was not any intention to create legal situations, but merely an informal dealing with the matter between the husband and wife which is common in daily life and which does not result in some legal transaction, but is merely a matter of convenience. Consequently it seems to me that this point is also fatal to the claim of the wife in the present case.'

Willmer LJ: 'I also agree, but in doing so I should like to make it clear that for my part I have found this a difficult case. In the end, however, I have come to the conclusion that it really falls to be decided on the ground already stated by Danckwerts LJ, viz, that the arrangement made by the parties falls within the principle enunciated in *Balfour* v *Balfour*, i.e., it was not intended to create legal relationships.'

However, it is possible to rebut the presumption.

Merritt v *Merritt*

[1970] 2 All ER 760 • Court of Appeal

The facts are stated in the judgment of Lord Denning MR.

Lord Denning MR: 'Early in 1966 [Mr and Mrs Merritt] came to an agreement whereby [their] house was to be put in joint names. That was done. It reflected the legal position when a house is acquired by a husband and wife by financial contributions of each. But, unfortunately, about that time the husband formed an attachment for another woman. He left the house and went to live with her. The wife then pressed the husband for some arrangement to be made for the future. On 25th May, they talked it over in the husband's car. The husband said that he would make the wife a monthly payment of £40 and told her that out of it she would have to make the outstanding payments to the building society. There was only £180 outstanding. He handed over the building society's mortgage book to the wife. She was herself going out to work, earning net £7 10s a week. Before she left the car she insisted that he put down in writing a further agreement. It forms the subject of the present action. He wrote these words on a piece of paper:

> "In consideration of the fact that you will pay all charges in connection with the house at 133, Clayton Road, Chessington, Surrey, until such time as the mortgage repayment has been completed, when the mortgage has been completed I will agree to transfer the property into your sole ownership.
> Signed. John B. Merritt 25.5.66."

The wife took that paper away with her. She did, in fact, over the ensuing months pay off the balance of the mortgage, partly, maybe, out of the money the husband gave her, £40 a month, and partly out of her own earnings. When the mortgage had been paid off, he reduced the £40 a month to £25 a month.

The wife asked the husband to transfer the house into her sole ownership. He refused to do so. She brought an action in the Chancery Division for a declaration that the house should belong to her and for an order that he should make the conveyance. The judge, Stamp J, made the order; but the husband now appeals to this court.

The first point taken on his behalf by counsel for the husband was that the agreement was not intended to create legal relations. It was, he says, a family arrangement such as was considered by the court in *Balfour* v *Balfour* and in *Jones* v *Padavatton*. So the wife could not sue on it. I do not think that those cases have any application here. The parties there were living together in amity. In such cases their domestic arrangements are ordinarily not intended to create legal relations. It is altogether different when the parties are not living in amity but are separated, or about to separate. They then bargain keenly. They do not rely on honourable understandings. They want everything cut and dried. It may safely be presumed that they intend to create legal relations.

Counsel for the husband then relied on the recent case of *Gould* v *Gould* when the parties had separated, and the husband agreed to pay the wife £12 a week "so long as he could manage it". The majority of the court thought that those words introduced such an element of uncertainty that the agreement was not intended to create legal relations. But for that element of uncertainty, I am sure that the majority would have held the agreement to be binding. They did not differ from the general proposition which I stated:

> "When . . . husband and wife, at arm's length, decide to separate and the husband promises to pay a sum as maintenance to the wife during the separation, the court does, as a rule, impute to them an intention to create legal relations."

In all these cases the court does not try to discover the intention by looking into the minds of the parties. It looks at the situation in which they were placed and asks itself: would reasonable people regard the agreements as intended to be binding?

Counsel for the husband sought to say that this agreement was uncertain because of the arrangement for £40 a month maintenance. That is obviously untenable. Next he said that there was no consideration for the agreement. That point is no good. The wife paid the outstanding amount to the building society. That was ample consideration. It is true that the husband paid her £40 a month which she may have used to pay the building society. But still her act in paying was good consideration. Counsel for the husband took a small point about rates. There was nothing in it. The rates were adjusted fairly between the parties afterwards. Finally, counsel for the husband said that, under s 17 of the Married Women's Property Act 1882, this house would be owned by the husband and the wife jointly; and that, even if this house were transferred to the wife, she should hold it on trust for them both jointly. There is nothing in this point either. The paper which the husband signed dealt with the beneficial ownership of the house. It was intended to belong entirely to the wife.

I find myself in entire agreement with the judgment of Stamp J. This appeal should be dismissed.'

Widgery LJ: 'When a husband and wife are living together in amity it is natural enough to presume that their discussions about money matters are not intended to create legally binding contracts . . .

But, of course, once that natural love and affection has gone, as it normally has when the marriage has broken up, there is no room at all for the application of such a presumption. Salmon LJ made this clear in *Jones* v *Padavatton* . . .

The experience of life and human nature which raises this presumption in the case of a husband and wife living together in amity does not support it when the affection which produces that relationship of confidence has gone.

I find it unnecessary to go so far as to say that there is a presumption in favour of the creation of legal relationships when the marriage is breaking up, but certainly there is no presumption against the creation of such legal relations as there is when the parties are living happily together.

I would dismiss this appeal.'

Parent and child

Again since such a relationship is a domestic one the general rule applies and therefore agreements between parent and child are not intended to be legally binding.

Jones v Padavatton

[1969] 2 All ER 616 • Court of Appeal

Mrs Jones suggested to her daughter, Mrs Padavatton, then resident in the USA, that she should go to England and read for the English Bar. Mrs Padavatton was at first reluctant to do this since she had a good job in Washington DC. Mrs Jones offered her daughter $200 (£42) per month maintenance if she would read for the Bar. Mrs Padavatton accepted her mother's offer and started the Bar course in November 1962. Then in 1964 Mrs Jones offered to buy a house in London so that Mrs Padavatton and her son could live there and let off the rest of the house to tenants so that the tenants' rents would provide maintenance for Mrs Padavatton in lieu of the £42 per month. In 1967 Mrs Jones claimed possession of the house from Mrs Padavatton; Mrs Padavatton claimed that Mrs Jones was bound by the two agreements. The issue before the court was whether Mrs Jones and Mrs Padavatton had intended either, or both, of the agreements to be legally binding.

Danckwerts LJ: '. . . There is no doubt that the daughter gave consideration for a promise by her mother to provide maintenance at the rate of £42 per month so long as she was reading for the Bar in England by giving up her job and her other advantages in Washington, and by reading for the Bar . . .

Before us a great deal of time was spent on discussions as to what were the terms of the arrangements between the parties, and it seemed to me that the further the discussions went, the more obscure and uncertain the terms alleged became. The acceptable duration of the daughter's studies was not finally settled, I think. There was a lack of evidence on the matter, and the members of the court were induced to supply suggestions based on their personal knowledge. At any rate, two questions emerged for argument: (i) Were the arrangements (such as they were) intended to produce legally binding agreements, or were they simply family arrangements depending for their fulfilment on good faith and trust, and not legally enforceable by legal proceedings? . . .

Counsel for the daughter argued strenuously for the view that the parties intended to create legally binding contracts. He relied on the old case of *Shadwell* v *Shadwell* and *Parker* v *Clark*. Counsel for the mother argued for the contrary view that there were no binding obligations, and that if there were they were too uncertain for the court to enforce. His stand-by was *Balfour* v *Balfour*. The principles involved are very well discussed in *Cheshire and Fifoot on Contract* (6th edn). Of course, there is no difficulty, if they so intend, in members of families entering into legally binding contracts in regard to family affairs. A competent equity draftsman would, if properly instructed, have no difficulty in drafting such a contract. But there is possibly in family affairs a presumption against such an intention (which, of course, can be rebutted). I would refer to Atkin LJ's magnificent exposition in regard to such arrangements in *Balfour* v *Balfour*.

There is no doubt that this case is a most difficult one, but I have reached a conclusion that the present case is one of those family arrangements which depend on the good faith of the promises which are made and are not intended to be rigid, binding agreements. *Balfour* v *Balfour* was a case of husband and wife, but there is no doubt that the same principles apply to dealings between other relations, such as father and son and daughter and mother. This, indeed, seems to me a compelling case. The mother and the daughter seem to have been on very good terms before 1967. The mother was arranging for a career for the daughter which she hoped would lead to success. This involved a visit to England in conditions which could not be wholly foreseen. What was required was an arrangement which was to be financed by the mother and was such as would be adaptable to circumstances, as it in fact was. The operation about the house was, in my view, not a completely fresh arrangement, but an adaptation of the mother's financial assistance to the daughter due to the situation which was found to exist in England. It was not a stiff contractual operation any more than the original arrangement.

In the result, of course, on this view, the daughter cannot resist the mother's rights as the owner of the house to the possession of which the mother is entitled . . .'

Social agreements

Generally speaking the presumption for social agreements is the same as for domestic agreements i.e. social agreements are not intended to be legally binding. However, it seems that in such circumstances it is easier to rebut the normal presumption.

Parker v *Clark*

[1960] 1 All ER 93 • Exeter Assizes

Mr and Mrs Clark were an elderly couple who lived in a house called Cramond. Mrs Parker was Mrs Clark's niece. The Parkers lived in a cottage called The Thimble. They were on very friendly terms with the Clarks and visited them from time to time. On 18 September 1955 Mr Clark proposed that the Parkers should join forces and live with them. Commander Parker said that it was a big thing and required much study. After thinking it over Commander Parker wrote to Mr Clark saying that if they went to live with the Clarks they would have to sell The Thimble. On 25 September Mr Clark replied by letter which stated 'Many thanks for your letter. The major difficulty re what is to happen to the "Thimble" can be solved by our leaving "Cramond" and its major contents . . . [to Mrs Parker, and Mrs Parker's daughter and sister] when we both pass away and if you cannot maintain it they can sell out. Its present value is £9000 to £12 000 without contents. Maintenance at present costs £200 . . . If we go fifty-fifty on maintenance of house it would cost you half of the £200 odd . . . and half the running expense of food, drinks, etc. but I think it would be fair if your share of the £200 was the same as you now pay at the "Thimble" if it is less than £200. I would pay for a daily woman four mornings a week, have a TV and a new car. You could sell out and pay off your mortgage and invest proceeds to increase your income.' The Parkers accepted this offer, sold their house and on 1 March 1956 moved in with the Clarks. Eventually the Parkers and Clarks fell out and in December 1957 the Parkers moved out of the house. They sued the Clarks for breach of contract claiming, *inter alia*, a third share of the house.

The issue before the court was whether the two families had intended to create a legal relationship.

Devlin J: 'The contract relied on by the plaintiffs is said to be contained in the defendants' letter of Sept. 25 and Commander Parker's acceptance thereof. In this part of the case, since Mr Clark and Commander Parker were the contractual protagonists, it is convenient to refer to them simply as plaintiff and defendant. The defendant's first submission in answer to the claim is that the letters, construed in the light of the surrounding circumstances, show no intention to enter into a legal relationship or to make a binding contract. No doubt a proposal between relatives to share a house and a promise to make a bequest of it may very well amount to no more than a family arrangement of the type considered in *Balfour* v *Balfour* which the courts will not enforce. But there is equally no doubt that arrangements of this sort, and in particular a proposal to leave property in a will, can be the subject of a binding contract. The letter proposal has been considered chiefly in relation to marriage contracts. In *Synge* v *Synge* it was held that the defendant, who promised in writing, as part of the terms of the marriage, to leave a house and land to the plaintiff, had thereby entered into a binding contract. Kay LJ, delivering the judgment of the Court of Appeal, quoted the dictum of Lord Lyndhurst LC, in *Hammersley* v *De Biel*, which is as follows:

"... the principle of law, at least of equity, is this – that if a party holds out inducements to another to celebrate a marriage, and holds them out deliberately and plainly, and the other party consents, and celebrates the marriage in consequence of them, if he had good reason to expect that it was intended that he should have the benefit of the proposal which was so held out, a court of equity will take care that he is not disappointed, and will give effect to the proposal."

That is the principle which I apply here; and, indeed, a contract of marriage is not dissimilar to an agreement by two families to live together for the rest of their joint lives.

The question must, of course, depend on the intention of the parties to be inferred from the language which they use and from the circumstances in which they use it. On the plaintiff's side, I accept his evidence that he considered that he was making a binding contract. An important factor in this was that he disposed of his own residence. It does not matter for this purpose whether it was or was not a term of the contract that he should sell The Thimble; the important thing is that the contract required him to give up his occupation of The Thimble and that he was always quite clear, and made it quite clear, that he would not give up occupation unless he also gave up the ownership and parted with the property. He would not have done that, he says (and I believe it), unless he thought that he was securing another permanent home. There is, undoubtedly, in the arrangement a lack of formality on which counsel for the defendants greatly relies. This, I think, is largely explained by the relationship between the parties; it is easier to demand formal documents from a stranger than it is from a relative and friend. It is clear that the plaintiff constantly relied on the letter of Sept. 25, 1955, as a sort of title to his rights; he kept it and referred to it whenever his rights were called in question. When, on Oct. 24, 1957, they were seriously threatened, he went forthwith and consulted a solicitor. He is not, in my judgment, the sort of man who would "think up" a legal action as an afterthought when he found that he was not getting what he wanted.

The plaintiff is not a moneyed man. On the strength of the defendant's promise he, so to speak, put down £672 10s. That is the figure which is agreed as the expense which he incurred in giving up The Thimble, on the assumption that he could re-purchase The Thimble or a cottage like it. In addition to that, he tied up £2000, so that he has never since been in a position to buy another property like The Thimble and has never in fact bought one. The defendant knew this and had plenty of time to reflect on it between Sept. 25, 1955, when he wrote his letter, and Mar. 1, 1956, when the plaintiffs arrived. If he had thought that all that his letter involved was an amicable arrangement terminable at will, I cannot believe that he would not have enlightened the plaintiff and, as a cautious man himself, have warned him against the folly of what he was doing. I cannot believe either that the defendant really thought that the law would leave him at liberty, if he so chose, to tell the plaintiffs when they arrived that he had changed his mind, that they could take their furniture away and that he was indifferent whether they found anywhere else to live or not. Yet this is what the defence means. The defendant gave several answers which show that this was not really his state of mind. He said that the object of the letter was to induce the plaintiffs to come to Cramond; and he agreed also that he made the will in fulfilment of the promise. I am satisfied that an arrangement binding in law was intended by both sides.'

Simpkins v Pays

[1955] 3 All ER 10 • Chester Assizes

The facts are stated in the judgment of Sellers J.

Sellers J: 'Happily this is an unusual type of case to come before a court of law, and it arises out of what seems to be a popular occupation of the public – competing in a competition in a Sunday newspaper. In this particular case there was a contest, No. 397, in the *Sunday Empire News* of June 27, 1954, a competition whereby readers were invited to place, in order of merit, eight fashions, or articles of attire. The plaintiff and the defendant, along with the defendant's grand-daughter, sent in a coupon with three forecasts on it. The middle line of the second forecast chanced to be successful, as appeared in the publication of the same newspaper on Sunday, July 4, 1954. This coupon won the prize of £750, being apparently the only coupon containing what was said to be the correct forecast, and this action is brought to recover one-third of that amount, £250.

The plaintiff had been living in the defendant's house from some time in 1950, since some six months after the defendant's husband died. The defendant, who gave evidence here, was a lady of some eighty-three years of age. The plaintiff was much younger. They lived together in harmony, the plaintiff paying a weekly sum for her board and lodging to the defendant . . .

. . . The substantial matter was, on what basis were these forecasts being made?

On each of the occasions when the plaintiff made out the coupon during those seven or eight weeks, she put down the forecasts in the way which I have indicated, and entered in the appropriate place on the coupon "Mrs Pays, 11, Trevor Street, Wrexham", that is to say, the defendant's name and address, as if the coupon had been the defendant's. There were, in fact, three forecasts on each coupon, and I accept the plaintiff's evidence that, when the matter first came to be considered, what was said, when they were going to do it in that way, was: "We will go shares", or words to that effect. Whether that was said by the plaintiff or by the defendant does not really matter. "Shares" was the word used, and I do not think anything very much more specific was said. I think that that was the basis of the arrangement; and it may well be that the plaintiff was right when she said in her evidence, that the defendant said: "You're lucky, May, and if we win we will go shares".

. . . Although the coupon sent in the defendant's name was successful, the competition was not, in fact, won by the forecast of either the plaintiff or the defendant, because the middle line was composed, not by either of the parties, but by the defendant's grand-daughter. The defendant's case involves that, whichever forecast won – whether it was the plaintiff's or the defendant's, or the grand-daughter's – the whole prize was to go to the defendant. I think that that is highly improbable.

On the finding of fact that the plaintiff's evidence is right as to what was said about the shares, learned counsel for the defendant not unnaturally said: "Even if that is so, the court cannot enforce this contract unless the arrangement made at the time was one which was intended to give rise to legal consequences". It may well be there are many family associations where some sort of rough and ready statement is made which would not, in a proper estimate of the circumstances, establish a contract which was contemplated to have legal consequences, but I do not so find here. I think that in the present case there was a mutuality in the arrangement between the parties. It was not very formal, but certainly it was, in effect, agreed that every week the forecast should go in in the name of the defendant, and that if there was success, no matter who won, all should share equally. It seems to be the implication from, or the interpretation of, what was said that this was in the nature of a very informal syndicate so that they should all get the benefit of success . . . [T]he plaintiff and the defendant entered into an agreement to share, and, accordingly the plaintiff was entitled to one-third. I so find and give judgment for the amount of £250.'

Gould v Gould

[1969] 3 All ER 728 • Court of Appeal

In May 1966 Mr Gould left his wife. He agreed to pay her £15 a week, but he qualified it by saying: '. . . so long as the business is OK', or 'so long as I can manage it'.

The issue before the court was whether that qualification meant that there was no enforceable agreement at all; did Mr and Mrs Gould intend to create a legal relationship?

Edmund Davies LJ: '. . . There can be no doubt that husband and wife can enter into a contract which binds them in law . . . [T]he recent decision of Stamp J, in *Merritt* v *Merritt* afford[s an] example of this. But it is on the spouse asserting that such a contract has been entered into to prove that assertion. (See the observations of Atkin LJ, in *Balfour* v *Balfour* and those of Salmon LJ, in *Jones* v *Padavatton*.) In the general run of cases the inclination would be against inferring that spouses intended to create a legal relationship. (See Lord Hodson in *Pettitt* v *Pettitt*.) The evidence establishing such an intention, needs, in my judgment, to be clear and convincing.

It is true that the facts of the present case differ from those of *Balfour* v *Balfour*, in that although the original agreement there relied on was entered into on the eve of the husband's leaving the wife to take up his governmental duties in Ceylon, at that time amity reigned between them; whereas here the arrangement sued on was made after the husband had left the wife. While I agree that in the present circumstances the probability that a legally-binding agreement was intended may be greater than in *Balfour* v *Balfour*, nevertheless the best key in my judgment to the parties' intention is the language they employed. The importance of this aspect of the case is not restricted simply to the question whether the agreement is bad for uncertainty, but extends to the initial question whether a legally binding agreement was ever intended within the parties' contemplation. According to the wife, the husband promised to pay her £15 a week "as long as he had it" and "as long as the business was OK". The husband's evidence was substantially to the same effect, namely,

> ". . . I suggested I would give her £15 each week; and she said for how long? and I said as long as I can manage it."

In my judgment those words import such uncertainty as to indicate strongly that legal relations were not contemplated. Furthermore, such uncertainty appears to my way of thinking to give rise to insoluble problems. How and by whom is it to be determined whether the business was "OK", or whether the husband could "manage" to keep up the payments? Furthermore, what was he getting in return for his alleged legal undertaking? There is nothing in the terms employed to indicate that as a *quid pro quo* the wife was surrendering any right – nothing, for example, to show that as long as the husband kept up the weekly payments of £15 under the oral arrangement the wife would not seek maintenance. Counsel for the wife accepts that the husband could terminate his payments at any time; but he submits that this could not be done capriciously and that if the court found that the husband had so acted, he would be liable. For my part I find it impossible to regard the language employed as having any such consequences in law. I have come to the conclusion that all that occurred here was that the parties entered into a purely domestic arrangement not intended to have legally-binding force and that the learned county court judge was in error in arriving at the contrary conclusion. I would therefore allow the husband's appeal.'

Commercial agreements

In commercial agreements (or agreements at 'arm's length') the general rule applies and therefore such agreements are intended to be legally binding. Again, however, the presumption can be rebutted.

'Honour' clauses

Rose & Frank Co v J R Crompton and Brothers Ltd

[1925] AC 445 • House of Lords

Two English companies entered into an agreement with an American company whereby the American company would be their sole agent for three years subject to six months' notice. The written agreement between the parties stated 'This arrangement is not entered into, nor is this memorandum written, as a formal or legal agreement, and shall not be subject to legal jurisdiction in the Law Courts either of the United States or England, but it is only a definite expression and record of the purpose and intention of the three parties concerned, to which they each honourably pledge themselves, with the fullest confidence – based on past business with each other – that it will be carried through by each of the three parties with mutual loyalty and friendly co-operation.' A dispute having arisen between the English companies and the American company the English companies cancelled their agreement with the American company without notice. The American company sued the English companies for breach of the main agreement and also for the non-delivery of goods it had ordered prior to the cancellation of the main agreement. The English companies had accepted the orders prior to the cancellation of the main agreement.

The issues before the court were firstly, whether the main agreement was a legally binding contract between the parties, and secondly, whether there was a legally binding agreement between the parties as to the goods ordered prior to the cancellation of the main agreement.

Lord Phillimore: 'With regard to the first and most important point, that of the legal force or want of force of the arrangement of 1913, your Lordships are, I conceive, of one mind with the Court of Appeal. I do not propose to repeat their reasoning, with which I venture to concur, but I wish to add one observation. I was for a time impressed by the suggestion that as complete legal rights had been created by the earlier part of the document in question, any subsequent clause nullifying those rights ought to be regarded as repugnant and ought to be rejected. This is what happened for instance in cases where an instrument *inter vivos* purports to pass the whole property in something either real or personal, and there follows a provision purporting to forbid the new owner from exercising the ordinary rights of ownership. In such cases this restriction is disregarded. But I think the right answer was made by Scrutton LJ. It is true that when the tribunal has before it for construction an instrument which unquestionably creates a legal interest, and the dispute is only as to the quality and extent of that interest, then later repugnant clauses in the instrument cutting down that interest which the earlier part of it has given are to be rejected, but this doctrine does not apply when the question is whether it is intended to create any legal interest at all. Here, I think, the overriding clause in the document is that which provides that it is to be a contract of honour only and unenforceable at law.

With regard to the next point – namely, the right of the plaintiffs to recover damages for non-delivery of the goods specified in the particular orders for the year 1919 . . .

According to the course of business between the parties which is narrated in the unenforceable agreement, goods were ordered from time-to-time, shipped, received, and paid for, under an established system; but the agreement being unenforceable, there was no obligation on the American company to order goods or upon the English companies to accept an order. Any actual transaction between the parties, however, gave rise to the ordinary legal rights; for the fact that it was not an obligation did not divest the transaction when done of its ordinary legal significance. This, my Lords, will, I think, be plain if we begin at the latter end of each transaction.

Goods were ordered, shipped, and received. Was there no legal liability to pay for them? One stage further back. Goods were ordered, shipped, and invoiced. Was there no legal liability to take delivery? I apprehend that in each of these cases the American company would be bound. If the goods were short-shipped or inferior in quality, or if the nature of them was such as to be deleterious to other cargo on board or illegal for the American company to bring into their country, the American company would have its usual legal remedies against the English companies or one of them. Business usually begins in some mutual understanding without a previous bargain.'

Jones v Vernon's Pools Ltd

[1938] 2 All ER 626 • Liverpool Spring Assizes

Jones alleged that he had sent in his football pools coupon which had won him £2137 14s 7d. Vernon's Pools denied that they had ever received his coupon. The coupon contained the words that any agreement entered into was 'binding in honour only'. The issue before the court was whether Jones and Vernon's Pools had ever intended to enter into a legal relationship.

Atkinson J: 'I am not going to decide the question of whether or not he posted it. I do not think that there is any need to do so. I would have to hear a good deal of evidence from the defendants, and there is no use wasting time deciding that question of fact when, even if I decided that the document was received by the defendants, I would still be satisfied that the plaintiff had no claim . . .

When all is said and done this coupon is sent in on certain terms which are printed on the back of every coupon, and the plaintiff admits that he knew perfectly well what these rules were, and that he read them, and if anybody can understand them he can. He makes no suggestion that there is anything in those rules which misled him in any way, or that he could not understand them, or that there was anything ambiguous about them, or that he thought they meant anything different from what in fact they do. It seems to me that the purpose of these rules is this. The defendants wish it to be made quite clear that they are conducting these pools on certain clear lines, and they intend to say by these conditions: "Everybody who comes into these pools must understand that there are no legal obligations either way in connection with these pools. We are going to do our best. Every care will be taken, and we employ accountants, but this money must be sent in on the clearest understanding that this is a gentlemen's agreement, an agreement which carries with it no legal obligations on either side, and confers no legal rights".

That there can be agreements of that kind, recognised by law, is perfectly clear from the case of *Rose & Frank Co* v *J R Crompton & Brothers Ltd*, where quite a complicated arrangement was made between an American firm and certain English companies relating to the method of doing business together, which was expressed to be a gentlemen's agreement, and to confer no legal rights. Disputes arose on that agreement, but it was held that those words governed the whole agreement. There is nothing unlawful or against the law in having a gentlemen's agreement, and the law would recognise to the full an agreement of that kind.

This purports to be an agreement of that kind, an agreement which is merely to confer rights short of legal rights, rights which cannot be enforced at law. The very first condition is this:

"This coupon is an entry form containing the conditions on which it may be completed and submitted to us and on which alone we are prepared to receive and, if we think fit, to accept it as an entry."

In other words, it is making quite clear that these conditions which follow govern the whole relationship between the defendants and anybody sending in coupons. Secondly:

"It is a basic condition of the sending in and the acceptance of this coupon that it is intended and agreed that the conduct of the pools and everything done in connection therewith and all arrangements relating thereto (whether mentioned in these rules or to be implied) and this coupon and any agreement or transaction entered into or payment made by or under it shall not be attended by or give rise to any legal relationship, rights, duties or consequences whatsoever or be legally enforceable or the subject of litigation, but such arrangements, agreements and transactions are binding in honour only."

That is a clause which seems to me to express in the fullest and clearest way that everything that follows in these rules is subject to that basic or overriding condition that everything that is promised, every statement made with relation to what a person sending the coupon may expect, or may be entitled to, is governed by that clause.

If it means what I think that they intend it to mean, and what certainly everybody who sent a coupon and who took the trouble to read it would understand, it means that they all trusted to the defendants' honour, and to the care they took, and that they fully understood that there should be no claim possible in respect of the transactions.

One can see at once the impossibility of any other basis. I am told that there are a million coupons received every week-end. Just imagine what it would mean if half the people in the country could come forward and suddenly claim that they had posted and sent in a coupon which they never had, bring actions against the pool alleging that, and calling evidence to prove that they had sent in a coupon containing the list of winning teams, and if Vernons had to fight case after case to decide whether or not those coupons had been sent in and received. The business could not be carried on for a day on terms of that kind. It could only be carried on on the basis that everybody is trusting them, and taking the risk themselves of things going wrong. It seems to me that, even if the plaintiff established that this coupon was received, it was received on the basis of these rules, and that he has agreed in the clearest way that, if anything does go wrong, he is to have no legal claim. In other words, he has agreed that the money which *prima facie* became due to him if that coupon reached them is not to be the subject of an action at law. There is to be no legal liability to pay. He has got to trust to them, and, if something goes wrong, as I say, it is his funeral, and not theirs. I am convinced that that is the position here, and, even if the coupon were received, he has failed to establish that he would have a claim which he could come to the courts to enforce. Therefore I give judgment for the defendants.'

'*Ex gratia*' compromise

Edwards v *Skyways Ltd*

[1964] 1 All ER 494 • Queen's Bench

Edwards worked as an airline pilot for Skyways. Skyways offered Edwards redundancy on terms that if he withdrew his pension contribution they would make him an *ex gratia* payment 'approximating to' their contributions. Edwards accepted the offer but Skyways refused to make its promised *ex gratia* payment to him.

Edwards sued for the promised *ex-gratia* payment. Skyways claimed that by using the term *ex gratia* they had intended not to create legal relations.

Megaw J: '[The] agreement is recorded as follows . . .

"To those pilots who are finally declared redundant, the company will make an ex-gratia payment equivalent to their (the company's) own contributions to the . . . Pension Scheme."

. . . The plaintiff has not been paid, because the obligation was merely, as I understood the defendant company's view, a moral one, which they repudiated. It is not necessary for me to set out the subsequent history, since it does not affect the issue, namely: was there a legal obligation on the part of the defendant company?

The defendant company admit, as I understand it, that at the meeting a promise was made on their behalf with their authority, although the actual word "promise" was not used. In the defence it was pleaded that no consideration moved from the plaintiff. That plea was expressly abandoned at the hearing. It was conceded that there was consideration. The defendant company admit that it was their intention to carry out their promise when they made it, and that the plaintiff's representatives, and the plaintiff himself, believed, and acted in the belief, that the promise would be fulfilled. Everyone, at the end of the meeting, believed that there was an agreement which would be carried out. But the defendant company say that the promise and the agreement have no legal effect, because there was no intention to enter into relations in respect of the promised payment.

It is clear from such cases as *Rose and Frank Co* v *J R Crompton & Bros, Ltd* and *Balfour* v *Balfour*, that there are cases in which English law recognises that an agreement, in other respects duly made, does not give rise to legal rights, because the parties have not intended that their legal relations should be affected. Where the subject-matter of the agreement is some domestic or social relationship or transaction, as in *Balfour* v *Balfour*, the law will often deny legal consequences to the agreement, because of the very nature of the subject-matter. Where the subject-matter of the agreement is not domestic or social, but is related to business affairs, the parties may, by using clear words, show that their intention is to make the transaction binding in honour only, and not in law; and the courts will give effect to the expressed intention. [See Scrutton LJ in *Rose and Frank Co* v *J R Crompton & Bros, Ltd*.]

In the present case, the subject-matter of the agreement is business relations, not social or domestic matters. There was a meeting of minds – an intention to agree. There was, admittedly, consideration for the defendant company's promise. I accept the propositions of counsel for the plaintiff that in a case of this nature the onus is on the party who asserts that no legal effect was intended, and the onus in a heavy one . . . [T]he defendant company say, first, as I understand it, that the mere use of the phrase "*ex gratia*" by itself, as a part of the promise to pay, shows that the parties contemplated that the promise, when accepted, should have no binding force in law. They say, secondly, that even if their first proposition is not correct as a general proposition, nevertheless here there was certain background knowledge, present in the minds of everyone, which gave unambiguous significance to "*ex gratia*" as excluding legal relationship.

As to the first proposition, the words "*ex gratia*" do not, in my judgment, carry a necessary, or even a probable, implication that the agreement is to be without legal effect. It is, I think, common experience amongst practitioners of the law that litigation or threatened litigation is frequently compromised on the terms that one party shall make to the other a payment described in express terms as "*ex gratia*" or "without admission of liability". The two phrases are, I think, synonymous. No one would imagine that a settlement, so made, is unenforceable at law. The words *"ex gratia"* or "without admission of liability" are used simply to indicate – it may be as a matter of amour propre, or it may be to avoid a precedent in subsequent cases – that the party agreeing to pay does not admit any pre-existing liability on his part; but he is certainly not seeking to preclude the legal enforceability of the settlement itself by describing the contemplated payment as *"ex gratia"*. So here, there are obvious reasons why the phrase might have been used by the defendant company in just such a way. They might have desired to avoid conceding that any such payment was due under the employers' contract of service. They might have wished – perhaps ironically in the event – to show, by using the phrase, their generosity in making a payment beyond what was required by the contract of service. I see nothing in the mere use of the words *"ex gratia"*, unless in the circumstances some very special meaning has to be given to them, to warrant the conclusion that this promise, duly made and accepted, for valid consideration, was not intended by the parties to be enforceable in law.'

Quasi-commercial agreements

There seem to be some contracts which, although appearing to be commercial agreements (or agreements at arm's length), are not contractually binding. Really all that can be said about these cases is that it is 'back to basics' – the court will look carefully to see what the parties *intended*: did they *intend* to be legally bound?

Letters of comfort

Kleinwort Benson Ltd v *Malaysia Mining Corp Bhd*

[1989] 1 All ER 785 • Court of Appeal

Malaysia Mining (MM) formed a wholly owned subsidiary company, M, to trade in tin on the London Metal Exchange. M's paid up capital of £1.5m was insufficient for it to trade on the London Metal Exchange so it sought to borrow up to £10m from Kleinwort Benson (KB). KB was only prepared to lend money to M if its parent company, MM, was willing to provide an assurance as to the responsibility of MM for the repayment by M of any sums lent by KB. MM provided KB with a 'Letter of Comfort' which stated 'It is our policy to ensure that the business of M is at all times in a position to meet its liabilities to you under the above arrangements'. In October 1985 the tin market collapsed and M went into liquidation. KB demanded repayment of the monies owed to it by M from MM. MM refused to pay.

The issue before the court was whether the 'comfort letter' was a legally binding agreement.

Ralph Gibson LJ: '. . . The statement in para 3, however, was not, it was submitted [by the defendants], a contractual promise and was not intended to have legal effect as such. It was nevertheless, in counsel's submission, not devoid of legal significance: it was a representation of fact as to the policy of the defendants at the time that the statement was made; and the plaintiffs were entitled to rely on it as a statement of the current policy of the defendants. If it were shown to have been untrue to the knowledge of the defendants at the time when it was made, the plaintiffs would have had a claim in deceit, but there has been no suggestion of that nature . . .

The main attack on the analysis and reasoning of the judge, which counsel for the defendants developed, was directed at the application by Hirst J of the proposition, illustrated by *Edwards* v *Skyways Ltd*, that a promise, made for consideration in a commercial transaction, will be taken to have been intended to have contractual effect in law, unless the contrary is clearly shown. The proposition was not disputed on behalf of the defendants before Hirst J, or this court. It was, however, submitted that the principle is of no assistance in deciding whether, on the evidence and on their true construction, the words in question are words of promise or not.

On that question, it was said, neither *Rose & Frank Co* v *J R Crompton & Bros Ltd* nor *Edwards* v *Skyways Ltd* laid down any relevant presumption in favour of the plaintiffs which the defendants were called on to displace. The judge, it was said, was led into the belief that, if he took the view that the defendants had failed to displace the presumption laid down in *Edwards* v *Skyways Ltd*, it followed that para 3 was to be given effect in law as a contractual promise . . .

For my part, I am persuaded that the main criticisms of the judgment of Hirst J advanced by counsel for the defendants are well founded and I would, for the reasons which follow, allow this appeal. In my judgment the defendants made a statement as to what their policy was, and did not in para 3 of the comfort letter expressly promise that such policy would be continued in future. It is impossible to make up for the lack of express promise by implying such a promise, and indeed, no such implied promise was pleaded. My conclusion rests on what, in my judgment, is the proper effect and meaning which, on the evidence, is to be given to para 3 of the comfort letters.

Before expressing my reasons for that conclusion, I should refer to the way in which the question of "intention of creating legal relation" was introduced into this case . . .

. . . [In] *Edwards* v *Skyways* Ltd . . . Megaw J was not dealing with the sort of question which is raised in this case, namely whether, given that the comfort letter was intended to express the legal relationship between the parties, the language of para 3 does or does not contain a contractual promise.

The central question in this case, in my judgment, is that considered in *Esso Petroleum Co Ltd* v *Mardon*, on which counsel for the plaintiffs relied in this court but which was not cited to Hirst J. That question is whether the words of para 3, considered in their context, are to be treated as a warranty or contractual promise. Paragraph 3 contains no express words of promise. Paragraph 3 is in its terms a statement of present fact and not a promise as to future conduct. I agree with the submission of counsel for the defendants that, in this regard, the words of para 3 are in sharp contrast with the words of para 2 of the letter: "We confirm that we will not" etc. The force of this point is not limited, as Hirst J stated it, to the absence from para 3 of the words "We confirm". The real contrast is between the words of promise, namely "We will not" in para 2, and the words of statement of fact, "It is our policy" in para 3. Hirst J held that, by the words of para 3, the defendants gave an undertaking that now and at all times in the future, so long as Metals should be under any liability to the plaintiffs under the facility arrangements, it is *and will be* the defendants' policy to ensure that Metals is in a position to meet their liabilities. To derive that meaning from the words it is necessary to add the words emphasised, namely "and will be", which do not appear in para 3. In short, the words of promise as to the future conduct of the defendants were held by Hirst J to be part of the necessary meaning of the words used in para 3. The question is whether that view of the words can be upheld.

The absence of express words of warranty as to present facts or the absence of express words of promise as to future conduct does not conclusively exclude a statement from the status of warranty or promise. According to the well-known dictum of Holt CJ, ". . . an affirmation can only be a warranty provided it appears on evidence to have been so intended": see Ormrod LJ in *Esso Petroleum Co Ltd* v *Mardon*, citing Viscount Haldane LC in *Heilbut Symons & Co* v *Buckleton* . . .

Counsel for the plaintiffs in this court placed reliance on the decision in *Esso Petroleum Co Ltd* v *Mardon*. It is, in my judgment, on the facts of this case, of no assistance to the plaintiffs. The evidence does not show that the words used in para 3 were intended to be a promise as to the future conduct of the defendants but, in my judgment, it shows the contrary.

. . . There is nothing in the evidence to show that, as a matter of commercial probability or common sense, the parties must have intended para 3 to be a contractual promise, which is not expressly stated, rather than a mere representation of fact which is so stated.

Next, the first draft of the comfort letter was produced by the plaintiffs. Paragraph 1 contained confirmation that the defendants knew of and approved of the granting of the facilities in question by the plaintiffs to Metals, and para 2 contained the express confirmation that the defendants would not reduce their current financial interest in Metals until (in effect) facilities had been paid or the plaintiffs consented. Both are relevant to the present and future moral responsibility of the defendants. If the words of para 3 are to be treated as intended to express a contractual promise by the defendants as to their future policy, which Hirst J held the words to contain, then the recitation of the plaintiffs' approval and the promise not to reduce their current financial interest in Metals, would be of no significance. If the defendants have promised that at all times in the future it will be the defendants' policy to ensure that Metals is in a position to meet its liabilities to the plaintiffs under the facility, it would not matter whether they had approved or disapproved, or whether they had disposed of their shares in Metals. Contracts may, of course, contain statements or promises which are caused to be of no separate commercial importance by the width of a later promise in the same document. Where, however, the court is examining a statement which is by its express words no more than a representation of fact, in order to consider whether it is shown to have been intended to be of the nature of a contractual promise or warranty, it seems to me to be a fact suggesting at least the absence of such intention if, as in this case, to read the statement as a contractual promise is to reduce to no significance two paragraphs included in the plaintiffs' draft, both of which have significance if the statement is read as a representation of fact only.

That point can be made more plainly thus: if para 3 in its original or in its final form was intended to contain a binding legal promise by the defendants to ensure the ability of Metals to pay the sums due under the facility, there was no apparent need or purpose for the plaintiffs, as bankers, to waste ink on paras 1 and 2 . . .

With that evidence before the court I find it impossible to hold that the words in para 3 were intended to have any effect between the parties other than in accordance with the express words used. For this purpose it seems to me that the onus of demonstrating that the affirmation appears on evidence to have been intended as a contractual promise must lie on the party asserting that it does, but I do not rest my conclusion on failure by the plaintiffs to discharge any onus. I think it is clear that the words of para 3 cannot be regarded as intended to contain a contractual promise as to the future policy of the defendants . . .'

Free gifts

Esso Petroleum Ltd v Commissioners of Customs and Excise

[1976] 1 All ER 117 • House of Lords

In 1970 Esso launched a World Cup promotion scheme whereby motorists could collect one World Cup coin for every four gallons of petrol that they purchased. The coins were advertised as 'Going free, at your Esso Action Station now', and: 'We are giving you a coin with every four gallons of Esso petrol you buy.' The Customs and Excise Commissioners claimed that the coins were subject to purchase tax since they had been 'produced in quantity for general sale' within the meaning of the Purchase Tax Act 1963.

One of the issues before the court was whether Esso had intended to create legal relations with the motorists.

Viscount Dilhorne: 'Was there any intention on the part of the garage proprietor and also on the part of the customer who bought four gallons, or multiples of that quantity, of petrol to enter into a legally binding contract in relation to a coin or coins?

The facts of [*Rose and Frank Co* v *J R Crompton & Bros Ltd*] were very different from those of this. In that case there was an agreement dealing with business matters. In this case the question has to be considered whether there was any agreement as to a coin or coins between the garage proprietor and the customers and also, if there was, was it intended on both sides to be one having legal relations? If a coin was just to be given to the motorist, it would not be necessary for there to have been any agreement between him and the garage proprietor with regard to it . . .

True it is that Esso are engaged in business. True it is that they hope to promote the sale of their petrol, but it does not seem to me necessarily to follow or to be inferred that there was any intention on their part that their dealers should enter into legally binding contracts with regard to the coins; or any intention on the part of the dealers to enter into any such contract or any intention on the part of the purchaser of four gallons of petrol to do so.

If on the facts of this case the conclusion is reached that there was any such intention on the part of the customer, of the dealer and of Esso, it would seem to exclude the possibility of any dealer ever making a free gift to any of his customers, however negligible its value, to promote his sales.

If what was described as being a gift which would be given if something was purchased was something of value to the purchaser, then it could readily be inferred that there was a common intention to enter into legal relations. But here, whatever the cost of production, it is clear that the coins were of little intrinsic value.

I do not consider that the offer of a gift of a free coin is properly to be regarded as a business matter in the sense in which that word was used by Scrutton LJ in the passage cited above [in *Rose and Frank Co* v *J R Crompton & Bros Ltd*]. Nor do I think that such an offer can be comprehended within the "business relations" which were in the *Skyways* case, as Megaw LJ said, "the subject matter of the agreement". I see no reason to imply any intention to enter into contractual relations from the statements on the posters that a coin would be given if four gallons of petrol were bought.

Nor do I see any reason to impute to every motorist who went to a garage where the posters were displayed to buy four gallons of petrol any intention to enter into a legally binding contract for the supply to him of a coin. On the acceptance of his offer to purchase four gallons there was no doubt a legally binding contract for the supply to him of that quantity of petrol, but I see again no reason to conclude that because such an offer was made by him, it must be held that, as the posters were displayed, his offer included an offer to take a coin. The gift of a coin might lead to a motorist returning to the garage to obtain another one, but I think the facts in this case negative any contractual intention on his part and on the part of the dealer as to the coin and suffice to rebut any presumption there may be to the contrary.

. . . [T]here was no legally binding contract as to the coins . . .'

Lord Russell of Killowen agreed with Viscount Dilhorne on this point.

Lord Simon of Glaisdale: 'I am, however, my Lords, not prepared to accept that the promotion material put out by Esso was not envisaged by them as creating legal relations between the garage proprietors who adopted it and the motorists who yielded to its blandishments. In the first place, Esso and the garage proprietors put the material out for their commercial advantage, and designed it to attract the custom of motorists. The whole transaction took place in a setting of business relations. In the second place, it seems to me in general undesirable to allow a commercial promoter to claim that what he has done is a mere puff, not intended to create legal relations (cf *Carlill* v *Carbolic Smoke Ball Co*). The coins may have been themselves of little intrinsic value; but all the evidence suggests that Esso contemplated that they would be attractive to motorists and that there would be a large commercial advantage to themselves from the scheme, an advantage in which the garage proprietors also would share. Thirdly, I think that authority [*Rose and Frank Co* v *J R Crompton & Bros Ltd and Edwards* v *Skyways Ltd*] supports the view that legal relations were envisaged.

I respectfully agree [with *Rose and Frank Co* v *J R Crompton & Bros Ltd* and *Edwards* v *Skyways Ltd*]. And I would venture to add that it begs the question to assert that no motorist who bought petrol in consequence of seeing the promotion material prominently displayed in the garage forecourt would be likely to bring an action in the county court if he were refused a coin. He might be a suburb Hampden who was not prepared to forgo what he conceived to be his rights or to allow a tradesman to go back on his word.

Believing as I do that Esso envisaged a bargain of some sort between the garage proprietor and the motorist, I must try to analyse the transaction. The analysis that most appeals to me is one of the ways in which Lord Denning MR considered the case [in the Court of Appeal], namely a collateral contract of the sort described by Lord Moulton in *Heilbut, Symons & Co* v *Buckleton*:

> ". . . there may be a contract the consideration for which is the making of some other contract. 'If you will make such and such a contract I will give you one hundred pounds', is in every sense of the word a complete legal contract. It is collateral to the main contract . . ."

So here. The law happily matches the reality. The garage proprietor is saying, "If you will buy four gallons of my petrol, I will give you one of these coins". None of the reasons which have caused the law to consider advertising or display material as an invitation to treat, rather than an offer, applies here. What the garage proprietor says by his placards is in fact and in law an offer of consideration to the motorist to enter into a contract of sale of petrol. Of course, not every motorist will notice the placard, but nor will every potential offeree of many offers be necessarily conscious that they have been made. However, the motorist who does notice the placard, and in reliance thereon drives in and orders the petrol, is in law doing two things at the same time. First, he is accepting the offer of a coin if he buys four gallons of petrol. Secondly, he is himself offering to buy four gallons of petrol: this offer is accepted by the filling of his tank.'

Lord Wilberforce agreed with Lord Simon.

Lord Fraser of Tullybelton held that the whole transaction was 'a simple operation of acquiring four gallons of petrol and a coin as a sale of both articles in one transaction' not 'two separate operations, a sale of the petrol and a collateral contract for acquiring the coin'.

SUMMARY

You should now be able to:

- Distinguish between social/domestic agreements and commercial agreements.
- Distinguish between different types of social and domestic agreements.
- Understand the significance of rebuttable presumptions.
- Know how to rebut a presumption.

If you have not mastered the above points you should go through this section again.

8 Privity

INTRODUCTION

The general rule is that no one but the parties to a contract can be bound by it, or entitled under it.

THE IMPOSITION OF CONTRACTUAL LIABILITIES UPON THIRD PARTIES

Two persons cannot, by any contract into which they have entered, impose liabilities upon a third party.

THE ACQUISITION OF CONTRACTUAL RIGHTS BY THIRD PARTIES

If Alice and Bob make a contract whereby they agree to do something for Cathy, and Cathy is not a party to the contract she cannot enforce it against Alice or Bob.

See *Tweddle* v *Atkinson* above (p 93).

Dunlop Pneumatic Tyre Co Ltd v *Selfridge & Co Ltd*

[1915] AC 847 • House of Lords

Dunlop sold car tyres to Dew & Co on condition that Dew & Co would not sell them below Dunlop's list price except to trade buyers who had to make a similar promise not to sell the tyres below Dunlop's list price. Dew & Co then sold the tyres to Selfridge & Co on condition that Selfridge & Co would not sell the tyres below Dunlop's list price. Selfridge & Co then sold tyres to members of the public at below Dunlop's list price. Dunlop sued Selfridge & Co for breach of their undertaking not to sell the tyres below Dunlop's list price. In order to circumvent the 'privity of contract' rule Dunlop argued that Dew & Co had acted as their agent. For the sake of the argument their Lordships assumed that Dew & Co had acted as agents for Dunlop.

The issue, therefore, before the court was whether Dunlop had provided consideration to Selfridge & Co for Selfridge & Co's promise not to sell the tyres below the list price.

Viscount Haldane LC: '. . . My Lords, in the law of England certain principles are fundamental. One is that only a person who is a party to a contract can sue on it. Our law knows nothing of a *jus quaesitum tertio* arising by way of contract. Such a right may be conferred by way of property, as, for example, under a trust, but it cannot be conferred on a stranger to a contract as a right to enforce the contract *in personam*. A second principle is that if a person with whom a contract not under seal has been made is to be able to enforce it consideration must have been given by him to the promisor or to some other person at the promisor's request. These two principles are not recognised in the same fashion by the jurisprudence of certain continental countries or of Scotland, but here they are well established. A third proposition is that a principal not named in the contract may sue upon it if the promisee really contracted as his agent. But again, in order to entitle him so to sue, he must have given consideration either personally or through the promisee, acting as his agent in giving it.

My Lords, in the case before us, I am of opinion that the consideration, the allowance of what was in reality part of the discount to which Messrs Dew, the promisees, were entitled as between themselves and the appellants, was to be given by Messrs Dew on their own account, and was not in substance, any more than in form, an allowance made by the appellant. The case for the appellant is that they permitted and enabled Messrs Dew, with the knowledge and by the desire of the respondents, to sell to the latter on the terms of the contract of January 2, 1912. But it appears to me that even if this is so the answer is conclusive. Messrs Dew sold to the respondents goods which they had a title to obtain from the appellants independently of this contract. The consideration by way of discount under the contract of January 2 was to come wholly out of Messrs Dew's pocket, and neither directly nor indirectly out of that of the appellants. If the appellants enabled them to sell to the respondents on the terms they did, this was not done as any part of the terms of the contract sued on.'

Lord Dunedin: 'My Lords, I confess that this case is to my mind apt to nip any budding affection which one might have had for the doctrine of consideration. For the effect of that doctrine in the present case is to make it possible for a person to snap his fingers at a bargain deliberately made, a bargain not in itself unfair, and which the person seeking to enforce it has a legitimate interest to enforce . . .

Now the agreement sued on is an agreement which on the face of it is an agreement between Dew and Selfridge . . . [I]n order to enforce it he must show consideration . . . moving from Dunlop to Selfridge.

In the circumstances, how can he do so? The agreement in question is not an agreement for sale. It is only collateral to an agreement for sale; but that agreement for sale is an agreement entirely between Dew and Selfridge. The tyres, the property in which upon the bargain is transferred to Selfridge, were the property of Dew, not of Dunlop, for Dew under his agreement with Dunlop held these tyres as proprietor, and not as agent. What then did Dunlop do, or forbear to do, in a question with Selfridge? The answer must be, nothing. He did not do anything, for Dew, having the right of property in the tyres could give a good title to any one he liked, subject, it might be, to an action of damages at the instance of Dunlop for breach of contract, which action, however, could never create a *vitium reale* in the property of the tyres. He did not forbear in anything, for he had no action against Dew which he gave up, because Dew had fulfilled his contract with Dunlop in obtaining, on the evasion of the sale, a contract from Selfridge in the terms prescribed.

To my mind, this ends the case. That there are methods of framing a contract which will cause persons in the position of Selfridge to become bound, I do not doubt. But that has not been done in this instance; and as Dunlop's advisers must have known of the law of consideration, it is their affair that they have not so drawn the contract.'

EQUITABLE EXCEPTIONS TO THE PRIVITY RULE

Specific performance in favour of the third party

Notwithstanding the fact that the third party cannot himself enforce the contract, the promisee under the contract may be able to obtain an order for specific performance against the promisor to compel him to carry out his promise in favour of the third party.

Beswick v Beswick

[1968] AC 58 • House of Lords

The facts are stated in the judgment of Lord Reid.

Lord Reid: 'My Lords, before 1962 the respondent's deceased husband carried on business as a coal merchant. By agreement of Mar 14, 1962, he assigned to his nephew, the appellant, the assets of the business and the appellant undertook first to pay to him £6 10s per week for the remainder of his life and then to pay to the respondent an annuity of £5 per week in the event of her husband's death. The husband died in November, 1963. Thereupon the appellant made one payment of £5 to the respondent, but he has refused to make any further payment to her. The respondent now sues for £175 arrears of the annuity and for an order for specific performance of the continuing obligation to pay the annuity . . .

It so happens that the respondent is administratrix of the estate of her deceased husband and she sues both in that capacity and in her personal capacity. So it is necessary to consider her rights in each capacity.

For clarity I think it best to begin by considering a simple case where, in consideration of a sale by A to B, B agrees to pay the price of £1000 to a third party X. Then the first question appears to me to be whether the parties intended that X should receive the money simply as A's nominee so that he would hold the money for behoof of A and be accountable to him for it, or whether the parties intended that X should receive the money for his own behoof and be entitled to keep it. That appears to me to be a question of construction of the agreement read in light of all the circumstances which were known to the parties. There have been several decisions involving this question . . . I think that *Re Schebsman, Ex p Official Receiver, The Trustee* v *Cargo Superintendents (London), Ltd* was rightly decided and that the reasoning of Uthwatt J, and the Court of Appeal supports what I have just said. In the present case I think it clear that the parties to the agreement intended that the respondent should receive the weekly sums of £5 in her own behoof and should not be accountable to her deceased husband's estate for them. Indeed the contrary was not argued.

Reverting to my simple example the next question appears to me to be, where the intention was that X should keep the £1000 as his own, what is the nature of B's obligation and who is entitled to enforce it? It was not argued that the law of England regards B's obligation as a nullity, and I have not observed in any of the authorities any suggestion that it would be a nullity. There may have been a time when the existence of a right depended on whether there was any means of enforcing it, but today the law would be sadly deficient if one found that, although there is a right, the law provides no means for enforcing it. So this obligation of B must be enforceable either by X or by A. I . . . consider the position at common law.

Lord Denning MR's view, expressed in this case not for the first time, is that X could enforce this obligation. But the view more commonly held in recent times has been that such a contract confers no right on X and that X could not sue for the £1000 . . .

. . . So for the purposes of this case I shall proceed on the footing that the commonly accepted view is right.

What then is A's position? I assume that A has not made himself a trustee for X, because it was not argued in this appeal that any trust had been created. So, if X has no right, A can at any time grant a discharge to B or make some new contract with B. If there were a trust the position would be different. X would have an equitable right and A would be entitled and indeed bound to recover the money and account for it to X. And A would have no right to grant a discharge to B. If there is no trust and A wishes to enforce the obligation how does he set about it? He cannot sue B for the £1000 because under the contract the money is not payable to him, and, if the contract were performed according to its terms, he would never have any right to get the money. So he must seek to make B pay X.

The argument for the appellant is that A's only remedy is to sue B for damages for B's breach of contract in failing to pay the £1000 to X. Then the appellant says that A can only recover nominal damages of 40s because the fact that X has not received the money will generally cause no loss to A: he admits that there may be cases where A would suffer damage if X did not receive the money, but says that the present is not such a case.

Applying what I have said to the circumstances of the present case, the respondent in her personal capacity has no right to sue, but she has a right as administratrix of her husband's estate to require the appellant to perform his obligation under the agreement. He has refused to do so and he maintains that the respondent's only right is to sue him for damages for breach of his contract. If that were so, I shall assume that he is right in maintaining that the administratrix could then recover only nominal damages, because his breach of contract has caused no loss to the estate of her deceased husband.

If that were the only remedy available the result would be grossly unjust. It would mean that the appellant keeps the business which he bought and for which he has only paid a small part of the price which he agreed to pay. He would avoid paying the rest of the price, the annuity to the respondent, by paying a mere 40s damages . . .

The respondent's second argument is that she is entitled in her capacity of administratrix of her deceased husband's estate to enforce the provision of the agreement for the benefit of herself in her personal capacity, and that a proper way of enforcing that provision is to order specific performance. That would produce a just result, and, unless there is some technical objection, I am of opinion that specific performance ought to be ordered. For the reasons given by your lordships I would reject the arguments submitted for the appellant that specific performance is not a possible remedy in this case.'

Lord Pearce: 'My Lords, if the annuity had been payable to a third party in the lifetime of Beswick, senior, and there had been default, he could have sued in respect of the breach. His administratrix is now entitled to stand in his shoes and to sue in respect of the breach which has occurred since his death.

It is argued that the estate can recover only nominal damages and that no other remedy is open, either to the estate or to the personal plaintiff. Such a result would be wholly repugnant to justice and common-sense. And if the argument were right it would show a very serious defect in the law.

In the first place, I do not accept the view that damages must be nominal. Lush LJ, in *Lloyd's* v *Harper* said:

"Then the next question which, no doubt, is a very important and substantial one, is, that Lloyd's, having sustained no damage themselves, could not recover for the losses sustained by third parties by reason of the default of Robert Henry Harper as an underwriter. That, to my mind, is a startling and alarming doctrine, and a novelty, because I consider it to be an established rule of law that where a contract is made with A for the benefit of B, A can sue on the contract for the benefit of B, and recover all that B could have recovered if the contract had been made with B himself."

(See also *Drimmie* v *Davies*.) I agree with the comment of Windeyer J, in *Bagot's Executor and Trustee Co, Ltd* v *Coulls* in the High Court of Australia that the words of Lush LJ, cannot be accepted without qualification and regardless of context, and also with his statement:

"I can see no reason why in such cases the damages which A would suffer upon B's breach of his contract to pay C $500 would be merely nominal: I think that in accordance with the ordinary rules for the assessment of damages for breach of contract they could be substantial. They would not necessarily be $500; they could I think be less or more."

In the present case I think that the damages, if assessed, must be substantial. It is not necessary, however, to consider the amount of damages more closely, since this is a case in which, as the Court of Appeal rightly decided, the more appropriate remedy is that of specific performance.

The administratrix is entitled, if she so prefers, to enforce the agreement rather than accept its repudiation, and specific performance is more convenient than an action for arrears of payment followed by separate actions as each sum falls due. Moreover, damages for breach would be a less appropriate remedy since the parties to the agreement were intending an annuity for a widow; and a lump sum of damages does not accord with this: and if (contrary to my view) the argument that a derisory sum of damages is all that can be obtained be right, the remedy of damages in this case is manifestly useless.

The present case presents all the features which led the equity courts to apply their remedy of specific performance. The contract was for sale of a business. The appellant could on his part clearly have obtained specific performance of it if Beswick senior or his administratrix had defaulted. Mutuality is a ground in favour of specific performance.

Moreover, the appellant on his side has received the whole benefit of the contract and it is a matter of conscience for the court to see that he now performs his part of it. Kay J said in *Hart* v *Hart*:

". . . when an agreement for valuable consideration . . . has been partially performed, the court ought to do its utmost to carry out that agreement by a decree for specific performance."

What, then, is the obstacle to granting specific performance?

It is argued that, since the respondent personally had no rights which she personally could enforce, the court will not make an order which will have the effect of enforcing those rights. I can find no principle to this effect. The condition as to payment of an annuity to the widow personally was valid. The estate (though not the widow personally) can enforce it. Why should the estate be barred from exercising its full contractual rights merely because in doing so it secures justice for the widow who, by a mechanical defect of our law, is unable to assert her own rights? Such a principle would be repugnant to justice and fulfil no other object than that of aiding the wrongdoer. I can find no ground on which such a principle should exist.'

Snelling v John G Snelling Ltd

[1972] 1 All ER 79 • Queen's Bench

In March 1966 three brothers, who were directors of John G Snelling Ltd (the company), had borrowed, on behalf of the company, £40 000 from Credit for Industry Ltd. Security for the loan was a mortgage on the properties of the company. On 22 March 1968 the brothers entered into an agreement between themselves whereby they agreed that in the event of any director voluntarily resigning he would immediately forfeit all moneys due to him from the company by way of loan account 'or similar'. This agreement was to remain in force until Credit for Industry Ltd's loan had been repaid. On 28 June 1968 Brian Snelling resigned as a director of the company and demanded repayment of the £15 268 owed to him by the company.

The issue before the court was whether the company, John G Snelling Ltd, could enforce the agreement against Brian Snelling since the company was not a party to the agreement of 22 March.

Ormrod J: 'I now turn to the position of the defendant company. Counsel for the plaintiff contends that it has no defence to this claim and relies on the well-known case, *Scruttons Ltd* v *Midland Silicones Ltd*, in which the House of Lords re-affirmed unequivocally the common law doctrine that in the absence of a trust or agency, a person cannot rely on a term in a contract to which he is not a party even if he is the person whom the contract is intended to benefit. Counsel contends, therefore, that the company cannot rely on the agreement between the brothers and claim that in the events which have happened the plaintiff's loan account has been forfeited, and consequently is no longer payable to him. There can be no doubt that this proposition is supported by the speeches in the *Midland Silicones* case. Counsel for the defendants, however, submits that some of the broad statements of principle in that case went too far and relies on the later case of *Beswick* v *Beswick* . . .

The critical difference between *Beswick* v *Beswick* and these other cases is that in all of them a person who was not a party to the contract from which the obligation in question arose, was attempting to enforce the contract. In *Beswick*, the widow in her capacity as the personal representative of her deceased husband's estate, was the promisee under the contract out of which the son's obligation to pay the annuity of £5 per week arose. She was therefore entitled to enforce the obligation. The fact that in her personal capacity she was the beneficiary of it was clearly irrelevant. The principle appears to be that if the right parties, that is, the promisee and the promisor, are before the court the action will be maintainable although the nature of the remedy which the court will grant will depend on the circumstances of each case. Thus in *Tweddle* v *Atkinson* the promisee was Mr Tweddle senior and, so he, or his personal representatives, could have enforced the agreement against Mr Guy's estate although Mr Tweddle junior was the beneficiary. On the principle of *Beswick* v *Beswick* the court would presumably have ordered the defendant to perform the obligation to pay the agreed sum to Mr Tweddle junior. In *Dunlop Pneumatic Tyre Co Ltd* v *Selfridge & Co Ltd* the wholesalers could have sued Selfridges for breach of contract in selling the tyres below the minimum price but in that case it seems probable that the court would have decided that nominal damages would be an adequate remedy . . .

The conclusion, therefore, is that the second and third defendants have proved the contract between the plaintiff and themselves and have proved a breach of it by the plaintiff . . . They are consequently entitled to judgment on the counterclaim . . . The defendant company, on the other hand, is not entitled to rely directly on the terms of this contract . . .

Counsel for the plaintiff has called my attention to *Gore* v *Van der Lann (Liverpool Corpn* intervening) in the Court of Appeal . . . [I]n the present case counsel for the plaintiff says that there was no specific promise by the plaintiff not to sue the defendant company and consequently the court should refuse to stay the plaintiff's action. I do not think that the Court of Appeal can have intended to lay down a general proposition of law that the court will not stay proceedings in such circumstances unless the plaintiff has expressly undertaken not to sue . . . I do not think that the Court of Appeal intended to go further than to say that the promise which is to be enforced by the granting of a stay must be clear and unambiguous. In this connection an observation by Kelly CB in *Slater* v *Jones* is of assistance. In that case, which concerned the effect of a resolution of creditors to accept a composition, he said:

"... I think that a person who is bound by such a resolution is also bound, by necessary implication, not to sue the debtor before the time for payment comes, and until default is made."

So here, it is a necessary implication of cl 4 of the agreement of 22nd March 1968 that the plaintiff will not sue the company.

In my judgment, therefore, the second and third defendants have made out an unambiguous case and have shown that the interests of justice require that the plaintiff be not permitted to recover against the defendant company. It follows that this is a proper case in which to grant a stay of all further proceedings in the plaintiff's action against the company.

Counsel for the defendants, however, has submitted that he is entitled to go further and ask for the plaintiff's claim against the company to be dismissed. He relies on three cases: *West Yorkshire Darracq Agency Ltd* v *Coleridge*, *Hirachand Punamchand* v *Temple* and *Re William Porter & Co Ltd*. In the West Yorkshire case all the directors of a company in liquidation agreed to forgo their respective claims to outstanding directors' fees. The liquidator was a party to an oral agreement to this effect. Horridge J held that the company was entitled to rely on the agreement as a good defence to a subsequent claim by one of the directors for his fees. The basis of the judgment was that the company, through the liquidator, was a party to the agreement, although no consideration moved from it to the plaintiff. In *Re William Porter & Co Ltd* the opposite situation arose. Following a resolution passed by the directors of a company that no directors' fees be paid until a further resolution was passed, the trustee in bankruptcy of the governing director submitted a proof in the liquidation of the company for subsequent fees due to the director. The liquidator rejected the proof. Simonds J held that the company was not a party to any agreement with the directors and that the *West Yorkshire* case did not apply. He went on to hold, however, that the directors, by assenting to the postponement or abrogation of their rights, had induced the company to a course of conduct from which it could have abstained. He, therefore, upheld the rejection of the proof by the liquidator.

In the present case the defendant company was not specifically mentioned as a party to the agreement of 22nd March 1968 which, in form at any rate, was an agreement between the three directors concerned. On the other hand, the minutes of the defendant company contain references to it and it was an important item on the agenda at two meetings of the board of directors. There being no liquidator there was no physical person other than the directors who could have been a party to it on behalf of the defendant company, and they themselves never applied their minds to the question whether the company was to be a party to it or not. They regarded the business, the company and its associated companies, and themselves as an amalgam for most purposes, and their intention was to act for the benefit of the amalgam. However, it is not possible to distinguish this case on its facts from *Re William Porter & Co Ltd* in this respect. I must, therefore, hold that the defendant company was not a party to the agreement. I have no evidence that the defendant company took any action in reliance on the agreement which it would not otherwise have done so that Simonds J's decision cannot be relied on to support the view that the company is entitled to have this action dismissed . . .

I am inclined to the view that in a case such as this where the promisees under the agreement and the party to be benefited by the agreement are all before the court and the promisees have succeeded against the plaintiff on their counterclaim, the right view is that the plaintiff's claim should be dismissed . . . If the action was left with no more than an order staying further proceedings on the claim, the plaintiff could start another action only to have it also stayed and so on *ad infinitum*. The reality of the matter is that the plaintiff's claim fails and the order of the court ought, if possible, clearly to reflect that fact.'

Jackson v Horizon Holidays Ltd

[1975] 3 All ER 92 • Court of Appeal

Mr Jackson booked a four week family holiday in Ceylon (now Sri Lanka) for himself, his wife and their three children with Horizon Holidays Ltd. The cost of the holiday was £1200. Mr Jackson stressed that the holiday was to be of the highest standard. In the event the holiday was very disappointing. Amongst other things the children's room was mildewed, there was fungus growing on the walls, the toilet was stained, the shower was dirty and there was no bath. Mr Jackson sued Horizon Holidays Ltd for breach of contract and claimed damages for himself, his wife and his children.

The issue before the court was whether Mr Jackson could recover damages on behalf of his wife and his children since they were not parties to the contract.

Lord Denning MR: 'On this question a point of law arises. The judge said that he could only consider the mental distress to Mr Jackson himself, and that he could not consider the distress to his wife and children. He said:

"... the damages are the Plaintiff's; that I can consider the effect upon his mind of his wife's discomfort, vexation and the like, although I cannot award a sum which represents her vexation."

Counsel for Mr Jackson disputes that proposition. He submits that damages can be given not only for the leader of the party, in this case, Mr Jackson's own distress, discomfort and vexation, but also for that of the rest of the party.

We have had an interesting discussion as to the legal position when one person makes a contract for the benefit of a party. In this case it was a husband making a contract for the benefit of himself, his wife and children. Other cases readily come to mind. A host makes a contract with a restaurant for a dinner for himself and his friends. The vicar makes a contract for a coach trip for the choir. In all these cases there is only one person who makes the contract. It is the husband, the host or the vicar, as the case may be. Sometimes he pays the whole price himself. Occasionally he may get a contribution from the others. But in any case it is he who makes the contract. It would be a fiction to say that the contract was made by all the family, or all the guests, or all the choir, and that he was only an agent for them. Take this very case. It would be absurd to say that the twins of three years old were parties to the contract or that the father was making the contract on their behalf as if they were principals. It would equally be a mistake to say that in any of these instances there was a trust. The transaction bears no resemblance to a trust. There was no trust fund and no trust property. No, the real truth is that in each instance, the father, the host or the vicar, was making a contract himself for the benefit of the whole party. In short, a contract by one for the benefit of third persons.

What is the position when such a contract is broken? At present the law says that the only one who can sue is the one who made the contract. None of the rest of the party can sue, even though the contract was made for their benefit. But when that one does sue, what damages can he recover? Is he limited to his own loss? Or can he recover for the others? Suppose the holiday firm puts the family into a hotel which is only half built and the visitors have to sleep on the floor? Or suppose the restaurant is fully booked and the guests have to go away, hungry and angry, having spent so much on fares to get there? Or suppose the coach leaves the choir stranded half-way and they have to hire cars to get home? None of them individually can sue. Only the father, the host or the vicar can sue. He can, of course, recover his own damages. But can he not recover for the others? I think he can. The case comes within the principle stated by Lush LJ in *Lloyd's* v *Harper*:

"... I consider it to be an established rule of law that where a contract is made with A for the benefit of B, A can sue on the contract for the benefit of B, and recover all that B could have recovered if the contract had been made with B himself."

It has been suggested that Lush LJ was thinking of a contract in which A was trustee for B. But I do not think so. He was a common lawyer speaking of the common law. His words were quoted with considerable approval by Lord Pearce in *Beswick* v *Beswick*. I have myself often quoted them. I think they should be accepted as correct, at any rate so long as the law forbids the third persons themselves to sue for damages. It is the only way in which a just result can be achieved. Take the instance I have put. The guests ought to recover from the restaurant their wasted fares. The choir ought to recover the cost of hiring the taxis home. There is no one to recover for them except the one who made the contract for their benefit. He should be able to recover the expense to which they have been put, and pay it over to them. Once recovered, it will be money had and received to their use. (They might even, if desired, be joined as plaintiffs.) If he can recover for the expense, he should also be able to recover for the discomfort, vexation and upset which the whole party have suffered by reason of the breach of contract, recompensing them accordingly out of what he recovers.'

Woodar Investment Development Ltd v Wimpey Construction UK Ltd

[1980] 1 All ER 571 • House of Lords

Woodar sold to Wimpey 14 acres of land for £850 000. As part of the contract Wimpey also agreed to pay £150 000 to Transworld Trade Ltd; Transworld was not a party to the contract. The contract further provided that Wimpey could rescind the contract if 'any Authority having a statutory power of compulsory acquisition shall have commenced' to purchase the land by compulsory purchase. Wimpey purported to rescind the contract under this provision but the High Court held that in the circumstances of the case Wimpey was not entitled to rescind the contract: Wimpey did not appeal on this point.

The issues before the court were, firstly, whether Wimpey by trying to invoke the above clause had repudiated the contract, and, secondly, whether Woodar could recover substantial damages on behalf of the third party, Transworld Trade Ltd.

The first issue is dealt with later in this book. On the second issue.

Lord Wilberforce: 'The second issue in this appeal is one of damages. Both courts below have allowed Woodar to recover substantial damages in respect of condition I under which £150 000 was payable by Wimpey to Transworld Trade Ltd on completion. On the view which I take of the repudiation issue, this question does not require decision, but in view of the unsatisfactory state in which the law would be if the Court of Appeal's decision were to stand I must add three observations.

(1) The majority of the Court of Appeal followed, in the case of Goff LJ with expressed reluctance, its previous decision in *Jackson* v *Horizon Holidays Ltd.* I am not prepared to dissent from the actual decision in that case. It may be supported either as a broad decision on the measure of damages (per James LJ) or possibly as an example of a type of contract, examples of which are persons contracting for family holidays, ordering meals in restaurants for a party, hiring a taxi for a group, calling for special treatment. As I suggested in *New Zealand Shipping Co Ltd* v *A M Satterthwaite & Co Ltd*, there are many situations of daily life which do not fit neatly into conceptual analysis, but which require some flexibility in the law of contract. *Jackson*'s case may well be one.

I cannot agree with the basis on which Lord Denning MR put his decision in that case. The extract on which he relied from the judgment of Lush LJ in *Lloyd's* v *Harper* was part of a passage in which Lush LJ was stating as an "established rule of law" that an agent (sc an insurance broker) may sue on a contract made by him on behalf of the principal (sc the assured) if the contract gives him such a right, and is no authority for the proposition required in *Jackson*'s case, still less for the proposition, required here, that, if Woodar made a contract for a sum of money to be paid to Transworld, Woodar can, without showing that it has itself suffered loss or that Woodar was agent or trustee for Transworld, sue for damages for non-payment of that sum. That would certainly not be an established rule of law, nor was it quoted as such authority by Lord Pearce in *Beswick* v *Beswick*.

(2) Assuming that *Jackson*'s case was correctly decided (as above), it does not carry the present case, where the factual situation is quite different. I respectfully think therefore that the Court of Appeal need not, and should not have followed it.

(3) Whether in a situation such as the present, viz where it is not shown that Woodar was agent or trustee for Transworld, or that Woodar itself sustained any loss, Woodar can recover any damages at all, or any but nominal damages, against Wimpey, and on what principle, is, in my opinion, a question of great doubt and difficulty, no doubt open in this House, but one on which I prefer to reserve my opinion.'

Trusts of contractual rights

A promisee may constitute a trust of the right to which he is entitled in favour of a third party. The third party can himself enforce that right in equity. This is because the third party's right *does not arise by way of contract*. It is not a right to enforce the contract directly, but *a right to enforce the trust* in his favour.

Generally the trustee must bring the action for it is he who has the legal right under the contract. If, however, the trustee refuses to sue, the beneficiary (i.e. the third party) can sue, joining the trustee as defendant.

Les Affréteurs Réunis Société Anonyme v *Leopold Walford (London) Ltd*

[1919] AC 801 • House of Lords

The facts are to be found in the judgment of Lord Birkenhead LC.

Lord Birkenhead LC: 'The facts are very simple. The charterers' brokers claim commission from the shipowners under a charterparty dated September 28, 1916 . . . by which the SS *Flora* was demised. The owners were Les Affréteurs Réunis Société Anonyme and the charterers were Lubricating and Fuel Oils, Ltd. The relevant clause in the charterparty is No 29, and is as follows: "A commission of three per cent on the estimated gross amount of hire is due to Leopold Walford (London), Ltd, on signing this charter (ship lost or not lost)."

. . . A charterparty is, of course, a contract between owners and charterers . . .; but the parties in the present case, by an interlocutory and very sensible arrangement, have agreed that the matter shall be dealt with as if the charterers were co-plaintiffs [with the brokers]. The question therefore is, can the charterers succeed in such circumstances as the present in such an action against owners?

My Lords, it was decided nearly seventy years ago in the case of *Robertson* v *Wait* that charterers can sue under an agreement of this character as trustees for the broker. I am unable to distinguish between the decision in *Robertson* v *Wait* and the conclusion which, in my view, should be reached in the present case. It was conceded by Mr Wright [counsel for the appellants] that unless there was a special and independent agreement in this case he was unable to distinguish the facts in this case from those which were considered in *Robertson* v *Wait.* In my opinion Mr Wright has failed to establish the existence of an independent agreement.

My Lords, so far as I am aware, that case has not before engaged the attention of this House, and I think it right to say plainly that I agree with that decision and I agree with the reasoning, shortly as it is expressed, upon which the decision was founded. In this connection I would refer to the well-known case of *In Re Empress Engineering Company.* In the judgment of Sir George Jessel MR the principle is examined which, in my view, underlies and is the explanation of the decision in *Robertson* v *Wait.* The Master of the Rolls uses this language: "So, again, it is quite possible that one of the parties to the agreement may be the nominee or trustee of the third person. As Lord Justice James suggested to me in the course of the argument, a married woman may nominate somebody to contract on her behalf, but then the person makes the contract really as trustee for somebody else, and it is because he contracts in that character that the *cestui que trust* can take the benefit of the contract."

It appears to me plain that for convenience, and under long-established practice, the broker in such cases, in effect, nominates the charterer to contract on his behalf, influenced probably by the circumstance that there is always a contract between charterer and owner in which this stipulation, which is to enure to the benefit of the broker, may very conveniently be inserted. In these cases the broker, on ultimate analysis, appoints the charterer to contract on his behalf. I agree therefore with the conclusion arrived at by all the learned judges in *Robertson* v *Wait,* that in such cases charterers can sue as trustees on behalf of the broker.'

Limits of trust

Did the promisee enter the contract as trustee?

It must be affirmatively proved that the promisee entered into the contract as a trustee.

Re Schebsman, ex parte The Official Receiver, The Trustee v *Cargo Superintendents (London) Limited and Schebsman*
[1944] 1 Ch 83 • Court of Appeal

In September 1940 Schebsman entered into an agreement with a Swiss company and its English subsidiary, for whom he used to work, whereby he would be paid £2000 immediately and a further sum of £5500 by instalments. The agreement further provided that if he died the remaining payments would be made to his widow and if she died, to his daughter. In March 1942 Schebsman was adjudicated bankrupt and in May that year he died. The Official Receiver claimed that the monies that the companies had promised to pay under the 1940 agreement formed part of Schebsman's estate. (If this had been the case the monies would have gone to pay Schebsman's creditors and his widow would have been left with nothing.)

One of the issues before the court was whether the 1940 agreement created a trust in favour of his widow and daughter.

Du Parcq LJ: 'It is, in my opinion, convenient to approach the problems raised in this appeal by first considering the position of the parties at common law. It is clear that Mrs Schebsman, who was not a party to the agreement of September 20, 1940, acquired no rights under it and has never been in a position to maintain an action on it. It is common ground, also, that the personal representatives of the debtor could not have recovered any sums which had been paid to Mrs Schebsman under the agreement as money had and received or by any process known to the common law. It is not disputed that the English company, which under the agreement was liable to make the payments, properly performed that agreement by paying into the hands of Mrs Schebsman those sums which it had bound itself to pay to Mrs Schebsman, and, at common law, could not be called on to pay them to the personal representatives of the debtor. Nor, I think, is it disputed, and it may be said to be self-evident, that the English company's agreement to pay these moneys into the hands of Mrs Schebsman was a valid agreement, a breach of which would be regarded by the courts as an "unlawful act" and a "legal wrong". I borrow these expressions from a well-known passage in the speech of Lord Lindley in *S Wales Miners' Federation* v *Glamorgan Coal Co.* The rules according to which damages for breach of contract are assessed sometimes allow a person guilty of the legal wrong constituted by the breach to escape very lightly, but that fact does not affect the illegality of his act.

So far there is general agreement. I may now express my own agreement with a proposition submitted by Mr Roxburgh. He said that the duty to pay into the hands of a nominated person is discharged when the money has been paid to that person, and that the party bound to make a payment has no control over its destination. As a general proposition, that is true and can hardly be questioned. In the case before us Mrs Schebsman, being no party to the contract, is clearly under no obligation to the English company to apply the money in any particular way, nor is the English company concerned with any agreement which she may choose to make with third parties binding herself to apply it in a particular manner, but the proposition, accurate as it is, may be misleading unless it is considered together with another proposition which I take to be equally unexceptionable and which I will now state.

It is open to parties to agree that, for a consideration supplied by one of them, the other will make payments to a third person for the use and benefit of that third person and not for the use and benefit of the contracting party who provides the consideration. Whether or not such an agreement has been made in a given case is clearly a question of construction, but, assuming that the parties have manifested their intention so to agree, it cannot, I think, be doubted that the common law would regard such an agreement as valid and as enforceable (in the sense of giving a cause of action for damages for its breach to the other party to the contract), and would regard the breach of it as an unlawful act. If the party from whom the consideration moved somehow succeeded in intercepting a payment intended for the named payee he would be guilty of a tort, and, in certain circumstances, of a crime, and he would also be breaking his contract, since it would be implicit in his agreement with the other party that he would do nothing to prevent the money paid from reaching the payee. If he sought to argue that because he had himself provided the consideration he alone was interested in the destination of the money, the answer would be that the other contracting party had not agreed (and, perhaps, might never have thought of agreeing) to make a payment either to him or for his benefit. If he can persuade the payee to hand the money over to him by lawful means, he is, of course, at liberty to do so, and there may be circumstance *dehors* [outside] the contract which gave him rights against the payee. Subject to that qualification, he can never, in the case of such a contract as I have supposed, lawfully claim payment of the money for himself while the contract remains unaltered. That the common law allows it to be varied nobody doubts. At any time the parties may agree that payment shall in future be made, not to the payee named in the contract, but to the party from whom the consideration moved, or, for that matter, to any other person, but in the case of such a contract there cannot be a variation at the will of one of the parties any more than a condition introduced into a contract for the benefit of both parties can be waived by only one of them.

I have said that the question whether a contract imposes a liability on one of the parties to confer a benefit on a third party, not privy to the contract, is always one of construction. From the point of view of the common law, with which alone I am now dealing, I have no doubt that the general rule of construction laid down by Blackburn J in *Burges* v *Wickham* must be applied. According to the general law of England the written record of a contract must not be varied or added to by oral evidence of what was the intention of the parties.

I now turn to the agreement in the present case to seek in the document itself the answer to the question whether the parties intended that, after the debtor's death, the company should be under an obligation to make payments to Mrs Schebsman for her own benefit, and the debtor's personal representatives should be under a corresponding obligation to accept payment to Mrs Schebsman for her own benefit as a fulfilment of the contract. It seems to me to be plain on the face of the contract that this was the intention of the parties. In this connection, the most striking feature of the agreement, in my opinion, is that after the deaths of Mrs and Miss Schebsman (assuming that the debtor were to predecease them, as, in fact, he did) all payments were to cease, even though a large part of the amount payable by the company might remain unpaid. This provision points clearly, as it seems to me, to the conclusion that both parties were concerned with benefiting Mrs Schebsman and the daughter, and that the company did not intend to bind itself to pay a penny for the benefit of the debtor's estate after the death of these ladies. It is impossible, in my judgment, to regard this as in effect an aleatory contract under which the amount of payments intended to accrue for the benefit of the debtor's estate was to be dependent on events so uncertain as the duration of the two lives. Further, it is, I think, proper to have regard to the fact that, in the circumstances disclosed by the agreement itself, both parties might be expected to wish to confer a benefit on the debtor's dependants. Lastly, I attach some importance to the language of cl 6 which speaks of payments "due to" Mrs and Miss Schebsman.

I may now summarise the position at common law as follows: (1) It is the right, as well as the duty, of the company to make the prescribed payments to Mrs Schebsman and to no other person. (2) Mrs Schebsman may dispose of the sums so received as she pleases and is not accountable for them to the personal representatives of the debtor or to anyone claiming to stand in the shoes of the debtor. (3) If anyone standing in the shoes of the debtor were to intercept the sums payable to Mrs Schebsman and refuse to account to her for them, he would be guilty of a breach of the debtor's contract with the company. (4) The obligation undertaken by the company cannot be varied at the will of the other party to the contract, but may be varied consensually at any time although the debtor is no longer living, as it could have been in his life-time.

It now remains to consider the question whether, and if so to what extent, the principles of equity affect the position of the parties. It was argued by Mr Denning that one effect of the agreement of September 20, 1940, was that a trust was thereby created, and that the debtor constituted himself trustee for Mrs Schebsman of the benefit of the covenant under which payments were to be made to her. Uthwatt J rejected this contention, and the argument has not satisfied me that he was wrong. It is true that, by the use possibly of unguarded language, a person may create a trust, as Monsieur Jourdain talked prose, without knowing it, but unless an intention to create a trust is clearly to be collected from the language used and the circumstances of the case, I think that the court ought not to be astute to discover indications of such an intention. I have little doubt that in the present case both parties (and certainly the debtor) intended to keep alive their common law right to vary consensually the terms of the obligation undertaken by the company, and if circumstances had changed in the debtor's life-time injustice might have been done by holding that a trust had been created and that those terms were accordingly unalterable. On this point, therefore, I agree with Uthwatt J [who held that Schebsman was not a trustee under the agreement].'

Green v Russell

[1959] 2 All ER 525 • Court of Appeal

Russell took out a personal accident insurance policy on behalf of his employees. Under the policy if any employee died at work as a result of an accident the deceased's estate would receive £1000. Green, an employee of Russell's, was killed in a fire whilst at work. The main issue before the court was a technical one which is not relevant for the purpose of this book. However, the court did discuss whether Russell could be considered a trustee of Green's rights under the contract of insurance, Green himself not being a party to the contract of insurance.

Romer LJ: 'The next question then which arises is whether Mr Green had an equitable interest in the policy, and in the sum which was paid on, and in respect of, his death. The plaintiff contends that Mr Russell constituted himself a trustee for the various employees (including Mr Green) named in the schedule to the policy in respect of the benefits attributable to each of them respectively. The learned judge rejected this contention and, in my opinion, rightly so. The suggestion that Mr Russell assumed the position and obligations of a trustee was based primarily on the recital to the policy . . . I take the following definition of a trust from *Underhill's Law of Trusts and Trustees* (10th edn):

> "A trust is an equitable obligation, binding a person (who is called a trustee) to deal with property over which he has control (which is called the trust property), for the benefit of persons (who are called the beneficiaries or *cestuis que trust*), of whom he may himself be one, and any one of whom may enforce the obligation. Any act or neglect on the part of a trustee which is not authorised or excused by the terms of the trust instrument, or by law, is called a breach of trust."

In my judgment no such conception as that described by Sir Arthur Underhill arises from the recital to the policy. An intention to provide benefits for someone else, and to pay for them, does not in itself give rise to a trusteeship; and yet that is all that emerges from the recital. Nor does the judge's finding that the existence of the policy was known to the employees in such a manner as to create in them a reasonable expectation of benefit affect the matter. There was nothing to prevent Mr Russell at any time, had he chosen to do so, from surrendering the policy and receiving back a proportionate part of the premium which he had paid. Nor was he under any obligation to pay the renewal premiums each year. The truth is that the benefits payable in pursuance of the policy were sums which the company would become contractually liable to Mr Russell to pay if the insured risks matured; and as Lord Greene MR, said in *Re Schebsman* to which the learned judge referred:

"It is not legitimate to import into the contract the idea of a trust when the parties have given no indication that such was their intention. To interpret this contract as creating a trust would, in my judgment, be to disregard the dividing line between the case of a trust and the simple case of a contract made between two persons for the benefit of a third." '

Contracts of insurance

Contracts of insurance even if made for the benefit of a third party cannot in principle be enforced by the third party unless a trust is created in favour of the third party.

However, legislation provides exceptions.

Road Traffic Act 1988

Section 148   Avoidance of certain exceptions to policies or securities

(7) Notwithstanding anything in any enactment, a person issuing a policy of insurance under section 145 of this Act shall be liable to indemnify the persons or classes of persons specified in the policy in respect of any liability which the policy purports to cover in the case of those persons or classes of persons.

Married Women's Property Act 1882

Section 11   Moneys payable under policy of assurance not to form part of estate of the insured

A married woman may . . . effect a policy upon her own life or the life of her husband for her [own benefit]; and the same and all benefit thereof shall enure accordingly.

A policy of assurance effected by any man on his own life, and expressed to be for the benefit of his wife, or of his children, or of his wife and children, or any of them, or by any woman on her own life, and expressed to be for the benefit of her husband, or of her children, or of her husband and children, or any of them, shall create a trust in favour of the objects therein named, and the moneys payable under any such policy shall not, so long as any object of the trust remains unperformed, form part of the estate of the insured, or be subject to his or her debts: Provided, that if it shall be proved that the policy was effected and the premiums paid with intent to defraud the creditors of the insured, they shall be entitled to receive, out of the moneys payable under the policy, a sum equal to the premiums so paid. The insured may by the policy, or by any memorandum under his or her hand, appoint a trustee or trustees of the moneys payable under the policy, and from time to time appoint a new trustee or new trustees thereof, and may make provision for the appointment of a new trustee or new trustees thereof, and for the investment of the moneys payable under such policy. In default of any such appointment of a trustee, such policy, immediately on its being effected, shall vest in the insured and his or her legal personal representatives, in trust for the purposes aforesaid . . .

The receipt of a trustee or trustees duly appointed, or in default of any such appointment, or in default of notice to the insurance office, the receipt of the legal personal representative of the insured shall be a discharge to the office for the sum secured by the policy, or for the value thereof, in whole or in part.

Marine Insurance Act 1906

Section 14   Quantum of interest

(2) A mortgagee, consignee, or other person having an interest in the subject-matter insured may insure on behalf and for the benefit of other persons interested as well as for his own benefit.

EXEMPTION CLAUSES AND THIRD PARTIES

A person may include in a contract an exclusion clause which purports to confer exemption not only upon himself but also on persons who are not parties to the contract. The general rule as discussed above still applies to these situations – *no one but the parties to a contract can be bound by it, or entitled under it.*

Adler v *Dickson*

[1954] 3 All ER 397 • Court of Appeal

Adler was a passenger travelling in a ship, the *Himalaya*, owned by P & O; Dickson was the master of the ship. Adler was walking up the gangway when the ship moved. This caused the gangway and Adler to fall sixteen feet to the wharf resulting in serious injury to Adler. The ticket issued to Adler contained the terms

'passengers . . . are carried at passengers' entire risk.

This ticket is issued by the company and accepted by the passenger subject to the following conditions and regulations,

The company will not be responsible for and shall be exempt from all liability in respect of any . . . injury whatsoever of or to the person of any passenger . . . whether such injury of or to the person of any passenger . . . shall occur on land, on shipboard or elsewhere . . . and whether the same shall arise from or be occasioned by the negligence of the company's servants on board the ship or on land in the discharge of their duties, or while the passenger is embarking or disembarking, or whether by the negligence of other persons directly or indirectly in the employment or service of the company, or otherwise, or by the act of God . . . dangers of the seas . . . or by accidents . . . or any acts, defaults or negligence of the . . . master, mariners, company's agents or servants of any kind under any circumstances whatsoever . . .'

Adler accepted that P & O's conditions exempted them from liability so she sued Dickson for his negligence in allowing the ship to move whilst she was on the gangway.

The issue before the court was whether Dickson could rely on P & O's conditions as exempting him from liability. For the purpose of the action in the Court of Appeal it was assumed that Dickson had been negligent.

Denning LJ reviewed the authorities and then said: 'My conclusion, therefore, is that, in the carriage of passengers as well as of goods, the law permits a carrier to stipulate for exemption from liability not only for himself but also for those whom he engages to carry out the contract: and this can be done by necessary implication as well as by express words. When such a stipulation is made, it is effective to protect those who render services under the contract, although they were not parties to it, subject, however, to this important qualification: The injured party must assent to the exemption of those persons. His assent may be given expressly or by necessary implication, but assent he must before he is bound: for it is clear law that an injured party is not to be deprived of his rights at common law except by a contract freely and deliberately entered into by him; and all the more so when the wrongdoer was not a party to the contract, but only participated in the performance of it. In all cases where the wrongdoer has escaped it will be found that the injured party assented expressly or by necessary implication to forgo his remedy against him. In the case of goods it is not difficult to infer an assent because the owner of the goods habitually insures them against loss or damage in transit. If the carrier is protected by an exemption clause, so should his servants be, leaving the owner to recover against the insurance company. As Scrutton LJ, said in the *Elder, Dempster* case:

"Were it otherwise there would be an easy way round the bill of lading";

and as Viscount Finlay said:

"It would be absurd that the owner of the goods could get rid of the protective clauses of the bill of lading . . . by suing . . . in tort".

In the case of passengers, however, it is not so easy to infer an assent. It was inferred in *Hall* v *North Eastern Ry Co* but not in *Cosgrove* v *Horsfall* even though the clause there purported expressly to exempt the servant. At least, that seems to me the correct explanation of those cases.

Applying those principles to the present case, the important thing to notice is that the steamship company only stipulated for exemption from liability for themselves. They did not in terms stipulate for exemption for their servants or agents, and I see no reason to imply any such exemption. The servants or agents are, therefore, not excused from the consequences of their personal negligence; see *City of Lincoln (Master & Owners)* v *Smith*. In any case, even if the company intended that the stipulation should cover their servants, nevertheless I see nothing whatever to suggest that the plaintiff knew of their intention or assented to it. If she read the conditions of the ticket (which she probably did not) and considered the possibility of being injured by the negligence or default of the company's servants (which I trust she thought unlikely) she might well think that her remedy against the company was barred, but she would not think her remedy against the servants was also barred. Suppose a steward on a liner were to strike a passenger or falsely to imprison her, or injure her by some wilful misconduct, then albeit it was done in the course of his employment, he could not claim the protection of the clause, for the simple reason that the passenger never agreed to his being exempted. She could sue the steward personally, even though her remedy against the company was barred. So also if the steward is negligent in the course of his employment, for there is no difference in principle between the cases. The passenger has not agreed to forgo his remedy against the actual wrongdoer and can still pursue it.

The result, in my opinion, is that the plaintiff can pursue her claim against the master and the boatswain without being defeated by the exemption clause. I think the appeal should be dismissed.'

Jenkins LJ: 'A good deal was said in the course of the argument before us about the absurdity of a stipulation relieving an employer of his liability for the negligence of his servant while leaving untouched the servant's liability for that same negligence. I do not follow this. If there is no exempting stipulation at all, then both master and servant are liable, and either can be sued at the option of the injured party. If there is a contract exempting the master but not the servant then the servant's liability remains as it was. The master may find this result inconvenient if he feels impelled either from motives of expediency or from a sense of moral obligation to indemnify the servant. If so, the answer is simple. He should have seen that the contract was so framed as to exempt his servant from liability as well as himself. To my mind it is far more absurd to impute to a passenger on a ship who has contracted with a shipowner for a given voyage in terms which exempt the shipowner from liability for his servants' negligence an intention thereby to deprive himself of all right to redress against the servants of the shipowner for any and every negligent act or omission which may be committed by such servants in the course of their duties, however gross the negligence and however grave the resulting damage to the passenger may be. Accordingly, if left free to do so by the authorities, I would dismiss the appeal.'

If the above case were to come before the courts today consider what effect the Unfair Contract Terms Act 1977 would have on the above exclusion clause, especially s 2.

Scruttons Ltd v Midland Silicones Ltd

[1962] AC 446 • House of Lords

A drum of chemicals was shipped in New York on a ship owned by United States Lines. The bill of lading (the contract of carriage) stated that 'Neither the carrier nor the ship shall in any event be . . . liable for any loss or damage . . . to goods in an amount exceeding $500 per package . . . ' The bill of lading further provided that the word 'carrier' included 'the ship . . . her owner, operator . . . , and also any . . . person to the extent bound by this bill of lading, whether acting as carrier or bailee'. Scruttons, a firm of stevedores employed by United States Lines to unload its ships, negligently dropped the drum of chemicals whilst loading Midland Silicones' lorry. The damage to the drum amounted to £593 12s 2d. Scruttons admitted negligence in handling the drum but contended that they were entitled to rely on the provisions in the bill of lading limiting liability for damage to the goods to $500, or £179 1s.

The issue before the court was whether Scruttons could rely on the limitation clause in the bill of lading bearing in mind that they were not parties to the bill of lading contract made between United States Lines and Midland Silicones Ltd.

Lord Reid: 'My Lords, the case for the respondents is simple. Goods which they had bought were damaged by the negligence of stevedores, who are the appellants. Before the damage occurred the property in the goods had passed to the respondents and they sue in tort for the amount of the loss to them caused by that damage. The appellants seek to take advantage of provisions in the bill of lading made between the sellers of the goods and the carrier. Those provisions in the circumstances of this case would limit liability to 500 dollars. They are expressed as being in favour of the carrier but the appellants maintain on a number of grounds that they can rely on these provisions with the result that, though the damage to the respondents' goods considerably exceeded 500 dollars, the respondents cannot recover more than the equivalent of that sum from them as damages. We were informed that questions of this kind frequently arise and that this action has been brought as a test case.

In considering the various arguments for the appellants I think it is necessary to have in mind certain established principles of the English law of contract. Although I may regret it I find it impossible to deny the existence of the general rule that a stranger to a contract cannot in a question with either of the contracting parties take advantage of provisions of the contract even where it is clear from the contract that some provision in it was intended to benefit him. That rule appears to have been crystallised a century ago in *Tweddle* v *Atkinson* and finally established in this House in *Dunlop Pneumatic Tyre Co, Ltd* v *Selfridge & Co, Ltd*. There are it is true certain well-established exceptions to that rule – though I am not sure that they are really exceptions and do not arise from other principles. But none of these in any way touches the present case.

The actual words used by Viscount Haldane LC in the *Dunlop* case were made the basis of an argument that, although a stranger to a contract may not be able to sue for any benefit under it, he can rely on the contract as a defence if one of the parties to it sues him in breach of his contractual obligation – that he can use the contract as a shield though not as a sword. I can find no justification for that. If the other contracting party can prevent the breach of contract well and good, but if he cannot I do not see how the stranger can. As was said in *Tweddle* v *Atkinson* the stranger cannot 'take advantage' from the contract.

It may be that in a roundabout way the stranger could be protected. If A, wishing to protect X, gives to X an enforceable indemnity, and contracts with B that B will not sue X, informing B of the indemnity, and then B does sue X in breach of his contract with A, it may be that A can recover from B as damages the sum which he has to pay X under the indemnity, X having had to pay it to B. But there is nothing remotely resembling that in the present case.

The appellants in this case seek to get round this rule in three different ways. In the first place they say that the decision in *Elder, Dempster & Co* v *Paterson, Zochonis & Co* establishes an exception to the rule sufficiently wide to cover the present case. I shall later return to consider this case. Secondly, they say that through the agency of the carrier they were brought into contractual relation with the shipper and that they can now found on that against the consignees, the respondents. And thirdly, they say that there should be inferred from the facts an implied contract, independent of the bill of lading, between them and the respondents. It was not argued that they had not committed a tort in damaging the respondents' goods.

I can see a possibility of success of the agency argument if (first) the bill of lading makes it clear that the stevedore is intended to be protected by the provisions in it which limit liability, (secondly) the bill of lading makes it clear that the carrier, in addition to contracting for these provisions on his own behalf, is also contracting as agent for the stevedore that these provisions should apply to the stevedore, (thirdly) the carrier has authority from the stevedore to do that, or perhaps later ratification by the stevedore would suffice, and (fourthly) that any difficulties about consideration moving from the stevedore were overcome. And then to affect the consignee it would be necessary to show that the provisions of the Bills of Lading Act, 1855, apply.

But again there is nothing of that kind in the present case. I agree with your Lordships that 'carrier' in the bill of lading does not include stevedore, and if that is so I can find nothing in the bill of lading which states or even implies that the parties to it intended the limitation of liability to extend to stevedores. Even if it could be said that reasonable men in the shoes of these parties would have agreed that stevedores should have this benefit that would not be enough to make this an implied term of the contract. And even if one could spell out of the bill of lading an intention to benefit the stevedores there is certainly nothing to indicate that the carrier was contracting as agent for the stevedores in addition to contracting on his own behalf. So it appears to me that the agency argument must fail.

And the implied contract argument seems to me to be equally unsound. From the stevedores' angle, they are employed by the carrier to deal with the goods in the ship. They can assume that the carrier is acting properly in employing them and they need not know to whom the goods belong. There was in their contract with the carrier a provision that they should be protected, but that could not by itself bind the consignee. They might assume that the carrier would obtain protection for them against the consignee and feel aggrieved when they found that the carrier did not or could not do that. But a provision in the contract between them and the carrier is irrelevant in a question between them and the consignee. Then from the consignees' angle they would know that stevedores would be employed to handle their goods but if they read the bill of lading they would find nothing to show that the shippers had agreed to limit the liability of the stevedores. There is nothing to show that they ever thought about this or that if they had they would have agreed or ought as reasonable men to have agreed to this benefit to the stevedores. I can find no basis in this for implying a contract between them and the stevedores. It cannot be said that such a contract was in any way necessary for business efficiency.

So this case depends on the proper interpretation of the *Elder, Dempster* case. What was there decided is clear enough. The ship was under time charter, the bill of lading made by the shippers and the charterers provided for exemption from liability in the event which happened and this exemption was held to enure to the benefit of the shipowners who were not parties to the bill of lading, but whose servant the master caused damage to the shippers' goods by his negligence. The decision is binding on us but I agree that the decision by itself will not avail the present appellants because the facts of this case are very different from those in the *Elder, Dempster* case. For the appellants to succeed it would be necessary to find from the speeches in this House a *ratio decidendi* which would cover this case and then to follow that *ratio decidendi* . . .

In such circumstances I do not think that it is my duty to pursue the unrewarding task of seeking to extract a *ratio decidendi* from what was said in this House in *Elder, Dempster*. Nor is it my duty to seek to rationalise the decision by determinating in any other way just how far the scope of the decision should extend. I must treat the decision as an anomalous and unexplained exception to the general principle that a stranger cannot rely for his protection on provisions in a contract to which he is not a party. The decision of this House is authoritative in cases of which the circumstances are not reasonably distinguishable from those which gave rise to the decision. The circumstances in the present case are clearly distinguishable in several respects. Therefore I must decide this case on the established principles of the law of England apart from that decision, and on that basis I have no doubt that this appeal must be dismissed.'

Another case in which attempts have been made to get around the privity restriction is *New Zealand Shipping Co Ltd* v *A M Satterthwaite & Co Ltd*, above (p 119).

Southern Water Authority v Carey

[1985] 2 All ER 1077 • Queen's Bench

Southern Water Authority claimed damages for negligence and/or breach of contract against the first defendants, Carey (the consulting engineers), the second defendants, Mather & Platt (Contracting) Ltd (the main contractors who had ceased trading), the third defendants, Simon-Hartley Ltd (sub-contractors), the fourth defendants, Vokes Ltd (sub-contractors), and the fifth defendants, Simon-Rosedowns Ltd (sub-contractors). The main contract made between Southern Water and Carey for the construction of sewage works contained clause 30 which provided:

'(vi) The Contractor's liability under this clause shall be in lieu of any condition or warranty implied by law as to the quality or fitness for any particular purpose of any portion of the Works taken over under Clause 28 (Taking-over) and save as in this Clause expressed neither the Contractor nor his Sub-Contractors, servants or agents shall be liable, whether in contract, tort or otherwise in respect of defects in or damage to such portion, or for any injury, damage or loss of whatsoever kind attributable to such defects or damage. For the purposes of this sub-clause the Contractor contracts on his own behalf and on behalf of and as trustee for his Sub-Contractors, servants and agents.'

The issue before the court was whether the sub-contractors could rely on clause 30 to exempt them from liability.

His Honour Judge David Smout QC: 'Counsel for the fourth defendants puts his argument in a number of ways. He points out that cl 30(vi) refers to the contractor contracting as trustee for the sub-contractor. But I can give no meaning to that phrase, for the conception of a trust attaching to a benefit under an exclusion clause extends far beyond conventional limits . . .

Counsel for the fourth defendants developed a further argument that cl 30(vi) reflects the terms of a unilateral contract, that is to say that it is tantamount to an offer or promise of immunity on certain conditions and that the sub-contractor in performing the works so that they become the subject of a taking-over certificate has accepted the offer or taken up the promise, and having complied with the condition has thereby entered into a binding contract. Reliance is placed on two decisions of the Privy Council, namely *New Zealand Shipping Co Ltd* v *A M Satterthwaite & Co Ltd* and *Port Jackson Stevedoring Pty Ltd* v *Salmond & Spraggon (Australia) Pty Ltd, the New York Star*. Both of these authorities relate to the liability of stevedores and involve the terms of a bill of lading. Both also contain an important agency element . . .

I must be cautious before extending into a wider field those decisions in so far as they apply the principle of unilateral contract to the specialised practice of carriers and stevedores in mercantile law. To my mind the principle of the unilateral contract does not, taken by itself, fit easily onto the accepted facts in the instant case and it strikes me as uncomfortably artificial.

It is, however, the agency element in *Satterthwaite*' s case that is much to the point.

[Lord Wilberforce] . . . went on to cite a passage from Lord Reid's judgment in

Scruttons Ltd v *Midland Silicones Ltd*, which has been referred to many times in argument in this case, and in which Lord Reid said:

"I can see a possibility of success of the agency argument if (first) the bill of lading makes it clear that the stevedore is intended to be protected by the provisions in it which limit liability, (secondly) the bill of lading makes it clear that the carrier, in addition to contracting for these provisions on his own behalf, is also contracting as agent for the stevedore that these provisions should apply to the stevedore, (thirdly) the carrier has authority from the stevedore to do that, or perhaps later ratification by the stevedore would suffice, and (fourthly) that any difficulties about consideration moving from the stevedore were overcome . . ."

Let us then consider the four propositions in the context of the instant case. First, does the main contract make it clear that the sub-contractors are intended to be protected by the provisions in it which limit liability? To my mind the answer must be Yes. Second, does it make it clear that the main contractor in addition to contracting for these provisions on his own behalf is also contracting as agent for the sub-contractors that the provisions should also apply to the sub-contractors? Again, I answer Yes: cl 30(vi) so states. The fourth proposition as to consideration poses no difficulty, for this is a contract under seal. It is the third proposition that is debatable in the instant case: had the main contractor authority from the sub-contractor, at the time of making the contract, and, if not, was there any later ratification that would suffice? Unlike *Satterthwaite's* case, there is no evidence here on which I could conclude that the main contractors had prior authority. What as to ratification? Counsel for the plaintiffs contends that there can be no ratification unless the principal was capable of being ascertained at the time when the act was done, i.e. when the deed was signed. Herein lies the defendants' difficulty. Counsel relies on *Watson* v *Swann* referring to the often cited *dicta* of Earle CJ and Willes J. They may be *obiter dicta* but they have been accepted for 100 years as expressing the basic principle . . . The fact that the fourth defendants were in the contemplation of the second defendants at the material time, as the documents show, and that it may be that the third defendants were also in contemplation, does not in my view suffice . . .

I turn now away from contract to the argument as it has been put in tort . . .

However, there are certain considerations in the modern development of the law of tort which go to the very heart of the matter. Counsel for the fourth defendants drew attention to them and counsel for the third defendants fully developed that line of argument. If there be any liability in tort on the third and fourth defendants or either of them, it must depend, of course, on an analysis of the scope of the duty of care. The modern starting point must be the propositions expressed by Lord Wilberforce in *Anns* v *Merton London Borough* . . .

No one would doubt that in an ordinary building case as between the sub-contractors and the building owner who has suffered damage there is a sufficient relationship of proximity that in the reasonable contemplation of the sub-contractor carelessness on his part may be likely to cause damage to the building owner. Thus a *prima facie* duty of care lies on the sub-contractor. So also in this case. But one has to go on to consider whether there are any considerations which ought to negative or to reduce or limit the scope of that duty. And merely to ask the question in the context of this case seems to me to foretell the answer. Did not the plaintiffs' predecessor as building owner, as it were, itself stipulate that the sub-contractors should have a measure of protection following on the issue of appropriate taking-over certificates? We must look to see the nature of such limitation clause to consider whether or not it is relevant in defining the scope of the duty in tort. The contractual setting may not necessarily be overriding, but it is relevant in the consideration of the scope of the duty in tort for it indicates the extent of the liability which the plaintiffs' predecessor wished to impose. To put it more crudely, and I hope I do no injustice to counsel for the third defendants to say that that is how he emphasised the matter, the contractual setting defines the area of risk which the plaintiffs' predecessor chose to accept and for which it may or may not have sought commercial insurance.

In *Junior Books Ltd* v *Veitchi Co Ltd* Lord Roskill cited the passage from Lord Wilberforce's speech in *Anns* v *Merton London Borough* . . . Significantly, Lord Roskill added this:

> "During the argument it was asked what the position would be in a case where there was a relevant exclusion clause in the main contract. My Lords, that question does not arise for decision in the instant appeal, but in principle I would venture the view that such a clause according to the manner in which it was worded might in some circumstances limit the duty of care just as in the *Hedley Byrne* case the plaintiffs were ultimately defeated by the defendants' disclaimer of responsibility."

The case has now arisen where there is such a limitation that is directly in point. While the terms of cl 30(vi) may, if literally interpreted, exceed the bounds of common sense the intent is clear, namely that the sub-contractor whose works have been so completed as to be the subject of a valid taking-over certificate should be protected in respect of those works from any liability in tort to the plaintiffs. As the plaintiffs' predecessor did so choose to limit the scope of the sub-contractors' liability, I see no reason why such limitation should not be honoured . . .'

Norwich City Council v Harvey

[1989] 1 WLR 828 • Court of Appeal

The facts are stated in the judgment of May LJ.

May LJ: '. . . The plaintiff, the building owner, owns and operates a swimming pool complex at St Augustines in Norwich. In March 1981 it entered into a contract with the main contractor, called Bush Builders (Norwich) Ltd, for an extension to the complex. The latter subcontracted certain felt roofing work to the second defendant. Unfortunately one of the latter's employees, the first defendant, while using a gas blow torch, set fire to both the existing buildings and the new extension causing damage, which gave rise to the claim in these proceedings.

The judge held that any duty of care which would otherwise have been owed by the defendants to the plaintiff had been qualified by the terms of the respective contracts between the parties, whereby the plaintiff accepted the risk of damage by fire and other perils to their property and that consequently it would not be just and reasonable to hold that the defendants owed any duty to the plaintiff to take reasonable care to avoid such damage. This is the fundamental issue in this case.

The contract between the plaintiff and Bush Builders (Norwich) Ltd, to which I shall refer as the "main contract", [contained clause] 20[C] [which states]:

> "20[C] The existing structures . . . owned by him or for which he is responsible and the works . . . shall be at the sole risk of the employer [i.e. the building owners] as regards loss or damage by fire . . . and the employer shall maintain adequate insurance against those risks."

Clearly therefore, as between the plaintiff and the main contractor, the former was solely liable in respect of any loss or damage to his premises caused by *inter alia* fire . . .

On the facts of this case it is not disputed that if the subcontractor owed any duty to take care to avoid damage to the plaintiff's property by fire, then it was in breach of that duty and the plaintiff is entitled to recover.

The judge held that there was no privity of contract between the plaintiff and the subcontractor; and also that there was no question of the main contractor acting either as the agent or trustee for the subcontractor (see His Honour Judge Smout QC in *Southern Water Authority* v *Carey*). The judge further declined to act upon any analogy with the bailment cases where, as in *Leigh and Sillavan Ltd* v *Aliakmon Shipping Co Ltd*, the contractual exemption is in the defendant sub-bailee's contract with the bailee. Having considered a number of recent authorities relating to the existence and extent of a duty of care he concluded:

"The matter must be approached as one of principle: is the duty owed by the defendant to the plaintiff qualified by the plaintiff's contract with the main contractor, or to put it more broadly, by the plaintiff's propounding a scheme whereby they accepted the risk of damage by fire and other perils to [its] own property – existing structures and contents – and some property which does not belong to it – unfixed materials and goods, the value of which has not been included in any certificate – while requiring the contractor to indemnify it against liabilities arising from the omission or default of both the contractor and of any subcontractor; then requiring the contractor to insure and to cause any subcontractor to insure against the liabilities included in the indemnity? I am left in no doubt that the duty in tort owed by the subcontractor to the employer is so qualified. This appears to me to follow from the passage to which I have referred in *Governors of the Peabody Donation Fund* v *Sir Lindsay Parkinson & Co Ltd* and to be consistent with the approach albeit on different facts in *Scottish Special Housing Association* v *Wimpey Construction UK Ltd* and *Mark Rowlands Ltd* v *Berni Inns Ltd* . . . Each case must turn both on its own facts, and on the authority of *Governors of the Peabody Donation Fund* v *Sir Lindsay Parkinson & Co Ltd*, what is just and reasonable."

I trust I do no injustice to the plaintiff's argument in this appeal if I put it shortly in this way. There is no dispute between the employer and the main contractor that the former accepted the risk of fire damage: see *James Archdale & Co Ltd* v *Comservices Ltd* and *Scottish Special Housing Association* v *Wimpey Construction UK Ltd*. However clause 20[C] does not give rise to any obligation on the employer to indemnify the subcontractor. That clause is primarily concerned to see that the works were completed. It was intended to operate only for the mutual benefit of the employer and the main contractor. If the judge and the subcontractor are right, the latter obtains protection which the rules of privity do not provide. Undoubtedly the subcontractor owed duties of care in respect of damage by fire to other persons and in respect of other property (for instance the lawful visitor, employees of the employer, or other buildings outside the site); in those circumstances it is impracticable juridically to draw a sensible line between the plaintiff on the one hand and others on the other to whom a duty of care was owed. The employer had no effective control over the terms upon which the relevant subcontract was let and no direct contractual control over either the subcontractor or any employee of its.

In addition, the plaintiff pointed to the position of the first defendant, the subcontractor's employee. *Ex hypothesi* he was careless and even if his employer be held to have owed no duty to the building employer, on what grounds can it be said that the employee himself owed no such duty? In my opinion, however, this particular point does not take the matter very much further. If in principle the subcontractor owed no specific duty to the building owner in respect of damage by fire, then neither in my opinion can any of its employees have done so.

In reply the defendants contend that the judge was right to hold that in all the circumstances there was no duty of care on the subcontractor in this case. Alternatively they submit that the employer's insurers have no right of subrogation to entitle them to maintain this litigation against the subcontractor.

The law relevant to the question whether or not a duty of care arises in given circumstances has been considered by the House of Lords and the Privy Council in a number of recent decisions. For present purposes one can start with the dictum from the speech of Lord Wilberforce in *Anns* v *Merton London Borough Council* . . .

In my opinion the present state of the law on the question whether or not a duty of care exists is that, save where there is already good authority that in the circumstances there is such a duty, it will only exist in novel situations where not only is there foreseeability of harm, but also such a close and direct relation between the parties concerned, not confined to mere physical proximity, to the extent contemplated by Lord Atkin in his speech in *Donoghue* v *Stevenson*. Further, a court should also have regard to what it considers just and reasonable in all the circumstances and facts of the case.

In the instant case it is clear that as between the plaintiff and the main contractor the former accepted the risk of damage by fire to its premises arising out of and in the course of the building works. Further, although there was no privity between the plaintiff and the subcontractor, it is equally clear from the documents passing between the main contractor and the subcontractor to which I have already referred that the subcontractor contracted on a like basis. In *Scottish Special Housing Association* v *Wimpey Construction UK Ltd* the House of Lords had to consider whether, as between the employer and main contractor under a contract in precisely the same terms as those of the instant case, it was in truth intended that the employer should bear the whole risk of damage by fire, even fire caused by the contractor's negligence. The position of subcontractors was not strictly in issue in the *Scottish Housing* case, which I cannot think the House did not appreciate, but having considered the terms of clauses 18, 19 and 20[C] of the same standard form as was used in the instant case Lord Keith of Kinkel, in a speech with which the remainder of their Lordships agreed, said:

> "I have found it impossible to resist the conclusion that it is intended that the employer shall bear the whole risk of damage by fire, including fire caused by the negligence of the contractor or that of subcontractors."

As Lord Keith went on to point out, a similar conclusion was arrived at by the Court of Appeal in England in *James Archdale & Co Ltd* v *Comservices Ltd* upon the construction of similarly but not identically worded corresponding clauses in a predecessor of the standard form used in *Scottish Special Housing Association* v *Wimpey Construction UK Ltd* and the instant case. Again the issue only arose in the earlier case as between employer and main contractor, but approaching the question on the basis of what is just and reasonable I do not think that the mere fact that there is no strict privity between the employer and the subcontractor should prevent the latter from relying upon the clear basis upon which all the parties contracted in relation to damage to the employer's building caused by fire, even when due to the negligence of the contractors or subcontractors.'

SUMMARY

You should now be able to:

- Understand that a person cannot have liabilities imposed upon him by a contract which he has not agreed to.

- Understand that even if a person has agreed to the terms of the contract he will *not be liable* under that contract unless he and the other parties to that contract have provided consideration.
- Understand that as a general rule a person cannot acquire rights under a contract *unless* he has provided consideration.
- Understand that in limited circumstances a person can acquire rights under a contract even though he has not agreed to the terms of the contract nor provided consideration.
- Understand how a person who is not a party to a contract can obtain the benefit of an exclusion clause contained in that contract.

If you have not mastered the above points you should go through this section again.

9 Contents of a contract

TERMS AND REPRESENTATIONS

Contract law distinguishes between terms and representations. A term is part of a contract; a representation is *not* part of a contract. The distinction is well put below.

Behn v Burness
(1863) 3 B & S 751 • Exchequer Chamber

> Williams J: '. . . Properly speaking, a representation is a statement, or assertion, made by one party to the other, before or at the time of the contract, of some matter or circumstance relating to it. Though it is sometimes contained in the written instrument, it is not an integral part of the contract; and, consequently the contract is not broken though the representation proves to be untrue . . .'

What the above quotation shows is that not everything that is said, before or at the time of making the contract, is intended to form part of the actual contract.

Difficulty of distinguishing terms from representations

Oscar Chess Ltd v Williams
[1957] 1 All ER 325 • Court of Appeal

In June 1955 Williams agreed to sell his 1948 Morris car for £290 to Oscar Chess who were car dealers. In return Williams bought a new Hillman Minx car from Oscar Chess for £650. The registration book showed that the Morris had been registered in 1948 and both parties honestly believed the car to be a 1948 model. In January 1956 Oscar Chess discovered that the Morris was in fact a 1939 model which was only worth £175. Oscar Chess sued Williams for breach of his alleged warranty that his car was a 1948 model.

The issue before the court was whether Williams had intended to warrant that the Morris was a 1948 model.

Denning LJ: 'The effect of such a mistake is this: It does not make the contract a nullity from the beginning, but it does in some circumstances enable the contract to be set aside in equity. If the buyer had come promptly, he might have succeeded in getting the whole transaction set aside in equity on the ground of this mistake (see *Solle* v *Butcher*), but he did not do so and it is now too late for him to do it (see *Leaf* v *International Galleries*). His only remedy is in damages, and to recover these he must prove a warranty.

In saying that he must prove a warranty, I use the word "warranty" in its ordinary English meaning to denote a binding promise. Everyone knows what a man means when he says, "I guarantee it", or "I warrant it", or "I give you my word on it". He means that he binds himself to it. That is the meaning which it has borne in English law for three hundred years from the leading case of *Chandelor* v *Lopus* onwards. During the last hundred years, however, the lawyers have come to use the word "warranty" in another sense. They use it to denote a subsidiary term in a contract as distinct from a vital term which they call a "condition". In so doing they depart from the ordinary meaning, not only of the word "warranty", but also of the word "condition". There is no harm in their doing this, so long as they confine this technical use to its proper sphere, namely, to distinguish between a vital term, the breach of which gives the right to treat the contract as at an end, and a subsidiary term which does not. The trouble comes, however, when one person uses the word "warranty" in its ordinary meaning and another uses it in its technical meaning . . . These different uses of the word seem to have been the source of confusion in the present case. The judge did not ask himself, "Was the representation (that the car was a 1948 Morris car) intended to be a warranty?" He asked himself, "Was it fundamental to the contract?" He answered it by saying that it was fundamental, and, therefore, it was a "condition" and not a "warranty". By concentrating on whether it was fundamental, he seems to me to have missed the crucial point in the case which is whether it was a term of the contract at all. The crucial question is: Was it a binding promise or only an innocent misrepresentation? The technical distinction between a "condition" and a "warranty" is quite immaterial in this case. (A condition is, as indicated above, a stipulation which is fundamental to a contract but a warranty is a provision which is collateral to the main purpose of the contract.) The practical distinction lies in the consequences; a breach of a condition will entitle the innocent party to treat the contract as being at an end, but a breach of warranty entitles the innocent party only to damages, because it is far too late for the buyer to reject the car. He can, at best, only claim damages. The material distinction here is between a statement which is a term of the contract and a statement which is only an innocent misrepresentation. This distinction is best expressed by the ruling of Holt CJ, "Was it intended as a warranty or not?", using the word "warranty" there in its ordinary English meaning: because it gives the exact shade of meaning that is required. It is something to which a man must be taken to bind himself.

In applying this test, however, some misunderstanding has arisen by the use of the word "intended". It is sometimes supposed that the tribunal must look into the minds of the parties to see what they themselves intended. That is a mistake. Lord Moulton made it quite clear, in *Heilbut, Symons & Co* v *Buckleton* that "The intention of the parties can only be deduced from the totality of the evidence . . .". The question whether a warranty was intended depends on the conduct of the parties, on their words and behaviour, rather than on their thoughts. If an intelligent bystander would reasonably infer that a warranty was intended, that will suffice. And this, when the facts are not in dispute, is a question of law . . .

It is instructive to take some recent instances to show how the courts have approached this question. When the seller states a fact which is or should be within his own knowledge and of which the buyer is ignorant, intending that the buyer should act on it and he does so, it is easy to infer a warranty; see *Couchman* v *Hill*, where a farmer stated that a heifer was unserved, and *Harling* v *Eddy*, where he stated that there was nothing wrong with her. So also if the seller makes a promise about something which is or should be within his own control; see *Birch* v *Paramount Estates, Ltd* decided on Oct 2, 1956, in this court, where the seller stated that the house would be as good as the show house. If, however, the seller, when he states a fact, makes it clear that he has no knowledge of his own but has got his information elsewhere, and is merely passing it on, it is not so easy to imply a warranty. Such a case as *Routledge* v *McKay* where the seller stated that a motor cycle combination was a 1942 model, and pointed to the corroboration of that statement to be found in the registration book, and it was held that there was no warranty.

Turning now to the present case, much depends on the precise words that were used. If the seller says: "I believe the car is a 1948 Morris. Here is the registration book to prove it", there is clearly no warranty. It is a statement of belief, not a contractual promise. If, however, the seller says: "I guarantee that it is a 1948 Morris. This is borne out by the registration book, but you need not rely solely on that. I give you my own guarantee that it is", there is clearly a warranty. The seller is making himself contractually responsible, even though the registration book is wrong.

In this case much reliance was placed by the judge on the fact that the buyer looked up *Glass's Guide* and paid £290 on the footing that the car was a 1948 model, but that fact seems to me to be neutral. Both sides believed the car to have been made in 1948 and in that belief the buyer paid £290. That belief can be just as firmly based on the buyer's own inspection of the log-book as on a contractual warranty by the seller.

Once that fact is put on one side, I ask myself: What is the proper inference from the known facts? It must have been obvious to both that the seller had himself no personal knowledge of the year when the car was made. He only became owner after a great number of changes. He must have been relying on the registration book. It is unlikely that such a person would warrant the year of manufacture. The most that he would do would be to state his belief, and then produce the registration book in verification of it. In these circumstances the intelligent bystander would, I suggest, say that the seller did not intend to bind himself so as to warrant that the car was a 1948 model. If the seller was asked to pledge himself to it, he would at once have said "I cannot do that. I have only the log-book to go by, the same as you".

The judge seems to have thought that there was a difference between written contracts and oral contracts. He thought that the reason why the buyer failed in *Heilbut, Symons & Co* v *Buckleton* and *Routledge* v *McKay* was because the sales were afterwards recorded in writing, and the written contracts contained no reference to the representation. I agree that that was an important factor in those cases. If an oral representation is afterwards recorded in writing, it is good evidence that it was intended as a warranty. If it is not put into writing, it is evidence against a warranty being intended; but it is by no means decisive. There have been many cases, such as *Birch* v *Paramount Estates, Ltd*, where the courts have found an oral warranty collateral to a written contract. When, however, the purchase is not recorded in writing at all, it must not be supposed that every representation made in the course of the dealing is to be treated as a warranty. The question then is still: Was it intended as a warranty? In the leading case of *Chandelor* v *Lopus* in 1603 a man by word of mouth sold a precious stone for £100 affirming it to be a bezoar stone whereas it was not. The declaration averred that the seller *affirmed* it to be a bezoar stone, but did not aver that he *warranted* it to be so. The declaration was held to be ill because: ". . . the bare affirmation that it was a bezoar stone, without warranting it to be so, is no cause of action . . .". That has been the law from that day to this and it was emphatically re-affirmed by the House of Lords in *Heilbut, Symons & Co* v *Buckleton*.

One final word. It seems to me clear that the plaintiffs, the motor dealers who bought the car, relied on the year stated in the log-book. If they had wished to make sure of it, they could have checked it then and there, by taking the engine number and chassis number and writing to the makers. They did not do so at the time, but only eight months later. They are experts, and, as they did not make that check at the time, I do not think that they should now be allowed to recover against the innocent seller who produced to them all the evidence which he had, namely, the registration book. I agree that it is hard on the plaintiffs to have paid more than the car is worth, but it would be equally hard on the seller to make him pay the difference. He would never have bought the Hillman car unless he had received the allowance of £290 for the Morris car. The best course in all these cases would be to "shunt" the difference down the train of innocent sellers until one reached the rogue who perpetrated the fraud; but he can rarely be traced, or if he can, he rarely has the money to pay the damages. Therefore, one is left to decide between a number of innocent people who is to bear the loss. That can only be done by applying the law about representations and warranties as we know it, and that is what I have tried to do. If the rogue can be traced, he can be sued by whosoever has suffered the loss: but, if he cannot be traced, the loss must lie where it falls. It should not be inflicted on innocent sellers, who sold the car many months, perhaps many years before, and have forgotten all about it and have conducted their affairs on the basis that the transaction was concluded. Such a seller would not be able to recollect after all this length of time the exact words which he used, such as whether he said "I believe it is a 1948 model", or "I warrant it is a 1948 model". The right course is to let the buyer set aside the transaction if he finds out the mistake quickly and comes promptly before other interests have irretrievably intervened, otherwise the loss must lie where it falls: and that is, I think, the course prescribed by law. I would allow this appeal accordingly.'

Morris LJ dissenting: 'The only point taken on behalf of the defendant was that the statement which was made did not form a part of the contract. The learned judge rejected this. He held that it was not only a term but an essential term. In my judgment he was correct. The statement that the car was a 1948 car was not a mere representation in respect of the subject-matter of the contract: the statement was adopted as the foundation of the contract which they made. The promise to pay £290 for that particular car (a figure arrived at by reference to the value of 1948 cars) was the counterpart of a term of the contract that that particular car was a 1948 model . . .

The plaintiffs do not allege that there was any collateral oral warranty. They submit that the statement of the defendant was not something detached from the contract, but was a part of the contract and was in legal terminology a condition. In my judgment, it was a stipulation of the contract which was a condition. But by the time that the plaintiffs ascertained that the car was a 1939 car, it was too late for them to take any other course than to treat the breach of condition as a breach of warranty (see Sale of Goods Act, 1893, s 11). On this basis the learned judge held that the plaintiffs were relegated to a right to claim damages, which he assessed at £115, being the difference between the value which the car would have had if it had been a 1948 car and its actual value, which he found was £175.

In deciding the case the learned judge applied his mind to the tests laid down in *Heilbut, Symons & Co v Buckleton*. In his speech in that case Lord Moulton spoke of the importance of maintaining in its full integrity the principle that a person is not liable in damages for an innocent misrepresentation and made it clear that it would be wrong to say that, merely because a representation is made in the course of a dealing and before completion of a bargain the representation amounts to a warranty. He approved the statement of Holt CJ, that an affirmation at the time of a sale is a warranty, provided that it appears on the evidence to have been so intended. The intention of the parties is to be deduced from the totality of the evidence . . .

The learned judge in the present case considered *Routledge v McKay* and correctly distinguished it from the present one. In the present case there was not, as in *Routledge v McKay*, an antecedent statement and then a later written contract which omitted any incorporation of or reference to the statement. *Routledge v McKay* is distinguishable on three grounds. In the present case there was a statement made at the time of the transaction: there was no written contract: and, in so far as there was a document brought into existence, the document consisted of an invoice addressed to the defendant which recorded the complete transaction and which expressly described the car for which an allowance of £290 was being made as a "1948 Morris 10 Saloon". The statement made which described the Morris car was, therefore, an integral part of the contract. It was, I consider, a condition of the contract, on which the plaintiffs contracted: compare *Bannerman v White*. In *Couchman v Hill* a statement was made that a heifer was "unserved". There was in that case a discussion whether the description "unserved" constituted a warranty or a condition. In his judgment, with which the other members of the court concurred, Scott LJ, said:

"... as a matter of law I think every item in a description which constitutes a substantial ingredient in the 'identity' of the thing sold is a condition, although every such condition can be waived by the purchaser who thereon becomes entitled to treat it as a warranty and recover damages. I think there was here an unqualified condition which, on its breach, the plaintiff was entitled to treat as a warranty and recover the damages claimed."

In the present case, on a consideration of the evidence which he heard, the learned judge came to the conclusion that the statement which he held to have been made by the defendant at the time of the making of the contract was a statement made contractually. It seems to me that the totality of the evidence points to that view. The statement related to a vitally important matter: it described the subject-matter of the contract then being made and directed the parties to, and was the basis of, their agreement as to the price to be paid or credited to the defendant. In the language of Scott LJ, it seems to me that the statement made by the defendant was "an item in [the] description" of what was being sold and that it constituted a substantial ingredient in the identity of the thing sold. It is with diffidence that I arrive at a conclusion differing from that of my Lords, but I cannot see that the learned judge in any way misdirected himself or misapplied any principle of law, and I see no reason for disturbing his conclusion.'

Dick Bentley Productions Ltd v Harold Smith (Motors) Ltd

[1965] 2 All ER 65 • Court of Appeal

The facts are stated in the judgment of Lord Denning MR.

Lord Denning MR: 'The second plaintiff, Mr Charles Walter Bentley, sometimes known as Dick Bentley, brings an action against Harold Smith (Motors) Ltd, for damages for breach of warranty on the sale of a car. Mr Bentley had been dealing with Mr Smith (to whom I shall refer in the stead of the defendant company) for a couple of years and told Mr Smith he was on the look-out for a well vetted Bentley car. In January 1960, Mr Smith found one and bought it for £1500 from a firm in Leicester. He wrote to Mr Bentley and said: "I have just purchased a Park Ward power operated hood convertible. It is one of the nicest cars we have had in for quite a long time". Mr Smith had told Mr Bentley earlier that he was in a position to find out the history of cars. It appears that with a car of this quality the makers do keep a complete biography of it.

Mr Bentley went to see the car. Mr Smith told him that a German baron had had this car. He said that it had been fitted at one time with a replacement engine and gearbox, and had done twenty thousand miles only since it had been so fitted. The speedometer on the car showed only twenty thousand miles. Mr Smith said the price was £1850, and he would guarantee the car for twelve months, including parts and labour. That was on the morning of Jan 23, 1960. In the afternoon Mr Bentley took his wife over to see the car. Mr Bentley repeated to his wife in Mr Smith's presence what Mr Smith had told him in the morning. In particular that Mr Smith said it had done only twenty thousand miles since it had been refitted with a replacement engine and gearbox. Mr Bentley took it for a short run. He bought the car for £1850, gave his cheque and the sale was concluded. The car was a considerable disappointment to him. He took it back to Mr Smith from time to time. Eventually he brought this action for breach of warranty. The county court judge found that there was a warranty, that it was broken, and that the damages were more than £400, but as the claim was limited to £400, he gave judgment for the plaintiffs for that amount.

The first point is whether this representation, namely that the car had done twenty thousand miles only since it had been fitted with a replacement engine and gearbox, was an innocent misrepresentation (which does not give rise to damages), or whether it was a warranty. It was said by Holt CJ [In *Crosse* v *Gardner* and *Medina* v *Stoughton*] . . .

"An affirmation at the time of the sale is a warranty, provided it appear on evidence to be so intended."

But that word "intended" has given rise to difficulties. I endeavoured to explain in *Oscar Chess Ltd* v *Williams* that the question whether a warranty was intended depends on the conduct of the parties, on their words and behaviour, rather than on their thoughts. If an intelligent bystander would reasonably infer that a warranty was intended, that will suffice. What conduct, then? What words and behaviour, lead to the inference of a warranty?

Looking at the cases once more, as we have done so often, it seems to me that if a representation is made in the course of dealings for a contract for the very purpose of inducing the other party to act on it, and it actually induces him to act on it by entering into the contract, that is *prima facie* ground for inferring that the representation was intended as a warranty. It is not necessary to speak of it as being collateral. Suffice it that the representation was intended to be acted on and was in fact acted on. But the maker of the representation can rebut this inference if he can show that it really was an innocent misrepresentation, in that he was in fact innocent of fault in making it, and that it would not be reasonable in the circumstances for him to be bound by it. In the *Oscar Chess* case the inference was rebutted. There a man had bought a second-hand car and received with it a log-book, which stated the year of the car, 1948. He afterwards resold the car. When he resold it he simply repeated what was in the log-book and passed it on to the buyer. He honestly believed on reasonable grounds that it was true. He was completely innocent of any fault. There was no warranty by him but only an innocent misrepresentation. Whereas in the present case it is very different. The inference is not rebutted. Here we have a dealer, Mr Smith, who was in a position to know, or at least to find out, the history of the car. He could get it by writing to the makers. He did not do so. Indeed it was done later. When the history of this car was examined, his statement turned out to be quite wrong. He ought to have known better. There was no reasonable foundation for it.

The county court judge found that the representations were not dishonest. Mr Smith was not guilty of fraud. But he made the statement as to twenty thousand miles without any foundation. And the judge was well justified in finding that there was a warranty. He said:

"I have no hesitation that as a matter of law the statement was a warranty. Mr Smith stated a fact that should be within his own knowledge. He had jumped to a conclusion and stated it as a fact. A fact that a buyer would act on."

That is ample foundation for the inference of a warranty. So much for this point.
I hold that the appeal fails and should be dismissed.'

Salmon LJ: 'I agree. I have no doubt at all that the learned county court judge reached a correct conclusion when he decided that Mr Smith gave a warranty to the second plaintiff, Mr Bentley, and that that warranty was broken. Was what Mr Smith said intended and understood as a legally binding promise? If so, it was a warranty and as such may be part of the contract of sale or collateral to it. In effect, Mr Smith said: "If you will enter into a contract to buy this motor car from me for £1850, I undertake that you will be getting a motor car which has done no more than twenty thousand miles since it was fitted with a new engine and a new gearbox". I have no doubt at all that what was said by Mr Smith was so understood and was intended to be so understood by Mr Bentley.

I accordingly agree that the appeal should be dismissed.'

Tests to distinguish between terms and representations

The following are points to be considered when trying to distinguish between *terms* and *representations*. No one point in itself is conclusive one way or another. In the end a balancing act of the various points has to be attempted.

Time between the making of the statement and the parties entering into the contract

Routledge v *McKay*

[1954] 1 All ER 855 • Court of Appeal

On 23 October the seller of a motor cycle combination told the buyer that it was a late 1941 or 1942 model. The registration book showed it to be first registered on 9 September 1941. The seller in fact knew that the model was a 1936 or 1938 model. A week later on 30 October the seller and buyer entered into a written contract drawn up by the buyer which did not refer to the date of the motor cycle combination. The buyer later discovered the true age of the motor cycle combination and sued the seller for breach of warranty.

Sir Raymond Evershed MR: 'The question is whether or not, on a sale of a motor bicycle with a sidecar combination, there was a warranty as to the date when the machine was originally put on the market. The classic exposition of the law in regard to warranties is to be found in the speech of Lord Moulton in *Heilbut, Symons & Co* v *Buckleton* . . .

. . . On the oral evidence, therefore, the judge found, in effect, that, before the bargain was eventually made, the [seller] specifically stated [on 23 October], in answer to a question, that it was a 1942 model, and pointed to the corroboration of that statement to be found in the registration book, and that he knew, from what the manufacturers told him, the true date to be 1936 or 1938. Of course, it does not follow that the [seller] was deliberately trying to deceive the [buyer], and in any case we are not here trying any action based on fraud.

The [buyer] had caused to be prepared a written memorandum or contract which was signed by himself and the fifth party on Oct. 30, 1949 . . . This written memorandum represents *prima facie* the record of what the parties intended to agree when the actual transaction took place. Counsel for the [seller] contended that the terms of it necessarily exclude any warranty, that is to say, any collateral bargain, either contemporary or earlier in date. I am not sure that I would go so far as that. But I think that as a matter of construction it would be difficult to say that such an agreement was consistent with a warranty being given at the same time so as to be intended to form a part of the bargain then made. I think, with counsel for the [seller], that the last words "It is understood that when the £30 is paid . . . this transaction is closed" would make such a contention difficult. But I will assume that the warranty was given, not when the bargain was struck, but on Oct. 23, 1949, on which date alone, according to the evidence, any representation about the date of the motor cycle combination was made at all.

If that representation is to be a warranty it has to be contractual in form. In other words, so far as I can see, once the existence of a warranty as part of the actual bargain is excluded, it must be a separate contract, and the overwhelming difficulty which faces the [buyer] is that when the representation was made there was then no bargain, and it is, therefore, in my view, impossible to say that it could have been collateral, to some other contract. Even apart from that, it seems to me that on the evidence there is nothing to support the conclusion, as a matter of law and bearing in mind Lord Moulton's observations, that in answering the question posed about the date of the motor cycle combination there was anything more intended than a mere representation.'

Birch v Paramount Estates (Liverpool) Ltd

[1956] 168 EG 396 • Court of Appeal

Birch alleged that by an oral warranty he was induced to purchase for £1825 a house to be built by Paramount Estates. He claimed that he was told his house would be of the same standard of workmanship as the company's show house. In fact the paintwork of his house was inferior to that in the show house and deteriorated faster. Paramount Estates denied any warranty.

The issue before the court was whether Paramount Estates had given a collateral warranty to Birch which became contractually binding when Birch agreed to buy the house.

Denning LJ: 'In 1954 Mr Birch visited a show house on the estate in question and then went to an incomplete house which he thought he might like to buy. A representative of the builders told him that the house would be just as good as the show house and would be built of materials of the same standard. On July 2, 1954, he signed a contract, a clause in which stated that the house would be built fit for occupation and habitation. The house was, however, very badly painted, much worse than the show house: and the builders had refused to repaint it. [Counsel for the builder] had argued that there was no oral contract and that everything was in the written contract. He had suggested the paintwork was completed by the date of the contract and that, however bad it was, Mr Birch could not complain. The judgment of the learned County Court judge was however unassailable. It did not matter whether the house was completed on July 2 or not. The oral contract was collateral with the written contract and the builders were liable.'

Morris LJ: 'The very purpose of having a show house was that a prospective purchaser might be attracted by what he saw and might have the opportunity of knowing what he was to get.'

In Birch's case there would have been a considerable period between Mr Birch viewing the show house and signing the contract to buy a house yet the Court of Appeal did not even comment on this point.

Importance of intention of parties

Bannerman v *White*

(1861) 10 CBNS 844 • Common Pleas

During the course of negotiations for the sale of hops by sample White asked Bannerman if any sulphur had been used in the growth or treatment of them, adding that he would not ask the price if sulphur had been used. Bannerman said that no sulphur had been used. After the hops had been delivered White discovered that sulphur had been used in the cultivation of a portion of the hops (5 acres out of 300). However, because the hops were so mixed up together, it was impossible to separate the sulphured from the unsulphured hops. White, therefore, rejected all the hops.

The issue before the court was whether the statement relating to the use of sulphur on the crops was intended to be a mere representation or term of the contract.

Erle CJ: 'Thus, the question was, – "Was the affirmation that no sulphur had been used intended between the parties to be part of the contract of sale, and a warranty by the plaintiff?"

As to this, it was contended on one side that the conversation relating to the sulphur was preliminary to entering on the contract, and no part thereof, both from the form of expression and also from the written guarantee which was shewn to have been given. On the other side it was contended that the whole interview was one transaction, that the intention of the parties was alone to be regarded, that the defendants had declared the importance they attached to the inquiry, and that the plaintiff must have known it. And the jury answered this question in the affirmative.

The effect of this finding of the jury, taken with the evidence, is now to be considered. We avoid the term "warranty", because it is used in two senses, and the term "condition", because the question is whether that term is applicable. Then, the effect is that the defendants required, and that the plaintiff gave his understanding, that no sulphur had been used. This undertaking was a preliminary stipulation; and if it had not been given, the defendants would not have gone on with the treaty which resulted in the sale. In this sense it was the condition upon which the defendants contracted; and it would be contrary to the intention expressed by this stipulation that the contract should remain valid if sulphur had been used.

The intention of the parties governs in the making and in the construction of all contracts. If the parties so intend, the sale may be absolute, with a warranty superadded; or the sale may be conditional, to be null if the warranty is broken. And, upon this statement of facts, we think that the intention appears that the contract should be null if sulphur had been used: and upon this ground we agree that the rule should be discharged.'

Later written document

Generally if, after a statement is made, the contract is put into writing and the representation does not appear in the written contract the conclusion will be that the parties did *not* intend the representation to be a *term* of the contract: if they had intended the representation to be a term of the contract surely they would have put it into the written contract?

See *Routledge* v *McKay* above (p 206).

Heilbut, Symons & Co v *Buckleton*

[1913] AC 30 • House of Lords

The facts are stated in the judgment of Lord Moulton.

Lord Moulton: 'My Lords, in this action the plaintiff sought relief in damages against the defendants in respect of two contracts whereby the defendants undertook to procure for the plaintiff, and the plaintiff undertook to accept, the allotment of 5000 and 1000 shares in a company called the Filisola Rubber and Produce Estates, Limited . . . [I]n the statement of claim an alternative claim for damages was included, based on the breach of an alleged warranty given by the defendants that the company was a rubber company . . .

The alleged warranty rested entirely upon the following evidence. The plaintiff got a friend to ring up on the telephone Mr Johnston (a representative of the defendants, for whose acts they accept the full responsibility) to tell him that the plaintiff wished to speak to him. The plaintiff's evidence continues thus: "I went to the telephone and I said 'Is that you, Johnston?' He said 'Yes'. I said 'I understand that you are bringing out a rubber company,' and he said 'we are'."

The material part of the evidence ends here . . .

There is no controversy between the parties as to certain points of fact and of law. It is not contested that the only company referred to was the Filisola Rubber and Produce Estates, Limited, or that the reply of Mr Johnston to the plaintiff's question over the telephone was a representation by the defendants that the company was a "rubber company", whatever may be the meaning of that phrase; nor is there any controversy as to the legal nature of that which the plaintiff must establish. He must show a warranty, i.e., a contract collateral to the main contract to take the shares, whereby the defendants in consideration of the plaintiff taking the shares promised that the company itself was a rubber company. The question in issue is whether there was any evidence that such a contract was made between the parties.

It is evident, both on principle and on authority, that there may be a contract the consideration for which is the making of some other contract. "If you will make such and such a contract I will give you one hundred pounds", is in every sense of the word a complete legal contract. It is collateral to the main contract, but each has an independent existence, and they do not differ in respect of their possessing to the full the character and status of a contract. But such collateral contracts must from their very nature be rare. The effect of a collateral contract such as that which I have instanced would be to increase the consideration of the main contract by 100l, and the more natural and usual way of carrying this out would be by so modifying the main contract and not by executing a concurrent and collateral contract. Such collateral contracts, the sole effect of which is to vary or add to the terms of the principal contract, are therefore viewed with suspicion by the law. They must be proved strictly. Not only the terms of such contracts but the existence of an *animus contrahendi* [an intention to enter into a contract] on the part of all the parties to them must be clearly shown. Any laxity on these points would enable parties to escape from the full performance of the obligations of contracts unquestionably entered into by them and more especially would have the effect of lessening the authority of written contracts by making it possible to vary them by suggesting the existence of verbal collateral agreements relating to the same subject-matter.

There is in the present case an entire absence of any evidence to support the existence of such a collateral contract. The statement of Mr Johnston in answer to plaintiff's question was beyond controversy a mere statement of fact, for it was in reply to a question for information and nothing more. No doubt it was a representation as to fact, and indeed it was the actual representation upon which the main case of the plaintiff rested. It was this representation which he alleged to have been false and fraudulent and which he alleged induced him to enter into the contracts and take the shares. There is no suggestion throughout the whole of his evidence that he regarded it as anything but a representation. Neither the plaintiff nor the defendants were asked any question or gave any evidence tending to show the existence of any *animus contrahendi* other than as regards the main contracts. The whole case for the existence of a collateral contract therefore rests on the mere fact that the statement was made as to the character of the company, and if this is to be treated as evidence sufficient to establish the existence of a collateral contract of the kind alleged the same result must follow with regard to any other statement relating to the subject-matter of a contract made by a contracting party prior to its execution. This would negative entirely the firmly established rule that an innocent representation gives no right to damages. It would amount to saying that the making of any representation prior to a contract relating to its subject-matter is sufficient to establish the existence of a collateral contract that the statement is true and therefore to give a right to damages if such should not be the case.

In the history of English law we find many attempts to make persons responsible in damages by reason of innocent misrepresentations, and at times it has seemed as though the attempts would succeed . . .

On the Common Law side of the Court the attempts to make a person liable for an innocent misrepresentation have usually taken the form of attempts to extend the doctrine of warranty beyond its just limits and to find that a warranty existed in cases where there was nothing more than an innocent misrepresentation. The present case is, in my opinion, an instance of this. But in respect of the question of the existence of a warranty the Courts have had the advantage of an admirable enunciation of the true principle of law which was made in very early days by Holt CJ with respect to the contract of sale. He says: "An affirmation at the time of the sale is a warranty, provided it appear on evidence to be so intended". So far as decisions are concerned, this has, on the whole, been consistently followed in the Courts of Common Law . . .

. . . The intention of the parties can only be deduced from the totality of the evidence, and no secondary principles of such a kind can be universally true.'

Couchman v Hill

[1947] 1 All ER 103 • Court of Appeal

The facts are stated in the judgment of Scott LJ.

Scott LJ: 'On December 15, 1945, the plaintiff purchased at an auction sale . . . a heifer, the property of the defendant, for the sum of £29. The heifer in question was . . . in the sale catalogue described as "unserved". There can be no question on the facts found by the county court judge but that, in the absence of some special agreement to the contrary, when the hammer fell the resulting contract was subject to the printed conditions of sale exhibited at the auction and to the stipulations contained in the sale catalogue. The latter document contained these words:

"Note. – The sale will be subject to the auctioneers' usual conditions, copies of which will be exhibited. The auctioneers will not be responsible for any error or misstatement in this catalogue, or in the dates of calving of any cattle. The information contained herein is supplied by the vendor and is believed to be correct, but its accuracy is not guaranteed, and all lots must be taken subject to all faults or errors of description (if any), and no compensation will be paid for the same."

No 3 of the printed conditions of sale was as follows:

"The lots are sold with all faults, imperfections, and errors of description, the auctioneers not being responsible for the correct description, genuineness, or authenticity of, or any fault or defect in, any lot, and giving no warranty whatever."

On February 6, 1946, a six months old foetus was removed from the heifer in question, and on February 26 the heifer died as a result of the strain of carrying a calf at too young an age for breeding. There was no suggestion that at the time of the sale either the defendant or the auctioneer did not honestly believe that the heifer was unserved. On the other hand, the plaintiff's evidence, which was accepted by the judge, was that he would not have bought it had he had any reason to doubt the accuracy of the description as he required an unserved heifer for service by his own bull at a time of his own choosing.

So far it is, in my opinion, clear that the plaintiff, by reason of the stipulations in the catalogue and conditions of sale, would have had no remedy by way of damages for breach of contract or warranty against the defendant . . . [I]t is, in my view, impossible to say that the words "the lots are sold with all faults, imperfections, and errors of description", and the words "and all lots must be taken subject to all faults or errors of description (if any), and no compensation will be paid for the same" are not to be incorporated as terms of the contract as between the vendor and purchaser when the hammer falls. Whether the word "unserved" amounts to a warranty or a condition is immaterial, because it is, I think, clear that it was, in any event, an error of description and as such expressly protected by the words to which I have referred. For these reasons it appears to me that, in so far as the plaintiff relied on the statement in the catalogue to support his claim for damages for breach of warranty, he necessarily failed.

The plaintiff, however, also alleged in his further particulars as follows: "The said warranty was also confirmed verbally both by the auctioneer and by the defendant on inquiry by the plaintiff prior to the sale". As to this the county court judge has accepted the plaintiff's evidence which was to the effect that at the sale and when the heifers were in the ring he asked both the defendant and the auctioneer: "Can you confirm heifers unserved?" and received from both the answer "Yes". There was no contract at that moment . . . There was no contract in existence until the hammer fell. The offer was defined, the auctioneer's authority was defined, but it was in law open to any would-be purchaser to intimate in advance before bidding for any particular heifer offered from the rostrum that he was not willing to bid for the lot unless the defendant modified the terms of sale contained in the two documents in some way specified by him. There is no doubt that the plaintiff did make some attempt of the kind in order to protect himself from the risk of buying an animal that was not of the kind described.

The real question is: What did the parties understand by the question addressed to and the answer received from both the defendant and the auctioneer? It is contended by the defendant that the question meant "having regard to the onerous stipulations which I know I shall have to put up with if I bid and the lot is knocked down to me, can you give me your honourable assurance that the heifers have in fact not been served? If so, I will risk the penalties of the catalogue". The alternative meaning is: "I am frightened of contracting on your published terms, but I will bid if you will tell me by word of mouth that you accept full responsibility for the statement in the catalogue that the heifers have not been served, or, in other words, give me a clean warranty. That is the only condition on which I will bid". If that was the meaning there was clearly an oral offer of a warranty which over-rode the stultifying condition in the printed terms, that offer was accepted by the plaintiff when he bid, and the contract was made on that basis when the lot was knocked down to him . . .'

One party an expert

See *Oscar Chess Ltd* v *Williams* and *Dick Bentley Productions Ltd* v *Harold Smith* above (pp 200 and 204).

Harling v *Eddy*

[1951] 2 All ER 212 • Court of Appeal

The facts are stated in the judgment of Sir Raymond Evershed MR.

Sir Raymond Evershed MR: 'The defendant is a substantial dealer in cattle, and on the relevant occasion he was offering for sale by auction a large number of Guernsey heifer cows. The catalogue describes them as tuberculin-tested Guernseys, and there is contained in the catalogue a number of conditions, including:

". . . (12) No animal, article, or thing is sold with a 'warranty' unless specially mentioned at the time of offering, and no warranty so given shall have any legal force of effect unless the terms thereof appear on the purchaser's account."

To complete my references to the catalogue, the particular animal in question was lot No. 9, and was described by the following words: "Non-pedigree Guernsey heifer, freshly calved. Earmark".

It appears from the findings of the judge that when this animal No. 9 came into the ring to be sold it received a somewhat frigid reception owing to its unpromising appearance. No one made any bid or evinced any desire to do so. Thereupon the defendant, the seller, who was present, made certain statements . . . The plaintiff said that the defendant stated that there was nothing wrong with the heifer, that he would absolutely guarantee her in every respect, and that he would be willing to take her back if she turned out not to be what he stated she was . . . On this vital matter it is plain that the judge . . . accepted the evidence of the plaintiff . . . defendant having given that description of his animal, the bidding was begun, and in the result the animal was knocked down to the plaintiff for £65.

. . . This animal died in October, and as the result of a post-mortem examination the cause of her death was found to be tuberculosis . . .

The question is: Does the statement which the defendant made at the sale immediately before the bidding entitle the plaintiff now to say: "The animal was not as you stated her to be, sound in every respect, and I now take advantage of the offer you made to me and claim from you the price I paid for the animal, or equivalent damages"? The difficulty arises from the circumstance that No. 12 of the conditions, which I have already read, *prima facie* seems intended to render nugatory any mere warranty given at the sale. But the first answer, in my judgment, to the defence based on condition No. 12 is that, in the circumstances, this statement by the defendant was a condition. It has been said many times, and particularly in *Wallis, Son & Wells* v *Pratt & Haynes*, that whether any statement is to be regarded as a condition or a warranty must depend on the intention to be properly inferred from the particular statement made. A statement that an animal is sound in every respect would, *prima facie*, be but a warranty, but in this case the learned judge found as a fact that the defendant went further and promised that he would take the animal back if she were no good . . . The defendant's statement having, therefore, included words to the effect: "If there is anything wrong I will take it back", it seems to me plain that the language he used could not have been intended merely as a warranty, for a warranty would give no right of rejection to the purchaser. The final words involve necessarily a right to the purchaser to reject, that is, to return the animal. They convert the statement, to my mind, from a warranty to a condition.

If, then, it is a condition, what would be the right of the plaintiff? Counsel for the defendant has argued forcibly that the plaintiff must at least exercise his right of rejection in due time. On Sept. 21, 1950, he plainly purported to do so. He called on the defendant to take the animal back. In my judgment, in the circumstances of the case the period between July 1, 1950, and the middle of September, 1950, would not be unreasonable. But, however that may be, it is plain also from *Wallis, Son & Wells* v *Pratt & Haynes* that a person entitled to the benefit of a condition, as was the plaintiff in this case, can turn the condition in effect into a warranty by claiming damages as for breach of warranty instead of exercising his right of rejection. By the time that this claim had been formulated the animal was dead, and the plaintiff could, in truth, do no other than claim damages, and, in my judgment, he was entitled to treat the condition to that extent as though it were a warranty . . . If that is right, the question still remains: Does No. 12 of the conditions apply? In my judgment, the answer is: No. Condition No. 12 is limited in its terms to a statement made which is a mere warranty and is not a condition, and the language in the second part of it, ". . . and no warranty so given shall have any legal force or effect . . ." can only refer to the warranty previously mentioned, viz, a statement which is a warranty and no more. In other words, in my judgment, condition No. 12 cannot be relied on by the defendant to defeat the right of the plaintiff to sue for damages for the breach of the condition under which he purchased.

Since this matter is of some importance, however, I think it is desirable that I should also express a view on the conclusion properly to be reached if this statement were a warranty merely. On that aspect of the matter I derive considerable assistance from the decision of this court in *Couchman* v *Hill* . . .

The terms of the printed conditions in the present case differ from the terms of the printed conditions in *Couchman* v *Hill*, and the language used by the respective defendants differs also, but I think the matter may be put precisely and properly, as it was suggested in the course of the argument, by Roxburgh J. I do not re-state the facts as found by the judge, but, bearing those facts in mind, and, in particular, the initial silence which greeted the entry of this animal into the ring and the fact that bidding only began when the statement had been made, the question may properly be formulated thus: Did the defendant imply by this statement that the animal should be sold on the faith of what he stated to the exclusion of the printed clause, condition No. 12, or of any other condition which might be found in the auction particulars which would of itself appear to exclude any oral statement made? Counsel for the defendant argued that neither party may have had in mind, when this particular incident occurred, what the exact terms of the conditions of sale were, though I should suppose that, both being experienced in the buying and selling of cattle, they would be aware, according to common practice, that there would be stultifying conditions of some kind in the auction particulars. If that were the question to be posed, in my judgment, it should be answered affirmatively on the facts as found by the judge. I, therefore, would hold that, even if the language used here were a warranty only and not a condition, still the plaintiff would be entitled to succeed.

Before leaving *Couchman* v *Hill*, I would like to say one further word about it. According to the report which I have, there is an editorial note referring to a much earlier case of a hundred years ago, *Hopkins* v *Tanqueray*, relating to the sale of a horse at Tattersalls. In that case the seller and the buyer met, not at the sale, but the day before the sale, and the conversation which is related in this note formed no part of the transaction which occurred at the sale itself. At the meeting between the seller and the buyer a statement was made about the soundness of the horse, and later the auction took place. The question was raised whether what had passed in the conversation could affect a stultifying condition in the auction particulars. The court in *Hopkins* v *Tanqueray* found that the promise made by the seller in his private conversation formed no part of the contract which was formed as a result of the sale at the auction and comprehended the conditions set out in the auction particulars. It is plain, therefore, that that case is wholly distinguishable from *Couchman* v *Hill*, and equally from this case. I say that because the note to which I have alluded suggests that, had *Hopkins* v *Tanqueray* been referred to at the time of the hearing in this court of *Couchman* v *Hill*, the decision in *Couchman* v *Hill* might have been different. I do not think so, and there is no reason for suggesting that *Couchman* v *Hill* was other than rightly decided. It binds this court in any case, but I desire to express my entire concurrence with the decision in *Couchman* v *Hill*. For the reasons which I have stated, therefore, it seems to me that the plaintiff's right to succeed is made good.'

Above tests not conclusive

In the event that the above tests are not conclusive, the main test is that of contractual intention.

In *Heilbut, Symons & Co* v *Buckleton*, above (p 209), Lord Moulton said '. . . The intention of the parties can only be deduced from the totality of the evidence, and no secondary principles of such a kind can be universally true.'

COLLATERAL WARRANTIES

As we have seen above generally if after a statement is made the contract is put into writing and the representation does not appear in the written contract the conclusion will be that the parties did *not* intend the representation to be a *term* of the contract: that being the case the courts will not allow parole evidence to be introduced so as to vary the terms of the written contract. This is known as the *parole evidence* rule.

In order to get around this rule a device known as a *collateral warranty* is sometimes applicable. A collateral warranty is an oral contract collateral to the written agreement: it is an oral contract which varies the terms of the written contract.

City & Westminster Properties (1934) Ltd v Mudd
[1958] 2 All 733 • Chancery Division

Mudd was the tenant of a shop which he also used as his home. He entered into a new lease with his landlords whereby he agreed 'not to use . . . the said premises except as the shop of [Mudd] for his business'; also 'not to do or suffer to be done anything . . . which may render the said premises . . . liable . . . to be assessed as a dwelling-house'. Mudd continued to sleep on the premises and the landlords, on discovering this, claimed that the lease was forfeited and that they were entitled to possession. Mudd argued that he had only signed the lease because the landlords' agent had promised him that if he signed the lease containing the above terms they would continue to let him live at his shop; he argued that the landlords were estopped from going back on their promise.

The issue before the court was whether the landlords had made a promise that was binding on them in law.

Harman J: 'There remains the so-called question of estoppel. This, in my judgment, is a misnomer and the present case does not raise the controversial issue of *Central London Property Trust Ltd* v *High Trees House Ltd*. This is not a case of a representation made after contractual relations existed between the parties to the effect that one party to the contract would not rely on his rights. If the tenant's evidence is to be accepted, as I hold that it is, it is a case of a promise made to him before the execution of the lease that if he would execute it in the form put before him, the landlords would not seek to enforce against him personally the covenant about using the property as a shop only. The tenant says that it was in reliance on this promise that he executed the lease and entered on the onerous obligations contained in it. He says, moreover, that but for the promise made he would not have executed the lease, but would have moved to other premises available to him at the time. If these be the facts, there was a clear contract acted on by the tenant to his detriment and from which the landlords cannot be allowed to resile. The case is truly analogous to *Re William Porter & Co, Ltd*. This is a decision of Simonds J. He said:

". . . I am entitled to apply the rule, stated nowhere better than in the old case of *Cairncross* v *Lorimer*. This was a Scottish appeal to the House of Lords, where Lord Campbell LC said . . . 'I am of opinion that, generally speaking, if a party having an interest to prevent an act being done, has full notice of its having been done, and acquiesces in it, so as to induce a reasonable belief that he consents to it, and the position of others is altered by their giving credit to his sincerity, he has no more right to challenge the act, to their prejudice, than he would have had if it had been done by his previous licence'."

In my judgment, the tenant's evidence is to be accepted on this point. No alternative explanation of his change of mind between the beginning and the end of December, 1947, is available, and I think that he was a witness of truth . . .

. . . The promise was that so long as the tenant personally was tenant, so long would the landlords forbear to exercise the rights which they would have as to residence if he signed the lease. He did sign the lease on this promise and is therefore entitled to rely on it so long as he is personally in occupation of the shop.'

Webster v *Higgin*

[1948] 2 All ER 127 • Court of Appeal

Prior to buying a second hand car the seller told the buyer that 'If you buy the [car] we will guarantee that it is in good condition and that you will have no trouble with it'. The buyer then entered into a hire-purchase contract for the purchase of the car. Clause 5 of the hire-purchase contract stated 'The hirer is deemed to have examined . . . the vehicle prior to this agreement and satisfied himself as to its condition, and no warranty, condition, description or representation on the part of the owner as to the state or quality of the vehicle is given or implied . . . any statutory or other warranty, condition, description or representation whether express or implied as to the state, quality, fitness or roadworthiness being hereby expressly excluded'. The car turned out to be 'a mass of second-hand and dilapidated ironmongery' and the buyer refused to pay for it.

The issue before the court was whether clause 5 rendered of no effect the seller's promise that the car was 'in good condition and that you will have no trouble with it'.

Lord Greene MR: '. . . In the course of a conversation which the defendant had with the plaintiff's foreman, whose authority is not in any way in dispute, the foreman said: "If you buy the Hillman 10 we will guarantee that it is in good condition and that you will have no trouble with it". Those words in the context are obviously an offer of a collateral guarantee. It is a guarantee to the defendant that, if he will enter into a contract of purchase, the guarantee will be given to him. I may say at once that that guarantee was broken as completely and thoroughly as any guarantee can possibly be broken. The evidence relating to the inside of that motor car, given by an expert whose testimony was accepted by the county court judge, amounted to a most deplorable description of what in effect was nothing but a mass of second-hand and dilapidated ironmongery.

. . . At a subsequent date the hire purchase agreement was signed, and, in my view, the signature on that hire purchase agreement was the act by which the defendant accepted the offer of a guarantee. The guarantee was: "If you buy this car, I will guarantee it". He bought the car when he put his signature to the hire purchase agreement, for I do not think he bought it before that date in the sense of being contractually bound to take it. It is said, however, that when the defendant signed the hire purchase agreement, the collateral offer of a guarantee which he accepted by signing that agreement was entirely abrogated and nullified by a term in the agreement itself.

We, therefore, have this curious position, analysing the words again: "If you, the purchaser, will sign this contract which contains an exclusion of every guarantee, I will guarantee the car". Of course, that is nonsense, but parties often make nonsensical arrangements. If the contract meant that, we should be bound to give it that meaning, but, whether or not it has that effect must, in my opinion, be a pure question of construction of the contract. The relevant clause in the contract, cl 5, was in these words:

> "The hirer is deemed to have examined (or caused to be examined) the vehicle prior to this agreement and satisfied himself as to its condition, and no warranty, condition, description or representation on the part of the owner as to the state or quality of the vehicle is given or implied . . ."

I pause there for a moment. To succeed the plaintiff must satisfy us that those words not merely exclude the giving of any warranty in the contract of sale itself, but that they are sufficient to exclude the operation of a warranty which was given in consideration of the purchaser entering into the contract. In my opinion, that is not the true construction of those words. It is to be noted that the words are "no warranty . . . is given or implied". What is the meaning of the present tense there? Is it to be read not only as incorporating something that is given or implied by or in this agreement, but also as extending to something which was given may be weeks, and, indeed, on the evidence some fortnight, before the agreement was signed? According to the plaintiff the present tense – "is given or implied" – has a meaning which it will not bear in the context. If the words had been, not merely "no warranty is given or implied", but "any warranty given collateral to this agreement is hereby extinguished", the position, no doubt, would have been different. If words to that effect had been given, the result would, as I have said, been farcical because the guarantee would then be offered in consideration of the purchaser signing a document by which he agreed that the guarantee should be of no value whatsoever. It seems to me that to produce such a result very clear words are wanted, and I do not find them in what I have read. The agreement continues:

". . . any statutory or other warranty, condition, description or representation whether express or implied as to the state, quality, fitness or roadworthiness being hereby expressly excluded . . ."

Again, I read those words as meaning a representation expressed in the document or implied from something in the document. The word "being" is, I think, important because it is the common way and the proper way of giving a definition or an elaboration of something that has already been said. If it was intended to carry the matter further, it would have been in the form of a separate sentence and not in the form of a present participle. If that be right, those words do not add anything to the exclusion by the earlier part of the clause of any representation which is given or implied in the document. The words of the clause are not sufficiently clear to abrogate a separate collateral agreement constituted by an offer of a guarantee and its acceptance by the signing of this document by the purchaser. It appears to me that on the evidence the proper and, indeed, the only conclusion to which the county court judge ought to have come was that there was a collateral guarantee which was broken and that there was nothing in the hire purchase agreement or in the order form to exclude or abrogate that guarantee . . .'

Collateral warranties and third parties

Shanklin Pier Ltd v Detel Products Ltd

[1951] 2 All ER 471 • King's Bench

The facts are stated in the judgment of McNair J.

McNair J: 'This case raises an interesting and comparatively novel question whether or not an enforceable warranty can arise as between parties other than parties to the main contract for the sale of the article in respect of which the warranty is alleged to have been given.

The plaintiffs, Shanklin Pier, Ltd, are and were at all material times the owners of a pier at Shanklin, in the Isle of Wight, which, during the war, was partly demolished and allowed to fall into disrepair. In or about July, 1946, they had in mind to have this pier repaired and re-painted, and for this purpose they entered into a contract with their contractors, George M Carter (Erectors), Ltd, to have the necessary repairs effected and to have the whole pier re-painted with two coats of bitumastic or bituminous paint. Under this contract they had the right to vary the specification. In these circumstances, their claim in this action against the defendants, Detel Products, Ltd, is that, in consideration of their specifying that this contractor should use for re-painting the pier two coats of a paint known as "DMU", manufactured by the defendants, the defendants warranted that the DMU paint would be suitable for re-painting the pier, would give a surface impervious to dampness, would prevent corrosion and the creeping of rust, and would have a life of seven to ten years. They further say that, in reliance on this warranty, they duly specified that their contractors should use DMU paint for re-painting the pier in lieu of the bituminous paint originally specified, and that their contractors bought quantities of the paint from the defendants and used it on the pier, that contrary to the warranty the paint was not suitable for re-painting the pier or for the protection of the pier from damp or corrosion or rust, and that its life was of a very short duration, with the result that the plaintiffs were put to extra expense amounting to £4127 10s. The defence, stated broadly, is that no such warranty was ever given, and that, if given, it would give rise to no cause of action between these parties. Accordingly, the first question which I have to determine is whether any such warranty was ever given.

[His Lordship reviewed the evidence and continued:] In the result, I am satisfied that, if a direct contract of purchase and sale of the DMU had then been made between the plaintiffs and the defendants, the correct conclusion on the facts would have been that the defendants gave to the plaintiffs the warranties substantially in the form alleged in the statement of claim. In reaching this conclusion, I adopt the principle, stated by Holt CJ in *Crosse* v *Gardner* and *Medina* v *Stoughton*, that an affirmation at the time of sale is a warranty, provided it appear on evidence to have been so intended. Before considering the question of law resulting from this finding, I can state the remainder of the narrative briefly. On the faith of these warranties, the plaintiffs in due course caused the specification in the original contract to be amended by the substitution of two coats of DMU without any superimposed decoration or finishing paint, in lieu of the two coats of bituminous paint originally specified, having obtained from their contractors estimates of the extra cost involved. The necessary DMU was purchased by the contractors, and, as the repairs were completed and the old work was prepared for re-painting, the DMU was applied and the property in the DMU then, if not before, passed to the plaintiffs. Within a short time it proved to be unsatisfactory, and it was decided to carry out an extensive process of flame cleaning of the old parts of the structure at a cost of £4127 10s, in order to remove all traces of bitumen. Notwithstanding this additional expenditure, the paint proved to be a complete failure.

Counsel for the defendants submitted that in law a warranty can give rise to no enforceable cause of action except between the same parties as the parties to the main contract in relation to which the warranty is given. In principle, this submission seems to me to be unsound. If, as is elementary, the consideration for the warranty in the usual case is the entering into of the main contract in relation to which the warranty is given, I see no reason why there may not be an enforceable warranty between A and B supported by the consideration that B should cause C to enter into a contract with A or that B should do some other act for the benefit of A . . .

. . . Accordingly, in my judgment, the plaintiffs are entitled to recover against the defendants £4127 10s, as damages for breach of the express warranties alleged.'

This principle also applies to hire-purchase cases.

Andrews v *Hopkinson*

[1956] 3 All ER 422 • Leeds Assizes

Andrews bought a car from Hopkinson on hire-purchase. Before buying the car Hopkinson said to Andrews 'It's a good little bus. I would stake my life on it. You will have no trouble with it'. The hire-purchase agreement provided that Andrews' acceptance of delivery should be conclusive that the vehicle was complete and in good order and condition and in every way satisfactory. On the same day Andrews signed a delivery note acknowledging that he had taken delivery of the car and was satisfied as to its condition. A week later Andrews was driving the car when it suddenly swerved and collided with a lorry. The car was wrecked and Andrews was seriously injured. When the police examined the car they found the steering mechanism to be seriously defective. Andrews sued Hopkinson for breach of an express warranty that the car was in good condition and reasonably safe and fit to use on the public highway.

The issue before the court was whether the clause in the hire-purchase agreement which stated that Andrews' acceptance of delivery should be conclusive that the vehicle was complete and in good order and condition and in every way satisfactory rendered of no effect Hopkinson's promise that the car was a 'good little bus' etc.

McNair J: 'In these circumstances the plaintiff brings his action against the defendant, basing his claim on three grounds. First he claims that the defendant warranted that the car was in good condition and reasonably safe and fit for use on the public highway, that the plaintiff acted on this warranty, and that damage was caused by breach of the warranty . . .

As to breach of warranty, in the first place it is clear that in law the relationship between the plaintiff and the defendant was not a relationship of seller and purchaser. The hire-purchase transaction, evidenced in the documents, was a reality and cannot be treated as a mere colourable transaction: see *Drury* v *Victor Buckland, Ltd.* Secondly, I am satisfied (i) applying the principle stated by Holt CJ, in *Crosse* v *Gardner*, and *Medina* v *Stoughton*, that, if the transaction between the plaintiff and the defendant had been in law a sale, the words deposed to by the plaintiff as being the words used by Mr Hopkinson junior could properly be held to be words of warranty, i.e., an affirmation made at the time of sale intended to be a warranty; (ii) that the words amounted at least to a warranty that the car was in good condition and reasonably safe and fit for use on a public highway; and (iii) that the plaintiff acted on this warranty in the sense that without it he would not have accepted delivery of the car or entered into the hire-purchase agreement.

On these findings I adopt the reasoning of Jones J, in *Brown* v *Sheen & Richmond Car Sales, Ltd*, and follow my own decision in *Shanklin Pier, Ltd* v *Detel Products*, where I set out at some length the reasons that led me to the conclusion (as they do in this case) that there may be an enforceable warranty between A, the intended purchaser of a car, and B, the motor dealer, supported by the consideration that B should cause the hire-purchase finance company to enter into a hire-purchase agreement with A, the intended purchaser.

It was rather faintly argued that even on these findings the defendant would only be liable for the difference in value between the car as delivered and the car as warranted. Although this may be the *prima facie* measure of damages in an ordinary case of breach of warranty in the sale of goods, I feel no doubt at all that on the facts of this case the whole of the damages can fairly be considered as loss directly and naturally resulting in the ordinary course of events from the breach of warranty and so recoverable as damages for breach. I hold, accordingly, that as damages for breach of warranty the plaintiff is entitled to judgment for £645 5s 6d.

Collateral warranties and tenders

See *Blackpool & Fylde Aero Club Ltd* v *Blackpool BC* above (p 17).

EXPRESS TERMS

Express terms are the terms expressly (actually) agreed between the parties, e.g. the sale of a specific pen for £5.

Conditions and warranties

Traditionally all express terms in a contract were classified as either a *condition* or a *warranty.* This was important when it came to breach of a contract term by one of the parties to the contract.

If the term that was broken was a condition then the innocent party could, if they wished, accept the breach as a repudiatory breach and thus the contract would be at an end; they could also sue for damages.

If the term that was broken was a warranty then the innocent party could only sue for damages; the contract continued in existence.

In practice it can be difficult to lay down a test so as to distinguish between conditions and warranties. Merely because a contract specifically states that a certain term is a condition does it automatically follow that it is a condition?

Schuler AG v Wickman Machine Tool Sales Ltd

[1973] 2 All ER 39 • House of Lords

A German company, Schuler, granted Wickman, an English company, the sole right to sell Schuler's products in the UK. Clause 7 of their agreement provided '(a) [Wickman] will use its best endeavours to promote and extend the sale of Schuler products in the [UK]. (b) It shall be condition of this Agreement that (i) [Wickman] shall send its representative to visit the six firms whose names are listed in the Schedule hereto at least once in every week for the purpose of soliciting orders for panel presses; (ii) that the same representative shall visit each firm on each occasion unless there are unavoidable reasons preventing the visit being made by that representative'. Clause 11 provided that the agreement could be determined forthwith if '(i) the other shall have committed a material breach of its obligations hereunder and shall have failed to remedy the same within 60 days of being required in writing so to do'. Wickman failed to make all the necessary visits required by clause 7(b). Schuler claimed that since Wickman had broken their obligations under clause 7 which was a condition of the contract that breach of the condition entitled them to treat Wickman's breach as a repudiatory breach.

The issue before the court was whether clause 7 was a condition of the contract.

Lord Reid: 'Clause 7 begins with the general requirement that Wickman shall "use its best endeavours" to promote sales of Schuler products. Then there is in cl 7(b)(i) specification of those best endeavours with regard to panel presses, and in cl 12(b) a much more general statement of what Wickman must do with regard to other Schuler products. This intention to impose a stricter obligation with regard to panel presses is borne out by the use of the word "condition" in cl 7(b). I cannot accept Wickman's argument that condition here merely means term. It must be intended to emphasise the importance of the obligations in sub-cll (b)(i) and (b)(ii). But what is the extent of that emphasis?

Schuler maintain that the word "condition" has now acquired a precise legal meaning; that, particularly since the enactment of the Sale of Goods Act 1893, its recognised meaning in English law is a term of a contract any breach of which by one party gives to the other party an immediate right to rescind the whole contract. Undoubtedly the word is frequently used in that sense. There may, indeed, be some presumption that in a formal legal document it has that meaning. But it is frequently used with a less stringent meaning. One is familiar with printed "conditions of sale" incorporated into a contract, and with the words "for conditions see back" printed on a ticket. There it simply means that the "conditions" are terms of the contract.

In the ordinary use of the English language "condition" has many meanings, some of which have nothing to do with agreements. In connection with an agreement it may mean a pre-condition: something which must happen or be done before the agreement can take effect. Or it may mean some state of affairs which must continue to exist if the agreement is to remain in force. The legal meaning on which Schuler rely is, I think, one which would not occur to a layman; a condition in that sense is not something which has an automatic effect. It is a term the breach of which by one party gives to the other an option either to terminate the contract or to let the contract proceed and, if he so desires, sue for damages for the breach.

Sometimes a breach of a term gives that option to the aggrieved party because it is of a fundamental character going to the root of the contract, sometimes it gives that option because the parties have chosen to stipulate that it shall have that effect. Blackburn J said in *Bettini* v *Gye*: "Parties may think some matter, apparently of very little importance, essential; and if they sufficiently express an intention to make the literal fulfilment of such a thing a condition precedent, it will be one".

In the present case it is not contended that Wickman's failures to make visits amounted in themselves to fundamental breaches. What is contended is that the terms of cl 7 "sufficiently express an intention" to make any breach, however small, of the obligation to make visits a condition so that any such breach shall entitle Schuler to rescind the whole contract if they so desire.

Schuler maintain that the use of the word "condition" is in itself enough to establish this intention. No doubt some words used by lawyers do have a rigid inflexible meaning. But we must remember that we are seeking to discover intention as disclosed by the contract as a whole. Use of the word "condition" is an indication – even a strong indication – of such an intention but it is by no means conclusive. The fact that a particular construction leads to a very unreasonable result must be a relevant consideration. The more unreasonable the result the more unlikely it is that the parties can have intended it, and if they do intend it the more necessary it is that they shall make that intention abundantly clear.

Clause 7(b) requires that over a long period each of the six firms shall be visited every week by one or other of two named representatives. It makes no provision for Wickman being entitled to substitute others even on the death or retirement of one of the named representatives. Even if one could imply some right to do this, it makes no provision for both representatives being ill during a particular week. And it makes no provision for the possibility that one or other of the firms may tell Wickman that they cannot receive Wickman's representative during a particular week. So if the parties gave any thought to the matter at all they must have realised the probability that in a few cases out of the 1,400 required visits a visit as stipulated would be impossible. But if Schuler's contention is right failure to make even one visit entitles them to terminate the contract however blameless Wickman might be. This is so unreasonable that it must make me search for some other possible meaning of the contract. If none can be found then Wickman must suffer the consequences. But only if that is the only possible interpretation.

If I have to construe cl 7 standing by itself then I do find difficulty in reaching any other interpretation. But if cl 7 must be read with cl 11 the difficulty disappears. The word "condition" would make any breach of cl 7(b), however excusable, a material breach. That would then entitle Schuler to give notice under cl 11(a)(i) requiring the breach to be remedied. There would be no point in giving such a notice if Wickman were clearly not in fault but if it were given Wickman would have no difficulty in shewing that the breach had been remedied. If Wickman were at fault then on receiving such a notice they would have to amend their system so that they could shew that the breach had been remedied. If they did not do that within the period of the notice then Schuler would be entitled to rescind.

In my view, that is a possible and reasonable construction of the contract and I would therefore adopt it. The contract is so obscure that I can have no confidence that this is its true meaning but for the reasons which I have given I think that it is the preferable construction. It follows that Schuler were not entitled to rescind the contract as they purported to do . . .'

Lord Wilberforce dissenting: 'The second legal issue which arises I would state in this way: whether it is open to the parties to a contract, not being a contract for the sale of goods, to use the word "condition" to introduce a term, breach of which *ipso facto* entitles the other party to treat the contract at an end.

The proposition that this may be done has not been uncriticised. It is said that this is contrary to modern trends which focus interest rather on the nature of the breach, allowing the innocent party to rescind or repudiate whenever the breach is fundamental, whether the clause breached is called a condition or not: that the affixing of the label "condition" cannot pre-empt the right of the court to estimate for itself the character of the breach. Alternatively it is said that the result contended for can only be achieved if the consequences of a breach of a "condition" (sc, that the other party may rescind) are spelt out in the contract. In support of this line of argument reliance is placed on the judgment of the Court of Appeal in *Hong Kong Fir Shipping Co Ltd* v *Kawasaki Kisen Kaisha Ltd.*

My Lords, this approach has something to commend it: it has academic support. The use as a promissory term of "condition" is artificial, as is that of "warranty" in some contexts. But in my opinion this use is now too deeply embedded in English law to be uprooted by anything less than a complete revision. I shall not trace the development of the term through 19th century cases, many of them decisions of Lord Blackburn, to the present time; this has been well done by academic writers. I would only add that the *Hong Kong Fir* case, even if it could, did not reverse the trend. What it did decide, and I do not think that this was anything new, was that although a term . . . was not a "condition" in the technical sense, it might still be a term breach of which if sufficiently serious could go to the root of the contract. Nothing in the judgments as I read them casts any doubt on the meaning or effect of "condition" where that word is technically used.

The alternative argument, in my opinion, is equally precluded by authority. It is not necessary for parties to a contract, when stipulating a condition, to spell out the consequences of breach: these are inherent in the (assumedly deliberate) use of the word (*Suisse Atlantique Société D'Armement Maritime SA* v *NV Rotterdamsche Kolen Centrale* per Lord Upjohn).

It is on this legal basis, as to which I venture to think that your Lordships are agreed, that this contract must be construed. Does cl 7(b) amount to a "condition" or a "term"? (to call it an important or material term adds, with all respect, nothing but some intellectual assuagement). My Lords, I am clear in my own mind that it is a condition, but your Lordships take the contrary view . . . I would only add that, for my part, to call the clause arbitrary, capricious or fantastic, or to introduce as a test of its validity the ubiquitous reasonable man (I do not know whether he is English or German) is to assume, contrary to the evidence, that both parties to this contract adopted a standard of easygoing tolerance rather than one of aggressive, insistent punctuality and efficiency. This is not an assumption I am prepared to make, nor do I think myself entitled to impose the former standard on the parties if their words indicate, as they plainly do, the latter. I note finally, that the result of treating the clause, so careful and specific in its requirements, as a term is, in effect, to deprive the appellants of any remedy in respect of admitted and by no means minimal breaches. The arbitrator's finding that these breaches were not "material" was not, in my opinion, justified in law in the face of the parties' own characterisation of them in their document: indeed the fact that he was able to do so, and so leave the appellants without remedy, argues strongly that the legal basis of his finding – that cl 7(b) was merely a term – is unsound.

I would allow this appeal.'

Innominate terms

The modern approach to classifying terms is not to pre-classify them at all but to 'wait and see' how serious the effect of the breach of contract is. If the effect of the breach is serious the term is a condition; if the effect of the breach is not very serious then the term is a warranty.

Hong Kong Fir Shipping Co Ltd v *Kawasaki Kisen Kaisha Ltd*
[1962] 1 All ER 474 • Court of Appeal

Kawasaki chartered the Hong Kong Fir from Hong Kong Fir Shipping Co for 24 months. The charter provided '1. . . . the vessel is delivered and placed at the disposal of the charterers . . . at Liverpool . . . she being in every way fitted for ordinary cargo service . . . 13. The owners only to be responsible for delay in delivery of the vessel or for delay during the currency of the charter . . . if such delay or loss has been caused by want of due diligence on the part of the owners . . . in making the vessel seaworthy and fitted for the voyage . . . '. The vessel was delivered to the charterers on 13 February 1957 and that day she sailed from Liverpool to Newport News in Virginia, USA, to pick up a cargo of coal and carry it to Osaka. She finally arrived at Osaka on 25 May. During this time she was at sea for about eight and a half weeks, off hire for about five weeks, and had £21 400 spent on her for repairs. Whilst at Osaka a further period of about fifteen weeks and an expenditure of £37 500 were required to make her ready for sea. In the meantime there had been a very steep fall in the freight market. By mid-June the rate had fallen from 47s to 24s per ton, and by mid-August there had been a further fall to 13s 6d per ton. On 5 June, when it was known that a very long time would be required to repair and test the vessel, the charterers wrote repudiating the charter and claiming damages for breach of contract. On 8 August the owners wrote intimating that they would treat the contract as cancelled by the charterers' wrongful repudiation and claim damages. Towards mid September the vessel was ready to sail. The owners sued the charterers for wrongful repudiation of contract. The charterers' defence was that the owners had broken a condition of the contract either by not delivering a seaworthy vessel or by delaying the vessel so long as to frustrate the commercial purpose of the charter.

Diplock LJ: '. . . Every synallagmatic contract contains in it the seeds of the problem: in what event will a party be relieved of his undertaking to do that which he has agreed to do but has not yet done? The contract may itself expressly define some of these events, as in the cancellation clause in a charterparty, but, human prescience being limited, it seldom does so exhaustively and often fails to do so at all. In some classes of contracts, such as sale of goods, marine insurance, contracts of affreightment evidenced by bills of lading and those between parties to bills of exchange, Parliament has defined by statute some of the events not provided for expressly in individual contracts of that class; but, where an event occurs the occurrence of which neither the parties nor Parliament have expressly stated will discharge one of the parties from further performance of his undertakings, it is for the court to determine whether the event has this effect or not. The test whether an event has this effect or not has been stated in a number of metaphors all of which I think amount to the same thing: does the occurrence of the event deprive the party who has further undertakings still to perform of substantially the whole benefit which it was the intention of the parties as expressed in the contract that he should obtain as the consideration for performing those undertakings? This test is applicable whether or not the event occurs as a result of the default of one of the parties to the contract, but the consequences of the event are different in the two cases. Where the event occurs as a result of the default of one party, the party in default cannot rely on it as relieving himself of the performance of any further undertakings on his part and the innocent party, although entitled to, need not treat the event as relieving him of the performance of his own undertakings. This is only a specific application of the fundamental legal and moral rule that a man should not be allowed to take advantage of his own wrong. Where the event occurs as a result of the default of neither party, each is relieved of the further performance of his own undertakings, and their rights in respect of undertakings previously performed are now regulated by the Law Reform (Frustrated Contracts) Act, 1943.

This branch of the common law has reached its present stage by the normal process of historical growth, and the fallacy in counsel for the charterers' contention that a different test is applicable when the event occurs as a result of the default of one party from that applicable in cases of frustration where the event occurs as a result of the default of neither party arises, in my view, from a failure to view the cases in their historical context. The problem: in what event will a party to a contract be relieved of his undertaking to do that which he has agreed to do but has not yet done? has exercised the English courts for centuries, probably ever since *assumpsit* emerged as a form of action distinct from covenant and debt, and long before even the earliest cases which we have been invited to examine; but, until the rigour of the rule in *Paradine* v *Jane* was mitigated in the middle of the last century by the classic judgments of Blackburn J, in *Taylor* v *Caldwell*, and Bramwell B, in *Jackson* v *Union Marine Insurance Co*, it was in general only events resulting from one party's failure to perform his contractual obligations which were regarded as capable of relieving the other party from continuing to perform that which he had undertaken to do . . .

Once it is appreciated that it is the event and not the fact that the event is a result of a breach of contract which relieves the party not in default of further performance of his obligations, two consequences follow: (i) The test whether the event relied on has this consequence is the same whether the event is the result of the other party's breach of contract or not, as Devlin J pointed out in *Universal Cargo Carriers Corpn* v *Citati*. (ii) The question whether an event which is their result of the other party's breach of contract has this consequence cannot be answered by treating all contractual undertakings as falling into one of two separate categories: "conditions", the breach of which gives rise to an event which relieves the party not in default of further performance of his obligations, and "warranties", the breach of which does not give rise to such an event. Lawyers tend to speak of this classification as if it were comprehensive, partly for the historical reasons which I have already mentioned, and partly because Parliament itself adopted it in the Sale of Goods Act, 1893, as respects a number of implied terms in contracts for the sale of goods and has in that Act used the expressions "condition" and "warranty" in that meaning. But it is by no means true of contractual undertakings in general at common law.

No doubt there are many simple contractual undertakings, sometimes express, but more often because of their very simplicity ("It goes without saying") to be implied, of which it can be predicated that every breach of such an undertaking must give rise to an event which will deprive the party not in default of substantially the whole benefit which it was intended that he should obtain from the contract. And such a stipulation, unless the parties have agreed that breach of it shall not entitle the non-defaulting party to treat the contract as repudiated, is a "condition". So, too, there may be other simple contractual undertakings of which it can be predicated that no breach can give rise to an event which will deprive the party not in default of substantially the whole benefit which it was intended that he should obtain from the contract; and such a stipulation, unless the parties have agreed that breach of it shall entitle the non-defaulting party to treat the contract as repudiated, is a "warranty". There are, however, many contractual undertakings of a more complex character which cannot be categorised as being "conditions" or "warranties" if the late nineteenth century meaning adopted in the Sale of Goods Act, 1893, and used by Bowen LJ, in *Bentsen* v *Taylor, Sons & Co*, be given to those terms. Of such undertakings, all that can be predicated is that some breaches will, and others will not, give rise to an event which will deprive the party not in default of substantially the whole benefit which it was intended that he should obtain from the contract; and the legal consequences of a breach of such an undertaking, unless provided for expressly in the contract, depend on the nature of the event to which the breach gives rise and do not follow automatically from a prior classification of the undertaking as a "condition" or a "warranty". For instance, to take the example of Bramwell B, in *Jackson* v *Union Marine Insurance Co*, by itself breach of an undertaking by a shipowner to sail with all possible despatch to a named port does not necessarily relieve the charterer of further performance of his obligation under the charterparty, but, if the breach is so prolonged that the contemplated voyage is frustrated, it does have this effect . . .

As my brethren have already pointed out, the shipowner's undertaking to tender a seaworthy ship has, as a result of numerous decisions as to what can amount to "unseaworthiness", become one of the most complex of contractual undertakings. It embraces obligations with respect to every part of the hull and machinery, stores and equipment and the crew itself. It can be broken by the presence of trivial defects easily and rapidly remediable as well as by defects which must inevitably result in a total loss of the vessel. Consequently, the problem in this case is, in my view, neither solved nor soluble by debating whether the owners' express or implied undertaking to tender a seaworthy ship is a "condition" or a "warranty". It is, like so many other contractual terms, an undertaking one breach of which may give rise to an event which relieves the charterer of further performance of his undertakings if he so elects, and another breach of which may not give rise to such an event but entitle him only to monetary compensation in the form of damages. It is, with all deference to counsel for the charterers' skilful argument, by no means surprising that, among the many hundreds of previous cases about the shipowner's undertaking to deliver a seaworthy ship, there is none where it was found profitable to discuss in the judgments the question whether that undertaking is a "condition" or a "warranty"; for the true answer, as I have already indicated, is that it is neither, but one of that large class of contractual undertakings, one breach of which may have the same effect as that ascribed to a breach of "condition" under the Sale of Goods Act, 1893, and a different breach of which may have only the same effect as that ascribed to a breach of "warranty" under that Act . . .

What the learned judge had to do in the present case as in any other case where one party to a contract relies on a breach by the other party as giving him a right to elect to rescind the contract, was to look at the events which had occurred as a result of the breach at the time at which the charterers purported to rescind the charterparty, and to decide whether the occurrence of those events deprived the charterers of substantially the whole benefit which it was the intention of the parties as expressed in the charterparty that the charterers should obtain from the further performance of their own contractual undertakings. One turns, therefore, to the contract, the Baltime 1939 Charter. Clause 13, the "due diligence" clause, which exempts the shipowners from responsibility for delay or loss or damage to goods on board due to unseaworthiness unless such delay or loss or damage has been caused by want of due diligence of the owners in making the vessel seaworthy and fitted for the voyage, is in itself sufficient to show that the mere occurrence of the events that the vessel was in some respect unseaworthy when tendered or that such unseaworthiness had caused some delay in performance of the charterparty would not deprive the charterer of the whole benefit which it was the intention of the parties he should obtain from the performance of his obligations under the contract – for he undertakes to continue to perform his obligations notwithstanding the occurrence of such events if they fall short of frustration of the contract and even deprives himself of any remedy in damages unless such events are the consequence of want of due diligence on the part of the shipowner.

The question which the learned judge had to ask himself was, as he rightly decided, whether or not, at the date when the charterers purported to rescind the contract, namely June 6, 1957, or when the owners purported to accept such rescission, namely Aug 8, 1957, the delay which had already occurred as a result of the incompetence of the engine-room staff, and the delay which was likely to occur in repairing the engines of the vessel and the conduct of the owners by that date in taking steps to remedy these two matters, were, when taken together, such as to deprive the charterers of substantially the whole benefit which it was the intention of the parties they should obtain from further use of the vessel under the charterparty. In my view, in his judgment – on which I would not seek to improve – the learned judge took into account and gave due weight to all the relevant considerations and arrived at the right answer for the right reasons.'

However, it is still possible to pre-classify terms as conditions.

Maredelanto Compania Naviera SA v Bergbau-Handel GmbH (The Mihalis Angelos)
[1970] 3 All ER 125 • Court of Appeal

The owners of the vessel *Mihalis Angelos* chartered it to the charterers for a voyage from Haiphong to Hamburg. In the charterparty the owners stated that the vessel was 'expected ready to load under this charter about 1 July 1965'. They had no reasonable grounds in saying that she was 'expected to load' on that date.

The issue before the court was whether the 'readiness' clause was a condition of the contract.

Megaw LJ: 'In my judgment, such a term in a charterparty ought to be regarded as being a condition of the contract, in the old sense of the word "condition", i.e. that when it has been broken, the other party can, if he wishes, by intimation to the party in breach, elect to be released from performance of his further obligations under the contract; and that he can validly do so without having to establish that, on the facts of the particular case, the breach has produced serious consequences which can be treated as "going to the root of the contract" or as being "fundamental", or whatever other metaphor may be thought appropriate for a frustration case.

I reach that conclusion for [several] reasons. First, it tends towards certainty in the law. One of the essential elements of law is some measure of uniformity. One of the important elements of the law is predictability. At any rate in commercial law, there are obvious and substantial advantages in having, where possible, a firm and definite rule for a particular class of legal relationship, e.g. as here, the legal categorisation of a particular, definable type of contractual clause in common use. It is surely much better, both for shipowners and charterers (and, incidentally, for their advisers) when a contractual obligation of this nature is under consideration, and still more when they are faced with the necessity for an urgent decision as to the effects of a suspected breach of it, to be able to say categorically: "If a breach is proved, then the charterer can put an end to the contract", rather than that they should be left to ponder whether or not the courts would be likely, in the particular case, when the evidence had been heard, to decide that in the particular circumstances the breach was or was not such as to go to the root of the contract. Where justice does not require greater flexibility, there is everything to be said for, and nothing against, a degree of rigidity in legal principle.

Secondly, it would, in my opinion, only be in the rarest case, if ever, that a shipowner could legitimately feel that he had suffered an injustice by reason of the law having given to a charterer the right to put an end to the contract because of the breach by the shipowner of a clause such as this. If a shipowner has chosen to assert contractually, but dishonestly or without reasonable grounds, that he expects his vessel to be ready to load on such and such a date, wherein does the grievance lie?

Thirdly, it is . . . clearly established by authority binding on this court that where a clause "expected ready to load" is included in a contract for the sale of goods to be carried by sea, that clause is a condition, in the sense that any breach of it enables the buyer to reject the goods without having to show that the dishonest or unreasonable expectation of the seller has in fact been prejudicial to the buyer . . .'

Cehave NV v Bremer Handelsgesellschaft GmbH (The Hansa Nord)

[1975] 3 All ER 739 • Court of Appeal

In September 1970 a German company sold citrus pulp pellets to a Dutch company for £100 000. Clause 7 of the contract of sale stated 'Shipment to be made in good condition'. On 14 May the buyers paid the price and got the shipping documents. When the cargo was unloaded from the *Hansa Nord* on 25 May it was discovered that the cargo in hold two, 2053 tons, was in good condition but that some of the cargo in hold one, 1260 tons, was damaged. By this time the market price for the cargo was only £86 000 and the buyers, looking for a way to get out of the contract, rejected the whole cargo (both holds one and two) on the ground that it was not shipped 'in good condition'; they also claimed repayment of the purchase price of £100 000. The sellers refused to accept the rejection of the cargo. Later the cargo was sold by order of the Rotterdam County Court. The cargo was bought by a third party for £33 000 who then sold it to the original buyers for £33 000. The buyers then used the entire cargo for its original purpose.

The issue before the court was whether the 'Shipment to be made in good condition' term in the contract was a condition.

Ormrod LJ: 'I now turn to the problems arising from cl 7 . . . Under this clause the sellers were under an obligation to ship the goods "in good condition" and to comply with other requirements which are not relevant. The [arbitrators] have found that the sellers were in breach of this stipulation but to a limited extent ... [T]hey concluded, by inference, that "not all the goods in hold no 1 were shipped in good condition" and that, in consequence, over-heating took place in this hold and caused further damage to that part of the cargo. The sellers now accept that they were in breach of contract to the extent found against them.

Counsel for the buyers submitted that cl 7 must be construed as a condition of the contract and that therefore his clients were entitled to reject the goods. Counsel for the sellers argued that it would be wrong to construe this stipulation as a condition. He argued that it should be regarded as a warranty, giving the buyers a right to damages or an allowance only; or, if the principles laid down in the judgments in the *Hong Kong Fir Shipping* case were applicable to contracts for the sale of goods, as he submitted they were, as an "intermediate" or "innominate" term. The learned judge accepted counsel for the buyers' submission and held that this stipulation must be construed as a condition.

Counsel for the buyers, relying on s 11(1)(b) [of the Sale of Goods Act 1893], argued that in a contract of sale the court was required to categorise all relevant stipulations as conditions or warranties, that this must be done by way of construction of the contract, and that, once done, the buyer's remedy for breach was determined; if a condition, he could reject, subject to the other provisions of the Act; if a warranty, he had no right to reject in any circumstances, his only remedy being damages. Construction, at least in theory, means ascertaining the intention of the parties in accordance with the general rules. If this submission is right, it means that a buyer can always reject for breach of a condition, however trivial the consequences, subject only to the so-called *de minimis* rule, and never reject for breach of warranty, however serious the consequences. So, on a falling market the buyer can take advantage of a minor breach of condition and, on a rising market, waive the breach and sue for damages. It also means, as Mocatta J pointed out in his judgment, that if breach of a stipulation could have potentially serious consequences for a buyer, the court may be obliged, whatever the results in the instant case, to construe the stipulation as a condition. Moreover, where the contract is in a standard form as in the case, a decision in one case will, in effect, categorise the stipulation for other cases in which the same form is used.

We have all been brought up since our student days to ask the question in the form: "Is this stipulation a condition or a warranty?" But before the Sale of Goods Act 1893 was passed the question was whether the buyer was bound to accept the goods. The answer depended, to use modern language, on whether the stipulation "went to the root of the contract", although it was differently phrased, e.g. "the buyer was entitled to get what he bargained for" or "the seller had failed to perform an essential term of the contract". The words "condition" and "warranty" were used in various senses in different cases but the distinction depended largely on the old rules of pleading. Section 11(1)(b) of the 1893 Act was clearly intended to remove this confusion of terminology but the essential dichotomy was not affected; it was and is, between the right to reject or the right to damages. The modern form of the question tends to put the cart before the horse and to obscure the issue.

If one asks oneself the question in the form, "Did the parties intend that the buyer should be entitled to reject the goods if they were not shipped in good condition?" the answer must be that it depends on the nature and effects of the breach. This is directly in line with Diplock LJ's approach in the *Hong Kong Fir Shipping* case; not surprisingly, since there can be very little difference in principle between whether the ship is seaworthy and whether goods are in good condition. There is obviously a strong case for applying the general principle of the *Hong Kong Fir Shipping* case to contracts for the sale of goods. The question remains, however, and it is the kernel of counsel for the buyers' submission, whether it is open to the court to do so. The parties themselves, of course, can do it by express agreement as, indeed, they have done in the present case in relation to quality. Clause 5 provides that breach of the terms as to quality shall entitle the buyer to an allowance, but that if the goods contain over five per cent of sand or in excess of 0.0005 per cent of castor seed husk, the buyer may reject the parcel. If it can be done expressly, it can be done by implication, unless it is in some way prohibited. Counsel for the buyers argues that s 11(1)(b) compels the court to choose between condition and warranty. I do not think that the subsection was intended to have any prohibitory effect. It is essentially a definition section, defining "condition" and "warranty" in terms of remedies. Nor is the classification absolutely rigid, for it provides that a buyer may treat a condition as a warranty if he wishes, by accepting the goods. It does not, however, envisage the possibility that a breach of warranty might go to the root of the contract, and so, in certain circumstances, entitle the buyer to treat the contract as repudiated. But the law has developed since the Act was passed. It is now accepted as a general principle since the *Hong Kong Fir Shipping* case that it is the events resulting from the breach, rather than the breach itself, which may destroy the consideration for the buyer's promise and so enable him to treat the contract as repudiated.

The problem is how to integrate this principle with s 11(1)(b). In practice it may not arise very often. Faced with a breach which has had grave consequences for a buyer, the court may be disposed to hold that he was entitled *ex post facto* to rescind or reject the goods, without categorising the broken stipulation, applying the general principles of the law of contract. The difficulty only arises if the court has already categorised the stipulation as a warranty. The present case provides an example. If the relevant part of cl 7 is construed as a warranty in this case, and later another dispute occurs in relation to another contract in the same form, between the same parties, for the sale of similar goods, in which the breach of cl 7 has produced much more serious consequences for the buyer, is the court bound by its decision in this case to hold that the buyer is precluded from rejecting the goods under the later contract because, as a matter of construction, it has already categorised the stipulation as a warranty? This is the converse of the *Mihalis Angelos* situation. If the answer is in the affirmative s 11(1)(b) has, by implication, excluded one of the general common law rules of contract. It was clearly not intended to have this effect and I agree with Lord Denning MR, for the reasons that he has given in his judgment, that the Act should not, if it can be avoided, be construed in this way. Section 61(2) seems to provide an answer. If this view is correct it is bound to have important repercussions on the way in which courts in future will approach the construction of stipulations in contracts for the sale of goods. It will no longer be necessary to place so much emphasis on the potential effects of a breach on the buyer, and to feel obliged, as Mocatta J did in this case, to construe a stipulation as a condition because in other cases or in other circumstances the buyer ought to be entitled to reject. Consequently, the court will be freer to regard stipulations, as a matter of construction, as warranties, if what might be called the "back-up" rule of the common law is available to protect buyers who ought to be able to reject in proper circumstances. I doubt whether, strictly speaking, this involves the creation of a third category of stipulations; rather, it recognises another ground for holding that a buyer is entitled to reject, namely that, *de facto*, the consideration for his promise has been wholly destroyed.

The result may be summarised in this way. When a breach of contract has taken place the question arises: is the party who is not in breach entitled in law to treat the contract as repudiated or, in the case of a buyer, to reject the goods? The answer depends on the answers to a series of other questions. Adopting Upjohn LJ's judgment in the *Hong Kong Fir Shipping* case, the first question is: does the contract expressly provide that in the event of the breach of the term in question the other party is entitled to terminate the contract or reject the goods? If the answer is No, the next question is: does the contract when correctly construed so provide? The relevant term, for example, may be described as a "condition". The question then arises whether this word is used as a code word for the phrase "shall be entitled to repudiate the contract or reject the goods", or in some other sense as in *Wickman Machine Tool Sales Ltd* v *Schuler AG*. The next question is whether the breach of the relevant term creates a right to repudiate or reject. This may arise either from statute or as a result of judicial decision on particular contractual terms. For example, if the requirements of s 14(1) or (2) of the Sale of Goods Act 1893 are fulfilled, the buyer will be entitled to reject the goods, as a result of this section read with s 11(1). In fact, in all those sections of the 1893 Act which create implied conditions the word "condition" by definition a code word for "breach of this term will entitle the buyer to reject the goods", subject to any other relevant provision of the Act. In other cases, the courts have decided that breach of some specific terms, such as, for example, an "expected ready to load stipulation", will *ipso facto* give rise to a right in the other party to repudiate the contract (the *Mihalis Angelos* per Lord Denning MR). In these two classes of case the consequences of the breach are irrelevant or, more accurately, are assumed to go to the root of the contract, and to justify repudiation. There remains the non-specific class where the events produced by the breach are such that it is reasonable to describe the breach as going to the root of the contract and so justifying repudiation.

If this approach is permissible in the present case I would unhesitatingly hold that the stipulation in cl 7 that the goods were to be shipped in good condition was not a condition, and that on the facts of this case the breach did not go to the root of the contract, and that, consequently, the buyers were not entitled to reject the goods.'

Bunge Corporation v Tradax Export SA

[1981] 2 All ER 513 • House of Lords

By a fob (free on board) contract Tradax agreed to sell to Bunge 5000 tons of soya bean meal, shipment to be made in June. Clause 7 of the contract provided that the buyer had to give 'at least 15 days' notice of probable readiness' of the vessel that was to carry the soya bean meal. This meant that the last day for giving notice was 12 June; in fact the buyer did not give notice until 17 June. Tradax claimed that this late nomination was a breach of a condition of the contract which entitled them to rescind the contract. Bunge argued that the term was an innominate term which, in the circumstances, only entitled Tradax to claim damages.

The issue before the court was whether the term, which was not called a condition in the contract, was a condition or an innominate term.

Lord Wilberforce: 'The appeal depends upon the construction to be placed upon clause 7 of GAFTA form 119 as completed by the special contract. It is not expressed as a "condition" and the question is whether, in its context and in the circumstances it should be read as such.

... [T]he main contention of counsel for the appellants was based on the decision of the Court of Appeal in *Hong Kong Fir Shipping Co Ltd* v *Kawasaki Kisen Kaisha Ltd*, as it might be applied to clause 7. Diplock LJ in his seminal judgment illuminated the existence in contracts of terms which were neither, necessarily, conditions nor warranties, but, in terminology which has since been applied to them, intermediate or innominate terms capable of operating, according to the gravity of the breach, as either conditions or warranties. Relying on this, counsel's submission was that the buyer's obligation under the clause, to "give at least [15] consecutive days' notice of probable readiness of (vessels) and of the approximate quantity required to be loaded", is of this character. A breach of it, both generally and in relation to this particular case, might be, to use counsel's expression, "inconsequential", i.e. not such as to make performance of the seller's obligation impossible. If this were so it would be wrong to treat it a breach of condition: *Hong Kong Fir* would require it to be treated as a warranty.

This argument, in my opinion, is based upon a dangerous misunderstanding, or misapplication, of what was decided and said in *Hong Kong Fir*. That case was concerned with an obligation of seaworthiness, breaches of which had occurred during the course of the voyage. The decision of the Court of Appeal was that this obligation was not a condition, a breach of which entitled the charterer to repudiate. It was pointed out that, as could be seen in advance the breaches, which might occur of it, were various. They might be extremely trivial, the omission of a nail; they might be extremely grave, a serious defect in the hull or in the machinery; they might be of serious but not fatal gravity, incompetence or incapacity of the crew. The decision, and the judgments of the Court of Appeal, drew from these facts the inescapable conclusion that it was impossible to ascribe to the obligation, in advance, the character of a condition.

Diplock LJ then generalised this particular consequence into the analysis which has since become classical. The fundamental fallacy of the appellants' argument lies in attempting to apply this analysis to a time clause such as the present in a mercantile contract, which is totally different in character. As to such a clause there is only one kind of breach possible, namely, to be late, and the questions which have to be asked are, first, what importance have the parties expressly ascribed to this consequence, and secondly, in the absence of expressed agreement, what consequence ought to be attached to it having regard to the contract as a whole.

The test suggested by the appellants was a different one. One must consider, they said, the breach actually committed and then decide whether that default would deprive the party not in default of substantially the whole benefit of the contract. They invoked even certain passages in the judgment of Diplock LJ in the *Hong Kong Fir* case to support it. One may observe in the first place that the introduction of a test of this kind would be commercially most undesirable. It would expose the parties, after a breach of one, two, three, seven and other numbers of days to an argument whether this delay would have left time for the seller to provide the goods. It would make it, at the time, at least difficult, and sometimes impossible, for the supplier to know whether he could do so. It would fatally remove from a vital provision in the contract that certainty which is the most indispensable quality of mercantile contracts, and lead to a large increase in arbitrations. It would confine the seller – perhaps after arbitration and reference through the courts – to a remedy in damages which might be extremely difficult to quantify. These are all serious objections in practice. But I am clear that the submission is unacceptable in law. The judgment of Diplock LJ does not give any support and ought not to give any encouragement to any such proposition; for beyond doubt it recognises that it is open to the parties to agree that, as regards a particular obligation, any breach shall entitle the party not in default to treat the contract as repudiated. Indeed, if he were not doing so he would, in a passage which does not profess to be more than clarificatory, be discrediting a long and uniform series of cases – at least from *Bowes* v *Shand* onwards which have been referred to by my noble and learned friend, Lord Roskill. It remains true, as Lord Roskill has pointed out in *Cehave NV* v *Bremer Handelsgesellschaft mbH* (*The Hansa Nord*), that the courts should not be too ready to interpret contractual clauses as conditions. And I have myself commended, and continue to commend, the greater flexibility in the law of contracts to which *Hong Kong Fir* points the way (*Reardon Smith Line Ltd* v *Yngvar*

Hansen-Tangen (trading as H E Hansen-Tangen)). But I do not doubt that, in suitable cases, the courts should not be reluctant, if the intentions of the parties as shown by the contract so indicate, to hold that an obligation has the force of a condition, and that indeed they should usually do so in the case of time clauses in mercantile contracts. To such cases the "gravity of the breach" approach of the *Hong Kong Fir* case would be unsuitable. I need only add on this point that the word "expressly" used by Diplock LJ in *Hong Kong Fir* should not be read as requiring the actual use of the word "condition": any term or terms of the contract, which, fairly read, have the effect indicated, are sufficient. Lord Diplock himself has given recognition to this in this House: *Photo Production Ltd* v *Securicor Transport Ltd*. I therefore reject that part of the appellants' argument which was based upon it, and I must disagree with the judgment of the learned trial judge in so far as he accepted it. I respectfully endorse, on the other hand, the full and learned treatment of this issue in the judgment of Megaw LJ in the Court of Appeal.

I would add that the argument above apples equally to the use which the appellants endeavoured to make of certain observations in *United Scientific Holdings Ltd* v *Burnley Borough Council*, a case on which I do not need to comment on this occasion.

In conclusion, the statement of the law in *Halsbury's Laws of England*, 4th edn, vol 9 . . . (generally approved in the House in the *United Scientific Holdings* case), appears to me to be correct, in particular in asserting (1) that the court will require precise compliance with stipulations as to time wherever the circumstances of the case indicate that this would fulfil the intention of the parties, and (2) that broadly speaking time will be considered of the essence in "mercantile" contracts – with footnote reference to authorities which I have mentioned.

The relevant clause falls squarely within these principles, and such authority as there is supports its status as a condition: see *Bremer Handelsgesellschaft mbH* v *J H Rayner & Co Ltd* and see *Turnbull (Peter) & Co Pty Ltd* v *Mundas Trading Co (Australasia) Pty Ltd*. In this present context it is clearly essential that both buyer and seller (who may change roles in the next series of contracts, or even in the same chain of contracts) should know precisely what their obligations are, most especially because the ability of the seller to fulfil his obligation may well be totally dependent on punctual performance by the buyer.

I would dismiss the appeal . . .'

IMPLIED TERMS

In addition to the terms expressly agreed between the parties there are sometimes terms implied into the contract. In such cases in order to determine what the exact contract (agreement) is between the parties the express terms *and the implied terms* must be *taken together*: together they constitute the *one* contract between the parties.

Terms implied by custom

See *Les Affréteurs Réunis Société Anonyme* v *Walford* above (p 184).

Terms implied by statute

Examples of terms implied into contracts by statute are to be found in the Sale of Goods Act 1979. For example s 14(2) provides that 'Where the seller sells goods in the course of a business, there is an implied term that the goods supplied under the contract are of satisfactory quality.'

Section 14(3) provides that 'Where the seller sells goods in the course of a business and the buyer, expressly or by implication, makes known – (a) to the seller ... any particular purpose for which the goods are being bought, there is an implied term that the goods supplied under the contract are reasonably fit for that purpose . . . '

Terms implied by the courts

As a general rule the courts are most reluctant to imply terms into any contract.

'Standard' implied terms

Lynch v Thorne

[1956] 1 All ER 744 • Court of Appeal

Under a written contract a builder agreed to sell to the buyer a house which was still being built. The builder covenanted to complete the building in accordance with a plan and specification attached to the agreement. Within two weeks of the buyer moving into the house, rain came in through some of the windows and a damp patch appeared in the south wall of a room on the first floor. The buyer alleged that it was an implied term of the contract that the house should be completed in a workmanlike manner, with proper materials, and should, when completed, be reasonably fit for human habitation.

The issue before the court was whether a term could be implied into a contract so as to contradict an express term of that contract.

Lord Evershed MR: '. . . I am, however, prepared to assume for the purposes of this judgment that, whether or not it can be said that any necessity so compels in the case where a vendor contracts to sell the land and also to complete the building, in such a case *prima facie* there is an implied covenant on the vendor builder's part that he will complete the house so as to make it habitable. Nevertheless, although such a term is *prima facie* to be implied, it must, according to well-established principle, always yield to the express letter of the bargain . . .

No one has sought to quarrel with the learned judge's findings of fact, and, so far as I can see, no one could quarrel with them. The judge, after referring to the plan and to the specification, said: "It is not disputed that the house has been built exactly in accordance with the drawings and specification . . ."

The effect of . . . those findings seems to me to be that, the contract having provided that the house should be built and completed in a particular way by the use of particular materials of particular characteristics, the defendant precisely and exactly complied with his obligation. He is also found to have shown, through his servants, a high standard of workmanship . . .

Counsel for the plaintiff . . . submitted, first, that, even though there was an express contract precisely prescribing the way in which the work was to be done, there was an overriding promise or warranty that the edifice, when built in strict accordance with those terms, would be a habitable house. That seems to me to involve an extension of the principle of implied terms for which I can find no authority, and which, indeed, seems to me to be in direct conflict with the authorities to which I have already referred. Secondly, counsel said, using this submission rather to emphasise and support his main contention which I have already stated, that the plaintiff, being no expert in the mysteries of architecture and house building, relies, and the judge found that he relied, on the skill and the judgment of the defendant, the builder. I am unable to derive from that fact the conclusion which commended itself to the judge. If a skilled person promises to do a job, that is, to produce a particular thing, whether a house or a motor car or a piece of machinery, and he makes no provision, as a matter of bargain, as to the precise structure or article which he will create, then it may well be that the buyer of the structure or article relies on the judgment and skill of the other party to produce that which he says he will produce. That, however, is only another way of formulating the existence in such circumstances of an implied warranty. On the other hand, if two parties elect to make a bargain which specifies in precise detail what one of them will do, then, in the absence of some other express provision, it would appear to me to follow that the bargain is that which they have made; and so long as the party doing the work does that which he has contracted to do, that is the extent of his obligation. One cannot help feeling a great deal of sympathy for the plaintiff, but an adult is, presumably, capable of taking competent skilled advice if he wants to, and, if he elects not to do so but to make a bargain in precise terms with someone else, then, although he does rely no doubt on the skill of the other party in a sense, he does so only in the sense that he assumes that the other party will do competently the job which the other party has promised to do (as was the fact in this case), and, at best, that he believes that the house which the other party is going to build will be a habitable house. That, however, is far short of importing into the transaction any such overriding condition or warranty as that for which counsel for the plaintiff contended. Counsel's contention would appear almost to involve the result that, because the plaintiff elected not to take advice himself, there was some duty of care thrust on the defendant which should more properly have been borne by someone engaged by the plaintiff. These considerations seem to me to find no place in the authorities, as I have understood them, and since there was here what Romer LJ, in *Perry* v *Sharon Development Co Ltd*, called an express contract as to the way in which the house was to be completed, I can find no room for an implied warranty, the only effect of the operation of which would, so far as I can see, be to create an inconsistency with the express language of the bargain made.'

'The Moorcock'

The courts will imply a term to give 'business efficacy' to the contract. This is on the basis of the 'presumed intention' of the parties. Remember the courts are most reluctant to imply a term into a contract and they will only imply a term into a contract on the *Moorcock* principle where the contract would otherwise fail.

The Moorcock

[1886–90] All ER Rep 530 • Court of Appeal

The appellant wharfingers owned a wharf and a jetty which extended into the River Thames. The respondent was the owner of the steamship *Moorcock*. In November 1887 it was agreed between the appellants and the respondent that the *Moorcock* should be discharged and loaded at the wharf and for that purpose should be moored alongside the jetty where she would take the ground at low water. No charge was made in respect of the vessel being moored alongside the jetty but the shipowner paid for the use of the cranes in discharging the cargo, and rates were payable to the appellants on all goods landed, shipped, or stored. Whilst the *Moorcock* was lying moored at the end of the jetty discharging her cargo, the tide ebbed and she grounded with the result that she sustained damage owing to the centre of the vessel settling on a ridge of hard ground beneath the mud.

The issue before the court was whether there should be implied into the contract a term that the wharfinger had taken reasonable care to ascertain that the bottom of the river at the jetty was in such a condition as not to endanger the vessel.

Bowen LJ: '. . . The question which arises in this case is whether, when a contract is made to let the use of this jetty to a ship which can only use it, as is known by both parties, by her taking the ground, there is any implied warranty on the part of the wharfingers [owners], and if so what is the extent of the warranty.

An implied warranty, or as it is called a covenant in law, as distinguished from an express contract or express warranty, really is in every instance founded on the presumed intention of the parties and upon reason. It is the implication which the law draws from what must obviously have been the intention of the parties, an implication which the law draws with the object of giving efficacy to the transaction and preventing such a failure of consideration as cannot have been within the contemplation of either of the parties. I believe if one were to take all the instances, which are many, of implied warranties and covenants in law which occur in the earlier cases . . . it will be seen that in all these cases the law is raising an implication from the presumed intention of the parties with the object of giving to the transaction such efficacy as both parties must have intended that it should have. If that is so, the reasonable implication which the law draws must differ according to the circumstances of the various transactions, and in business transactions what the law desires to effect by the implication is to give such business efficacy to the transaction as must have been intended by both parties; not to impose on one side all the perils of the transaction, or to emancipate one side from all the burdens, but to make each party promise in law as much, at all events, as it must have been in the contemplation of both parties that he should be responsible for.

What did each party in the present case know? because, if we are examining into their presumed intention, we must examine into their minds as to what the transaction was. Both parties knew that this jetty was let for the purpose of profit, and knew that it could only be used by the ship taking the ground and lying on the ground. They must have known that it was by grounding that she would use the jetty. They must have known, both of them, that unless the ground was safe the ship would be simply buying an opportunity of danger and buying no convenience at all, and that all consideration would fail unless the ground was safe. In fact, the business of the jetty could not be carried on unless, I do not say the ground was safe, it was supposed to be safe. The master and crew of the ship could know nothing, whereas the defendants or their servants might, by exercising reasonable care, know everything. The defendants or their servants were on the spot at high and low tide, morning and evening. They must know what had happened to the ships that had used the jetty before, and with the slightest trouble they could satisfy themselves in case of doubt whether the berth was or not safe. The ship's officers, on the other hand, had no means of verifying the state of the berth, because, for aught I know, it might be occupied by another ship at the time the *Moorcock* got there.

The question is how much of the peril or the safety of this berth is it necessary to assume in order to get the minimum of efficacy to the business consideration of the transaction which the ship consented to bear, and which the defendants took upon themselves. Supposing that the berth had been actually under the control of the defendants, they could, of course, have repaired it and made it fit for the purpose of loading and unloading. It seems to me that *Mersey Docks Trustees* v *Gibbs* shows that those who own a jetty, who take money for its use, and who have under their control the *locus in quo*, are bound to take all reasonable care to prevent danger to those using the jetty, either to make the berth good or else not to invite ships to go to the jetty, i.e. either to make it safe or to advise ships not to go there. But there is a distinction between that case and the present. The berth here was not under the actual control of the defendants . . .

Applying that modification, which is a reasonable modification, to this case, it may well be said that the law will not imply that the defendants, who had not control of the place, ought to have taken reasonable care to make the berth good, but it does not follow that they are relieved from all responsibility, a responsibility which depends not merely on the control of the place, which is one element as to which the law implies a duty, but on other circumstances. The defendants are on the spot. They must know the jetty cannot be safely used unless reasonable care is taken. No one can tell whether reasonable safety has been secured except themselves, and I think that, if they let out their jetty for use, they at all events imply that they have taken reasonable care to see that the berth, which is the essential part of the use of the jetty, is safe, and, if it is not safe, and if they have not taken such reasonable care, it is their duty to warn persons with whom they have dealings that they have not done so . . .'

Liverpool City Council v *Irwin*

[1976] 2 All ER 39 • House of Lords

The Irwins were tenants of a flat owned by Liverpool City Council. The tenancy agreement imposed many obligations on the tenants but none on the landlord, Liverpool City Council. The tenants complained of continual failure of the lifts, lack of lighting on the stairs, the dangerous condition of the staircase and frequent blockage of the rubbish chutes. Eventually the tenants considered that they had suffered enough problems and refused to pay their rent. In response to this the landlords sought an order for possession of the tenants' flats. The tenants counter-claimed alleging that the landlord was in breach of an implied term to keep the common parts of the flats in repair and properly lighted.

The issue before the court was whether a term could be implied into the tenancy agreement and, if so, on what basis.

Lord Wilberforce: 'I consider first the appellants' claim insofar as it is based on contract. The first step must be to ascertain what the contract is. This may look elementary, even naive, but it seems to me to be the essential step and to involve, from the start, an approach different, if simpler, from that taken by the members of the Court of Appeal. We look first at documentary material. As is common with council lettings there is no formal demise or lease or tenancy agreement. There is a document headed "Liverpool Corporation, Liverpool City Housing Department" and described as "Conditions of Tenancy". This contains a list of obligations on the tenant – he shall do this, he shall not do that, or he shall not do that without the corporation's consent. This is an amalgam of obligations added to from time to time, no doubt, to meet complaints, emerging situations, or problems as they appear to the council's officers. In particular there have been added special provisions relating to multi-storey flats which are supposed to make the conditions suitable to such dwellings. We may note under "Further special notes" some obligations not to obstruct staircases and passages, and not to permit children under ten to operate any lifts. I mention these as a recognition of the existence and relevance of these facilities.

At the end there is a form for signature by the tenant stating that he accepts the tenancy. On the landlords' side there is nothing, no signature, no demise, no covenant; the contract takes effect as soon as the tenants sign the form and are let into possession.

We have then a contract which is partly, but not wholly, stated in writing. In order to complete it, in particular to give it a bilateral character, it is necessary to take account of the actions of the parties and the circumstances. As actions of the parties, we must note the granting of possession by the corporation and reservation by it of the "common parts" – stairs, lifts, chutes etc. As circumstances we must include the nature of the premises, viz a maisonette for family use on the ninth floor of a high block, one which is occupied by a large number of other tenants, all using the common parts and dependent on them, none of them having any expressed obligation to maintain or repair them.

To say that the construction of a complete contract out of these elements involves a process of "implication" may be correct: it would be so if implication means the supplying of what is not expressed. But there are varieties of implications which the courts think fit to make and they do not necessarily involve the same process. Where there is, on the face of it, a complete, bilateral contract, the courts are sometimes willing to add terms to it, as implied terms; this is very common in mercantile contracts where there is an established usage; in that case the courts are spelling out what both parties know and would, if asked, unhesitatingly agree to be part of the bargain. In other cases, where there is an apparently complete bargain, the courts are willing to add a term on the ground that without it the contract will not work – this is the case, if not of the *Moorcock* itself on its facts, at least of the doctrine of the *Moorcock* as usually applied. This is, as was pointed out by the majority in the Court of Appeal, a strict test – though the degree of strictness seems to vary with the current legal trend, and I think that they were right not to accept it as applicable here. There is a third variety of implication, that which I think Lord Denning MR favours, or at least did favour in this case, and that is the implication of reasonable terms. But though I agree with many of his instances, which in fact fall under one or other of the preceding heads, I cannot go so far as to endorse his principle; indeed, it seems to me, with respect, to extend a long, and undesirable, way beyond sound authority.

The present case, in my opinion, represents a fourth category or, I would rather say, a fourth shade on a continuous spectrum. The court here is simply concerned to establish what the contract is, the parties not having themselves fully stated the terms. In this sense the court is searching for what must be implied.

What then should this contract be held to be? There must first be implied a letting, i.e. a grant of the right of exclusive possession to the tenants. With this there must, I would suppose, be implied a covenant for quiet enjoyment, as a necessary incident of the letting. The difficulty begins when we consider the common parts. We start with the fact that the demise is useless unless access is obtained by the staircase; we can add that, having regard to the height of the block, and the family nature of the dwellings, the demise would be useless without a lift service; we can continue that there being rubbish chutes built in to the structures and no other means of disposing of light rubbish there must be a right to use the chutes. The question to be answered – and it is the only question in this case – is what is to be the legal relationship between landlord and tenant as regards these matters?

There can be no doubt that there must be implied (i) an easement for the tenants and their licensees to use the stairs, (ii) a right in the nature of an easement to use the lifts and (iii) an easement to use the rubbish chutes.

But are these easements to be accompanied by any obligation on the landlord, and what obligation? There seem to be two alternatives. The first, for which the corporation contends, is for an easement coupled with no legal obligation, except such as may arise under the Occupiers' Liability Act 1957 as regards the safety of those using the facilities, and possibly such other liability as might exist under the ordinary law of tort. The alternative is for easements coupled with some obligation on the part of the landlords as regards the maintenance of the subject of them, so that they are available for use.

My Lords, in order to be able to choose between these, it is necessary to define what test is to be applied, and I do not find this difficult. In my opinion such obligation should be read into the contract as the nature of the contract itself implicitly requires, no more, no less; a test in other words of necessity. The relationship accepted by the corporation is that of landlord and tenant; the tenant accepts obligations accordingly, in relation, *inter alia*, to the stairs, the lifts and the chutes. All these are not just facilities, or conveniences provided at discretion; they are essentials of the tenancy without which life in the dwellings, as a tenant, is not possible. To leave the landlord free of contractual obligation as regards these matters, and subject only to administrative or political pressure, is, in my opinion, totally inconsistent with the nature of this relationship. The subject-matter of the lease (high-rise blocks) and the relationship created by the tenancy demands, of its nature, some contractual obligation on the landlord.

I do not think that this approach involves any innovation as regards the law of contract. The necessity to have regard to the inherent nature of a contract and of the relationship thereby established was stated in this House in *Lister* v *Romford Ice & Cold Storage Co Ltd.* That was a case between master and servant and of a search for an "implied term". Viscount Simonds made a clear distinction between a search for an implied term such as might be necessary to give "business efficacy" to the particular contract and a search, based on wider considerations, for such a term as the nature of the contract might call for, or as a legal incident of this kind of contract. If the search were for the former, he said: "I should lose myself in the attempt to formulate it with the necessary precision". We see an echo of this in the present case, when the majority in the Court of Appeal, considering a "business efficacy term", i.e. a *Moorcock* term, found themselves faced with five alternative terms and therefore rejected all of them. But that is not, in my opinion, the end, or indeed the object, of the search.

We have some guidance in authority for the kind of term which this typical relationship (of landlord and tenant in multi-occupational dwellings) requires . . .

[Lord Wilberforce then examined the authorities for examples of terms typically found in contracts between landlords and tenants.]

These are all reflections of what necessarily arises whenever a landlord lets portions of a building for multiple occupation, retaining essential means of access . . .

It remains to define the standard. My Lords, if, as I think, the test of the existence of the term is necessity the standard must surely not exceed what is necessary having regard to the circumstances. To imply an absolute obligation to repair would go beyond what is a necessary legal incident and would indeed be unreasonable. An obligation to take reasonable care to keep in reasonable repair and usability is what fits the requirements of the case. Such a definition involves – and I think rightly – recognition that the tenants themselves have their responsibilities. What it is reasonable to expect of a landlord has a clear relation to what a reasonable set of tenants should do for themselves . . .

I would hold therefore that the corporation's obligation is as I have described. And in agreement, I believe, with your Lordships, I would hold that it has not been shown in this case that there was any breach of that obligation. On the main point therefore I would hold that the appeal fails.

My Lords, it will be seen that I have reached exactly the same conclusion as that of Lord Denning MR, with most of whose thinking I respectfully agree. I must only differ from the passage in which, more adventurously, he suggested that the courts had power to introduce into contracts any terms they thought reasonable or to anticipate legislative recommendations of the Law Commission. A just result can be reached, if I am right, by a less dangerous route.'

Trollope & Colls Ltd v North West Metropolitan Regional Hospital Board
[1973] 2 All ER 260 • House of Lords

The Hospital Board engaged Trollope to build phase III of a hospital project. The date for the completion of the contract was stated in the contract to be 30 April 1972. Phase I was 59 weeks late in being completed and the Hospital Board claimed that the date for the completion of phase III should be extended to take account of the overrun. Trollope insisted that the date for completion of phase III remained 30 April 1972.

The issue before the court was whether a term could be implied into the contract so as to extend the time for the completion of phase III.

Lord Pearson: 'In that situation a dispute arose as to the contractual position, and there was a curious reversal of the usual attitudes in such cases. The appellants were claiming that the express provisions of the contract were to be read literally and no implied term could be introduced, and so the appellants were not entitled to any extension of time and were bound to complete phase III by the specified date. They professed to be able to complete their part of the work by the specified date, and they called on the respondents to nominate sub-contractors who would enter into sub-contracts conforming to that time schedule. This the respondents were unable to do. The appellants were turning the situation to their own advantage, because, if the contract could not be carried out, a new arrangement would have to be made for the work to be done at the prices prevailing in or about 1971, which were considerably higher than the contract prices. The difference between the contract prices and the prices prevailing in or about 1971 is said to be in the region of one million pounds.

The respondents, on the other hand, wished to have the work carried out at the contract prices. They contended that the appellants were entitled to an extension of the time for completion of phase III by 47 weeks . . .

. . . The court will not even improve the contract which the parties have made for themselves, however desirable the improvement might be. The court's function is to interpret and apply the contract which the parties have made for themselves. If the express terms are perfectly clear and free from ambiguity, there is no choice to be made between different possible meanings: the clear terms must be applied even if the court thinks some other terms would have been more suitable. An unexpressed term can be implied if and only if the court finds that the parties must have intended that term to form part of their contract: it is not enough for the court to find that such a term would have been adopted by the parties as reasonable men if it had been suggested to them: it must have been a term that went without saying, a term necessary to give business efficacy to the contract, a term which, although tacit, formed part of the contract which the parties made for themselves. The relevant express term is entirely clear and free from ambiguity: the date for completion of phase III is the date stated in the appendix to conditions "C", which is 30th April 1972. That term in itself can have only one meaning.

As to the alleged implied term, I am by no means convinced that the parties overlooked the possible effect of an "overrun" of phase I on the time for completing phase III . . . The parties were making the timetable which they considered suitable for the particular case. It is reasonable to suppose that they knew what they were doing, and that the appellants were taking the risk of an "overrun" of phase I curtailing the time for phase III . . .'

Gardner v Coutts & Co

[1967] 3 All ER 1064 • Chancery

In July 1948 in return for a payment of 10s Jekyll granted Lawson an option to purchase a freehold property known as Munstead Hut if, during his lifetime, he desired to sell the property. In January 1963 Jekyll gave Munstead Hut to his sister. Gardner, Lawson's successor in title, claimed that it was an implied term of the agreement that Jekyll should not during his lifetime make a gift of the property without first giving to Lawson, or her successor in title, the option of purchasing Munstead Hut.

The issue before the court was whether such a term could be implied into the option.

Cross J: 'The agreement does not provide expressly for the event of Mr Jekyll giving away Munstead Hut in his lifetime. The whole question is whether there ought to be implied in the agreement a provision to [that] effect . . .

When one hears the words "implied term" one thinks at once of MacKinnon LJ and his officious bystander. It appears, however, that that individual, though not yet so characterised, first made his appearance as long ago as 1918 in a judgment of Scrutton LJ. I shall read a passage from that judgment and then the well-known passage from the judgment of MacKinnon LJ in a later case. In *Reigate* v *Union Manufacturing Co (Ramsbottom) Ltd*, Scrutton LJ said:

"The first thing is to see what the parties have expressed in the contract; and then an implied term is not to be added because the court thinks it would have been reasonable to have inserted it in the contract. A term can only be implied if it is necessary in the business sense to give efficacy to the contract; that is, if it is such a term that it can confidently be said that if at the time the contract was being negotiated someone had said to the parties, 'What will happen in such a case', they would both have replied, 'Of course, so and so will happen; we did not trouble to say that; it is too clear'. Unless the court comes to some such conclusion as that, it ought not to imply a term which the parties themselves have not expressed.

In the case of *Shirlaw* v *Southern Foundries (1926), Ltd and Federated Foundries, Ltd*, MacKinnon LJ said:

"I recognise that the right or duty of a court to find the existence of an implied term or implied terms in a written contract is a matter to be exercised with care, and a court is too often invited to do so upon vague and uncertain grounds. Too often, also, such an invitation is backed by the citation of a sentence or two from the judgment of Bowen LJ in *The Moorcock*. They are sentences from an *extempore* judgment as sound and sensible as are all the utterances of that great judge, but I fancy that he would have been rather surprised if he could have foreseen that these general remarks of his would come to be a favourite citation of a supposed principle of law, and I even think that he might sympathise with the occasional impatience of his successors when the *Moorcock* is so often flashed before them in that guise. For my part, I think that there is a test that may be at least as useful as such generalities. If I may quote from an essay which I wrote some years ago, I then said: '*Prima facie* that which in any contract is left to be implied and need not be expressed is something so obvious that it goes without saying'. Thus, if, while the parties were making their bargain, an officious bystander were to suggest some express provision for it in their agreement, they would testily suppress him with a common: 'Oh, of course!' At least it is true, I think, that if a term were never implied by a judge unless it could pass that test, he could not be held to be wrong."

I agree wholeheartedly that a judge ought to be very cautious over implying terms in contracts. It is so easy to say to oneself. "That is an eminently reasonable provision. If the parties had thought of it they would certainly have put it in, and so I ought to imply it." That sort of approach is, of course, quite wrong. If Mr. Jekyll's reaction to the question "What if you want to give the property away?" would have been "Well, that is a new point; and I do not suppose that in fact I will ever want to give it away, but as you have raised this point I am prepared to agree to offer it to Mrs Lawson for £3000 if I do want to give it away. So put that in too", then as I see it the plaintiff must fail. For him to succeed I must be reasonably confident that on the question being raised Mr Jekyll would have agreed with Mrs Lawson in saying "Oh, but of course that event is included too. What goes for a projected sale goes also for a projected gift".

. . . Nevertheless, viewing this matter apart from authority, I think that it is implicit in a grant of first refusal that the person who has to offer the property to the other party, should not be entitled to give it away without offering it and so to defeat the first refusal. That being the way that I view the matter, if I apply the test laid down by Scrutton LJ, and MacKinnon LJ, I am confident that at the time, whatever views Mr Jekyll may have formed later, if somebody had said to him "You have not expressly catered for the possibility of your wanting to give away the property", he would have said, as undoubtedly Mrs Lawson would have said, "Oh, of course that is implied. What goes for a contemplated sale must go for a contemplated gift" . . .'

Moorcock – strict test

The *Moorcock* is a strict test. The test is not only what is a *reasonable* term but whether it is also a *necessary* term.

If a term is implied as a legal incident of a particular kind of contract, the court is not trying to imply a term into a *concluded* contract but rather it is trying to establish what the full contract is: see *Liverpool CC* v *Irwin* above (p 236).

The *Liverpool CC* v *Irwin* approach has been followed by the Court of Appeal in the following case.

Ferguson v John Dawson & Partners (Contractors) Ltd

[1976] 3 All ER 817 • Court of Appeal

Ferguson was employed by John Dawson & Partners 'on the lump' [a device, now prohibited by statute, for avoiding the payment of national insurance and income tax]. Whilst working on the roof of a building Ferguson fell 15 feet and was seriously injured. He claimed damages from John Dawson & Partners for his injuries. In order to be able to claim damages from John Dawson & Partners he had to show that he was an employee of theirs; they claimed that he was self-employed and that, therefore, they were not liable for his injuries.

The issue before the court was what terms governed the contract between Ferguson and John Dawson & Partners.

Megaw LJ: 'The defendants, as I have said, contend that the contract which governed the legal relationship between the plaintiff and the defendants for the three months up to the time of the accident was a single-term contract. The single term, derived from Mr Murray's words "I did inform him that there were no cards, we were purely working as a lump labour force", was that the plaintiff's status *vis-à-vis* the defendants was to be, or was to be deemed to be, "a self-employed labour only sub-contractor". I shall assume for present purposes, though counsel for the plaintiff was not disposed to accept the assumption, that this is a correct interpretation of the intended, and understood, meaning of the delphic words which were spoken by Mr Murray and tacitly accepted by the plaintiff.

I am not, however, prepared to accept the defendants' further contention that there were no other terms of the contract. Indeed, if there were no other terms, the only conclusion in law, I think, would be the absurd conclusion that there was no contract at all during the three months in which the plaintiff was working for the defendants. Counsel for the defendants, when this was put to him, was disposed to accept that there must have been a contractual term as to remuneration. There must, as I think, have been many other contractual terms, also necessarily to be implied, even though they were not mentioned in the brief conversation when Mr Murray and the plaintiff agreed that the plaintiff should start work on the following Monday. This is so, whether the contract was a contract of service or for services. For example, what sort of work could the defendants require the plaintiff to do? Was he to work in his own time or during stated hours and, if so, what hours? Where could he be required to work? What notice, if any, was required by either side for the termination of the contract? What control could the defendants through Mr Murray exercise over the order in which the plaintiff did such work as he might be required to do, or the manner of doing it?

In my opinion, the law is not so divorced from reality as to assume that the same considerations as to the ascertainment of the relevant contractual terms, if a legal analysis of the terms has to be made for any purpose, applies to a contract of the nature with which we are here concerned, the taking on of a labourer on casual application to a site agent on a building site, as applies to commercial contracts between business men, whether made orally after discussion of terms or made in writing with elaborate provisions. The terms – even the essential terms – of a contract of the present nature would often not be spoken or written at the time when the workman is taken on. They would be understood by reference to the known circumstances and the existing practices and conventions of a particular trade or a particular contractor or a particular site. Moreover, if and insofar as they were not implied, by common knowledge of what the practice was, at the time when the labourer was first taken on – the date when the legal analysis would regard the contract as being made – terms could well be added thereafter, as particular questions of the rights and obligations of the parties arose during the progress of the work. Again, to apply legal analysis, such terms would be treated as having been added, or the contract as being varied.

In this context of the implication of terms, I would refer to what was so helpfully said by Lord Wilberforce in the recent House of Lords case, *Liverpool City Council* v *Irwin*:

"The present case, in my opinion, represents a fourth category or, I would rather say, a fourth shade on a continuous spectrum. The court here is simply concerned to establish what the contract is, the parties not having themselves fully stated the terms. In this sense the court is searching for what must be implied."

So also in this case with we are concerned.

Accordingly, I reject the defendants' contention that on legal analysis there were no contractual terms governing the relationship between the plaintiff and the defendants other than a term "self-employed labour only sub-contractor". There were such other contractual terms . . .

. . . [W]e are not here concerned with construing a contract, but with evidence as to what the terms of a contract were – the implication of terms within Lord Wilberforce's fourth category or fourth "shade of the spectrum" . . .

In my judgment, on the tests laid down in the authorities, all of this indicates beyond doubt that the reality of the relationship was employer and employee: a contract of service . . .

My own view would have been that a declaration by the parties, even if it be incorporated in the contract, that the workman is to be, or is to be deemed to be, self-employed, an independent contractor, ought to be wholly disregarded – not merely treated as not being conclusive – if the remainder of the contractual terms, governing the realities of the relationship, show the relationship of employer and employee . . . '

Way in which to apply the Moorcock test

The first thing the court sets out to do is to see if there is a 'term which the typical relationship requires', i.e. the necessary term.

Shell UK Ltd v Lostock Garage Ltd

[1977] 1 All ER 481 • Court of Appeal

Lostock Garage entered into an agreement with Shell whereby in return for Shell making a loan to Lostock Garage, Lostock Garage would sell only Shell petrol. In December 1975 there was a petrol price war. Shell reduced the price of the petrol that it supplied to two garages who were close to Lostock Garage. Neither of these two garages were tied to Shell. Shell refused to reduce the price of the petrol it supplied to Lostock Garage. This caused Lostock Garage to trade at a loss. Lostock Garage then, in breach of its agreement with Shell, purchased petrol from another supplier. Shell brought an action against Lostock Garage claiming damages for breach of contract. Lostock Garage claimed that Shell was in breach of an implied term in the contract that 'Shell would not abnormally discriminate against' them in favour of competing and neighbouring garages.

The issue before the court was whether the court could, and if so should, imply such a term into the contract.

Lord Denning MR: Implied terms. 'It was submitted by counsel for Lostock that there was to be implied in the solus agreement a term that Shell, as the supplier, should not abnormally discriminate against the buyer and/or should supply petrol to the buyer on terms which did not abnormally discriminate against him. He said that Shell had broken that implied term by giving support to the two Shell garages and refusing it to Lostock; that, on that ground, Shell were in breach of the solus agreement; and that Lostock were entitled to terminate it.

This submission makes it necessary once again to consider the law as to implied terms. I ventured with some trepidation to suggest that terms implied by law could be brought within one comprehensive category, in which the courts could imply a term such as was just and reasonable in the circumstances: see *Greaves & Co (Contractors) Ltd* v *Baynham Meikle & Partners*; *Liverpool City Council* v *Irwin*. But, as I feared, the House of Lords have rejected it as quite unacceptable. As I read the speeches, there are two broad categories of implied terms.

(i) The first category

The first category comprehends all those relationships which are of common occurrence, such as the relationship of seller and buyer, owner and hirer, master and servant, landlord and tenant, carrier by land or by sea, contractor for building works, and so forth. In all those relationships the courts have imposed obligations on one party or the other, saying they are implied terms. These obligations are not founded on the intention of the parties, actual or presumed, but on more general considerations: see *Luxor (Eastbourne) Ltd* v *Cooper* per Lord Wright; *Lister* v *Romford Ice and Cold Storage Co* per Viscount Simonds and Lord Tucker (both of whom give interesting illustrations); *Liverpool City Council* v *Irwin* per Lord Cross of Chelsea and Lord Edmund-Davis. In such relationships the problem is not solved by asking: what did the parties intend? or, would they have unhesitatingly agreed to it, if asked? It is to be solved by asking: has the law already defined the obligation or the extent of it? If so, let it be followed. If not, look to see what would be reasonable in the general run of such cases (see per Lord Cross of Chelsea) and then say what the obligation shall be. The House in *Liverpool City Council* v *Irwin* went through that very process. They examined the existing law of landlord and tenant, in particular that relating to easements, to see if it contained the solution to the problem; and, having found that it did not, they imposed an obligation on the landlord to use reasonable care. In these relationships the parties can exclude or modify the obligation by express words, but unless they do so, the obligation is a legal incident of the relationship which is attached by the law itself and not by reason of any implied term.

Likewise, in the general law of contract, the legal effect of frustration does not depend on an implied term. It does not depend on the presumed intention of the parties, nor on what they would have answered, if asked, but simply on what the court itself declares to amount to a frustration: see *Davis Contractors* v *Fareham Urban District Council* per Lord Radcliffe; *Ocean Tramp Tankers Corpn* v *V/O Sovfracht, The Eugenia*.

(ii) The second category

The second category comprehends those cases which are not within the first category. These are cases, not of common occurrence, in which from the particular circumstances a term is to be implied. In these cases the implication is based on an intention imputed to the parties from their actual circumstances: see *Luxor (Eastbourne) Ltd* v *Cooper* per Lord Wright. Such an imputation is only to be made when it is necessary to imply a term to give efficacy to the contract and make it a workable agreement in such manner as the parties would clearly have done if they had applied their mind to the contingency which has arisen. These are the "officious bystander" type of case: see *Lister* v *Romford Ice & Cold Storage Co* per Lord Tucker. In such cases a term is not to be implied on the ground that it would be reasonable, but only when it is necessary and can be formulated with a sufficient degree of precision. This was the test applied by the majority of this court in *Liverpool City Council* v *Irwin*; and they were emphatically upheld by the House on this point; see per Lord Cross of Chelsea and Lord Edmund-Davies.

There is this point to be noted about *Liverpool City Council* v *Irwin*. In this court the argument was only about an implication in the second category. In the House of Lords that argument was not pursued. It was only the first category.

Into which of the two categories does the present case come? I am tempted to say that a solus agreement between supplier and buyer is of such common occurrence nowadays that it could be put into the first category; so that the law could imply a term based on general considerations. But I do not think this would be found acceptable. Nor do I think the case can be brought within the second category. If Shell had been asked at the beginning: "Will you agree not to discriminate abnormally against the buyer?" I think they would have declined. It might be a reasonable term, but it is not a necessary term. Nor can it be formulated with sufficient precision. On this point I agree with Kerr J. It should be noticed that in *Esso Petroleum Co Ltd* v *Harper's Garage (Stourport) Ltd* Mocatta J also refused to make such an implication and there was no appeal from his decision.

In the circumstances, I do not think any term can be implied.'

SUMMARY

You should now be able to:

- Distinguish between *terms* and *representations.*
- Understand how a *collateral warranty* can modify a written agreement.
- Distinguish between *conditions*, *warranties* and *innominate terms.*
- Understand how *implied terms* form part of a contract.

If you have not mastered the above points you should go through this section again.

10 Exemption clauses: the common law

EXEMPTION CLAUSES

An exemption (exclusion) clause in one whereby one party to a contract inserts into a contract a term excluding or limiting his potential liability for any future breach of contract by him.

Although there are now statutory provisions (see Unfair Contract Terms Act 1977 below) it is still important to consider the common law relating to exemption clauses because not all exemption clauses are covered by the Unfair Contract Terms Act 1977.

INCORPORATION OF AN EXEMPTION CLAUSE INTO THE CONTRACT

The exemption clause must be incorporated into the contract otherwise it will not form part of the agreement between the parties and therefore will not bind them.

Ways in which exemption clauses can be incorporated into a contract

Is the document intended to have contractual effect?

An exemption clause will not be incorporated into a contract if the document containing the exemption clause was not intended to have contractual force.

Chapelton v Barry UDC

[1940] 1 KB 532 • Court of Appeal

The facts are stated in the judgment of Slesser LJ.

Slesser LJ: 'This appeal arises out of an action brought by Mr David Chapelton against the Barry Urban District Council, and it raises a question of some importance to the very large number of people who are in the habit of using deck chairs to sit by the seaside at holiday resorts.

On June 3, 1939, Mr Chapelton went on to the beach at a place called Cold Knap, which is within the area of the Barry Urban District Council, and wished to sit down in a deck chair. On the beach, by the side of a café, was a pile of deck chairs belonging to the defendants, and by the side of the deck chairs there was a notice put up in these terms: "Barry Urban District Council. Cold Knap. Hire of chairs, 2d per session of 3 hours". Then followed words which said that the public were respectfully requested to obtain tickets for their chairs from the chair attendants, and that those tickets must be retained for inspection.

Mr Chapelton, having taken two chairs from the attendant, one for himself and one for a Miss Andrews, who was with him, received two tickets from the attendant, glanced at them, and slipped them into his pocket. He said in the court below that he had no idea that there were any conditions on those tickets and that he did not know anything about what was on the back of them. He took the chairs to the beach and put them up in the ordinary way, setting them up firmly on a flat part of the beach, but when he sat down he had the misfortune to go through the canvas, and, unfortunately, had a bad jar, the result of which was that he suffered injury and had to see a doctor, and in respect of that he brought his action.

The learned county court judge has found that if he had been satisfied that the plaintiff had had a valid legal claim, he would have awarded him the sum of £50 in addition to the special damages claimed.

The learned county court judge also found that the accident to the plaintiff was due to the negligence on the part of the defendants in providing a chair for him which was unfit for its use which gave way in the manner which I have stated. But he nevertheless found in favour of the defendants by reason of the fact that on the ticket which was handed to Mr Chapelton when he took the chair appeared these words: "Available for 3 hours. Time expires where indicated by cut-off and should be retained and shown on request. The Council will not be liable for any accident or damage arising from hire of chair".

As I read the learned county court judge's judgment . . . he said that the plaintiff had sufficient notice of the special contract printed on the ticket and was, accordingly, bound thereby – that is to say, as I understand it, that the learned county court judge has treated this case as similar to the many cases which have been tried in reference to conditions printed on tickets, and more particularly, on railway tickets – and he came to the conclusion that the local authority made an offer to hire out his chair to Mr Chapelton only on certain conditions, which appear on the ticket, namely, that they, the council, would not be responsible for any accident which arose from the use of the chair, and they say that Mr Chapelton hired the chair on the basis that that was one of the terms of the contract between him and themselves, the local authority.

Questions of this sort are always questions of difficulty and are very often largely questions of fact. In the class of case where it is said that there is a term in the contract freeing railway companies, or other providers of facilities, from liabilities which they would otherwise incur at common law, it is a question as to how far that condition has been made a term of the contract and whether it has been sufficiently brought to the notice of the person entering into the contract with the railway company, or other body, and there is a large number of authorities on that point. In my view, however, the present case does not come within that category at all. I think that the contract here, as appears from a consideration of all the circumstances, was this: The local authority offered to hire chairs to persons to sit upon on the beach, and there was a pile of chairs there standing ready for use by any one who wished to use them, and the conditions on which they offered persons the use of those chairs were stated in the notice which was put up by the pile of chairs, namely, that the sum charged for the hire of a chair was 2d per session of three hours. I think that was the whole of the offer which the local authority made in this case. They said, in effect: "We offer to provide you with a chair, and if you accept that offer and sit in the chair, you will have to pay for that privilege 2d per session of three hours".

I think that Mr Chapelton, in common with other persons who used these chairs, when he took the chair from the pile (which happened to be handed to him by an attendant, but which, I suppose, he might have taken from the pile of chairs himself if the attendant had been going on his rounds collecting money, or was otherwise away) simply thought that he was liable to pay 2d for the use of the chair. No suggestion of any restriction of the council's liability appeared in the notice which was near the pile of chairs. That, I think, is the proper view to take of the nature of the contract in this case. Then the notice contained these further words: "The public are respectfully requested to obtain tickets properly issued from the automatic punch in their presence from the Chair Attendants." The very language of that "respectful request" shows clearly, to my mind, that for the convenience of the local authority the public were asked to obtain from the chair attendants tickets, which were mere vouchers or receipts showing how long a person hiring a chair is entitled to use that chair. It is wrong, I think, to look at the circumstances that the plaintiff obtained his receipt at the same time as he took his chair as being in any way a modification of the contract which I have indicated. This was a general offer to the general public, and I think it is right to say that one must take into account here that there was no reason why anybody taking one of these chairs should necessarily obtain a receipt at the moment he took his chair – and, indeed, the notice is inconsistent with that, because it "respectfully requests" the public to obtain receipts for their money. It may be that somebody might sit in one of these chairs for one hour, or two hours, or, if the holiday resort was a very popular one, for a longer time, before the attendant came round for his money, or it may be that the attendant would not come to him at all for payment for the chair, in which case I take it there would be an obligation upon the person who used the chair to search out the attendant, like a debtor searching for his creditor, in order to pay him the sum of 2d for the use of the chair and to obtain a receipt for the 2d paid.

I think the learned count court judge has misunderstood the nature of the agreement. I do not think that the notice excluding liability was a term of the contract at all, and I find it unnecessary to refer to the different authorities which were cited to us, save that I would mention a passage in the judgment of Mellish LJ in *Parker* v *South Eastern Ry Co*, where he points out that it may be that a receipt or ticket may not contain terms of the contract at all, but may be a mere voucher, where he says: "For instance, if a person, driving through a turnpike-gate received a ticket upon paying the toll, he might reasonably assume that the object of the ticket was that by producing it he might be free from paying toll at some other turnpike-gate, and might put it in his pocket unread". I think the object of the giving and taking of this ticket was that the person taking it might have evidence at hand by which he could show that the obligation he was under to pay 2d for the use of the chair for three hours had been duly discharged, and I think it is altogether inconsistent, in the absence of any qualification of liability in the notice put up near the pile of chairs, to attempt to read into it the qualification contended for. In my opinion, this ticket is no more than a receipt, and is quite different from a railway ticket which contains upon it the terms upon which a railway company agrees to carry the passenger. This, therefore, is not, I think, as Mr Ryder Richardson has argued, a question of fact for the learned county court judge. I think the learned county court judge as a matter of law has misconstrued this contract, and looking at all the circumstances of the case, has assumed that this condition on the ticket, or the terms upon which the ticket was issued, has disentitled the plaintiff to recover. The class of case which Sankey LJ dealt with in *Thompson* v *London, Midland and Scottish Ry Co*, which seems to have influenced the learned county court judge in his decision, is entirely different from that which we have to consider in the present appeal.

This appeal should be allowed.'

Burnett v *Westminster Bank Ltd*

[1965] 3 All ER 81 • Queen's Bench

Burnett, who had been banking with Westminster Bank for several years, had two accounts with them; one was with the Borough branch and the other was with the Bromley branch. He wrote a cheque for £2300 on a cheque from his Borough branch cheque book but he crossed out Borough and its address and substituted Bromley and its address. He initialled the alterations. He then decided to stop the cheque. He telephoned the Bromley branch and told them the correct number and date of the cheque and its amount and also that it was a Borough cheque altered to Bromley and instructed them not to pay the cheque. He confirmed these instructions by letter to the Bromley branch. However, the bank did not stop the cheque and his account was debited with £2300. Burnett claimed £2300 stating that the bank acted without his authority when they debited his account at the Borough branch. The bank's defence was that it was an express term of contract between themselves and Burnett that cheques issued by the Borough branch would be applied only to that account and no other account. The bank claimed that these terms were incorporated into the contract between themselves and Burnett from the notice printed on the front cover of the cheque book which stated 'the cheques in this book will be applied to the account for which they have been prepared. Customers must not, therefore, permit their use on any other account'. The bank argued that notwithstanding the alterations Burnett had made to the cheque it must be read as a mandate to the Borough branch with which they had complied.

The issue before the court was whether the notice in the cheque book had been incorporated into the contract between the bank and Burnett.

Mocatta J: 'It is plain . . . that the defendants could not unilaterally so restrict the plaintiff's rights and the contrary was not contended. The restriction could only be made effective by agreement between the plaintiff and the defendants. In some cases, no doubt, express agreement on a similar restriction may be reached between banker and customer, such as, for example, by exchange of letters or the signature on some form by the customer. The defendants were not here in a position to rely on any such express written agreement evidence by any document signed by the plaintiff. They argued, however, that the plaintiff had, by his conduct in using a cheque or cheques taken from the new cheque book containing on the front of its cover the two sentences which I have set out, agreed to the restriction in question.

I was referred by both counsel to the well-known case of *Parker* v *South Eastern Ry Co, Gabell* v *Same*, and it was suggested, particularly by counsel for the defendants, that the three general rules therein laid down in relation to ticket cases, were applicable here. Counsel for the defendants based himself on the rules as stated in *Anson's Law of Contract* (22nd edn):

"(1) If the person receiving the ticket did not see or know that there was any writing on the ticket, then he is not bound by the conditions.

(2) If he knew there was writing, and knew or believed that the writing contained conditions, then he is bound by the conditions, even though he did not read them and did not know what they were.

(3) If he knew that there was writing on the ticket, but did not know or believe that the writing contained conditions, nevertheless he will be bound if the party delivering the ticket has done all that can reasonably be considered necessary to give notice of the term to persons of the class to which he belongs."

On the facts here counsel submitted that as the plaintiff had seen that the front cover of the new cheque book bore printed words, it did not matter that he had not read them and did not know or believe that they contained conditions affecting the use he was entitled to make of the cheques in the book, provided that the defendants had done all that could reasonably be considered necessary to give him notice of the conditions. Counsel for the defendants submitted that the two sentences on the new cheque book cover constituted in the circumstances such reasonable notice. They were easily legible, the new cheque book both in its cover and contents was noticeably different from the old one previously issued and it was next to impossible for the defendants by writing letters or issuing forms for signature to secure that the customers read the letters or signed the forms. The defendants had therefore given the plaintiff reasonable notice. . .

I do not consider that the ticket cases afford exact parallels with the circumstances here, since those cases relate to printed documents being handed contemporaneously with the making of the relevant contract. Here the plaintiff and defendants had been in contractual relationship, since the plaintiff first opened his account with the defendants at their Borough branch. If two sentences on the face of the cheque book are to have contractual effect that must be by way of variation of the already existing contract between the parties. The effect of this distinction, however, is in my judgment merely to emphasise the importance of the notice to be given by the defendants to their customer before they can be in a position to plead successfully that he has accepted the proposed variation by using a cheque from the new book.

Despite counsel for the defendants' able argument I am unable to treat the two sentences on the cheque book cover as adequate notice. Whilst it is true that the new cheque book differed materially from previous ones in format, the differences were not very marked. Cheque book covers had never previously been used for the purpose of containing contractual terms and I think that they fall into the category of documents which the recipients could reasonably assume contained no conditions; see, for example, per Mellish LJ, in *Parker* v *South Eastern Ry Co* and *Chapelton* v *Barry Urban District Council*. The position might have been different had the new cheque book been the first issued to the plaintiff on his opening the account. But in the case of a customer like the plaintiff who has had an account for some time under the system prevailing down to the issue of the new cheque book, I am of the opinion that the mere presence of the two sentences on the new cheque book cover is inadequate to affect the pre-existing contractual relationship. In such circumstances I do not consider that the defendants could establish that they had given adequate notice to their customer to bind him to the new restricted use of the cheques unless they could show that he had read the sentences in question, or had signed some document indicating his agreement to their effect. I would be prepared to accept as the equivalent of the latter the signature of the customer on a cheque provided that the cheque form itself bore words limiting its use to the bank, branch and account shown in print on it. The present cheque bore no such words.

Since I have reached the conclusion that on the facts here the defendants cannot bring themselves within the third of the rules which I have cited from *Anson*, the defence in this action must fail . . .

I accordingly declare that the plaintiff is entitled to have his Borough account with the defendants credited by them with £2300.'

Incorporation by signature

L'Estrange v *Graucob Ltd*

[1934] 2 KB 394 • King's Bench

L'Estrange signed an agreement to purchase a cigarette vending machine from Graucob. The agreement contained a term which said 'This agreement contains all the terms and conditions under which I agree to purchase the machine specified above, and any express or implied condition, statement, or warranty, statutory or otherwise not stated herein is hereby excluded'. When the machine was delivered to L'Estrange it was found to be faulty so L'Estrange rejected it claiming that it was not fit for the purpose for which it was sold. Graucob claimed that the agreement expressly provided for the exclusion of all implied warranties. L'Estrange said although she did not read the agreement she did sign it intentionally.

Scrutton LJ: 'The main question raised in the present case is whether that clause formed part of the contract. If it did, it clearly excluded any condition or warranty.

In the course of the argument in the county court reference was made to the railway passenger and cloak-room ticket cases, such as *Richardson, Spence & Co* v *Rowntree*. In that case Lord Herschell LC laid down the law applicable to these cases and stated the three questions which should there be left to the jury. In the present case the learned judge asked himself the three questions appropriate to these cases, and in answering them has found as facts: (i) that the plaintiff knew that there was printed material on the document which she signed, (ii) that she did not know that the document contained conditions relating to the contract, and (iii) that the defendants did not do what was reasonably sufficient to bring these conditions to the notice of the plaintiff.

The present case is not a ticket case, and it is distinguishable from the ticket cases. In *Parker* v *South Eastern Ry Co* Mellish LJ laid down in a few sentences the law which is applicable to this case. He there said (1): "In an ordinary case, where an action is brought on a written agreement which is signed by the defendant, the agreement is proved by proving his signature, and, in the absence of fraud, it is wholly immaterial that he has not read the agreement and does not know its contents". Having said that, he goes on to deal with the ticket cases, where there is no signature to the contractual document, the document being simply handed by the one party to the other: "The parties may, however, reduce their agreement into writing, so that the writing constitutes the sole evidence of the agreement, without signing it; but in that case there must be evidence independently of the agreement itself to prove that the defendant has assented to it. In that case, also, if it is proved that the defendant has assented to the writing constituting the agreement between the parties, it is, in the absence of fraud, immaterial that the defendant had not read the agreement and did not know its contents". In cases in which the contract is contained in a railway ticket or other unsigned document, it is necessary to prove that an alleged party was aware, or ought to have been aware, of its terms and conditions. These cases have no application when the document has been signed. When a document containing contractual terms is signed, then, in the absence of fraud, or, I will add, misrepresentation, the party signing it is bound, and it is wholly immaterial whether he has read the document or not. . .

In this case the plaintiff has signed a document headed "Sales Agreement", which she admits had to do with an intended purchase, and which contained a clause excluding all conditions and warranties. That being so, the plaintiff, having put her signature to the document and not having been induced to do so by any fraud or misrepresentation, cannot be heard to say that she is not bound by the terms of the document because she has not read them.'

Incorporation by reasonable notice

An exemption clause will be incorporated into a contract if the party seeking to rely on it gives reasonable notice that the document contains conditions.

Parker v *South Eastern Railway Co*

[1874–80] All ER Rep 166 • Court of Appeal

Parker had deposited his bag in the cloakroom at the defendant's railway station. He paid the clerk 2d and was given a ticket which on the face of it said 'See back'. On the other side were several clauses one of which said 'The company will not be responsible for any package exceeding the value of £10'. On returning to the cloakroom Parker presented his ticket to the clerk but the bag could not be found. Parker claimed £24 10s as the value of his bag. The company pleaded that Parker had accepted the goods on the condition that they would not be responsible for the value if it exceeded £10. At the trial Pollock B asked the jury (1) Did Parker read, or was he aware of, the special condition upon which the articles were deposited? (2) Was he, in the circumstances, under any obligation, in the exercise of reasonable and proper caution, to read or make himself aware of the condition? The jury answered both questions in the negative and judgment was given for Parker.

On appeal the issue before the court was whether the clause on the back of the ticket had been incorporated into the contract between Parker and the railway company.

Mellish LJ: '. . . The question then is, whether the plaintiff was bound by the conditions contained in the ticket . . . Now if in the course of making a contract one party delivers to another a paper containing writing, and the party receiving the paper knows that the paper contains conditions which the party delivering it intends to constitute the contract, I have no doubt that the party receiving the paper does, by receiving and keeping it, assent to the conditions contained in it, although he does not read them, and does not know what they are, and therefore in my opinion, the case of *Harris* v *Great Western Ry Co* was rightly decided, because in that case the plaintiff admitted, on cross-examination, that he believed there were some conditions on the ticket. On the other hand, the case of *Henderson* v *Stevenson* is a conclusive authority that if the person receiving the ticket does not know that there is any writing upon the back of the ticket, he is not bound by a condition printed on the back.

The facts in the case before us differs from those in both *Henderson* v *Stevenson* and *Harris* v *Great Western Ry Co*, because in [the case which has] been argued before us, though the plaintiff admitted that [he] knew there was writing on the back of the ticket, [he] swore not only that [he] did not read it, but that [he] did not know or believe that the writing contained conditions, and we are to consider whether, under those circumstances, we can lay down as a matter of law either that the plaintiff is bound or that he is not bound by the conditions contained in the ticket, or whether his being bound depends on some question of fact to be determined by the jury, and if so, whether the right question was left to the jury in the present case.

Now I am of opinion that we cannot lay down, as a matter of law, either that the plaintiff was bound, or that he was not bound, by the conditions printed on the ticket, from the mere fact that he knew there was writing on the ticket, but did not know that the writing contained conditions. I think there may be cases in which a paper containing writing is delivered by one party to another in the course of a business transaction, where it would be quite reasonable that the party receiving it should assume that the writing contained in it no condition, and should put it in his pocket unread; as for instance, if a person driving through a turnpike gate received a ticket upon paying the toll, he might reasonably assume that the object of the ticket was that by producing it he might be free from paying toll at some other turnpike gate, and might put it in his pocket unread. On the other hand, if a person who ships goods to be carried on a voyage by sea receives a bill of lading signed by the master he would plainly be bound by it, although in an action afterwards against the shipowner for the loss of the goods he might swear that he had never read the bill of lading, and that he did not know that it contained the terms of the contract of carriage, and that the shipowner was protected by the exceptions contained in it. Now the reason why the person receiving the bill of lading would be bound seems to me to be because, in the great majority of cases, persons shipping goods do know that the bill of lading contains the terms of the contract of carriage, and the shipbroker or the master delivering the bill of lading is entitled to assume that the person shipping goods has that knowledge, although it is quite possible to suppose that a person who is neither a man of business nor a lawyer, might on some particular occasion ship goods without the least knowledge of what a bill of lading was; but in my opinion, such a person must bear the consequences of his own exceptional ignorance, it being plainly impossible that business could be carried on, if every person who delivers a bill of lading had to stop to explain what a bill of lading was. Now the question we have to consider is whether the railway company were entitled to assume that the person depositing luggage, and receiving a ticket in such a way that he could see that some writing was printed on it, were entitled to assume that the person receiving it would understand that the writing contained the conditions of contract, and this seems to me to depend upon whether people in general would, in fact and naturally, draw that inference. The railway company, as it seems to me, must be entitled to make some assumptions respecting the person who deposits luggage with them. I think they are entitled to assume that he can read, and that he understands the English language, and that he pays such attention to what he is about as may be reasonably expected from a person in such a transaction as that of depositing luggage in a cloakroom. The railway company must, however, take mankind as they find them, and if what they do is sufficient to inform people in general that the ticket contains conditions, I think that a particular plaintiff ought not to be in a better position than other persons on account of his exceptional ignorance or stupidity or carelessness; but if what the railway company do is not sufficient to convey to the minds of people in general that the ticket contains conditions, then they have received goods on deposit without obtaining the consent of the persons depositing them to the conditions limiting their liability.

I am of opinion, therefore, that the proper direction to leave to the jury in these cases is, that if the person receiving the ticket did not see or know that there was any writing on the ticket, he is not bound by the conditions; that if he knew there was writing, and knew or believed that the writing contained conditions, that then he is bound by the conditions, that if he knew there was writing on the ticket, but did not know or believe that the writing contained conditions, nevertheless he would be bound, if the delivering of the ticket to him in such a manner that he could see there was writing upon it, was, in the opinion of the jury, reasonable notice that the writing contained conditions. I have lastly to consider whether the direction of the learned Judge, namely, was the plaintiff, under the circumstances, under any obligation, in the exercise of reasonable and proper caution to read or to make himself aware of the conditions, correct?

I think that this direction was not strictly accurate, and was calculated to mislead the jury. The plaintiff was certainly under no obligation to read the ticket, but was entitled to leave it unread if he pleased, and the question does not appear to me to direct the attention of the jury to the real question, namely, whether the railway company did what was reasonably sufficient to give the plaintiff notice of the condition. On the whole, I am of opinion that there ought to be a new trial.'

[Baggalley LJ delivered a judgment agreeing with Mellish LJ]

Bramwell LJ: 'It is clear that if the plaintiffs in these actions had read the conditions on the tickets and not objected, they would have been bound by them. No point was or could be made that the contract was complete before the ticket was given . . . We have it, then, that if the plaintiffs knew that what was printed was the contract which the defendants were willing to enter into, the plaintiffs, not objecting, are bound by its terms, though they did not inform themselves what they were. The plaintiffs have sworn that they did not know that the printing was the contract, and we must act as though that was true and we believed it, at least as far as entering the verdict for the defendants is concerned. Does this make any difference? The plaintiffs knew of the printed matter; both admit they knew it concerned them in some way. Though they said they did not know what it was, yet neither pretends that he knew or believed it was not the contract. Neither pretends he thought it had nothing to do with the business in hand, that he thought it was an advertisement or other matter unconnected with his deposit of a parcel at the defendants' cloak room. They admit that for anything they knew or believed, it might be, only they did not know or believe it was, the contract. Their evidence is very much that they did not think, or thinking did not care much about it. Now they claim to charge the company; to have the benefit of their own indifference. Is this just? Is it reasonable? Is it the way in which any other business is allowed to be conducted? Is it even allowed to a man to "think", "judge", "guess", "chance" a matter, without informing himself when he can, and then when his "thought", "judgment", "guess", or "chance" turns out wrong or unsuccessful, claim to impose a burden or duty on another which he could not have done had he informed himself as he might?. . . Could the defendants practically do more than they did? Had they not a right to suppose either that the plaintiffs knew the conditions, or that they were content to take on trust whatever is printed?. . . Has not the giver of the paper a right to suppose that the receiver is content to deal on the terms in the paper? What more can be done? Must he say, "Read that"? As I have said, he does so in effect when he puts it into the other's hands . . .

The difficulty I feel as to what I have written is that it is too demonstrative, but, put in practical language, it is this – the defendants put into the hands of the plaintiffs a paper with printed matter on it, which in all good sense and reason must be supposed to relate to the matter in hand. This printed matter the plaintiff sees, and is either bound to read it and object if he does not agree to it, or if he does read it and not object, or does not read it, he must be held to consent to its terms. Therefore, on the facts, the Judge should have directed verdicts for the defendants.

. . . No one can read the evidence in this case without seeing the mischief of encouraging claims so unconscientious as this.'

Have reasonable steps been taken to draw the notice to the attention of the other party?

The party seeking to rely on the exemption clause need not show that he has actually brought it to the notice of the other party, but only that he took reasonable steps to do so.

See *Parker* v *South Eastern Railway Co* above.

Thompson v London, Midland and Scottish Railway Company

[1930] 1 KB 41 • Court of Appeal

Aldcroft, Thompson's niece, bought a half day excursion ticket for her aunt who was illiterate. On the face of the ticket were printed the words 'Excursion. For conditions see back', and on the back of the ticket were printed the words 'Issued subject to the conditions and regulations in the company's time tables . . .'. In the company's time table (which had to be bought for 6d) were printed the words 'Excursion tickets . . . are issued subject to the general regulations and to the condition that the holders . . . shall have no rights of action against the company . . . in respect of . . . injury (fatal or otherwise) . . . however caused'. Thompson was injured as a result of the alleged negligence of the railway company. The railway company relied on the exemption from liability provisions contained in the time table.

The issue before the court was whether the railway company had taken reasonable steps to bring the conditions to the notice of Thompson.

Lord Hanworth MR: 'Dealing with the condition, I must just say a word or two more as to its nature. The ticket issued to the plaintiff had in plain and unmistakable terms in type as large as the other words upon the face of the ticket: "Excursion, For conditions see back". There is no difficulty in reading those words any more than there is a difficulty in reading the words "Third Class" or "Manchester" down below. Then on the back of the ticket is printed also in type, which if small is easily legible: "Issued subject to the conditions and regulations of the company's time tables and notices and excursion and other bills. Return as per bill". In the time table at p 552 there is this condition, which is relied upon and which I have read. The condition on the back makes the first reference to the company's time tables, but it also refers to notices and excursion and other bills. In the excursion bills, which contain some notes as to the tickets to be issued and the charges to be made and the dates on which passengers can travel at a single fare for a double journey, there is a reference to the conditions and the inquirer is directed to the time table. Ultimately therefore the time table is the place where this particular condition is found. Any person who took the trouble to follow out the plain and legible words on the ticket, "See Conditions", would be directed without difficulty to the source of the conditions and would be able to find it. Obviously persons who are minded to go for a day journey of this sort do not take the trouble to make an examination of all the conditions, but two things are plain, first, that any person who takes this ticket is conscious that there are some conditions on which it is issued and also, secondly, that it is priced at a figure far below the ordinary price charged by the railway company, and from that it is a mere sequence of thought that one does not get from the railway company the ticket which they do provide at the higher figure of 5s. 4d.

The plaintiff in this case cannot read; but, having regard to the authorities, and the condition of education in this country, I do not think that avails her in any degree. The ticket was taken for her by her agent. The time of the train was ascertained for her by Miss Aldcroft's father, and he had made the specific inquiry in order to see at what time and under what circumstances there was an excursion train available for the intending travellers. He ascertained, therefore, and he had the notice put before him before ever the ticket was taken, that there were conditions on the issue of excursion and other reduced-fare tickets.

It appears to me that the right way of considering such notices is put by Swift J in *Nunan* v *Southern Ry Co*. After referring to a number of cases which have been dealt with in the Courts he says: "I am of opinion that the proper method of considering such a matter is to proceed upon the assumption that where a contract is made by the delivery, by one of the contracting parties to the other, of a document in a common form stating the terms upon which the person delivering it will enter into the proposed contract, such a form constitutes the offer of the party who tenders it, and if the form is accepted without objection by the person to whom it is tendered this person is as a general rule bound by its contents and his act amounts to an acceptance of the offer to him whether he reads the document or otherwise informs himself of its contents or not, and the conditions contained in the document are binding upon him". In law it seems to me that that is right. The railway company is to be treated as having made an offer to intending travellers that if they will accept the conditions on which the railway company make the offer they can be taken at suitable times, on suitable days and by indicated trains from Darwen to Manchester and back at a price largely reduced from the common price; but upon certain conditions which can be ascertained, and of the existence of which there can be no doubt, for they are indicated clearly upon the ticket which is issued.

Whether or not the father of Miss Aldcroft took the trouble to search out the conditions, or to con them over or not, it appears to me that when that ticket was taken it was taken with the knowledge that the conditions applied, and that the person who took the ticket was bound by those conditions. If that be so, the conditions render it impossible for the plaintiff to succeed in her action. It is, however, argued that it is a question of fact for the jury, whether or not sufficient notice was given of these conditions, and whether or not, therefore, the plaintiff ought to be held bound by the conditions; for it said that the conditions are, I will not say past finding out, but difficult to ascertain. The learned Commissioner who tried the case appreciated that the verdict of the jury was based probably on the fact that you have to make a considerable search before you find out the conditions. I think he is right in saying that in the line of cases, and there are many, under which this case falls, it has not ever been held that the mere circuity which has to be followed to find the actual condition prevents the passenger having notice that there was a condition . . .

Now there is the present case. It was quite clear, and everybody understood and knew that there would have to be a ticket issued. Without such ticket, which is the voucher showing the money has been paid, it would not be possible for the lady to go on the platform to take her train, or on reaching the end of her transit to leave the platform without giving up a ticket. It is quite clear, therefore, that it was intended there should be a ticket issued; and on that ticket plainly on its face is a reference made to the conditions under which it is issued.

. . . So here the giving of the ticket in plain terms indicated that there are conditions, and that one of the conditions is that the person shall find them at a certain place and accept them, and that is I think quite a plain indication that the carrier has made that offer upon terms and conditions only, and that any answer that he had not brought the conditions sufficiently to the notice of the person accepting the offer must be set aside as perverse.'

Thornton v Shoe Lane Parking Ltd
[1971] 1 All ER 686 • Court of Appeal

Thornton drove his car up to the barrier of a multi-storey car park which he had not parked in before. Outside the car park was a notice which said at the bottom 'All Cars Parked At Owners Risk'. Thornton took a parking ticket from the machine at the barrier; on the ticket was printed 'This ticket is issued subject to the conditions of issue as displayed on the premises'. He looked at the ticket to see the time on it. He saw that there was printing on the ticket, but he did not read it. If he had read the ticket he would have had to walk around the car park to search for the conditions. He then drove into the car park. When he returned he paid the car park charge. Whilst putting his belongings into the boot of his car there was an accident and he was severely injured. One of the conditions displayed in the car park said that Shoe Lane Parking 'shall not be responsible . . . for any . . . injury to the Customer . . . occurring when the Customer's motor vehicle is in the Parking Building howsoever that . . . injury shall be caused'. Shoe Lane Parking claimed that this clause exempted them from any liability to Thornton.

The issue before the court was whether the clause was incorporated into the contract.

Lord Denning MR: 'We have been referred to the ticket cases of former times from *Parker v South Eastern Ry Co* to *McCutcheon v David MacBrayne Ltd*. They were concerned with railways, steamships and cloakrooms where booking clerks issued tickets to customers who took them away without reading them. In those cases the issue of the ticket was regarded as an offer by the company. If the customer took it and retained it without objection, his act was regarded as an acceptance of the offer: see *Watkins v Rymill* and *Thompson v London, Midland and Scottish Ry Co*. These cases were based on the theory that the customer, on being handed the ticket, could refuse it and decline to enter into a contract on those terms. He could ask for his money back. That theory was, of course, a fiction. No customer in a thousand ever read the conditions. If he had stopped to do so, he would have missed the train or the boat.

None of those cases has any application to a ticket which is issued by an automatic machine. The customer pays his money and gets a ticket. He cannot refuse it. He cannot get his money back. He may protest to the machine, even swear at it; but it will remain unmoved. He is committed beyond recall. He was committed at the very moment when he put his money into the machine. The contract was concluded at that time. It can be translated into offer and acceptance in this way. The offer is made when the proprietor of the machine holds it out as being ready to receive the money. The acceptance takes place when the customer puts his money into the slot. The terms of the offer are contained in the notice placed on or near the machine stating what is offered for the money. The customer is bound by those terms as long as they are sufficiently brought to his notice beforehand, but not otherwise. He is not bound by the terms printed on the ticket if they differ from the notice, because the ticket comes too late. The contract has already been made: see *Olley v Marlborough Court Ltd*. The ticket is no more than a voucher or receipt for the money that has been paid (as in the deckchair case, *Chapelton v Barry Urban District Council*), on terms which have been offered and accepted before the ticket is issued. In the present case the offer was contained in the notice at the entrance giving the charges for garaging and saying "at owners risk", i.e. at the risk of the owner so far as damage to the car was concerned. The offer was accepted when the plaintiff drove up to the entrance and, by the movement of his car, turned the light from red to green, and the ticket was thrust at him. The contract was then concluded, and it could not be altered by any words printed on the ticket itself. In particular, it could not be altered so as to exempt the company from liability for personal injury due to their negligence.

Assuming, however, that an automatic machine is a booking clerk in disguise, so that the old fashioned ticket cases still apply to it, we then have to go back to the three questions put by Mellish LJ in *Parker v South Eastern Ry* . . . It is no use telling the customer that the ticket is issued subject to some "conditions" or other, without more; for he may reasonably regard "conditions" in general as merely regulatory, and not as taking away his rights, unless the exempting condition is drawn specifically to his attention . . . Telescoping the three questions, they come to this: the customer is bound by the exempting condition if he knows that the ticket is issued subject to it; or, if the company did what was reasonably sufficient to give him notice of it. Counsel for the defendants admitted here that the defendants did not do what was reasonably sufficient to give the plaintiff notice of the exempting condition. That admission was properly made. I do not pause to enquire whether the exempting condition is void for unreasonableness. All I say is that it is so wide and so destructive of rights that the court should not hold any man bound by it unless it is drawn to his attention in the most explicit way. It is an instance of what I had in mind in *J Spurling Ltd* v *Bradshaw*. In order to give sufficient notice, it would need to be printed in red ink with a red hand pointing to it, or something equally startling.

However, although reasonable notice of it was not given, counsel for the defendants said that this case came within the second question propounded by Mellish LJ, namely that the plaintiff "knew or believed that the writing contained conditions". There was no finding to that effect. The burden was on the defendants to prove it, and they did not do so. Certainly there was no evidence that the plaintiff knew of this exempting condition. He is not, therefore, bound by it . . .

I do not think the defendants can escape liability by reason of the exempting condition. I would, therefore, dismiss the appeal.'

Time of notice

Was the exclusion clause brought to the attention of the other party before or after the making of the contract?

Olley v Marlborough Court Ltd

[1949] 1 All ER 127 • Court of Appeal

Olley had reserved a room at the Marlborough Court hotel. On registering at the hotel she paid for a week's accommodation in advance. In her bedroom was a notice which stated 'The proprietors will not hold themselves responsible for articles lost or stolen unless handed to the manageress for safe custody. Valuables should be deposited for safe custody in a sealed package and a receipt obtained.' Whilst she was out of her room, various articles of hers worth £329 were stolen.

Having decided that Marlborough Court were negligent, the issue before the court was whether the exclusion clause had been incorporated into the contract.

Singleton LJ: '. . . Counsel for the defendants raised a question of the true effect of a document exhibited in the bedroom occupied by the plaintiff and her husband. That document was inside some sort of cupboard which hid the washstand in the bedroom. It began thus:

> "The proprietors will not hold themselves responsible for articles lost or stolen unless handed to the manageress for safe custody. Valuables should be deposited for safe custody in a sealed packet and a receipt obtained."

. . . Counsel for the defendants submitted that the words that I have read should be read into the contract between the plaintiff and the defendants, and that, if they were so read, they must be regarded as freeing the defendants from their own negligence. He cited a number of authorities in support of that proposition, the most useful of which, perhaps, was a case in the Court of Appeal in 1922, *Rutter* v *Palmer*, where Scrutton LJ, dealing with a somewhat similar question, said:

"In construing an exemption clause certain general rules may be applied: First the defendant is not exempted from liability for the negligence of his servants unless adequate words are used; secondly, the liability of the defendant apart from the exempting words must be ascertained; then the particular clause in question must be considered; and if the only liability of the party pleading the exemption is a liability for negligence, the clause will more readily operate to exempt him."

. . . I am more attracted, I confess, in considering this matter by the earlier words of Scrutton LJ: "First, the defendant is not exempted from liability for the negligence of his servants unless adequate words are used". If the defendants, who would *prima facie* be liable for their own negligence, seek to exempt themselves by words of some kind, they must show (i) that those words form part of the contract between the parties and (ii) that they are so clear that they must be understood by the parties in the circumstances as absolving the defendants from the results of their own negligence. On both those points it seems to me that the defendants' argument fails. It is clear when the plaintiff and her husband went to the hotel they had not seen the notice. Apparently, by the custom of the hotel, they were asked to pay a week in advance, and when they went to the bedroom for the first time they had not seen the notice and the words at the head of the notice could not be part of the contract between the parties . . . I do not think it is open to the defendants to place reliance on that clause or, at least, I do not think they are exempted from their liability for negligence by the words at the beginning of that notice. I agree with what my Lord said on the subject and I attach even more importance to the fact that this was no part of the contract at the time when the parties first went into the bedroom and there is no evidence to show that there was ever any alteration in the terms of that contract. I agree with the submission which counsel for the plaintiff made, that it is for the defendants to show that these words form part of the contract and that they have only one clear meaning. I think they are ambiguous in more ways than one. That is all I need say upon that side of the case.'

Denning LJ: 'The only other point is whether the defendants are protected by the notice which they put in the plaintiff's bedroom providing:

"The proprietors will not hold themselves responsible for articles lost or stolen unless handed to the manageress for safe custody."

The first question is whether that notice formed part of the contract. People who rely on a contract to exempt themselves from their common law liability must prove that contract strictly. Not only must the terms of the contract be clearly proved, but also the intention to create legal relations – the intention to be legally bound – must also be clearly proved. The best way of proving it is by a written document signed by the party to be bound. Another way is by handing him, before or at the time of the contract, a written notice specifying certain terms and making it clear to him that the contract is in those terms. A prominent public notice which is plain for him to see when he makes the contract would, no doubt, have the same effect, but nothing short of one of these three ways will suffice. It has been held that mere notices put on receipts for money do not make a contract: see *Chapelton* v *Barry UDC*. So, also, in my opinion, notices put up in bedrooms do not of themselves make a contract. As a rule, the guest does not see them until after he has been accepted as a guest. The hotel company, no doubt, hope that the guest will be held bound by them, but the hope is vain unless they clearly show that he agreed to be bound by them, which is rarely the case.'

See *Thornton* v *Shoe Lane Parking Ltd* above.

Reasonableness of notice depends on extent of exclusion

Interfoto Picture Library Ltd v Stiletto Visual Programmes Ltd

[1988] 1 All ER 348 • Court of Appeal

Stiletto telephoned Interfoto, who ran a photographic transparency lending library, to enquire if they had any photographs of the 1950s. Interfoto, who had not done business with Stiletto before, said they would research Stiletto's request. Later that day Interfoto sent 47 transparencies packed in a jiffy bag to Stiletto. The bag contained a delivery note which stated in condition 2 'All transparencies must be returned to us within 14 days from the date of posting/delivery/collection. A holding fee of £5 plus VAT per day will be charged for each transparency which is retained by you longer than the said period of 14 days . . .' Stiletto did not read the delivery note. Four weeks later Stiletto returned the transparencies to Interfoto. Interfoto then invoiced Stiletto for £3783.50. Stiletto refused to pay and Interfoto brought an action against them to recover the £3783.50.

The usual charge in the transparency lending business was less than £3.50 per slide per week.

The issues before the court were whether condition 2 had been incorporated into the contract and if so could Stiletto be relieved from liability under it.

Dillon LJ: 'An alternative argument for the defendants, in this court as below, was to the effect that any contract between the parties was made before the defendants knew of the existence of the delivery note viz either in the course of the preliminary telephone conversation between [Stiletto] and [Interfoto], or when the jiffy bag containing the transparencies was received in the defendants' premises but before the bag was opened. I regard these submissions as unrealistic and unarguable. The original telephone call was merely a preliminary inquiry and did not give rise to any contract. But the contract came into existence when the plaintiffs sent the transparencies to the defendants and the defendants, after opening the bag, accepted them by [Stiletto's] phone call to the plaintiffs at 3.10 on 5 March. The question is whether condition 2 was a term of that contract.

There was never any oral discussion of terms between the parties before the contract was made. In particular there was no discussion whatever of terms in the original telephone conversation when [Stiletto] made his preliminary inquiry. The question is therefore whether condition 2 was sufficiently brought to the defendants' attention to make it a term of the contract which was only concluded after the defendants had received, and must have known that they had received the transparencies *and* the delivery note.

This sort of question was posed, in relation to printed conditions, in the ticket cases, such as *Parker* v *South Eastern Railway Co*, in the last century. At that stage the printed conditions were looked at as a whole and the question considered by the courts was whether the printed conditions as a whole had been sufficiently drawn to a customer's attention to make the whole set of conditions part of the contract; if so the customer was bound by the printed conditions even though he never read them.

More recently the question has been discussed whether it is enough to look at a set of printed conditions as a whole. When for instance one condition in a set is particularly onerous does something special need to be done to draw customers' attention to that particular condition? In an *obiter dictum* in *J Spurling Ltd* v *Bradshaw* Denning LJ stated:

"Some clauses which I have seen would need to be printed in red ink on the face of the document with a red hand pointing to it before the notice could be held to be sufficient."

Then in *Thornton* v *Shoe Lane Parking Ltd* both Lord Denning MR and Megaw LJ held as one of their grounds of decision, as I read their judgments, that where a condition is particularly onerous or unusual the party seeking to enforce it must show that that condition, or an unusual condition of that particular nature, was fairly brought to the notice of the other party . . .

Condition 2 of these plaintiffs' conditions is in my judgment a very onerous clause. The defendants could not conceivably have known, if their attention was not drawn to the clause, that the plaintiffs were proposing to charge a "holding fee" for the retention of the transparencies at such a very high and exorbitant rate.

At the time of the ticket cases in the last century it was notorious that people hardly ever troubled to read printed conditions on a ticket or delivery note or similar document. That remains the case now. In the intervening years the printed conditions have tended to become more and more complicated and more and more one-sided in favour of the party who is imposing them, but the other parties, if they notice that there are printed conditions at all, generally still tend to assume that such conditions are only concerned with ancillary matters of form and are not of importance. In the ticket cases the courts held that the common law required that reasonable steps be taken to draw the other parties' attention to the printed conditions or they would not be part of the contract. It is, in my judgment, a logical development of the common law into modern conditions that it should be held, as it was in *Thornton* v *Shoe Lane Parking Ltd*, that, if one condition in a set of printed conditions is particularly onerous or unusual, the party seeking to enforce it must show that that particular condition was fairly brought to the attention of the other party.

In the present case, nothing whatever was done by the plaintiffs to draw the defendants' attention particularly to condition 2; it was merely one of four columns' width of conditions printed across the foot of the delivery note. Consequently condition 2 never, in my judgment, became part of the contract between the parties.

I would therefore allow this appeal and reduce the amount of the judgment which the judge awarded against the defendants to the amount which he would have awarded on a *quantum meruit* on his alternative findings, i.e. the reasonable charge of £3.50 per transparency per week for the retention of the transparencies beyond a reasonable period, which he fixed at 14 days from the date of their receipt by the defendants.'

Bingham LJ: 'The tendency of the English authorities has, I think, been to look at the nature of the transaction in question and the character of the parties to it; to consider what notice the party alleged to be bound was given of the particular condition said to bind him; and to resolve whether in all the circumstances it is fair to hold him bound by the condition in question. This may yield a result not very different from the civil law principle of good faith, at any rate so far as the formation of the contract is concerned.

Turning to the present case, I am satisfied for reasons which Dillon LJ has given that no contract was made on the telephone when the defendants made their initial request. I am equally satisfied that no contract was made on delivery of the transparencies to the defendants before the opening of the jiffy bag in which they were contained. Once the jiffy bag was opened and the transparencies taken out with the delivery note, it is in my judgment an inescapable inference that the defendants would have recognised the delivery note as a document of a kind likely to contain contractual terms and would have seen that there were conditions printed in small but visible lettering on the face of the document. To the extent that the conditions so displayed were common form or usual terms regularly encountered in this business, I do not think the defendants could successfully contend that they were not incorporated into the contract.

The crucial question in the case is whether the plaintiffs can be said fairly and reasonably to have brought condition 2 to the notice of the defendants. The judge made no finding on the point, but I think that it is open to this court to draw an inference from the primary findings which he did make. In my opinion the plaintiffs did not do so. They delivered 47 transparencies, which was a number the defendants had not specifically asked for. Condition 2 contained a daily rate per transparency after the initial period of 14 days many times greater than was usual or (so far as the evidence shows) heard of. For these 47 transparencies there was to be a charge for each day of delay of £235 plus value added tax. The result would be that a venial period of delay, as here, would lead to an inordinate liability. The defendants are not to be relieved of that liability because they did not read the condition, although doubtless they did not; but in my judgment they are to be relieved because the plaintiffs did not do what was necessary to draw this unreasonable and extortionate clause fairly to their attention. I would accordingly allow the defendants' appeal and substitute for the judge's award the sum which he assessed upon the alternative basis of *quantum meruit*.'

Incorporation by course of dealing

Notice may be inferred from previous dealings.

Spurling Ltd v *Bradshaw*

[1956] 2 All ER 121 • Court of Appeal

The facts are to be found in the judgment of Denning LJ.

The issue before the court was whether an exemption clause exempting Spurling had been incorporated into the contract.

Denning LJ: 'In the first part of June, 1953, the defendant bought eight wooden casks of orange juice, containing sixty gallons apiece. He bought them "to clear for £120", and he sent them to some warehousemen, the plaintiffs, J Spurling, Ltd, who on June 10, 1953, sent a receipt for them, called a "landing account", which said:

> "We have pleasure in advising you that these goods consigned to you arrived at our premises this day and are subject to either warehouse, wharfage, demurrage or other charges . . . The company's conditions as printed on the back hereof cover the goods held in accordance with this notice. Goods will be insured if you instruct us accordingly; otherwise they are not insured."

On the back there were "Contract conditions" and many lines of small print, which included, towards the end, these words:

> "We will not in any circumstances when acting either as warehousemen, wharfingers, contractors, stevedores, carriers by land, or agents, or in any other capacity, be liable for any loss, damage or detention howsoever, whensoever, or wheresoever occasioned in respect of any goods entrusted to or carried or handled by us in the course of our business, even when such loss, damage or detention may have been occasioned by the negligence, wrongful act or default of ourselves or our servants or agents or others for whose acts we would otherwise be responsible."

On the same date, June 10, 1953, the plaintiffs sent an invoice to the defendant: "To receiving, warehousing and redelivery, £4", and there was a note at the bottom of it:

"All goods are handled by us in accordance with the conditions as over and warehoused at owner's risk and not insured unless specially instructed."

There were no conditions "as over". The defendant paid the £4 due on the invoice and he also paid the warehouse rent on these goods for a time, but he afterwards fell into arrear on these and other goods. On Mar 9, 1954, the plaintiffs sent to him an account for the balance owing by him which was, they said, rather old. Within three days the defendant issued a delivery order in favour of a Mr Tuscon directed to the plaintiffs, asking them to release to him the eight barrels of orange juice; and on Apr 23, 1954, Mr Tuscon, who was a cartage contractor, collected these eight barrels. I will refer a little later to what Mr Tuscon said was their condition when he collected them; but so far as the correspondence is concerned, there was not a word of complaint about the barrels for a long time. The plaintiffs wrote letters asking the defendant to pay their account, but he failed to do so. Over £60 was due to them and they wrote time and again, and received no reply. They put it into the hands of a debt collecting agency who wrote twice demanding the money. At last on Dec 17, 1954, there was a reply. The defendant by his solicitors then said that he had a counterclaim for damages in respect of the storage of these barrels. Thus it was eight months after the goods were collected before there was any written complaint. The plaintiffs issued a writ for their charges amounting to £61 12s 6d. The defendant put in a defence admitting the charges, but he also set up a counterclaim for £180 which, as I read it, was a counterclaim for negligence in the storage of the goods. He said that, when collected, five barrels were empty and without lids, one barrel contained dirty water, and two barrels were leaking badly. The plaintiffs put in a defence to the counterclaim in which they denied the charge of negligence and further said it was an express term of the contract that they should not be liable for any loss or damage of or to in connection with the barrels, and they relied on the "landing account" for that purpose. In all the circumstances, it was not surprising that the plaintiffs relied on the exempting clause . . .

This brings me to the question whether this clause was part of the contract. Counsel for the defendant urged us to hold that the plaintiffs did not do what was reasonably sufficient to give notice of the conditions within *Parker* v *South Eastern Ry Co.* I agree that the more unreasonable a clause is, the greater the notice which must be given of it. Some clauses which I have seen would need to be printed in red ink on the face of the document with a red hand pointing to it before the notice could be held to be sufficient. The clause in this case, however, in my judgment, does not call for such exceptional treatment, especially when it is construed, as it should be, subject to the proviso that it only applies when the warehouseman is carrying out his contract and not when he is deviating from it or breaking it in a radical respect. So construed, the judge was, I think, entitled to find that sufficient notice was given. It is to be noticed that the landing account on its face told the defendant that the goods would be insured if he gave instructions; otherwise they were not insured. The invoice, on its face, told him they were warehoused "at owner's risk". The printed conditions, when read subject to the proviso which I have mentioned, added little or nothing to those explicit statements taken together. Next it was said that the landing account and invoice were issued after the goods had been received and could not therefore be part of the contract of bailment: but the defendant admitted that he had received many landing accounts before. True he had not troubled to read them. On receiving this account, he took no objection to it, left the goods there, and went on paying the warehouse rent for months afterwards. It seems to me that by the course of business and conduct of the parties, these conditions were part of the contract.

In these circumstances, the plaintiffs were entitled to rely on this exempting condition. I think, therefore, that the counterclaim was properly dismissed, and this appeal also should be dismissed.'

McCutcheon v *David MacBrayne Ltd*

[1964] 1 All ER 430 • House of Lords

The facts are stated in the judgment of Lord Reid.

The issue before the court was whether an exemption clause was incorporated into the contract by a course of previous dealings.

Lord Reid: 'My Lords, the appellant is a farm grieve in Islay. While on the mainland in October, 1960, he asked his brother-in-law, Mr McSporran, a farmer in Islay, to have his car sent by the respondents to West Loch Tarbert. Mr McSporran took the car to Port Askaig. He found in the respondents' office there the purser of their vessel *Lochiel*, who quoted the freight for a return journey for the car. He paid the money, obtained a receipt and delivered the car to the respondents. It was shipped on the *Lochiel* but the vessel never reached West Loch Tarbert. She sank owing to negligent navigation by the respondents' servants, and the car was a total loss. The appellant sues for its value, agreed at £480.

The question is, what was the contract between the parties? The contract was an oral one. No document was signed or changed hands until the contract was completed. I agree with the unanimous view of the learned judges of the Court of Session that the terms of the receipt which was made out by the purser and handed to Mr McSporran after he paid the freight cannot be regarded as terms of the contract. So the case is not one of the familiar ticket cases where the question is whether conditions endorsed on or referred to in a ticket or other document handed to the consignor in making the contract are binding on the consignor. If conditions, not mentioned when this contract was made, are to be added to or regarded as part of this contract it must be for some reason different from those principles which are now well settled in ticket cases. If this oral contract stands unqualified there can be no doubt that the respondents are liable for the damage caused by the negligence of their servants.

The respondents' case is that their elaborate printed conditions form part of this contract. If they do, then admittedly they exclude liability in this case. I think that I can fairly summarise the evidence on this matter. The respondents exhibit copies of these conditions in their office, but neither the appellant nor his agent Mr McSporran had read these notices, and I agree that they can play no part in the decision of this case. The respondents' practice was to require consignors to sign risk notes, which included these conditions, before accepting any goods for carriage, but on this occasion no risk note was signed. The respondents' clerkess, knowing that Mr McSporran was bringing the car for shipment, made out a risk note for his signature, but when he arrived she was not there and he dealt with the purser of the *Lochiel*, who was in the office. He asked for a return passage for the car. The purser quoted a charge of some £6. He paid that sum and then the purser made out and gave him a receipt which he put in his pocket without looking at it. He then delivered the car. The purser forgot to ask him to sign the risk note. The Lord Ordinary believed the evidence of Mr McSporran and the appellant. Mr McSporran had consigned goods of various kinds on a number of previous occasions. He said that sometimes he had signed a note, sometimes he had not. On one occasion he had sent his own car. A risk note for that consignment was produced signed by him. He had never read the risk notes signed by him. He says – "I sort of just signed it at the time as a matter of form". He admitted that he knew that he was signing in connexion with some conditions, but he did not know what they were. In particular, he did not know that he was agreeing to send the goods at owner's risk. The appellant had consigned goods on four previous occasions. On three of them he was acting on behalf of his employer. On the other occasion he had sent his own car. Each time he had signed a risk note. He also admitted that he knew that there were conditions, but said that he did not know what they were.

The respondents contend that, by reason of the knowledge thus gained by the appellant and his agent in these previous transactions, the appellant is bound by their conditions. But this case differs essentially from the ticket cases. There, the carrier in making the contract hands over a document containing or referring to conditions which he intends to be part of the contract. So if the consignor or passenger, when accepting the document, knows or ought as a reasonable man to know that that is the carrier's intention, he can hardly deny that the conditions are part of the contract, or claim, in the absence of special circumstances, to be in a better position than he would be if he had read the document. But here, in making the contract neither party referred to, or indeed had in mind, any additional terms, and the contract was complete and fully effective without any additional terms. If it could be said that when making the contract Mr McSporran knew that the respondents always required a risk note to be signed and knew that the purser was simply forgetting to put it before him for signature, then it might be said that neither he nor his principal could take advantage of the error of the other party of which he was aware. But counsel frankly admitted that he could not put his case as high as that. The only other ground on which it would seem possible to import these conditions is that based on a course of dealing. If two parties have made a series of similar contracts each containing certain conditions, and then they make another without expressly referring to those conditions it may be that those conditions ought to be implied. If the officious bystander had asked them whether they had intended to leave out the conditions this time, both must, as honest men, have said "of course not". But again the facts here will not support that ground. According to Mr McSporran, there had been no consistent course of dealing; sometimes he was asked to sign and sometimes not. And, moreover, he did not know what the conditions were. This time he was offered an oral contract without any reference to conditions, and he accepted the offer in good faith.

The respondents also rely on the appellant's previous knowledge. I doubt whether it is possible to spell out a course of dealing in his case. In all but one of the previous cases he had been acting on behalf of his employer in sending a different kind of goods and he did not know that the respondents always sought to insist on excluding liability for their own negligence. So it cannot be said that, when he asked his agent to make a contract for him, he knew that this or, indeed, any other special term would be included in it. He left his agent a free hand to contract, and I see nothing to prevent him from taking advantage of the contract which his agent in fact made.

The judicial task is not to discover the actual intentions of each party: it is to decide what each was reasonably entitled to conclude from the attitude of the other.

In this case I do not think that either party was reasonably bound or entitled to conclude from the attitude of the other as known to him that these conditions were intended by the other party to be part of this contract.'

Lord Devlin: 'This is a matter that is relevant to the way in which the respondents put their case. They say that the previous dealings between themselves and the appellant, being always on the terms of their "risk note", as they call their written conditions, the contract between themselves and the appellant must be deemed to import the same conditions. In my opinion, the bare fact that there have been previous dealings between the parties does not assist the respondents at all. The fact that a man has made a contract in the same form ninety-nine times (let alone three or four times which are here alleged) will not of itself affect the hundredth contract, in which the form is not used. Previous dealings are relevant only if they prove knowledge of the terms, actual and not constructive, and assent to them. If a term is not expressed in a contract, there is only one other way in which it can come into it and that is by implication. No implication can be made against a party of a term which was unknown to him. It previous dealings show that a man knew of and agreed to a term on ninety-nine occasions, there is a basis for saying that it can be imported into the hundredth contract without an express statement. It may or may not be sufficient to justify the importation, – that depends on the circumstances; but at least by proving knowledge the essential beginning is made. Without knowledge there is nothing.'

CONSTRUCTION

As a general rule the courts do not like exemption clauses and will, therefore, generally construe exemption clauses in such a way that they do not exclude the thing claimed by the party who is in breach.

Contra proferentem rule

Under the *contra proferentem rule* exemption clauses are strictly construed against the parties who rely on them. See *Harling* v *Eddy* above, p 212.

Andrews Brothers (Bournemouth) Ltd v Singer and Co Ltd
[1934] 1 KB 17 • Court of Appeal

Singer sold a car, described in the contract as new, to Andrews Brothers. The car was not new within the meaning of the contract so Andrews Brothers sued Singer for damages for breach of contract. Singer contended that they were exempted from liability by reason of clause 5 of the contract which read 'All cars sold by the company are subject to the terms of the warranty set out in Schedule No 3 of this agreement and all conditions, warranties and liabilities implied by statute, common law or otherwise are excluded'. Singer argued that their obligation to supply a car complying with the description in the contract was a condition implied by statute, and as Andrews Brothers had accepted the car under the agreement containing clause 5 they could not bring an action in respect of the supplying of a car which was not a new one.

The issue before the court was whether an exemption clause which purported to exclude liability for 'implied terms' also excluded liability for the 'express term' that the car supplied was a new car.

Scrutton LJ: '. . . The question therefore is whether the defendants have succeeded in excluding liability in this case – whether they can tender under the contract goods not complying with the description in the contract and say that the plaintiffs having accepted the car cannot now sue for breach of contract.

In my opinion this was a contract for the sale of a new Singer car. The contract continually uses the phrase "new Singer cars". At the end of the agreement I find this: "In the event of the dealer having purchased from the Company during the period of this agreement 250 new cars of current season's models"; and in the very beginning of the agreement I find this: "The Company hereby appoint the dealer their sole dealer for the sale of new Singer cars". The same phrase also occurs in other parts of the agreement, and the subject-matter is therefore expressly stated to be "new Singer cars". The judge has found, and his view is not now contested, that the car tendered in this case was not a new Singer car. Does then clause 5 prevent the vendors being liable in damages for having tendered and supplied a car which is not within the express terms of the contract? Clause 5 says this: "All conditions, warranties and liabilities implied by statute, common law or otherwise are excluded". There are well-known obligations in various classes of contracts which are not expressly mentioned but are implied. During the argument Greer LJ mentioned an apt illustration, namely, where an agent contracts on behalf of A he warrants that he has authority to make the contract on behalf of A although no such warranty is expressed in the contract. Mr Pritt relied on s 13 of the Sale of Goods Act, 1893, which provides that "where there is a contract for the sale of goods by description, there is an implied condition that the goods shall correspond with the description . . .", and from that he says it follows that this particular condition comes within the words employed by the section. That, I think, is putting a very strained meaning on the word "implied" in the section. Where goods are expressly described in the contract and do not comply with that description, it is quite inaccurate to say that there is an implied term; the term is expressed in the contract. Suppose the contract is for the supply of a car of 1932 manufacture, and a car is supplied which is of 1930 manufacture, there has not been a breach of an implied term; there has been a breach of an express term of the contract. It leads to a very startling result if it can be said that clause 5 allows a vendor to supply to a purchaser an article which does not comply with the express description of the article in the contract, and then, though the purchaser did not know of the matter which prevented the article supplied from complying with the express terms of the contract, to say, "We are under no liability to you because this is a condition implied by statute and we have excluded such liability".

In my view there has been in this case a breach of an express term of the contract. If a vendor desires to protect himself from liability in such a case he must do so by much clearer language than this, which, in my opinion, does not exempt the defendants from liability where they have failed to comply with the express term of the contracts. For these reasons I think Goddard J came to a correct conclusion, and this appeal therefore fails.'

Ambiguous words are construed in the least favourable way.

Houghton v Trafalgar Insurance Company Ltd
[1953] 2 All ER 1409 • Court of Appeal

Houghton, the assured, claimed against the Trafalgar Insurance under an insurance policy in respect of a car accident which resulted in his car becoming a total loss. At the time of the accident the five seater car contained six people – the driver and one passenger in the front seats, and four passengers in the back of the car, three being seated on the back seat and one on the knees of another. The policy contained a clause which excluded Trafalgar Insurance's liability for 'Loss, damage, and/or liability caused or arising whilst any such car is . . . conveying any load in excess of that for which it was constructed.'

The issue before the court was whether the exclusion clause excluded Trafalgar Insurance's liability when the car was carrying too many people.

Somervell LJ: 'If there is any ambiguity in cl (d) of the exclusion clauses it will be resolved in favour of the assured. In my opinion, the words relied on, "any load in excess of that for which it was constructed", clearly cover cases only where there is a weight specified in respect of the load of the vehicle, be it lorry or van. I agree that the earlier words in the clause are obviously applicable to an ordinary private car in respect of which there is no such specified load weight, but there was no evidence whether this was a form which was used for lorries as well as private cars. However, I do not think that is material. We have to construe the words in their ordinary meaning, and I think that they clearly cover only the cases which I have mentioned. If that be right, they cannot avail the insurers in the present case.

I would only add that the present suggestion that the words apply here is, to me, remarkable. I think the plainest possible words would be necessary if it were desired to exclude the insurance cover because in the back of the car there was one passenger more than seating accommodation was provided for. All sorts of obscurities and difficulties might arise. I would like to add that, if this or any other insurance company wishes to put forward a policy which will be inapplicable when an extra passenger is carried, I hope they will print that provision in red ink so that the assured will have it drawn to his particular attention. In my opinion, this appeal should be dismissed.'

Beck & Co v Szymanowski & Co
[1923] AC 43 • House of Lords

Beck sold reels of cotton sewing thread to Szymanowski. Clause 5 of the contract stated 'The goods delivered shall be deemed to be in all respects in accordance with the Contract and the buyers shall be bound to accept and pay for the same accordingly unless the sellers shall within 14 days after arrival of the goods at their destination receive from the buyers notice of any matter or thing by reason whereof they may allege that the goods are not in accordance with the Contract'. When the cotton was delivered it was discovered that the cotton on the reels was 6% shorter than it should have been. Szymanowski sued Beck for short delivery. Beck contended that clause 5 excluded their liability for short delivery.

Lord Shaw of Dunfermline: 'My Lords, my opinion on this case can be expressed in a few sentences.

I think that this was a transaction in the cotton trade and that this was a contract for the sale of cotton thread.

The make up of the thread was agreed to be in lengths of 200 yards, wound on reels.

The number of reels delivered was correct, but it is admitted that large quantities of the reels delivered contained lengths not of 200 yards but of about 188 yards. The average shortage was 6 per cent, amounting to millions of yards of cotton thread.

Payment of damages for short delivery is refused by the sellers, because, particularly, of cl 5 of the printed conditions incorporated into the contract. I note the terms of that clause again only that I may indicate the exact words which, in my humble opinion, make the clause inapplicable as a bar to the present claim. The clause applies to "the goods delivered", saying that they shall be deemed to be in all respects according to contract.

But one may stop there; for the damages are claimed not in respect of the goods delivered but in respect of goods which were not delivered. And when fourteen days are given for notice of any "matter or thing of reason whereof they may allege that the goods are not in accordance with the contract" the expression "the goods" can only mean "the goods delivered", to which alone the clause applies.

Anything else would mean that the sale was in substance a sale of reels and was not in substance a sale of cotton thread. I think this is to confound make up with substance.

And the results would be extraordinary; if a seller innocently sent forward the number of reels with only half the thread that should be upon them, the clause would cover that portion, and the seller would, barring objection within fourteen days, keep the price for the whole thread, although he had only supplied half. Learned counsel admitted this. *Prima facie*, such a construction seems unreasonable.

The contract itself does not, it is granted, expressly provide for the case of short delivery. It can, however, and very properly, apply with regard to actual deliveries and to objections to these on the points, say, of quality, colour, weight or tensile strength.

But in my opinion the clause can never be used so as to convert goods undelivered into goods delivered or to warrant an implication to the effect that non-delivery in length or small measure was included in the objections which should, within the time fixed, be made to goods delivered. I am totally unable to make such an implication out of anything in the bargain between these parties – an implication which would seriously affect the security of business dealings.

I think that the appeal should be dismissed, with costs.'

Negligence

Clear words are required to exempt a party from liability for negligence.

White v *John Warwick & Co Ltd*
[1953] 1 WLR 1285 • Court of Appeal

The facts are stated in the judgment of Denning LJ.

Denning LJ: 'In this case the defendants supplied a cycle on hire to the plaintiff, who was a news vendor, intending that he and his servants should ride it. The cycle was defective and, in consequence of the defect, the plaintiff was thrown off and injured, and he now claims damages for breach of contract or for negligence. The defendants claim to be protected by the printed clause of the agreement which . . . read ["Nothing in this agreement shall render the owners liable for any personal injuries . . ."].

In this type of case two principles are well settled. The first is that if a person desires to exempt himself from a liability which the common law imposes on him, he can only do so by a contract freely and deliberately entered into by the injured party in words that are clear beyond the possibility of misunderstanding. The second is: if there are two possible heads of liability on the part of [the] defendant, one for negligence, and the other a strict liability, an exemption clause will be construed, so far as possible, as exempting the defendant only from his strict liability and not as relieving him from his liability for negligence.

In the present case there are two possible heads of liability on the defendants, one for negligence, the other for breach of contract. The liability for breach of contract is more strict than the liability for negligence. The defendants may be liable in contract for supplying a defective machine, even though they were not negligent. (See *Hyman* v *Nye*.) In these circumstances, the exemption clause must, I think, be construed as exempting the defendants only from their liability in contract, and not from their liability for negligence.

Mr Gibbens [counsel for the owners] admitted that if the negligence was a completely independent tort, the exemption clause would not avail; but he said that the negligence here alleged was a breach of contract, not an independent tort. The facts which gave rise to the tort were, he said, the same as those which gave rise to the breach of contract, and the plaintiff should not be allowed to recover merely by framing his action in tort instead of contract. That was the view which appealed to Parker J, but I cannot agree with it.

In my opinion, the claim for negligence in this case is founded in tort and not on contract . . .

. . . In my judgment, [the exemption clause] exempts the defendants from liability in contract, but not from liability in tort. If the plaintiff can make out his cause of action in negligence, he is, in my opinion, entitled to do so, although the same facts also give a cause of action in contract from which the defendants are exempt.'

Archdale & Co Ltd v *Comservices Ltd*

[1954] 1 All ER 210 • Court of Appeal

Archdale employed Comservices to redecorate their factory under a Royal Institute of British Architects standard form contract. Clause 14(b) of the contract stated 'Injury to property. [Comservices] shall be liable for and shall indemnify [Archdale] against . . . any liability, loss . . . in respect of any injury or damage whatsoever to any property . . . in so far as such injury or damage arises out of . . . the execution of the works, and provided always that the same is due to any negligence . . . of the contractor, his servants or agents . . . and subject also as regards loss or damage by fire to the provisions contained in cl 15 of these conditions'. Clause 15(b) of the contract stated 'The existing structures and the works and unfixed materials . . . shall be at the sole risk of [Archdale] as regards loss or damage by fire and [Archdale] shall maintain a proper policy of insurance against that risk . . . and, if any loss or damage affecting the works is so occasioned by fire, [Archdale] shall pay to the [Comservices] the full value of all work and materials then executed . . .' Comservices negligently caused a fire which resulted in Archdale's premises being damaged. Archdale claimed that Comservices were liable under clause 14(b) and claimed £2858 in respect of the cost of repairs to the building. Comservices replied that Archdale were prevented from recovering such sums because clause 14(b) was expressly, in respect of fire risk, made subject to clause 15(b) which placed on Archdale the duty to insure against fire.

The issue before the court was whether the contract should be construed *contra proferentem* so as to make Comservices liable for their own negligence.

Somervell LJ: '. . . [T]he natural construction of these two clauses, read together, is that, in so far as loss or damage by fire come within the earlier words of cl 14(b), that is to be taken out of cl 14(b) altogether. It is then dealt with by cl 15(b) under which the sole risk is on the employer, and he must insure.

These questions do not bear of much elaboration, but I think the phrase contained in cl 15(b) which was referred to in argument, viz,

". . . the employer shall maintain a proper policy of insurance against that risk . . .",

tends . . . to reinforce the conclusion to which I have come.'

Denning LJ: 'This is not the ordinary case of a clause simply providing which party is to bear the loss. The clauses in this case are directed to the additional question: Which party is to insure? The Contractor is to insure against the risk of injury to persons. He is also to insure against the risk of injury to property, save for this – cl 14(b) expressly says that loss or damage by fire is in a category by itself. The employer is to insure against the risk of fire. When viewed in relation to insurance it is quite plain that the risk of fire is on the employer however it is caused (even though caused by the negligence of the contractor's servants) and he is the person who must insure against it.'

Romer LJ: 'I also agree. The principle which was established or recognised by the cases to which counsel for the plaintiffs referred can and ought to be invoked wherever the parties to a contract leave their intention in doubt. But when the parties have clearly expressed what their intention is, there is no necessity to refer to the principle. The principle is one of construction and no more, and it is not entitled to the status of a rule of law.

Construing cl 14(b) and cl 15(b) of this contract by themselves I have little doubt that they bear the meaning which Somervell LJ, has attributed to them, for the reasons which he has given. If so, it would be quite wrong to attribute a different meaning simply by reason of a principle of construction which has been evolved for the solution of cases of a similar type, but where the parties have not expressed themselves sufficiently clearly.'

Alderslade v *Hendon Laundry Ltd*
[1945] 1 All ER 244 • Court of Appeal

Hendon Laundry negligently lost Alderslade's handkerchiefs which he had left with them for laundering. A clause in the contract between Hendon Laundry and Alderslade stated 'The maximum amount allowed for lost or damaged articles is 20 times the charge made for laundering'. Hendon Laundry sought to rely on this clause so as to limit their liability.

Since the clause did not specifically exclude their liability for negligence the issue before the court was whether the clause limited Hendon Laundry's liability for articles that they had negligently lost.

Lord Greene MR: '. . . The effect of those authorities can I think be stated as follows: where the head of damage in respect of which limitation of liability is sought to be imposed by such a clause is one which rests on negligence and nothing else, the clause must be construed as extending to that head of damage, because if it were not so construed it would lack subject-matter. Where, on the other hand, the head of damage may be based on some ground other than that of negligence, the general principle is that the clause must be confined to loss occurring through that other cause to the exclusion of loss arising through negligence. The reason for that is that if a contracting party wishes in such a case to limit his liability in respect of negligence, he must do so in clear terms, and in the absence of such clear terms the clause is to be construed as relating to a different kind of liability and not to liability based on negligence . . .

. . . It must be remembered that a limitation clause of this kind only applies where the damage, in respect of which the limitation clause is operative, takes place within the four corners of the contract. A contracting party who goes outside his contract cannot rely upon the clause if the loss occurs during operations outside the contract as distinct from operations which the contract contemplates. But there is no room for the application of that principle in the present case because there is no material for finding that the loss of these handkerchiefs was due to some act by the laundry company outside what it had contracted to do. How and where they were lost is unknown.

It was argued by counsel on behalf of the respondent that the clause must be construed in the present case so as to exclude loss by negligence, and the county court judge so held. It was said that the loss of a customer's property might take place for one of two reasons, namely, negligence and mere breach of contract, and, that being so, in the absence of clear words referring to negligence, loss through negligence cannot be taken to be covered by the clause. In my opinion that argument fails. It is necessary to analyse the legal relationship between the customer and the laundry. What I may call the hard core of the contract, the real thing to which the contract is directed, is the obligation of the laundry company to launder. That is the primary obligation; it is the contractual obligation which must be performed according to its terms, and no question of taking due care enters into it. The laundry company undertakes, not to exercise due care in laundering the customer's goods, but to launder them, and if it fails to launder them it is no use saying, "I did my best, I exercised due care and took reasonable precautions, and I am very sorry if as a result the linen is not properly laundered". But in addition to that, which is the essence of the contract, there are certain ancillary obligations into which the laundry company enters if it accepts goods from a customer to be laundered. The first one relates to the safe custody of the goods while they are in the possession of the company. The customer's goods may be waiting in the laundry premises to be washed; while they are so waiting there is an obligation to take care of them, but it is in my opinion not the obligation of an insurer but the obligation to take reasonable care for the protection of the goods. If while they are waiting to be washed in the laundry a thief, through no fault of the laundry company, steals them, the laundry company is not liable. The only way in which the company could be made liable for the loss of articles which are awaiting their turn to be washed would, I think, quite clearly be if it could be shown that the company had been guilty of negligence in performing their duty to take care of the goods. Now that is one ancillary obligation which is inherent in a contract of this kind. Another relates to the delivery of the goods. The laundry company in most cases, and indeed in this case, makes a practice of delivering the goods to the customer, and in the ordinary case the customer expects to receive that service. But what is the precise obligation of the laundry in respect of the return of the goods after the laundering has been completed? In my opinion it stands on the same footing as the other ancillary obligation that I have mentioned, namely, the obligation to take reasonable care in looking after and safeguarding the goods. It cannot, I think, be suggested that the obligation of the laundry company in the matter of returning the goods after they have been laundered is the obligation of an insurer. To say that they have undertaken by contract an absolute obligation to see that they are returned seems to me to go against one's common sense. Supposing the laundry is returning the goods by van to its customer and while the van is on its way a negligent driver of a lorry drives into it and overturns it with the result that it is set on fire and the goods destroyed. No action would lie by the customer for damages for the loss of those goods . . . To hold otherwise would mean that in respect of that clearly ancillary service the laundry company were undertaking an absolute obligation that the goods would, whatever happened, be returned to the customer. It seems to me therefore that the only obligation on the company in the matter of returning the goods is an obligation to take reasonable care.

In the present case all that we know about the goods is that they are lost. There seems to me to be no case in which goods can be lost, in respect of which it would be necessary to limit liability, unless it be a case where the goods are lost by negligence. Goods sent to the laundry will not be lost in the act of washing them. On the other hand, they may be lost while they are in the custody of the laundry company before washing or after washing has been completed. They may be lost in the process of returning them to the customer after they have been washed, but in each of those two cases, if my view is right, the obligation of the laundry company is an obligation to take reasonable care and nothing else. Therefore, the claim of a customer that the company is liable to him in respect of articles that have been lost must, I think, depend upon the issue of due care on the part of the company. If that be right, to construe this clause, so far as it relates to loss, in such a way as to exclude loss occasioned by lack of proper care would be to leave the clause so far as loss is concerned – I say nothing about damage – without any content at all. The result, in my opinion, is that the clause must be construed as applying to the case of loss through negligence and, accordingly, it has its *prima facie* meaning which is comprehensive and clear.'

MacKinnon LJ: 'I agree . . . In the case of a bailment, where the bailee is liable only for loss or damage by reason of negligence, the position is very different. The rule or principle is very admirably stated by Scrutton LJ . . . in a short passage in *Rutter* v *Palmer*, where he said:

> "in construing an exemption clause certain general rules may be applied: First, the defendant is not exempted from liability for the negligence of his servants unless adequate words are used; secondly, the liability of the defendant apart from the exempting words must be ascertained; then the particular clause in question must be considered; and if the only liability of the party pleading the exemption is a liability for negligence, the clause will more readily operate to exempt him."

Applying that principle to the facts of this case, I think that this clause does avail to protect the proprietor of the laundry in respect of liability for negligence, which must be assumed to be the cause of these handkerchiefs having disappeared.'

Hollier v *Rambler Motors (AMC) Ltd*

[1972] 1 All ER 399 • Court of Appeal

In March 1970 Hollier telephoned Rambler to see if they could repair his car. He was told that if he brought the car in they would repair it later in the week. Whilst Hollier's car was on Rambler's premises it was destroyed by a fire which was caused through the negligence of Rambler. Hollier had had his car repaired or serviced at Rambler's garage on three or four previous occasions over a period of five years. It was Rambler's practice to have an 'invoice' signed by the customer. At the bottom of the invoice was a clause which stated 'The company is not responsible for damage caused by fire to customers' cars on the premises. Customers' cars are driven by staff at owners' risk.' Hollier signed the invoice on at least two occasions. He never read the invoices. Hollier brought an action against Rambler for breach of contract and claimed damages for the loss of his car.

Salmon LJ: '[Hollier] says that there was a course of dealing which constituted the three or four occasions over five years – that is, on an average, not quite one dealing a year – from which it is to be implied that what he called "the condition" at the bottom of the contract should be imported into the oral agreement made in the middle of March 1970. I am bound to say that, for my part, I do not know of any other case in which it has been decided or even argued that a term could be implied into an oral contract on the strength of a course of dealing (if it can be so called) which consisted at the most of three or four transactions over a period of five years . . .

It seems to me that if it was impossible to rely on a course of dealing in *McCutcheon* v *David MacBrayne Ltd*, still less would it be possible to do so in this case, when the so-called course of dealing consisted only of three or four transactions in the course of five years . . . The speeches of the other members of the House on the decision itself in

McCutcheon's case make it plain that the clause upon which the defendants seek to rely cannot in law be imported into the oral contract they made in March 1970.

That really disposes of this appeal, but in case I am wrong on the view that I have formed, without any hesitation, I may say, that the course of dealing did not import the so-called exclusion clause, I think I should deal with the point as to whether or not the words on the bottom of the form, had they been incorporated in the contract, would have excluded the defendants' liability to compensate the plaintiff for damage caused to the plaintiff's car by a fire which in turn had been caused by the defendants' own negligence. It is well settled that a clause excluding liability for negligence should make its meaning plain on its face to any ordinarily literate and sensible person. The easiest way of doing that, of course, is to state expressly that the garage, tradesman or merchant, as the case may be, will not be responsible for any damage caused by his own negligence. No doubt merchants, tradesmen, garage proprietors and the like are a little shy of writing in an exclusion clause quite so bluntly as that. Clearly it would not tend to attract customers, and might even put many off. I am not saying that an exclusion clause cannot be effective to exclude negligence unless it does so expressly, but in order for the clause to be effective the language should be so plain that it clearly bears that meaning. I do not think that defendants should be allowed to shelter behind language which might lull the customer into a false sense of security by letting him think – unless perhaps he happens to be a lawyer – that he would have redress against the man with whom he was dealing for any damage which he, the customer, might suffer by the negligence of that person.

The principles are stated by Scrutton LJ with his usual clarity in *Rutter* v *Palmer*:

> "For the present purposes a rougher test will serve. In construing an exemption clause certain general rules may be applied: First the defendant is not exempted from liability for the negligence of his servants unless adequate words are used, secondly, the liability of the defendant apart from the exempting words must be ascertained; then the particular clause in question must be considered; and if the only liability of the party pleading the exemption is a liability for negligence, the clause will more readily operate to exempt him."

Scrutton LJ was far too great a lawyer, and had far too much robust common sense, if I may be permitted to say so, to put it higher than that "if the only liability of the party pleading the exemption is a liability for negligence, the clause will more readily operate to exempt him". He does not say that "if the only liability of the party pleading the exemption is a liability for negligence, the clause will necessarily exempt him". After all, there are many cases in the books dealing with exemption clauses, and in every case it comes down to a question of construing the alleged exemption clause which is then before the court. It seems to me that in *Rutter* v *Palmer*, although the word "negligence" was never used in the exemption clause, the exemption clause would have conveyed to any ordinary, literate and sensible person that the garage in that case was inserting a clause in the contract which excluded their liability for the negligence of their drivers. The clause being considered in that case – and it was without any doubt incorporated in the contract – was: "Customers' cars are driven by our staff at customers' sole risk". Any ordinary man knows that when a car is damaged it is not infrequently damaged because the driver has driven it negligently. He also knows, I suppose, that if he sends it to a garage and a driver in the employ of the garage takes the car on the road for some purpose in connection with the work which the customer has entrusted the garage to do, the garage could not conceivably be liable for the car being damaged in an accident unless the driver was at fault. It follows that no sensible man could have thought that the words in that case had any meaning except that the garage would not be liable for the negligence of their own drivers. That is a typical case where, on the construction of the clause in question, the meaning for which the defendant was there contending was the obvious meaning of the clause.

The next case to which I wish to refer is the well-known case of *Alderslade* v *Hendon Laundry Ltd.* In that case articles were sent by the plaintiff to the defendants' laundry to be washed, and they were lost. In an action by the plaintiff against the defendants for damages, the defendants relied on the following condition to limit their liability: "The maximum amount allowed for lost or damaged articles is 20 times the charge made for laundering". Again, this was a case where negligence was not expressly excluded. The question was: what do the words mean? I have no doubt that they would mean to the ordinary housewife who was sending her washing to the laundry that, if the goods were lost or damaged in the course of being washed through the negligence of the laundry, the laundry would not be liable for more than 20 times the charge made for the laundering. I say that for this reason. It is, I think, obvious that when a laundry loses or damages goods it is almost invariably because there has been some neglect or default on the part of the laundry. It is said that thieves break in and steal, and the goods (in that case handker-chiefs) might have been stolen by thieves. That of course is possible, but I should hardly think that a laundry would be a great allurement to burglars. It is a little far-fetched to think of burglars breaking into a laundry to steal the washing when there are banks, jewellers, post offices, factories, offices and homes likely to contain money and articles far more attractive to burglars. I think that the ordinary sensible housewife, or indeed anyone else who sends washing to the laundry, who saw that clause must have appreciated that almost always goods are lost or damaged because of the laundry's negligence, and therefore this clause could apply only to limit the liability of the laundry, when they were in fault or negligent.

But counsel for [Rambler] has drawn our attention to the way in which the matter was put by Lord Greene MR in delivering the leading judgment in this court, and he contends that Lord Greene MR was in fact making a considerable extension to the law as laid down by Scrutton LJ in the case to which I have referred. For this proposition he relies on the following passage in Lord Greene MR's judgment:

> "The effect of those authorities can I think be stated as follows: Where the head of damage in respect of which limitation of liability is sought to be imposed by such a clause is one which rests on negligence and nothing else, the clause must be construed as extending to that head of damage, because it would otherwise lack subject matter."

If one takes that word "must" *au pied de la lettre* that passage does support Mr Tuckey's contention. However, we are not here construing a statute, but a passage in an unreserved judgment of Lord Greene MR, who was clearly intending no more than to re-state the effect of the authorities as they then stood. It is to be observed that MacKinnon LJ, who gave the other judgment in this court, set out the rule or principle which he said was very admirably stated by Scrutton LJ in *Rutter* v *Palmer*. He said:

> "Applying that principle to the facts of the case, I think that the clause in question does avail to protect the proprietors of the laundry in respect of liability for negligence which must be assumed to be the cause of these handkerchiefs having disappeared."

And clearly it did, for the reasons that I have already given. I do not think that Lord Greene MR was intending to extend the law in the sense for which Mr Tuckey contends. If it were so extended, it would make the law entirely artificial by ignoring that rules of construction are merely our guides and not our masters; in the end you are driven back to construing the clause in question to see what it means. Applying the principles laid down by Scrutton

LJ, they lead to the result at which the court arrived in *Alderslade* v *Hendon Laundry Ltd*. In my judgment these principles lead to a very different result in the present case. The words are: "The company is not responsible for damage caused by fire to customers' cars on the premises". What would that mean to any ordinarily literate and sensible car owner? I do not suppose that any such, unless he is a trained lawyer, has an intimate or indeed any knowledge of the liability of bailees in law. If you asked the ordinary man or woman: "Supposing you send your car to the garage to be repaired, and there is a fire, would you suppose that the garage would be liable?" I should be surprised if many of them did not answer, quite wrongly: "Of course they are liable if there is a fire". Others might be more cautious and say: "Well, I had better ask my solicitor", or, "I do not know. I suppose they may well be liable". That is the crucial difference, to my mind, between the present case and *Alderslade* v *Hendon Laundry Ltd* and *Rutter* v *Palmer*. In those two cases, any ordinary man or woman reading the conditions would have known that all that was being excluded was the negligence of the laundry, in the one case, and the garage, in the other. But here I think the ordinary man or woman would be equally surprised and horrified to learn that if the garage was so negligent that a fire was caused which damaged their car, they would be without remedy because of the words in the condition. I can quite understand that the ordinary man or woman would consider that, because of these words, the mere fact that there was a fire would not make the garage liable. Fires can occur from a large variety of causes, only one of which is negligence on the part of the occupier of the premises, and that is by no means the most frequent cause. The ordinary man would I think say to himself: "Well, what they are telling me is that if there is a fire due to any cause other than their own negligence they are not responsible for it". To my mind, if the defendants were seeking to exclude their responsibility for a fire caused by their own negligence, they ought to have done so in far plainer language than the language here used. In my view the words of the condition would be understood as being meant to be a warning to the customer that if a fire does occur at the garage which damages the car, and it is not caused by the negligence of the garage owner, then the garage is not responsible for damage.

There is another case which I think throws some light upon the problem before us, and that is *Olley* v *Marlborough Court Ltd*. In that case there was a notice in the bedroom of a private residential hotel to this effect: 'Proprietors will not hold themselves responsible for articles lost or stolen, unless handed to manageress for safe custody.' Owing to the negligence of the hotel, a thief managed to get into a room, which had been taken by the plaintiff, and stole a quantity of articles. The plaintiff brought an action against the proprietors of the hotel, and succeeded in this court. In that case there was a question as to whether the notice to which I have referred formed part of the contract between the plaintiff and the hotel proprietors; and there was also some question as to whether the hotel was an inn, in which case they would have been to some extent insurers of the goods, and another question as to whether the hotel was only a private hotel. This court considered the case on the basis that the notice did form part of the contract between the parties, and that the hotel was a private hotel, and came to the conclusion, as I have already indicated, that the plaintiff was entitled to recover. Denning LJ said:

> "Ample content can be given to the notice by construing it as a warning that the hotel company is not liable, in the absence of negligence. As such it serves a useful purpose. It is a warning to the guest that he must do his part to take care of his things himself, and, if needs be, insure them. It is unnecessary to go further and to construe the notice as a contractual exemption of the hotel company from their common law liability for negligence."

Similarly, I think, in this case the words at the bottom of this form can be given ample content by construing them as a warning in the sense that I have already indicated. It seems plain that if the notice in the bedroom of the hotel had read as follows: "Proprietors will not hold themselves responsible for articles lost or stolen, or for the damage or destruction of articles caused by fire", and then there had been a full stop, and the notice went on to say that to avoid articles being lost or stolen they should be handed to the manageress for safe custody, by a parity of reasoning the court must have come to the conclusion that the notice would not have excluded the hotel proprietors from liability for the loss of articles by a fire caused by their own negligence.'

Although the clause will be strictly interpreted, this interpretation must not be a strained one

Ailsa Craig Fishing Co Ltd v *Malvern Fishing Co Ltd and Securicor (Scotland)*

[1983] 1 All ER 101 • House of Lords

Securicor had been hired to provide a security service for Ailsa Craig. As a result of Securicor's negligence, Ailsa Craig's boat was lost. Ailsa Craig claimed damages of £55 000 against Securicor, alleging negligence and breach of contract. Securicor sought to rely on a limitation clause in its contract with Ailsa Craig that limited its liability to £1000.

The issue before the court was whether Securicor could rely on the limitation of liability clause.

Lord Wilberforce: 'Whether a condition limiting liability is effective or not is a question of construction of that condition in the context of the contract as a whole. If it is to exclude liability for negligence, it must be most clearly and unambiguously expressed, and, in such a contract as this, must be construed *contra proferentem*. I do not think that there is any doubt so far. But I venture to add one further qualification, or at least clarification: one must not strive to create ambiguities by strained construction, as I think the appellants have striven to do. The relevant words must be given, if possible, their natural, plain meaning. Clauses of limitation are not regarded by the courts with the same hostility as clauses of exclusion; this is because they must be related to other contractual terms, in particular to the risks to which the defending party may be exposed, the remuneration which he receives and possibly also the opportunity of the other party to insure.'

Lord Fraser of Tullybelton: 'The question whether Securicor's liability has been limited falls to be answered by construing the terms of the contract in accordance with the ordinary principles applicable to contracts of this kind. The argument for limitation depends on certain special conditions attached to the contract prepared on behalf of Securicor and put forward in their interest. There is no doubt that such conditions must be construed strictly against the *proferens*, in this case Securicor, and that in order to be effective they must be "most clearly and unambiguously expressed": see *W & S Pollock & Co* v *Macrae* per Lord Dunedin . . .

There are later authorities which lay down very strict principles to be applied when considering the effect of clauses of exclusion or of indemnity: see particularly the Privy Council case of *Canada Steamship Lines Ltd* v *R* where Lord Morton, delivering the advice of the Board, summarised the principles in terms which have recently been applied by this House in *Smith* v *UMB Chrysler (Scotland) Ltd*. In my opinion these principles are not applicable in their full rigour when considering the effect of conditions merely limiting liability. Such conditions will of course be read *contra proferentem* and must be clearly expressed, but there is no reason why they should be judged by the specially exacting standards which are applied to exclusion and indemnity clauses. The reason for imposing such standards on these conditions is the inherent improbability that the other party to a contract including such a condition intended to release the *proferens* from a liability that would otherwise fall on him. But there is no such high degree of improbability that he would agree to a limitation of the liability of the *proferens*, especially when, as explained in condition 4(i) of the present contract, the potential losses that might be caused by the negligence of the *proferens* or its servants are so great in proportion to the sums that can reasonably be charged for the services contracted for. It is enough in the present case that the condition must be clear and unambiguous.'

George Mitchell (Chesterhall) Ltd v Finney Lock Seeds Ltd

[1983] 2 All ER 737 • House of Lords

Finney Lock sold cabbage seed to George Mitchell for £201. The contract contained a clause which stated '[1] In the event of any seeds . . . proving defective . . . we will, at our option, replace the defective seeds . . . free of charge to the buyer or will refund all payments made to us by the buyer . . . [2] We hereby exclude all liability for any loss or damage arising from the use of any seeds . . . supplied by us and for any consequential loss or damage . . .' George Mitchell planted 63 acres with the seeds. The crop was useless and had to be ploughed in. George Mitchell brought an action against Finney Lock claiming damages of £61 513 for breach of contract.

The issues before the court were whether the exemption clause applied to the breach in question and if it did was it 'fair or reasonable' within s 55 of the Sale of Goods Act 1979 for Finney Lock to rely on it.

Lord Bridge of Harwich: 'The *Photo Production* case gave the final quietus to the doctrine that a 'fundamental breach' of contract deprived the party in breach of the benefit of clauses in the contract excluding or limiting his liability. The Ailsa Craig case drew an important distinction between exclusion and limitation clauses. This is clearly stated by Lord Fraser:

"There are later authorities which lay down very strict principles to be applied when considering the effect of clauses of exclusion or of indemnity: see particularly the Privy Council case of *Canada Steamship Lines Ltd* v *R* where Lord Morton, delivering the advice of the Board, summarised the principles in terms which have recently been applied by this House in *Smith* v *UMB Chrysler (Scotland) Ltd*. In my opinion these principles are not applicable in their full rigour when considering the effect of conditions merely limiting liability. Such conditions will of course be read *contra proferentem* and must be clearly expressed, but there is no reason why they should be judged by the specially exacting standards which are applied to exclusion and indemnity clauses."

My Lords, it seems to me, with all due deference, that the judgments of the trial judge and of Oliver LJ on the common law issue come dangerously near to reintroducing by the back door the doctrine of "fundamental breach" which this House in the *Photo Production* case had so forcibly evicted by the front. The judge discusses what I may call the "peas and beans" or "chalk and cheese" cases, i.e. those in which it has been held that exemption clauses do not apply where there has been a contract to sell one thing, e.g. a motor car, and the seller has supplied quite another thing, e.g. a bicycle . . .

. . . The relevant condition, read as a whole, unambiguously limits the appellants' liability to replacement of the seeds or refund of the price. It is only possible to read an ambiguity into it by the process of strained construction which was deprecated by Lord Diplock in the *Photo Production* case and by Lord Wilberforce in the *Ailsa Craig* case.

. . . Having once reached a conclusion in the instant case that the relevant condition unambiguously limited the appellants' liability, I know of no principle of construction which can properly be applied to confine the effect of the limitation to breaches of contract arising without negligence on the part of the appellants. In agreement with Lord Denning MR, I would decide the common law issue in the appellants' favour.

The statutory issue turns, as already indicated, on the application of the provisions of the modified s 55 of the Sale of Goods Act 1979 . . .

The relevant subsections of the modified s 55 provide as follows: . . .

"(4) In the case of a contract of sale of goods, any term of that or any other contract exempting from all or any of the provisions of section 13, 14 or 15 above is void in the case of a consumer sale and is, in any other case, not enforceable to the extent that it is shown that it would not be fair or reasonable to allow reliance on the term.

(5) In determining for the purposes of subsection (4) above whether or not reliance on any such term would be fair or reasonable regard shall be had to all the circumstances of the case and in particular to the following matters – (a) the strength of the bargaining positions of the seller and buyer relative to each other, taking into account, among other things, the availability of suitable alternative products and sources of supply (b) whether the buyer received an inducement to agree to the term or in accepting it had an opportunity of buying the goods or suitable alternatives without it from any source of supply (c) whether the buyer knew or ought reasonably to have known of the existence and extent of the term (having regard, among other things, to any previous course of dealing between the parties) . . ."

My Lords, at long last I turn to the application of the statutory language to the circumstances of the case. Of the particular matters to which attention is directed by paras (a) to (e) of s 55(5), only those in paras (a) to (c) are relevant. As to para (c), the respondents admittedly knew of the relevant condition (they had dealt with the appellants for many years) and, if they had read it, particularly cl 2, they would, I think, as laymen rather than lawyers, have had no difficulty in understanding what it said. This and the magnitude of the damages claimed in proportion to the price of the seeds sold are factors which weigh in the scales in the appellants' favour.

The question of relative bargaining strength under para (a) and of the opportunity to buy seeds without a limitation of the seedsman's liability under para (b) were interrelated. The evidence was that a similar limitation of liability was universally embodied in the terms of trade between seedsmen and farmers and had been so for very many years. The limitation had never been negotiated between representative bodies but, on the other hand, had not been the subject of any protest by the National Farmers' Union. These factors, if considered in isolation, might have been equivocal. The decisive factor, however, appears from the evidence of four witnesses called for the appellants, two independent seedsmen, the chairman of the appellant company, and a director of a sister company (both being wholly-owned subsidiaries of the same parent). They said that it had always been their practice, unsuccessfully attempted in the instant case, to negotiate settlements of farmers' claims for damages in excess of the price of the seeds, if they thought that the claims were "genuine" and "justified". This evidence indicated a clear recognition by seedsmen in general, and the appellants in particular, that reliance on the limitation of liability imposed by the relevant condition would not be fair or reasonable.

Two further factors, if more were needed, weigh the scales in favour of the respondents. The supply of autumn, instead of winter, cabbage seed was due to the negligence of the appellants' sister company. Irrespective of its quality, the autumn variety supplied could not, according to the appellants' own evidence, be grown commercially in East Lothian. Finally, as the trial judge found, seedsmen could insure against the risk of crop failure caused by supply of the wrong variety of seeds without materially increasing the price of seeds.

. . . I should conclude without hesitation that it would not be fair or reasonable to allow the appellants to rely on the contractual limitation of their liability.'

INVALID OR INOPERATIVE EXEMPTION CLAUSES

Even though an exemption clause exists one of the parties to the contract can themselves negate its effect.

Misrepresentation

Curtis v Chemical Cleaning & Dyeing Co Ltd

[1951] 1 KB 805 • Court of Appeal

Curtis took a white satin wedding dress to the Chemical Cleaning and Dyeing Co's shop for cleaning. The shop assistant handed her a document headed 'Receipt' which she was asked to sign. Before doing so Curtis asked the assistant why her signature was required. She was told that it was because the shop would not accept liability for certain specified risks, including the risk of damage by or to the beads and sequins with which the dress was trimmed. Curtis then signed the 'receipt', which in fact stated 'This . . . article is accepted on condition that the company is not liable for any damage howsoever arising'. When the dress was returned to Curtis there was a stain on it. Curtis claimed that the shop had been negligent and brought an action against the shop claiming damages of £32 10s. The shop sought to rely on the exemption clause contained in the signed receipt.

The issue before the court was whether the oral assurance given by the shop assistant overrode the written agreement so as to negate or modify the exemption clause.

Lord Denning: 'This case is of importance because of the many cases nowadays when people sign printed forms without reading them, only to find afterwards that they contain stringent clauses exempting the other side from their common-law liabilities. In every such case it must be remembered that, if a person wishes to exempt himself from a liability which the common law imposes on him, he can only do it by an express stipulation brought home to the party affected, and assented to by him as part of the contract: *Olley* v *Marlborough Court.* If the party affected signs a written document, knowing it to be a contract which governs the relations between them, his signature is irrefragable evidence of his assent to the whole contract, including the exempting clauses, unless the signature is shown to be obtained by fraud or misrepresentation: *L'Estrange* v *Graucob.* But what is a sufficient misrepresentation for this purpose? That is the point which Mr Geoffrey Lawrence has raised in this appeal.

In my opinion any behaviour, by words or conduct, is sufficient to be a misrepresentation if it is such as to mislead the other party about the existence or extent of the exemption. If it conveys a false impression, that is enough. If the false impression is created knowingly, it is a fraudulent misrepresentation; if it is created unwittingly, it is an innocent misrepresentation; but either is sufficient to disentitle the creator of it to the benefit of the exemption ... When one party puts forward a printed form for signature, failure by him to draw attention to the existence or extent of the exemption clause may in some circumstances convey the impression that there is no exemption at all, or at any rate not so wide an exemption as that which is in fact contained in the document. The present case is a good illustration. The customer said in evidence: "When I was asked to sign the document I asked 'why?' The assistant said I was to accept any responsibility for damage to beads and sequins. I did not read it all before I signed it". In those circumstances, by failing to draw attention to the width of the exemption clause, the assistant created the false impression that the exemption only related to the beads and sequins, and that it did not extend to the material of which the dress was made. It was done perfectly innocently, but nevertheless a false impression was created ... [I]t was a sufficient misrepresentation to disentitle the cleaners from relying on the exemption, except in regard to beads and sequins.

In the present case the customer knew, from what the assistant said, that the document contained conditions. If nothing was said she might not have known it. In that case the document might reasonably be understood to be, like a boot repairer's receipt, only a voucher for the customer to produce when collecting the goods, and not understood to contain conditions exempting the cleaners from their common-law liability for negligence. In that case it would not protect the cleaners: see *Chapelton* v *Barry Urban District Council*. I say this because I do not wish it to be supposed that the cleaners would have been better off if the assistant had simply handed over the document to the customer without asking her to sign it; or if the customer were not so inquiring as the plaintiff, but were an unsuspecting person who signed whatever she was asked without question. In those circumstances the conduct of the cleaners might well be such that it conveyed the impression that the document contained no conditions, or, at any rate, no condition exempting them from their common-law liability, in which case they could not rely on it.

... In my opinion when the signature to a condition, purporting to exempt a person from his common-law liabilities, is obtained by an innocent misrepresentation, the party who has made that misrepresentation is disentitled to rely on the exemption ...'

Overriding oral undertaking

See *Couchman* v *Hill* above.

Evans & Son (Portsmouth) Ltd v Andrea Merzario Ltd
[1976] 2 All ER 930 • Court of Appeal

For many years Evans had employed Andrea, who were forwarding agents, to arrange for their goods to be transported by sea to England. Up until 1967 Andrea had always had Evans' goods shipped below deck. In 1967 Andrea suggested to Evans that in future Evans' goods should be transported in containers. Evans agreed to this provided that their goods continued to be shipped below decks. Andrea gave Evans an oral assurance that the containers would be so shipped. A container containing Evans' goods was wrongly shipped on deck. During the voyage the container was lost overboard. Evans claimed damages against Andrea for loss of their goods alleging that Andrea was in breach of contract in not having had the goods shipped below decks. The written agreement between Evans and Andrea contained Condition 11 which stated that Andrea would not be liable for loss or damage unless it occurred whilst in their actual custody and then only if they were guilty of wilful neglect or default. Condition 13 of the agreement stated that Andrea's liability was not to exceed the value of the goods or a sum at the rate of £50 per ton of 20 cwt.

The issue before the court was whether Andrea could rely on conditions 11 and 13.

Lord Denning MR: '. . . But even in respect of promises as to the future, we have a different approach nowadays to collateral contracts. When a person gives a promise, or an assurance to another, intending that he should act on it by entering into a contract, and he does act on it by entering into the contract, we hold that it is binding: see *Dick Bentley Productions Ltd* v *Harold Smith (Motors) Ltd*. That case was concerned with a representation of fact, but it applies also to promises as to the future. Following this approach, it seems to me plain that [Andrea] gave an oral promise or assurance that the goods in this new container traffic would be carried under deck. He made the promise in order to induce [Evans] to agree to the goods being carried in containers. On the faith of it, [Evans] accepted the quotations and gave orders for transport. In those circumstances the promise was binding. There was a breach of that promise and the forwarding agents are liable – unless they can rely on the printed conditions.

It is common ground that the course of dealing was on the standard conditions of the forwarding trade. Those conditions were relied on. Condition 4 which gives the company complete freedom in respect of means, route and procedure in the transportation of goods. Condition 11 which says that the company will not be liable for loss or damage unless it occurs whilst in their actual custody and then only if they are guilty of wilful neglect or default. Condition 13 which says that their liability shall not exceed the value of the goods or a sum at the rate of £50 per ton of 20 cwt. The question is whether the company can rely on those exemptions. I do not think so. The cases are numerous in which oral promises have been held binding in spite of written exempting conditions; such as *Couchman* v *Hill*, *Harling* v *Eddy*, *City & Westminster Properties (1934) Ltd* v *Mudd*. The most recent is *Mendelssohn* v *Normand Ltd* where I said: "The printed condition is rejected because it is repugnant to the express oral promise or representation". Following these authorities, it seems to me that the forwarding agents cannot rely on the condition. There was a plain breach of the oral promise by the forwarding agents. I would allow the appeal.'

Roskill LJ: '. . . The real question, as I venture to think, is not whether one calls this an assurance or a guarantee, but whether that which was said amounted to an enforceable contractual promise by the defendants to the plaintiffs that any goods thereafter entrusted by the plaintiffs to the defendants for carriage from Milan to the United Kingdom via Rotterdam and thence by sea to England would be shipped under deck. The matter was apparently argued before the learned judge on behalf of the plaintiffs on the basis that the defendants' promise (if any) was what the lawyers sometimes call a collateral oral warranty. That phrase is normally only applicable where the original promise was external to the main contract, the main contract being a contract in writing, so that usually parole evidence cannot be given to contradict the terms of the written contract. The basic rule is clearly stated in the latest edition of *Benjamin on Sale* to which I refer but which I will not repeat. But that doctrine, as it seems to me, has little or no application where one is not concerned with a contract in writing (with respect, I cannot accept counsel for the defendants' argument that there was here a contract in writing) but with a contract which, as I think, was partly oral, partly in writing and partly by conduct. In such a case the court does not require to have recourse to lawyers' devices such as collateral oral warranty in order to seek to adduce evidence which would not otherwise be admissible. The court is entitled to look at and should look at all the evidence from start to finish in order to see what the bargain was that was struck between the parties. That is what we have done in this case and what, with great respect, I think the learned judge did not do in the course of his judgment. I unreservedly accept counsel for the defendants' submission that one must not look at one or two isolated answers given in evidence; one should look at the totality of the evidence. When one does that, one finds first, as I have already mentioned, that these parties had been doing business in transporting goods from Milan to England for some time before; secondly, that transportation of goods from Milan to England was always done on trailers which were always under deck; thirdly, that the defendants wanted a change in the practice – they wanted containers used instead of trailers; fourthly, that the plaintiffs were only willing to agree to that change if they were promised by the defendant that those containers would be shipped under deck, and would not have agreed to the change but for that promise. The defendants gave such a promise which to my mind against this background plainly amounted to an enforceable contractual promise. In those circumstances it seems to me that the contract was this: "If we continue to give you our business, you will ensure that those goods in containers are shipped under deck"; and the defendants agreed that this would be so. Thus there was a breach of that contract by the defendants when this container was shipped on deck; and it seems to me to be plain that the damage which the plaintiffs suffered resulted from that breach. That being the position, I think that counsel for the defendants' first argument fails.

I will deal very briefly with the second point, with which Lord Denning MR has already dealt fully. It is suggested that even so these exemption clauses apply. I ventured to ask counsel for the defendants what the position would have been if when the defendants' first quotation had come along there had been stamped on the face of that quotation: "No containers to be shipped on deck"; and this container had then been shipped on deck. He bravely said that the exemption clauses would still have applied. With great respect, I think that is an impossible argument. In the words which Devlin J used in *Firestone Tyre & Rubber Co Ltd* v *Vokins & Co Ltd*, and approved by Lord Denning MR in *Mendelssohn* v *Normand Ltd*, the defendants' promise that the container would be shipped on deck would be wholly illusory. This is not a case of fundamental breach. It is a question of construction. Interpreting the contract as I find it to have been, I feel driven to the conclusion that none of these exemption clauses can be applied, because one has to treat the promise that no container would be shipped on deck as overriding any question of exempting condition. Otherwise, as I have already said, the promise would be illusory.'

FUNDAMENTAL BREACH: DOES IT EXIST?

Photo Production Ltd v *Securicor Transport Ltd*

[1980] 1 All ER 556 • House of Lords

The facts are set out in the judgment of Lord Wilberforce.

Lord Wilberforce: 'My Lords, this appeal arises from the destruction by fire of a factory owned by the respondents ('Photo Production') involving loss and damage agreed to amount to £615 000. The question is whether the appellants ('Securicor') are liable to the respondents for this sum.

Securicor are a company which provides security services. In 1968 they entered into a contract with Photo Production by which for a charge of £8 15s 0d (old currency) per week it agreed to "provide their Night Patrol Service whereby four visits per night shall be made seven nights per week and two visits shall be made during the afternoon of Saturday and four visits shall be made during the day of Sunday". The contract incorporated printed standard conditions which, in some circumstances, might exclude or limit Securicor's liability. The questions in this appeal are (i) whether these conditions can be invoked at all in the events which happened and (ii) if so, whether either the exclusion provision, or a provision limiting liability, can be applied on the facts . . .

What happened was that on a Sunday night the duty employee of Securicor was one Musgrove. It was not suggested that he was unsuitable for the job or that Securicor were negligent in employing him. He visited the factory at the correct time, but when inside he deliberately started a fire by throwing a match onto some cartons. The fire got out of control and a large part of the premises was burnt down. Though what he did was deliberate, it was not established that he intended to destroy the factory. The judge's finding was in these words:

> "Whether Musgrove intended to light only a small fire (which was the very least he meant to do) or whether he intended to cause much more serious damage, and, in either case, what was the reason for his act, are mysteries I am unable to solve."

This, and it is important to bear it in mind when considering the judgments in the Court of Appeal, falls short of a finding that Musgrove deliberately burnt or intended to burn Photo Production's factory.

The condition on which Securicor relies reads, relevantly, as follows:

> "Under no circumstances shall the Company [Securicor] be responsible for any injurious act or default by any employee of the Company unless such act or default could have been foreseen and avoided by the exercise of due diligence on the part of the Company as his employer; nor, in any event, shall the Company be held responsible for; (a) Any loss suffered by the customer through burglary, theft, fire or any other cause, except insofar as such loss is solely attributable to the negligence of the Company's employees acting within the course of their employment . . ."

There are further provisions limiting to stated amounts the liability of Securicor on which it relies in the alternative if held not to be totally exempt.

It is first necessary to decide on the correct approach to a case such as this where it is sought to invoke an exception or limitation clause in the contract. The approach of Lord Denning MR in the Court of Appeal was to consider first whether the breach was "fundamental". If so, he said, the court itself deprives the party of the benefit of an exemption of limitation clause. Shaw and Waller LJJ substantially followed him in this argument.

Lord Denning MR in this was following the earlier decision of the Court of Appeal, and in particular his own judgment in *Harbutt's Plasticine Ltd* v *Wayne Tank and Pump Co Ltd*. In that case Lord Denning MR distinguished two cases: (a) the case where as the result of a breach of contract the innocent party has, and exercises, the right to bring the contract to an end; and (b) the case where the breach automatically brings the contract to an end, without the innocent party having to make an election whether to terminate the contract or to continue it. In the first case Lord Denning MR, purportedly applying this House's decision in *Suisse Atlantique Société d'Armement Maritime SA* v *NV Rotterdamsche*

Kolen Centrale, but in effect two citations from two of their Lordships' speeches, extracted a rule of law that the "termination" of the contract brings it, and with it the exclusion clause, to an end. The *Suisse Atlantique* case in his view –

> "affirms the long line of cases in this court that when one party has been guilty of a fundamental breach of the contract . . . and the other side accepts it, so that the contract comes to an end . . . then the guilty party cannot rely on an exception or limitation clause to escape from his liability for the breach.' See (*Harbutt*'s case). He then applied the same principle to the second case.

My Lords, whatever the intrinsic merit of this doctrine, as to which I shall have something to say later, it is clear to me that so far from following this House's decision in the *Suisse Atlantique* case it is directly opposed to it and that the whole purpose and tenor of the *Suisse Atlantique* case was to repudiate it. The lengthy, and perhaps I may say sometimes indigestible speeches of their Lordships, are correctly summarised in the headnote –

> '(3) That the question whether an exceptions clause was applicable where there was a fundamental breach of contract was one of the true construction of the contract.' "

That there was any rule of law by which exception clauses are eliminated, or deprived of effect, regardless of their terms, was clearly not the view of Viscount Dilhorne, Lord Hodson or myself. The passages invoked for the contrary view of a rule of law consist only of short extracts from two of the speeches, on any view a minority. But the case for the doctrine does not even go so far as that. Lord Reid, in my respectful opinion, and I recognise that I may not be the best judge of this matter, in his speech read as a whole, cannot be claimed as a supporter of a rule of law. Indeed he expressly disagreed with Lord Denning MR's observations in two previous case (*Karsales (Harrow) Ltd* v *Wallis* and *UGS Finance Ltd* v *National Mortgage Bank of Greece*) in which he had put forward the "rule of law" doctrine. In order to show how close the disapproved doctrine is to that sought to be revived in *Harbutt*'s case I shall quote one passage from the *Karsales* case:

> "Notwithstanding earlier cases which might suggest the contrary, it is now settled that exempting clauses of this kind, no matter how widely they are expressed, only avail the party when he is carrying out his contract in its essential respects. He is not allowed to use them as a cover for misconduct or indifference or to enable him to turn a blind eye to his obligations. They do not avail him when he is guilty of a breach which goes to the root of the contract."

Lord Reid comments as to this that he could not deduce from the authorities cited in the *Karsales* case that the proposition stated in the judgments could be regarded as in any way "settled law". His conclusion is stated thus: "In my view no such rule of law ought to be adopted", adding that there is room for legislative reform.

My Lords, in the light of this, the passage from the *Suisse Atlantique* case cited by Lord Denning MR has to be considered. For convenience I restate it:

> "If fundamental breach is established, the next question is what effect, if any, that has on the applicability of other terms of the contract. This question has often arisen with regard to clauses excluding liability, in whole or in part, of the party in breach. I do not think that there is generally much difficulty where the innocent party has elected to treat the breach as a repudiation, bring the contract to an end and sue for damages. Then the whole contract has ceased to exist including the exclusion clause, and I do not see how that clause can then be used to exclude an action for loss which will be

suffered by the innocent party after it has ceased to exist, such as loss of the profit which would have accrued if the contract had run its full term."

It is with the utmost reluctance that, not forgetting the "beams" that may exist elsewhere, I have to detect here a mote of ambiguity or perhaps even of inconsistency. What is referred to is "loss which will be suffered by the innocent party after [the contract] has ceased to exist" and I venture to think that all that is being said, rather elliptically, relates only to what is to happen in the future, and is not a proposition as to the immediate consequences caused by the breach; if it were, that would be inconsistent with the full and reasoned discussion which follows.

It is only because of Lord Reid's great authority in the law that I have found it necessary to embark on what in the end may be superfluous analysis. For I am convinced that, with the possible exception of Lord Upjohn whose critical passage, when read in full, is somewhat ambiguous, their Lordships, fairly read, can only be taken to have rejected those suggestions for a rule of law which had appeared in the Court of Appeal and to have firmly stated that the question is one of construction, not merely of course of the exclusion clause alone, but of the whole contract.

Much has been written about the *Suisse Atlantique* case. Each speech has been subjected to various degrees of analysis and criticism, much of it constructive. Speaking for myself I am conscious of imperfections of terminology, though sometimes in good company. But I do not think that I should be conducing to the clarity of the law by adding to what was already too ample a discussion a further analysis which in turn would have to be interpreted. I have no second thoughts as to the main proposition that the question whether, and to what extent, an exclusion clause is to be applied to a fundamental breach, or a breach of a fundamental term, or indeed to any breach of contract, is a matter of construction of the contract. Many difficult questions arise and will continue to arise in the infinitely varied situations in which contracts come to be breached: by repudiatory breaches, accepted or not, anticipatory breaches, by breaches of conditions or of various terms and whether by negligent, or deliberate, action, or otherwise. But there are ample resources in the normal rules of contract law for dealing with these without the superimposition of a judicially invented rule of law. I am content to leave the matter there with some supplementary observations.

(1) The doctrine of "fundamental breach" in spite of its imperfections and doubtful parentage has served a useful purpose. There were a large number of problems, productive of injustice, in which it was worse than unsatisfactory to leave exception clauses to operate. Lord Reid referred to these in the *Suisse Atlantique* case, pointing out at the same time that the doctrine of fundamental breach was a dubious specific. But since then Parliament has taken a hand: it has passed the Unfair Contract Terms Act 1977. This Act applies to consumer contracts and those based on standard terms and enables exception clauses to be applied with regard to what is just and reasonable. It is significant that Parliament refrained from legislating over the whole field of contract. After this Act, in commercial matters generally, when the parties are not of unequal bargaining power, and when risks are normally borne by insurance, not only is the case for judicial intervention undemonstrated, but there is everything to be said, and this seems to have been Parliament's intention, for leaving the parties free to apportion the risks as they think fit and for respecting their decisions.

At the stage of negotiation as to the consequences of a breach, there is everything to be said for allowing the parties to estimate their respective claims according to the contractual provisions they have themselves made, rather than for facing them with a legal complex so uncertain as the doctrine of fundamental breach must be. What, for example, would have been the position of Photo Production's factory if instead of being destroyed it had been damaged, slightly or moderately or severely? At what point does the doctrine (with what logical justification I have not understood) decide, *ex post facto*, that the breach was (factually) fundamental before going on to ask whether legally it is to be regarded as fundamental? How is the date of "termination" to be fixed? Is it the date of the incident causing the damage, or the date of the innocent party's election, or some other date? All these difficulties arise from the doctrine and are left unsolved by it.

At the judicial stage there is still more to be said for leaving cases to be decided straightforwardly on what the parties have bargained for rather than on analysis, which becomes progressively more refined, of decisions in other cases leading to inevitable appeals. The learned judge was able to decide this case on normal principles of contractual law with minimal citation of authority. I am sure that most commercial judges have wished to be able to do the same (cf the *Angelia, Trade and Transport Inc* v *Iino Kaiun Kaisha Ltd*, per Kerr J). In my opinion they can and should.

(2) *Harbutt's Plasticine Ltd* v *Wayne Tank and Pump Co Ltd* must clearly be overruled. It would be enough to put that on its radical inconsistency with the *Suisse Atlantique* case. But even if the matter were *res integra* I would find the decision to be based on unsatisfactory reasoning as to the "termination" of the contract and the effect of "termination" on the plaintiffs' claim for damage. I have, indeed, been unable to understand how the doctrine can be reconciled with the well-accepted principle of law, stated by the highest modern authority, that when in the context of a breach of contract one speaks of "termination" what is meant is no more than that the innocent party or, in some cases, both parties are excused from further performance. Damages, in such cases, are then claimed under the contract, so what reason in principle can there be for disregarding what the contract itself says about damages, whether it "liquidates" them, or limits them, or excludes them? These difficulties arise in part from uncertain or inconsistent terminology. A vast number of expressions are used to describe situations where a breach has been committed by one party of such character as to entitle the other party to refuse further performance: discharge, rescission, termination, the contract is at an end, or dead, or displaced; clauses cannot survive, or simply go. I have come to think that some of these difficulties can be avoided; in particular the use of "rescission", even if distinguished from rescission *ab initio*, as an equivalent for discharge, though justifiable in some contexts (see *Johnson* v *Agnew*) may lead to confusion in others. To plead for complete uniformity may be to cry for the moon. But what can and ought to be avoided is to make use of these confusions in order to produce a concealed and unreasoned legal innovation: to pass, for example, from saying that a party, victim of a breach of contract, is entitled to refuse further performance, to saying that he may treat the contract as at an end, or as rescinded, and to draw from this the proposition, which is not analytical but one of policy, that all or (arbitrarily) some of the clauses of the contract lose, automatically, their force, regardless of intention.

If this process is discontinued the way is free to use such words as "discharge" or "termination" consistently with principles as stated by modern authority which *Harbutt's* case disregards. I venture with apology to relate the classic passages. In *Heyman* v *Darwins Ltd* Lord Porter said:

> "To say that the contract is rescinded or has come to an end or has ceased to exist may in individual cases convey the truth with sufficient accuracy, but the fuller expression that the injured party is thereby absolved from future performance of his obligations under the contract is a more exact description of the position. Strictly speaking, to say that, upon acceptance of the renunciation of a contract, the contract is

rescinded is incorrect. In such a case the injured party may accept the renunciation as a breach going to the root of the whole of the consideration. By that acceptance he is discharged from further performance and may bring an action for damages, but the contract itself is not rescinded."

Similarly Lord Macmillan; see also *Boston Deep Sea Fishing and Ice Co Ltd* v *Ansell* per Bowen LJ. In *Moschi* v *Lep Air Services Ltd* my noble and learned friend Lord Diplock drew a distinction (relevant for that case) between primary obligations under a contract, which on "rescission" generally come to an end, and secondary obligations which may then arise. Among the latter he included an obligation to pay compensation, i.e. damages. And he stated in terms that this latter obligation "is just as much an obligation arising from the contract as are the primary obligations that it replaces". My noble and learned friend has developed this line of thought in an enlightening manner in his opinion which I have now had the benefit of reading.

These passages I believe to state correctly the modern law of contract in the relevant respects; they demonstrate that the whole foundation of *Harbutt's* case is unsound. *A fortiori*, in addition to Harbutt's case there must be overruled *Wathes (Western) Ltd* v *Austine (Menswear) Ltd* which sought to apply the doctrine of fundamental breach to a case where, by election of the innocent party, the contract had not been terminated, an impossible acrobatic, yet necessarily engendered by the doctrine. Similarly, *Charterhouse Credit Co Ltd* v *Tolly* must be overruled, though the result might have been reached on construction of the contract . . .

(4) It is not necessary to review fully the numerous cases in which the doctrine of fundamental breach has been applied or discussed. Many of these have now been superseded by the Unfair Contract Terms Act 1977. Others, as decisions, may be justified as depending on the construction of the contract (cf *Levison* v *Patent Steam Carpet Cleaning Co Ltd* in the light of well-known principles such as that stated in *Alderslade* v *Hendon Laundry Ltd*.

In this situation the present case has to be decided. As a preliminary, the nature of the contract has to be understood. Securicor undertook to provide a service of periodical visits for a very modest charge which works out at 26p per visit. It did not agree to provide equipment. It would have no knowledge of the value of Photo Production's factory; that, and the efficacy of their fire precautions, would be known to Photo Production. In these circumstances nobody could consider it unreasonable that as between these two equal parties the risk assumed by Securicor should be a modest one, and that Photo Production should carry the substantial risk of damage or destruction.

The duty of Securicor was, as stated, to provide a service. There must be implied an obligation to use care in selecting their patrolmen, to take care of the keys and, I would think, to operate the service with due and proper regard to the safety and security of the premises. The breach of duty committed by Securicor lay in a failure to discharge this latter obligation. Alternatively it could be put on a vicarious responsibility for the wrongful act of Musgrove, viz, starting a fire on the premises; Securicor would be responsible for this on the principle stated in *Morris* v *C W Martin & Sons Ltd*. This being the breach, does condition 1 apply? It is drafted in strong terms, "Under no circumstances, any injurious act or default by any employee". These words have to be approached with the aid of the cardinal rules of construction that they must be read *contra proferentem* and that in order to escape from the consequences of one's own wrongdoing, or that of one's servant, clear words are necessary. I think that these words are clear. Photo Production in fact relied on them for an argument that since they exempted from negligence they must be taken as not exempting from the consequence of deliberate acts. But this is a perversion of the rule that if a clause can cover something other than negligence it will not be applied to negligence. Whether, in addition to negligence, it covers other, e.g. deliberate, acts, remains a matter of construction requiring, of course, clear words. I am of opinion that it does and, being free to construe and apply the clause, I must hold that liability is excluded . . .'

SUMMARY

You should now be able to:

- Appreciate the common law aspects of exemption clauses.
- Determine whether an exemption clause has been *incorporated* into a contract.
- Determine if an exemption clause is actually effective.
- Determine if an exemption clause has been rendered *invalid* or *inoperative*.

If you have not mastered the above points you should go through this section again.

11 Exemption clauses: the Unfair Contract Terms Act 1977

THE UNFAIR CONTRACT TERMS ACT 1977

Section 1 Scope of Part I

(1) For the purposes of this Part of this Act, 'negligence' means the breach –
    (a) of any obligation, arising from the express or implied terms of a contract, to take reasonable care to exercise reasonable skill in the performance of the contract;
    (b) of any common law duty to take reasonable care or exercise reasonable skill (but not any stricter duty);
    (c) of the common duty of care imposed by the Occupiers' Liability Act 1957 . . .

(2) This Part of this Act is subject to Part III; and in relation to contracts, the operation of sections 2 to 4 and 7 is subject to the exceptions made by Schedule 1.

(3) In the case of both contract and tort, sections 2 to 7 apply (except where the contrary is stated in section 6(4)) only to business liability, that is liability for breach of obligations or duties arising –
    (a) from things done or to be done by a person in the course of a business (whether his own business or another's); or
    (b) from the occupation of premises used for business purposes of the occupier;
and references to liability are to be read accordingly but liability of an occupier of premises for breach of an obligation or duty towards a person obtaining access to the premises for recreational or educational purposes, being liability for loss or damage suffered by reason of the dangerous state of the premises, is not a business liability of the occupier unless granting that person such access for the purposes concerned falls within the business purposes of the occupier.

(4) In relation to any breach of duty or obligation, it is immaterial for any purpose of this Part of this Act whether the breach was inadvertent or intentional, or whether liability for it arises directly or vicariously.

Section 2 Negligence liability

(1) A person cannot by reference to any contract term or to a notice given to persons generally or to particular persons exclude or restrict his liability for death or personal injury resulting from negligence.

(2) In the case of other loss or damage, a person cannot so exclude or restrict his liability for negligence except in so far as the term or notice satisfies the requirement of reasonableness.

(3) Where a contract term or notice purports to exclude or restrict liability for negligence a person's agreement to or awareness of it is not of itself to be taken as indicating his voluntary acceptance of any risk.

Section 3   Liability arising in contract

(1) This section applies as between contracting parties where one of them deals as consumer or on the other's written standard terms of business.

(2) As against that party, the other cannot by reference to any contract term –
(a) when himself in breach of contract, exclude or restrict any liability of his in respect of the breach; or
(b) claim to be entitled –
(i) to render a contractual performance substantially different from that which was reasonably expected of him, or
(ii) in respect of the whole or any part of his contractual obligation, to render no performance at all,
except in so far as (in any of the cases mentioned above in this subsection) the contract term satisfies the requirement of reasonableness.

Section 4   Unreasonable indemnity clauses

(1) A person dealing as consumer cannot by reference to any contract term be made to indemnify another person (whether a party to the contract or not) in respect of liability that may be incurred by the other for negligence or breach of contract, except in so far as the contract term satisfies the requirement of reasonableness.

(2) This section applies whether the liability in question –
(a) is directly that of the person to be indemnified or is incurred by him vicariously;
(b) is to the person dealing as consumer or to someone else.

Section 5   'Guarantee' of consumer goods

(1) In the case of goods of a type ordinarily supplied for private use or consumption, where loss or damage –
(a) arises from the goods proving defective while in consumer use; and
(b) results from the negligence of a person concerned in the manufacture or distribution of the goods,
liability for the loss or damage cannot be excluded or restricted by reference to any contract term or notice contained in or operating by reference to a guarantee of the goods.

(2) For these purposes –
(a) goods are to be regarded as 'in consumer use' when a person is using them, or has them in his possession for use, otherwise than exclusively for the purposes of a business; and
(b) anything in writing is a guarantee if it contains or purports to contain some promise or assurance (however worded or presented) that defects will be made good by complete or partial replacement, or by repair, monetary compensation or otherwise.

(3) This section does not apply as between the parties to a contract under or in pursuance of which possession or ownership of the goods passed.

Section 6   Sale and hire-purchase

(1) Liability for breach of the obligations arising from –
   (a) section 12 of the Sale of Goods Act 1979 (seller's implied undertakings as to title, etc);
   (b) section 8 of the Supply of Goods (Implied Terms) Act 1973 (the corresponding thing in relation to hire-purchase),
cannot be excluded or restricted by reference to any contract term.

(2) As against a person dealing as consumer, liability for breach of the obligations arising from –
   (a) section 13, 14 or 15 of the 1979 Act (seller's implied undertakings as to conformity of goods with description or sample, or as to their quality or fitness for a particular purpose);
   (b) section 9, 10 or 11 of the 1973 Act (the corresponding things in relation to hire-purchase),
cannot be excluded or restricted by reference to any contract term.

(3) As against a person dealing otherwise than as consumer, the liability specified in subsection (2) above can be excluded or restricted by reference to a contract term, but only in so far as the term satisfies the requirement of reasonableness.

(4) The liabilities referred to in this section are not only the business liabilities defined by section 1(3), but include those arising under any contract of sale of goods or hire-purchase agreement.

Section 7   Miscellaneous contracts under which goods pass

(1) Where the possession or ownership of goods passes under or in pursuance of a contract not governed by the law of sale of goods or hire-purchase, subsections (2) to (4) below apply as regards the effect (if any) to be given to contract terms excluding or restricting liability for breach of obligation arising by implication of law from the nature of the contract.

(2) As against a person dealing as consumer, liability in respect of the goods' correspondence with description or sample, or their quality or fitness for any particular purpose, cannot be excluded or restricted by reference to any such term.

(3) As against a person dealing otherwise than as consumer, that liability can be excluded or restricted by reference to such a term, but only in so far as the term satisfies the requirement of reasonableness.

(3A) Liability for breach of the obligations arising under section 2 of the Supply of Goods and Services Act 1982 (implied terms about title etc in certain contracts for the transfer of the property in goods) cannot be excluded or restricted by reference to any such term.

(4) Liability in respect of –
    (a) the right to transfer ownership of the goods, or give possession; or
    (b) the assurance of quiet possession to a person taking goods in pursuance of the contract,
cannot (in a case to which subsection (3A) above does not apply) be excluded or restricted by reference to any such term except in so far as the term satisfies the requirement of reasonableness.

(5) This section does not apply in the case of goods passing on a redemption of trading stamps within the Trading Stamps Act 1964 . . .

Section 9   Effect of breach

(1) Where for reliance upon it a contract term has to satisfy the requirement of reasonableness, it may be found to do so and be given effect accordingly notwithstanding that the contract has been terminated either by breach or by a party electing to treat it as repudiated.

(2) Where on a breach the contract is nevertheless affirmed by a party entitled to treat it as repudiated, this does not of itself exclude the requirement of reasonableness in relation to any contract term.

Section 10   Evasion by means of secondary contract

A person is not bound by any contract term prejudicing or taking away rights of his which arise under, or in connection with the performance of, another contract, so far as those rights extend to the enforcement of another's liability which this Part of this Act prevents that other from excluding or restricting.

Section 11   The 'reasonableness' test

(1) In relation to a contract term, the requirement of reasonableness for the purposes of this Part of this Act, section 3 of the Misrepresentation Act 1967 . . . is that the term shall have been a fair and reasonable one to be included having regard to the circumstances which were, or ought reasonably to have been, known to or in the contemplation of the parties when the contract was made.

(2) In determining for the purposes of section 6 or 7 above whether a contract term satisfies the requirement of reasonableness, regard shall be had in particular to the matters specified in Schedule 2 to this Act; but this subsection does not prevent the court or arbitrator from holding, in accordance with any rule of law, that a term which purports to exclude or restrict any relevant liability is not a term of the contract.

(3) In relation to a notice (not being a notice having contractual effect), the requirement of reasonableness under this Act is that it should be fair and reasonable to allow reliance on it, having regard to all the circumstances obtaining when the liability arose or (but for the notice) would have arisen.

(4) Where by reference to a contract term or notice a person seeks to restrict liability to a specified sum of money, and the question arises (under this or any other Act) whether the term or notice satisfies the requirement of reasonableness, regard shall be had in particular (but without prejudice to subsection (2) above in the case of contract terms) to –
(a) the resources which he could expect to be available to him for the purpose of meeting the liability should it arise; and
(b) how far it was open to him to cover himself by insurance.

(5) It is for those claiming that a contract term or notice satisfies the requirement of reasonableness to show that it does.

Section 12 'Dealing as consumer'

(1) A party to a contract 'deals as consumer' in relation to another party if –
(a) he neither makes the contract in the course of a business nor holds himself out as doing so; and
(b) the other party does make the contract in the course of a business; and
(c) in the case of a contract governed by the law of sale of goods or hire-purchase, or by section 7 of this Act, the goods passing under or in pursuance of the contract are of a type ordinarily supplied for private use or consumption.

(2) But on a sale by auction or by competitive tender the buyer is not in any circumstances to be regarded as dealing as consumer.

(3) Subject to this, it is for those claiming that a party does not deal as consumer to show that he does not.

Section 13 Varieties of exemption clause

(1) To the extent that this Part of this Act prevents the exclusion or restriction of any liability it also prevents –
(a) making the liability or its enforcement subject to restrictive or onerous conditions;
(b) excluding or restricting any right or remedy in respect of the liability, or subjecting a person to any prejudice in consequence of his pursuing any such right or remedy;
(c) excluding or restricting rules of evidence or procedure;
and (to that extent) sections 2 and 5 to 7 also prevent excluding or restricting liability by reference to terms and notices which exclude or restrict the relevant obligation or duty.

(2) But an agreement in writing to submit present or future differences to arbitration is not to be treated under this Part of this Act as excluding or restricting any liability.

Section 14 Interpretation of Part I

In this Part of this Act –

'business' includes a profession and the activities of any government department or local or public authority;

'goods' has the same meaning as in the Sale of Goods Act 1979:

'hire-purchase agreement' has the same meaning as in the Consumer Credit Act 1974;

'negligence' has the meaning given by section 1(1);

'notice' includes an announcement, whether or not in writing, and any other communication or pretended communication; and

'personal injury' includes any disease and any impairment of physical or mental condition.

Schedule 1   Scope of sections 2 to 4 and 7

1. Sections 2 to 4 of this Act do not extend to –
    (a) any contract of insurance (including a contract to pay an annuity on human life);
    (b) any contract so far as it relates to the creation or transfer of an interest in land, or to the termination of such an interest, whether by extinction, merger, surrender, forfeiture or otherwise;
    (c) any contract so far as it relates to the creation or transfer of a right or interest in any patent, trade mark, copyright or design right, registered design, technical or commercial information or other intellectual property, or relates to the termination of any such right or interest;
    (d) any contract so far as it relates –
        (i) to the formation or dissolution of a company (which means any body corporate or unincorporated association and includes a partnership), or
        (ii) to its constitution or the rights or obligations of its corporators or members;
    (e) any contract so far as it relates to the creation or transfer of securities or of any right or interest in securities.

2. Section 2(1) extends to –
    (a) any contract of marine salvage or towage;
    (b) any charterparty of a ship or hovercraft; and
    (c) any contract for the carriage of goods by ship or hovercraft;
but subject to this sections 2 to 4 and 7 do not extend to any such contract except in favour of a person dealing as consumer.

3. Where goods are carried by ship or hovercraft in pursuance of a contract which either –
    (a) specifies that as the means of carriage over part of the journey to be covered, or
    (b) makes no provision as to the means of carriage and does not exclude that means,
then sections 2(2), 3 and 4 do not, except in favour of a person dealing as consumer, extend to the contract as it operates for and in relation to the carriage of the goods by that means.

4. Section 2(1) and (2) do not extend to a contract of employment, except in favour of the employee.

Schedule 2   'Guidelines' for application of reasonableness test

The matters to which regard is to be had in particular for the purposes of sections 6(3), 7(3) and (4), 20 and 21 are any of the following which appear to be relevant –
    (a) the strength of the bargaining positions of the parties relative to each other, taking into account (among other things) alternative means by which the customer's requirements could have been met;

(b) whether the customer received an inducement to agree to the term, or in accepting it had an opportunity of entering into a similar contract with other persons, but without having to accept a similar term;

(c) whether the customer knew or ought reasonably to have known of the existence and extent of the term (having regard, among other things, to any custom of the trade and any previous course of dealing between the parties);

(d) where the term excludes or restricts any relevant liability if some condition is not complied with, whether it was reasonable at the time of the contract to expect that compliance with that condition would be practicable;

(e) whether the goods were manufactured, processed or adapted to the special order of the customer.

SCOPE OF THE ACT

1   The Act applies to exclusion of liability in tort as well as in contract: see s 1(3).

2   The Act does not apply to regulate any contract term but generally only those that attempt to exclude or restrict liability.

3   Most provisions of the Act only apply to the exclusion of 'business liability' as defined in s 1(3).

4   Certain contracts are not covered by the Act's provisions e.g. contracts of employment, contracts of insurance, carriage of goods by sea: see Sch 1.

If the Act does apply, some exclusion clauses are rendered void by the Act while some are merely subjected to a requirement of reasonableness.

Exclusion clauses rendered void

1   A contract term which purports to exclude liability for death or personal injury due to negligence is void: see s 2(1). But remember the Act only applies to business liability: see s 1(3).

2   A contract term which purports to exclude liability for breach of implied conditions in ss 12–15 of the Sale of Goods Act 1979 (description, satisfactory quality, fitness for purpose, correspondence with sample) where the buyer deals as a consumer is void: see s 6(1) and (2).

Clauses subject to reasonableness test

1   A contract term which purports to exclude liability for negligence (other than death or personal injury) has to satisfy the test of reasonableness: see s 2(2).

2   A contract term which purports to exclude liability for description, quality, fitness, sample where the other does not deal as a consumer has to satisfy the test of reasonableness: see s 6(3)

3   Where one party deals as a consumer or on the other's written standard terms of business a contract term which purports to exclude the liability of the other party for his breach of contract has to satisfy the test of reasonableness: see s 6(3).

Dealing as a consumer

R & B Customs Brokers Co Ltd v *United Dominions Trust Ltd*

[1988] 1 WLR 321 • Court of Appeal

R & B Customs Brokers (a two-man company) bought a second hand Colt Shogun car from United Dominions Trust Ltd. The car turned out to suffer from a serious leak which could not be repaired. R & B Customs Brokers sought to reject the car on the ground that the car was not of merchantable quality within the meaning of s 14(2) of the Sale of Goods Act 1979 or fit for the purpose within the meaning of s 14(3) of the same Act. The Court of Appeal having decided that the car was not fit for its purpose then had to decide whether an exclusion clause in the contract excluding United Dominions Trust Ltd's liability was effective. This depended on whether R & B Customs Brokers, a company, had dealt 'as a consumer'.

Dillon LJ: 'I come therefore to the Act of 1977 and the defendant's printed conditions on their form of contract with the company. It is not in dispute that those conditions were sufficiently drawn to Mr Bell's attention, although he did not trouble to read them, and therefore, in so far as they were applicable and valid, they are part of the conditional sale agreement of 3 November between the defendants and the company.

The relevant condition of the defendants, printed on the back of the form of conditional sale agreement, reads:

"If the buyer deals as a consumer within the meaning of section 12 of the Unfair Contract Terms Act 1977 or any statutory modification or re-enactment thereof . . . the buyer's statutory rights are not affected by sub-clause (a) of the following clause.

Exclusion of warranties and conditions – 2(a). The Seller not being the manufacturer of the goods nor at any time prior to the making of this agreement being in actual possession or control of them does not let the goods subject to any warranty or condition whether express or implied as to condition description quality or fitness for any particular purpose or at all."

The Act of 1977 provides by section 6 . . .

"(2) As against a person dealing as consumer, liability for breach of the obligations arising from – (a) section 13, 14 or 15 of the 1979 Act (seller's implied undertakings as to conformity of goods with description or sample, or as to their quality or fitness for a particular purpose); (b) section 9, 10 or 11 of the 1973 Act (the corresponding things in relation to hire-purchase), cannot be excluded or restricted by reference to any contract terms. (3) As against a person dealing otherwise than as a consumer, the liability specified in subsection (2) but only in so far as the term satisfies the requirement of reasonableness."

Two questions therefore arise, and success on either of them is sufficient for the company's purpose, viz: (1) In entering into the conditional sale agreement with the defendants, was the company "dealing as consumer"? If it was, then, on the wording of the defendants' printed conditions, the condition 2(a) did not apply, no doubt because under section 6(2) of the Act of 1977 the liability could not be excluded. (2) If the company was dealing otherwise than as a consumer, does the defendant's condition 2(a) excluding liability under section 14(3) satisfy "the requirement of reasonableness"?

"Dealing as a consumer" is defined in section 12 of the Act of 1977, which provides:

"(1) A party to a contract 'deals as consumer' in relation to another party if – (a) he neither makes the contract in the course of a business nor holds himself out as doing so; and (b) the other party does make the contract in the course of a business; and (c) in the case of a contract governed by the law of sale of goods or hire-purchase, or by section 7 of this Act, the goods passing under or in pursuance of the contract are of a type ordinarily supplied for private use or consumption. (2) But on a sale by auction or by competitive tender the buyer is not in any circumstances to be regarded as dealing as consumer. (3) Subject to this, it is for those claiming that a party does not deal as consumer to show that he does not."

It is accepted that the conditions (b) and (c) in section 12(1) are satisfied. This issue turns on condition (a). Did the company neither make the contract with the defendants in the course of a business nor hold itself out as doing so?

In the present case there was no holding out beyond the mere facts that the contract and the finance application were made in the company's corporate name, and in the finance application the section headed "Business Details" was filled in to the extent of giving nature of the company's business as that of shipping brokers, giving the number of years trading and the number of employees, and giving the names and addresses of the directors. What is important is whether the contract was made in the course of a business.

In a certain sense, however, from the very nature of a corporate entity, where a company which carries on a business makes a contract, it makes that contract in the course of its business, otherwise the contract would be *ultra vires* and illegal. Thus, where a company which runs a grocer's shop buys a new delivery van, it buys it in the course of its business. Where a merchant bank buys a car as a "company car" as a prerequisite for a senior executive, it buys it in the course of its business. Where a farming company buys a Land Rover for the personal and company use of a farm manager, it again does so in the course of its business. Possible variations are numerous. In each case it would not be legal for the purchasing company to buy the vehicle in question otherwise than in the course of its business. Section 12 does not require that the business in the course of which the one party, referred to in condition (a), makes the contract must be of the same nature as the business in the course of which the other party, referred to in condition (b), makes the contract, e.g. that they should both be motor dealers.

We have been referred to one decision at first instance under the Act of 1977, *Peter Symmons & Co* v *Cook*, but the note of the judgment is too brief to be of real assistance. More helpfully, we have been referred to decisions under the Trade Descriptions Act 1968, and in particular to the decision of the House of Lords in *Davies* v *Sumner*.

Under the Trade Descriptions Act 1968 any person who in the course of a trade or business applies a false trade description to goods is, subject to the provisions of the Act, guilty of an offence. It is a penal Act whereas the Act of 1977 is not, and it is accordingly submitted that decisions on the construction of the Trade Descriptions Act 1968 cannot assist on the construction of section 12 of the Act of 1977. Also the legislative purposes of the two Acts are not the same. The primary purpose of the Trade Descriptions Act 1968 is consumer protection, and the course of business referred to is the course of business of the alleged wrongdoer. But the provisions as to dealing as a consumer in the Act of 1977 are concerned with differentiating between two classes of innocent contracting party – those who deal as consumers and those who do not – for whom differing degrees of protection against unfair contract terms are afforded by the Act of 1977. Despite these distinctions however, it would, in my judgment, be unreal and unsatisfactory to conclude that the fairly ordinary words "in the course of business" bear a significantly different meaning in, on the one hand, the Trade Descriptions Act 1968, and on the other hand, section 12 of the Act of 1977. In particular I would be very reluctant to conclude that these words bear a significant wider meaning in section 12 than in the Trade Descriptions Act 1968.

I turn therefore to *Davies* v *Sumner*. That case was not concerned with a company, but with an individual who had used a car for the purposes of his business as a self-employed courier. When he sold the car by trading it in part exchange for a new one, he had applied a false trade description to it by falsely representing the mileage the car had travelled to have been far less than it actually was. Lord Keith of Kinkel, who delivered the only speech in the House of Lords, commented that it was clear that the transaction – sc of trading in the car on the purchase of a new one – was reasonably incidental to the carrying on of the business, but he went on to say:

> "Any disposal of a chattel held for the purposes of a business may, in a certain sense, be said to have been in the course of that business, irrespective of whether the chattel was acquired with a view to resale or for consumption or as a capital asset. But in my opinion section 1(1) of the Act is not intended to cast such a wide net as this. The expression 'in the course of a trade or business' in the context of an Act having consumer protection as its primary purpose conveys the concept of some degree of regularity, and it is to be observed that the long title to the Act refers to 'misrepresentations of goods, services, accommodation and facilities provided in the course of trade'. Lord Parker CJ in the Havering case clearly considered that the expression was not used in the broadest sense. The reason why the transaction there in issue was caught was that in his view it was 'an integral part of the business carried on as a car hire firm'. That would not cover the sporadic selling off of pieces of equipment which were no longer required for the purposes of a business. The vital feature of the Havering case appears to have been, in Lord Parker's view, that the defendant's business *as part of its normal practice* bought and disposed of cars. The need for some degree of regularity does not, however, involve that a one-off adventure in the nature of trade, carried through with a view to profit, would not fall within section 1(1) because such a transaction would itself constitute a trade."

Lord Keith then held that the requisite degree of regularity had not been established on the facts of *Davies* v *Sumner* because a normal practice of buying and disposing of cars had not yet been established at the time of the alleged offence. He pointed out for good measure that the disposal of the car was not a disposal of stock in trade but could be a disposal in the course of a trade or business.

Lord Keith emphasised the need for some degree of regularity, and he found pointers to this in the primary purpose and long title of the Trade Descriptions Act 1968. I find pointers and to a similar need for regularity under the Act of 1977, where matters merely incidental to the carrying on of a business are concerned, both in the words which I would emphasise, "in the course of" in the phrase "in the course of a business" and in the concept, or legislative purpose, which must undertake the dichotomy under the Act of 1977 between those who deal with consumers and those who deal otherwise than as consumers.

This reasoning leads to the conclusion that, in the Act of 1977 also, the words "in the course of business" are not used in what Lord Keith called "the broadest sense". I also find helpful the phrase used by Lord Parker CJ and quoted by Lord Keith, "an integral part of the business carried on". The reconciliation between the phrase and the need for some degree of regularity is, as I see it, as follows; there are some transactions which are clearly integral parts of the businesses concerned, and these should be held to have been carried out in the course of those businesses; this would cover, apart from much else, the instance of a one-off adventure in the nature of trade, where the transaction itself would constitute a trade or business. There are other transactions, however, such as the purchase of the car in the present case, which are at highest only incidental to the carrying on of the relevant business; here a degree of regularity is required before it can be said that they are an integral part of the business carried on, and so entered into in the course of that business.

Applying the test thus indicated to the facts of the present case, I have no doubt that the requisite degree of regularity is not made out on the facts. Mr Bell's evidence that the car was the second or third vehicle acquired on credit terms was in my judgment and in the context of this case not enough. Accordingly, I agree with the judge that, in entering into the conditional sale agreement with the defendants, the company was "dealing as consumer". The defendants' condition 2(a) is thus inapplicable and the defendants are not absolved from liability under section 14(3).'

The Chester Grosvenor Hotel Company Ltd v Alfred McAlpine Management Ltd

(1991) 56 Build LR 115 • Queen's Bench

Clause 17 in a contract between Grosvenor and McAlpine purported to limit McAlpine's liability. Clause 17 stated

"a) Where the Project Manager is liable to the Client for breach of this Agreement (including a liability for liquidated damages for delay) by reason of any act or omission of a Construction Contractor:

(i) the Project Manager shall, in consultation with the Client, take all practical steps to enforce the terms of the Construction Contractor's Contract, including action or arbitration, in the Client's name and at the Client's expense, if necessary, to secure the performance of the Construction Contractor's obligations and to recover damages in respect of any loss or expense directly or indirectly incurred by the Project Manager and/or the Client as a result of the breach.

(ii) The Client shall not be entitled to recover from the Project Manager whether under this Agreement or by set off or other actions any sums

(1) in excess of such sums if any, as the Project Manager shall have recovered and received by judgment or arbitration award or by agreement with the Client's consent from such Construction Contractor.

(2) before recovery and receipt of such sums."

The court, as a preliminary issue, had to decide firstly, if Grosvenor had 'dealt as a consumer'; secondly, whether Grosvenor had entered into a contract on McAlpine's 'written standard terms of business'; and thirdly, whether Clause 17 satisfied the 'reasonableness' test.

Note: Issues two and three are dealt with below.

Judge Stannard: The Unfair Contract Terms Act 1977
'. . . Grosvenor [claim] that clause 17 is struck down by section 3 of the Unfair Contract Terms Act 1977 . . .

It is common ground that clause 17 attracts the terms of paragraph (a) of sub-section (2) of the section. However, there are issues as to whether Grosvenor "(dealt) as a consumer" within the terms of sub-section (1); whether the terms of the management contracts were McAlpine's "written standard terms of business" within the meaning of the same provision; and whether, if either the first or second issue is to be resolved in Grosvenor's favour, clause 17 satisfies the requirement of reasonableness referred to by the sub-section. The onus of proof is on McAlpine in regard to the first and third issues: see sections 11(5) and 12(3) of the 1977 Act, and is on Grosvenor with reference to the second issue.

"Deals as consumer"

Section 12 of the Act of 1977 provides in its material terms that:

"(1) A party to a contract 'deals as consumer' in relation to another party if –
(a) he neither makes the contract in the course of a business nor holds himself out as doing so; and
(b) the other party does make the contract in the course of a business."

The issue which arises is whether Grosvenor made the management contracts in the course of a business, or held themselves out as doing so, within the terms of paragraph (a).

In *R & B Customs Brokers Co Ltd* v *United Dominions Trust Ltd*, the Court of Appeal held that a private company, which carried on business as shipping and freight forwarding agents, was not "dealing as consumer" within the terms of sections 6 and 12 of the Act of 1977 when purchasing a motor car for the personal and business use of one of its two directors, who were a married couple. Dillon LJ held:

"There are some transactions which are clearly integral parts of the businesses concerned, and these should be held to have been carried out in the course of those businesses; this would cover, apart from much else, the instance of a one-off adventure in the nature of trade, where the transaction itself would constitute a trade or business. There are other transactions, however, such as the purchase of the car in the present case, which are at highest only incidental to the carrying on of the relevant business; here a degree of regularity is required before it can be said that they are an integral part of the business carried on, and so entered into in the course of that business."

The only other member of the court, Neill LJ, gave judgment in similar terms.

In *Rasbora Ltd* v *JCL Marine Ltd* the same conclusion was reached by Lawson J with reference to the term "a consumer sale" in section 55(4) of the Sale of Goods Act 1893 (as amended) in its application to the purchase of a boat by a company for the private use of the owner of the whole of its issued share capital.

It was pointed out on behalf of Grosvenor that their business was that of hoteliers, and submitted that the management contracts were entered into as isolated transactions and not as an integral part of their business.

The Grosvenor Hotel is a luxury hotel. In order to maintain that status it was necessary that it should be constantly refurbished. In 1963 and 1973 large-scale rebuilding and refurbishment were undertaken at the hotel, on the latter occasion following a fire. In 1976 Grosvenor contracted for minor works at the hotel. The contracts which are immediately relevant to these proceedings were entered into as part of this systematic programme of refurbishment. In the interim periods lesser works of refurbishment were carried out continually. These were performed by a small maintenance team comprised of Grosvenor's own staff, and by local tradesmen. In these circumstances I conclude that

Grosvenor entered into the management contracts as an essential part of their business by way of providing hotel facilities. Further, these contracts were entered into as part of Grosvenor's established practice of refurbishing the hotel. In these circumstances I conclude that these contracts were an integral part of Grosvenor's business, and that in entering into them it did not deal as consumer within the terms of the statute . . .'

Dealing on the other's written standard terms of business

The Chester Grosvenor Hotel Company Ltd v *Alfred McAlpine Management Ltd*

(1991) 56 Build LR 115 • Queen's Bench

The facts appear above.

Judge Stannard: "Written standard terms of business"

'In *McCrone* v *Boots Farm Sales Ltd* in the Outer House Lord Dunpark considered the term "standard form contract" which appears in section 17 of the Act of 1977 with reference to Scottish law. He held:

> "The Act does not define 'standard form contract' but its meaning is not difficult to comprehend. In some cases there may be difficulty in deciding whether the phrase properly applies to a particular contract. I have no difficulty in deciding that, upon the assumption that the defenders prove that their general conditions of sale were set out in all their invoices and that they were incorporated by implication in their contract with the pursuer, the contract was a standard form contract within the meaning of the said section 17.
>
> Since Parliament saw fit to leave the phrase to speak for itself, far be it from me to attempt to formulate a comprehensive definition of it. However, the terms of section 17 in the context of this Act make it plain to me that the section is designed to prevent one party to a contract from having his contractual rights, against a party who is in breach of contract, excluded or restricted by a term or condition, which is one of a number of fixed terms or conditions invariably incorporated in contracts of the kind in question by the party in breach, and which have been incorporated in the particular contract in circumstances in which it would be unfair and unreasonable for the other party to have his rights so excluded or restricted. If the section is to achieve its purpose, the phrase 'standard form contract' cannot be confined to written contracts in which both parties use standard forms. It is, in my opinion, wide enough to include any contract, whether wholly written or partly oral, which includes a set of fixed terms or conditions which the proponer applies, without material variation, to contracts of the kind in question."

It is to be noted that in this passage Lord Dunpark expressly disclaimed any attempt to formulate a comprehensive definition of the phrase "standard form contract".

I accept that where a party invariably contracts in the same written terms without material variation, those terms will become its "standard form contract" or "written standard terms of business". However, it does not follow that because terms are not employed invariably, or without material variation, they cannot be standard terms. If this were not so the statute would be emasculated, since it could be excluded by showing that, although the same terms had been employed without modification on a multitude of occasions, and were employed on the occasion in question, previously on one or more isolated occasions they had been modified or not employed at all. In my judgment the question is one of fact and degree. What are alleged to be standard terms may be used so infrequently in comparison with other terms that they cannot realistically be regarded as standard, or on any particular occasion may be so added to or mutilated that they must be regarded as having lost their essential identity. What is required for terms to be standard is that they should be regarded by the party which advances them as its standard terms and that it should habitually contract in those terms. If it contracts also in other terms, it must be determined in any given case, and as a matter of fact, whether this has occurred so frequently that the terms in question cannot be regarded as standard, and if on any occasion a party has substantially modified its prepared terms, it is a question of fact whether those terms have been so altered that they must be regarded as not having been employed on that occasion. Having applied these principles to the present case, I conclude that the two management contracts which were entered into between Grosvenor and McAlpine were on McAlpine's written standard terms of business.'

Application of the reasonableness test

See *George Mitchell Ltd* v *Finney Lock Seeds Ltd* above (p 278).

R W Green Ltd v *Cade Bros Farms*

[1978] 1 Lloyd's Rep 602 • Queen's Bench

Green sold 20 tons of uncertified seed potatoes to Cade for £634. When the potatoes began to grow, it became obvious that they were infected with a potato virus. As a result of this virus infection the crop was very poor. Cade claimed that the seed potatoes had not been of merchantable quality or fit for their purpose within the meaning of s 14 of the Sale of Goods Act 1893 and claimed damages for loss of profit of £6000. Green replied that their liability was limited to the price of the potatoes – £634 – by clause 5 of the contract of sale which provided:

"... Time being the essence of this Contract ... notification of rejection, claim or complaint must be made to the Seller giving a statement of the grounds for such rejection claim or complaint within three days ... after the arrival of the seed at its destination ... It is specifically provided and agreed that compensation and damages payable under any claim or claims arising out of this Contract under whatsoever pretext shall not under any circumstances amount in aggregate to more than the Contract price of the potatoes forming the subject of the claim or claims."

Cade argued that clause 5 was not enforceable because it was not fair and reasonable within the meaning of s 55(4) of the Sale of Goods Act 1893.

The issues before the court were firstly whether clause 5 covered the alleged breach of contract and, secondly, if it did, was it fair and reasonable for Green to rely on it?

Griffiths J: 'This contract, like any commercial contract, must be considered and construed against the background of the trade in which it operates. The plaintiffs' conditions are based upon a standard form of conditions produced by the National Association of Seed Potato Merchants. They are used by a large majority of seed potato merchants and, apart from amendments to accommodate a change to metrication, they have been in use in their present form for over 20 years. They have evolved over a much longer period as the result both of trade practice and discussions between the Association and the National Farmers' Union. They are therefore not conditions imposed by the strong upon the weak; but are rather a set of trading terms upon which both sides are apparently content to do business.

It is also important to have in mind the distinction between certified and uncertified seed. The Ministry of Agriculture provides a service whereby its inspectors will inspect a potato crop during the growing season, and if it appears healthy will issue a certificate to that effect. There are various grades of certificate indicating the percentage of virus infected plants in the growing crop, ranging from an H certificate based on a tolerance of 2 per cent, to an FS certificate, based on a tolerance of 0.001 per cent. If a farmer buys certified seed, he pays a little more for it to cover the costs of the inspection and certification. The certificate cannot be an absolute guarantee that the seed will not be infected, but according to Mr Cock it is on the whole a fairly reliable system, and I have no doubt provides a very real safeguard against buying an infected batch of seed. The farmer who buys uncertified seed does not have this safeguard which is provided by the independent examination of the Ministry, and must as a general rule be taking a greater risk of buying infected seed, but of course he gets it at a cheaper price . . .

On my findings no complaint was made about the potatoes until 13 days after delivery. The plaintiffs therefore say that the claim is out of time and barred by the condition that it must be made within three, or in certain cases 10, days of delivery. The plaintiffs' directors, in their evidence, explained that such a term was necessary in the trade because potatoes are a very perishable commodity and may deteriorate badly after delivery, particularly if they are not properly stored. So it was thought reasonable to give the farmer three days to inspect and make his complaint, and in the case of certain specific types of damage which might take longer to become apparent, 10 days. This appears to me to be a very reasonable requirement in the case of damage that is discoverable by reasonable inspection. But the presence of virus Y in the potatoes was not discoverable by inspection, and the complaint that was made did not relate to this defect, which neither the farmer nor the potato merchant suspected . . .

At the time this contract was made no one would expect it to have been practicable for the farmer to complain of virus Y in the potatoes within three days of delivery, for the simple reason that he would not know of its presence. It would therefore, in my judgment, not be fair or reasonable that this claim should be defeated because no complaint was made within three or 10 days of delivery. I therefore declare that that part of cl 5 is unenforceable in this action and provides no defence to the plaintiffs.

Is the claim to be limited to the contract price of the potatoes? Mr Harvey submits that upon its true construction, cl 5 applies only to patent defects; he argues that as that part of the condition that deals with notification of complaints could only have been intended to apply to patent – that is, to reasonably discoverable – defects, it follows that the limitation of the damages in the latter part of the condition must also be similarly restricted to patent defects. I cannot accept this construction. In the first place I doubt if, as a matter of construction, the parts of the condition dealing with complaints is restricted to patent defects; it appears, as drafted, to cover all complaints, but the Court has avoided the harsh consequences of this construction by declaring it unenforceable pursuant to its statutory power. However, even assuming that is should be construed as limited to complaints in respect of patent defects, I can see no reason to read a similar restriction into the very wide wording of the final sentence of the condition, which I now repeat:

"... It is specifically provided and agreed that compensation and damages payable under any claim or claims arising out of this contract under whatsoever pretext shall not under any circumstances amount in aggregate to more than the contract price of the potatoes forming the subject of the claim or claims."

This is clear language, easily intelligible, and I do not believe that any farmer who read it would say to himself "Ah; now that only applies to patent defects".

Furthermore, it is made clear by the terms of cl 3(a) that the condition is intended to cover defects not patent at the time of delivery, for that condition provides:

"Seed potatoes sometimes develop diseases after delivery. It being impossible to ascertain the presence of such diseases by the exercise of reasonable skill and judgment the Seller cannot accept any responsibility should any disease develop after delivery other than as provided under clause 5."

In my judgment, as a matter of construction cl 5 limits the defendants' claim to the contract price of the potatoes.

Should I exercise my discretion under s 55, as amended, of the Sale of Goods Act and declare it to be unenforceable, because it would not be fair or reasonable to let the plaintiffs rely upon it?

I have considered the matters to which I am particularly directed to have regard by s 55(5), in so far as they are relevant in this case. The parties were of equal bargaining strength; the buyer received no inducement to accept the term. True, it appears that he could not easily have bought potatoes without this term in the contract, but he had had the protection of the National Farmers' Union to look after his interests as the contract evolved and he knew that he was trading on these conditions.

No moral blame attaches to either party; neither of them knew, nor could be expected to know, that the potatoes were infected. There was of course a risk; it was a risk that the farmer could largely have avoided by buying certified seed, but he chose not to do so. To my mind the contract in clear language places the risk in so far as damage may exceed the contract price, on the farmer. The contract has been in use for many years with the approval of the negotiating bodies acting on behalf of both seed potato merchants and farmers, and I can see no grounds upon which it would be right for the Court to say in the circumstances of this case that such a term is not fair or reasonable.'

Smith v *Eric S Bush*

[1989] 2 All ER 514 • House of Lords

The House of Lords held that a valuer who was instructed by a building society to value a house, knowing that his valuation would probably be relied upon by the prospective purchaser, owed a duty to the purchaser to exercise reasonable skill and care in carrying out the valuation. The House of Lords having found that the valuer had been negligent in this particular case then had to decide whether an exemption clause printed in red lettering and in the clearest terms which purported to exclude liability for negligence of the valuer was a fair and reasonable one within the meaning of s 2(2) of the Unfair Contract Terms Act 1977.

Lord Griffiths: 'Finally, the question is whether the exclusion of liability contained in the disclaimer satisfies the requirement of reasonableness provided by section 2(2) of the 1977 Act. The meaning of reasonableness and the burden of proof are both dealt with in s 11(3) which provides:

"In relation to a notice (not being a notice having contractual effect), the requirement of reasonableness under this Act is that it should be fair and reasonable to allow reliance on it, having regard to all the circumstances obtaining when the liability arose or (but for the notice) would have arisen."

It is clear, then, that the burden is upon the surveyor to establish that in all the circumstances it is fair and reasonable that he should be allowed to rely upon his disclaimer of liability.

I believe that it is impossible to draw up an exhaustive list of the factors which must be taken into account when a judge is faced with this very difficult decision. Nevertheless, the following matters should, in my view, always be considered.

(1) Were the parties of equal bargaining power. If the court is dealing with a one-off situation between parties of equal bargaining power the requirement of reasonableness would be more easily discharged than in a case such as the present where the disclaimer is imposed upon the purchaser who has no effective power to object.

(2) In the case of advice would it have been reasonably practicable to obtain the advice from an alternative source taking into account considerations of costs and time. In the present case it is urged on behalf of the surveyor that it would have been easy for the purchaser to have obtained his own report on the condition of the house, to which the purchaser replies, that he would then be required to pay twice for the same advice and that people buying at the bottom end of the market, many of whom will be young first-time buyers, are likely to be under considerable financial pressure without the money to go paying twice for the same service.

(3) How difficult is the task being undertaken for which liability is being excluded. When a very difficult or dangerous undertaking is involved there may be a high risk of failure which would certainly be a pointer towards the reasonableness of excluding liability as a condition of doing the work. A valuation, on the other hand, should present no difficulty if the work is undertaken with reasonable skill and care. It is only defects which are observable by a careful visual examination that have to be taken into account and I cannot see that it places any unreasonable burden on the valuer to require him to accept responsibility for the fairly elementary degree of skill and care involved in observing, following-up and reporting on such defects. Surely it is work at the lower end of the surveyor's field of professional expertise.

(4) What are the practical consequences of the decision on the question of reasonableness. This must involve the sums of money potentially at stake and the ability of the parties to bear the loss involved, which, in its turn, raises the question of insurance. There was once a time when it was considered improper even to mention the possible existence of insurance cover in a lawsuit. But those days are long past. Everyone knows that all prudent, professional men carry insurance, and the availability and cost of insurance must be a relevant factor when considering which of two parties should be required to bear the risk of a loss. We are dealing in this case with a loss which will be limited to the value of a modest house and against which it can be expected that the surveyor will be insured. Bearing the loss will be unlikely to cause significant hardship if it has to be borne by the surveyor but it is, on the other hand, quite possible that it will be a financial catastrophe for the purchaser who may be left with a valueless house and no money to buy another. If the law in these circumstances denies the surveyor the right to exclude his liability, it may result in a few more claims but I do not think so poorly of the surveyor's profession as to believe that the floodgates will be opened. There may be some increase in surveyor's insurance premiums which will be passed on to the public, but I cannot think that it will be anything approaching the figures involved in the difference between the Abbey National's offer of a valuation without liability and a valuation with liability discussed in the speech of my noble and learned friend, Lord Templeman. The

result of denying a surveyor, in the circumstances of this case, the right to exclude liability, will result in distributing the risk of his negligence among all house purchasers through an increase in his fees to cover insurance, rather than allowing the whole of the risk to fall upon the one unfortunate purchaser.

I would not, however, wish it to be thought that I would consider it unreasonable for professional men in all circumstances to seek to exclude or limit their liability for negligence. Sometimes breathtaking sums of money may turn on professional advice against which it would be impossible for the advisor to obtain adequate insurance cover and which would ruin him if he were to be held personally liable. In these circumstances it may indeed be reasonable to give the advice upon a basis of no liability or possibly of liability limited to the extent of the adviser's insurance cover.

In addition to the foregoing four factors, which will always have to be considered, there is in this case the additional feature that the surveyor is only employed in the first place because the purchaser wishes to buy the house and the purchaser in fact provides or contributes to the surveyor's fees. No one has argued that if the purchaser had employed and paid the surveyor himself, it would have been reasonable for the surveyor to exclude liability for negligence, and the present situation is not far removed from that of a direct contract between the surveyor and the purchaser. The evaluation of the foregoing matters leads me to the clear conclusion that it would not be fair and reasonable for the surveyor to be permitted to exclude liability in the circumstances of this case. I would therefore dismiss this appeal. It must, however, be remembered that this is a decision in respect of a dwelling house of modest value in which it is widely recognised by surveyors that purchasers are in fact relying on their care and skill. It will obviously be of general application in broadly similar circumstances. But I expressly reserve my position in respect of valuations of quite different types of property for mortgage purposes, such as industrial property, large blocks of flats or very expensive houses. In such cases it may well be that the general expectation of the behaviour of the purchaser is quite different. With very large sums of money at stake prudence would seem to demand that the purchaser obtain his own structural survey to guide him in his purchase and, in such circumstances with very much larger sums of money at stake, it may be reasonable for the surveyors valuing on behalf of those who are providing the finance either to exclude or limit their liability to the purchaser.'

The Chester Grosvenor Hotel Company Ltd v Alfred McAlpine Management Ltd

(1991) 56 Build LR 115 • Queen's Bench

The facts appear above (p 300).

Judge Stannard: "Reasonableness"
   'In regard to the statutory requirement of reasonableness, sub-section (1) of section 11 of the Act of 1977 provides:

"(1) In relation to a contract term, the requirement of reasonableness for the purposes of this Part of this Act . . . is that the term shall have been a fair and reasonable one to be included having regard to the circumstances which were, or ought reasonably to have been, known to or in the contemplation of the parties when the contract was made."

The following are the salient factors.

(1) It is common ground that the parties were of equal bargaining power. In *Stag Line Ltd v Tyne Shiprepair Group Ltd and Others (the Zinnia)* Staughton J . . . held that an exemption clause was fair and reasonable within the terms of section 11 of the Act of 1977 when agreed upon by parties which had bargaining positions which were broadly equal. He held:

> "As Lord Wilberforce said in *Photo Production Ltd v Securicor Transport Ltd*:
>
> '. . . in commercial matters generally, when the parties are not of unequal bargaining power, and when risks are normally borne by insurance, not only is the case for judicial intervention undemonstrated, but there is everything to be said, and this seems to have been Parliament's intention, for leaving the parties free to apportion the risks as they think fit and for respecting their decisions.'
>
> . . . The passage is, of course, subject to the point that Parliament has required the test of reasonableness to be applied, even in such a case, where one party seeks to rely on his written standard terms of business. Nevertheless, the sentiment which it conveys seems to me entirely appropriate to the circumstances of the present case."

In my judgment this consideration also has very considerable weight in the present case.

(2) The management contracts were entered into between substantial commercial concerns bargaining at arm's length, and effected a division of risks between them. Since the management contracts did not deprive Grosvenor of their right to proceed directly against the construction contractors in the event of their being in breach of the construction contracts, the only risk which was allotted to Grosvenor by clause 17 was, in practical terms, the risk of insolvency in the construction contractors. It was pointed out by Mr Steynor that where clause 17 applied it deprived Grosvenor of the option of choosing to sue McAlpine rather than the construction contractors, but this consideration is unimportant if the construction contractors were of good financial standing. This allocation of risk was reflected in McAlpine's remuneration. By virtue of clauses 1(c) and 16 of the management contracts, Grosvenor had the right to control the risk by disapproving the selection of construction contractors. It was of course possible for Grosvenor to make enquiries into the financial status of the proposed construction contractors, and McAlpine did in fact do so. At the time of contracting it was within the reasonable contemplation of the parties that if the risk was to be realised, disregarding the possibility of insurance and having regard to their respective financial resources, the financial consequences for the party which bore it, although serious, would probably not be disastrous.

(3) The management contracts were not "take-it-or-leave-it" contracts in the sense that Grosvenor could not have contracted on other terms. There were many other contractors with whom they might have contracted, and on various alternative terms.

(4) Grosvenor had ample opportunity of considering the terms of the management contracts before accepting them. The first management contract was submitted to Grosvenor on 30 November 1984 and read by Mr Richard Edwards, who was then their Managing Director, and Mr Ronald McCahill, their Secretary and Finance Director, before it was entered into on 6 December 1984. During the interim period Grosvenor had the opportunity of obtaining advice either from independent sources or from other companies within the group of companies of which it was a member, which included a development company. As to Mr Steynor's contention that McAlpine should specifically have drawn Grosvenor's attention to clause 17, in my judgment this submission is unrealistic having regard to the fact that this was not a "consumer contract", and to Grosvenor's commercial standing. Nor do I accept Mr Steynor's submission that the meaning of clause 17 was so

obscure that Grosvenor's officers could not reasonably have been expected to appreciate its general import and importance.

(5) Mr Steynor pointed out that McAlpine were experts who were being paid for the exercise of their specialist skills, that Grosvenor obviously relied upon them to apply those skills carefully, and that nevertheless by clause 17 they sought to avoid liability for a vital application of their expertise. However, this consideration applies to many situations in which exemption clauses are relied upon. The Act of 1977 permits experts, including professional men, to contract out of liability subject to the statutory criterion of reasonableness. Accordingly this aspect of the case cannot be regarded as conclusive. However, I have given it due weight against the other relevant factors.

(6) . . . Section 11(1) of the Act 1977 refers to "the circumstances which were, or ought reasonably to have been, known to or in the contemplation of the parties when the contract was made". Since it is not suggested that existing insurance was disclosed during the antecedent negotiations, the material question is not whether the parties were insured against the relevant risk, but whether such insurance was reasonably available to them at the date of contracting. It is clear from the evidence that if McAlpine had agreed to bear the risk, insurance against it would have been available to them, perhaps under their existing professional indemnity policy, and that insurance was also available to Grosvenor in the form of cover against default by the construction contractors. It is also established by the evidence that if either party had obtained additional insurance against the relevant risk, the cost of doing so would have fallen on Grosvenor. In the event, although Grosvenor bore the risk under clause 17, at the time of contracting they chose not to obtain insurance against it, notwithstanding that such insurance was available and they could have afforded to obtain it.

In these circumstances I have no doubt that clause 17 satisfied the statutory requirement of reasonableness.'

Stag Line Ltd v *Tyne Shiprepair Group Ltd and Others (The Zinnia)*

[1984] 2 Lloyd's Rep 211 • Queen's Bench

The facts in this case are not really relevant since the court held that the defendants, Tyne Shiprepair Group Ltd, were only liable for nominal damages to Stag Line Ltd.

One of the issues before the court was whether the Unfair Contract Terms Act 1977 rendered of no effect the exclusion clause in the contract which purported to limit the defendant's liability.

Staughton J: 'I would have been tempted to hold that all the conditions are unfair and unreasonable for two reasons: first, they are in such small print that one can barely read them; secondly, the draughtsmanship is so convoluted and prolix that one almost needs an LLB to understand them. However, neither of those arguments was advanced before me, so I say no more about them.

The requirement of reasonableness here arises by reason of s 2 (liability for negligence), s 3 (written standard terms of business), and s 7 (correspondence of goods with description). For the purposes of s 7, I am required by s 11(2) to have regard to the matters specified in schedule 2 of the Act; but not for the purposes of ss 2 and 3. There being an overlap in the present case, it was agreed that I should have regard to the matters so specified.

The point which was most discussed was the strength of the bargaining positions of the parties relative to each other. This I find to have been, in broad terms, equal. The owners could, and apparently did, obtain tenders from a number of other yards. The defendants did from time to time relax some of their standard terms at the request of a particular customer, but that had only happened in the past at the request of customers with more economic power than the present owners. They had never in the past relaxed the exclusion in cl 8(9) of economic loss, or modified cl 8 otherwise than by extending the period of guarantee. But they had never been asked to do so. I do not find that surprising. Commercial men negotiating a contract for the future are not too concerned about the small print if they can secure a guarantee clause which seems to them satisfactory. It is only after a breach has occurred that they may take a different view . . .

Viewing the matter as a whole, and taking account of the other matters that are mentioned in schedule 2 in so far as they apply, I do not find the exclusion of economic loss to be unfair or unreasonable. As Lord Wilberforce said in *Photo Production Ltd* v *Securicor Transport Ltd*:

> ". . . in commercial matters generally, when the parties are not of unequal bargaining power, and when risks are normally borne by insurance, not only is the case for judicial intervention undemonstrated, but there is everything to be said, and this seems to have been Parliament's intention, for leaving the parties free to apportion the risks as they think fit and for respecting their decisions."

. . . That passage is, of course, subject to the point that Parliament has required the test of reasonableness to be applied, even in such a case, where one party seeks to rely on his written standard terms of business. Nevertheless, the sentiment which it conveys seems to me entirely appropriate to the circumstances of the present case.

I would take a different view of cl 8(4), if it provides that the owner shall have no remedy unless he returns his vessel to the yard for repair, or to such other place as the yard may direct. (In the case of negligent breach of contract, I have held that the remedy is not so limited). There is no alternative provision, such as I have seen in a good many similar contracts, that the yard will bear the cost to the owner of repair elsewhere, up to the amount which repair would have cost the yard. The result is capricious, both for the owner and the yard; the apportionment of risk is made to depend upon where a casualty happens to occur, and whether the owner happens to find it convenient and economic to return his vessel to the yard. Those matters seem to me to be relevant, as also is para (d) of the guidelines in schedule 2 of the Act: where the term excludes or restricts any relevant liability if some condition is not complied with, whether it was reasonable at the time of the contract to expect that compliance with that condition would be practicable.

I would have held that cl 8(4) was unfair and unreasonable, if it deprived the owners of all remedy because they did not return the vessel to Wallsend's yard. Whether it would have been open to the Court to effect any modification of the clause is a point which I do not, in the event, have to decide.

Exclusion clauses purporting to exclude liability for misrepresentation

This topic is dealt with below in the section on Misrepresentation.

Evasion of liability by means of a secondary contract

Tudor Grange Holdings Ltd v *Citibank NA*

[1991] 4 All ER 1 • Chancery Division

Tudor Grange, who owed money to Citibank, made certain general allegations that they had claims against Citibank although they refused to specify what those claims were. However, Tudor Grange entered into a 'release agreement' with Citibank whereby they agreed to release Citibank 'from all claims, demands and causes of action whether or not presently known or suspected' by Tudor Grange in return for Citibank making them a further loan. Citibank's loans to Tudor Grange were secured on Tudor Grange's assets. Later Tudor Grange claimed that the release was of no effect since it was contrary to s 10 of the Unfair Contract Terms Act 1977. The court, therefore, had to decide whether s 10 applied to the release.

Sir Nicolas Browne-Wilkinson VC: The Unfair Contract Terms Act 1977

'Mr Sheridan [counsel for Tudor Grange] accepts that the 1977 Act is normally regarded as applying to exemption clauses in the strict sense, namely clauses in a contract exempting prospectively against a future liability. However, he submits that s 10 of the Act according to its plain meaning operates so as to make subsequent compromises and waivers of accrued claims subject to the tests of reasonableness introduced by the 1977 Act. Section 10 reads as follows:

"A person is not bound by any contract term prejudicing or taking away rights of his which arise under, or in connection with the performance of another contract, so far as those rights extend to the enforcement of another's liability which this Part of this Act prevents that other from excluding or restricting."

Mr Sheridan puts his case in this way. He says what the banks were under contractual duties of care to the plaintiffs under the banking contracts. The release purports to take away the plaintiffs' rights to complain of breaches of the banking contracts and the duty of care contained in it. Therefore, says Mr Sheridan, the case comes directly within the words of the section. Reading the section with the interpolation of the characters in this case, he said it would read like this:

"A person [i.e. the plaintiffs] is not bound by any contract term [i.e. the release] taking away rights of [the plaintiffs], which arise under another contract [i.e. the banking contracts], so far as those rights [i.e. the rights under the banking contracts] extend to the enforcement of another's [i.e. the bank's] liability which this Part of this Act prevents that other [i.e. the bank] from excluding or restricting."

He submits, in my view correctly, that under s 2(2) of the Act, the bank could not itself by contract exclude or restrict its liability for breach of its contractual duty of care unless such exclusion or restriction was reasonable. Therefore, he says, the release is only binding if it satisfies the requirement of reasonableness, a matter which requires full investigation of all the facts and cannot be the subject matter of a striking-out application.

This argument that s 10 of the Act may apply to compromises or settlement of existing disputes has been foreseen by a number of textbook writers as an unfortunate possibility. They are unanimous in their hope that the courts will be robust in resisting it. If Mr Sheridan's construction is correct, the impact will be very considerable. The 1977 Act is normally regarded as being aimed at exemption clauses in the strict sense, that is to say clauses in a contract which aim to cut down prospective liability arising in the course of the performance of the contract in which the exemption clause is contained. If Mr Sheridan's argument is correct, the Act will apply to all compromises or waivers of existing claims arising from past actions. Any subsequent agreement to compromise contractual disputes falling within s 2 or s 3 of the Act will itself be capable of being put in question on the grounds that the compromise or waiver is not reasonable. Even an action settled at the door of the court on the advice of solicitors and counsel could be reopened on the grounds that the settlement was not reasonable within the meaning of the Act.

If I am forced to that conclusion by the words of s 10 properly construed, so be it. But, in my judgment, it is improbable that Parliament intended that result: it would be an end to finality in seeking to resolve disputes.

The starting point in construing s 10 is, in my judgment, to determine the mischief aimed at by the Act itself. For this purpose, it is legitimate to look at the second report of the Law Commission on Exemption Clauses (Law Com no 69) (see per Lord Griffiths in *Smith* v *Eric S Bush* (a firm). This report was the genesis of the 1977 Act. The report is wholly concerned with remedying injustices which are caused by exemption clauses in the strict sense. So far as I can see, the report makes no reference of any kind to any mischief relating to agreements to settle disputes.

Next, the marginal note to s 10 reads as follows: "Evasion by means of secondary contract". Although the marginal note to a section cannot control the language used in the section, it is permissible to have regard to it in considering what is the general purpose of the section and the mischief at which it is aimed: see *Stephens* v *Cuckfield RDC*. This sidenote clearly indicates that it is aimed at devices intended to evade the provisions of Pt 1 of the 1977 Act by the use of another contract. In my judgment, a contract to settle disputes which have arisen concerning the performance of an earlier contract cannot be described as an evasion of the provisions in the Act regulating exemption clauses in the earlier contract. Nor is the compromise contract "secondary" to the earlier contract.

The textbooks, to my mind correctly, identify at least one case which s 10 is designed to cover. Under contract 1, the supplier (S) contracts to supply a customer (C) with a product. Contract 1 contains no exemption clause. However, C enters into a servicing contract, contract 2, with another party (X). Under contract 2, C is precluded from exercising certain of his rights against S under contract 1. In such a case s 10 operates to preclude X from enforcing contract 2 against C so as to prevent C enforcing his rights against S under contract 1. The extent of the operation of s 10 in such circumstances may be doubtful (see Treitel *Law of Contract* (7th edn, 1987)). But there is no doubt that such a case falls squarely within the terms of s 10.

In the case that I have just postulated, the references in s 10 to "another's liability" and "that other" are references to someone other than X, i.e. to the original supplier, S. On Mr Sheridan's construction the words "another" and "that other" are taken as referring to someone other than C, the customer whose rights are restricted, so as to make the section apply to a case such as the present where there is no third party, X. Although as a matter of language the words of the section are capable of referring to anyone other than C, in my judgment, read in context and having regard to the purpose both of the Act and of the section itself, the reference to "another" plainly means someone other than X, that is to say someone other than the party to the secondary contract. In my judgment, s 10 does not apply where the parties to both contracts are the same.

This view is reinforced by a further factor. If the Act were intended to apply to terms in subsequent compromise agreements between the same parties as the original contract, s 10 would be quite unnecessary. Under ss 2 and 3 there is no express requirement that the contract term excluding or restricting S's liability to C has to be contained in the same contract as that giving rise to S's liability to C. If S and C enter into two contracts, it makes no difference if the exemption clause is contained in a different contract from that under which the goods are supplied. Sections 2 and 3 by themselves will impose the test of reasonableness. Why then should Parliament have thought that in s 10 there was some possibility of evasion in such circumstances?

In my judgment, the 1977 Act is dealing solely with exemption clauses in the strict sense (i.e. clauses in a contract modifying prospective liability) and does not affect retrospective compromises of existing claims. Section 10 is dealing only with attempts to evade the Act's provisions by the introduction of such an exemption clause into a contract with a third party. This view does not in any way conflict with the construction of s 23 of the Act, which has similar application to Scottish law.

My only doubt is raised by Sch 1, para 5. Schedule 1 provides that ss 2 to 4 of the Act are not to extend to various matters. Paragraph 5 reads as follows:

"Section 2(1) does not affect the validity of any discharge and indemnity given by a person, on or in connection with an award to him of compensation for pneumoconiosis attributable to employment in the coal industry, in respect of any further claim arising from his contracting that disease."

At first sight, the express exclusion from the operation of the Act of one category of compromise agreement suggests that other compromise agreements are within the Act. However, I am not persuaded of this. Paragraph 5 shows all the signs of a provision inserted at the insistence of one lobby, the coal industry, out of an abundance of caution. Why should Parliament have intended to exclude only one type of latent damage, pneumoconiosis, but leave all compromises involving other types of latent damage subject to the test of reasonableness? Moreover, para 5 only excludes from the test of reasonableness the provision barring future claims. On Mr Sheridan's construction, this would leave the other terms of settlement in the pneumoconiosis claim subject to the test of reasonableness imposed by the Act. That is not a conclusion that I think Parliament can have intended.

Accordingly, for those reasons, s 10 cannot apply to the release of 13 March 1989.'

Varieties of exemption clause

Stewart Gill Ltd v *Horatio Myer & Co Ltd*

[1992] 2 All ER 257 • Court of Appeal

Horatio Myer entered into a contract with Stewart Gill for the delivery, installation and testing of an overhead conveyor system. By the terms of the contract 5 per cent of the price was payable on completion of installation and 5 per cent 30 days following completion. Stewart Gill sued Horatio Myer for the 10 per cent of the price due on completion or 30 days thereafter. Horatio Myer alleged that Stewart Gill had breached the contract and counterclaimed claiming to set off the 10 per cent of the price it owed against the damages owed to it by Stewart Gill. Stewart Gill denied the counterclaim and argued that a term in the contract prevented Horatio Myer from withholding payment. The relevant clause was cl 12.4 which read:

"The Customer shall not be entitled to withhold payment of any amount due to the Company under the Contract by reason of any payment credit set off counterclaim allegation of incorrect or defective Goods or for any other reason whatsoever which the Customer may allege excuses him from performing his obligations hereunder."

The issues before the court were whether clause 12.4 of Stewart Gill's standard conditions of contract was caught by s 13(1)(b) of the Unfair Contract Terms 1977 Act, and, if so, did the clause satisfy the requirement of reasonableness?

Lord Donaldson of Lymington MR: 'Section 3 of the 1977 Act applies where, as here, one party to a contract deals with the other on that other's written standard terms of business. However, it is limited to terms excluding or restricting liability or entitling the party concerned to render no contractual performance or a performance which is substantially different from that which was reasonably expected of him. Clause 12.4 is not such a clause, but the section is relevant to a consideration of s 13, although it is not there referred to in express terms.

Section 7 applies where, as here, the contract transfers the ownership of goods otherwise than under a contract for the sale or hire purchase of goods. Unlike s 3, it is referred to in s 13 but, like s 3, it is concerned with exclusion or restriction of liability.

This leaves s 13, which is in the following terms . . .

It is trite fact (as contrasted with being trite law) that there are more ways than one of killing a cat. Section 13 addresses this problem. On behalf of the plaintiffs it was submitted that it only did so to the extent of rendering ineffective any unreasonable term which by, for example, introducing restrictive or onerous conditions indirectly achieved the exclusion or restriction of liability which, if achieved directly, would fall within the scope of other sections. The plaintiffs rightly say that cl 12.4 does not have this effect. On behalf of the defendants it was submitted that it had a wider scope.

The answer is, of course, to be found in the wording of the section, but it does not exactly leap out of the print and hit one between the eyes. Analysing the section and disregarding words which are irrelevant, it seems to deal with the matter as follows:

"(1) To the extent that this Part of this Act prevents the exclusion or restriction of any liability it also prevents . . ."

This seems to me to do no more than give expression to the "cat" approach. Both ss 3 and 7 would render ineffective any clause in the plaintiffs' written standard terms of business which excluded or restricted liability in respects which are here material and s 13 extends this in some way. In order to find out in what way, one must read on:

"it also prevents – (a) making the liability or its enforcement subject to restrictive or onerous conditions; (b) excluding or restricting any right or remedy in respect of the liability . . . (c) excluding or restricting rules of . . . procedure . . ."

Now cl 12.4 can perhaps be said to make the enforcement of the plaintiffs' liability subject to a condition that the defendants shall not have sought to set off their own claims against their liability to pay the price and this might well be said to be onerous. However, I do not think it necessary to pursue this, because it is quite clear that cl 12.4 excludes the defendants' "right" to set off their claims against the plaintiffs' claim for the price and further excludes the remedy which they would otherwise have of being able to enforce their claims against the plaintiffs by means of a set-off (see para (b)). It also excludes or restricts the procedural rules as to set off (see para (c)). Thus far, therefore, the defendants can bring themselves within the section.

We then get to the words:

"and (to that extent) sections 2 and 5 to 7 also prevent excluding or restricting liability by reference to terms and notices which exclude or restrict the relevant obligation or duty."

Although I find this obscure, I do not think that these words restrict the ambit of the preceding words. I think that they constitute an extension and that what is intended to be covered is an exclusion or restriction of liability not by contract but by reference to notices or terms of business which are not incorporated in a contract. If this is correct, it is irrelevant to the present case.

On this construction of s 13 the defendants succeed because, whatever the reasonableness of a clause which excludes or restricts a right of set-off, nothing could *prima facie* be more unreasonable than that the defendants should not be entitled to withhold payment to the plaintiffs of any amount due to the plaintiffs under the contract by reason of a "credit" owing by the plaintiffs to the defendants and, *a fortiori*, a "payment" made by the defendants to the plaintiffs. In this context "payment" must I think mean overpayment under another contract and credit mean "credit note" or admitted liability again under another contract, because otherwise it would be doubtful whether it could be said by the plaintiffs that any amount was due to them under the contract. Mr David Joseph appearing for the plaintiffs did not seriously gainsay this, but he submitted that, as the defendants were not seeking to rely upon a payment or credit, this part of the clause could be ignored. In support of my view that cl 12.4 as a whole completely fails the test of reasonableness, I gratefully adopt the additional considerations based upon its concluding words and Sch 2 to the Act discussed in the judgment of Stuart-Smith LJ, which I have read in draft.

Whether or not it is possible to sever parts of the clause depends upon s 11(1), which is in these terms:

"The 'reasonableness' test. – (1) In relation to a contract term, the requirement of reasonableness for the purposes of this Part of this Act . . . is that the term shall have been a fair and reasonable one to be included having regard to the circumstances which were, or ought reasonably to have been, known to or in the contemplation of the parties when the contract was made."

In the face of this wording it seems to me to be impossible to contend that we should look only at the part of the clause which is relied upon. The issue is whether "the term [the whole term and nothing but the term] shall have been a fair and reasonable one to be included". This has to be determined as at the time when the contract is made and without regard to what particular use one party may subsequently wish to make of it. I would unhesitatingly answer this in the negative and accordingly would dismiss the appeal.'

Stuart-Smith LJ: 'In my judgment it is the term as a whole that has to be reasonable and not merely some part of it. Throughout the Act the expression used is "by reference to any contract term", "the [contract] term satisfies the requirement of reasonableness" (see ss 3 and 7). And in s 11(1) the reasonableness test is laid down as:

"In relation to a contract term, the requirement for reasonableness . . . is that the term shall have been a fair and reasonable one to be included having regard to the circumstances which were, or ought reasonably to have been, known to or in the contemplation of the parties when the contract was made."

Although the question of reasonableness is primarily one for the court when the contract term is challenged, it seems to me that the parties must also be in a position to judge this at the time the contract is made. If this is so, I find it difficult to see how such an appreciation can be made if the customer has to guess whether some, and if so which, part of the term will alone be relied upon.

Section 11(2) of the Act requires the court which is determining the question of reasonableness for the purpose of ss 6 and 7 to have regard in particular to the matters specified in Sch 2. Although Sch 2 does not apply in the present case, the considerations there set out are usually regarded as being of general application to the question of reasonableness. Two paragraphs of these guidelines would in my judgment be unworkable unless the whole term is being considered.

Paragraph (b) provides:

"whether the customer received an inducement to agree to the term, or in accepting it had an opportunity of entering into a similar contract with other persons, but without having to accept a similar term."

If there was an inducement, it would I think be quite impossible in most cases to say that it related only to the words which the party seeking to establish reasonableness relies upon as opposed to those he wishes to delete. It is equally unreal to suppose that the customer could divine which part the vendor will ultimately seek to rely upon so as to decide whether other persons are willing to contract without the term.

Paragraph (c) provides:

"whether the customer knew or ought reasonably to have known of the existence and extent of the term (having regard, among other things, to any custom of the trade and any previous course of dealing between the parties)."

In my judgment the customer would be most unlikely ever to know the extent of the term if the vendor is entitled, when it is questioned as to reasonableness, to rely on only part of it.

These examples in my judgment support the construction of the word "term" as being the whole term or clause as drafted, and not merely that part of it which may eventually be taken to be relevant to the case in point.

Nor does it appear to me to be consistent with the policy and purpose of the Act to permit a contractor to impose a contractual term, which taken as a whole is completely unreasonable, to put a blue pencil through the most offensive parts and say that what is left is reasonable and sufficient to exclude or restrict his liability in a manner relied upon.'

UNFAIR TERMS IN CONSUMER CONTRACTS REGULATIONS 1994

SI 1994 No 3159
Made 8 December 1994 under the European Communities Act 1972, s 2(2)

Introduction to the Regulations
Article 1   Citation and commencement
Article 2   Interpretation
Article 3   Terms to which these Regulations apply
Article 4   Unfair terms
Article 5   Consequence of including unfair terms
Article 6   Construction of written contracts
Article 7   Choice of law clauses
Article 8   Prevention of continued use of unfair terms
Schedule 1   Contracts and particular terms excluded from the scope of these Regulations

Schedule 2   Assessment of good faith
Schedule 3   Unfair terms

Introduction to the Regulations

The Regulations apply, with certain exceptions, to any term which has not been individually negotiated in contracts concluded between a consumer and a seller or supplier (Regulation 3). Schedule 1 contains a list of contracts and particular terms which are excluded from the scope of the Regulations. In addition, those terms which define the main subject matter of the contract or concern the adequacy of the price or remuneration as against the goods or services supplied are not to be subject to assessment for fairness, provided that they are in plain, intelligible language (Regulation 3(2)).

The Regulations provide that an unfair term is one which contrary to the requirement of good faith causes a significant imbalance in the parties' rights and obligations under the contract to the detriment of the consumer (Regulation 4(1)). Schedule 2 contains a list of some of the matters which shall be considered when making an assessment of good faith. Unfair terms are not binding on the consumer (Regulation 5).

The Regulations provide that the Director General of Fair Trading shall consider any complaint made to him about the fairness of any contract term drawn up for general use. He may, if he considers it appropriate to do so, seek an injunction to prevent the continued use of that term or a term having like effect in contracts drawn up for general use by a party to the proceedings (Regulation 8). In addition, the Director General is given the power to arrange for the dissemination of information and advice concerning the operation of the Regulations (Regulation 8(7)).

Article 1   Citation and commencement

These Regulations may be cited as the Unfair Terms in Consumer Contracts Regulations 1994 and shall come into force on 1st July 1995.

Article 2   Interpretation

(1) In these Regulations –

"business" includes a trade or profession and the activities of any government department or local or public authority;

"the Community" means the European Economic Community and the other States in the European Economic Area;

"consumer" means a natural person who, in making a contract to which these Regulations apply, is acting for purposes which are outside his business;

"court" in relation to England and Wales and Northern Ireland means the High Court;

"Director" means the Director General of Fair Trading;

"EEA Agreement" means the Agreement on the European Economic Area signed at Oporto on 2 May 1992 as adjusted by the protocol signed at Brussels on 17 March 1993;

"member State" shall mean a State which is a contracting party to the EEA Agreement but until the EEA Agreement comes into force in relation to Liechtenstein does not include the State of Liechtenstein;

"seller" means a person who sells goods and who, in making a contract to which these Regulations apply, is acting for purposes relating to his business; and "supplier" means a person who supplies goods or services and who, in making a contract to which these Regulations apply, is acting for purposes relating to his business.

Article 3   Terms to which these Regulations apply

(1) Subject to the provisions of Schedule 1, these Regulations apply to any term in a contract concluded between a seller or supplier and a consumer where the said term has not been individually negotiated.

(2) In so far as it is in plain, intelligible language, no assessment shall be made of the fairness of any term which –

    (a) defines the main subject matter of the contract, or

    (b) concerns the adequacy of the price or remuneration, as against the goods or services sold or supplied.

(3) For the purposes of these Regulations, a term shall always be regarded as not having been individually negotiated where it has been drafted in advance and the consumer has not been able to influence the substance of the term.

(4) Notwithstanding that a specific term or certain aspects of it in a contract has been individually negotiated, these Regulations shall apply to the rest of a contract if an overall assessment of the contract indicates that it is a pre-formulated standard contract.

(5) It shall be for any seller or supplier who claims that a term was individually negotiated to show that it was.

Article 4   Unfair terms

(1) In these Regulations, subject to paragraphs (2) and (3) below, "unfair term" means any term which contrary to the requirement of good faith causes a significant imbalance in the parties' rights and obligations under the contract to the detriment of the consumer.

(2) An assessment of the unfair nature of a term shall be made taking into account the nature of the goods or services for which the contract was concluded and referring, as at the time of the conclusion of the contract, to all circumstances attending the conclusion of the contract and to all the other terms of the contract or of another contract on which it is dependent.

(3) In determining whether a term satisfies the requirement of good faith, regard shall be had in particular to the matters specified in Schedule 2 to these Regulations.

(4) Schedule 3 to these Regulations contains an indicative and non exhaustive list of the terms which may be regarded as unfair.

Article 5   Consequence of inclusion of unfair terms in contracts

(1) An unfair term in a contract concluded with a consumer by a seller or supplier shall not be binding on the consumer.

(2) The contract shall continue to bind the parties if it is capable of continuing in existence without the unfair term.

Article 6   Construction of written contracts

A seller or supplier shall ensure that any written term of a contract is expressed in plain, intelligible language, and if there is doubt about the meaning of a written term, the interpretation most favourable to the consumer shall prevail.

Article 7   Choice of law clauses

These Regulations shall apply notwithstanding any contract term which applies or purports to apply the law of a non member State, if the contract has a close connection with the territory of the member States.

Article 8   Prevention of continued use of unfair terms

(1) It shall be the duty of the Director to consider any complaint made to him that any contract term drawn up for general use is unfair, unless the complaint appears to the Director to be frivolous or vexatious.

(2) If having considered a complaint about any contract term pursuant to paragraph (1) above the Director considers that the contract term is unfair he may, if he considers it appropriate to do so, bring proceedings for an injunction (in which proceedings he may also apply for an interlocutory injunction) against any person appearing to him to be using or recommending use of such a term in contracts concluded with consumers.

(3) The Director may, if he considers it appropriate to do so, have regard to any undertakings given to him by or on behalf of any person as to the continued use of such a term in contracts concluded with consumers.

(4) The Director shall give reasons for his decision to apply or not to apply, as the case may be, for an injunction in relation to any complaint which these Regulations require him to consider.

(5) The court on an application by the Director may grant an injunction on such terms as it thinks fit.

(6) An injunction may relate not only to use of a particular contract term drawn up for general use but to any similar term, or a term having like effect, used or recommended for use by any party to the proceedings.

(7) The Director may arrange for the dissemination in such form and manner as he considers appropriate of such information and advice concerning the operation of these Regulations as may appear to him to be expedient to give to the public and to all persons likely to be affected by these Regulations.

Schedule 1   Contracts and particular terms excluded from the scope of these Regulations

These Regulations do not apply to –

(a) any contract relating to employment;

(b) any contract relating to succession rights;

(c) any contract relating to rights under family law;

(d) any contract relating to the incorporation and organisation of companies or partnerships; and

(e) any term incorporated in order to comply with or which reflects –

(i) statutory or regulatory provisions of the United Kingdom; or

(ii) the provisions or principles of international conventions to which the member States or the Community are party.

Schedule 2   Assessment of good faith

In making an assessment of good faith, regard shall be had in particular to –

(a) the strength of the bargaining positions of the parties;

(b) whether the consumer had an inducement to agree to the term;

(c) whether the goods or services were sold or supplied to the special order of the consumer, and

(d) the extent to which the seller or supplier has dealt fairly and equitably with the consumer.

Schedule 3

1 Terms which have the object or effect of –

(a) excluding or limiting the legal liability of a seller or supplier in the event of the death of a consumer or personal injury to the latter resulting from an act or omission of that seller or supplier;

(b) inappropriately excluding or limiting the legal rights of the consumer vis-à-vis the seller or supplier or another party in the event of total or partial non performance or inadequate performance by the seller or supplier of any of the contractual obligations, including the option of offsetting a debt owed to the seller or supplier against any claim which the consumer may have against him;

(c) making an agreement binding on the consumer whereas provision of services by the seller or supplier is subject to a condition whose realisation depends on his own will alone;

(d) permitting the seller or supplier to retain sums paid by the consumer where the latter decides not to conclude or perform the contract, without providing for the consumer to receive compensation of an equivalent amount from the seller or supplier where the latter is the party cancelling the contract;

(e) requiring any consumer who fails to fulfil his obligation to pay a disproportionately high sum in compensation;

(f) authorising the seller or supplier to dissolve the contract on a discretionary basis where the same facility is not granted to the consumer, or permitting the seller or supplier to retain the sums paid for services not yet supplied by him where it is the seller or supplier himself who dissolves the contract;

(g) enabling the seller or supplier to terminate a contract of indeterminate duration without reasonable notice except where there are serious grounds for doing so;

(h) automatically extending a contract of fixed duration where the consumer does not indicate otherwise, when the deadline fixed for the consumer to express this desire not to extend the contract is unreasonably early;

(i) irrevocably binding the consumer to terms with which he had no real opportunity of becoming acquainted before the conclusion of the contract;

(j) enabling the seller or supplier to alter the terms of the contract unilaterally without a valid reason which is specified in the contract;

(k) enabling the seller or supplier to alter unilaterally without a valid reason any characteristics of the product or service to be provided;

(l) providing for the price of goods to be determined at the time of delivery or allowing a seller of goods or supplier of services to increase their price without in both cases giving the consumer the corresponding right to cancel the contract if the final price is too high in relation to the price agreed when the contract was concluded;

(m) giving the seller or supplier the right to determine whether the goods or services supplied are in conformity with the contract, or giving him the exclusive right to interpret any term of the contract;

(n) limiting the seller's or supplier's obligation to respect commitments undertaken by his agents or making his commitments subject to compliance with a particular formality;

(o) obliging the consumer to fulfil all his obligations where the seller or supplier does not perform his;

(p) giving the seller or supplier the possibility of transferring his rights and obligations under the contract, where this may serve to reduce the guarantees for the consumer, without the latter's agreement;

(q) excluding or hindering the consumer's right to take legal action or exercise any other legal remedy, particularly by requiring the consumer to take disputes exclusively to arbitration not covered by legal provisions, unduly restricting the evidence available to him or imposing on him a burden of proof which, according to the applicable law, should lie with another party to the contract.

2 Scope of subparagraphs 1(g), (j) and (l)

(a) Subparagraph 1(g) is without hindrance to terms by which a supplier of financial services reserves the right to terminate unilaterally a contract of indeterminate duration without notice where there is a valid reason, provided that the supplier is required to inform the other contracting party or parties thereof immediately.

(b) Subparagraph 1(j) is without hindrance to terms under which a supplier of financial services reserves the right to alter the rate of interest payable by the consumer or due to the latter, or the amount of other charges for financial services without notice where there is a valid reason, provided that the supplier is required to inform the other contracting party or parties thereof at the earliest opportunity and that the latter are free to dissolve the contract immediately.

Subparagraph 1(j) is also without hindrance to terms under which a seller or supplier reserves the right to alter unilaterally the conditions of a contract of indeterminate duration, provided that he is required to inform the consumer with reasonable notice and that the consumer is free to dissolve the contract.

(c) Subparagraphs 1(g), (j) and (l) do not apply to –

transactions in transferable securities, financial instruments and other products or services where the price is linked to fluctuations in a stock exchange quotation or index or a financial market rate that the seller or supplier does not control;

contracts for the purchase or sale of foreign currency, traveller's cheques or international money orders denominated in foreign currency;

(d) Subparagraph 1(l) is without hindrance to price indexation clauses, where lawful, provided that the method by which prices vary is explicitly described.

SUMMARY

You should now be able to:

- Appreciate how the Unfair Contract Terms Act 1977 applies to some exemption clauses but not all.
- Distinguish between exemption clauses rendered void and those needing to satisfy the *reasonableness test*.
- Apply the reasonableness test.
- Identify when one of the parties is 'dealing as a consumer'.
- Identify when one party is dealing on the other's written standard terms of business.

If you have not mastered the above points you should go through this section again.

12 Misrepresentation

THE MISREPRESENTATION ACT 1967

Section 1   Removal of certain bars to rescission for innocent misrepresentation

Where a person has entered into a contract after a misrepresentation has been made to him, and –
   (a) the misrepresentation has become a term of the contract; or
   (b) the contract has been performed;
or both, then, if otherwise he would be entitled to rescind the contract without alleging fraud, he shall be so entitled, subject to the provisions of this Act, notwithstanding the matters mentioned in paragraphs (a) and (b) of this section.

Section 2   Damages for misrepresentation

(1) Where a person has entered into a contract after a misrepresentation has been made to him by another party thereto and as a result thereof he has suffered loss, then, if the person making the misrepresentation would be liable to damages in respect thereof had the misrepresentation been made fraudulently, that person shall be so liable notwithstanding that the misrepresentation was not made fraudulently, unless he proves that he had reasonable ground to believe and did believe up to the time the contract was made that the facts represented were true.

(2) Where a person has entered into a contract after a misrepresentation has been made to him otherwise than fraudulently, and he would be entitled, by reason of the misrepresentation, to rescind the contract, then, if it is claimed, in any proceedings arising out of the contract, that the contract ought to be or has been rescinded the court or arbitrator may declare the contract subsisting and award damages in lieu of rescission, if of opinion that it would be equitable to do so, having regard to the nature of the misrepresentation and the loss that would be caused by it if the contract were upheld, as well as to the loss that rescission would cause to the other party.

(3) Damages may be awarded against a person under subsection (2) of this section whether or not he is liable to damages under subsection (1) thereof, but where he is so liable any award under the said subsection (2) shall be taken into account in assessing his liability under the said subsection (1).

Section 3　Avoidance of provision excluding liability for misrepresentation

If a contract contains a term which would exclude or restrict –
    (a) any liability to which a party to a contract may be subject by reason of any misrepresentation made by him before the contract was made; or
    (b) any remedy available to another party to the contract by reason of such a misrepresentation,
that term shall be of no effect except in so far as it satisfies the requirement of reasonableness as stated in section 11(1) of the Unfair Contract Terms Act 1977; and it is for those claiming that the term satisfies that requirement to show that it does.

WHAT IS MISREPRESENTATION?

A misrepresentation is *not* part of a contract. A misrepresentation is made before the contract is made. Really misrepresentation is the *tort of deceit*.

An operative misrepresentation consists of a false statement of existing or past fact made by one party before or at the time of making the contract, which is addressed to the other party and which induces the other party to enter into the contract.

THE REPRESENTATION

There must be a false representation

There must be some positive statement or conduct in order to amount to an operative misrepresentation.

There is no duty to disclose anything to the other party: see *Smith* v *Hughes* below, p 2.

A half-truth may be a misrepresentation.

Dimmock v Hallett

(1866) LR 2 Ch App 21 • Chancery Appeals

Hallett purchased an estate from Dimmock. The particulars of sale described a farm called Bull Hassocks Farm, containing 300 acres, as 'Lately in the occupation of Mr R Hickson, at an annual rent of £290 15s Now in hand.' Another farm, called Creyke's Hundreds, containing 115 acres, was mentioned as 'let to Mr R Hickson, a yearly Lady Day tenant (old style) at £130 per annum'. Another farm, Misson Springs, containing 131 acres, was mentioned to be 'let to Mr F Wigglesworth, a yearly Lady Day tenant (new style) at £160 per annum'. On taking possession of the estate Hallett found that the land was not 'fertile and improvable' but was almost a wilderness and in part abandoned. Hallett also found that Bull Hassocks Farm could not be let for anything like £290 15s a year. Furthermore two of the tenants who had been described as continuing tenants had given notice to quit their farms, which formed a large part of the estate. Hallett claimed that these misstatements amounted to a misrepresentation by Dimmock and that, therefore, the contract of sale should be rescinded on the grounds of misrepresentation.

The issue before the court was whether the statements made by Dimmock amounted to a misrepresentation which entitled Hallett to have the contract annulled.

Turner LJ: 'The next alleged misrepresentation is much more important. A farm called Bull Hassocks, containing 300 acres, or nearly a third of the property put up for sale, is described as "lately in the occupation of Mr R Hickson, at an annual rent of £290 15s. Now in hand." The facts are, that this farm had been let at a higher rent than £290 15s before Hickson became tenant. Hickson took the farm at Midsummer, 1863, at the rent of £290 15s. At Michaelmas, 1864, he left it, and there appears never to have been any actual tenancy between his leaving and the time of the sale. Mr Dimmock, however, being in possession, agreed with a Mr Nelson to let him Bull Hassocks Farm, and another farm called Creyke's Hundreds, containing 115 acres, at 15s per acre, which would bring the rent of Bull Hassocks Farm to £225 at most. That agreement was not carried into effect, for Nelson desired to be relieved of the farm, paid £20 to be off his bargain. Was it then fair and honest to describe the farm in the particulars as late in the occupation of Hickson at a rent of £290 15s, when Hickson had been out of possession nearly a year and a half, within which period there had been an agreement to let the farm at a rent less by £65 than that paid by him. Such a description amounts to a representation to the purchaser that he will come into possession of a farm which will let for £290 15s, whereas Mr Dimmock, who had agreed to let it for so much less, knew that nothing near that rent could be obtained for it. But the matter does not rest there, for even the representation that the farm had been let to Hickson at £290 15s was not correct. He had occupied it for it a year and a quarter, paying only £1 for the first quarter; and this took place at a time of year when the occupation must have been beneficial; for the farm contained about 150 acres of pastures, which Hickson thus held at a nominal rent from Midsummer to Michaelmas. I am of opinion, therefore, that the particulars contain representations which were untrue, and calculated materially to increase the apparent value of the property. The Court requires good faith in conditions of sale, and looks strictly at the statements contained in them.

Again, Creyke's Hundred's, containing 115 acres, is described as let to R Hickson, a yearly Lady Day tenant, at £130 per annum; and another farm, Misson Springs, containing 131 acres, is mentioned as let to Wigglesworth, a yearly Lady Day tenant, at £160 per annum. Now the sale took place on the 25th of January, 1866, and there is no reference made in the particulars to the fact that each of these tenants had given a notice to quit, which would expire at Lady Day. The purchaser, therefore, would be led to suppose, as to these farms, that he was purchasing with continuing tenancies at fixed rents, whereas he would, in fact, have to find tenants immediately after the completion of his purchase. I refer particularly to this, because as to some of the other farms it is stated in the particulars that the tenants had given notice to quit; so that the purchaser must have been led to believe that the tenants of Creyke's Hundreds and Misson Springs were continuing tenants. This again, as it seems to me, is a material misrepresentation . . .

I am of opinion, therefore, that [Hallett] is entitled to be discharged.'

However, a mere silence is not a misrepresentation.

Keates v The Earl of Cadogan

(1851) 20 LJCP 76 • Common Pleas

The Earl of Cadogan let a house which he knew to be 'in such a ruinous and dangerous state and condition as to be dangerous to enter, occupy, or dwell in, and was likely wholly or in part to fall down, and thereby do damage and injury to persons and property therein' to Keates for three years at an annual rent of £5. Keates argued that the contract should be set aside on the ground that the Earl of Cadogan should have warned him of the state of the house before he agreed to rent it.

Jervis CJ: '. . . I do not think that this declaration discloses a sufficient cause of action. It is not contended that there was any warranty that the house was fit for immediate occupation: but it is said, that because the defendant knows it is in a ruinous state, and does nothing to inform the plaintiff of that fact, therefore the action is maintainable. It is consistent with the state of things disclosed in the declaration, that, the defendant knowing the state of things, the plaintiff may have come to him and said, "Will you lease that house to me?" and the defendant may have answered "Yes, I will". It is not contended by the plaintiff that any misrepresentation was made; nor was it alleged that the plaintiff was acting on the impression produced by the conduct of the defendant as to the state of the house, or that he was not to make investigations before he began to reside in it. I think, therefore, that the defendant is entitled to our judgment, there being no obligation on the defendant to say anything about the state of the house, and no allegation of deceit. It is an ordinary case of letting.'

What if circumstances change?

What if something is true when it is first said but because of changed circumstances it becomes untrue?

With v *O'Flanagan*
[1936] 1 Ch 575 • Court of Appeal

In January 1934 With entered into negotiations with Dr O'Flanagan to purchase his medical practice. At that time Dr O'Flanagan said that the business had takings of £2000 per year. However, when With purchased the business in May 1934 the takings had fallen to £5 per week due to the illness of Dr O'Flanagan; this fact had not been disclosed to With. On discovering this fact, With sought to have the contract rescinded on the grounds of Dr O'Flanagan's misrepresentation.

The issue before the court was whether Dr O'Flanagan's failure to inform With of the changes in circumstances amounted to a misrepresentation.

Lord Wright MR: 'As to the law, which has been challenged, I want to say this. I take the law to be as it was stated by Fry J in *Davies* v *London and Provincial Marine Insurance Co* where it is perhaps most fully expressed. In that case certain friends of an agent had agreed to deposit a sum of money for what was alleged to have been defaults on his part. The company who had employed him were under the belief and were advised that the default of the agent constituted felony, but they were later advised that these acts did not amount to felony and they withdrew the order for his arrest, and then still later in the day the friends of the agent agreed to deposit a sum of money on the footing of what they had been told earlier in the day before the arrest had been withdrawn – these statements had not been corrected – and on that footing it was held by Fry J "that the change of circumstances ought to have been stated to the intending sureties, and that the agreement must be rescinded and the money returned to the sureties". I need not read the whole of the passage in the judgment, but I need only refer to one or two points. The learned judge points out: "Where parties are contracting with one another, each may, unless there be a duty to disclose, observe silence even in regard to facts which he believes would be operative upon the mind of the other; and it rests upon those who say that there was a duty to disclose, to shew that the duty existed". Then the learned judge points out that in many cases there is such a duty as between persons in a confidential or a fiduciary relationship where the preexisting relationship involves the duty of entire disclosure. Then his Lordship says: "In the next place, there are certain contracts which have been called contracts *uberrimae fidei* where, from their nature, the Court requires disclosure from one of the contracting parties". The learned judge refers to contracts of partnership and marine insurance. Then he goes on: "Again, in ordinary contracts the duty may arise from circumstances which occur during the negotiation. Thus, for instance, if one of the negotiating parties has made a statement which is false in fact, but which he believes to be true and which is material to the contract, and during the course of the negotiation he discovers the falsity of that statement, he is under an obligation to correct his erroneous statement; although if he had said nothing he very likely might have been entitled to hold his tongue throughout". Then he adds what was material in that case and what is material in this case: "So, again, if a statement has been made which is true at the time, but which during the course of the negotiations becomes untrue, then the person who knows that it has become untrue is under an obligation to disclose to the other the change of circumstances".

Very much the same was said by the same learned judge, when a Lord Justice, in *In re Scottish Petroleum Co*. The facts there were very simple. A man took shares in a company on the faith of a statement that the company had four directors, one of whom was personally known to him and in whom he had confidence. That was a representation of the existing fact, perfectly true at the time. He applied for shares on the faith of that representation, but before that application was made the particular director, and one other had ceased to be directors and he claimed to be entitled to withdraw his application and he claimed an order rescinding the allotment of shares which had been made to him on his application. Fry LJ held that *prima facie* the applicant had a right to repudiate his bargain by reason of the change of circumstances. A complication arose because the allotment had been made and the applicant, instead of claiming at once to be relieved and to have his name taken from the list of members of the company, stood by for some time and then applied at a later stage. His claim failed because of that delay. Fry LJ says in terms that apart from that delay he would have had the right to be relieved. The learned Lord Justice quotes at length a very important passage from a judgment of Turner LJ in *Traill* v *Baring* in confirmation of his view. Perhaps I ought to read that passage. This is what Turner LJ says: "I take it to be quite clear, that if a person makes a representation by which he induces another to take a particular course, and the circumstances are afterwards altered to the knowledge of the party making the representation, but not to the knowledge of the party to whom the representation is made, and are so altered that the alteration of the circumstances may affect the course of conduct which may be pursued by the party to whom the representation is made, it is the imperative duty of the party who has made the representation to communicate to the party to whom the representation has been made the alteration of those circumstances; and that this Court will not hold the party to whom the representation has been made bound unless such a communication has been made". In these cases – I need not refer to others on this point – the position is based upon the duty to communicate the change of circumstances.

The matter, however, may be put in another way though with the same effect, and that is on the ground that a representation made as a matter of inducement to enter into a contract is to be treated as a continuing representation. That view of the position was put in *Smith* v *Kay* by Lord Cranworth. He says of a representation made in negotiation some time before the date of a contract: "It is a continuing representation. The representation does not end for ever when the representation is once made; it continues on. The pleader who drew the bill, or the young man himself, in stating his case, would say, Before I executed the bond I had been led to believe, and I therefore continued to believe, that it was executed pursuant to the arrangement."

The underlying principle is also stated again in a slightly different application by Lord Blackburn in *Brownlie* v *Campbell.* I need only quote a very short passage. Lord Blackburn says: ". . . when a statement or representation has been made in the *bona fide* belief that it is true, and the party who has made it afterwards comes to find out that it is untrue, and discovers what he should have said, he can no longer honestly keep up that silence on the subject after that has come to his knowledge, thereby allowing the other party to go on, and still more, inducing him to go on, upon a statement which was honestly made at the time when it was made, but which he has not now retracted when he has become aware that it can be no longer honestly persevered in". The learned Lord goes on to say that would be fraud, though nowadays the Court is more reluctant to use the word "fraud" and would not generally use the word "fraud" in that connection because the failure to disclose, though wrong and a breach of duty, may be due to inadvertence or a failure to realize that the duty rests upon the party who has made the representation not to leave the other party under an error when the representation has become falsified by a change of circumstances. This question only occurs when there is an interval of time between the time when the representation is made and when it is acted upon by the party to whom it was made, who either concludes the contract or does some similar decisive act; but the representation remains in effect and it is because that is so, and because the Court is satisfied in a proper case on the facts that it remained operative in the mind of the representee, that the Court holds that under such circumstances the represented should not be bound.

I have discussed the law at some little length because the cases to which I have referred show, I think, that this doctrine is not limited to a case of contracts *uberrimae fidei* or to any cases in which owing to confidential relationship there is a peculiar duty of disclosure; on the contrary, the passage which I read from the judgment of Fry J shows quite clearly that he distinguishes this consequence as one which arises in cases in which if the party was silent, there would be no duty to disclose at all . . .

On these grounds . . . I . . . have come to the conclusion that [With having] established [his] case . . . there ought to be a declaration rescinding the contract . . .'

Romer LJ: 'I agree. The only principle invoked by the appellants in this case is as follows. If A with a view to inducing B to enter into a contract makes a representation as to a material fact, then if at a later date and before the contract is actually entered into, owing to a change of circumstances, the representation then made would to the knowledge of A be untrue and B subsequently enters into the contract in ignorance of that change of circumstances and relying upon that representation, A cannot hold B to the bargain. There is ample authority for that statement and, indeed, I doubt myself whether any authority is necessary, it being, it seems to me, so obviously consistent with the plainest principles of equity.'

The representation must be one of fact

Opinion is not fact

Bisset v *Wilkinson*

[1927] AC 177 • Privy Council

Wilkinson agreed to buy a farm from Bisset. During the negotiations Bisset, who had only used a small part of the farm as a sheep farm, told Wilkinson 'that if the place was worked as I was working it . . . my idea was that it would carry two thousand sheep'. Before the court Bisset said 'I do not dispute that [Wilkinson] bought it believing it would carry the two thousand sheep'. Wilkinson claimed that Bisset's statement as to the carrying capacity of the farm was a misrepresentation and that, therefore, he was entitled to have the contract rescinded.

Lord Merrivale: 'Sheep-farming was the purpose for which the respondents purchased the lands of the plaintiff. One of them had no experience of farming. The other had been before the war in charge of sheep on an extensive sheep-farm carried on by his father, who had accompanied and advised him in his negotiation with the appellant and had carefully inspected the lands at Avondale. In the course of coming to his agreement with the respondents the appellant made statements as to the property which, in their defence and counter-claim, the respondents alleged to be misrepresentations . . .

In an action for rescission, as in an action for specific performance of an executory contract, when misrepresentation is the alleged ground of relief of the party who repudiates the contract, it is, of course, essential to ascertain whether that which is relied upon is a representation of a specific fact, or a statement of opinion, since an erroneous opinion stated by the party affirming the contract, though it may have been relied upon and have induced the contract on the part of the party who seeks rescission, gives no title to relief unless fraud is established. The application of this rule, however, is not always easy, as is illustrated in a good many reported cases, as well as in this. A representation of fact may be inherent in a statement of opinion and, at any rate, the existence of the opinion in the person stating it is a question of fact. In *Karberg's Case* Lindley LJ, in course of testing a representation which might have been, as it was said to be by interested parties, one of opinion or belief, used this inquiry: 'Was the statement of expectation a statement of things not really expected?' The Court of Appeal applied this test and rescinded the contract which was in question. In *Smith* v *Land and House Property Corporation* there came in question a vendor's description of the tenant of the property sold as "a most desirable tenant" – a statement of his opinion, as was argued on his behalf in an action to enforce the contract of sale. This description was held by the Court of Appeal to be a misrepresentation of fact, which, without proof of fraud, disentitled the vendor to specific performance of the contract of purchase. "It is often fallaciously assumed", said Bowen LJ, "that a statement of opinion cannot involve the statement of fact. In a case where the facts are equally well known to both parties, what one of them says to the other is frequently nothing but an expression of opinion. The statement of such opinion is in a sense a statement of fact, about the condition of the man's own mind, but only of an irrelevant fact, for it is of no consequence what the opinion is. But if the facts are not equally well known to both sides, then a statement of opinion by one who knows the facts best involves very often a statement of a material fact, for he impliedly states that he knows facts which justify his opinion." The kind of distinction which is in question is illustrated again in a well known case of *Smith* v *Chadwick*. There the words under consideration involved the inquiry in relation to the sale of an industrial concern whether a statement of "the present value of the turnover or output" was of necessity a statement of fact that the produce of the works was of the amount mentioned, or might be and was a statement that the productive power of the works was estimated at so much. The words were held to be capable of the second of these meanings. The decisive inquiries came to be: what meaning was actually conveyed to the party complaining; was he deceived, and, as the action was based on a charge of fraud, was the statement in question made fraudulently?

In the present case, as in those cited, the material facts of the transaction, the knowledge of the parties respectively, and their relative positions, the words of representation used, and the actual condition of the subject-matter spoken of, are relevant to the two inquiries necessary to be made: What was the meaning of the representation? Was it true?

In ascertaining what meaning was conveyed to the minds of the now respondents by the appellant's statement as to the two thousand sheep, the most material fact to be remembered is that, as both parties were aware, the appellant had not and, so far as appears, no other person had at any time carried on sheep-farming upon the unit of land in question. That land as a distinct holding had never constituted a sheep-farm. The two blocks comprised in it differed substantially in character. Hogan's block was described by one of the respondents' witnesses as "better land". "It might carry", he said, "one sheep or perhaps two or even three sheep to the acre". He estimated the carrying capacity of the land generally as little more than half a sheep to the acre. And Hogan's land had been allowed to deteriorate during several years before the respondents purchased. As was said by Sim J: "In ordinary circumstances, any statement made by an owner who has been occupying his own farm as to its carrying capacity would be regarded as a statement of fact . . . This, however, is not such a case. The defendants knew all about Hogan's block and knew also what sheep the farm was carrying when they inspected it. In these circumstances . . . the defendants were not justified in regarding anything said by the plaintiff as to the carrying capacity as being anything more than an expression of his opinion on the subject." In this view of the matter their Lordships concur.

Whether the appellant honestly and in fact held the opinion which he stated remained to be considered. This involved examination of the history and condition of the property. If a reasonable man with the appellant's knowledge could not have come to the conclusion he stated, the description of that conclusion as an opinion would not necessarily protect him against rescission for misrepresentation. But what was actually the capacity in competent hands of the land the respondents purchased had never been, and never was, practically ascertained. The respondents, after two years' trial of sheep-farming, under difficulties caused in part by their inexperience, found themselves confronted by a fall in the values of sheep and wool which would have left them losers if they could have carried three thousand sheep. As is said in the judgment of Ostler J: "Owing to sheep becoming practically valueless, they reduced their flock and went in for cropping and dairy-farming in order to make a living".

The opinions of experts and of their neighbours, on which the respondents relied, were met by the appellant with evidence of experts admitted to be equally competent and upright with those of his opponents, and his own practical experience upon part of the land, as to which his testimony was unhesitatingly accepted by the judge of first instance. It is of dominant importance that Sim J negatived the respondents' charge of fraud.

After attending to the close and very careful examination of the evidence which was made by learned counsel for each of the parties their Lordships entirely concur in the view which was expressed by the learned judge who heard the case. The defendants failed to prove that the farm if properly managed was not capable of carrying two thousand sheep.'

A statement of opinion can constitute a representation of fact

Smith v Land and House Property Corporation

(1884) 28 ChD 7 • Court of Appeal

Smith advertised an hotel for sale. It was described as 'now held by a very desirable tenant, Mr Frederick Fleck, for an unexpired term of twenty-eight years, at a rent of

£400 per annum'. In fact Fleck, who had been a tenant from 1880, had paid no rent until January 1882. Further, Fleck had only paid part of the last quarter's rent and then only under threat of distress. On discovering the true character of Fleck the Land and House Property Corporation, who had agreed to buy the hotel, refused to complete. Smith sued them for specific performance and the Land and House Property Corporation claimed that the contract should be rescinded on the ground of Smith's misrepresentation as to the character of Fleck.

Bowen LJ: '. . . The action is by vendors for specific performance, and the purchasers allege that there is in the particulars a misrepresentation which disentitles the Plaintiffs to specific performance. To sustain this defence the Defendants must prove that there was a material misrepresentation, and that they entered into the contract on the faith of the representation.

Was there then a misrepresentation of a specific fact? This partly depends on the question, whether on the construction of the particulars, what they say as to Fleck is a representation of a specific fact, a question which the Court of Appeal has the same means of deciding as the Judge in the Court below. Whether the purchasers relied upon it is a question of fact which the Judge of the Court below had better means of deciding than we have, for he saw and heard the witnesses.

In considering whether there was a misrepresentation, I will first deal with the argument that the particulars only contain a statement of opinion about the tenant. It is material to observe that it is often fallaciously assumed that a statement of opinion cannot involve the statement of a fact. In a case where the facts are equally well known to both parties, what one of them says to the other is frequently nothing but an expression of opinion. The statement of such opinion is in a sense a statement of a fact, about the condition of the man's own mind, but only of an irrelevant fact, for it is of no consequence what the opinion is. But if the facts are not equally known to both sides, then a statement of opinion by the one who knows the facts best involves very often a statement of a material fact, for he impliedly states that he knows facts which justify his opinion. Now a landlord knows the relations between himself and his tenant, other persons either do not know them at all or do not know them equally well, and if the landlord says that he considers that the relations between himself and his tenant are satisfactory, he really avers that the facts peculiarly within his knowledge are such as to render that opinion reasonable. Now are the statements here statements which involve such a representation of material facts? They are statements on a subject as to which *prima facie* the vendors know everything and the purchasers nothing. The vendors state that the property is let to a most desirable tenant, what does that mean? I agree that it is not a guarantee that the tenant will go on paying his rent, but it is to my mind a guarantee of a different sort, and amounts at least to an assertion that nothing has occurred in the relations between the landlords and the tenant which can be considered to make the tenant an unsatisfactory one. That is an assertion of a specific fact. Was it a true assertion? Having regard to what took place between Lady Day and Midsummer, I think that it was not. On the 25 March, a quarter's rent became due. On 1 May, it was wholly unpaid and a distress was threatened. The tenant wrote to ask for time. The Plaintiffs replied that the rent could not be allowed to remain over Whitsuntide. The tenant paid on 6 May £30, on 13 June £40, and the remaining £30 shortly before the auction. Now could it at the time of the auction, be said that nothing had occurred to make Fleck an undesirable tenant? In my opinion a tenant who had paid his last quarter's rent by driblets under pressure must be regarded as an undesirable tenant.

Treating this then as a misrepresentation, did it induce the purchasers to buy? It appears to me that it is in every case a question of fact whether a person is induced to buy by a particular representation. We may obtain valuable hints from reported cases, but none of the cases appear to me to impugn the proposition that the question is one of fact to be decided on the circumstances of each particular case. A representation in the particulars must be taken as made for the purpose of influencing the purchaser's mind. Then did the purchaser rely upon it? I cannot quite agree with the remark of the late Master of the Rolls in *Redgrave* v *Hurd* that if a material representation calculated to induce a person to enter into a contract is made to him it is an inference of law that he was induced by the representations to enter into it, and I think that probably his Lordship hardly intended to go so far as that, though there may be strong reason for drawing, such an inference as an inference of fact. But here we are not left to inference. The chairman of the company was called and swore in the most distinct and positive way that it did influence him, and that but for the representation he would not have purchased. The Judge was at liberty to disbelieve him, but I see no reason why he was bound so to do. His evidence was not shaken on cross-examination, and the Judge believed him. He uses the very argument that the property had been examined on behalf of the company as strengthening the statement that the company relied on the representation, for he says the report of the secretary was so unfavourable that but for the representation as to the tenant they would not have bought. *Redgrave* v *Hurd* shews that a person who has made a misrepresentation cannot escape by saying, "You had means of information, and if you had been careful you would not have been misled". It was urged that Alderman Knight would not have relied on the representation had he not put on it a construction that it will not bear, viz, that it was a guarantee that the tenant would go on paying the rent. I do not think that he understood it so. I think he merely understood it as a representation that, so far as the vendors knew, the tenant was likely to go on paying the rent for the rest of the term. If we had merely to deal with the evidence of Alderman Knight on paper, I should not feel quite satisfied that we ought to treat it as satisfactory, but as the Judge who heard and saw him was satisfied, I think that we ought not to differ from his conclusion.'

In the above case the 'opinion' was based on existing fact – that the rent had not been paid – and that opinion could not have been logically reached from those facts.

Advertising 'puffs' are not representations of fact

Dimmock v *Hallett*

(1866) LR 2 Ch App 21 • Chancery Appeals

The facts are stated above (p 323).

The particulars of sale described the estate as 'fertile and improvable land'.

Turner LJ: 'The purchaser further grounds his case on misrepresentation in the particulars. Some of the instances alleged appear to me to be unimportant. Thus I think that a mere general statement that land is fertile and improvable, whereas part of it has been abandoned as useless, cannot, except in extreme cases – as, for instance, where a considerable part is covered with water, or otherwise irreclaimable – be considered such a misrepresentation as to entitle a purchaser to be discharged. In the present case, I think the statement is to be looked at as a mere flourishing description by an auctioneer.'

Expression of intention

An expression of future intention is not a representation of existing fact. If, therefore, the expressed intention is not followed through then generally an action for misrepresentation will not succeed. If, however, the person expressing his future intention knows at the time of making the statement that he has no real intention to do that thing then this will amount to a misrepresentation.

Edgington v *Fitzmaurice*
(1885) 29 ChD 459 • Court of Appeal

The directors of a company issued a prospectus inviting subscriptions for debentures, and stating that the objects of the issue of debentures were '1. To enable the society to complete the present alterations and additions to the buildings and to purchase their own horses and vans, whereby a large saving will be effected in the cost of transport; and 2. To further develop the arrangements at present existing for the direct supply of cheap fish from the coast, which are still in their infancy.' However, the real object of the issue of debentures was to pay off pressing liabilities of the company, and not to complete the buildings or to purchase horses and vans or to develop the business of the company. On the strength of the prospectus (and also on his own mistaken belief that the debentures would give him a charge on the company) Edgington bought shares in the company. The company having become insolvent, Edgington brought an action against the directors of the company asking for the repayment by them of a sum of £1500 advanced by him on debentures of the company, on the ground that he was induced to advance the money by the fraudulent misrepresentations of the defendants.

The issues before the court were firstly, whether the directors had made a fraudulent misrepresentation of fact or had merely given an opinion of how the money raised by the issue of the debentures was to be used, and, secondly, whether the fact that Edgington had misled himself meant that the directors had not induced him to enter into the contract.

Bowen LJ: 'This is an action for deceit, in which the Plaintiff complains that he was induced to take certain debentures by the misrepresentations of the Defendants, and that he sustained damage thereby. The loss which the Plaintiff sustained is not disputed. In order to sustain his action he must first prove that there was a statement as to facts which was false; and secondly, that it was false to the knowledge of the Defendants, or that they made it not caring whether it was true or false. For it is immaterial whether they made the statement knowing it to be untrue, or recklessly, without caring whether it was true or not, because to make a statement recklessly for the purpose of influencing another person is dishonest. It is also clear that it is wholly immaterial with what object the lie is told. That is laid down in Lord Blackburn's judgment in *Smith* v *Chadwick*, but it is material that the defendant should intend that it should be relied on by the person to whom he makes it. But, lastly, when you have proved that the statement was false, you must further shew that the plaintiff has acted upon it and has sustained damage by so doing: you must shew that the statement was either the sole cause of the plaintiff's act, or materially contributed to his so acting. So the law is laid down in *Clarke* v *Dickson*, and that is the law which we have now to apply . . .

But when we come to the third alleged misstatement I feel that the Plaintiff's case is made out. I mean the statement of the objects for which the money was to be raised. These were stated to be to complete the alterations and additions to the buildings to purchase horses and vans, and to develop the supply of fish. A mere suggestion of possible purposes to which a portion of the money might be applied would not have formed a basis for an action of deceit. There must be a misstatement of an existing fact: but the state of a man's mind is as much a fact as the state of his digestion. It is true that it is very difficult to prove what the state of a man's mind at a particular time is, but if it can be ascertained it is as much a fact as anything else. A misrepresentation as to the state of a man's mind is, therefore, a misstatement of fact. Having applied as careful consideration to the evidence as I could, I have reluctantly come to the conclusion that the true objects of the Defendants in raising the money were not those stated in the circular. I will not go through the evidence, but looking only to the cross-examination of the Defendants, I am satisfied that the objects for which the loan was wanted were misstated by the Defendants, I will not say knowingly, but so recklessly as to be fraudulent in the eye of the law.

Then the question remains – Did this misstatement contribute to induce the Plaintiff to advance his money. Mr Davey's argument has not convinced me that they did not. He contended that the Plaintiff admits that he would not have taken the debentures unless he had thought they would give him a charge on the property, and therefore he was induced to take them by his own mistake, and the misstatement in the circular was not material. But such misstatement was material if it was actively present to his mind when he decided to advance his money. The real question is, what was the state of the Plaintiff's mind, and if his mind was disturbed by the misstatement of the Defendants, and such disturbance was in part the cause of what he did, the mere fact of his also making a mistake himself could make no difference . . .'

The representation must be addressed to the party misled

Peek v *Gurney*

(1873) LR 6 HL 377 • House of Lords

A company issued a prospectus in July 1865 to the general public inviting them to subscribe for shares in the company. The prospectus contained material misrepresentations. Peek, who was not an original allottee, bought his shares in the company on the stock market in October and December 1865. The company having gone into liquidation, Peek became liable as a contributory and paid £100 000 on his shares in the winding up. Peek sought an indemnity from the directors of the company on the ground that their misrepresentations in the prospectus had caused him to buy the shares.

The issue before the court was whether the prospectus was addressed to Peek or only to the original allottees of the company; viz did the directors of the company intend the prospectus only to invite persons to become allottees of the shares?

Lord Chelmsford: 'The last question to be considered is, whether the Appellant, who alleges that he purchased his shares upon the faith of the prospectus, has a remedy against the Respondents for the misrepresentations which it contains. The Appellant contends that the prospectus being addressed to the public for the purpose of inducing them to join the proposed company, any one of the public who is led by it to take shares, whether originally as an allottee, or by purchase of allotted shares upon the market, is entitled to relief against the persons who issued the prospectus. The Respondents on the other hand insist that the prospectus, not being an invitation to the public ultimately to become holders of shares, but to join the company at once by obtaining allotments of shares, those only who were drawn in by the misrepresentations in the prospectus to become allottees, can have a remedy against the Respondents . . .

But the learned counsel for the Appellant, not denying the original purpose of the prospectus, contended, upon the authority of decided cases, that the prospectus, having reached the hands of the Appellant, and he, relying upon the truth of the statement it contained, having been induced to purchase shares, the Respondents were liable as for a misrepresentation made to him personally . . .

. . . It appears to me that there must be something to connect the directors making the representation with the party complaining that he has been deceived and injured by it; as in *Scott* v *Dixon*, by selling a report containing the misrepresentations complained of to a person who afterwards purchases shares upon the faith of it, or as suggested in *Gerhard* v *Bates*, by delivering the fraudulent prospectus to a person who thereupon becomes a purchaser of shares, or by making an allotment of shares to a person who has been induced by the prospectus to apply for such allotment. In all these cases the parties in one way or other are brought into direct communication; and in an action the misrepresentation would be properly alleged to have been made by the Defendant to the Plaintiff; but the purchaser of shares in the market upon the faith of a prospectus which he has not received from those who are answerable for it, cannot by action upon it so connect himself with them as to render them liable to him for the misrepresentations contained in it, as if it had been addressed personally to himself. I therefore think that the Appellant cannot make the Respondents responsible to him for the loss he has sustained by trusting to the prospectus issued by them inviting the public to apply for allotments of shares . . .

The representation must induce the contract

Misrepresentation need not be sole inducement. See *Edgington* v *Fitzmaurice* above (p 332).

Opportunities for inspection

The mere fact that the party misled has had the opportunity of investigating and ascertaining whether the representation is true or false will not necessarily deprive him of his right to allege that he was deceived by it.

Redgrave v Hurd

(1881) 20 ChD 1 • Court of Appeal

Redgrave, an elderly solicitor, advertised for a partner 'who would not object to purchase advertiser's suburban residence, suitable for a family, value £1600'. Hurd answered the advertisement and enquired as to the income of the practice. Redgrave told him that the business brought in about £300 per year and showed him receipts amounting to about £200. When Hurd asked how the remaining £100 was made up Redgrave showed him a number of papers which he said related to other business not included in the summaries. These papers, which Hurd did not examine, showed only a most trifling amount of business. Hurd shortly afterwards signed an agreement to purchase the house for £1600, and paid a deposit. Hurd took possession, but finding that the business was worthless, refused to complete. Redgrave brought an action for specific performance against Hurd. Hurd put in a defence, in which he disputed the right to specific performance on the ground of misrepresentations as to the business, and by counter-claim claimed on the same ground to have the contract rescinded, and to have damages on the ground of the expenses he had been put to and the loss incurred by giving up his own practice.

The issue before the court was whether Hurd could be said to have relied on Redgrave's representation as to the income of the practice since he had the means of discovering, and might, with reasonable diligence, have discovered, that Redgrave's representation was untrue.

Sir George Jessel MR: '. . . As regards the rescission of a contract, there was no doubt a difference between the rules of Courts of Equity and the rules of Courts of Common Law – a difference which of course has now disappeared by the operation of the Judicature Act, which makes the rules of equity prevail. According to the decisions of Courts of Equity it was not necessary, in order to set aside a contract obtained by material false representation, to prove that the party who obtained it knew at the time when the representation was made that it was false. It was put in two ways, either of which was sufficient. One way of putting the case was, "A man is not to be allowed to get a benefit from a statement which he now admits to be false. He is not to be allowed to say, for the purpose of civil jurisdiction, that when he made it he did not know it to be false; he ought to have found that out before he made it." The other way of putting it was this: "Even assuming that moral fraud must be shewn in order to set aside a contract, you have it where a man, having obtained a beneficial contract by a statement which he now knows to be false, insists upon keeping that contract. To do so is a moral delinquency: no man ought to seek to take advantage of his own false statements." The rule in equity was settled, and it does not matter on which of the two grounds it was rested. As regards the rule of Common Law there is no doubt it was not quite so wide. There were, indeed, cases in which, even at Common Law, a contract could be rescinded for misrepresentation, although it could not be shewn that the person making it knew the representation to be false. They are variously stated, but I think, according to the later decisions, the statement must have been made recklessly and without care, whether it was true or false, and not with the belief that it was true. But, as I have said, the doctrine in equity was settled beyond controversy, and it is enough to refer to the judgment of Lord Cairns in the *Reese River Silver Mining Company* v *Smith*, in which he lays it down in the way which I have stated.

There is another proposition of law of very great importance which I think it is necessary for me to state, because, with great deference to the very learned Judge from whom this appeal comes, I think it is not quite accurately stated in his judgment. If a man is induced to enter into a contract by a false representation it is not a sufficient answer to him to say, "If you had used due diligence you would have found out that the statement was untrue. You had the means afforded you of discovering its falsity, and did not choose to avail yourself of them." I take it to be a settled doctrine of equity, not only as regards specific performance but also as regards rescission, that this is not an answer unless there is such delay as constitutes a defence under the *Statute of Limitations*. That, of course, is quite a different thing. Under the statute delay deprives a man of his right to rescind on the ground of fraud, and the only question to be considered is from what time the delay is to be reckoned. It had been decided, and the rule was adopted by the statute, that the delay counts from the time when by due diligence the fraud might have been discovered. Nothing can be plainer, I take it, on the authorities in equity than that the effect of false representation is not got rid of on the ground that the person to whom it was made has been guilty of negligence. One of the most familiar instances in modern times is where men issue a prospectus in which they make false statements of the contracts made before the formation of a company, and then say that the contracts themselves may be inspected at the offices of the solicitors. It has always been held that those who accepted those false statements as true were not deprived of their remedy merely because they neglected to go and look at the contracts. Another instance with which we are familiar is where a vendor makes a false statement as to the contents of a lease, as for instance, that it contains no covenant preventing the carrying on of the trade which the purchaser is known by the vendor to be desirous of carrying on upon the property. Although the lease itself might be produced at the sale, or might have been open to the inspection of the purchaser long previously to the sale, it has been repeatedly held that the vendor cannot be allowed to say, "You were not entitled to give credit to my statement". It is not sufficient, therefore, to say that the purchaser had the opportunity of investigating the real state of the case, but did not avail himself of that opportunity. It has been apparently supposed by the learned Judge in the Court below that the case of *Attwood* v *Small* conflicts with that proposition. He says this: "He inquired into it to a certain extent, and if he did that carelessly and inefficiently it is his own fault. As in *Attwood* v *Small*, those directors and agents of the company who made ineffectual inquiry into the business which was to be sold to the company were nevertheless held by their investigation to have bound the company, so here, I think, the Defendant who made a cursory investigation into the position of things on the 17th of February must be taken to have accepted the statements which were in those papers." I think that those remarks are inaccurate in law, and are not borne out by the case to which the learned Judge referred . . .

. . . In no way, as it appears to me, does the decision, or any of the grounds of decision, in *Attwood* v *Small*, support the proposition that it is a good defence to an action for rescission of a contract on the ground of fraud that the man who comes to set aside the contract inquired to a certain extent, but did it carelessly and inefficiently, and would, if he had used reasonable diligence, have discovered the fraud.

. . . Then the common case of the Plaintiff and the Defendant is that in answer to an inquiry from the Defendant, the Plaintiff said there was other business which was not entered upon those papers. Now that inquiry as I understand it was this, "You were doing £300 a year, you shew in those papers only £200 a year, where is the rest?" And the answer was, "Oh, there is a lot of papers here containing business which will account for the rest". Well, it appears to me, that that being the common case of both parties, it shews that Hurd, though still relying on the representation that the business was at least £300 a year, when he found that the papers shewed only a gross £200 a year, wanted to know where the business was that made up the £300 a year, and he is told, "Oh there are a lot of papers there; I have not made out my bills of costs fully, but you will find the business if you look through those papers"; but he did not look through them. The learned Judge continues: "I cannot attribute much weight to that other business, and for this reason, that in my judgment if the Defendant had meant to rely upon this extraneous business, which was not mentioned in the papers, he would have made some inquiry about it". I am sorry to say I differ from every word of that. The Defendant did make an inquiry. All that the Plaintiff had prepared for him were these summaries. He says, "Where is the rest of the business?" "Oh it is in that parcel of papers." How could the Defendant make out bills of costs from the parcel of papers? He could do nothing but rely on the Plaintiff's statement that the parcel of papers did contain the business. Then the learned Judge goes on to say: "According to the conclusion which I come to upon the evidence, the books were there before the Defendant, and although he did not trouble to look into them he had the opportunity of doing so. In my judgment if he had intended to rely upon that parol representation of business beyond that which appeared in the papers, having the materials before him, he would have made some inquiry into it. But he did nothing of the sort." Now in that respect I am sorry to say that the learned Judge was not correct. There were no books which shewed the business done. The Plaintiff did not keep any such books, and had nothing but his diaries, and some letter books; and therefore, it is a mistake to suppose that there were any books before the Defendant which he could look into to ascertain the correctness of the statements made by the Plaintiff; and the whole foundation of the judgment on this part of the case, even if it had been well founded in law, fails in fact, because the Defendant was not guilty of negligence in not doing that which it was impossible to do, no books being in existence which would shew the amount of business done. Then the learned Judge continues: "He did nothing of the sort: I think the true result of the evidence is this, that the Defendant thought that if he could have even such a nucleus of business as these papers disclosed, he could by the energy and skill which he possessed make himself good business in Birmingham". Then that being so the learned Judge came to the conclusion either that the Defendant did not rely on the statement, or that if he did rely upon it he had shewn such negligence as to deprive him of his title to relief from this Court. I have already said, the latter proposition is in my opinion not founded in law, and the former part is not founded in fact; I think also it is not founded in law, for when a person makes a material representation to another to induce him to enter into a contract, and the other enters into that contract, it is not sufficient to say that the party to whom the representation is made does not prove that he entered into the contract, relying upon the representation. If it is a material representation calculated to induce him to enter into the contract, it is an inference of law that he was induced by the representation to enter into it, and in order to take away his title to be relieved from the contract on the ground that the representation was untrue, it must be shewn either that he had knowledge of the facts contrary to the representation, or that he stated in terms, or shewed clearly by his conduct, that he did not rely on the representation. If you tell a man, "You may enter into partnership with me, my business is bringing in between £300 and £400 a year", the man who makes that representation must know that it is a material inducement to the other to enter into the partnership, and you cannot investigate as to whether it was more or less probable that the inducement would operate on the mind of the party to whom the representation was made. Where you have neither evidence that he knew facts to shew that the statement was untrue, nor that he said or did anything to shew that he did not actually rely upon the statement, the inference remains that he did so rely, and the statement being a material statement, its being untrue is a sufficient ground for rescinding the contract. For these reasons I am of opinion that the judgment of the learned Judge must be reversed and the appeal allowed.

As regards the form of the judgment, as the appellant succeeds on the counter-claim, I think it would be safer to make an order both in the action and the counter-claim, rescinding the contract and ordering the deposit to be returned. As I have already said, it is not a case in which damages should be given.'

NB: everything above relates to *all* types of misrepresentation.

EFFECT OF MISREPRESENTATION

A contract is *voidable* (as opposed to *void*) at the option of the misled person.

A person who has been misled can:

- refuse to carry out his undertaking;
- resist any claim for specific performance;
- if necessary have the contract set aside by means of the equitable remedy of rescission.

In addition the misled person may be able to claim damages.

Further, if misrepresentation is:

- *fraudulent*, the misled person can sue for damages for deceit;
- *negligent*, the misled person can sue for damages but a defence is available.

What follows are the three types of misrepresentation – *fraudulent, negligent* and *innocent misrepresentation* – and the remedies available to the misled party depending on which type of misrepresentation has been made.

FRAUDULENT MISREPRESENTATION

What constitutes a fraud?

Derry v *Peek*

(1889) 14 App Cas 337 • House of Lords

A special Act provided that a tramway company might be permitted to move its carriages by steam power if the Board of Trade gave its permission. Mistakenly thinking they had the right to use steam power instead of horses, the directors of the tramway company issued a prospectus which stated that they had the right to use steam power instead of horses. Peek took shares on the faith of this statement. Afterwards the Board of Trade refused to let the company use steam power and the company was wound up. Peek brought an action of deceit against the directors founded upon the false statement contained in the prospectus.

Lord Herschell: 'My Lords, in the statement of claim in this action [Peek] alleges that the appellants made in a prospectus issued by them certain statements which were untrue, that they well knew that the facts were not as stated in the prospectus, and made the representations fraudulently, and with the view to induce the plaintiff to take shares in the company.

. . . I think the authorities establish the following propositions: First, in order to sustain an action of deceit, there must be proof of fraud, and nothing short of that will suffice. Secondly, fraud is proved when it is shewn that a false representation has been made (1) knowingly, or (2) without belief in its truth, or (3) recklessly, careless whether it be true or false. Although I have treated the second and third as distinct cases, I think the third is but an instance of the second, for one who makes a statement under such circumstances can have no real belief in the truth of what he states. To prevent a false statement being fraudulent, there must, I think, always be an honest belief in its truth. And this probably covers the whole ground, for one who knowingly alleges that which is false, has obviously no such honest belief. Thirdly, if fraud be proved, the motive of the person guilty of it is immaterial. It matters not that there was no intention to cheat or injure the person to whom the statement was made . . .

In my opinion making a false statement through want of care falls far short of, and is a very different thing from, fraud, and the same may be said of a false representation honestly believed though on insufficient grounds . . . But the whole current of authorities, with which I have so long detained your Lordships, shews to my mind conclusively that fraud is essential to found an action of deceit, and that it cannot be maintained where the acts proved cannot properly be so termed . . . But for the reasons I have given I am unable to hold that anything less than fraud will render directors or any other persons liable to an action of deceit . . .

It now remains for me to apply what I believe to be the law to the facts of the present case. The charge against the defendants is that they fraudulently represented that by the special Act of Parliament which the company had obtained they had a right to use steam or other mechanical power instead of horses. The test which I propose employing is to inquire whether the defendants knowingly made a false statement in this respect, or whether, on the contrary, they honestly believed what they stated to be a true and fair representation of the facts . . .

As I have said, Stirling J gave credit to these witnesses [the directors], and I see no reason to differ from him. What conclusion ought to be drawn from their evidence? I think they were mistaken in supposing that the consent of the Board of Trade would follow as a matter of course because they had obtained their Act. It was absolutely in the discretion of the Board whether such consent should be given. The prospectus was therefore inaccurate. But that is not the question. If they believed that the consent of the Board of Trade was practically concluded by the passing of the Act, has the plaintiff made out, which it was for him to do, that they have been guilty of a fraudulent misrepresentation? I think not. I cannot hold it proved as to any one of them that he knowingly made a false statement, or one which he did not believe to be true, or was careless whether what he stated was true or false. In short, I think they honestly believed that what they asserted was true, and I am of opinion that the charge of fraud made against them has not been established . . .

Adopting the language of Jessel MR in *Smith* v *Chadwick* I conclude by saying that on the whole I have come to the conclusion that the statement, "though in some respects inaccurate and not altogether free from imputation of carelessness, was a fair, honest and *bona fide* statement on the part of the defendants, and by no means exposes them to an action for deceit".'

Negligence does not amount to fraud

See *Derry* v *Peek* above (p 338).

Measure of damage for fraudulent misrepresentation

Damages are based on tort principles (out of pocket) not on contract principles (loss of profit).

Smith New Court Securities Ltd v Scrimgeour Vickers (Asset Management) Ltd

[1996] 4 All ER 769 • House of Lords

SNC purchased shares in Ferranti from SVAM, who acted as agents for Citibank, at 82.25p per share. SNC were originally only willing to pay 78p per share but were persuaded to pay the higher price by the fraudulent misrepresentation of SVAM that there was another buyer who was willing to pay more for the shares; there was, in fact, no such other buyer. The total price paid for the shares was £23 146 321. Soon after the purchase of the shares the share price slumped to 44p per share because of a fraud that had been perpetrated on Ferranti by a third party, Guerin; this fraud was unconnected with the share purchase. Having established there had been a fraudulent misrepresentation the issue before the House of Lords was the measure of damages payable to SNC.

Lord Browne-Wilkinson: 'The damages issue which is the subject matter of the appeal raises for decision for the first time in your Lordships' House the question of the correct measure of damages where a plaintiff has acquired property in reliance on a fraudulent misrepresentation made by the defendant . . .

. . . [T]he only claim by Smith has been for damages for deceit. Both before the trial judge, Chadwick J, and the Court of Appeal, Nourse, Rose and Hoffmann LJJ, the argument proceeded on the basis that, where a fraudulent misrepresentation has induced the plaintiff to enter into a contract of purchase, the measure of damages is, in general, the difference between the contract price and the true open market value of the property purchased, valued as at the date of the contract of purchase. This was the law as laid down in a series of cases decided at the end of the 19th century, usually in relation to shares purchased in reliance on a fraudulent prospectus: see *Twycross* v *Grant*; *Waddell* v *Blockey*; *Peek* v *Derry* and subsequently treated as settled law by the Court of Appeal in *McConnel* v *Wright*. It was common ground that there was one exception to this general rule: where the open market at the transaction date was a false market, in the sense that the price was inflated because of a misrepresentation made to the market generally by the defendant, the market value is not decisive: in such circumstances the "true" value as at the transaction date has to be ascertained but with the benefit of hindsight: *McConnel* v *Wright* . . .

As to the second rule referred to by the Court of Appeal – the rule requiring damages to be assessed as at the date of the transaction – Mr Grabiner, for Smith, submitted that the basis on which the 19th century cases were decided was erroneous and that later decisions show the right approach to the assessment of damages. I agree with those submissions and rather than consider the sterilities of the argument surrounding the 19th century cases proceed at once to consider the more modern law . . .

The decision which restated the law correctly is *Doyle* v *Olby (Ironmongers) Ltd* . . .

Doyle v *Olby (Ironmongers) Ltd* establishes four points. First, that the measure of damages where a contract has been induced by fraudulent misrepresentation is reparation for all the actual damage directly flowing from (i.e. caused by) entering into the transaction. Second, that in assessing such damages it is not an inflexible rule that the plaintiff must bring into account the value as at the transaction date of the asset acquired: although the point is not adverted to in the judgments, the basis on which the damages were computed shows that there can be circumstances in which it is proper to require a defendant only to bring into account the actual proceeds of the asset provided that he has acted reasonably in retaining it. Third, damages for deceit are not limited to those which were reasonably foreseeable. Fourth, the damages recoverable can include consequential loss suffered by reason of having acquired the asset.

In my judgment *Doyle* v *Olby (Ironmongers) Ltd* was rightly decided on all these points . . .

In sum, in my judgment the following principles apply in assessing the damages payable where the plaintiff has been induced by a fraudulent misrepresentation to buy property:

(1) The defendant is bound to make reparation for all the damage directly flowing from the transaction;

(2) although such damage need not have been foreseeable, it must have been directly caused by the transaction;

(3) in assessing such damage, the plaintiff is entitled to recover by way of damages the full price paid by him, but he must give credit for any benefits which he has received as a result of the transaction;

(4) as a general rule, the benefits received by him include the market value of the property acquired as at the date of acquisition; but such general rule is not to be inflexibly applied where to do so would prevent him obtaining full compensation for the wrong suffered;

(5) although the circumstances in which the general rule should not apply cannot be comprehensively stated, it will normally not apply where either (a) the misrepresentation has continued to operate after the date of the acquisition of the asset so as to induce the plaintiff to retain the asset or (b) the circumstances of the case are such that the plaintiff is, by reason of the fraud, locked into the property.

(6) In addition, the plaintiff is entitled to recover consequential losses caused by the transaction;

(7) the plaintiff must take all reasonable steps to mitigate his loss once he has discovered the fraud . . .

How then do those principles apply in the present case? First, there is no doubt that the total loss incurred by Smith was caused by the Roberts fraud, unless it can be said that Smith's own decision to retain the shares until after the revelation of the Guerin fraud was a causative factor. The Guerin fraud had been committed before Smith acquired the shares on 21 July 1989. Unknown to everybody, on that date the shares were already pregnant with disaster. Accordingly when, pursuant to the Roberts fraud, Smith acquired the Ferranti shares they were induced to purchase a flawed asset. This is not a case of the difficult kind that can arise where the depreciation in the asset acquired between the date of acquisition and the date of realisation may be due to factors affecting the market which have occurred after the date of the defendant's fraud. In the present case the loss was incurred by reason of the purchasing of the shares which were pregnant with the loss and that purchase was caused by the Roberts fraud.

Can it then be said that the loss flowed not from Smith's acquisition but from Smith's decision to retain the shares? In my judgment it cannot. The judge found that the shares were acquired as a market-making risk and at a price which Smith would only have paid for an acquisition as a market-making risk. As such, Smith could not dispose of them on 21 July 1989 otherwise than at a loss. Smith were in a special sense locked into the shares having bought them for a purpose and at a price which precluded them from sensibly disposing of them. It was not alleged or found that Smith acted unreasonably in retaining the shares for as long as they did or in realising them in the manner in which they did.

In the circumstances, it would not in my judgment compensate Smith for the actual loss they have suffered (i.e. the difference between the contract price and the resale price eventually realized) if Smith were required to give credit for the shares having a value of 78p on 21 July 1989. Having acquired the shares at 82p for stock Smith could not commercially have sold on that date at 78p. It is not realistic to treat Smith as having received shares worth 78p each when in fact, in real life, they could not commercially have sold or realised the shares at that price on that date. In my judgment, this is one of those cases where to give full reparation to Smith, the benefit which Smith ought to bring into account to be set against its loss for the total purchase price paid should be the actual resale price achieved by Smith when eventually the shares were sold . . .

For these reasons I would hold that the damages recoverable amount to £11 352 220 being the difference between the contract price and the amount actually realised by Smith on the resale of the shares. However, as there was no appeal by Smith against the judge's assessment of the damages at £10 764 005, Smith's claim must be limited to that latter amount. I would therefore allow the appeal and restore the judge's order.'

NEGLIGENT MISREPRESENTATION

Although this type of misrepresentation is commonly known as negligent misrepresentation it is more accurately and solemnly referred to as 'misrepresentation under *s 2(1) of the Misrepresentation Act 1967* '.

Misrepresentation Act 1967: Section 2(1) Damages for misrepresentation

(1) Where a person has entered into a contract after a misrepresentation has been made to him by another party thereto and as a result thereof he has suffered loss, then, if the person making the misrepresentation would be liable to damages in respect thereof had the misrepresentation been made fraudulently, that person shall be so liable notwithstanding that the misrepresentation was not made fraudulently, unless he proves that he had reasonable ground to believe and did believe up to the time the contract was made that the facts represented were true.

Howard Marine & Dredging Co Ltd v *Ogden & Sons (Excavations) Ltd*
[1978] 2 All ER 1134 • Court of Appeal

During negotiations between Ogden and Howard Marine, O'Loughlin, Howard Marine's marine manager, told Ogden that their barges would each carry about 1600 tonnes subject to various factors. Relying on this statement Ogden hired the two barges from Howard Marine. In fact the barges would only carry 1055 tonnes. In making his statement O'Loughlin was relying on the figure he remembered seeing in Lloyd's Register. In fact the figure in Lloyd's Register was wrong. The barges' own shipping documents, of which O'Loughlin had possession and had read, clearly showed that the barges would only carry 1055 tonnes. On discovering the misrepresentation Ogden refused to pay the hire and Howard Marine withdrew the barges and sued for the outstanding payments. Ogden counterclaimed and claimed damages under s 2(1) Misrepresentation Act 1967.

Bridge LJ: '. . . I will consider first the position under [s 2(1) of] the statute.

The first question then is whether Howards would be liable in damages in respect of Mr O'Loughlin's misrepresentation if it had been made fraudulently, that is to say, if he had known that it was untrue. An affirmative answer to that question is inescapable. The judge found in terms that what Mr O'Loughlin said about the capacity of the barges was said with the object of getting the hire contract for Howards, in other words with the intention that it should be acted on. This was clearly right. Equally clearly the misrepresentation was in fact acted on by Ogdens. It follows, therefore, on the plain language of the 1967 Act that, although there was no allegation of fraud, Howards must be liable unless they proved that Mr O'Loughlin had reasonable ground to believe what he said about the barges' capacity.

. . . If the representee proves a misrepresentation which, if fraudulent, would have sounded in damages, the onus passes immediately to the representor to prove that he had reasonable ground to believe the facts represented. In other words the liability of the representor does not depend on his being under a duty of care the extent of which may vary according to the circumstances in which the representation is made. In the course of negotiations leading to a contract the 1967 Act imposes an absolute obligation not to state facts which the representor cannot prove he had reasonable ground to believe.

. . . [I]t is to be assumed that Mr O'Loughlin was perfectly honest throughout. But the question remains whether his evidence, however benevolently viewed, is sufficient to show that he had an objectively reasonable ground to disregard the figure in the ship's documents and to prefer the Lloyd's Register figure. I think it is not . . . Accordingly I conclude that Howards failed to prove that Mr O'Loughlin had reasonable ground to believe the truth of his misrepresentation to [Ogden].'

Lord Denning MR (Dissenting): 'This enactment imposes a new and serious liability on anyone who makes a representation of fact in the course of negotiations for a contract If that representation turns out to be mistaken, then, however innocent he may be, he is just as liable as if he had made it fraudulently . . . [W]ith this Act he is made liable, unless he proves, and the burden is on him to prove, that he had reasonable ground to believe and did in fact believe that it was true.

Section 2(1) certainly applies to the representation made by Mr O'Loughlin on 11 July 1974 when he told Ogdens that each barge could carry 1600 tonnes. The judge found that it was a misrepresentation, that he said it with the object of getting the hire contract for Howards. They got it; and, as a result, Ogdens suffered loss. But the judge found that Mr O'Loughlin was not negligent, and so Howards were not liable for it.

The judge's finding was criticised before us, because he asked himself the question: was Mr O'Loughlin negligent? whereas he should have asked himself: did Mr O'Loughlin have reasonable ground to believe that the representation was true? I think that criticism is not fair to the judge. By the word "negligent" he was only using shorthand for the longer phrase contained in s 2(1) which he had before him. And the judge, I am sure, had the burden of proof in mind, for he had come to the conclusion that Mr O'Loughlin was not negligent. The judge said in effect: "I am satisfied that Mr O'Loughlin was not negligent"; and being so satisfied, the burden need not be further considered . . .

It seems to me that, when one examines the details, the judge's view was entirely justified. He found that Mr O'Loughlin's state of mind was this. Mr O'Loughlin had examined Lloyd's Register and had seen there that the deadweight capacity of each barge was 1800 tonnes. That figure stuck in his mind. The judge found that "the 1600 tonnes was arrived at by knocking off what he considered a reasonable margin for fuel, and so on, from the 1800 tonnes summer deadweight figure in Lloyd's Register, which was in the back of his mind". The judge said that Mr O'Loughlin had seen at some time the German shipping documents and had seen the deadweight figure of 1055.135 tonnes, but it did not register. All that was in his mind was the 1800 tonnes in Lloyd's Register which was regarded in shipping circles as the bible. That afforded reasonable ground for him to believe that the barges could each carry 1600 tonnes payload; and that is what Mr O'Loughlin believed.

So on this point, too, I do not think we should fault the judge. It is not right to pick his judgment to pieces, by subjecting it (or the shorthand note) to literal analysis. Viewing it fairly, the judge (who had s 2(1) in front of him) must have been of opinion that the burden of proof was discharged.'

Measure of damages

East v *Maurer*

[1991] 1 WLR 461 • Court of Appeal

Maurer sold one of two neighbouring hairdressing salons which he owned to East for £20 000. Maurer told East deliberately and falsely, before the sale of the business was agreed, that he would not work at the other salon except in cases of emergency. This statement was particularly important since it meant that his clientele would not follow him to the neighbouring business. After the sale was completed East discovered that Maurer was working full time at his other neighbouring business. East brought an action in deceit against Maurer. The trial judge awarded damages of £33 328 which included £15 000 for loss of profit. Maurer appealed against the award of damages for loss of profit.

The issue before the court was whether, in an action for deceit, damages could be awarded for loss of profit.

Beldam LJ: '[The judge's] award was made up in this way. First, he took the capital expenditure by taking the cost price of the business, £20,000, and deducting from it the amount realised on the sale, thus arriving at the figure of £12,500. Secondly, he awarded the plaintiffs the fees and expenses incurred by them in buying and selling the business, and in carrying out improvements in an attempt to make it profitable. The figures awarded there amounted in total to £2,390. Next, he awarded trading losses incurred during the 3¼ years during which the plaintiffs attempted to run the business. Those amounted to £2,438.

The next head of damages he awarded has led the defendants to appeal to this court against the amount of the damages. In addition to the sums already mentioned, he awarded the plaintiffs loss of profits during the 3¼-year period arriving at a figure of £15,000. Finally he awarded the figure of £1,000 as general damages for disappointment and inconvenience of the plaintiffs in their attempt to establish this business. It is against the award of £15,000 for loss of profit that the defendants now appeal . . .

That the measure of damages for the tort of deceit and for breach of contract are different, no longer needs support from authority. Damages for deceit are not awarded on the basis that the plaintiff is to be put in as good a position as if the statement had been true; they are to be assessed on a basis which would compensate the plaintiff for all the loss he has suffered, so far as money can do it.

This was confirmed in *Doyle* v *Olby (Ironmongers) Ltd*, to which both the judge and this court were referred and was a case in which the facts were similar to those of the present case. In the course of his judgment Lord Denning MR said:

"The second question is what is the proper measure of damages for fraud, as distinct from damages for breach of contract. It was discussed during the argument in *Hadley* v *Baxendale* . . . But in *McConnel* v *Wright*, Lord Collins MR pointed out the difference. It was an action for fraudulent statements in a prospectus whereby a man was induced to take up shares. Lord Collins said of the action for fraud: 'It is not an action for breach of contract, and, therefore, no damages in respect of prospective gains which the person contracting was entitled by his contract to expect to come in, but it is an action of tort – it is an action for a wrong done whereby the plaintiff was tricked out of certain money in his pocket, and, therefore, *prima facie*, the highest limit of his damages is the whole extent of his loss, and that loss is measured by the money which was in his pocket and is now in the pocket of the company.' But that statement was the subject of comment by Lord Atkin in *Clark* v *Urquhart*. He said: 'I find it difficult to suppose that there is any difference in the measure of damages in an action of deceit depending upon the nature of the transaction into which the plaintiff is fraudulently induced to enter. Whether he buys shares or buys sugar, whether he subscribes for shares, or agrees to enter into a partnership, or in any other way alters his position to his detriment, in principle, the measure of damages should be the same, and whether estimated by a jury or a judge. I should have thought it would be based on the actual damage directly flowing from the fraudulent inducement. The formula in *McConnel* v *Wright* may be correct or it may be expressed in too rigid terms.

I think that Lord Collins did express himself in too rigid terms. He seems to have overlooked consequential damages. On principle the distinction seems to be this: in contract, the defendant has made a promise and broken it. The object of damages is to put the plaintiff in as good a position, as far as money can do it, as if the promise had been performed. In fraud, the defendant has been guilty of a deliberate wrong by inducing the plaintiff to act to his detriment. The object of damages is to compensate the plaintiff for all the loss he has suffered, so far, again, as money can do it. In contract, the damages are limited to what may reasonably be supposed to have been in the contemplation of the parties. In fraud, they are not so limited. The defendant is bound to make reparation for all the actual damages directly flowing from the fraudulent inducement. The person who has been defrauded is entitled to say: 'I would not have entered into this bargain at all but for your representation. Owing to your fraud, I have not only lost all the money I paid you, but, what is more, I have been put to a large amount of extra expense as well and suffered this or that extra damages.' All such damages can be recovered: and it does not lie in the mouth of the fraudulent person to say that they could not reasonably have been foreseen. For instance, in this very case Mr Doyle has not only lost the money which he paid for the business, which he would never have done if there had been no fraud: he put all that money in and lost it; but also he has been put to expense and loss in trying to run a business which has turned out to be a disaster for him. He is entitled to damages for all his loss, subject, of course to giving credit for any benefit that he has received. There is nothing to be taken off in mitigation: for there is nothing more that he could have done to reduce his loss. He did all that he could reasonably be expected to do."

In the present case it seems to me that the difference can be put in this way. The first defendant did not warrant to the plaintiffs that all the customers with whom he had a professional rapport would remain customers of the salon at Exeter Road. He represented that he would not be continuing to practise as a stylist in the immediate area.

The observations of Lord Denning MR, to which I have referred, are supported by an earlier judgment of Dixon J in *Toteff* v *Antonas*, a decision of the High Court of Australia . . .

Mr Shawcross has pointed out that both in *Doyle* v *Olby (Ironmongers) Ltd* and in *Toteff* v *Antonas*, none of the judgments referred to loss of profit as a recoverable head of damage; it may well be that the facts of each of those cases and the period involved before the claims were made, may not have made loss of profit a considerable head of damage. But as to the statements of principle to which I have referred, it seems to me clear that there is no basis upon which one could say that loss of profits incurred whilst waiting for an opportunity to realise to its best advantage a business which has been purchased, are irrecoverable. It is conceded that losses made in the course of running the business of a company, are recoverable. If in fact the plaintiffs lost the profits which they could reasonably have expected from running a business in the area of a kind similar to the business in this case, I can see no reason why those do not fall within the words of Lord Atkin in *Clark* v *Urquhart*, "actual damage directly flowing from the fraudulent inducement".

So I consider that on the facts found by the judge in the present case, the plaintiffs did establish that they had suffered a loss due to the defendants' misrepresentation which arose from their inability to earn the profits in the business which they hoped to buy in the Bournemouth area.

I would therefore reject the submission of Mr Shawcross that loss of profits is not a recoverable head of damage in cases of this kind.

However, I am not satisfied that in arriving at the figure of £15,000 the judge approached the quantification of those damages on the correct basis . . .

It seems to me that he should have begun by considering the kind of profit which the second plaintiff might have made if the representation which induced her to buy the business at Exeter Road had not been made, and that involved considering the kind of profits which she might have expected to make in another hairdressing business bought for a similar sum. Mr Nicholson has argued that on the evidence of Mr Knowles, an experienced accountant, the judge could have arrived at the same or an equivalent figure on that basis. I do not agree. The judge left out of account the fact that the second plaintiff was moving into an entirely different area and one in which she was, comparatively speaking, a stranger. Secondly, that she was going to deal with a different clientele. Thirdly, that there were almost certainly in that area of Bournemouth other smart hairdressing salons which represented competition and which, in any event, if the first defendant had, as he had represented, gone to open a salon on the Continent, could have attracted the custom of his former clients.

The judge, as Mr Nicholson has pointed out, had two clear starting points. First, that any person investing £20,000 in a business would expect a greater return than if the sum was left safely in the bank or in a building society earning interest, and a reasonable figure for that at the rates then prevailing would have been at least £6,000. Secondly, that the salary of a hairdresser's assistant in the usual kind of establishment was at this time £40 per week and that the assistant could expect tips in addition. That would produce a figure of over £7,000, but the proprietor of a salon would clearly expect to earn more, having risked his money in the business. It seems to me that those are valid points from which to start to consider what would be a reasonable sum to award for loss of profits of a business of this kind. As was pointed out by Winn LJ, in *Doyle* v *Olby (Ironmongers) Ltd*, this is not a question which can be considered on a mathematical basis. It has to be considered essentially, in the round, making what he described as a "jury assessment". Taking all the factors into account, I think that the judge's figure was too high; for my part I would have awarded a figure of £10,000 for that head of damage, and to this extent I would allow the appeal.'

Royscot Trust Ltd v *Rogerson*

[1991] 3 All ER 294 • Court of Appeal

The facts are stated in the judgment of Balcombe LJ.

Balcombe LJ: 'The second defendant to the action and the appellant in this court. Maidenhead Honda Centre Ltd ("the dealer"), is a motor car dealer. At the beginning of

May 1987 the first defendant, Mr Andrew Jeffrey Rogerson ("the customer"), agreed with the dealer to buy on hire-purchase a second hand Honda Prelude motor car for the price of £7,600, of which a deposit of £1,200 was to be paid, leaving a balance of £6,400. The plaintiff and the respondent to this appeal, Royscot Trust Ltd ("the finance company"), is a company which finances hire-purchase sales. It does so in the usual way, that is by purchasing the car which is the subject of the sale from the dealer and then entering into a hire-purchase agreement with the customer.

The finance company has a policy that it will not accept a hire-purchase transaction unless the deposit paid represents at least 20 per cent of the total cash price. On 5 May 1987 the dealer submitted a proposal to the finance company in relation to the customer's proposed purchase of the car, by which the dealer represented to the finance company that the total cash price payable was £8,000 and that a deposit of £1,600 had been paid by the customer. It will be observed that the balance under these figures, £6,400, is the same as that which was truly payable by the customer. It is common ground that this was a misrepresentation and that in reliance upon it the finance company entered into a hire-purchase agreement with the customer dated 5 May 1987 under which the customer agreed to pay a total price (including the deposit) of £9,878.92, of which the balance of £8,278.92 was to be paid by 36 monthly instalments of £229.97. At no time has it been pleaded or claimed by the finance company that in making this representation the dealer was acting fraudulently. Accordingly, in making its claim for damages the finance company relies on innocent misrepresentation under s 2(1) of the Misrepresentation Act 1967. In fact the customer paid the dealer a deposit of £1,200, and the finance company paid the dealer the sum of £6,400.

The customer paid to the finance company under the hire-purchase agreement monthly instalments amounting in all to £2,774.76. In August 1987 the customer dishonestly sold the car to a private purchaser for the sum of £7,200; that purchaser acquired a good title to the car under the provisions of the Hire-Purchase Act 1964. The customer told the finance company in August 1988 that he had wrongfully disposed of the car a year previously and on 28 September 1988 made his last monthly payment to the finance company. The car was then said to be worth at least £6,325.

On 22 September 1989 the finance company issued proceedings against both the customer and the dealer in the Uxbridge County Court and on 23 November 1989 entered judgment in default against both defendants for damages to be assessed. It was that assessment of damages which came before Judge Barr on 22 February 1990.

As against the customer the judge assessed the finance company's damages as £5,504.16 (the balance of £8,278.92 less the instalments paid of £2,774.76), and judgment in that sum was entered against him. There has been no appeal against that judgment.

Before the judge, counsel for the finance company submitted that its loss was the difference between the sum of £6,400 which it paid to the dealer and the sum of £2,774.76 paid by the customer, viz £3,625.24 . . .

So I turn to the issue on this appeal which the dealer submits raises a pure point of law: where (a) a motor dealer innocently misrepresents to a finance company the amount of the sale price of, and the deposit paid by the intended purchaser of, the car, and (b) the finance company is thereby induced to enter into a hire-purchase agreement with the purchaser which it would not have done if it had known the true facts, and (c) the purchaser thereafter dishonestly disposes of the car and defaults on the hire-purchase agreement, can the finance company recover all or part of its losses on the hire-purchase agreement from the motor dealer?

The finance company's cause of action against the dealer is based on s 2(1) of the Misrepresentation Act 1967 . . .

As a result of some dicta by Lord Denning MR in two cases in the Court of Appeal – *Gosling* v *Anderson* and *Jarvis* v *Swans Tours Ltd* – and the decision at first instance in *Watts* v *Spence* there was some doubt whether the measure of damages for an innocent misrepresentation giving rise to a cause of action under the Act of 1967 was the tortious measure, so as to put the representee in the position in which he would have been if he had never entered into the contract, or the contractual measure, so as to put the representee in the position in which he would have been if the misrepresentation had been true, and thus in some cases give rise to a claim for damages for loss of bargain. Lord Denning MR's remarks in *Gosling* v *Anderson* were concerned with an amendment to a pleading, while his remarks in *Jarvis* v *Swans Tours Ltd* were clearly *obiter*. *Watts* v *Spence* was disapproved by this court in *Sharneyford Supplies Ltd* v *Edge*. However, there is now a number of decisions which make it clear that the tortious measure of damages is the true one. Most of these decisions are at first instance . . . One at least, *Chesneau* v *Interhome Ltd*, is a decision of this court. The claim was one under s 2(1) of the Act of 1967 and the appeal concerned the assessment of damages. In the course of his judgment Eveleigh LJ said:

> ". . . [damages] should be assessed in a case like the present one on the same principles as damages are assessed in tort. The subsection itself says: '. . . if the person making the misrepresentation would be liable to damages in respect thereof had the misrepresentation been made fraudulently, that person shall be so liable . . .' By 'so liable' I take it to mean liable as he would be if the misrepresentation had been made fraudulently."

In view of the wording of the subsection it is difficult to see how the measure of damages under it could be other than the tortious measure and, despite the initial aberrations referred to above, that is now generally accepted. Indeed counsel before us did not seek to argue the contrary.

The first main issue before us was: accepting that the tortious measure is the right measure, is it the measure where the tort is that of fraudulent misrepresentation, or is it the measure where the tort is negligence at common law? The difference is that in cases of fraud a plaintiff is entitled to any loss which flowed from the defendant's fraud, even if the loss could not have been foreseen: see *Doyle* v *Olby (Ironmongers) Ltd.* In my judgment the wording of the subsection is clear: the person making the innocent misrepresentation shall be "so liable", i.e. liable to damages as if the representation had been made fraudulently. This was the conclusion to which Walton J came in *F & B Entertainments Ltd* v *Leisure Enterprises Ltd.* See also the decision of Sir Douglas Frank QC, sitting as a High Court judge, in *McNally* v *Welltrade International Ltd.* In each of these cases the judge held that the basis for the assessment of damages under s 2(1) of the Act of 1967 is that established in *Doyle* v *Olby (Ironmongers) Ltd.* This is also the effect of the judgment of Eveleigh LJ in *Chesneau* v *Interhome Ltd* already cited: "By 'so liable' I take it to mean liable as he would be if the misrepresentation had been made fraudulently."

This was also the original view of the academic writers. In an article, 'The Misrepresentation Act 1967' (1967) 30 MLR by P S Atiyah and G H Treitel, the authors say:

> "The measure of damages in the statutory action will apparently be that in an action of deceit . . . But more probably the damages recoverable in the new action are the same as those recoverable in an action of deceit . . ."

Professor Treitel has since changed his view. In Treitel, *The Law of Contract*, 7th edn, he says:

"Where the action is brought under s 2(1) of the Misrepresentation Act, one possible view is that the deceit rule will be applied by virtue of the fiction of fraud. But the preferable view is that the severity of the deceit rule can only be justified in cases of actual fraud and that remoteness under s 2(1) should depend, as in actions based on negligence, on the test of foreseeability."

The only authority cited in support of the "preferable" view is *Shepheard* v *Broome*, a case under s 38 of the Companies Act 1867, which provided that in certain circumstances a company director, although not in fact fraudulent, should be "deemed to be fraudulent". As Lord Lindley said: ". . . To be compelled by Act of Parliament to treat an honest man as if he were fraudulent is at all times painful", but he went on to say: "but the repugnance which is naturally felt against being compelled to do so will not justify your Lordships in refusing to hold the appellant responsible for acts for which an Act of Parliament clearly declares he is to be held liable . . .". The House of Lords so held.

It seems to me that that case, far from supporting Professor Treitel's view, is authority for the proposition that we must follow the literal wording of s 2(1), even though that has the effect of treating, so far as the measure of damages is concerned, an innocent person as if he were fraudulent. *Chitty on Contracts* says:

". . . it is doubtful whether the rule that the plaintiff may recover even unforeseeable losses suffered as the result of fraud would be applied; it is an exceptional rule which is probably justified only in cases of actual fraud."

No authority is cited in support of that proposition save the passage in Professor Treitel's book cited above.

Professor Furmston in Cheshire, Fifoot and Furmston's *Law of Contract* says:

"It has been suggested [and the reference is to the passage in Atiyah and Treitel's article cited above] that damages under s 2(1) should be calculated on the same principles as govern the tort of deceit. This suggestion is based on a theory that s 2(1) is based on a 'fiction of fraud'. We have already suggested that this theory is misconceived. On the other hand the action created by s 2(1) does look much more like an action in tort than one in contract and it is suggested that the rules for negligence are the natural ones to apply."

The suggestion that the "fiction of fraud" theory is misconceived occurs in a passage which includes the following:

"Though it would be quixotic to defend the drafting of the section, it is suggested that there is no such 'fiction of fraud' since the section does not say that a negligent misrepresentor shall be treated for all purposes as if he were fraudulent. No doubt the wording seeks to incorporate by reference some of the rules relating to fraud but, for instance, nothing in the wording of the subsection requires the measure of damages for deceit to be applied to the statutory action."

With all respect to the various learned authors whose works I have cited above, it seems to me that to suggest that a different measure of damage applies to an action for innocent misrepresentation under the section than that which applies to an action for fraudulent misrepresentation (deceit) at common law is to ignore the plain words of the subsection and is inconsistent with the cases to which I have referred. In my judgment, therefore, the finance company is entitled to recover from the dealer all the losses which it suffered as a result of its entering into the agreements with the dealer and the customer, even if those losses were unforeseeable, provided that they were not otherwise too remote . . .

Accordingly, I would dismiss the dealer's appeal. I would allow the finance company's cross-appeal, set aside the judgment of 22 February 1990, and direct that in its place judgment be entered for the finance company against the dealer in the sum of £3,625.24 together with interest. The finance company accepts that it will have to give credit for any sums that it may receive from its judgment against the customer.'

INNOCENT MISREPRESENTATION

An innocent misrepresentation is a misrepresentation where no element of fraud or negligence is present.

Remedies available to misled person

Rescission

See *Redgrave* v *Hurd* above (p 334).

Indemnity

Whittington v Seale-Hayne

(1900) 82 Law Times 49 • Chancery

The Whittingtons leased a house and premises from Seale-Hayne for the purpose of breeding prize poultry. The Whittingtons claimed that they had entered into the lease on the representation made to them by Seale-Hayne that the premises were in a thoroughly sanitary condition and were also in a good state of repair. The lease contained a provision that the Whittingtons would 'execute all such works as are . . . required by any local . . . authority'. As a result of the house and premises being in an insanitary condition the Whittingtons' manager and family became very ill and the poultry either died or became valueless for the purpose of breeding. Further, the local authority required the drains to be put in order and the house rendered fit for human habitation. The Whittingtons claimed, firstly, rescission and cancellation of the lease; secondly, damages; and thirdly, an indemnity against all costs and charges incurred by them in respect of the matters alleged in paragraph 11 of the statement of claim which included value of stock lost, £750; loss of breeding season, £500; removal of storage and rent, £75; services on behalf of their manager, £100; incidental damages, £100.

Seale-Hayne having admitted making the misrepresentation the issue before the court was which remedies were available to the Whittingtons?

Farwell J: 'The point is one of some nicety. The plaintiffs' action is one for the rescission of a lease on the ground of innocent misrepresentation, and the claim also asks for damages and an indemnity against all costs and charges incurred by the plaintiffs in respect of the lease and the insanitary condition of the premises. The suggestion was made that I should assume for the purpose of argument that innocent misrepresentations were made sufficient to entitle the plaintiffs to rescission. The question then arises to what extent the doctrine, that a plaintiff who succeeds in an action for rescission on the ground of innocent misrepresentation is entitled to be placed in *status quo ante*, is to be applied. Counsel for the plaintiffs say that in such a case the successful party is to be placed in exactly the same position as if he had never entered into the contract. The defendant admits liability so far as regards anything which was paid under the contract, but not in respect of any damages incurred by reason of the contract; and I think the defendant's view is the correct one . . . This brings me back to the case of *Newbigging* v *Adam*, and the difficulty which I have is that the judgments in the Court of Appeal do not agree, and I have therefore to choose between them. I think Bowen LJ's is the correct view. He says: "But when you come to consider what is the exact relief to which a person is entitled in a case of misrepresentation, it seems to me to be this, and nothing more, that he is entitled to have the contract rescinded and is entitled accordingly to all the incidents and consequences of such rescission. It is said that the injured party is entitled to be placed *in status quo*. It seems to me that when you are dealing with innocent misrepresentation that you must understand that proposition that he is to be placed in status quo with this limitation – that he is not to be replaced in exactly the same position in all respects, otherwise he would be entitled to recover damages, but is to be replaced in his position so far as regards the rights and obligations which have been created by the contract into which he has been induced to enter. That seems to me to be the true doctrine, and I think it is put in the neatest way in *Redgrave* v *Hurd*." That case decided that you cannot recover damages for innocent misrepresentation . . . The Lord Justice goes on to say: "Speaking only for myself, I should not like to lay down the proposition that a person is to be restored to the position which he held before the misrepresentation was made, nor that the person injured must be indemnified against loss which arises out of the contract, unless you place upon the words 'out of the contract' the limited and special meaning which I have endeavoured to shadow forth. Loss arising out of the contract is a term which would be too wide. It would embrace damages at common law, because damages at common law are only given upon the supposition that they are damages which would naturally and reasonably follow from the injury done." With respect, if I may say so, I agree with every word the Lord Justice said . . . I have here to consider is what is the limit of the liabilities which are within the indemnity. Mr Hughes [counsel for Seale-Hayne] admits that the rents, rates, and repairs under the covenants in the lease ought to be made good; but he disputes, and I agree with him, that the plaintiff is entitled to what is claimed by paragraph 11 of the statement of claim, which is really damage pure and simple.'

The right to rescind

A misrepresentation renders the contract *voidable* – not void.

As with a breach of contract the innocent person (the party misled) can choose to affirm the contract.

Mode of rescission

Where a person has a right to rescind a contract rescission takes place by that person communicating his rescission to the other party. However, what happens if that other party cannot be found?

Car & Universal Finance Co Ltd v Caldwell

[1964] 1 All ER 290 • Court of Appeal

Caldwell sold his car to Norris for £975. Norris, who took the car away, paid £10 in cash and the balance by cheque. When Caldwell tried to bank the cheque he discovered that the cheque was worthless and that he had been deceived and defrauded. Norris's deception amounted to a fraudulent misrepresentation which meant he gained a voidable title to the car. Eventually the car was sold to the Car and Universal Finance Co Ltd.

The issue before the court was whether Caldwell had rescinded the contract and therefore regained the title to the car before the Car and Universal Finance Co Ltd had obtained the car and thus title to the car.

Sellers LJ: 'This appeal raises a primary point in the law of contract. The question has arisen whether a contract which is voidable by one party can in any circumstances be terminated by that party without his rescission being communicated to the other party. Lord Denning MR, from whom this appeal comes from a trial in the Queen's Bench, has held in the circumstances of this case that there can be rescission without communication where the seller of a motor car who admittedly had the right to rescind the contract of sale on the ground of fraudulent misrepresentation terminated the contract by an unequivocal act of election which demonstrated clearly that he had elected to rescind it and to be no longer bound by it.

The general rule, no doubt, is that where a party is entitled to rescind a contract and wishes to do so the contract subsists until the opposing party is informed that the contract has been terminated. The difficulty of the seller in this case was that, when he learnt of the fraud and therefore ascertained his right to terminate the bargain, he could not without considerable delay find either the fraudulent buyer or the car which had been sold . . .

This is what he did. As soon as he learnt from the bank manager that the cheque in payment for the car could not be met and that there had been a similar transaction previously and that the police were looking for Norris, the defendant went at once to the police. The police produced a photograph of Norris, whom the defendant identified as the man to whom he had sold his car. A warrant was out for the arrest of this man in the name of Rowley. His house had been watched and endeavours had been made to find him. Through the police and the organisation of the Automobile Association to defendant made every endeavour to find and recover the car forthwith and to discover the absconding and elusive Norris. The defendant clearly wished to terminated the contract of sale and take back the car and acted as far as he could to that end . . .

. . . An affirmation of a voidable contract may be established by any conduct which unequivocally manifests an intention to affirm it by the party who has the right to affirm or disaffirm . . . [I]n circumstances such as the present case the other contracting party, a fraudulent rogue who would know that the vendor would want his car back as soon as he knew of the fraud, would not expect to be communicated with as a matter of right or requirement and would deliberately, as here, do all he could to evade any such communication being made to him. In such exceptional contractual circumstances, it does not seem to me appropriate to hold that a party so acting can claim any right to have a decision to rescind communicated to him before the contract is terminated. To hold that he could would involve that the defrauding party, if skilful enough to keep out of the way, could deprive the other party to the contract of his right to rescind, a right to which he was entitled and which he would wish to exercise as the defrauding party would well know or at least confidently suspect. The position has to be viewed, as I see it, between the two contracting parties involved in the particular contract in question. That another innocent party or parties may suffer does not in my view of the matter justify imposing on a defrauded seller an impossible task. He has to establish clearly and unequivocally that he terminates the contract and is no longer to be bound by it. If he cannot communicate his decision he may still satisfy a judge or jury that he had made a final and irrevocable decision and ended the contract.

I am in agreement with the Master of the Rolls, who asked:

"How is a man in the position of defendant ever to be able to rescind the contract when a fraudulent person absconds as Norris did here?"

and answered that he can do so

"if he at once, on discovering the fraud, takes all possible steps to regain the goods, even though he cannot find the rogue nor communicate with him".'

Limits to the right to rescind

If any of the following situations occur the misled party will loose his right to rescind and since (generally speaking) the only remedy available to a misled person is the right to rescind the misled party will be left without any remedy.

- Affirmation
- Lapse of time
- Right of third parties
- Ability to restore
- Damages in lieu of rescission.

Affirmation

If after becoming aware of the misrepresentation the misled party affirms the contract, either by express words or by an act which shows an intention to affirm it, rescission cannot be obtained.

Long v Lloyd

[1958] 2 All ER 402 • Court of Appeal

Lloyd advertised his lorry for sale at £850 and described it as in 'exceptional condition'. When Long telephoned Lloyd to ask about the lorry Lloyd said that it was 'in first-class condition'. Long said he would buy the lorry for £750 if he was satisfied on a trial run. When Long collected the lorry for the trial run Lloyd told him that it would do eleven miles to the gallon. On the trial run it became apparent that the speedometer was not working and a spring was missing from the accelerator pedal; further, Long had difficulty with the top gear. Long then and there agreed to buy the lorry for £750. He paid £375 immediately and it was agreed that he could pay the balance at a later date. The following Wednesday Long went to pick up a small load in the lorry. On the journey Long noticed an oil leak, a crack in one of the wheels, and that he had used eight gallons of fuel for about forty miles; further the dynamo ceased to function. That night he told Lloyd of these defects. Lloyd offered to pay for half the cost of a reconstructed dynamo and Long agreed. The following day the dynamo was fitted and the lorry was driven by Long's brother to Middlesborough. However, the lorry broke down on its journey. Long wrote to Lloyd complaining of the various defects and asked for his money back. The court of first instance held that Lloyd had honestly made the misrepresentations complained of.

The issue before the Court of Appeal was whether Long was still entitled to reject the lorry.

Pearce LJ: 'As to the facts of the present case, counsel for the plaintiff contrasts the period of only a few days between the delivery of the lorry to the plaintiff and his purported rescission of the contract with the period of five years in Leaf's case. He says the plaintiff was entitled to a reasonable time within which to ascertain the true condition of the lorry and to exercise (if so advised) the right of rescission which for the present purpose he must be assumed to have had. It is of course obvious that so far as time is concerned this case bears no resemblance to Leaf's case. Nevertheless, a strict application to the facts of the present case of Denning LJ's view to the effect that the right (if any) to rescind after completion on the ground of innocent misrepresentation is barred by acceptance of the goods must necessarily prove fatal to the plaintiff's case. Apart from special circumstances, the place of delivery is the proper place for examination and for acceptance. It was open to the plaintiff to have the lorry examined by an expert before driving it away but he chose not to do so. It is true, however, that the truth of certain of the representations, for example, that the lorry would do eleven miles to the gallon could not be ascertained except by user and therefore the plaintiff should have a reasonable time to test it. Until he had had such an opportunity it might well be said that he had not accepted the lorry, always assuming, of course, that he did nothing inconsistent with the ownership of the seller. An examination of the facts, however, shows that on any view he must have accepted the lorry before he purported to reject it.

Thus, to recapitulate the facts, after the trial run the plaintiff drove the lorry home from Hampton Court to Sevenoaks, a not inconsiderable distance. After that experience he took it into use in his business by driving it on the following day to Rochester and back to Sevenoaks with a load. By the time he returned from Rochester he knew that the dynamo was not charging, that there was an oil seal leaking, that he had used eight gallons of fuel for a journey of forty miles and that a wheel was cracked. He must also, as we think, have known by this time that the vehicle was not capable of forty miles per hour. As to oil consumption, we should have thought that, if it was so excessive that the sump was practically dry after three hundred miles, the plaintiff could have reasonably been expected to discover that the rate of consumption was unduly high by the time he had made the journey from Hampton Court to Sevenoaks and thence to Rochester and back. On his return from Rochester the plaintiff telephoned to the defendant and complained about the dynamo, the excessive fuel consumption, the leaking oil seal and the cracked wheel. The defendant then offered to pay half the cost of the reconstructed dynamo which the plaintiff had been advised to fit, and the plaintiff accepted the defendant's offer. We find this difficult to reconcile with the continuance of any right of rescission which the plaintiff might have had down to that time.

The matter does not rest there. On the following day the plaintiff, knowing all that he did about the condition and performance of the lorry, despatched it, driven by his brother, on a business trip to Middlesbrough. That step, at all events, appears to us to have amounted, in all the circumstances of the case, to a final acceptance of the lorry by the plaintiff for better or for worse, and to have conclusively extinguished any right of rescission remaining to the plaintiff after completion of the sale . . .'

Lapse of time

Lapse of time may be treated as affirmation. Knowledge of misrepresentation is usually, but not always, required before lapse of time is treated as affirmation.

Leaf v *International Galleries*

[1950] 1 All ER 693 • Court of Appeal

The facts are stated in the judgment of Denning LJ.

Denning LJ: 'In March, 1944, the buyer bought from the sellers an oil painting of Salisbury Cathedral. On the back of the picture there was a label indicating that it had been exhibited as a Constable, and during the negotiations for the purchase the sellers represented that it was a painting by Constable. That representation, the judge has found, was incorporated as one of the terms of the contract. The receipt for the price, £85, was given in these terms: "Mar. 6, 1944. One original oil painting Salisbury Cathedral by J Constable, £85". Nearly five years later the buyer was minded to sell the picture. He took it to Christie's to be put into an auction, and he was then advised that it was not a Constable. So he took it back to the sellers and told them he wanted to return it and get his money back. They did take the picture back temporarily for investigation, and they still adhered to the view that it was a Constable. Eventually the buyer brought a claim in the county court claiming rescission of the contract. In his particulars of claim he pleaded that the picture had been represented to be a Constable, and that he had paid £85 in reliance on that representation. The sellers resisted the claim. After hearing expert evidence the judge found as a fact, and this must be accepted, that the painting was not by Constable and was worth little.

The question is whether the buyer is entitled to rescind the contract on that account. I emphasise that this is a claim to rescind only. There is no claim in this action for damages for breach of condition or breach of warranty. The claim is simply one for rescission . . . The way in which the case is put by counsel for the buyer is this. He says this was an innocent misrepresentation and that in equity he is entitled to claim rescission even of an executed contract of sale on that account. He points out that the judge has found that it is quite possible to restore the parties to the same position that they were in originally, by the buyer simply handing back the picture to the sellers in return for the repayment of the purchase price.

In my opinion, this case is to be decided according to the well known principles applicable to the sale of goods. This was a contract for the sale of goods. There was a mistake about the quality of the subject-matter, because both parties believed the picture to be a Constable, and that mistake was in one sense essential or fundamental. Such a mistake, however, does not avoid the contract. There was no mistake about the subject-matter of the sale. It was a specific picture of "Salisbury Cathedral". The parties were agreed in the same terms on the same subject-matter, and that is sufficient to make a contract: see *Solle* v *Butcher*. There was term in the contract as to the quality of the subject-matter, namely, as to the person by whom the picture was painted – that it was by Constable. That term of the contract was either a condition or a warranty. If it was a condition, the buyer could reject the picture for breach of the condition at any time before he accepted it or was to be deemed to have accepted it, whereas, if it was only a warranty, he could not reject it but was confined to a claim for damages.

I think it right to assume in the buyer's favour that this term was a condition, and that, if he had come in proper time, he could have rejected the picture, but the right to reject for breach of condition has always been limited by the rule that once the buyer has accepted, or is deemed to have accepted, the goods in performance of the contract, he cannot thereafter reject, but is relegated to his claim for damages: see s 11(1)(c) of the Sale of Goods Act . . . The circumstances in which a buyer is deemed to have accepted goods in performance of the contract are set out in s 35 of the Act which provides that the buyer is deemed to have accepted the goods, among other things,

". . . when after the lapse of a reasonable time, he retains the goods without intimating to the seller that he has rejected them."

In this case this buyer took the picture into his house, and five years passed before he intimated any rejection. That, I need hardly say, is much more than a reasonable time. It is far too late for him at the end of five years to reject this picture for breach of any condition. His remedy after that length of time is for damages only, a claim which he has not brought before the court.

Is it to be said that the buyer is in any better position by relying on the representation, not as a condition, but as an innocent misrepresentation? I agree that on a contract for the sale of goods an innocent material misrepresentation may in a proper case be a ground for rescission even after the contract has been executed . . . It is unnecessary, however, to pronounce finally on these matters because, although rescission may in some cases be a proper remedy, nevertheless it is to be remembered that an innocent misrepresentation is much less potent than a breach of condition. A condition is a term of the contract of a most material character, and, if a claim to reject for breach of condition is barred, it seems to me a fortiori that a claim to rescission on the ground of innocent misrepresentation is also barred. So, assuming that a contract for the sale of goods may be rescinded in a proper case for innocent misrepresentation, nevertheless, once the buyer has accepted, or is deemed to have accepted, the goods, the claim is barred. In this case the buyer must clearly be deemed to have accepted the picture. He had ample opportunity to examine it in the first few days after he bought it. Then was the time to see if the condition or representation was fulfilled, yet he has kept it all this time and five years have elapsed without any notice of rejection. In my judgment, he cannot now claim to rescind, and the appeal should be dismissed.'

Right of third parties
Section 23 Sale of Goods Act 1979

'When the seller of goods has a voidable title thereto, but this title has not been avoided at the time of the sale, the buyer acquires a good title to the goods, provided he buys them in good faith and without notice of the seller's defect of title.'

See also *Car & Universal Finance Co Ltd* v *Caldwell* above (p 351).

Ability to restore (restitutio in integrum) impossible

Clarke v *Dickson*
(1858) EB & E 148

Clarke was induced by representations made by Dickson to buy shares in the Welsh Potosi Lead and Copper Mining Company. Later when the company was being wound up Clarke discovered for the first time that the representations by which he was induced to buy the shares were false and fraudulent on the part of Dickson. Clarke therefore brought an action to recover the deposits which he had paid for the shares. The issue before the court was whether it was possible for the court to order restitutio in integrum given that Clarke's shares were now worthless.

Crompton J: 'When once it is settled that a contract induced by fraud is not void, but voidable at the option of the party defrauded, it seems to me to follow that, when that party exercises his option to rescind the contract, he must be in a state to rescind; that is, he must be in such a situation as to be able to put the parties into their original state before the contract. Now here I will assume, what is not clear to me, that the plaintiff bought his shares from the defendants and not from the Company, and that he might at one time have had a right to restore the shares to the defendants if he could, and demand the price from them. But then what did he buy? Shares in a partnership with others. He cannot return those; he has become bound to those others. Still stronger, he has changed their nature: what he now has and offers to restore are shares in a quasi corporation now in process of being wound up. That is quite enough to decide this case. The plaintiff must rescind *in toto* or not at all; he cannot both keep the shares and recover the whole price. That is founded on the plainest principles of justice. If he cannot return the article he must keep it, and sue for his real damage in an action on the deceit. Take the case I put in the argument, of a butcher buying live cattle, killing them, and even selling the meat to his customers. If the rule of law were as the plaintiff contends, that butcher might, upon discovering a fraud on the part of the grazier who sold him the cattle, rescind the contract and get back the whole price: but how could that be consistent with justice? The true doctrine is, that a party can never repudiate a contract after, by his own act, it has become out of his power to restore the parties to their original condition.'

Damages in lieu of rescission – Section 2(2) & (3) Misrepresentation Act 1967

An issue that arises under s 2(2) Misrepresentation Act 1967 is whether the damages are calculated on the tort principle (out of pocket) or on the contract principle (loss of profit).

William Sindall plc v *Cambridgeshire County Council*

[1994] 3 All ER 932 • Court of Appeal

Sindall bought a piece of land from Cambridgeshire CC for £5m. Later it was discovered that a foul sewer ran under the land. By this time the land had fallen in value to £2.5m. Sindall sought rescission of the contract on the grounds of misrepresentation and mistake. The Court of Appeal held that there was no operative mistake nor was there a misrepresentation. However, the court did discuss the operation of s 2(2) of the Misrepresentation Act 1967.

Hoffmann LJ: Discretion. 'My conclusion that there are no grounds for rescission, either for misrepresentation or mistake, mean that it is unnecessary to consider whether the judge correctly exercised his discretion under section 2(2) of the Misrepresentation Act 1967 not to award damages in lieu of rescission. But in case this case goes further, I should say that in my judgment the judge approached this question on a false basis, arising from his mistake about the seriousness of the defect. This vitiated the exercise of the discretion and would have made it necessary, if we thought that Sindall would otherwise have been entitled to rescind for misrepresentation, to exercise our own discretion under section 2(2) . . .

The discretion conferred by section 2(2) is a broad one, to do what is equitable. But there are three matters to which the court must in particular have regard.

The first is the nature of the misrepresentation. It is clear from the Law Reform Committee's report that the court was meant to consider the importance of the representation in relation to the subject-matter of the transaction. I have already said that in my view, in the context of a £5m sale of land, a misrepresentation which would have cost £18,000 to put right and was unlikely seriously to have interfered with the development or resale of the property was a matter of relatively minor importance.

The second matter to which the court must have regard is "the loss that would be caused by [the misrepresentation] if the contract were upheld". The section speaks in terms of loss suffered rather than damages recoverable but clearly contemplates that if the contract is upheld, such loss will be compensated by an award of damages. Section 2(2) therefore gives a power to award damages in circumstances in which no damages would previously have been recoverable. Furthermore, such damages will be compensation for loss caused by the misrepresentation, whether it was negligent or not. This is made clear by section 2(3), which provides:

"Damages may be awarded under subsection (2) of this section whether or not he is liable to damages under subsection (1) thereof, but where he is so liable any award under subsection (2) shall be taken into account in assessing his liability under the said subsection (1)."

Damages under section 2(2) are therefore damages for the misrepresentation as such. What would be the measure of such damages? This court is not directly concerned with quantum, which would be determined at an inquiry. But since the court, in the exercise of its discretion, needs to know whether damages under section 2(2) would be an adequate remedy and to be able to compare such damages with the loss which rescission would cause to Cambridgeshire, it is necessary to decide in principle how the damages would be calculated . . .

Under section 2(1), the measure of damages is the same as for fraudulent misrepresentation, i.e. all loss caused by the plaintiff having been induced to enter into the contract: *Cemp Properties (UK) Ltd* v *Dentsply Research & Development Corporation*. This means that the misrepresentor is invariably deprived of the benefit of the bargain (e.g. any difference between the price paid and the value of the thing sold) and may have to pay additional damages for consequential loss suffered by the representee on account of having entered into the contract. In my judgment, however, it is clear that this will not necessarily be the measure of damages under section 2(2).

First, section 2(1) provides for damages to be awarded to a person who "has entered into a contract after a misrepresentation has been made to him by another party and as a result thereof" – sc of having entered into the contract – "he has suffered loss". In contrast, section 2(2) speaks of "the loss which would be caused by it" – sc the misrepresentation – "if the contract were upheld". In my view, section 2(1) is concerned with the damage flowing from having entered into the contract, while section 2(2) is concerned with damage caused by the property not being what it was represented to be.

Secondly, section 2(3) contemplates that damages under section 2(2) may be less than damages under section 2(1) and should be taken into account when assessing damages under the latter subsection. This only makes sense if the measure of damages may be different.

Thirdly, the Law Reform Committee report makes it clear that section 2(2) was enacted because it was thought that it might be a hardship to the representor to be deprived of the whole benefit of the bargain on account of a minor misrepresentation. It could not possibly have intended the damages in lieu to be assessed on a principle which would invariably have the same effect.

The Law Reform Committee drew attention to the anomaly which already existed by which a minor misrepresentation gave rise to a right of rescission whereas a warranty in the same terms would have grounded no more than a claim for modest damages. It said that this anomaly would be exaggerated if its recommendation for abolition of the bar on rescission after completion were to be implemented. I think that section 2(2) was intended to give the court a power to eliminate this anomaly by upholding the contract and compensating the plaintiff for the loss he has suffered on account of the property not having been what it was represented to be. In other words, damages under section 2(2) should never exceed the sum which would have been awarded if the representation had been a warranty. It is not necessary for present purposes to discuss the circumstances in which they may be less.

If one looks at the matter when Sindall purported to rescind, the loss which would be caused if the contract were upheld was relatively small: the £18 000 it would have cost to divert the sewer, the loss of a plot and interest charges on any consequent delay at the rate of £2000 a day. If one looks at the matter at the date of trial, the loss would have been nil because the sewer had been diverted.

The third matter to be taken into account under section 2(2) is the loss which would be caused to Cambridgeshire by rescission. This is the loss of the bargain at the top of the market (cf *the Lucy*) having to return about £8m in purchase price and interest in exchange for land worth less than £2m.

Having regard to these matters, and in particular the gross disparity between the loss which would be caused to Sindall by the misrepresentation and the loss which would be caused to Cambridgeshire by rescission, I would have exercised my discretion to award damages in lieu of rescission.'

Misrepresentation Act 1967: Section 1 Removal of certain bars to rescission for innocent misrepresentation

Where a person has entered into a contract after a misrepresentation has been made to him, and –
  (a) the misrepresentation has become a term of the contract; or
  (b) the contract has been performed;
or both, then, if otherwise he would be entitled to rescind the contract without alleging fraud, he shall be so entitled, subject to the provisions of this Act, notwithstanding the matters mentioned in paragraphs (a) and (b) of this section.

MISREPRESENTATION ACT 1967: SECTION 3 EXCLUSION OF LIABILITY

Section 3, as substituted by s 8(1) of the Unfair Contract Terms Act 1977, of the Misrepresentation Act 1967 provides that

If a contract contains a term which would exclude or restrict –
  (a) any liability to which a party to a contract may be subject by reason of any misrepresentation made by him before the contract was made; or
  (b) any remedy available to another party to the contract by reason of such a misrepresentation,
that term shall be of no effect except in so far as it satisfies the requirement of reasonableness as stated in section 11(1) Unfair Contract Terms Act 1977; and it is for those claiming that the term satisfies that requirement to show that it does.

NB: Section 3 is not only limited to business liability; s 2(1) Unfair Contract Terms Act 1977 only applies to ss 2–7.

Defining liability

Section 3 does not invalidate a contractual provision that the contract contains the entire terms of the contract.

McGrath v *Shah*

(1989) 57 P&CR 452 • Chancery Division

The McGraths agreed to sell their house to the Shahs. The Shahs claimed that the McGraths had made statements to them before the contract was made that the house would contain a 40 foot playroom and built-in oven and hob and that these statements had become contractual terms. The McGraths claimed that the contract between themselves and the Shahs was contained solely in the written contract between them; they relied on condition 9 which stated

> "This contract constitutes the entire contract between the parties, and may be varied (whether by way of collateral contract or otherwise) only in writing under the hands of the parties or their solicitors. The purchaser hereby admits that save in respect of such of the written statements of the vendor's solicitors prior to the date hereof as were not capable of independent verification (whether by inspection or by search or inquiry of any local or other public authority, whether or not such inspection, search or inquiry has been made, or otherwise) no representation, whether oral or written, has been made to him by or on behalf of the vendor concerning the property on which he has relied or which has influenced, induced or persuaded him to enter into this contract."

The Shahs replied that condition 9 was contrary to s 8(1) of the Unfair Contract Terms Act 1977 and therefore of no effect since it did not satisfy the requirement of reasonableness.

Judge Chadwick QC: 'The second point taken by Mr Eyre is that certain statements made before the exchange of contracts on June 18 became themselves contractual terms . . .

The two particular statements which are said to have become contractual terms are these: first, that the property would include a playroom on the top or attic floor of some 40 feet in length . . .

In relation to those two complaints, it seems to me that the question which I have to consider is whether there is a serious question that the contract made on June 18 contained contractual warranties as to the continued existence of a 40-foot room on the top floor, and the continued existence of the hob and cooker in the kitchen; or whether the true position was that the defendants purchased the property in the actual condition in which it was on June 18.

It seems to me that an insuperable hurdle in the way of the defendants on this point is raised in the first sentence in Special Condition 9 in the contract of June 18. That sentence provides in terms that:

> ". . . This contract constitutes the entire contract between the parties, and may be varied only in writing under the hands of the parties or their solicitors . . ."

One can see why such a provision is included in a contract for the sale and purchase of land. All material terms of a contract for the sale of land must be evidenced by some memorandum in writing signed by the party to be charged – see section 40(1) of the Law of Property Act 1925. Accordingly, it is highly undesirable to have any scope for argument whether the written terms of a contract for the sale of land do, in fact, constitute the entire contract.

Mr Eyre is driven, I think, to say that the first sentence of Special Condition 9 can be disregarded as being struck down by the Unfair Contract Terms Act 1977 . . .

The relevant provision of the Unfair Contract Terms Act 1977 is section 8(1) which amends section 3 of the Misrepresentation Act 1967. The section reads:

". . . If a contract contains a term which would exclude or restrict

(a) any liability to which a party to a contract may be subject by reason of any misrepresentation made by him before the contract was made, or

(b) any remedy available to another party to the contract by reason of such a misrepresentation, that term shall be of no effect except in so far as it satisfies the requirement of reasonableness as stated in section 11(1) of the Unfair Contract Terms Act 1977, and it is for those claiming that the term satisfies that requirement to show that it does."

In my judgment, that provision, which is in terms directed to the exclusion or restriction of liability for misrepresentation, or of remedies arising by reason of misrepresentation, is not apt to cover a contractual provision which seeks to define where the contractual terms are actually to be found. But if I am wrong in that, then it seems to me that far from it being unfair or unreasonable for the parties to include in that contract a term in the form of the first sentence in Special Condition 9, it is eminently fair and reasonable that they should do so where the contract is a contract relating to the sale of land. By doing so, as it seems to me, they are attempting to avoid the problems which could arise in the absence of such a term – in particular, the problems arising from section 40 of the Law of Property Act 1925.

If the first sentence of Special Condition 9 has the effect which is clearly intended, then statements made prior to the contract on June 18 cannot, in my judgment, form terms of that contract . . .

. . . I can see no reason why a party should not put forward particulars of his property upon the term that ". . . these particulars do not constitute, nor constitute any part of, an offer or contract . . ." It seems to me that what the party is seeking to do by such a term is to disclaim any intention of contracting in the terms of the particulars; and the formation of a contract being dependent upon the existence of mutual contractual intention, it seems to me necessarily to follow that the absence of such intention in one party communicated to the other is fatal to the formation of any contract between them in those terms.

If that be right, then the Unfair Contract Terms Act 1977 can have no application to a disclaimer of the kind that I have mentioned, because section 8 of that Act only applies where a contract contains a term which would exclude or restrict liability. If the disclaimer is contained in a pre-contractual document, and is apt to prevent a contract from coming into existence at all, then it seems to me that the condition precedent in section 8 of the 1977 Act cannot be satisfied, and the section cannot have effect.'

This case can be contrasted with *Walker* v *Boyle* below (p 363). Judge Chadwick QC distinguished the cases by saying

'The first point raised on behalf of the defendants by Mr Eyre is that there were serious misrepresentations made prior to June 18 which would have entitled the purchasers to rescind the contract before completion, and that in those circumstances the vendors were not entitled to serve a notice to complete. He draws support for that proposition from dicta in the judgment of Dillon J in the case of *Walker* v *Boyle*. The judge said this:

"... The position as to this notice to complete is, as I see it, quite simply this: if Mr Walker was entitled to rescind the contract for misrepresentation, then the notice to complete cannot have any effect. If, however, Mr Walker was not entitled to rescind the contract, then the notice to complete was a valid notice with which Mr Walker failed to comply ..."

In my judgment, those dicta must be read in the context of the facts upon which Dillon J had to decide. Put briefly, the facts in that case were that in the course of answering preliminary inquiries, the vendor had failed to disclose the existence of a boundary dispute with her neighbour. The judge was satisfied that failure to disclose that boundary dispute was a material misrepresentation; such that if the purchaser, Mr Walker, had known of it he would never have entered into the contract. A meeting took place in an attempt to resolve the dispute, but without result. Thereupon the purchaser, Mr Walker, gave notice of his intention to rescind the contract and claimed the return of his deposit. He followed that by the issue of a writ seeking rescission and the return of deposit. On the same day that the writ was issued, the vendor's solicitors served a notice to complete under Condition 22 of the National Conditions of Sale (19th edn). The purchaser failed to comply with that notice, and the vendor's solicitors purported to treat that failure to comply as a breach of contract, forfeited the deposit, and issued a writ in a second action claiming damages.

So that the facts before Dillon J were such that by the time the notice to complete had been issued, not only had the purchaser already sought to rescind the contract and claim the return of his deposit, but indeed he had issued proceedings for that purpose. In that context, it is easy to see why the judge expressed himself as he did in that passage on which Mr Eyre relies. If Mr Walker was entitled to rescind the contract for misrepresentation, then he had done so effectively before the notice to complete was served; and so it would necessarily follow that the notice to complete could not have any effect, there being no longer any contract between the parties. On the other hand, if he had not been entitled to rescind the contract, then the contract was still on foot and the notice to complete was valid.

I do not find anything in that case which supports the proposition which Mr Eyre urges on behalf of the defendant purchasers, namely, that whenever the circumstances are such that the purchaser is or may be entitled to rescind a contract for misrepresentation, the vendor is not entitled to serve a notice to complete. The position in my judgment is that the vendor is entitled to rely upon Condition 22 of the national conditions, and serve a notice to complete, if at the time that he does so the contract has not been rescinded. Of course, if after the notice to complete has been served the purchaser decides that he does not wish to complete the contract, he is still able to rely on his right to rescind: the service of the notice to complete will not have affected that right. But, if the purchaser chooses not to rescind the contract, the contract remains in force with all its incidents, including the provisions of National Condition 22 and the effect of any notice that may have been served under that condition. In the present case the purchasers have expressly disclaimed any intention to rescind the contract. They wish to enforce it. Indeed, that is the basis upon which they seek to uphold the caution.'

Application of Misrepresentation Act 1967 section 3

An exemption clause is *prima facie* invalid (not the whole contract) unless it is shown to be reasonable within s 11(1) of UCTA 1977 by the person who relies upon it.

Walker v *Boyle*

[1982] 1 All ER 634 • Chancery Division

Boyle, in the course of selling his wife's house to Walker, told Walker that there were no disputes regarding the boundaries of the property. This turned out not to be true and amounted to an innocent misrepresentation. Contracts were exchanged between Boyle and Walker. The standard form contract, the National Conditions of Sale, contained condition 17(1) which stated that

> 'no error, mis-statement or omission in any preliminary answer concerning the property . . . shall annul the sale'.

When Walker learnt of the misrepresentation he brought an action against Boyle claiming rescission of the contract and the return of his deposit. Boyle claimed that condition 17(1) exempted him from liability for any misrepresentation he may have made. The issue before the court was whether condition 17 was caught by s 3 of the Misrepresentation Act 1967 and, if so, was it a fair and reasonable term within s 11(1)(c) of the Unfair Contract Terms Act 1977.

Dillon J: '. . . [T]he extent to which an exclusion clause can be valid is now governed by s 3 of the Misrepresentation Act 1967. As substituted by s 8 of the Unfair Contract Terms Act 1977 . . .

If condition 17 has any validity or relevance in the circumstances of this case, it is a term which would exclude liabilities to which Mrs Boyle would be subject by reason of misrepresentation, and so s 3 of the 1967 Act is applicable . . .

I do not regard condition 17 as satisfying that requirement in the circumstances of this case. Another way of putting it is that Mrs Boyle has not shown that it does satisfy that requirement.

It has been submitted by counsel for Mrs Boyle that as there were solicitors acting for both parties, it would be a very strong thing to say that any term of the contract which resulted is not a fair and reasonable one in the circumstances. That argument would have great force, no doubt, if the solicitors had specifically directed their minds to the problem and had evolved the clause which was under attack. In fact, however, neither solicitor directed his mind to condition 17, and they have both told me, and they are men of not inconsiderable experience as conveyancing solicitors, that they have never come across a case where any question under condition 17 has arisen. It was submitted that it was the duty of the purchaser's solicitor to advise his client, Mr Walker, of the implications of condition 17 and of the other terms of the contract which Mr Walker was going to enter into, and he must be taken to have discharged that duty and satisfied himself and Mr Walker that the terms were reasonable. It is, of course, the duty of a solicitor to advise his client about any abnormal or unusual term in a contract, but I think it is perfectly normal and proper for a solicitor to use standard forms of conditions of sale such as the National Conditions of Sale. I do not think he is called on to go through the small print of those somewhat lengthy conditions with a tooth-comb every time he is advising a purchaser or to draw the purchaser's attention to every problem which on a careful reading of the conditions might in some circumstance or other conceivably arise. I cannot believe that purchasers of house property throughout the land would be overjoyed at having such lengthy explanations of the National Conditions of Sale ritually foisted on them.

It has also been submitted by counsel for Mrs Boyle that the court should be very slow to hold that a common-form clause like condition 17 is not fair and reasonable. Of course it is true that there are common-form clauses which have been evolved by negotiation between trade associations, associations of merchants or associations of growers or trade unions or other such bodies concerned to protect the rights of their members, which can be regarded as representing what consensus in the trade regards as fair and reasonable. Again, the National Conditions of Sale are not the product of negotiation between such bodies and it is plain from the conditions I have cited in the *Nottingham Patent Brick and Tile Co* case and Clauson J's case of *Charles Hunt Ltd* v *Palmer* that what now appears in condition 17 has come down through the ages despite very drastic limitations imposed on it by the courts. I do not think it can be said that its precarious survival until 1977 entitles it to the automatic accolade of fairness and reasonableness.

It follows that Mr Walker succeeds in my judgment in his claim to the return of his deposit . . .'

Overbrooke Estates Ltd v *Glencombe Properties Ltd*

[1974] 3 All ER 511 • Chancery Division

Overbrooke instructed auctioneers to sell one of their properties. On 8 November 1973 Glencombe purchased the property at an auction held by the auctioneers. Condition R(b) of the contract, set out in the auction catalogue, stated that 'The Vendors do not make or give and neither the Auctioneers nor any person in the employment of the Auctioneers has any authority to make or give any representation or warranty in relation to [the property]'. Prior to bidding for the property the auctioneers, who were the agents of Overbrooke, told Glencombe in response to its enquiry that neither 'the Local Authority nor the Greater London Council had any schemes or plans for the said property nor were interested in the property for compulsory purchase or any other purpose'. Later, Glencombe, having discovered that the property might become subject to a slum clearance scheme, refused to complete the purchase. Overbrooke sued Glencombe for specific performance and Glencombe counterclaimed and sought rescission of the contract on the grounds of the misrepresentation that Overbrooke's agents, the auctioneers, had made to them.

One of the issues before the court was whether condition R(b) was 'fair and reasonable within the circumstances of the case' within s 3 of the Misrepresentation Act 1967.

Brightman J: 'Counsel's argument for [Glencombe] is based on s 3 of the Misrepresentation Act 1967 . . .

The argument of counsel is as follows. The words in s 3(a), "misrepresentation made by him before the contract was made" must include a misrepresentation made by the contracting party's agent. The authority of the contracting party's agent in such a case is a necessary ingredient of any liability sought to be imposed on such contracting party. Therefore a provision restricting the ostensible authority of the agent is a provision which restricts the liability of the contracting party for the misrepresentation. Therefore, if such a provision is relied on to negative the principal's liability for the misrepresentation, the court has to consider what is fair and reasonable in the circumstances of the case and that can only be done in the course of the trial of the action. To put the matter more shortly, condition R(b) excludes, or restricts, liability because it excludes, or restricts, an essential ingredient of liability, namely, the ostensible authority of Willmotts.

In my judgment s 3 of the 1967 Act will not bear the load which counsel for the defendant company seeks to place on it. In my view the section only applies to a provision which would exclude or restrict liability for a misrepresentation made by a party or his duly authorised agent, including of course an agent with ostensible authority. The section does not, in my judgment, in any way qualify the right of a principal publicly to limit the otherwise ostensible authority of his agent. The second argument of the defendant company fails.'

Cremdean Properties Ltd v *Nash*

244 EG 547 • Court of Appeal

Nash sold, by tender, a block of property to Cremdean Properties. The tender documents, on which Cremdean Properties relied, stated that 'these premises are for sale by tender, with the benefit of planning consent for approximately 17 900 sq ft of offices'. A footnote to the special conditions of sale by tender stated 'Messrs Lalonde Bros & Parham [Nash's estate agents in relation to the sale of the block of property] for themselves, for the vendors or landlord whose agents they are give notice that (a) These particulars are prepared for the convenience of an intending purchaser or tenant and although they are believed to be correct their accuracy is not guaranteed and any error, omission or misdescription shall not annul the sale or be grounds on which compensation may be claimed and neither do they constitute any part of an offer of a contract (b) Any intending purchaser or tenant must satisfy himself by inspection or otherwise as to the correctness of each of the statements contained in these particulars'. On discovering that the block of property would not provide the stated square footage of office space stated in the tender documents Cremdean Properties issued a writ claiming rescission of the contract on the ground of misrepresentation and, in the alternative, damages. Nash claimed that the footnote to the special conditions was effective so as to exclude any liability for misrepresentation. Cremdean Properties argued that even if the footnote was a contractual term the footnote was not fair and reasonable within s 3 of the Misrepresentation Act 1967.

Bridge LJ: 'Prior to 1967, there being no allegation of fraud or anything like it against the defendants in the plaintiffs' pleading, the plaintiffs could not have succeeded in rescinding the contract with the first defendant because . . . it had been completed by conveyance before the writ was issued. But the plaintiffs in that regard are newly entitled to rely, and do rely, on the provisions of section 1 of the Misrepresentation Act 1967, which, so far as is material, provides as follows: "Where a person has entered into a contract after a misrepresentation has been made to him, and . . . (b) the contract has been performed . . . then, if otherwise he would be entitled to rescind the contract without alleging fraud, he shall be so entitled, subject to the provisions of this Act, notwithstanding the matters mentioned in paragraph (b) of this section". I also mention in passing, though it is not directly relevant for the purposes of the present appeal, that section 2 of the Act of 1967 creates a novel creature in the law in the shape of a liability upon a representor who makes an innocent misrepresentation in the course of negotiation which results in the conclusion of a contract which may, in the circumstances indicated in this section, found in damages . . .

If the Act of 1967 stopped short at section 2 it might very well follow without argument that the terms of the footnote to the special conditions are effective to exclude any liability for misrepresentation which would otherwise fall upon the first defendant. But the heart of the matter turns upon the provisions of section 3 of the Misrepresentation Act . . .

The argument for the plaintiffs before the learned judge, which the learned judge accepted, was that subject to the exception . . . that section is operative to invalidate the terms of the footnote relied upon by the first defendants in so far as that footnote would otherwise be effective to exclude any liability under the Misrepresentation Act, for an innocent misrepresentation leading to the contract.

Mr Newsom's [counsel for Nash] able argument on behalf of the defendant can really be summarised very shortly. In effect what he says is this. The terms of the footnote are not simply, if contractual at all, a contractual exclusion either of any liability to which the defendant would otherwise be subject for any misrepresentation in the document, or of any remedy otherwise available on that ground to the plaintiff. The footnote is effective, so the argument runs, to nullify any representation in the document altogether; it is effective, so it is said, to bring about a situation in law as if no representation at all had ever been made. For my part, I am quite unable to accept that argument. I reject it primarily on the simple basis that on no reading of the language of the footnote could it have the remarkable effect contended for. One may usefully analyse the footnote by dividing it into three parts. The first part is embodied in the words: "These particulars are prepared for the convenience of an intending purchaser or tenant and although they are believed to be correct their accuracy is not guaranteed . . .". That is something quite different from saying "any representation in this document shall be deemed not to be a representation". On the contrary, this part of the footnote is clearly intended to exclude contractual liability for the accuracy of any representation; so far from saying that there has been no representation, it is reinforcing the fact that there have been representations by indicating that they are believed to be correct.

The second part of the footnote is embodied in the words: ". . . any error, omission or misdescription shall not annul the sale or be grounds on which compensation may be claimed" – that, I think Mr Newsom concedes, is nothing more or less than a purported exclusion of liability which would otherwise accrue on the ground of any misrepresentation in the statements to be found elsewhere in the document.

Finally, the third part of the footnote is embodied in the words: "Any intending purchaser or tenant must satisfy himself by inspection or otherwise as to the correctness of each of the statements contained in these particulars". That part of the footnote may have considerable importance when this action comes to trial, as bearing upon the question of fact that will arise at the trial, as to whether the plaintiffs relied upon any misrepresentation. But for present purposes we, of course, have to assume the truth of what is pleaded, namely, that the representation as to office space was false and that the plaintiffs relied upon the alleged misrepresentation. Clearly the third part of this footnote, again on any reading of its language, does not amount even to a purported annulment of the very existence of any representation embodied in the earlier parts of this document.

In support of his argument Mr Newsom relied upon a decision of Brightman J in a case called *Overbrooke Estates Ltd* v *Glencombe Properties Ltd* . . .

Brightman J [states]: "In my judgment section 3 of the Act will not bear the load which Mr Irvine seeks to place upon it. In my view the section only applies to a provision which would exclude or restrict liability for a misrepresentation made by a party or his duly authorised agent, including of course an agent with ostensible authority. The section does not, in my judgment, in any way qualify the right of a principal publicly to limit the otherwise ostensible authority of his agent. The defendants' second argument fails."

I respectfully agree entirely with the whole of that reasoning. With respect to Mr Newsom's argument I am unable to see that it has any application at all to the facts of the present case, because there never was any question here but that the agents acting for the first defendant and the other defendants, when they published the document on which the plaintiffs rely as embodying the relevant misrepresentation, had the full authority of their principals to say what they did say in the document. It is one thing to say that section 3 does not inhibit a principal from publicly giving notice limiting the ostensible authority of his agents; it is quite another thing to say that a principal can circumvent the plainly intended effect of section 3 by a clause excluding his own liability for a representation which he has undoubtedly made.

I am quite content to found my judgment in this case on the proposition that the language of the footnote relied upon by Mr Newsom simply does not, on its true interpretation, have the effect contended for. But I would go further and say that if the ingenuity of a draftsman could devise language which would have that effect, I am extremely doubtful whether the court would allow it to operate so as to defeat section 3. Supposing the vendor included a clause which the purchaser was required to, and did, agree to in some such terms as "notwithstanding any statement of fact included in these particulars the vendor shall be conclusively deemed to have made no representation within the meaning of the Misrepresentation Act 1967", I should have thought that that was only a form of words the intended and actual effect of which was to exclude or restrict liability, and I should not have thought that the courts would have been ready to allow such ingenuity in forms of language to defeat the plain purpose at which section 3 is aimed.'

SUMMARY

You should now be able to:

- Identify a *false* representation.
- Distinguish between, and appreciate the difference between, a representation of *fact* and a representation of *opinion*.
- Understand the person to whom the misrepresentation must be addressed.
- Appreciate that the misrepresentation must *induce* the contract.
- Appreciate the significance of *opportunities for inspection*.
- Distinguish between the various types of misrepresentation.
- Understand the various effects of misrepresentation and the remedies available for the different types of misrepresentation.
- Understand the relationship between misrepresentation and exclusion of liability.

If you have not mastered the above points you should go through this section again.

13 Mistake

MISTAKE AT COMMON LAW

The two broad terms used in this section are *common mistake* and *unilateral mistake*. You will find these terms used by some text book writers but other writers will use different terms or the same terms but in a different way which can prove confusing. If you find it easier, just forget the two terms and concentrate on the way in which the cases are grouped.

The two classes of common law mistake are known as *operative mistakes* (i.e. they render a contract *void*).

There are two types of operative mistake:

- *Common mistake*: cases in which the parties, though genuinely in agreement, have both contracted in the mistaken belief that some fact which lies at the root of the contract is true.
- *Unilateral mistake*: cases where, although to all outward appearances the parties are in agreement, there is in fact no *genuine* agreement between them, and the law, therefore, does not regard a contract as having come into existence.

For a mistake to be operative at common law the mistake must be one of fact not of law.

Mistake must exist when the contract was made

In order for a mistake to be an operative mistake it must exist when the contract was made.

Amalgamated Investment & Property Co Ltd v John Walker & Sons Ltd
[1976] 3 All ER 509 • Court of Appeal

John Walker's (JW) estate agents advertised some of their property for sale describing it as 'For occupation or redevelopment'. In July 1973 Amalgamated Investment (AI) wrote to JW's estate agents and made an offer of £1 710 000 for the property; the offer was made subject to contract. Enquiries were made before contract in the ordinary way, and amongst other questions asked was 'the Vendor is asked specifically to state whether he is aware of any order, designation or proposal of any local or other authority or body having compulsory powers involving any of the following ... The designation of the property as a building of special architectural or historic interest.' JW replied that they were not aware of any order etc. On 25 September 1973 the contract was signed. A day later the Department of the Environment wrote a letter to JW notifying them that the property, the subject-matter of the contract, had been selected for inclusion in the statutory list of buildings of special architectural or historic interest compiled by the Secretary of State, and that that list was about to be given legal effect. The list was given legal effect on 22 August 1973. The judge at first instance found as a fact that the value of the property with no redevelopment potential was probably £1 500 000 less than the contract price. On 12 December 1973 AI issued their writ against JW claiming rescission of the agreement on the ground of common mistake. On 14 December JW issued a writ against AI claiming specific performance of the contract or alternatively a declaration that AI had wrongly repudiated the contract, and forfeiture of the deposit and damages, with ancillary relief.

The issue before the Court of Appeal was whether the contract between AI and JW was void for common mistake.

Buckley LJ: 'It has been contended before us that there was here a common mistake of fact on a matter of fundamental importance, in consequence of which the contract ought to be set aside. Reliance has been placed on the decision of this court in *Solle* v *Butcher* and the decision of Goff J in *Grist* v *Bailey*.

Counsel for the plaintiffs says that they bought the property as property which was ripe for development and that the defendants sold on the same basis, and that by reason of the decision to list the property the property was not in fact ripe for development. Therefore he says there was a common mistake as to the nature of the property, and the purchaser is entitled to rescission.

The actual pleading of the common mistake that is alleged is in these terms, to be found in paras 2, 3 and 4 of the statement of claim:

> "2. At the time of the execution of the Agreement both the Plaintiff and the Defendant believed that the property was suitable for and capable of being redeveloped, and the said purchase price was determined by the said belief.
> 3. Unknown to the Plaintiff and to the Defendant the Department of the Environment had on or before 25th September 1973 selected the property for inclusion in the statutory list of buildings of special architectural or historic interest compiled by the Secretary of State for the Environment.
> 4. The selection of the property for inclusion in the said list prevents the property from being suitable for or capable of being redeveloped, or alternatively substantially reduces the potentiality of the said property for redevelopment."

So the alleged common mistake was that the property was property suitable for and capable of being developed.

For the application of the doctrine of mutual mistake as a ground for setting the contract aside, it is of course necessary to show that the mistake existed at the date of the contract . . . The crucial date, in my judgment, is the date when the list was signed. It was then that the building became a listed building, and it was only then that the expectations of the parties (who no doubt both expected that this property would be capable of being developed, subject always of course to obtaining planning permission, without it being necessary to obtain listed building permission) were disappointed. For myself, I entirely agree with the conclusion which the learned judge reached on this part of the case. In my judgment, there was no mutual mistake as to the circumstances surrounding the contract at the time when the contract was entered into. The only mistake that there was one which related to the expectation of the parties. They expected that the building would be subject only to ordinary town planning consent procedures, and that expectation has been disappointed. But at the date when the contract was entered into I cannot see that there is any ground for saying that the parties were then subject to some mutual mistake of fact relating to the circumstances surrounding the contract. Accordingly, for my part, I think that the learned judge's decision on that part of the case is one which should be upheld.'

COMMON MISTAKE

In this type of mistake, the parties, though genuinely in agreement, contract on the basis of an assumption which lies at the root of a contract and subsequently proves to be false. In such a case the contract may be avoided for common mistake. Typically common mistake arises when the subject-matter of the contract has, at the time of the contract, and unknown to the parties, ceased to exist, or it has never existed.

Bell v *Lever Brothers Ltd*
[1932] AC 161 • House of Lords

Bell was employed by Lever Brothers to act as chairman of the Niger Company. In 1929 the Niger Company merged with another company. As a result of this the Niger Company no longer required a chairman. Lever Brothers therefore negotiated a redundancy settlement with Bell whereby he agreed to be made redundant in return for £30 000. After the money had been paid Lever Brothers discovered that Bell, when chairman of the Niger Company, had secretly entered into certain speculative transactions in cocoa on his own account. If Lever Brothers had known of these transactions before it made Bell redundant it could have dismissed him summarily and determined his employment contract without notice and without payment of compensation. Lever Brothers commenced an action claiming rescission of the agreement of settlement and repayment of the compensation on the ground of mistake.

At first instance Wright J gave judgment for Lever Brothers on the ground of mutual mistake as to the fundamental basis of the agreements of settlement, being of opinion that both parties entered into those agreements in the common belief that the agreements of employment could not be brought to an end without the consent of the appellants.

The Court of Appeal (Scrutton, Lawrence and Greer LJJ), in affirming the judgment of Wright J, held that the agreement of settlement should be set aside on the ground of mutual mistake.

NB: the term 'mutual mistake' is used throughout the judgments. These days the term 'common mistake' would more probably be used.

Lord Atkin: 'Mistake as to quality of the thing contracted for raises more difficult questions. In such a case a mistake will not affect assent unless it is the mistake of both parties, and is as to the existence of some quality which makes the thing without the quality essentially different from the thing as it was believed to be. Of course it may appear that the parties contracted that the article should possess the quality which one or other or both mistakenly believed it to possess. But in such a case there is a contract and the inquiry is a different one, being whether the contract as to quality amounts to a condition or a warranty, a different branch of the law. The principles to be applied are to be found in two cases which, as far as my knowledge goes, have always been treated as authoritative expositions of the law. The first is *Kennedy* v *Panama Royal Mail Co* . . .

The next case is *Smith* v *Hughes*, the well known case as to new and old oats . . .

In these cases I am inclined to think that the true analysis is that there is a contract, but that the one party is not able to supply the very thing, whether goods or services, that the other party contracted to take; and therefore the contract is unenforceable by the one if executory, while if executed the other can recover back money paid on the ground of failure of the consideration.

We are now in a position to apply to the facts of this case the law as to mistake so far as it has been stated . . .

The agreement which is said to be void is the agreement contained in the letter of March 19, 1929, that Bell would retire from the Board of the Niger Company and its subsidiaries, and that in consideration of his doing so Levers would pay him as compensation for the termination of his agreements and consequent loss of office the sum of £30 000 in full satisfaction and discharge of all claims and demands of any kind against Lever Brothers, the Niger Company or its subsidiaries. The agreement, which as part of the contract was terminated, had been broken so that it could be repudiated. Is an agreement to terminate a broken contract different in kind from an agreement to terminate an unbroken contract, assuming that the breach has given the one party the right to declare the contract at an end? I feel the weight of the plaintiffs' contention that a contract immediately determinable is a different thing from a contract for an unexpired term, and that the difference in kind can be illustrated by the immense price or release from the longer contract as compared with the shorter. And I agree that an agreement to take an assignment of a lease for five years is not the same thing as to take an assignment of a lease for three years, still less a term for a few months. But, on the whole, I have come to the conclusion that it would be wrong to decide that an agreement to terminate a definite specified contract is void if it turns out that the agreement had already been broken and could have been terminated otherwise. The contract released is the identical contract in both cases, and the party paying for release gets exactly what he bargains for. It seems immaterial that he could have got the same result in another way, or that if he had known the true facts he would not have entered into the bargain. A buys B's horse; he thinks the horse is sound and he pays the price of a sound horse; he would certainly not have bought the horse if he had known as the fact is that the horse is unsound. If B has made no representation as to soundness and has not contracted that the horse is sound, A is bound and cannot recover back the price. A buys a picture from B; both A and B believe it to be the work of an old master, and a high price is paid. It turns out to be a modern copy. A has no remedy in the absence of representation or warranty. A agrees to take on lease or to buy from B an unfurnished dwelling-house. The house is in fact uninhabitable. A would never have entered into the bargain if he had known the fact. A has no remedy, and the position is the same whether B knew the facts or not, so long as he made no representation or gave no warranty. A buys a roadside garage business from B abutting on a public thoroughfare: unknown to A, but known to B, it has already been decided to construct a bypass road which will divert substantially the whole of the traffic from passing A's garage. Again A has no remedy. All these cases involve hardship on A and benefit B, as most people would say, unjustly. They can be supported on the ground that it is of paramount importance that contracts should be observed, and that if parties honestly comply with the essentials of the formation of contracts – i.e., agree in the same terms on the same subject-matter – they are bound, and must rely on the stipulations of the contract for protection from the effect of facts unknown to them.

This brings the discussion to the alternative mode of expressing the result of a mutual mistake. It is said that in such a case as the present there is to be implied a stipulation in the contract that a condition of its efficacy is that the facts should be as understood by both parties – namely, that the contract could not be terminated till the end of the current term. The question of the existence of conditions, express or implied, is obviously one that affects not the formation of contract, but the investigation of the terms of the contract when made. A condition derives its efficacy from the consent of the parties, express or implied. They have agreed, but on what terms. One term may be that unless the facts are or are not of a particular nature, or unless an event has or has not happened, the contract is not to take effect. With regard to future facts such a condition is obviously contractual. Till the event occurs the parties are bound. Thus the condition (the exact terms of which need not here be investigated) that is generally accepted as underlying the principle of the frustration cases is contractual, an implied condition. Sir John Simon formulated for the assistance of your Lordships a proposition which should be recorded: "Whenever it is to be inferred from the terms of a contract or its surrounding circumstances that the consensus has been reached upon the basis of a particular contractual assumption, and the assumption is not true, the contract is avoided: i.e., it is void *ab initio* if the assumption is of present fact and it ceases to bind if the assumption is of future fact."

I think few would demur to this statement, but its value depends upon the meaning of "a contractual assumption", and also upon the true meaning to be attached to "basis", a metaphor which may mislead. When used expressly in contracts, for instance, in policies of insurance, which state that the truth of the statements in the proposal is to be the basis of the contract of insurance, the meaning is clear. The truth of the statements is made a condition of the contract, which failing, the contract is void unless the condition is waived. The proposition does not amount to more than this that, if the contract expressly or impliedly contains a term that a particular assumption is a condition of the contract; the contract is avoided if the assumption is not true. But we have not advanced far on the inquiry how to ascertain whether the contract does contain such a condition. Various words are to be found to define the state of things which make a condition. "In the contemplation of both parties fundamental to the continued validity of the contract", "a foundation essential to its existence", "a fundamental reason for making it", are phrases found in the important judgment of Scrutton LJ in the present case. The first two phrases appear to me to be unexceptionable. They cover the case of a contract to serve in a particular place, the existence of which is fundamental to the service, or to procure the services of a professional vocalist, whose continued health is essential to performance. But "a fundamental reason for making a contract" may, with respect, be misleading. The reason of one party only is presumably not intended, but in the cases I have suggested above, of the sale of a horse or of a picture, it might be said that the fundamental reason for making the contract was the belief of both parties that the horse was sound or the picture an old master, yet in neither case would the condition as I think exist. Nothing is more dangerous than to allow oneself liberty to construct for the parties contracts which they have not in terms made by importing implications which would appear to make the contract more businesslike or more just. The implications to be made are to be no more than are "necessary" for giving business efficacy to the transaction, and it appears to me that, both as to existing facts and future facts, a condition would not be implied unless the new state of facts makes the contract something different in kind from the contract in the original state of facts . . .

We therefore get a common standard for mutual mistake and implied conditions whether as to existing or as to future facts. Does the state of the new facts destroy the identity of the subject-matter as it was in the original state of facts? To apply the principle to the infinite combinations of facts that arise in actual experience will continue to be difficult, but if this case results in establishing order into what has been a somewhat confused and difficult branch of the law it will have served a useful purpose.

I have already stated my reasons for deciding that in the present case the identity of the subject-matter was not destroyed by the mutual mistake, if any, and need not repeat them.'

MISTAKE AS TO SUBSTANCE OR QUALITY

Is there a distinction to be drawn between a mistake as to *substance* (or essence) and a mistake as to *quality* (or attributes)? Does the former avoid a contract whereas the latter does not?

Kennedy v Panama, New Zealand and Australian Royal Mail Co Ltd
(1867) LR 2 QB 580 • Queen's Bench

The Panama, New Zealand and Australian Royal Mail Co Ltd (the company) issued a prospectus which stated that they were 'prepared to receive applications for new shares in order to enable the company to perform the contract recently entered into with the government of New Zealand, for a monthly mail service between Sydney, New Zealand, and Panama, in correspondence with the West Indian Mail Company's steamers between Southampton and Panama'. Kennedy, induced by this statement in the prospectus, applied for and obtained some of the new shares. The contract alluded to in the prospectus had been made by the company with the agent of the New Zealand government, both parties *bona fide* believing that he had authority to make it; but it turned out that he had no such authority, and the government refused to ratify the contract. On discovering the misrepresentation Kennedy sued to recover the instalments he had paid on the shares.

Blackburn J: 'The only remaining question is one of much greater difficulty. It was contended by Mr Mellish, on behalf of Lord Gilbert Kennedy, that the effect of the prospectus was to warrant to the intended shareholders that there really was such a contract as is there represented, and not merely to represent that the company *bona fide* believed it; and that the difference in substance between shares in a company with such a contract and shares in a company whose supposed contract was not binding, was a difference in substance in the nature of the thing; and that the shareholder was entitled to return the shares as soon as he discovered this, quite independently of fraud, on the ground that he had applied for one thing and got another. And, if the invalidity of the contract really made the shares he obtained different things in substance from those which he applied for, this would, we think, be good law. The case would then resemble *Gompertz* v *Bartlett* and *Gurney* v *Wormersley*, where the person, who had honestly sold what he thought a bill without recourse to him, was nevertheless held bound to return the price on its turning out that the supposed bill was a forgery in the one case, and void under the stamp laws in the other; in both cases the ground of the decision being that the thing handed over was not the thing paid for. A similar principle was acted upon in *Ship's Case*. There is, however, a very important difference between cases where a contract may be rescinded on account of fraud, and those in which it may be rescinded on the ground that there is a difference in substance between the thing bargained for and that obtained. It is enough to shew that there was a fraudulent representation as to *any part* of that which induced the party to enter into the contract which he seeks to rescind; but where there has been an innocent misrepresentation or misapprehension, it does not authorize a rescission unless it is such as to shew that there is a complete difference in substance between what was supposed to be and what was taken, so as to constitute a failure of consideration . . .

The principle is well illustrated in civil law . . . There, – after laying down the general rule, that where the parties are not one as to the subject of the contract there is no agreement, and that this applies where the parties have misapprehended each other as to the corpus, as where an absent slave was sold and the buyer thought he was buying Pamphilus and the vendor thought he was selling Stichus, and pronouncing the judgment that in such a case there was no bargain because there was "*error in corpore*", . . . and the answers given by the great jurists quoted are to the effect, that if there be misapprehension as to the substance of the thing there is no contract; but if it be only a difference in some quality or accident, even though the misapprehension may have been the actuating motive to the purchaser, yet the contract remains binding . . . And, as we apprehend, the principle of our law is the same as that of the civil law; and the difficulty in every case is to determine whether the mistake or misapprehension is as to the substance of the whole consideration, going, as it were, to the root of the matter, or only to some point, even though a material point, an error as to which does not affect the substance of the whole consideration . . .

In the present case the prospectus states that the issue of the new shares was authorized by a meeting. Had that been a mistake, we think it would have been in the substance, as the applicant would not have had shares at all; but that statement was quite accurate, and he got shares in the company. It was stated in the prospectus that the motive for the increase of the capital was to enable the company to work the new contract. That also was strictly accurate. It was, by implication, stated that the contract was binding, and this was a mis-statement, though an innocent one; but we do not think that it affected the substance of the matter, for the applicant actually got shares in the very company for shares in which he had applied; and that company has, by means of the invalid contract, got the benefit, and is now carrying the mails on terms, not the same as those they supposed, and perhaps not so profitable, but still on profitable terms; and the shares obtained in the company, such as it is, are far from being of no value: indeed, the fall of £2 per share, which is stated in the case to be the discount at the time of action brought, is not greater than may be very well accounted for by the change of times, quite independently of the dispute about the contract. We think there was a misapprehension as to that which was a material part of the motive inducing the applicant to ask for the shares, but not preventing the shares from being in substance those he applied for . . .

But if the question be, as we think it is, whether the misapprehension as to the contract goes to the root and substance of the matter, so as to make the shares which the applicant has obtained in a company with this questionable contract substantially different things from shares in a company with a valid contract, we think those considerations are legitimate; and they lead us to the conclusion that the case is analogous to that of the horse supposed to be sound and not really so, and not to the case of a thing substantially different.

It follows that in our opinion the judgment in both actions should be for the company.'

Does mistake as to substance avoid the contract?

The following cases show that mistake as to substance does not always avoid the contract.

Solle v *Butcher*

[1950] 1 KB 671 • Court of Appeal

Butcher let a flat to Solle for £250 per year. Both parties believed at the time of letting that the flat was not subject to the Rent Restriction Acts. If it had been subject to the Rent Restriction Acts the appropriate rent would have been £140 per year. Butcher claimed that he relied on Solle's assurances that the flat was not subject to the Rent Restriction Acts. Later Solle brought an action in the County Court claiming that the flat was subject to the Rent Restriction Acts and that, therefore, his rent should only be £140 per year. Butcher claimed that the lease was either void at common law for mistake or voidable in equity.

Denning LJ: 'In this plight the landlord seeks to set aside the lease. He says, with truth, that it is unfair that the tenant should have the benefit of the lease for the outstanding five years of the term at £140 a year, when the proper rent is £250 a year. If he cannot give a notice of increase now, can he not avoid the lease? The only ground on which he can avoid it is on the ground of mistake. It is quite plain that the parties were under a mistake. They thought that the flat was not tied down to a controlled rent, whereas in fact it was. In order to see whether the lease can be avoided for this mistake it is necessary to remember that mistake is of two kinds: first, mistake which renders the contract void, that is, a nullity from the beginning, which is the kind of mistake which was dealt with by the courts of common law; and, secondly mistake which renders the contract not void, but voidable, that is, liable to be set aside on such terms as the court thinks fit, which is the kind of mistake which was dealt with by the courts of equity. Much of the difficulty which has attended this subject has arisen because, before the fusion of law and equity, the courts of common law, in order to do justice in the case in hand, extended this doctrine of mistake beyond its proper limits and held contracts to be void which were really only voidable, a process which was capable of being attended with much injustice to third persons who had bought goods or otherwise committed themselves on the faith that there was a contract. (In the well-known case of *Cundy* v *Lindsay*, Cundy suffered such an injustice. He bought the handkerchiefs from the rogue, Blenkarn, before the Judicature Acts came into operation.) Since the fusion of law and equity, there is no reason to continue this process, and it will be found that only those contracts are now held void in which the mistake was such as to prevent the formation of any contract at all.

Let me first consider mistakes which render a contract a nullity. All previous decisions on this subject must now be read in the light of *Bell* v *Lever Bros Ltd.* The correct interpretation of that case, to my mind, is that, once a contract has been made, that is to say, once the parties, whatever their inmost states of mind, have to all outward appearances agreed with sufficient certainty in the same terms on the same subject matter, then the contract is good unless and until it is set aside for failure of some condition on which the existence of the contract depends, or for fraud, or on some equitable ground. Neither party can rely on his own mistake to say it was a nullity from the beginning, no matter that it was a mistake which to his mind was fundamental, and no matter that the other party knew that he was under a mistake. *A fortiori*, if the other party did not know of the mistake, but shared it. The cases where goods have perished at the time of sale, or belong to the buyer, are really contracts which are not void for mistake but are void by reason of an implied condition precedent, because the contract proceeded on the basic assumption that it was possible of performance . . .

Applying these principles, it is clear that here there was a contract. The parties agreed in the same terms on the same subject-matter. It is true that the landlord was under a mistake which was to him fundamental: he would not for one moment have considered letting the flat for seven years if it meant that he could only charge £140 a year for it. He made the fundamental mistake of believing that the rent he could charge was not tied down to a controlled rent; but, whether it was his own mistake or a mistake common to both him and the tenant, it is not a ground for saying that the lease was from the beginning a nullity. Any other view would lead to remarkable results, for it would mean that, in the many cases where the parties mistakenly think a house is outside the Rent Restriction Acts when it is really within them, the tenancy would be a nullity, and the tenant would have to go; with the result that the tenants would not dare to seek to have their rents reduced to the permitted amounts lest they should be turned out.

Let me next consider mistakes which render a contract voidable, that is, liable to be set aside on some equitable ground. Whilst presupposing that a contract was good at law, or at any rate not void, the court of equity would often relieve a party from the consequences of his own mistake, so long as it could do so without injustice to third parties. The court, it was said, had power to set aside the contract whenever it was of opinion that it was unconscientious for the other party to avail himself of the legal advantage which he had obtained: *Torrance* v *Bolton* per James LJ.

The court had, of course, to define what it considered to be unconscientious, but in this respect equity has shown a progressive development. It is now clear that a contract will be set aside if the mistake of the one party has been induced by a material misrepresentation of the other, even though it was not fraudulent or fundamental; or if one party, knowing that the other is mistaken about the terms of an offer, or the identity of the person by whom it is made, lets him remain under his delusion and concludes a contract on the mistaken terms instead of pointing out the mistake. That is, I venture to think, the ground on which the defendant in *Smith* v *Hughes* would be exempted nowadays, and on which, according to the view by Blackburn J of the facts, the contract in *Lindsay* v *Cundy*, was voidable and not void; and on which the lease in *Sowler* v *Potter*, was, in my opinion, voidable and not void.

A contract is also liable in equity to be set aside if the parties were under a common misapprehension either as to facts or as to their relative and respective rights, provided that the misapprehension was fundamental and that the party seeking to set it aside was not himself at fault . . .

. . . [T]he House of Lords in 1867 in the great case of *Cooper* v *Phibbs*, affirmed the doctrine there acted on as correct. In that case an uncle had told his nephew, not intending to misrepresent anything, but being in fact in error, that he (the uncle) was entitled to a fishery; and the nephew, after the uncle's death, acting in the belief of the truth of what the uncle had told him, entered into an agreement to rent the fishery from the uncle's daughters, whereas it actually belonged to the nephew himself. The mistake there as to the title to the fishery did not render the tenancy agreement a nullity. If it had done, the contract would have been void at law from the beginning and equity would have had to follow the law. There would have been no contract to set aside and no terms to impose. The House of Lords, however, held that the mistake was only such as to make it voidable, or, in Lord Westbury's words, "liable to be set aside" on such terms as the court thought fit to impose; and it was so set aside.

The principle so established by *Cooper* v *Phibbs* has been repeatedly acted on . . .

Applying that principle to this case, the facts are that the plaintiff, the tenant, was a surveyor who was employed by the defendant, the landlord, not only to arrange finance for the purchase of the building and to negotiate with the rating authorities as to the new rateable values, but also to let the flats. He was the agent for letting, and he clearly formed the view that the building was not controlled. He told the valuation officer so. He advised the defendant what were the rents which could be charged. He read to the defendant an opinion of counsel relating to the matter, and told him that in his opinion he could charge £250 and that there was no previous control. He said that the flats came outside the Act and that the defendant was "clear". The defendant relied on what the plaintiff told him, and authorized the plaintiff to let at the rentals which he had suggested. The plaintiff not only let the four other flats to other people for a long period of years at the new rentals, but also took one himself for seven years at £250 a year. Now he turns round and says, quite unashamedly, that he wants to take advantage of the mistake to get the flat at £140 a year for seven years instead of the £250 a year, which is not only the rent he agreed to pay but also the fair and economic rent; and it is also the rent permitted by the Acts on compliance with the necessary formalities. If the rules of equity have become so rigid that they cannot remedy such an injustice, it is time we had a new equity, to make good the omissions of the old. But, in my view, the established rules are amply sufficient for this case . . .

In the ordinary way, of course, rescission is only granted when the parties can be restored to substantially the same position as that in which they were before the contract was made; but, as Lord Blackburn said in *Erlanger* v *New Sombrero Phosphate Co*: "The practice has always been for a court of equity to give this relief whenever, by the exercise of its powers, it can do what is practically just, though it cannot restore the parties precisely to the state they were in before the contract". That indeed was what was done in *Cooper* v *Phibbs*. Terms were imposed so as to do what was practically just. What terms then, should be imposed here? If the lease were set aside without any terms being imposed, it would mean that the plaintiff, the tenant, would have to go out and would have to pay a reasonable sum for his use and occupation. That would, however, not be just to the tenant.

The situation is similar to that of a case where a long lease is made at the full permitted rent in the common belief that notices of increase have previously been served, whereas in fact they have not. In that case, as in this, when the lease is set aside, terms must be imposed so as to see that the tenant is not unjustly evicted. When Sir John Romilly MR was faced with a somewhat similar problem, he gave the tenant the option either to agree to pay the proper rent or to go out . . . If the mistake here had not happened, a proper notice of increase would have been given and the lease would have been executed at the full permitted rent. I think that this court should follow these examples and should impose terms which will enable the tenant to choose either to stay on at the proper rent or to go out.'

In *Leaf* v *International Galleries*, above (p 355), although there was a mistake as to substance the mistake was discovered too late to avoid the contract.

Frederick E Rose (London) Ltd v *William H Pim Jnr & Co Ltd*
[1953] 2 All ER 739 • Court of Appeal

Rose received an inquiry from a third party for the supply of feveroles. Rose did not know what feveroles were so he asked Pim. Pim replied that feveroles and horsebeans were the same thing. On the understanding by both Rose and Pim that feveroles and horsebeans were the same thing Rose entered into an oral contract to purchase 500 tons of Tunisian horsebeans from Pim. The oral agreement was later incorporated into a written contract. Later it turned out that feveroles and horsebeans were *not* the same thing. Rose brought an action whereby he sought to have the contract set aside on the grounds of mistake.

Denning LJ: 'The facts which I have stated raise nice questions on the law of mistake. It is quite clear on the evidence that the parties . . . were under a common mistake. The sellers [and] the buyers . . . all thought that "feveroles" meant horsebeans, and that horsebeans meant "feveroles". They thought that if they got horsebeans they would get the "feveroles" which they wanted. It was under the influence of that mistake that they entered into those contracts for horsebeans . . .

What is the effect in law of this common mistake on the contract between the buyers and the sellers? Counsel for the sellers quoted *Bell* v *Lever Bros Ltd* and suggested that the contract was a nullity and void from the beginning, though he shuddered at the thought of the consequences of so holding. I am clearly of opinion that the contract was not a nullity. It is true that both parties were under a mistake, and that the mistake was of a fundamental character with regard to the subject-matter. The goods contracted for – horsebeans – were essentially different from what they were believed to be – "feveroles". Nevertheless, the parties to all outward appearances were agreed. They had agreed with quite sufficient certainty on a contract for the sale of goods by description, namely, horsebeans. Once they had done that, nothing in their minds could make the contract a nullity from the beginning, though it might, to be sure, be a ground in some circumstances for setting the contract aside in equity. In *Ryder* v *Woodley*, where a buyer contracted to buy a commodity described "St Gilles Marais wheat", believing that it was wheat when it was not, the contract was held to be binding on him and not a nullity. In *Harrison & Jones, Ltd* v *Bunten & Lancaster, Ltd* where parties contracted for the supply of "Calcutta Kapok 'Sree' brand", both believing it to be pure kapok containing no cotton, whereas it in fact contained ten to twelve per cent of cotton, Pilcher J held that their mistake, although fundamental, did not make the contract a nullity . . .

At the present day, since the fusion of law and equity, the position appears to be that, when the parties to a contract are to all outward appearances in full and certain agreement, neither of them can set up his own mistake, or the mistake of both of them, so as to make the contract a nullity from the beginning. Even a common mistake as to the subject-matter does not make it a nullity. Once the contract is outwardly complete, the contract is good unless and until it is set aside for failure of some condition on which the existence of the contract depends, or for fraud, or on some equitable ground: see *Solle* v *Butcher*. Could this contract, then, have been set aside? I think it could, if the parties had acted in time. This contract was made under a common mistake as to the meaning of "feveroles" and "horsebeans". This mistake was induced by the innocent misrepresentation of the sellers, made to the buyers and passed on to the sub-buyers. As soon as the buyers and sub-buyers discovered the mistake they could, I think, have rejected the goods and asked for their money back. The fact that the contract was executed would not be a bar to rescission. But once the buyers and subbuyers accepted the goods, and treated themselves as the owners of them, they could no longer claim rescission: see *Leaf* v *International Galleries*.'

There are, however, cases which show that a mistake as to substance will avoid the contract. In *Bell* v *Lever Brothers Ltd* Lord Thankerton said that a mistake as to the subject-matter must relate to 'something which both must necessarily have accepted in their minds as an *essential and integral* element of the subject-matter'.

Nicholson & Venn v *Smith-Marriott*

(1947) 177 LT 189 • King's Bench

Venn bought a set of linen napkins and tablecloths which bore a royal coat of arms from Smith at auction for 750 guineas. The linen set had been described in the auction catalogue as 'all with the crest and arms of Charles I and . . . the authentic property of that monarch'. The linen turned out not to be Carolean but Georgian and worth only £105. One of the arguments put forward by Venn was that he was entitled to have his price repaid since the contract was void for mistake.

Hallett J: '. . . [If the plaintiffs are] right and there was a mutual mistake vitiating the contract, they will be entitled to . . . the price of the goods if they are entitled to reject them. Therefore, two questions appeared at one time to arise. The first and major question was whether here the mutual mistake was of such a character as to vitiate the assent of the parties to the contract of sale. Counsel for the defendants never disputed that there was a mistake and that it was mutual, in that both parties contracted on the basis and in the belief, which was mistaken, that this table linen bore the crest and arms of Charles I . . . For the defendants it was contended that the mutual mistake was not of such a character as to vitiate the assent of the parties to the contract. Counsel for the plaintiffs contended the contrary . . .

In *Bell* v *Lever Brothers Ltd* Lord Atkin throws some light upon the problem, saying, "Mistake as to quality of the thing contracted for raises more difficult questions. In such a case a mistake will not affect assent unless it is the mistake of both parties" – as here it was – "and is as to the existence of some quality which makes the thing without the quality essentially different from the thing as it was believed to be. Of course it may appear that the parties contracted that the article should posses the quality which one or other or both mistakenly believed it to possess. But in such a case there is a contract and the inquiry is a different one, being whether the contract as to quality amounts to a condition or a warranty, a different branch of the law." I profited from those words of Lord Atkin to try and keep clear in my head the two different aspects of the matter, the contractual aspect . . . and the aspect of mutual mistake.

Lord Atkin further says: "If the invalidity of the contract really made the shares he obtained different things in substance from those which he applied for, this . . . would, we think, be good law". So the question first posed by Lord Atkin is whether what is missing is a quality which makes the thing essentially different from the thing that it was believed to be and is a quality which, if present, would make the thing essentially different from that which was supplied, while the second test is whether the things obtained were different in substance from those which the plaintiffs had sought to buy . . .

Clearly, in this case, as it seems to me, what the defendants were intending to sell and the plaintiffs intending to buy was not two fine table cloths and twelve fine table napkins as such, but something which I will describe as a Carolean relic. Using the language of Lord Atkin, I am disposed to the view that a Georgian relic, if there be such a thing – which I have no reason to suppose there is – is an "essentially different" thing from a Carolean relic. I think that the absence of the crest and arms of Charles I – the absence of anything attesting or appearing to attest a connection between this table linen and that monarch . . . – did make the goods obtained different things in substance from those which the plaintiffs sought to buy and believed that they had bought. I should be disposed therefore, though recognising the great difficulties of the point and without any undue confidence in the correctness of any judgment, to hold if necessary that here there was a mutual mistake of the kind or category calculated to vitiate the assent of the parties and therefore to enable the plaintiffs to treat themselves as not bound by the contract.'

The transaction could be regarded in two ways:

1 The parties may have intended to buy and sell table linen: in this case a mistake as to its age or value would be irrelevant – it would be a mistake as to quality and therefore not an operative mistake.
2 The parties may have intended to buy and sell a Carolean relic, i.e. a mistake as to substance; in that case their mistake would be fundamental and make the contract void.

Does mistake as to the quality of the thing contracted for avoid the contract?

In *Bell* v *Lever Brothers Ltd* Lord Atkin said that mistake as to quality 'will not affect assent unless it is the mistake of both parties, and is as to the existence of some quality which makes the thing without the quality *essentially different* from the thing as it was believed to be'.

Mistake as to quality will not generally avoid the contract.

Smith v Hughes

(1871) 40 LJQB 221 • Queen's Bench

The facts are stated in the judgment of Cockburn CJ.

Cockburn CJ: 'This was an action brought in the County Court of Surrey upon a contract for the sale of a quantity of oats by the plaintiff to the defendant, which contract the defendant had refused to complete, on the ground that the contract had been for the sale and purchase of old oats, whereas the oats tendered by the plaintiff had been oats of the last crop, and therefore not in accordance with the contract.

The plaintiff was a farmer, the defendant a trainer of race horses. And it appeared that the plaintiff, having some good winter oats to sell, had applied to the defendant's manager, to know if he wanted to buy oats, and having received for answer that the manager was always ready to buy good oats, exhibited to him a sample, saying at the same time that he had forty or fifty quarters of the same oats for sale at the price of 35s per quarter. The manager took the sample, and on the following day wrote to say that he would take the whole quantity at the price of 34s a quarter.

Thus far the parties were agreed, but there was a conflict of evidence between them as to whether anything passed at the interview between the plaintiff and defendant's manager on the subject of the oats being old oats, the defendant asserting that he had expressly said that he was ready to buy old oats, and that the plaintiff had replied that the oats were old oats, while the plaintiff denied that any reference had been made to the oats being old or new.

The plaintiff having sent in a portion of the oats, the defendant, on meeting him afterwards, said "Why those were new oats you sent me", to which the plaintiff having answered, "I knew they were; I had none other"; the defendant replied, "I thought I was buying old oats; new oats are useless to me, you must take them back". This the plaintiff refused to do, and brought this action.

It was stated by the defendant's manager that trainers, as a rule, always used old oats, and that his own practice was never to buy new oats if he could get old. But the plaintiff denied having known that defendant never bought new oats, or that trainers did not use them, and, on the contrary, asserted that a trainer had recently offered him a price for new oats. Evidence was given for the defendant that 34*s* a quarter was a very high price for new oats, and such as a prudent man of business would not have given. On the other hand, it appeared that oats were at the time very scarce and dear.

The learned Judge of the County Court left two questions to the jury: first, whether the word "old" had been used with reference to the oats in the conversation between the plaintiff and the defendant's manager; secondly, whether the plaintiff had believed that the defendant believed, or was under the impression, that he was contracting for old oats; in either of which cases he directed the jury to find for the defendant.

It is to be regretted that the jury were not required to give specific answers to the questions so left to them. For it is quite possible that their verdict may have been given for the defendant on the first ground, in which case there could, I think, be no doubt as to the propriety of the Judge's direction; whereas now, as it is possible that the verdict of the jury, or at all events of some of them, may have proceeded on the second ground, we are called upon to consider and decide whether the ruling of the learned Judge, with reference to the second question, was right.

For this purpose, we must assume that nothing was said on the subject of the defendant's manager desiring to buy *old* oats, or of the oats having been said to be *old.* On the other hand, we must assume that the defendant's manager believed the oats to be *old* oats, and that the plaintiff was conscious of the existence of such belief, but did nothing directly or indirectly to bring it about, simply offering his oats, and exhibiting his sample, remaining perfectly passive as to what was passing in the mind of the other party. The question is, whether under such circumstances the passive acquiescence of the seller in the self-deception of the buyer, will entitle the latter to avoid the contract. I am of opinion that it will not . . .

I take the true rule to be, that where a specific article is offered for sale without express warranty, or without circumstances from which the law will imply a warranty – as where, for instance, an article is ordered for a specific purpose – and the buyer has full opportunity of inspecting and forming his own judgment, if he chooses to act on his own judgment, the rule *caveat emptor* applies. If he gets the article he contracted to buy, and that article corresponds with what it was sold as, he gets all he is entitled to, and is bound by the contract. Here the defendant agreed to buy a specific parcel of oats. The oats were what they were sold as, namely, good oats according to the sample. The buyer persuaded himself that they were old oats when they were not so, but the seller neither said nor did anything to contribute to his deception. He has himself to blame. The question is, not what a man of scrupulous morality or nice honour would do under such circumstances. The case put of the purchase of an estate in which there is a mine under the surface, but the fact is unknown to the seller, is one in which a man of tender conscience or high honour would be unwilling to take advantage of the ignorance of the seller, but there could be no doubt that the contract for the sale of the estate would be binding . . .

Now, in this case, there was plainly no legal obligation in the plaintiff, in the first instance, to state whether the oats were new or old. He offered them for sale according to the sample, as he had a perfect right to do, and gave the buyer the fullest opportunity of inspecting the sample, which practically was equivalent to an inspection of the oats themselves. What then was there to create any trust or confidence between the parties, so as to make it incumbent on the plaintiff to communicate the fact that the oats were not, as the defendant assumed them to be, old oats? If, indeed, the buyer, instead of acting on his own opinion, had asked the question whether the oats were old or new, or had said anything which intimated his understanding that the seller was selling the oats as old oats, the case would have been wholly different; or even if he had said anything which shewed that he was not acting on his own inspection and judgment, but assumed as the foundation of the contract that the oats were old, the silence of the seller as a means of misleading him, might have amounted to a fraudulent concealment, such as would have entitled the buyer to avoid the contract. Here, however, nothing of the sort occurs. The buyer in no way refers to the seller but acts entirely on his own judgment . . .

It only remains to deal with an argument which was pressed upon us, that, as the defendant, in the present case, intended to buy old oats, and the plaintiff to sell new, the two minds were not *ad idem*, and that consequently there was no contract. This argument proceeds on the fallacy of confounding what was merely a motive operating on the buyer to induce him to buy, with one of the essential conditions of the contract. Both parties were agreed as to the sale and purchase of this particular parcel of oats. The defendant believed the oats to be old, and was thus induced to agree to buy them, but he omitted to make their age a condition of the contract. All that can be said is that the two minds were not *ad idem* as to the age of the oats; they certainly were *ad idem* as to the sale and purchase of them. Suppose a person to buy a horse without a warranty, believing him to be sound, and the horse turns out unsound, could it be contended that it would be open to him to say that, as he had intended to buy a sound horse, and the seller to sell an unsound one, the contract was void, because the seller must have known from the price the buyer was willing to give, or from his general habits, as a buyer of horses, that he thought the horse was sound? The cases are exactly parallel.

The result is that, in my opinion, the learned Judge of the County Court was wrong in leaving the second question to the jury, and that consequently the case must go down to a new trial.'

Blackburn J: 'But I have more difficulty about the second point raised in the case. I apprehend that if one of the parties intends to make a contract on one set of terms, and the other intends to make a contract on another set of terms; or, as it is sometimes expressed, if the parties are not *ad idem*, there is no contract, unless the circumstances are such as to preclude one of the parties from denying that he has agreed to the terms of the other. The rule of law is that stated in *Freeman* v *Cooke*.

If, whatever a man's real intention may be, he so conducts himself that a reasonable man would believe that he was assenting to the terms proposed by the other party, and that other party, upon that belief, enters into the contract with him, the man thus conducting himself would be equally bound as if he had intended to agree to that party's terms.

The jury were directed that if they believed that the word "old" was used, they should find for the defendant; and this was right, for if that was the case, it is obvious that neither did the defendant intend to enter into a contract on the plaintiff's terms, that is, to buy this parcel of oats without any stipulation as to their quality, nor could the plaintiff have been led to believe that he was intending to do so.

But the second direction raises the difficulty. I think that if from that direction the jury would understand that they were first to consider whether they were satisfied that the defendant intended to buy this parcel of oats, on the terms that it was part of his contract with the plaintiff that they were old oats, so as to have the warranty of the plaintiff to that effect; they were properly told that if that was so, the defendant could not be bound to a contract without any such warranty, unless the plaintiff was misled. But I doubt whether the direction would bring to the minds of the jury the distinction between agreeing to take the oats under the belief that they were old, and agreeing to take the oats under the belief that the plaintiff contracted that they were old.

The difference is the same as that between buying a horse believed to be sound, and buying one believed to be warranted sound; but I doubt if it was made obvious to the jury. And I doubt this the more, because I do not see much evidence to justify a finding for the defendant, on this latter ground, if the word "old" was not used. There may have been more evidence than is stated in the case, and the demeanour of the witnesses may have strengthened the impression produced by the evidence there was, but it does not seem a very satisfactory verdict if it proceeded on this latter ground.

I agree, therefore, in the result, that there should be a new trial.'

Failure of consideration

If a 'contract' is held to be void because of an operative mistake then this will result in a total failure of consideration. In such a case the seller of goods could not claim or retain the purchase money. It does not matter whether the contract was valid or not. However, when a buyer brings an action for damages for non-delivery the *validity* of the contract will arise.

The problem is this: if you have spent money in pursuance of a 'contract' which turns out to be void you will have no contract on which to base an action. Instead you need to be able to say that there is a contract in existence but it has been broken by the other party.

McRae v *Commonwealth Disposals Commission*
(1951) 84 CLR 377 • High Court of Australia

The Commonwealth Disposals Commission invited tenders 'for the purchase of an oil tanker lying on Jourmaund Reef, which is approximately 100 miles north of Samarai. The vessel is said to contain oil.' McRae's tender was accepted by the Commission. A condition of the sale stated that the goods 'are sold as and where they lie with all faults' and no warranty was given as to 'condition description quality or otherwise'. Unable to locate Jourmaund Reef on a map McRae was supplied by the Commission with the alleged location of the tanker. At considerable expense McRae fitted out a salvage expedition and proceeded to the location given to him by the Commission but he was unable to find any tanker there. McRae sued the Commission for breach of contract. The Commission argued that no contract had come into existence because any such agreement was void for mistake.

Dixon and Fullagar JJ: 'The first question to be determined is whether a contract was made between the plaintiffs and the Commission. The argument that the contract was void, or, in other words, that there was no contract, was based, as has been observed, on *Couturier* v *Hastie* . . . No occasion seems to have arisen for a close examination of *Couturier* v *Hastie* but such an occasion does now arise.

In considering *Couturier* v *Hastie* . . . [the] question thus raised would seem to depend entirely on the construction of the contract, and it appears really to have been so treated throughout . . .

In *Bell* v *Lever Bros Ltd* Lord Atkin, though he does not mention *Couturier* v *Hastie* itself, discusses *Gompertz* v *Bartlett* and *Gurney* v *Womersley* and other cases which have sometimes been regarded as turning on mistake avoiding a contract *ab initio*, and His Lordship concludes the discussion with a very important observation. He says: – "In these cases I am inclined to think that the true analysis is that there is a contract, but that the one party is not able to supply the very thing, whether goods or services, that the other party contracted to take; and therefore the contract is unenforceable by the one if executory, while, if executed, the other can recover back money paid on the ground of failure of the consideration . . ."

The observation of Lord Atkin in *Bell* v *Lever Bros Ltd* seems entirely appropriate to *Couturier* v *Hastie*. In that case there was a failure of consideration, and the purchaser was not bound to pay the price: if he had paid it before the truth was discovered, he could have recovered it back as money had and received. The construction of the contract was the vital thing in the case because, and only because, on the construction of the contract depended the question whether the consideration had really failed, the vendor maintaining that, since he was able to hand over the shipping documents, it had not failed. The truth is that the question whether the contract was void, or the vendor excused from performance by reason of the non-existence of the supposed subject matter, did not arise in *Couturier* v *Hastie* . . .

If the view so far indicated be correct, as we believe it to be, it seems clear that the case of *Couturier* v *Hastie* does not compel one to say that the contract in the present case was void. But, even if the view that *Couturier* v *Hastie* was a case of a void contract be correct, we would still think that it could not govern the present case. Denning LJ indeed says in *Solle* v *Butcher*: – "Neither party can rely on his own mistake to say it was a nullity from the beginning, no matter that it was a mistake which to his mind was fundamental, and no matter that the other party knew he was under a mistake. *A fortiori* if the other party did not know of the mistake, but shared it." But, even if this be not wholly and strictly correct, yet at least it must be true to say that a party cannot rely on mutual mistake where the mistake consists of a belief which is, on the one hand, entertained by him without any reasonable ground, and, on the other hand, deliberately induced by him in the mind of the other party. It does not seem possible on the evidence to say that Bowser or Sheehan was guilty of fraud in the sense that either knew at the date of the contract that the Commission had no tanker to sell. And even at the later stage, after the receipt of the message from Misima, it is difficult to impute to them actual knowledge that there was no tanker at Jourmaund Entrance. The message should have conveyed to them the fact that the only vessel lying in the vicinity was almost certainly worthless, and ordinary commonsense and decency would have suggested that the contents of the message ought to be communicated to the plaintiffs. But the message referred to a "barge type tanker", and it is quite possible that this description would fail to bring home to their minds that there was no tanker. A finding of actual knowledge that they had nothing to sell does not seem justified by the evidence, though it is difficult to credit them at the time of the publication of the advertisements with any honest affirmative belief that a tanker existed. The confusion as to locality in the description advertised is almost enough to exclude the inference of any such affirmative belief. But, even if they be credited with a real belief in the existence of a tanker, they were guilty of the grossest negligence. It is impossible to say that they had any reasonable ground for such a belief. Having no reasonable grounds for such a belief, they asserted by their advertisement to the world at large, and by their later specification of locality to the plaintiffs, that they had a tanker to sell. They must have known that any tenderer would rely implicitly on their assertion of the existence of a tanker, and they must have known that the plaintiffs would rely implicitly on their later assertion of the existence of a tanker in the latitude and longitude given. They took no steps to verify what they were asserting, and any "mistake" that existed was induced by their own culpable conduct. In these circumstances it seems out of the question that they should be able to assert that no contract was concluded. It is not unfair or inaccurate to say that the only "mistake" the plaintiffs made was that they believed what the Commission told them.

The position so far, then, may be summed up as follows. It was not decided in *Couturier* v *Hastie* that the contract in that case was void. The question whether it was void or not did not arise. If it had arisen, as in an action by the purchaser for damages, it would have turned on the ulterior question whether the contract was subject to an implied condition precedent. Whatever might then have been held on the facts of *Couturier* v *Hastie* it is impossible in this case to imply any such term. The terms of the contract and the surrounding circumstances clearly exclude any such implication. The buyers relied upon, and acted upon, the assertion of the seller that there was a tanker in existence. It is not a case in which the parties can be seen to have proceeded on the basis of a common assumption of fact so as to justify the conclusion that the correctness of the assumption was intended by both parties to be a condition precedent to the creation of contractual obligations. The officers of the Commission made an assumption, but the plaintiffs did not make an assumption in the same sense. They knew nothing except what the Commission had told them. If they had been asked, they would certainly not have said: "Of course, if there is no tanker, there is no contract". They would have said: "We shall have to go and take possession of the tanker. We simply accept the Commission's assurance that there is a tanker and the Commission's promise to give us that tanker." The only proper construction of the contract is that it included a promise by the Commission that there was a tanker in the position specified. The Commission contracted that there was a tanker there. "The sale in this case of a ship implies a contract that the subject of the transfer did exist in the character of a ship" (*Barr* v *Gibson*). If, on the other hand, the case of *Couturier* v *Hastie* and this case ought to be treated as cases raising a question of "mistake", then the Commission cannot in this case rely on any mistake as avoiding the contract, because any mistake was induced by the serious fault of their own servants, who asserted the existence of a tanker recklessly and without any reasonable ground. There was a contract, and the Commission contracted that a tanker existed in the position specified. Since there was no such tanker, there has been a breach of contract, and the plaintiffs are entitled to damages for that breach.

Before proceeding to consider the measure of damages, one other matter should be briefly mentioned. The contract was made in Melbourne, and it would seem that its proper law is Victorian law. Section 11 of the Victorian Goods Act 1928 corresponds to s 6 of the English Sale of Goods Act 1893, and provides that "where there is a contract for the sale of specific goods, and the goods without the knowledge of the seller have perished at the time when the contract is made the contract is void". This has been generally supposed to represent the legislature's view of the effect of *Couturier* v *Hastie*. Whether it correctly represents the effect of the decision in that case or not, it seems clear that the section has no application to the facts of the present case. Here the goods never existed, and the seller ought to have known that they did not exist . . .

For these reasons we are of opinion that the plaintiffs were entitled to recover damages in this case for breach of contract, and that their damages are to be measured by reference to expenditure incurred and wasted in reliance on the Commission's promise that a tanker existed at the place specified.'

Is there a doctrine of common mistake?

Associated Japanese Bank (International) Ltd v *Credit du Nord SA*

[1988] 3 All ER 902 • Queen's Bench

The facts are stated in the judgment of Steyn J.

Steyn J: 'Throughout the law of contract two themes regularly recur: respect for the sanctity of contract and the need to give effect to the reasonable expectations of honest men. Usually, these themes work in the same direction. Occasionally, they point to opposite solutions. The law regarding common mistake going to the root of a contract is a case where tension arises between the two themes. That is illustrated by the circumstances of this extraordinary case.

In broad but necessarily imprecise terms the shape of this case is as follows. In February 1984 Mr Jack Bennett concluded a sale and leaseback transaction with Associated Japanese Bank (International) Ltd (AJB) in respect of four machines which were described by serial numbers. In other words, Mr Bennett sold the machines to AJB, and AJB then leased the machines to Mr Bennett. AJB had been unwilling to enter into the transaction unless the lessee's obligations were guaranteed by an acceptable guarantor. Credit du Nord SA (CDN) proved to be an acceptable guarantor, and for a guarantee fee CDN guaranteed the obligations of the lessee under the lease agreement. AJB paid a sum in excess of £1m to Mr Bennett. Out of the proceeds of the sale Mr Bennett paid the first quarterly rental. But in May 1984 he was arrested. The second quarterly rental was never paid and it was subsequently discovered that the machines which were the subject matter of the sale and lease did not exist. Mr Bennett had committed a fraud on both AJB and CDN. Pursuant to the terms of the lease, AJB claimed the total outstanding balance from Mr Bennett. In July 1984 Mr Bennett was adjudged bankrupt. AJB sued CDN on the guarantee . . .

The central remaining question to be resolved is whether AJB is entitled under the guarantee to judgment in the sum of £1 012 000 together with interest. The principal issues to which most of counsel's submissions were directed related to . . . whether the guarantee was void *ab initio* by reason of a common mistake affecting the guarantee, viz the existence of the machines . . .

Mistake

The common law regarding mutual or common mistake

There was a lively debate about the common law rules governing a mutual or common mistake of the parties as to some essential quality of the subject matter of the contract. Counsel for CDN submitted that *Bell* v *Lever Bros Ltd* authoritatively established that a mistake by both parties as to the existence of some quality of the subject matter of the contract, which makes the subject matter of the contract without the quality essentially different from the subject matter as it was believed to be, renders the contract void *ab initio*. Counsel for AJB contested this proposition. He submitted that at common law a mistake even as to an essential quality of the subject matter of the contract will not affect the contract unless it resulted in a total failure of consideration. It was not clear to me that this formulation left any meaningful and independent scope for the application of common law rules in this area of the law. In any event, it is necessary to examine the legal position in some detail.

The landmark decision is undoubtedly *Bell* v *Lever Bros Ltd*. Normally a judge of first instance would simply content himself with applying the law stated by the House of Lords.

There has, however, been substantial controversy about the rule established in that case. It seems right therefore to examine the effect of that decision against a somewhat wider framework. In the early history of contract law, the common law's preoccupation with consideration made the development of a doctrine of mistake impossible. Following the emergence in the nineteenth century of the theory of consensus *ad idem* it became possible to treat misrepresentation, undue influence and mistake as factors vitiating consent. Given that the will theory in English contract law was cast in objective form, judging matters by the external standard of the reasonable man, both as to contract formation and contractual interpretation, it nevertheless became possible to examine in what circumstances mistake might nullify or negative consent. But even in late Victorian times there was another powerful policy consideration militating against upsetting bargains on the ground of unexpected circumstances which occurred before or after the contract. That was the policy of *caveat emptor* which held sway outside the field of contract law subsequently codified by the Sale of Goods Act in 1893. Nevertheless, principles affecting the circumstances in which consent may be vitiated gradually emerged. The most troublesome areas proved to be two related areas, viz common mistake as to an essential quality of the subject matter of the contract and post-contractual frustration. Blackburn J, an acknowledged master of the common law, who yielded to no one in his belief in the sanctity of contract, led the way in both areas.

In *Taylor* v *Caldwell* Blackburn J first stated the doctrine of frustration in terms which eventually led to the adoption of the "radical change in obligation" test of commercial frustration in modern law: see *Davis Contractors Ltd* v *Fareham UDC* and *National Carriers Ltd* v *Panalpina (Northern) Ltd*. In the field of mistake as to the essential quality of the subject matter Blackburn J also gave the lead. In *Kennedy* v *Panama, New Zealand and Australian Royal Mail Co Ltd* the issue was whether a contract for the purchase of shares was vitiated by an untrue representation that the company had secured a contract to carry mail for the New Zealand government. The court upheld the contract. In passing it must be noted that the case was decided on a restrictive approach as to the circumstances in which a contract can be rescinded for innocent misrepresentation that, of course, was remedied in due course by equity. But in the present context the importance of the case lies in the remarks of Blackburn J about mistakes as to quality. Given the fact that there was no direct authority on the point (and certainly none which could not be explained on other grounds) he turned to the civil law. He referred to the civilian doctrine of *error in substantia*. That doctrine seeks to categorise mistakes into two categories, viz mistakes as to the substance of the subject matter or mistakes as to attributes (sometimes classified as mistakes in motive). Blackburn J, delivering the judgment of the court, held:

> ". . . the principle of our law is the same as that of the civil law and the difficulty in every case is to determine whether the mistake or misapprehension is as to the substance of the whole consideration, going, as it were, to the root of the matter, or only to some point, even though a material point, an error as to which does not affect the substance of the whole consideration."

That test did not avail the plaintiff, for it was held that he got what he bought.

None of the cases between the decisions in *Kennedy* v *Panama, New Zealand and Australian Royal Mail Co Ltd* and *Bell* v *Lever Bros Ltd* significantly contributed to the development of this area of the law. But *Bell* v *Lever Bros Ltd* was a vitally important case. The facts of that case are so well known as to require no detailed exposition. Lever Bros had, in the modern phrase, given two employees "golden handshakes" of £30 000 and £20 000 in consideration of the early termination of their service contracts. Subsequently,

Lever Bros discovered that the contracts of service had been voidable by reason of the two employees' breach of fiduciary duties in trading for their own account. Lever Bros argued that the contracts pursuant to which the service agreements were terminated were void *ab initio* for common mistake, and sought recovery of the sums paid to the employees. The claim succeeded at first instance and in the Court of Appeal but by a three to two majority the House of Lords held that the claim failed. Lord Atkin held:

> ". . . a mistake will not affect assent unless it is the mistake of both parties, and is as to the existence of some quality which makes the thing without the quality essentially different from the thing as it was believed to be."

In my view none of the other passages in Lord Atkin's speech detract from that statement of the law. Lord Thankerton came to a similar conclusion. He held that common mistake "can only properly relate to something which both must necessarily have accepted in their minds as an essential and integral part of the subject-matter".

That seems to me exactly the same test as Lord Atkin enunciated. Clearly, Lord Atkin did not conceive of any difference between his formulation and that of Lord Thankerton, for he observed:

> "To apply the principle to the infinite combinations of facts that arise in actual experience will continue to be difficult, but if this case results in establishing order into what has been a somewhat confused and difficult branch of the law it will have served a useful purpose."

Lord Blanesburgh's speech proceeded on different lines. It must not be forgotten that the issue of common mistake was only put forward at the eleventh hour. Lord Blanesburgh would have refused the necessary amendment, but he expressed his "entire accord" with the substantive views of Lord Atkin and Lord Thankerton. The majority were therefore in agreement about the governing principle.

It seems to me that the better view is that the majority in *Bell* v *Lever Bros Ltd* had in mind only mistake at common law. That appears to be indicated by the shape of the argument, the proposed amendment placed before the House of Lords and the speeches of Lord Atkin and Lord Thankerton. But, if I am wrong on this point, it is nevertheless clear that mistake at common law was in the forefront of the analysis in the speeches of the majority.

The law has not stood still in relation to mistake in equity. Today, it is clear that mistake in equity is not circumscribed by common law definitions. A contract affected by mistake in equity is not void but may be set aside on terms: see *Solle* v *Butcher, Magee* v *Pennine Insurance Co Ltd, Grist* v *Bailey*. It does not follow, however, that *Bell* v *Lever Bros Ltd* is no longer an authoritative statement of mistake at common law. On the contrary, in my view the principles enunciated in that case clearly still govern mistake at common law. It is true that in *Solle* v *Butcher* Denning LJ interpreted *Bell* v *Lever Bros Ltd* differently. He said that a common mistake, even on a most fundamental matter, does not make the contract void at law. That was an individual opinion. Neither Bucknill LJ (who agreed in the result) nor Jenkins LJ (who dissented) even mentioned *Bell* v *Lever Bros Ltd*. In *Magee* v *Pennine Insurance Co Ltd* Lord Denning MR returned to the point. About *Bell* v *Lever Bros Ltd* he simply said: "I do not propose . . . to go through the speeches in that case. They have given enough trouble to commentators already." He then repeated his conclusion in *Solle* v *Butcher*. Winn LJ dissented. Fenton Atkinson LJ agreed in the result but it is clear from his judgment that he did not agree with Lord Denning MR's interpretation of *Bell* v *Lever Bros Ltd*. Again, Lord Denning MR's observation represented only his own view. With the profoundest respect to the former Master of the Rolls, I am constrained to say that in my view his interpretation of *Bell* v *Lever Bros Ltd* does not do justice to the speeches of the majority.

When Lord Denning MR referred in *Magee* v *Pennine Insurance Co Ltd* to the views of commentators he may have had in mind comments in Cheshire and Fifoot *Law of Contract* (6th edn). In substance the argument was that the actual decision in *Bell* v *Lever Bros Ltd* contradicts the language of the speeches. If the test was not satisfied there, so the argument runs, it is difficult to see how it could ever be satisfied: see the latest edition of this valuable textbook for the same argument (Cheshire, Fifoot and Furmston *Law of Contract* (11th edn)). This is a point worth examining because at first glance it may seem persuasive. *Bell* v *Lever Bros Ltd* was a quite exceptional case; all their Lordships were agreed that common mistake had not been pleaded and would have required an amendment in the House of Lords if it were to succeed. The speeches do not suggest that the employees were entitled to keep both the gains secretly made and the golden handshakes. The former were clearly recoverable from them. Nevertheless, the golden handshakes were very substantial. But there are indications in the speeches that the so-called "merits" were not all in favour of Lever Bros. The company was most anxious, because of a corporate merger, to terminate the two service agreements. There was apparently a doubt whether the voidability of the service agreements if revealed to the company at the time of the severance contract would have affected the company's decision. Lord Thankerton said:

"... I do not find sufficient material to compel the inference that the appellants, at the time of the contract, regarded the indefeasibility of the service agreements as an essential and integral element in the subject-matter of the bargain."

Lord Atkin clearly regarded it as a hard case on the facts, but concluded "on the whole" that the plea of common mistake must fail. It is noteworthy that Lord Atkin commented on the scarcity of evidence as to the subsidiaries from the boards of which the two employees resigned. Lord Blanesburgh's speech was directed to his conclusion that the amendment ought not to be allowed. He did, however, make clear that "the mistake must go to the whole consideration", and pointed to the advantages (other than the release from the service agreements) which Lever Bros received. Lord Blanesburgh emphasised that Lever Bros secured the future co-operation of the two employees for the carrying through of the amalgamation. And the burden, of course, rested squarely on Lever Bros. With due deference to the distinguished authors who have argued that the actual decision in *Bell* v *Lever Bros Ltd* contradicts the principle enunciated in the speeches it seems to me that their analysis is altogether too simplistic, and that the actual decision was rooted in the particular facts of the case. In my judgment there is no reason to doubt the substantive reasons emerging from the speeches of the majority.

No one could fairly suggest that in this difficult area of the law there is only one correct approach or solution. But a narrow doctrine of common law mistake (as enunciated in *Bell* v *Lever Bros Ltd*), supplemented by the more flexible doctrine of mistake in equity (as developed in *Solle* v *Butcher* and later cases), seems to me to be an entirely sensible and satisfactory state of the law: see *Sheikh Bros Ltd* v *Ochsner*. And there ought to be no reason to struggle to avoid its application by artificial interpretations of *Bell* v *Lever Bros Ltd*.

It might be useful if I now summarised what appears to me to be a satisfactory way of approaching this subject. Logically, before one can turn to the rules as to mistake, whether at common law or in equity, one must first determine whether the contract itself, by express or implied condition precedent or otherwise, provides who bears the risk of the relevant mistake. It is at this hurdle that many pleas of mistake will either fail or prove to have been unnecessary. Only if the contract is silent on the point is there scope for invoking mistake. That brings me to the relationship between common law mistake and mistake in equity. Where common law mistake has been pleaded, the court must first consider this plea. If the contract is held to be void, no question of mistake in equity arises. But, if the contract is held to be valid, a plea of mistake in equity may still have to be considered: see *Grist* v *Bailey* and the analysis in *Anson's Law of Contract* (26th edn). Turning now to the approach to common law mistake, it seems to me that the following propositions are valid although not necessarily all entitled to be dignified as propositions of law.

The first imperative must be that the law ought to uphold rather than destroy apparent contracts. Second, the common law rules as to a mistake regarding the quality of the subject matter, like the common law rules regarding commercial frustration, are designed to cope with the impact of unexpected and wholly exceptional circumstances on apparent contracts. Third, such a mistake in order to attract legal consequences must substantially be shared by both parties, and must relate to facts as they existed at the time the contract was made. Fourth, and this is the point established by *Bell* v *Lever Bros Ltd*, the mistake must render the subject matter of the contract essentially and radically different from the subject matter which the parties believed to exist. While the civilian distinction between the substance and attributes of the subject matter of a contract has played a role in the development of our law (and was cited in the speeches in *Bell* v *Lever Bros Ltd*), the principle enunciated in *Bell* v *Lever Bros Ltd* is markedly narrower in scope than the civilian doctrine. It is therefore no longer useful to invoke the civilian distinction. The principles enunciated by Lord Atkin and Lord Thankerton represent the *ratio decidendi* of *Bell* v *Lever Bros Ltd*. Fifth, there is a requirement which was not specifically discussed in *Bell* v *Lever Bros Ltd*. What happens if the party who is seeking to rely on the mistake had no reasonable grounds for his belief? An extreme example is that of the man who makes a contract with minimal knowledge of the facts to which the mistake relates but is content that it is a good speculative risk. In my judgment a party cannot be allowed to rely on a common mistake where the mistake consists of a belief which is entertained by him without any reasonable grounds for such belief: cf *McRae* v *Commonwealth Disposals Commission*. That is not because principles such as estoppel or negligence require it, but simply because policy and good sense dictate that the positive rules regarding common mistake should be so qualified. Curiously enough this qualification is similar to the civilian concept where the doctrine of *error in substantia* is tempered by the principles governing *culpa in contrahendo*. More importantly, a recognition of this qualification is consistent with the approach in equity where fault on the part of the party adversely affected by the mistake will generally preclude the granting of equitable relief: see *Solle* v *Butcher*.

Applying the law to the facts

It is clear, of course, that in this case both parties, the creditor and the guarantor, acted on the assumption that the lease related to existing machines. If they had been informed that the machines might not exist, neither AJB nor CDN would for one moment have contemplated entering into the transaction. That, by itself, I accept, is not enough to sustain the plea of common law mistake. I am also satisfied that CDN had reasonable grounds for believing that the machines existed. That belief was based on CDN's discussions with Mr Bennett, information supplied by National Leasing, a respectable firm of lease brokers, and the confidence created by the fact that AJB were the lessors.

The real question is whether the subject matter of the guarantee (as opposed to the sale and lease) was essentially different from what it was reasonably believed to be. The real security of the guarantor was the machines. The existence of the machines, being profit-earning chattels, made it more likely that the debtor would be able to service the debt. More importantly, if the debtor defaulted and the creditor repossessed the machines, the creditor had to give credit for 97.5% of the value of the machines. If the creditor sued the guarantor first, and the guarantor paid, the guarantor was entitled to be subrogated to the creditor's rights in respect of recovery against the debtor: see Goff and Jones *Law of Restitution* (3rd edn). No doubt the guarantor relied to some extent on the credit-worthiness of Mr Bennett. But I find that the prime security to which the guarantor looked was the existence of the four machines as described to both parties. For both parties the guarantee of obligations under a lease with non-existent machines was essentially different from a guarantee of a lease with four machines which both parties at the time of the contract believed to exist. The guarantee is an accessory contract. The non-existence of the subject matter of the principal contract is therefore of fundamental importance. Indeed the analogy of the classic *res extincta* cases, so much discussed in the authorities, is fairly close. In my judgment, the stringent test of common law mistake is satisfied the guarantee is void *ab initio* . . .

Equitable mistake

Having concluded that the guarantee is void *ab initio* at common law, it is strictly unnecessary to examine the question of equitable mistake. Equity will give relief against common mistake in cases where the common law will not, and it provides more flexible remedies, including the power to set aside the contract on terms. It is not necessary to repeat my findings of fact save to record again the fundamental nature of the common mistake, and that CDN was not at fault in any way. If I had not decided in favour of CDN on construction and common law mistake, I would have held that the guarantee must be set aside on equitable principles. Unfortunately, and counsel are not to blame for that, the question of the terms (if any) to be imposed (having regard particularly to sums deposited by Mr Bennett with CDN) were not adequately explored in argument. If it becomes necessary to rule on this aspect, I will require further argument.'

William Sindall plc v Cambridgeshire County Council

[1994] 3 All ER 932 • Court of Appeal

The facts are given above (p 357).

Hoffmann LJ: 5. Mistake
'The judge found that in the absence of any actionable misrepresentation, Sindall was entitled to rescind the contract for a common mistake as to the existence of a sewer. This is at first sight a startling result. As Steyn J said in *Associated Japanese Bank (International) Ltd* v *Credit du Nord SA*:

> "Logically, before one can turn to the rules as to mistake, whether at common law or in equity, one must first determine whether the contract itself, by express or implied condition precedent or otherwise, provides who bears the risk of the relevant mistake. It is at this hurdle that many pleas of mistake will either fail or prove to have been unnecessary. Only if the contract is silent on the point, is there scope for invoking mistake."

When the judge speaks of the contract allocating risk "by express or implied condition precedent or otherwise" I think he includes rules of general law applicable to the contract and which, for example, provide that, in the absence of express warranty, the law is *caveat emptor.* This would, in my view, allocate the risk of an unknown defect in goods to the buyer, even though it is not mentioned in the contract. Similarly, the rule in *Hill* v *Harris* that a lessor or vendor does not impliedly warrant that the premises are fit for any particular purpose means that the contract allocates the risk of the premises being unfit for such purpose. I should say that neither in *Grist* v *Bailey* nor in *Laurence* v *Lexcourt Holdings Ltd* did the judges who decided those cases at first instance advert to the question of contractual allocation of risk. I am not sure that the decisions would have been the same if they had.

In this case the contract says in express terms that it is subject to all easements other than those of which the vendor knows or has the means of knowledge. This allocates the risk of such incumbrances to the buyer and leaves no room for rescission on the grounds of mistake.'

Evans LJ: 'This could be a textbook case on the law of mistake in contract . . .

First, mistake. There are certain circumstances in which the courts will hold that an agreement made between two parties, each labouring under a fundamental mistake, is invalid as a contract, that is to say, it has no legal effect. The judge applied the test established by the majority judgments of the House of Lords in *Bell* v *Lever Brothers* as defined by Steyn J in *Associated Japanese Bank (International) Ltd* v *Credit du Nord SA*, and he reached the following conclusion:

> "there are undoubtedly important differences between what was contracted for and what was purchased. They do not, as it seems to me, meet the essential test of being essentially and radically different."

There is no appeal against that finding or against the judge's conclusion that the builders failed to establish any common law remedy on the basis of mistake. I would add merely this, that the concept of a factual situation "essentially and radically different" from that by reference to which the parties made their agreement is the same concept, in my view, as that which may lead to frustration of the contract where there has been a change in circumstances due to a supervening event. Before 1956, there was much debate as to the legal basis for the discharge of contracts by frustration, but this was authoritatively settled by the House of Lords in *Davis Contractors Ltd* v *Fareham Urban District Council* and in particular by the speech of Viscount Radcliffe:

> "frustration occurs whenever the law recognises that without default of either party a contractual obligation has become incapable of being performed because the circumstances in which performance is called for would render it a thing radically different from that which was undertaken by the contract. *Non haec in foedera veni.* It was not this that I promised to do."

The judge proceeded to consider Sindall's claim for rescission on the ground of mutual mistake, that is to say, for the equitable remedy which is available in circumstances like those described by Denning LJ in *Solle* v *Butcher.* He found in this context that there was "such a mistake as would entitle equity to order rescission". This implies that the mistake was "fundamental" (per Denning LJ) and the question arises whether simultaneously the mistake can be fundamental yet the land not "essentially and radically different" from what it was supposed to be. But it is unnecessary and inappropriate, in my judgment, to consider this issue at this stage, because on any view of the matter, as Mr Sher I think accepts, the first question is whether the contract on its true construction covers the new situation which has arisen by reason of a change of circumstances (frustration) or the emergence of a factual situation different from that which was assumed (mutual mistake).

If the scope of the contract is wide enough to cover the new, or newly discovered, situation, then there is no room either for discharge by frustration or for rescission in equity on the grounds of mistake. Put another way, if the agreed terms provide for this situation, then the parties have "allocated the risk" as between themselves, as Mr Etherton submits that they did in the present case . . .

Equitable mistake

Logically, there remains the question whether the contract, notwithstanding that on its true construction it covers the situation which has arisen, and that it cannot be set aside for misrepresentation, nevertheless may be rescinded on the ground of equitable mistake, as defined by Denning LJ in *Solle* v *Butcher*. It must be assumed, I think, that there is a category of mistake which is "fundamental", so as to permit the equitable remedy of rescission, which is wider than the kind of "serious and radical" mistake which means that the agreement is void and of no effect in law: see *Chitty on Contracts*, 26th edn; Treitel, *The Law of Contract*, 8th edn; and Cheshire, Fifoot and Furmston's *Law of Contract*, 11th edn. The difference may be that the common law rule is limited to mistakes with regard to the subject matter of the contract, whilst equity can have regard to a wider and perhaps unlimited category of "fundamental" mistake. However that may be, I am satisfied that the judge's finding in the present case was vitiated by his assumption that the presence of the sewer and of the city's easement had serious consequences for the proposed development, even if the sewer was incorporated into the public sewer that was envisaged for the development itself (option 2A). This would not involve the loss of seven houses and three flats, as the judge appears to have thought, but, at most, of one three-bedroomed house. The additional cost of the alterations to the sewer would not have exceeded about £20,000. Given the breadth of the contract terms, in particular condition no 14 which on its face was intended to cover precisely such a situation as this, and the relatively minor consequences of the discovery of the sewer, even if some period of delay as well as additional cost was involved it is impossible to hold, in my judgment, that there is scope for rescission here.'

UNILATERAL MISTAKE

The 'objective test'

In this type of 'contract' there is no genuine agreement between the parties – the parties are not *ad idem* because one of the parties is mistaken.

This type of mistake is not often a ground for rendering a contract void because of the 'objective test' as established in *Smith* v *Hughes*, above (p 380), where Blackburn J said 'If, whatever a man's real intention may be, he so conducts himself that a reasonable man would believe that he was assenting to the terms proposed by the other party, and that other party, upon that belief, enters into the contract with him, the man thus conducting himself would be equally bound as if he had intended to agree to that party's terms.'

Four exceptions to the objective test

The following are *void* for unilateral mistake:

- where, despite outward appearances, there is no real coincidence between the terms of the offer and those of the acceptance;
- where there is a mistake as to the promise known to the other party;
- where there is a mistake as to the identity of the person with whom the contract is made;
- where there is a mistake in relation to a written document.

Offer and acceptance not coincident

These cases could be looked at as 'formation of the contract' cases: is the 'agreement' in both cases *void for uncertainty*?

Raffles v Wichelhaus

(1864) 2 H & C 906 • Exchequer

'Declaration. For that it was agreed between the plaintiff and the defendants, to wit, at Liverpool, that the plaintiff should sell to the defendants, and the defendants buy of the plaintiff, certain goods, to wit, 125 bales of Surat cotton, guaranteed middling fair merchant's Dhollorah, to arrive ex *Peerless* from Bombay; and that the cotton should be taken from the quay, and that the defendants would pay the plaintiff for the same at a certain rate, to wit, at the rate of 17¼d per pound, within a certain time when agreed upon after the arrival of the said goods in England. Averments: that the said goods did arrive by the said ship from Bombay in England, to wit, at Liverpool, and the plaintiff was then and there ready, and willing and offered to deliver the said goods to the defendants, &c. Breach: that the defendants refused to accept the said goods or pay the plaintiff for them.

Plea. That the said ship mentioned in the said agreement was meant and intended by the defendants to be the ship called the *Peerless*, which sailed from Bombay, to wit, in October; and that the plaintiff was not ready and willing and did not offer to deliver to the defendants any bales of cotton which arrived by the last mentioned ship, but instead thereof was only ready and willing and offered to deliver to the defendants 125 bales of Surat cotton which arrived by another and different ship, which was also called the *Peerless*, and which sailed from Bombay, to wit, in December.

Demurrer, and joinder therein.

Milward, in support of the demurrer. The contract was for the sale of a number of bales of cotton of a particular description, which the plaintiff was ready to deliver. It is immaterial by what ship the cotton was to arrive, so that it was a ship called the *Peerless*. The words "to arrive ex *Peerless*", only mean that if the vessel is lost on the voyage, the contract is to be at an end. [Pollock CB, It would be a question for the jury whether both parties meant the same ship called the *Peerless*.] That would be so if the contract was for the sale of a ship called the *Peerless*; but it is for the sale of cotton on board a ship of that name. [Pollock CB, The defendant only bought that cotton which was to arrive by a particular ship. It may as well be said, that if there is a contract for the purchase of certain goods in warehouse A, that is satisfied by the delivery of goods of the same description in warehouse B.] In that case there would be goods in both warehouses; here it does not appear that the plaintiff had any goods on board the other *Peerless*. [Martin B, It is imposing on the defendant a contract different from that which he entered into. Pollock CB, It is like a contract for the purchase of wine coming from a particular estate in France or Spain, where there are two estates of that name.] The defendant has no right to contradict by parol evidence a written contract upon the face of it. He does not impute misrepresentation or fraud, but only says that he fancied the ship was a different one.

Intention is of no avail, unless stated at the time of the contract. [Pollock CB, One vessel sailed in October and the other in December.] The time of sailing is no part of the contract.

Mellish (Cohen with him), in support of the plea. There is nothing on the face of the contract to shew that any particular ship called the *Peerless* was meant; but the moment it appears that two ships called the *Peerless* were about to sail from Bombay there is a latent ambiguity, and parol evidence may be given for the purpose of shewing that the defendant meant one *Peerless*, and the plaintiff another. That being so, there was no consensus *ad idem*, and therefore no binding contract. He was then stopped by the Court.

Per Curiam Pollock CB, Martin B and Pigott B. There must be judgment for the defendants.'

Judgment for the defendants.

Scriven Brothers & Co v Hindley & Co

(1913) 3 KB 564 • King's Bench

Northcott was employed by Scriven Brothers to sell a large quantity of Russian hemp and tow. The catalogue, prepared by Northcott, contained the shipping mark 'S.L.' and the numbers of the bales in two lots, namely, 63 to 67, 47 bales, and 68 to 79, 176 bales. The former were hemp and the latter were tow but the catalogue did not disclose this difference. At the showrooms bales from each of these two lots were on view, and on the floor of the room in front of the bales was written in chalk 'S.L. 63 to 67' opposite the samples of hemp, and 'S.L. 68 to 79' opposite the samples of tow. Macgregor, Hindley's buyer, bid for the 47 bales of hemp and these were knocked down to him at £24 0s 6d per ton. The 176 bales of tow were then put up and Macgregor bid £17 per ton (an extravagant price for tow). The 176 bales were immediately knocked down to him. The auctioneer said that he announced this lot as 'mixed tow', but this was denied. It was admitted at the trial that Macgregor bid under the belief that the goods were hemp. It was stated by witnesses on both sides that in their experience Russian hem and Russian tow were never landed from the same ship under the same shipping marks.

Scriven Brothers contended that the mistake was only a mistake as to value and was not one as to the subject-matter of the apparent contract.

The jury found: (1) That hemp and tow are different commodities in commerce. (2) That the auctioneer intended to sell 176 bales of tow. (3) That Macgregor intended to bid for 176 bales of hemp. (4) That the auctioneer believed that the bid was made under a mistake when he knocked down the lot. (5) That the auctioneer had reasonable ground for believing that the mistake was merely one as to value. (6) That the form of the catalogue contributed to cause the mistake that occurred.

Lawrence J: In this case the plaintiffs brought an action for £476 12s 7d, the price of 560 cwt 2 qrs 27 lbs of Russian tow, as being due for goods bargained and sold. The defendants by their defence denied that they agreed to buy this Russian tow, and alleged that they bid for Russian hemp and that the tow was knocked down to them under a mistake of fact as to the subject-matter of the supposed contract . . .

The jury have found that hemp and tow are different commodities in commerce. I should suppose that no one can doubt the correctness of this finding. The second and third findings of the jury shew that the parties were never *ad idem* as to the subject-matter of the proposed sale; there was therefore in fact no contract of bargain and sale. The plaintiffs can recover from the defendants only if they can shew that the defendants are estopped from relying upon what is now admittedly the truth . . .

I must, of course, accept for the purposes of this judgment the findings of the jury, but I do not think they create any estoppel . . .

Once it was admitted that Russian hemp was never before known to be consigned or sold with the same shipping marks as Russian tow from the same cargo, it was natural for the person inspecting the "S.L." goods and being shewn hemp to suppose that the "S.L." bales represented the commodity hemp. Inasmuch as it is admitted that some one had perpetrated a swindle upon the bank which made advances in respect of this shipment of goods it was peculiarly the duty of the auctioneer to make it clear to the bidder either upon the face of his catalogue or in some other way which lots were hemp and which lots were tow.

To rely upon a purchaser's discovering chalk marks upon the floor of the show-room seems to me unreasonable as demanding an amount of care upon the part of the buyer which the vendor had no right to exact. A buyer when he examines a sample does so for his own benefit and not in the discharge of any duty to the seller; the use of the word "negligence" in such a connection is entirely misplaced, it should be reserved for cases of want of due care where some duty is owed by one person to another. No evidence was tendered of the existence of any such duty upon the part of buyers of hemp . . . In my view it is clear that the finding of the jury upon the sixth question [that the plaintiff had contributed to the mistake] prevents the plaintiffs from being able to insist upon a contract by estoppel. Such a contract cannot arise when the person seeking to enforce it has by his own negligence or by that of those for whom he is responsible caused, or contributed to cause, the mistake.

I am therefore of opinion that judgment should be entered for the defendants.'

Mistake as to the promise known to the other party

Again these cases could be looked at as 'formation of the contract' cases: can it be said that in these cases the parties are *ad idem*?

The general rule is that although the conduct of one party is such that a reasonable man would assume that he was assenting to the offer of the other party, yet if that other party knows that he does not really assent there will be no genuine agreement.

However, the mistake must *relate* to the promise – *the actual offer* – any other mistake, e.g. as to the quality or nature of the thing contracted for will not act as an operative mistake. This rule is known as the rule in *Smith* v *Hughes*, above.

Hartog v Colin & Shields

[1939] 3 All ER 566 • King's Bench

Colin & Shields claimed that they had mistakenly offered 30 000 Argentine hare skins to Hartog at so much per pound instead of so much per piece and that Hartog knew that they had made a mistake. They argued that because Hartog knew of the mistake in the offer no contract had come into existence.

Singleton J: 'In this case, the plaintiff, a Belgian subject, claims damages against the defendants because he says they broke a contract into which they entered with him for the sale of Argentine hare skins. The defendants' answer to that claim is: "There really was no contract, because you knew that the document which went forward to you, in the form of an offer, contained a material mistake. You realised that, and you sought to take advantage of it."

Counsel for the defendants took upon himself the onus of satisfying me that the plaintiff knew that there was a mistake and sought to take advantage of that mistake. In other words, realising that there was a mistake, the plaintiff did that which James LJ, in *Tamplin* v *James*, described as "snapping up the offer". It is important, I think, to realise that in the verbal negotiations which took place in this country, and in all the discussions there had ever been, the prices of Argentine hare skins had been discussed per piece, and later, when correspondence took place, the matter was always discussed at the price per piece, and never at a price per pound . . . [T]he way in which Argentine hare skins are bought and sold is generally per piece. That is shown by the discussions which took place between the parties in this country, and by the correspondence. Then on Nov 23 came the offer upon which the plaintiff relies. It was an offer of 10 000 Argentine hares . . . at 10¼d per lb; 10 000 half hares at 6¾d per lb; 10 000 summer hares at 5d per lb. Those prices correspond, roughly, in the case of the winter hares, to 3¾d per piece, half hares 2d per piece, and summer hares 1¾d per piece. The last offer prior to this, in which prices were mentioned, was on Nov 3 from the defendants; and the price then quoted for winter hares was 10¾d per piece. Even allowing that the market was bound to fall a little, I find it difficult to believe that anyone could receive an offer for a large quantity of Argentine hares at a price so low as 3¾d per piece without having the gravest doubts of it.

. . . I am satisfied, however, from the evidence given to me, that the plaintiff must have realised, and did in fact know, that a mistake had occurred . . .

I cannot help thinking that, when this quotation in pence per pound reached Mr Hartog, the plaintiff, he must have realised, and that Mr Caytan, too, must have realised, that there was a mistake. Otherwise I cannot understand the quotation. There was an absolute difference from anything which had gone before – a difference in the manner of quotation, in that the skins are offered per pound instead of per piece.

I am satisfied that it was a mistake on the part of the defendants or their servants which caused the offer to go forward in that way, and I am satisfied that anyone with any knowledge of the trade must have realised that there was a mistake . . . The offer was wrongly expressed, and the defendants by their evidence, and by the correspondence, have satisfied me that the plaintiff could not reasonably have supposed that that offer contained the offerers' real intention. Indeed, I am satisfied to the contrary. That means that there must be judgment for the defendants.'

Mistake as to the identity of the person with whom the contract is made

Again these cases could be looked at as 'formation of the contract' cases: can it be said that in these cases the parties are *ad idem*?

This can only occur where A contracts with B, believing him to be C; i.e., where A has in contemplation a definite and identifiable person with whom he intends to contract. The identity of the other party must be of *vital importance*.

Offeror makes a mistake as to identity

An offer can only be accepted by the person to whom it is addressed.

Boulton v Jones

(1857) 2 H & N 564 • Exchequer

The plaintiff had been foreman and manager to one Brocklehurst, a hose pipe manufacturer, with whom the defendants had been in the habit of dealing, and with whom they had a running account. On the morning of the 13 January 1857 the plaintiff bought Brocklehurst's stock, fixtures, and business, and paid for them. In the afternoon of the same day, the defendant's servant brought a written order, addressed to Brocklehurst, for three 50-feet leather hose 2½ in. The goods were supplied by the plaintiff. The plaintiff's book keeper struck out the name of Brocklehurst and inserted the name of the plaintiff in the order. An invoice was afterwards sent in by the plaintiff to the defendants who said they knew nothing of him.

Pollock CB: 'The point raised is, whether the facts proved did no shew an intention on the part of the defendants to deal with Brocklehurst. The plaintiff, who succeeded Brocklehurst in business, executed the order without any intimation of the change that had taken place, and brought this action to recover the price of the goods supplied. It is a rule of law, that if a person intends to contract with A, B cannot give himself any right under it. Here the order in writing was given to Brocklehurst. Possibly Brocklehurst might have adopted the act of the plaintiff in supplying the goods, and maintained an action for their price. But since the plaintiff has chosen to sue, the only course the defendants could take was to plead that there was no contract with him.'

Bramwell B: 'The admitted facts are, that the defendants sent to a shop an order for goods, supposing they were dealing with Brocklehurst. The plaintiff, who supplied the goods, did not undeceive them. If the plaintiff were now at liberty to sue the defendants, they would be deprived of their right of set-off as against Brocklehurst. When a contract is made, in which the personality of the contracting party is or may be of importance, as a contract with a man to write a book, or the like, or where there might be a set-off, no other person can interpose and adopt the contract. As to the difficulty that the defendants need not pay anybody, I do not see why they should, unless they have made a contract either express or implied. I decide the case on the ground that the defendants did not know that the plaintiff was the person who supplied the goods, and that allowing the plaintiff to treat the contract as made with him would be a prejudice to the defendants.'

Offeree makes a mistake as to identity

No contract will be formed if a person accepting an offer believes on reasonable grounds that he is accepting an offer from someone other than the person by whom it has in fact been made and this fact is known to the offeror.

Cundy v Lindsay

(1878) 3 App Cas 459 • House of Lords

Blenkarn, who occupied a room in a house looking into Wood Street, Cheapside, wrote to Lindsay offering to purchase a considerable quantity of Lindsay's goods. In his letter he used the address '37 Wood Street, Cheapside'. He signed the letters in such a way that his name appeared to be 'Blenkiron & Co'. At 123 Wood Street there was a respectable firm of the name, 'W Blenkiron & Co'. Lindsay supplied goods to 'Messrs Blenkiron & Co, 37 Wood Street'. Blenkarn received the goods at that address and then sold them to Cundy who was entirely ignorant of the fraud.

The issue before the court was whether property in the goods, however temporary, had passed to Blenkarn. This depended on whether the contract between Blenkarn and Lindsay was void for mistake.

Lord Cairns LC: 'My Lords, the question, therefore, in the present case, as your Lordships will observe, really becomes the very short and simple one which I am about to state. Was there any contract which, with regard to the goods in question in this case, had passed the property in the goods from the Messrs Lindsay to Alfred Blenkarn? If there was any contract passing that property, even although, as I have said, that contract might afterwards be open to a process of reduction, upon the ground of fraud, still, in the meantime, Blenkarn might have conveyed a good title for valuable consideration to the present Appellants.

Now, my Lords, there are two observations bearing upon the solution of that question which I desire to make. In the first place, if the property in the goods in question passed, it could only pass by way of contract; there is nothing else which could have passed the property . . .

Now, my Lords, discharging that duty and answering that inquiry, what the jurors have found is in substance this: it is not necessary to spell out the words, because the substance of it is beyond all doubt. They have found that by the form of the signatures to the letters which were written by Blenkarn, by the mode in which his letters and his applications to the Respondents were made out, and by the way in which he left uncorrected the mode and form in which, in turn, he was addressed by the Respondents; that by all those means he led, and intended to lead, the Respondents to believe, and they did believe, that the person with whom they were communicating was not Blenkarn, the dishonest and irresponsible man, but was a well known and solvent house of Blenkiron & Co, doing business in the same street. My Lords, those things are found as matters of fact, and they are placed beyond the range of dispute and controversy in the case.

If that is so, what is the consequence? It is that Blenkarn – the dishonest man, as I call him – was acting here just in the same way as if he had forged the signature of Blenkiron & Co, the respectable firm, to the applications for goods, and as if, when, in return, the goods were forwarded and letters were sent, accompanying them, he had intercepted the goods and intercepted the letters, and had taken possession of the goods, and of the letters which were addressed to, and intended for, not himself but, the firm of Blenkiron & Co. Now, my Lords, stating the matter shortly in that way, I ask the question, how is it possible to imagine that in that state of things any contract could have arisen between the Respondents and Blenkarn, the dishonest man? Of him they knew nothing, and of him they never thought. With him they never intended to deal. Their minds never, even for an instant of time rested upon him, and as between him and them there was no consensus of mind which could lead to any agreement or any contract whatever. As between him and them there was merely the one side to a contract, where, in order to produce a contract, two sides would be required. With the firm of Blenkiron & Co of course there was no contract, for as to them the matter was entirely unknown, and therefore the pretence of a contract was a failure.

The result, therefore, my Lords, is this, that your Lordships have not here to deal with one of those cases in which there is *de facto* a contract made which may afterwards be impeached and set aside, on the ground of fraud; but you have to deal with a case which ranges itself under a completely different chapter of law, the case namely in which the contract never comes into existence. My Lords, that being so, it is idle to talk of the property passing. The property remained, as it originally had been, the property of the Respondents, and the title which was attempted to be given to the Appellants was a title which could not be given to them.'

Mistake as to the attributes of a person ineffective

If the mistake is not one of identity but only of a person's attributes (in other words a mistake as to the person's quality – as above) e.g. his solvency, the mistake is ineffective.

King's Norton Metal Co Ltd v Edridge, Merrett & Co Ltd

(1897) 14 TLR 98 • Court of Appeal

King's Norton received a letter purporting to come from Hallam and Co, Sheffield, at the head of which was a representation of a large factory with a number of chimneys, and in one corner was a printed statement that Hallam and Co had depots and agencies at Belfast, Lille, and Ghent. The letter contained a request by Hallam and Co for a quotation of prices for brass rivet wire. In reply King's Norton quoted prices, and Hallam and Co then, by letter, ordered some goods which were sent off to them. These goods were never paid for. It turned out that a man named Wallis had adopted the name of Hallam and Co in order to fraudulently obtain goods. Wallis sold the goods that he had obtained from King's Norton to Edridge who bought them *bona fide*, and with no notice of any defect of title in Wallis. It appeared that King's Norton had been paid for some goods previously ordered by Hallam and Co, by a cheque drawn by 'Hallam and Co'. King's Norton brought an action to recover damages for the conversion of their goods. At the trial, the learned Judge found against King's Norton upon the ground that the property in the goods had passed to Wallis, who sold them to Edridge before King's Norton had avoided the contract.

The issue before the court was whether the contract between King's Norton and Wallis was void for mistake or merely voidable.

Smith LJ said that the case was a plain one. The question was whether the plaintiffs, who had been cheated out of their goods by a rogue called Wallis, or the defendants were to bear the loss. The law seemed to him to be well settled. If a person, induced by false pretences, contracted with a rogue to sell goods to him and the goods were delivered the rogue could until the contract was disaffirmed give a good title to the goods to a *bona fide* purchaser for value. The facts here were that Wallis, for the purpose of cheating, set up in business as Hallam and Co, and got note-paper prepared for the purpose, and wrote to the plaintiffs representing that he was carrying on business as Hallam and Co. He got the goods in question and sold them to the defendants, who bought them *bona fide* for value. The question was, With whom, upon this evidence, which was all one way, did the plaintiffs contract to sell the goods? Clearly with the writer of the letters. If it could have been shown that there was a separate entity called Hallam and Co and another entity called Wallis then the case might have come within the decision in *Cundy* v *Lindsay*. In his opinion there was a contract by the plaintiffs with the person who wrote the letters, by which the property passed to him. There was only one entity, trading it might be under an alias, and there was a contract by which the property passed to him.

Contracts inter praesentes

This means that the parties are contracting in each other's presence i.e. face to face.

Phillips v *Brooks Ltd*

[1919] 2 KB 243

On 15 April 1918 North entered Phillips's shop and asked to see some pearls and some rings. He selected pearls at the price of £2550 and a ring at the price of £450. He produced a cheque book and wrote out a cheque for £3000. In signing it, he said: 'You see who I am, I am Sir George Bullough', and he gave an address in St James's Square. Phillips knew that there was such a person as Sir George Bullough, and finding on reference to a directory that Sir George lived at the address mentioned, he said, 'Would you like to take the articles with you?' to which the man replied: 'You had better have the cheque cleared first, but I should like to take the ring as it is my wife's birthday to-morrow,' whereupon Phillips let him have the ring. The cheque was dishonoured. North was subsequently convicted of obtaining the ring by false pretences. In the meantime on 16 April 1918, North, in the name of Firth, had pledged the ring with Brooks who, *bona fide* and without notice, advanced £350 upon it. Phillips sued Brooks, who were pawnbrokers, for the return of a ring or, alternatively, its value, and damages for its detention.

The issue before the court was whether the contract between Phillips and North was void for mistake or merely voidable.

Horridge J: '. . . I have carefully considered the evidence of the plaintiff, and have come to the conclusion that, although he believed the person to whom he was handing the ring was Sir George Bullough, he in fact contracted to sell and deliver it to the person who came into his shop, and who was not Sir George Bullough, but a man of the name of North, who obtained the sale and delivery by means of the false pretence that he was Sir George Bullough . . .

After obtaining the ring the man North pledged it in the name of Firth with the defendants, who *bona fide* and without notice advanced £350 upon it. The question, therefore, in this case is whether or not the property had so passed to the swindler as to entitle him to give a good title to any person who gave value and acted *bona fide* without notice. This question seems to have been decided in an American case of *Edmunds* v *Merchants' Despatch Transportation Co.* The headnote in that case contains two propositions, which I think adequately express my view of the law. They are as follows: (1) "If A, fraudulently assuming the name of a reputable merchant in a certain town, buys, in person, goods of another, the property in the goods passes to A." (2) "If A, representing himself to be a brother of a reputable merchant in a certain town, buying for him, buys, in person, goods of another, the property in the goods does not pass to A."

The following expressions used in the judgment of Morton CJ seem to me to fit the facts in this case: "The minds of the parties met and agreed upon all the terms of the sale, the thing sold, the price and time of payment, the person selling and the person buying. The fact that the seller was induced to sell by fraud of the buyer made the sale voidable, but not void. He could not have supposed that he was selling to any other person; his intention was to sell to the person present, and identified by sight and hearing; it does not defeat the sale because the buyer assumed a false name or practised any other deceit to induce the vendor to sell." Further on, Morton CJ says: "In the cases before us, there was a *de facto* contract, purporting, and by which the plaintiffs intended, to pass the property and possession of the goods to the person buying them; and we are of opinion that the property did pass to the swindler who bought the goods." . . .

. . . I think, there was a passing of the property and the purchaser had a good title, and there must be judgment for the defendants with costs.'

Ingram v *Little*

[1960] 3 All ER 332 • Court of Appeal

Three elderly ladies advertised their car for sale. A fraudster, who called himself Hutchinson, agreed to buy their car for £717. When he offered to pay by cheque the ladies refused to go ahead with the sale. In order to persuade them that he was a reputable person he gave his name as a Mr P G M Hutchinson; he said he lived at Stanstead House, Stanstead Road, Caterham. In order to verify his statements one of the sisters went to the local post office which was two minutes from her house and checked his name and address in the local telephone directory. Having confirmed that a Mr P G M Hutchinson did live at the address given by the fraudster the sisters decided to accept the cheque. The cheque was dishonoured. In the meantime the fraudster had sold the car to the innocent third party Little.

The issue before the Court of Appeal was whether the contract between the three ladies and the fraudster was void for mistake in which case there being no contract no property in the car would have passed to the fraudster.

Pearce LJ: '. . . The question here is whether there was any contract, whether offer and acceptance met . . .

The real problem in the present case is whether the plaintiffs were in fact intending to deal with the person physically present who had fraudulently endowed himself with the attributes of some other identity or whether they were intending only to deal with that other identity. If the former, there was a valid but voidable contract and the property passed. If the latter, there was no contract and the property did not pass . . .

An apparent contract made orally *inter praesentes* raises particular difficulties. The offer is apparently addressed to the physical person present. *Prima facie*, he, by whatever name he is called, is the person to whom the offer is made. His physical presence identified by sight and hearing preponderates over vagaries of nomenclature. "*Praesentia corporis tollit errorem nominis*" [Physical presence does not raise a mistake of identity] said Lord Bacon. Yet clearly, though difficult, it is not impossible to rebut the *prima facie* presumption that the offer can be accepted by the person to whom it is physically addressed. To take two extreme instances. If a man orally commissions a portrait from some unknown artist who had deliberately passed himself off, whether by disguise or merely by verbal cosmetics, as a famous painter, the imposter could not accept the offer. For, though the offer is made to him physically, it is obviously, as he knows, addressed to the famous painter. The mistake in identity on such facts is clear and the nature of the contract makes it obvious that identity was of vital importance to the offeror. At the other end of the scale, if a shopkeeper sells goods in a normal cash transaction to a man who misrepresents himself as being some well known figure, the transaction will normally be valid. For the shopkeeper was ready to sell goods for cash to the world at large, and the particular identity of the purchaser in such a contract was not of sufficient importance to override the physical presence identified by sight and hearing. Thus the nature of the proposed contract must have a strong bearing on the question whether the intention of the offeror (as understood by his offeree) was to make his offer to some other particular identity rather than to the physical person to whom it was orally offered.

In our case the facts lie in the debatable area between the two extremes. At the beginning of the negotiations, always an important consideration, the name or personality of the false Hutchinson were of no importance and there was no other identity competing with his physical presence. The plaintiffs were content to sell the car for cash to any purchaser. The contractual conversation was orally addressed to the physical identity of the false Hutchinson. The identity was the man present, and his name was merely one of his attributes. Had matters continued thus there would clearly have been a valid but voidable contract.

I accept the learned judge's view that there was no contract at the stage when the man pulled out his cheque book. From a practical point of view negotiations reached an impasse at that stage. For the vendor refused to discuss the question of selling on credit. It is argued that there was a contract as soon as the price was agreed at £717 and that from that moment either party could have sued on the contract with implied terms as to payment and delivery. That may be theoretically arguable, but in my view the judge's more realistic approach was right. Payment and delivery still needed to be discussed and the parties would be expecting to discuss them. Immediately they did discuss them it became plain that they were not *ad idem* and that no contract had yet been created. But, even if there had been a concluded agreement before discussion of a cheque, it was rescinded. The man tried to make Miss Ingram take a cheque. She declined and said that the deal was off. He did not demur but set himself to reconstruct the negotiations. For the moment had come which he must all along have anticipated as the crux of the negotiations, the vital crisis of the swindle. He wanted to take away the car on credit against his worthless cheque but she refused. Thereafter the negotiations were of a different kind from what the vendor had mistakenly believed them to be hitherto. The parties were no longer concerned with a cash sale of goods where the identity of the purchaser was *prima facie* unimportant. They were concerned with a credit sale in which both parties knew that the identity of the purchaser was of the utmost importance. She now realised that she was being asked to give to him possession of the car on the faith of his cheque.

This was an important stage of the transaction, because it demonstrated quite clearly that she was not prepared to sell on credit to the mere physical man in her drawing room, though he represented himself as a man of substance . . . He tried to persuade her to sell to him as P G M Hutchinson, of Stanstead House, a personality which no doubt he had selected for the purpose of inspiring confidence into his victim. This was unsuccessful. Only when she had ascertained (through her sister's short excursion to the local post office and investigation of the telephone directory) that there was a P G M Hutchinson, of Stanstead House, in the directory did she agree to sell on credit. The fact that the man wrote the name and address on the back of the cheque is an additional indication of the importance attached by the parties to the individuality of P G M Hutchinson, of Stanstead House.

It is not easy to decide whether the vendor was selling to the man in her drawing room (fraudulently misrepresented as being a man of substance with the attributes of the real Hutchinson) or to P G M Hutchinson, of Stanstead House (fraudulently misrepresented as being the man in her drawing room). Did the individuality of P G M Hutchinson, of Stanstead House, or the physical presence of the man in the room preponderate? Can it be said that the *prima facie* predominance of the physical presence of the false

Hutchinson identified by sight and hearing was overborne by the identity of the real Hutchinson on the particular facts of this case?

The learned judge said:

"I have not the slightest hesitation in reaching the conclusion that the offer which the plaintiffs through the Misses Ingram made to accept the cheque for £717 was one made solely to, and one which was capable of being accepted only by, the honest Mr Hutchinson – i.e., Mr Philip Gerald Morpeth Hutchinson, of Stanstead House, Stanstead Road, Caterham, Surrey, and that it was incapable of being accepted by the rogue Hutchinson."

. . . I should hesitate long before interfering with that finding of fact . . .

Each case must be decided on its own facts. The question in such cases is this. Has it been sufficiently shown in the particular circumstances that, contrary to the *prima facie* presumption, a party was not contracting with the physical person to whom he uttered the offer, but with another individual whom (to the other party's knowledge) he believed to be the physical person present. The answer to that question is a finding of fact . . .

The court is naturally reluctant to accept the argument that there has been a mistake in such a case as this, since it creates hardship on subsequent *bona fide* purchasers. The plaintiffs' unguarded transaction has caused loss to another; and unfortunately when the contract is void at common law the court cannot (as the law stands now) by its equitable powers impose terms that would produce a fairer result. However, in this case the subsequent purchasers, although the judge found that there was no *mala fides*, were no more wise or careful than the plaintiffs. The regrettable ease with which a dishonest person can accomplish such a fraud is partially due to the unfortunate fact that registration books are not documents of title and that registration and legal ownership are so loosely connected.'

Lewis v Averay

[1971] 3 All ER 907 • Court of Appeal

The facts are stated in the judgment of Lord Denning MR. The facts are very similar to *Phillips* v *Brooks* and *Ingram* v *Little* and the issue is the same: was the contract void for mistake?

Lord Denning MR: 'This is another case where one of two innocent persons has to suffer for the fraud of a third. It will no doubt interest students and find its place in the textbooks.

Mr Lewis is a young man who is a post-graduate student of chemistry. He lives at Clifton near Bristol. He had an Austin Cooper motor car. He decided to sell it. He put an advertisement in the newspaper offering it for £450. On May 8, 1969, in reply to the advertisement a man – I will simply call him the "rogue", for so he was – telephoned and asked if he could come and see the car. He did not give his name. He said he was speaking from Wales, in Glamorganshire. Mr Lewis said that he could come and see it. He came in the evening to Mr Lewis's flat. Mr Lewis showed him the car, which was parked outside. The rogue drove it and tested it. He said he liked it. They then went along to the flat of Mr Lewis's fiancée, Miss Kershaw (they have since married). He told them he was Richard Green and talked much about the film world. He led both of them to believe that he was the well-known film actor, Richard Greene, who played Robin Hood in the "Robin Hood" series. They talked about the car. He asked to see the logbook. He was shown it and seemed satisfied. He said he would like to buy the car. They agreed a price of £450. The rogue wrote out a cheque for £450 on the Beckenham branch of the Midland Bank.

He signed it "RA Green". He wanted to take the car at once. But Mr Lewis was not willing for him to have it until the cheque was cleared. To hold him off, Mr Lewis said that there were one or two small jobs he would like to do on the car before letting him have it, and that would give time for the cheque to be cleared. The rogue said: "Don't worry about those small jobs. I would like to take the car now." Mr Lewis said: "Have you anything to prove that you are Mr Richard Green?" The rogue thereupon brought out a special pass of admission to Pinewood Studios, which had an official stamp on it. It bore the name of Richard A Green and the address, and also a photograph which was plainly the photograph of this man, who was the rogue. On seeing this pass, Mr Lewis was satisfied. He thought that this man was really Mr Richard Greene, the film actor. By that time it was 11 o'clock at night. Mr Lewis took the cheque and let the rogue have the car and the logbook and the Ministry of Transport test certificate. Each wrote and signed a receipt evidencing the transaction. Mr Lewis wrote:

> "Received from, Richard A Green, 59 Marsh Rd, Beckenham, Kent, the sum of £450 in return for Austin Cooper S Reg No AHT 484B chassis No CA257 – 549597. Keith Lewis"

The rogue wrote: "Received logbook No 771835 and MOT for Mini-Cooper S No AHT 484B. RA Green."

Next day, May 9, 1969, Mr Lewis put the cheque into the bank. A few days later the bank told him it was worthless. The rogue had stolen a cheque book and written this £450 on a stolen cheque.

Meanwhile, whilst the cheque was going through, the rogue sold the car to an innocent purchaser. He sold it to a young man called Mr Averay. He was at the time under 21. He was a music student in London at the Royal College of Music. His parents live at Bromley. He was keen to buy a car. He put an advertisement in the *Exchange and Mart*, seeking a car for £200. In answer he had a telephone call from the rogue. He said that he was speaking from South Wales. He said that he was coming to London to sell a car. Mr Averay arranged to meet him on May 11, 1969. The rogue came with the car. Young Mr Averay liked it, but wanted to get the approval of his parents. They drove it to Bromley. The parents did approve. Young Mr Averay agreed to buy it for £200. The rogue gave his name as Mr Lewis. He handed over the car and logbook to young Mr Averay. The logbook showed the owner as Mr Lewis. In return Mr Averay, in entire good faith, gave the rogue a cheque for £200. The rogue signed this receipt:

> "Sale of Cooper S to AJ Averay. Received £200 for the Cooper S Registration No AHT 484B, the said car being my property absolutely, there being no hire purchase charges outstanding or other impediment to selling the car. Keith Lewis May 13, 1969."

A fortnight later, on May 29, 1969, Mr Averay wanted the workshop manual for the car. So his father on his behalf wrote to the name and address of the seller as given in the logbook – that is, to Mr Lewis. Then, of course, the whole story came to light. The rogue had cashed the cheque and disappeared. The police have tried to trace him, but without success.

Now Mr Lewis, the original owner of the car, sues young Mr Averay. Mr Lewis claims that the car is still his. He claims damages for conversion. The judge found in favour of Mr Lewis and awarded damages of £330 for conversion.

The real question in the case is whether on May 8, 1969, there was a contract of sale under which the property in the car passed from Mr Lewis to the rogue. If there was such a contract, then, even though it was voidable for fraud, nevertheless Mr Averay would get a good title to the car. But if there was no contract of sale by Mr Lewis to the rogue –

either because there was, on the face of it, no agreement between the parties, or because any apparent agreement was a nullity and void *ab initio* for mistake, then no property would pass from Mr Lewis to the rogue. Mr Averay would not get a good title because the rogue had no property to pass to him.

There is no doubt that Mr Lewis was mistaken as to the identity of the person who handed him the cheque. He thought that he was Richard Greene, a film actor of standing and worth: whereas in fact he was a rogue whose identity is quite unknown. It was under the influence of that mistake that Mr Lewis let the rogue have the car. He would not have dreamed of letting him have it otherwise.

What is the effect of this mistake? There are two cases in our books which cannot, to my mind, be reconciled the one with the other. One of them is *Phillips* v *Brooks*, where a jeweller had a ring for sale. The other is *Ingram* v *Little*, where two ladies had a car for sale. In each case the story is very similar to the present. A plausible rogue comes along. The rogue says that he likes the ring, or the car, as the case may be. He asks the price. The seller names it. The rogue says that he is prepared to buy it at that price. He pulls out a cheque book. He writes or prepares to write, a cheque for the price. The seller hesitates. He has never met this man before. He does not want to hand over the ring or the car not knowing whether the cheque will be met. The rogue notices the seller's hesitation. He is quick with his next move. He says to the jeweller, in *Phillips* v *Brooks*: "I am Sir George Bullough of 11 St James's Square"; or to the ladies in *Ingram* v *Little* "I am P G M Hutchinson of Stanstead House, Stanstead Road, Caterham"; or to the post-graduate student in the present case: "I am Richard Greene, the film actor of the Robin Hood series". Each seller checks up the information. The jeweller looks up the directory and finds there is a Sir George Bullough at 11 St James's Square. The ladies check up too. They look at the telephone directory and find there is a "PGM Hutchinson of Stanstead House, Stanstead Road, Caterham". The post-graduate student checks up too. He examines the official pass of the Pinewood Studios and finds that it is a pass for "Richard A Green" to the Pinewood Studios with this man's photograph on it. In each case the seller feels that this is sufficient confirmation of the man's identity. So he accepts the cheque signed by the rogue and lets him have the ring, in the one case, and the car and logbook in the other two cases. The rogue goes off and sells the goods to a third person who buys them in entire good faith and pays the price to the rogue. The rogue disappears. The original seller presents the cheque. It is dishonoured. Who is entitled to the goods? The original seller? Or the ultimate buyer? The courts have given different answers. In *Phillips* v *Brooks Ltd*, the ultimate buyer was held to be entitled to the ring. In *Ingram* v *Little* the original seller was held to be entitled to the car. In the present case the deputy county court judge has held the original seller entitled.

It seems to me that the material facts in each case are quite indistinguishable the one from the other. In each case there was, to all outward appearance, a contract: but there was a mistake by the seller as to the identity of the buyer. This mistake was fundamental. In each case it led to the handing over of the goods. Without it the seller would not have parted with them.

This case therefore raises the question: What is the effect of a mistake by one party as to the identity of the other? It has sometimes been said that if a party makes a mistake as to the identity of the person with whom he is contracting there is no contract, or, if there is a contract, it is a nullity and void, so that no property can pass under it. This has been supported by a reference to the French jurist Pothier; but I have said before, and I repeat now, his statement is no part of English law. I know that it was quoted by Lord Haldane in *Lake* v *Simmons*, and, as such, misled Tucker J in *Sowler* v *Potter*, into holding that a lease was void whereas it was really voidable. But Pothier's statement has given rise to such refinements that it is time it was dead and buried altogether.

For instance, in *Ingram* v *Little* the majority of the court suggested that the difference between *Phillips* v *Brooks* and *Ingram* v *Little* was that in *Phillips* v *Brooks* the contract of sale was concluded (so as to pass the property to the rogue) before the rogue made the fraudulent misrepresentation: whereas in *Ingram* v *Little* the rogue made the fraudulent misrepresentation before the contract was concluded. My own view is that in each case the property in the goods did not pass until the seller let the rogue have the goods.

Again it has been suggested that a mistake as to the identity of a person is one thing: and a mistake as to his attributes is another. A mistake as to identity, it is said, avoids a contract: whereas a mistake as to attributes does not. But this is a distinction without a difference. A man's very name is one of his attributes. It is also a key to his identity. If then, he gives a false name, is it a mistake as to his identity? or a mistake as to his attributes? These fine distinctions do no good to the law.

As I listened to the argument in this case, I felt it wrong that an innocent purchaser (who knew nothing of what passed between the seller and the rogue) should have his title depend on such refinements. After all, he has acted with complete circumspection and in entire good faith: whereas it was the seller who let the rogue have the goods and thus enabled him to commit the fraud. I do not, therefore, accept the theory that a mistake as to identity renders a contract void.

I think the true principle is that which underlies the decision of this court in *King's Norton Metal Co Ltd* v *Edridge, Merrett & Co Ltd* and of Horridge J in *Phillips* v *Brooks*, which has stood for these last 50 years. It is this: When two parties have come to a contract – or rather what appears, on the face of it, to be a contract – the fact that one party is mistaken as to the identity of the other does not mean that there is no contract, or that the contract is a nullity and void from the beginning. It only means that the contract is voidable, that is, liable to be set aside at the instance of the mistaken person, so long as he does so before third parties have in good faith acquired rights under it.

Applied to the cases such as the present, this principle is in full accord with the presumption stated by Pearce LJ and also by Devlin LJ in *Ingram* v *Little*. When a dealing is had between a seller like Mr Lewis and a person who is actually there present before him, then the presumption in law is that there is a contract, even though there is a fraudulent impersonation by the buyer representing himself as a different man than he is. There is a contract made with the very person there, who is present in person. It is liable no doubt to be avoided for fraud, but it is still a good contract under which title will pass unless and until it is avoided. In support of that presumption, Devlin LJ quoted, not only the English case of *Phillips* v *Brooks*, but other cases in the United States where

> "the Courts hold that if A appeared in person before B, impersonating C, an innocent purchaser from A gets the property in the goods against B."

That seems to me to be right in principle in this country also.

In this case Mr Lewis made a contract of sale with the very man, the rogue, who came to the flat. I say that he "made a contract" because in this regard we do not look into his intentions, or into his mind to know what he was thinking or into the mind of the rogue. We look to the outward appearances. On the face of the dealing, Mr Lewis made a contract under which he sold the car to the rogue, delivered the car and the logbook to him, and took a cheque in return. The contract is evidenced by the receipts which were signed. It was, of course, induced by fraud. The rogue made false representations as to his identity. But it was still a contract, though voidable for fraud. It was a contract under which this property passed to the rogue, and in due course passed from the rogue to Mr Averay, before the contract was avoided.

Although I very much regret that either of these good and reliable gentlemen should suffer, in my judgment it is Mr Lewis who should do so. I think the appeal should be allowed and judgment entered for the defendant.'

No third person in existence

In this case the argument is that you must intend to contract with someone: if there is only one person in existence – even if it is not the one you really intended to contract with – that is the person with whom you have contracted.

See *King's Norton Metal Co Ltd* v *Edridge, Merrett & Co Ltd* above.

MISTAKE IN RELATION TO A WRITTEN DOCUMENT

Non est factum is a common law defence which permits one who has signed a written document, which is *essentially different* from that which he intended to sign, to plead that, notwithstanding his signature, 'it is not his deed'. If the plea of *non est factum* is successful the contract is void.

A person cannot rely upon the defence of *non est factum* merely because he is too lazy or too busy to read through a document before signing it, or because it contains objectionable terms or terms the legal effect of which, he is unaware.

Essentially different transaction

In order for the defence to succeed, the person executing the document must show that the transaction which the document purports to effect is essentially different in substance or in kind from the transaction intended.

Saunders v Anglia Building Society (sub nom Gallie v Lee)

[1970] 3 All ER 961 • House of Lords

Mrs Gallie, aged 78, executed an assignment of her leasehold interest in her house to Lee. By signing the deed of assignment Mrs Gallie believed that it was a deed of gift in effect giving her house to her nephew Parkin on condition that he was to permit her to reside there for the rest of her life. In this belief she handed the title deeds to Parkin believing that the house thereupon became his property. On obtaining the deed of assignment Lee mortgaged the house to the Anglia Building Society who advanced him £2000. Eventually Lee defaulted on the mortgage repayments and the Anglia Building Society sought possession of the house. Mrs Gallie pleaded that the deed was void on the basis of *non est factum*.

Lord Reid: '... In my opinion this appeal must fail however one states the law. The existing law seems to me to be in a state of some confusion. I do not think that it is possible to reconcile all the decisions, let alone all the reasons given for them. In view of some general observations made in the Court of Appeal I think that it is desirable to try to extract from the authorities the principles on which most of them are based. When we are trying to do that my experience has been that there are dangers in there being only one speech in this House. Then statements in it have often tended to be treated as definitions and it is not the function of a court or of this House to frame definitions; some latitude should be left for future developments. The true ratio of a decision generally appears more clearly from a comparison of two or more statements in different words which are intended to supplement each other.

The plea of *non est factum* obviously applies when the person sought to be held liable did not in fact sign the document. But at least since the sixteenth century it has also been held to apply in certain cases so as to enable a person who in fact signed a document to say that it is not his deed. Obviously any such extension must be kept within narrow limits if it is not to shake the confidence of those who habitually and rightly rely on signatures when there is no obvious reason to doubt their validity. Originally this extension appears to have been made in favour of those who were unable to read owing to blindness or illiteracy and who therefore had to trust someone to tell them what they were signing. I think that it must also apply in favour of those who are permanently or temporarily unable through no fault of their own to have without explanation any real understanding of the purport of a particular document, whether that be from defective education, illness or innate incapacity.

But that does not excuse them from taking such precautions as they reasonably can. The matter generally arises where an innocent third party has relied on a signed document in ignorance of the circumstances in which it was signed, and where he will suffer loss if the maker of the document is allowed to have it declared a nullity. So there must be a heavy burden of proof on the person who seeks to invoke this remedy. He must prove all the circumstances necessary to justify its being granted to him, and that necessarily involves his proving that he took all reasonable precautions in the circumstances. I do not say that the remedy can never be available to a man of full capacity. But that could only be in very exceptional circumstances; certainly not where his reason for not scrutinising the document before signing it was that he was too busy or too lazy. In general I do not think that he can be heard to say that he signed in reliance on someone he trusted. But, particularly when he was led to believe that the document which he signed was not one which affected his legal rights, there may be cases where this plea can properly be applied in favour of a man of full capacity.

The plea cannot be available to anyone who was content to sign without taking the trouble to try to find out at least the general effect of the document. Many people do frequently sign documents put before them for signature by their solicitor or other trusted advisers without making any enquiry as to their purpose or effect. But the essence of the plea *non est factum* is that the person signing believed that the document he signed had one character or one effect whereas in fact its character or effect was quite different. He could not have such a belief unless he had taken steps or been given information which gave him some grounds for his belief. The amount of information he must have and the sufficiency of the particularity of his belief must depend on the circumstances of each case. Further the plea cannot be available to a person whose mistake was really a mistake as to the legal effect of the document, whether that was his own mistake or that of his adviser. That has always been the law and in this branch of the law at least I see no reason for any change.

We find in many of the authorities statements that a man's deed is not his deed if his mind does not go with his pen. But that is far too wide. It would cover cases where the man had taken no precautions at all, and there was no ground for his belief that he was signing something different from that which in fact he signed. I think that it is the wrong approach to start from that wide statement and then whittle it down by excluding cases where the remedy will not be granted. It is for the person who seeks the remedy to show that he should have it.

Finally, there is the question to what extent or in what way must there be a difference between that which in fact he signed and that which he believed he was signing. In an endeavour to keep the plea within bounds there have been many attempts to lay down a dividing line. But any dividing line suggested has been difficult to apply in practice and has sometimes led to unreasonable results. In particular I do not think that the modern division between the character and the contents of a document is at all satisfactory. Some of the older authorities suggest a more flexible test so that one can take all factors into consideration. There was a period when here as elsewhere in the law hard and fast dividing lines were sought, but I think that experience has shown that often they do not produce certainty but do produce unreasonable results.

I think that in the older authorities difference in practical result was more important than difference in legal character. If a man thinks that he is signing a document which will cost him £10 and the actual document would cost him £1000 it could not be right to deny him this remedy simply because the legal character of the two was the same. It is true that we must then deal with questions of degree but that is a familiar task for the courts and I would not expect it to give rise to a flood of litigation.

There must I think be a radical difference between what he signed and what he thought he was signing – or one could use the words "fundamental" or "serious" or "very substantial". But what amounts to a radical difference will depend on all the circumstances. If he thinks he is giving property to A whereas the document gives it to B the difference may often be of vital importance, but in the circumstances of the present case I do not think that it is. I think that it must be left to the courts to determine in each case in light of all the facts whether there was or was not a sufficiently great difference. The plea *non est factum* is in sense illogical when applied to a case where the man in fact signed the deed. But it is none the worse for that if applied in a reasonable way.'

Lord Pearson: '*The degree of difference required.* The judgments in the older cases used a variety of expressions to signify the degree or kind of difference that, for the purposes of the plea of *non est factum*, must be shown to exist between the document as it was and the document as it was believed to be. More recently there has been a tendency to draw a firm distinction between: (a) a difference in character or class, which is sufficient for the purposes of the plea; and (b) a difference only in contents, which is not sufficient. This distinction has been helpful in some cases, but, as the judgments of the Court of have shown, it would produce wrong results if it were applied as a rigid rule for all cases. In my opinion, one has to use a more general phrase, such as "fundamentally different" or "radically different" or "totally different".

Negligence

Is the plea of *non est factum* available to a person who through his own negligence signs a document? As a normal rule if a person of full understanding and capacity forbears, or carelessly omits, to read what he signs, the defence of *non est factum* will not be available.

Saunders v *Anglia Building Society* (sub nom *Gallie* v *Lee*)
[1970] 3 All ER 961 • House of Lords

The facts appear above (p 408).

Lord Pearson: '*Negligence.* It is clear that by the law as it was laid down in *Foster* v *Mackinnon* a person who had signed a document differing fundamentally from what he believed it to be would be disentitled from successfully pleading *non est factum* if his signing of the document was due to his own negligence. The word "negligence" in this connection had no special, technical meaning. It meant carelessness, and in each case it was a question of fact for the jury to decide whether the person relying on the plea had been negligent or not. In *Forster* v *Mackinnon* Bovill CJ had told the jury that, if the endorsement was not the defendant's signature, or if, being his signature, it was obtained on a fraudulent representation that it was a guarantee, and the defendant signed it without knowing that it was a bill, and under the belief that it was a guarantee and if the defendant was not guilty of any negligence in so signing the paper, the defendant was entitled to the verdict. On appeal this direction was held to be correct. In *Vorley* v *Cooke* Sir John Stuart V-C said:

> "It cannot be said that Cooke's conduct was careless or rash. He was deceived, as anyone with the ordinary amount of intelligence and caution would have been deceived, and he is therefore entitled to be relieved."

Whatever may be thought of the merits of the decision in that case, this passage illustrates the simple approach to the question whether the signer of the deed had been negligent or not. Similarly, in *Lewis* v *Clay* Lord Russell of Killowen CJ left to the jury the question: "Was the defendant, in signing his name as he did, recklessly careless, and did he thereby enable Lord William Nevill to perpetrate the fraud?" '

MISTAKE IN EQUITY

Equity may be prepared to grant relief where the common law refuses to intervene.
Three remedies are available:

- refusal of an order for specific performance;
- rectification of a written document;
- rescission.

Note, however, that at the most Equity renders a contract *voidable*, not void.

Refusal of an order for specific performance

Tamplin v *James*
(1880) 15 ChD 215 • Court of Appeal

Property was put up for sale by auction under the description of 'All that well-accustomed inn with the brewhouse, outbuildings, and premises known as *The Ship*, together with the messuage, saddler's shop, and premises adjoining thereto . . . No 454 and 455 on the said tithe map, and containing by admeasurement twenty perches more or less.' The property was not sold at the auction but bought by the defendant for £750 immediately after the auction. The defendant mistakenly thought he was buying the property plus two gardens that adjoined it. However, the tithe map, which the defendant had not inspected, clearly showed that the property offered for sale did not include the two gardens. On discovering his mistake the defendant refused to go ahead with the purchase of the property. The plaintiff sued for specific performance.

James LJ: 'In my opinion, the order under appeal is right. The vendors did nothing tending to mislead. In the particulars of sale they described the property as consisting of Nos 454 and 455 on the tithe map, and this was quite correct. The purchaser says that the tithe map is on so small a scale as not to give sufficient information, but he never looked at it. He must be presumed to have looked at it, and at the particulars of sale. He says he knew the property, and was aware that the gardens were held with the other property in the occupation of the tenants, and he came to the conclusion that what was offered for sale was the whole of what was in the occupation of the tenants, but he asked no question about it. If a man will not take reasonable care to ascertain what he is buying, he must take the consequences. The defence on the ground of mistake cannot be sustained. It is not enough for a purchaser to swear, "I thought the farm sold contained twelve fields which I knew, and I find it does not include them all", or, "I thought it contained 100 acres and it only contains eighty". It would open the door to fraud if such a defence was to be allowed. Perhaps some of the cases on this subject go too far, but for the most part the cases where a Defendant has escaped on the ground of a mistake not contributed to by the Plaintiff, have been cases where a hardship amounting to injustice would have been inflicted upon him by holding him to his bargain, and it was unreasonable to hold him to it. *Webster* v *Cecil* is a good instance of that, being a case where a person snapped at an offer which he must have perfectly well-known to be made by mistake, and the only fault I find with the case is that, in my opinion, the bill ought to have been dismissed with costs. It is said that it is hard to hold a man to a bargain entered into under a mistake, but we must consider the hardship on the other side. Here are trustees realizing their testator's estate, and the reckless conduct of the Defendant may have prevented their selling to somebody else. If a man makes a mistake of this kind without any reasonable excuse he ought to be held to his bargain.'

Rectification

Rectification only applies to written contracts (or deeds). If the written contract does not accurately reflect the oral agreement the court can rectify the written contract.

Requirements for rectification

There must be full and final agreement but not necessarily a concluded contract.

Joscelyne v *Nissen*
[1970] 1 All ER 1213 • Court of Appeal

A daughter, with the help of a mortgage, bought her parents' house to help them out of financial difficulties. She and her husband moved into the house. Her mother became seriously ill and her father had to devote much of his time to looking after his wife. As a result his business started to suffer and he felt that he could not really carry on. Because of this he and the daughter discussed a scheme by which, if the business and its assets were made over to the daughter, she should in return pay him a weekly pension to supplement his old age pension and in addition pay the expenses in connection with the parents' part of the house; these expenses were to include the gas, electricity and coal bills and also the cost of the necessary home help. The father and the daughter continued in this expressed accord thereafter and when they signed the agreement still intended that it should provide for such payment. However, the contract signed did not provide for payment of these matters.

The father sought rectification of the contract. The daughter argued that since there was no complete concluded agreement before the contract was signed then in point of law the remedy of rectification was not available to her father.

Russell LJ: 'For the daughter it is argued that the law is that the father cannot get rectification of the written instrument save to accord with a complete antecedent concluded oral contract with the daughter, and, as was found by the judge, there was none. For the father it is argued that if in the course of negotiation a firm accord has been expressly reached on a particular term of the proposed contract, and both parties continued minded that the contract should contain appropriate language to embrace that term, it matters not that the accord was not part of a complete antecedent concluded oral contract.

The point of law has a curious judicial history . . .

Next we have *Crane* v *Hegeman-Harris Co Inc* decided by Simonds J . . . Simonds J said:

"Before I consider the facts and come to a conclusion whether the defendants are right in their contention, it is necessary to say a few words upon the principles which must guide me in this matter. I am clear that I must follow the decision of Clauson J, as he then was, in *Shipley Urban District Council* v *Bradford Corpn*, the point of which is that, in order that this court may exercise its jurisdiction to rectify a written instrument, it is not necessary to find a concluded and binding contract between the parties antecedent to the agreement which it is sought to rectify. The judge held, and I respectfully concur with his reasoning and his conclusion, that it is sufficient to find a common continuing intention in regard to a particular provision or aspect of the agreement. If one finds that, in regard to a particular point, the parties were in agreement up to the moment when they executed their formal instrument, and the formal instrument does not conform with that common agreement, then this court has jurisdiction to rectify, although it may be that there was, until the formal instrument was executed, no concluded and binding contract between the parties. That is what the judge decided, and, as I say, with his reasoning I wholly concur, and I can add nothing to his authority in the matter, except that I would say that, if it were not so, it would be a strange thing, for the result would be that two parties binding themselves by a mistake to which each had equally contributed, by an instrument which did not express their real intention, would yet be bound by it. That is a state of affairs which I hold is not the law, and, until a higher court tells me it is the law, I shall continue to exercise the jurisdiction which Clauson J, as I think rightly, held might be entertained by this court. Secondly, I want to say this upon the principle of the jurisdiction. It is a jurisdiction which is to be exercised only upon convincing proof that the concluded instrument does not represent the common intention of the parties. That is particularly the case where one finds prolonged negotiations between the parties eventually assuming the shape of a formal instrument in which they have been advised by their respective skilled legal advisers. The assumption is very strong in such a case that the instrument does represent their real intention, and it must be only upon proof which Lord Eldon, I think, in a somewhat picturesque phrase described as 'irrefragable' that the court can act. I would rather, I think, say that the court can only act if it is satisfied beyond all reasonable doubt that the instrument does not represent their common intention, and is further satisfied as to what their common intention was. For let it be clear that it is not sufficient to show that the written instrument does not represent their common intention unless positively also one can show what their common intention was. It is in light of those principles that I must examine the facts of this somewhat complicated case . . ."

In our judgment the law is as expounded by Simonds J in *Crane's* case with the qualification that some outward expression of accord is required. We do not wish to attempt to state in any different phrases that with which we entirely agree, except to say that it is in our view better to use only the phrase "convincing proof" without echoing an old fashioned word such as "irrefragable" and without importing from the criminal law the phrase "beyond all reasonable doubt". Remembering always the strong burden of proof that lies on the shoulders of those seeking rectification, and that the requisite accord and continuance of accord of intention may be the more difficult to establish if a complete antecedent concluded contract be not shown, it would be a sorry state of affairs if when that burden is discharged a party to a written contract could, on discovery that the written language chosen for the document did not on its true construction reflect the accord of the parties on a particular point, take advantage of the fact.

The contention in law for the daughter would, we apprehend, involve this proposition, that if all the important terms of an agreement were set out in correspondence with clarity, but expressly "subject to contract", and the contract by a slip of the copyist unnoticed by either party, departed from what had been "agreed", there could not be rectification . . .

. . . [The contract] shall be rectified so as to read:

"[The daughter] shall until she sells the business and out of the proceeds of the business discharge [the father's] expenses in respect of gas, coal, electricity and home help incurred by him while occupying 'Martindale' . . . " '

Where a literal disparity has occurred in the contract, the courts have not ordered rectification, unless error has occurred.

Frederick E Rose (London) Ltd v William H Pim Jnr & Co Ltd

[1953] 2 All ER 739 • Court of Appeal

The facts appear above (p 377). In the judgment below Denning LJ deals with the issue of whether the court should rectify the written contract to read feveroles instead of horsebeans.

Denning LJ: '. . . It is quite plain that . . . the buyers could [not] claim damages under the written contracts, because those contracts were contracts for horsebeans and the goods delivered were in fact horsebeans, and that has been so found by arbitrators in London. In those circumstances the buyers seek in this action to have their contract with the sellers rectified so as to make it refer to "feveroles" instead of horsebeans. If they get the contract rectified, they will claim damages for failure to deliver "feveroles" . . .

The buyers now, after accepting the goods, seek to rectify the contract. Instead of its being a contract for "horsebeans" *simpliciter*, they seek to make it a contract for "horsebeans described in Egypt as feveroles" or, in short, a contract for "feveroles". The judge has granted their request. He has found that there was "a mutual and fundamental mistake" and that the sellers and the buyers, through their respective market clerks, "intended to deal in horsebeans of the feverole type". And he has held that, because that was their intention − their continuing common intention − the court could rectify their contract to give effect to it. In this I think he was wrong. Rectification is concerned with contracts and documents, not with intentions. In order to get rectification, it is necessary to show that the parties were in complete agreement on the terms of their contract, but by an error wrote them down wrongly. And in this regard, in order to ascertain the terms of their contract, you do not look into the inner minds of the parties – into their intentions – any more than you do in the formation of any other contract. You look at their outward acts, i.e., at what they said or wrote to one another in coming to their agreement, and then compare it with the document which they have signed. If you can predicate with certainty what their contract was, and that it is, by a common mistake, wrongly expressed in the document, then you rectify the document. But nothing less will suffice. It is not necessary that all the formalities of the contract should have been executed so as to make it enforceable at law: see *Shipley Urban District Council* v *Bradford Corpn*; but, formalities apart, there must have been a concluded contract. There is a passage in *Crane* v *Hegeman-Harris Co Inc* which suggests that a continuing common intention alone will suffice, but I am clearly of opinion that a continuing common intention is not sufficient unless it has found expression in outward agreement. There could be no certainty at all in business transactions if a party who had entered into a firm contract could afterwards turn round and claim to have it rectified on the ground that the parties intended something different. He is allowed to prove, if he can, that they agreed something different: see *Lovell & Christmas, Ltd* v *Wall* per Lord Cozens-Hardy MR, and per Buckley LJ; but not that they intended something different.'

The present case is a good illustration of the distinction. The parties, no doubt, intended that the goods should satisfy the inquiry of the Egyptian buyers, namely, "horsebeans described in Egypt as feveroles". They assumed that they would do so, but they made no contract to that effect. Their agreement, as outwardly expressed, both orally and in writing, was for "horsebeans". That is all that the sellers ever committed themselves to supply, and all they should be bound to. There was, no doubt, an erroneous assumption underlying the contract – an assumption for which it might have been set aside on the ground of misrepresentation or mistake – but that is very different from an erroneous expression of the contract, such as to give rise to rectification . . .'

Rectification for unilateral mistake

Rectification has been extended to cases of unilateral mistake where the document fails to reflect one party's intention at the time of 'making the contract'.

Thomas Bates & Son Ltd v *Wyndham's (Lingerie) Ltd*

[1981] 1 All ER 1077 • Court of Appeal

The original lease between Bates, who were the landlords, and Wyndham's, who were the tenants, contained a provision for fixing the rent by arbitration in default of agreement between the parties. A new lease which was prepared by the landlords omitted to include the arbitration provision. The tenants, who were aware of the omission, signed the new lease without drawing the omission to the attention of the landlord. On discovering the omission the landlords brought an action for rectification of the lease so as to include the arbitration provision.

Buckley LJ: 'The landlords claim rectification in the present case on the basis of a principle enunciated by Pennicuick J in *A Roberts & Co, Ltd* v *Leicestershire County Council*:

"The second ground rests on the principle that a party is entitled to rectification of a contract on proof that he believed a particular term to be included in the contract and that the other party concluded the contract with the omission or a variation of that term in the knowledge that the first party believed the term to be included . . . The principle is stated in *Snell's Principles of Equity* as follows: 'By what appears to be a species of equitable estoppel, if one party to a transaction knows that the instrument contains a mistake in his favour but does nothing to correct it, he (and those claiming under him) will be precluded from resisting rectification on the ground that the mistake is unilateral and not common'."

Of course if a document is executed in circumstances in which one party realises that in some respect it does not accurately reflect what down to that moment had been the common intention of the parties, it cannot be said that the document is executed under a common mistake, because the party who has realised the mistake is no longer labouring under the mistake. There may be cases in which the principle enunciated by Pennicuick J applies although there is no prior common intention, but we are not, I think, concerned with such a case here, for it seems to me, on the facts that I have travelled through, that it is established that the parties had a common intention down to the time when Mr Avon realised the mistake in the terms of the lease, a common intention that the rent in respect of any period after the first five years should be agreed or, in default of agreement, fixed by an arbitrator.

The principle so enunciated by Pennicuick J was referred to with approval in this court in *Riverlate Properties Ltd* v *Paul* where Russell LJ, reading the judgment of the court, said:

"It may be that the original conception of reformation of an instrument by rectification was based solely on common mistake: but certainly in these days rectification may be based on such knowledge on the part of the defendant: see for example *A Roberts & Co Ltd* v *Leicestershire County Council*. Whether there was in any particular case knowledge of the intention and mistake of the other party must be a question of fact to be decided on the evidence. Basically it appears to us that it must be such as to involve the lessee in a degree of sharp practice."

In that case the lessee against whom the lessor sought to rectify a lease was held to have had no such knowledge as would have brought the doctrine into play. The reference to "sharp practice" may thus be said to have been an *obiter dictum*. Undoubtedly I think in any such case the conduct of the defendant must be such as to make it inequitable that he should be allowed to object to the rectification of the document. If this necessarily implies "some measure" of sharp practice, so be it; but for my part I think that the doctrine is one which depends more on the equity of the position. The graver the character of the conduct involved, no doubt the heavier the burden of proof may be; but, in my view, the conduct must be such as to affect the conscience of the party who has suppressed the fact that he has recognised the presence of a mistake.

For this doctrine (that is to say the doctrine of *A Roberts* v *Leicestershire County Council*) to apply I think it must be shown: first, that one party, A, erroneously believed that the document sought to be rectified contained a particular term or provision, or possibly did not contain a particular term or provision which, mistakenly, it did contain; second, that the other party, B, was aware of the omission or the inclusion and that it was due to a mistake on the part of A; third, that B has omitted to draw the mistake to the notice of A. And I think there must be a fourth element involved, namely that the mistake must be one calculated to benefit B. If these requirements are satisfied, the court may regard it as inequitable to allow B to resist rectification to give effect to A's intention on the ground that the mistake was not, at the time of execution of the document, a common mistake.

Thomas Bates & Son Ltd v *Wyndham's (Lingerie) Ltd* shows that rectification for unilateral mistake will be allowed if:

- The other party must have known of the mistaken party's intentions and of the mistake.
- The other party must have failed to draw the mistaken party's attention to the mistake.
- The mistake must be such that he would suffer a detriment if the inaccuracy in the document were to remain uncorrected.

Rescission

Rescission is a discretionary remedy and the court has power in equity to attach to the rescission such terms as justice may require in order to effect a *restitutio in integrum*.

RELATIONSHIP OF EQUITY TO COMMON LAW MISTAKE

It would seem that although some 'mistakes' do not invalidate a contract at common law, nevertheless, in certain cases the contract will be rescinded (equity).

See *Solle* v *Butcher* above (p 375).

Magee v *Pennine Insurance Co Ltd*

[1969] 2 All ER 891 • Court of Appeal

In 1961 Magee signed a proposal form for the insurance of a motor car. In it he said that he held a provisional driving licence when, in fact, he had never held a driving licence. His real purpose in applying for the insurance was to obtain insurance for his 18 year old son who would have had to pay a much higher premium for car insurance if he had applied only in his own name. The trial judge found that Magee's misrepresentation in the proposal form was not fraudulent; the form having being filled in by the man at the garage who had sold him the car. In 1965 his son was involved in an accident whilst driving the car. The insurance company decided that the car was a write off and offered Magee £385 in full settlement of the claim. Magee orally accepted the offer. Then the insurance company discovered that Magee had made a misstatement in the original proposal form. They then told Magee that they were not liable on the insurance policy because of Magee's misstatement. The trial judge held that the insurance company was entitled to repudiate the policy on the ground of the misstatement but that they were liable on a contract of compromise which had been formed when Magee had accepted their offer of £385 in full settlement of the claim.

The issue before the Court of Appeal was whether the 'compromise contract' was void for mistake.

Lord Denning MR: '. . . Accepting that the agreement to pay £385 was an agreement of compromise, is it vitiated by mistake? The insurance company was clearly under a mistake. It thought that the policy was good and binding. It did not know, at the time of that letter, that there had been misrepresentations in the proposal form. If the plaintiff knew of its mistake – if he knew that the policy was bad – he certainly could not take advantage of the agreement to pay £385. He would be "snapping at an offer which he knew was made under a mistake"; and no man is allowed to get away with that. But I prefer to assume that the plaintiff was innocent. I think we should take it that both parties were under a common mistake. Both parties thought that the policy was good and binding. The letter of 12th May 1965, was written on the assumption that the policy was good whereas it was in truth voidable.

What is the effect in law of this common mistake? Counsel for the plaintiff said that the agreement to pay £385 was good, despite this common mistake. He relied much on *Bell* v *Lever Brothers Ltd* and its similarity to the present case. He submitted that, inasmuch as the mistake there did not vitiate that contract, the mistake here should not vitiate this one. I do not propose today to go through the speeches in that case. They have given enough trouble to commentators already. I would say simply this: A common mistake, even on a most fundamental matter, does not make a contract void at law; but it makes it voidable in equity. I analysed the cases in *Solle* v *Butcher* and I would repeat what I said there:

> "A contract is also liable in equity to be set aside if the parties were under a common misapprehension either as to facts or as to their relative and respective rights, provided that the misapprehension was fundamental and that the party seeking to set it aside was not himself at fault."

Applying that principle here, it is clear that, when the insurance company and the plaintiff made this agreement to pay £385, they were both under a common mistake which was fundamental to the whole agreement. Both thought that the plaintiff was entitled to claim under the policy of insurance, whereas he was not so entitled. That common mistake does not make the agreement to pay £385 a nullity, but it makes it liable to be set aside in equity.

This brings me to a question which has caused me much difficulty. Is this a case in which we ought to set the agreement aside in equity? I have hesitated on this point, but I cannot shut my eyes to the fact that the plaintiff had no valid claim on the insurance policy; and, if he had no claim on the policy, it is not equitable that he should have a good claim on the agreement for the insurance company to pay £385 which it would not have dreamt of making if it had not been under a mistake. I would, therefore, allow the appeal and give judgment for the insurance company.'

SUMMARY

You should now be able to:

- Distinguish between mutual and unilateral mistakes.

As regards common mistake you should be able to:

- Appreciate the difference between mistake as to the *quality* of a thing contracted for and mistake as to the *substance* of the thing contracted for.
- Appreciate the importance of *total failure of consideration* and the validity of the contract.

As regards unilateral mistake you should be able to:

- Determine when offer and acceptance do not coincide.

- Deal with problems relating to mistakes as to *identity*.
- Deal with problems in relation to mistakes in connection with written documents.

As regards mistake in equity you should be able to:

- Understand the remedies available.

If you have not mastered the above points you should go through this section again.

14 Duress, undue influence and inequality of bargaining power

DURESS

A contract which has been obtained by illegitimate forms of pressure or intimidation is *voidable* at common law or equity on the ground of duress.

Duress at common law

Occidental Worldwide Investment Corp v *Skibs A/S Avanti, Skibs A/S Glarona, Skibs A/S Navalis (The 'Siboen' and The 'Sibotre')*

[1976] 1 Lloyd's Rep 293 • Queen's Bench

Kerr J: Duress

'. . . [Counsel] [f]irst . . . submitted that English law only knows duress to the person and duress to goods, and that a case like the present falls into neither category, with the result that this defence must fail *in limine*. Secondly, he submitted that although money paid under duress to goods is recoverable, a contract can only be set aside for duress to the person but not in any other case of duress. He said that in every case in which a party enters into a contract otherwise than under duress to the person, any payment or forbearance pursuant to such contract is regarded as voluntary, whatever may have been the nature or degree of compulsion, short of violence to the person, which may have caused him to enter into the contract. He relied mainly on a line of authority in which *Skeate* v *Beale* is the leading case.

I do not think that English law is as limited as submitted by [Counsel] . . . For instance, if I should be compelled to sign a lease or some other contract for a nominal but legally sufficient consideration under an imminent threat of having my house burnt down or a valuable picture slashed, though without any threat of physical violence to anyone, I do not think that the law would uphold the agreement. I think that a plea of coercion or compulsion would be available in such cases. The latter is the term used in a line of Australian cases of strong persuasive authority to which I was referred . . . These judgments also state that the degree of compulsion or duress is not necessarily limited to cases of threats to the person or duress in relation to goods. Further, I think that there are indications in *Skeate* v *Beale* itself and in other cases that the true question is ultimately whether or not the agreement in question is to be regarded as having been concluded voluntarily; but it does not follow that every agreement concluded under some form of compulsion is ipso facto to be regarded as voluntary with the solitary exception of cases involving duress to the person. In *Wakefield* v *Newton* Lord Denman referred to cases such as *Skeate* v *Beale* as

"... that class where the parties have come to a voluntary settlement of their concerns, and have chosen to pay what is found due."

In *Kaufman* v *Gerson* the Court of Appeal refused to enforce a written contract signed by the defendant which was valid under French law because the consideration for the defendant's promise to pay sums of money to the plaintiff had been that the plaintiff would not prosecute the defendant's husband in France, he having apparently committed a criminal offence under French law. The reason for the refusal to enforce the contract was duress or coercion. The Judge at first instance held the contract to be enforceable because there was no threat of physical violence. But this was reversed unanimously, and Sir Richard Henn Collins MR significantly asked: "What does it matter what particular form of coercion is used as long as the will is coerced?" The same approach is strongly supported by the judgments of Lord Denning MR and Lord Justice Danckwerts in *D&C Builders Ltd* v *Rees* [who held] . . . that there was no "true accord" because (in the words of Lord Denning) "no person can insist on a settlement procured by intimidation". It is true that in that case, and in all the three Australian cases, it was held that there had been no consideration for the settlement which the Courts reopened. But I do not think that it would have made any difference if the defendants in these cases had also insisted on some purely nominal but legally sufficient consideration. If the contract is void the consideration would be recoverable in quasi-contract; if it is voidable equity could rescind the contract and order the return of the consideration . . .

But even assuming, as I think, that our law is open to further development in relation to contracts concluded under some form of compulsion not amounting to duress to the person, the Court must in every case at least be satisfied that the consent of the other party was overborne by compulsion so as to deprive him of any *animus contrahendi*. This would depend on the facts of each case. One relevant factor would be whether the party relying on duress made any protest at the time or shortly thereafter. Another would be to consider whether or not he treated the settlement as closing the transaction in question and as binding upon him, or whether he made it clear that he regarded the position as still open. All these considerations are mentioned in the Australian judgments, and the question whether or not there was any intention to close the transaction is also referred to in the judgments of Lord Reading CJ and Lord Justice Buckley in *Maskell* v *Horner* . . .

Economic duress – does it exist?

Since *The Siboen* there have been cases where one party to a contract has threatened to break his side of the bargain, i.e. not to carry on with the contract, because he has found that the contract is no longer advantageous to him.

He promises the innocent party that he will only continue with the contract provided the contract is renegotiated in terms more favourable to himself. The innocent party is thus forced into a new contract. Does this amount to economic duress?

It is clear that the courts are prepared to recognise economic duress but only where such duress amounts to a coercion of will.

Pao On v Lau Yiu

[1979] 3 All ER 65 • Privy Council

The facts appear above (p 96).

Lord Scarman: 'Duress, whatever form it takes, is a coercion of the will so as to vitiate consent. Their Lordships agree with the observation of Kerr J in *The Siboen and The*

Sibotre that in a contractual situation commercial pressure is not enough. There must be present some factor 'which could in law be regarded as a coercion of his will so as to vitiate his consent' . . .. In determining whether there was a coercion of will such that there was no true consent, it is material to enquire whether the person alleged to have been coerced did or did not protest; whether, at the time he was allegedly coerced into making the contract, he did or did not have an alternative course open to him such as an adequate legal remedy; whether he was independently advised; and whether after entering the contract he took steps to avoid it. All these matters are, as was recognised in *Maskell* v *Horner*, relevant in determining whether he acted voluntarily or not.

In the present case there is unanimity amongst the judges below that there was no coercion of Lau's will. In the Court of Appeal the trial judges finding . . . that Lau considered the matter thoroughly, chose to avoid litigation, and formed the opinion that the risk in giving the guarantee was more apparent than real was upheld. In short, there was commercial pressure, but no coercion. Even if this Board was disposed, which it is not, to take a different view, it would not substitute its opinion for that of the judges below on this question of fact.

It is, therefore, unnecessary for the Board to embark on an enquiry into the question whether English law recognises a category of duress known as "economic duress". But, since the question has been fully argued in this appeal, their Lordships will indicate very briefly the view which they have formed. At common law money paid under economic compulsion could be recovered in an action for money had and received: see *Astley* v *Reynolds*. The compulsion had to be such that the party was deprived of "his freedom of exercising his will". It is doubtful, however, whether at common law and duress other than duress to the person sufficed to render a contract voidable; see Blackstone's *Commentaries* and *Skeate* v *Beale*. American law (*Williston on Contracts*) now recognises that a contract may be avoided on the ground of economic duress. The commercial pressure alleged to constitute such duress must, however, be such that the victim must have entered the contract against his will, must have had no alternative course open to him, and must have been confronted with coercive acts by the party exerting the pressure: see *Williston on Contracts*. American judges pay great attention to such evidential matters as the effectiveness of the alternative remedy available, the fact or absence of protest, the availability of independent advice, the benefit received, and the speed with which the victim has sought to avoid the contract. Recently two English judges have recognised that commercial pressure may constitute duress the pressure of which can render a contract voidable: see Kerr J in *The Siboen and The Sibotre* and Mocatta J in *North Ocean Shipping Co Ltd* v *Hyundai Construction Co Ltd*. Both stressed that the pressure must be such that the victim's consent to the contract was not a voluntary act on his part. In their Lordships' view, there is nothing contrary to principle in recognising economic duress as a factor which may render a contract voidable, provided always that the basis of such recognition is that it must amount to a coercion of will, which vitiates consent. It must be shown that the payment made or the contract entered into was not a voluntary act.'

Establishing economic duress

In *The Siboen* Kerr J raised two questions:

1   Did the victim protest at the time or shortly thereafter?
2   Did the victim regard whatever settlement was reached as closing the transaction or did he seek to reopen it?

North Ocean Shipping Co Ltd v *Hyundai Construction Co Ltd (The Atlantic Baron)*

[1978] 3 All ER 1170 • Queen's Bench Division

The facts of this case appear above (p 111).

Mocatta J: 'Having reached the conclusion that there was consideration for the agreement made on 28th and 29th June 1973 I must next consider whether even if that agreement, varying the terms of the original shipbuilding contract of 10th April 1972, was made under a threat to break that original contract and the various increased instalments were made consequentially under the varied agreement, the increased sums can be recovered as money had and received. Counsel for the owners submitted that they could be, provided they were involuntary payments and not made, albeit perhaps with some grumbling, to close the transaction.

Certainly this is the well-established position if payments are made, for example, to avoid the wrongful seizure of goods where there is no prior agreement to make such payments. The best known English case to this effect is probably *Maskell* v *Horner* . . .

There has been considerable discussion in the books whether, if an agreement is made under duress of goods to pay a sum of money and there is some consideration for the agreement, the excess sum can be recovered. The authority for this suggested distinction is *Skeate* v *Beale*. It was there said by Lord Denman CJ that an agreement was not void because it was made under duress of goods, the distinction between that case and the cases of money paid to recover goods wrongfully seized being said to be obvious in that the agreement was not compulsorily but voluntarily entered into. In the slightly later case of *Wakefield* v *Newbon*, Lord Denman CJ referred to cases such as *Skeate* v *Beale* as "that class where the parties have come to a voluntary settlement of their concerns, and have chosen to pay what is found due". Kerr J in *The Siboen and The Sibotre*, gave strong expression to the view that the suggested distinction based on *Skeate* v *Beale* would not be observed today. He said, though *obiter*, that *Skeate* v *Beale* would not justify a decision that –

> "if, for instance, I should be compelled to sign a lease or some other contract for a nominal but legally sufficient consideration under an imminent threat of having my house burnt down or a valuable picture slashed, though without any threat of physical violence to anyone, I do not think the law would uphold the agreement."

. . . It would seem, therefore, that the Australian courts would be prepared to allow the recovery of excess money paid, even under a new contract, as the result of a threat to break an earlier contract, since the threat or compulsion would be applied to the original contractual right of the party subject to the compulsion or economic duress. This also seems to be the view in the United States, where this was one of the grounds of decision in *King Construction Company* v *Smith Electric Co*. This view also accords with what was said in *D&C Builders Ltd* v *Rees* per Lord Denning MR: "No person can insist on a settlement procured by intimidation." . . .

I may here usefully cite a further short passage from the valuable remarks of Kerr J in *The Siboen and The Sibotre*, where after referring to three of the Australian cases I have cited he said:

> "It is true that in that case, and in all the three Australian cases, it was held that there had been no consideration for the settlement which the Courts reopened. But I do not think that it would have made any difference if the defendants in these cases had also insisted on some purely nominal but legally sufficient consideration. If the contract is

void the consideration would be recoverable in quasi-contract: if it is voidable equity could rescind the contract and order the return of the consideration."

Before proceeding further it may be useful to summarise the conclusions I have so far reached. First, I do not take the view that the recovery of money paid under duress other than to the person is necessarily limited to duress to goods falling within one of the categories hitherto established by the English cases. I would respectfully follow and adopt the broad statement of principle laid down by Isaacs J cited earlier and frequently quoted and applied in the Australian cases. Secondly, from this it follows that the compulsion may take the form of "economic duress" if the necessary facts are proved. A threat to break a contract may amount to such "economic duress". Thirdly, if there has been such a form of duress leading to a contract for consideration, I think that contract is a voidable one which can be avoided and the excess money paid under it recovered.

I think the facts found in this case do establish that the agreement to increase the price by ten per cent reached at the end of June 1973 was caused by what may be called "economic duress". The yard were adamant in insisting on the increased price without having any legal justification for so doing and the owners realised that the yard would not accept anything other than an unqualified agreement to the increase. The owners might have claimed damages in arbitration against the yard with all the inherent unavoidable uncertainties of litigation, but in view of the position of the owners *vis-à-vis* their relations with Shell it would be unreasonable to hold that this is the course they should have taken: see *Astley* v *Reynolds*. The owners made a very reasonable offer of arbitration coupled with security for any award in the yard's favour that might be made, but this was refused. They then made their agreement, which can truly I think be said to have been made under compulsion, by the telex of 28th June without prejudice to their rights. I do not consider the yard's ignorance of the Shell charter material. It may well be that had they known of it they would have been even more exigent.

If I am right in the conclusion reached with some doubt earlier that there was consideration for the ten per cent increase agreement reached at the end of June 1973 and if it be right to regard this as having been reached under a kind of duress in the form of economic pressure, then what is said in *Chitty on Contracts*, to which both counsel referred me, is relevant, namely that a contract entered into under duress is voidable and not void –

> "that a person who has entered into the contract may either affirm or avoid such contract after the duress has ceased; and if he has so voluntarily acted under it with a full knowledge of all the circumstances he may be held bound on the ground of ratification, or if, after escaping from the duress, he takes no steps to set aside the transaction, he may be found to have affirmed it."

On appeal in *Ormes* v *Beadel* and in Kerr J's case there was on the facts action which was held to amount to affirmation or acquiescence in the form of taking part in an arbitration pursuant to the impugned agreement. There is nothing comparable to such action here.

On the other hand, the findings of fact in the special case present difficulties whether one is proceeding on the basis of a voidable agreement reached at the end of June 1973 or whether such agreement was void for want of consideration, and it were necessary in consequence to establish that the payments were made involuntarily and not with the intention of closing the transaction.

I have already stated that no protest of any kind was made by the owners after their telex of 28th June 1973, before their claim in this arbitration on 30th July 1975, which was shortly after, in July of that year, the *Atlantic Baroness*, a sister ship of the *Atlantic Baron*, had been tendered, though, as I understand it, she was not accepted and arbitration proceedings in regard to her are in consequence taking place. There was therefore a delay between 27th November 1974, when the *Atlantic Baron* was delivered and 30th July 1975, before the owners put forward their claim.

The owners were, therefore, free from the duress on 27th November 1974 and took no action by way of protest or otherwise between the important telex of 28th June 1973 and their formal claim for the return of the excess ten per cent paid of 30th July 1975, when they nominated their arbitrator. One cannot dismiss this delay as of no significance, though I would not consider it conclusive by itself. I do not attach any special importance to the lack of protest made at the time of the assignment, since the documents made no reference to the increased ten per cent. However by the time the *Atlantic Baron* was due for delivery in November 1974 market conditions had changed radically, as is found in the special case and the owners must have been aware of this. The special case finds, as stated earlier, that the owners did not believe that if they made any protest in the protocol of delivery and acceptance the yard would have refused to deliver the vessel or the *Atlantic Baroness* and had no reason so to believe. Counsel for the owners naturally stressed that in the rather carefully expressed findings in the special case, there is no finding that if at the time of the final payments the owners had withheld payment of the additional ten per cent, the yard would not have delivered the vessel. However, after careful consideration, I have come to the conclusion that the important points here are that (i) since there was no danger at this time in registering a protest, (ii) the final payments were made without any qualification, and (iii) were followed by a delay until 31st July 1975 before the owners put forward their claim, the correct inference to draw, taking an objective view of the facts, is that the action and inaction of the owners can only be regarded as an affirmation of the variation in June 1973 of the terms of the original contract by the agreement to pay the additional ten per cent. In reaching this conclusion I have not, of course, overlooked the findings in the special case [that the owners never intended to affirm the agreement for extra payments] but I do not think that an intention on the part of the owners not to affirm the agreement for the extra payments, not indicated to the yard, can avail them in view of their overt acts. As was said in *Deacon* v *Transport Regulation Board* in considering whether a payment was made voluntarily or not: "No secret mental reservation of the doer is material. The question is – what would his conduct indicate to a reasonable man as his mental state." I think this test is equally applicable to the decision this court has to make whether a voidable contract has been affirmed or not and I have applied this test in reaching the conclusion I have just expressed.

I think I should add very shortly that having considered the many authorities cited, even if I had come to a different conclusion on the issue about consideration, I would have come to the same decision adverse to the owners on the question whether the payments were made voluntarily in the sense of being made to close the transaction.'

Judgment for the yard.

Universe Tankships Inc of Monrovia v *International Transport Workers Federation*

[1982] 2 WLR 803 • House of Lords

ITF blacked a ship belonging to Universe Tankships as part of its policy to improve the wages and conditions of crews on ships flying flags of convenience. As a result of the blacking Universe Tankships agreed to pay $6480 to ITF's welfare fund. After the ship had sailed Universe Tankships brought an action claiming the return of the $6480 on the basis that they had paid it under duress.

Lord Diplock: 'My Lords, I turn to the second ground on which repayment of the $6480 is claimed, which I will call the duress point. It is not disputed that the circumstances in which ITF demanded that the shipowners should enter into the special agreement and the typescript agreement and should pay the moneys of which the latter documents acknowledge receipt, amounted to economic duress upon the shipowners; that is to say, it is conceded that the financial consequences to the shipowners of the Universe Sentinel continuing to be rendered off-hire under her time charter to Texaco, while the blacking continued, were so catastrophic as to amount to a coercion of the shipowners' will which vitiated their consent to those agreements and to the payments made by them to ITF. This concession makes it unnecessary for your Lordships to use the instant appeal as the occasion for a general consideration of the developing law of economic duress as a ground for treating contracts as voidable and obtaining restitution of money paid under economic duress as money had and received to the plaintiffs' use. That economic duress may constitute a ground for such redress was recognised, albeit obiter, by the Privy Council in *Pao On* v *Lau Yiu Long*. The Board in that case referred with approval to two judgments at first instance in the commercial court which recognised that commercial pressure may constitute duress: one by Kerr J in *Occidental Worldwide Investment Corporation* v *Skibs A/S Avanti*, the other by Mocatta J in *North Ocean Shipping Co Ltd* v *Hyundai Construction Co Ltd*, which traces the development of this branch of the law from its origin in the 18th and early 19th century cases.

It is, however, in my view crucial to the decision of the instant appeal to identify the rationale of this development of the common law. It is not that the party seeking to avoid the contract which he has entered into with another party, or to recover money that he has paid to another party in response to a demand, did not know the nature or the precise terms of the contract at the time when he entered into it or did not understand the purpose for which the payment was demanded. The rationale is that his apparent consent was induced by pressure exercised upon him by that other party which the law does not regard as legitimate, with the consequence that the consent is treated in law as revocable unless approbated either expressly or by implication after the illegitimate pressure has ceased to operate on his mind. It is a rationale similar to that which underlies the avoidability of contracts entered into and the recovery of money exacted under colour of office, or under undue influence or in consequence of threats of physical duress.

Commercial pressure, in some degree, exists wherever one party to a commercial transaction is in a stronger bargaining position than the other party. It is not, however, in my view, necessary, nor would it be appropriate in the instant appeal, to enter into the general question of the kinds of circumstances, if any, in which commercial pressure, even though it amounts to a coercion of the will of a party in the weaker bargaining position, may be treated as legitimate and, accordingly, as not giving rise to any legal right of redress. In the instant appeal the economic duress complained of was exercised in the field of industrial relations to which very special considerations apply.'

Lord Scarman (dissenting): 'It is, I think, already established law that economic pressure can in law amount to duress; and that duress, if proved, not only renders voidable a transaction into which a person has entered under its compulsion but is actionable as a tort, if it causes damage or loss: *Barton* v *Armstrong* and *Pao On* v *Lao Yiu Long*. The authorities upon which these two cases were based reveal two elements in the wrong of duress: (1) pressure amounting to compulsion of the will of the victim; and (2) the illegitimacy of the pressure exerted. There must be pressure, the practical effect of which is compulsion or the absence of choice. Compulsion is variously described in the authorities as coercion or the vitiation of consent. The classic case of duress is, however, not the lack of will to [resist] but the victim's intentional submission arising from the realisation that there is no other practical choice open to him. This is the thread of principle which links the early law of duress (threat to life or limb) with later developments when the law came also to recognise as duress first the threat to property and now the threat to a man's business or trade. The development is well traced in Goff and Jones, *The Law of Restitution*, 2nd edn.

The absence of choice can be proved in various ways, e.g. by protest, by the absence of independent advice, or by a declaration of intention to go to law to recover the money paid or the property transferred: see *Maskell* v *Horner*. But none of these evidential matters goes to the essence of duress. The victim's silence will not assist the bully, if the lack of any practicable choice but to submit is proved. The present case is an excellent illustration. There was no protest at the time, but only a determination to do whatever was needed as rapidly as possible to release the ship. Yet nobody challenges the judge's finding that the owner acted under compulsion. He put it thus:

> "It was a matter of the most urgent commercial necessity that the plaintiffs should regain the use of their vessel. They were advised that their prospects of obtaining an injunction were minimal, the vessel would not have been released unless the payment was made, and they sought recovery of the money with sufficient speed once the duress had terminated."

The real issue in the appeal is, therefore, as to the second element in the wrong duress: was the pressure applied by the ITF in the circumstances of this case one which the law recognises as legitimate? For, as Lord Wilberforce and Lord Simon of Glaisdale said in *Barton* v *Armstrong*: "the pressure must be one of a kind which the law does not regard as legitimate".

As the two noble and learned Lords remarked, in life, including the life of commerce and finance, many acts are done "under pressure, sometimes overwhelming pressure": but they are not necessarily done under duress. That depends on whether the circumstances are such that the law regards the pressure as legitimate.

In determining what is legitimate two matters may have to be considered. The first is as to the nature of the pressure. In many cases this will be decisive, though not in every case. And so the second question may have to be considered, namely, the nature of the demand which the pressure is applied to support.

The origin of the doctrine of duress in threats to life or limb, or to property, suggests strongly that the law regards the threat of unlawful action as illegitimate, whatever the demand. Duress can, of course, exist even if the threat is one of lawful action: whether it does so depends upon the nature of the demand. Blackmail is often a demand supported by a threat to do what is lawful, e.g. to report criminal conduct to the police. In many cases, therefore, "What [one] has to justify is not the threat, but the demand . . . ": see per Lord Atkin in *Thorne* v *Motor Trade Association*.

The present is a case in which the nature of the demand determines whether the pressure threatened or applied, i.e. the blacking, was lawful or unlawful. If it was unlawful, it is conceded that the owner acted under duress and can recover. If it was lawful, it is conceded that there was no duress and the sum sought by the owner is irrecoverable. The lawfulness or otherwise of the demand depends upon whether it was an act done in contemplation or furtherance of a trade dispute . . .

For these reasons I conclude that the demand for contributions related to the terms and conditions of employment on the ship, and, if it had been resisted by the owner, would have led to a trade dispute. Blacking the ship in support of the demand was . . . accordingly, a legitimate exercise of pressure and did not constitute duress. The owner cannot recover the contributions.'

Atlas Express Ltd v Kafco (Importers and Distributors) Ltd

[1989] 1 All ER 641 • Queen's Bench

Kafco had obtained a valuable contract to supply basketware to Woolworth shops in the UK. In order to distribute its goods to the various Woolworth shops Kafco entered into a contract with Atlas, a national road carrier, whereby Atlas would carry Kafco's cartons at £1.10 per carton. Kafco, using its own expertise, had agreed this price on the basis that it would carry at least 400 cartons per load. In fact the first load contained only 200 cartons. Atlas, realising its mistake, refused to carry any more of Kafco's cartons unless Kafco agreed to pay £440 per load. Fearful of losing its contract with Woolworth and finding it impossible to find another carrier in such a short time Kafco reluctantly agreed to pay the £440 per load. Later, however, Kafco refused to pay the extra charges and Atlas sued to recover the money owed to them by Kafco based on the figure of £440 per load.

The issue before the court was whether Kafco had paid the money under economic duress.

Tucker J: 'The issue which I have to determine is whether the defendants are bound by the agreement signed on their behalf on 18 November 1986. The defendants contend that they are not bound, for two reasons: first, because the agreement was signed under duress, second because there was no consideration for it.

The first question raises an interesting point of law, i.e. whether economic duress is a concept known to English law.

Economic duress must be distinguished from commercial pressure, which on any view is not sufficient to vitiate consent. The borderline between the two may in some cases be indistinct. But the authors of *Chitty on Contracts* and of Goff and Jones on the *Law of Restitution* appear to recognise that in appropriate cases economic duress may afford a defence, and in my judgment it does. It is clear to me that in a number of English cases judges have acknowledged the existence of this concept . . .

Reverting to the case before me, I find that the defendants' apparent consent to the agreement was induced by pressure which was illegitimate and I find that it was not approbated. In my judgment that pressure can properly be described as economic duress, which is a concept recognised by English law, and which in the circumstances of the present case vitiates the defendants' apparent consent to the agreement.

In any event, I find that there was no consideration for the new agreement. The plaintiffs were already obliged to deliver the defendants' goods at the rates agreed under the terms of the original agreement. There was no consideration for the increased minimum charge of £440 per trailer.

Accordingly, I find that the plaintiffs' claim fails, and there will be judgment for the defendants with costs.'

Williams v Roffey Bros & Nicholls (Contractors) Ltd

[1990] 1 All ER 512 • Court of Appeal

The facts appear above (p 113).

Glidewell LJ: 'There is, however, another legal concept of relatively recent development which is relevant, namely, that of economic duress. Clearly if a subcontractor has agreed to undertake work at a fixed price, and before he has completed the work declines to continue with it unless the contractor agrees to pay an increased price, the subcontractor may be held guilty of securing the contractor's promise by taking unfair advantage of the difficulties he will cause if he does not complete the work. In such a case an agreement to pay an increased price may well be voidable because it was entered into under duress. Thus this concept may provide another answer in law to the question of policy which has troubled the courts since before *Stilk* v *Myrick* and no doubt led at the date of that decision to a rigid adherence to the doctrine of consideration.'

Note that duress was not pleaded in this case.

CTN Cash and Carry Ltd v *Gallaher Ltd*

[1994] 4 All ER 714 • Court of Appeal

Gallaher by mistake sent £17 000 worth of cigarettes to CTN's warehouse in Burnley. Before the cigarettes could be collected they were stolen. Gallaher, mistakenly, but in good faith, claimed that CTN were responsible for the loss and invoiced them for the stolen cigarettes. When CTN refused to pay Gallaher said that it would withdraw CTN's credit facilities if CTN did not pay. CTN then paid the £17 000. Later CTN issued a writ claiming the return of the £17 000 on the ground that they had paid the money under duress.

Steyn LJ: 'The present dispute does not concern a protected relationship. It also does not arise in the context of dealings between a supplier and a consumer. The dispute arises out of arm's length commercial dealings between two trading companies. It is true that the defendants were the sole distributors of the popular brands of cigarettes. In a sense the defendants were in a monopoly position. The control of monopolies is, however, a matter for Parliament. Moreover, the common law does not recognise the doctrine of inequality of bargaining power in commercial dealings (see *National Westminster Bank plc* v *Morgan*). The fact that the defendants were in a monopoly position cannot therefore by itself convert what is not otherwise duress into duress.

A second characteristic of the case is that the defendants were in law entitled to refuse to enter into any future contracts with the plaintiffs for any reason whatever or for no reason at all. Such a decision not to deal with the plaintiffs would have been financially damaging to the defendants, but it would have been lawful. *A fortiori*, it was lawful for the defendants, for any reason or for no reason, to insist that they would no longer grant credit to the plaintiffs. The defendants' demand for payment of the invoice, coupled with the threat to withdraw credit, was neither a breach of contract nor a tort.

A third, and critically important, characteristic of the case is the fact that the defendants *bona fide* thought that the goods were at the risk of the plaintiffs and that the plaintiffs owed the defendants the sum in question. The defendants exerted commercial pressure on the plaintiffs in order to obtain payment of a sum which they *bona fide* considered due to them. The defendants' motive in threatening withdrawal of credit facilities was commercial self-interest in obtaining a sum that they considered due to them . . .

I also readily accept that the fact that the defendants have used lawful means does not by itself remove the case from the scope of the doctrine of economic duress. Professor Birks, in *An Introduction to the Law of Restitution*, lucidly explains:

"Can lawful pressures also count? This is a difficult question, because, if the answer is that they can, the only viable basis for discriminating between acceptable and unacceptable pressures is not positive law but social morality. In other words, the judges must say what pressures (though lawful outside the restitutionary context) are improper as contrary to prevailing standards. That makes the judges, not the law or the legislature, the arbiters of social evaluation. On the other hand, if the answer is that lawful pressures are always exempt, those who devise outrageous but technically lawful means of compulsion must always escape restitution until the legislature declares the abuse unlawful. It is tolerably clear that, at least where they can be confident of a general consensus in favour of their evaluation, the courts are willing to apply a standard of impropriety rather than technical unlawfulness."

And there are a number of cases where English courts have accepted that a threat may be illegitimate when coupled with a demand for payment even if the threat is one of lawful action . . . On the other hand, Goff and Jones' *Law of Restitution* observed that English courts have wisely not accepted any general principle that a threat not to contract with another, except on certain terms, may amount to duress.

We are being asked to extend the categories of duress of which the law will take cognisance. That is not necessarily objectionable, but it seems to me that an extension capable of covering the present case, involving "lawful act duress" in a commercial context in pursuit of a *bona fide* claim, would be a radical one with far-reaching implications. It would introduce a substantial and undesirable element of uncertainty in the commercial bargaining process. Moreover, it will often enable *bona fide* settled accounts to be reopened when parties to commercial dealings fall out. The aim of our commercial law ought to be to encourage fair dealing between parties. But it is a mistake for the law to set its sights too highly when the critical inquiry is not whether the conduct is lawful but whether it is morally or socially unacceptable. That is the inquiry in which we are engaged. In my view there are policy considerations which militate against ruling that the defendants obtained payment of the disputed invoice by duress.

Outside the field of protected relationships, and in a purely commercial context, it might be a relatively rare case in which "lawful act duress" can be established. And it might be particularly difficult to establish duress if the defendant *bona fide* considered that his demand was valid. In this complex and changing branch of the law I deliberately refrain from saying "never". But as the law stands, I am satisfied that the defendants' conduct in this case did not amount to duress.

It is an unattractive result, inasmuch as the defendants are allowed to retain a sum which at the trial they became aware was not in truth due to them. But in my view the law compels the result.'

Sir Donald Nicholls VC: '. . . When the defendant company insisted on payment, it did so in good faith. It believed the risk in the goods had passed to the plaintiff company, so it considered it was entitled to be paid for them. The defendant company took a tough line. It used its commercial muscle. But the feature underlying and dictating this attitude was a genuine belief on its part that it was owed the sum in question. It was entitled to be paid the price for the goods. So it took the line: the plaintiff company must pay in law what it owed, otherwise its credit would be suspended.

Further, there is no evidence that the defendant's belief was unreasonable. Indeed, we were told by the defendant's counsel that he had advised his client that on the risk point the defendant stood a good chance of success. I do not see how a payment demanded and made in those circumstances can be said to be vitiated by duress.'

Duress in equity

Relief is wider than at common law, but the limits of relief are not clearly defined.

A threat to prosecute is a ground for relief

Williams v *Bayley*
[1866] LR 1 HL 200 • House of Lords

Bayley's son, William, had forged his father's signature on several promissory notes. On discovering the forgeries the bank arranged a meeting of all the parties. At the meeting Williams said to Bayley 'If the bills are yours we are all right; if they are not, we have only one course to pursue; we cannot be parties to compounding a felony'. During further discussions Williams' solicitor said it was 'a serious matter' and Bayley's solicitor added, 'a case of transportation for life'. After further discussion Bayley said to his solicitor 'What be I to do? How can I help myself? You see these men will have their money.' In the end Bayley reached a settlement with the bank by which in return for him mortgaging his property to them they would return the forged notes to him.

The issue before the court was whether the agreement should be set aside on the ground that Bayley had not freely consented to the agreement.

Lord Cranworth LC: '. . . Now is that a transaction which a Court of equity will tolerate, or is it not? I agree very much with a good deal of the argument of Sir Hugh Cairns as to this doctrine of pressure. Many grounds on which a Court of equity has acted in such cases do not apply in this case . . . But here was a pressure of this nature. We have the means of prosecuting, and so transporting your son. Do you choose to come to his help and take on yourself the amount of his debts – the amount of these forgeries? If you do we will not prosecute; if you do not, we will. That is the plain interpretation of what passed. Is that, or is it not, legal? In my opinion, my Lords, I am bound to go the length of saying that I do not think it is legal. I do not think that a transaction of that sort would have been legal even if, instead of being forced on the father, it had been proposed by him and adopted by the bankers; and I come to that conclusion upon this short ground, that in *Wallace* v *Hardacre* . . . Lord Ellenborough positively states that which has always been understood to be the correct view of the law upon this subject, namely, that although in that case there was no reason for treating the agreement as invalid, yet it would have been otherwise if the agreement had been substantially an agreement to stifle a criminal prosecution . . . Now, is the agreement in question, or is it not, one the object of which is to stifle a criminal prosecution? If there be really a case in which that character can be properly given to an agreement I think that this is such a case, and therefore, in my opinion, the decree is perfectly right . . .'

UNDUE INFLUENCE

Undue influence is an *equitable doctrine*.

Undue influence consists of pressure less direct or substantial than coercion as in duress.

Two situations in which courts will recognise undue influence:

(1) Where the party charged has exercised undue influence, in the sense of domination, over the other party;

(2) where there is an abuse of the duties of care and confidence which may be

imposed on one party towards another as a result of the particular relationship which emerges from the special circumstances of the association.

In (1) evidence of express influence must be proved. In (2) undue influence is presumed in the absence of evidence to the contrary.

Presumption of undue influence

Allcard v *Skinner*

(1887) 36 ChD 145 • Court of Appeal

In 1868 Miss Allcard was introduced by the Rev Nihill, her spiritual director and confessor, to Miss Skinner, who was the lady superior of a Protestant institution known as 'The Sisters of the Poor' which had been founded by Nihill and Skinner. Allcard joined the sisterhood and became a professed member of the sisterhood in 1871. By the rules of the sisterhood Allcard bound herself to observe the rules of poverty, chastity, and obedience. The rules further provided 'that the voice of thy Superior is the voice of God', that 'no Sister [should] seek advice of any extern without the Superior's leave', and that all individual property had to be given up and that if it were given up to the sisterhood it should not be required or reclaimed by the members on leaving. Shortly after joining the sisterhood in 1870 Allcard made a will leaving all her property to Skinner. Whilst she was a member of the sisterhood she gave Skinner £1050 plus stocks and shares worth £5870. In 1879 Allcard left the sisterhood and immediately revoked her will but she did not reclaim any of her property until 1885 which at that date was worth £1671. Allcard brought an action for the return of her property claiming that she was induced to make over her property whilst acting under the direction and paramount influence of Skinner, and without any separate or independent advice.

The issue before the court was whether Allcard was under undue influence when she gave her property to Skinner.

Cotton LJ: 'Is the Plaintiff entitled to recall the stock now in question and still in hand? There is no decision in point with reference to a case like the present. For, although in the case of *Whyte* v *Meade* a deed of gift by a nun was set aside, there were in that case special circumstances which prevent it being treated as an authority in favour of the Plaintiff. The question is – Does the case fall within the principles laid down by the decisions of the Court of Chancery in setting aside voluntary gifts executed by parties who at the time were under such influence as, in the opinion of the Court, enabled the donor afterwards to set the gift aside? These decisions may be divided into two classes: First, where the Court has been satisfied that the gift was the result of influence expressly used by the donee for the purpose; second, where the relations between the donor and donee have at or shortly before the execution of the gift been such as to raise a presumption that the donee had influence over the donor. In such a case the Court sets aside the voluntary gift, unless it is proved that in fact the gift was the spontaneous act of the donor acting under circumstances which enabled him to exercise an independent will and which justifies the Court in holding that the gift was the result of a free exercise of the donor's will. The first class of cases may be considered as depending on the principle that no one shall be allowed to retain any benefit arising from his own fraud or wrongful act. In the second class of cases the Court interferes, not on the ground that any wrongful act has in fact been committed by the donee, but on the ground of public policy, and to prevent the relations which existed between the parties and the influence arising therefrom being abused.

Both the Defendant and Mr Nihill have stated that they used no influence to induce the Plaintiff to make the gift in question, and there is no suggestion that the defendant acted from any selfish motive, and it cannot be contended that this case comes under the first class of decisions to which I have referred. The question is whether the case comes within the principle of the second class, and I am of opinion that it does. At the time of the gift the Plaintiff was a professed sister, and, as such, bound to render absolute submission to the Defendant as superior of the sisterhood. She had no power to obtain independent advice, she was in such a position that she could not freely exercise her own will as to the disposal of her property, and she must be considered as being (to use the words of Lord Justice Knight Bruce in *Wright* v *Vanderplank*) "not, in the largest and amplest sense of the term – not, in mind as well as person – an entirely free agent".

But it is contended . . . that she had competent advice, that of her brother, before she joined the sisterhood, and that she then formed the resolution . . . to give everything to the sisterhood, and that this prevents the subsequent transfer being set aside. In my opinion, even if there were evidence that she had, before she joined the sisterhood, advice on the question of how she should deal with her property, that would not be sufficient. The question is, I think, whether at the time when she executed the transfer she was under such influences as to prevent the gift being considered as that of one free to determine what should be done with her property . . . In my opinion, when the Plaintiff left the sisterhood in 1879, she was entitled to set aside the transfer, and to have re-transferred to her the fund still held by the Defendant. Has she lost this right by delay?'

Note: in the end the Court of Appeal held (Cotton LJ dissenting), that under the circumstances Allcard's claim was barred by her laches (delay) and acquiescence.

Special relationship between the parties

Even if the plaintiff cannot prove that his mind was a 'mere channel through which the will of defendant operated' he may yet succeed if there existed between the parties some special relationship of confidence which the defendant has abused.

Lloyds Bank Ltd v Bundy

[1974] 3 All ER 757 • Court of Appeal

Bundy, an elderly farmer, and his son both banked with the same branch of Lloyds Bank. The son's company also banked at the same branch. In 1966 when the son's company got into financial difficulties Bundy guaranteed his son's company's overdraft for £1500 and charged his farm, Yew Tree Farm, to Lloyds to secure the £1500. In 1967 Bundy, after legal advice, extended the charge to £7500 to guarantee his son's company's increasing overdraft. In 1969, the son's company's financial position having got worse, the assistant bank manager, Head, and the son visited Bundy. At a meeting with the family Head told them that the bank had given serious thought whether they could continue to support the son's company but that the bank was prepared to do so if Bundy extended the charge on the house to £11 000, the house only being worth £10 000 at that time. Bundy agreed and Head produced the agreement which had already been filled in. Bundy signed the agreement and Head witnessed it there and then. Head did not leave the forms with Bundy nor did Bundy have any independent advice. In 1970, the son's company having ceased to trade, Lloyds claimed possession of Bundy's house.

Bundy sought to have the charges set aside on the ground of undue influence.

Sir Eric Sachs: 'The first and most troublesome issue which here falls for consideration is whether on the particular and somewhat unusual facts of the case the bank was, when obtaining his signatures on 17 December 1969, in a relationship with the defendant that entailed a duty on their part of what can for convenience be called fiduciary care. (The phrase "fiduciary care" is used to avoid the confusion with the common law duty of care – a different field of our jurisprudence.)

As was pointed out in *Tufton* v *Sperni* the relationships which result in such a duty must not be circumscribed by reference to defined limits; it is necessary to – "refute the suggestion that, to create the relationship of confidence, the person owing a duty must be found clothed in the recognisable garb of a guardian, trustee, solicitor, priest, doctor, manager, or the like".

Everything depends on the particular facts, and such a relationship has been held to exist in unusual circumstances as between purchaser and vendor, as between great uncle and adult nephew, and in other widely differing sets of circumstances. Moreover, it is neither feasible nor desirable to attempt closely to define the relationship, or its characteristics, or the demarcation line showing the exact transition point where a relationship that does not entail that duty passes into one that does (cf Ungoed-Thomas J in *Re Craig*).

On the other hand, whilst disclaiming any intention of seeking to catalogue the elements of such a special relationship, it is perhaps of a little assistance to note some of those which have in the past frequently been found to exist where the court had been led to decide that this relationship existed as between adults of sound mind. Such cases tend to arise where someone relies on the guidance or advice of another, where the other is aware of that reliance and where the person on whom reliance is placed obtains, or may well obtain, a benefit from the transaction or has some other interest in it being concluded. In addition, there must, of course, be shown to exist a vital element which in this judgment will for convenience be referred to as confidentiality. It is this element which is so impossible to define and which is a matter for the judgment of the court on the facts of any particular case.

Confidentiality, a relatively little used word, is being here adopted, albeit with some hesitation, to avoid the possible confusion that can arise through referring to "confidence". Reliance on advice can in many circumstances be said to import that type of confidence which only results in a common law duty to take care – a duty which may co-exist with but is not coterminous with that of fiduciary care. "Confidentiality" is intended to convey that extra quality in the relevant confidence that is implicit in the phrase "confidential relationship" (cf per Lord Chelmsford LC in *Tate* v *Williamson*, Lindley LJ in *Allcard* v *Skinner* and Wright J in *Moreley* v *Loughnan*) and may perhaps have something in common with "confiding" and also "confidant", when, for instance, referring to someone's "man of affairs". It imports some quality beyond that inherent in the confidence that can well exist between trustworthy persons who in business affairs deal with each other at arm's length. It is one of the features of this element that once it exists, influence naturally grows out of it (cf Evershed MR in *Tufton* v *Sperni*, following Lord Chelmsford LC in *Tate* v *Williamson*).

It was inevitably conceded on behalf of the bank that the relevant relationship can arise as between banker and customer. Equally, it was inevitably conceded on behalf of the defendant that in the normal course of transactions by which a customer guarantees a third party's obligations, the relationship does not arise. The onus of proof lies on the customer who alleges that in any individual case the line has been crossed and the relationship has arisen.

Before proceeding to examine the position further, it is as well to dispose of some points on which confusion is apt to arise. Of these the first is one which plainly led to misapprehension on the part of the learned county court judge. Undue influence is a phrase which is commonly regarded – even in the eyes of a number of lawyers – as relating solely to occasions when the will of one person has become so dominated by that of another that, to use the learned county court judge's words, "the person acts as the mere puppet of the dominator". Such occasions, of course, fall within what Cotton LJ in *Allcard* v *Skinner* described as the first class of cases to which the doctrine on undue influence applies. There is, however, a second class of such cases. This is referred to by Cotton LJ as follows:

> "In the second class of cases the Court interferes, not on the ground that any wrongful act has in fact been committed by the donee, but on the ground of public policy, and to prevent the relations which existed between the parties and the influence arising therefrom being abused."

It is thus to be emphasised that as regards the second class the exercise of the court's jurisdiction to set aside the relevant transaction does not depend on proof of one party being "able to dominate the others as though a puppet" (to use the words again adopted by the learned county court judge when testing whether the defence was established) nor any wrongful intention on the part of the person who gains a benefit from it, but on the concept that once the special relationship has been shown to exist, no benefit can be retained from the transaction unless it has been positively established that the duty of fiduciary care has been entirely fulfilled. To this second class, however, the learned judge never averted and plainly never directed his mind.

It is also to be noted that what constitutes fulfilment of that duty (the second issue in the case now under consideration) depends again on the facts before the court. It may in the particular circumstances entail that the person in whom confidence has been reposed should insist on independent advice being obtained or ensuring in one way or another that the person being asked to execute a document is not insufficiently informed of some factor which could affect his judgment. The duty has been well stated as being one to ensure that the person liable to be influenced has formed "an independent and *informed* judgment", or to use the phraseology of Lord Evershed MR in *Zamet* v *Hyman* "after full, free *and informed* thought" . . .

Stress was placed in argument for the bank on the effect of the word "abused" as it appears in the above cited passage in the judgment of Cotton LJ and in other judgments and textbooks. As regards the second class of undue influence, however, that word in the context means no more than that once the existence of a special relationship has been established, then any possible use of the relevant influence is, irrespective of the intentions of the persons possessing it, regarded in relation to the transaction under consideration as an abuse – unless and until the duty of fiduciary care has been shown to be fulfilled or the transaction is shown to be truly for the benefit of the person influenced. This approach is a matter of public policy . . .

. . . [I]t is now convenient to turn to the evidence relating to the first of them – whether the special relationship has here been shown to exist at the material time . . .

It is, of course, plain that when Mr Head was asking the defendant to sign the documents, the bank would derive benefit from the signature, that there was a conflict of interest as between the bank and the defendant, that the bank gave him advice, that he relied on that advice, and that the bank knew of the reliance. The further question is whether on the evidence concerning the matters already recited there was also established that element of confidentiality which has been discussed. In my judgment it is thus established. Moreover reinforcement for that view can be derived from some of the material which it is more convenient to examine in greater detail when considering what the resulting duty of fiduciary care entailed.

What was required to be done on the bank's behalf once the existence of that duty is shown to have been established? The situation of the defendant in his sitting-room at Yew Tree Farm can be stated as follows. He was faced by three persons anxious for him to sign. There was his son Michael, the overdraft of whose company had been, as is shown by the correspondence, escalating rapidly; whose influence over his father was observed by the judge – and can hardly not have been realised by the bank; and whose ability to overcome the difficulties of his company was plainly doubtful, indeed its troubles were known to Mr Head to be "deep-seated". There was Mr Head, on behalf of the bank, coming with the documents designed to protect the bank's interest already substantially made out and in his pocket. There was Michael's wife asking Mr Head to help her husband.

The documents which Mr Bundy was being asked to sign could result, if the company's troubles continued, in Mr Bundy's sole asset being sold, the proceeds all going to the bank, and his being left penniless in his old age. That he could thus be rendered penniless was known to the bank – and in particular to Mr Head. That the company might come to a bad end quite soon with these results was not exactly difficult to deduce (less than four months later, on 3 April 1970, the bank were insisting that Yew Tree Farm be sold).

The situation was thus one which to any reasonably sensible person, who gave it but a moment's thought, cried aloud the defendant's need for careful independent advice. Over and above the need any man has for counsel when asked to risk his last penny on even an apparently reasonable project, was the need here for informed advice as to whether there was any real chance of the company's affairs becoming viable if the documents were signed. If not, there arose questions such as, what is the use of taking the risk of becoming penniless without benefiting anyone but the bank; is it not better both for you and your son that you, at any rate, should still have some money when the crash comes; and should not the bank at least bind itself to hold its hand for some given period? The answers to such questions could only be given in the light of a worthwhile appraisement of the company's affairs – without which the defendant could not come to an *informed judgment* as to the wisdom of what he was doing.

No such advice to get an independent opinion was given; on the contrary, Mr Head chose to give his own views on the company's affairs and to take this course, though he had at trial to admit: "I did not explain the company's affairs very fully I had only just taken over". (Another answer that escaped entry in the learned judge's original notes.)

On the above recited facts, the breach of the duty to take fiduciary care is manifest . . .

. . . In my judgment, however, a breach by the bank of their duty to take fiduciary care has, on the evidence, as a whole been so affirmatively established that this court can and should make an order setting aside the guarantee and the charge of 17 December 1969 . . .

The conclusion that the defendant has established that as between himself and the bank the relevant transaction fell within the second category of undue influence cases referred to by Cotton LJ in *Allcard* v *Skinner* . . .'

National Westminster Bank plc v *Morgan*

[1985] 2 WLR 588 • House of Lords

The facts appear below (p 438).

Lord Scarman: 'I turn, therefore, to consider the *ratio decidendi* for Sir Eric Sachs's judgment [in *Lloyds Bank Ltd* v *Bundy*]. In so far as Sir Eric appears to have accepted the "public policy" principle formulated by Cotton LJ in *Allcard* v *Skinner*, I think for the reasons which I have already developed that he fell into error if he is to be understood as also saying that it matters not whether the transaction itself was wrongful in the sense explained by Lindley LJ, in *Allcard* v *Skinner*, by Lord Macnaghten in *Bank of Montreal* v *Stuart* and by Lord Shaw of Dunfermline in the *Poosathurai* case. But in the last paragraph of his judgment where Sir Eric turned to consider the nature of the relationship necessary to give rise to the presumption of undue influence in the context of a banking transaction, he got it absolutely right. He said:

> "There remains to mention that Mr Rankin, whilst conceding that the relevant special relationship could arise as between banker and customer, urged in somewhat doom-laden terms that a decision taken against the bank on the facts of this particular case would seriously affect banking practice. With all respect to that submission, it seems necessary to point out that nothing in this judgment affects the duties of a bank in the normal case where it is obtaining a guarantee, and in accordance with standard practice explains to the person about to sign its legal effect and the sums involved. When, however, a bank, as in the present case, goes further and advises on more general matters germane to the wisdom of the transaction, that indicates that it may – not necessarily must – be crossing the line into the area of confidentiality so that the court may then have to examine all the facts including, of course, the history leading up to the transaction, to ascertain whether or not that line has, as here, been crossed. It would indeed be rather odd if a bank which *vis-à-vis* a customer attained a special relationship in some ways akin to that of a 'man of affairs' – something which can be a matter of pride and enhance its local reputation – should not, where a conflict of interest has arisen as between itself and the person advised, be under the resulting duty now under discussion. Once, as was inevitably conceded, it is possible for a bank to be under that duty, it is, as in the present case, simply a question for 'meticulous examination' of the particular facts to see whether that duty has arisen. On the special facts here it did arise and it has been broken."

This is good sense and good law, though I would prefer to avoid the term "confidentiality" as a description of the relationship which has to be proved. In truth, as Sir Eric recognised, the relationships which may develop a dominating influence of one over another are infinitely various. There is no substitute in this branch of the law for "meticulous examination of the facts".

A meticulous examination of the facts of the present case reveals that Mr Barrow never "crossed the line". Nor was the transaction unfair to Mrs Morgan. The bank was, therefore, under no duty to ensure that she had independent advice. It was an ordinary banking transaction whereby Mrs Morgan sought to save her home; and she obtained an honest and truthful explanation of the bank's intention which, notwithstanding the terms of the mortgage deed which in the circumstances the trial judge was right to dismiss as "essentially theoretical", was correct: for no one has suggested that Mr Barrow or the bank sought to make Mrs Morgan liable, or to make her home the security, for any debt of her husband other than the loan and interest necessary to save the house from being taken away from them in discharge of their indebtedness to the building society.'

National Westminster Bank plc v *Morgan*

[1985] 2 WLR 588 • House of Lords

Mr Morgan's business was in financial trouble and as a result he fell into arrears with his mortgage repayments to the Abbey National Building Society who took proceedings for possession of his house. His bank, National Westminster Bank, offered to help him out of his financial difficulties by offering him a £14 500 bridging loan subject to a legal charge on his and his wife's house. Mr Morgan signed the charge but in order to get his wife's signature, Barrow, the assistant bank manager, called on Mrs Morgan at the house. Mrs Morgan was concerned that the document which she was being asked to sign might enable the husband to borrow from the bank for business purposes. She wanted the charge confined to paying off the Abbey National and to the provision of bridging finance for about five weeks. She told Barrow that she had no confidence in her husband's business ability and did not want the mortgage to cover his business liabilities. Mr Barrow advised her that the cover was so limited. She expressed her gratitude to the bank for saving their home and she signed the document. Mr Morgan failed to repay the loan and the bank took proceedings for possession of the house. Mrs Morgan claimed that the charge should be set aside on the grounds of undue influence.

Lord Scarman: 'Such was the interview in which it is said that Mr Barrow crossed the line which divides a normal business relationship from one of undue influence. I am bound to say that the facts appear to me to be a far cry from a relationship of undue influence or from a transaction in which an unfair advantage was obtained by one party over the other. The trial judge clearly so thought: for he stated his reasons for rejecting Mrs Morgan's case with admirable brevity. He made abundantly clear his view that the relationship between Mr Barrow and Mrs Morgan never went beyond that of a banker and customer, that Mrs Morgan had made up her own mind that she was ready to give the charge, and that the one piece of advice (as to the legal effect of the charge) which Mr Barrow did give, though erroneous as to the terms of the charge, correctly represented his intention and that of the bank . . .

The Court of Appeal disagreed. The two Lords Justices who constituted the court, Dunn and Slade LJJ (surely it should have been a court of three?) put an interpretation upon the facts very different from that of the judge: they also differed from him on the law.

As to the facts, I am far from being persuaded that the trial judge fell into error when he concluded that the relationship between the bank and Mrs Morgan never went beyond the normal business relationship of banker and customer. Both Lord Justices saw the relationship between the bank and Mrs Morgan as one of confidence in which she was relying on the bank manager's advice. Each recognised the personal honesty, integrity, and good faith of Mr Barrow. Each took the view that the confidentiality of the relationship was such as to impose upon him a "fiduciary duty of care". It was his duty, in their view, to ensure that Mrs Morgan had the opportunity to make an independent and informed decision: but he failed to give her any such opportunity. They, therefore, concluded that it was a case for the presumption of undue influence.

My Lords, I believe that the Lords Justices were led into a misinterpretation of the facts by their use, as is all too frequent in this branch of the law, of words and phrases such as "confidence", "confidentiality", "fiduciary duty". There are plenty of confidential relationships which do not give rise to the presumption of undue influence (a notable example is that of husband and wife, *Bank of Montreal* v *Stuart*; and there are plenty of non-confidential relationships in which one person relies upon the advice of another, e.g. many contracts for the sale of goods. Nor am I persuaded that the charge, limited as it was by Mr Barrow's declaration to securing the loan to pay off the Abbey National debt and interest during the bridging period, was disadvantageous to Mrs Morgan. It meant for her the rescue of her home upon the terms sought by her – a short-term loan at a commercial rate of interest. The Court of Appeal has not, therefore, persuaded me that the judge's understanding of the facts was incorrect.

But, further, the view of the law expressed by the Court of Appeal was, as I shall endeavour to show, mistaken. Dunn LJ, while accepting that in all the reported cases to which the court was referred the transactions were disadvantageous to the person influenced, took the view that in cases where public policy requires the court to apply the presumption of undue influence there is no need to prove a disadvantageous transaction. Slade LJ also clearly held that it was not necessary to prove a disadvantageous transaction where the relationship of influence was proved to exist. Basing himself on the judgment of Cotton LJ in *Allcard* v *Skinner*. . .

Like Dunn LJ, I know of no reported authority where the transaction set aside was not to the manifest disadvantage of the person influenced. It would not always be a gift: it can be a "hard and inequitable" agreement (*Ormes* v *Beadel*); or a transaction "immoderate and irrational" (*Bank of Montreal* v *Stuart*) or "unconscionable" in that it was a sale at an undervalue (*Poosathurai* v *Kannappa Chettiar*). Whatever the legal character of the transaction, the authorities show that it must constitute a disadvantage sufficiently serious to require evidence to rebut the presumption that in the circumstances of the relationship between the parties it was procured by the exercise of undue influence. In my judgment, therefore, the Court of Appeal erred in law in holding that the presumption of undue influence can arise from the evidence of the relationship of the parties without also evidence that the transaction itself was wrongful in that it constituted an advantage taken of the person subjected to the influence which, failing proof to the contrary, was explicable only on the basis that undue influence had been exercised to procure it.

The principle justifying the court in setting aside a transaction for undue influence can now be seen to have been established by Lindley LJ in *Allcard* v *Skinner*. It is not a vague "public policy" but specifically the victimisation of one party by the other. It was stated by Lindley LJ in a famous passage:

> "The principle must be examined. What then is the principle? Is it that it is right and expedient to save persons from the consequences of their own folly? or is it that it is right and expedient to save them from being victimised by other people? In my opinion the doctrine of undue influence is founded upon the second of these two principles. Courts of equity have never set aside gifts on the ground of the folly, imprudence, or want of foresight on the part of donors. The courts have always repudiated any such jurisdiction. *Huguenin* v *Baseley* is itself a clear authority to this effect. It would obviously be to encourage folly, recklessness, extravagance and vice if persons could get back property which they foolishly made away with, whether by giving it to charitable institutions or by bestowing it on less worthy objects. On the other hand, to protect people from being forced, tricked or misled in any way by others into parting with their property is one of the most legitimate objects of all laws; and all equitable doctrine of undue influence has grown out of and been developed by the necessity of grappling with insidious forms of spiritual tyranny and with the infinite varieties of fraud." . . .

Subsequent authority supports the view of the law as expressed by Lindley LJ in *Allcard* v *Skinner*. The need to show that the transaction is wrongful in the sense explained by

Lindley LJ before the court will set aside a transaction whether relying on evidence or the presumption of the exercise of undue influence has been asserted in two Privy Council cases . . .

The wrongfulness of the transaction must, therefore, be shown: it must be one in which an unfair advantage has been taken of another. The doctrine is not limited to transactions of gift. A commercial relationship can become a relationship in which one party assumes a role of dominating influence over the other. In *Poosathurai*'s case, the Board recognised that a sale at an undervalue could be a transaction which a court could set aside as unconscionable if it was shown or could be presumed to have been procured by the exercise of undue influence. Similarly a relationship of banker and customer may become one in which the banker acquires a dominating influence. If he does and a manifestly disadvantageous transaction is proved, there would then be room for the court to presume that it resulted from the exercise of undue influence.'

Is lender affected by influence?

CIBC Mortgages plc v *Pitt*

[1993] 4 All ER 433 • House of Lords

In 1986 Mr Pitt told his wife that he wished to borrow some money on the security of their house to buy shares. Mrs Pitt was not happy with this suggestion and made her feelings known to her husband. As a result Mr Pitt embarked on a course of conduct putting pressure on his wife which the trial judge held amounted to actual undue influence. In consequence, Mrs Pitt eventually agreed to the suggestion. Mr and Mrs Pitt then applied to CIBC for a loan stating that the purpose of the loan was to buy a holiday home; they both signed the application form. Mrs Pitt did not read any of the pages of the application which had been filled in by somebody else. CIBC then offered them a loan of £150 000 by way of a remortgage secured on their house. Mr and Mrs Pitt signed the mortgage offer to indicate their acceptance, but Mrs Pitt did not read it before signing. In all the transactions CIBC's solicitors acted for all the parties. At no stage did Mrs Pitt receive separate advice about the transaction nor did anyone suggest that she should do so. Having received the loan Mr Pitt used the money to buy shares. At first Mr Pitt's investments proved most successful but in October 1987 the stock market crashed and Mr Pitt found he could no longer keep up the mortgage repayments. CIBC thus sought possession of the Pitts' house. Mrs Pitt claimed that the charge could not be enforced against her on the ground of misrepresentation and undue influence.

Lord Browne-Wilkinson: *Manifest disadvantage* . . .

'My Lords, I am unable to agree with the Court of Appeal decision in *BCCI* v *Aboody*. I have no doubt that the decision in *Morgan* does not extend to cases of actual undue influence. Despite two references in Lord Scarman's speech to cases of actual undue influence, as I read his speech he was primarily concerned to establish that disadvantage had to be shown, not as a constituent element of the cause of action for undue influence, but in order to raise a presumption of undue influence within class 2. That was the only subject matter before the House of Lords in *Morgan* and the passage I have already cited was directed solely to that point. With the exception of a passing reference to *Ormes* v *Beadel* all the cases referred to by Lord Scarman were cases of presumed undue influence. In the circumstances, I do not think that this House can have been intending to lay down any general principle applicable to all claims of undue influence, whether actual or presumed.

Whatever the merits of requiring a complainant to show manifest disadvantage in order to raise a class 2 presumption of undue influence, in my judgment there is no logic in imposing such a requirement where actual undue influence has been exercised and proved. Actual undue influence is a species of fraud. Like any other victim of fraud, a person who has been induced by undue influence to carry out a transaction which he did not freely and knowingly enter into is entitled to have that transaction set aside as of right. No case decided before *Morgan* was cited (nor am I aware of any) in which a transaction proved to have been obtained by actual undue influence has been upheld nor is there any case in which a court has even considered whether the transaction was, or was not, advantageous. A man guilty of fraud is no more entitled to argue that the transaction was beneficial to the person defrauded than is a man who has procured a transaction by misrepresentation. The effect of the wrongdoer's conduct is to prevent the wronged party from bringing a free will and properly informed mind to bear on the proposed transaction which accordingly must be set aside in equity as a matter of justice.

I therefore hold that a claimant who proves actual undue influence is not under the further burden of proving that the transaction induced by undue influence was manifestly disadvantageous: he is entitled as of right to have it set aside . . .

Notice

Even though, in my view, Mrs Pitt is entitled to set aside the transaction as against Mr Pitt, she has to establish that in some way the plaintiff is affected by the wrongdoing of Mr Pitt so as to be entitled to set aside the legal charge as against the plaintiff.

. . . Applying the decision of this House in *O'Brien*, Mrs Pitt has established actual undue influence by Mr Pitt. The plaintiff will not however be affected by such undue influence unless Mr Pitt was, in a real sense, acting as agent of the plaintiff in procuring Mrs Pitt's agreement or the plaintiff had actual or constructive notice of the undue influence. The judge has correctly held that Mr Pitt was not acting as agent for the plaintiff. The plaintiff had no actual notice of the undue influence. What, then, was known to the plaintiff that could put it on inquiry so as to fix it with constructive notice?

So far as the plaintiff was aware, the transaction consisted of a joint loan to the husband and wife to finance the discharge of an existing mortgage on 26 Alexander Avenue and, as to the balance, to be applied in buying a holiday home. The loan was advanced to both husband and wife jointly. There was nothing to indicate to the plaintiff that this was anything other than a normal advance to a husband and wife for their joint benefit.

Mr Price QC for Mrs Pitt argued that the invalidating tendency which reflects the risk of there being class 2B undue influence was, in itself, sufficient to put the plaintiff on inquiry. I reject this submission without hesitation. It accords neither with justice nor with practical common sense. If third parties were to be fixed with constructive notice of undue influence in relation to every transaction between husband and wife, such transactions would become almost impossible. On every purchase of a home in joint names, the building society or bank financing the purchase would have to insist on meeting the wife separately from her husband, advise her as to the nature of the transaction and recommend her to take legal advice separate from that of her husband. If that were not done, the financial institution would have to run the risk of a subsequent attempt by the wife to avoid her liabilities under the mortgage on the grounds of undue influence or misrepresentation. To establish the law in that sense would not benefit the average married couple and would discourage financial institutions from making the advance.

What distinguishes the case of the joint advance from the surety case is that, in the latter, there is not only the possibility of undue influence having been exercised but also the increased risk of it having in fact been exercised because, at least on its face, the guarantee by a wife of her husband's debts is not for her financial benefit. It is the combination of these two factors that puts the creditor on inquiry.'

Barclays Bank plc v O'Brien

[1993] 4 All ER 417 • House of Lords

The facts of the case are stated in the judgment of Lord Browne-Wilkinson.

Lord Browne-Wilkinson: 'My Lords, in this appeal your Lordships for the first time have to consider a problem which has given rise to reported decisions of the Court of Appeal on no less than 11 occasions in the last eight years and which has led to a difference of judicial view. Shortly stated the question is whether a bank is entitled to enforce against a wife an obligation to secure a debt owed by her husband to the bank where the wife has been induced to stand as surety for her husband's debt by the undue influence or misrepresentation of the husband.

The facts

... Mr and Mrs O'Brien were husband and wife. The matrimonial home, 151 Farnham Lane, Slough, was in their joint names subject to a mortgage of approximately £25 000 to a building society. Mr O'Brien was a chartered accountant and had an interest in a company, Heathrow Fabrications Ltd. The company's bank account was at the Woolwich branch of Barclays Bank. In the first three months of 1987 the company frequently exceeded its overdraft facility of £40 000 and a number of its cheques were dishonoured on presentation. In discussions in April 1981 between Mr O'Brien and the manager of the Woolwich branch, Mr Tucker, Mr O'Brien told Mr Tucker that he was remortgaging the matrimonial home: Mr Tucker made a note that Mrs O'Brien might be a problem. The overdraft limit was raised at that stage to £60 000 for one month. Even though no additional security was provided, by 15 June 1987 the company's overdraft had risen to £98 000 and its cheques were again being dishonoured.

On 22 June 1987 Mr O'Brien and Mr Tucker agreed (1) that the company's overdraft limit would be raised to £135 000 reducing to £120 000 after three weeks, (2) that Mr O'Brien would guarantee the company's indebtedness and (3) that Mr O'Brien's liability would be secured by a second charge on the matrimonial home.

The necessary security documents were prepared by the bank. They consisted of an unlimited guarantee by Mr O'Brien of the company's liability and a legal charge by both Mr and Mrs O'Brien of the matrimonial home to secure any liability of Mr O'Brien to the bank. Mr Tucker arranged for the documents, together with a side letter, to be sent to the Burnham branch of the bank for execution by Mr and Mrs O'Brien. In a covering memorandum Mr Tucker requested the Burnham branch to advise the O'Briens as to the current level of the facilities afforded to the bank (£107 000) and the projected increase to £135 000. The Burnham branch was also asked to ensure that the O'Briens were "fully aware of the nature of the documentation to be signed and advised that if they are in any doubt they should contact their solicitors before signing".

Unfortunately the Burnham branch did not follow Mr Tucker's instructions. On 1 July Mr O'Brien alone signed the guarantee and legal charge at the Burnham branch, the document simply being produced for signature and witnessed by a clerk. On the following day Mrs O'Brien went to the branch with her husband. There were produced for signature by Mrs O'Brien the legal charge on the matrimonial home together with a side letter, which reads:

> "We hereby agree acknowledge and confirm as follows: (1) That we have each received from you a copy of the guarantee dated 3 July 1987 (a copy of which is attached hereto) under which Nicholas Edward O'Brien guarantees the payment and discharge of all moneys and liabilities now or hereafter due owing or incurred by Heathrow Fabrications Ltd to you. (2) That the liability of the said Nicholas Edward O'Brien to you pursuant to the said guarantee is and will be secured by the legal charge dated 3 July 1987 over the property described above made between (1) Nicholas Edward O'Brien (2) Nicholas Edward O'Brien and Bridget Mary O'Brien and (3) Barclays Bank Plc. (3) That you recommended that we should obtain independent legal advice before signing this letter."

In fact the Burnham branch gave Mrs O'Brien no explanation of the effect of the documents. No one suggested that she should take independent legal advice. She did not read the documents or the side letter. She simply signed the legal charge and side letter and her signature was witnessed by the clerk. She was not given a copy of the guarantee.

The company did not prosper and by October 1987 its indebtedness to the bank was over £154 000. In November 1987 demand was made against Mr O'Brien under his guarantee. When the demand was not met possession proceedings under the legal charge were brought by the bank against Mr and Mrs O'Brien. Mrs O'Brien seeks to defend these proceedings by alleging that she was induced to execute the legal charge on the matrimonial home by the undue influence of Mr O'Brien and by his misrepresentation. The trial judge, Judge Marder QC, and the Court of Appeal rejected the claim based on undue influence: on the appeal to this House the claim based on undue influence is not pursued. However, the judge did find that Mr O'Brien had falsely represented to Mrs O'Brien that the charge was to secure only £60 000 and that even this liability would be released in a short time when the house was remortgaged. On those findings of fact the trial judge granted an order for possession against Mrs O'Brien holding that the bank could not be held responsible for the misrepresentation made by Mr O'Brien.

The decision of the Court of Appeal

The Court of Appeal (Purchas, Butler-Sloss and Scott LJJ) reversed his decision. The leading judgment in the Court of Appeal was given by Scott LJ, who found that there were two lines of authority. One line would afford no special protection to married women: the rights of the creditor bank could only be adversely affected by the wrongful acts of the principal debtor, the husband, in procuring the surety's liability if the principal debtor was acting as the agent of the creditor in procuring the surety to join or the creditor had knowledge of the relevant facts. I will call this theory "the agency theory". The other line of authority (which I will call "the special equity theory") detected by Scott LJ considers that equity affords special protection to a protected class of surety, viz those where the relationship between the debtor and the surety is such that influence by the debtor over the surety and reliance by the surety on the debtor are natural features of the relationship. In cases where a surety is one of this protected class, the surety obligation is unenforceable by the creditor bank if (1) the relationship between the debtor and the surety was known to the creditor, (2) the surety's consent was obtained by undue influence or by misrepresentation or without "an adequate understanding of the nature and effect of the transaction" and (3) the creditor had failed to take reasonable steps to ensure that the surety had given a true and informed consent to the transaction. The Court of Appeal preferred the special equity principle. They held that the legal charge on the O'Briens' matrimonial home was not enforceable by the bank against Mrs O'Brien save to the extent of the £60 000 which she had thought she was agreeing to secure.

Policy considerations

The large number of cases of this type coming before the courts in recent years reflects the rapid changes in social attitudes and the distribution of wealth which have recently occurred. Wealth is now more widely spread. Moreover a high proportion of privately owned wealth is invested in the matrimonial home. Because of the recognition by society of the equality of the sexes, the majority of matrimonial homes are now in the joint names of both spouses. Therefore in order to raise finance for the business enterprises of one or other of the spouses, the jointly owned home has become a main source of security. The provision of such security requires the consent of both spouses.

In parallel with these financial developments, society's recognition of the equality of the sexes has led to a rejection of the concept that the wife is subservient to the husband in the management of the family's finances. A number of the authorities reflect an unwillingness in the court to perpetuate law based on this outmoded concept. Yet, as Scott LJ in the Court of Appeal rightly points out, although the concept of the ignorant wife leaving all financial decisions to the husband is outmoded, the practice does not yet coincide with the ideal. In a substantial proportion of marriages it is still the husband who has the business experience and the wife is willing to follow his advice without bringing a truly independent mind and will to bear on financial decisions. The number of recent cases in this field shows that in practice many wives are still subjected to, and yield to, undue influence by their husbands. Such wives can reasonably look to the law for some protection when their husbands have abused the trust and confidence reposed in them.

On the other hand, it is important to keep a sense of balance in approaching these cases. It is easy to allow sympathy for the wife who is threatened with the loss of her home at the suit of a rich bank to obscure an important public interest, viz the need to ensure that the wealth currently tied up in the matrimonial home does not become economically sterile. If the rights secured to wives by the law renders vulnerable loans granted on the security of matrimonial homes, institutions will be unwilling to accept such security, thereby reducing the flow of loan capital to business enterprises. It is therefore essential that a law designed to protect the vulnerable does not render the matrimonial home unacceptable as security to financial institutions.

With these policy considerations in mind I turn to consider the existing state of the law. The whole of the modern law is derived from the decision of the Privy Council in *Turnbull & Co* v *Duval* which, as I will seek to demonstrate, provides an uncertain foundation. Before considering that case however, I must consider the law of undue influence which (though not directly applicable in the present case) underlies both *Turnbull* v *Duval* and most of the later authorities.

Undue influence

A person who has been induced to enter into a transaction by the undue influence of another (the wrongdoer) is entitled to set that transaction aside as against the wrongdoer. Such undue influence is either actual or presumed. In *Bank of Credit and Commerce International SA* v *Aboody* the Court of Appeal helpfully adopted the following classification.

Class 1: actual undue influence. In these cases it is necessary for the claimant to prove affirmatively that the wrongdoer exerted undue influence on the complainant to enter into the particular transaction which is impugned.

Class 2: presumed undue influence. In these cases the complainant only has to show, in the first instance, that there was a relationship of trust and confidence between the complainant and the wrongdoer of such a nature that it is fair to presume that the wrongdoer abused that relationship in procuring the complainant to enter into the impugned transaction. In class 2 cases therefore there is no need to produce evidence that actual undue influence was exerted in relation to the particular transaction impugned: once a confidential relationship has been proved, the burden then shifts to the wrongdoer to prove that the complainant entered into the impugned transaction freely, for example by showing that the complainant had independent advice. Such a confidential relationship can be established in two ways, viz:

Class 2A. Certain relationships (for example solicitor and client, medical advisor and patient) as a matter of law raise the presumption that undue influence has been exercised.

Class 2B. Even if there is no relationship falling within class 2A, if the complainant proves the *de facto* existence of a relationship under which the complainant generally reposed trust and confidence in the wrongdoer, the existence of such relationship raises the presumption of undue influence. In a class 2B case therefore, in the absence of evidence disproving undue influence, the complainant will succeed in setting aside the impugned transaction merely by proof that the complainant reposed trust and confidence in the wrongdoer without having to prove that the wrongdoer exerted actual undue influence or otherwise abused such trust and confidence in relation to the particular transaction impugned.

As to dispositions by a wife in favour of her husband, the law for long remained in an unsettled state. In the nineteenth century some judges took the view that the relationship was such that it fell into class 2A, i.e. as a matter of law undue influence by the husband over the wife was presumed. It was not until the decisions in *Howes* v *Bishop* and *Bank of Montreal* v *Stuart* that it was finally determined that the relationship of husband and wife did not as a matter of law raise a presumption of undue influence within class 2A. It is to be noted therefore that when *Turnbull* v *Duval* was decided in 1902 the question whether there was a class 2A presumption of undue influence as between husband and wife was still unresolved.

An invalidating tendency?

Although there is no class 2A presumption of undue influence as between husband and wife, it should be emphasised that in any particular case a wife may well be able to demonstrate that *de facto* she did leave decisions on financial affairs to her husband thereby bringing herself within class 2B, i.e. that the relationship between husband and wife in the particular case was such that the wife reposed confidence and trust in her husband in relation to their financial affairs and therefore undue influence is to be presumed. Thus, in those cases which still occur where the wife relies in all financial matters on her husband and simply does what he suggests, a presumption of undue influence within class 2B can be established solely from the proof of such trust and confidence without proof of actual undue influence.

In the appeal in *CIBC Mortgages plc* v *Pitt* (judgment in which is to be given immediately after that in the present appeal) Mr Price QC for the wife argued that in the case of transactions between husband and wife there was an "invalidating tendency", i.e. although there was no class 2A presumption of undue influence, the courts were more ready to find that a husband had exercised undue influence over his wife than in other cases. Scott LJ in the present case also referred to the law treating married women "more tenderly" than others. This approach is based on dicta in early authorities. In *Grigby* v *Cox* Lord Hardwicke LC, whilst rejecting any presumption of undue influence, said that a court of equity "will have more jealousy" over dispositions by a wife to a husband. In *Yerkey* v *Jones* Dixon J refers to this "invalidating tendency". He also refers to the court recognising "the opportunities which a wife's confidence in her husband gives him of unfairly or improperly procuring her to become surety".

In my judgment this special tenderness of treatment afforded to wives by the courts is properly attributable to two factors. First, many cases may well fall into the class 2B category of undue influence because the wife demonstrates that she placed trust and confidence in her husband in relation to her financial affairs and therefore raises a presumption of undue influence. Second, the sexual and emotional ties between the parties provide a ready weapon for undue influence: a wife's true wishes can easily be overborne because of her fear of destroying or damaging the wider relationship between her and her husband if she opposes his wishes.

For myself, I accept that the risk of undue influence affecting a voluntary disposition by a wife in favour of a husband is greater than in the ordinary run of cases where no sexual or emotional ties affect the free exercise of the individual's will.

Undue influence, misrepresentation and third parties

Up to this point I have been considering the right of a claimant wife to set aside a transaction as against the wrongdoing husband when the transaction has been procured by his undue influence. But in surety cases the decisive question is whether the claimant wife can set aside the transaction, not against the wrongdoing husband, but against the creditor bank. Of course, if the wrongdoing husband is acting as agent for the creditor bank in obtaining the surety from the wife, the creditor will be fixed with the wrongdoing of its own agent and the surety contract can be set aside as against the creditor. Apart from this, if the creditor bank has notice, actual or constructive, of the undue influence exercised by the husband (and consequentially of the wife's equity to set aside the transaction) the creditor will take subject to that equity and the wife can set aside the transaction against the creditor (albeit a purchaser for value) as well as against the husband: see *Bainbrigge* v *Browne* and *BCCI* v *Aboody*. Similarly, in cases such as the present where the wife has been induced to enter into the transaction by the husband's misrepresentation, her equity to set aside the transaction will be enforceable against the creditor if either the husband was acting as the creditor's agent or the creditor had actual or constructive notice . . .

The subsequent authorities

The authorities in which the principle derived from *Turnbull* v *Duval* has been applied are fully analysed in the judgment of Scott LJ and it is unnecessary to review them fully again.

Scott LJ analyses the cases as indicating that down to 1985 there was no decision which indicated that the agency theory, rather than the special equity theory, was the basis of the decision in *Turnbull* v *Duval*. I agree. But that is attributable more to the application of the *Turnbull* v *Duval* principle than to any analysis of its jurisprudential basis . . .

From 1985 down to the decision of the Court of Appeal in the present case the decisions have all been based on the agency theory, i.e. that the principal debtor has acted in breach of duty to his wife, the surety, and that, if the principal debtor was acting as the creditor's agent but not otherwise, the creditor cannot be in any better position than its agent, the husband. In all the cases since 1985 the principal debtor has procured the agreement of the surety by a legal wrong (undue influence or misrepresentation). In all the cases emphasis was placed on the question whether the creditor was infected by the debtor's wrongdoing because the debtor was acting as the agent of the creditor in procuring the wife's agreement to stand as surety . . .

However, in four of the cases since 1985 attention has been drawn to the fact that, even in the absence of agency, if the debtor has been guilty of undue influence or misrepresentation the creditor may not be able to enforce the surety contract if the creditor had notice, actual or constructive, of the debtor's conduct: see *Avon Finance Co Ltd* v *Bridger* per Brandon LJ, *Coldunell Ltd* v *Gallon, Midland Bank plc* v *Shephard* and *BCCI* v *Aboody*. As will appear, in my view it is the proper application of the doctrine of notice which provides the key to finding a principled basis for the law.

Accordingly, the present law is built on the unsure foundations of *Turnbull* v *Duval*. Like most law founded on obscure and possibly mistaken foundations it has developed in an artificial way, giving rise to artificial distinctions and conflicting decisions. In my judgment your Lordships should seek to restate the law in a form which is principled, reflects the current requirements of society and provides as much certainty as possible.

Conclusions

(a) Wives

My starting point is to clarify the basis of the law. Should wives (and perhaps others) be accorded special rights in relation to surety transactions by the recognition of a special equity applicable only to such persons engaged in such transactions? Or should they enjoy only the same protection as they would enjoy in relation to their other dealings? In my judgment, the special equity theory should be rejected. First, I can find no basis in principle for affording special protection to a limited class in relation to one type of transaction only. Second, to require the creditor to prove knowledge and understanding by the wife in all cases is to reintroduce by the back door either a presumption of undue influence of class 2A (which has been decisively rejected) or the *Romilly* heresy (which has long been treated as bad law). Third, although Scott LJ found that there were two lines of cases one of which supported the special equity theory, on analysis although many decisions are not inconsistent with that theory the only two cases which support it are *Yerkey* v *Jones* and the decision of the Court of Appeal in the present case. Finally, it is not necessary to have recourse to a special equity theory for the proper protection of the legitimate interests of wives as I will seek to show.

In my judgment, if the doctrine of notice is properly applied, there is no need for the introduction of a special equity in these types of cases. A wife who has been induced to stand as a surety for her husband's debts by his undue influence, misrepresentation or some other legal wrong has an equity as against him to set aside that transaction. Under the ordinary principles of equity, her right to set aside that transaction will be enforceable against third parties (e.g. against a creditor) if either the husband was acting as the third party's agent or the third party had actual or constructive notice of the facts giving rise to her equity. Although there may be cases where, without artificiality, it can properly be held that the husband was acting as the agent of the creditor in procuring the wife to stand as surety, such cases will be of very rare occurrence. The key to the problem is to identify the circumstances in which the creditor will be taken to have had notice of the wife's equity to set aside the transaction.

The doctrine of notice lies at the heart of equity. Given that there are two innocent parties, each enjoying rights, the earlier right prevails against the later right if the acquirer of the later right knows of the earlier right (actual notice) or would have discovered it had he taken proper steps (constructive notice). In particular, if the party asserting that he takes free of the earlier rights of another knows of certain facts which put him on inquiry as to the possible existence of the rights of that other and he fails to make such inquiry or take such other steps as are reasonable to verify whether such earlier right does or does not exist, he will have constructive notice of the earlier right and take subject to it. Therefore where a wife has agreed to stand surety for her husband's debts as a result of undue influence or misrepresentation, the creditor will take subject to the wife's equity to set aside the transaction if the circumstances are such as to put the creditor on inquiry as to the circumstances in which she agreed to stand surety.

It is at this stage that, in my view, the "invalidating tendency" or the law's "tender treatment" of married women, becomes relevant. As I have said above in dealing with undue influence, this tenderness of the law towards married women is due to the fact that, even today, many wives repose confidence and trust in their husbands in relation to their financial affairs. This tenderness of the law is reflected by the fact that voluntary dispositions by the wife in favour of her husband are more likely to be set aside than other dispositions by her: a wife is more likely to establish presumed undue influence of class 2B by her husband than by others because, in practice, many wives do repose in their husbands' trust and confidence in relation to their financial affairs. Moreover the informality of business dealings between spouses raises a substantial risk that the husband has not accurately stated to the wife the nature of the liability she is undertaking, i.e. he has misrepresented the position, albeit negligently.

Therefore, in my judgment a creditor is put on inquiry when a wife offers to stand surety for her husband's debts by the combination of two factors: (a) the transaction is on its face not to the financial advantage of the wife; and (b) there is a substantial risk in transactions of that kind that, in procuring the wife to act as surety, the husband has committed a legal or equitable wrong that entitles the wife to set aside the transaction.

It follows that, unless the creditor who is put on inquiry takes reasonable steps to satisfy himself that the wife's agreement to stand surety has been properly obtained, the creditor will have constructive notice of the wife's rights.

What, then are the reasonable steps which the creditor should take to ensure that it does not have constructive notice of the wife's rights, if any? Normally the reasonable steps necessary to avoid being fixed with constructive notice consist of making inquiry of the person who may have the earlier right (i.e. the wife) to see whether such right is asserted. It is plainly impossible to require of banks and other financial institutions that they should inquire of one spouse whether he or she has been unduly influenced or misled by the other. But in my judgment the creditor, in order to avoid being fixed with constructive notice, can reasonably be expected to take steps to bring home to the wife the risk she is running by standing as surety and to advise her to take independent advice. As to past transactions, it will depend on the facts of each case whether the steps taken by the creditor satisfy this test. However for the future in my judgment a creditor will have satisfied these requirements if it insists that the wife attend a private meeting (in the absence of the husband) with a representative of the creditor at which she is told of the extent of her liability as surety, warned of the risk she is running and urged to take independent legal advice. If these steps are taken in my judgment the creditor will have taken such reasonable steps as are necessary to preclude a subsequent claim that it had constructive notice of the wife's rights. I should make it clear that I have been considering the ordinary case where the creditor knows only that the wife is to stand surety for her husband's debts. I would not exclude exceptional cases where a creditor has knowledge of further facts which render the presence of undue influence not only possible but probable. In such cases, the creditor to be safe will have to insist that the wife is separately advised.

I am conscious that in treating the creditor as having constructive notice because of the risk of class 2B undue influence or misrepresentation by the husband I may be extending the law as stated by Fry J in *Bainbrigge* v *Browne* and the Court of Appeal in *BCCI* v *Aboody*. Those cases suggest that for a third party to be affected by constructive notice of presumed undue influence the third party must actually know of the circumstances which give rise to a presumption of undue influence. In contrast, my view is that the risk of class 2B undue influence or misrepresentation is sufficient to put the creditor on inquiry. But my statement accords with the principles of notice: if the known facts are such as to indicate the possibility of an adverse claim that is sufficient to put a third party on inquiry.

If the law is established as I have suggested, it will hold the balance fairly between on the one hand the vulnerability of the wife who relies implicitly on her husband and, on the other hand, the practical problems of financial institutions asked to accept a secured or unsecured surety obligation from the wife for her husband's debts. In the context of suretyship, the wife will not have any right to disown her obligations just because subsequently she proves that she did not fully understand the transaction: she will, as in all other areas of her affairs, be bound by her obligations unless her husband has, by misrepresentation, undue influence or other wrong, committed an actionable wrong against her. In the normal case, a financial institution will be able to lend with confidence in reliance on the wife's surety obligation provided that it warns her (in the absence of the husband) of the amount of her potential liability and of the risk of standing surety and advises her to take independent advice.

Mr Jarvis QC for the bank urged that this is to impose too heavy a burden on financial institutions. I am not impressed by this submission. The report by Professor Jack's Review Committee on Banking Services: *Law and Practice* (1989), (Cmnd 622) recommended that prospective guarantors should be adequately warned of the legal effects and possible consequences of their guarantee and of the importance of receiving independent advice. Pursuant to this recommendation, the Code of Banking Practice (adopted by banks and building societies in March 1992) provides in para 12.1 as follows:

"Banks and building societies will advise private individuals proposing to give them a guarantee or other security for another person's liabilities that: (i) by giving the guarantee or third party security he or she might become liable instead of or as well as that other person; (ii) he or she should seek independent legal advice before entering into the guarantee or third party security. Guarantees and other third party security forms will contain a clear and prominent notice to the above effect."

Thus good banking practice (which applies to all guarantees, not only those given by a wife) largely accords with what I consider the law should require when a wife is offered as surety. The only further substantial step required by law beyond that good practice is that the position should be explained by the bank to the wife in a personal interview. I regard this as being essential because a number of the decided cases show that written warnings are often not read and are sometimes intercepted by the husband. It does not seem to me that the requirement of a personal interview imposes such an additional administrative burden as to render the bank's position unworkable.

(b) Other persons

I have hitherto dealt only with the position where a wife stands surety for her husband's debts. But in my judgment the same principles are applicable to all other cases where there is an emotional relationship between cohabitees. The "tenderness" shown by the law to married women is not based on the marriage ceremony but reflects the underlying risk of one cohabitee exploiting the emotional involvement and trust of the other. Now that unmarried cohabitation, whether heterosexual or homosexual, is widespread in our society, the law should recognise this. Legal wives are not the only group which are now exposed to the emotional pressure of cohabitation. Therefore if, but only if, the creditor is aware that the surety is cohabiting with the principal debtor, in my judgment the same principles should apply to them as apply to husband and wife.

In addition to the cases of cohabitees, the decision of the Court of Appeal in *Avon Finance Co Ltd* v *Bridger* shows (rightly in my view) that other relationships can give rise to a similar result. In that case a son, by means of misrepresentation, persuaded his elderly parents to stand surety for his debts. The surety obligation was held to be unenforceable by the creditor *inter alia* because to the bank's knowledge the parents trusted the son in their financial dealings. In my judgment that case was rightly decided: in a case where the creditor is aware that the surety reposes trust and confidence in the principal debtor in relation to his financial affairs, the creditor is put on inquiry in just the same way as it is in relation to husband and wife.

Summary

I can therefore summarise my views as follows. Where one cohabitee has entered into an obligation to stand as surety for the debts of the other cohabitee and the creditor is aware that they are cohabitees: (1) the surety obligation will be valid and enforceable by the creditor unless the suretyship was procured by the undue influence, misrepresentation or other legal wrong of the principal debtor; (2) if there has been undue influence, misrepresentation or other legal wrong by the principal debtor, unless the creditor has taken reasonable steps to satisfy himself that the surety entered into the obligation freely and in knowledge of the true facts, the creditor will be unable to enforce the surety obligation because he will be fixed with constructive notice of the surety's right to set aside the transaction; (3) unless there are special exceptional circumstances, a creditor will have taken such reasonable steps to avoid being fixed with constructive notice if the creditor warns the surety (at a meeting not attended by the principal debtor) of the amount of her potential liability and of the risks involved and advises the surety to take independent legal advice.

I should make it clear that in referring to the husband's debts I include the debts of a company in which the husband (but not the wife) has a direct financial interest.

The decision of this case

Applying those principles to this case, to the knowledge of the bank Mr and Mrs O'Brien were man and wife. The bank took a surety obligation from Mrs O'Brien, secured on the matrimonial home, to secure the debts of a company in which Mr O'Brien was interested but in which Mrs O'Brien had no direct pecuniary interest. The bank should therefore have been put on inquiry as to the circumstances in which Mrs O'Brien had agreed to stand as surety for the debt of her husband. If the Burnham branch had properly carried out the instructions from Mr Tucker of the Woolwich branch, Mrs O'Brien would have been informed that she and the matrimonial home were potentially liable for the debts of a company which had an existing liability of £107 000 and which was to be afforded an overdraft facility of £135 000. If she had been told this, it would have counteracted Mr O'Brien's misrepresentation that the liability was limited to £60 000 and would last for only three weeks. In addition according to the side letter she would have been recommended to take independent legal advice.

Unfortunately Mr Tucker's instructions were not followed and to the knowledge of the bank (through the clerk at the Burnham branch) Mrs O'Brien signed the documents without any warning of the risks or any recommendation to take legal advice. In the circumstances the bank (having failed to take reasonable steps) is fixed with constructive notice of the wrongful misrepresentation made by Mr O'Brien to Mrs O'Brien. Mrs O'Brien is therefore entitled as against the bank to set aside the legal charge on the matrimonial home securing her husband's liability to the bank.

For these reasons I would dismiss the appeal with costs.'

Midland Bank plc v *Massey*

[1995] 1 All ER 929 • Court of Appeal

Massey had a long-standing and stable emotional and sexual relationship with Potts and, though they did not live together, she had had two children by him. Potts fraudulently persuaded Massey to grant a legal charge over her house in favour of the Midland Bank.

The issue before the court was whether Massey could rely on the doctrine of constructive notice as outlined in *Barclays Bank plc* v *O'Brien*.

Steyn LJ: 'Taking the law enunciated, as opposed to the guidance offered in *Barclays Bank plc* v *O'Brien*, it is clear that two questions must be considered, namely (a) Was the bank put on inquiry as to the circumstances in which Miss Massey agreed to provide the security and (b) if so, did the bank take reasonable steps to ensure the agreement of Miss Massey to the charge was properly obtained?

Was the bank put on inquiry?
In *Barclays Bank plc* v *O'Brien* Lord Browne-Wilkinson observed:

> " . . . in my judgment a creditor is put on inquiry when a wife offers to stand surety for her husband's debts by the combination of two factors: (a) the transaction is on its face not to the financial advantage of the wife; and (b) there is a substantial risk in transactions of that kind that, in procuring the wife to act as surety, the husband has committed a legal or equitable wrong that entitles the wife to set aside the transaction."

. . . In my view it would have been clear to Mr Dixon, acting for the bank, that the transaction on its face was not to the financial advantage of Miss Massey. For my part I am also willing to accept that, in the circumstances, there was a substantial risk that Mr Potts had committed a wrong which entitled Miss Massey to set aside the transaction.

I would therefore hold that the bank was put on inquiry as to the possible existence of rights in Miss Massey to set aside the transaction.

Did the bank take reasonable steps to ensure that Miss Massey's agreement to the charge was properly obtained?
That brings me to the question whether the bank took reasonable steps to ensure itself that Miss Massey's agreement to grant the charge was properly obtained. If so, the bank will avoid being fixed with constructive notice. If not, the bank cannot avoid the setting aside of the charge.

How should the question of what constitutes reasonable steps be approached in the context of a case such as the present? In *Barclays Bank plc* v *O'Brien* Lord Browne-Wilkinson gave the following guidance:

" . . . in my judgment the creditor, in order to avoid being fixed with constructive notice, can reasonably be expected to take steps to bring home to the wife the risk she is running by standing as surety and to advise her to take independent advice. As to the past transactions it will depend on the facts of each case whether the steps taken by the creditor satisfy this test. However for the future in my judgment a creditor will have satisfied these requirements if it insists that the wife attend a private meeting (in the absence of the husband) with a representative of the creditor at which she is told of the extent of her liability as surety, warned of the risk she is running and urged to take independent legal advice. If these steps are taken in my judgment the creditor will have taken such reasonable steps as are necessary to preclude a subsequent claim that it had constructive notice of the wife's rights. I should make it clear that I have been considering the ordinary case where the creditor knows only that the wife is to stand surety for her husband's debts. I would not exclude exceptional cases where a creditor has knowledge of further facts which render the presence of undue influence not only possible but probable. In such cases, the creditor to be safe will have to insist that the wife is separately advised."

In the present case the bank required Miss Massey to be independently advised. The bank had been put in touch with a reputable firm of solicitors to whom it sent the charge. When the solicitors returned the duly executed charge to the bank they confirmed that they had explained the document to Miss Massey.

. . . I would respectfully put that guidance [offered by Lord Browne-Wilkinson] in context by two observations. First, the guidance was clearly not intended to be exhaustive, as indeed the facts of the present case demonstrate. Secondly, the guidance was intended to strike a fair balance between the need to protect wives (and others in a like position) whose judgmental capacity was impaired and the need to avoid unnecessary impediments to using the matrimonial home as security. The guidance ought therefore not to be mechanically applied. The relief is after all equitable relief. It is the substance that matters. If, as far as the creditor is concerned, the objective of independent advice for the wife (or somebody in a like position) is realised, the fact that there was not an interview between a representative of the creditor and the surety, unattended by the debtor, ought not by itself to be fatal to the creditor's case. In the present case Mr Dixon did not see Miss Massey alone. That was not good practice. But fortunately she did receive independent legal advice. I would therefore hold that in this case the bank complied with the substance of the guidance . . .

The bank did not know what happened between Mr Jones and Miss Massey, or how the interview was conducted. And it was under no duty to inquire. But the bank had every reason to believe (as was the case on the judge's findings) that Miss Massey had received independent advice. Relying on observations of Dillon LJ in *Bank of Baroda* v *Shah* the judge observed that the bank was entitled to assume that the solicitors would act honestly and give proper advice to Miss Massey. I agree. How far the solicitor's advice went was essentially a matter for Miss Massey and Mr Jones. The law does not generally require the creditor to stipulate the nature and extent of the advice. It will be for the solicitor to discuss with the wife (or a surety in an equivalent position) what further advice, if any, she ought to take. In any event, Mr Jones did explain the nature of the charge to Miss Massey and satisfied himself that she entered into it willingly . . .

I conclude that the bank took reasonable steps to ensure that Miss Massey's agreement to the charge was properly obtained. I would dismiss the appeal.'

Bank of Baroda v Rayarel
[1995] 2 FLR 376 • Court of Appeal

The facts are similar to those of the Massey case above.

Hirst LJ: '. . . Here the bank knew throughout that all three defendants, including the third defendant, were being advised by a solicitor throughout all the relevant stages of the transaction. It follows that, in my judgment, they were entitled to assume that each of those three clients individually (that is each of the three defendants) would be properly and separately advised, in accordance with the duty of Mr Bird as the solicitor to each of them, and in particular the bank were entitled to assume that the solicitor would properly advise the third defendant as to the risk she was running and as to the advisability of her obtaining separate legal advice. In other words, put in a nutshell, the bank were entitled to assume that Mr Bird was doing his job properly, and that of course would include furnishing proper separate advice, clearly communicated to the third defendant if there was any linguistic difficulty or other problem of communication.

Here, indeed, the matter goes even further because of the terms of the certificate which was proffered by the bank to all three defendants, including the third defendant, and which was signed individually by each of them and witnessed by Mr Bird. It is in my judgment important to note that it was the bank who were requiring the certificate to be signed by all three defendants as part of the overall transaction. By its terms it states, and I quote it again because it is so important:

"The chargor [and she is one of the three chargors] acknowledges to have received a copy of this deed and to have been advised of the effect of this deed and of the right to have independent legal advice on its effect."

I emphasise particularly those last few words, "have been advised of the . . . right to have independent legal advice on its effect". The bank there were clearly requiring a certificate that such advice had been given. That was signed by the third defendant and her signature was effectively countersigned by Mr Bird. On that basis the bank must have been reinforced in their assumption that they could rely on Mr Bird to advise the third defendant properly, including advising her to obtain independent legal advice.

When that came back to the bank, duly signed, any doubt as to its correctness would have involved, in effect, questioning the probity and honesty of the solicitor, Mr Bird. There is, in my judgment, no obligation on the bank to proceed on such an unreasonable degree of suspicion as to a solicitor's honesty . . .

For the reasons I have given . . . I am satisfied that the bank have satisfied [the] burden [of showing that it took reasonable steps to ensure that the wife was being separately advised] and for all these reasons I would dismiss this appeal.'

INEQUALITY OF BARGAINING POWER

Inequality of bargaining power – is there such a doctrine?

Lloyds Bank Ltd v Bundy
[1974] 3 All ER 757 • Court of Appeal

The facts appear above (p 433).

Lord Denning MR: *The general rule*

'Now let me say at once that in the vast majority of cases a customer who signs a bank guarantee or a charge cannot get out of it. No bargain will be upset which is the result of the ordinary interplay of forces. There are many hard cases which are caught by this rule. Take the case of a poor man who is homeless. He agrees to pay a high rent to a landlord just to get a roof over his head. The common law will not interfere. It is left to Parliament. Next take the case of a borrower in urgent need of money. He borrows it from the bank at high interest and it is guaranteed by a friend. The guarantor gives his bond and gets nothing in return. The common law will not interfere. Parliament has intervened to prevent moneylenders charging excessive interest. But it has never interfered with banks.

Yet there are exceptions to this general rule. There are cases in our books in which the courts will set aside a contract, or a transfer of property, when the parties have not met on equal terms, when the one is so strong in bargaining power and the other so weak that, as a matter of common fairness, it is not right that the strong should be allowed to push the weak to the wall. Hitherto those exceptional cases have been treated each as a separate category in itself. But I think the time has come when we should seek to find a principle to unite them. I put on one side contracts or transactions which are voidable for fraud or misrepresentation or mistake. All those are governed by settled principles. I go only to those where there has been inequality of bargaining power, such as to merit the intervention of the court.

4. The categories

The first category is that of "duress of goods". A typical case is when a man is in a strong bargaining position by being in possession of the goods of another by virtue of a legal right, such as, by way of pawn or pledge or taken in distress. The owner is in a weak position because he is in urgent need of the goods. The stronger demands of the weaker more than is justly due, and he pays it in order to get the goods. Such a transaction is voidable. He can recover the excess: see *Astley* v *Reynolds* and *Green* v *Duckett*. To which may be added the cases of "*colore officii*", where a man is in a strong bargaining position by virtue of his official position or public profession. He relies on it so as to gain from the weaker – who is urgently in need – more than is justly due: see *Pigott's Case* cited by Lord Kenyon CJ; *Parker* v *Bristol and Exeter Railway Co* and *Steele* v *William*. In such cases the stronger may make his claim in good faith honestly believing that he is entitled to make his demand. He may not be guilty of any fraud or misrepresentation. The inequality of bargaining power – the strength of the one versus the urgent need of the other – renders the transaction voidable and the money paid to be recovered back: see *Maskell* v *Horner*.

The second category is that of the "unconscionable transaction". A man is so placed as to be in need of special care and protection and yet his weakness is exploited by another far stronger than himself so as to get his property at a gross undervalue. The typical case is that of the "expectant heir". But it applies to all cases where a man comes into property, or is expected to come into it, and then being in urgent need another gives him ready cash for it, greatly below its true worth, and so gets the property transferred to him: see *Evans* v *Llewellin*. Even though there be no evidence of fraud or misrepresentation, nevertheless the transaction will be set aside: see *Fry* v *Lane* where Kay J said:

> "The result of the decisions is that where a purchase is made from a poor and ignorant man at a considerable undervalue, the vendor having no independent advice, a Court of Equity will set aside the transaction."

This second category is said to extend to all cases where an unfair advantage has been gained by an unconscientious use of power by a stronger party against a weaker: see the cases cited in *Halsbury's Laws of England* and in Canada, *Morrison* v *Coast Finance Ltd* and *Knupp* v *Bell*.

The third category is that of "undue influence" usually so called. These are divided into two classes as stated by Cotton LJ in *Allcard* v *Skinner*. The first are those where the stronger has been guilty of some fraud or wrongful act – expressly so as to gain some gift or advantage from the weaker. The second are those where the stronger has not been guilty of any wrongful act, but has, through the relationship which existed between him and the weaker, gained some gift or advantage for himself. Sometimes the relationship is such as to raise a presumption of undue influence, such as parent over child, solicitor over client, doctor over patient, spiritual adviser over follower. At other times a relationship of confidence must be proved to exist. But to all of them the general principle obtains which was stated by Lord Chelmsford LC in *Tate* v *Williamson*:

> "Wherever the persons stand in such a relation that, while it continues, confidence is necessarily reposed by one, and the influence which naturally grows out of that confidence is possessed by the other, and this confidence is abused, or the influence is exerted to obtain an advantage at the expense of the confiding party, the person so availing himself of his position will not be permitted to retain the advantage, although the transaction could not have been impeached if no such confidential relation had existed."

Such a case was *Tufton* v *Sperni*.

The fourth category is that of "undue pressure". The most apposite of that is *Williams* v *Bayley* where a son forged his father's name to a promissory note, and, by means of it, raised money from the bank of which they were both customers. The bank said to the father, in effect: "Take your choice – give us security for your son's debt. If you do take that on yourself, then it will all go smoothly; if you do not, we shall be bound to exercise pressure." Thereupon the father charged his property to the bank with payment of the note. The House of Lords held that the charge was invalid because of undue pressure exerted by the bank. Lord Westbury said:

> "A contract to give security for the debt of another, which is a contract without consideration, is, above all things, a contract that should be based upon the free and voluntary agency of the individual who enters into it."

Other instances of undue pressure are where one party stipulates for an unfair advantage to which the other has no option but to submit. As where an employer – the stronger party – had employed a builder – the weaker party – to do work for him. When the builder asked for payment of sums properly due (so as to pay his workmen) the employer refused to pay unless he was given some added advantage. Stuart V-C said:

> "Where an agreement, hard and inequitable in itself, has been exacted under circumstances of pressure on the part of the person who exacts it this Court will set it aside":

see *Ormes* v *Beadel*; *D&C Builders Ltd* v *Rees* . . .

5. The general principles

Gathering all together, I would suggest that through all these instances there runs a single thread. They rest on "inequality of bargaining power". By virtue of it, the English law gives relief to one who, without independent advice, enters into a contract on terms which are very unfair or transfers property for a consideration which is grossly inadequate, when his bargaining power is grievously impaired by reason of his own needs or desires, or by his own ignorance or infirmity, coupled with undue influences or pressures brought to bear on him by or for the benefit of the other. When I use the word "undue" I do not mean to suggest that the principle depends on proof of any wrongdoing. The one who stipulates for an unfair advantage may be moved solely by his own self-interest, unconscious of the distress he is bringing to the other. I have also avoided any reference to the will of the one being "dominated" or "overcome" by the other. On who is in extreme need may knowingly consent to a most improvident bargain, solely to relieve the straits in which he finds himself. Again, I do not mean to suggest that every transaction is saved by independent advice. But the absence of it may be fatal. With these explanations, I hope this principle will be found to reconcile the cases. Applying it to the present case, I would notice these points.

(1) The consideration moving from the bank was grossly inadequate. The son's company was in serious difficulty. The overdraft was at its limit of £10 000. The bank considered that their existing security was insufficient. In order to get further security, they asked the father to charge the house – his sole asset – to the uttermost. It was worth £10 000. The charge was for £11 000. That was for the benefit of the bank. But not at all for the benefit of the father, or indeed for the company. The bank did not promise to continue the overdraft or to increase it. On the contrary, they required the overdraft to be reduced. All that the company gained was a short respite from impending doom.

(2) The relationship between the bank and the father was one of trust and confidence. The bank knew that the father relied on them implicitly to advise him about the transaction. The father trusted the bank. This gave the bank much influence on the father. Yet the bank failed in that trust. They allowed the father to charge the house to his ruin.

(3) The relationship between the father and the son was one where the father's natural affection had much influence on him.

(4) He would naturally aspire to accede to his son's request. He trusted his son. There was a conflict of interest between the bank and the father. Yet the bank did not realise it. Nor did they suggest that the father should get independent advice. If the father had gone to his solicitor – or to any man of business – there is no doubt that any one of them would say: "You must not enter into this transaction. You are giving up your house, your sole remaining asset, for no benefit to you. The company is in such a parlous state that you must not do it."

These considerations seem to me to bring this case within the principles I have stated. But, in case that principle is wrong, I would also say that the case falls within the category of undue influence of the second class stated by Cotton LJ in *Allcard* v *Skinner*. I have no doubt that the assistant bank manager acted in the utmost good faith and was straightforward and genuine. Indeed the father said so. But beyond doubt he was acting in the interests of the bank – to get further security for a bad debt. There was such a relationship of trust and confidence between them that the bank ought not to have swept up his sole remaining asset into their hands – for nothing – without his having independent advice . . .'

Sir Eric Sachs: '. . . As regards the wider areas covered in masterly survey in the judgment of Lord Denning MR, but not raised *arguendo*, I do not venture to express an opinion – though having some sympathy with the views that the courts should be able to give relief to a party who has been subject to undue pressure as defined in the concluding passage of his judgment on that point.'

National Westminster Bank plc v Morgan

[1985] 2 WLR 588 • House of Lords

The facts appear above (p 438).

Lord Scarman: 'Lord Denning MR believed that the doctrine of undue influence could be subsumed under a general principle that English courts will grant relief where there has been "inequality of bargaining power". He deliberately avoided reference to the will of one party being dominated or overcome by another. The majority of the court did not follow him; they based their decision on the orthodox view of the doctrine as expounded in *Allcard* v *Skinner*. The opinion of the Master of the Rolls, therefore, was not the ground of the court's decision, which was to be found in the view of the majority, for whom Sir Eric Sachs delivered the leading judgment.

Nor has counsel for the respondent sought to rely on Lord Denning MR's general principle: and, in my view, he was right not to do so. The doctrine of undue influence has been sufficiently developed not to need the support of a principle which by its formulation in the language of the law of contract is not appropriate to cover transactions of gift where there is no bargain. The fact of an unequal bargain will, of course, be a relevant feature in some cases of undue influence. But it can never become an appropriate basis of principle of an equitable doctrine which is concerned with transactions "not to be reasonably accounted for on the ground of friendship, relationship, charity, or other ordinary motives on which ordinary men act" (Lindley LJ in *Allcard* v *Skinner*). And even in the field of contract I question whether there is any need in the modern law to erect a general principle of relief against inequality of bargaining power. Parliament has undertaken the task – and it is essentially a legislative task – of enacting such restrictions upon freedom of contract as are in its judgment necessary to relieve against the mischief: for example, the hire-purchase and consumer protection legislation, of which the Supply of Goods (Implied Terms) Act 1973, Consumer Credit Act 1974, Consumer Safety Act 1978, Supply of Goods and Services Act 1982 and Insurance Companies Act 1982 are examples. I doubt whether the courts should assume the burden of formulating further restrictions.'

SUMMARY

You should now be able to:

- Recognise duress at common law.
- Determine whether economic duress exists.
- Apply the concept of economic duress.
- Identify duress in equity.
- Recognise domination by one party over another.
- Identify special relationships between parties.
- Determine whether there is such a doctrine as inequality of bargaining power.

If you have not mastered the above points you should go through this section again.

15 Discharge by performance and breach

DISCHARGE OF THE CONTRACT BY PERFORMANCE

Despite the somewhat jaundiced view that law students get from studying the law of contract – *that all contracts end by one party or the other breaking the contract* – most contracts come to an end when both parties perform their part of the contract e.g. when one delivers the goods and the other pays for them.

In order for a contract to be discharged by performance *the performance of the contract must be precise and exact*. If this was not the case there would be a breach of contract. For example, if there is a contract between Max and Christine for the sale of his red pen to her for £5 and he delivers a black pen then the performance of the contract would not be precise and exact and therefore Max would have broken the contract.

Partial performance of an entire contract

Some (very few) contracts ('entire' contracts) make it clear from the intentions of the parties that no payment will be made until the other party has entirely (completely) performed his part of the contract. In such a case if a party does not completely perform his part of the contract he will not be entitled to any monies whatsoever.

In other words payment is *conditional* on *entire* and *complete* performance.

Cutter v Powell (1795)

[1775–1802] All ER Rep 159 • King's Bench

Powell promised Cutter that if he acted as his second mate for a voyage from Jamaica to Liverpool he would 'pay to Cutter the sum of thirty guineas, provided he proceeds, continues and does his duty as second mate in the said ship from hence to the port of Liverpool'. The ship sailed on 2 August 1793 and arrived at Liverpool on 9 October 1793. Unfortunately Cutter died at sea on 20 September.

Cutter's widow sued Powell to recover a proportionate part of her husband's wages on a *quantum meruit* for work and labour done by her husband during that part of the voyage that he lived and served Powell.

Lord Kenyon CJ: 'Here the defendant expressly promised to pay the intestate 30 guineas, provided he proceeded, continued and did his duty as second mate in the ship from Jamaica to Liverpool, and the accompanying circumstances disclosed in the case are that the common rate of wages is 4 pounds per month when the party is paid in proportion to the time he serves, and that this voyage is generally performed in two months. Therefore, if there had been no contract between these parties, all that the intestate could have recovered on a *quantum meruit* for the voyage would have been £8, whereas here the defendant contracted to pay 30 guineas provided the mate continued to do his duty as mate during the whole voyage, in which case the latter would have received nearly four times as much as if he were paid for the number of months he served. He stipulated to receive the larger sum if the whole duty were performed, and nothing unless the whole of that duty were performed. It was a kind of insurance . . .'

Ashhurst J: 'We cannot collect that there is any custom prevailing among merchants on these contracts, and, therefore we have nothing to guide us but the terms of the contract itself. This is a written contract, and it speaks for itself. As it is entire and, as the defendant's promise depends on a condition precedent to be performed by the other party, the condition must be performed before the other party is entitled to receive any thing under it. It has been argued, however, that the plaintiff may now recover on a *quantum meruit*, but she has no right to desert the agreement for wherever there is an express contract the parties must be guided by it, and one party cannot relinquish or abide by it as it may suit his advantage. Here the intestate was by the terms of his contract to perform a given duty before he could call upon the defendant to pay him anything; it was a condition precedent, without performing which the defendant is not liable. That seems to me to conclude the question. The intestate did not perform the contract on his part; he was not indeed to blame for not doing it; but still as this was a condition precedent, and as he did not perform it, his representative is not entitled to recover.'

Sumpter v Hedges

(1898) 1 QB 673 • Court of Appeal

The plaintiff builder had contracted with the defendant to build two houses and stables on the defendant's land for the sum of £565. The plaintiff did part of the work, amounting in value to about £333, and had received payment of part of the price. He then informed the defendant that he had no money and could not go on with the work. The learned judge found that he had abandoned the contract. The defendant thereupon finished the buildings himself using the building materials which the plaintiff had left on the ground. The judge gave judgment for the plaintiff for the value of the materials so used but allowed him nothing in respect of the work which he had done upon the buildings.

Collins LJ: '. . . I think the case is really concluded by the finding of the learned judge to the effect that the plaintiff had abandoned the contract. If the plaintiff had merely broken his contract in some way so as not to give the defendant the right to treat him as having abandoned the contract, and the defendant had then proceeded to finish the work himself, the plaintiff might perhaps have been entitled to sue on a *quantum meruit* on the ground that the defendant had taken the benefit of the work done. But that is not the present case. There are cases in which, though the plaintiff has abandoned the performance of a contract, it is possible for him to raise the inference of a new contract to pay for the work done on a *quantum meruit* from the defendant's having taken the benefit of that work, but, in order that that may be done, the circumstances must be such as to give an option to the defendant to take or not to take the benefit of the work done. It is only where the circumstances are such as to give that option that there is any evidence on which to ground the inference of a new contract. Where, as in the case of work done on land, the circumstances are such as to give the defendant no option whether he will take the benefit of the work or not, then one must look to other facts than the mere taking the benefit of the work in order to ground the inference of a new contract. In this case I see no other facts on which such an inference can be founded. The mere fact that a defendant is in possession of what he cannot help keeping, or even has done work upon it, affords no ground for such an inference. He is not bound to keep unfinished a building which in an incomplete state would be a nuisance on his land. I am therefore of opinion that the Plaintiff was not entitled to recover for the work which he had done.'

Hoenig v Isaacs

[1952] 2 All ER 176 • Court of Appeal

The defendant employed the plaintiff to decorate his flat and to provide it with some furniture for a sum of £750. The terms of payment were 'net cash, as the work proceeds; and balance on completion'. The defendant having paid the plaintiff £400 moved into his flat and used the furniture. When the plaintiff requested payment of the balance the defendant refused to pay. He claimed that it was an entire contract which the plaintiff had failed to complete because of faulty design and bad workmanship. The official referee held that there had been a substantial compliance with the contract and that the defendant was liable for £750 less the cost of remedying the defects which he assessed at £56 and he gave judgment for £294.

The issue before the Court of Appeal was whether the contract was an entire contract.

Denning LJ: 'This case raises the familiar question: Was entire performance a condition precedent to payment? That depends on the true construction of the contract. In this case the contract was made over a period of time and was partly oral and partly in writing, but I agree with the official referee that the essential terms were set down in the letter of Apr. 25, 1950. It describes the work which was to be done and concludes with these words:

"The foregoing, complete, for the sum of £750 net. Terms of payment are net cash, as the work proceeds; and balance on completion".

The question of law that was debated before us was whether the plaintiff was entitled in this action to sue for the £350 balance of the contract price as he had done. The defendant said that he was only entitled to sue on a *quantum meruit*. The defendant was anxious to insist on a *quantum meruit*, because he said that the contract price was unreasonably high. He wished, therefore, to reject that price altogether and simply to pay a reasonable price for all the work that was done. This would obviously mean an inquiry into the value of every item, including all the many items which were in compliance with the contract as well as the three which fell short of it. That is what the defendant wanted. The plaintiff resisted this course and refused to claim on a *quantum meruit*. He said that he was entitled to the balance of £350 less a deduction for the defects.

In determining this issue the first question is whether, on the true construction of the contract, entire performance was a condition precedent to payment. It was a lump sum contract, but that does not mean that entire performance was a condition precedent to payment. When a contract provides for a specific sum to be paid on completion of specified work, the courts lean against a construction of the contract which would deprive the contractor of any payment at all simply because there are some defects or omissions.

The promise to complete the work is, therefore, construed as a term of the contract, but not as a condition. It is not every breach of that term which absolves the employer from his promise to pay the price, but only a breach which goes to the root of the contract, such as an abandonment of the work when it is only half done. Unless the breach does go to the root of the matter, the employer cannot resist payment of the price. He must pay it and bring a cross-claim for the defects and omissions, or, alternatively, set them up in diminution of the price. The measure is the amount which the work is worth less by reason of the defects and omissions, and is usually calculated by the cost of making them good: see *Mondel* v *Steel; H Dakin & Co, Ltd* v *Lee*, and the notes to *Cutter* v *Powell* in *Smith's Leading Cases*. It is, of course, always open to the parties by express words to make entire performance a condition precedent. A familiar instance is when the contract provides for progress payments to be made as the work proceeds, but for retention money to be held until completion. Then entire performance is usually a condition precedent to payment of the retention money, but not, of course, to the progress payments. The contractor is entitled to payment *pro rata* as the work proceeds, less a deduction for retention money. But he is not entitled to the retention money until the work is entirely finished, without defects or omissions. In the present case the contract provided for 'net cash, as the work proceeds; and balance on completion'. If the balance could be regarded as retention money, then it might well be that the contractor ought to have done all the work correctly, without defects or omissions, in order to be entitled to the balance. But I do not think the balance should be regarded as retention money. Retention money is usually only ten per cent, or fifteen per cent, whereas this balance was more than fifty per cent. I think this contract should be regarded as an ordinary lump sum contract. It was substantially performed. The contractor is entitled, therefore, to the contract price, less a deduction for the defects.

Even if entire performance was a condition precedent, nevertheless the result would be the same, because I think the condition was waived. It is always open to a party to waive a condition which is inserted for his benefit. What amounts to a waiver depends on the circumstances. If this was an entire contract, then, when the plaintiff tendered the work to the defendant as being a fulfilment of the contract, the defendant could have refused to accept it until the defects were made good, in which case he would not have been liable for the balance of the price until they were made good. But he did not refuse to accept the work. On the contrary, he entered into possession of the flat and used the furniture as his own, including the defective items. That was a clear waiver of the condition precedent. Just as in a sale of goods the buyer who accepts the goods can no longer treat a breach of condition as giving a right to reject but only a right to damages, so also in a contract for work and labour an employer who takes the benefit of the work can no longer treat entire performance as a condition precedent, but only as a term giving rise to damages . . .

Bolton v *Mahadeva*

[1972] 2 All ER 1322 • Court of Appeal

The plaintiff agreed to install central heating in the defendant's house for a lump sum of £560. When the work was complete the defendant refused to pay because of defects to the heating system which would have cost £174 to put right. The plaintiff claimed that although the contract was for a lump sum he had substantially performed it and was therefore entitled to the balance of the price less the £174.

Cairns LJ: 'The main question in the case is whether the defects in workmanship found by the judge to be such as to cost £174 to repair – i.e. between one-third and one-quarter of the contract price – were of such a character and amount that the plaintiff could not be said to have substantially performed his contract. That is, in my view, clearly the legal principle which has to be applied to cases of this kind.

The rule which was laid down many years ago in *Cutter* v *Powell*, in relation to lump sum contracts was that, unless the contracting party had performed the whole of his contract, he was not entitled to recover anything. That strong rule must now be read in the light of certain more recent cases to which I shall briefly refer. The first of those cases is *H Dakin & Co Ltd* v *Lee*, a decision of the Court of Appeal, in which it was held that, where the amount of work which had not been carried out under a lump sum contract was very minor in relation to the contract as a whole, the contractor was entitled to be paid the lump sum, subject to such deduction as might be proper in respect of the uncompleted work . . . The basis on which the Court of Appeal did decide *H Dakin & Co Ltd* v *Lee* is to be found in a passage of the judgment of Lord Cozens-Hardy MR. I do not think it is necessary to read it in full, but I read this short passage:

> "But to say that a builder cannot recover from a building owner merely because some item of the work has been done negligently or inefficiently or improperly is a proposition which I should not listen to unless compelled by a decision of the House of Lords. Take a contract for a lump sum to decorate a house; the contract provides that there shall be three coats of oil paint, but in one of the rooms only two coats of paint are put on. Can anybody say that under these circumstances the building owner could go and occupy the house and take the benefit of all the decorations which had been done in the other rooms without paying a penny for all the work done by the builder, just because only two coats of paint had been put on in one room where there ought to have been three?" . . .

In considering whether there was substantial performance I am of opinion that it is relevant to take into account both the nature of the defects and the proportion between the cost of rectifying them and the contract price. It would be wrong to say that the contractor is only entitled to payment if the defects are so trifling as to be covered by the *de minimis* rule.

. . . The judge came to the conclusion that, because of a defective flue, there were fumes which affected the condition of the air in the living rooms, and he further held that the amount of heat given out was such that, on the average, the house was less warm than it should have been with the heating system on, to the extent of 10 per cent. But, while that was the average over the house as a whole, the deficiency in warmth varied very much as between one room and another. The figures that were given in evidence and, insofar as we heard, were not contradicted, were such as to indicate that in some rooms the heat was less than it should have been by something between 26 and 30 per cent . . .

Now, certainly it appears to me that the nature and amount of the defects in this case were far different from those which the court had to consider in *H Dakin & Co Ltd* v *Lee* and *Hoenig* v *Isaacs*. For my part, I find it impossible to say that the judge was right in reaching the conclusion that in those circumstances the contract had been substantially performed. The contract was a contract to install a central heating system. If a central heating system when installed is such that it does not heat the house adequately and is such, further, that fumes are given out, so as to make living rooms uncomfortable, and if the putting right of those defects is not something which can be done by some slight amendment of the system, then I think that the contract is not substantially performed.

The actual amounts of expenditure which the judge assessed as being necessary to cure those particular defects were £40 in each case. Taking those matters into account and the other matters making up the total of £174, I have reached the conclusion that the judge was wrong in saying that this contract had been substantially completed; and, on my view of the law, it follows that the plaintiff was not entitled to recover under that contract.

Doctrine of 'substantial performance'

In cases other than 'entire contracts' if there has been a *minor departure* in the performance of a party's obligations under a contract then the law provides that if the contract is *substantially performed*, the injured party cannot treat himself as discharged from his obligation to pay, although he will have a claim for any loss which he may have sustained by reason of the incomplete performance.

The general rule is that substantial performance occurs when actual performance falls not far short of the required performance and the cost of remedying the defect is small in comparison with the contract price.

NB: a party who incompletely performs his obligation cannot as a right claim payment but the injured party may accept partial performance which is less than substantial performance. Once this is done the party in default may be able to claim payment for work actually done. This issue is dealt with later under the topic of *Quantum meruit.*

TIME OF PERFORMANCE

Time is not normally the essence of a contract

The Law of Property Act 1925 s 41 provides that time is not normally the essence of a contract.

Section 41 states

'Stipulations in a contract, as to time or otherwise, which according to rules of equity are not deemed to be or to have become of the essence of the contract, are also construed and have effect at law in accordance with the same rules.'

Circumstances in which time will be of the essence

Bunge Corporation v *Tradax Export SA*

[1981] 2 All ER 513 • House of Lords

Lord Wilberforce: 'In conclusion, the statement of the law in *Halsbury's Laws of England* (generally approved in the House in the *United Scientific Holdings* case), appears to me to be correct, in particular in asserting (1) that the court will require precise compliance with stipulations as to time wherever the circumstances of the case indicate that this would fulfil the intention of the parties, and (2) that broadly speaking time will be considered of the essence in "mercantile" contracts . . .'

An example of time being of the essence is found in *Charles Rickards Ltd* v

Oppenheim, above (p 151), where Denning LJ said 'It is clear on the findings of the judge that there was an initial stipulation making time of the essence of the contract between the plaintiffs and the defendant, namely, that it was to be completed "in six, or, at the most, seven months".'

Although Lord Wilberforce states in *Bunge Corporation* v *Tradax Export SA*, above, that 'broadly speaking time will be considered of the essence in "mercantile" contracts' the Sale of Goods Act 1979 s 10(1) and (2) provides that payment is not deemed to be of essence unless stated in the contract.

Sale of Goods Act 1979: Section 10 Stipulations about time

(1)   Unless a different intention appears from the terms of the contract, stipulations as to time of payment are not of the essence of a contract of sale.
(2)   Whether any other stipulation as to time is or is not of the essence of the contract depends on the terms of the contract.

Time not originally 'of the essence'

It was seen in *Charles Rickards Ltd* v *Oppenheim* that if a party is late in performing their side of the contract the innocent party can, on giving reasonable notice, make time the essence of the contract. The question arises as to how late in performing the contract must the defaulter be before the innocent party can make time of the essence?

Behzadi v *Shaftesbury Hotels Ltd*

[1991] 2 All ER 477 • Court of Appeal

Purchas LJ: 'What, then, is the effect of serving a so-called notice "making time of the essence"? It certainly does not make time of the essence so far as the obligations in the contract of sale are concerned, since one party cannot unilaterally vary the terms of the contract. It cannot be served until after there has been a breach by the defaulting party either of the term fixing the date for compliance, or of the implied term where the contract is silent as to the date for performance. The notice has in law no contractual import. With the modern practice of including standard conditions into contracts for sale of land, occasions when a date is not prescribed for completion or for the performance of intermediate steps . . . have become increasingly rare. It is only in such cases that the reasonable time for performance term can be imported into the contract. In most cases, therefore, the effect of the notice will be to give the defaulting party an opportunity to perform his obligations under the contract. However, I see no reason for the imposition of any further period of delay after the breach of contract has been established by non-performance in accordance with its terms before it is open to a party to serve such a notice. The important matter is that the notice must in all the circumstances of the case give a reasonable opportunity for the other party to perform his part of the contract. However, one who elects to serve a notice immediately upon the breach of the contract will be well advised to be cautious in his selection of the period to be included in the notice before he reserves the right to repudiate.'

DISCHARGE BY BREACH

This topic relates to contents of the contract (conditions, warranties and innominate terms).

A breach of contract by one party *always* entitles the other to sue for damages. However, not every breach operates as a *discharge* – in other words not every breach entitles the innocent party to accept the breach and treat the contract as at an end. In order to have this effect the breach must be such as to constitute a repudiation by the party in default of his obligations under the contract.

Discharge at option of the injured party

Breach does not itself terminate the contract. The injured party must *elect* (choose) to treat the contract as discharged; he can choose to continue with (affirm) the contract.

White & Carter (Councils) Ltd v McGregor

[1961] 3 All ER 1178 • House of Lords

White & Carter entered into a contract with McGregor for the display of advertisements of McGregor's business on White & Carter's litter bins for a period of three years. On the day on which the contract was made, and before White & Carter had taken any steps to carry the contract into effect, McGregor repudiated the contract but White & Carter refused to accept the repudiation and went on to advertise McGregor's business on their litter bins for the full three years.

The issue before the House of Lords was whether, in these circumstances, White & Carter were entitled to carry out the contract and sue for the contract price or whether their only remedy was to sue for damages for breach of the contract.

Lord Reid: 'The general rule cannot be in doubt. It was settled in Scotland at least as early as 1848 and it has been authoritatively stated time and again in both Scotland and England. If one party to a contract repudiates it in the sense of making it clear to the other party that he refuses or will refuse to carry out his part of the contract, the other party, the innocent party, has an option. He may accept that repudiation and sue for damages for breach of contract whether or not the time for performance has come; or he may if he chooses disregard or refuse to accept it and then the contract remains in full effect . . .

I need not refer to the numerous authorities. They are not disputed by the respondent but he points out that in all of them the party who refused to accept the repudiation had no active duties under the contract. The innocent party's option is generally said to be to wait until the date of performance and then to claim damages estimated as at that date. There is no case in which it is said that he may, in face of the repudiation, go on and incur useless expense in performing the contract and then claim the contract price. The option, it is argued, is merely as to the date as at which damages are to be assessed. Developing this argument, the respondent points out that in most cases the innocent party cannot complete the contract himself without the other party doing, allowing or accepting something, and that it is purely fortuitous that the appellants can do so in this case. In most cases by refusing co-operation the party in breach can compel the innocent party to restrict his claim to damages. Then it was said that even where the innocent party can complete the contract without such co-operation it is against the public interest that he should be allowed to do so. An example was developed in argument. A company might engage an expert to go abroad and prepare an elaborate report and then repudiate the contract before anything was done. To allow such an expert then to waste thousands of pounds in preparing the report cannot be right if a much smaller sum of damages would give him full compensation for his loss. It would merely enable to expert to extort a settlement giving him far more than reasonable compensation.

The respondent founds on the decision of the First Division in *Langford & Co Ltd* v *Dutch.* There an advertising contractor agreed to exhibit a film for a year. Four days after this agreement was made the advertiser repudiated it but, as in the present case, the contractor refused to accept the repudiation and proceeded to exhibit the film and sue for the contract price. The sheriff-substitute dismissed the action as irrelevant and his decision was affirmed on appeal. In the course of a short opinion the Lord President (Lord Cooper) said:

> "It appears to me that, apart from wholly exceptional circumstances of which there is no trace in the averments on this record, the law of Scotland does not afford to a person in the position of the pursuers the remedy which is here sought. The pursuers could not force the defender to accept a year's advertisement which she did not want, though they could of course claim damages for her breach of contract. On the averments the only reasonable and proper course, which the pursuers should have adopted, would have been to treat the defender as having repudiated the contract and as being on that account liable in damages, the measure of which we are, of course, not in a position to discuss."

The Lord President cited no authority and I am in doubt what principle he had in mind . . .

Langford & Co Ltd v Dutch is indistinguishable from the present case . . . We must now decide whether that case was rightly decided. In my judgment it was not. It could only be supported on one or other of two grounds. It might be said that, because in most cases the circumstances are such that an innocent party is unable to complete the contract and earn the contract price without the assent or co-operation of the other party, therefore in cases where he can do so he should not be allowed to do so. I can see no justification for that.

The other ground would be that there is some general equitable principle or element of public policy which requires this limitation of the contractual rights of the innocent party. It may well be that, if it can be shown that a person has no legitimate interest, financial or otherwise, in performing the contract rather than claiming damages, he ought not to be allowed to saddle the other party with an additional burden with no benefit to himself. If a party has no interest to enforce a stipulation he cannot in general enforce it: so it might be said that if a party has no interest to insist on a particular remedy he ought not to be allowed to insist on it. And, just as a party is not allowed to enforce a penalty, so he ought not to be allowed to penalise the other party by taking one course when another is equally advantageous to him. If I may revert to the example which I gave of a company engaging an expert to prepare an elaborate report and then repudiating before anything was done, it might be that the company could show that the expert had no substantial or legitimate interest in carrying out the work rather than accepting damages: I would think that the *de minimis* principle would apply in determining whether his interest was substantial and that he might have a legitimate interest other than an immediate financial interest. But if the expert had no such interest then that might be regarded as a proper case for the exercise of the general equitable jurisdiction of the court. But that is not this case. Here the respondent did not set out to prove that the appellants had no legitimate interest in completing the contract and claiming the contract price rather than claiming damages, there is nothing in the findings of fact to support such a case, and it seems improbable that any such case could have been proved. It is, in my judgment, impossible to say that the appellants should be deprived of their right to claim the contract price merely because the benefit to them as against claiming damages and reletting their advertising space might be small in comparison with the loss to the respondent: that is the most that could be said in favour of the respondent. Parliament has on many occasions relieved parties from certain kinds of improvident or oppressive contracts, but the common law can only do that in very limited circumstances. Accordingly, I am unable to avoid the conclusion that this appeal must be allowed and the case remitted so that decree can be pronounced as craved in the initial writ.'

Lord Tucker: 'My Lords, I have had the advantage of reading the opinion prepared by my noble and learned friend, Lord Hodson. I am in complete agreement with the reasons he gives for allowing the appeal.'

Lord Hodson: '. . . It is settled as a fundamental rule of the law of contract that repudiation by one of the parties to a contract does not itself discharge it. See the speech of Viscount Simon LC in *Heyman* v *Darwins, Ltd* citing with approval the following sentence from a judgment of Scrutton LJ in *Golding* v *London & Edinburgh Insurance Co, Ltd*:

> "I have never been able to understand what effect repudiation by one party has unless the other party accepts [the repudiation]."

In *Howard* v *Pickford Tool Co, Ltd* Asquith LJ said: "An unaccepted repudiation is a thing writ in water and of no value to anybody: it confers no legal rights of any sort or kind" . . .

It follows that, if, as here, there was no acceptance, the contract remains alive for the benefit of both parties and the party who has repudiated can change his mind but it does not follow that the party at the receiving end of the proffered repudiation is bound to accept it before the time for performance and is left to his remedy in damages for breach.

Counsel for the respondent did not seek to dispute the general proposition of law to which I have referred but sought to argue that if at the date of performance by the innocent party the guilty party maintains his refusal to accept performance and the innocent party does not accept the repudiation, although the contract still survives, it does not survive so far as the right of the innocent party to perform it is concerned but survives only for the purpose of enforcing remedies open to him by way of damages or specific implement. This produces an impossible result; if the innocent party is deprived of some of his rights it involves putting an end to the contract except in cases, unlike this, where, in the exercise of the court's discretion, the remedy of specific implement is available.

The true position is that the contract survives and does so not only where specific implement is available. When the assistance of the court is not required the innocent party can choose whether he will accept repudiation and sue for damages for anticipatory breach or await the date of performance by the guilty party. Then, if there is failure in performance, his rights are preserved.

It may be unfortunate that the appellants have saddled themselves with an unwanted contract causing an apparent waste of time and money. No doubt this aspect impressed the Court of Session but there is no equity which can assist the respondent. It is trite that equity will not rewrite an improvident contract where there is no disability on either side. There is no duty laid on a party to a subsisting contract to vary it at the behest of the other party so as to deprive himself of the benefit given to him by the contract. To hold otherwise would be to introduce a novel equitable doctrine that a party was not to be held to his contract unless the court in a given instance thought it reasonable so to do. In this case it would make an action for debt a claim for a discretionary remedy. This would introduce an uncertainty into the field of contract which appears to be unsupported by authority either in English or Scottish law save for the one case (viz, *Langford & Co, Ltd* v *Dutch*) on which the Court of Session founded its opinion and which must, in my judgment, be taken to have been wrongly decided . . .

I would allow the appeal.'

Lord Morton of Henryton (dissenting): 'My Lords, I think that this is a case of great importance, although the claim is for a comparatively small sum. If the appellants are right, strange consequences follow in any case in which, under a repudiated contracts, services are to be performed by the party who has not repudiated it, so long as he is able to perform these services without the co-operation of the repudiating party. Many examples of such contracts could be given. One, given in the course of the argument and already mentioned by my noble and learned friend, Lord Reid, is the engagement of an expert to go abroad and write a report on some subject for a substantial fee plus his expenses. If the appellants succeed in the present case, it must follow that the expert is entitled to incur the expense of going abroad, to write his unwanted report, and then to recover the fee and expenses, even if the other party has plainly repudiated the contract before any expense has been incurred.

It is well established that repudiation by one party does not put an end to a contract. The other party can say "I hold you to your contract, which still remains in force". What, then, is his remedy if the repudiating party persists in his repudiation and refuses to carry out his part of the contract? The contract has been broken. The innocent party is entitled to be compensated by damages for any loss which he has suffered by reason of the breach, and in a limited class of cases the court will decree specific implement. The law of Scotland provides no other remedy for a breach of contract, and there is no reported case which decides that the innocent party may act as the appellants have acted. The present case is one in which specific implement could not be decreed, since the only obligation of the respondent under the contract was to pay a sum of money for services to be rendered by the appellants. Yet the appellants are claiming a kind of inverted specific implement of the contract. They first insist on performing their part of the contract, against the will of the other party, and then claim that he must perform his part and pay the contract price for unwanted services. In my opinion, my Lords, the appellants' only remedy was damages, and they were bound to take steps to minimise their loss, according to a well-established rule of law. Far from doing this, having incurred no expense at the date of the repudiation, they made no attempt to procure another advertiser, but deliberately went on to incur expense and perform unwanted services with the intention of creating a money debt which did not exist at the date of the repudiation . . .

I would dismiss the appeal.'

Lord Keith of Avonholm (dissenting): 'I find the argument advanced for the appellants a somewhat startling one. If it is right it would seem that a man who has contracted to go to Hong Kong at his own expense and make a report, in return for a remuneration of £10 000, and who, before the date fixed for the start of the journey and perhaps before he has incurred any expense, is informed by the other contracting party that he has cancelled or repudiates the contract, is entitled to set off for Hong Kong and produce his report in order to claim in debt the stipulated sum. Such a result is not, in my opinion, in accordance with principle or authority and cuts across the rule that where one party is in breach of contract the other must take steps to minimise the loss sustained by the breach . . .

I would dismiss the appeal.'

Clea Shipping Corporation v *Bulk Oil International Ltd* (*The Alaskan Trader*)

[1984] 1 All ER 129 • Queen's Bench

The facts are stated in the judgment of Lloyd J.

Lloyd J: 'On Oct 19, 1979, *Alaskan Trader* was chartered by the respondents as disponent owners to the claimants for a period of 24 months 15 days more or less . . . She was delivered under the charter on Dec 20, 1979, and thereafter performed services on short Mediterranean voyages carrying gas oil from Haifa. On Oct 19, 1980 . . . the vessel suffered a serious engine breakdown. It was clear that the repairs would take many months. The charterers indicated that they had no further use for the vessel. The market had turned against them. At the time of the charter the market rate was £13–£14 per ton. By October, 1980, it had declined to £8–£9 per ton. Nevertheless the owners went ahead with the repairs at a cost of £800 000. Throughout the period of the repairs the vessel was, of course, off-hire. The repairs were completed on Apr 7, 1981. The owners thereupon informed the charterers that the vessel was again at their disposal. But the charterers declined to give the master any orders. They regarded the charter-party as having come to an end. The owners could have treated the charterers' conduct as a repudiation of the charter-party. But they did not do so. They anchored the vessel off Piraeus, where she remained with a full crew on board, ready to sail, but idle, until the time charter expired on Dec 5, 1981. She was then sold for scrap . . .

Lord Reid [in *White and Carter* v *McGregor*] agreed with Lord Hodson and Lord Tucker that on the facts the plaintiffs' claim in debt must succeed. But his speech contains two important observations on the law. First, he pointed out that it is only in rare cases that the innocent party will be able to complete performance of his side of the contract, without the assent or co-operation of the party in breach. Obviously if the innocent party cannot complete performance, he is restricted to his claim for damages. A buyer who refuses to accept delivery of the goods, and thereby prevents property passing, cannot, in the ordinary case, be made liable for the price. The peculiarity of *White and Carter* v *McGregor*, as Lord Reid pointed out, was that the plaintiffs could completely fulfil their part of the contract without any co-operation from the defendant.

The second observation as to the law was that a party might well be unable to enforce his contractual remedy if "he had no legitimate interest, financial or otherwise, in performing the contract rather than claiming damages" . . .

The next case is *Hounslow London Borough Council* v *Twickenham Garden Developments*, a case relied on strongly by Mr Cooke for the charterers. That case concerned a building contract between a firm of contractors and the local borough council. The council sought to determine the contract, but the contractors refused to accept the repudiation. They relied on *White and Carter* v *McGregor*. Mr Justice Megarry analysed the speeches in that case, and drew attention to the two observations, or limitations, in the speech of Lord Reid. He described both limitations as important. As to the first, he held that the building contract in the case before him contemplated the passive, if not active, co-operation of both parties in its performance. Accordingly, the case fell within the first of Lord Reid's limitations . . .

In the light of these authorities, I must return to the facts of the present case. It may be convenient to repeat a few sentences from para 30 of the award:

"I am satisfied that this commercial absurdity is not justified by a proper interpretation of the decided cases. I consider that the analogy of a contract between Master and servant applies more closely to a timecharter than the analogy of a simple debt. The

Owner supplies the vessel and crew; the Charterer supplies fuel oil, pays disbursements and gives orders. The Charterers were also able to satisfy me that at that stage the Owners had no legitimate interest in pursuing their claim for hire rather than a claim for damages. In these respects the present case differs materially from the case of *White and Carter* v *McGregor*, and is more closely analogous to the case of *The Puerto Buitrago*, where the judgments of Lord Denning and Lord Orr are particularly in point."

It seems to me that the arbitrator is here distinguishing clearly between the two observations or limitations on the general principle to which Lord Reid had drawn attention in his speech. He is saying that a time charter is more analogous to a contract between master and servant than a simple debt, i.e., that it is a contract which calls for co-operation between both parties. He is also saying ("The charterers were *also* able to satisfy me") that the owners had no legitimate interest in pursuing their claim for hire as distinct from damages. I will take the legitimate interest point first.

In addition to arguing that what Lord Reid had said about legitimate interest was only a quotation from Counsel, and in any event *obiter* – arguments with which I have already dealt – Mr Colman submitted that Lord Reid was, quite simply, wrong. It seems to me that it would be difficult for me to take that view in the light of what was said by all three members of the Court of Appeal in *The Puerto Buitrago*. Whether one takes Lord Reid's language, which was adopted by Lords Justices Orr and Browne in *The Puerto Buitrago*, or Lord Denning MR's language in that case ("in all reason"), or Mr Justice Kerr's language in *The Odenfeld* ("wholly unreasonable, quite unrealistic, unreasonable and untenable"), there comes a point at which the Court will cease, on general equitable principles, to allow the innocent party to enforce his contract according to its strict legal terms. How one defines that point is obviously a matter of some difficulty; for it involves drawing a line between conduct which is merely unreasonable (see per Lord Reid in *White and Carter* v *McGregor* criticising the Lord President in *Langford Co Ltd* v *Dutch*) and conduct which is wholly unreasonable: see per Mr Justice Kerr in *The Odenfeld*. But however difficult it may be to define the point, that there is such a point seems to me to have been accepted both by the Court of Appeal in *The Puerto Buitrago* and by Mr Justice Kerr in *The Odenfeld*.

I appreciate that the House of Lords has recently re-emphasised the importance of certainty in commercial contracts, when holding that there is no equitable jurisdiction to relieve against the consequences of the withdrawal clause in a time charter: *Scandinavian Trading Tanker Co AB* v *Flota Petrolera Ecuatoriana (The Scaptrade)*. I appreciate, too, that the importance of certainty was one of the main reasons urged by Lord Hodson in *White and Carter* v *McGregor* in upholding the innocent party's unfettered right to elect. But for reasons already mentioned, it seems to me that this Court is bound to hold that there is some fetter, if only in extreme cases; and for want of a better way of describing that fetter, it is safest for this Court to use the language of Lord Reid, which, as I have already mentioned, was adopted by a majority of the Court of Appeal in *The Puerto Buitrago* . . .

In the present case, by contrast, the arbitrator has found, and found clearly, that the owners had *no* legitimate interest in pursuing their claim for hire. In my view that finding is conclusive of this appeal.'

But remember if the innocent party does choose to affirm the contract *he still has his right to sue for damages.*

In limited circumstances the innocent party has no choice but to treat the contract as discharged, e.g. if he cannot carry out the contract without the co-operation of the other party e.g. a contract of employment.

Acceptance of breach must be made clear to the contract breaker

Vitol SA v *Norelf Ltd* ; *the Santa Clara*

[1996] 3 All ER 193 • House of Lords

In February 1991 Norelf sold to Vitol a cargo of propane cif (cost, insurance, freight) north-west Europe. The price of the propane was US$400 per tonne. Payment was to be made by telegraphic transfer within 30 days of the bill of lading date. Throughout March 1991 there was a consistent and marked downturn of the propane market cif north-west Europe. The fall in prices confronted Vitol with a large loss if the transaction proceeded. Conversely, if the transaction collapsed, Norelf faced a large loss. On 8 March 1991 when the *Santa Clara* was loading the cargo Vitol sent a telex to Norelf saying:

'It was a condition of the contract that delivery would be effected 1–7 March 1991 . . . We are advised that the vessel is not likely to complete loading now until sometime on 9 March – well outside the agreed contractual period. In view of the breach of this condition we must reject the cargo and repudiate the contract.'

On 11 March the rejection telex came to the notice of Norelf. In the meantime the vessel had completed loading and had sailed on 9 March. Vitol never retracted nor attempted to retract their repudiation of the contract. Norelf did nothing to affirm or perform the contract. On the contrary, Norelf resold on 15 March, at a price of $170 per tonne.

Then on 9 August 1991 Norelf's solicitors claimed about $1m as damages, calculated by reference to the difference between the contract price of $400 per tonne and a resale price of $170 per tonne.

The issue that came before the court was whether Norelf had ever accepted Vitol's repudiation.

Lord Steyn: 'My Lords, the question of law before the House does not call for yet another general re-examination of the principles governing an anticipatory breach of a contract and the acceptance of the breach by an aggrieved party. For present purposes I would accept as established law the following propositions: (1) Where a party has repudiated a contract the aggrieved party has an election to accept the repudiation or to affirm the contract: *Fercometal SARL* v *Mediterranean Shipping Co SA, the Simona*. (2) An act of acceptance of a repudiation requires no particular form: a communication does not have to be couched in the language of acceptance. It is sufficient that the communication or conduct clearly and unequivocally conveys to the repudiating party that that aggrieved party is treating the contract as at an end. (3) It is rightly conceded by counsel for the buyers that the aggrieved party need not personally, or by an agent, notify the repudiating party of his election to treat the contract as at an end. It is sufficient that the fact of the election comes to the repudiating party's attention, for example notification by an unauthorised broker or other intermediary may be sufficient: *Wood Factory Pty Ltd* v *Kiritos Pty Ltd* per McHugh J, *Majik Markets Pty Ltd* v *S & M Motor Repairs Pty Ltd (No 1)* per Young J and Carter and Harland, *Contract Law in Australia*.

The arbitrator did not put forward any heterodox general theory of the law of repudiation. On the contrary, he expressly stated that unless the repudiation was accepted by the sellers and the acceptance was communicated to the buyers the election was of no effect. It is plain that the arbitrator directed himself correctly in accordance with the governing general principle. The criticism of the arbitrator's reasoning centres on his conclusion that "the failure of [the sellers] to take any further step to perform the contract which was apparent to [the buyers] constituted sufficient communication of acceptance". By that statement the arbitrator was simply recording a finding that the buyers knew that the sellers were treating the contract as at an end. That interpretation is reinforced by the paragraph in his award read as a whole. The only question is whether the relevant holding of the arbitrator was wrong in law.

It is now possible to turn directly to the first issue posed, namely whether non-performance of an obligation is ever as a matter of law capable of constituting an act of acceptance. On this aspect I found the judgment of Phillips J entirely convincing. One cannot generalise on the point. It all depends on the particular contractual relationship and the particular circumstances of the case. But, like Phillips J, I am satisfied that a failure to perform may sometimes signify to a repudiating party an election by the aggrieved party to treat the contract as at an end. Postulate the case where an employer at the end of a day tells a contractor that he, the employer, is repudiating the contract and that the contractor need not return the next day. The contractor does not return the next day or at all. It seems to me that the contractor's failure to return may, in the absence of any other explanation, convey a decision to treat the contract as at an end. Another example may be an overseas sale providing for shipment on a named ship in a given month. The seller is obliged to obtain an export licence. The buyer repudiates the contract before loading starts. To the knowledge of the buyer the seller does not apply for an export licence with the result that the transaction cannot proceed. In such circumstances it may well be that an ordinary businessman, circumstanced as the parties were, would conclude that the seller was treating the contract as at an end. Taking the present case as illustrative, it is important to bear in mind that the tender of a bill of lading is the pre-condition to payment of the price. Why should an arbitrator not be able to infer that when, in the days and weeks following loading and the sailing of the vessel, the seller failed to tender a bill of lading to the buyer, he clearly conveyed to a trader that he was treating the contract as at an end? In my view therefore the passage from the judgment of Kerr LJ in the *Golodetz* case, if it was intended to enunciate a general and absolute rule, goes too far. It will be recalled, however, that Kerr LJ spoke of a continuing failure to perform. One can readily accept that a continuing failure to perform, i.e. a breach commencing before the repudiation and continuing thereafter, would necessarily be equivocal. In my view too much has been made of the observation of Kerr LJ. Turning to the observation of Nourse that a failure to perform a contractual obligation is necessarily and always equivocal, I respectfully disagree. Sometimes in the practical world of businessmen an omission to act may be as pregnant with meaning as a positive declaration. While the analogy of offer and acceptance is imperfect, it is not without significance that while the general principle is that there can be no acceptance of an offer by silence, our law does in exceptional cases recognise acceptance of an offer by silence. Thus in *Rust* v *Abbey Life Assurance Co Ltd* the Court of Appeal held that a failure by a proposed insured to reject a proffered insurance policy for seven months justified on its own an inference of acceptance. See also Treitel, *The Law of Contract*. Similarly, in the different field of repudiation, a failure to perform may sometimes be given a colour by special circumstances and may only be explicable to a reasonable person in the position of the repudiating party as an election to accept the repudiation.

My Lords, I would answer the question posed by this case in the same way as Phillips J did. In truth the arbitrator inferred an election, and communication of it, from the tenor of the rejection telex and the failure *inter alia* to tender the bill of lading. That was an issue of fact within the exclusive jurisdiction of the arbitrator.

For these reasons I would allow the appeal of the sellers.'

Effect of election to accept repudiation

Both parties' future obligations (those not performed) are discharged. However, the defaulter becomes liable to pay damages.

Moschi v *Lep Air Services Ltd*

[1972] 2 All ER 393 • House of Lords

Lord Reid: '. . . I am unable to accept some of [the Court of Appeal's] reasoning as to what happens when a contract is broken. In particular I cannot agree that after accepted repudiation the contractual obligations still exist as obligations. For the breach of any contract the normal remedy is damages in money. The contract may have been to deliver say 100 tons of wheat. If the party fails to deliver somehow that obligation disappears and by operation of law is replaced by an obligation to pay money. So it appears to me that when a contract is brought to an end by repudiation accepted by the other party all the obligations in the contract come to an end and they are replaced by operation of law by an obligation to pay money damages. The damages are assessed by reference to the old obligations but the old obligations no longer exist as obligations. Were it otherwise there would be in existence simultaneously two obligations, one to perform the contract and the other to pay damages. But that could not be right. The only legal nexus remaining is the obligation to pay the damages; so here when the respondents elected to end the company's contract by treating their fundamental breach as a repudiation and accepting it, their right against the company became a right to get damages . . .'

Lord Diplock: 'My Lords, it has become usual to speak of the exercise by one party to a contract of his right to treat the contract as rescinded in circumstances such as these, as an "acceptance" of the wrongful repudiation of the contract by the other party as a rescission of the contract. But it would be quite erroneous to suppose that any fresh agreement between the parties or any variation of the terms of the original contract is involved when the party who is not in default elects to exercise his right to treat the contract as rescinded because of a repudiatory breach of the contract by the other party. He is exercising a right conferred on him by law of which the sole source is the original contract. He is not varying that contract; he is enforcing it.

It is no doubt convenient to speak of a contract as being terminated or coming to an end when the party who is not in default exercises his right to treat it as rescinded. But the law is concerned with the effect of that election on those obligations of the parties of which the contract was the source, and this depends on the nature of the particular obligation and on which party promised to perform it.

Generally speaking, the rescission of the contract puts an end to the primary obligations of the party not in default to perform any of his contractual promises which he has not already performed by the time of the rescission. It deprives him of any right as against the other party to continue to perform them. It does not give rise to any secondary obligation in substitution for a primary obligation which has come to an end. The primary obligations of the party in default to perform any of the promises made by him and remaining unperformed likewise come to an end as does his right to continue to perform them. But for his primary obligations there is substituted by operation of law a secondary obligation to pay to the other party a sum of money to compensate him for the loss he has sustained as a result of the failure to perform the primary obligations. This secondary obligation is just as much an obligation arising from the contract as are the primary obligations that it replaces (see *R V Ward Ltd* v *Bignall*).

Although this is the general rule as to the effect of rescission of the contract on obligations of which it was the source, there may be exceptional primary obligations which continue to exist notwithstanding that the contract has been rescinded. These are obligations that are ancillary to the main purpose of the contract – which is, of course, that the parties should perform their primary obligations voluntarily. Mutual promises to submit to arbitration disputes arising as to the performance by the parties of their other obligations arising from the contract may be expressed in terms which make it clear that it was the common intention of the parties that their primary obligation to continue to perform these promises should continue notwithstanding that their other primary obligations had come to an end (*Heyman* v *Darwins Ltd*).

Photo Production Ltd v *Securicor Transport Ltd*

[1980] 1 All ER 556 • House of Lords

The facts appear above (p 283).

Lord Diplock: 'My Lords, it is characteristic of commercial contracts, nearly all of which today are entered into not by natural legal persons, but by fictitious ones, i.e. companies, that the parties promise to one another that something will be done, for instance, that property and possession of goods will be transferred, that goods will be carried by ship from one port to another, that a building will be constructed in accordance with agreed plans, that services of a particular kind will be provided. Such a contract is the source of primary legal obligations on each party to it to procure that whatever he has promised will be done is done. (I leave aside arbitration clauses which do not come into operation until a party to the contract claims that a primary obligation has not been observed.)

Where what is promised will be done involves the doing of a physical act, performance of the promise necessitates procuring a natural person to do it; but the legal relationship between the promisor and the natural person by whom the act is done, whether it is that of master and servant, or principal and agent, or of parties to an independent subcontract, is generally irrelevant. If that person fails to do it in the manner in which the promisor has promised to procure it to be done, as, for instance, with reasonable skill and care, the promisor has failed to fulfil his own primary obligation. This is to be distinguished from "vicarious liability", a legal concept which does depend on the existence of a particular legal relationship between the natural person by whom a tortious act was done and the person sought to be made vicariously liable for it. In the interests of clarity the expression should, in my view, be confined to liability for tort.

A basic principle of the common law of contract, to which there are no exceptions that are relevant in the instant case, is that parties to a contract are free to determine for them-selves what primary obligations they will accept. They may state these in express words in the contract itself and, where they do, the statement is determinative; but in practice a commercial contract never states all the primary obligations of the parties in full; many are left to be incorporated by implication of law from the legal nature of the contract into which the parties are entering. But if the parties wish to reject or modify primary obligations which would otherwise be so incorporated, they are fully at liberty to do so by express words.

Leaving aside those comparatively rare cases in which the court is able to enforce a primary obligation by decreeing specific performance of it, breaches of primary obligations give rise to substituted secondary obligations on the part of the party in default, and, in some cases, may entitle the other party to be relieved from further performance of his own primary obligations. These secondary obligations of the contract breaker and any concomitant relief of the other party from his own primary obligations also arise by implication of law, generally common law, but sometimes statute, as in the case of codifying statutes passed at the turn of the century, notably the Sale of Goods Act 1893. The contract, however, is just as much the source of secondary obligations as it is of primary obligations; and like primary obligations that are implied by law secondary obligations too can be modified by agreement between the parties, although, for reasons to be mentioned later, they cannot, in my view, be totally excluded. In the instant case, the only secondary obligations and concomitant reliefs that are applicable arise by implication of the common law as modified by the express words of the contract.

Every failure to perform a primary obligation is a breach of contract. The secondary obligation on the part of the contract breaker to which it gives rise by implication of the common law is to pay monetary compensation to the other party for the loss sustained by him in consequence of the breach; but, with two exceptions, the primary obligations of both parties so far as they have not yet been fully performed remain unchanged. This secondary obligation to pay compensation (damages) for non-performance of primary obligations I will call the "general secondary obligation". It applies in the cases of the two exceptions as well.

The exceptions are: (1) where the event resulting from the failure by one party to perform a primary obligation has the effect of depriving the other party of substantially the whole benefit which it was the intention of the parties that he should obtain from the contract, the party not in default may elect to put an end to all primary obligations of both parties remaining unperformed (if the expression "fundamental breach" is to be retained, it should, in the interests of clarity, be confined to this exception); (2) where the contracting parties have agreed, whether by express words or by implication of law, that any failure by one party to perform a particular primary obligation ("condition" in the nomenclature of the Sale of Goods Act 1893), irrespective of the gravity of the event that has in fact resulted from the breach, shall entitle the other party to elect to put an end to all primary obligation of both parties remaining unperformed (in the interests of clarity, the nomenclature of the Sale of Goods Act 1893, "breach of condition", should be reserved for this exception).

Where such an election is made (a) there is substituted by implication of law for the primary obligations of the party in default which remain unperformed a secondary obligation to pay monetary compensation to the other party for the loss sustained by him in consequence of their non-performance in the future and (b) the unperformed primary obligations of that other party are discharged. This secondary obligation is additional to the general secondary obligation; I will call it "the anticipatory secondary obligation".

In cases falling within the first exception, fundamental breach, the anticipatory secondary obligation arises under contracts of all kinds by implication of the common law, except to the extent that it is excluded or modified by the express words of the contract. In cases falling within the second exception, breach of condition, the anticipatory secondary obligation generally arises under particular kinds of contracts by implication of statute law; though in the case of "deviation" from the contract voyage under a contract of carriage of goods by sea it arises by implication of the common law. The anticipatory secondary obligation in these cases too can be excluded or modified by express words.

When there has been a fundamental breach or breach of condition, the coming to an end of the primary obligations of both parties to the contract at the election of the party not in default is often referred to as the "determination" or "rescission" of the contract or, as in the Sale of Goods Act 1893, "treating the contract as repudiated". The first two of these expressions, however, are misleading unless it is borne in mind that for the unperformed primary obligations of the party in default there are substituted by operation of law what I have called the secondary obligations.

The bringing to an end of all primary obligations under the contract may also leave the parties in a relationship, typically that of bailor and bailee, in which they owe to one another by operation of law fresh primary obligations of which the contract is not the source; but no such relationship is involved in the instant case.

I have left out of account in this analysis as irrelevant to the instant case an arbitration or choice of forum clause. This does not come into operation until a party to the contract claims that a primary obligation of the other party has not been performed; and its relationship to other obligations of which the contract is the source was dealt with by this House in *Heyman* v *Darwins Ltd.*'

However, merely bringing an action for breach of contract does not 'rescind the contract *ab initio*'.

Johnson v Agnew

[1979] 1 All ER 883 • House of Lords

A typical factual situation with which this case deals is described in the judgment of Lord Wilberforce.

Lord Wilberforce. 'My Lords, this appeal arises in a vendors' action for specific performance of a contract for the sale of land, the appellant being the purchaser and the vendors the respondents. The factual situation is commonplace, indeed routine. An owner of land contracts to sell it to a purchaser; the purchaser fails to complete the contract; the vendor goes to the court and obtains an order that the contract be specifically performed; the purchaser still does not complete; the vendor goes back to the court and asks for the order for specific performance to be dissolved, for the contract to be terminated or "rescinded", and for an order for damages. One would think that the law as to so typical a set of facts would be both simple and clear. It is no credit to our law that it is neither. Learned judges in the Chancery Division and in the Court of Appeal have had great difficulty in formulating a rule and have been obliged to reach differing conclusions. That this is so is due partly to the mystification which has been allowed to characterise contracts for the sale of land, as contrasted with other contracts, partly to an accumulated debris of decisions and textbook pronouncements which has brought semantic confusion and misunderstandings into an area capable of being governed by principle. I hope that this may be an opportunity for a little simplification . . .

In this situation it is possible to state at least some uncontroversial propositions of law. First, in a contract for the sale of land, after time has been made, or has become, of the essence of the contract, if the purchaser fails to complete, the vendor can either treat the purchaser as having repudiated the contract, accept the repudiation, and proceed to claim damages for breach of the contract, both parties being discharged from further performance of the contract; or he may seek from the court an order for specific performance with damages for any loss arising from delay in performance. (Similar remedies are of course available to purchasers against vendors.) This is simply the ordinary law of contract applied to contracts capable of specific performance. Secondly, the vendor may proceed by action for the above remedies (viz specific performance or damages) in the alternative. At the trial he will however have to elect which remedy to pursue. Thirdly, if the vendor treats the purchaser as having repudiated the contract and accepts the repudiation, he cannot thereafter seek specific performance. This follows from the fact that, the purchaser having repudiated the contract and his repudiation having been accepted, both parties are discharged from further performance.

At this point it is important to dissipate a fertile source of confusion and to make clear that although the vendor is sometimes referred to in the above situation as "rescinding" the contract, this so-called "rescission" is quite different from rescission *ab initio*, such as may arise for example in cases of mistake, fraud or lack of consent. In those cases, the contract is treated in law as never having come into existence. (Cases of a contractual right to rescind may fall under this principle but are not relevant to the present discussion.) In the case of an accepted repudiatory breach the contract has come into existence but has been put an end to or discharged. Whatever contrary indications may be disinterred from old authorities, it is now quite clear, under the general law of contract, that acceptance of a repudiatory breach does not bring about "rescission *ab initio*". I need only quote one passage to establish these propositions. In *Heyman* v *Darwins Ltd* Lord Porter said:

> "To say that the contract is rescinded or has come to an end or has ceased to exist may in individual cases convey the truth with sufficient accuracy, but the fuller expression that the injured party is thereby absolved from future performance of his obligations under the contract is a more exact description of the position. Strictly speaking, to say that, upon acceptance of the renunciation of a contract, the contract is rescinded is incorrect. In such a case the injured party may accept the renunciation as a breach going to the root of the whole of the consideration. By that acceptance he is discharged from further performance and may bring an action for damages, but the contract itself is not rescinded."

See also *Boston Deep Sea Fishing & Ice Co Ltd* v *Ansell* per Bowen LJ, *Mayson* v *Clouet* per Lord Dunedin and *Moschi* v *Lep Air Services Ltd* per Lord Reid and Lord Diplock. I can see no reason, and no logical reason has ever been given, why any different result should follow as regards contracts for the sale of land, but a doctrine to this effect has infiltrated into that part of the law with unfortunate results. I shall return to this point when considering *Henty* v *Schroder* and cases which have followed it down to *Barber* v *Wolfe* and *Horsler* v *Zorro*.

Fourthly, if an order for specific performance is sought and is made, the contract remains in effect and is not merged in the judgment for specific performance. This is clear law, best illustrated by the judgment of Greene MR in *Austins of East Ham Ltd* v *Macey*, in a passage which deals both with this point and with that next following. It repays quotation in full:

> "The contract is still there. Until it is got rid of, it remains as a blot on the title, and the position of the vendor, where the purchaser has made default, is that he is entitled, not to annul the contract by aid of the court, but to obtain the normal remedy of a party to a contract which the other party has repudiated. He cannot, in the circumstances, treat it as repudiated except by order of the court and the effect of obtaining such an order is that the contract, which until then existed, is brought to an end. The real position, in my judgment, is that, so far from proceeding to the enforcement of an order for specific performance, the vendor, in such circumstances is choosing a remedy which is alternative to the remedy of proceeding under the order for specific performance. He could attempt to enforce that order and could levy an execution which might prove

completely fruitless. Instead of doing that, he elects to ask the court to put an end to the contract, and that is an alternative to an order for enforcing specific performance."

Fifthly, if the order for specific performance is not complied with by the purchaser, the vendor may either apply to the court for enforcement of the order, or may apply to the court to dissolve the order and ask the court to put an end to the contract. This proposition is as stated in *Austins of East Ham Ltd* v *Macey* (and see also *Sudagar Singh* v *Nazeer* per Megarry V-C) and is in my opinion undoubted law, both on principle and authority. It follows, indeed, automatically from the facts that the contract remains in force after the order for specific performance and that the purchaser has committed a breach of it of a repudiatory character which he has not remedied, or as Megarry V-C put it, that he is refusing to complete.

These propositions being, as I think they are, uncontrovertible, there only remains the question whether, if the vendor takes the latter course, i.e. of applying to the court to put an end to the contract, he is entitled to recover damages for breach of the contract. On principle one may ask "Why ever not?" If, as is clear, the vendor is entitled (after and notwithstanding that an order for specific performance has been made) if the purchaser still does not complete the contract, to ask the court to permit him to accept the purchaser's repudiation and to declare the contract to be terminated, why, if the court accedes to this, should there not follow the ordinary consequences, undoubted under the general law of contract, that on such acceptance and termination the vendor may recover damages for breach of contract? . . .

Then, in *McKenna* v *Richey*, a case very similar to the present, it was decided by O'Bryan J in the Supreme Court of Victoria that, after an order for specific performance had been made, which in the event could not be carried into effect, even though this was by reason of delay on the part of the plaintiff, the plaintiff could still come to the court and ask for damages on the basis of an accepted repudiation. The following passage is illuminating:

"The apparent inconsistency of a plaintiff suing for specific performance and for common law damages in the alternative arises from the fact that, in order to avoid circuity of action, there is vested in one Court jurisdiction to grant either form of relief. The plaintiff, in effect, is saying: 'I don't accept your repudiation of the contract but am willing to perform my part of the contract and insist upon your performing your part – but if I cannot successfully insist on your performing your part, I will accept the repudiation and ask for damages'. Until the defendant's repudiation is accepted the contract remains on foot, with all the possible consequences of that fact. But if, from first to last, the defendant continues unwilling to perform her part of the contract, then, if for any reason the contract cannot be specifically enforced, the plaintiff may, in my opinion, turn round and say: 'Very well, I cannot have specific performance; I will now ask for my alternative remedy of damages at common law'. This, in my opinion, is equally applicable both before and after decree whether the reason for the refusal or the failure of the decree of specific performance is due to inability of the defendant to give any title to the property sold, or to the conduct of the plaintiff which makes it inequitable for the contract to be specifically enforced."

Later the judge said of the case:

"It is an appropriate case for a Court of Equity to say: 'As a matter of discretion, this contract should not now be enforced specifically, but, in lieu of the decree for specific performance, the Court will award the plaintiff such damages as have been suffered by her in consequence of the defendant's breach. That is the best justice that can be done in this case'."

The judge in his judgment fully discusses and analyses the English cases but nevertheless reaches this view.

My Lords, I am happy to follow the latter case . . .'

Forms of discharge by breach

The right to treat a contract as discharged arises where one party

1   Renounces his liability under it; or
2   By his own act makes it impossible that he should fulfil his obligations, or
3   Fails to perform that which he promised.

1–3 amount to a repudiation of the contract. 1 and 2 can occur *either* before performance begins (known as *anticipatory breach*) or during performance.

Renunciation

In order for the breach to amount to renunciation the defaulter must evince an intention not to go on with the contract. The conduct of the defaulter must be such as to lead the innocent party to the conclusion that the defaulter no longer intends to be bound by the contract.

Federal Commerce and Navigation Ltd v Molena Alpha Inc; The Nanfri, The Benfri, The Lorfri

[1979] 1 All ER 307 • House of Lords

In November 1974 Molena time chartered three boats to Federal Commerce. Clause 9 of the charters provided that 'the Master to be under the orders of the Charterers as regards employment, agency, or other arrangements'. This meant that the master could issue freight prepaid bills of lading. A dispute having arisen between the parties, Molena, after taking legal advice in London and New York, threatened, on 4 October 1977, to revoke the master's authority to issue freight prepaid bills of lading and also threatened to instruct the master to issue bills of lading stating that they were subject to a lien. The arbitrator found that if these threats had been carried out they would have resulted in dire consequences for Federal Commerce.

The issue before the House of Lords was whether this threat amounted to a repudiatory breach by Molena.

Lord Wilberforce: 'I come then to the issue of repudiation. It is first necessary to see whether the owners' conduct on 4th October 1977 was a breach of contract at all . . .

. . . It must be clear that the owners cannot require bills of lading to be claused so as to incorporate the terms of the time charter: such a requirement would be contrary to the whole commercial purpose of the charterers . . .

. . . If the masters had in the present case acted on the owners' instructions, an actual breach would, in my view, have been committed; they did not in fact do so because the without prejudice agreement was immediately made. But the owners' instructions (communicated to the charterers) clearly constituted a threat of a breach or an anticipatory breach of the contract.

Was this then such a threatened or anticipatory breach as to entitle the charterers to put an end to the charters? It was argued for the charterers that cl 9 of the charters amounted to a condition of the contract, so that any breach of it automatically gave the charterers the right to put an end to it. I do not agree with this. The clause is not drafted as a condition, and on its face it admits of being breached in a number of ways some of which might be far from serious and would certainly not go to the root of the contract. I regard the clause as one breaches of which must be examined on their individual demerits. Was this breach, or threatened breach, repudiatory or not? . . . [T]he modern position is clear. The form of the critical question may differ slightly as it is put in relation to varying situations: per Lord Coleridge CJ in *Freeth* v *Burr*, as –

". . . an intimation of an intention to abandon and altogether to refuse performance of the contract [or to] evince an intention no longer to be bound by the contract."

Or, per Lord Wright in *Ross T Smyth & Co Ltd* v *T D Bailey, Son & Co*:

"I do not say that it is necessary to show that the party alleged to have repudiated should have an actual intention not to fulfil the contract. He may intend in fact to fulfil it, but may be determined to do so only in a manner substantially inconsistent with his obligations, and not in any other way."

Or, per Diplock LJ in *Hong Kong Fir Shipping Co Ltd* v *Kawasaki Kisen Kaisha Ltd*, such as to deprive –

"the charters of substantially the whole benefit which it was the intention of the parties . . . that the charterers should obtain from the further performance of their own contractual undertakings."

Or, per Buckley LJ in *Decro-Wall International SA* v *Practitioners in Marketing Ltd* :

"To constitute repudiation, the threatened breach must be such as to deprive the injured party of a substantial part of the benefit to which he is entitled under the contract . . . will the consequences of the breach be such that it would be unfair to the injured party to hold him to the contract and leave him to the remedy in damages . . . ?"

The difference in expression between these two last formulations does not, in my opinion, reflect a divergence of principle, but arises from and is related to the particular contract under consideration. They represent, in other words, applications to different contracts of the common principle that to amount to repudiation a breach must go to the root of the contract.

My Lords, I do not think there can be any doubt that the owners' breach or threatened breach in the present case, consisting in their announcement that their masters would refuse to issue bills of lading freight pre-paid and not "claused" so as to refer to the charters, *prima facie* went to the root of the contract as depriving the charterers of substantially the whole benefit of the contract . . . It was in fact the owners' intention to put irresistible pressure on the charterers ("to compel the Charterers to pay over all sums deducted from hire by the Charterers which the Owners disputed, irrespective of whether such deductions should ultimately be determined to be valid or invalid": see the award, para 27), through the action they threatened to take. If the charterers had not given way, the charters would have become useless for the purpose for which they were granted. I do not think that this was disputed by the owners; in any event it was not disputable. What was said was that the action of the owners, in the circumstances in which it was taken, should not be taken to be repudiatory. They had, on 21st September 1977, referred the whole question of deductions to arbitration; in a short time the whole issue would be cleared up one way or another, after which the charters would continue to be operated in accordance with the arbitrators' decision. The owners' action was of an interim character designed to have effect only until the position as to deductions could be clarified. The owners' interest was strongly in the direction of maintaining the charters; their move was simply a tactical one designed to resolve a doubtful situation. The sums which they were forcing the charterers to pay were inconsiderable. The charterers had already offered to pay them in "escrow".

My Lords, with genuine respect for the judgment of Kerr J who in substance agreed with this argument, I find myself obliged to reject it. Even if I were prepared to accept the assumption that arbitration proceedings set in motion on 21st September 1977 would be rapidly concluded through an early and speedy hearing, without a case being stated and without appeals in the courts (all of which must in fact be speculative), even so the owners' action must be regarded as going to the root of the contract. The issue of freight pre-paid bills of lading in respect of each of the three vessels was an urgent, indeed an immediate, requirement. The *Nanfri* completed loading a cargo, shipped by Continental Grain for Europe, on 5th October 1977; the *Benfri*, on passage to Chicago, was to load a cargo in Duluth for Europe; the *Lorfri* had loaded one parcel of grain for Continental Grain on 3rd October in respect of which a separate bill of lading was to be issued, and thereafter she was scheduled to load the balance of her capacity from Continental Grain at other Great Lakes ports.

These were pending transactions, and "The Charterers were likely to incur very substantial liabilities to Continental Grain if the cargoes which were being loaded or which were about to be loaded on 5th October were not completed and if freight pre-paid unclaused bills of lading were not issued promptly" (see the award, para 28). Blacklisting by Continental Grain was likely to follow (*ibid*). Thus the resolution of the deductions issue by arbitration, however soon this might be achieved, would still have left the charterers in a position where they might have lost the whole benefit of the time charters. That a "without prejudice" agreement was in fact entered into which averted these consequences is of course irrelevant though the fact that it was made does underline the extent of the pressure on the charterers. It is also irrelevant that the steps the charterers were being compelled, under threat of a breach of contract, to take were not very serious for them. A threat to commit a breach, having radical consequences, is nonetheless serious because it is disproportionate to the intended effect. It is thirdly irrelevant that it was in the owners' real interest to continue the charters rather than put an end to them. If a party's conduct is such as to amount to a threatened repudiatory breach, his subjective desire to maintain the contract cannot prevent the other party from drawing the consequences of his actions . . .

For these reasons I agree with the decision of the Court of Appeal that the charterers were entitled to determine the contracts . . .'

Woodar Investment Development Ltd v Wimpey Construction UK Ltd

[1980] 1 All ER 571 • House of Lords

The facts of this case are set out earlier in this book (p 182).

Lord Wilberforce: 'My Lords, I have used the words "in the circumstances" to indicate, as I think both sides accept, that in considering whether there has been a repudiation by one party, it is necessary to look at his conduct as a whole. Does this indicate an intention to abandon and to refuse performance of the contract? In the present case, without taking Wimpey's conduct generally into account, Woodar's contention, that Wimpey had repudiated, would be a difficult one. So far from repudiating the contract, Wimpey were relying on it and invoking one of its provisions, to which both parties had given their consent. And unless the invocation of that provision were totally abusive, or lacking in good faith (neither of which is contended for), the fact that it has proved to be wrong in law cannot turn it into a repudiation. At the lowest, the notice of rescission was a neutral document consistent either with an intention to preserve, or with an intention to abandon, the contract, and I will deal with it on this basis, more favourable to Woodar. In order to decide which is correct Wimpey's conduct has to be examined . . .

The facts indicative of Wimpey's intention must now be summarised. It is clear in the first place that, subjectively, Wimpey in 1974 wanted to get out of the contract. Land prices had fallen, and they thought that if the contract was dissolved, they could probably acquire it at a much lower price. But subjective intention is not decisive: it supplied the motive for serving the notice of rescission; there remains the question whether, objectively regarded, their conduct showed an intention to abandon the contract.

. . . Wimpey's advisers arranged a meeting with a Mr Cornwell, who was acting for Woodar . . . to discuss the matter. This took place on 7th March 1974 and is recorded as a disclosed *aide memoire* dated the next day . . . After recording each side's statement of position, the document contained, *inter alia*, these passages: "He [Mr Cornwell] stated that if we attempted to rescind the contract, then he would take us to court and let the judge decide whether the contract could be rescinded on the point we were making" . . . The *aide memoire* continues:

> "I told him that our Legal Department would be serving the Notice to Rescind the Contract within a short while – this would ensure that the company was fully protected and was prudent. He assured me that he would accept it on that basis and not regard it as a hostile act."

The notice was then served on 20th March 1974. On 22nd March Woodar's solicitors wrote that they did not accept its validity. On 30th May 1974 Mr Cornwell wrote a long letter to Sir Godfrey Mitchell, president of Wimpey. I refer to one passage:

> ". . . within a few days of the original meeting, a notice of rescission was served upon the vendor company by your organisation that the contract was to be rescinded. Simultaneously with that notice of rescission, proceedings were instituted and there the matter remains so far as the legal situation is concerned and both parties, from the legal point of view, must now await the decision of the court as to the validity of the claim made by Messrs George Wimpey & Co Limited that they are entitled to rescind this contract upon the grounds which they have so stated."

On 4th June 1974 Mr Cornwell wrote again: "All I need say now is that we will retire to our battle stations and it goes without saying I am sure that you will abide by the result as I will."

My Lords, I cannot find anything which carries the matter one inch beyond, on Wimpey's part an expressed reliance on the contract, . . . on Woodar's side an intention to take the issue of the validity of the notice (nothing else) to the courts, and an assumption, not disputed by Wimpey, that both sides would abide by the decision of the court. This is quite insufficient to support the case for repudiation . . .

My Lords, in my opinion, it follows, as a clear conclusion of fact, that Wimpey manifested no intention to abandon, or to refuse future performance of, or to repudiate the contract. And the issue being one of fact, citation of other decided cases on other facts is hardly necessary. I shall simply state that the proposition that a party who takes action relying simply on the terms of the contract and not manifesting by his conduct an ulterior intention to abandon it is not to be treated as repudiating it . . .

In my opinion, therefore, Wimpey are entitled to succeed on the repudiation issue, and I would only add that it would be a regrettable development of the law of contract to hold that a party who *bona fide* relies on an express stipulation in a contract in order to rescind or terminate a contract should, by that fact alone, be treated as having repudiated his contractual obligations if he turns out to be mistaken as to his rights. Repudiation is a drastic conclusion which should only be held to arise in clear cases of a refusal, in a matter going to the root of the contract, to perform contractual obligations. To uphold Woodar's contentions in this case would represent an undesirable contention of the doctrine.'

Vaswani v *Italian Motors (Sales and Services) Ltd*

[1996] 1 WLR 270 • Privy Council

In May 1989 Vaswani agreed to buy a Ferrari Testarossa from Italian Motors for £179 500 and paid a 25% deposit of £44 875. When the car was ready for delivery in June 1990 the price of the car had increased to £218 800. Italian Motors requested Vaswani to pay the balance of the price based on the new price. This they claimed they were entitled to do under the terms of the contract. Vaswani was reluctant to pay and on 6 July Italian Motors gave notice to Vaswani that unless he paid the balance by 10 July they would treat the contract as at an end and that his deposit would be forfeited. On 10 July, the balance still not having been paid, Italian Motors forfeited the deposit.

The Privy Council having decided that on the proper construction of the contract Italian Motors were not entitled to demand the increased price the issue was whether Italian Motors had repudiated the contract by demanding the increased price.

Lord Woolf: *The repudiation issue*

'. . . There are here features of this case which make this issue by no means straightforward. There is the fact that the sellers were acting *bona fide* in seeking the higher price . . . The other feature is that it appears to be reasonably clear that even if the sellers had demanded the correct balance of the purchase price this would not have been paid by the buyer . . .

If the sellers had demanded the payment of the correct sum then they would have had the right to forfeit the deposit and resell the car. The sellers having demanded a sum in excess of that due their primary argument is based on the proposition that it does not amount to a repudiation of a contract to assert a genuinely held but erroneous view as to the effect of the contract. That this can be the position is good sense and already subject to considerable judicial support. The position is accurately set out by Lord Wilberforce in *Woodar Investment Development Ltd* v *Wimpey Construction UK Ltd*, where he also warned that: "Repudiation is a drastic conclusion which should only be held to arise in clear cases of a refusal, in a matter going to the root of the contract, to perform contractual obligations".

While therefore here the request for the payment of an excessive price would not in itself amount to a repudiation, if the conduct relied on went beyond the assertion of a genuinely held view of the effect of the contract the conduct could amount to a repudiation. This is the position if the conduct is inconsistent with the continuance of the contract. Then the *bona fide* motives of the party responsible do not prevent the conduct being repudiatory. Again the position is clearly expressed by Lord Wilberforce, this time in a case concerning a charterparty, *Federal Commerce & Navigation Co Ltd* v *Molena Alpha Inc.* Lord Wilberforce, having described how the owners subjected the charterers to irresistible pressure to pay over sums of money that the charterers had deducted pending the outcome of an arbitration, states the position in these terms:

> "It is thirdly irrelevant that it was in the owners' real interest to continue the charters rather than to put an end to them. If a party's conduct is such as to amount to a threatened repudiatory breach, his subjective desire to maintain the contract cannot prevent the other party from drawing the consequences of his actions . . . They went, in fact, far beyond this when they threatened a breach of the contract with serious consequences."

Nor is conduct, if it is repudiatory, excused because it occurs in consequence of legal advice as may be the case with the sellers' actions in this case. The position is correctly set out by Lord Denning MR in the *Federal Commerce* case in the Court of Appeal in a passage of his judgment cited by Lord Scarman in *Woodar Investment Development Ltd* v *Wimpey Construction UK Ltd* which is in these terms:

> "I have yet to learn that a party who breaks a contract can excuse himself by saying that he did it on the advice of his lawyers: or that he was under an honest misapprehension . . . I would go by the principle . . . that if the party's conduct ' "contract" must be a misprint' – objectively considered in its impact on the other party – is such as to evince an intention no longer to be bound by his contractual obligations, then it is open to the other party to accept his repudiation and treat the contract as discharged from that time onwards."

In this case while the sellers did indicate to the buyer that he should pay a sum which was excessive or the deposit would be forfeited they never went so far as to indicate to the buyer that it would be purposeless to pay the correct sum as required by condition 8. This was not therefore a case like the *Norway*, where the sellers had made it clear that it was pointless to tender a lesser sum. All they had done was to put forward their calculation which had gone unchallenged. There was nothing to prevent the buyer paying the sum he calculated was due. Until he at least tendered the sum he considered was due the sellers were not required to deliver the vehicle. However in fact the buyer never called for delivery by the sellers. This was no doubt because he had made no further payment and never intended to attempt to test their willingness to deliver. The sellers did not threaten "a breach of the contract with serious consequences" as in *Federal Commerce & Navigation Co Ltd* v *Molena Alpha Inc* and there was no conduct by them which was totally inconsistent with the continuance of the contract until after the buyer had made it clear that he was not going to make any further payment. This being the situation their Lordships are of the opinion the sellers did not repudiate the contract.'

Renunciation before performance due – (anticipatory breach)

NB: anticipatory breach does not automatically bring a contract to an end.

Parties to a wholly executory contract have a right to the maintenance of the contractual relation right up to the time of performance, as well as to the performance of the contract when due.

If the injured party does not *accept* the renunciation and insists on the defaulter performing the contract he loses his right to rely on the anticipatory breach.

Fercometal SARL v *Mediterranean Shipping Co SA*; *The Simona*

[1988] 2 All ER 742 • House of Lords

Mediterranean Shipping chartered a ship, the *Simona*, to Fercometal for the carriage of steel from Durban to Bilbao. Clause 10 of the charterparty provided 'Should the vessel not be ready to load . . . on or before the [9 July], Charterers have the option of cancelling this contract . . . ' On 2 July Fercometal wrongfully repudiated the charter and chartered another ship, the *Leo Tornado*, from another company. Mediterranean Shipping refused to accept Fercometal's repudiation. On 5 July Mediterranean Shipping informed Fercometal that the *Simona* would be ready to load on 8 July. In fact the *Simona* was not ready to load on 9 July which meant that Mediterranean Shipping were in breach of the charterparty; Fercometal therefore cancelled the contract and loaded their steel onto the *Leo Tornado*. Mediterranean Shipping sued Fercometal for its repudiatory breach. Mediterranean Shipping argued that Fercometal's earlier breach excused them from complying with their obligation to provide a ship that was ready to load on 9 July.

The issue before the House of Lords was what was the effect of Fercometal's repudiation of 2 July.

Lord Ackner: *The effect of a repudiation*

'The earlier authorities, when faced with a wrongful neglect or refusal, were concerned to absolve the "innocent party" from the need to render useless performance, which the repudiating buyer had indicated he no longer wanted. In *Jones* v *Barkley* one finds the seeds of the later doctrine of accepted anticipatory breach. Lord Mansfield CJ said:

> "One need only state what the agreement, tender, and discharge, were, as set forth in the declaration. It charges, that the plaintiffs offered to assign, and to execute and deliver a general release, and tendered a draft of an assignment and release, and offered to execute and deliver such assignment, but the defendant absolutely discharged them from executing the same, *or any assignment and release whatsoever*. The defendant pleads, that the plaintiff did not actually execute an assignment and release and the question is, whether there was a sufficient performance. Take it on the reason of the thing. The party must shew he was ready but, if the other stops him on the ground of an intention not to perform his part, it is not necessary for the first to go farther, and do a nugatory act." (Lord Mansfield CJ's emphasis.)

In *Cort and Gee* v *Ambergate Nottingham and Boston and Eastern Junction Rly Co* the plaintiffs agreed to manufacture a quantity of iron chairs for the defendant's railway. The defendant, having accepted some of the chairs, informed the plaintiffs that it had as many chairs as it required and that no further chairs would be accepted. The plaintiffs thereupon treated themselves as discharged from all further obligations and commenced proceedings against the defendant for wrongfully refusing to accept the chairs. They pleaded that from the time of making of the contract until the defendant's refusal they were ready and willing to perform their obligations, but that they had been discharged from further performance of the contract by the defendant's repudiation. The defendant denied that an oral renunciation prior to the time for performance excused the plaintiffs from the need to show that they were ready and willing to perform at the time set for performance. Thus, the question was: what sort of readiness and willingness (if any) does a plaintiff have to show in order to maintain an action for wrongful repudiation? It was held that the plaintiffs' averment was sufficient and Lord Campbell CJ said:

"In common sense the meaning of such an averment of *readiness and willingness* must be that noncompletion of the contract was not the fault of the plaintiffs, and that they were disposed and able to complete it if it had not been renounced by the defendants." (Lord Campbell CJ's emphasis.)

The above case and some of the earlier ones were considered in *Hochster* v *De la Tour*, where a courier sued his employer who had written in before the time for performance had arrived that his services were no longer required. This was a clear anticipatory breach since, before the time had arrived at which the defendant was bound to perform his contractual obligation, he had evinced an intention no longer to be bound by his contractual obligations. At the conclusion of his judgment Lord Campbell CJ said:

"If it should be held that, upon a contract to do an act on a future day, a renunciation of the contract by one party dispenses with a condition to be performed in the meantime by the other, there seems no reason for requiring that other to wait till the day arrives before seeking his remedy by action: and the only ground on which the condition can be dispensed with seems to be, that the renunciation may be treated as a breach of the contract."

Frost v *Knight* was a case of a breach of promise to marry the plaintiff as soon as his (the defendant's) father should die. During the father's lifetime the defendant refused absolutely to marry the plaintiff and the plaintiff sued him, his father still being alive. When the case was argued before the Court of Exchequer Kelly CB concluded that there could be no actual breach of a contract by reason of non-performance so long as the time for the performance had not yet arrived. On appeal to the Exchequer Chamber Cockburn CJ said:

"The promisee has an inchoate right to the performance of the bargain, which becomes complete when the time for performance has arrived. In the mean time he has the right to have the contract kept open as a subsisting and effective contract. Its unimpaired and unimpeached efficacy may be essential to his interests. His rights acquired under it may be dealt with by him in various ways for his benefit and advantage. Of all such advantage the repudiation of the contract by the other party, and the announcement that it never will be fulfilled, must of course deprive him. It is therefore quite right to hold that such an announcement amounts to a violation of the contract in omnibus, and that upon it the promisee, if so minded, may at once treat it as a breach of the entire contract, and bring his action accordingly."

The innocent party's option

When one party wrongly refuses to perform obligations, this will not automatically bring the contract to an end. The innocent party has an option. He may either accept the wrongful repudiation as determining the contract and sue for damages or he may ignore or reject the attempt to determine the contract and affirm its continued existence. Cockburn CJ in *Frost* v *Knight* put the matter thus:

"The law with reference to a contract to be performed at a future time, where the party bound to performance announces prior to the time his intention not to perform it, as established by the cases of *Hochster* v *De la Tour* and *The Danube and Black Sea Co* v *Xenos* on the one hand, and *Avery* v *Bowden*, *Reid* v *Hoskins*, and *Barwick* v *Buba* on the other, may be thus stated. The promisee, if he pleases, may treat the notice of intention as inoperative, and await the time when the contract is to be executed, and then hold the other party responsible for all the consequences of non-performance: but in that case he keeps the contract alive for the benefit of the other party as well as his own he remains subject to all his own obligations and liabilities under it, and enables the other party not only to complete the contract, if so advised, notwithstanding his previous repudiation of it, but also to take advantage of any supervening circumstance which would justify him in declining to complete it. On the other hand, the promisee may, if he thinks proper, treat the repudiation of the other party as a wrongful putting an end to the contract, and may at once bring his action as on a breach of it and in such action he will be entitled to such damages as would have arisen from the non-performance of the contract at the appointed time, subject, however, to abatement in respect of any circumstances which may have afforded him the means of mitigating his loss."

This passage was adopted by Cotton LJ in *Johnstone* v *Milling* (1886). In that case Lord Esher MR described the situation thus:

". . . a renunciation of a contract, or, in other words, a total refusal to perform it by one party before the time for performance arrives, does not, by itself, amount to a breach of contract but may be so acted upon and adopted by the other party as a rescission of a contract as to give an immediate right of action. When one party assumes to renounce the contract, that is, by anticipation refuses to perform it, he thereby, so far as he is concerned, declares his intention then and there to rescind the contract . . . The other party may adopt such renunciation of the contract by so acting upon it as in effect to declare that he too treats the contract as at an end, except for the purpose of bringing an action upon it for the damages sustained by him in consequence of such renunciation."

The way in which a "supervening circumstance" may turn out to be to the advantage of the party in default, thus relieving him from liability, is illustrated by *Avery* v *Bowden*, where the outbreak of the Crimean war between England and Russia made performance of the charterparty no longer legally possible. The defendant, who prior to the outbreak of the war had in breach of contract refused to load, was provided with a good defence to an action for breach of contract, since his repudiation had been ignored. As pointed out by Parker LJ in his judgment, the law as stated in *Frost* v *Knight* and *Johnstone* v *Milling* has been reasserted in many cases since, and in particular in *Heyman* v *Darwins Ltd*, where Viscount Simon LC said:

"The first head of claim in the writ appears to be advanced on the view that an agreement is automatically terminated if one party 'repudiates' it. That is not so. As Scrutton LJ said in *Golding* v *London & Edinburgh Insurance Co, Ltd*: "I have never been able to understand what effect the repudiation by one party has unless the other accepts it". If one party so acts or so expresses himself, as to show that he does not mean to accept and discharge the obligations of a contract any further, the other party has an option as to the attitude he may take up. He may, notwithstanding the so-called repudiation, insist on holding his co-contractor to the bargain and continue to tender due performance on his part. In that event, the co-contractor *has the opportunity of withdrawing from his false position, and, even if he does not, may escape ultimate liability because of some supervening event not due to this own fault which excuses or puts an end to further performance.*" (Parker LJ's emphasis.)

If an unaccepted repudiation has no legal effect ("a thing writ in water and of no value to anybody": per Asquith LJ in *Howard* v *Pickford Tool Co Ltd*, how can the unaccepted acts of repudiation by the charterers in this case provide the owners with any cause of action?

It was accepted in the Court of Appeal by counsel then appearing for the owners that it was an inevitable inference from the findings made by the arbitrators that the *Simona* was not ready to load the charterers' steel at any time prior to the charterers' notice of cancellation on 12 July. Counsel who has appeared before your Lordships for the owners has not been able to depart from this concession. Applying the well-established principles set out above, the anticipatory breaches by the charterers not having been accepted by the owners as terminating the contract, the charterparty survived intact with the right of cancellation unaffected. The vessel was not ready to load by close of business on the cancelling date, viz 9 July, and the charterers were therefore entitled to and did give what on the face of it was an effective notice of cancellation.'

SUMMARY

You should now be able to:

- Understand that most contracts are satisfactorily performed without any problems.
- Distinguish between a *partial performance of an entire contract* and a *substantial performance*.
- Appreciate the significance of *time* in the performance of contracts.
- Distinguish between breaches of contract which entitle the innocent party to treat the contract as at an end and those breaches which only entitle the innocent party to damages.
- Appreciate that even if there is a breach of contract that entitles the innocent party to treat the contract as at an end the innocent party can choose to keep the contract alive.
- Recognise those breaches of contract that entitle the innocent party to treat the contract as at an end viz *renunciation, impossibility created by the contract breaker,* and *failure of performance*.
- Identify, and appreciate the significance of, *anticipatory breaches* of contract.

If you have not mastered the above points you should go through this section again.

16 Discharge by frustration

INTRODUCTION

Frustration discharges a contract where a change of circumstances renders the contract legally or physically impossible of performance.

The important point to remember about frustration is that if a frustrating event occurs, that event itself, without any action by either or both of the parties to a contract, discharges the contract, that is brings it to an end.

In commercial contracts the parties to a contract usually expressly provide against the risk of frustrating events by inserting a *force majeure* clause into the contract. In the absence of such a clause the courts will often imply such a clause into the contract.

Taylor v *Caldwell*

(1863) B&S 826 • Queen's Bench

The facts are stated in the judgment of Blackburn J.

Blackburn J: 'In this case the plaintiffs and defendants had, on the 27th May, 1861, entered into a contract by which the defendants agreed to let the plaintiff have the use of The Surrey Gardens and Music Hall on four days then to come, viz., the 17th June, 15th July, 5th August and 19th August, for the purpose of giving a series of four grand concerts, and day and night fetes at the Gardens and Hall on those days respectively; and the plaintiffs agreed to take the Gardens and Hall on those days and pay 100l. for each day.

. . . The agreement then proceeds to set out various stipulations between the parties as to what each was to supply for these concerts and entertainments, and as to the manner in which they should be carried on. The effect of the whole is to shew that the existence of the Music Hall in the Surrey Gardens in a state fit for a concert was essential for the fulfilment of the contract – such entertainment as the parties contemplated in their agreement could not be given without it.

After the making of the agreement, and before the first day on which a concert was to be given the Hall was destroyed by fire. This destruction, we must take it on the evidence, was without the fault of either party, and was so complete that in consequence the concerts could not be given as intended. And the question we have to decide is whether, under these circumstances, the loss which the plaintiffs have sustained is to fall upon the defendants. The parties when framing their agreement evidently had not present to their minds the possibility of such a disaster, and have made no express stipulation with reference to it, so that the answer to the question must depend upon the general rules of law applicable to such a contract.

There seems no doubt that where there is a positive contract to do a thing, not in itself unlawful, the contractor must perform it or pay damages for not doing it although in consequence of unforeseen accidents, the performance of his contract has become unexpectedly burthensome or even impossible . . . But this rule is only applicable when the contract is positive and absolute, and not subject to any condition either express or implied: and there are authorities which, as we think, establish the principle that where, from the nature of the contract, it appears that the parties must from the beginning have known that it could not be fulfilled unless when the time for the fulfilment of the contract arrived some particular specified thing continued to exist, so that, when entering into the contract, they must have contemplated such continuing existence as the foundation of what was to be done; there, in the absence of any express or implied warranty that the thing shall exist, the contract is not to be construed as a positive contract but as subject to an implied condition that the parties shall be excused in case, before breach, performance becomes impossible from the perishing of the thing without default of the contractor.

There seems to be little doubt that this implication tends to further the great object of making the legal construction such as to fulfil the intention of those who entered into the contract. For in the course of affairs men in making such contracts in general would, if it were brought to their minds, say that there should be such a condition . . .

There is a class of contracts in which a person binds himself to do something which requires to be performed by him in person and such promises e.g. promises to marry, or promises to serve for a certain time, are never in practice qualified by an express exception of the death of the party; and therefore in such cases the contract is in terms broken if the promisor dies before fulfilment. Yet it was very early determined that, if the performance is personal, the executors are not liable; *Hyde* v *The Dean of Windsor* . . . where a very apt illustration is given. "Thus," says the learned author, "if an author undertakes to compose a work, and dies before completing it, his executors are discharged from this contract: for the undertaking is merely personal in its nature, and by the intervention of the contractor's death, has become impossible to be performed. For this he cites a dictum of Lord Lyndhurst in *Marshall* v *Broadhurst*, and a case mentioned by Patteson J in *Wentworth* v *Cock*. In *Hall* v *Wright*, Crompton J, in his judgment, puts another case. Where a contract depends upon personal skill and the act of God renders it impossible, as, for instance, in the case of a painter employed to paint a picture who is struck blind, it may be that the performance might be excused".

It seems that in those cases the only ground on which the parties or their executors, can be excused from the consequences of the breach of the contract is that from the nature of the contract there is an implied condition of the continued existence of the life of the contractor, and, perhaps in the case of the painter of his eyesight . . .

. . . The principle seems to us to be that, in contracts in which the performance depends on the continued existence of a given person or thing, a condition is implied that the impossibility of performance arising from the perishing of the person or thing shall excuse the performance.

In none of these cases is the promise in words other than positive, nor is there any express stipulation that the destruction of the person or thing shall excuse the performance; but that excuse is by law implied, because from the nature of the contract it is apparent that the parties contracted on the basis of the continued existence of the particular person or chattel. In the present case, looking at the whole contract, we find that the parties contracted on the basis of the continued existence of the Music Hall at the time when the concerts were to be given; that being essential to their performance.

We think, therefore that the Music Hall having ceased to exist, without default of either party, both parties are excused, the plaintiffs from taking the gardens and paying the money, the defendants from performing their promise to give the use of the Hall and Gardens and other things . . .'

EXTENSION OF PRINCIPLE TO 'FRUSTRATION OF THE ADVENTURE' AS OPPOSED TO 'LITERAL IMPOSSIBILITY'

Jackson v Union Marine Insurance Co Ltd

(1874) 44 LJCP 27 • Exchequer Chamber

Jackson chartered a ship to Rathbone. Under the terms of the charter party the ship was 'to proceed with all convenient speed from Liverpool to Newport, and there load a cargo of iron rails for San Francisco'. Jackson insured himself with Union Marine Insurance against the possible loss of business with Rathbone. Before the ship got to Newport she ran aground and remained there for a considerable time. When she was eventually got off such time had elapsed that the charter party had come to an end in the commercial sense. Rathbone therefore abandoned his contract with Jackson and chartered another ship to carry his rails to San Francisco. Jackson then claimed under his policy of insurance for the loss of his business with Rathbone. The issue before the court was whether, under these circumstances, Rathbone was released from his contract to load under the charter party. If this was the case then there would have been a total loss of business within the meaning of the insurance policy.

Bramwell B: 'The first question in this case is, whether the plaintiff could have maintained an action against the charterers for not loading, for if he could, there certainly has not been a loss of the chartered freight by any of the perils insured against. In considering this question, the finding of the jury, that "the time necessary to get the ship off and repair her, so as to be a cargo carrying ship, was so long as to put an end in a commercial sense to the commercial speculation entered into by the shipowner and charterers" is all important. I do not think the question could have been left in better terms, but it may be paraphrased or amplified. I understand that the jury have found that the voyage the parties had contemplated had become impossible; that a voyage undertaken after the ship was sufficiently repaired would have been a different voyage; not, indeed, different as to the ports of loading and discharge, but different as a different adventure; a voyage for which, at the time of the charter, the plaintiff had not in intention engaged the ship, nor the charterers the cargo; a voyage as different as though it had been described as intended to be a spring voyage, while the one after the repair would be an autumn voyage. It is manifest that, if a definite voyage had been contracted for, and became impossible by perils of the seas, that that voyage would have been prevented, and the freight to be carried thereby would have been lost by the perils of the seas. The power which undoubtedly would exist to perform, say, an autumn voyage, in lieu of a spring voyage, *if both parties were willing*, would be a power to enter into a new agreement, and would no more prevent the loss of the spring voyage and its freight than would the power which would exist if both parties were willing to perform a voyage between different ports with a different cargo.

But the defendants say that here the contract was not to perform a definite voyage, but was at some and any future time, however distant, provided it was by no default in the shipowner and only postponed by perils of the seas, to carry a cargo of rails from Newport to San Francisco; that, no matter at what distance of time, at what loss to the shipowner, whatever might be the ship's engagements, however freights might have risen or seamen's wages, though the voyage, at the time when the ship was ready, might be twice as dangerous, and, possibly, twice as long, from fogs, ice and other perils, though war might have broken out meanwhile between the country to whose port she was to sail, and some other, still she was bound to take and had the right to demand the cargo of the shippers, who in like way had a right to have carried, and was bound to find, the agreed cargo, or, if that had been sent on already, a cargo of the same description, no matter at what loss to them, and however useless the transport of the goods might be to them. This is so inconvenient that, though fully impressed with the considerations so forcibly put by Mr Aspland, and retaining the opinion I expressed in *Tarrabochia* v *Hickie*, I think that, unless the rules of law prohibit it, we ought to hold the contrary.

The question turns on the construction and effect of the charter. By it the vessel is to sail to Newport with all possible despatch, perils of the seas excepted. It is said this constitutes the only agreement as to time, and provided all possible despatch is used, it matters not when she arrives at Newport. I am of a different opinion. If this charterparty be read as a charter for a definite voyage or adventure, then it follows that there is *necessarily* an implied condition that the ship shall arrive at Newport in time for it . . .

The two stipulations to use all possible despatch and arrive in time for the voyage are not repugnant, nor is either superfluous or useless. The shipowner, in the case put, expressly agrees to use all possible despatch; that is not a condition precedent, the sole remedy for and right consequent on the breach of it is an action. He also impliedly agrees that the ship shall arrive in time for the voyage; that is a condition precedent, as well as an agreement, and its non-performance not only gives the charterers a cause of action but also releases them. Of course if these stipulations, owing to excepted perils, are not performed there is no cause of action, but there is the same release of the charterers. The same reasoning would apply if the terms were, to "use all possible despatch, and further, and as a condition precedent, to be ready at the port of loading on June 1st". That reasoning also applies to the present case. If the charter party be read, as for a voyage or adventure not precisely defined by time or otherwise, but still for a particular voyage, arrival at Newport in time for it is necessarily a condition precedent. It seems to me it must be so read. I should say reason and good sense require it. The difficulty is supposed to be that there is some rule of law to the contrary. This I cannot see, and its seems to me that in this case the shipowner undertook to use all possible despatch to arrive at the port of loading, and also agreed that the ship should arrive "there at such a time that, in a commercial sense, the commercial speculation entered into by the shipowner and charterers should not be at an end but in existence". That latter agreement is also a condition precedent. Not arriving at such a time puts an end to the contract, though, as it arises from an excepted peril, it gives no cause of action. And the same result is arrived at by what is the same argument differently put. Where no time is named for the doing of anything the law attaches a reasonable time. Now, let us suppose this charter party had said nothing about arriving with all possible despatch. In that case, had the ship not arrived at Newport in a reasonable time, owing to the default of the shipowner, the charterers would have had a right of action against the owner, and would have had a right to withdraw from the contract. It is impossible to hold that in that case the owner would have a right to say, "I came a year after the time I might have come, because, meanwhile, I have been profitably employing my ship, you must load me, and bring your action for damages". The charterers would be discharged, because the implied condition to arrive in a reasonable time was not performed. Now, let us suppose the charter party contains, as here, that the ship shall arrive with all possible despatch. I ask again, is that so inconsistent with or repugnant to a further condition that, at all events, she shall arrive within a reasonable time? or is that so needless a condition that it is not to be implied? I say certainly not. I must repeat the foregoing reasoning. Let us suppose them both expressed, and it will be seen they are not inconsistent nor needless. Thus, "I will use all possible despatch to get the ship to Newport, but, at all events, she shall arrive in a reasonable time for the adventure contemplated". I hold, therefore, that the implied condition of a reasonable time exists in this charter party. Now, what is the effect of the exception of perils of the seas, and of delay being caused thereby? Suppose it was not there, and not implied, the shipowner would be subject to an action for not arriving in a reasonable time, and the charterers would be discharged . . .

The words are there, what is their effect? I think this: they excuse the shipowner, but give him no right. The charterers have no cause of action, but are released from the charter. Both, therefore, the shipowner and charterers are released. The condition precedent has not been performed but by default of neither . . . The exception is an excuse for him who is to do the act and operates to save him from an action and makes his non-performance not a breach of contract; but does not operate to take away the right the other party would have had if the non-performance had been a breach of contract to retire from the engagement, and if one party may, so may the other. Thus A, enters the service of B, and is ill and cannot perform his work. No action will lie against him; but B may hire a fresh servant, and not wait his recovery if his illness would put an end, in a business sense, to their business engagement, and would frustrate the object of that engagement. A short illness would not suffice if consistent with the object they had in view . . . There is then a condition precedent that the vessel shall arrive in a reasonable time. On failure of this the contract is at an end, and the charterer discharged, though he has no cause of action, as the failure arose from an excepted peril. The same result follows, then, whether the implied condition is treated as one that the vessel shall arrive in time for that adventure, or one that it shall arrive in a reasonable time, that time being in time for the adventure contemplated. And in either case, as in the express cases supposed, and in the analogous cases put, non-arrival and incapacity by that time ends the contract. The principle being that though non-performance of a condition may be excused, it does not take away the right reserved from him for whose benefit the condition was introduced. On these grounds I think that in reason, on principle, and for the convenience of both parties, it ought to be held in this case that the charterers were on the finding of the jury discharged.'

Examples of frustration

Destruction of subject-matter

The essential specific thing destroyed: see *Taylor* v *Caldwell* above (p 489).

Non-occurrence of a particular event

Krell v *Henry*

[1903] 2 KB 740 • Court of Appeal

Henry agreed to hire Krell's flat, which was in Pall Mall, on June 26 and 27 1902 for £75. Henry's purpose in hiring the flat on these two days was to view the coronation procession of the King; however, the contract of hire made no mention of this fact. Henry paid a deposit of £25. The procession was cancelled owing to the serious illness of the King. When Henry refused to carry out the contract Krell sued him for the outstanding £50. Henry claimed that the contract had been frustrated and counterclaimed for the return of his £25: he argued that the procession having been cancelled there had been a total failure of consideration.

Vaughan Williams LJ: 'The real question in this case is the extent of the application in English law of the principle of the Roman law which has been adopted and acted on in many English decisions, and notably in the case of *Taylor* v *Caldwell*. That case at least makes it clear that "where, from the nature of the contract, it appears that the parties must from the beginning have known that it could not be fulfilled unless, when the time for the fulfilment of the contract arrived, some particular specified thing continued to exist, so that when entering into the contract they must have contemplated such continued existence as the foundation of what was to be done; there, in the absence of any express or implied warranty that the thing shall exist, the contract is not to be considered a positive contract, but as subject to an implied condition that the parties shall be excused in case, before breach, performance becomes impossible from the perishing of the thing without default of the contractor". Thus far it is clear that the principle of the Roman law has been introduced into the English law. The doubt in the present case arises as to how far this principle extends . . . [T]he case of *Nickoll* v *Ashton* makes it plain that the English law applies the principle not only to cases where the performance of the contract becomes impossible by the cessation of existence of the thing which is the subject-matter of the contract, but also to cases where the event which renders the contract incapable of performance is the cessation or non-existence of an express condition or state of things, going to the root of the contract, and essential to its performance . . . I do not think that the principle of the civil law as introduced into the English law is limited to cases in which the event causing the impossibility of performance is the destruction or non- existence of some thing which is the subject-matter of the contract or of some condition or state of things expressly specified as a condition of it. I think that you first have to ascertain, not necessarily from the terms of the contract, but, if required, from necessary inferences, drawn from surrounding circumstances recognised by both contracting parties, what is the substance of the contract, and then to ask the question whether that substantial contract needs for its foundation the assumption of the existence of a particular state of things. If it does, this will limit the operation of the general words, and in such case, if the contract becomes impossible of performance by reason of the non-existence of the state of things assumed by both contracting parties as the foundation of the contract, there will be no breach of the contract thus limited. Now what are the facts of the present case? The contract is contained in two letters of June 20 which passed between the defendant and the plaintiff's agent, Mr Cecil Bisgood. These letters do not mention the coronation, but speak merely of the taking of Mr Krell's chambers, or, rather, of the use of them, in the daytime of June 26 and 27, for the sum of £75, £25 then paid, balance £50 to be paid on the 24th. But the affidavits, which by agreement between the parties are to be taken as stating the facts of the case, shew that the Plaintiff exhibited on his premises, third floor, 56A, Pall Mall, an announcement to the effect that windows to view the Royal coronation procession were to be let, and that the defendant was induced by that announcement to apply to the house-keeper on the premises, who said that the owner was willing to let the suite of rooms for the purpose of seeing the Royal procession for both days, but not nights, of June 26 and 27. In my judgment the use of the rooms was let and taken for the purpose of seeing the Royal procession. It was not a demise of the rooms, or even an agreement to let and take the rooms. It is a licence to use rooms for a particular purpose and none other. And in my judgment the taking place of those processions on the days proclaimed along the proclaimed route, which passed 56A, Pall Mall, was regarded by both contracting parties as the foundation of the contract; and I think that it cannot reasonably be supposed to have been in the contemplation of the contracting parties, when the contract was made, that the coronation would not be held on the proclaimed days, or the processions not take place on those days along the proclaimed route; and I think that the words imposing on the defendant the obligation to accept and pay for the use of the rooms for the named days, although general and unconditional, were not used with reference to the possibility of the particular contingency which afterwards occurred. It was suggested in the course of the argument that if the occurrence, on the proclaimed days, of the coronation and the procession in this case were the foundation of the contract, and if the general words are thereby limited or qualified, so that in the event of the non-occurrence of the coronation and procession along the proclaimed route they would discharge both parties from further performance of the contract, it would follow that if a cabman was engaged to take some-one to Epsom on Derby Day at a suitable enhanced price for such a journey, say £10, both parties to the contract would be discharged in the contingency of the race at Epsom for some reason becoming impossible; but I do not think this follows, for I do not think that in the cab case the happening of the race would be the foundation of the contract. No doubt the purpose of the engager would be to go to see the Derby, and the price would be proportionately high; but the cab had no special qualifications for the purpose which led to the selection of the cab for this particular occasion. Any other cab would have done as well. Moreover, I think that, under the cab contract, the hirer, even if the race went off, could have said, "Drive me to Epsom; I will pay you the agreed sum; you have nothing to do with the purpose for which I hired the cab", and that if the cabman refused he would have been guilty of a breach of contract, there being nothing to qualify his promise to drive the hirer to Epsom on a particular day. Whereas in the case of the coronation, there is not merely the purpose of the hirer to see the coronation procession, but it is the coronation procession and the relative position of the rooms which is the basis of the contract as much for the lessor as the hirer; and I think that if the King, before the coronation day and after the contract, had died, the hirer could not have insisted on having the rooms on the days named. It could not in the cab case be reasonably said that seeing the Derby race was the foundation of the contract, as it was of the licence in this case. Whereas in the present case, where the rooms were offered and taken, by reason of their peculiar suitability from the position of the rooms for a view of the coronation procession, surely the view of the coronation procession was the foundation of the contract, which is a very different thing from the purpose of the man who engaged the cab – namely, to see the race – being held to be the foundation of the contract. Each case must be judged by its own circumstances. In each case one must ask oneself, first, what, having regard to all the circumstances, was the foundation of the contract? Secondly, was the performance of the contract prevented? Thirdly, was the event which prevented the performance of the contract of such a character that it cannot reasonably be said to have been in the contemplation of the parties at the date of the contract? If all these questions are answered in the affirmative (as I think they should be in this case), I think both parties are discharged from further performance of the contract. I think that the coronation procession was the foundation of this contract, and that the non-happening of it prevented the performance of the contract; and, secondly, I think that the non-happening of the procession, to use the words of Sir James Hannen in *Baily* v *De Crespigny* was an event "of such a character that it cannot reasonably be supposed to have been in the contemplation of the contracting parties when the contract was made, and that they are not to be held bound by general words which, though large enough to include, were not used with reference to the possibility of the particular contingency which afterwards happened" . . . I myself am clearly of opinion that in this case, where we have to ask ourselves whether the object of the contract was frustrated by the non-happening of the coronation and its procession on the days proclaimed, parol evidence is admissible to shew that the subject of the contract was rooms to view the coronation procession, and was so to the knowledge of both parties. When once this is established, I see no difficulty whatever in the case. It is not essential to the application of the principle of *Taylor* v *Caldwell* that the direct subject of the contract should perish or fail to be in existence on the date of performance of the contract. It is sufficient if a state of things or condition expressed in the contract and essential to its performance perishes or fails to be in existence at that time. In the present case the condition which fails and prevents the achievement of that which was, in the contemplation of both parties, the foundation of the contract, is not expressly mentioned either as a condition of the contract or the purpose of it; but I think for the reasons which I have given that the principle of *Taylor* v *Caldwell* ought to be applied. This disposes of the plaintiff's claim for £50 unpaid balance of the price agreed to be paid for the use of the rooms.'

W J Tatem Ltd v *Gamboa*

[1939] 1 KB 132 • King's Bench

Tatem chartered the steamship *Molton* to Gamboa, who was an agent of the Republican Government of Spain, for thirty days from 1 July 1937 in order to help evacuate the 'civil population from North Spain'. The hire rate was £250 per day 'until her redelivery to the owners'. On 1 July 1937, the *Molton* was duly delivered to Gamboa at Santander. On 14 July she was seized by a Nationalist ship off Santander, taken to Bilbao, and kept in custody there until 7 September when she was released. She was redelivered to Tatem on 11 September. Gamboa had paid in advance the agreed hire up to 31 July. On 18 August Gamboa wrote to Tatem declining to have any further concern with the ship. Tatem then commenced proceedings claiming payment of hire at the rate of £250 a day from 1 August until 11 September. Gamboa denied liability on the ground that the adventure had been frustrated by the seizure of the ship.

Goddard J: 'It is said on behalf of the defendant that so soon as this ship was seized there was a frustration of the contract and that the contract became impossible of performance as from that date, and, therefore, that all rights and liabilities under the contract ceased. He admits that he cannot reclaim any part of the hire he paid in advance, but contends that he is not liable to pay any further additional hire, that is to say, for the time during which the ship was in the hands of the insurgents. Sir Robert Aske, on the other hand, has argued very strongly that the enterprise in this case cannot be said to have been frustrated, because both sides must be taken to have contemplated when they made this contract that the ship might be seized – indeed, that the risk of seizure was plain and obvious to everybody – and that it must be taken that that was one of the risks which the ship was running . . .

I will assume that the parties contemplated that the ship might be seized and detained as she was. It is difficult to reconcile all the judgments and speeches which have been made on this difficult subject of frustration, which was very little discussed in the books before the war . . . Viscount Finlay said . . . in *Larrinaga & Co, Ltd* v *Société Franco Americaine des Phosphates de Médulla, Paris*: "When certain risks are foreseen the contract may contain conditions providing that in certain events the obligation shall cease to exist. But even when there is no express condition in the contract, it may be clear that the parties contracted on the basis of the continued existence of a certain state of facts, and it is with reference to cases alleged to be of this kind that the doctrine of 'frustration' is most frequently invoked. If the contract be one which for its performance depends on the continued existence of certain buildings or other premises, it is an implied condition that the premises should continue to be in existence, and their total destruction by fire without fault on the part of those who have entered into the contract will be a good defence. Such a contract does not as a matter of law imply a warranty that the buildings or other property shall continue to exist."

Sir Robert Aske meets this point by saying there cannot be frustration where the circumstances must have been contemplated by the parties. By "circumstances" I mean circumstances which are afterwards relied on as frustrating the contract. It is true that in many of the cases there is found the expression "unforeseen circumstances", and it is argued that "unforeseen circumstances" must mean circumstances which could not have been foreseen. But it seems to me, with respect, that, if the true doctrine be that laid down by Lord Haldane, frustration depends on the absolute disappearance of the contract; or, if the true basis be, as Lord Finlay put it, "the continued existence of a certain state of facts", it makes very little difference whether the circumstances are foreseen or not. If the foundation of the contract goes, it goes whether or not the parties have made a provision for it. The parties may make provision about what is to happen in the event of this destruction taking place, but if the true foundation of the doctrine is that once the subject-matter of the contract is destroyed, or the existence of a certain state of facts has come to an end, the contract is at an end, that result follows whether or not the event causing it was contemplated by the parties. It seems to me, therefore, that when one uses the expression "unforeseen circumstances" in relation to the frustration of the performance of a contract one is really dealing with circumstances which are unprovided for, circumstances for which (and in the case of a written contract one only has to look at the document) the contract makes no provision.

In support of that I think I need only further refer to the words of Lord Haldane in the *Tamplin* case . . . I regard the learned Lord as saying there that, unless the contrary intention is made plain, the law imposes this doctrine of frustration in the events which have been described. If the foundation of the contract goes, either by the destruction of the subject-matter or by reason of such long interruption or delay that the performance is really in effect that of a different contract, and the parties have not provided what in that event is to happen, the performance of the contract is to be regarded as frustrated.

To the same effect, I think, are the cases which deal with this doctrine in relation to the requisitioning of ships. When the war had proceeded but a very short time the Admiralty Requisitioning Board was set up. Ships were requisitioned freely, and I suppose it is not putting it too high to say that no shipowner knew when his ship would be requisitioned. Accordingly, one finds, for instance, in *Bank Line, Ltd* v *Arthur Capel & Co* that the charterparty actually provided for requisition. It provided that the charterers were to have the option of cancelling the charterparty should the steamer be commandeered by the Government during the charter, and yet for reasons which appear in the speeches in the House of Lords it was held that it did not prevent the doctrine of frustration of performance applying. It seems to me that the parties must have had before them the possibility, or the probability if you will, of requisition every bit as much as the parties had of seizure in this case. I think, therefore, that that case and other cases . . . show in effect that, although the parties may have had or must be deemed to have had the matter in contemplation, the doctrine of frustration is not prevented from applying.

To apply the doctrine as I understand it to this case, what do we find? We find that there is a charter for a month only, a charter at a very high rate of freight. Although it is a time charter, the limits in which it is to trade are very narrow – from the northern ports in the hands of the Republican Government of Spain to ports in France – and the specific purpose of the charter is made plain. It is the evacuation of the civil population from north Spain. It must be obvious, therefore, that the foundation of that contract was destroyed as soon as the insurgent war vessel had seized the ship, which it did after it had performed one voyage and when the period of the charter had but half expired. No more could be done with the ship. The owners were unable to leave it under the control of the charterer. The charterer was unable to make use of it or to return it to the owners. The charterer had paid his month's hire, and that he not only cannot get back but does not seek to get back. In my opinion, the performance of the charter was frustrated from the time of the seizure, and consequently the reasoning of the cases to which I have referred applies . . .'

But such non-occurrence does not necessarily discharge the contract.

Herne Bay Steam Boat Co v Hutton

[1903] 2 KB 683 • Court of Appeal

Hutton agreed to hire a boat, the *Cynthia*, from the Herne Bay Steam Boat Co for £250. Hutton paid £50 deposit and agreed to pay the balance before he took possession of the ship. The agreement provided that the *Cynthia* would be at Hutton's disposal on June 28 and 29 to take passengers from Herne Bay "for the purpose of viewing the naval review and for a day's cruise round the fleet". On June 25 the review was officially cancelled although the fleet remained anchored at Spithead and was still at anchor on June 28 and 29. On hearing of the cancellation the Herne Bay Steam Boat Co wired to Hutton and requested payment of the remaining £200. Hutton did not reply. On June 28 and 29 the Herne Bay Steam Boat Co used their ship themselves. On June 29 Hutton informed the Herne Bay Steam Boat Co that since the review had been cancelled, he did not require the use of the ship, and that therefore he was not going to pay the balance of £200 nor was he going to have anything more to do with the agreement. The Herne Bay Steam Boat Co brought an action against Hutton to recover the balance of £200 less the profit they had made by using the *Cynthia* on June 28 and 29. Hutton claimed that his contract with the Herne Bay Steam Boat Co had been frustrated when the review was officially cancelled and counter-claimed for the £50 he had paid by way of deposit on the basis that there had been a total failure of consideration.

Vaughan Williams LJ: '. . . Mr Hutton, in hiring this vessel, had two objects in view: first, of taking people to see the naval review, and, secondly, of taking them round the fleet. Those, no doubt, were the purposes of Mr Hutton, but it does not seem to me that because, as it is said, those purposes became impossible, it would be a very legitimate inference that the happening of the naval review was contemplated by both parties as the basis and foundation of this contract, so as to bring the case within the doctrine of *Taylor* v *Caldwell*. On the contrary, when the contract is properly regarded, I think the purpose of Mr Hutton, whether of seeing the naval review or of going round the fleet with a party of paying guests, does not lay the foundation of the contract within the authorities.

Having expressed that view, I do not know that there is any advantage to be gained by going on in any way to define what are the circumstances which might or might not constitute the happening of a particular contingency as the foundation of a contract. I will content myself with saying this, that I see nothing that makes this contract differ from a case where, for instance, a person has engaged a brake to take himself and a party to Epsom to see the races there, but for some reason or other, such as the spread of an infectious disease, the races are postponed. In such a case it could not be said that he could be relieved of his bargain. So in the present case it is sufficient to say that the happening of the naval review was not the foundation of the contract.'

Romer LJ: '. . . In my opinion . . . it is a contract for the hiring of a ship by the defendant for a certain voyage, though having, no doubt, a special object, namely, to see the naval review and the fleet; but it appears to me that the object was a matter with which the defendant, as hirer of the ship, was alone concerned, and not the plaintiffs, the owners of the ship.

The case cannot, in my opinion, be distinguished in principle from many common cases in which, on the hiring of a ship, you find the objects of the hiring stated. Very often you find the details of the voyage stated with particularity, and also the nature and details of the cargo to be carried. If the voyage is intended to be one of pleasure, the object in view may also be stated, which is a matter that concerns the passengers. But this statement of the objects of the hirer of the ship would not, in my opinion, justify him in saying that the owner of the ship had those objects just as much in view as the hirer himself. The owner would say, "I have an interest in the ship as a passenger or cargo carrying machine, and I enter into the contract simply in that capacity; it is for the hirer to concern himself about the objects." . . .

The view I have expressed with regard to the general effect of the contract before us is borne out by the following considerations. The ship (as a ship) had nothing particular to do with the review or the fleet except as a convenient carrier of passengers to see it: any other ship suitable for carrying passengers would have done equally as well. Just as in the case of the hire of a cab or other vehicle, although the object of the hirer might be stated, that statement would not make the object any the less a matter for the hirer alone, and would not directly affect the person who was letting out the vehicle for hire. In the present case I may point out that it cannot be said that by reason of the failure to hold the naval review there was a total failure of consideration. That cannot be so. Nor is there anything like a total destruction of the subject-matter of the contract. Nor can we, in my opinion, imply in this contract any condition in favour of the defendant which would enable him to escape liability. A condition ought only to be implied in order to carry out the presumed intention of the parties, and I cannot ascertain any such presumed intention here. It follows that, in my opinion, so far as the plaintiffs are concerned, the objects of the passengers on this voyage with regard to sight-seeing do not form the subject-matter or essence of this contract . . .'

Stirling LJ: 'It is said that, by reason of the reference in the contract to the "naval review", the existence of the review formed the basis of the contract, and that as the review failed to take place the parties became discharged from the further performance of the contract, in accordance with the doctrine of *Taylor* v *Caldwell*. I am unable to arrive at that conclusion. It seems to me that the reference in the contract to the naval review is easily explained; it was inserted in order to define more exactly the nature of the voyage, and I am unable to treat it as being such a reference as to constitute the naval review the foundation of the contract as to entitle either party to the benefit of the doctrine in *Taylor* v *Caldwell*. I come to this conclusion the more readily because the object of the voyage is not limited to the naval review, but also extends to a cruise round the fleet. The fleet was there, and passengers might have been found willing to go round it. It is true that in the event which happened the object of the voyage became limited, but, in my opinion, that was the risk of the defendant whose venture the taking the passengers was.

For these reasons I am unable to agree with the learned judge in holding that in the contemplation of the parties the taking place of the review was the basis for the performance of the contract, and I think that the defendant is not discharged from its performance.'

Charterparties

Has the supervening event frustrated the object of both parties by so changing the circumstances that to hold the promisor to it would be to hold him to something which though not impossible, is something different from that which he originally promised to do?

F A Tamplin Steamship Co Ltd v *Anglo-Mexican Petroleum Products Co Ltd*

[1916] 2 AC 397 • House of Lords

The facts are stated in the judgment of Lord Loreburn. The issue before the court was whether a charterparty had been frustrated when the ship that was the subject of the charterparty was requisitioned for use by the government.

Earl Loreburn: '. . . This ship was chartered for five years. She was to be managed and controlled by the owners, but the use to be made of her in carrying merchandise within prescribed limitations depended upon the direction of the charterers. From December, 1912, till December, 1914, she was employed accordingly. From that date till the hearing of the case she has been employed by His Majesty's Government for purposes connected with the war. There are therefore nineteen months of the five years unexpired. No one knows how long the Government will continue to use this vessel, but, so long as they do use her, neither party to the contract can carry out their common adventure.

It may be as well to say that the first requisition of this ship was in December, 1914, and the second in February, 1915, but she was not released from the day she was first taken over.

In these circumstances the owners maintain that Mr Leck's award, holding that this charterparty came to an end when the steamer was requisitioned in February, 1915, is right.

In order to decide this question it is necessary to ascertain the principle of law which underlies the authorities. I believe it to be as follows: When a lawful contract has been made and there is no default, a Court of law has no power to discharge either party from the performance of it unless either the rights of someone else or some Act of Parliament give the necessary jurisdiction. But a Court can and ought to examine the contract and the circumstances in which it was made, not of course to vary, but only to explain it, in order to see whether or not from the nature of it the parties must have made their bargain on the footing that a particular thing or state of things would continue to exist. And if they must have done so, then a term to that effect will be implied, though it be not expressed in the contract. In applying this rule it is manifest that such a term can rarely be implied except where the discontinuance is such as to upset altogether the purpose of the contract. Some delay or some change is very common in all human affairs, and it cannot be supposed that any bargain has been made on the tacit condition that such a thing will not happen in any degree . . .

Applying the principle to the present case, I find that these contracting parties stipulated for the use of this ship during a period of five years, which would naturally cover the duration of many voyages. Certainly both sides expected that these years would be years of peace. They also expected, no doubt, that they would be left in joint control of the ship, as agreed, and that they would not be deprived of it by any act of State. But I cannot say that the continuance of peace or freedom from an interruption in their use of the vessel was a tacit condition of this contract. On the contrary, one at all events of the parties might probably have thought, if he thought of it at all, that war would enhance the value of the contract, and both would have been considerably surprised to be told that interruption for a few months was to release them both from a time charter that was to last five years. On the other hand, if the interruption can be pronounced, in the language of Lord Blackburn already cited, "so great and long as to make it unreasonable to require the parties to go on with the adventure", then it would be different. Both of them must have contracted on the footing that such an interruption as that would not take place, and I should imply a condition to that effect. Taking into account, however, all that has happened, I cannot infer that the interruption either has been or will be in this case such as makes it unreasonable to require the parties to go on. There may be many months during which this ship will be available for commercial purposes before the five years have expired. It might be a valuable right for the charterer during those months to have the use of this ship at the stipulated freight. Why should he be deprived of it? No one can say that he will or that he will not regain the use of the ship, for it depends upon contingencies which are incalculable. The owner will continue to receive the freight he bargained for so long as the contract entitles him to it, and if, during the time for which the charterer is entitled to the use of the ship, the owner received from the Government any sums of money for the use of her, he will be accountable to the charterer. Should the upshot of it all be loss to either party – and I do not suppose it will be so – then each will lose according as the action of the Crown has deprived either of the benefit he would otherwise have derived from the contract. It may be hard on them as it was on the plaintiff in *Appleby* v *Myers*. The violent interruption of a contract always may damage one or both of the contracting parties. Any interruption does so. Loss may arise to some one whether it be decided that these people are or that they are not still bound by the charterparty. But the test for answering that question is not the loss that either may sustain. It is this: Ought we to imply a condition in the contract that an interruption such as this shall excuse the parties from further performance of it? I think not. I think they took their chance of lesser interruptions, and the condition I should imply goes no further than that they should be excused if substantially the whole contract became impossible of performance, or in other words impracticable, by some cause for which neither was responsible. Accordingly I am of opinion that this charterparty did not come to an end when the steamer was requisitioned and that the requisition did not suspend it or affect the rights of the owners or charterers under it, and that the appeal fails.'

Tsakiroglou & Co Ltd v *Noblee & Thorl GmbH*

[1961] 2 All ER 179 • House of Lords

Tsakiroglou agreed to sell to Noblee 300 tons of Sudan groundnuts at £50 per ton cif Hamburg. This meant that the groundnuts had to be shipped from Port Sudan to Hamburg. The usual and normal route at the date of the contract was via Suez Canal. On the date that the groundnuts were to be shipped the Suez Canal was closed. This meant that in order to have carried out the contract Tsakiroglou would have had to send the goods via the Cape. The freight via Suez would have been about £7 10s per ton whereas the freight via the Cape was £15 per ton. Tsakiroglou refused to ship the goods via the Cape. Noblee responded by giving notice of their intention to buy groundnuts elsewhere. The issue before the court was whether the contract had been frustrated by reason of the closing of the Suez.

Lord Reid: 'The appellants' first argument was that it was an implied term of the contract that shipment should be via Suez. It is found in the Case that both parties contemplated that shipment would be by that route, but I find nothing in the contract or in the Case to indicate that they intended to make this a term of the contract, or that any such term should be implied; they left the matter to the ordinary rules of law. Admittedly, the ordinary rule is that a shipper must ship by the usual and customary route, or, if there is no such route, then by a practicable and reasonable route. But the appellants' next contention was that this means the usual and customary route at the date of the contract, while the respondents maintain that the rule refers to the time of performance . . . Regarding the question as an open one, I would ask which is the more reasonable interpretation of the rule.

. . . [I]f the rule is to ascertain the route at the time of performance, then the question whether the seller is still bound to ship the goods by the new route does depend on the circumstances as they affect him and the buyer; whether or not they are such as to infer frustration of the contract. That appears to me much more just and reasonable and, in my opinion, that should be held to be the proper interpretation of the rule.

I turn, then, to consider the position after the canal was closed, and to compare the rights and obligations of the parties thereafter, if the contract still bound them, with what their rights and obligations would have been if the canal had remained open. As regards the sellers, the appellants, the only difference to which I find reference in the Case – and, indeed, the only difference suggested in argument – was that they would have had to pay £15 per ton freight instead of £7 10s. They had no concern with the nature of the voyage. In other circumstances that might have affected the buyers, and it is necessary to consider the position of both parties because frustration operates without being invoked by either party and, if the market price of groundnuts had fallen instead of rising, it might have been the buyers who alleged frustration. There might be cases where damage to the goods was a likely result of the longer voyage which twice crossed the Equator, or, perhaps, the buyer could be prejudiced by the fact that the normal duration of the voyage via Suez was about three weeks, whereas the normal duration via the Cape was about seven weeks. But there is no suggestion in the Case that the longer voyage could damage the groundnuts or that the delay could have caused loss to these buyers of which they could complain. Counsel for the appellants rightly did not argue that this increase in the freight payable by the appellants was sufficient to frustrate the contract, and I need not, therefore, consider what the result might be if the increase had reached an astronomical figure. The route by the Cape was certainly practicable. There could be, on the findings in the Case, no objection to it by the buyers, and the only objection to it from the point of view of the sellers was that it cost them more. And it was not excluded by the contract. Where, then, is there any basis for frustration? It appears to me that the only possible way of reaching a conclusion that this contract was frustrated would be to concentrate on the altered nature of the voyage. I have no means of judging whether, looking at the matter from the point of view of a ship whose route from Port Sudan was altered from via Suez to via the Cape, the difference would be so radical as to involve frustration, and I express no opinion about that. As I understood the argument, it was based on the assumption that the voyage was the manner of performing the sellers' obligations and that, therefore, its nature was material. I do not think so. What the sellers had to do was simply to find a ship proceeding by what was a practicable and now a reasonable route – if, perhaps, not yet a usual route – to pay the freight and obtain a proper bill of lading, and to furnish the necessary documents to the buyer. That was their manner of performing their obligations, and, for the reasons which I have given, I think that such changes in these matters as were made necessary fell far short of justifying a finding of frustration . . .'

In *Jackson* v *Union Marine Insurance Co Ltd*, above (p 491), Bramwell B said that the delay must be such as 'to put an end in a commercial sense to the commercial speculation entered into by the [parties]'.

Building contracts

Delay itself insufficient to constitute frustration.

Davis Contractors Ltd v Fareham Urban District Council

[1956] 2 All ER 145 • House of Lords

In July 1946 Davis Contractors entered into a contract with Fareham UDC to build 78 houses in eight months for a fixed sum of £85 836. Because of a shortage of skilled labour and of certain materials the contract took 22 months to complete and cost Davis Contractors £115 000. Davis Contractors contended that the contract had been frustrated and that they were entitled to claim on a *quantum meruit* for the cost actually incurred.

Lord Reid: 'Frustration has often been said to depend on adding a term to the contract by implication: for example, Earl Loreburn in *F A Tamplin SS Co, Ltd* v *Anglo-Mexican Petroleum Products Co, Ltd*, after quoting language of Lord Blackburn, said:

> "That seems to me another way of saying that from the nature of the contract it cannot be supposed the parties, as reasonable men, intended it to be binding on them under such altered conditions. Were the altered conditions such that, had they thought of them, they would have taken their chance of them, or such that as sensible men they would have said 'if that happens, of course, it is all over between us'? What, in fact, was the true meaning of the contract? Since the parties have not provided for the contingency, ought a court to say it is obvious they would have treated the thing as at an end?"

I find great difficulty in accepting this as the correct approach, because it seems to me hard to account for certain decisions of this House in this way. I cannot think that a reasonable man in the position of the seaman in *Horlock* v *Beal* would readily have agreed that the wages payable to his wife should stop if his ship was caught in Germany at the outbreak of war, and I doubt whether the charterers in *Bank Line, Ltd* v *A Capel & Co* could have been said to be unreasonable if they had refused to agree to a term that the contract was to come to an end in the circumstances which occurred. These are not the only cases where I think it would be difficult to say that a reasonable man in the position of the party who opposes unsuccessfully a finding of frustration would certainly have agreed to an implied term bringing it about.

I may be allowed to note an example of the artificiality of the theory of an implied term given by Lord Sands in *Scott & Sons* v *Del Sel*:

> "A tiger has escaped from a travelling menagerie. The milkgirl fails to deliver the milk. Possibly the milkman may be exonerated from any breach of contract; but, even so, it would seem hardly reasonable to base that exoneration on the ground that 'tiger days excepted' must be held as if written into the milk contract."

I think that there is much force in Lord Wright's criticism in *Denny, Mott & Dickson, Ltd* v *James B Fraser & Co, Ltd*:

"The parties did not anticipate fully and completely, if at all, or provide for what actually happened. It is not possible to my mind to say that, if they had thought of it, they would have said, 'Well, if that happens, all is over between us'. On the contrary, they would almost certainly on the one side or the other have sought to introduce reservations or qualifications or compensations."

It appears to me that frustration depends, at least in most cases, not on adding any implied term but on the true construction of the terms which are, in the contract, read in light of the nature of the contract and of the relevant surrounding circumstances when the contract was made . . .

In a contract of this kind, the contractor undertakes to do the work for a definite sum, and he takes the risk of the cost being greater or less than he expected. If delays occur through no one's fault, that may be in the contemplation of the contract and there may be provision for extra time being given. To that extent, the other party takes the risk of delay. But he does not take the risk of the cost being increased by such delay. It may be that delay could be of a character so different from anything contemplated that the contract was at an end, but in this case, in my opinion, the most that could be said is that the delay was greater in degree than was to be expected. It was not caused by any new and unforeseeable factor or event; the job proved to be more onerous but it never became a job of a different kind from that contemplated in the contract.'

Lord Radcliffe: 'Before I refer to the facts, I must say briefly what I understand to be the legal principle of frustration. It is not always expressed in the same way, but I think that the points which are relevant to the decision of this case are really beyond dispute. The theory of frustration belongs to the law of contract and it is represented by a rule which the courts will apply in certain limited circumstances for the purpose of deciding that contractual obligations, *ex facie* binding, are no longer enforceable against the parties. The description of the circumstances that justify the application of the rule and, consequently, the decision whether, in a particular case, those circumstances exist are, I think, necessarily questions of law. It has often been pointed out that the descriptions vary from one case of high authority to another. Even as long ago as 1918, Lord Sumner was able to offer an anthology of different tests directed to the factor of delay alone, and delay, though itself a frequent cause of the principle of frustration being invoked, is only one instance of the kind of circumstance to which the law attends see *Bank Line, Ltd* v *A Capel & Co*. A full current anthology would need to be longer yet. But the variety of description is not of any importance, so long as it is recognised that each is only a description and that all are intended to express the same general idea. I do not think that there has been a better expression of that idea than the one offered by Earl Loreburn in *F A Tamplin SS Co, Ltd* v *Anglo-Mexican Petroleum Products Co, Ltd*. It is shorter to quote than to try to paraphrase it:

". . . a court can and ought to examine the contract and the circumstances in which it was made, not of course to vary, but only to explain it, in order to see whether or not from the nature of it the parties must have made their bargain on the footing that a particular thing or state of things would continue to exist. And if they must have done so, then a term to that effect will be implied, though it be not expressed in the contract . . . no court has an absolving power, but it can infer from the nature of the contract and the surrounding circumstances that a condition which is not expressed was a foundation on which the parties contracted."

So expressed, the principle of frustration, the origin of which seems to lie in the development of commercial law, is seen to be a branch of a wider principle which forms part of the English law of contract as a whole. But, in my opinion, full weight ought to be given to the requirement that the parties "must have made" their bargain on the particular footing. Frustration is not to be lightly invoked as the dissolvent of a contract.

Lord Loreburn ascribes the dissolution to an implied term of the contract that was actually made. This approach is in line with the tendency of English courts to refer all the consequences of a contract to the will of those who made it. But there is something of a logical difficulty in seeing how the parties could even impliedly have provided for something which, *ex hypothesi*, they neither expected nor foresaw; and the ascription of frustration to an implied term of the contract has been criticised as obscuring the true action of the court which consists in applying an objective rule of the law of contract to the contractual obligations that the parties have imposed on themselves. So long as each theory produces the same result as the other, as normally it does, it matters little which theory is avowed (see *British Movietonews, Ltd* v *London & District Cinemas, Ltd* per Viscount Simon). But it may still be of some importance to recall that, if the matter is to be approached by way of implied term, the solution of any particular case is not to be found by inquiring what the parties themselves would have agreed on had they been, as they were not, forewarned. It is not merely that no one can answer that hypothetical question; it is also that the decision must be given "irrespective of the individuals concerned, their temperaments and failings, their interest and circumstances" (*Hirji Mulji* v *Cheong Yue SS Co*). The legal effect of frustration "does not depend on their intention or their opinions, or even knowledge, as to the event". On the contrary, it seems that, when the event occurs, the

"meaning of the contract must be taken to be, not what the parties did intend (for they had neither thought nor intention regarding it), but that which the parties, as fair and reasonable men, would presumably have agreed upon if, having such possibility in view, they had made express provision as to their several rights and liabilities in the event of its occurrence . . . " (*Dahl* v *Nelson, Donkin & Co* per Lord Watson).

By this time, it might seem that the parties themselves have become so far disembodied spirits that their actual persons should be allowed to rest in peace. In their place there rises the figure of the fair and reasonable man. And the spokesman of the fair and reasonable man, who represents after all no more than the anthropomorphic conception of justice, is, and must be, the court itself. So, perhaps, it would be simpler to say at the outset that frustration occurs whenever the law recognises that, without default of either party, a contractual obligation has become incapable of being performed because the circumstances in which performance is called for would render it a thing radically different from that which was undertaken by the contract. *Non haec in foedera veni*. It was not this that I promised to do. There is, however, no uncertainty as to the materials on which the court must proceed.

"The data for decision are, on the one hand, the terms and construction of the contract, read in the light of the surrounding circumstances, and, on the other hand, the events which have occurred . . . " (*Denny, Mott & Dickson, Ltd* v *James B Fraser & Co, Ltd* per Lord Wright).

In the nature of things there is often no room for any elaborate inquiry. The court must act on a general impression of what its rule requires. It is for that reason that special importance is necessarily attached to the occurrence of any unexpected event that, as it were, changes the face of things. But, even so, it is not hardship or inconvenience or material loss itself which calls the principle of frustration into play. There must be as well such a change in the significance of the obligation that the thing undertaken would, if performed, be a different thing from that contracted for.

I am bound to say that, if this is the law, the appellants' case seems to me a long way from a case of frustration. Here is a building contract entered into by a housing authority and a big firm of contractors in all the uncertainties of the post-war world. Work was begun shortly before the formal contract was executed, and continued, with impediments and minor stoppages but without actual interruption, until the seventy-eight houses contracted for had all been built. After the work had been in progress for a time, the appellants raised the claim, which they repeated more than once, that they ought to be paid a larger sum for their work than the contract allowed; but the respondents refused to admit the claim and, so far as appears, no conclusive action was taken by either side which would make the conduct of one or the other a determining element in the case. That is not, in any obvious sense, a frustrated contract . . .'

LIMITATIONS ON THE DOCTRINE

Self-induced frustration

Maritime National Fish Ltd v Ocean Trawlers Ltd

[1935] AC 524 • Privy Council

The facts are stated in the judgment of Lord Wright. The issue before the court was whether the appellants could rely on their own 'self-induced' frustration.

Lord Wright: 'The appellants were charterers of a steam trawler the *St Cuthbert* which was the property of the respondents . . .

By letters dated July 6 and 8, 1932, exchanged between the appellants and respondents, it was agreed that the charterparty as then existing should be renewed for one year from October 25, 1932 . . .

When the parties entered into the new agreement in July, 1932, they were well aware of certain legislation . . . which in substance made it a punishable offence to leave or depart from any port in Canada with intent to fish with a vessel that uses an otter or other similar trawl for catching fish, except under licence from the Minister . . .

The *St Cuthbert* was a vessel which was fitted with, and could only operate as a trawler with an otter trawl.

The appellants, in addition to the *St Cuthbert*, also operated four other trawlers, all fitted with otter trawling gear.

On March 11, 1933, the appellants applied to the Minister of Fisheries for licences for the trawlers they were operating . . . but on April 5, 1933, the Acting Minister replied that it had been decided . . . that licences were only to be granted to three of the five trawlers operated by the appellants: he accordingly requested the appellants to advise the Department for which three of the five trawlers they desired to have licences. The appellants thereupon gave the names of three trawlers other than the *St Cuthbert*, and for these three trawlers licences were issued, but no licence was granted for the *St Cuthbert*. In consequence, as from April 30, 1933, it was no longer lawful for the appellants to employ the *St Cuthbert* as a trawler in their business. On May, 1 1933, the appellants gave notice that the *St Cuthbert* was available for re-delivery to the respondents; they claimed that they were no longer bound by the charter.

On June 19, 1933, the respondents commenced their action claiming $590.97 as being hire due under the charter for the month ending May 25, 1933 . . .

The main defence was that through no fault, act or omission on the part of the appellants, the charterparty contract became impossible of performance on and after April 30, 1933, and thereupon the appellants were wholly relieved and discharged from the contract, including all obligations to pay the monthly hire which was stipulated.

. . . [The Supreme Court of Nova Scotia] thought that if there was frustration of the adventure, it resulted from the deliberate act of the appellants in selecting the three trawlers for which they desired licences to be issued

Their Lordships are of opinion that the latter ground is sufficient to determine this appeal. Great reliance was placed in the able argument of Mr Smith for the appellants on *Bank Line Ltd* v *Arthur Capel & Co*, and in particular on the judgment of Lord Sumner in that case. That case was in principle very different from this, because the vessel which was chartered in that case was actually taken from the control of the shipowners for a period such as to defeat the contemplated adventure: it was in consequence impossible during that time for the shipowners to place the vessel at the charterers' disposal at all. In the present case the *St Cuthbert* was not requisitioned: it remained in the respondents' control, who were able and willing to place it at the appellants' disposal: what happened was that the appellants could not employ the *St Cuthbert* for trawling with an otter trawl . . . This case is more analogous to such a case as *Krell* v *Henry*, where the contract was for the hire of a window for a particular day: it was not expressed but it was mutually understood that the hirers wanted the window in order to view the Coronation procession: when the procession was postponed by reason of the unexpected illness of King Edward, it was held that the contract was avoided by that event: the person who was letting the window was ready and willing to place it at the hirer's disposal on the agreed date; the hirer, however, could not use it for the purpose which he desired. It was held that the contract was dissolved, because the basis of the contract was that the procession should take place as contemplated. The correctness of that decision has been questioned, for instance, by Lord Finlay LC in *Larrinaga* v *Société Franco-Américaine des Phosphates*: Lord Finlay observes: "It may be that the parties contracted in the expectation that a particular event would happen, each taking his chance, but that the actual happening of the event was not made the basis of the contract."

The authority is certainly not one to be extended: it is particularly difficult to apply where, as in the present case, the possibility of the event relied on as constituting a frustration of the adventure (here the failure to obtain a licence) was known to both parties when the contract was made, but the contract entered into was absolute in terms so far as concerned that known possibility. It may be asked whether in such causes there is any reason to throw the loss on those who have undertaken to place the thing or service for which the contract provides at the other parties' disposal and are able and willing to do so. In *Hirji Mulji* v *Cheong, Yue Steamship Co* Lord Sumner speaks of frustration as "a device, by which the rules as to absolute contracts are reconciled with a special exception which justice demands". In a case such as the present it may be questioned whether the Court should imply a condition resolutive of the contract (which is what is involved in frustration) when the parties might have inserted an express condition to that effect but did not do so, though the possibility that things might happen as they did, was present in their minds when they made the contract.

This was one of the grounds on which the judges of the Supreme Court were prepared to decide this case. Their Lordships do not indicate any dissent from the reasoning of the Supreme Court on this point, but they did not consider it necessary to hear a full argument, or to express any final opinion about it, because in their judgment the case could be properly decided on the simple conclusion that it was the act and election of the appellants which prevented the *St Cuthbert* from being licensed for fishing with an otter trawl. It is clear that the appellants were free to select any three of the five trawlers they were operating and could, had they willed, have selected the *St Cuthbert* as one, in which event a licence would have been granted to her. It is immaterial to speculate why they preferred to put forward for licences the three trawlers which they actually selected. Nor is it material, as between the appellants and the respondents, that the appellants were operating other trawlers to three of which they gave the preference. What matters is that they could have got a licence for the *St Cuthbert* if they had so minded. If the case be figured as one in which the *St Cuthbert* was removed from the category of privileged trawlers, it was by the appellants' hand that she was so removed, because it was their hand that guided the hand of the Minister in placing the licences where he did and thereby excluding the *St Cuthbert*. The essence of "frustration" is that it should not be due to the act or election of the party. There does not appear to be any authority which has been decided directly on this point. There is, however, a reference to the question in the speech of Lord Sumner in *Bank Line Ltd* v *Arthur Capel & Co*. What he says is: "One matter I mention only to get rid of it. When the shipowners were first applied to by the Admiralty for a ship they named three, of which the *Quito* was one and intimated that she was the one they preferred to give up. I think it is now well settled that the principle of frustration of an adventure assumes that the frustration arises without blame or fault on either side. Reliance cannot be placed on a self-induced frustration; indeed, such conduct might give the other party the option to treat the contract as repudiated. Nothing, however, was made of this in the courts below, and I will not now pursue it."

. . . [T]heir Lordships are of opinion that the loss of the *St Cuthbert*'s licence can correctly be described, *quoad* the appellants, as "a self induced frustration".'

J Lauritzen AS v *Wijsmuller BV, The Super Servant Two*

[1990] 1 Lloyds Rep 1 • Court of Appeal

Wijsmuller agreed to transport Lauritzen's drilling rig, the *Dan King*, from Japan to Rotterdam on one of their barges; either the *Super Servant One* or *Super Servant Two*. In fact, Wijsmuller intended to use the *Super Servant Two* to transport the *Dan King* because the *Super Servant One* was committed to other contracts. Before the *Dan King* was due to be carried the *Super Servant Two* sank. The issue before the court was whether the *Dan King* contract had been frustrated by the sinking of the *Super Servant Two*.

Bingham LJ: *Question 2: general* [Was the contract frustrated?]

'The argument in this case raises important issues on the English law of frustration. Before turning to the specific questions I think it helpful to summarise the established law so far as relevant to this case.

The classical statement of the modern law is that of Lord Radcliffe in *Davis Contractors Ltd* v *Fareham Urban District Council*,

". . . frustration occurs whenever the law recognises that without default of either party a contractual obligation has become incapable of being performed because the circumstances in which performance is called for would render it a thing radically different from that which was undertaken by the contract. *Non haec in foedera veni*. It was not this that I promised to do."

As Lord Reid observed in the same case:

". . . there is no need to consider what the parties thought or how they or reasonable men in their shoes would have dealt with the new situation if they had foreseen it. The question is whether the contract which they did make is, on its true construction, wide enough to apply to the new situation: if it is not, then it is at an end."

Certain propositions, established by the highest authority, are not open to question:

(1) The doctrine of frustration was evolved to mitigate the rigour of the common law's insistence on literal performance of absolute promises (*Hirji Mulji* v *Cheong Yue Steamship Co Ltd; Denny Mott and Dickson Ltd* v *James B Fraser & Co Ltd; Joseph Constantine Steamship Line Ltd* v *Imperial Smelting Corporation Ltd*). The object of the doctrine was to give effect to the demands of justice, to achieve a just and reasonable result, to do what is reasonable and fair, as an expedient to escape from injustice where such would result from enforcement of a contract in its literal terms after a significant change in circumstances (*Hirji Mulji; Joseph Constantine Steamship Line Ltd; National Carriers Ltd* v *Panalpina (Northern) Ltd*).

(2) Since the effect of frustration is to kill the contract and discharge the parties from further liability under it, the doctrine is not to be lightly invoked, must be kept within very narrow limits and ought not to be extended (*Bank Line Ltd* v *Arthur Capel & Co; Davis Contractors Ltd; Pioneer Shipping Ltd* v *BTP Tioxide Ltd (the Nema)*).

(3) Frustration brings the contract to an end forthwith, without more ado and automatically (*Hirji Mulji; Maritime National Fish Ltd* v *Ocean Trawlers Ltd; Joseph Constantine Steamship Line Ltd; Denny Mott & Dickson Ltd*).

(4) The essence of frustration is that it should not be due to the act or election of the party seeking to rely on it (*Hirji Mulji; Maritime National Fish Ltd; Joseph Constantine Steamship Ltd; Denny Mott & Dickson; Davis Contractors Ltd*). A frustrating event must be some outside event or extraneous change of situation (*Paal Wilson & Co A/S v Partenreederi Hannah Blumenthal (the Hannah Blumenthal)*).

(5) A frustrating event must take place without blame or fault on the side of the party seeking to rely on it (*Bank Line Ltd; Joseph Constantine Steamship Ltd; Davis Contractors Ltd supra; The Hannah Blumenthal*).

Question 2(a) [Was the contract frustrated (a) if the loss of the *Super Servant Two* occurred without the negligence of the Defendants their servants or agents?]

Mr Clarke for Wijsmuller submitted that the extraneous supervening event necessary to found a plea of frustration occurred when *Super Servant Two* sank on 29 Jan 1981. The *Dan King* contract was not, however, thereupon frustrated but remained alive until Wijsmuller decided a fortnight later that that contract could not be, or would not be, performed. There was, he submitted, factually, no break in the chain of causation between the supervening event and the non-performance of the contract. He acknowledged that *Maritime National Fish Ltd*, contained observations on their face inimical to his argument, but distinguished that as a decision on causation confined to its own peculiar facts and laying down no general rule. For authoritative support Mr Clarke relied on cases dealing with the application of *force majeure* clauses in commodity contracts, and in particular on an unreported judgment of Mr Justice Robert Goff, as he then was, adopted with approval by the Court of Appeal in *Bremer Handelsgesellschaft GmbH* v *Continental Grain Co*:

"... the question resolves itself into a question of causation; in my judgment, at least in a case in which a seller can (as in the present case) claim the protection of a clause which protects him where fulfilment is hindered by the excepted peril, subsequent delivery of his available stock to other customers will not be regarded as an independent cause of shortage, provided that in making such delivery the seller acted reasonably in all the circumstances of the case . . ."

A similar approach was reflected in other cases: see, for example, *Intertradex SA v Lesieur-Tourteaux SARL*, per Mr Justice Donaldson as he then was; per Lord Denning MR. Reliance was also placed on passages in *The Law of Contract* by Professor Treitel, which the Judge quoted in his judgment. Thus, Mr Clarke urged, this was a case in which Wijsmuller could not perform all their contracts once *Super Servant Two* was lost; they acted reasonably (as we must assume) in treating the *Dan King* contract as one they could not perform; so the sinking had the direct result of making that contract impossible to perform . . .

Had the *Dan King* contract provided for carriage by *Super Servant Two* with no alternative, and that vessel had been lost before the time for performance, then assuming no negligence by Wijsmuller (as for purposes of this question we must), I feel sure the contract would have been frustrated. The doctrine must avail a party who contracts to perform a contract of carriage with a vessel which, though no fault of his, no longer exists. But that is not this case. The *Dan King* contract did provide an alternative. When that contract was made one of the contracts eventually performed by *Super Servant One* during the period of contractual carriage of *Dan King* had been made, the other had not, at any rate finally. Wijsmuller have not alleged that when the *Dan King* contract was made either vessel was earmarked for its performance. That, no doubt, is why an option was contracted for. Had it been foreseen when the *Dan King* contract was made that *Super Servant Two* would be unavailable for performance, whether because she had been deliberately sold or accidentally sunk. Lauritzen at least would have thought it no matter since the carriage could be performed with the other. I accordingly accept Mr Legh-Jones' submission that the present case does not fall within the very limited class of cases in which the law will relieve one party from an absolute promise he has chosen to make.

But I also accept Mr Legh-Jones' submission that Wijsmuller's argument is subject to other fatal flaws. If, as was argued, the contract was frustrated when Wijsmuller made or communicated their decision on 16 Feb, it deprives language of all meaning to describe the contract as coming to an end automatically. It was, indeed, because the contract did not come to an end automatically on 29 Jan, that Wijsmuller needed a fortnight to review their schedules and their commercial options. I cannot, furthermore, reconcile Wijsmuller's argument with the reasoning or the decision in *Maritime National Fish Ltd supra*. In that case the Privy Council declined to speculate why the charterers selected three of the five vessels to be licensed but, as I understand the case, regarded the interposition of human choice after the allegedly frustrating event as fatal to the plea of frustration. If Wijsmuller are entitled to succeed here, I cannot see why the charterers lost there. The cases on frustrating delay do not, I think, help Wijsmuller since it is actual and prospective delay (whether or not recognised as frustrating by a party at the time) which frustrates the contract, not a party's election or decision to treat the delay as frustrating. I have no doubt that *force majeure* clauses are, where their terms permit, to be construed and applied as in the commodity cases on which Wijsmuller relied, but it is in my view inconsistent with the doctrine of frustration as previously understood on high authority that its application should depend on any decision, however reasonable and commercial, of the party seeking to rely on it . . .

Question 2(b) [(2) Was the contract frustrated (b) if the loss of the *Super Servant Two* was caused by the negligence of the Defendants their servants or agents?]

The issue between the parties was short and fundamental: what is meant by saying that a frustrating event, to be relied on, must occur without the fault or default, or without blame attaching to, the party relying on it?

Mr Clarke's answer was that a party was precluded from relying on an event only when he had acted deliberately or in breach of an actionable duty in causing it. Those conditions were not met here since it was not alleged Wijsmuller sank *Super Servant Two* deliberately and at the material time Wijsmuller owed Lauritzen no duty of care . . .

Wijsmuller's test would, in my judgment, confine the law in a legalistic strait-jacket and distract attention from the real question, which is whether the frustrating event relied upon is truly an outside event or extraneous change of situation or whether it is an event which the party seeking to rely on it had the means and opportunity to prevent but nevertheless caused or permitted to come about. A fine test of legal duty is inappropriate; what is needed is a pragmatic judgment whether a party seeking to rely on an event as discharging him from a contractual promise was himself responsible for the occurrence of that event.

Lauritzen have pleaded in some detail the grounds on which they say that *Super Servant Two* was lost as a result of the carelessness of Wijsmuller, their servants or agents. If those allegations are made good to any significant extent Wijsmuller would (even if my answer to Question 2(a) is wrong) be precluded from relying on their plea of frustration.'

EVENT MUST DEFEAT COMMON INTENTION OF THE PARTIES

Frustration cannot be one-sided.

Blackburn Bobbin Co Ltd v T W Allen & Sons Ltd

[1918] 2 KB 467 • Court of Appeal

The facts are stated in the judgment of Pickford LJ. The issue before the court was whether the outbreak of war had frustrated the contract.

Pickford LJ: '. . . [T]he point raised is whether an implication is to be read into the contract the performance of which has been interfered with or prevented by matters arising out of the war. The contract, which contained no exceptions, was for the sale by the defendants to the plaintiffs of 70 standards of Finland birch timber at the price of £10 15s per standard free on rail at Hull. Before the war it was the regular practice to load the timber on vessels at ports in Finland for direct sea carriage to English ports, and not to send it by rail across Scandinavia and ship it from a Scandinavian port to England. When war broke out the Germans declared timber to be contraband, but, even before that declaration, sailings from Finnish ports had entirely ceased, and therefore the ordinary and normal method of supplying Finland timber came to an end I will assume that it was not possible, at first at any rate, to get Finland birch timber to England at all, although it is true that in 1916 a certain amount was sent across Scandinavia and shipped from ports there. In August, 1914, and the following months some correspondence took place between the plaintiffs and the defendants as to the timber, the former asking for supplies, and the defendants talking up the position that all pre-war contracts had been cancelled by the war.

The defendants contend that the contract was at an end because it was in the contemplation of both parties that the defendants should be able to supply the timber according to the ordinary method of supplying it in the trade, and that when that became impossible both parties were discharged from their obligations. We have had a most interesting discussion of the numerous cases where this doctrine has been dealt with, and it is from no disrespect to Mr MacKinnon's argument that I refrain from going through them, but I refrain from doing so because I accept the principle for which those cases were cited. The principle was thus stated by Lord Haldane in *Tamplin Steamship Co* v *Anglo-Mexican Petroleum Products Co* : "The occurrence itself", i.e. the occurrence preventing the performance of the contract, "may yet be of a character and extent so sweeping that the foundation of what the parties are deemed to have had in contemplation has disappeared, and the contract itself has vanished with that foundation". It was also stated thus by Lord Shaw in *Horlock* v *Beal* : "The underlying ratio is the failure of something which was the basis of the contract in the mind and intention of the contracting parties". In my opinion McCardie J was right in saying that the principle of these cases did not apply to discharge the defendants in this case. He has found that the plaintiffs were unaware at the time of the contract of the circumstance that the timber from Finland was shipped direct from a Finnish port to Hull, and that they did not know whether the transport was or was not partly by rail across Scandinavia, nor did they know that timber merchants in this country did not hold stocks of Finnish birch. I accept the finding that in fact the method of dispatching this timber was not known to the plaintiffs. But there remains the question, must they be deemed to have contracted on the basis of the continuance of that method although they did not in fact know of it? I see no reason for saying so. Why should a purchaser of goods, not specific goods, be deemed to concern himself with the way in which the seller is going to fulfil his contract by providing the goods he has agreed to sell? The sellers in this case agreed to deliver the timber free on rail at Hull, and it was no concern of the buyers as to how the sellers intended to get the timber there. I can see no reason for saying and to free the defendants from liability this would have to be said – that the continuance of the normal mode of shipping the timber from Finland was a matter which both parties contemplated necessary for the fulfilment of the contract. To dissolve the contract the matter relied on must be something which both parties had in their minds when they entered into the contract, such for instance as the existence of the music-hall in *Taylor* v *Caldwell*, or the continuance of the vessel in readiness to perform the contract, as in *Jackson* v *Union Marine Insurance Co*. Here there is nothing to show that the plaintiffs contemplated, and there is no reason why they should be deemed to have contemplated, that the sellers should continue to have the ordinary facilities for dispatching the timber from Finland. As I have said, that was a matter which to the plaintiffs was wholly immaterial. It was not a matter forming the basis of the contract they entered into . . .

For the reasons I have given the defendants have failed on the facts to make out their case that the contract was dissolved. The appeal will be dismissed.'

EFFECTS OF FRUSTRATION
Contract determined automatically

Hirji Mulji v *Cheong Yue SS Co Ltd*
[1926] AC 497 • Privy Council

Lord Sumner: 'Language is occasionally used in the cases which seems to show that frustration is assimilated in the speaker's mind to repudiation or rescission of contracts. The analogy is a false one. Rescission (except by mutual consent or by a competent Court) is the right of one party, arising upon conduct by the other, by which he intimates his intention to abide by the contract no longer. It is a right to treat the contract as at an end if he chooses, and to claim damages for its total breach, but it is a right in his option and does not depend in theory on any implied term providing for its exercise, but is given by the law in vindication of a breach. Frustration, on the other hand, is explained in theory as a condition or term of contract, implied by the law *ab initio*, in order to supply what the parties would have inserted had the matter occurred to them, on the basis of what is fair and reasonable, having regard to the mutual interests concerned and of the main objects of the contract . . .'

Future obligations discharged

At common law future obligations are discharged but rights and obligations accrued before the event remain intact.

Appleby v *Meyers*
(1867) 36 LJCP 331 • Court of Common Pleas

Appleby contracted with Meyers to erect certain machinery on Meyers's premises. When the machinery was only partly erected a fire accidentally broke out in the buildings and destroyed the machinery. The issue before the court was whether Appleby could claim anything in respect of any portion of the machinery which had been erected and destroyed, as the whole work contracted to be done by them had not been completed.

Blackburn J: '. . . We think that where, as in the present case, the premises are destroyed without fault on either side, it is a misfortune equally affecting both parties; excusing both from further performance of the contract, but giving a cause of action to neither . . .

But though this is the *prima facie* contract between those who enter into contracts for doing work and supplying materials, there is nothing to render it either illegal or absurd in the workman to agree to complete the whole, and be paid when the whole is complete, and not till then; and we think that the plaintiffs in the present case had entered into such a contract. Had the accidental fire left the defendant's premises untouched, and only injured a part of the work which the plaintiffs had already done, we apprehend that it is clear the plaintiffs, under such a contract as the present, must have done that part over again, in order to fulfil their contract to complete the whole, and "put it to work for the sums above named respectively". As it is, they are, according to the principle laid down in *Taylor* v *Caldwell*, excused from completing the work; but they are not therefore entitled to any compensation for what they have done, but which has, without any fault of the defendant, perished. The case is in principle like that of a shipowner who has been excused from the performance of his contract to carry goods to their destination because his ship has been disabled by one of the excepted perils, but who is not therefore entitled to any payment on account of the part performance of the voyage . . . [W]e think that on the principles of English law laid down in *Cutter* v *Powell, Jesse* v *Roy, Munro* v *Butt, Sinclair* v *Bowles*, and other cases, the plaintiffs, having contacted to do an entire work for a specific sum, can receive nothing unless the work be done, or it can be shewn that it was the defendant's fault that the work was incomplete, or that there is something to justify the conclusion that the parties have entered.'

Fibrosa Spolka Akcyjna v *Fairbairn Lawson Combe Barbour Ltd*
[1942] 2 All ER 122 • House of Lords

In July 1939 Fairbairn Lawson contracted to manufacture and deliver certain textile machinery to Fibrosa, whose business was in Poland, for a price of £4800. The contract provided that £1600 should be paid at the time when the order was given;

in fact Fibrosa only paid £1000. In September 1939 Poland became enemy-occupied territory. Fibrosa claimed the return of their £1000 on the basis that their contract with Fairbairn Lawson had been frustrated when Poland became enemy-occupied territory. The issue before the House of Lords was whether Fibrosa could reclaim the £1000 given that there had been a total failure of consideration on the part of Fairbairn Lawson.

Viscount Simon LC: '. . . The application of *Taylor* v *Caldwell* to the actual problem with which he had to deal in *Chandler* v *Webster*, by Sir Richard Collins MR, deserves close examination. He said:

> "The plaintiff contends that he is entitled to recover the money which he has paid on the ground that there has been a total failure of consideration. He says that the condition on which he paid the money was that the procession should take place, and that, as it did not take place, there has been a total failure of consideration. That contention does no doubt raise a question of some difficulty, and one which has perplexed the courts to a considerable extent in several cases. The principle on which it has been dealt with is that which was applied in *Taylor* v *Caldwell* – namely, that, where, from causes outside the volition of the parties, something which was the basis of, or essential to the fulfilment of, the contract has become impossible, so that, from the time when the fact of that impossibility has been ascertained, the contract can no further be performed by either party, it remains a perfectly good contract up to that point, and everything previously done in pursuance of it must be treated as rightly done, but the parties are both discharged from further performance of it. If the effect were that the contract were wiped out altogether, no doubt the result would be that the money paid under it would have to be repaid as on a failure of consideration. But that is not the effect of the doctrine; it only releases the parties from further performance of the contract. Therefore, the doctrine of failure of consideration does not apply."

It appears to me that the reasoning in this crucial passage is open to two criticisms: –

(a) The claim of a party who has paid money under a contract to get the money back, on the ground that the consideration for which he paid it has totally failed, is not based upon any provision contained in the contract, but arises because, in the circumstances which have happened, the law gives a remedy in quasi-contract to the party who has not got that for which he bargained. It is a claim to recover money to which the defendant has no further right because in the circumstances which have happened, the money must be regarded as received to the plaintiff's use. It is true that the effect of frustration is that, while the contract can no further be performed, "it remains a perfectly good contract up to that point, and everything previously done in pursuance of it must be treated as rightly done"; but it by no means follows that the situation existing at the moment of frustration is one which leaves the party that has paid money and has not received the stipulated consideration without any remedy. To claim the return of money paid on the ground of total failure of consideration is not to vary the terms of the contract in any way. The claim arises not because the right to be repaid is one of the stipulated conditions of the contract, but because, in the circumstances which have happened, the law gives the remedy. It is the failure to distinguish between the action of *assumpsit* for money had and received in a case where the consideration has wholly failed, and an action on the contract itself, which explains the mistake which I think has been made in applying English law to this subject-matter . . . it does not follow that because the plaintiff cannot sue "on the contract", he cannot sue *dehors* the contract for the recovery of a payment in respect of which consideration has failed . . .

(b) There is, no doubt, a distinction between cases in which a contract is "wiped out altogether", e.g., because it is void as being illegal from the start, or as being due to fraud which the innocent party has elected to treat as avoiding the contract, and cases in which intervening impossibility "only releases the parties from further performance of the contract". Does the distinction between these two classes of case, however, justify the deduction of Sir Richard Collins MR, that "the doctrine of failure of consideration does not apply" where the contract remains a perfectly good contract up to the date of frustration? This conclusion seems to be derived from the view that, if the contract remains good and valid up to the moment of frustration, money which has already been paid under it cannot be regarded as having been paid for a consideration which has wholly failed. The party who has paid the money has had the advantage, whatever it may be worth, of the promise of the other party. That is true, but it is necessary to draw a distinction. In English law, an enforceable contract may be formed by an exchange of a promise for a promise, or by the exchange of a promise for an act – I am excluding contracts under seal – and thus, in the law relating to the formation of contract, the promise to do a thing may often be the consideration; but, when one is considering the law of failure of consideration and of the quasi-contractual right to recover money on that ground, it is, generally speaking not the promise which is referred to as the consideration, but the performance of the promise. The money was paid to secure performance and, if performance fails, the inducement which brought about the payment is not fulfilled.

If this were not so, there could never be any recovery of money, for failure of consideration, by the payer of the money in return for a promise of future performance. Yet there are endless examples which show that money can be recovered, as for a complete failure of consideration, in cases where the promise was given but could not be fulfilled: . . .

I can see no valid reason why the right to recover pre-paid money should not equally arise on frustration arising from supervening circumstances as it arises on frustration from destruction of a particular subject-matter.

The conclusion is that the rule in *Chandler* v *Webster* is wrong, and that the appellants can recover their £1,000.

While this result obviates the harshness with which the previous view in some instances treated the party who had made a prepayment, it cannot be regarded as dealing fairly between the parties in all cases, and must sometimes have the result of leaving the recipient who has to return the money at a grave disadvantage. He may have incurred expenses in connection with the partial carrying out of the contract which are equivalent, or more than equivalent, to the money which he prudently stipulated should be prepaid, but which he now has to return for reasons which are no fault of his. He may have to repay the money, though he has executed almost the whole of the contractual work, which will be left on his hands. These results follow from the fact that the English common law does not undertake to apportion a prepaid sum in such circumstances . . . It must be for the legislature to decide whether provision should be made for an equitable apportionment of prepaid monies which have to be returned by the recipient in view of the frustration of the contract in respect of which they were paid.

Unsatisfactory position at common law

After the *Fibrosa* case the law was still not satisfactory, for the party who had to return the prepayment might have incurred expenses, or he might be left with goods on his hands which were made valueless by the failure of the contract.

Further, if the party seeking recovery of the money had received any part, however small, of the performance of the contract, there could be no total failure of consideration, and the rule in the *Fibrosa* case did not apply.

To remedy the situation the Law Reform (Frustrated Contracts) Act 1943 was passed.

LAW REFORM (FRUSTRATED CONTRACTS) ACT 1943

An Act to amend the law relating to the frustration of contracts

Section 1 Adjustment of rights and liabilities of parties to frustrated contracts

(1) Where a contract governed by English law has become impossible of performance or been otherwise frustrated, and the parties thereto have for that reason been discharged from the further performance of the contract, the following provisions of this section shall, subject to the provisions of section two of this Act, have effect in relation thereto.

(2) All sums paid or payable to any party in pursuance of the contract before the time when the parties were so discharged (in this Act referred to as "the time of discharge") shall, in the case of sums so paid, be recoverable from him as money received by him for the use of the party by whom the sums were paid, and, in the case of sums so payable, cease to be so payable:

Provided that, if the party to whom the sums were so paid or payable incurred expenses before the time of discharge in, or for the purpose of, the performance of the contract, the court may, if it considers it just to do so having regard to all the circumstances of the case, allow him to retain or, as the case may be, recover the whole or any part of the sums so paid or payable, not being an amount in excess of the expenses so incurred.

(3) Where any party to the contract has, by reason of anything done by any other party thereto in, or for the purpose of, the performance of the contract, obtained a valuable benefit (other than a payment of money to which the last foregoing subsection applies) before the time of discharge, there shall be recoverable from him by the said other party such sum (if any), not exceeding the value of the said benefit to the party obtaining it, as the court considers just, having regard to all the circumstances of the case and, in particular, –

(a) the amount of any expenses incurred before the time of discharge by the benefited party in, or for the purpose of, the performance of the contract, including any sums paid or payable by him to any other party in pursuance of the contract and retained or recoverable by that party under the last foregoing subsection, and
(b) the effect, in relation to the said benefit, of the circumstances giving rise to the frustration of the contract.

(4) In estimating, for the purposes of the foregoing provisions of this section, the amount of any expenses incurred by any party to the contract, the court may, without prejudice to the generality of the said provisions, include such sum as appears to be reasonable in respect of overhead expenses and in respect of any work or services performed personally by the said party.

(5) In considering whether any sum ought to be recovered or retained under the foregoing provisions of this section by any party to the contract, the court shall not take into account any sums which have, by reason of the circumstances giving rise to the frustration of the contract, become payable to that party under any contract of insurance unless there was an obligation to insure imposed by an express term of the frustrated contract or by or under any enactment.

(6) Where any person has assumed obligations under the contract in consideration of the conferring of a benefit by any other party to the contract upon any other person, whether a party to the contract or not, the court may, if in all the circumstances of the case it considers it just to do so, treat for the purposes of subsection (3) of this section any benefit so conferred as a benefit obtained by the person who has assumed the obligations as aforesaid.

Section 2   Provision as to application of this Act

(1) This Act shall apply to contracts, whether made before or after the commencement of this Act, as respects which the time of discharge is on or after the first day of July, nineteen hundred and forty-three, but not to contracts as respects which the time of discharge is before the said date.

(2) This Act shall apply to contracts to which the Crown is a party in like manner as to contracts between subjects.

(3) Where any contract to which this Act applies contains any provision which, upon the true construction of the contract, is intended to have effect in the event of circumstances arising which operate, or would but for the said provision operate, to frustrate the contract, or is intended to have effect whether such circumstances arise or not, the court shall give effect to the said provision and shall only give effect to the foregoing section of this Act to such extent, if any, as appears to the court to be consistent with the said provision.

(4) Whether it appears to the court that a part of any contract to which this Act applies can properly be severed from the remainder of the contract, being a part wholly performed before the time of discharge, or so performed except for the payment in respect of that part of the contract of sums which are or can be ascertained under the contract, the court shall treat that part of the contract as if it were a separate contract and had not been frustrated and shall treat the foregoing section of this Act as only applicable to the remainder of that contract.

(5) This Act shall not apply –
   (a) to any charterparty, except a time charterparty or a charterparty by way of demise, or to any contract (other than a charterparty) for the carriage of goods by sea; or
   (b) to any contract of insurance, save as is provided by subsection (5) of the foregoing section; or
   (c) to any contract to which section 7 of the Sale of Goods Act 1979 (which avoids contracts for the sale of specific goods which perish before the risk has passed to the buyer) applies, or to any other contract for the sale, or for the sale and delivery, of specific goods, where the contract is frustrated by reason of the fact that the goods have perished.

NB Section 1(2) embodies the *Fibrosa* rule, although it is now no longer necessary to prove total failure of consideration.

By s 1(3) either party can recover compensation for any valuable benefit conferred upon the other party under the contract.

Does s 1(3) apply to cases like *Appleby* v *Meyers*?

BP Exploration Co (Libya) Ltd v *Hunt (No 2)*

[1982] 1 All ER 925 • Queen's Bench

The facts of this case are very complex but in brief in 1960 BP and Hunt entered into an agreement whereby Hunt granted BP a half share in an oil exploration concession that had been granted to him by the Libyan government. Under the agreement BP were to bear all the costs and risks of the exploration. However, if the exploration turned out to be successful (which it did) Hunt was to repay BP their costs of exploration out of his profits. In 1971 the Libyan government expropriated BP's half share of the concession. BP claimed successfully (i) that their contract with Hunt had been frustrated when the Libyan government expropriated their half share of the concession; and (ii) a 'just sum' under s 1(3) of the Law Reform (Frustrated Contracts) Act 1943.

The extract that follows is from the judgment of Robert Goff J. His judgment was upheld by both the Court of Appeal and the House of Lords. In the extract Robert Goff J explains the general way in which s 1(2) and (3) of the Law Reform (Frustrated Contracts) Act 1943 are to be applied.

Robert Goff J: 'I turn, therefore, to the construction of the Act itself. Much argument was directed towards the problem of construction, and in particular to the effect to be given to s 1(2) and (3) and s 2(3) of the Act. I shall now set out my conclusions on the effect to be given to these subsections.

(1) The principle of recovery

The principle, which is common to both s 1(2) and (3), and indeed is the fundamental principle underlying the Act itself, is prevention of the unjust enrichment of either party to the contract at the other's expense. It was submitted by counsel, on behalf of BP that the principle common to both subsections was one of restitution for net benefits received, the net benefit being the benefit less an appropriate deduction for expenses incurred by the defendant. This is broadly correct so far as s 1(2) is concerned; but under s 1(3) the net benefit of the defendant simply provides an upper limit to the award: it does not measure the amount of the award to be made to the plaintiff. This is because in s 1(3) a distinction is drawn between the plaintiff's performance under the contract, and the benefit which the defendant has obtained by reason of that performance, a distinction about which I shall have more to say later in this judgment; and the net benefit obtained by the defendant from the plaintiff's performance may be more than a just sum payable in respect of such performance, in which event a sum equal to the defendant's net benefit would not be an appropriate sum to award to the plaintiff. I therefore consider it better to state the principle underlying the Act as being the principle of unjust enrichment, which underlies the right of recovery in very many cases in English law, and indeed is the basic principle of the English law of restitution, of which the Act forms part.

Although s 1(2) and (3) is concerned with restitution in respect of different types of benefit, it is right to construe the two subsections as flowing from the same basic principle and therefore, so far as their different subject matters permit, to achieve consistency between them. Even so, it is always necessary to bear in mind the difference between awards of restitution in respect of money payments and awards where the benefit conferred by the plaintiff does not consist of a payment of money. Money has the peculiar character of a universal medium of exchange. By its receipt, the recipient is inevitably benefited; and (subject to problems arising from such matters as inflation, change of position and the time value of money) the loss suffered by the plaintiff is generally equal to the defendant's gain, so that no difficulty arises concerning the amount to be repaid. The same cannot be said of other benefits, such as goods or services. By their nature, services cannot be restored; nor in many cases can goods be restored, for example where they have been consumed or transferred to another. Furthermore the identity and value of the resulting benefit to the recipient may be debatable. From the very nature of things, therefore, the problem of restitution in respect of such benefits is more complex than in cases where the benefit takes the form of a money payment; and the solution of the problem has been made no easier by the form in which the legislature has chosen to draft s 1(3) of the Act.

The Act is *not* designed to do certain things. (i) It is not designed to apportion the loss between the parties. There is no general power under either s 1(2) or s 1(3) to make any allowance for expenses incurred by the plaintiff (except, under the proviso to s 1(2), to enable him to enforce *pro tanto* payment of a sum payable but unpaid before frustration); and expenses incurred by the defendant are only relevant in so far as they go to reduce the net benefit obtained by him and thereby limit any award to the plaintiff. (ii) It is not concerned to put the parties in the position in which they would have been if the contract had been performed. (iii) It is not concerned to restore the parties to the position they were in before the contract was made. A remedy designed to prevent unjust enrichment may not achieve that result; for expenditure may be incurred by either party under the contract which confers no benefit on the other, and in respect of which no remedy is available under the Act.

An award under the Act may have the effect of rescuing the plaintiff from an unprofitable bargain. This may certainly be true under s 1(2), if the plaintiff has paid the price in advance for an expected return which, if furnished, would have proved unprofitable; if the contract is frustrated before any part of that expected return is received, and before any expenditure is incurred by the defendant, the plaintiff is entitled to the return of the price he has paid, irrespective of the consideration he would have recovered had the contract been performed. Consistently with s 1(2), there is nothing in s 1(3) which necessarily limits an award to the contract consideration. But the contract consideration may nevertheless be highly relevant to the assessment of the just sum to be awarded under s 1(3); this is a matter to which I will revert later in this judgment.

(2) Claims under s 1(2)

Where an award is made under s 1(2), it is, generally speaking, simply an award for the repayment of money which has been paid to the defendant in pursuance of the contract, subject to an allowance in respect of expenses incurred by the defendant. It is not necessary that the consideration for the payment should have wholly failed: claims under s 1(2) are not limited to cases of total failure of consideration, and cases of partial failure of consideration can be catered for by a cross-claim by the defendant under s 1(2) or s 1(3) or both. There is no discretion in the court in respect of a claim under s 1(2), except in respect of the allowance for expenses; subject to such an allowance (and, of course, a cross-claim) the plaintiff is entitled to repayment of the money he has paid. The allowance for expenses is probably best rationalised as a statutory recognition of the defence of change of position. True, the expenses need not have been incurred by reason of the plaintiff's payment; but they must have been incurred in, or for the purpose of, the performance of the contract under which the plaintiff's payment has been made, and for that reason it is just that they should be brought into account. No provision is made in the subsection for any increase in the sum recoverable by the plaintiff, or in the amount of expenses to be allowed to the defendant, to allow for the time value of money. The money may have been paid, or the expenses incurred, many years before the date of frustration; but the cause of action accrues on that date, and the sum recoverable under the Act as at that date can be no greater than the sum actually paid, though the defendant may have had the use of the money over many years, and indeed may have profited from its use. Of course, the question whether the court may award interest from the date of the accrual of the cause of action is an entirely different matter, to which I shall refer later in this judgment.

(3) Claims under s 1(3)(a)

General. In contract, where an award is made under s 1(3), the process is more complicated, First, it has to be shown that the defendant has, by reason of something done by the plaintiff in, or for the purpose of, the performance of the contract, obtained a valuable benefit (other than a payment of money) before the time of discharge. That benefit has to be identified, and valued, and such value forms the upper limit of the award. Secondly, the court may award to the plaintiff such sum, not greater than the value of such benefit, as it considers just having regard to all the circumstances of the case, including in particular the matters specified in s 1(3)(a) and (b). In the case of an award under s 1(3) there are, therefore, two distinct stages: the identification and valuation of the benefit, and the award of the just sum. The amount to be awarded is the just sum, unless the defendant's benefit is less, in which event the award will be limited to the amount of that benefit. The distinction between the identification and valuation of the defendant's benefit, and the assessment of the just sum, is the most controversial part of the Act. It represents the solution adopted by the legislature of the problem of restitution in cases where the benefit does not consist of a payment of money; but the solution so adopted has been criticised by some commentators as productive of injustice, and it certainly gives rise to considerable problems, to which I shall refer in due course.

Identification of the defendant's benefit. In the course of the argument before me, there was much dispute whether, in the case of services, the benefit should be identified as the services themselves, or as the end product of the services. One example canvassed (because it bore some relationship to the facts of the present case) was the example of prospecting for minerals. If minerals are discovered, should the benefit be regarded (as counsel for Mr Hunt contended) simply as the services of prospecting, or (as counsel for BP contended) as the minerals themselves being the end product of the successful exercise? Now, I am satisfied that it was the intention of the legislature, to be derived from s 1(3) as a matter of construction, that the benefit should in an appropriate case be identified as the end product of the services. This appears, in my judgment, not only from the fact that s 1(3) distinguishes between the plaintiff's performance and the defendant's benefit, but also from s 1(3)(b) which clearly relates to the product of the plaintiff's performance. Let me take the example of a building contract. Suppose that a contract for work on a building is frustrated by a fire which destroys the building and which, therefore, also destroys a substantial amount of work already done by the plaintiff. Although it might be thought just to award the plaintiff a sum assessed on a *quantum meruit* basis, probably a rateable part of the contract price, in respect of the work he has done, the effect of s 1(3)(b) will be to reduce the award to nil, because of the effect, in relation to the defendant's benefit, of the circumstances giving rise to the frustration of the contract. It is quite plain that, in s 1(3)(b), the word "benefit" is intended to refer, in the example I have given, to the actual improvement to the building, because that is what will be affected by the frustrating event; the subsection therefore contemplates that, in such a case, the benefit is the end product of the plaintiff's services, not the services themselves. This will not be so in every case, since in some cases the services will have no end product; for example, where the services consist of doing such work as surveying, or transporting goods. In each case, it is necessary to ask the question: what benefit has the defendant obtained by reason of the plaintiff's contractual performance? But it must not be forgotten that in s 1(3) the relevance of the value of the benefit is to fix a ceiling to the award. If, for example, in a building contract, the building is only partially completed, the value of the partially completed building (i.e. the product of the services) will fix a ceiling for the award; the stage of the work may be such that the uncompleted building may be worth less than the value of the work and materials that have gone into it, particularly as completion by another builder may cost more than completion by the original builder would have cost. In other cases, however, the actual benefit to the defendant may be considerably more than the appropriate or just sum to be awarded to the plaintiff, in which event the value of the benefit will not in fact determine the quantum of the award. I should add, however, that, in a case of prospecting, it would usually be wrong to identify the discovered mineral as the benefit. In such a case there is always (whether the prospecting is successful or not) the benefit of the prospecting itself, i.e. of knowing whether or not the land contains any deposit of the relevant minerals; if the prospecting is successful, the benefit may include also the enhanced value of the land by reason of the discovery; if the prospector's contractual task goes beyond discovery and includes development and production, the benefit will include the further enhancement of the land by reason of the installation of the facilities, and also the benefit of in part transforming a valuable mineral deposit into a marketable commodity.

I add by way of footnote that all these difficulties would have been avoided if the legislature had thought it right to treat the services themselves as the benefit. In the opinion of many commentators, it would be more just to do so; after all, the services in question have been requested by the defendant, who normally takes the risk that they may prove worthless, from whatever cause. In the example I have given of the building destroyed by fire, there is much to be said for the view that the builder should be paid for the work he has done, unless he has (for example by agreeing to insure the works) taken upon himself the risk of destruction by fire. But my task is to construe the Act as it stands. On the true construction of the Act, it is in my judgment clear that the defendant's benefit must, in an appropriate case, be identified as the end product of the plaintiff's services, despite the difficulties which this construction creates, difficulties which are met again when one comes to value the benefit.

Apportioning the benefit. In all cases, the relevant benefit must have been obtained by the defendant by reason of something done by the plaintiff. Accordingly, where it is appropriate to identify the benefit with an end product and it appears that the defendant has obtained the benefit by reason of work done both by the plaintiff and by himself, the court will have to do its best to apportion that benefit, and to decide what proportion is attributable to the work done by the plaintiff. That proportion will then constitute the relevant benefit for the purposes of s 1(3) of the Act.

Valuing the benefit. Since the benefit may be identified with the product of the plaintiff's performance, great problems arise in the valuation of the benefit. First, how does one solve the problem which arises from the fact that a small service may confer an enormous benefit, and conversely, a very substantial service may confer only a very small benefit? The answer presumably is that at the stage of valuation of the benefit (as opposed to assessment of the just sum) the task of the court is simply to assess the value of the benefit to the defendant. For example, if a prospector after some very simple prospecting discovers a large and unexpected deposit of a valuable mineral, the benefit to the defendant (namely, the enhancement in the value of the land) may be enormous; it must be valued as such, always bearing in mind that the assessment of a just sum may very well lead to a much smaller amount being awarded to the plaintiff. But conversely, the plaintiff may have undertaken building work for a substantial sum which is, objectively speaking, of little or no value, for example, he may commence the redecoration, to the defendant's execrable taste, of rooms which are in good decorative order. If the contract is frustrated before the work is complete, and the work is unaffected by the frustrating event, it can be argued that the defendant has obtained no benefit, because the defendant's property has been reduced in value by the plaintiff's work; but the partial work must be treated as a benefit to the defendant, since he requested it, and valued as such. Secondly, at what point in time is the benefit to be valued? . . . However, does this mean that, for the purposes of s 1(3), the benefit is always to be valued as at the date of frustration? For example, if goods are transferred and retained by the defendant till frustration when they have appreciated or depreciated in value, are they to be valued as at the date of frustration? The answer must, I think, generally speaking, be in the affirmative, for the sake of consistency . . .

Other problems can arise from the valuation of the defendant's benefit as the end product; I shall come to these later in the consideration of the facts of the present case. But there is a further problem which I should refer to, before leaving this topic. Section 1(3)(a) requires the court to have regard to the amount of any expenditure incurred before the time of discharge by the benefited party in, or for the purpose of, the performance of the contract. The question arises: should this matter be taken into account at the stage of valuation of the benefit, or of assessment of the just sum? Take a simple example. Suppose that the defendant's benefit is valued at £150, and that a just sum is assessed at £100, but that there remain to be taken into account defendant's expenses of £75: is the award to be £75 or £25? The clue to this problem lies, in my judgment, in the fact that the allowance for expenses is a statutory recognition of the defence of change of position. Only to the extent that the position of the defendant has so changed that it would be unjust to award restitution, should the court make an allowance for expenses. Suppose that the plaintiff does work for the defendant which produces no valuable end product, or a benefit no greater in value than the just sum to be awarded in respect of the work; there is then no reason why the whole of the relevant expenses should not be set off against the just sum. But suppose that the defendant has reaped a large benefit from the plaintiff's work, far greater in value than the just sum to be awarded for the work. In such circumstances it would be quite wrong to set off the whole of the defendant's expenses against the just sum. The question whether the defendant has suffered a change of position has to be judged in the light of all the circumstances of the case. Accordingly, on the Act as it stands, under s 1(3) the proper course is to deduct the expenses from the value of the benefit, with the effect that only in so far as they reduce the value of the benefit below the amount of the just sum which would otherwise be awarded will they have any practical bearing on the award.

Finally, I should record that the court is required to have regard to the effect, in relation to the defendant's benefit, of the circumstances giving rise to the frustration of the contract. I have already given an example of how this may be relevant, in the case of building contracts; and I have recorded the fact that this provision has been the subject of criticism. There may, however, be circumstances where it would not be just to have regard to this fact or, for example, if, under a building contract, it was expressly agreed that the work in progress should be insured by the building-owner against risks which include the event which had the effect of frustrating the contract and damaging or destroying the work.

Assessment of the just sum. The principle underlying the Act is prevention of the unjust enrichment of the defendant at the plaintiff's expense. Where, as in cases under s 1(2), the benefit conferred on the defendant consists of payment of a sum of money, the plaintiff's expense and the defendant's enrichment are generally equal; and, subject to other relevant factors, the award of restitution will consist simply of an order for repayment of a like sum of money. But where the benefit does not consist of money, then the defendant's enrichment will rarely be equal to the plaintiff's expense. In such cases, where (as in the case of a benefit conferred under a contract thereafter frustrated) the benefit has been requested by the defendant, the basic measure of recovery in restitution is the reasonable value of the plaintiff's performance: in a case of services, a *quantum meruit* or reasonable remuneration, and in a case of goods, a *quantum valebat* or reasonable price. Such cases are to be contrasted with cases where such a benefit has not been requested by the defendant. In the latter class of case, recovery is rare in restitution; but if the sole basis of recovery was that the defendant had been incontrovertibly benefited, it might be legitimate to limit recovery to the defendant's actual benefit, a limit which has (perhaps inappropriately) been imported by the legislature into s 1(3) of the Act. However, under s 1(3) as it stands, if the defendant's actual benefit is less than the just or reasonable sum which would otherwise be awarded to the plaintiff, the award must be reduced to a sum equal to the amount of the defendant's benefit.

A crucial question, upon which the Act is surprisingly silent, is this: what bearing do the terms of the contract, under which the plaintiff has acted, have upon the assessment of the just sum? First, the terms upon which the work was done may serve to indicate the full scope of the work done, and so be relevant to the sum awarded in respect of such work. For example, if I do work under a contract under which I am to receive a substantial prize if successful, and nothing if I fail, and the contract is frustrated before the work is complete but not before a substantial benefit has been obtained by the defendant, the element of risk taken by the plaintiff may be held to have the effect of enhancing the amount of any sum to be awarded. Secondly, the contract consideration is always relevant as providing some evidence of what will be a reasonable sum to be awarded in respect of the plaintiff's work. Thus if a prospector, employed for a fee, discovers a gold mine before the contract under which he is employed is frustrated (for example, by illegality or by his illness or disablement) at a time when his work was incomplete, the court may think it just to make an award in the nature of a reasonable fee for what he has done (though of course the benefit obtained by the defendant will be far greater), and a rateable part of the contract fee may provide useful evidence of the level of sum to be awarded. If, however, the contract had provided that he was to receive a stake in the concession, then the just sum might be enhanced on the basis that, in all the circumstances, a reasonable sum should take account of such a factor: cf. *Way* v *Latilla*. Thirdly, however, the contract consideration, or a rateable part of it, may provide a limit to the sum to be awarded. To take a fairly extreme example, a poor householder or a small businessman may obtain a contract for building work to be done to his premises at considerably less than the market price, on the basis that he cannot afford to pay more. In such a case, the court may consider it just to limit the award to a rateable part of the contract price, on the ground that it was the understanding of the parties that in no circumstances (including the circumstances of the contract being frustrated) should the plaintiff recover more than the contract price or a rateable part of it. Such a limit may properly be said to arise by virtue of the operation of s 2(3) of the Act. But it must not be forgotten that, unlike money, services can never be restored, nor usually can goods, since they are likely to have been either consumed or disposed of, or to have depreciated in value; and since, *ex hypothesi*, the defendant will only have been prepared to contract for the goods or services on the basis that he paid no more than the contract consideration, it may be unjust to compel him, by an award under the Act, to pay more than that consideration, or a rateable part of it, in respect of the services or goods he has received. It is unnecessary for me to decide whether this will always be so; but it is likely that in most cases this will impose an important limit upon the sum to be awarded: indeed it may well be the most relevant limit to an award under s 1(3) of the Act. The legal basis of the limit may be s 2(3) of the Act; but even if that subsection is inapplicable, it is open to the court, in an appropriate case, to give effect to such a limit in assessing the just sum to be awarded under s 1(3), because in many cases it would be unjust to impose upon the defendant an obligation to make restitution under the subsection at higher than the contract rate.'

SUMMARY

You should now be able to:

- Appreciate the nature of the doctrine of frustration.
- Appreciate the extension of the 'frustration of the adventure' principle to the 'literal impossibility' principle.
- Identify examples of frustration.
- Understand the limitations to the doctrine of frustration.
- Understand the effects of frustration.

If you have not mastered the above points you should go through this section again.

17 Remedies for breach of contract

INTRODUCTION

The following remedies are open to a person injured by the breach, whether the breach is of such a kind as to justify him in treating the contract as discharged or not.

Damages Every breach of contract entitles the injured party to damages for the loss he has suffered.

Quantum meruit If the injured party, when the breach occurs, has already done part, though not all, of what he was bound to do under the contract, he may be entitled to claim the value of what he has done. In that case he is said to sue upon a *quantum meruit*.

Specific performance and injunction In certain circumstances the injured party may obtain an order for the specific performance of the contract, or an injunction to restrain its breach. These are equitable remedies and are generally granted at the discretion of the court.

DAMAGES

Remoteness of damage

Damages are the normal remedy at common law. In order to get damages it must be shown that the loss was caused by the breach. However, *the loss must not be too remote.*

Hadley v Baxendale
(1854) 23 LJ Ex 179 • Exchequer

This was an action by the plaintiffs, owners of a steam grist mill, against the defendant, a carrier, for delay in delivering two pieces of iron, being the broken shaft of the plaintiffs' mill, by reason of which delay the engineer, to whom they were to be delivered, was unable to supply a new shaft, the mill was stopped, and the plaintiffs lost certain profits by the delay of their business, which was laid in the declaration as special damage. The defendant paid £25 into court.

At the trial, before Crompton J, at the Summer Assizes for Gloucester, 1853, it appeared that the broken shaft was to be sent to the engineer as a model for a new one, and at the time of the contract for the carriage being made, the defendant's clerk was informed that the mill was stopped and that the shaft must be sent immediately. It further appeared that its delivery at its destination was delayed for several days, and, consequently, the plaintiffs did not receive the new shaft back as they expected, and their mill was kept idle.

Alderson B: 'We think the proper rule in such a case as the present is this: – where two parties have made a contract which one of them has broken, the damages which the other party ought to receive in respect of such breach of contract should be, either such as may fairly and reasonably be considered arising naturally, i.e., according to the usual course of things, from such breach of contract itself, or such as may reasonably be supposed to have been in the contemplation of both parties at the time they made the contract, as the probable result of the breach of it. Now, if the special circumstances under which the contract was actually made were communicated by the plaintiff to the defendant, and thus known to both parties, the damages resulting from the breach of such a contract which they would reasonably contemplate would be the amount of injury which would ordinarily follow from a breach of contract under those special circumstances, so known and communicated. But, on the other hand, if those special circumstances were wholly unknown to the party breaking the contract, he at the most could only be supposed to have had in his contemplation the amount of injury which would arise generally, and in the great multitude of cases not affected by any special circumstances, from such a breach of contract. For had the special circumstances been known, the parties might have especially provided for the breach of contract by special terms as to the damages in that case, and of this advantage it would be very unjust to deprive them . . .

Now, in the present case, if we are to apply the principles above laid down, we find that the only circumstances here communicated by the plaintiff to the defendant at the time the contract was made were, that the article to be carried was the broken shaft of a mill, and that the plaintiff was the miller of that mill. But how do these circumstances reasonably shew that the profits of the mill must be stopped by an unreasonable delay in the delivery of the broken shaft by the carrier to the third person? Suppose the plaintiff had another shaft in his possession put up or putting up at the time, and that he only wished to send back the broken shaft to the engineer who made it, it is clear that this would be quite consistent with the above circumstances, and yet the unreasonable delay in the delivery would have no effect upon the intermediate profits of the mill. Or, again, suppose that at the time of the delivery to the carrier the machinery of the mill had been in other respects defective, then also the same results will follow. Here it is true that the shaft was actually sent back to serve as a model for a new one, and that the want of a new one was the only cause of the stoppage of the mill, and that the loss of profits really arose from not sending down the new shaft in proper time, and that this arose from the delay in delivering the broken one to serve as a model. But it is obvious that in the great multitude of cases of millers sending off broken shafts to third persons by a carrier under ordinary circumstances such consequences would not in all probability have occurred, and these special circumstances were never communicated by the plaintiff to the defendant. It follows, therefore, that the loss of profit here cannot reasonably be considered such a consequence of a breach of contract as could have been fairly and reasonably contemplated by both these parties when they made this contract; for such loss would neither have flowed naturally from the breach of this contract in the great multitude of such cases occurring under ordinary circumstances, nor were the special circumstances, which perhaps would have made it a reasonable and natural consequence of such breach of contract, communicated to or known by the defendant.'

Victoria Laundry (Windsor) Ltd v *Newman Industries Ltd*
[1949] 1 All ER 997 • Court of Appeal

The facts are stated in the judgment of Asquith LJ.

Asquith LJ: 'This is an appeal by the plaintiffs against a judgment of Streatfeild J, in so far as that judgment limited the damages to £110 in respect of an alleged breach of contract by the defendants which is now uncontested. The breach of contract consisted in the delivery of a boiler sold by the defendants to the plaintiffs some twenty odd weeks after the time fixed by the contract for delivery. The short point is whether, in addition to the £110 awarded, the plaintiffs were entitled to claim in respect of loss of profits which they say they would have made if the boiler had been delivered punctually . . .

The ground of the learned judge's decision, which we consider more fully later, may be summarised as follows. He took the view that the loss of profit claimed was due to special circumstances, and, therefore, recoverable, if at all, only under the second rule in *Hadley v Baxendale*, and not recoverable in the present case because such special circumstances were not at the time of the contract communicated to the defendants. He also attached much significance to the fact that the object supplied was not a self-sufficient profit-making article, but part of a larger profit-making whole, and cited in this connection *Portman v Middleton* and *British Columbia, etc, Saw Mill Co v Nettleship*. Before commenting on the learned judge's reasoning, we must refer to some of the authorities . . .

What propositions applicable to the present case emerge from the authorities as a whole, including those analysed above? We think they include the following: (1) It is well settled that the governing purpose of damages is to put the party whose rights have been violated in the same position, so far as money can do so, as if his rights had been observed: *Wertheim v Chicoutimi Pulp Co*. This purpose, if relentlessly pursued, would provide him with a complete indemnity for all loss *de facto* resulting from a particular breach, however improbable, however unpredictable. This, in contract at least, is recognised as too harsh a rule. Hence, (2): In cases of breach of contract the aggrieved party is only entitled to recover such part of the loss actually resulting as was at the time of the contract reasonably foreseeable as liable to result from the breach. (3) What was at that time reasonably foreseeable depends on the knowledge then possessed by the parties, or, at all events, by the party who later commits the breach. (4) For this purpose, knowledge "possessed" is of two kinds – one imputed, the other actual. Everyone, as a reasonable person, is taken to know the "ordinary course of things" and consequently what loss is liable to result from a breach in that ordinary course. This is the subject-matter of the "first rule" in *Hadley v Baxendale*, but to this knowledge, which a contract-breaker is assumed to possess whether he actually possesses it or not, there may have to be added in a particular case knowledge which he actually possesses of special circumstances outside the "ordinary course of things" of such a kind that a breach in those special circumstances would be liable to cause more loss. Such a case attracts the operation of the "second rule" so as to make additional loss also recoverable. (5) In order to make the contract-breaker liable under either rule it is not necessary that he should actually have asked himself what loss is liable to result from a breach. As has often been pointed out, parties at the time of contracting contemplate, not the breach of the contract, but its performance. It suffices that, if he had considered the question, he would as a reasonable man have concluded that the loss in question was liable to result: see certain observations of Lord Du Parcq in *Monarch Steamship Co Ltd v A/B Karlshamns Oljefrabriker*. (6) Nor, finally, to make a particular loss recoverable, need it be proved that on a given state of knowledge the defendant could, as a reasonable man, foresee that a breach must necessarily result in that loss. It is enough if he could foresee it was likely so to result. It is enough, to borrow from the language of Lord Du Parcq in the same case, if the loss (or some factor without which it would not have occurred) is a "serious possibility" or a "real danger". For short, we have used the word "liable" to result. Possibly the colloquialism "on the cards" indicates the shade of meaning with some approach to accuracy.

If these, indeed, are the principles applicable, what is the effect of their application to the facts of the present case? We have, at the beginning of this judgment, summarised the main relevant facts. The defendants were an engineering company supplying a boiler to a laundry. We reject the submission for the defendants that an engineering company knows no more than the plain man about boilers or the purposes to which they are commonly put by different classes of purchasers, including laundries . . . Of the uses or purposes to which boilers are put, they would clearly know more than the uninstructed layman. Again, they knew they were supplying the boiler to a company carrying on the business of laundrymen and dyers, for use in that business. The obvious use of a boiler, in such a business, is surely to boil water for the purpose of washing or dyeing . . . [This] is the obvious purpose which, in the case of a laundry, leaps to the average eye. If the purpose then be to wash or dye, why does the company want to wash or dye, unless for purposes of business advantage, in which term we, for the purposes of the rest of this judgment, include maintenance or increase of profit or reduction of loss? We shall speak henceforward not of loss of profit, but of "loss of business". No commercial concern commonly purchases for the purposes of its business a very large and expensive structure like this – a boiler nineteen feet high and costing over £2000 – with any other motive, and no supplier, let alone an engineering company, which has promised delivery of such an article by a particular date with knowledge that it was to be put into use immediately on delivery, can reasonably contend that it could not foresee that loss of business (in the sense indicated above) would be liable to result to the purchaser from a long delay in the delivery thereof. The suggestion that, for all the supplier knew, the boiler might have been needed simply as a "stand-by", to be used in a possibly distant future, is gratuitous and was plainly negatived by the terms of the letter of Apr 26, 1946 . . .

. . . [W]e would wish to add, first, that the learned judge appears to infer that because certain "special circumstances" were, in his view, not "drawn to the notice of" the defendants, and, therefore, in his view, the operation of the "second rule" was excluded, ergo, nothing in respect of loss of business can be recovered under the "first rule". This inference is, in our view, no more justified in the present case than it was in *Cory* v *Thames Ironworks Co*. Secondly, while it is not wholly clear what were the "special circumstances" on the non-communication of which the learned judge relied, it would seem that they were or included the following: – (a) the "circumstance" that delay in delivering the boiler was going to lead "necessarily" to loss of profits, but the true criterion is surely not what was bound "necessarily" to result, but what was likely or liable to do so, and we think that it was amply conveyed to the defendants by what was communicated to them (plus what was patent without express communication) that delay in delivery was likely to lead to "loss of business"; (b) the "circumstance" that the plaintiffs needed the boiler "to extend their business". It was surely not necessary for the defendants to be specifically informed of this as a precondition of being liable for loss of business. Reasonable persons in the shoes of the defendants must be taken to foresee, without any express intimation, that a laundry which, at a time when there was a famine of laundry facilities, was paying £2000 odd for plant and intended at such a time to put such plant "into use" immediately, would be likely to suffer in pocket from five months' delay in delivery of the plant in question, whether they intended by means of it to extend their business, or merely to maintain it, or to reduce a loss; (c) the "circumstance" that the plaintiffs had the assured expectation of special contracts, which they could only fulfil by securing punctual delivery of the boiler. Here, no doubt, the learned judge had in mind the particularly lucrative dyeing contracts to which the plaintiffs looked forward and which they mention in para 10 of the statement of claim. We agree that in order that the plaintiffs should recover specifically and as such the profits expected on these contracts, the defendants would have had to know, at the time of their agreement with the plaintiffs, of the prospect and terms of such contracts. We also agree that they did not, in fact, know these things. It does not, however, follow that the plaintiffs are precluded from recovering some general (and perhaps conjectural) sum for loss of business in respect of dyeing contracts to be reasonably expected any more than in respect of laundering contracts to be reasonably expected . . .

We are, therefore, of opinion that the appeal should be allowed and the issue referred to an official referee as to what damage, if any, is recoverable in addition to the £110 awarded by the learned trial judge. The official referee would assess those damages in consonance with the findings in this judgment as to what the defendants knew or must be taken to have known at the material time, either party to be at liberty to call evidence as to the quantum of the damage in dispute.'

In *The Heron II*, below, Asquith LJ's 'reasonable foresight' test was disapproved of by the House of Lords. The House of Lords held that a higher degree of probability is required to satisfy the test of remoteness in contract than in tort.

Koufos v *C Czarnikow Ltd, the Heron II*

[1967] 3 All ER 686 • House of Lords

Lord Reid: 'My Lords, by charterparty of Oct 15, 1960, the respondents chartered the appellant's vessel, *Heron II*, to proceed to Constanza, there to load a cargo of three thousand tons of sugar; and to carry it to Basrah, or, in the charterers' option, to Jeddah. The vessel left Constanza on Nov 1. The option was not exercised and the vessel arrived at Basrah on Dec 2. The umpire has found that "a reasonably accurate prediction of the length of the voyage was twenty days". But the vessel had in breach of contract made deviations which caused a delay of nine days.

It was the intention of the respondent charterers to sell the sugar "promptly after arrival at Basrah and after inspection by merchants". The appellant shipowner did not know this, but he was aware of the fact that there was a market for sugar at Basrah. The sugar was in fact sold at Basrah in lots between Dec 12 and 22 but shortly before that time the market price had fallen partly by reason of the arrival of another cargo of sugar. It was found by the umpire that if there had not been this delay of nine days the sugar would have fetched £32 10s per ton. The actual price realised was only £31 2s 9d per ton. The charterers claim that they are entitled to recover the difference as damage for breach of contract. The shipowner admits that he is liable to pay interest for nine days on the value of the sugar and certain minor expenses but denies that fall in market value can be taken into account in assessing damages in this case.

McNair J, following the decision in *The Parana*, decided this question in favour of the appellant. He said:

"In those circumstances it seems to me almost impossible to say that the shipowner must have known that the delay in prosecuting the voyage would probably result, or be likely to result, in this kind of loss."

The Court of Appeal by a majority (Diplock and Salmon LJJ, Sellers LJ dissenting) reversed the decision of the trial judge. The majority held that *The Parana* laid down no general rule and, applying the rule (or rules) in *Hadley* v *Baxendale*, as explained in *Victoria Laundry (Windsor), Ltd* v *Newman Industries, Ltd*, they held that the loss due to fall in market price was not too remote to be recoverable as damages.

It may be well first to set out the knowledge and intention of the parties at the time of making the contract so far as relevant or argued to be relevant. The charterers intended to sell the sugar in the market at Basrah on arrival of the vessel. They could have changed their mind and exercised their option to have the sugar delivered at Jeddah, but they did not do so. There is no finding that they had in mind any particular date as the likely date of arrival at Basrah or that they had any knowledge or expectation that in late November or December there would be a rising or a falling market. The shipowner was given no information about these matters by the charterers. He did not know what the charterers intended to do with the sugar. But he knew there was a market in sugar at Basrah, and it appears to me that, if he had thought about the matter, he must have realised that at least it was not unlikely that the sugar would be sold in the market at market price on arrival. He must also be held to have known that in any ordinary market prices are apt to fluctuate from day to day: but he had no reason to suppose it more probable that during the relevant period such fluctuation would be downwards rather than upwards – it was an even chance that the fluctuation would be downwards.

So the question for decision is whether a plaintiff can recover as damages for breach of contract a loss of a kind which the defendant, when he made the contract, ought to have realised was not unlikely to result from a breach of contract causing delay in delivery. I use the words "not unlikely" as denoting a degree of probability considerably less than an even chance but nevertheless not very unusual and easily foreseeable.

For over a century everyone has agreed that remoteness of damage in contract must be determined by applying the rule (or rules) laid down by a court including Parke, Martin and Alderson BB, in *Hadley* v *Baxendale*; but many different interpretations of that rule have been adopted by judges at different times. So I think that one ought first to see just what was decided in that case, because it would seem wrong to attribute to that rule a meaning which, if it had been adopted in that case, would have resulted in a contrary decision of that case.

In *Hadley* v *Baxendale* the owners of a flour mill at Gloucester, which was driven by a steam engine, delivered to common carriers, Pickford & Co, a broken crank shaft to be sent to engineers in Greenwich. A delay of five days in delivery there was held to be in breach of contract, and the question at issue was the proper measure of damages. In fact the shaft was sent as a pattern for a new shaft and until it arrived the mill could not operate. So the owners claimed £300 as loss of profit for the five days by which resumption of work was delayed by this breach of contract; but the carriers did not know that delay would cause loss of this kind. Alderson B, delivering the judgment of the court said:

" . . . we find that the only circumstances here communicated by the plaintiffs to the defendants at the time the contract was made were that the article to be carried was the broken shaft of a mill and that the plaintiffs were the millers of that mill. But how do these circumstances show reasonably that the profits of the mill must be stopped by an unreasonable delay in the delivery of the broken shaft by the carrier to the third person? Suppose the plaintiffs had another shaft in their possession put up or putting up at the time, and that they only wished to send back the broken shaft to the engineer who made it; it is clear that this would be quite consistent with the above circumstances, and yet the unreasonable delay in the delivery would have no effect upon the intermediate profits of the mill. Or, again, suppose that at the time of the delivery to the carrier the machinery of the mill had been in other respects defective, then, also the same results would follow."

Then, having said that in fact the loss of profit was caused by the delay, he continued:

"But it is obvious that, in the great multitude of cases of millers sending off broken shafts to third persons by a carrier under ordinary circumstances, such consequences would not, in all probability, have occurred . . . "

Alderson B clearly did not and could not mean that it was not reasonably foreseeable that delay might stop the resumption of work in the mill. He merely said that in the great multitude – which I take to mean the great majority – of cases this would not happen. He was not distinguishing between results which were foreseeable or unforeseeable, but between results which were likely because they would happen in the great majority of cases, and results which were unlikely because they would only happen in a small minority of cases. He continued:

> "It follows, therefore, that the loss of profits here cannot reasonably be considered such a consequence of the breach of contract as could have been fairly and reasonably contemplated by both the parties when they made this contract."

He clearly meant that a result which will happen in the great majority of cases should fairly and reasonably be regarded as having been in the contemplation of the parties, but that a result which, though foreseeable as a substantial possibility, would happen only in a small minority of cases should not be regarded as having been in their contemplation. He was referring to such a result when he continued:

> "For such loss would neither have flowed naturally from the breach of this contract in the great multitude of such cases occurring under ordinary circumstances, nor were the special circumstances, which perhaps, would have made it a reasonable and natural consequence of such breach of contract, communicated to or known by the defendants."

I have dealt with the latter part of the judgment before coming to the well known rule, because the court were there applying the rule and the language which was used in the latter part appears to me to throw considerable light on the meaning which they must have attached to the rather vague expressions used in the rule itself. The rule is that the damages

> " ... should be such as may fairly and reasonably be considered either arising naturally, i.e., according to the usual course of things, from such breach of contract itself, or such as may reasonably be supposed to have been in the contemplation of both parties at the time they made the contract as the probable result of the breach of it."

I do not think that it was intended that there were to be two rules or that two different standards or tests were to be applied. The last two passages which I quoted from the end of the judgment applied to the facts before the court, which did not include any special circumstances communicated to the defendants; and the line of reasoning there is that, because in the great majority of cases loss of profit would not in all probability have occurred, it followed that this could not reasonably be considered as having been fairly and reasonably contemplated by both the parties, for it would not have flowed naturally from the breach in the great majority of cases.

I am satisfied that the court did not intend that every type of damage which was reasonably foreseeable by the parties when the contract was made should either be considered as arising naturally, i.e., in the usual course of things, or be supposed to have been in the contemplation of the parties. Indeed the decision makes it clear that a type of damage which was plainly foreseeable as a real possibility but which would only occur in a small minority of cases cannot be regarded as arising in the usual course of things or be supposed to have been in the contemplation of the parties: the parties are not supposed to contemplate as grounds for the recovery of damage any type of loss or damage which, on the knowledge available to the defendant, would appear to him as only likely to occur in a small minority of cases.

In cases like *Hadley* v *Baxendale* or the present case it is not enough that in fact the plaintiff's loss was directly caused by the defendant's breach of contract. It clearly was so caused in both. The crucial question is whether, on the information available to the defendant when the contract was made, he should, or the reasonable man in his position would, have realised that such loss was sufficiently likely to result from the breach of contract to make it proper to hold that the loss flowed naturally from the breach or that loss of that kind should have been within his contemplation.

The modern rule in tort is quite different and it imposes a much wider liability. The defendant will be liable for any type of damage which is reasonably foreseeable as liable to happen even in the most unusual case, unless the risk is so small that a reasonable man would in the whole circumstances feel justified in neglecting it; and there is good reason for the difference. In contract, if one party wishes to protect himself against a risk which to the other party would appear unusual, he can direct the other party's attention to it before the contract is made, and I need not stop to consider in what circumstances the other party will then be held to have accepted responsibility in that event. In tort, however, there is no opportunity for the injured party to protect himself in that way, and the tortfeasor cannot reasonably complain if he has to pay for some very unusual but nevertheless foreseeable damage which results from his wrongdoing. I have no doubt that today a tortfeasor would be held liable for a type of damage as unlikely as was the stoppage of Hadley's Mill for lack of a crank shaft: to any one with the knowledge the carrier had that may have seemed unlikely, but the chance of it happening would have been seen to be far from negligible. But it does not at all follow that *Hadley* v *Baxendale* would today be differently decided . . .

It may be that there was nothing very new in this, but I think that *Hall*'s case must be taken to have established that damages are not to be regarded as too remote merely because, on the knowledge available to the defendant when the contract was made, the chance of the occurrence of the event which caused the damage would have appeared to him to be rather less than an even chance. I would agree with Lord Shaw that it is generally sufficient that that event would have appeared to the defendant as not unlikely to occur. It is hardly ever possible in this matter to assess probabilities with any degree of mathematical accuracy. But I do not find in that case, or in cases which preceded it, any warrant for regarding as within the contemplation of the parties any event which would not have appeared to the defendant, had he thought about it, to have a very substantial degree of probability.

Then it has been said that the liability of defendants has been further extended by *Victoria Laundry (Windsor), Ltd* v *Newman Industries, Ltd*. I do not think so. The plaintiffs bought a large boiler from the defendants and the defendants were aware of the general nature of the plaintiffs' business and the plaintiffs' intention to put the boiler into use as soon as possible. Delivery of the boiler was delayed in breach of contract and the plaintiffs claimed as damages loss of profit caused by the delay. A large part of the profits claimed would have resulted from some specially lucrative contracts which the plaintiffs could have completed if they had had the boiler: that was rightly disallowed because the defendants had no knowledge of these contracts. Asquith LJ said:

> "It does not, however, follow that the plaintiffs are precluded from recovering some general (and perhaps conjectural) sum for loss of business in respect of dyeing contracts to be reasonably expected, any more than in respect of laundering contracts to be reasonably expected."

It appears to me that this was well justified on the earlier authorities. It was certainly not unlikely on the information which the defendants had when making the contract that delay in delivering the boiler would result in loss of business: indeed it would seem that that was more than an even chance. And there was nothing new in holding that damages should be estimated on a conjectural basis. This House had approved of that as early as 1813 in *Hall* v *Ross*.

What is said to create a "landmark", however, is the statement of principles by Asquith LJ. This does to some extent go beyond the older authorities and in so far as it does so, I do not agree with it. In para (2) it is said that the plaintiff is entitled to recover "such part of the loss actually resulting as was at the time of the contract reasonably foreseeable as liable to result from the breach". To bring in reasonable foreseeability appears to me to be confusing measure of damages in contract with measure of damages in tort. A great many extremely unlikely results are reasonably foreseeable: it is true that Asquith LJ may have meant foreseeable as a likely result, and if that is all he meant I would not object farther than to say that I think that the phrase is liable to be misunderstood. For the same reason I would take exception to the phrase "liable to result" in para (5). Liable is a very vague word, but I think that one would usually say that when a person foresees a very improbable result he foresees that it is liable to happen.

I agree with the first half of para (6). For the best part of a century it has not been required that the defendant could have foreseen that a breach of contract must necessarily result in the loss which has occurred; but I cannot agree with the second half of para (6). It has never been held to be sufficient in contract that the loss was foreseeable as "a serious possibility" or "a real danger" or as being "on the cards". It is on the cards that one can win £100 000 or more for a stake of a few pence – several people have done that; and anyone who backs a hundred to one chance regards a win as a serious possibility – many people have won on such a chance. Moreover *The Wagon Mound (No 2) Overseas Tankship (UK), Ltd* v *Miller Steamship Co Pty, Ltd* could not have been decided as it was unless the extremely unlikely fire should have been foreseen by the ship's officer as a real danger. It appears to me that in the ordinary use of language there is a wide gulf between saying that some event is not unlikely or quite likely to happen and saying merely that it is a serious possibility, a real danger, or on the cards. Suppose one takes a well-shuffled pack of cards, it is quite likely or not unlikely that the top card will prove to be a diamond: the odds are only three to one against; but most people would not say that it is quite likely to be the nine of diamonds for the odds are then fifty-one to one against. On the other hand I think that most people would say that there is a serious possibility or a real danger of its being turned up first and, of course, it is on the cards. If the tests of "real danger" or "serious possibility" are in future to be authoritative, then the *Victoria Laundry* case would indeed be a landmark because it would mean that *Hadley* v *Baxendale* would be differently decided today. I certainly could not understand any court deciding that, on the information available to the carrier in that case, the stoppage of the mill was neither a serious possibility nor a real danger. If those tests are to prevail in future, then let us cease to pay lip service to the rule in *Hadley* v *Baxendale*. But in my judgment to adopt these tests would extend liability for breach of contract beyond what is reasonable or desirable. From the limited knowledge which I have of commercial affairs I would not expect such an extension to be welcomed by the business community, and from the legal point of view I can find little or nothing to recommend it . . .

It appears to me that, without relying in any way on the *Victoria Laundry* case, and taking the principle that had already been established, the loss of profit claimed in this case was not too remote to be recoverable as damages. So it remains to consider whether the decision in *The Parana* established a rule which, though now anomalous, should nevertheless still be followed. In that case owing to the defective state of the ship's engines a voyage which ought to have taken sixty-five to seventy days took 127 days, and as a result a cargo of hemp fetched a much smaller price than it would have done if there had been no breach of contract. The Court of Appeal held, however, that the plaintiffs could not recover this loss as damages. The vital part of their judgment was as follows:

> "In order that damages may be recovered, we must come to two conclusions – first, that it was reasonably certain that the goods would not be sold until they did arrive; and secondly, that it was reasonably certain that they would be sold immediately after they arrived, and that that was known to the carrier at the time when the bills of lading were signed."

If that was the right test then the decision was right, and I think that that test was in line with a number of cases decided before or about that time (1877); but, as I have already said, so strict a test has long been obsolete; and, if one substitutes for "reasonably certain" the words "not unlikely" or some similar words denoting a much smaller degree of probability, then the whole argument in the judgment collapses.'

Parsons (H) (Livestock) Ltd v Uttley Ingham & Co Ltd

[1978] 1 All ER 525 • Court of Appeal

The facts are stated in the judgment of Scarman LJ.

Orr LJ: 'I agree with Lord Denning MR and also with Scarman LJ, whose judgment I have had the opportunity of reading, that this appeal should be dismissed, but with respect to Lord Denning MR I would dismiss it for the reasons to be given by Scarman LJ and not on the basis that a distinction is to be drawn for the present purposes between loss of profits and physical damage cases. I have not been satisfied that such a distinction is sufficiently supported by the authorities.'

Scarman LJ: 'The plaintiffs, who are pig farmers, claim damages of more than £36 000 for breach of contract. The defendants admit a breach of contract but say that the plaintiffs are entitled to no more than £18 damages. The judge found for the plaintiffs and ordered an inquiry to determine the amount of damages. The litigation arises out of the sale of a hopper for the storage in bulk of food to be fed to the plaintiffs' pigs. Some of the food went mouldy and poisoned some of the pigs. The judge found that the food poisoning was caused by bad storage conditions in the hopper and resulted in the plaintiffs suffering substantial business loss. It was on the basis of this finding that he gave judgment for the plaintiffs. The issue in this court is one of remoteness of damage. Plainly, it is of great importance to the parties. It also poses some difficult questions for the court. Lord Denning MR would decide the case upon the basis of a distinction which he suggests the law recognises between a breach of contract causing physical damage and one which causes loss of profit. He treats the famous trilogy of remoteness of damage cases (*Hadley v Baxendale; Victoria Laundry (Windsor) Ltd v Newman Industries Ltd* and *The Heron II, Koufos v C Czarnikow Ltd*) as limited in application to the loss of business profits and takes the view that in cases of physical damage the test is the same in tort as in contract. He accordingly concludes that in the class of contract cases in which he puts this case the test is the *Wagon Mound* test, reasonable foreseeability.

My conclusion in the present case is the same as that of Lord Denning MR but I reach it by a different route. I would dismiss the appeal. I agree with him in thinking it absurd that the test for remoteness of damage should, in principle, differ according to the legal classification of the cause of action, though one must recognise that parties to a contract have the right to agree on a measure of damages which may be greater, or less, than the law would offer in the absence of agreement. I also agree with him in thinking that, notwithstanding the interpretation put on some dicta in *The Heron II, Koufos* v *C Czarnikow Ltd*, the law is not so absurd as to differentiate between contract and tort save in situations where the agreement, or the factual relationship, of the parties with each other requires it in the interests of justice. I differ from him only to this extent: the cases do not, in my judgment, support a distinction in law between loss of profit and physical damage. Neither do I think it necessary to develop the law judicially by drawing such a distinction. Of course (and this is a reason for refusing to draw the distinction in law) the type of consequence, loss of profit or market or physical injury, will always be an important matter of fact in determining whether in all the circumstances the loss or injury was of a type which the parties could reasonably be supposed to have in contemplation . . .

A formidable volume of expert evidence upon this point was deployed for the consideration of the judge. His findings as to the contemplatability of E coli was as follows:

". . . I would not consider that I would be justified in finding that in the spring of 1971 at the time of the contract either a farmer in the position of the plaintiffs or a hopper manufacturer in the position of the defendants would reasonably have contemplated that there was either a very substantial degree of possibility or a real danger or serious possibility that the feeding of mouldy pignuts in the condition described by Mr Parsons would cause illness in the pigs that ate them, even on an intensive farm such as that of the plaintiffs."

The plaintiffs, by their respondent's notice, challenge this finding. I have done my best to study the evidence as it appears from the detailed and lucid judgment under appeal. I confess that I think I might well have reached a different conclusion, but bearing in mind the inevitable limitations upon an appellate court's consideration of such a question and the great advantages available to the judge, and most assuredly used to the full by him, I think it would be wrong to disturb his finding.

But it is necessary to note the essence – and the limits – of the finding. It is a finding that the parties could not reasonably be supposed to have had in contemplation that there was a serious possibility of mouldy nuts causing illness in the plaintiffs' pigs. It is not a finding that they could not reasonably have had in contemplation that a hopper unfit for its purpose of storing food in a condition suitable for feeding to the pigs might well lead to illness . . .

. . . [The judge] stated his conclusion in these words:

"On this interpretation the inevitable conclusion from the findings I have already made would be that this hopper was not reasonably fit for that purpose and that this caused the nuts to become toxic and that the illness of the pigs was a direct and natural consequence of such breach and toxicity, and that the plaintiffs do not have to prove that the toxicity or its results were foreseeable to either party. To put it another way, once the question of foreseeability of the breach is eliminated, as it is by the absolute warranty, the consequences of the breach flow naturally from it."

Counsel for the defendants criticises strongly this part of the judgment. He says it is based on a misunderstanding of *Hadley* v *Baxendale*; and he referred us to the well-known passage in Lord Reid's speech *The Heron II, Koufos* v *C Czarnikow Ltd* where he said that it is not enough that in fact the plaintiff's loss was directly caused by the defendant's breach of contract. Lord Reid said:

"The crucial question is whether, on the information available to the defendant when the contract was made, he should, or the reasonable man in his position would, have realised that such loss was sufficiently likely to result from the breach of contract to make it proper to hold that the loss flowed naturally from the breach or that loss of that kind should have been within his contemplation."

Notwithstanding his choice of language, I think the judge was making the approach which, according to Lord Reid, is the correct one. He was saying, in effect, that the parties to this contract must have appreciated that, if, as happened in the event, the hopper, unventilated, proved not to be suitable for the storage of pignuts to be fed to the plaintiffs' pigs, it was not unlikely, there was a serious possibility, that the pigs would become ill. The judge put it in this way:

"The *natural* result of feeding toxic food to animals is damage to their health and may be death, which is what occurred, albeit from a hitherto unknown disease and to particularly susceptible animals. There was therefore no need to invoke the question of *reasonable* contemplation in order to make the defendant liable" (my emphasis).

The judge in this critical passage is contrasting a natural result, i.e. one which people placed as these parties were would consider as a serious possibility, with a special, specific result, i.e. E coli disease, which, as he later found, the parties could not at the time of contract reasonably have contemplated as a consequence. He distinguished between "presumed contemplation" based on a special knowledge from ordinary understanding based upon general knowledge and concludes that the case falls within the latter category. He does so because he has held that the assumption, or hypothesis, to be made is that the parties had in mind at the time of contract not a breach of warranty limited to the delivery of mouldy nuts but a warranty as to the fitness of the hopper for its purpose. The assumption is of the parties asking themselves not what is likely to happen if the nuts are mouldy but what is likely to happen to the pigs if the hopper is unfit for storing nuts suitable to be fed to them. While, on his finding, nobody at the time of contract could have expected E coli to ensue from eating mouldy nuts, he is clearly, and, as a matter of common sense, rightly, saying that people would contemplate, upon the second assumption, the serious possibility of injury and even death among the pigs.

And so the question becomes: was he right to make the assumption he did? In my judgment, he was (see *Grant* v *Australian Knitting Mills Ltd*, and particularly the well-known passage in the speech of Lord Wright).

I would agree with *McGregor on Damages* that –

"in contract as in tort, it should suffice that, if physical injury or damage is within the contemplation of the parties, recovery is not to be limited because the degree of physical injury or damage could not have been anticipated."

This is so, in my judgment, not because there is, or ought to be, a specific rule of law governing cases of physical injury but because it would be absurd to regulate damages in such cases upon the necessity of supposing the parties had a prophetic foresight as to the exact nature of the injury that does in fact arise. It is enough if upon the hypothesis predicated physical injury must have been a serious possibility. Though in loss of market or loss of profit cases the factual analysis will be very different from cases of physical injury, the same principles, in my judgment, apply. Given the situation of the parties at the time of contract, was the loss of profit, or market, a serious possibility, something that would have been in their minds had they contemplated breach?

It does not matter, in my judgment, if they thought that the chance of physical injury, loss of profit, loss of market, or other loss as the case may be, was slight, or that the odds were against it, provided they contemplated as a serious possibility the type of consequence, not necessarily the specific consequence, that ensued upon breach.

Making the assumption as to breach that the judge did, no more than common sense was needed for them to appreciate that food affected by bad storage conditions might well cause illness in the pigs fed upon it.'

Compensatory nature of damages

Damages are to put the injured party into the position he would have been had the contract been performed. This can also include *loss of profit*.

Damages are *not* punitive or exemplary, they are compensation for loss suffered – not a punishment for wrong inflicted.

For what can damages be recovered?

Damages can be given for 'the disappointment, the distress, the upset and frustration caused by the breach'.

Jarvis v *Swans Tours Ltd*
[1973] 1 All ER 71 • Court of Appeal

The facts are stated in the judgment of Lord Denning MR.

Lord Denning MR. 'The plaintiff, Mr Jarvis, is a solicitor employed by a local authority at Barking. In 1969 he was minded to go for Christmas to Switzerland. He was looking forward to a skiing holiday. It is his one fortnight's holiday in the year. He prefers it in the winter rather than in the summer.

Mr Jarvis read a brochure issued by Swans Tours Ltd. He was much attracted by the description of Morlialp, Giswil, Central Switzerland. I will not read the whole of it, but just pick out some of the principal attractions:

> "House Party Centre with special resident host . . . Morlialp is a most wonderful little resort on a sunny plateau . . . Up there you will find yourself in the midst of beautiful alpine scenery, which in winter becomes a wonderland of sun, snow and ice, with a wide variety of fine ski-runs, a skating-rink and an exhilarating toboggan run . . . Why did we choose the Hotel Krone . . . mainly and most of all, because of the "Gemutlichkeit" and friendly welcome you will receive from Herr and Frau Weibel . . . The Hotel Krone has its own Alphutte Bar which will be open several evenings a week . . . No doubt you will be in for a great time, when you book this houseparty holiday . . . Mr Weibel, the charming owner, speaks English."

On the same page, in a special yellow box, it was said:

> "Swans Houseparty In Morlialp. All these Houseparty arrangements are included in the price of your holiday. Welcome party on arrival. Afternoon tea and cake for 7 days. Swiss Dinner by candlelight. Fondue-party. Yodler evening. Chali farewell party in the 'Alphutte Bar'. Service of representative."

Alongside on the same page there was a special note about ski-packs: "Hire of Skis, Sticks and Boots . . . 12 days £11.10".

In August 1969, on the faith of that brochure, Mr Jarvis booked a 15 day holiday, with ski-pack. The total charge was £63.45, including Christmas supplement. He was to fly from Gatwick to Zurich on 20th December 1969 and return on 3rd January 1970.

The plaintiff went on the holiday, but he was very disappointed. He was a man of about 35 and he expected to be one of a houseparty of some 30 or so people. Instead, he found there were only 13 during the first week. In the second week there was no houseparty at all. He was the only person there. Mr Weibel could not speak English. So there was Mr Jarvis, in the second week, in this hotel with no houseparty at all, and no one could speak English, except himself. He was very disappointed, too, with the skiing. It was some distance away at Giswil. There were no ordinary length skis. There were only mini-skis, about 3 ft long. So he did not get his skiing as he wanted to. In the second week he did get some longer skis for a couple of days, but then, because of the boots, his feet got rubbed and he could not continue even with the long skis. So his skiing holiday, from his point of view, was pretty well ruined . . .

. . . The matter was summed up by the learned judge:

". . . during the first week he got a holiday in Switzerland which was to some extent inferior . . . and, so too the second week he got a holiday which was very largely inferior [to what he was led to expect]."

What is the legal position? I think that the statements in the brochure were representations or warranties. The breaches of them give Mr Jarvis a right to damages. It is not necessary to decide whether they were representations or warranties; because, since the Misrepresentation Act 1967, there is a remedy in damages for misrepresentation as well as for breach of warranty.

The one question in the case is: what is the amount of damages? The judge seems to have taken the difference in value between what he paid for and what he got. He said that he intended to give "the difference between the two values and no other damages" under any other head. He thought that Mr Jarvis had got half of what he paid for. So the judge gave him half the amount which he had paid, namely, £31.72. Mr Jarvis appeals to this court. He says that the damages ought to have been much more . . .

What is the right way of assessing damages? It has often been said that on a breach of contract damages cannot be given for mental distress. Thus in *Hamlin* v *Great Northern Railway Co* Pollock CB said that damages cannot be given "for the disappointment of mind occasioned by the breach of contract". And in *Hobbs* v *London & South Western Railway Co* Mellor J said that –

". . . for the mere inconvenience, such as annoyance and loss of temper, or vexation, or for being disappointed in a particular thing which you have set your mind upon, without real physical inconvenience resulting, you cannot recover damages."

The courts in those days only allowed the plaintiff to recover damages if he suffered physical inconvenience, such as, having to walk five miles home, as in Hobbs's case; or to live in an overcrowded house: see *Bailey* v *Bullock*.

I think that those limitations are out of date. In a proper case damages for mental distress can be recovered in contract, just as damages for shock can be recovered in tort. One such case is a contract for a holiday, or any other contract to provide entertainment and enjoyment. If the contracting party breaks his contract, damages can be given for the disappointment, the distress, the upset and frustration caused by the breach. I know that it is difficult to assess in terms of money, but it is no more difficult than the assessment which the courts have to make every day in person injury cases for loss of amenities. Take the present case. Mr Jarvis has only a fortnight's holiday in the year. He books it far ahead, and looks forward to it all that time. He ought to be compensated for the loss of it.

A good illustration was given by Edmund Davis LJ in the course of the argument. He put the case of a man who has taken a ticket for Glyndebourne. It is the only night on which he can get there. He hires a car to take him. The car does not turn up. His damages are not limited to the mere cost of the ticket. He is entitled to general damages for the disappointment he has suffered and the loss of the entertainment which he should have had. Here, Mr Jarvis's fortnight's winter holiday has been a grave disappointment. It is true that he was conveyed to Switzerland and back and had meals and bed in the hotel. But that is not what he went for. He went to enjoy himself with all the facilities which the defendants said he would have. He is entitled to damages for the lack of those facilities, and for his loss of enjoyment.

A similar case occurred in 1951. It was *Stedman* v *Swan's Tours*. A holiday-maker was awarded damages because he did not get the bedroom and the accommodation which he was promised. The county court judge awarded him £13 15s. This court increased it to £50.

I think the judge was in error in taking the sum paid for the holiday, £63.45, and halving it. The right measure of damages is to compensate him for the loss of entertainment and enjoyment which he was promised, and which he did not get. Looking at the matter quite broadly, I think the damages in this case should be the sum of £125. I would allow the appeal accordingly.'

Damages can also be recovered for 'mental distress'.

Watts v *Morrow*

[1991] 4 All ER 937 • Court of Appeal

Mr and Mrs Watts engaged Morrow, a surveyor, to survey a house that they were interested in buying. They made it clear that they wanted a 'trouble free' house. Morrow negligently surveyed the house. Mr and Mrs Watts, relying on Morrow's survey, purchased the house for £177 500. Later they discovered serious defects in the house which cost Mr and Mrs Watts £33 961 to repair. At the trial of the action the value of the house in its defective condition was established to be £162 500. The judge awarded Mr and Mrs Watts £33 961 being the cost of repairs rather than £15 000 being the difference between the price paid for the house and the price that would have been paid for the house had the defects been known. In addition the judge awarded Mr and Mrs Watts £4000 each for 'distress and inconvenience'. The issues before the Court of Appeal were (i) whether damages should have been awarded for the cost of repair or whether damages should have been awarded on the difference in value between the price paid for the house and the price that would have been paid for the house had the defects been known; and (ii) whether damages should have been awarded for 'distress and inconvenience'.

Bingham LJ: *(1) Diminution in value or cost of repairs*
'The restitutory or compensatory principle which underlies the award of damages in contract is not open to question. Since it is ultimately a question of fact what sum of money is necessary to put a particular plaintiff in the position he would have been in if the particular defendant had properly performed the contract in question, I would accept Mr Naughton's contention that the measure of damages cannot be governed by an inflexible rule of law to be applied in all cases irrespective of the particular facts and regardless of whether or not such measure gives effect to the underlying principle. But this does not mean that there may not be sound *prima facie* rules to be applied in the ordinary run of cases . . . In the present field, by which I mean the purchase of houses by private buyers

in reliance on a negligent survey of structure or condition, *Philips* v *Ward* has been generally thought to lay down and in my view did lay down a *prima facie* rule for measuring damages. The crucial question is whether that *prima facie* rule was, as the judge held, inapplicable to the facts of the present case.

I do not think so. In *Philips* v *Ward*, as in the present case, the cost of repairs exceeded the diminution in value. The Court of Appeal there pointed out that if the plaintiff received the house (for which he had paid £25,000) and £7,000 (the cost of repairs) he would in effect have obtained the house for £18,000. But the value of the house in the defective state in which it had actually been was £21,000, and had the defendant properly performed his contract the plaintiff could not have bought at any lower price. An award of £7,000 would not therefore have put him in the same position as if the defendant had properly performed his contract. It would have improved his position to the extent of £3,000 and thus put him in an advantageous position he could never have enjoyed had the defendant properly performed.

The same simple approach applies here. The plaintiffs paid £177,500, the value of the house as it was represented to be. The value of the house in its actual condition was £162,500, a difference of £15,000. The actual cost of repairs was (in rounded up figures) £34,000. If the plaintiff were to end up with the house and an award of £34,000 damages he would have obtained the house for £143,500. But even if the defendant had properly performed his contract this bargain was never on offer. The effect of the award is not to put the plaintiffs in the same position as if the defendant had properly performed but in a much better one.

I would be willing to accept, as Romer LJ did in *Philips* v *Ward*, that if, on learning of the true state of the house, the plaintiffs had at once moved out and sold, they might well have been able to recover the costs thrown away in addition to the diminution in value. But these plaintiffs, no doubt for good reason, did not do that. They stayed and did the repairs. But the quantum of their claim would in theory be the same whether they had actually done and paid for the repairs or not, and if they had not the figures demonstrate a clear windfall profit. If, on learning of the defects which should have been but were not reported, a purchaser decides (for whatever reason) to retain the house and not move out and sell, I would question whether any loss he thereafter suffers, at least in the ordinary case, can be laid at the door of the contract-breaker . . .

(2) Damages for distress and inconvenience
A contract-breaker is not in general liable for any distress, frustration, anxiety, displeasure, vexation, tension or aggravation which his breach of contract may cause to the innocent party. This rule is not, I think, founded on the assumption that such reactions are not foreseeable, which they surely are or may be, but on considerations of policy.

But the rule is not absolute. Where the very object of a contract is to provide pleasure, relaxation, peace of mind or freedom from molestation, damages will be awarded if the fruit of the contract is not provided or if the contrary result is procured instead. If the law did not cater for this exceptional category of case it would be defective. A contract to survey the condition of a house for a prospective purchaser does not, however, fall within this exceptional category.

In cases not falling within this exceptional category, damages are in my view recoverable for physical inconvenience and discomfort caused by the breach and mental suffering directly related to that inconvenience and discomfort. If those effects are foreseeably suffered during a period when defects are repaired I am prepared to accept that they are sound in damages even though the cost of the repairs is not recoverable as such. But I also agree that awards should be restrained, and that the awards in this case far exceeded a reasonable award for the injury shown to have been suffered. I agree with the [£750] figures which Ralph Gibson LJ proposes to substitute.'

No damages will be awarded for injury to reputation.

Addis v *Gramophone Co Ltd*

[1908–10] All ER Rep 1 • House of Lords

The facts are stated in the judgment of Lord Loreburn LC.

Lord Loreburn LC: 'The plaintiff was employed by the defendants as manager of their business at Calcutta at £15 per week as salary, and a commission on the trade done. He could be dismissed by six months' notice. In October, 1905, the defendants gave him six months' notice, but at the same time they appointed Mr Gilpin to act as his successor, and took steps to prevent the plaintiff from acting any longer as manager. In December, 1905, the plaintiff came back to England. At that time the exact state of accounts between the plaintiff and the defendants was not ascertained. There had been debits and credits, and apparently no definite or periodical payments on account either of salary or commission. Thus there was a disputed account, though the limits of the dispute appear very narrow. In these circumstances the plaintiff brought this action in 1906, claiming an account and damages for breach of contract. That there was a breach of contract is quite clear. If what happened in October, 1905, did not amount to a wrongful dismissal it was, at all events, a breach of the plaintiff's right to act as manager during the six months and to earn the best commission he could make. Still another cause of action was included. The plaintiff had deposited some securities as guarantee of his good faith while absent from headquarters. In 1906 he demanded their return. The defendants unwarrantably refused to return the securities, and so the claim for detinue was included . . .

As to the damages of £600 for wrongful dismissal, a controversy ensued whether the £600 was intended to include salary for the six months or merely damages, because of the abrupt and oppressive way in which the plaintiff's services were discontinued and the loss he sustained from the discredit thus thrown upon him. Finally, a question of law was argued whether or not such damages could be recovered in law.

To my mind, it signifies nothing in the present case whether the claim is to be treated as for wrongful dismissal or not. In any case there was a breach of contract in not allowing the plaintiff to discharge his duties as manager, and the damages are exactly the same in either view. They are, in my opinion, the salary to which the plaintiff was entitled for the six months between October, 1905, and April, 1906, together with the commission which the jury think he would have earned had he been allowed to manage the business himself. I cannot agree that the manner of dismissal affects these damages. Such considerations have never been allowed to influence damages in this kind of case. An expression of Lord Coleridge CJ (*Maw* v *Jones*), has been quoted as authority to the contrary. I doubt if the learned Lord Chief Justice so intended it. If he did, I cannot agree with him. If there be a dismissal without notice the employer must pay an indemnity; but, that indemnity cannot include compensation either for the injured feelings of the servant or for the loss he may sustain from the fact that his having been dismissed or itself makes it more difficult for him to obtain fresh employment. The cases relating to a refusal by a banker to honour cheques, when he has funds in hand, have, in my opinion, no bearing. That class of case has always been regarded as exceptional. And the rule as to damages in wrongful dismissal, or in breach of contract to allow a man to continue in a stipulated service, has always been, I believe, what I have stated. It is too inveterate to be altered now, even if it were desirable to alter it.'

No damages will lie for a profit made by the contract breaker.

Surrey County Council v Bredero Homes Ltd
[1993] 1 WLR 1361 • Court of Appeal

Surrey CC sold a piece of land to Bredero. As part of the sale agreement Bredero covenanted to build only 72 houses on the land. In breach of the agreement Bredero built 77 houses. Surrey CC sued Bredero for breach of covenant. The judge at first instance only awarded nominal damages. Surrey CC appealed claiming substantial damages.

Steyn LJ: '. . . The issue in this appeal was defined by Sir William Goodhart, appearing for the plaintiffs, as the correct measure of damages in a case where the following three circumstances are satisfied. (a) There has been a deliberate breach of contract, (b) the party in breach has made a profit from that breach and (c) the innocent party is in financial terms in the same position as if the contract had been fully performed. It is an important issue with considerable implications for the shape of our law of obligations, and I therefore add a few remarks of my own.

Dillon LJ has reviewed the relevant case law. It would not be a useful exercise for me to try to navigate through those much travelled waters again. Instead, it seems to me that it may possibly be useful to consider the question from the point of view of the application of first principles.

An award of compensation for breach of contract serves to protect three separate interests. The starting principle is that the aggrieved party ought to be compensated for loss of his positive or expectation interests. In other words, the object is to put the aggrieved party in the same financial position as if the contract had been fully performed. But the law also protects the negative interest of the aggrieved party. If the aggrieved party is unable to establish the value of a loss of bargain he may seek compensation in respect of his reliance losses. The object of such an award is to compensate the aggrieved party for expenses incurred and losses suffered in reliance on the contract. These two complementary principles share one feature. Both are pure compensatory principles. If the aggrieved party has suffered no loss he is not entitled to be compensated by invoking these principles. The application of these principles to the present case would result in an award of nominal damages only.

There is, however, a third principle which protects the aggrieved party's restitutionary interest. The object of such an award is not to compensate the plaintiff for a loss, but to deprive the defendant of the benefit he gained by the breach of contract. The classic illustration is a claim for the return of goods sold and delivered where the buyer has repudiated his obligation to pay the price. It is not traditional to describe a claim for restitution following a breach of contract as damages. What matters is that a coherent law of obligations must inevitably extend its protection to cover certain restitutionary interests. How far that protection should extend is the essence of the problem before us. In my view *Wrotham Park Estate Co Ltd v Parkside Homes Ltd* is only defensible on the basis of the third or restitutionary principle: see *MacGregor on Damages*, and Professor P B H Birks, "Civil wrongs: a new world", *Butterworth Lectures* (1990–1991).

The plaintiffs' argument that the *Wrotham Park* case can be justified on the basis of a loss of bargaining opportunity is a fiction. The object of the award in the *Wrotham Park* case was not to compensate the plaintiffs for financial injury, but to deprive the defendants of an unjustly acquired gain. Whilst it must be acknowledged that the *Wrotham Park* case represented a new development, it seems to me that it was based on a principled legal theory, justice and sound policy. In the defendant's skeleton argument some doubt was cast, by way of alternative submission, on the correctness of the award of damages for breach of covenant in the *Wrotham Park* case. In my respectful view, it was rightly decided and represents a useful development in our law. In *Tito* v *Waddell (No 2)*, Sir Robert Megarry V-C interpreted the *Wrotham Park* case and *Bracewell* v *Appleby*, which followed the *Wrotham Park* case, as cases of invasion of property rights. I respectfully agree. The *Wrotham Park* case is analogous to cases where a defendant has made use of the aggrieved party's property and thereby saved expense: see *Penarth Dock Engineering Co Ltd* v *Pounds*. I readily accept that "property" in this context must be interpreted in a wide sense. I would also not suggest that there is no scope for further development in this branch of the law.

But, in the present case, we are asked to extend considerably the availability of restitutionary remedies for breach of contract. I question the desirability of any such development. The acceptance of the plaintiffs' primary or alternative submission, as outlined by Dillon LJ, will have a wide-ranging impact on our commercial law. Even the alternative and narrower submission will, for example, cover charterparties and contracts of affreightment where the remedy of a negative injunction may be available. Moreover, so far as the narrower submission restricts the principle to cases where the remedies of specific performance and injunction would have been available, I must confess that that seems to me a bromide formula without any rationale in logic or common sense. Given a breach of contract, why should the availability of a restitutionary remedy, as a matter of legal entitlement, be dependent on the availability of the wholly different and discretionary remedies of injunction and specific performance? If there is merit in the argument I cannot see any sense in restricting a compensatory remedy which serves to protect restitutionary interests to cases where there would be separate remedies of specific performance and injunction designed directly and indirectly to enforce payment.

For my part I would hold that if Sir William Goodhart's wider proposition fails the narrower one must equally fail. Both submissions hinge on the defendant's breach being deliberate. Sir William invoked the principle that a party is not entitled to take advantage of his own wrongdoing. Despite Sir William's disclaimer it seems to me that the acceptance of the propositions formulated by him will inevitably mean that the focus will be on the motive of the party who committed the breach of contract. That is contrary to the general approach of our law of contract and, in particular, to rules governing the assessment of damages.

In my view there are also other policy reasons which militate against adopting Sir William's primary or narrower submission. The introduction of restitutionary remedies to deprive cynical contract breakers of the fruits of their breaches of contract will lead to greater uncertainty in the assessment of damages in commercial and consumer disputes. It is of paramount importance that the way in which disputes are likely to be resolved by the courts must be readily predictable. Given the premise that the aggrieved party has suffered no loss, is such a dramatic extension of restitutionary remedies justified in order to confer a windfall in each case on the aggrieved party? I think not. In any event such a widespread availability of restitutionary remedies will have a tendency to discourage economic activity in relevant situations. In a range of cases such liability would fall on underwriters who have insured relevant liability risks. Inevitably underwriters would have to be compensated for the new species of potential claims. Insurance premiums would have to go up. That, too, is a consequence which mitigates against the proposed extension. The recognition of the proposed extension will in my view not serve the public interest. It is sound policy to guard against extending the protection of the law of obligations too widely. For these substantive and policy reasons I regard it as undesirable that the range of restitutionary remedies should be extended in the way in which we have been invited to do so.

The present case involves no breach of fiduciary obligations. It is a case of breach of contract. The principles governing expectation or reliance losses cannot be invoked. Given the fact of the breach of contract the only question is whether restitution is an appropriate remedy for this wrong. The case does not involve any invasion of the plaintiffs' property interests even in the broadest sense of that word, nor is it closely analogous to the *Wrotham Park* position. I would therefore rule that no restitutionary remedy is available and there is certainly no other remedy available. I would dismiss the appeal.'

A plaintiff cannot recover twice in respect of the same breach, that is for loss of profit and also capital loss.

Cullinane v British 'Rema' Manufacturing Co Ltd
[1953] 2 All ER 1257 • Court of Appeal

The defendants agreed to sell a pulverising and drying plant to the plaintiff for £6578. A term of the contract provided that the plant would be capable of producing dry clay powder at the rate of six tons per hour. In fact the plant was only capable of producing dry clay powder at the rate of two tons per hour. The plaintiff claimed £7370 damages for the loss of capital value of the plant (i.e. the difference between a plant that could produce dry clay powder at the rate of six tons per hour and a plant that produced dry clay powder at the rate of two tons per hour) and also £8913 damages for loss of profit it would have made had it been able to produce clay at six tons per hour instead of two tons per hour. The court of first instance awarded damages under both heads. The defendant appealed arguing that the plaintiff was entitled to damages either for loss of capital value or loss of profit but not both.

Sir Raymond Evershed MR: 'As a matter of principle again, it seems to me that a person who has obtained a machine such as the plaintiff here obtained, which was mechanically in exact accordance with the order given, but was unable to perform a particular function which it was warranted to perform, may adopt one of two courses. He may, when he discovers its incapacity and that it is not what he wanted and is useless to him, claim to recover the capital cost he has incurred less anything he can obtain by disposing of the material that he got. A claim of that kind puts the plaintiff in the same position as though he had never made the contract at all. He is, in other words, back where he started, and, if it were shown that the profit-earning capacity was, in fact, very small, the plaintiff would probably elect so to base his claim. Alternatively, he may, where the warranty in question relates to performance, make his claim on the basis of the profit he has lost, because the machine as delivered fell short in its performance of that which it was warranted to do. If he chooses to base his claim on that footing, depreciation has nothing whatever to do with it.

During the course of the argument many analogies were taken, and I find assistance from the simple agricultural analogy of the cow. For example, A sells to B a cow for £100, and warrants that for its next five lactations it will produce milk at the rate of four gallons a day and it is discovered that the cow's performance is at the rate, not of four gallons, but one gallon a day, and that a one-gallon-a-day cow is worth not £100 but £10. The buyer might then elect either to claim the difference between the £100 that he had paid for a four-gallon-a-day cow and £10, the true value of the one-gallon-a-day cow, and recover the difference, £90, which puts him in the same position as if he had intended to buy what in fact he bought. Alternatively, he might say: "I keep this cow and I shall sue you for the loss I have suffered because her performance was not as warranted. I am getting, not four gallons, but one gallon, a day, and, therefore, I am losing what I would have made on the sales (less necessary expenditure) of an extra thousand gallons a year." If the latter course is chosen, then, as I have indicated, it seems to me that the depreciated or depreciating value of the cow has nothing whatever to do with the claim. So much, I think, is conceded, and it has, therefore, seemed to us that it would be impossible to combine in this case a claim for the capital loss and a claim for the total loss of profit, just as it would be impossible to recover both the £90, being the capital loss on the cow and the full amount of the loss due to the shortage of milk . . .

But, whatever be the answer to these problems, I come back to the same point, namely, that the plaintiff can choose either to claim on the basis that he had wasted capital and that he ought to be put in the position he would have been in if he had never bought this machine, or to say: "I have got the machine. What I am claiming is the loss I have suffered because its performance falls short of that which was warranted, and, therefore, I have not made the profitable sales which I would have made, and I claim, accordingly, the loss of resultant profits". The second alternative being the larger, he is entitled to choose that, but, in my judgment, he should be limited to it. He is not, in my judgment . . . able to claim . . . both for loss of capital and for loss of profit . . .'

Calculation of damages – difference in value or cost of restoration

Ruxley Electronics and Construction Ltd v Forsyth

[1995] 3 All ER 268 • House of Lords

The facts are stated in the judgment of Lord Jauncey.

Lord Jauncey of Tullichettle: 'My Lords, the respondent entered into a contract with the appellant for the construction by them of a swimming pool at his house in Kent. The contract provided for the pool having a maximum depth of 7 ft 6 in but, as built, its maximum depth was only 6 ft. The respondent sought to recover as damages for breach of contract the cost of demolition of the existing pool and construction of a new one of the required depth. The trial judge made the following findings which are relevant to this appeal: (1) the pool as constructed was perfectly safe to dive into; (2) there was no evidence that the shortfall in depth had decreased the value of the pool; (3) the only practicable method of achieving a pool of the required depth would be to demolish the existing pool and reconstruct a new one at a cost of £21,560; (4) he was not satisfied that the respondent intended to build a new pool at such a cost; (5) in addition such cost would be wholly disproportionate to the disadvantage of having a pool of a depth of only 6 ft as opposed to 7 ft 6 in and it would therefore be unreasonable to carry out the works; and (6) that the respondent was entitled to damages for loss of amenity in the sum of £2,500.

The Court of Appeal by a majority (Staughton and Mann LJ; Dillon LJ dissenting) allowed the appeal, holding that the only way in which the respondent could achieve his contractual objective was by reconstructing the pool at a cost of £21,560 which was accordingly a reasonable venture.

The general principles applicable to the measure of damages for breach of contract are not in doubt. In a very well-known passage Parke B in *Robinson* v *Harman* said:

"The next question is: What damages is the plaintiff entitled to recover? The rule of the common law is that where a party sustains a loss by reason of a breach of contract, he is, so far as money can do it, to be placed in the same situation, with respect to damages, as if the contract had been performed."

In *British Westinghouse Electric and Manufacturing Co Ltd* v *Underground Electric Railways Co of London Ltd* Viscount Haldane LC said:

"The quantum of damage is a question of fact, and the only guidance the law can give is to lay down general principles which afford at times but scanty assistance in dealing with particular cases . . . Subject to these observations I think that there are certain broad principles which are quite well settled. The first is that, as far as possible, he who has proved a breach of a bargain to supply what he contracted to get is to be placed, as far as money can do it, in as good a situation as if the contract had been performed. The fundamental basis is thus compensation for pecuniary loss naturally flowing from the breach; but this first principle is qualified by a second, which imposes on a plaintiff the duty of taking all reasonable steps to mitigate the loss consequent on the breach . . ."

More recently, in what is generally accepted as the leading authority on the measure of damages for defective building work, Lord Cohen in *East Ham BC* v *Bernard Sunley & Sons Ltd* said:

". . . the learned editors of *Hudson's Building and Engineering Contracts* (8th edn) say, that there are in fact three possible bases of assessing damages, namely, (a) the cost of reinstatement; (b) the difference in cost to the builder of the actual work done and work specified; or (c) the diminution in value of the work due to the breach of contract. They go on (ibid): 'There is no doubt that wherever it is reasonable for the employer to insist upon re-instatement the courts will treat the cost of re-instatement as the measure of damage.' In the present case it could not be disputed that it was reasonable for the employers to insist on re-instatement and in these circumstances it necessarily follows that on the question of damage the trial judge arrived at the right conclusion."

Lord Upjohn likewise stated that in a case of defective building work reinstatement was the normal measure of damages.

Mr McGuire QC for the appellant argued that the cost of reinstatement was only allowable where (1) the employer intended as a matter of probability to rebuild if damages were awarded, and (2) that it was reasonable as between him and the contractor so to do. Since the judge had found against the respondent on both these matters the appeal should be allowed. Mr Jacob on the other hand maintained that reasonableness only arose at the stage when a real loss had been established to exist and that where that loss could only be met by damages assessed on one basis there was no room for consideration of reasonableness. Such was the case where a particular personal preference was part of the contractual objective – a situation which did not allow damages to be assessed on a diminution of value basis.

I start with the question of reasonableness in the context of reinstatement. There is a considerable body of authority dealing with this matter. Lord Cohen in the passage in *East Ham BC* v *Bernard Sunley & Sons Ltd* quoted above referred to the reasonableness of insisting on reinstatement. In *Imodco Ltd* v *Wimpey Major Projects Ltd* Glidewell LJ stated that the cost of work to put pipes in the position contracted for would be recoverable if there was an intention to carry out the work and if it was reasonable so to do. In *Minscombe Properties Ltd* v *Sir Alfred McAlpine & Sons Ltd* O'Connor LJ applied the test of reasonableness in determining whether the cost of reinstatement of land to its contracted for condition should be recoverable as damages. In *Radford* v *De Froberville* Oliver J said:

> "In the instant case, the plaintiff says in evidence that he wishes to carry out the work on his own land and there are, as it seems to me, three questions that I have to answer. First, am I satisfied on the evidence that the plaintiff has a genuine and serious intention of doing the work? Secondly, is the carrying out of the work on his own land a reasonable thing for the plaintiff to do? Thirdly, does it make any difference that the plaintiff is not personally in occupation of the land but desires to do the work for the benefit of his tenants?"

In *C R Taylor (Wholesale) Ltd* v *Hepworths Ltd* May J referred with approval to a statement in *McGregor On Damages* (13th edn) that in deciding between diminution in value and cost of reinstatement the appropriate test was the reasonableness of the plaintiff's desire to reinstate the property and remarked that the damages to be awarded were to be reasonable as between plaintiff and defendant. He concluded that in the case before him to award the notional cost of reinstatement would be unreasonable since it would put the plaintiffs in a far better financial position than they would have been before the fire occurred. In *McGregor* (15th edn), after a reference to the cost of reinstatement being the normal measure of damages in a case of defective building, it is stated:

> "If, however, the cost of remedying the defect is disproportionate to the end to be attained, the damages fall to be measured by the value of the building had it been built as required by the contract less its value as it stands."

In *Bellgrove* v *Eldridge* the High Court of Australia in a judgment of the court, after referring with approval to the rule stated in *Hudson on Building Contracts* (7th edn) that –

> "The measure of the damages recoverable by the building owner for the breach of a building contract is . . . the difference between the contract price of the work or building contracted for and the cost of making the work or building conform to the contract . . ."

and referring to a number of cases supporting this proposition, continued:

> "In none of these cases is anything more done than that work which is required to achieve conformity and the cost of the work, whether it be necessary to replace only a small part, or a substantial part, or, indeed, the whole of the building is, subject to the qualification which we have already mentioned and to which we shall refer, together with any appropriate consequential damages, the extent of the building owner's loss. The qualification, however, to which this rule is subject is that, not only must the work undertaken be necessary to produce conformity, but that also, it must be a reasonable course to adopt."

A similar approach to reasonableness was adopted by Cardozo J delivering the judgment of the majority of the Court of Appeals of New York in *Jacob & Youngs Inc* v *Kent*.

Damages are designed to compensate for an established loss and not to provide a gratuitous benefit to the aggrieved party, from which it follows that the reasonableness of an award of damages is to be linked directly to the loss sustained. If it is unreasonable in a particular case to award the cost of reinstatement it must be because the loss sustained does not extend to the need to reinstate. A failure to achieve the precise contractual objective does not necessarily result in the loss which is occasioned by a total failure. This was recognised by the High Court of Australia in the passage in *Bellgrove* v *Eldridge* cited above where it was stated that the cost of reinstatement work subject to the qualification of reasonableness was the extent of the loss, thereby treating reasonableness as a factor to be considered in determining what was that loss rather than, as the respondents argued, merely a factor in determining which of two alternative remedies were appropriate for a loss once established. Further support for this view is to be found in the following passage in the judgment of Megarry V-C in *Tito* v *Waddell (No 2)*:

> "*Per contra*, if the plaintiff has suffered little or no monetary loss in the reduction of value of his land, and he has no intention of applying any damages towards carrying out the work contracted for, or its equivalent, I cannot see why he should recover the cost of doing work which will never be done. It would be a mere pretence to say that this cost was a loss and so should be recoverable as damages."

Megarry V-C was, as I understand it, there saying that it would be unreasonable to treat as a loss the cost of carrying out work which would never in fact be done.

I take the example suggested during argument by my noble and learned friend Lord Bridge of Harwich. A man contracts for the building of a house and specifies that one of the lower courses of brick should be blue. The builder uses yellow brick instead. In all other respects the house conforms to the contractual specification. To replace the yellow bricks with blue would involve extensive demolition and reconstruction at a very large cost. It would clearly be unreasonable to award to the owner the cost of reconstructing because his loss was not the necessary cost of reconstruction of his house, which was entirely adequate for its design purpose, but merely the lack of aesthetic pleasure which he might have derived from the sight of blue bricks. Thus in the present appeal the respondent has acquired a perfectly serviceable swimming pool, albeit one lacking the specified depth. His loss is thus not the lack of a usable pool with consequent need to construct a new one. Indeed were he to receive the cost of building a new one and retain the existing one he would have recovered not compensation for loss but a very substantial gratuitous benefit, something which damages are not intended to provide.

What constitutes the aggrieved party's loss is in every case a question of fact and degree. Where the contract breaker has entirely failed to achieve the contractual objective it may not be difficult to conclude that the loss is the necessary cost of achieving that objective. Thus if a building is constructed so defectively that it is of no use for its designed purpose the owner may have little difficulty in establishing that his loss is the necessary cost of reconstructing. Furthermore, in taking reasonableness into account in determining the extent of loss it is reasonableness in relation to the particular contract and not at large. Accordingly, if I contracted for the erection of a folly in my garden which shortly thereafter suffered a total collapse it would be irrelevant to the determination of my loss to argue that the erection of such a folly which contributed nothing to the value of my house was a crazy thing to do. As Oliver J said in *Radford* v *De Froberville* :

> "If he contracts for the supply of that which he thinks serves his interests, be they commercial, aesthetic or merely eccentric, then if that which is contracted for is not supplied by the other contracting party I do not see why, in principle, he should not be compensated by being provided with the cost of supplying it through someone else or in a different way, subject to the proviso, of course, that he is seeking compensation for a genuine loss and not merely using a technical breach to secure an uncovenanted profit."

However, where the contractual objective has been achieved to a substantial extent the position may be very different.

It was submitted that where the objective of a building contract involved satisfaction of a personal preference the only measure of damages available for a breach involving failure to achieve such satisfaction was the cost of reinstatement. In my view this is not the case. Personal preference may well be a factor in reasonableness and hence in determining what loss has been suffered but it cannot *per se* be determinative of what that loss is.

My Lords, the trial judge found that it would be unreasonable to incur the cost of demolishing the existing pool and building a new and deeper one. In so doing he implicitly recognised that the respondent's loss did not extend to the cost of reinstatement. He was, in my view, entirely justified in reaching that conclusion. It therefore follows that the appeal must be allowed.

It only remains to mention two further matters. The appellant argued that the cost of reinstatement should only be allowed as damages where there was shown to be an intention on the part of the aggrieved party to carry out the work. Having already decided that the appeal should be allowed I no longer find it necessary to reach a conclusion on this matter. However, I should emphasise that in the normal case the court has no concern with the use to which a plaintiff puts an award of damages for a loss which has been established. Thus, irreparable damage to an article as a result of a breach of contract will entitle the owner to recover the value of the article irrespective of whether he intends to replace it with a similar one or to spend the money on something else. Intention, or lack of it, to reinstate can have relevance only to reasonableness and hence to the extent of the loss which has been sustained. Once that loss has been established intention as to the subsequent use of the damages ceases to be relevant.

The second matter relates to the award of £2500 for loss of amenity made by the trial judge. The respondent argued that he erred in law in making such award. However, as the appellant did not challenge it, I find it unnecessary to express any opinion on the matter.'

Difficulty of assessment no bar

Difficulty in assessing damages does not disentitle a plaintiff from having an attempt made to assess them, unless they depend altogether on remote and hypothetical possibilities.

Chaplin v *Hicks*
[1911–13] All ER Rep 224 • Court of Appeal

Chaplin, along with 6000 others, entered a nationwide beauty contest and got through to the final stage where only 50 contestants were left. Hicks was to select the twelve winners from these remaining contestants. The winners were to be given theatrical engagement by him for three years at £5 per week. Hicks, in breach of his contract with Chaplin, prevented her from taking part in the final selection stage. The judge and jury awarded her damages of £100 for the opportunity she lost in being prevented from taking part in the final selection stage.

Fletcher Moulton LJ: 'For the purposes of this appeal we must take it that the contract was entered into, and that the defendant did not keep his engagement with the plaintiff by failing to give her an opportunity of appearing before him for selection, with the result that she was excluded from the limited competition and had no chance of securing one of the appointments. Counsel for the defendant did not deny the existence of the contract, or its terms, or the fact that it was a contract which the law would enforce, or the breach of it by the defendant, but he said that the damages sustained by the plaintiff could only be nominal – namely, the amount of the fee (1s) which the plaintiff had paid upon entering for the competition. He said further that in a case where the expectation of the plaintiff depended upon a contingency the law would give him nothing but nominal damages for a breach of the contract . . .

At common law contracts were never enforced specifically as in equity. It considered only that the contract was broken and that there must be a *solatium* to the sufferer by the breach. It knew no other principle than that it was the aim of the law to give the injured party such damages as if the contract had not been broken. To do this might in some cases be extremely difficult, because the loss occasioned to the plaintiff might depend on matters which had no real connection with the breach. Thus, for example, if a man furnished a post-chaise to drive a son to see his father before he died and the chaise broke down, the result might be that the father would cut the son out of his will, but it would not be fair to include in the damages compensation for the loss of the son's expectations. Therefore, the law required this limitation, that the damages must be such as may reasonably be supposed to have been in the contemplation of the parties to the contract, and must not be extraneous to the contract. Counsel for the defendant contended that damages arising from this breach of contract were too remote, because they were never intended to have any connection with it, but that contention is clearly unsustainable. The very object and scope of the contract was that the plaintiff should have the chance of being selected by the defendant for one of the theatrical engagements he offered, and his refusal to fulfil his part of the contract is the breach complained of. Damages are, therefore, a fair compensation to the plaintiff for being excluded from the limited class of candidates. It seems to me that nothing more direct or more intimately connected with the contract could be found.

But then counsel for the defendant went on to say that these damages were very difficult, if not altogether incapable, of assessment, because no one could say, even if the plaintiff had had a chance of submitting herself for selection, whether she would have obtained one of these situations. That raises what is really the only point of importance in the case – namely, whether it is reasonable to say that the fact that the plaintiff was excluded from the limited class amounted to what may be described as an injury done to her? I think it did, and it may be a very substantial injury. According to the theory of the law which tries to give an equivalent for loss actually sustained, the plaintiff starts here with an unchallengeable case. But it is said that, as there was a possibility that the plaintiff might not be chosen, it is impossible to assess the damages. It is, however, clear that where in the minds of reasonable men there has been a *de facto* loss, the jury have to do their best to estimate it. It is not necessary that there should be an accepted measure of damages. The recognised rules as to the measure of damages only apply in cases of frequent occurrence where the court is well acquainted with the surrounding circumstances, for instance, in an action for damages for breach of a contract for sale of goods. In most cases there is no recognised rule, and the jury must assess what they think would be an adequate *solatium*. I ask myself whether in a case where the results of the contract depend upon the volition of an independent person, the law in the event of a breach shuts its eyes to the wrong and refuses to give damages? During the argument I put the case of a contract of service by which the employer became bound to employ the clerk as one of five second class clerks at a salary of £200 a year, and afterwards to select from among these five two first class clerks at £500 a year each. I am satisfied that any person accepting that engagement would be entitled to say: "I may be one of the five second class clerks from whom the two first class clerks are to be chosen". He would be entitled to look at that as a valuable part of the consideration for his services, and, if he were deprived of his position, he would be entitled to ask a jury to estimate the value of that of which he had been deprived.

I have come to the conclusion that where a man has a right to belong to a limited class of competitors for something of value, and that right is taken away from him, it is always open to the jury, and in fact their duty, to assess the damage he has sustained. The present case is a typical one. The plaintiff, from being one of 6000 competitors, had become one of fifty who were entitled to twelve prizes to be distributed among them; and, seeing she had lost all advantages of being one of the competitors, the jury were entitled to estimate her loss. This is not a case in which I can lay down any measure of damages. The jury must be entirely guided by their good sense, and I cannot say that they assessed the damages on an extravagant scale. Twelve engagements of considerable pecuniary value were offered as prizes, and no doubt there would be considerable consequential advantages to the plaintiff if she was successful in the competition. I think the jury were entitled to say that it was of considerable pecuniary value to her that she should get into the limited class, and they could award her damages accordingly.'

Penalty clauses and liquidated damages clauses

Assessment of damages by the parties

Often a clause will be incorporated into the contract which assesses the damages at which the parties rate a breach of contract by one or both of them. The clause must be a genuine attempt to assess damages – a *liquidated damages clause* – rather than a true *penalty clause*. English law does not accept *penalty* clauses.

Whether a clause is a liquidated damages clause or a penalty clause is a matter of construction judged at the time of making the contract: see *Dunlop Pneumatic Tyre Co Ltd* v *New Garage & Motor Co Ltd* below.

Limiting sum

Liquidated damages clauses can act as a type of 'exclusion clause' – not excluding liability but limiting liability; this the courts will accept: see *Cellulose Acetate Silk Co Ltd* v *Widnes Foundry (1925) Ltd* below.

Cellulose Acetate Silk Co Ltd v Widnes Foundry (1925) Ltd

[1933] AC 20 • House of Lords

Widnes Foundry contracted with the Silk Company to deliver and erect an acetone recovery plant. The contract stated that the work would be completed in 18 weeks. Clause 10 of the agreement stated 'If this period of 18 weeks is exceeded [Widnes Foundry] to pay by way of penalty the sum of £20 per working week for every week you exceed the 18 weeks'. Widnes Foundry were 30 weeks late in completing their work. The Silk Company sued Widnes Foundry for £5850 which, they claimed, was the actual loss they had suffered through the delay. Widnes Foundry claimed that their liability was limited by clause 10 to £600 only.

Lord Atkin: 'What then is the effect of clause 10? . . . I entertain no doubt that what the parties meant was that in the event of delay the damages and the only damages were to be £20 a week, no less and no more. It has to be remembered that the Foundry Company's business in this respect was to supply an accessory to a large business plant for which they had no responsibility. The extent of the purchasers' business might be enormous; their expenses were beyond the sellers' control; and it would be a very ordinary business precaution for the sellers in such a case to say: "we will name a date for delivery but we will accept no liability to pay damages for not observing the date; for if we were by our default to stop the whole of your business the damages might be overwhelming in relation to our possible profit out of the transaction. We won't incur any such risk." This precaution the prospective sellers took in their printed Condition 10. They definitely negative any liability for delay. The purchasers have ample notice of this in the first quotation form sent to them on February 16. The purchasers pressed for an earlier date; they got it, and getting it without more they would still only have a business firm's assurance of delivery by that date; they would still be unable to claim damages from them for breach. The sellers ask for an addition to the price in order to enable them to give the earlier delivery; the buyers ask for some compensation if they do not get the delivery they want. It is agreed at £20 per week of delay. It appears to me that such sum is provided as compensation in place of the no compensation at all which would otherwise have been the result. Except that it is called a penalty, which on the cases is far from conclusive, it appears to be an amount of compensation measured by the period of delay. I agree that it is not a pre-estimate of actual damage. I think it must have been obvious to both the parties that the actual damage would be much more than £20 a week; but it was intended to go towards the damage, and it was all that the sellers were prepared to pay. I find it impossible to believe that the sellers who were quoting for delivery at nine months without any liability, undertook delivery at eighteen weeks, and in so doing, when they engaged to pay £20 a week, in fact made themselves liable to pay full compensation for all loss.

For these reasons I think the Silk Company are only entitled to recover £20 a week as agreed damages.'

Rules for ascertaining whether a clause is a penalty clause or a liquidated damages clause

The rules are summarised by Lord Dunedin in

Dunlop Pneumatic Tyre Company v New Garage and Motor Company

[1915] AC 79 • House of Lords

The facts are stated in the judgment of Lord Dunedin.

Lord Dunedin: 'My Lords, the appellants, through an agent, entered into a contract with the respondents under which they supplied them with their goods, which consisted mainly of motor-tyre covers and tubes. By this contract, in respect of certain concessions as to discounts, the respondents bound themselves not to do several things, which may be shortly set forth as follows: . . . not to sell to any private customer or co-operative society at prices less than the current price list issued by the Dunlop Company; . . . Finally, the agreement concluded (clause 5), "we agree to pay to the Dunlop Pneumatic Tyre Company, Ltd the sum of £5 for each and every tyre, cover or tube sold or offered in breach of this agreement, as and by way of liquidated damages and not as a penalty".

The appellants, having discovered that the respondents had sold covers and tubes at under the current list price, raised action and demanded damages. The case was tried and the breach in fact held proved. An inquiry was directed before the Master as to damages. The Master inquired, and assessed the damages at £250, adding this explanation "I find that it was left open to me to decide whether the £5 fixed in the agreement was penalty or liquidated damages. I find that it was liquidated damages."

The respondents appealed to the Court of Appeal, when the majority of that Court, Vaughan Williams and Swinfen Eady LJ, held, Kennedy LJ dissenting, that the said sum of £5 was a penalty, and entered judgment for the plaintiffs for the sum of £2 as nominal damages. Appeal from that decision is now before your Lordships' House.

. . . I do not think it advisable to attempt any detailed review of the various cases, but I shall content myself with stating succinctly the various propositions which I think are deducible from the decisions which rank as authoritative: –

(1) Though the parties to a contract who use the words "penalty" or "liquidated damages" may *prima facie* be supposed to mean what they say, yet the expression used is not conclusive. The Court must find out whether the payment stipulated is in truth a penalty or liquidated damages. This doctrine may be said to be found passim in nearly every case.

(2) The essence of a penalty is a payment of money stipulated as *in terrorem* of the offending party; the essence of liquidated damages is a genuine covenanted pre-estimate of damage (*Clydebank Engineering and Shipbuilding Co* v *Don Jose Ramos Yzquierdo y Castaneda*).

(3) The question whether a sum stipulated is penalty or liquidated damages is a question of construction to be decided upon the terms and inherent circumstances of each particular contract, judged of as at the time of the making of the contract, not as at the time of the breach (*Public Works Commissioner* v *Hills* and *Webster* v *Bosanquet*).

(4) To assist this task of construction various tests have been suggested, which if applicable to the case under consideration may prove helpful, or even conclusive. Such are:

(a) It will be held to be penalty if the sum stipulated for is extravagant and unconscionable in amount in comparison with the greatest loss that could conceivably be proved to have followed from the breach. (Illustration given by Lord Halsbury in *Clydebank* Case).

(b) It will be held to be a penalty if the breach consists only in not paying a sum of money, and the sum stipulated is a sum greater than the sum which ought to have been paid (*Kemble* v *Farren*). This though one of the most ancient instances is truly a corollary to the last test. Whether it had its historical origin in the doctrine of the common law that where A promised to pay B a sum of money on a certain day and did not do so, B could only recover the sum with, in certain cases, interest, but could never recover further damages for non-timeous payment, or whether it was a survival of the time when equity reformed unconscionable bargains merely because they were unconscionable, – a subject which much exercised Jessel MR in *Wallis* v *Smith* – is probably more interesting than material.

(c) There is a presumption (but no more) that it is penalty when "a single lump sum is made payable by way of compensation, on the recurrence of one or more or all of several events some of which may occasion serious and others but trifling damage" (Lord Watson in *Lord Elphinstone* v *Monkland Iron and Coal Co*).

On the other hand:

(d) It is no obstacle to the sum stipulated being a genuine pre-estimate of damage, that the consequences of the breach are such as to make precise pre-estimation almost an impossibility. On the contrary, that is just the situation when it is probable that pre-estimated damage was the true bargain between the parties (*Clydebank* Case, Lord Halsbury; *Webster* v *Bosanquet*, Lord Mersey).

Turning now to the facts of the case, it is evident that the damage apprehended by the appellants owing to the breaking of the agreement was an indirect and not a direct damage. So long as they got their price from the respondents for each article sold, it could not matter to them directly what the respondents did with it. Indirectly it did. Accordingly, the agreement is headed "Price Maintenance Agreement", and the way in which the appellants would be damaged if prices were cut is clearly explained in evidence by Mr Baisley, and no successful attempt is made to controvert that evidence. But though damage as a whole from such a practice would be certain, yet damage from any one sale would be impossible to forecast. It is just, therefore, one of those cases where it seems quite reasonable for Parties to contract that they should estimate that damage at a certain figure, and provided that figure is not extravagant there would seem no reason to suspect that it is not truly a bargain to assess damages, but rather a penalty to be held *in terrorem.*'

QUANTUM MERUIT

Quantum meruit is an alternative to, rather than a form of, damages.

Requirements for *quantum meruit*

1   *Quantum meruit* is only available if the original contract has been discharged.
2   The contract breaker must have broken the contract so as to entitle the innocent party to treat the contract as discharged.
3   The innocent party must have elected to treat the contract as discharged.
4   Only the innocent party can bring an action.

If conditions 1 to 4 are satisfied the innocent party can either sue for breach of contract or rescind the contract and sue on a *quantum meruit* for work actually done.

Assessment of *quantum meruit*

Quantum meruit is to recompense the innocent party *for work actually done* – to restore him to the position which he would have been in if the contract had never been made.

Damages, on the other hand, are to place the innocent party in position he would have been in had the contract been performed.

Planché v Colburn

[1824–34] All ER Rep 94 • Common Pleas

Colburn had commenced a periodical publication called *The Juvenile Library* and had engaged Planché for £100 to write a volume on costume and ancient armour for it. Planché had written part of the volume and was ready and willing to complete and deliver the whole for insertion in *The Juvenile Library* but Colburn in breach of contract would not publish it and refused to pay Planché the sum of £100 as previously agreed. Planché sued on a *quantum meruit* for work and labour he had expended on preparing his volume. Colburn said that Planché entered into a new contract. The trial judge left it to the jury to say whether the work had been abandoned by Colburn, and whether Planché had entered into any new contract. A verdict was found for Planché with £50 damages.

Tindal CJ: 'In this case a contract had been entered into for the publication of a work on costume and ancient armour in *The Juvenile Library*. The considerations by which an author is generally actuated in undertaking to write a work are pecuniary profit and literary reputation. It is clear that the latter may be sacrificed if an author who has engaged to write a volume of a popular nature, to be published in a work intended for a juvenile class of readers, should be subject to have his writings published as a separate and distinct work and, therefore, liable to be judged of by more severe rules than would be applied to a familiar work intended merely for children. The defendants not only suspended, but actually put an end to, *The Juvenile Library*. They had broken their contract with the plaintiff and an attempt was made, unsuccessfully, to show that the plaintiff had afterwards entered into a new contract to allow them to publish his book as a separate work. I agree that when a special contract is in existence and open the plaintiff cannot sue on a *quantum meruit*. Part of the question here, therefore, was whether the contract did exist or not. It distinctly appeared that the work was finally abandoned and the jury found that no new contract had been entered into. In these circumstances the plaintiff ought not to lose the fruit of his labour and there is no ground for the application which has been made.

Quasi contract subject to the contract

Regalian Properties plc v London Dockland Development Corp

[1995] 1 All ER 1005 • Chancery Division

In 1986 Regalian offered to buy residential development land from LDDC for £18.5m. LDDC accepted Regalian's offer 'subject to contract'. Various delays occurred in concluding the contract and in 1988 the proposed project was abandoned. Regalian brought an action to recover by way of restitution some £3m representing monies they had expended in respect of the proposed development and in preparation for the intended contract. Regalian argued 'that where parties to a proposed contract had a mutual understanding that there would be a contract between them and, pursuant to that understanding, one party incurred expense which benefited the other party, then if the intended contract failed to materialise through no fault of the party incurring expense, that party could recover his wasted costs from the other'.

Rattee J: 'Such are the facts in the context of which I must now consider Regalian's claim in this action. In essence that claim (as amended at the trial) is for reimbursement by LDDC of disbursements amounting to £2.891m-odd, representing fees paid by Regalian to various professional firms in respect of the proposed development. As I have already said, Regalian accepts that it has no contractual right to recover such costs because no contract ever came into being between Regalian and LDDC. The claim is based on what Mr Coulson, in his very eloquent submissions on behalf of Regalian, asserted was a principle of the law of restitution. The principle he asserted was that where parties to a proposed contract have a mutual understanding that there will be a contract between them and pursuant to that understanding one party incurs expense which benefits the other party, then if the intended contract fails to materialise through no fault of the party who has incurred expense, that party can recover the wasted costs from the other.

Mr Coulson realistically accepted that his submission is not free from difficulty. He referred to *Goff and Jones on Restitution* (4th edn) . . . in which, in a chapter entitled "Anticipated Contracts Which Do Not Materialise", it is said:

"The problem arises most acutely when parties enter into negotiations which they confidently expect will mature into a binding contract. The negotiations break down in circumstances where one of the parties has incurred considerable expense, which may or may not have benefited the other. Can he recover all or any of this wasted expenditure? There is, of course, no contract, and consequently no claim for damages for reliance loss arising from its breach. Moreover, English law does not recognise, at least in name, any doctrine of good faith bargaining, *culpa in contrahendo*, as it is known in civilian jurisdictions, which can form the basis of a collateral contract; a gentleman's agreement to pay for services does not bind any gentleman (cf *J H Milner & Son* v *Percy Bilton Ltd* per Fenton Atkinson J). And it has consistently been held that a contract to negotiate is a contract which is not known to English law. The relative paucity of the case law provides no clear and consistent answer to the question whether a party can be recompensed for what he has lost."

The learned editor then goes on to consider some of the case law there is. Mr Coulson, on behalf of Regalian, relies in particular on three cases as establishing the proposition for which he contends in the present context.

The first of the cases particularly relied on by Mr Coulson is *William Lacey (Hounslow) Ltd* v *Davis* . . .

. . . the result [of that case] seems to me to make perfectly good sense on the facts of that case. At the request of the defendant the plaintiff had done work which had clearly benefited the defendant quite outside the ambit of the anticipated contract and had only not charged for it separately, as one would otherwise have expected him to do, because he thought he would be sufficiently recompensed by what he would be paid by the plaintiff under the contract. In those circumstances it is not surprising that the law of restitution found a remedy for the plaintiff when the contract did not materialise. I do not consider that the decision lends any real support to the claim made by Regalian in the present case for compensation for expenditure incurred by it for the purpose of enabling itself to obtain and perform the intended contract at a time when the parties had in effect expressly agreed by the use of the words "subject to contract" that there should be no legal obligation by either party to the other unless and until a formal contract had been entered into. It was frankly accepted by Mr Goldstone of Regalian that he knew and intended that this should be the effect of the use of the phrase "subject to contract", and indeed Regalian admits in its pleadings that those words were not intended to have any unusual meaning in the present case. As Mr Goldstone, whom I found an honest and indeed impressive witness, put it in his evidence, he knew that either party was free to walk away from the negotiations, although he confidently expected that this would not happen . . .

The second authority on which Mr Coulson relied was a decision of the Supreme Court of New South Wales in *Sabemo Pty Ltd* v *North Sydney Municipal Council* . . .

The learned judge appears from other passages in his judgment to have considered that he was applying the decision in the *William Lacey* case. In my judgment, Sabemo's claim was distinguishable from that in *William Lacey* on similar grounds to those on which I have already explained, I think Regalian's claim in the present case is distinguishable, namely that in *William Lacey* the work, the subject matter of the claim, was quite outside the ambit of the intended contract . . .

I referred a little earlier to the . . . dictum of Goff J in *British Steel Corp* v *Cleveland Bridge and Engineering Co Ltd*. I should say a little more about that case. The defendant had successfully tendered for the fabrication of steelwork to be used in the construction of a building. It entered into negotiations with the plaintiff for a sub-contract, whereunder the plaintiff would supply certain steel nodes that would form part of the relevant steelwork. It was proposed that the sub-contract would be in a standard form used by the defendant. The defendant requested the plaintiff to commence work on the steel nodes immediately "pending the preparation and issuing to you of the official form of sub-contract". The intended formal contract was not entered into, because the parties failed to agree certain terms to go into it. The plaintiff produced and delivered to the defendant all but one of the steel nodes. The defendant refused to pay for them, and instead sought to recover from the plaintiff damages for late delivery of the nodes. The plaintiff sued for the value of the nodes it had supplied by way of *quantum meruit*. The defendant counterclaimed for damages for, *inter alia*, late delivery of the nodes, alleging that a binding contract came into being between the parties.

Robert Goff J rejected the defendant's argument that a contract existed between the parties. He then considered the plaintiff's *quantum meruit* claim in these terms:

> "In my judgment, the true analysis of the situation is simply this. Both parties confidently expected a formal contract to eventuate. In these circumstances, to expedite performance under that anticipated contract, one requested the other to commence the contract work, and the other complied with that request. If thereafter, as anticipated, a contract was entered into, the work done as requested will be treated as having been performed under that contract; if, contrary to their expectation, no contract was entered into, then the performance of the work is not referable to any contract the terms of which can be ascertained, and the law simply imposes an obligation on the party who made the request to pay a reasonable sum for such work as has been done pursuant to that request, such an obligation sounding in quasi contract or, as we now say, in restitution. Consistently with that solution, the party making the request may find himself liable to pay for work which he would not have had to pay for as such if the anticipated contract had come into existence, e.g. preparatory work which will, if the contract is made, be allowed for in the price of the finished work (cf *William Lacey (Hounslow) Ltd* v *Davis*."

I do not consider that this decision lends any real support to Regalian's claim in the present case. I can well understand why Goff J concluded that where one party to an expected contract expressly requests the other to perform services or supply goods that would have been performable or suppliable under the expected contract when concluded in advance of the contract, that party should have to pay a *quantum meruit* if the contract does not materialise. The present case is not analogous. The costs for which Regalian seeks reimbursement were incurred by it not by way of accelerated performance of the anticipated contract at the request of LDDC, but for the purpose of putting itself in a position to obtain and then perform the contract.

Mr Coulson relied on the last part of the dictum of Robert Goff J which I have cited, in which he pointed out that the application of the principle of restitution, which he applied in that case, can result in one party to an anticipated contract which does not materialise finding himself liable to pay the other party for preparatory work for which he would not have had to pay under the contract, because under the contract it would have been allowed for in the overall contract price. I do not think the judge had in mind (because he was not concerned with such a claim) that a landowner intending to contract to grant a building lease could find itself liable to pay the intending lessee developer for preparatory work done by the lessee for the purpose of putting itself in a position to obtain and perform the contract.

I must return now to the statement of principle made by Sheppard J in the *Sabemo* case, which I have cited earlier. For the essence of Mr Coulson's submissions, on behalf of Regalian, is that that principle should be applied in the present case. For convenience I repeat here the relevant passage from the judgment of Sheppard J in the *Sabemo* case:

> "In my opinion, the better view of the correct application of the principle in question is that, where two parties proceed upon the joint assumption that a contract will be entered into between them, and one does work beneficial for the project, and thus in

the interests of the two parties, which work he would not be expected, in other circumstances, to do gratuitously, he will be entitled to compensation or restitution, if the other party unilaterally decides to abandon the project, not for any reason associated with *bona fide* disagreement concerning the terms of the contract to be entered into, but for reasons which, however valid, pertain only to his own position and do not relate at all to that of the other party."

I have already said that the principle as so stated would not, in my judgment, apply in any event to the facts of this case, because the reason the contract did not materialise was that the parties could not agree on the price, and not that either party decided to abandon the project. However, in case I am wrong on this, I should say that in my respectful opinion the principle enunciated by Sheppard J in the last passage I have cited from his judgment is not established by any English authority. I appreciate that the English law of restitution should be flexible and capable of continuous development. However, I see no good reason to extend it to apply some such principle as adopted by Sheppard J in the *Sabemo* case to facts such as those of the present case, where, however much the parties expect a contract between them to materialise, both enter negotiations expressly (whether by use of the words "subject to contract" or otherwise) on terms that each party is free to withdraw from the negotiations at any time. Each party to such negotiations must be taken to know (as in my judgment Regalian did in the present case) that pending the conclusion of a binding contract any cost incurred by him in preparation for the intended contract will be incurred at his own risk in the sense that he will have no recompense for those costs if no contract results. In other words, I accept in substance the submission made by Mr Naughton QC, counsel for LDDC, to the effect that, by deliberate use of the words "subject to contract" with the admitted intention that they should have their usual effect, LDDC and Regalian each accepted that in the event of no contract being entered into, any resultant loss should lie where it fell.

Regalian, under the leadership of Mr Goldstone, was a very experienced operator in the property development market. To his considerable credit Mr Goldstone did not pretend that he was not aware that LDDC, like any other party to negotiations "subject to contract", was free to walk away from those negotiations, however little he expected it to do so. Regalian incurred the costs concerned in that knowledge. Though it is perhaps not strictly relevant, I see nothing inequitable in those circumstances in the loss resulting from the breakdown of negotiations lying where it fell, particularly bearing in mind that, in the light of the slump in the residential property market that followed the attempt by LDDC in May 1988 to renegotiate the price for the proposed building leases, Regalian has good reason to be thankful that it did not find itself having to take those leases on the terms previously proposed.

In my judgment, Regalian has failed to make good its claim based on the principles of restitution. It having, rightly, in my view, abandoned its alternative pleaded claim based on alleged misrepresentation, its action fails and must be dismissed.'

SPECIFIC PERFORMANCE

Specific performance is an equitable remedy. Equitable remedies are available only in exceptional circumstances and when damages are not an adequate remedy.

Specific performance is an order by which the Court directs the contract breaker to perform the contract which he has made in accordance with the terms of the contract.

Specific performance is *supplementary* and *discretionary*

Supplementary

- Specific performance is supplementary to the common law remedy of damages.
- Specific performance is not normally granted where damages provide adequate relief.
- Specific performance is not normally granted for personal property.
- Specific performance is normally granted for the sale of land.

Discretionary

Specific performance is not necessarily granted merely because damages are not an adequate remedy. The Court has a discretion. The Court looks at the general fairness of the situation e.g. has the 'innocent party' been guilty of undue influence, misrepresentation or induced mistake. The Court can refuse specific performance on the ground that it would cause undue hardship.

When will specific performance be refused?

Want of mutuality

The Court will not grant specific performance to one party when it could not do so at the suit of the other. The time to test *mutuality* is the date of trial.

Price v Strange

[1977] 3 All ER 371 • Court of Appeal

Strange agreed to grant a sublease of a maisonette to Price provided Price carried out certain works to the interior and exterior of the maisonette. After Price had completed the interior works Strange repudiated the agreement and prevented Price from completing the works to the exterior of the maisonette; she had the works to the exterior completed at her own expense. Price sued for specific performance of the agreement. Strange pleaded that specific performance could not be granted because the remedy was not mutual at the date of the contract.

NB: Fry on *Specific Performance* states that 'A contract to be specifically enforced by the court must, as a general rule, be mutual, – that is to say, such that it might, at the time it was entered into, have been enforced by either of the parties against the other of them . . . The mutuality of a contract is, as we have seen, to be judged of at the time it is entered into.'

Goff LJ: 'In my judgment, therefore, the proposition in Fry is wrong and the true principle is that one judges the defence of want of mutuality on the facts and circumstances as they exist at the hearing, albeit in the light of the whole conduct of the parties in relation to the subject matter, and in the absence of any other disqualifying circumstances the court will grant specific performance if it can be done without injustice or unfairness to the defendant . . .

If, therefore, the plaintiff had been allowed to finish the work and had done so, I am clearly of opinion that it would have been right to order specific performance, but we have to consider what is the proper order, having regard to the fact that he was allowed to do an appreciable part and then not allowed to finish. Even so, in my judgment, the result is still the same for the following reasons.

First, the defendant by standing by and allowing the plaintiff to spend time and money in carrying out an appreciable part of the work created an equity against herself. This is supported, first, by *Hart* v *Hart* and *Parker* v *Taswell* which show that where there has been part performance the court will struggle against difficulties to secure total performance, but much more strongly by the principles laid down in *Chalmers* v *Pardoe*. That case shows that where A encourages or permits B to build on or improve A's land on the faith of an understanding or assurance, short of a binding contract, that he will permit him to have it or use it for B's own benefit, equity will in a proper case not merely give B a lien for recovering his expenditure but compel A to implement the understanding. *A fortiori* must it be so where, as here, the plaintiff was allowed to start work on the defendant's property on the faith of an actual contract which, notwithstanding the want of writing, was by the very act of part performance made enforceable in equity.

Secondly, the work has in fact been finished. The court will not be deterred from granting specific performance in a proper case, even though there remain obligations still to be performed by the plaintiff if the defendant can be properly protected: see *Langen & Wind Ltd* v *Bell* . . .

Still more readily should it act where the work has been done so that the defendant is not at risk of being ordered to grant the underlease and having no remedy except in damages for subsequent non-performance of the plaintiff's agreement to put the premises in repair.

Thirdly, the defendant can be fully recompensed by a proper financial adjustment for the work she has had carried out.

I am fully satisfied that the law is as I have stated it to be . . .

For these reasons I would allow this appeal and order specific performance but upon terms that the plaintiff do pay to the defendant proper compensation for the work done by her . . .'

Contracts for personal service

The Court will not grant specific performance for contracts for personal services such as contracts of employment.

Page One Records Ltd v *Britton (trading as 'The Troggs')*

[1967] 3 All ER 822 • Chancery

In 1966 the Troggs entered into a written agreement with Page One Records under which they appointed Page One Records to be their manager. The agreement which extended world-wide was to continue for a period of five years. It provided that during the period of agreement The Troggs would not 'engage any other person . . . to act as managers . . . for [The Troggs]'. The agreement provided that The Troggs would pay the first plaintiff a sum representing 20% of all moneys received by The Troggs during the period of the agreement.

In 1967 Page One Records received a letter signed by each of The Troggs which purported to terminate the agreement.

Page One Records sought (i) an injunction to restrain The Troggs from engaging a new manager; and (ii) an injunction to restrain The Troggs acting as a group from publishing any music.

Stamp J: 'The defendants have not, in my judgment, established a *prima facie* case for the view that there were such breaches by the first plaintiff of its duty to The Troggs as to justify The Troggs in repudiating the agreements which they made with the first plaintiff. If all that I had to do was to determine whether the first plaintiff had made out a *prima facie* case of breach of contract entitling it to damages, I would hold that it had, entitling the plaintiffs to make a heavy claim for damages against the defendants. It does not follow, however, that because the plaintiffs have made out a *prima facie* case for succeeding in recovering damages in the action, that they have made out a *prima facie* case, or any case, for an interlocutory or any injunction. The plaintiffs, relying on *Lumley* v *Wagner* and the cases which have followed it, claim . . . an order that the [The Troggs] be restrained until trial from engaging as their managers . . . any person firm or corporation other than the first plaintiff . . .

Counsel for The Troggs submits that even if the plaintiffs had throughout acted impeccably towards The Troggs, no such injunction as is asked for ought to be granted. He advances three propositions on behalf of The Troggs. (i) That specific performance is never granted to enforce a contract for personal services. (ii) That an injunction is never granted which would have the effect of preventing an employer discharging an agent who is in a fiduciary position *vis-à-vis* the employer. He emphasises that here the first plaintiff, as manager and agent of The Troggs, is in the position of an employee. (iii) That an injunction is never granted at the suit of the party against whom the party to be restrained could not obtain specific performance. It is urged – and, in my judgment, correctly – that The Troggs could have no action for specific performance of the management or agency agreements against the first plaintiff.

The present case is clearly distinguished, in principle, from such cases as *Lumley* v *Wagner*, for there the only obligation on the part of the plaintiffs seeking to enforce the negative stipulation was an obligation to pay remuneration and an obligation which could clearly be enforced by the defendants. Here, however, the obligations to the first plaintiff, involving personal services, were obligations of trust and confidence and were obligations which, plainly, could not be enforced at the suit of The Troggs. Here, indeed, so it seems to me, the totality of the obligations between the parties are more a joint venture almost approaching the relationship of partners than anything else, involving mutual confidence and reciprocal obligations on all sides.

For the purposes of consideration of equitable relief, I must, I think, look at the totality of the arrangements, and the negative stipulations on which the plaintiffs rely, are, in my judgment, no more or less than stipulations designed to tie the parties together in a relationship of mutual confidence, mutual endeavour and reciprocal obligations. These considerations, in the view of Knight Bruce LJ, in *Johnson* v *Shrewsbury and Birmingham Ry Co*, and *Pickering* v *Bishop of Ely*, on which he relied in the former case, distinguish *Lumley* v *Wagner*. I quote from the judgment of Knight Bruce LJ:

"It is clear in the present case that, had the defendants been minded to compel the plaintiffs to perform their duties against their will, it could not have been done. Mutuality therefore is out of the question, and, according to the rules generally supposed to exist in courts of equity, that might have been held sufficient to dispose of the matter; cases however have existed where, though the defendant could not have been compelled to do all he had undertaken to do by the contract, yet as he had contracted to abstain from doing a certain thing the court has interfered reasonably enough.

A case, lately much referred to on this point is that of a German singer, who, having found probably that more could be obtained by breaking her promise than by keeping it, determined to obtain the larger sum and accordingly to break her promise. She could not be compelled to sing as she had contracted to do, but as she had contracted not to sing at any other place than the one specified in the agreement, she was (and very properly in my opinion) restrained from singing at any other place. There all the obligations on the part of the plaintiff could have been satisfied by the payment of money, but not so those of the defendant. Here the parties are reversed. Here all the obligations of the defendants can be satisfied by paying money; but not so the obligations of the plaintiffs, who come here for the purpose in effect of compelling the defendants, by a prohibitory or mandatory injunction, to do or abstain from doing certain acts, while the correlative acts are such as the plaintiffs could not be compelled to do."

Apart altogether, however, from the lack of mutuality of the right of enforcement, this present case, in my judgment, fails on the facts at present before me on a more general principle, the converse of which was conveniently stated in the judgment of Branson J, in *Warner Brothers Pictures Inc* v *Nelson*. Branson J stated the converse of the proposition and the proposition, correctly stated, is, I think, this, that where a contract of personal service contains negative covenants, the enforcement of which will amount either to a degree of specific performance of the positive covenants of the contract or to the giving of a decree under which the defendant must either remain idle or perform those positive covenants, the court will not enforce those negative covenants.

In the *Warner Brothers* case Branson J, felt able to find that the injunction sought would not force the defendant to perform her contract or remain idle. He said:

"It was also urged that the difference between what the defendant can earn as a film artiste and what she might expect to earn by any other form of activity is so great that she will in effect be driven to perform her contract. That is not the criterion adopted in any of the decided cases. The defendant is stated to be a person of intelligence, capacity and means, and no evidence was adduced to show that, if enjoined from doing the specified acts otherwise than for the plaintiffs, she will not be able to employ herself both usefully and remuneratively in other spheres of activity, though not as remuneratively as in her special line. She will not be driven, although she may be tempted, to perform the contract, and the fact that she may be so tempted is no objection to the grant of an injunction."

So it was said in this case, that if an injunction is granted The Troggs could, without employing any other manager or agent, continue as a group on their own or seek other employment of a different nature. So far as the former suggestion is concerned, in the first place, I doubt whether consistently with the terms of the agreements which I have read, The Troggs could act as their own managers; and, in the second place, I think that I can and should take judicial notice of the fact that these groups, if they are to have any great success, must have managers. Indeed, it is the plaintiffs' own case that The Troggs are simple persons, of no business experience, and could not survive without the services of a manager. As a practical matter on the evidence before me, I entertain no doubt that they would be compelled, if the injunction were granted on the terms that the plaintiffs seek, to continue to employ the first plaintiff as their manager and agent and it is, I think, on this point that this case diverges from the *Lumley* v *Wagner* case and the cases which have followed it, including the *Warner Brothers* case: for it would be a bad thing to put pressure on The Troggs to continue to employ as a manager and agent in a fiduciary capacity one, who, unlike the plaintiff in those cases who had merely to pay the defendant money, has duties of a personal and fiduciary nature to perform and in whom The Troggs, for reasons good, bad or indifferent, have lost confidence and who may, for all I know, fail in its duty to them.

On the facts before me on this interlocutory motion, I should, if I granted the injunction, be enforcing a contract for personal services in which personal services are to be performed by the first plaintiff. In *Lumley* v *Wagner*, Lord St Leonards LC, in his judgment, disclaimed doing indirectly what he could not do directly; and in the present case, by granting an injunction I would, in my judgment, be doing precisely that. I must, therefore, refuse the injunction which the first plaintiff seeks. The claim of the second plaintiff seems to me to be inextricably mixed up with the claim by the first plaintiff and no separate argument has really been addressed to me on the basis that the second plaintiff might succeed although the first plaintiff failed to obtain an injunction at the trial.'

Warren v *Mendy*

[1989] 3 All ER 103 • Court of Appeal

Nigel Benn entered into an agreement with Frank Warren whereby Warren was to act as Benn's manager for three years. Clause 4 of the agreement stated 'The boxer agrees and undertakes: (i) during the continuance of this agreement to be managed and directed exclusively by the manager and not to enter into any agreement or arrangement with any other manager or person for any of the above-mentioned purposes without obtaining the prior written consent of the manager ... ' A few months later Benn and Warren fell out and Benn asked Mendy to act 'as my agent to advise me on all matters concerning my career'. Warren sought an injunction against Mendy to restrain him from inducing Benn to breach his contract with Warren.

Nourse LJ: 'It is well settled that an injunction to restrain a breach of contract for personal services ought not to be granted where its effect will be to decree performance of the contract. Speaking generally, there is no comparable objection to the grant of an injunction restraining the performance of particular services for a third party, because, by not prohibiting the performance of other services, it does not bind the servant to his contract. But a difficulty can arise, usually in the entertainment or sporting worlds, where the services are inseparable from the exercise of some special skill or talent, whose continued display is essential to the psychological and material, and sometimes to the physical well-being of the servant. The difficulty does not reside in any beguilement of the court into looking more tenderly on such who breach their contracts, glamorous though they often are. It is that the human necessity of maintaining the skill or talent may practically bind the servant to the contract, compelling him to perform it.

The best known of the authorities on this subject are *Lumley* v *Wagner* (impresario and opera singer) and *Warner Brothers Pictures Inc* v *Nelson* (film producer and actress), where injunctions were granted, and *Page One Records Ltd* v *Britton* (manager and pop group), where an injunction was refused. Here we have the case of manager and boxer. It is in one respect unusual, in that the manager has brought the action not against the boxer but against a third party who seeks to replace him, at all events in some respects. The manager claims that the third party has induced a breach of his contract with the boxer. He seeks an injunction only against the third party . . .

This consideration of the authorities has led us to believe that the following general principles are applicable to the grant or refusal of an injunction to enforce performance of the servant's negative obligations in a contract for personal services inseparable from the exercise of some special skill or talent. (We use the expressions "master" and "servant" for ease of reference and not out of any regard for the reality of the relationship in many of these cases.) In such a case the court ought not to enforce the performance of the negative obligations if their enforcement will effectively compel the servant to perform his positive obligations under the contract. Compulsion is a question to be decided on the facts of each case, with a realistic regard for the probable reaction of an injunction on the psychological and material, and sometimes the physical, need of the servant to maintain the skill or talent. The longer the term for which an injunction is sought, the more readily will compulsion be inferred. Compulsion may be inferred where the injunction is sought not against the servant but against a third party, if either the third party is the only other available master or if it is likely that the master will seek relief against anyone who attempts to replace him. An injunction will less readily be granted where there are obligations of mutual trust and confidence, more especially where the servant's trust in the master may have been betrayed or his confidence in him has genuinely gone.

In stating the principles as we have, we are not to be taken as intending to pay anything less than a full and proper regard to the sanctity of contract. No judge would wish to detract from his duty to enforce the performance of contracts to the very limit which established principles allow him to go. Nowhere is that duty better vindicated than in the words of Lord St Leonards LC. To that end the judge will scrutinise most carefully, even sceptically, any claim by the servant that he is under the human necessity of maintaining the skill or talent and thus will be compelled to perform the contract, or that his trust in the master has been betrayed or that his confidence in him has genuinely gone. But if, having done that, the judge is satisfied that the grant of an injunction will effectively compel performance of the contract, he ought to refuse it. To do otherwise would be to disregard the authoritative observations which were made in this court in *Whitwood Chemical Co* v *Hardman . . .*'

Despite the above, the Court may be prepared to grant an injunction *preventing* a party breaking a contract for personal services.

Warner Brothers Pictures Inc v Nelson

[1936] 3 All ER 160 • King's Bench

Nelson entered into a contract with Warner Brothers whereby she agreed to render her exclusive services as a motion picture actress solely and exclusively to Warner Brothers. She also agreed, by way of negative stipulation, that: 'she will not, during [the term of the contract] render any services for or in any other photographic, stage or motion picture production or productions, or business of any other person or engage in any other occupation without the written consent of the producer being first had and obtained'.

Later, Nelson, for no discoverable reason, except that she wanted more money, declined to be further bound by the agreement, left the United States and entered into an agreement in England with a third person.

Warner Brothers commenced an action against Nelson and claimed declaration that the contract was valid and binding, an injunction to restrain her from acting in breach of it, and damages.

Branson J: 'I turn then to the consideration of the law applicable to this case on the basis that the contract is a valid and enforceable one. It is conceded that our courts will not enforce a positive covenant of personal service; and specific performance of the positive covenants by the defendant to serve the plaintiffs is not asked in the present case.

The practice of the court of chancery in relation to the enforcement of negative covenants is stated on the highest authority by Lord Cairns LC, in the House of Lords in *Doherty* v *Allman*. His Lordship says:

"My Lords, if there had been a negative covenant, I apprehend, according to well settled practice, a court of equity would have had no discretion to exercise. If parties, for valuable consideration, with their eyes open, contract that a particular thing shall not be done, all that a court of equity has to do is to say, by way of injunction, that which the parties have already said by way of covenant, that the thing shall not be done; and in such case the injunction does nothing more than give the sanction of the process of the court to that which already is the contract between the parties. It is not then a question of the balance of convenience or inconvenience, or of the amount of damage or of injury – it is the specific performance, by the court, of that negative bargain which the parties have made, with their eyes open, between themselves."

That was not a case of a contract of personal service; but the same principle had already been applied to such a contract by Lord St Leonards LC, in *Lumley* v *Wagner*. [In that case] Lord St Leonards LC, used the following language:

"Wherever this court has not proper jurisdiction to enforce specific performance, it operates to bind men's consciences, as far as they can be bound, to a true and literal performance of their agreements; and it will not suffer them to depart from their contracts at their pleasure, leaving the party with whom they have contracted to the mere chance of any damages which a jury may give. The exercise of this jurisdiction has, I believe, had a wholesome tendency towards the maintenance of that good faith which exists in this country to a much greater degree perhaps than in any other; and although the jurisdiction is not to be extended, yet a judge would desert his duty who did not act up to what his predecessors have handed down as the rule for his guidance in the administration of such an equity."

This passage was cited as a correct statement of the law in the opinion of a strong board of the Privy Council in the case of *Lord Strathcona SS Co* v *Dominion Coal Co*, and I not only approve it, if I may respectfully say so, but am bound by it.

The defendant, having broken her positive undertakings in the contract without any cause or excuse which she was prepared to support in the witness box, contends that she cannot be enjoined from breaking the negative covenants also. The mere fact that a covenant, which the court would not enforce if expressed in positive form, is expressed in the negative instead, will not induce the court to enforce it. That appears, if authority is needed for such a proposition, from *Davis* v *Foreman, Kirchner* v *Gruban*, and *Chapman* v *Westerby*. The court will attend to the substance and not to the form of the covenant. Nor will the court, true to the principle that specific performance of a contract of personal service will never be ordered, grant an injunction in the case of such a contract to enforce negative covenants if the effect of so doing would be to drive the defendant either to starvation or to specific performance of the positive covenants: see *Whitwood Chemical Co* v *Hardman* . . .

. . . An injunction is a discretionary remedy, and the court in granting it may limit it to what the court considers reasonable in all the circumstances of the case. This appears from the judgment of the Court of Appeal in *William Robinson & Co Ltd* v *Heuer*. The particular covenant in that case [provided] that

"Heuer shall not during this engagement, without the previous consent in writing of the said W Robinson & Co, Ltd, carry on or be engaged either directly or indirectly as principal, agent, servant, or otherwise, in any trade, business, or calling, either relating to goods of any description sold or manufactured by the said W Robinson & Co, Ltd . . . or in any other business whatsoever." . . .

Before parting with that case, I should say that the court proceeded to sever the covenants in that case and to grant an injunction, not to restrain the defendant from carrying on any other business whatsoever, but framed so as to give what was felt to be a reasonable protection to the plaintiffs and no more. The plaintiffs waived an option which they possessed to extend the period of service for an extra 5 years and the injunction then was granted for the remaining period of unextended time.

It is said that this case is no longer the law, but that *Attwood* v *Lamont* has decided that no such severance is permissible. I do not agree. *Attwood* v *Lamont* was a case where the covenants were held void as in restraint of trade. There is all the difference in the world between declining to make an illegal covenant good by neglecting that which makes it contrary to law and exercising a discretion as to how far the court will enforce a valid covenant by injunction. The latter was done in the Court of Appeal in *Robinson* v *Heuer*, the former in *Attwood* v *Lamont*.

The case before me is therefore one in which it would be proper to grant an injunction unless to do so would in the circumstances be tantamount to ordering the defendant to perform her contract or remain idle or unless damages would be the more appropriate remedy.

With regard to the first of these considerations, it would, of course, be impossible to grant an injunction covering all the negative covenants in the contract. That would, indeed, force the defendant to perform her contract or remain idle; but this objection is removed by the restricted form in which the injunction is sought. It is confined to forbidding the defendant, without the consent of the plaintiffs, to render any services for or in any motion picture or stage production for anyone other than the plaintiffs.

It was also urged that the difference between what the defendant can earn as a film artiste and what she might expect to earn by any other form of activity is so great that she will in effect be driven to perform her contract. That is not the criterion adopted in any of the decided cases. The defendant is stated to be a person of intelligence, capacity and means, and no evidence was adduced to show that, if enjoined from doing the specified acts otherwise than for the plaintiffs, she will not be able to employ herself both usefully and remuneratively in other spheres of activity, though not as remuneratively as in her special line. She will not be driven, although she may be tempted, to perform the contract, and the fact that she may be so tempted is no objection to the grant of an injunction . . .

With regard to the question whether damages is not the more appropriate remedy, I have the uncontradicted evidence of the plaintiffs as to the difficulty of estimating the damages which they may suffer from the breach by the defendant of her contract. I think it is not inappropriate to refer to the fact that, in the contract between the parties, in clause 22, there is a formal admission by the defendant that her services, being "of a special, unique, extraordinary and intellectual character" gives them a particular value, "the loss of which cannot be reasonably or adequately compensated in damages" and that a breach may "cost the producer great and irreparable injury and damage", and the artiste expressly agrees that the producer shall be entitled to the remedy of injunction. Of course, parties cannot contract themselves out of the law; but it assists, at all events, on the question of evidence as to the applicability of an injunction in the present case, to find the parties formally recognising that which is now before the court as a matter of evidence, that in cases of this kind injunction is a more appropriate remedy than damages.

Furthermore, in the case of *Grimston* v *Cuningham*, which was also a case in which a theatrical manager was attempting to enforce against an actor a negative stipulation against going elsewhere, Wills J, granted an injunction, . . . he used the following language:

"This is an agreement of a kind which is pre-eminently subject to the interference of the court by injunction, for in cases of this nature it very often happens that the injury suffered in consequence of the breach of the agreement would be out of all proportion to any pecuniary damages which could be proved or assessed by a jury. This circumstance affords a strong reason in favour of exercising the discretion of the court by granting an injunction."

I think that that applies to the present case also, and that an injunction should be granted in regard to the specified services.

Then comes the question as to the period for which the injunction should operate. The period of the contract, now that the plaintiffs have undertaken not as from 16 October 1936, to exercise the rights of suspension conferred upon them by cl 23 thereof, will, if they exercise their options to prolong it, extend to about May 1942. As I read the judgment of the Court of Appeal in *Robinson* v *Heuer*, the court should make the period such as to give reasonable protection and no more to the plaintiffs against the ill effects to them of the defendant's breach of contract. The evidence as to that was perhaps necessarily somewhat vague. The main difficulty that the plaintiffs apprehend is that the defendant might appear in other films whilst the films already made by them and not yet shown are in the market for sale or hire and thus depreciate their value. I think that, if the injunction is in force during the continuance of the contract or for three years from now, whichever period is the shorter, that will substantially meet the case.'

Specific performance is sometimes available if damages are not an adequate remedy

Sky Petroleum Ltd v *VIP Petroleum Ltd*

[1974] 1 All ER 954 • Chancery

The facts are stated in the judgment of Goulding J.

Goulding J: 'This is a motion for an injunction brought by the plaintiff company, Sky Petroleum Ltd, as buyer, under a contract dated 11th March 1970 made between the defendant company, VIP Petroleum Ltd, as seller, of the one part and the plaintiff company of the other part. That contract was to operate for a period of ten years, subject to certain qualifications, and thereafter on an annual basis unless terminated by either party giving to the other not less than three months' written notice to that effect. It was a contract at fixed prices, subject to certain provisions which I need not now mention. Further, the contract obliged the plaintiff company – and this is an important point – to take its entire requirement of motor gasoline and diesel fuel under the contract, with certain stipulated minimum yearly quantities.

After the making of the agreement, it is common knowledge that the terms of trade in the market for petroleum and its different products changed very considerably, and I have little doubt that the contract is now disadvantageous to the defendant company. After a long correspondence, the defendant company, by telegrams dated 15th and 16th November 1973, has purported to terminate the contract under a clause therein providing for termination by the defendant company if the plaintiff company fails to conform with any of the terms of the bargain. What is alleged is that the plaintiff company has exceeded the credit provisions of the contract and has persistently been, and now is, indebted to the defendant company in larger amounts than were provided for. So far as that dispute relates, as for the purposes of this motion it must, to the date of the purported termination of the contract, it is impossible for me to decide it on the affidavit evidence. It involves not only a question of construction of the contract, but also certain disputes on subsequent arrangements between the parties and on figures in the accounts. I cannot decide it on motion and the less I say about it the better.

What I have to decide is whether any injunction should be granted to protect the plaintiff company in the meantime. There is trade evidence that the plaintiff company has no great prospect of finding any alternative source of supply for the filling stations which constitute its business. The defendant company has indicated its willingness to continue to supply the plaintiff company, but only at prices which, according to the plaintiff company's evidence, would not be serious prices from a commercial point of view. There is, in my judgment, so far as I can make out on the evidence before me, a serious danger that unless the court interferes at this stage the plaintiff company will be forced out of business. In those circumstances, unless there is some specific reason which debars me from doing so, I should be disposed to grant an injunction to restore the former position under the contract until the rights and wrongs of the parties can be fully tried out.

It is submitted for the defendant company that I ought not to do so for a number of reasons. It is said that, on the facts, the defendant company was entitled to terminate and the plaintiff company was in the wrong. That, of course, is the very question in the action, and I have already expressed my inability to resolve it even provisionally on the evidence now before me. Then it is said that there are questions between the parties as to arrangements subsequent to the making of the contract, in particular regarding the price to be paid, and that they give rise to uncertainties which would make it difficult to enforce any order made by way of interlocutory relief. I do not think I ought to be deterred by that consideration, though I can see it has some force. In fact, during September and October, to go no further back, the defendant company has gone on supplying and the plaintiff company has gone on paying. There has been nothing apparently impracticable in the contract, although the defendant company says, of course, that the plaintiff company has not been paying large enough sums quickly enough.

Now I come to the most serious hurdle in the way of the plaintiff company which is the well-known doctrine that the court refuses specific performance of a contract to sell and purchase chattels not specific or ascertained. That is a well-established and salutary rule and I am entirely unconvinced by counsel for the plaintiff company when he tells me that an injunction in the form sought by him would not be specific enforcement at all. The matter is one of substance and not of form and it is, in my judgment, quite plain that I am for the time being specifically enforcing the contract if I grant an injunction. However the ratio behind the rule is, as I believe, that under the ordinary contract for the sale of non-specific goods, damages are a sufficient remedy. That, to my mind, is lacking in the circumstances of the present case. The evidence suggests, and indeed it is common knowledge, that the petroleum market is in an unusual state in which a would-be buyer cannot go out into the market and contract with another seller, possibly at some sacrifice as to price. Here, the defendant company appears for practical purposes to be the plaintiff company's sole means of keeping its business going, and I am prepared so far to depart from the general rule as to try to preserve the position under the contract until a later date. I therefore propose to grant an injunction.'

Contracts requiring constant supervision by court

Ryan v *Mutual Tontine Westminster Chambers Association*

[1893] 1 Ch 116 • Court of Appeal

The lease of a residential flat contained a covenant by which the landlord agreed to appoint a resident porter who would perform certain services specified in the lease. The landlord appointed a resident porter but he spent several hours every weekday acting as chef at a neighbouring club. The tenants brought an action against the landlord for breach of his covenant to appoint a full time resident porter. The issue before the Court was whether the Court could grant an injunction to prevent continuance of the breach of the covenant or order specific performance of it.

Lord Esher MR: '. . . It seems to me that this case comes within one or other, according to the point of view from which it is regarded, of two well-recognised rules of Chancery practice, which prevent the application of the remedy by compelling specific performance. I do not myself put this case as coming within any rule as to contracts to perform personal services. It is not necessary for me therefore to express any opinion as to such a rule. The contract sought to be enforced here is not a contract with a person employed as a servant. It is a contract between a person who has to employ a servant and a person for whose benefit the employment of such servant is to take place. It is a contract between a landlord and his tenant, by which the former undertakes to employ a porter to perform certain services for the benefit of the latter. The contract therefore, is not merely that the landlord shall employ a porter, but that he shall employ a porter who shall do certain specified work for the benefit of the tenant. That is, in my opinion, one indivisible contract. The performance of what is suggested to be the first part of the contract, viz, the agreement to employ a porter, would be of no use whatever to the tenant unless he performed the services specified. The right of the tenant under the contract is really an entirety, viz, to have a porter employed by whom these services shall be performed; and the breach of the contract substantially is that these services were not performed. The contract is that these services shall be performed during the whole term of the tenancy; it is therefore a long-continuing contract, to be performed from day to day, and under which the circumstances of non-performance might vary from day to day. I apprehend, therefore, that the execution of it would require that constant superintendence by the Court, which the Court in such cases has always declined to give. Therefore, if the contract is regarded as a whole, there is good ground for saying that it is not one of which the court could compel specific performance.'

However, in *Posner* v *Scott-Lewis*, below, whose facts were very similar to *Ryan* v *Mutual Tontine Westminster Chambers Assn*, Mervyn Davies J did grant an order of specific performance.

Posner v Scott-Lewis

[1986] 3 All ER 513 • Chancery

Mervyn Davies J: 'Drawing attention to these differences between Ryan and the present case, Mr Tager for the plaintiffs submitted that Ryan should be distinguished. In short, he said that since the resident porter's functions at Danes Court were already obligations of the lessor to the lessees, there were no duties on the part of the porter towards the tenants that the tenants were seeking to enforce. All that was required was the appointment of a resident porter, whereas in Ryan the plaintiff was in effect seeking to enforce performance of duties said to be owed by the porter to the plaintiff. I do not accept or reject Mr Tager's able argument. I suspect that it is difficult to distinguish the Ryan case. However that may be, the Ryan case has been remarked upon in many later authorities.

In *C H Giles & Co* v *Morris* Megarry J, after referring to Ryan's case, said:

"One day, perhaps, the courts will look again at the so-called rule that contracts for personal services or involving the continuous performance of services will not be specifically enforced. Such a rule is plainly not absolute and without exception, nor do I think that it can be based on any narrow consideration such as difficulties of constant superintendence by the court. Mandatory injunctions are by no means unknown, and there is normally no question of the court having to send its officers to supervise the performance of the order of the court. Prohibitory injunctions are common, and again there is no direct supervision by the court. Performance of each type of injunction is normally secured by the realisation of the person enjoined that he is liable to be punished for contempt if evidence of his disobedience to the order is put before the court; and if the injunction is prohibitory, actual committal will usually, so long as it continues, make disobedience impossible. If instead the order is for specific performance of a contract for personal services, a similar machinery of enforcement could be employed, again without there being any question of supervision by any officer of the court. The reasons why the court is reluctant to decree specific performance of a contract for personal services (and I would regard it as a strong reluctance rather than a rule) are, I think, more complex and more firmly bottomed on human nature. If a singer contracts to sing, there could no doubt be proceedings for committal if, ordered to sing, the singer remained obstinately dumb. But if instead the singer sang flat, or sharp, or too fast, or too slowly, or too loudly, or too quietly, or resorted to a dozen of the manifestations of temperament traditionally associated with some singers, the threat of committal would reveal itself as a most unsatisfactory weapon: for who could say whether the imperfections of performance were natural or self-induced? To make an order with such possibilities of evasion would be in vain; and so the order will not be made. However, not all contracts of personal service or for the continuous performance of services are as dependent as this on matters of opinion and judgment, nor do all such contracts involve the same degree of the daily impact of person upon person. In general, no doubt, the inconvenience and mischief of decreeing specific performance of most of such contracts will greatly outweigh the advantages, and specific performance will be refused. But I do not think that it should be assumed that as soon as any element of personal service or continuous services can be discerned in a contract the court will, without more, refuse specific performance. Of course, a requirement for the continuous performance of services has the disadvantage that repeated breaches may engender repeated applications to the court for enforcement. But so may many injunctions; and the prospects of repetition, although an important consideration, ought not to be allowed to negative a right. As is so often the case in equity, the matter is one of the balance of advantage and disadvantage in relation to the particular obligations in question; and the fact that the balance will usually lie on one side does not turn this probability into a rule. The present case, of course, is *a fortiori*, since the contract of which specific performance has been decreed requires not the performance of personal services or any continuous series of acts, but merely procuring the execution of an agreement which contains a provision for such services or acts."

Those observations do not of themselves enable me to disregard *Ryan* v *Mutual Tontine Westminster Chambers Assoc*. But then one comes to *Shiloh Spinners* v *Harding*. Lord Wilberforce seems to say that "the impossibility for the courts to supervise the doing of work" may be rejected as a reason against granting relief. Finally there is *Tito* v *Waddell*. Megarry V-C said:

"In cases of this kind it was at one time said that an order for the specific performance of the contract would not be made if there would be difficulty in the court supervising its execution: see, e.g. *Ryan* v *Mutual Tontine Westminster Chambers Association*. Sir Archibald Smith MR subsequently found himself unable to see the force of this objection (see *Wolverhampton Corporation* v *Emmons*); and after it had been discussed and questioned in *C H Giles & Co Ltd* v *Morris*, the House of Lords disposed of it (I hope finally) in *Shiloh Spinners Ltd* v *Harding*. The real question is whether there is a sufficient definition of what has to be done in order to comply with the order of the court. That definition may be provided by the contract itself, or it may be supplied by the terms of the order, in which case there is the further question whether the court considers that the terms of the contract sufficiently support, by implication or otherwise, the terms of the proposed order."

In the light of those authorities it is, I think, open to me to consider the making of an order for specific performance in this case; particularly since the order contemplated is in the *a fortiori* class referred to by Mr Justice Megarry (as he then was) in the last sentence of the extract from the *Giles* case quoted above. Damages here could hardly be regarded as an adequate remedy.

Whether or not a specific performance order should be made seems to me to depend on the following considerations: (a) is there a sufficient definition of what has to be done in order to comply with the order of the court (b) will enforcing compliance involve superintendence by the court to an unacceptable degree (c) what are the respective prejudices or hardships that will be suffered by the parties if the order is made or not made?

As to (a), one may in this case sufficiently define what has to be done by the defendants by ordering the defendants, within say two months, to employ a porter to be resident at Danes Court for the purpose of carrying out the . . . duties . . . As to (b) I do not see that such an order will occasion any protracted superintendence by the court. If the defendants without good cause fail to comply with the order in due time, then the plaintiffs can take appropriate enforcement proceedings against the defendants. As to (c), I see no hardship or prejudice resulting to the defendants from the order. They will simply be performing what they have promised to do and what has been carried out by the lessors over the past 20 years. On the other hand I see considerable inconvenience, if not exactly hardship, for the plaintiffs if, having bargained for a resident porter and paid a premium and having enjoyed his presence for 20 years, they are to be expected for the future to be content with a porter who simply walks up and down the stairs for two hours only during the day doing his cleaning and refuse collection. It follows that there should be an order for specific performance.'

SUMMARY

You should now be able to:

- Appreciate that damages are the normal remedy available to the injured party.
- Understand that in order to get damages it must be shown that the loss was caused by the breach i.e. *the loss must not be too remote*.
- Appreciate that damages are compensatory in nature and are *not* punitive or exemplary.

- Distinguish between penalty clauses and liquidated damages.
- Appreciate the significance of *quantum meruit* as an alternative to damages.
- Understand the equitable remedy of specific performance.

If you have not mastered the above points you should go through this section again.

18 Restitution

INTRODUCTION

Restitution is a topic that has developed over the last 50 years or so. You will have noticed on reading through this book that the term 'restitution' has cropped up in several topics such as mistake, frustration and *quantum meruit*. It is not intended here to revisit all those topics in detail although reference will be made to them where necessary.

UNJUST ENRICHMENT: TOTAL FAILURE OF CONSIDERATION

Typically in cases where there is an operative mistake at common law which renders the contract void then any monies that have been paid by one party to the other party may be recovered on the basis of the total failure of consideration; the action is for monies 'had and received'. In such cases the party is permitted to recover his money on the basis that it would be unjust to allow the other party to retain it since that other party has given nothing in return for it. Similar provisions apply where the contract has been frustrated; see, for example, *Fibrosa Spolka Akcyjna* v *Fairbairn Lawson Combe Barbour Ltd* above.

EQUITABLE RESCISSION

We have seen that sometimes, even if a mistake is not sufficient to render a contract void at common law, equity will intervene so as to allow the contract to be rescinded. In such circumstances the courts, in theory, will only order rescission where *restitutio in integrum* is possible: see *Clarke* v *Dickson* above (p 356). However, where *restitutio in integrum* is not possible, the courts have a discretion to order rescission on certain terms: see, for example, *Cooper* v *Phibbs* cited in *Solle* v *Butcher* above (p 375), and *Solle* v *Butcher* itself.

INDEMNITY AS A RESTITUTIONARY REMEDY

Newbigging v *Adam*

(1886) 34 ChD 582 • Court of Appeal

Newbigging entered into a partnership with Adams and paid £9700 into the partnership. Newbigging also paid £324 2s 7d to discharge the liabilities of the partnership. The partnership proved to be a failure and Newbigging sought to have the partnership agreement set aside on the grounds of Adams' misrepresentations. He also sought an indemnity 'against all claims and demands whatsoever in respect of the said partnership or partnerships, or any of the debts or liabilities thereof'.

Bowen LJ: . . . 'The second conclusion of fact which I do not hesitate to draw is that there was a misrepresentation . . .

If we turn to the question of misrepresentation, damages cannot be obtained at law for misrepresentation which is not fraudulent, and you cannot, as it seems to me, give in equity any indemnity which corresponds with damages. If the mass of authority there is upon the subject were gone through I think it would be found that there is not so much difference as is generally supposed between the view taken at common law and the view taken in equity as to misrepresentation. At common law it has always been considered that misrepresentations which strike at the root of the contract are sufficient to avoid the contract on the ground explained in *Kennedy* v *Panama, New Zealand, and Australian Royal Mail Co*; but when you come to consider what is the exact relief to which a person is entitled in a case of misrepresentation it seems to me to be this, and nothing more, that he is entitled to have the contract rescinded, and is entitled accordingly to all the incidents and consequences of such rescission. It is said that the injured party is entitled to be replaced *in statu quo*. It seems to me that when you are dealing with innocent misrepresentation you must understand that proposition that he is to be replaced *in statu quo* with this limitation – that he is not to be replaced in exactly the same position in all respects, otherwise he would be entitled to recover damages, but is to be replaced in his position so far as regards the rights and obligations which have been created by the contract into which he has been induced to enter. That seems to me to be the true doctrine, and I think it is put in the neatest way in *Redgrave* v *Hurd*. In that case there was a misrepresentation, but, though there was a suggestion of fraud in the pleadings, the Court of Appeal thought that fraud was not so expressly pleaded as to enable the Court to treat the case as one of fraud, and that the relief given must depend on misrepresentation alone. The Master of the Rolls, so treating it, says: "Before going into the details of the case I wish to say something about my view of the law applicable to it, because in the text-books, and even in some observations of noble Lords in the House of Lords, there are remarks which I think, according to the course of modern decisions, are not well founded, and do not accurately state the law. As regards the rescission of a contract, there was no doubt a difference between the rules of Courts of Equity and the rules of Courts of Common Law – a difference which of course has now disappeared by the operation of the Judicature Act, which makes the rules of equity prevail. According to the decisions of Courts of Equity it was not necessary, in order to set aside a contract obtained by material false representation, to prove that the party who obtained it knew at the time when the representation was made that it was false. It was put in two ways, either of which was sufficient. One way of putting the case was, 'A man is not to be allowed to get a benefit from a statement which he now admits to be false. He is not to be allowed to say, for the purpose of civil jurisdiction, that when he made it he did not know it to be false; he ought to have found that out before he made it.' The other way of putting it was this, 'Even assuming that moral fraud must be shewn in order to set aside a contract, you have it where a man, having obtained a beneficial contract by a statement which he now knows to be false, insists upon keeping that contract. To do so is a moral delinquency: no man ought to seek to take advantages of his own false statement.' The rule in equity was settled, and it does not matter on which of the two grounds it was rested. As regards the rule of common law there is no doubt it was not quite so wide. There were, indeed, cases in which, even at common law, a contract could be rescinded for misrepresentation, although it could not be shewn that the person making it knew the representation to be false. They are variously stated, but I think, according to the later decisions, the statement must have been made recklessly, and without care whether it was true or false, and not with the belief that it was true." With great respect for the shadow and memory of that great name I cannot help saying that this is not a perfect exposition of what the common law was, but, so far as the rule of equity goes, I must assume that the Master of the Rolls spoke with full knowledge of the equity authorities, and he treats the relief as being the giving back by the party who made the misrepresentation of the advantages he obtained by the contract. Now those advantages may be of two kinds. He may get an advantage in the shape of an actual benefit, as when he receives money; he may also get an advantage if the party with whom he contracts assumes some burthen in consideration of the contract. In such a case it seems to me that complete rescission would not be effected unless the misrepresenting party not only hands back the benefits which he has himself received – but also re-assumes the burthen which under the contract the injured person has taken upon himself. Speaking only for myself I should not like to lay down the proposition that a person is to be restored to the position which he held before the misrepresentation was made, nor that the person injured must be indemnified against loss which arises out of the contract, unless you place upon the words "out of the contract" the limited and special meaning which I have endeavoured to shadow forth. Loss arising out of the contract is a term which would be too wide. It would embrace damages at common law, because damages at common law are only given upon the supposition that they are damages which would naturally and reasonably follow from the injury done. I think *Redgrave* v *Hurd* shews that it would be too wide, because in that case the Court excluded from the relief which was given the damages which had been sustained by the plaintiff in removing his business, and other similar items. There ought, as it appears to me, to be a giving back and a taking back on both sides, including the giving back and taking back of the obligations which the contract has created, as well as the giving back and the taking back of the advantages. There is nothing in the case of *Rawlins* v *Wickham* which carries the doctrine beyond that. In that case, one of three partners having retired, the remaining partners introduced the plaintiff into the firm, and he, under his contract with them, took upon himself to share with them the liabilities which otherwise they would have borne in their entirety. That was a burthen which he took under the contract and in virtue of the contract. It seems to me, therefore, that upon this principle indemnity was rightly decreed as regards the liabilities of the new firm. I have not found any case which carries the doctrine further, and it is not necessary to carry it further in order to support the order now appealed from. A part of the contract between the Plaintiff and Adam & Co was that the Plaintiff should become and continue for five years partner in a new firm and bring in £10 000. By this very contract he was to pledge his credit with his partners in the new firm for the business transactions of the new firm. It was a burthen or liability imposed on him by the very contract. It seems to me that the £9000 odd, and, indeed, all the moneys brought in by him or expended by him for the new firm up to the £10 000, were part of the actual moneys which he undertook by the true contract with Adam & Co to pay. Of course he ought to be indemnified as regards that. I think, also, applying the same doctrine, he ought to be indemnified against all the liabilities of the firm, because they were liabilities which under the contract he was bound to take upon himself. It seems to me upon those grounds that the decision of the Vice-Chancellor ought to be supported.'

IS RESTITUTION AVAILABLE FOR BREACH OF CONTRACT?

If one party to a contract deliberately breaks the contract and in so doing makes a profit from that breach can the innocent party claim, by way of unjust enrichment, damages for that deliberate breach? This situation was dealt with in *Surrey County Council* v *Bredero Homes Ltd* above (p 542) where in breach of its agreement with Surrey CC Bredero built 77 houses instead of 72. Surrey CC sued Bredero for breach of covenant. Steyn LJ said '. . . The introduction of restitutionary remedies to deprive cynical contract breakers of the fruits of their breaches of contract will lead to greater uncertainty in the assessment of damages in commercial and consumer disputes. It is of paramount importance that the way in which disputes are likely to be resolved by the courts must be readily predictable. Given the premise that the aggrieved party has suffered no loss, is such a dramatic extension of restitutionary remedies justified in order confer a windfall in each case on the aggrieved party? I think not . . . The recognition of the proposed extension will in my view not serve the public interest. It is sound policy to guard against extending the protection of the law of obligations too widely. For these substantive and policy reasons I regard it as undesirable that the range of restitutionary remedies should be extended in the way in which we have been invited to do so.'

SUMMARY

You should now be able to:

• Explain the position and role of restitution within the law of contract.

If you have not mastered the above point you should go through this section again.